COMPOSING KNOWLEDGE
Readings for College Writers

Holding: Defendant's mark infringed plaintiff's mark. One factor courts consider in determining infringement is intent. Here, defendant "conducted absolutely no search" prior to adopting the infringing mark and performed no search until after trial commenced. This carelessness is a factor weighing in favor of a finding of infringement.

CASE STUDY AND ACTIVITIES

Case Study.   Watson Inc. has decided to introduce a variety of new toys and stuffed animals to be sold at the amusement park, each of which will bear a different trademark. One of the toys, which is intended to be sold only during the next month, will be called PUPPY LOVE. Another toy will be called TAYLOR TIGER. Watson hopes that TAYLOR TIGER will be so successful that it will spin off a series of books and videos for children. Finally, Watson will market PUP TENT, a stuffed dog equipped with some camping gear, such as a compass.

Activities.   Describe the types of searches that should be conducted for each mark. Assume that the search for PUP TENT discloses a canceled registration for PUPPY TENT for stuffed animals. What should Watson do?

ROLE OF PARALEGAL

Paralegals play a significant role in the clearance and availability stage of a trademark application. Although legal advice can be given only by attorneys, there are numerous activities in which paralegals will be involved:

- obtaining information about the client's proposed mark;
- conducting a preliminary in-house knockout search to eliminate bars to registration;
- ordering and reviewing a comprehensive search;
- consulting with the IP team regarding potentially conflicting marks disclosed in searches; and
- conducting investigations of potentially conflicting marks.

INTERNET RESOURCES

PTO TESS and TARR databases: http://www.uspto.gov (select "Trademarks" and then select either "Search trademarks" (TESS) or "Check status" (TARR))

COMPOSING KNOWLEDGE
Readings for College Writers

Rolf Norgaard
University of Colorado at Boulder

Bedford/St. Martin's

Boston ◆ New York

For Bedford/St. Martin's

Senior Developmental Editor: John E. Sullivan III
Production Editor: Kendra LeFleur
Senior Production Supervisor: Nancy Myers
Marketing Manager: Karita dos Santos
Editorial Assistant: Jennifer Lyford
Production Assistants: Lidia MacDonald and Amy Derjue
Copyeditor: Mary Lou Wilshaw-Watts
Text Design: Anne Carter
Cover Design: Wiley Design Studio
Cover Art: Particular Times. Painting courtesy of Martina Nehrling, © Martina Nehrling.
Photo courtesy of Zg Gallery, Chicago.
Composition: Pine Tree Composition
Printing and Binding: R.R. Donnelly & Sons Company

President: Joan E. Feinberg
Editorial Director: Denise B. Wydra
Editor in Chief: Karen S. Henry
Director of Marketing: Karen Melton Soeltz
Director of Editing, Design, and Production: Marcia Cohen
Managing Editor: Elizabeth M. Schaaf

Library of Congress Control Number: 2006933435

Manufactured in the United States of America.

1 0 9 8 7
f   e   d   c   b

For information, write: Bedford/St. Martin's, 75 Arlington Street, Boston, MA 02116
(617-399-4000)

ISBN-10: 0–312–15313–9
ISBN-13: 978–0–312–15313–7

Acknowledgments

David Bartholomae. "Inventing the University." From *When A Writer Can't Write* by David Bartholomae. Copyright © 1985. Reprinted by permission of the Guilford Press.

Charles Bazerman. "Where Is the Classroom?" From *English Basics*, Winter 1992. A Houghton Mifflin newsletter. Copyright © 1992 by Houghton Mifflin Company. Reprinted with permission.

Acknowledgments and copyrights are continued at the back of the book on pages 791–95, which constitute an extension of the copyright page. It is a violation of the law to reproduce these selections by any means whatsoever without the written permission of the copyright holder.

PREFACE

Higher education has its own rules — rules about who is heard, what counts as knowledge, what works as persuasion. For students who don't know these rules, college can be a confusing place. In college courses, students learn more than facts or topics in a discipline. They are exposed, often indirectly, to assumptions and conventions about how language and inquiry work together. Writing courses afford a special opportunity to explore this process. With its focus on the role of writing in inquiry, and its goal of helping students join a community of inquiring minds, *Composing Knowledge* embraces this challenge and enables you to make this process of education more explicit for your students.

Composing Knowledge first asks students to step back and examine their assumptions about learning. Then it provides them with a training ground for higher education, giving them tools with which to think deeply about and understand their learning experiences. By considering how we "compose" knowledge, this anthology also helps students gain some "composing knowledge." That is, it helps them become better thinkers and writers, able to join the conversations that shape what we know and how we know it. Ultimately, students are better positioned to contribute to the many conversations of academic and civic life.

Students often wonder what holds their college education together. Aware that facts or topics in this or that course do not make for an education, students are eager to explore questions that might connect their academic experience and integrate their intellectual lives. Initially, these questions are straightforward: How do we read a syllabus? How do we respond to a sophisticated piece of writing? The questions progress in complexity: How do we enter the college community, the community of our chosen discipline, civic communities, or for that matter electronic communities? How are ways of knowing shaped by communities, and how are those communities themselves shaped by language? And as we enter those communities, how do we connect our work to the larger discussions of civic life? Taking up these questions, *Composing Knowledge* offers provocative, wide-ranging readings and apparatus that help students explore and understand their experiences in higher education.

The organization of *Composing Knowledge* encourages students to reflect on writing their way into — and beyond — a community. Chapters One and Two, "Joining the Conversation," and "Inventing the University," take up the

challenge faced by so many students, even the best: that of joining a conversation where that very conversation is precisely what "invents" a university.
Chapter Three, "Persuading Each Other," takes a closer look at those conversations and their hidden (and often perplexing) discursive moves. The
remaining chapters bring into the classroom current discussions that are
changing the ways we learn and write in communities: Chapter Four,
"Engagements," encourages discussions about our collaborative way of working; Chapter Five, "(En)gendering Knowledge," examines issues surrounding gender and knowing; Chapter Six, "Learning Technology," takes on
debates about technology as it shapes our learning and writing; and Chapter
Seven, "Seeing and Believing," explores new interest in visual rhetoric.

Composing Knowledge supports fruitful classroom instruction in a number
of distinctive ways:

- It helps students to master the habits of reflective thinking, active reading, and critical writing essential to success in college and professional
  life.
- It offers our best current thinking on writing and learning in communities — communities that are themselves organized through language.
- It addresses contemporary issues that are reshaping the writing and
  learning we do in those communities.
- It encourages students to reflect on ways of knowing from across the
  curriculum, and to connect those ways to broader issues of literacy and
  community.
- It lends relevance to the writing classroom by having students develop
  writing projects that take them "into the field" to reflect on and respond
  to their own situated learning and writing experiences.
- It links the college writing classroom to professional and civic life by
  having students write in genres that extend beyond the academic essay
  to include letters, editorials, and proposals.

Provocative Readings from Experts and Insiders

The readings in *Composing Knowledge* differ in some respects from standard
anthology fare. Open most any composition reader, and you are likely to find
selections driven by topical concerns. The text operates on a "field coverage"
principle, with essays on this or that topic, from one or another discipline or
area of life. Such anthologies reinforce the assumption, common in other
courses, that knowledge is a given, that what students consume is a bundle
of views or information on certain topics. Even controversy tends to come
prepackaged as a static set of opposing opinions on a given subject.

The readings in *Composing Knowledge* are driven by a different concern:
open questions grounded in the lived learning experience of students as they

find their way in new communities. Moreover, the readings are not meant to be consumed but rather engaged. Each invites reflection, interaction, and response — that is, each invites the work of readers. The readings are also provocations in that they ask students to test insights in and through their own writing and learning experiences.

The questions that drive *Composing Knowledge* are explored in essays that vary in both style and difficulty. Each section opens with short, accessible — and often personal — essays and then moves to essays of greater length, complexity, and range. Many of the authors, renowned writers and prominent intellectuals, will be welcomingly familiar: Amy Tan, Stephen Jay Gould, George Orwell, Katha Pollitt, Jared Diamond, Malcolm Gladwell, Susan Sontag, and Neil Postman, to name but a few. Others, less likely to be known to students, will help them participate in discussions now shaping the academy: Mary Louise Pratt, Deborah Tannen, bell hooks, Gerald Graff, Paulo Freire, Louis Menand, Mike Rose, George Lakoff, Kenneth A. Bruffee, Thomas S. Kuhn, and Jane Tompkins. Still others will be our own voices, the voices of our colleagues in rhetoric and composition, who broach issues of compelling interest and relevance to undergraduates themselves: Nancy Sommers, David Bartholomae, Wayne C. Booth, Lisa Ede, Andrea Lunsford, Charles Bazerman, David Russell, Gregory G. Colomb, and Joseph Williams. All too often withheld from the very students taking our courses, these voices remind students that our own knowledge in and of composition is, like their own, always constructed, always "composed," and provide a uniquely informed perspective on the way knowledge is produced in the writing classroom.

Flexible Organization

Composing Knowledge is designed to assist you in composing your own course. Because each of the seven chapters is made up of two smaller units of readings, for a total of fourteen sets, the book is eminently adaptable. Students might be asked to sample several essays from each unit, or to delve into several chapters in depth, or to link sets of readings in novel ways. This flexible text is thus meant to serve the several ways you might organize your own course:

- **Courses that focus on critical reading** will find a range of selections, some quite challenging, that encourage students to read both with and against the grain of the text. The book's apparatus supports this focus through headnotes, questions and short assignments, and longer writing projects that help students interact with texts on several levels and in several ways.
- **Courses that focus on academic writing** will find a wide array of readings (many of which are documented) that exemplify or discuss the

multifaceted nature of academic writing. The book's own writing instruction supports this focus with questions, short assignments, and writing projects that address those skills critical to academic writing, among them defining, summarizing, analyzing, and arguing.

- **Courses that include extensive research and writing projects** will find a host of innovative project ideas that connect readings with ethnographic fieldwork that has students exploring engaging issues drawn from their own situated learning and writing experiences.

- **Courses that focus on writing across the curriculum** will find a wide range of readings that set academic, professional, and civic issues in the context of disciplinary communities. Questions associated with the readings and a host of writing projects encourage students to develop the kinds of documents that speak to various disciplines and to professional and civic audiences, among them letters and memos, proposals, reports, executive summaries, newsletters, commentaries, and reviews.

Rich Editorial Apparatus

A number of editorial and pedagogical features complement the readings themselves, supporting their effective use in writing classrooms. These features help you compose a classroom that encourages critical reading and engaged discussion, leading to innovative writing projects. They include:

A CHAPTER-LONG GENERAL INTRODUCTION. The general introduction to *Composing Knowledge* establishes the rhetorical context for the book and the student's own work. The first of three parts in the introduction acquaints students with the several ways in which literacy, community, and inquiry intersect. It reveals how contested those terms are and makes the case why exploring those intersections matters in their development as mature writers. The second section helps students view the readings themselves and their critical engagement with them as conversations that occur in a community. It outlines specific strategies (from previewing and annotating to uncovering argumentative structure) that help students both honor and challenge texts as they work with the readings in the collaborative setting of the writing classroom. The final section helps students see their own lived experience in academic and civic communities as an important dimension of this collection. It introduces the concept of writing projects as "fieldwork" and offers specific "how to" strategies for conducting various kinds of fieldwork projects. This work connects the readings with students' own sustained reflection on how they compose — and are composed by — writing and learning in the academy and beyond.

INTRODUCTIONS TO EACH UNIT OF READINGS. For each of the fourteen units of readings, a short introduction sets the stage for the various concerns raised in and by the selections.

PREWRITING ACTIVITIES. Each unit introduction is followed by a group of questions under the heading "Reflecting on Prior Knowledge." Designed to encourage prewriting activities, the questions remind students that they do not come to the readings "cold"; their own experiences in and out of college have been shaped by the very issues they will soon engage in the readings.

HEADNOTES. Contextual information prior to each selection introduces the readers to the author and places the reading as a contribution to an ongoing conversation.

WRITING ON READINGS. Two sets of questions and writing assignments follow each reading selection, offering an opportunity to build rhetorically informed writing instruction into the students' engagement with the readings. The first set of questions and short assignments, "Working with the Text," encourages students to uncover core issues and arguments in ways that prepare them for a closer second reading. The second set of questions and short assignments, "From Text to Field," raises connections and intersections with other texts in the collection and with contemporary issues on campus and in the community. This second set of activities often prepares the ground for the more extensive "Into the Field: Options for Writing Projects."

FIELDWORK PROJECTS. These assignments, titled "Into the Field: Options for Writing Projects," are located at the end of each of the fourteen units of readings. Here, students are encouraged to engage in their own fieldwork. Approximately ten to twelve questions and scenarios at the end of each chapter prompt students to develop more extended writing projects that link the issues raised in the readings with their own experience in academic and civic communities.

Often drawing on local documents and students' own close observation, these options for writing projects have students reflect on courses and curricula, teaching and learning, syllabi and assignments, disciplines and departments, classroom and workplace cultures. Students might examine their own required curriculum to uncover the assumptions that drive how their college constructs their education. Or they might analyze recruiting and admissions materials from their own and other colleges to analyze what images they construct of college living and learning.

You might think of the various "Into the Field" options as helping students to pursue their own ethnographic projects, to explore their college, their newly chosen discipline, and their immediate community as an ethnographer might explore an unfamiliar and fascinating culture.

RESOURCES FOR TEACHING *COMPOSING KNOWLEDGE.* This instructor's manual includes a sample syllabus and teaching tips for each of the four kinds of courses noted above. Entries for each of the readings provide guidance and anticipate possible classroom issues.

COMPANION WEB SITE. Located at bedfordstmartins.com/composingknowledge, the site provides research links for each unit in *Composing Knowledge,* helping students to make connections among the text, their academic and personal lives, and issues in the world at large.

Acknowledgments

This book would not have seen the light of day were it not for the sustained interest, friendly persistence, and Job-like patience of John Sullivan, development editor at Bedford/St. Martin's. He continued to support the project, even when personal and professional lives intervened (everything from hand surgery to heavy administrative duties as I helped establish a new Program for Writing and Rhetoric on our campus). His insightful and creative suggestions and his attention to detail have made this a far better book than I could have produced on my own.

I would also like to thank others at Bedford/St. Martin's who believed in and worked on *Composing Knowledge,* in particular Jimmy Fleming, humanities specialist, who signed the project; Joan Feinberg, president; Chuck Christensen, president emeritus; Denise Wydra, editorial director; Karen Henry, editor in chief; Steve Scipione, executive editor; and Jennifer Lyford, editorial assistant, who helped during its development; Kendra LeFleur, production editor, and Elizabeth Schaaf, managing editor, who saw the book through production; Martha Friedman and Naomi Kornhauser, for handling art permissions; Sandy Schechter and Diane Kraut, for clearing text permission; and Karita dos Santos, marketing manager.

I would also like to thank those reviewers who examined portions of the manuscript and provided helpful feedback on it: Valerie Balester, Texas A&M; William A. Covino, Florida Atlantic University; Van Hillard, Duke University; Roxanne Mountford, University of Arizona; Christine Murray, University of Texas, Arlington; and Thomas A. Wallis, North Carolina State University. I am also grateful to those reviewers who have chosen to remain anonymous.

The support and interest of my colleagues in the Program for Writing and Rhetoric at the University of Colorado at Boulder have enriched me intellectually and sustained me personally, and thus served, in ways too numerous to mention, as midwives for this book. I owe a special debt of gratitude to Paula Wenger, whose invaluable assistance on headnotes and text questions kept the project moving forward when administrative duties threatened to overwhelm me. Faculty and graduate students in a campuswide Rhetoric Workshop offered a forum for scholarly discussion and writing that enriched the conception and pedagogy of this book. Administrators on campus helped support this project through their renewed commitment to writing and rhetoric as cornerstones for educational excellence.

First and last, I owe an enormous debt to my students over the years. Their spirited discussion, insightful comments, and engaged writing have taught me even as I was teaching them. Born in the classroom, not the private study, this book is as much theirs as mine. My thanks to you all.

Thus, the history of my debts becomes the tale of my good fortune. Nowhere more so than at home. Andrea has been at once my most perceptive reader and my unfailing muse. Stefan and Lara have come to share my passion for ideas and language, growing inch by inch as this book grew chapter by chapter.

free to talk with her about anything that is important to you. Her being there to help you is not directed by some special interests of her own. She is willing to spend time helping you to deal with some non-academic issues in order to create a safe learning environment for you.

(2) Have the capacity to help with your major concerns. The ideal advisor should have the experience, skills, and resources such as information and credibility to address the problems you have. Some students might emphasize the power position of an advisor in an institution. However, a politically powerful advisor is not necessarily good for you if you are not good at dealing with big powers.

(3) Trust you and be able to appreciate your achievements. The ideal advisor will make sure that you are on the right tack. However, if you come up with some conclusions that are different from or even to the contrary of his own ideas, he will still be happy to give your work the credit it deserves.

In practice, the selection of one's advisor may involve some other factors that do not appear to be purely academic. For example, because of their pressing financial needs, some students would first target those faculty members who have the potential to provide some financial support (such as paid employment in their funded research projects). We can hardly say this consideration is inappropriate, since such students may turn out to be very serious about their academic undertaking once they are able to survive the financial challenges. In reality, many of such students work extremely hard to prove themselves both financially and academically. They sincerely wish that they could contribute something in exchange for the paid job opportunity. Sometimes they are indeed very helpful to the faculty, although we tend to understand the process of financial support as a one-way phenomenon. The student, on the other hand, would learn a great deal assisting faculty members with their projects. As a student, however, you must understand that a job opportunity like this is not simply a source of financial aid to you. For that purpose you should work in the college cafeteria, in the university bookstore, or as a library assistant, even though those jobs pay you much less than working as a research assistant. To stay in a research position, you must prove yourself with extraordinary skills and competence.

In contrast to the above, many students emphasize the academic reputation of their advisors. Choosing your advisor simply by her fame, however, may not be to your best interest. You will see why this is the case. As we have talked about the ideal advisor, it might also be helpful to discuss a little about what kinds of people on campus you should avoid considering as your advisor. Generally

INTERNET RESOURCES (cont'd)

Trademark search tips: http://lexis.nexis.com/associates/searchtips/
                                  (tips on trademark searching offered by
                                  LEXIS)

Searching trademarks on the Internet: http://www.ubc.ca/scieng/patents/tmnet_e1.htm

DIALOG tutorial: http://training.dialog.com/onlinecourses/
                                  trademarks

DISCUSSION QUESTIONS

1. Assume that a client intends to use the mark STRATOTECH for computer consulting services to be offered on a nationwide basis. Discuss the search strategy that should be used to ensure the mark is available for use and registration.
2. If a client intends to use the mark PRICE CUT MONSTER MONTH for a local month-long promotion for selling cars, what kind of search should be conducted?
3. Assume that a client wishes to use the mark TRICLEAN for a cleaning product. A search of the PTO records discloses that a previous registration for TRICLEAN has expired. Discuss the risks to the client of using TRICLEAN without further investigation.
4. If a client wishes to use the mark NUTRICREAM for hand lotion and discovers a series of marks used for cosmetics with the prefix *Nutri,* what does this suggest?
5. If a search of PTO records for NUTRICREAM discloses a reference for NUTRIKREEM, what should the client do?

For additional resources, go to www.westlegalstudies.com.

CONTENTS

1. Joining the Conversation   *33*

2. Inventing the University   *147*

5. (En)gendering Knowledge   *491*

making and breaking of social links, people are beginning to function as elements in a hypertextual network of affiliations."

7. Seeing and Believing   *675*

MIND'S EYE   *677*

Annie Dillard, Seeing   *679*

"The secret of seeing is, then, the pearl of great price. . . . But although the pearl may be found, it may not be sought. The literature of illumination reveals this above all: although it comes to those who wait for it, it is always, even to the most practiced and adept, a gift and a total surprise."

John Berger, The White Bird   *684*

"Art does not imitate nature, it imitates a creation, sometimes to propose an alternative world, sometimes simply to amplify, to confirm, to make social the brief hope offered by nature. Art is an organized response to what nature allows us to glimpse occasionally."

Susan Sontag, In Plato's Cave   *690*

"In teaching us a new visual code, photographs alter and enlarge our notions of what is worth looking at and what we have a right to observe. They are a grammar and, even more importantly, an ethics of seeing."

E. H. Gombrich, Truth and Stereotype   *709*

Exploring works of art that purport to represent the world faithfully, a famous art historian identifies a curious puzzle: "The familiar will always remain the likely starting point for the rendering of the unfamiliar. . . . The artist, no less than the writer, needs a vocabulary before he can embark on a 'copy' of reality."

WITNESSING THE IMAGE   *725*

David Levi Strauss, Photography and Belief   *728*

"Photography materialized seeing in a new way, and significantly changed the relation between seeing and believing. Photography as mechanical reproduction almost immediately altered the aura of the work of art, and over the next 150 years photography acquired its own aura — the aura of believability."

John Durham Peters, Witnessing   *736*

"To witness thus has two faces: the passive one of seeing and the active one of saying. Herein lies the fragility of witnessing: the difficult juncture between experience and discourse. The journey from experience (the seen) into words (the said) is precarious."

CHAPTER 4

The Trademark Registration Process

CHAPTER OVERVIEW

From the discussion in Chapter 2, it is clear that federal registration of a mark offers a trademark owner distinct advantages over mere reliance on common law or state trademark rights. There are two primary paths to registration for U.S.-based applications: a use-based application (alleging use in interstate commerce) and an intent-to-use application (alleging a bona fide intent to so use the mark in the future). Both types of applications share many common features and progress through the registration process in a fairly similar fashion. The process for federal registration of a mark can be expensive and can take as long as twelve to eighteen months, even if there are no significant problems or delays.

PREPARING THE APPLICATION

Introduction

Once a mark has been selected and evaluated for use and registrability, an application for federal registration of the mark should be prepared and filed. The written application comprises a request for registration, the name of the applicant, the citizenship of the applicant, the address of the applicant, an identification of the goods and/or services offered under the mark, a drawing of the mark, a verification or declaration signed by the applicant or agent or attorney, and, usually, the basis for filing the application, namely, whether the application is based on actual use of the mark or the owner's intent to use the mark. The process of moving an application through the PTO is called **prosecution.**

The application must be in English. Forms for electronically filed applications are provided by the PTO. If the form provided by the PTO is not used, the application should be on lettersize (namely 8 1/2 inches by 11 inches) paper, type-written, double-spaced, with margins of at least 1 1/2 inches at the left and top of the pages. The application should be written on only one side of the paper. (See Appendix D, Form 1, Trademark Application.)

The PTO prefers but does not generally require that the documents submitted be

"*Fascinated and excited, tens of millions of Americans stared at their screens, sharing the experience of these missiles and bombs unerringly guided by the wonders of American technology to a target identified by a narrator as an important military installation. The generation raised in video arcades and on Nintendo could hardly be more satisfied.*"

"*The globalization of terror is something new. It goes hand in hand with the globalization of the media. The creation of new media technology has created a public space in which political actors may perform: terrorists are some of the actors who can now play on a global stage.*"

CONTENTS BY THEMES AND DISCIPLINES

DISCOURSE CONVENTIONS

EDUCATION

GENDER STUDIES AND RHETORICS OF DIFFERENCE

LANGUAGE AND LITERACY

MEDIA AND TECHNOLOGY

SCIENCE AND ENGINEERING

COMPOSING KNOWLEDGE
Readings for College Writers

INTRODUCTION

> Imagine that you enter a parlor. You come late. When you arrive, others have long preceded you, and they are engaged in a heated discussion, a discussion too heated for them to pause and tell you exactly what it is about. In fact, the discussion had already begun long before any of them got there, so no one present is qualified to retrace all the steps that had gone before. You listen for a while, until you decide that you have caught the tenor of the argument; then you put in your oar. Someone answers; you answer him; another comes to your defense; another aligns himself against you. . . . However, the discussion is interminable. The hour grows late, you must depart. And you do depart, with the discussion still vigorously in progress.
>
> — KENNETH BURKE, *The Philosophy of Literary Form*

Knowing and Composing

When you enter the university, or enter advanced course work in your major, you are entering the sort of parlor that Kenneth Burke describes. While the conversation can certainly be engaging, and the ideas stimulating, the experience of entering a new setting can be quite unsettling. Who are these folks who are deep in conversation, and what are they getting so worked up about? On what basis are they taking sides? What does it take to join the conversation and become one of "them"? And what are the "moves" involved in having a voice in the conversation and in having that voice heard?

We would do well to think of the university as a kind of Burkean parlor or rather a set of overlapping parlors, for no one parlor could ever be sufficient to capture all of the conversations that go on in various disciplines or on campus. Although we may think of a college or university as a collection of buildings, or our own education as a list of courses completed or of expertise gained, the conversational metaphor is actually quite apt. The university is a house of argument. The university represents an ongoing conversation about questions that are genuinely at issue. An essential part of your college education is not just learning facts but also learning how to make sense of and join that conversation—a conversation that is not limited to classrooms but also extends to larger civic spaces. This book, and the writing course you are taking, can play a helpful role in that process.

originals. Photocopies may be submitted (except for foreign registrations and certain other special documents for which certified copies are required). Thus, if a client signs an application and returns it to your office by facsimile (fax), you may photocopy the signature page, attach it to the application, and file it with the PTO, as long as the signature is legible.

The PTO permits the filing by fax of most papers and documents; however, trademark applications are not acceptable by fax. They must be hand-delivered to the PTO, filed by mail, or submitted electronically.

All of the requirements relating to the filing and prosecution of trademark applications are governed by the **Trademark Manual of Examining Procedure (TMEP),** an excellent source of materials with numerous examples and case citations. Most trademark practitioners keep the TMEP handy at all times. The TMEP is also available on the PTO web site at http://www.uspto.gov/web/offices/tac/tmep/index.html.

The PTO introduced an electronic filing system in 1998. The **Trademark Electronic Application System (TEAS)** permits applicants to file numerous documents electronically. For example, applicants can now fill out a trademark application form electronically and submit it directly to the PTO over the Internet, paying by credit card or PTO deposit account. In addition to trademark applications, documents relating to renewals of trademarks and responses to PTO inquiries and office actions can be filed electronically. Documents can be transmitted electronically or prepared using the PTO online forms, printed out, and then mailed to the PTO using its system called PrinTEAS.

When a document is filed electronically, the PTO receives it within seconds after filing and immediately issues a confirmation of filing via e-mail. These electronically filed documents are examined more quickly than their paper counterparts. Documents submitted electronically using TEAS® are considered filed on the date the PTO receives the transmission.

Documents requiring signatures use a symbol adopted by the applicant as a signature, for example, /john h. taylor/ or /jht/. Similarly, if a drawing, image, or specimen is required, the applicant must submit a digitized image in .gif or .jpg form.

The PTO prefers that applicants file documents electronically using TEAS, and in 2002, 38 percent of initial applications were filed electronically. The PTO's goal is to perform nearly all communications with customers electronically by the end of 2004. The TEAS system can be accessed at http://www.uspto.gov/teas/index.html.

The Applicant

An application to register a mark can be made only by the owner of the mark or, in the case of an intent-to-use application, by a person who has a bona fide intent to use the mark in commerce. Applicants may be natural persons or business entities such as corporations, partnerships, associations, unions, or other organizations. Government entities such as nations, states, municipalities, and other governmental bodies also can apply to register marks that they own. For example, the U.S. Army Recruiting Department is the owner of the registered mark BE ALL YOU CAN BE®, and the New York State Department of Economic Development is the owner of the famous mark I LOVE NY® (with a heart design replacing the word *love*).

The applicant's name must be in correct legal form. Thus, a corporation that owns a mark should be identified in the application by

If we look more closely at Burke's parlor, we find three concerns in play. Those three concerns, and the various intersections among them, inform the readings in the chapters that lie ahead. By exploring the intersections of literacy, community, and inquiry, this collection can help you enter the many conversations of academic and civic life.

LITERACY. Although Burke's description of the parlor foregrounds conversation, we can hardly imagine that this conversation could be effective without reading and writing—without, in short, literacy. Indeed, conversation itself— the give and take among various voices—becomes a way of better understanding how and why we read and write. Yet literacy is a vexed concept. Does Burke's parlor, and your own first attempts to participate in it, presume the mere ability to read and write (that is, functional literacy) or some kind of critical engagement or critical literacy?

COMMUNITY. On a first reading, Burke's description of parlor conversation might suggest that those in the room form a cohesive, homogeneous community. But the more we look about in that parlor, the more fraught that term *community* becomes. The community of your own writing class may be a case in point. Although community may first seem a warm and fuzzy concept, membership also implies exclusion. Who is silenced in Burke's parlor? Who decides when and whether you can "put in your oar"? And how do the conversations in one parlor intersect with those in the next room?

INQUIRY. Heated conversation seems to be the norm in Burke's parlor, yet participants seem to be doing more than *having* an argument. They are *making* arguments. What does that distinction mean for your own reading and writing? How do you know how to participate if no one ever pauses and shows you the hidden moves needed to foster and support genuine inquiry and to develop and shape an argument?

Composing Knowledge locates you at the crossroads of these three contested concepts, most especially at the site of your own practice. The readings in this collection help you reflect on your own situated writing and learning experiences. Those readings, and above all your own writing, suggest that knowledge doesn't come prepackaged. It's not something to consume and then regurgitate. *Knowledge is composed.* Knowledge is shaped by language and by communities of knowers that organize themselves through language. And as we work together to explore this notion, we will also uncover *knowledge that can help you compose.*

But first, let's consider a bit more closely the three contested terms at play in Burke's parlor and how they intersect with each other and with your own writing and reading experiences in college, the site of our practice.

Literacy

When my son Stefan entered kindergarten and began to engage writing and reading in a school setting, he took a greater interest in my own work. "What do you do at the university?" he asked one day. "I teach writing," I replied. Flush with the self-confidence that only a precocious kindergartner can have, he offered, "I can do that!" "Well, it's a bit more complicated," I said. He paused, and then his eyes grew large. "Oh, you mean cursive!"

Writing and reading are indeed complicated acts, and at the university we have no foolproof Palmer Method for learning the strokes. Yet the tendency to reduce the advanced literacy needed for college work back to a basic mechanical skill—the ability to read and write—persists to this day. Some still presume, for example, that a first-year writing course is but a prelude to the real intellectual work of college.

Literacy has traditionally been seen as a neutral, mechanical skill, an ability one picks up, much like riding a bike, that requires little further development or nuanced application. No wonder more than a few students chafe at college writing courses, especially when they are required. Standard definitions of *literacy* tend to stress this focus on basic competence, implying that literacy is a rather unproblematic term and that it can be easily measured—and just as easily learned or taught. But even as levels of literacy have changed over the centuries, the focus on measurement and competence persists. This perception is reinforced with each election cycle, when we hear cries that our country is in the midst of a "literacy crisis." Johnny, we are told, cannot read. And if schools haven't done the job, college must step in to remediate.

College writing courses suffer from this legacy, from definitions of literacy that are themselves far too literal—and remedial. That needn't be the case. Through this book, and through your collaboration with fellow readers and writers in class, I hope you will begin to explore—and question—what it means to read and write in the Burkean parlors of your college or university.

One move that can help you get under way is to look beyond writing and reading as merely individual or private acts. That is, literacy sheds light on how individual acts of writing are connected to larger cultural, historical, social, and political systems. Paulo Freire, the Brazilian educator who spurred much of the discussion of literacy in this century, put it this way: "Reading the word" cannot be separated from "reading the world." If literacy involves reading the world, then we need to look beyond mere individual competence in encoding and decoding texts. Far from being a merely personal matter, literacy involves cultural contexts. These cultural contexts are often multiple and can overlap or even become fraught with tensions.

One such context is the culture of the university itself. By familiarizing students with academic discourse, professors seek to help students understand and participate in the conversations that shape the university. The goal here is to "learn the language" and master the secret handshake of this community. Yet the term *academic literacy* remains highly contested even inside the ivory tower. How broadly or narrowly can or should one define academic writing? Can a focus on academic writing draw on your own experiences beyond the academy and on other avenues for literacy development, such as civic discourse or home and community discourse? How can one accommodate disciplinary differences in academic writing? And does an interest in socializing you to academic literacy amount at some point to exerting undue influence on or authority over you?

Asking such questions requires not just literacy in the usual sense but a "critical literacy," one that helps you become aware of how authority and power work in and through language. Literacy is inherently tied to membership and belonging, with all their implications regarding exclusion and access. To be critical of the heated discussions in Burke's parlor, one still has to get inside the door and join the conversation.

Traditional literacy models all too often assume a print culture—the culture of the book—that is seen in isolation from broader and alternative experiences with literacy. Recent advances in electronic communication, for example, raise a host of questions about how the supposed primacy of the written word is mediated by, or at times supplanted by, multimedia environments. Computers and the Web have changed in some fundamental ways how we read, write, and circulate the written word—and how such words interact with the world of images. We need today a "cyberliteracy" that encourages critical reflection on the role of technology in literacy, just as that same critical reflection is needed in discussions of traditional print literacy.

In your own writing class, and in other classes across campus, you will find invoked, directly or perhaps subtly, one or more of these competing and contested definitions of *literacy*. This book and especially your own literate activities in this and other courses offer an opportunity to question those definitions yourself. Whatever consequences literacy brings will be the result of the social practices with which it is associated. Those social practices have to do with the nitty gritty of your own situated writing, reading, and learning experiences. In short, *what literacy does to you depends on what you do with literacy*. That is the challenge afforded in and through this book.

For Writing and Discussion

During the course of one day, inventory your own literacy practices. In other words, create a "literacy log." What do you count as literacy, and what do others seem to value? What various (and perhaps competing) definitions of *literacy* are implied in your log?

Community

Let's slip once again into Burke's parlor. The heated discussion that goes on in the parlor can help us distinguish several elements of that context. We have, of course, the speakers or writers. And once we have caught the tenor of the arguments in play, we can "put in [our] oar" and join that discussion. We also have an audience: those to whom the speakers address their comments. As the conversation evolves, they will, in turn, take up their own roles as speakers. And we have the forum itself, the parlor, the place or context for this discussion. Several general terms have been used to describe this constellation of elements: speech community, interpretive community, or, perhaps best for our purposes, *discourse community*. By that term we mean the site or social group that is shaped and defined by shared assumptions about communicative practices such as speaking or writing. The boundaries and character of that site or group are set by those communicative practices, along with the shared norms and values of its members.

Discourse communities are not static. Recall that at some point every participant in Burke's parlor slips in and slips out. But the conversation continues — and evolves. The norms or ground rules for that discussion are not set once and for all but take shape in and through the conversation. Moreover, discourse communities are not exclusive. We can belong to several such communities simultaneously, and they can overlap. Discourse communities can be relatively local, such as the discourse community of your writing classroom or the English department on your campus or the corporate office down the road. In such communities, the day-to-day contact of its members helps shape shared norms of behavior and habits of thought. But discourse communities can also be much more global, as in the worldwide community of physicists who study subatomic particles. These participants may never actually meet everyone in the community, but that community is held together through a commitment to a shared intellectual enterprise and through a set of common expectations and methods. Recent advances in electronic communication make virtual communities more real by the day. The term *discourse community* reminds us that society is held together by discourse and that, in turn, discourse has a social dimension.

Implicit in all this talk about community is a warm, comforting sense of like-mindedness. Indeed, *community* is one of the very few terms that does not seem to have any negative connotations. Just think of all the instances in which this term has come up in your life: community center, campus community, community of friends, community fund-raiser, community values. The list can go on, but what is common among these phrases is a sense of homogeneity, a sense of cohesiveness, of shared values and purposes. For this reason, community is a seductive and powerful concept. Hear it mentioned and it tugs at you. And for that very reason, it is a concept that we ought to interrogate.

The discourse communities in which we participate are often invisible or transparent to us, so second nature do they become. Only when we are thrust into a new setting do such communities become opaque and puzzling. Consider the disorienting first few weeks on your college campus, for example, or that difficult course in your new academic major. Although the term *community* would have us believe that everybody is of like mind, that everybody lives in a shared community, the concept becomes a bit problematic when we notice just how many communities we participate in and how they overlap and conflict.

Because of its relatively small size, your own writing class may seem to offer your best shot at a like-minded, cohesive academic community. Or so it might seem. Look about you, and it doesn't take long for the internal tensions to emerge. You and your classmates have been thrown together in one room, or parlor, through course requirements and the luck of academic scheduling. As the term progresses, many of you will surely become friends, perhaps close friends. Even so, membership in this classroom community becomes problematic. In your classroom dealings, who is included, and who may be subtly excluded? What counts as authority and expertise in this setting? What is foregrounded in the conversation, and what are the taboos, the things you cannot speak about openly? What kind of social ethos or character is it best to adopt? Who are the insiders and the outsiders? And what are the subtle and not so subtle forms of academic and social gatekeeping? Much of your work in the writing classroom will surely call upon good-spirited collaboration, the sort of cooperation that is essential when writers share work in progress. Even so, these sorts of questions alert us to an aspect of community that is often hidden beneath the more public focus on consensus and shared norms. Community can also be a site where competing beliefs intersect and come into conflict.

Our brief reflection on community in the writing classroom can point us to some general observations about this strange academic culture in which you are trying to find your way. Whether we think of the university as one monolithic community or as a "multiversity," a group of somewhat fragmented disciplinary communities, that community is not just about subject matter. True, we often think of the university as a collection of subject-matter communities, with biology here, sociology across the way, and engineering over on the other side of campus. But beneath these tidy, received distinctions, we can begin to see how language practices define the activities of social groups, including disciplines.

As a venue for overlapping (and sometimes competing) language practices, the university is really a stage for various styles of interacting with questions, claims, and evidence. It offers a kaleidoscope of manifestations of authority and expertise, each manifestation dependent on specific traditions or ways of knowing. Knowledge appears less and less to be a given, something you merely consume. Linguistic formations drive and direct the organization and production of knowledge. Seen in this light, your college education shouldn't end with mastering the facts in this or that course. Your college education is just as much about figuring out Burke's parlor, about knowing how to join the heated conversations themselves. Knowledge emerges as something composed—something that you yourself can and must compose.

As you try to orient yourself to this new setting, you may face pressure (from the institution, from your instructors, and perhaps from your parents or peers) to take up and make your own the voice of the academy. You want to talk the talk but not if it becomes an unnatural act of ventriloquism. You want to appropriate new ways of writing and thinking but without becoming appropriated by the university. The challenge is how to find new aspects of yourself without losing yourself—to try on new voices without losing your voice.

This book offers a way to negotiate these competing claims as you enter the Burkean parlor that is the university. In the chapters that follow, you will read and write about the very community you find yourself in, with all its contradictions and tensions. (And if you haven't noticed yet, it can be a very strange community.) In a sense, you will explore this community as if you were an ethnographer trying to figure out the culture on some South Seas island. With this critical and purposeful awareness of community, and of the ways literate practices shape community, this book and your writing course can also serve as an introduction to college learning. Welcome to University 101.

For Writing and Discussion

Team up with one or two other members of your writing class and exchange your perceptions about what makes a community in this and other classes. How and why might your perceptions of community differ from those of your classmates? Explore both the "seams" and the "ruptures" that lie along the borders between, and even within, communities.

Inquiry

At heart, inquiry is a process of asking questions and trying out answers. The "heated conversations" in the Burkean parlor might first give the impression that participants are *having* arguments. But to be true to the process of inquiry, they must be *making* arguments—that is, crafting both questions and answers in ways that have us test and revise our ideas. If, in the spirit of Burke's parlor, we might see the university as a house of argument, inquiry lies at its center. For this very reason, surely all of your professors will exhort you to think critically. Writing instructors especially will press you at each turn, for the great virtue of writing is that it makes thinking visible.

If critical thinking is the capacity to see relationships methodically, it is little wonder that teachers have sought a way to teach that kind of seeing. For some years, the focus was on developing critical thinking through skills that could be objectified, codified, and easily taught. Yet a series of "steps" or measurable subskills had the effect of making critical thinking into a mechanical calculus. It also translated critical thinking into the pursuit of "true" knowledge, of stable if not eternal truths that remain unsullied by the uncertainty around us. If mention of critical thinking or inquiry makes your eyes glaze over, you are experiencing firsthand the legacy of making thinking into some abstract skill, remote from your immediate writing, reading, and learning, remote from your daily life, your communities, your language.

Composing Knowledge invites you, by contrast, to ground inquiry in literacy and community. Your own knowledge is "composed" through language and through the conversations that shape and maintain your communities. These conversations often have to do not with absolute truth or verifiable fact but with knowledge that is to some degree contingent, uncertain, rooted in particular contexts and in the transactions we have with others. Knowledge becomes something that is not "out there" in the material and social world, just as it is not "in here" in the personal or private world of the individual. It emerges only through the interactions among material, social, and personal worlds. The vehicle for that interaction is rhetoric, the available means of persuasion that we find as we converse in and among communities.

Especially when linked to inquiry, such conversations should not be viewed as a "shouting match" or a "debate" whose purpose is to "win" by "pounding the opposition into the ground." These characterizations have in common a rather simplistic confrontational understanding of argument. That's not to say that argument doesn't involve some degree of conflict or the presence of a skeptical audience. Yet if the university is a house of argument, we should argue about questions at issue in ways that offer the best possible response to shared concerns, with reasons that will prompt our audience to consider, accept, and act on our claims. In this sense, argument has an inherently social dimension, one grounded in belief and assent. Claims are not merely *claims that* something is so but rather *claims on* us and on our fellow citizens to believe that something is so.

To garner that belief, that assent, we had best not be too hasty to write from preconceived positions. If writing is an avenue for making thinking visible, accessible, and revisable, we should not just believe and defend but also ask and inquire. If our work in the university is about reaching conclusions, we need to make and defend those conclusions in ways that permit us, throughout, to test and revise them. We also need to make them in ways that speak to the communities (disciplinary and otherwise) in which we find ourselves. Your education in college consists not just of the facts you learn about certain subjects but also of the conversations you join. That is, your education is not just topical; it is also rhetorical.

Conversations, however, are inherently unstable and uncertain, making inquiry a risky business. It's not so much that you may be proven wrong (although that possibility is always there). Rather, it's that you—and your positions—must certainly grow and evolve. The test of true inquiry is that it doesn't stop, just as the heated conversations in Burke's parlor precede us and continue long after we are gone. Inquiry grounded in literacy and community, in language and conversation, can meet this test. After all, as Burke's parlor suggests, good argument and good inquiry have all the virtues of good conversation.

Composing Knowledge seeks to support your conversations by having you explore your own situated writing, reading, and learning experiences. The readings in the chapters, and the fieldwork they can launch, are offered as provocations and opportunities.

For Writing and Discussion

At the opening of every term, professors usually offer some statements about the importance of inquiry, critical thinking, or argument in their courses. Catalog a few of these statements—garnered from classroom lectures or conversations, assignment sheets, and syllabi—and share them with your classmates. What commonalities do you detect? To what extent do expectations differ among the disciplines?

Reading the Conversation

To enter and take an active role in Burke's parlor, or in the conversations on your campus and in your discipline, you'll need to figure out the implicit, unstated rules for how people go about talking and arguing. In college, as in the professional world, much of this conversation occurs in and through written texts. Although there are surely general patterns or guidelines to academic conversations, you'll need to alert yourself to the subtle but telling differences between how conversation partners handle themselves in different contexts or disciplinary spaces. Beyond the obvious differences in topic, conversations in the science parlor proceed in a slightly different way than those in the humanities parlor. All the more reason, then, that you read the conversation before you step into it. "Reading the conversation" means reading texts in what might be new and unfamiliar ways.

As you enter college or your particular major, you already have a long and rich reading life behind you. What's more, you are already familiar with various kinds of reading. There's beach reading, of course, where you delight in the page-turner. And you have also become well practiced in what we might call sponge reading: soaking up as much information as you can prior to a test. You've become adept at focused reading, as when you study a bus schedule for the exact information you need. And of course you have often skimmed reading material, as when you flip through a magazine to find an article that interests you.

Yet for all of the variety in your reading habits, they tend to focus on using or consuming texts. The academic conversations you are now entering into require something more: savvy reading, rhetorical reading. You'll need to read texts *as* conversations, noting not just what is being said but also how and why the conversation proceeds as it does.

Savvy Reading, Rhetorical Reading

Academic reading distinguishes itself not only by the sheer volume and difficulty of the texts but also by the expectations that accompany reading tasks and assignments. You've braced yourself for a lot of reading, and difficult reading it will be, but what may be unexpected is that you'll need to read in new and different ways.

Nearly all of the reading you do for research and for course work requires that you work simultaneously at two levels. On one level, the level you are probably most familiar with, you'll need to read for content. We can think of this kind of knowledge as *conceptual knowledge*. Here, your focus is on understanding terms, concepts, and formulas—the body of knowledge itself. This kind of reading focuses on the mastery of domain content, on the facts of the discipline. Most introductory textbooks for a discipline work primarily at this level.

But a good deal of academic reading also requires you to work at a second level. Here, your focus is not only on the body of knowledge but also on how bodies of knowers—people in that discipline—use this body of knowledge to pose new questions or to apply their expertise to new problems. We might think of this second kind of knowledge as *procedural knowledge*. Reading at this second level helps you to understand disciplinary "ways of knowing"—how people in a disciplinary community wrap their minds around problems. You are not only learning *what* biologists or sociologists know but also *how* biologists or sociologists think—not just *what* experts say in texts but *how* experts do their work in and through texts and *why* they construct their texts as they do. To become a savvy academic reader means reading rhetorically, with an eye to purpose and persuasion. It means reading not just for the "what" but also for the "how" and the "why." It means reading in two dimensions at once.

To enter Burke's parlor as a fully participating member, you need to know the conversational and textual "moves." The best way to become attuned to those moves and to begin to make them your own is to understand reading as a conversation—a conversation that you will join. Although the mute and static words on the printed page might first give you quite a different impression, reading is in fact a layered and dynamic exchange.

The first and most immediate layer lies in your interaction with the text itself. It's tempting to presume that the process of reading black marks on a white page is entirely passive or that it is a one-way process of decoding. But even as you seem to be consuming or devouring a text, you are also constructing a mental model of the text and its meaning. We tend to think of composing a text as something that the author does, but as a reader you are also sharing in that act of composition. In reading a text, you are composing a reading *of* the text. You are bringing your understanding and contextual awareness to the text in order to construct its meaning. Among the many joys of reading is that the words on the page may prompt you to make private associations, based on your own individual experiences. However, as a rhetorical reader, you must focus, first and foremost, on the public meaning of a text — a meaning that must be accessible to and shared by many readers, based on the text you have in common. Even as you compose a reading of the text, you need to be able to test and defend that reading within and before a community of readers.

What also makes reading such a layered and dynamic exchange is that the text you have in front of you is the result of the author's choices. Those choices are driven by the author's purposes and are shaped by the rhetorical context in which he or she writes. To read a text is, then, to read the rhetorical context in which the text was first written and read. As you compose your reading of a text, you'll need to understand and respect the potential difference between the author's purposes for writing and your purposes for reading. When you read a text, you find yourself in and responding to a rhetorical situation that may not be identical to the one in which the author wrote. This double focus on the author's situation and your own situation is part of what makes academic reading both challenging and engaging.

A third layer in the dynamic exchange has to do with the text's place in a larger conversation of texts. The author's voice is invariably calling upon, engaging, and responding to a variety of voices. Although words on a page may give the impression of a monologue, reading in a savvy, rhetorical fashion means picking up on the various clues about the hidden conversation that is going on. These clues can be found in the way a text may quote or reference other authors or previous works or even in the way a text may make the name set forth in its articles of incorporation. Clients often abbreviate their corporate names or make mistakes in the punctuation of their corporate names. Because the certificate of registration will issue in the name of the applicant as set forth in the application, errors in an owner's name will result in errors in the certificate of registration. Therefore, the secretary of state in the state in which the corporation was incorporated may need to be contacted to verify the precise spelling and punctuation of the corporate name.

If the application is a person or business that conducts business under a fictitious business name, for example, "Sam Smith, doing business as 'Sam's Cheesecake Factory,'" the application should include the assumed name.

If the applicant is a partnership, for example, "Balboa Gardens Partnership," the application should be made by the partnership itself and should identify the state in which the partnership was organized.

Identifying an applicant as a "company" will result in rejection of an application because the term *company* does not have a specific meaning; the applicant must be expressly identified as a corporation, a partnership, a joint venture, a limited liability company, and so forth.

A trademark or service mark application is usually filed in the name of one party. Historically, the PTO has been reluctant to accept applications by joint applicants because ownership by more than one party seems to be contrary to the function of a trademark to identify a single commercial source. Although an application by joint applicants is acceptable in some instances, for example, by a husband and wife who share joint ownership of a mark, an examining attorney at the PTO will carefully scrutinize applications by joint applicants to ensure that both parties own the mark in common. A joint venture or a partnership cannot be joint applicants. A joint venture or a partnership is a single business applicant that owns a mark.

The application must specify the applicant's citizenship. For an individual, it is sufficient to state that the applicant is a citizen of the United States, France, or some other country. For a corporation or other business entity, the state or country of organization must be identified. Thus, a statement that the applicant is "ABC Inc., a corporation organized under the laws of the State of California" is acceptable.

The written application must provide the address of the applicant, including the zip code number. An individual may identify a residence or business address. Corporations and other business entities should set forth their business addresses.

Identification of Goods or Services

The application must identify the goods and/or services offered or to be offered under the mark that is the subject of the application. Careful consideration must be given to drafting this part of the application. Goods and services are categorized by the PTO into forty-five separate classes, called **International Classes** because many other nations use this same classification system established by WIPO. Until 1973, the PTO used a different classification scheme, called the United States Classification Scheme. Each class requires a filing fee of $335. Thus, an application for the mark RALPH LAUREN® to be used in connection with paint in International Class (I.C.) 2, cosmetics in I.C. 3, stationery in I.C. 16, beverage glasses in I.C. 21, and clothing in I.C. 25, for a total of five classes, would require a filing fee of $1,675. A registered mark only receives protection for those classes in which it is registered. Thus, if in an effort to save $335, the application for the RALPH LAUREN mark does not include beverage glasses in I.C. 21, there will be no registration for the mark for those goods. Preparing the application requires careful analysis of all of the goods/services for which subtle allusions to history or culture. A rhetorical reading means appreciating a text's place in and use of a web of texts. Given your many years of schooling, you may be accustomed to thinking of references in a text as an author's way of signaling his or her debt and thus of avoiding plagiarism. But that is only part of the complex ways references to texts and authors are deployed. Writers cite other authors to convince us that their reading is broad and current; they signal alliances and disagreements; they establish the problem or identify the research gap they are filling; they frame issues and contending positions; they engage skeptical questions and counterarguments; and they marshal support and credibility for their own position. Savvy reading enables you to understand how authors make rhetorical use of this larger web of texts.

Reading for the conversation has its real payoff in preparing you to join that conversation—to extend it, disagree with it, or take it in new directions. Reading becomes a prelude to and an invitation for your own writing. Having paid attention to the rhetoric of reading, you are now in a much better position to write in rhetorically effective ways for other readers. Your own purposes, and the rhetorical situation in which you write, may well be quite different from those of the authors whom you have read. But your reflection on your own reading process and on the nature of the conversation you are joining will surely make your contributions all the more valuable.

For Writing and Discussion

Working in small groups, discuss your prior reading life and the training (or lack of training) you have had in academic reading. What misconceptions, old habits, fears, or worries seem to plague your reading life in college?

Dialogue, Argument, Collaboration

To develop and apply specific strategies for reading rhetorically, let's consider in some detail how you might approach one particular text. Deborah Tannen's short article "Agonism in the Academy: Surviving Higher Learning's Argument Culture" provides an interesting opportunity, in that the author is discussing her views on the kinds of conversations students and faculty have in academic settings. So, not only will we be practicing how to read Tannen's text as a kind of conversation, but we will also be considering Tannen's views on academic conversations.

It's tempting to start reading by . . . well, starting to read the text's first paragraph. But in the very first moments when we come upon and enter a text, we are making crucial—if sometimes unconscious—decisions about our reading strategies. The more we can become conscious of and reflect on these first moments, the more likely it is that we can become savvy rhetorical readers. Five strategies are crucial in these early moments.

DEVELOP A CONTEXT FOR YOUR READING BY LOOKING FOR TEXTUAL CUES. Savvy readers don't dive into their reading without first surveying the rhetorical landscape. Where was the article published, and when? Tannen's piece first appeared in March of 2000 in the *Chronicle of Higher Education*, a weekly newspaper whose audience is college faculty and administrators. Who is the author? With a quick glance you should try to identify who the author is (Deborah Tannen) and to locate any information about the author (the brief note at the end of the article identifies her as a professor at Georgetown University and the author of a book titled *The Argument Culture*). The most important cue is perhaps the article's title. Because titles often signal the focus or even the central claim of a text, you can use titles to help shape your reading process and to make early predictions about the text's meaning. In the case of Tannen's article, you know that she will address "argument culture" and that it is something one must "survive." Even at this early stage, before reading that first paragraph, you can begin developing questions that can guide your inquiry. What, for example, does *agonism* mean? By beginning to survey the rhetorical context of the text, you are able to call upon and better utilize whatever background or prior knowledge you may have.

A second strategy follows from the first. Having glanced at the text and considered where it was published, you already have some important clues about the kind of text it is—its *genre*—and thus the general kind of reading required.

LINK YOUR READING STRATEGY TO THE GENRE OF THE TEXT. Although we tend to think of genre as the outward appearance of a text (poems and novels and academic articles do look a bit different, after all), genre is actually an important indicator of how readers and writers carry on their conversations. Before diving in to read sentence after sentence, you'll want to consider how the structure and the style of the piece, and what use it makes of evidence or citations, offer guidance on ways the selection is best read. For example, Tannen's article is relatively short and offers no footnotes or bibliography. It was published in a newspaper about higher education that often presents opinion pieces or short, nontechnical articles that capture the leading ideas of a longer work or book. By understanding its genre, you can adapt your reading strategies appropriately. In this case, you can expect that the article will try to interest and address a fairly wide academic audience with arguments drawn from a more detailed study. In your college and professional career, you will encounter any number of different textual genres, from literary analysis to scientific research articles, each with its own conventions, its own distinctive conversational handshake.

How, then, should you read Tannen's article? It all depends on your immediate purpose in reading. And thus we come to a third strategy.

UNDERSTAND AND ADAPT YOUR READING STRATEGY IN LIGHT OF YOUR OWN CHANGING PURPOSES. Your purposes and goals for reading any text can vary, from a quick skim to determine your interest in reading further to a moderately paced reading to understand the gist of the argument to a detailed study of the text in preparation for your writing. Because no one style of reading can meet very different goals, you'll want to become accustomed to rereading material. Rereading doesn't mean that you somehow didn't "get" the article. It means that what you did get on a first reading can now prepare you to read again in a somewhat new fashion, with different and more specific goals and questions in mind. Savvy readers are readers who adapt.

Because the words on the page are your crucial resource for composing a reading of the text, it's important to stay close to those words. Here is a further strategy.

WORK WITH (AND ON) THE PAGE BY ANNOTATING YOUR TEXT. Annotating a text with your notes, comments, and queries is a way to make the text your own, to talk back to the text even as it talks to you. For a text to make an impression on us, it is often helpful to make an impression (literally) on the text. (If you are working from a library copy, you will of course need to keep the text clean and record your annotations in a reading notebook.) Annotations are a way to focus your attention, to probe and question, and to record the evolution of your reading of the text over time. You'll need to adopt your own annotation style, but be sure that your annotations are helpful and informative for future readings. Simple underlining, especially of whole passages, may not tell you enough when you return to the text. Likewise, broad swatches of text highlighted in some neon color may look impressive but may do little to enlighten you about the text or your own response to it. When annotating, focus on some of the following: key or unfamiliar terms and concepts, formulations of the issue, statements of purpose, indications about the organization or structure of the text or its line of reasoning, connections among ideas, and, of course, questions about or objections to the author's views.

In general, annotations, like the reading process itself, should reflect the two basic movements or rhythms of any conversation: We both listen and respond.

BALANCE SYMPATHETIC LISTENING TO THE TEXT WITH SKEPTICAL QUESTIONING OF THE TEXT. Annotations can help you read both with and against the grain of the text. They can prompt you to listen attentively as you seek to understand the text. In turn, annotations can help you interrogate the text as you develop avenues for responding to it. You'll need to balance both approaches, and each is enriched by the other. Only by listening can you ask more probing questions. And those very questions can help send you back to the text for a closer and more informed reading of what the author is saying. Savvy, rhetorical reading has all of the give-and-take qualities of good conversation.

To illustrate these strategies for listening and responding, I have annotated Tannen's article. It's important to remember that annotations aren't all made on a first reading. In fact, most evolve from continued rereading and the ongoing give and take of listening and responding.

> **For Writing and Discussion**
> Locate your reading notes or annotations for an article you read in another course from a previous semester or from high school. Coming back to these annotations, what do you find to be helpful or unhelpful about them? What would you like to change or adapt as you refine how you interact with texts on the page?

Agonism in the Academy: Surviving Higher Learning's Argument Culture

Key term — look this up.

Deborah Tannen

A reading group that I belong to, composed of professors, recently discussed a memoir by an academic. I came to the group's meeting full of anticipation, eager to examine the insights I'd gained from the book and to be enlightened by those that had intrigued my fellow group members. As the meeting began, one member announced that she hadn't read the book; four, including me, said they'd read and enjoyed it; and one said she hadn't liked it because she does not like academic memoirs. She energetically criticized the book. "It's written in two voices," she said, "and the voices don't interrogate each other."

Quickly, two other members joined her critique, their point of view becoming a chorus. They sounded smarter, seeing faults that the rest of us had missed, making us look naive. We credulous three tried in vain to get the group talking about what we had found interesting or important in the book, but our suggestions were dull compared to the game of critique.

I know how this feels.

Effective phrase

I left the meeting disappointed because I had learned nothing new about the book or its subject. All I had learned about was the acumen of the critics. I was especially struck by the fact that one of the most talkative and influential critics was the member who had

Engaging story. What's its rhetorical function?

not read the book. Her unfamiliarity with the work had not hindered her, because the critics had focused more on what they saw as faults of the genre than on faults of the particular book.

The turn that the discussion had taken reminded me of the subject of my most recent book, *The Argument Culture*. The phenomenon I'd observed at the book-group meeting was an example of what the cultural linguist Walter Ong calls "agonism," which he defines in *Fighting for Life* as "programmed contentiousness" or "ceremonial combat." Agonism does not refer to disagreement, conflict, or vigorous dispute. It refers to ritualized opposition—for instance, a debate in which the contestants are assigned opposing positions and one party wins, rather than an argument that arises naturally when two parties disagree.

Key term/ concept

Can't debate be helpful and instructive?

Need more on naturally; arising argument; Tannen doesn't follow up on this.

In *The Argument Culture*, I explored the role and effects of agonism in three domains of public discourse: journalism, politics, and the law. But the domain in which I first identified the phenomenon and began thinking about it is the academic world. I remain convinced that agonism is endemic in academe—and bad for it.

Sounds like this could be Tannen's claim—check out "endemic."

The way we train our students, conduct our classes and our research, and exchange ideas at meetings and in print are all driven by our ideological assumption that intellectual inquiry is a metaphorical battle. Following from that is a second assumption, that the best way to demonstrate intellectual prowess is to criticize, find fault, and attack.

Many aspects of our academic lives can be described as agonistic. For example, in our scholarly papers, most of us follow a conventional framework that requires us to position our work in opposition to someone else's, which we prove wrong. The framework tempts—almost requires—us to oversimplify or even misrepresent others' positions; cite the weakest example to make a generally reasonable work appear less so; and ignore facts that support others' views, citing only evidence that supports our own positions.

General road map for Tannen's article?

The way we train our students frequently reflects the battle metaphor as well. We assign scholarly work for them to read, then invite them to tear it apart. That is helpful to an extent, but it often means that they don't learn to do the harder work of integrating ideas, or of considering the work's historical and disciplinary context. Moreover, it fosters in students a stance of arrogance and narrow-mindedness, qualities that do not serve the fundamental goals of education.

Yes, I've seen this happen. Well put!

In the classroom, if students are engaged in heated debate, we believe that education is taking place. But in a 1993 article in *The*

History Teacher, Patricia Rosof, who teaches at Hunter College High School in New York City, advises us to look more closely at what's really happening. If we do, she says, we will probably find that only a few students are participating; some other students may be paying attention, but many may be turned off. Furthermore, the students who are arguing generally simplify the points they are making or disputing. To win the argument, they ignore complexity and nuance. They refuse to concede a point raised by their opponents, even if they can see that it is valid, because such a concession would weaken their position. Nobody tries to synthesize the various views, because that would look indecisive, or weak.

If the class engages in discussion rather than debate—adding such intellectual activities as exploring ideas, uncovering nuances, comparing and contrasting different interpretations of a work—more students take part, and more of them gain a deeper, and more accurate, understanding of the material. Most important, the students learn a stance of respect and open-minded inquiry.

Academic rewards—good grades and good jobs—typically go to students and scholars who learn to tear down others' work, not to those who learn to build on the work of their colleagues. In *The Argument Culture*, I cited a study in which communications researchers Karen Tracy and Sheryl Baratz examined weekly colloquia attended by faculty members and graduate students at a large university. As the authors reported in a 1993 article in *Communication Monographs*, although most people said the purpose of the colloquia was to "trade ideas" and "learn things," faculty members in fact were judging the students' competence based on their participation in the colloquia. And the professors didn't admire students who asked "a nice little supportive question," as one put it —they valued "tough and challenging questions."

One problem with the agonistic culture of graduate training is that potential scholars who are not comfortable with that kind of interaction are likely to drop out. As a result, many talented and creative minds are lost to academe. And, with fewer colleagues who prefer different approaches, those who remain are more likely to egg each other on to even greater adversarial heights. Some scholars who do stay in academe are reluctant to present their work at conferences or submit it for publication because of their reluctance to take part in adversarial discourse. The cumulative effect is that nearly everyone feels vulnerable and defensive, and thus less willing to suggest new ideas, offer new perspectives, or question received wisdom.

Marginal notes:

I've had this experience, but is Tannen overgeneralizing? Isn't Tannen being agonistic in her own attack on agonism? She offers few concessions.

Is debate all that bad? I've learned a lot from debate experiences.

My best classes use inquiry. But I've sat through really lame discussions too. Much depends on the teacher.

Can't challenging questions also play a helpful and supportive role?

Yes. Self-selection. Cultures include & exclude people.

But ideas do need to be tested. And American culture is competitive.

Although scholarly attacks are ritual—prescribed by the conventions of academe—the emotions propelling them can be real. Jane Tompkins, a literary critic who has written about the genre of the western in modern fiction and film, has compared scholarly exchanges to shootouts. In a 1988 article in the *Georgia Review*, she noted that her own career took off when she published an essay that "began with a frontal assault on another woman scholar. When I wrote it I felt the way the hero does in a western. Not only had this critic argued *a, b,* and *c,* she had held *x, y,* and *z!* It was a clear case of outrageous provocation." Because her opponent was established and she was not, Tompkins felt "justified in hitting her with everything I had."

Note use of war/battle metaphors.

Later in her career, as she listened to a speaker at a conference demolish another scholar's work, she felt that she was witnessing "a ritual execution of some sort, something halfway between a bullfight, where the crowd admires the skill of the matador and enjoys his triumph over the bull, and a public burning, where the crowd witnesses the just punishment of a criminal. For the academic experience combined the elements of admiration, bloodlust, and moral self-congratulation."

Again, concepts of ritual and game.

At a deeper level, the conceptual metaphor of intellectual argument as a battle leads us to divide researchers into warring camps. Just about any field can provide examples. For instance, many disciplines are affected—and disfigured—by a stubborn nature/nurture dichotomy, although both biology and culture obviously influence all of us. Such divisiveness encourages both students and scholars to fight about others' work rather than trying to understand it. And those whose work is misrepresented end up using creative energy to defend their past work—energy that they could use more productively in other ways.

Interesting. Effects go beyond individuals to whole disciplines.

Agonism has still another serious effect: It is one of the reasons scholars have a hard time getting policymakers to pay attention to their research. Policymakers who come across relevant academic research immediately encounter opposing research. Lacking the expertise to figure out who's right, they typically conclude that they cannot look to academe for guidance.

Yes. Academics seem never to agree. True of global-warming debate?

Our agonistic ideology seems so deeply embedded in academe that one might wonder what alternatives we have. In *Embracing Contraries*, the English professor Peter Elbow calls the ways we approach ideas a "doubting game"—a method for sniffing out faults. What we need, he says, is an additional approach—a "believing game," to sniff out strengths. The two games would complement

Note that both games needed.

each other. Although we wouldn't end up agreeing with all the authors we read, by suspending disbelief we would be more likely to learn something from them.

In my view, we need new metaphors through which to think about our academic enterprise, or to conceptualize intellectual interchange. We could learn much more if we thought of theories not as static structures to be shot down or falsified, but as sets of understandings to be questioned and reshaped. The sociologist Kerry Daly, in the introduction to his book *Families and Time*, suggests that "theories should be treated like bread dough that rises with a synergetic mix of ingredients only to be pounded down with the addition of new ingredients and human energy."

In the realm of teaching, Don McCormick and Michael Kahn, in a 1982 article in *Exchange: The Organizational Behavior Teaching Journal*, suggest that critical thinking can be taught better if we use the metaphor of a barn raising, instead of that of a boxing match. We should think of "a group of builders constructing a building, or a group of artists fabricating a creation together."

McCormick and Kahn make another point that, as I wrote in *The Argument Culture*, I came to believe is the most crucial and damaging aspect of the culture of agonism. Living, working, and thinking in ways shaped by the battle metaphor produces an atmosphere of animosity that poisons our relations with each other at the same time that it corrupts the integrity of our research. Not only is the agonistic culture of academe not the best path to truth and knowledge, but it also is corrosive to the human spirit.

After my reading group had discussed the academic memoir, I expressed my frustration to a group member. She commented, "It turns out that book wasn't the best example of the genre."

"But we didn't read an example of a genre," I protested. "We read a book by a person."

Refocusing our attention in that way is the greatest gain in store if we can move beyond critique in its narrow sense. We would learn more from each other, be heard more clearly by others, attract more varied talents to the scholarly life, and restore a measure of humanity to ourselves, our endeavor, and the academic world we inhabit.

Deborah Tannen is a university professor at Georgetown University. Her most recent book is The Argument Culture *(Random House, 1998; Ballantine paperback, 1999).*

Marginal annotations:

Suspend— when and for how long? Don't we need doubt?

Transition— focus now on metaphors.

Nice metaphor!

Another effective metaphor. What do these new metaphors have in common?

Well put. But is all of academe agonistic in bad ways? Are all disciplines the same? Don't sciences combine debate with collaboration and teamwork?

Return to opening story. Story serves as bookends for article.

Effective summary statement.

Look up Tannen on Georgetown Website for more info.

Rhetorical Deep Structure

As you work with the text and experience its tug and pull through your own listening and questioning, you are doing more than reading word for word. Looking beyond the surface features of the text, you are locating and assessing what we might think of as the text's "rhetorical deep structure." Your annotations can help you uncover this deep structure, as can developing a rhetorical outline of the text or writing a brief summary.

To join the conversation that this text has initiated for you, you'll need to look beyond the flow of words and the array of topics covered to find core arguments and underlying reasoning. Here are some of the issues or concerns that you'll want to be alert to. Use the following questions as an informal checklist that can help develop more depth and nuance in your reading process.

WHAT IS THE QUESTION AT ISSUE? WHAT PROBLEM IS BEING ADDRESSED? Although most textbooks do a good job of hiding from your view the open issues that drive current work in a particular discipline, much of the actual writing and reading that gets done in the university is really about finding, framing, and pursuing questions at issue. Review your reading text to see how the author states or frames the question at issue. What kind of question is it? Does it concern issues of definition or questions about consequences and results? Or do the questions concern issues of value or issues of policy and action? Note that the question at issue may be implied. For example, Deborah Tannen does not pose her question at issue in blunt or direct terms, but as you read and reread her article, it becomes clear that the question or problem that motivates her is the presumption that agonism is the appropriate and preferred approach to teaching, learning, and scholarship. Her article seeks to question that presumption.

WHO IS THE AUDIENCE? HOW DOES THE TEXT CONSTRUCT OR POSITION ITS AUDIENCE? WHAT KIND OF CONVERSATION IS BEING PRESUMED BY THE TEXT? Questions at issue are rarely abstract and disembodied. Depending on how they are framed, questions at issue become questions for someone. In some of your reading, you'll find that the author addresses a very specific audience. In other texts, you may find that the audience is a bit more general. You should also be alert that some texts will have both a primary and a secondary audience. Rarely, however, will the audience simply be "the general reader." Consider where or by what means the text has been published, and you'll quickly get a handle on matters of audience. Given that it was published in the *Chronicle of Higher Education*, Tannen's article, for example, speaks to college faculty and administrators but has a broader secondary audience that can include students and all those interested in education. In the texts that you read, ask yourself if you are an insider or an outsider to the community addressed by the text. Beyond identifying who the audience is, you'll want to consider how the text positions or characterizes the audience. Is the audience assumed to be sympathetic, hostile, uncommitted, or skeptical? How is the audience expected to react, or what action does the text presume the audience should take? What is the audience's role in the conversation, and what use will it make of the text? Tannen, for example, encourages her audience to think more broadly about teaching and learning and to question the presumed virtues of agonism. Her examples and stories are intended to establish a common bond of experience with her audience.

WHAT IS THE AUTHOR'S PURPOSE? Authors have aims that they set for themselves, and those aims are forged out of the relationship that authors have to the subject matter and the audience. Some aims can be pursued through several different genres, other aims lend themselves to certain kinds of genres. Some purposes can overlap, and some texts can have multiple purposes, each one building or laying the foundation for the next. Here are some of the common purposes you will encounter in your college reading:

> expressing or reflecting
> inquiring or exploring
> explaining or informing
> analyzing or interpreting
> arguing, deliberating, or taking a stand
> evaluating, judging, or critiquing
> proposing solutions
> finding common ground or consensus building

Tannen's article focuses on evaluating, judging, or critiquing, even as it may pursue other purposes in specific paragraphs to help support her critique and even as she touches on possible solutions.

WHAT IS THE AUTHOR'S CLAIM OR THESIS? WHAT LINE OF REASONING DOES THE AUTHOR PURSUE? DOES THE AUTHOR ENGAGE SKEPTICAL QUESTIONS? If much of the work in the university centers on finding, framing, and pursuing questions at issue, then it follows that many of the texts will offer and support answers to such questions. Some of the texts you will read in college will be very explicit about the claim being made; others will only offer such a claim implicitly; and still others, depending on the author's purpose, will not stake the mark will be used to ensure that the mark receives all the protection it needs. A detailed listing of the international classes with numerous examples is found in Chapter 1400 of TMEP, available on the PTO's web site. (See Exhibit 4–1 for a list of the international classes and explanation of the goods/services in each class.)

EXHIBIT 4–1
List of International Classes

International Class	Goods/Services	Explanatory Note
Goods		
1	Chemicals	Includes chemicals used in industry, science, photography, manures, adhesives used in industry
2	Paints	Includes paints, varnishes, lacquers, raw natural resins
3	Cosmetics and cleaning preparations	Includes bleaching preparations and other substances for laundry use, soaps, cleaning preparations, perfumery, cosmetics, hair lotions
4	Lubricants and fuels	Includes industrial oils and greases, lubricants, candles, and wicks
5	Pharmaceuticals	Includes pharmaceuticals and other preparations for medical use, disinfectants, materials for dressings, food for babies
6	Metal goods	Common metals and their alloys, metal building materials, pipes and tubes made of metal, safes
7	Machinery	Machines and machine tools, motors and engines (except for land vehicles), agricultural implements
8	Hand tools	Hand tools, cutlery, sidearms, razors
9	Electrical and scientific apparatus	Scientific, nautical, surveying, photographic, optical apparatus and instruments, cash registers, apparatus for recording, transmission, or reproduction of sound or images, magnetic data carriers, recording discs, calculating machines, data processing equipment and computers, computer games, computer software
10	Medical apparatus	Surgical, medical, dental, and veterinary apparatus and instruments, suture materials
11	Environmental control apparatus	Apparatus for lighting, heating, steam generating, cooking, drying, refrigerating, water supply, and sanitary purposes
12	Vehicles	Vehicles, apparatus for locomotion by land, air, or water, engines for land vehicles

out one particular claim. A claim or thesis is an arguable opinion; it not only states a proposition but also makes a claim on our belief. Given that they are arguable, claims are potentially refutable (they can't be merely personal expressions of preference or self-evident statements) and thus demand explanation, support, and a consideration of potential skeptical questions or counterarguments. So, as a rhetorically savvy reader, your job is to ask what the author wishes you to believe, how the author attempts to elicit or persuade you of that belief, and what assumptions are made in the process. In much academic writing and reading, those attempts are grounded in reasoning and evidence and are pursued through lines of reasoning that build or work toward the author's conclusions. Specific disciplines, however, have differing conventions and expectations about what kinds of evidence are acceptable and how such evidence is to be collected and presented. Tannen's article claims that "agonism is endemic in academe—and bad for it." She pursues this claim through a line of reasoning that she summarizes in paragraph six, which in turn gives us some clues about the organizational structure of her article. But along with the obligation to explain herself and support her claim comes the obligation (perhaps only partially met) to consider skeptical questions about her own positions.

HOW DOES THE AUTHOR ENGAGE THE INTERESTS, EMOTIONS, VALUES, AND COMMITMENTS OF THE AUDIENCE? Although academic writing and reading place a high premium on appeals to reason and evidence, we can ill afford to overlook the ways in which texts appeal to our interests, emotions, and commitments. In many respects, such appeals can be very powerful, for they have to do with the often hidden ways in which we and others identify with certain experiences, values, and beliefs, and with certain communities and causes. In Tannen's article, she calls on stories and examples that appeal to the audience's potentially negative prior experiences with agonism. Emotionally laden terms and the careful choice of evidence tend to paint agonism in a very negative light and collaborative learning in a very positive light.

HOW DOES THE AUTHOR ESTABLISH HIS OR HER CREDIBILITY? Authors elicit our belief not only by the reasoning they offer but also by who they are and by the character that they establish for themselves on the page. Academic credentials and positions, the nature of the publication in which their work appears, and references to their own research and the work of others are among the many ways that authors win your belief. The voice of the author in the text and the degree to which the text exhibits evenhandedness and fairness all contribute to the judgments a reader invariably makes about the author—and what the author is saying. In the case of Tannen's article, we know from the note about the author that she is a professor at Georgetown University (and as it turns out a well-published and highly regarded sociolinguist). Although the *Chronicle of Higher Education* is not a place where authors publish new research, she does gain credibility by mentioning her full-length book on the subject. She also gains credibility by mentioning other well-regarded scholars (among them Walter Ong, Karen Tracy, and Peter Elbow), thereby demonstrating how her work builds on the efforts of others. Tannen demonstrates, in short, that she is active in and is advancing an ongoing conversation. But her voice and style also indicate that she is successful in reaching beyond a merely academic audience (her books are popular well beyond the classroom). She is an insider in Burke's parlor who has also developed a knack for welcoming newbies to the conversation.

WHAT WORLDVIEW OR IDEOLOGY DOES THE TEXT SUBSCRIBE TO? WHAT HAS BEEN FOREGROUNDED OR EMPHASIZED, AND WHAT HAS BEEN DE-EMPHASIZED OR OMITTED? Texts do more than present ideas; they offer a glimpse into a worldview out of which those ideas have grown. Individual ideas and beliefs are invariably part of a network or system of truth claims—what we might call an ideology. As a savvy, rhetorical reader, you will want to locate a given text within such a larger system. You can thereby gain a sense of the premises or beliefs that inform an author's view but are rarely announced or questioned themselves. You might think of worldviews or ideologies as filters that highlight some issues and concerns, while screening out others. Asking what a text neglects or omits altogether is often as important as focusing on what is written on the page. In the article on agonism, we gain insight into a set of pedagogical commitments and values that Tannen seems to have, although she may not discuss such commitments directly. For example, we can gather that her pedagogical worldview places high priority on teamwork and collaborative teaching and learning.

Two preliminary writing activities can help you build on your annotations and answer the questions that were enumerated above.

DEVELOP A RHETORICAL OUTLINE OF THE TEXT. You are surely familiar with outlines, especially as a way of organizing information prior to and during your own writing process. But a reverse outline—an outline of an already written text or draft—can help you refine both your reading and your writing skills. A rhetorical outline has two parts describing what is happening in each paragraph or section of a text. The first part describes what the author *says*. Here your focus is on identifying the content or topic of that section of text. The second part of a rhetorical outline describes what the author *does* in that section. Here your focus is on how what the author is saying does something rhetorically. Examples of *does* statements might include the following: frames the question at issue, summarizes prior research; offers his or her claim, provides evidence for an assertion, answers a skeptical question or counterargument; signposts the organization of the text, provides a transition from one section of the text to the next, and so on. A rhetorical outline can help you look beyond the content of a text so that you can uncover how the author orchestrates the conversation. This strategy can also help you as a writer, especially when you have a promising but unruly and chaotic rough draft. The *does* statements help you clarify in your own mind what you hope to accomplish at each stage in your own writing as you join and sustain a conversation.

WRITE A SUMMARY OF THE TEXT. Summaries challenge you to portray the ideas of another piece of writing in a brief text that must itself acquire shape and serve a purpose. Although summaries seem merely descriptive, they challenge even the most accomplished writers because they ask you to comprehend and render the rhetorical deep structure of what you summarize. Summaries must be fair, balanced, concise, and accurate. Most importantly, you must discern what is essential to the line of argument and how individual statements relate to the thrust and function of the whole. The rhetorical deep structure of the source text can help you shape your summary of it, as you reflect the author's question, claim, and line of reasoning in your own text. Summaries can serve as powerful aids for reading rhetorically. Moreover, because they help you identify key rhetorical issues, they can also invite you to assess texts and join the conversation. Summaries can take many forms in your academic and professional life. To be sure, a common assignment might be to write a summary or to write a summary that is followed up by a short response. But summaries also have further and varied applications. Summaries can help you write an annotated bibliography or a review of research on a particular question. You will often see summaries serve as abstracts for a published article. In the business world, an executive summary offers a nontechnical, action-oriented condensation of a long report to busy managers and executives. Promissory abstracts serve as summaries for long works still on the drawing board. Summaries most often appear not as stand-alone documents but as integral elements in your own writing. Any time you are responding to or critiquing a text, or calling on another text to further your own point, you owe it to your audience to first summarize it in a fair manner. As you stand on the shoulders of other authors and build on their research, you need to characterize their work even as you draw on it for your own rhetorical purposes.

For Writing and Discussion

Drawing on a reading in this collection, try your hand at annotating the text, answering questions about its rhetorical structure, developing a rhetorical outline, and writing a summary. These tools will serve you well in a variety of coming reading and writing assignments. Circulate copies of your summary in small groups, each of whose members have worked with the same text. Compare each other's work and discuss the challenges of writing a summary. Given that you read the same text, how similar are your summaries? What might account for the differences? What can you learn about your writing and about your reading habits by reviewing the summaries written by others in your group?

Joining the Conversation

When you enter the parlor that Kenneth Burke describes—the house of argument that is the university—you must first "read" the conversation in order to understand its ebb and flow and its conversational rules. But the larger purpose of reading the conversation is to participate, to add your voice. As Burke notes, "You listen for a while, until you decide that you have caught the tenor of the argument; then you put in your oar."

"Putting in your oar" requires that you think of yourself a bit differently than many high school and college courses may have thought of you. Other courses often position you as a consumer of what other people already know. *Composing Knowledge* and the course you may be using it in serve as an invitation to think of yourself as a writer in a community of writers and most especially as a producer of knowledge. Writing becomes an opportunity to compose knowledge both for yourself and for others. Through your own acts of reading and writing, criticism and research, you learn firsthand the ways that knowledge is composed, beliefs are formed, values are sustained, and a corner of the world is transformed. I hope you learn, above all, that your own voice can make a difference.

For your voice to make a difference, you need to establish your authority even as you work with and call on the authority of others. The texts you are reading may loom as authoritative, the authors as beyond question. But as you read closely and are drawn into conversation with the texts, you will find opportunities to make claims about the texts, to extend the conversation, and to apply insights to your own situated learning experience. You will find, in short, your own voice, and you will discover the grounds for your own authority. Such authority can be won through the manner in which you engage the text, through your ability to integrate other voices and texts into your conversation, and through your own expertise and experience. But even as you "author-ize" your own voice, you will want to keep in play and rely on the voices of others. You'll discover that the tug and pull between your voice and the voices of others, your authority and the authority of others, is part of what makes conversation productive and genuinely worthwhile.

Strategies for Engaging the Conversation

Your own contributions to an ongoing conversation don't start with a long and full-blown speech. They often start with a question, a comment, and, perhaps only in response to someone else's comment, a somewhat longer reply. It's much the same with your writing. Your formal written essays in college often find their most productive early moments in informal writing. These moments, in turn, can give you the impetus to develop more formal essays that analyze or argue with the text or that extend or apply insight you have about the text in new ways. Here are three strategies for engaging the conversation in ways that can lead you to make valuable contributions and produce work that you are especially proud of.

START WITH INFORMAL WRITING THAT CAN SPUR RHETORICAL INVENTION. Informal writing can often help you find your best ideas because it gives you permission not to censor them prematurely. What is known as "freewriting" is one such kind of informal exercise in invention. After freewriting for, let's say, ten or fifteen minutes, you can then return to the rambling text you have produced to locate issues and ideas that you can then develop in a more systematic manner. A reading log or a learning log can help you ground your response to specific moments in the text, preparing you to then develop that response into a fuller and more ambitious text. One specific kind of reading log is what is known as a double-entry notebook, in which you literally draw a line down the middle of the page as a way of connecting specific quotes or passages from the text, recorded in one column, with your responses and reflections, noted in the parallel column. Short response papers (sometimes preceded by a summary) allow you to build on informal and often private exploratory writing in a more systematic and formal way. These response papers can in turn become a prelude to a longer project.

Composing Knowledge supports your informal writing by inviting you to "reflect on your prior knowledge" at the beginning of each chapter. Each selection, in turn, poses questions for "Working with the Text" that can draw on your textual annotations and send you back into the text for a second reading with new questions and perspectives.

MAKE AND REFINE CLAIMS ABOUT THE TEXT THAT LEAD TO ANALYSIS OR ARGUMENT. Having worked closely with a text through annotations and through informal exploratory writing, you will have developed a sharper sense of the way the text is crafted and whether or not you agree or disagree with the claims made by the author. A common college writing assignment is to advance a claim about a written text because in many disciplines (literature, history, religion, and law, among them) close, critical reading of a text is a fundamental skill. Your focus will be on the rhetorical methods and strategies employed by the author; in turn, you will call upon rhetorical strategies of your own as you support the thesis or claim you are making, drawing on textual evidence and analysis. Having looked for the rhetorical deep structure of the text, you are in a good position to draft your own text that calls upon those very features: an engaging question at issue, an arguable claim, a line of reasoning that explores and supports that claim, and a willingness to engage skeptical questions that may seem to be inconvenient to the very case you are building.

Accompanying each reading in *Composing Knowledge*, you will find questions that can help you in the section "Working with the Text." These questions by no means exhaust the interesting issues you can pose about a text, but they do offer you a start and represent an invitation for you to pose—and answer—such questions on your own.

EXTEND OR APPLY THE CONVERSATION, OFTEN TO YOUR OWN SITUATED EXPERIENCES. Another common writing assignment in college calls for you to draw on texts as part of a larger conversation—one in which you take the primary role. Here the focus is on your contribution and on your ability to extend or apply the voices of others to a new issue or problem. College research papers have received a deservedly bad reputation, especially when they are produced simply to describe the arguments of others. But at heart, such assignments call on much more creative work than may seem apparent. You must read and synthesize the work of others and evaluate what contributions they might make to your own new argument, one that addresses a question you have formulated. In essence, the work of others serves as a provocation or springboard for your own ideas. You will use the voices of others to frame questions, to position yourself in the conversation, and to raise questions regarding and offer support for your own line of reasoning. As you extend or apply the work of others, you must draw on your own specialized knowledge and fieldwork. For this reason, projects that address your own lived experience or areas of expertise are especially appropriate.

Following each reading in *Composing Knowledge*, you will find questions under the heading "From Text to Field" that help you shift your focus from the text itself to questions or issues that invite you to extend or apply the conversation. At the end of each of the seven chapters in the book, you will find a large portfolio of more ambitious project ideas, "Into the Field," that can launch you into your own original work.

For Writing and Discussion

1. As you meet in small groups, reflect back on a writing opportunity in high school or college, in whatever discipline, in which you felt you most successfully engaged texts and composed knowledge. Discuss what it was in your reading and writing that helped to account for this success. How do the keys for your prior success relate to the strategies discussed here, and how might these strategies build on and refine some techniques you may already be using? How do you think you can leverage your prior successful experience and take your work to the next higher level?

2. Now that you have read and considered the annotations on Tannen's short article on "Agonism in the Academy," ask yourself what your own opinion on the matter is. Do you agree or disagree with Tannen? Is there one aspect of her argument that you'd like to consider in detail? Or would you like to extend or apply Tannen's work in light of your own learning experiences? You can work through a series of short papers that draw on the progression from informal writing to analysis and argument and on to essays that apply or extend the issues raised in her essay. Alternatively, you can focus on just one kind of academic assignment as you consider your own response to Tannen's views on the kinds of conversations we have in the academy.

Into the Field

Composing Knowledge takes seriously the proposition that you are far more than a consumer of knowledge—a role that many of your courses may unwittingly have you adopt. As a writer, you are shaping, composing, and sharing knowledge. You draw on the work of others, to be sure, but also on your own close observation and experience. Little wonder, then, that the writing projects suggested in this book place a premium on original fieldwork—fieldwork that invites you to reflect on, extend, and apply the various readings in this volume.

Why fieldwork? Issues broached in the readings come alive as you see their connection to your own situated learning experience in college. And the writing process itself becomes more relevant as you include not only library research but also close observation of your own classrooms, curricula, and campus. Fieldwork positions you not as a novice but as an expert-in-the-making. Moreover, because you bring to bear experience and observation that is situated and drawn from local contexts, you can make distinctive and original contributions to a larger, ongoing conversation.

Varieties of Fieldwork

Composing Knowledge offers fieldwork that draws on various disciplines and on the varied settings, methods, and issues that arise in your own education.

Each of the seven chapters in the book takes on a different facet of compos-ing knowledge in college.

We begin where you begin: with the challenges inherent in entering the college community and joining its many conversations. These challenges include "learning the language" (academic and otherwise) of your campus and figuring out how to "dance" with your professors as you engage with them in the classes you take. Here, fieldwork may involve a profile of the very rituals and traditions you need to learn if you are to become an insider on campus or an examination of the various texts (cartoons, announcements, and so on) that are displayed on or near the doors of your professors' offices.

The second chapter of *Composing Knowledge* invites you to consider how, through your own activities, you are inventing the university for yourself. We'll look at how classrooms, courses, and curricula are constructed and what role language and writing have in shaping the university. Fieldwork will include studying documents that you may not immediately recognize as hav-ing archival value. Syllabi, for example, can tell you a good deal not just about the course you are taking but also about how the course positions you as a student and about what kind of teaching and learning will be valued. You might also read the physical classroom as a kind of text, observing how learning spaces are designed and how they distribute authority and power. Alternatively, you may find yourself looking into historical documents that describe the evolution of any writing requirements on your campus.

In Chapter 3, you'll consider how we go about persuading each other in an academic setting. It turns out that frames of reference or the kinds of con-ceptual glasses we wear on our noses go a long way in influencing what and how we see. In turn, we'll consider how arguments occur in the contexts of communities, each of which has slightly different conventions and expecta-tions about how members talk to each other. Your fieldwork will encourage you to think about what academic research methods both include and exclude and about the metaphors we use when describing that work. You'll also consider whether the various academic disciplines on your campus con-tribute to one common academic community or fracture your campus into a series of academic fiefdoms.

Although we may be tempted at times to think of academic life in college as essentially solitary, even lonely, Chapter 4 makes the argument that col-lege requires of us a series of ongoing engagements with others. Our work is inherently social. We find ourselves collaborating at every turn and crossing a variety of cultural borders. Your fieldwork will invite you to explore the benefits—and the tensions—in such collaborations, whether in a writing class or in your particular major. You might also find yourself exploring the cultural divides on your campus and the ways in which college forces us to reflect on various borderland experiences.

Chapter 5—"(En)gendering Knowledge"—explores how the creation and communication of knowledge invariably raises issues of gender and identity. The first unit of the chapter, "Speaking of Gender," addresses issues of gender and language. The second unit, "Minding Gender," asks us to pay attention to how gender roles and concepts influence us at a very deep level, affecting our minds and emotions, even our scientific study of brains and biology. This chapter will send you into the field to study the dynamics of classroom conversation and gendered roles as captured by campus graffiti. You'll consider how histories of your academic field are gendered and assess the role of gender issues in shaping the very climate of your campus.

The sixth chapter explores the role of technology in education. Even as we focus on learning the latest technology, we all too easily forget just how much influence technology has as we learn about and encounter the world. By loosening the bonds of time and place, technology lets us rethink our notions of community. Likewise, we must be mindful that technology can influence and even create new tools for thinking. Fieldwork opportunities include assessing the role of technology in wired classrooms and in the creation of a sense of community on campus. You'll take a critical look at how PowerPoint is used—or misused—in your classes, and you'll ponder how your campus library is reconceiving itself in the late age of print.

The final chapter of *Composing Knowledge* explores how, in our increasingly visual culture, text and image are intertwined. Here we explore the connections between seeing and believing and how our "mind's eye" contributes to our vision. And we'll ponder what it means to witness our world and to witness the images by which we sometimes know our world. Fieldwork will send you out on your campus to see its nooks and crannies and even its famous landmarks afresh. We'll consider how schemas (visual and otherwise) influence what we see and know. We'll even explore how campus image making influences high school students and has itself become a big business. We'll ask ourselves why we tend to believe images, and we'll ponder the global reach of an image-saturated media.

These many opportunities for fieldwork will lead to far more than the usual academic essay. Based on your fieldwork and involvement in actual communities, you will find yourself writing diverse documents (from profiles to reports to proposals). Most importantly, based on your fieldwork, you'll find real audiences and discover that your voice and your writing matter. You'll come to know that by composing your knowledge well you can contribute to and even change what and how we know.

Launching Your Fieldwork

Although you won't need a pith helmet to carry out the fieldwork that *Composing Knowledge* invites, you will need to be savvy about your work in the field. This book invites you to become aware of your own situated learning and living environment. It asks that you become more aware as you observe, participate in, reflect on, and question the world of your college experience— and the larger world beyond. You'll come to look closely at your everyday experiences in class, on campus, and in the community. And in so doing, you'll discover texts, artifacts, and resources that may have escaped your notice.

How can you work effectively in the field and draw on that experience as you read and write? Here are some tips:

- Be willing to observe and question what might at first seem normal or habitual. Consider how events and artifacts become part of a culture— part of a web of behaviors, patterns, and (often unspoken) rules that a group of people or a community shares.
- Keep detailed and accurate field notes on what you observe and on the artifacts that you are analyzing. Expand on those field notes when you are not in the field or at your research site.
- Draw on the evidence of the everyday. Although you may be tackling large issues, everyday artifacts of the classroom, campus, or community can often be telling and invaluable resources.
- Question your assumptions. What untested attitudes, beliefs, or cultural values might you project onto your work in the field?
- Acknowledge your role as both a participant and an observer. You are both looking at a culture or community and participating in that culture or community. Be aware of your own position or stance in relation to what you are studying.
- Be willing to step outside of a group or situation with which you may be quite familiar. Likewise, be willing to step into a group or situation that may seem foreign. Be willing to make the familiar strange and the strange familiar.
- Respect your fellow students and the various citizens on your campus and in your community. Consult with your instructor as you engage in your fieldwork to determine if any special permission or approval may be needed.

Composing Knowledge invites you to explore your own learning, the teaching and learning cultures of college, and the connections of your college experience to the larger community. The readings in the coming

EXHIBIT 4–1
List of International
Classes (continued)

International Class	Goods/Services	Explanatory Note
13	Firearms	Firearms, ammunition and projectiles, explosives, fireworks
14	Jewelry	Precious metals and goods in precious metals, jewelry, precious stones, clocks, watches, chronometric instruments
15	Musical instruments	Includes mechanical pianos, musical boxes, electrical and electronic music instruments
16	Paper goods and printed matter	Paper, cardboard, printed matter, photographs, stationery, artists' materials, typewriters and office requisites (except furniture), instructional and teaching material, magazines, books
17	Rubber goods	Rubber, gum, plastics in extruded form, packing material, flexible pipes (not of metal)
18	Leather goods	Leather and imitations of leather, trunks, traveling bags, umbrellas, whips, saddlery
19	Nonmetallic building materials	Building materials (nonmetallic), asphalt, pitch, nonmetallic rigid pipes for building
20	Furniture and articles not otherwise classified	Furniture, mirrors, picture frames, goods of wood, cork, wicker, bone, cane, amber, and substitutes for all these materials
21	Housewares and glass	Household or kitchen utensils and containers (not of precious metal), combs and sponges, brushes, articles for cleaning purposes, glassware, porcelain, earthenware
22	Cordage and fibers	Ropes, string, nets, tents, awnings, tarpaulins, sails, sacks
23	Yarns and threads	Yarns and threads, for textile use
24	Fabrics	Textile goods not in other classes, bed and table covers
25	Clothing	Clothing, footwear, headgear
26	Fancy goods	Lace and embroidery, ribbons, braid, buttons, pins, needles, artificial flowers
27	Floor coverings	Carpets, rugs, mats, linoleum, wall hangings (nontextile)
28	Toys and sporting goods	Games and playthings, sporting goods, decorations for Christmas trees

(continues)

chapters will help you make sense of the many conversations that occur in the Burkean parlor that is your college or university. Those readings will also serve as provocations for your own response and invitations for extending and applying the issues discussed to your own lived experience. Framed by these readings, the original fieldwork you conduct positions you not as the novice but as the expert-in-the-making. Even as you draw on the work of others, you have your own knowledge to compose. Your journey through the following chapters will offer you knowledge for composing well.

1

Joining the Conversation

LEARNING THE LANGUAGE

You and I belong to a community to the extent that we are able to join in its conversations. But to join those conversations, we need to learn the language of that community. That process, explored in this chapter's readings, is not nearly as straightforward as it may seem.

Learning a language surely conjures up memories of our French or German or Spanish classes. We recall the vocabulary quizzes and the grammar tests and our early, awkward attempts to carry on the most basic of conversations. Yet if we think of "learning the language" at this level, the level of verb endings and subjunctives, we surely miss the vital connection between language and community or culture. Even as we slog through the daily homework routine of learning a foreign language, we know that in time learning this language will allow us to participate in the conversations of a community at a far deeper level. We may try to imitate cultural practices or wear our French beret at just the right slight angle. But only through learning a language can we understand the common, but unspoken, assumptions and the hidden attitudes and beliefs that hold a community together. And in so doing, we hope to enter that community without immediately being singled out as the newcomer, the foreigner.

As a college student, you too are joining a community or, to be more precise a whole host of communities—some disciplinary, some social, each overlapping with others. The process is at once exciting and challenging, all the more so because to join these communities you must learn their languages. Here, too, no one wants to be singled out as the newcomer, the foreigner. The common language seems to be English: the academic version of English. You expect to be inundated with new technical vocabulary, especially in the sciences. But what may come as a particular surprise is that each disciplinary community, even composition, has something of its own language. It would be relatively easy if learning this language were simply a matter of learning the buzzwords, the jargon. But at a deeper level, the languages you are encountering carry with them new attitudes and behaviors, new assumptions and values, new ways of thinking about and seeing the world.

Writing class holds a special place among the various classes in that it offers an opportunity to reflect on—and not merely to use or imitate—the languages of the academy. A writing class has us look *at* language and literacy, not merely *through* them, to the concerns of this or that field. And as we become more aware of our own continuing attempts to learn the language, we become more aware of our several identities and of our hopes and fears and likewise more aware of how we move in and between several communities.

The six readings included in this chapter explore the process of learning the language from several perspectives. Each perspective bears in some way on your own entry into language and community on campus.

Because life in the academy assumes advanced literacy, it is important to begin by recalling that an assumption even about basic literacy does not hold for millions of our fellow citizens. In the chapter's first selection, Jonathan Kozol reveals what is the enormous human cost of illiteracy.

Perri Klass recalls her education in medical school as being an education in a new language and, through that language, an initiation into a new community. In addition to learning a host of new technical terms, she also picks up on the attitudes and behaviors carried in the language she now hears in the hospital corridors.

Our entry into a community has not only to do with language but also with rituals and traditions. As David Berreby reminds us, "Students don't just attend a college; they join its tribes." And in so doing, they become involved in a process that, at whatever level, separates "us" from "them."

For novelist Amy Tan, knowing more than one language and more than one culture means that we begin to realize that social settings are easily misunderstood in translation. As we learn new languages and join new communities, we become more aware that language becomes "the peg and the shelf that enables us to sort out and categorize the world."

The language that holds us together, that creates commonalities, say, in high school classrooms across the country, is not what many educators might presume. Formal academic learning—the literacy we acquire in school—has far less influence than we might realize. More important by far, argues Theodore Sizer, is the public literacy that shapes our national culture.

For Barbara Mellix, learning the new language of the academy is also an occasion for reflecting on our cultural roots. As we learn that new language, we will never quite have the same relationship with our other voices. Like the other five authors, Mellix comes to realize that the languages we learn and the conversations we join shape who we are.

Reflecting on Prior Knowledge

1. In a journal entry, recall the experience of being an outsider joining a new group. What was unfamiliar in the language—and behavior—of that group? How did your own attitudes and behavior begin to change as you grew to be accepted within that new community? How was that change captured in your language?

2. Think back to a time when you modified how you spoke or wrote given the particular setting or audience. In a journal entry, recall the scenario and begin exploring why you changed your language behavior. What was your relationship to your audience that prompted this change?

3. In a journal entry, recall the experience of some newcomer trying to enter your community or trying to appropriate and use your language. How did you feel or react? What does it mean to "own" language, and what is entailed in "taking" or "adopting" a language or a set of rituals and traditions?

4. Recall an experience when some misunderstanding occurred in a bicultural or multicultural context despite everyone trying to be well intentioned and polite. In a journal entry, explore what it was about the social context that failed "in translation."

5. Describe the "proper" way to act, speak, or write in a particular situation, be it social or academic, on campus or off. How do we come to learn such proprieties, especially if there are no explicit rules?

The Human Cost
of an Illiterate Society

Jonathan Kozol

An activist and well-known writer on issues of education and home-lessness, Jonathan Kozol has stirred the conscience of America with his incisive and moving critiques. For some four decades, Kozol has sought to end illiteracy, to put a human face on homelessness, to draw attention to continuing segregation in America's schools, and through such issues to prick the conscience of an affluent America that squanders its wealth and ingenuity by failing to address these issues.

Educated at Harvard University, where he graduated summa cum laude, and chosen as a Rhodes scholar, Kozol found that his career plans took a turn in 1964, when the political and social tumult of the 1960s moved him to become a public-school teacher in some of our nation's poorest schools. His account of teaching in a segregated school system, *Death at an Early Age: The Destruction of the Hearts and Minds of Negro Children in the Boston Public Schools,* won the National Book Award in 1968. *Illiterate America* (1985) offers a profoundly troubling exposé of the ways in which millions of Americans are excluded from our society because they cannot read or write. In *Rachel and Her Children: Homeless Families in America* (1988), Kozol offers a moving, detailed portrait of homeless families living in a New York City shelter. In 1991, in what is arguably his most well-known book, *Savage Inequalities: Children in America's Schools,* Kozol reveals the fundamental disparities in school quality from district to district. Two books then followed that offer a personal portrait of children growing up in Mott Haven, the poorest neighborhood in New York City: *Amazing Grace: The Lives of Children and the Conscience of a Nation* (1995) and *Ordinary Resurrections: Children in the Years of Hope* (2000). In his latest book, *Shame of a Nation: The Restoration of Apartheid Schooling in America* (2005), Kozol delivers a scathing indictment of public-education policy that preserves inequities along lines of race and class.

"The Human Cost of an Illiterate Society" is a chapter from *Illiterate America.* Here Kozol discusses how illiteracy forecloses worlds of possibility and renders millions at best "half-citizens."

PRECAUTIONS. READ BEFORE USING.
Poison: Contains sodium hydroxide (caustic soda-lye).
Corrosive: Causes severe eye and skin damage, may cause blindness.
Harmful or fatal if swallowed.
If swallowed, give large quantities of milk or water.
Do not induce vomiting.
Important: Keep water out of can at all times to prevent contents from violently erupting. . . .

— Warning on a Can of Drāno

We are speaking here no longer of the dangers faced by passengers on Eastern Airlines or the dollar costs incurred by U.S. corporations and taxpayers. We are speaking now of human suffering and of the ethical dilemmas that are faced by a society that looks upon such suffering with qualified concern but does not take those actions which its wealth and ingenuity would seemingly demand.

Questions of literacy, in Socrates' belief, must at length be judged as matters of morality. Socrates could not have had in mind the moral compromise peculiar to a nation like our own. Some of our Founding Fathers did, however, have this question in their minds. One of the wisest of those Founding Fathers (one who may not have been most compassionate but surely was more prescient than some of his peers) recognized the special dangers that illiteracy would pose to basic equity in the political construction that he helped to shape.

"A people who mean to be their own governors," James Madison wrote, "must arm themselves with the power knowledge gives. A popular government without popular information or the means of acquiring it, is but a prologue to a farce or a tragedy, or perhaps both."

Tragedy looms larger than farce in the United States today. Illiterate citizens seldom vote. Those who do are forced to cast a vote of questionable worth. They cannot make informed decisions based on serious print information. Sometimes they can be alerted to their interests by aggressive voter education. More frequently, they vote for a face, a smile, or a style, not for a mind or character or body of beliefs.

The number of illiterate adults exceeds by 16 million the entire vote cast for ⁵ the winner in the 1980 presidential contest. If even one-third of all illiterates could vote, and read enough and do sufficient math to vote in their self-interest, Ronald Reagan would not likely have been chosen president. There is, of course, no way to know for sure. We do know this: Democracy is a mendacious term when used by those who are prepared to countenance the forced exclusion of one-third of our electorate. So long as 60 million people are denied significant participation, the government is neither of, nor for, nor by, the people. It is a government, at best, of those two-thirds whose wealth, skin color, or parental privilege allows them opportunity to profit from the provocation and instruction of the written word.

The undermining of democracy in the United States is one "expense" that sensitive Americans can easily deplore because it represents a contradiction that endangers citizens of all political positions. The human price is not so obvious at first.

Since I first immersed myself within this work I have often had the following dream: I find that I am in a railroad station or a large department store within a city that is utterly unknown to me and where I cannot understand the printed words. None of the signs or symbols is familiar. Everything looks strange: like mirror writing of some kind. Gradually I understand that I am in the Soviet Union. All the letters on the walls around me are Cyrillic. I look for my pocket dictionary but I find that it has been mislaid. Where have I left it? Then I recall that I forgot to bring it with me when I packed my bags in Boston. I struggle to remember the name of my hotel. I try to ask somebody for directions. One person stops and looks at me in a peculiar way. I lose the nerve to ask. At last I reach into my wallet for an ID card. The card is missing. Have I lost it? Then I remember that my card was confiscated for some reason, many years before. Around this point, I wake up in a panic.

This panic is not so different from the misery that millions of adult illiterates experience each day within the course of their routine existence in the U.S.A.

Illiterates cannot read the menu in a restaurant.

They cannot read the cost of items on the menu in the *window* of the   10 restaurant before they enter.

Illiterates cannot read the letters that their children bring home from their teachers. They cannot study school department circulars that tell them of the courses that their children must be taking if they hope to pass the SAT exams. They cannot help with homework. They cannot write a letter to the teacher. They are afraid to visit in the classroom. They do not want to humiliate their child or themselves.

Illiterates cannot read instructions on a bottle of prescription medicine. They cannot find out when a medicine is past the year of safe consumption; nor can they read of allergenic risks, warnings to diabetics, or the potential sedative effect of certain kinds of nonprescription pills. They cannot observe preventive health care admonitions. They cannot read about "the seven warning signs of cancer" or the indications of blood-sugar fluctuations or the risks of eating certain foods that aggravate the likelihood of cardiac arrest.

Illiterates live, in more than literal ways, an uninsured existence. They cannot understand the written details on a health insurance form. They cannot read the waivers that they sign preceding surgical procedures. Several women I have known in Boston have entered a slum hospital with the intention of obtaining a tubal ligation and have emerged a few days later after having been subjected to a hysterectomy. Unaware of their rights, incognizant of jargon, intimidated by the unfamiliar air of fear and atmosphere of ether that so many of us find oppressive in the confines even of the most attractive and expensive medical facilities, they have signed their names to documents they could not read and which nobody, in the hectic situation that prevails so often in those overcrowded hospitals that serve the urban poor, had even bothered to explain.

Childbirth might seem to be the last inalienable right **We are speaking now of** of any female citizen within a civilized society. Illiterate **human suffering.** mothers, as we shall see, already have been cheated of the power to protect their progeny against the likelihood of demolition in deficient public schools and, as a result, against the verbal servitude within which they themselves exist. Surgical denial of the right to bear that child in the first place represents an ultimate denial, an unspeakable metaphor, a final darkness that denies even the twilight gleamings of our own humanity. What greater violation of our biological, our biblical, our spiritual humanity could possibly exist than that which takes place nightly, perhaps hourly these days, within such overburdened and benighted institutions as the Boston City Hospital? Illiteracy has many costs; few are so irreversible as this.

Even the roof above one's head, the gas or other fuel for heating that pro- 15 tects the residents of northern city slums against the threat of illness in the winter months become uncertain guarantees. Illiterates cannot read the lease that they must sign to live in an apartment which, too often, they cannot afford. They cannot manage check accounts and therefore seldom pay for anything by mail. Hours and entire days of difficult travel (and the cost of bus or other public transit) must be added to the real cost of whatever they consume. Loss of interest on the check accounts they do not have, and could not manage if they did, must be regarded as another of the excess costs paid by the citizen who is excluded from the common instruments of commerce in a numerate society.

"I couldn't understand the bills," a woman in Washington, D.C., reports, "and then I couldn't write the checks to pay them. We signed things we didn't know what they were."

EXHIBIT 4–1
List of International
Classes (continued)

International Class	Goods/Services	Explanatory Note
29	Meats and processed foods	Meat, fish, poultry, game, preserved and cooked fruits and vegetables, jams and jellies, eggs, milk and milk products, edible oils and fats
30	Staple foods	Coffee, tea, sugar, rice, flour and preparations made from cereals, bread, pastry and confectionery, honey, mustard, salt, yeast, spices
31	Natural agricultural products	Agricultural, horticultural, forestry products, and grains not in other classes, living animals, fresh fruits and vegetables, seeds, natural plants and flowers
32	Light beverages	Beers, mineral and aerated waters, and other nonalcoholic drinks, fruit drinks and juices, syrups
33	Wine and spirits	Alcoholic beverages (except beers)
34	Smokers' articles	Tobacco, smokers' articles, matches

Services

International Class	Goods/Services	Explanatory Note
35	Advertising and business	Advertising, business management, business administration, office functions
36	Insurance and financial	Insurance, financial affairs, monetary affairs, real estate affairs
37	Building construction and repair	Building construction, repair, installation services
38	Telecommunications	Includes services allowing at least one person to communicate with another by sensory means
39	Transportation and storage	Transport, packaging and storage of goods, travel arrangement
40	Treatment of materials	Includes mainly services rendered by the mechanical or chemical processing or transformation of objects or substances, for example, dyeing a garment or destruction of trash
41	Education and entertainment	Education, providing of training, entertainment, sporting, and cultural activities
42	Computer, scientific, and legal	Scientific and technological services and research and design relating thereto, industrial analysis and research services, design and development of computer hardware and software, legal services

Illiterates cannot read the notices that they receive from welfare offices or from the IRS. They must depend on word-of-mouth instruction from the welfare worker—or from other persons whom they have good reason to mistrust. They do not know what rights they have, what deadlines and requirements they face, what options they might choose to exercise. They are half-citizens. Their rights exist in print but not in fact.

Illiterates cannot look up numbers in a telephone directory. Even if they can find the names of friends, few possess the sorting skills to make use of the yellow pages; categories are bewildering and trade names are beyond decoding capabilities for millions of nonreaders. Even the emergency numbers listed on the first page of the phone book—"Ambulance," "Police," and "Fire"—are too frequently beyond the recognition of nonreaders.

Many illiterates cannot read the admonition on a pack of cigarettes. Neither the Surgeon General's warning nor its reproduction on the package can alert them to the risks. Although most people learn by word of mouth that smoking is related to a number of grave physical disorders, they do not get the chance to read the detailed stories which can document this danger with the vividness that turns concern into determination to resist. They can see the handsome cowboy or the slim Virginia lady lighting up a filter cigarette; they cannot heed the words that tell them that this product is (not "may be") dangerous to their health. Sixty million men and women are condemned to be the unalerted, high-risk candidates for cancer.

Illiterates do not buy "no-name" products in the supermarkets. They must 20 depend on photographs or the familiar logos that are printed on the packages of brand-name groceries. The poorest people, therefore, are denied the benefits of the least costly products.

Illiterates depend almost entirely upon label recognition. Many labels, however, are not easy to distinguish. Dozens of different kinds of Campbell's soup appear identical to the nonreader. The purchaser who cannot read and does not dare to ask for help, out of the fear of being stigmatized (a fear which is unfortunately realistic), frequently comes home with something which she never wanted and her family never tasted.

Illiterates cannot read instructions on a pack of frozen food. Packages sometimes provide an illustration to explain the cooking preparations; but illustrations are of little help to someone who must "boil water, drop the food—*within* its plastic wrapper—in the boiling water, wait for it to simmer, instantly remove."

Even when labels are seemingly clear, they may be easily mistaken. A woman in Detroit brought home a gallon of Crisco for her children's dinner. She thought that she had bought the chicken that was pictured on the label. She had enough Crisco now to last a year—but no more money to go back and buy the food for dinner.

Recipes provided on the packages of certain staples sometimes tempt a semiliterate person to prepare a meal her children have not tasted. The longing to vary the uniform and often starchy content of low-budget meals provided to the family that relies on food stamps commonly leads to ruinous results. Scarce funds have been wasted and the food must be thrown out. The same applies to distribution of food-surplus produce in emergency conditions. Government inducements to poor people to "explore the ways" by which to make a tasty meal from tasteless noodles, surplus cheese, and powdered milk are useless to nonreaders. Intended as benevolent advice, such recommendations mock reality and foster deeper feelings of resentment and of inability to cope. (Those, on the other hand, who cautiously refrain from "innovative" recipes in preparation of their children's meals must suffer the opprobrium of "laziness," "lack of imagination. . . .")

Illiterates cannot travel freely. When they attempt to do so, they encounter   25
risks that few of us can dream of. They cannot read traffic signs and, while they often learn to recognize and to decipher symbols, they cannot manage street names which they haven't seen before. The same is true for bus and subway stops. While ingenuity can sometimes help a man or woman to discern directions from familiar landmarks, buildings, cemeteries, churches, and the like, most illiterates are virtually immobilized. They seldom wander past the streets and neighborhoods they know. Geographical paralysis becomes a bitter metaphor for their entire existence. They are immobilized in almost every sense we can imagine. They can't move up. They can't move out. They cannot see beyond. Illiterates may take an oral test for drivers' permits in most sections of America. It is a questionable concession. Where will they go? How will they get there? How will they get home? Could it be that some of us might like it better if they stayed where they belong?

Travel is only one of many instances of circumscribed existence. Choice, in almost all of its facets, is diminished in the life of an illiterate adult. Even the printed TV schedule, which provides most people with the luxury of preselection, does not belong within the arsenal of options in illiterate existence. One consequence is that the viewer watches only what appears at moments when he happens to have time to turn the switch. Another consequence, a lot more common, is that the TV set remains in operation night and day. Whatever the program offered at the hour when he walks into the room will be the nutriment that he accepts and swallows. Thus, to passivity, is added frequency—indeed, almost uninterrupted continuity. Freedom to select is no more possible here than in the choice of home or surgery or food.

"You don't choose," said one illiterate woman. "You take your wishes from somebody else." Whether in perusal of a menu, selection of highways, purchase of groceries, or determination of affordable enjoyment, illiterate

Americans must trust somebody else: a friend, a relative, a stranger on the street, a grocery clerk, a TV copywriter.

"All of our mail we get, it's hard for her to read. Settin' down and writing a letter, she can't do it. Like if we get a bill . . . we take it over to my sister-in-law. . . . My sister-in-law reads it."

Billing agencies harass poor people for the payment of the bills for purchases that might have taken place six months before. Utility companies offer an agreement for a staggered payment schedule on a bill past due. "You have to trust them," one man said. Precisely for this reason, you end up by trusting no one and suspecting everyone of possible deceit. A submerged sense of distrust becomes the corollary to a constant need to trust. "They are cheating me . . . I have been tricked . . . I do not know. . . ."

Not knowing: This is a familiar theme. Not knowing the right word for the   30 right thing at the right time is one form of subjugation. Not knowing the world that lies concealed behind those words is a more terrifying feeling. The longitude and latitude of one's existence are beyond all easy apprehension. Even the hard, cold stars within the firmament above one's head begin to mock the possibilities for self-location. Where am I? Where did I come from? Where will I go?

"I've lost a lot of jobs," one man explains. "Today, even if you're a janitor, there's still reading and writing. . . . They leave a note saying, 'Go to room so-and-so. . . . 'You can't do it. You can't read it. You don't know."

"The hardest thing about it is that I've been places where I didn't know where I was. You don't know where you are. . . . You're lost."

"Like I said: I have two kids. What do I do if one of my kids starts choking? I go running to the phone. . . . I can't look up the hospital phone number. That's if we're at home. Out on the street, I can't read the sign. I get to a pay phone. 'Okay, tell us where you are. We'll send an ambulance.' I look at the street sign. Right there, I can't tell you what it says. I'd have to spell it out, letter for letter. By that time, one of my kids would be dead. . . . These are the kinds of fears you go with, every single day. . . .

"Reading directions, I suffer with. I work with chemicals. . . . That's scary to begin with. . . ."

"You sit down. They throw the menu in front of you. Where do you go   35 from there? Nine times out of ten you say, 'Go ahead. Pick out something for the both of us.' I've eaten some weird things, let me tell you!"

Menus. Chemicals. A child choking while his mother searches for a word she does not know to find assistance that will come too late. Another mother speaks about the inability to help her kids to read: "I can't read to them. Of course that's leaving them out of something they should have. Oh, it matters. You *believe* it matters! I ordered all these books. The kids belong to a book club. Donny wanted me to read a book to him. I told Donny: 'I can't read.' He said: 'Mommy, you sit down. I'll read it to you.' I tried it one day, reading from the pictures. Donny looked at me. He said, 'Mommy, that's not right.' He's only five. He knew I couldn't read. . . .

A landlord tells a woman that her lease allows him to evict her if her baby cries and causes inconvenience to her neighbors. The consequence of challenging his words conveys a danger which appears, unlikely as it seems, even more alarming than the danger of eviction. Once she admits that she can't read, in the desire to maneuver for the time in which to call a friend, she will have defined herself in terms of an explicit impotence that she cannot endure. Capitulation in this case is preferable to self-humiliation. Resisting the definition of oneself in terms of what one cannot do, what others take for granted, represents a need so great that other imperatives (even one so urgent as the need to keep one's home in winter's cold) evaporate and fall away in face of fear. Even the loss of home and shelter, in this case, is not so terrifying as the loss of self.

"I come out of school. I was sixteen. They had their meetings. The directors meet. They said that I was wasting their school paper. I was wasting pencils. . . ."

Another illiterate, looking back, believes she was not worthy of her teacher's time. She believes that it was wrong of her to take up space within her school. She believes that it was right to leave in order that somebody more deserving could receive her place.

Children choke. Their mother chokes another way: on more than 40 chicken bones.

People eat what others order, know what others tell them, struggle not to see themselves as they believe the world perceives them. A man in California speaks about his own loss of identity, of self-location, definition:

"I stood at the bottom of the ramp. My car had broke down on the freeway. There was a phone. I asked for the police. They was nice. They said to tell them where I was. I looked up at the signs. There was one that I had seen before. I read it to them: ONE WAY STREET. They thought it was a joke. I told them I couldn't read. There was other signs above the ramp. They told me to try. I looked around for somebody to help. All the cars was going by real fast. I couldn't make them understand that I was lost. The cop was nice. He told me: 'Try once more.' I did my best. I couldn't read. I only knew the sign above my head. The cop was trying to be nice. He knew that I was trapped. 'I can't send out a car to you if you can't tell me where you are.' I felt afraid. I nearly cried. I'm forty-eight years old. I only said: 'I'm on a one-way street. . . .'"

Perhaps we might slow down a moment here and look at the realities described above. This is the nation that we live in. This is a society that most of us did not create but which our President and other leaders have been willing to sustain by virtue of malign neglect. Do we possess the character and courage to address a problem which so many nations, poorer than our own, have found it natural to correct?

The answers to these questions represent a reasonable test of our belief in the democracy to which we have been asked in public school to swear allegiance.

Working with the Text

1. Jonathan Kozol opens this chapter from *Illiterate America* by citing the set of warnings on a can of Drāno. Why do you think Kozol chooses this strategy? What effect do you think he is hoping to achieve? How did this opening affect you as a reader? How does your ability to read the warnings bring home to you the dangers that might be encountered by someone who can't read those warnings?

2. For the first six paragraphs of this chapter, Kozol focuses on the costs of illiteracy to democratic institutions and to political and civic participation. He then transitions to a perspective that highlights the "human price" of illiteracy, a perspective that he maintains for much of the chapter. Then, in the final two paragraphs, Kozol again returns to a broader perspective and calls on us to act—in ways both civic and political—on our growing awareness of the "human price" that he has revealed. What purposes lie behind Kozol's structural decisions in his organization of this chapter? What does Kozol accomplish by framing specific examples of the human cost of illiteracy with broader reflections on democracy and ethics?

3. Kozol's discussion of the human costs of illiteracy relies in large measure on specific examples. Indeed, the very cascade of examples, their sheer number, carries an important rhetorical effect. How does the ever-increasing number of examples contribute to the persuasiveness of Kozol's argument? Does the copiousness of evidence contribute to a sense of the magnitude and scope of the problem?

From Text to Field

1. As Jonathan Kozol turns to catalog the "human price" of illiteracy, he recounts a dream. "I find that I am in a railroad station or a large department store within a city that is utterly unknown to me and where I cannot understand the printed words" (par. 7). Kozol argues that the panic he experiences from this dream is "not so different from the misery that millions of adult illiterates experience each day within the course of their routine existence in the U.S.A." Reflect on your experiences and nightmares, and recall a situation (real or

dreamt) in which you experienced panic of the kind Kozol describes. To what extent does that situation parallel the plight of illiterate Americans? Why does Kozol relate a dream to his audience? Does the dream story succeed in personalizing the succeeding real-life examples, which may be beyond the immediate experience of those in his audience?

2. Kozol's discussion of illiteracy relies on examples and concrete scenarios. What additional examples or stories might you contribute to those Kozol has offered? Consider offering examples that stem from your immediate surroundings: your campus and your community. How would someone who is illiterate handle even the most basic of jobs on your campus? Likewise, find a consumer item in a store that would prove difficult for an illiterate to understand, or describe an activity or task not mentioned by Kozol that would prove daunting for someone who cannot read. In a short essay, discuss what aspects of Kozol's argument your own examples have reinforced or what new perspectives your examples might shed light on.

3. The experience of being in a foreign country where you do not know even the most basic aspects of the language is at best an imperfect analogue to the experiences of being illiterate. If you have traveled abroad in countries where you did not know the language, or perhaps even the alphabet, what was the experience like? To what extent is such an experience helpful in understanding illiteracy? Likewise, in what ways is such an experience fundamentally different from the experiences encountered by those who are illiterate?

Learning the Language

Perri Klass

As a medical student, Perri Klass had to learn a new code, a new language, a new set of attitudes and behaviors. Although most of us will never learn that particular language, her initiation into the language of the medical community parallels what happens when any one of us enters a new group. Whether that new group is a family or a fraternity/sorority, a discipline or profession, or a new workplace culture, Perri Klass calls to our attention both the rewards and dangers of "learning the language." To use a medical euphemism, she might say the process is "a not entirely benign procedure."

With her own diverse background as a pediatrician, writer, and mother, Perri Klass is sensitive to the ways in which we come into language. She was born in Trinidad in 1958, where her father (an anthropologist) and her mother (a writer) lived at the time. She received her MD from Harvard Medical School in 1986 and has gone on to specialize in pediatric medicine. Even with the demands of medical training and practice, not to mention family, she has published three novels, *Recombinations* (1985), *Other Women's Children* (1990), and *The Mystery of Breathing* (2004), as well as two short-story collections, *I Am Having an Adventure* (1986) and *Love and Modern Medicine: Stories* (2001). She has also written two collections of essays about medical training, *Baby Doctor: A Pediatrician's Training* (1992) and *A Not Entirely Benign Procedure: Four Years as a Medical Student* (1987), in which the following selection appears as a chapter. Her latest book, written with Eileen Costello, is *Quirky Kids* (2004). Perri Klass's interest in "learning the language" continues, as she now serves as the medical director of the national literacy program Reach Out and Read, dedicated to promoting literacy as part of pediatric primary care.

"Mrs. Tolstoy is your basic LOL in NAD, admitted for a soft rule-out MI," the intern announces. I scribble that on my patient list. In other words, Mrs. Tolstoy is a Little Old Lady in No Apparent Distress who is in the hospital to make sure she hasn't had a heart attack (rule out a Myocardial Infarction). And we think it's unlikely that she has had a heart attack (a *soft* rule-out).

If I learned nothing else during my first three months of working in the hospital as a medical student, I learned endless jargon and abbreviations. I started out in a state of primeval innocence, in which I didn't even know that "sCP, SOB, N/V" meant "without chest pain, shortness of breath, or nausea and vomiting." By the end I took the abbreviations so much for granted that I would complain to my mother the English professor, "And can you believe I had to put down *three* NG tubes last night?"

"You'll have to tell me what an NG tube is if you want me to sympathize properly," my mother said. NG, nasogastric — isn't it obvious?

I picked up not only the specific expressions but also the patterns of speech and the grammatical conventions; for example, you never say that a patient's blood pressure fell or that his cardiac enzymes rose. Instead, the patient is always the subject of the verb: "He dropped his pressure." "He bumped his enzymes." This sort of construction probably reflects the profound irritation of the intern when the nurses come in the middle of the night to say that Mr. Dickinson has disturbingly low blood pressure. "Oh, he's gonna hurt me bad tonight," the intern might say, inevitably angry at Mr. Dickinson for dropping his pressure and creating a problem.

When chemotherapy fails to cure Mrs. Bacon's cancer, what we say is, 5 "Mrs. Bacon failed chemotherapy."

"Well, we've already had one hit today, and we're up next, but at least we've got mostly stable players on our team." This means that our team (group of doctors and medical students) has already gotten one new admission today, and it is our turn again, so we'll get whoever is admitted next in emergency, but at least most of the patients we already have are fairly stable; that is, unlikely to drop their pressures or in any other way get suddenly sicker and hurt us bad. Baseball metaphor is pervasive. A no-hitter is a night without any new admissions. A player is always a patient — a nitrate player is a patient on nitrates, a unit player is a patient in the intensive care unit, and so on, until you reach the terminal player.

It is interesting to consider what it means to be winning, or doing well, in this perennial baseball game. When the intern hangs up the phone and announces, "I got a hit," that is not cause for congratulations. The team is not scoring points; rather, it is getting hit, being bombarded with new patients. The object of the game from the point of view of the doctors, considering the players for whom they are already responsible, is to get as few new hits as possible.

This special language contributes to a sense of closeness and professional spirit among people who are under a great deal of stress. As a medical student,

I found it exciting to discover that I'd finally cracked the code, that I could understand what doctors said and wrote, and could use the same formulations myself. Some people seem to become enamored of the jargon for its own sake, perhaps because they are so deeply thrilled with the idea of medicine, with the idea of themselves as doctors.

I knew a medical student who was referred to by the interns on the team as Mr. Eponym because he was so infatuated with eponymous terminology, the more obscure the better. He never said "capillary pulsations" if he could say "Quincke's pulses." He would lovingly tell over the multinamed syndromes—Wolff-Parkinson-White, Lown-Ganong-Levine, Schönlein-Henoch—until the temptation to suggest Schleswig-Holstein or Stevenson-Kefauver or Baskin-Robbins became irresistible to his less reverent colleagues.

You move closer and closer to being a doctor instead of just talking like one.

And there is the jargon that you don't ever want to hear yourself using. You know that your training is changing you, but there are certain changes you think would be going a little too far.   10

The resident was describing a man with devastating terminal pancreatic cancer. "Basically he's CTD," the resident concluded. I reminded myself that I had resolved not to be shy about asking when I didn't understand things. "CTD?" I asked timidly.

The resident smirked at me. "Circling The Drain."

The images are vivid and terrible. "What happened to Mrs. Melville?"

"Oh, she boxed last night." To box is to die, of course.

Then there are the more pompous locutions that can make the beginning   15
medical student nervous about the effects of medical training. A friend of mine was told by his resident, "A pregnant woman with sickle-cell represents a failure of genetic counseling."

Mr. Eponym, who tried hard to talk like the doctors, once explained to me, "An infant is basically a brainstem preparation." The term "brainstem preparation," as used in neurological research, refers to an animal whose higher brain functions have been destroyed so that only the most primitive reflexes remain, like the sucking reflex, the startle reflex, and the rooting reflex.

And yet at other times the harshness dissipates into a strangely elusive euphemism. "As you know, this is a not entirely benign procedure," some doctor will say, and that will be understood to imply agony, risk of complications, and maybe even a significant mortality rate.

The more extreme forms aside, one most important function of medical jargon is to help doctors maintain some distance from their patients. By reformulating a patient's pain and problems into a language that the patient doesn't even speak, I suppose we are in some sense taking those pains and problems under our jurisdiction and also reducing their emotional impact. This linguistic separation between doctors and patients allows conversations to go on at the bedside that are unintelligible to the patient. "Naturally, we're worried about adeno-CA," the intern can say to the medical student, and lung cancer need never be mentioned.

I learned a new language this past summer. At times it thrills me to hear myself using it. It enables me to understand my colleagues, to communicate effectively in the hospital. Yet I am uncomfortably aware that I will never again notice the peculiarities and even atrocities of medical language as keenly as I did this summer. There may be specific expressions I manage to avoid, but even as I remark them, promising myself I will never use them, I find that this language is becoming my professional speech. It no longer sounds strange in my ears—or coming from my mouth. And I am afraid that as with any new language, to use it properly you must absorb not only the vocabulary but also the structure, the logic, the attitudes. At first you may notice these new and alien assumptions every time you put together a sentence, but with time and increased fluency you stop being aware of them at all. And as you lose that awareness, for better or for worse, you move closer and closer to being a doctor instead of just talking like one.

Working with the Text

1. Why do doctors use medical jargon? Perri Klass offers several reasons in her essay. First list those reasons, and then write a short response essay in which you tease out how those reasons might be related. From your perspective as a patient, are there reasons that Klass might have neglected to mention?

2. Klass reflects on both the benefits and the drawbacks of specialized medical language. Develop a two-column list of those benefits and drawbacks. Whose interests and perspectives does that list represent? Are there other benefits and drawbacks you would add to that list? Working from your lists, write a short response essay on whether the language of any community is inevitably partial and inevitably speaks to certain interests. Does specialized language imply a user's particular view of the world?

3. Two figures make cameo appearances in the essay: the mother and a fellow medical student whom Klass names "Mr. Eponym." What functions do these two characters serve? How do the mother and Mr. Eponym relate to the implied reader of the essay? In what ways are groups defined as much by outsiders as by members? Write a short analysis of the essay in which you tease out connections between the structure of Klass's essay and the dynamics of entering a community.

International Class	Goods/Services	Explanatory Note
43	Hotels and restaurants	Services for providing food and drink, temporary accommodations
44	Medical, beauty, and agricultural	Medical services, veterinary services, hygienic and beauty care for human beings or animals, horticulture and forestry services
45	Personal	Personal and social services rendered by others to meet the needs of individuals, security services for the protection of property and individuals

EXHIBIT 4-1
List of International
Classes (continued)

If a mark is used for more than one class of goods or services, the applicant may either file a combined (or multiple class) application, listing all of the goods and services in the same application, or file entirely separate (or single) applications for each class of goods/services. The filing fees will be identical. Some attorneys prefer to file separate applications, believing that a defect in regard to one class of goods or services in a combined application will hold up registration for the mark in all classes. For example, if three separate applications are filed for goods in I.C. 3, 21, and 25, and there is a delay with regard to the goods in I.C. 25, the other applications may proceed to registration, thereby allowing the applicant to secure a registration for the mark at least in regard to some goods. The final decision on whether to file a combined application or separate applications is one of tactics and strategy.

The PTO requires that the identification of goods or services be as clear, accurate, and concise as possible. The accuracy of identification language is of particular importance because, while an identification may be limited or clarified, no addition to, or expansion of, an identification is permitted after an application is filed. Thus, if an application is filed on January 1 for women's clothing in I.C. 25 and the applicant later wishes to add perfume (in I.C. 3) to the application, such an amendment would not be allowed. The applicant would be required to file an additional application that would then have a later filing date than the first application filed January 1. The applicant may, however, amend the original application to clarify that the clothing to be offered consists of blouses, skirts, and pants. An applicant cannot attempt a blanket filing for "all the goods in I.C. 9." Such an application would be refused by the PTO. If an applicant incorrectly classifies clothing in I.C. 26 rather than in I.C. 25, the PTO will allow correction of this error.

Typically, the PTO requires that the applicant use terms such as *namely* and *consisting of* when identifying goods. Thus, an identification of "cosmetics, *namely* lipstick and deodorant" is acceptable, while an identification of "cosmetics, *including* lipstick and deodorant" will be refused as indefinite and overbroad inasmuch as a reader cannot tell the exact goods that will be offered under the mark from reading the identification.

Finally, due to the increased volume of applications for computer-related goods in I.C. 9, the PTO expressly requires that identifications of goods for computer software or comparable goods must specify the purpose or function of the program. For example, the following descriptions would be acceptable to the

From Text to Field

1. Reflecting on her medical education, Klass says "you must absorb not only the vocabulary but also the structure, the logic, the attitudes" (par. 19). What do you think Klass means by this statement? What arguments do you think Klass is making by telling her story as she does? In a brief autobiographical essay, analyze your own early apprenticeship in an academic field or in an area of interest, such as sports or music or a hobby. Consider what the veiled argument might be behind your own story.

2. Klass ends her essay by commenting on the relationship between "talking like" a doctor and "being a doctor." How do you see this relationship between language and identity in your own college life? How does that relationship change as you move from home to campus, from friends to class, even from discipline to discipline? Write a short exploratory or reflective essay on language and identity from your perspective as a student.

3. Consider some specialty, discipline, or sphere of activity with a language of its own, perhaps one far removed from your own interests. You may refer to books (even essays in this book) or to your experiences in the classroom. As you offer examples of that specialized language, write an essay in which you consider what uses of jargon are appropriate or inappropriate and for whom. Is jargon natural or even beneficial, or does it offer an unwelcome barrier? Does jargon offer a means for regulation or control, for the "disciplining" of a community's members?

It Takes a Tribe

David Berreby

What is it about the human mind that makes us believe in categories like race, gender, and ethnicity? Why is it that we form groups, dividing ourselves into "us" and "them"?

These are the questions that sent David Berreby on a quest that resulted in his recent book *Us and Them: Understanding Your Tribal Mind* (2005). Berreby pursues answers to those questions by spanning a number of disciplines and drawing on a wide range of sources, from classical texts to the most current research. A science journalist and nonfiction writer, David Berreby has written regularly about science and culture for such publications as the *New York Times,* the *New Republic,* the *Sciences, Discover,* and *Slate.*

In his article "It Takes a Tribe," which appeared in the *New York Times* in 2004, David Berreby explores why and how we become so thoroughly identified with the universities we attend. What Berreby discovers is that "[s]tudents don't just attend a college; they join its tribes." It turns out that we want to live in tribes, and we are keen on figuring out the rules of membership, initiation, and exclusion. We're eager to belt out the school song—just as soon as we learn what the words are.

When the budding pundit Walter Lippmann coined the term *stereotype* back in 1922, he offered several examples from the America of his time: *Agitator. Intellectual. South European. From the Back Bay.* You know, he told the reader, when a glimpse and a word or two create a full mental picture of a whole group of people. As in *plutocrat.* Or *foreigner.* Or *Harvard man.*

Harvard man? We know, thanks to Lippmann, that stereotypes are part of serious problems like racism, prejudice, and injustice. What is Lippmann's alma mater doing on such a list? (He even added: "How different from the statement, 'He is a Yale man.'")

Spend time on a campus in coming weeks, though, and you'll see what he meant.

At colleges across the country, from Ivy League to less exclusive state schools, students who are mispronouncing the library's name this month will soon feel truly and deeply a part of their college. They'll be singing their school songs and cherishing the traditions (just as soon as they learn what they are). They'll talk the way "we" do. (Going to Texas A & M? Then greet people with a cheerful "howdy.") They'll learn contempt for that rival university—Oklahoma to their Texas, Sacramento State to their UC Davis, Annapolis to their West Point.

They may come to believe, too, that an essential trait separates them from   5 the rest of humanity—the same sort of feeling most Americans have about races, ethnic groups, and religions. As the writer Christopher Buckley said recently in his college's alumni magazine: "When I run into a Yale man I somehow feel that I am with a kindred spirit. A part of that kindred-ness comes from his gentility and his not being all jumped up about it. It's a certain sweetness of character."

All this sentiment comes on fast (a study last year at Ivy League campuses found freshmen even more gung-ho than older students). Yet college loyalty, encouraged by alumni relations offices, can last a lifetime—as enduring as the Princeton tiger tattooed on the buttock of former Secretary of State George P. Shultz, or the Yale sweater sported by evil Mr. Burns on *The Simpsons*, a number of whose writers went to Harvard.

New identities are forged within the university as well, in elite groups like Skull and Bones at Yale or the Corps of Cadets at Texas A & M, or Michigamua at the University of Michigan; in sororities and fraternities; even in particular majors and particular labs. Students don't just attend a college; they join its tribes.

"What endlessly impresses me is people losing sight of how arbitrary it is," says Robert M. Sapolsky, a Stanford biologist who specializes in the links between social life and stress. "Students understand how readily they could have wound up at another school or wound up in another lab." Yet every year, he adds, "they fall for it." For most, what Professor Sapolsky calls that "nutty but palpable" onset of college tribalism is just a part of campus life. For social scientists, it's an object of research, offering clues to a fundamental and puzzling aspect of human nature: People need to belong, to feel a part of *us*. Yet a sense of *us* brings with it a sense of *them*.

Human beings will give a lot, including their lives, for a group they feel part of—for *us*, as in *our nation* or *our religion*. They will also harm those labeled "them," including taking their lives. Far as genocide and persecution seem from fraternity hazings and Cal versus Stanford, college tribes may shed light on the way the mind works with those other sorts of groups, the ones that shape and misshape the world, like nation, race, creed, caste, or culture.

After all, a college campus is full of people inventing a sense of *us* and a sense of *them*. As one junior at the University of California, Los Angeles, told her school paper before a game against the University of Southern California: "School spirit is important because it gives us a sense of belonging and being a part of something bigger. Besides," she said, "USC sucks in every way."

In an e-mail interview, Professor Sapolsky writes that "Stanford students (and faculty) do tons of this, at every possible hierarchical level." For instance, he says, they see Stanford versus Harvard, and Stanford versus the University of California at Berkeley. "Then, within Stanford, all the science wonks doing tribal stuff to differentiate themselves from the fuzzies—the humanities/social science types. Then within the sciences, the life science people versus the chemistry/physics/math geeks." Within the life sciences, he adds, the two tribes are "bio majors and majors in what is called 'human biology'—former deprecated as being robotic premeds, incapable of thinking, just spitting out of factoids; latter as fuzzies masquerading as scientists."

Recent research on students suggests these changes in perception aren't trivial. A few years ago, a team of social psychologists asked students at the University of California at Santa Barbara to rank various collections of people in terms of how well they "qualify as a group." In their answers, "students at a university" ranked above "citizens of a nation." "Members of a campus committee" and "members of a university social club" ranked higher than "members of a union" or "members of a political party," "romantic couples," or "office colleagues working together on a project." For that matter, "students at a university" and "members of a campus committee" ranked well above blacks and Jews in the students' estimation of what qualifies as a group.

Students . . . will soon feel truly and deeply a part of their college.

Much of this thinking, researchers have found, is subconscious. We may think we care about our college ties for good and sensible reasons—wonderful classes! dorm-room heart-to-hearts! job connections!—when the deeper causes are influences we didn't notice.

Some twenty years ago, researchers asked students at Rutgers to describe themselves using only words from a set of cards prepared in advance. Some cards contained words associated with Rutgers, like *scarlet*, the school color, and *knight*, the name of its athletic teams. Others, like *orange*, were associated with archrival Princeton. Some students took the test in a room decorated with a Rutgers pennant; others took it under a Princeton flag. A third group saw only a New York Yankees banner.

Students who saw a Princeton or Rutgers emblem were more likely to use   15
Rutgers-related words to describe themselves. They also mentioned that they
were students at Rutgers earlier than those who saw only the neutral flag.
They didn't consciously decide to stand up for Rutgers. Outside their conscious minds, though, that identity was in place, ready to be released by symbols of the tribe.

More recently, three social psychologists at Harvard looked at another
example of subconscious tribal beliefs. Mahzarin R. Banaji, who led the
study, argues that people in similar, equivalent groups will place those groups
into a hierarchy, from best to worst, even when there is no rational basis for
ranking them. The psychologists tested Yale sophomores, juniors, and seniors,
who live and eat together in "residential colleges." Students know that these
colleges are effectively all alike and that people are assigned to them at random. Still, the team found, Yalies did indeed rank them from best to worst.
(In the interests of peace and comity, the colleges were kept anonymous.)
Moreover, students assigned to the less prestigious units were less enthusiastic about their homes than those from the ones with a better reputation.

What this suggests, Professor Banaji says, is that taking one's place in a tribe
and accepting the tribe's place in a larger society are mental acts that happen
regardless of the group's purpose or meaning. Once people see that they've
been divided into groups, they'll act accordingly, even if they know that the
divisions are as meaningless as, oh, the University of Arizona versus Arizona
State. "We know that human beings identify with social groups, sometimes
sufficiently to kill or die on their behalf," she says. "What is not as well known
is that such identity between self and group can form rapidly, often following
a psychological route that is relatively subconscious. That is, like automata,
we identify with the groups in which we are accidentally placed."

Not all researchers agree that people care about so-called nonsense groups
with the same passion they give to religion, politics, or morals. Another theory holds that the subconscious mind can distinguish which groups matter
and how much. One example comes from a much-cited experiment, performed, naturally, on college students.

In 1959, the social psychologists Elliot Aronson and Judson Mills asked
undergraduate women to join a discussion group after a short initiation. For
one set of participants the initiation required reciting a few mild sexual
words. The other group had to say a list of much saltier words about sex,
which embarrassed them to no end (remember, this was 1959). The discussion group was dull as dishwater, but the women who suffered to join rated
it as much more valuable than those who had a mild initiation (and higher
than a control group that didn't have to do anything).

A subconscious clue for perceiving a tribe as real and valuable, then, may   20
be expending sweat, tears, and embarrassment to get in. The political activist

Tom Hayden recently recalled just such a rite at the University of Michigan, in an article on the left-wing Web site alternet.org. He was complaining about the lock that Skull and Bones has on November's election (President Bush and the Democratic nominee, Senator John Kerry, are members).

"As a junior, I was tapped for the Druids," Mr. Hayden wrote about his own campus clan, "which involved a two-day ritual that included being stripped to my underpants, pelted with eggs, smeared with red dye, and tied to a campus tree. These humiliations signified my rebirth from lowly student journalist to Big Man on Campus."

As for Professor Aronson, had he not wanted tight control over the experiment, he writes in his widely used textbook, *The Social Animal*, he and Professor Mills could simply have studied an initiation outside the lab—at a campus fraternity or sorority.

That kind of lumping together—studying one group to explain another—drives scholars in other fields to distraction. To them, a pep rally is different from a political rally. Historians, trained to see big generalizations as meaningless, are often aghast at the way psychologists' theories about groups ignore the difference between, say, today's two-gendered, multiethnic, and meritocratic Harvard College and the one that gave Lippmann his degree in 1909. And anthropologists for generations have disdained psychology for ignoring cultural differences.

But one fact is clear, and college groups exemplify it well: While many creatures live in groups, humanity's are unlike anything else found in nature. Peter Richerson, a biologist at Sacramento State's rival, the University of California at Davis, likes to point out that his students, sitting quietly together on the first day of class, are an amazing exception to the general rules of animal behavior. Put chimpanzees or monkeys that don't know one another in a room, and they would be in hysterics. People team up with strangers easily.

Professor Richerson and his longtime collaborator, Robert Boyd, an   25 anthropologist at USC's hated enemy, UCLA, argue that we will sign up for membership in tribelike groups for the same reason birds sing: It feels right because we evolved to do it. "We want to live in tribes," Professor Richerson says. Humans are "looking to be told what group they belong to, and then once they do that, they want to know, 'What are the rules?'"

The tricky part, says Professor Sapolsky of Stanford, Cal-Berkeley's bitter rival, is that humans alone among animals can think about what a tribe is and who belongs. "Humans actually think about who is an 'us' and who is a 'them' rather than just knowing it," he says. "The second it becomes a cognitive process, it is immensely subject to manipulation."

And, of course, studying the phenomenon won't make you immune. "I'm true blue," says Professor Banaji, who taught at Yale from 1986 until 2002, when she joined the Harvard faculty. "I was physically unable to sit through a women's basketball game between Harvard and Yale on the Harvard side."

Working with the Text

1. Although the subject of group allegiance in college may lend itself to anecdotal treatment, David Berreby organizes this article by citing various experts and moving from one research study to the next. What advantages does this strategy hold? Given the subject of the article, why does Berreby lend his voice to the voices of others? Are there any disadvantages to Berreby's strategy?

2. Many of the examples and research studies cited by Berreby highlight the early moments when tribal affiliations are formed. What is distinctive and important about these early moments? Why does the nature of our initiation into a group carry such continuing significance?

3. College rituals and traditions do more than create a sense of community and belonging. They also function as a means of exclusion—a way not just to foster a sense of "us" but also to create a sense of "them," a sense of the "other." Review Berreby's article for references to this us/them dichotomy. Why is the creation of a sense of "us" implicated in the creation of "them"?

4. Berreby suggests at several points that the distinctions that help us create a tribal identity are often not terribly real or essential. Indeed, some distinctions seem to be fictions of our own creation. In what ways do our tribal impulses lead us to create questionable distinctions among ourselves? According to Berreby, what accounts for this impulse?

From Text to Field

1. In his article, David Berreby makes frequent references to the rituals and traditions of campus life. What rituals and traditions on your campus seem to be most important to you and your fellow students? How might these compare to the rituals and traditions important to faculty members and alumni?

2. As you recall the first several weeks you spent on campus, what role did orientation programs or dorm life or sports have in fostering a sense of belonging? Berreby notes that studies have shown that first-year students are especially "gung-ho" about college loyalty. Why do you think this may be the case?

3. On your own campus, do you observe instances when tribal loyalties and initiation into a particular "tribe" seem to have gotten out of hand? To what extent are hazing and other initiation rituals driven by this tribal impulse? Do various groups on your campus—sororities and fraternities among them—balance the impulse to form tribes with an awareness of its possible dangers?

4. Berreby notes that we do more than place ourselves and others in tribes; we also place these tribes in hierarchies. What kind of hierarchies exist on your campus—whether among majors, dorms or residential colleges, and clubs? How did you learn about these hierarchies, and how did they evolve?

5. In this particular article, David Berreby focuses exclusively on tribal instincts on college campuses. Are campuses unique or distinctive in this respect, or do such instincts play themselves out in other arenas, such as in the business world or in community and social activities? Discuss examples of tribalism that are not tied to a college campus. Do you see these examples as supporting essentially the same arguments that Berreby makes, or do these examples raise new issues?

The Language of Discretion

Amy Tan

Raised in California by her immigrant parents from China, Amy Tan understands firsthand the issues of language use and translation that come from living in a bicultural or multicultural environment. A good part of learning any language (even the academic languages of various disciplines) involves understanding "the language of discretion." You might think of discretion as "cautious reserve in speech" or, in the context of Tan's essay, the set of expectations and understandings that needn't be verbalized in speech because they are shared within a community. Learning those silent or tacit expectations is a challenge for all of us, as we move in and among communities.

Tan began writing short stories while working as a freelance writer in San Francisco specializing in corporate communications. Those stories were collected in her immensely popular first novel, *The Joy Luck Club* (1989), which was later produced as a motion picture. Tan's other fiction includes *The Kitchen God's Wife* (1991), *The Hundred Secret Senses* (1995), and most recently *Saving Fish from Drowning* (2005) as well as two children's books, *The Moon Lady* (1992) and *The Chinese Siamese Cat* (1994). She has also published a collection of essays, *The Opposite of Fate* (2003). In "The Language of Discretion" (1989) you hear Tan's voice as an essayist, reflecting on the very issues that drive her works of fiction.

At a recent family dinner in San Francisco, my mother whispered to me: "Sau-sau [Brother's Wife] pretends too hard to be polite! Why bother? In the end, she always takes everything."

My mother thinks like a *waixiao*, an expatriate, temporarily away from China since 1949, no longer patient with ritual courtesies. As if to prove her point, she reached across the table to offer my elderly aunt from Beijing the last scallop from the Happy Family seafood dish.

Sau-sau scowled. *"B'yao, zhen b'yao!"* (I don't want it, really I don't!) she cried, patting her plump stomach.

"Take it! Take it!" scolded my mother in Chinese.

"Full, I'm already full," Sau-sau protested weakly, eyeing the beloved scallop.

"Ai!" exclaimed my mother, completely exasperated. "Nobody else wants it. If you don't take it, it will only rot!"

At this point, Sau-sau sighed, acting as if she were doing my mother a big favor by taking the wretched scrap off her hands.

My mother turned to her brother, a high-ranking communist official who was visiting her in California for the first time: "In America a Chinese person could starve to death. If you say you don't want it, they won't ask you again forever."

My uncle nodded and said he understood fully: Americans take things quickly because they have no time to be polite.

I thought about this misunderstanding again—of social contexts failing in translation—when a friend sent me an article from the *New York Times Magazine* (24 April 1988). The article, on changes in New York's Chinatown, made passing reference to the inherent ambivalence of the Chinese language.

Language enables us to sort out and categorize the world.

Chinese people are so "discreet and modest," the article stated, there aren't even words for "yes" and "no."

That's not true, I thought, although I can see why an outsider might think that. I continued reading.

If one is Chinese, the article went on to say, "One compromises, one doesn't hazard a loss of face by an overemphatic response."

My throat seized. Why do people keep saying these things? As if we truly were those little dolls sold in Chinatown tourist shops, heads bobbing up and down in complacent agreement to anything said!

I worry about the effect of one-dimensional statements on the unwary and guileless. When they read about this so-called vocabulary deficit, do they also conclude that Chinese people evolved into a mild-mannered lot because the language only allowed them to hobble forth with minced words?

Something enormous is always lost in translation. Something insidious seeps into the gaps, especially when amateur linguists continue to compare, one-for-one, language differences and then put forth notions wide open to misinterpretation: that Chinese people have no direct linguistic means to make decisions, assert or deny, affirm or negate, just say no to drug dealers, or behave properly on the witness stand when told, "Please answer yes or no."

Yet one can argue, with the help of renowned linguists, that the Chinese are indeed up a creek without "yes" and "no." Take any number of variations

PTO: "computer software for word processing" or "database management software for use by financial advisers." A broad description such as "computer programs in the field of medicine" is not acceptable. See Exhibit 4–2 for examples of identifications of goods and services.

EXHIBIT 4–2
Samples of Identifications of Goods and Services

Type of Mark	Mark	International Class	Goods/Services	Other Data
Trademark	POLO RALPH LAUREN	I.C. 14	Watches	Registration notes that "the name 'Ralph Lauren' identifies a particular living individual whose consent is of record."
Trademark (with disclaimer)	RAISIN BRAN CRUNCH	I.C. 30	Processed cereal	Registration notes the following disclaimer: "No claim is made to the exclusive right to use 'Raisin Bran' apart from the mark as shown."
Service mark	PARAMOUNT (& DESIGN)	I.C. 41	Entertainment services, namely production of motion pictures	Registration notes, "The mark consists of the word 'Paramount' in stylized letters about five shadow mountain with an arc of stars surrounding it all."
Design mark	[Design of Hat] registered to Walt Disney Company	I.C. 25	Hats	The registration notes, "The mark consists of the configuration of round mouse ears attached to a beanie."
Service mark (with disclaimer)	JURASSIC PARK RIVER ADVENTURE	I.C. 41	Amusement park services	The registration notes the following disclaimer: "No claim is made to the exclusive right to use 'River Adventure' apart from the mark as shown."
Certification mark	U2 (& DESIGN)	I.C. A (previous classification for certification marks)	Pressure vessels intended for high-pressure application	The registration notes, "The certification mark is used by persons authorized by applicant to certify that the products on which the certification mark is stamped meet applicant's standards for the material, design, construction and workmanship of said products."

on the old language-and-reality theory stated years ago by Edward Sapir: "Human beings . . . are very much at the mercy of the particular language which has become the medium for their society. . . . The fact of the matter is that the 'real world' is to a large extent built up on the language habits of the group."[1]

This notion was further bolstered by the famous Sapir-Whorf hypothesis, which roughly states that one's perception of the world and how one functions in it depends a great deal on the language used. As Sapir, Whorf, and new carriers of the banner would have us believe, language shapes our thinking, channels us along certain patterns embedded in words, syntactic structures, and intonation patterns. Language has become the peg and the shelf that enables us to sort out and categorize the world. In English, we see "cats" and "dogs"; what if the language had also specified *glatz,* meaning "animals that leave fur on the sofa," and *glotz,* meaning "animals that leave fur and drool on the sofa"? How would language, the enabler, have changed our perceptions with slight vocabulary variations?

And if this were the case—of language being the master of destined thought—think of the opportunities lost from failure to evolve two little words, *yes* and *no,* the simplest of opposites! Ghenghis Khan could have been sent back to Mongolia. Opium wars might have been averted. The Cultural Revolution could have been sidestepped.

There are still many, from serious linguists to pop psychology cultists, who view language and reality as inextricably tied, one being the consequence of the other. We have traversed the range from the Sapir-Whorf hypothesis to est° and neurolinguistic programming, which tell us "you are what you say."

I too have been intrigued by the theories. I can summarize, albeit badly, ages-old empirical evidence: of Eskimos and their infinite ways to say "snow," their ability to *see* the differences in snowflake configurations, thanks to the richness of their vocabulary, while non-Eskimo speakers like myself founder in "snow," "more snow," and "lots more where that came from."

I too have experienced dramatic cognitive awakenings via the word. Once I added "mauve" to my vocabulary I began to see it everywhere. When I learned how to pronounce *prix fixe,* I ate French food at prices better than the easier-to-say *à la carte* choices.

But just how seriously are we supposed to take this?

Sapir said something else about language and reality. It is the part that often gets left behind in the dot-dot-dots of quotes: ". . . No two languages are ever sufficiently similar to be considered as representing the same social reality. The worlds in which different societies live are distinct worlds, not merely the same world with different labels attached."

20

---

est: Erhard Seminars Training, a program for large group awareness training founded by Werner Erhard and popular in the 1970s.

When I first read this, I thought, Here at last is validity for the dilemmas I 25
felt growing up in a bicultural, bilingual family! As any child of immigrant
parents knows, there's a special kind of double bind attached to knowing two
languages. My parents, for example, spoke to me in both Chinese and
English; I spoke back to them in English.

"Amy-ah!" they'd call to me.

"What?" I'd mumble back.

"Do not question us when we call," they scolded me in Chinese. "It is not
respectful."

"What do you mean?"

"Ai! Didn't we just tell you not to question?" 30

To this day, I wonder which parts of my behavior were shaped by
Chinese, which by English. I am tempted to think, for example, that if I am
of two minds on some matter it is due to the richness of my linguistic experiences, not to any personal tendencies toward wishy-washiness. But which
mind says what?

Was it perhaps patience—developed through years of deciphering my
mother's fractured English—that had me listening politely while a woman
announced over the phone that I had won one of five valuable prizes? Was
it respect—pounded in by the Chinese imperative to accept convoluted
explanations—that had me agreeing that I might find it worthwhile to
drive seventy-five miles to view a time-share resort? Could I have been at
a loss for words when asked, "Wouldn't you like to win a Hawaiian cruise
or perhaps a fabulous Star of India designed exclusively by Carter and Van
Arpels?"

And when this same woman called back a week later, this time complaining that I had missed my appointment, obviously it was my type A language that kicked into gear and interrupted her. Certainly, my blunt
denial—"Frankly I'm not interested"—was as American as apple pie. And
when she said, "But it's in Morgan Hill," and I shouted, "Read my lips. I
don't care if it's Timbuktu," you can be sure I said it with the precise intonation expressing both cynicism and disgust.

It's dangerous business, this sorting out of language and behavior. Which
one is English? Which is Chinese? The categories manifest themselves: passive and aggressive, tentative and assertive, indirect and direct. And I realize
they are just variations of the same theme: that Chinese people are discreet
and modest.

Reject them all! 35

If my reaction is overly strident, it is because I cannot come across as too
emphatic. I grew up listening to the same lines over and over again, like so
many rote expressions repeated in an English phrasebook. And I too almost
came to believe them.

Yet if I consider my upbringing more carefully, I find there was nothing discreet about the Chinese language I grew up with. My parents made everything abundantly clear. Nothing wishy-washy in their demands, no compromises accepted: "Of course you will become a famous neurosurgeon," they told me. "And yes, a concert pianist on the side."

In fact, now that I remember, it seems that the more emphatic outbursts always spilled over into Chinese: "Not that way! You must wash rice so not a single grain spills out."

I do not believe that my parents—both immigrants from mainland China—are an exception to the modest-and-discreet rule. I have only to look at the number of Chinese engineering students skewing minority ratios at Berkeley, MIT, and Yale. Certainly they were not raised by passive mothers and fathers who said, "It is up to you, my daughter. Writer, welfare recipient, masseuse, or molecular engineer—you decide."

And my American mind says, See, those engineering students weren't able to say no to their parents' demands. But then my Chinese mind remembers: Ah, but those parents all wanted their sons and daughters to be *pre-med*.

And my American mind says, See, those engineering students weren't 40 able to say no to their parents' demands. But then my Chinese mind remembers: Ah, but those parents all wanted their sons and daughters to be *pre-med*.

Having listened to both Chinese and English, I also tend to be suspicious of any comparisons between the two languages. Typically, one language—that of the person doing the comparing—is often used as the standard, the benchmark for a logical form of expression. And so the language being compared is always in danger of being judged deficient or superfluous, simplistic or unnecessarily complex, melodious or cacophonous. English speakers point out that Chinese is extremely difficult because it relies on variations in tone barely discernible to the human ear. By the same token, Chinese speakers tell me English is extremely difficult because it is inconsistent, a language of too many broken rules, of Mickey Mice and Donald Ducks.

Even more dangerous to my mind is the temptation to compare both language and behavior *in translation*. To listen to my mother speak English, one might think she has no concept of past or future tense, that she doesn't see the difference between singular and plural, that she is gender blind because she calls my husband "she." If one were not careful, one might also generalize that, based on the way my mother talks, all Chinese people take a circumlocutory route to get to the point. It is, in fact, my mother's idiosyncratic behavior to ramble a bit.

Sapir was right about differences between two languages and their realities. I can illustrate why word-for-word translation is not enough to translate meaning and intent. I once received a letter from China which I read to non-Chinese-speaking friends. The letter, originally written in Chinese, had been translated by my brother-in law in Beijing. One portion described the time when my uncle at age ten discovered his widowed mother (my grandmother) had remarried—as a number three concubine, the ultimate disgrace for an honorable family. The translated version of my uncle's letter read in part:

> In 1925, I met my mother in Shanghai. When she came to me, I didn't have greeting to her as if seeing nothing. She pull me to a corner secretly and asked me why didn't have greeting to her. I couldn't control myself and cried, "Ma! Why did you leave us? People told me: one day you ate a beancake yourself. Your sister in-law found it and sweared at you, called your names. So . . . is it true?" She clasped my hand and answered immediately, "It's not true, don't say what like this." After this time, there was a few chance to meet her.

"What!" cried my friends. "Was eating a beancake so terrible?"

Of course not. The beancake was simply a euphemism; a ten-year-old boy 45 did not dare question his mother on something as shocking as concubinage. Eating a beancake was his equivalent for committing this selfish act, something inconsiderate of all family members, hence, my grandmother's despairing response to what seemed like a ludicrous charge of gluttony. And sure enough, she was banished from the family, and my uncle saw her only a few times before her death.

While the above may fuel people's argument that Chinese is indeed a language of extreme discretion, it does not mean that Chinese people speak in secrets and riddles. The contexts are fully understood. It is only to those on the *outside* that the language seems cryptic, the behavior inscrutable.

I am, evidently, one of the outsiders. My nephew in Shanghai, who recently started taking English lessons, has been writing me letters in English. I had told him I was a fiction writer, and so in one letter he wrote, "Congratulate to you on your writing. Perhaps one day I should like to read it." I took it in the same vein as "Perhaps one day we can get together for lunch." I sent back a cheery note. A month went by and another letter arrived from Shanghai. "Last one perhaps I hadn't writing distinctly," he said. "In the future, you'll send a copy of your works for me."

I try to explain to my English-speaking friends that Chinese language use is more *strategic* in manner, whereas English tends to be more direct; an American business executive may say, "Let's make a deal," and the Chinese manager may reply, "Is your son interested in learning about your widget business?" Each to his or her own purpose, each with his or her own linguistic path. But I hesitate to add more to the pile of generalizations, because no matter how many examples I provide and explain, I fear that it appears defensive and only reinforces the image: that Chinese people are "discreet and modest"—and it takes an American to explain what they really mean.

Why am I complaining? The description seems harmless enough (after all, the *New York Times Magazine* writer did not say "slippery and evasive"). It is precisely the bland, easy acceptability of the phrase that worries me.

I worry that the dominant society may see Chinese people from a limited 50 —and limiting—perspective. I worry that seemingly benign stereotypes may be part of the reason there are few Chinese in top management positions, in mainstream political roles. I worry about the power of language: that if one says anything enough times—in *any* language—it might become true.

Could this be why Chinese friends of my parents' generation are willing to accept the generalization?

"Why are you complaining?" one of them said to me. "If people think we are modest and polite, let them think that. Wouldn't Americans be pleased to admit they are thought of as polite?"

And I do believe anyone would take the description as a compliment — at first. But after a while, it annoys, as if the only things that people heard one say were phatic remarks: "I'm so pleased to meet you. I've heard many wonderful things about you. For me? You shouldn't have!"

These remarks are not representative of new ideas, honest emotions, or considered thought. They are what is said from the polite distance of social contexts: of greetings, farewells, wedding thank-you notes, convenient excuses, and the like.

It makes me wonder though. How many anthropologists, how many soci- 55 ologists, how many travel journalists have documented so-called "natural interactions" in foreign lands, all observed with spiral notebook in hand? How many other cases are there of the long-lost primitive tribe, people who turned out to be sophisticated enough to put on the stone-age show that ethnologists had come to see?

And how many tourists fresh off the bus have wandered into Chinatown expecting the self-effacing shopkeeper to admit under duress that the goods are not worth the price asked? I have witnessed it.

"I don't know," the tourist said to the shopkeeper, a Cantonese woman in her fifties. "It doesn't look genuine to me. I'll give you three dollars."

"You don't like my price, go somewhere else," said the shopkeeper.

"You are not a nice person," cried the shocked tourist, "not a nice person at all!"

"Who say I have to be nice," snapped the shopkeeper. 60

"So how does one say 'yes' and 'no' in Chinese?" ask my friends a bit warily.

And here I do agree in part with the *New York Times Magazine* article. There is no one word for "yes" or "no"—but not out of necessity to be discreet.

If anything, I would say the Chinese equivalent of answering "yes" or "no" is *discrete*, that is, specific to what is asked.

Ask a Chinese person if he or she has eaten, and he or she might say *chrle* (eaten already) or perhaps *meiyou* (have not).

Ask, "So you had insurance at the time of the accident?" and the response would be *dwei* (correct) or *meiyou* (did not have).

Ask, "Have you stopped beating your wife?" and the answer refers directly to the proposition being asserted or denied: stopped already, still have not, never beat, have no wife.

What could be clearer?

As for those who are still wondering how to translate the language of discretion, I offer this personal example.

My aunt and uncle were about to return to Beijing after a three-month visit to the United States. On their last night I announced I wanted to take them out to dinner.

"Are you hungry?" I asked in Chinese.

"Not hungry," said my uncle promptly, the same response he once gave me ten minutes before he suffered a low-blood-sugar attack.

"Not too hungry," said my aunt. "Perhaps you're hungry?"

"A little," I admitted.

"We can eat, we can eat," they both consented.

"What kind of food?" I asked.

"Oh, doesn't matter. Anything will do. Nothing fancy, just some simple food is fine."

"Do you like Japanese food? We haven't had that yet," I suggested.

They looked at each other.

"We can eat it," said my uncle bravely, this survivor of the Long March.

"We have eaten it before," added my aunt. "Raw fish."

"Oh, you don't like it?" I said. "Don't be polite. We can go somewhere else."

"We are not being polite. We can eat it," my aunt insisted.

So I drove them to Japantown and we walked past several restaurants featuring colorful plastic displays of sushi.

"Not this one, not this one either," I continued to say, as if searching for a Japanese restaurant similar to the last. "Here it is," I finally said, turning into a restaurant famous for its Chinese fish dishes from Shandong.

"Oh, Chinese food!" cried my aunt, obviously relieved.

My uncle patted my arm. "You think Chinese."

"It's your last night here in America," I said. "So don't be polite. Act like an American."

And that night we ate a banquet.

Note

1. Edward Sapir, *Selected Writings*, ed. D. G. Mandelbaum (Berkeley and Los Angeles, 1949).

Working with the Text

1. In "The Language of Discretion," Amy Tan remarks that "the Chinese equivalent of answering 'yes' or 'no' is dis*crete*, that is, specific to what is asked" (par. 62). Look up the terms *discreet* and *discrete* in a college dictionary. Then review the essay with these two terms in mind, and consider what ideas and arguments those two terms enable her to develop. Write a short one-page summary of the essay that casts its argument in terms of those two words.

2. Early in the essay, Tan clarifies that her focus is on "social contexts failing in translation." Drawing on her discussions elsewhere in the essay, clarify what she means. Then write a short response essay in which you analyze the connection between "social context" and "translation" (language use as it moves across communities). Why do social contexts necessarily raise issues of translation and language?

3. Tan writes, "As any child of immigrant parents knows, there's a special kind of double bind attached to knowing two languages" (par. 25). What does Tan mean by "double bind"? In a journal or together with a classmate, use your own acquaintance with two languages (two dialects of English, English and a foreign language, or your native language and the English you have acquired) to come up with one or more scenarios of the sort that Tan describes. In one paragraph, offer that scenario. In a second paragraph, analyze your scenario in light of the arguments that Tan makes.

From Text to Field

1. After Tan writes "language has become the peg and the shelf that enables us to sort out and categorize the world" (par. 18), she goes on to offer a whimsical example: a new way of talking about cats and dogs. As you survey your own initiation into one aspect of the college community, have you stumbled across some important distinctions or categories that our existing language fails to capture? Write your own humorous, whimsical, or satirical essay in which you develop the new vocabulary to capture one such distinction. As you draft and revise this essay, think about the underlying argumentative point you are making and about the audience to whom you are making it.

2. Tan discusses what we might think of as "complimentary" stereotypes about the Chinese. In an essay, explore the problems associated with naïve characterizations of a group that you belong to or a discipline you are studying. Think about how stereotypes arise and why they persist with such strength.

3. Discretion is as much about silence as it is about overt language use. That is, discretion has to do with what needn't or shouldn't be said. Discretion involves expectations, rules or conventions that often become visible only when they are violated. Reflect on such "silent" conventions in a particular community or group or in a particular discipline or classroom. Write an essay in which you articulate the unspoken, in which you reveal the often puzzling "discretions" of a community you belong to or are now just entering.

Public Literacy: Puzzlements of a High School Watcher

Theodore R. Sizer

A paradox of American culture is that even as we place so much emphasis on diversity, we bemoan the fact that our cities, interstates, and institutions tend to look very much alike. For all of our emphasis on local control, our public schools are themselves astonishingly similar to one another. Public literacy—the shared experience expressed in our language, images, and symbols—has become a common subject of academic study in recent years, but when Theodore Sizer delivered his "Public Literacy" presentation in 1988, academics were largely silent on the issue. The following essay is based on Sizer's presentation at the Modern Language Association's "Right to Literacy" Conference, where the focus was on addressing illiteracy. In his essay, Sizer addresses the question, "But what of the shared symbol systems, the public literacy, that we already have? It is shaping, in an unprecedented way, a national culture."

Theodore Sizer has spent most of his academic career "watching" education, particularly secondary education. In the early 1980s, he led a study of the practices in American high schools. After teaching at Harvard and serving as dean of the Harvard Graduate School of Education, he was headmaster of Phillips Academy. Currently Sizer is University Professor Emeritus at Brown University and has been chairman of the Coalition of Essential Schools as well as visiting professor of education at Harvard. Among a number of publications focusing on secondary education is his 1999 book, *The Students Are Watching: Schools and the Moral Contract,* which he wrote with his wife, Nancy Sizer.

To visit among American high schools is to be struck by how similar these venerable social institutions are. Certainly, there is variety, best explained by differences in social class and, to a small extent, the race and the ethnicity of the students. The feel of a school serving the poor is profoundly different from the feel of its cousin in a Gold Coast suburb. However, it is the similarities that impress—the ubiquitous routines, the seven-period day, the bells, home-coming, school defined as English-math-science-social studies-language, each purveyed to students in isolation from every other. There are the texts, the sequence of topics, the testing, and, most important, the assumptions about learning and teaching and schooling that undergird these practices and the wry, usually genial cynicism of the teachers. In a nation priding itself on its local schooling, the consistencies are surprising. And the consistencies are exhibited by the students themselves—their clothing, lingo, enthusiasms, symbols. Again, class counts here, as does geography. But the wonder is why the differences are not far greater. Americans are mesmerized by their differences. Perhaps they should reflect a bit more on their similarities.

There is a wealth of shared knowledge reflected in high school regimens. Kids can move from Bangor to Butte and lose few steps. Not only are the language and the school routines relatively the same, but the nuances and the gestures of getting along remarkably transcend geography. The starker differences among Americans portrayed in basic training barrack scenes from World War II movies seem quaint today to most of us. The fact is that we clearly have a pervasive and powerful public literacy, a set of widely accepted symbols and ideas that give meaning to being American.

At a recent seminar my Brown University colleague Robert Scholes neatly demonstrated this public literacy by asking us to examine carefully what we must already know if we are to understand a twenty-eight-second Budweiser beer television commercial. The spot portrayed a fledgling black baseball umpire. In the half minute he moves from a scruffy minor-league ballpark to a major-league stadium to a close play at third and the resultant tirade from an offended, beefy white manager to the predictable smoke-filled bar where, with a glamorous black woman dutifully at his side, he accepts the tip of a bottle across the room from that same manager. It's all about making it, with Bud. The segment is redolent with assumed meanings. Most foreigners would miss most of it, as Scholes found. We Americans share a culture so completely that we are barely aware of it.

During the week of 19 June 1988, a typical early-summer span, the television sets that reside in more than 95 percent of America's 89 million homes were on some seven hours a day; 14.5 million households tuned in to *Night Court* and *Cheers*; *The Cosby Show* and *Sixty Minutes* drew barely fewer. Earlier that year, 37 million households watched the football Super Bowl. Shared experience, necessarily articulated in widely shared language and symbols, is a stunning reality. This shared experience shapes our expectations and discourse. It is no wonder that our adolescents are so much more

EXHIBIT 4–2
Samples of
Identification
of Goods and
Services
(continued)

Type of Mark	Mark	International Class	Goods/ Services	Other Data
Sound mark registered to Harlem Globetrotters	Sound mark	I.C. 41	Entertainment services in the nature of basketball exhibitions	Registration notes, "The mark consists of the melody 'Sweet Georgia Brown.'"
Collective membership mark	AMERICAN BAR ASSOCIATION	I.C. 200 (previous classification system for collective marks)	Indicating membership in applicant	No other data noted

Basis for Filing Application and Method of Use

The application submitted to the PTO usually specifies one of the following bases for the application (and usually states the manner in which the mark is used):

- actual use of the mark in commerce, specifying a date of first use in commerce and specifying the method of use, such as stating that the mark is affixed to the goods offered under the mark (15 U.S.C. § 1051(a));
- a bona fide intent to use the mark in commerce and specifying the mode or manner in which the mark is intended to be used, such as stating the mark will be used in advertising offering the services (15 U.S.C. § 1051(b));
- a bona fide intent to use the mark in commerce and a claim that the mark is the subject of a prior foreign application (15 U.S.C. § 1126(d)); or
- a bona fide intent to use the mark in commerce and a claim that the mark is the subject of a prior foreign registration (15 U.S.C. § 1126(e)). Applications based on foreign applications and registrations are discussed in Chapter 8.

If the basis for filing the application is not set forth in the application, it can be supplied during examination of the application.

Drawing of Mark

One of the most critical parts of the application is the **drawing** or the display of the mark. Because the drawing is entered into the automated records of the PTO and is available to the public through TESS discussed in Chapter 3 and because the drawing is used when the mark is ultimately published in the PTO publication *Official Gazette* and is reproduced in the actual certificate of registration, the drawing must conform with specific PTO requirements.

There are two types of drawings: typed form drawings and special form drawings. A *typed form drawing* is simply a typewritten display of the mark in uppercase type. For example, the word KRAFT® constitutes a typed drawing. In reality, the display is not a "drawing" at all. A typed form drawing is used when the mark consists solely of words, letters, or numbers with no pictorial or graphical element. If the application uses any special characteristics such as bolding or italicizing of the mark, the mark will be registered in such fashion.

alike than we, considering the expanse and the heterogeneous ethnicity of this country, might otherwise expect.

One might easily mock the results of this shared experience, this 5 American public literacy. It is better to test it undefensively and perhaps try to harness it. Our public literacy is characterized by at least four properties. First, it is centrally driven, usually for purposes of merchandising. Whether with jeans or biology textbooks, the name of the commercial game is national saturation. Only large companies survive in this big league, even if they appear to be little companies. For example, in the textbook field, Silver Burdett, Ginn, Allyn and Bacon, Simon and Schuster, and Prentice Hall are all Gulf and Western satraps. National symbols are expertly crafted. We have a substantial national curriculum, one with few professional educators' or elected school boards' fingerprints on it.

Second, our public literacy is commercial. The vehicle for our shared culture emerges from the selling of things, usually products or services of some sort but also people, in electoral campaigns, and even ideas, as Jim and Tammy Bakker and their kin would have us believe. Much of the message is about demands in the making, provoking us to want things we previously didn't even know about. Thus, it's expansive, broadening. If you've never tried oat bran, you haven't lived. Move up to a Buick.

Third, our public literacy simplifies, synthesizes, unifies, focuses. *USA Today.* The McDonald's arches. Stylized logos. The *Harpers* short-essay format. The point is to be made simply, easily, quickly, and, above all, effectively. The sound bite. The powerful metaphor: an iron curtain. The utterly memorable modern version of Confucian analects. The reduction of a full life-style to the snapshot of a celebrity: *People* magazine.

Finally, our public literacy is pedagogically sophisticated, using understandings about human learning and a range of technologies far beyond the school-teacher's ken. There are tie-ins—film to video to books to T-shirts. Clustered media characterize this pedagogy, the carefully coordinated use of sight and sound and print in artful, powerful combination. It is tough for your average French teacher to compete with MTV. As teachers, we school and college folk limp far behind our cousins in the communications industry.

We clearly have a pervasive and powerful public literacy.

The questions all this provokes are as demanding as they are obvious. Is this shared experience, this public literacy, a good thing? Is it tasteless? Is some of it, in fact, a vicious form of "acceptable" lying? Or is it modestly more benign, merely purveying corrupting fictions? Does it, with an artfulness that provokes acceptance and passivity, undermine habits of thoughtfulness? Is it undemocratic?

Why do we have it? Or, put more cogently, who wants it? (Public accept- 10 ance to date seems to be almost universal.) Should it be changed? That is, should there be rules of public discourse, as well as rules of the road, or is the First Amendment the inevitable protector of tawdriness and dishonesty, as well as free expression? Can, in fact, a public literacy be changed? What are the costs in trying to change it? Who should change it? Government? If so, by direct regulation, a national assessment of all the educating media? Or by indirection, through the tax code, with great business advantages given to alternative or public (not-for-profit) enterprises? Or do we leave change to the market, hoping that an aroused public will clean up mindlessness and worse in the common domain, somewhat as it appears to be doing to rid publicly shared air of cigarette-smoke pollution?

There must be answers to these questions. My concern here, however, is not to pursue these but to express some puzzlements. Why aren't we talking much about this ubiquitous public literacy? The intense and visible concern for illiteracy, for the inability of many to read and to find meaning in that reading—as reflected in this conference—is as sincere and important as it is conventional; folks have to be able to read, understand, and articulate to survive in this society. But what of the shared symbol systems, the public literacy, that we already have? It is shaping, in an unprecedented way, a national culture. Its power seems greater in some important respects than the formal teaching in schools and colleges.

The academy itself accepts the megaculture, the machine for public literacy, in a revealing way: It barely studies the matter. Higher education has been largely mute, for example, about the threat to academic freedom implicit in national testing or a de facto nationalized and virtually monopolistic textbook industry. The effects of television on American thought are remarkably little studied. We accept cultural gigantism, little reflecting on its meaning. By contrast, our savage little debates about critical theory rarely focus on the texts that saturate our cultural life but turn around intense little obscurities that, while perhaps of intellectual merit, have no cultural significance.

I am puzzled by how easily we rely on quick fixes in these matters— acceptance of a single score on a forty-minute machine-graded test to rate a school or to rank a student against hundreds of thousands of others; a glib dismissal of the mass media, one resting on precious little empirical data; an avoidance of that army of people in the communications industry who are, in fact, teaching our people their shared values; concession to the encroachments on individual freedom implicit in the increasingly centralized character of our institutions. We aren't paying enough attention, and a charge of myopia against the academy is not too strong. However, there is not just inattention; there is in all too many quarters active hostility to studying the popular culture in general, much less its aspect as a form of literacy. Such concerns are considered soft, unworthy activity for the bright person seeking tenure. It is both strange and sad.

The academy must recognize the reality of a public literacy, see it in perspective, and study it carefully. We must adopt a rich definition of this public literacy. As E. D. Hirsch has reminded us, it has a content, and we must see it as a content in context—gregarious, changeable, reflected and used in a rich variety of media. But content is only a part; no functioning literacy is merely facts; it is the ways of using those facts, of using style, of exhibiting habits. This use or exhibition arises from incentives, and the incentives that a culture presents its citizens shape their willingness to use and to be in the habit of using the values, content, and symbols that tie that culture together. Incentives arise from politics, both formal and informal, and the social system in which those politics proceed. Americans need to know more about the real content of our literacy, about its exhibition, and about the incentives and the politics that produce such incentives, that provoke that exhibition. It is the duty of the academy to pursue these complex issues.

In sum, we have an unprecedented wide public literacy in this country. All those adolescents roiling through their schools' standardized routines and responding collectively to mass media's messages are evidence enough of that. Let us pay close attention to this new phenomenon, this product of affluence and technology. And if we find it wanting, let us be about changing it.   15

Working with the Text

1. The title of Theodore Sizer's essay presents an odd combination: It mixes the public with the academic. Write a brief essay in which you comment on Sizer's strategic use of his title. How does his "puzzlement" provide a key to a fresher understanding of why academics should pay more attention to public literacy?

2. To illustrate how "pervasive and powerful" our public literacy is, Sizer describes an exercise led by Brown University's Robert Scholes, in which he asked his colleagues to identify "what we must already know . . . to understand" a beer commercial (par. 3). To reflect on the point Scholes wanted to make, choose a commercial that you find especially effective or entertaining. With Sizer's essay in mind, write a brief essay in which you identify what a viewer would have to already know to interpret the message of the commercial. What images, actions, phrases, and assumed values would only an American be likely to understand?

3. Sizer analyzes our public literacy by claiming that it is "characterized by at least four properties" (par. 5). As you reread the essay, review those properties. In a brief essay, use the properties to analyze an artifact in our culture—an image,

an object, a phrase, a gesture, an icon—that you consider to be part of our "public literacy."

4. The purpose of Sizer's argument, which was originally an address for a Modern Language Association conference, is to persuade his colleagues to study and critique our public literacy. Reread the final segment of the essay, starting with "The academy itself accepts the megaculture, the machine for public literacy, in a revealing way: It barely studies the matter" (par. 12). From your perspective as a student, write a brief proposal to academics persuading them to study an aspect of our public literacy that raises an issue or issues identified by Sizer that are also concerns for you.

From Text to Field

1. Sizer challenges his audience to analyze our public literacy by asserting, "The questions all this provokes are as demanding as they are obvious" (par. 9). What follows are two paragraphs of those questions. Based on your own knowledge, observations, and experience, write an essay in which you answer one or more of the questions that interest you most.

2. One of Sizer's deepest concerns is that the power of our public literacy "seems greater in some important respects than the formal teaching in schools and colleges" (par. 11). From your perspective as a student, write an essay in which you reflect on whether this has been the case for you. If aspects of our public literacy have been more powerful for you than your formal education, what are they, and why have they had a greater influence? If your formal education has been more powerful, in what ways, and why?

3. Sizer indicts academics for accepting "quick fixes" in the face of what he considers to be serious challenges from the "megaculture." Review the examples of issues that concern Sizer along these lines, listed in the paragraph that begins, "I am puzzled by how easily we rely on quick fixes in these matters" (par. 13). Write an essay in which you explore how one of these "matters" is manifesting itself in our culture. For example, you might explore a way or ways in which the "army of people in the communications industry" are "teaching our people their shared values." Or you might analyze particular "encroachments on individual freedom implicit in the increasingly centralized character of our institutions."

From Outside, In

Barbara Mellix

Each one of us, at varying points in life and career, will find ourselves moving, as in the title of this essay, "From Outside, In." This entry can also be, in some sense, a leave-taking, and as such can involve several communities. It also may involve complicated relationships between language and power and may require a new awareness of what is "proper" in each community. No easy move, this stepping "from outside, in." It forces us to rethink who we are and may prompt us to discover both the limits and the resourcefulness of language.

Raised in Greeleyville, South Carolina, Barbara Mellix draws on her own vexed relationship to multiple languages and communities in this essay, published in the *Georgia Review* in 1987. The essay recounts her experiences from early childhood through her first college writing courses that she took as a working mother. Mellix went on to receive her MFA in creative writing in 1986 from the University of Pittsburgh. In addition to teaching writing in the English department at the University of Pittsburgh, she serves as executive assistant dean in the College of Arts and Sciences, where she edits the college's alumni magazine.

Two years ago, when I started writing this paper, trying to bring order out of chaos, my ten-year-old daughter was suffering from an acute attack of boredom. She drifted in and out of the room complaining that she had nothing to do, no one to "be with" because none of her friends were at home. Patiently I explained that I was working on something special and needed peace and quiet, and I suggested that she paint, read, or work with her computer. None of these interested her. Finally, she pulled up a chair to my desk and watched me, now and then heaving long, loud sighs. After two or three minutes (nine or ten sighs), I lost my patience. "Looka here, Allie," I said, "you are too old for this kinda carryin' on. I done told you this is important. You wronger than dirt to be in here haggin' me like this and you know it. Now git on outta here and leave me off before I put my foot all the way down."

I was at home, alone with my family, and my daughter understood that this way of speaking was appropriate in that context. She knew, as a matter of fact, that it was almost inevitable; when I get angry at home, I speak some of my finest, most cherished black English. Had I been speaking to my daughter in this manner in certain other environments, she would have been shocked and probably worried that I had taken leave of my sense of propriety.

Like my children, I grew up speaking what I considered two distinctly different languages—black English and standard English (or as I thought of them then, the ordinary everyday speech of "country" coloreds and "proper" English)—and in the process of acquiring these languages, I developed an understanding of when, where, and how to use them. But unlike my children, I grew up in a world that was primarily black. My friends, neighbors, minister, teachers—almost everybody I associated with every day—were black. And we spoke to one another in our own special language: *That sho is a pretty dress you got on. If she don' soon leave me off I'm gon tell her head a mess. I was so mad I could'a pissed a blue rod. He all the time trying to low-rate somebody. Ain't that just about the nastiest thing you ever set ears on?*

Then there were the "others," the "proper" blacks, transplanted relatives and one-time friends who came home from the city for weddings, funerals, and vacations. To these we spoke standard English. "Ain't?" my mother would yell at me when I used the term in the presence of "others." "You *know* better than that." And I would hang my head in shame and say the "proper" word.

I remember one summer sitting in my grandmother's house in ₅ Greeleyville, South Carolina, when it was full of the chatter of city relatives who were home on vacation. My parents sat quietly, only now and then volunteering a comment or answering a question. My mother's face took on a strained expression when she spoke. I could see that she was being careful to say just the right words in just the right way. Her voice sounded thick, muffled. And when she finished speaking, she would lapse into silence, her proper smile on her face. My father was more articulate, more aggressive. He spoke quickly, his words sharp and clear. But he held his proud head higher, a signal that he, too, was uncomfortable. My sisters and brothers and I stared at our aunts, uncles, and cousins, speaking only when prompted. Even then, we hesitated, formed our sentences in our minds, then spoke softly, shyly.

My parents looked small and anxious during those occasions, and I waited impatiently for our leave-taking when we would mock our relatives the moment we were out of their hearing. "Reeely," we would say to one another, flexing our wrists and rolling our eyes, "how dooo you stan' this heat? Chile, it just too hyooo-mid for words." Our relatives had made us feel "country," and this was our way of regaining pride in ourselves while getting a little revenge in the bargain. The words bubbled in our throats and rolled across our tongues, a balming.

As a child I felt this same doubleness in uptown Greeleyville where the whites lived. "Ain't that a pretty dress you're wearing!" Toby, the town police-man, said to me one day when I was fifteen. "Thank you very much," I replied, my voice barely audible in my own ears. The words felt wrong in my mouth, rigid, foreign. It was not that I had never spoken that phrase before—it was common in black English, too—but I was extremely conscious that this was an occasion for proper English. I had taken out my English and put it on as I did my church clothes, and I felt as if I were wearing my Sunday best in the middle of the week. It did not matter that Toby had not spoken grammatically correct English. He was white and could speak as he wished. I had something to prove. Toby did not.

Speaking standard English to whites was our way of demonstrating that we knew their language and could use it. Speaking it to standard-English-speaking blacks was our way of showing them that we, as well as they, could "put on airs." But when we spoke stan-dard English, we acknowledged (to ourselves and to others—but primarily to ourselves) that our custom-ary way of speaking was inferior. We felt foolish, embarrassed, somehow diminished because we were ashamed to be our real selves. We were reserved, shy in the presence of those who owned and/or spoke *the* language.

> I write and continually give birth to myself.

My parents never set aside time to drill us in standard English. Their forms of instruction were less formal. When my father was feeling particu-larly expansive, he would regale us with tales of his exploits in the outside world. In almost fluent English, complete with dialogue and flavored with gestures and embellishment, he told us about his attempt to get a haircut at a white barbershop; his refusal to acknowledge one of the town merchants until the man addressed him as "Mister"; the time he refused to step off the sidewalk uptown to let some whites pass; his airplane trip to New York City (to visit a sick relative) during which the stewardess and porters—recognizing that he was a "gentleman"—addressed him as "Sir." I did not realize then—nor, I think, did my father—that he was teaching us, among other things, standard English and the relationship between language and power.

My mother's approach was different. Often, when one of us said, "I'm gon wash off my feet," she would say, "And what will you walk on if you wash them off?" Everyone would laugh at the victim of my mother's "proper" mood. But it was different when one of us children was in a proper mood. "You think you are so superior," I said to my oldest sister one day when we were arguing and she was winning. "Superior!" my sister mocked. "You mean I am acting 'biggidy'?" My sisters and brothers sniggered, then joined in teasing me. Finally, my mother said, "Leave your sister alone. There's

10

nothing wrong with using proper English." There was a half-smile on her face. I had gotten "uppity," had "put on airs" for no good reason. I was at home, alone with the family, and I hadn't been prompted by one of my mother's proper moods. But there was also a proud light in my mother's eyes; her children were learning English very well.

Not until years later, as a college student, did I begin to understand our ambivalence toward English, our scorn of it, our need to master it, to own and be owned by it—an ambivalence that extended to the public-school classroom. In our school, where there were no whites, my teachers taught standard English but used black English to do it. When my grammar-school teachers wanted us to write, for example, they usually said something like, "I want y'all to write five sentences that make a statement. Anybody get done before the rest can color." It was probably almost those exact words that led me to write these sentences in 1953 when I was in the second grade:

The white clouds are pretty.
There are only 15 people in our room.
We will go to gym.
We have a new poster.
We may go out doors.

Second grade came after "Little First" and "Big First," so by then I knew the implied rules that accompanied all writing assignments. Writing was an occasion for proper English. I was not to write in the way we spoke to one another: The white clouds pretty; There ain't but 15 people in our room; We going to gym; We got a new poster; We can go out in the yard. Rather I was to use the language of "other": clouds *are*, there *are*, we *will*, we *may*.

My sentences were short, rigid, perfunctory, like the letters my mother wrote to relatives:

Dear Papa,
How are you? How is Mamie? Fine I hope. We are fine. We will come to see you Sunday. Cousin Ned will give us a ride.
    Love,
    Daughter

The language was not ours. It was something from outside us, something we used for special occasions.

But my coloring on the other side of that second-grade paper is different. I drew three hearts and a sun. The sun has a smiling face that radiates and envelops everything it touches. And although the sun and its world are enclosed in a circle, the colors I used—red, blue, green, purple, orange, yellow, black—indicates that I was less restricted with drawing and coloring than I was with writing standard English. My valentines were not just red. My sun was not just a yellow ball in the sky.

By the time I reached the twelfth grade, speaking and writing standard English had taken on new importance. Each year, about half of the newly graduated seniors of our school moved to large cities—particularly in the North—to live with relatives and find work. Our English teacher constantly corrected our grammar: "Not 'ain't,' but 'isn't.'" We seldom wrote papers, and even those few were usually plot summaries of short stories. When our teacher returned the papers, she usually lectured on the importance of using standard English: "I *am*; you *are*; he, she, or it *is*," she would say, writing on the chalkboard as she spoke. "How you gon git a job talking about 'I is,' or 'I isn't' or 'I ain't'?"

In Pittsburgh, where I moved after graduation, I watched my aunt and 15 uncle—who had always spoken standard English when in Greeleyville — switch from black English to standard English to a mixture of the two, according to where they were or who they were with. At home and with certain close relatives, friends, and neighbors, they spoke black English. With those less close, they spoke a mixture. In public and with strangers, they generally spoke standard English.

In time, I learned to speak standard English with ease and to switch smoothly from black to standard or a mixture, and back again. But no matter where I was, no matter what the situation or occasion, I continued to write as I had in school:

> Dear Mommie,
> How are you? How is everybody else? Fine I hope. I am fine. So are Aunt and Uncle. Tell everyone I said hello. I will write again soon.
> Love,
> Barbara

At work, at a health insurance company, I learned to write letters to customers. I studied form letters and letters written by coworkers, memorizing the phrases and the ways in which they were used. I dictated:

> Thank you for your letter of January 5. We have made the changes in your coverage you requested. Your new premium will be $150 every three months. We are pleased to have been of service to you.

In a sense, I was proud of the letters I wrote for the company: They were proof of my ability to survive in the city, the outside world—an indication of my growing mastery of English. But they also indicate that writing was still mechanical for me, something that didn't require much thought.

Reading also became a more significant part of my life during those early years in Pittsburgh. I had always liked reading, but now I devoted more and more of my spare time to it. I read romances, mysteries, popular novels. Looking back, I realized that the books I liked best were simple, unambiguous: good versus bad and right versus wrong with right rewarded and wrong punished, mysteries unraveled and all set right in the end. It was how I remembered life in Greeleyville.

Of course I was romanticizing. Life in Greeleyville had not been so very uncomplicated. Back there I had been—first as a child, then as a young woman with limited experience in the outside world—living in a relatively closed-in society. But there were implicit and explicit principles that guided our way of life and shaped our relationships with one another and the people outside—principles that a newcomer would find elusive and baffling. In Pittsburgh, I had matured, become more experienced: I had worked at three different jobs, associated with a wider range of people, married, had children. This new environment with different prescripts for living required that I speak standard English much of the time, and slowly, imperceptibly, I had ceased seeing a sharp distinction between myself and "others." Reading romances and mysteries, characterized by dichotomy, was a way of shying away from change, from the person I was becoming.

But that other part of me—that part which took great pride in my ability to hold a job writing business letters—was increasingly drawn to the new developments in my life and the attending possibilities, opportunities for even greater change. If I could write letters for a nationally known business, could I not also do something better, more challenging, more important? Could I not, perhaps, go to college and become a school teacher? For years, afraid and a little embarrassed, I did no more than imagine this different me, this possible me. But sixteen years after coming north, when my younger daughter entered kindergarten, I found myself unable—or unwilling—to resist the lure of possibility. I enrolled in my first college course: Basic Writing, at the University of Pittsburgh.

For the first time in my life, I was required to write extensively about 20 myself. Using the most formal English at my command, I wrote these sentences near the beginning of the term:

> One of my duties as a homemaker is simply picking up after others. A day seldom passes that I don't search for a mislaid toy, book, or gym shoe, etc. I change the Ty-D-Bol, fight "ring around the collar," and keep our laundry smelling "April fresh." Occasionally, I settle arguments between my children and suggest things to do when they're bored. Taking telephone messages for my oldest daughter is my newest (and sometimes most aggravating) chore. Hanging the toilet paper is my most insignificant.

My concern was to use "appropriate" language, to sound as if I belonged in a college classroom. But I felt separate from the language—as if it did not and could not belong to me. I couldn't think and feel genuinely in that language, couldn't make it express what I thought and felt about being a housewife. A part speaking, you should shun those faculty members, no matter how famous they might be, who tend to:

(1) Make you feel that you or your problems are unwelcome. Some people simply cannot rule out the influence of certain prejudices, which could be applied as some invisible discrimination against you for nothing of your fault. Some others may just not want to get involved in some of your problems. Still some others may merely care too much about themselves. If one of them becomes your advisor, it is unlikely that you will get the full assistance and support you need. Rather, this person might even become an important source of your disappointment, stress, and frustration. One situation could be that she would approve your proposal, but later says you should not study that subject after all.

(2) Appear very stressed or unstable themselves. People, even very nice people, cannot function well or just act normally when they get overwhelmed. This sometimes happens, for instance, when a new faculty member is driven crazy by expectations on himself to publish or perish. Your advisor must be able to commit certain amount of time to help you. On the other hand, you do not want to be forced to switch your advisor someday because the advisor you chose is leaving for good.

(3) Have a rigid academic style. Here "rigid" is used in a negative sense, meaning that some persons cannot take different viewpoints or new ideas easily. They tend to be very picky about details, and if they find something they do not like they will become impatient reading the rest of your thesis or dissertation, no matter what great work it is or could be. People are sometimes autocratic and would impose their ideas on others, especially on those who are at their disposal, before they understand what the others mean. If this forms a personality trait, you should try not to become a victim of it. Nevertheless, you must not confuse this situation with anything that just appears to be academically strict to you, which is actually what you need as a student. In any case, taking advice gracefully will benefit your academic growth as well as your personal health.

The guide books you can find in your library usually stress the importance of matching your research interests with those of your advisor's. Yet faculty members who remember their experience as either students or advisors in the thesis/dissertation process might not regard this as crucial as it appears to be. Some might even declare that they can supervise a research project on any topic in their field since what the student needs, they believe, is mainly a methodological guide. In the above we have seen some of the things even beyond that. To find your ideal advisor is not that straightforward indeed. It is also a matter of

Such a mark (or one displaying letters in script or some other unique font or display) is referred to as "stylized." A *special form drawing* presents a mark that consists solely of a pictorial or design element or words and numbers together with a pictorial or design element. For example, the well-known display of actor Paul Newman on various food products is an example of a special form or design mark. As long as the special form will reproduce satisfactorily, it may be photocopied for the PTO. If the mark will not reproduce satisfactorily, an artist or draftsperson may have to be hired to produce a pen and ink drawing. Across the top of the drawing sheet, the applicant must include a typewritten heading providing basic information, specifically, the name and address of the applicant, the goods or services offered under the mark, and the date the mark was first used and was first used in commerce (if the application is based on actual use of the mark).

The drawing should be set forth on a separate drawing page, a single sheet of lettersize paper. The drawing should be between 2½ inches and 4 inches high and/or wide. Thus, there may be a need to photocopy the mark several times to reduce it to the appropriate size for the PTO.

The precise and exacting requirements for the drawing page correlate to the method for searching conducted in the PTO Trademark Search Library. If individuals could display marks in any format they desired, searching the PTO records to determine if a confusingly similar mark exists would be nearly impossible. Moreover, the PTO ultimately publishes the marks in the *Official Gazette*. Conformity in display of marks allows for ready review of the published marks.

Because applications filed under 15 U.S.C. § 1051(b) are based on an intent to use the mark in the future, an applicant may not have made a final determination on the exact appearance of a mark at the time an application is filed. For intent-to-use applications, the PTO will allow some minor variation between the drawing submitted at the time the application is filed and the mark as actually used. Nevertheless, the drawing must be a substantially exact representation of the mark as it will eventually be used.

If an applicant wishes to claim color as a feature of the mark, the application must so specify. For example, the applicant will be required to state "the mark is shown in the color blue." If color is not claimed, the mark may be displayed in any color. Generally, therefore, color is claimed only when such a feature is critical to recognition of the mark, such as the golden color of McDonald's "golden arches" mark.

No drawing is required if the mark consists only of a sound, scent, or other nonvisual matter. For these types of marks, the applicant must submit a detailed written description of the mark.

Specimens

If the application is made under 15 U.S.C. § 1051(a) and alleges that the mark has been used in commerce, the PTO will require that the applicant submit proof of such use by providing a **"specimen"** of the mark showing exactly how the mark is seen by the public. One specimen must be filed for each class of goods named in the application. Thus, if the application is for HELENA (& SWAN DESIGN) for soap in I.C. 3 and sweaters in I.C. 25, two specimens must be submitted.

Actual tags, bags, labels, and other similar items are highly preferred over photocopies. For example, the best specimen for the soap just described would be a wrapper for the soap, clearly showing the mark HELENA (& SWAN DESIGN). An appropriate specimen for the sweaters would be an actual tag that is sewn into the back of the garments. If the mark appears on a bulky item, such as a refrigerator or park bench, it would be ludicrous to send in the of me resented, among other things, being judged by such things as the appearance of my family's laundry and toilet bowl, but in that language I could only imagine and write about a conventional housewife.

For the most part, the remainder of the term was a period of adjustment, a time of trying to find my bearings as a student in a college composition class, to learn to shut out my black English whenever I composed, and to prevent it from creeping into my formulations; a time for trying to grasp the language of the classroom and reproduce it in my prose; for trying to talk about myself in that language, reach others through it. Each experience of writing was like standing naked and revealing my imperfection, my "otherness." And each new assignment was another chance to make myself over in language, reshape myself, make myself "better" in my rapidly changing image of a student in a college composition class.

But writing became increasingly unmanageable as the term progressed, and by the end of the semester, my sentences sounded like this:

> My excitement was soon dampened, however, by what seemed like a small voice in the back of my head saying that I should be careful with my long awaited opportunity. I felt frustrated and this seemed to make it difficult to concentrate.

There is a poverty of language in these sentences. By this point, I knew that the clichéd language of my Housewife essay was unacceptable, and I generally recognized trite expressions. At the same time, I hadn't yet mastered the language of the classroom, hadn't yet come to see it as belonging to me. Most notable is the lifelessness of the prose, the apparent absence of a person behind the words. I wanted those sentences—and the rest of the essay—to convey the anguish of yearning to, at once, become something more and yet remain the same. I had the sensation of being split in two, part of me going into a future the other part didn't believe possible. As that person, the student writer at that moment, I was essentially mute. I could not—in the process of composing—use the language of the old me, yet I couldn't imagine myself in the language of "others."

I found this particularly discouraging because at midsemester I had been writing in a much different way. Note the language of this introduction to an essay I had written then, near the middle of the term:

> Pain is a constant companion to the people in "Footwork." Their jobs are physically damaging. Employers are insensitive to their feelings and in many cases add to their problems. The general public wounds them further by treating them with disgrace because of what they do for a living. Although the workers are as diverse as they are similar, there is a definite link between them. They suffer a great deal of abuse.

The voice here is stronger, more confident, [with] appropriate terms like "physically damaging," "wounds them further," "insensitive," "diverse"—terms I couldn't have imagined using when writing about my own experience—and shaping them into sentences like "Although the workers are as diverse as they are similar, there is a definite link between them." And there is the sense of a personality behind the prose, someone who sympathizes with the workers. "The general public wounds them further by treating them with disgrace because of what they do for a living."

What causes these differences? I was, I believed, explaining other people's thoughts and feelings, and I was free to move about in the language of "others" so long as I was speaking *of* others. I was unaware that I was transforming into my best classroom language my own thoughts and feelings about people whose experiences and ways of speaking were in many ways similar to mine.

The following year, unable to turn back or to let go of what had become   25 something of an obsession with language (and hoping to catch and hold the sense of control that had eluded me in Basic Writing), I enrolled in a research writing course. I spent most of the term learning how to prepare for and write a research paper. I chose sex education as my subject and spent hours in libraries, searching for information, reading, taking notes. Then (not without messiness and often demoralizing frustration) I organized my information into categories, wrote a thesis statement, and composed my paper—a series of paragraphs and quotations spaced between carefully constructed transitions. The process and results felt artificial, but as I would later come to realize I was passing through a necessary stage. My sentences sounded like this:

> This reserve becomes understandable with examination of who the abusers are. In an overwhelming number of cases, they are people the victims know and trust. Family members, relatives, neighbors, and close family friends commit seventy-five percent of all reported sex crimes against children, and parents, parent substitutes, and relatives are the offenders in thirty to eighty percent of all reported cases. While assault by strangers does occur, it is less common, and is usually a single episode. But abuse by family members, relatives, and acquaintances may continue for an extended period of time. In cases of incest, for example, children are abused repeatedly for an average of eight years. In such cases, "the use of physical force is rarely necessary because of the child's trusting, dependent relationship with the offender. The child's cooperation is often facilitated by the adult's position of dominance, an offer of material goods, a threat of physical violence, or a misrepresentation of moral standards."

The completed paper gave me a sense of profound satisfaction, and I read it often after my professor returned it. I know now that what I was pleased with was the language I used and the professional voice it helped me maintain. "Use better words," my teacher had snapped at me one day after reading the notes I'd begun accumulating from my research, and slowly I began taking on the language of my sources. In my next set of notes, I used the word "vacillating"; my professor applauded. And by the time I composed the final draft, I felt at ease with terms like "overwhelming number of cases," "single episode," and "reserve," and I shaped them into sentences similar to those of my "expert" sources.

If I were writing the paper today, I would of course do some things differently. Rather than open with an anecdote—as my teacher suggested—I would begin simply with a quotation that caught my interest as I was researching my paper (and which I scribbled, without its source, in the margin of my notebook): "Truth does not do so much good in the world as the semblance of truth does evil." The quotation felt right because it captured what was for me the central idea of my essay—an idea that emerged gradually during the making of my paper—and expressed it in a way I would like to have said it. The anecdote, a hypothetical situation I invented to conform to the information in the paper, felt forced and insincere because it represented—to a great degree—my teacher's understanding of the essay, *her* idea of what in it was most significant. Improving upon my previous experiences with writing, I was beginning to think and feel in the language I used, to find my own voices in it, to sense that how one speaks influences how one means. But I was not yet secure enough, comfortable enough with the language to trust my intuition.

Now that I know that to seek knowledge, freedom, and autonomy means always to be in the concentrated process of becoming—always to be venturing into new territory, feeling one's way at first, then getting one's balance, negotiating, accommodating, discovering one's self in ways that previously defined "others"—I sometimes get tired. And I ask myself why I keep on participating in this highbrow form of violence, this slamming against perplexity. But there is no real futility in the question, no hint of that part of the old me who stood outside standard English, hugging to herself a disabling mistrust of a language she thought could not represent a person with her history and experience. Rather, the question represents a person who feels the consequences of her education, the weight of her possibilities as a teacher and writer and human being, a voice in society. And I would not change that person, would not give back the good burden that accompanies my growing expertise, my increasing power to shape myself in language and share that self with "others."

"To speak," says Frantz Fanon, "means to be in a position to use a certain syntax, to grasp the morphology of this or that language, but it means above all to assume a culture, to support the weight of civilization."[1] To write means to do the same, but in a more profound sense. However, Fanon also says that to achieve mastery means to "get" in a position of power, to "grasp," to "assume." This I have learned both as a student and subsequently as a teacher—can involve tremendous emotional and psychological conflict for those attempting to master academic disclosure. Although as a beginning student writer I had a fairly good grasp of ordinary spoken English and was proficient at what Labov calls "code-switching" (and what John Baugh in *Black Street Speech* terms "style shifting"), when I came face to face with the demands of academic writing, I grew increasingly self-conscious, constantly aware of my status as a black and a speaker of one of the many black English vernaculars—a traditional outsider. For the first time, I experienced my sense of doubleness as something menacing, a built-in enemy. Whenever I turned inward for salvation, the balm so available during my childhood, I found instead this new fragmentation which spoke to me in many voices. It was the voice of my desire to prosper, but at the same time it spoke of what I had relinquished and could not regain: a safe way of being, a state of powerlessness which exempted me from responsibility for who I was and might be. And it accused me of betrayal, of turning away from blackness. To recover balance, I had to take on the language of the academy, the language of "others." And to do that, I had to learn to imagine myself as a part of the culture of that language, and therefore someone free to manage that language, to take liberties with it. Writing and rewriting, practicing, experimenting, I came to comprehend more fully the generative power of language. I discovered—with the help of some especially sensitive teachers—that through writing one can continually bring new selves into being, each with new responsibilities and difficulties, but also with new possibilities. Remarkable power, indeed. I write and continually give birth to myself.

Note

1. *Black Skin, White Masks* (1952; rpt. New York: Grove Press, 1967), pp. 17–18.

Working with the Text

1. Even as Barbara Mellix tells us a story, she is making an argument. How would you rephrase her argument as one core assertion? As you reread the essay, try out several such assertions. Choose one that seems to capture her argument and build a one-paragraph summary of the essay's argument (not its chronological story) around that statement. In a second paragraph, reflect on what the summary has brought to light and what it now hides from view. What is persuasive about the narrative or story that is difficult to capture in a summary of the argument?

2. Early in the essay, Mellix uses the term *propriety*, a term that continues to be central throughout her essay. Look up *propriety* in a college dictionary, and

then reread Mellix in light of this concept. In a short essay, clarify what you think to be Mellix's attitude toward propriety. What is the relationship between propriety and community? propriety and power?

3. Given the title of Mellix's essay, "From Outside, In," write a one-page characterization of her rhetorical situation. That is, consider how Mellix has incorporated her speaking "selves" into the essay, who her intended audience seems to be, and how both affect her take on the subject of advanced literacy.

From Text to Field

1. Underlying much of Mellix's essay is the complex relationship between speaking and writing, between orality and literacy. Write an essay in which you analyze the difficulties of developing more advanced literacy in a world that leaves less time for books and accords more prominence to oral/spoken technologies such as television and radio.

2. At several points in her essay, Mellix raises the connection between language and power. Review the essay in light of that relationship. What several dimensions of power (institutional, social, pedagogical, personal) come into play? Can power both constrain and empower? Given your reading of Mellix's essay, turn your attention to the role of writing in your own college education. Write an essay in which you analyze the several ways power exerts itself over your writing or develops through your writing.

3. Mellix speaks of a "doubleness," of both a loss and a gain, that she experiences as she learns standard English. She also notes an "ambivalence toward English, our scorn of it, our need to master it, to own and be owned by it" (par. 11). In a short essay, comment on that doubleness, the reasons that occasion it, and the consequences of it. How is this doubleness related to the role of the mature Mellix as narrator or to your own role as a college student as you look back on your development as a writer? What are her, and your, challenges in dealing with several communities at once, each one bleeding into others? Can one distinguish "outside" and "inside" as clearly as Mellix's title seems to suggest?

INTO THE FIELD: Options for Writing Projects

1. The Languages of Community: An Ethnographic Report

Consider a nonacademic community to which you belong that is organized around some activity—a volunteer organization, for example, or perhaps a fraternity or sorority. How does language help constitute or regulate that community? Given your community, what is the relationship between language and consensus? Between language and social activity? Does language identify insiders and outsiders and thus serve a kind of "gatekeeping" function, a kind of "secret handshake"?

Describe and analyze this community as if you were an ethnographer who came upon this culture on some remote island. (An ethnographer is a field researcher who lives, observes, describes, and analyzes the daily life, behaviors, and language of a group of people over a period of time.) You may wish to focus on one particular social event or one "text" to help focus your analysis.

2. Literacy and Illiteracy in Your Community

Illiteracy is a difficult problem to address because it is invisible: No outward signs will single out this or that person. But illiteracy is also difficult to address because our ignorance of the prevalence of the issue can render it invisible. We might assume, for example, that our college town—because it is a "college" town—couldn't possibly have a literacy problem among its residents. But even the most prosperous communities often have a hidden problem with literacy.

This field project invites you to learn more about literacy and illiteracy in your hometown or in the community where you go to college. The local public library or your university's community outreach office can probably provide information about existing literacy programs, the literacy demographics of your community, and opportunities for volunteer work or service learning that can aid literacy efforts.

For this project, you may find it useful to write a profile of community efforts to improve literacy or you may wish to write a proposal for an initiative to help students become involved in literacy education in the community.

3. Insider's Guide to a Course

Recently you may have taken a class in a discipline previously unfamiliar to you, perhaps for general-education requirements or as a gateway course into your major. Analyze what might be the seemingly "foreign" language of a specific "text" in that course: the remarks made by your professor during one class, the preface or introduction to a textbook, the syllabus for the course, or a particular assignment. How does that language reflect the community you are entering, be it the disciplinary community or the classroom community? What are the means of exclusion and inclusion that separate insiders from outsiders? How does the language used imply a particular view of the world? How does language serve as a means of exerting power?

For your project, write an "Insider's Guide" to the text you have chosen from that course. Your goal is to help a student not otherwise familiar with the hidden assumptions present in the language.

4. Codes of Speech and Conduct

Explore whether your college or university has a code of conduct, some statement about civility, or some codes regulating speech. Examine the actual language of the document and the relationships it suggests among language, conduct, and community. You might also examine statements in course syllabi, or comments by your instructor or by classmates, that communicate expectations about conduct in the classroom community. You may also wish to examine documents circulated in your dorm by your resident advisor or by the campus housing office. Be sure to discuss the language of the document in the context of actual behavior in the dorms, classrooms, or on campus. You may also wish to conduct an interview with faculty or officials who may have had a hand in drafting the documents so that you better understand their intentions and the purposes of the documents.

For your project, write an analysis of one such document. What assumptions does it make about the role of language in building community and regulating behavior? In what ways is language a means to regulate and form a community?

Or, if your fieldwork uncovers problems with the document or problems in its enforcement or acceptance, consider writing a letter to the appropriate campus office in which you analyze those problems and propose changes to the document.

5. Literacy Narrative

The essay "From Outside, In" (p. 76), by Barbara Mellix, offers what amounts to her own "literacy narrative." Perri Klass (p. 48) likewise offers, albeit in more abbreviated fashion, her own story about learning a new language. For your project, offer your own literacy narrative.

Think about what goes into constructing such a narrative. In what respect is it a "construction," shaped by your mature, literate self? What is the argument behind your narrative? Consider writing a second, parallel essay that articulates those very argumentative issues more directly. You may also wish to examine literacy narratives in literature (e.g., *Pygmalion*) or in film (e.g., *Educating Rita, Wild Child, Children of a Lesser God*).

6. An Assignment "Rule Book"

At one point in her essay, Barbara Mellix (p. 76) speaks of the "rules of assignments." Take a close look at the "rules of assignments" in your composition course or in a course you are taking in a different discipline. For your project, develop an assignment rule book. Your goal is to develop a set of rules, conventions, or procedures for the assignment that may not be explicit but nonetheless inform the purpose and evaluation of the assignment. In that respect, your goal is to develop a document that could help the professor explain the assignment in more detail the next time he or she gives it or that can help future students meet the challenge of that assignment.

Here are some questions you may wish to consider: Are the rules explicit or only implied? What status and function do those rules have? Are they absolute or relative and flexible? For whom are those rules written? When can they be broken and by whom? What purpose do they serve? What is the connection between a set of specific rules and what we might call the "literacy activities" in that field? That is, does the assignment serve as a kind of miniapprenticeship, socializing you to the ways of that community? If so, why and how? In what ways do the tacit rules for the assignment reflect the culture of that particular discipline—its ways of knowing, thinking, and arguing?

7. Social Contexts in Translation

Amy Tan (p. 60) points out that social contexts often fail in translation. Choose from among the following three scenarios and explore the connection between language and community, focusing on difficulties in translation.

- If you are bilingual or if you are a literature or foreign-language major, consider analyzing the difficulties in translating a particular passage from a literary or nonliterary text. If you can, compare several translations. Write an essay in which you analyze the manner in which issues of translation often involve social assumptions or hidden understandings about culture.
- If you are a business major or if you are interested in new technologies, consider exploring handheld electronic translators or Web site services that promise to translate documents. Imagine that you have been hired as a consultant by a company that is expanding its international operations. Write a consultant's report in which you analyze the ability of pocket translating machines and/or Web sites to capture the social contexts of business practices.
- Find out if your campus has an ESL or English as a second language program. Interview one or more nonnative speakers of English, or volunteer as a "conversation partner" for the program (you'll find it immensely rewarding). Focus on a specific country of origin and write an analysis of some of the difficulties that foreign students encounter as they try to "learn the

language" of social contexts on your campus. You may wish to focus on just one particular aspect of social context (for example, interactions between students and professors).

8. "Tribalism" on Campus

David Berreby's article "It Takes a Tribe" (p. 53) invites you to take stock of rituals and traditions on your campus. How does one become an insider on campus—a "Spartan," or an "Aggie," or a "Buffalo"? Likewise, how does one become identified with one or the other group or club, fraternity or sorority, on campus?

This field project asks you to consider what prompts students—especially new students—to form such affiliations and to examine the means and methods of initiation. You may also wish to explore how various groups maintain themselves over time. You can focus on sports as a key means for identity formation, but don't forget academic majors or, for that matter, the role of the alumni office.

Develop your research and ethnographic fieldwork into a profile of tribal rituals and traditions on your campus, one that could be submitted as a chapter in a (hypothetical) book *Alma Mater: An Insider's Guide to College Rituals and Traditions*.

9. Curricular Narratives

In the course of Barbara Mellix's essay (p. 76), she comments on several different writing classes that she has taken and on the expectations and writing processes involved in each. For your project, become familiar with the writing courses your college offers. Be sure to consult course catalogs and syllabi; you also may wish to interview several instructors. Once you become familiar with those course offerings, analyze the implied narrative or the expected path of intellectual or career development that those writing courses may assume. Do those assumptions or expectations hold true most of the time? Or does the implied literacy narrative governing those courses pose some problem for students and faculty? For additional context, you may wish to consider what assumptions other courses in your university make about your development as a writer.

Your project may take one of several forms. You may wish to write a document that explains to students entering the course what they might expect during the first few weeks and how this course might fit into their other writing courses or college courses with a substantial commitment to writing. This document could take the form of a letter to new students or a preface to a handbook your writing program might provide its students.

If, during your fieldwork, you uncover problems or tensions in the way one or more courses are conceived, consider writing a letter to the department's curriculum committee in which, from your perspective as a student, you offer your views and recommendations. If you choose this option, be sure you are well informed and that you understand the "state of the conversation" about these courses and what agendas and values may be in play.

10. Dramatic Cognitive Awakenings

At one point in her essay, Amy Tan speaks of her own "dramatic cognitive awakenings via the word" (par. 22). This project asks you to focus on one key term or concept of interest to you that has importance to your field of study. It is especially helpful if you choose a term that is somehow "contested" or that is subject to varying interpretations.

For this project, write an essay in which you analyze both your chosen term and your cognitive awakening to it. First, consider naïve or uninformed interpretations of the term or how a newcomer to the field might misunderstand the complexities surrounding the term. Next, offer a fuller interpretation of the term that captures its contested life. How does the term fit into disciplinary conversations? What hidden agendas or values might accompany various interpretations of the term? Finally, reflect on your own "cognitive awakening" to the term. What has enabled you to see the term in a richer, more complex context? In what ways did "learning this language" require you to learn or adopt certain attitudes or behaviors of your disciplinary community?

11. Taking Stock of Your Literacy: Academic and Public

When it comes to literacy in narrow terms (reading and writing), we tend to think of our literacy education as something that happens at home or in school. And yet, our reading and writing, and especially the cultural knowledge that informs our reading and writing, tend to be influenced by a broader social and public literacy.

This field project invites you to take an introspective look at the influences that have guided your growth as a reader and writer. Drawing on Theodore Sizer's article (p. 70) in this chapter, consider whether school literacy or public literacy has had more influence in your life. Can one cleanly and clearly separate the two? Do these two kinds of literacy reinforce one another, or do they compete and potentially undermine one another?

You may wish to frame your project as a personal essay that responds to Sizer's article.

12. The Language of Community on the Net

Entering a community requires that you learn its language and with that language a host of attitudes, assumptions, and expectations. As we become habituated to moving from this to that community in real life, we tend not to notice refrigerator or bench itself. Even its packaging would be cumbersome. In such cases, the PTO will accept a photograph as long as the mark can be readily seen as being affixed to the item.

Advertising material is generally not acceptable as a specimen for *goods*. Thus, merely including a brochure or ad about products such as soap or clothing is insufficient. Similarly, letterhead displaying the mark and other similar materials such as invoices and business cards are not acceptable. The PTO wishes to ensure that the mark is in actual use on the goods in question. Thus, mere promotional materials do not show use of goods.

Such advertising materials may, however, be sufficient to show use of a mark in connection with *services*. Thus, if the mark CHUCKY'S FUN TIME is used for restaurant services, an advertisement, coupon, brochure, direct-mail leaflet, and menu would be acceptable specimens inasmuch as there will be no actual product or good displaying the CHUCKY'S FUN TIME mark. An audio cassette or compact disc is submitted as a specimen for a sound mark.

A specimen need not be submitted at the time of filing an application. An appropriate specimen must be submitted, however, during the examination process for an application based on actual use of mark and after the PTO approves the application and when a statement alleging use is submitted by an applicant whose application is based on an intent to use the mark. Until October 30, 1999, the PTO required three specimens for each class to be submitted at the time of filing of a use-based application. At present, one specimen per class is required, and although applicants may submit specimens during examination, the PTO expects most applicants will continue to submit the specimen with their use-based applications.

Declaration and Signature

The application must be signed by and include a declaration or verification by the applicant or its agent or attorney. The **declaration** is a statement placed at the end of the application whereby the signatory acknowledges that the statements in the application are true and that the signatory understands that willful false statements are punishable by fine or imprisonment and may jeopardize the validity of the application or any registration resulting from the application. (See Exhibit 4–3 for form of declaration.)

The undersigned being warned that willful false statements and the like are punishable by fine or imprisonment, or both, under 18 U.S.C. 1001, and that such willful false statements and the like may jeopardize the validity of the application or document or any registration resulting therefrom, declares that all statements made of his/her own knowledge are true; and that all statements made on information and belief are believed to be true.

_____
(Signature)

_____
(Print or Type Name and Position)

_____
(Date)

EXHIBIT 4–3
Declaration for
Trademark Application

their distinctive language behaviors. The Internet provides an interesting vehicle for exploring the connections between language, behavior, and community precisely because so much of the interaction is explicitly verbal.

For this project, choose one Internet site or one community with a presence on the Web. Monitor and analyze how this community uses language to maintain itself. What accommodation does this site or this community make for newcomers? Or does the site or community presume to speak only to "true believers"? How does language function on this site or in this community to uphold certain beliefs, assumptions, or agendas. To what extent does the language of this site or community welcome debate or criticism? You will probably find that the language of community on the Net becomes more pronounced as the community adopts what are regarded as more radical or extreme positions.

Write your project as an ethnographic report. That is, based on the specific language of this community as available on an Internet site, what can you infer about its practices and beliefs, its attitudes and values?

DANCING WITH PROFESSORS

The title for this unit is drawn from one of the readings, an essay by historian Patricia Nelson Limerick. Writing in the *New York Times Book Review*, she wonders why it is that so many professors "write bad prose." For Limerick, the apt answer can be found in a remark she recalls being made by a classics professor some years ago: "We must remember that professors are the ones nobody wanted to dance with in high school."

Now that you are in college, however, you do find yourself dancing with professors—intellectually, at least—be it in the seminar room or the lecture hall. Gone are the crepe-paper streamers in the high school gym, yet the notion that you might have to "dance" with your professor, or that he or she might have to dance with you, remains unsettling. Instead of eyeing each other warily from across the gym floor, you'll find that the seminar room and the lecture hall now become the venues for those sometimes awkward steps together.

What can we make of this "dance" between student and professor, and why might it be helpful to step out onto the dance floor and try out a few basic steps? It's tempting to think of your education as a solo number, as something you do by and for yourself. After all, you're the one who's getting the grade. Yet the dance metaphor holds and can shed some light on your experience in college and in the writing classroom.

Teaching and learning occur together and influence each other in often unexpected ways. Moreover, both teaching and learning are inherently social. We think and write at our best in the company of others. Although no one may literally strike the dance-floor pose, there is surely a good deal of dancing going on. You might be tempted to think of your professor as the one who is "leading," and often times he or she is, but the expected roles, the assumed positions, can change. You might take the lead as you work on a project, and surely, especially in smaller classes, you may find that your partner is a fellow student or a group of students.

We dance with each other—at times awkwardly, but surely with ever-increasing confidence—because college is all about learning "the moves." We might think that our days are filled with the demands of teaching and learning what might be called "domain content"—the factual information of any one field. But beyond or underlying that explicit and visible education is a more subtle but telling one: You are learning the moves of thinking and writing so essential to success in college and in your chosen field. You are imitating, practicing, and trying out—on your own and with each other—a variety of dance steps that show a mind in action.

The dance floor, in this respect, can extend well beyond the classroom. We are dancing in the library or in our respective dorms and offices. We are dancing when we read or listen attentively, not just when we write or speak. We are dancing when we engage each other and ourselves. We are, all of us, dancing in and with our minds.

The writing classroom has a special role in helping you learn those moves, those habits of mind that inform your work with professors and with each other. Because writing renders visible and malleable the ways in which we think, a writing class can help you reflect on the connections between language and inquiry. Moreover, because writing classes are inherently collaborative, they offer an opportunity for all of us, as we entertain different ideas and various audiences, to step out of our own skins. You may not find black footprints placed on the classroom floor as a guide to the latest swing or salsa, but you will be learning nevertheless some key moves.

The four readings included on this unit's "dance card" touch on the different kinds of partnerships that come into play as you write and learn in college. For Mike Rose, entering the conversation that is college relied in good measure on the support of faculty mentors. Coming as he did from South L.A., Rose encountered a very different set of expectations on campus. His mentors—the ones you yourself might find—played a crucial role in helping to explain the moves that occur, but are often not explained, in the college classroom.

Gerald Graff found his favorite dance partner not in books themselves— he found he disliked them at an early age—but in the critical debates that swirled around the famous books he felt he was obliged to like. Those critical debates offered a chance to join a conversation that was not always readily apparent in the books themselves.

Patricia Nelson Limerick explores the very metaphor of the dance and questions why it is that college professors seem to neglect the needs of their partners, be they the readers of their own prose or the students they are teaching. Limerick offers, in the end, a useful reminder that, for all of us, professors and students alike, egos can get in the way of a good dance.

Nancy Sommers reminds us that we are our own best—and severest— partners. In an essay that explores the interplay between personal and external authority that unfolds in our written drafts, Sommers challenges us never to leave ourselves behind, even as we write academic essays.

Reflecting on Prior Knowledge

1. In a journal entry, or working collaboratively in a small group, recall why you first became interested in going to college. What role did an academic program, sports, mentor, or teacher have in developing this interest? What have been your own expectations—or those of your family and high school friends—about the role of college in your life and career?

2. In what you might title "A Brief Personal History of the Book," reflect on the role of books in your life. You may wish to focus on one key period in your reading life or on one kind of book. Have you ever disliked books or a certain kind of book? If so, what might have accounted for that attitude? Have you found your relationship with books changing for better or for worse? What instigated that change—a teacher, an issue or a debate, a friend, or a particular book?

3. In American culture, certain stereotypes tend to define the image of the college professor. Briefly recall what you see as the most salient of those stereotypes, and then describe an encounter or a situation (in college or in the past) in which those stereotypes were either confirmed or challenged.

4. In a journal entry, reflect on what you see as the ideal educational relationship (intellectual and/or interpersonal) with a professor. In short, what kind of "dance" would you like to have? Consider what would need to change—in professors, in yourself, in the institution—in order for that educational relationship to come about. What rewards do you see in your idealized relationship, and what risks or challenges?

5. Reflect on an opportunity you might have had in the past to connect your academic and personal commitments. Did that opportunity lead to the kind of successful integration that you hoped for? What might have accounted for that success or for an outcome that was short, perhaps well short, of being successful? How did you handle the competing claims of establishing your academic authority and calling upon the authority of lived experience?

Entering the Conversation

Mike Rose

School, especially a college or a university, can make students feel
unintelligent, threatened, and angry when they encounter conversations that use unfamiliar terms and foreign-sounding logic. It was only
through the insight and effort of his teachers that Mike Rose moved
from the language and culture of South L.A., where he grew up, into
the conversations of his liberal-arts course work at Loyola University.

The importance of his mentors, and the worlds they helped him
enter, led Rose first into teaching then into the study of teaching. With
degrees from Loyola University, the University of Southern California,
and UCLA, Rose has taught public school, undergraduate, and graduate
students. His research into effective teaching focuses on recognizing
the social, cultural, linguistic, and cognitive factors that influence how
students learn. His books on language and learning include *Possible
Lives: The Promise of Public Education in America* (1995), based on four
years of searching across the nation for public school classrooms that
work. "Entering the Conversation" is from his landmark book, *Lives on
the Boundary: The Struggles and Achievements of America's
Underprepared* (1989). The range of his interests is reflected in two
recent publications, *Widening the Lens on Standardized Patient
Assessment: What the Encounter Can Reveal about the Development
of Clinical Competence* (2001) and *The Working Life of a Waitress:
Mind, Culture, and Activity* (2001). His most recent book is *The Mind at
Work* (2004).

Mike Rose is currently a professor of social research methodology
in the UCLA graduate school of education and an instructor for the
UCLA writing program.

It is an unfortunate fact of our psychic lives that the images that surround
us as we grow up—no matter how much we may scorn them later—give

shape to our deepest needs and longings. Every year Loyola men elected a homecoming queen. The queen and her princesses were students at the Catholic sister schools: Marymount, Mount St. Mary's, St. Vincent's. They had names like Corinne and Cathy, and they came from the Sullivan family or the Mitchells or the Ryans. They were taught to stand with toe to heel, their smiles were inviting, and the photographer's flash illuminated their eyes. Loyola men met them at fraternity parties and mixers and "CoEd Day," met them according to rules of manner and affiliation and parental connection as elaborate as a Balinese dance. John and I drew mustaches on their photographs, but something about them reached far back into my life.

Growing up in South L.A. was certainly not a conscious misery. My neighborhood had its diversions and its mysteries, and I felt loved and needed at home. But all in all there was a dreary impotence to the years, and isolation, and a deep sadness about my father. I protected myself from the harsher side of it all through a life of the mind. And while that interior life included spaceships and pink chemicals and music and the planetary moons, it also held the myriad television images of the good life that were piped into my home: Robert Young sitting down to dinner, Ozzie Nelson tossing the football with his sons, the blond in a Prell commercial turning toward the camera. The images couldn't have been more trivial—all sentimental phosphorescence—but as a child tucked away on South Vermont, they were just about the only images I had of what life would be without illness and dead ends. I didn't realize how completely their message had seeped into my being, what loneliness and sorrow was being held at bay—didn't realize it until I found myself in the middle of Loyola's social life without a guidebook, feeling just beyond the superficial touch of the queen and her princesses, those smiling incarnations of a television promise. I scorned the whole silly show and ached to be embraced by one of these mythic females under the muted light of a paper moon.

So I went to school and sat in class and memorized more than understood and whistled past the academic graveyard. I vacillated between the false potency of scorn and feelings of ineptitude. John and I would get in his car and enjoy the warmth of each other and laugh and head down the long strip of Manchester Boulevard, away from Loyola, away from the palms and green, green lawns, back to South L.A. We'd throw the ball in the alley or lag pennies on Vermont or hit Marty's Liquor. We'd leave much later for a movie or a football game at Mercy High or the terrible safety of downtown Los Angeles. Walking, then, past the *discotecas* and pawnshops, past the windows full of fried chicken and yellow lamps, past the New Follies, walking through hustlers and lost drunks and prostitutes and transvestites with rouge the color of bacon—stopping, finally, before the musty opening of a bar where two silhouettes moved around a pool table as though they were underwater.

I don't know what I would have found if the flow of events hadn't changed dramatically. Two things happened. Jack MacFarland privately influenced my course of study at Loyola, and death once again ripped through our small family.

The coterie of MacFarland's students—Art Mitz, Mark Dever, and me— were still visiting our rumpled mentor. We would stop by his office or his apartment to mock our classes and the teachers and all that "'Loyola man' bullshit." Nobody had more appreciation for burlesque than Jack MacFarland, but I suppose he saw beneath our caustic performances and knew we were headed for trouble. Without telling us, he started making phone calls to some of his old teachers at Loyola—primarily to Dr. Frank Carothers, the chairman of the English Department—and, I guess, explained that these kids needed to be slapped alongside the head with a good novel. Dr. Carothers volunteered to look out for us and agreed to some special studies courses that we could substitute for a few of the more traditional requirements, courses that would enable us to read and write a lot under the close supervision of a faculty member. In fact, what he promised were tutorials—and that was exceptional, even for a small college. All this would start up when we returned from summer vacation. Our sophomore year, Jack MacFarland finally revealed, would be different.

When Lou Minton rewired the trailer, he rigged a phone line from the front house: A few digits and we could call each other. One night during the summer after my freshman year, the phone rang while I was reading. It was my mother and she was screaming. I ran into the house to find her standing in the kitchen hysterical—both hands pressed to her face—and all I could make out was Lou's name. I didn't see him in the front of the house, so I ran back through the kitchen to the bedroom. He had fallen back across the bed, a hole right at his sideburn, his jaw still quivering. They had a fight, and some ugly depth of pain convulsed within him. He left the table and walked to the bedroom. My mother heard the light slam of a .22. Nothing more.

That summer seems vague and distant. I can't remember any specifics, though I had to take care of my mother and handle the affairs of the house. I probably made do by blunting a good deal of what I saw and navigating with intuitive quadrants. But though I cannot remember details, I do recall feelings and recognitions: Lou's suicide came to represent the sadness and dead time I had protected myself against, the personal as well as public oppressiveness of life in South Los Angeles. I began to see that my escape to the trailer and my isolationist fantasies of the demimonde would yield another kind of death, a surrender to the culture's lost core. An alternative was somehow starting to take shape around school and knowledge. Knowledge seemed . . . was it empowering? No, that's a word I would use now. Then I felt freed, as if I were untying fetters. There simply were times when the pain and confusion of that summer would give way to something I felt more than I knew: a lightness to my body, an ease in breathing. Three or four months later I took an art history course, and one day during a slide show on Gothic architecture I felt myself rising up within the interior light of Mont-Saint-Michel. I wanted to be released from the despair that surrounded me on South Vermont and from my own troubled sense of exclusion.

Jack MacFarland had saved me at one juncture—caught my fancy and revitalized my mind—what I felt now was something further, some tentative recognition that an engagement with ideas could foster competence and lead me out into the world. But all this was very new and fragile, and given what I know now, I realize how easily it could have been crushed. My mother, for as long as I can remember, always added onto any statement of intention— hers or others'—the phrase *se vuol Dio*, if God wants it. The fulfillment of desire, no matter how trivial, required the blessing of the gods, for the world was filled with threat. "I'll plant the seeds this weekend," I might say. "Se vuol Dio," she would add. *Se vuol Dio*. The phrase expressed several lifetimes of ravaged hope: my grandfather's lost leg, the failure of the Rose Spaghetti House, my father laid low, Lou Minton, the landscapes of South L.A. *Se vuol Dio*. For those who live their lives on South Vermont, tomorrow doesn't beckon to be defined from a benign future. It's up to the gods, not you, if any old thing turns out right. I carried within me no history of assurances that what I was feeling would lead to anything.

> **Words piled up like cars in a serial wreck.**

Because of its size and because of the kind of teacher who is drawn to small liberal arts colleges, Loyola would turn out to be a very good place for me. For even with MacFarland's yearlong tour through ideas and language, I was unprepared. English prose written before the twentieth century was difficult, sometimes impossible, for me to comprehend. The kind of reasoning I found in logic was very foreign. My writing was okay, but I couldn't hold a candle to Art Mitz or Mark Dever or to those boys who came from good schools. And my fears about science and mathematics prevailed: Pereira Hall, the Math and Engineering Building, was only forty to fifty yards from the rear entrance to the English Department but seemed an unfriendly mirage, a malevolent castle floating in the haze of a mescaline dream.

We live, in America, with so many platitudes about motivation and self- 10
reliance and individualism—and myths spun from them, like those of Horatio Alger—that we find it hard to accept the fact that they are serious nonsense. To live your early life on the streets of South L.A.—or Homewood or Spanish Harlem or Chicago's South Side or any one of hundreds of other depressed communities—and to journey up through the top levels of the

American educational system will call for support and guidance at many, many points along the way. You'll need people to guide you into conversations that seem foreign and threatening. You'll need models, lots of them, to show you how to get at what you don't know. You'll need people to help you center yourself in your own developing ideas. You'll need people to watch out for you. There is much talk these days about the value of a classical humanistic education, a call for an immersion in the humanities, a return to the great books. These appeals raise lots of suspicions, for such curricula have traditionally served to exclude working-class people from the classroom. It doesn't, of necessity, have to be that way. The teachers that fate and Jack MacFarland's crisis intervention sent my way worked at making the humanities truly human. What transpired between us was the essence of humane liberal education, and it enabled me to move far beyond the cognitive charade of my freshman year.

From the midpoint of their freshman year, Loyola students had to take one philosophy course per semester: Logic, Philosophy of Nature, Philosophy of Man, General Ethics, Natural Theology, and so on. Logic was the first in the series, and I had barely gotten a C. The rest of the courses looked like a book fair of medieval scholasticism with the mold scraped off the bindings, and I dreaded their advent. But I was beginning my sophomore year at a time when the best and brightest of the Jesuit community were calling for an intellectually panoramic, socially progressive Catholicism, and while this lasted, I reaped the benefits. Sections of the next three courses I had to take would be taught by a young man who was studying for the priesthood and who was, himself, attempting to develop a personal philosophy that incorporated the mind and the body as well as the spirit.

Mr. Johnson could have strolled off a Wheaties box. Still in his twenties and a casting director's vision of those good looks thought to be all-American, Don Johnson had committed his very considerable intelligence to the study and teaching of philosophy. Jack MacFarland had introduced me to the Greeks, to Christian scholasticism, eighteenth-century deism, and French existentialism, but it was truly an introduction, a curtsy to that realm of the heavens where the philosophers dwell. Mr. Johnson provided a fuller course. He was methodical and spoke with vibrance and made connections between ancients and moderns with care. He did for philosophy what Mr. MacFarland had done for literary history: He gave me a directory of key names and notions.

We started in a traditional way with the Greek philosophers who preceded Socrates—Thales, Heraclitus, Empedocles—and worked our way down to Kant and Hegel. We read a little Aquinas, but we also read E. A. Burtt's *The Metaphysical Foundations of Modern Science*, and that gave me entry to Kepler, Copernicus, Galileo (which I was then spelling *Galelao*), and Newton.

As he laid out his history of ideas, Mr. Johnson would consider aloud the particular philosophical issue involved, so we didn't, for example, simply get an outline of what Hegel believed, but we watched and listened as Don Johnson reasoned like Hegel and then raised his own questions about the Hegelian scheme. He was a working philosopher, and he was thinking out loud in front of us.

The Metaphysical Foundations of Modern Science was very tough going. It assumed not only a familiarity with Western thought but, as well, a sophistication in reading a theoretically rich argument. It was, in other words, the kind of book you encounter with increased frequency as you move through college. It combined the history of mathematics and science with philosophical investigation, and when I tried to read it, I'd end up re-scanning the same sentences over and over, not understanding them, and, finally, slamming the book down on the desk—swearing at this golden boy Johnson and angry with myself. Here's a typical passage, one of the many I marked as being hopeless:

> We begin now to glimpse the tremendous significance of what these fathers of modern science were doing, but let us continue with our questions. What further specific metaphysical doctrines was Kepler led to adopt as a consequence of this notion of what constitutes the real world? For one thing, it led him to appropriate in his own way the distinction between primary and secondary qualities, which had been noted in the ancient world by the atomist and skeptical schools, and which was being revived in the sixteenth century in varied form by such miscellaneous thinkers as Vives, Sanchez, Montaigne, and Campanella. Knowledge as it is immediately offered the mind through the senses is obscure, confused, contradictory, and hence untrustworthy; only those features of the world in terms of which we get certain and consistent knowledge open before us what is indubitably and permanently real. Other qualities are not real qualities of things, but only signs of them. For Kepler, of course, the real qualities are those caught up in this mathematical harmony underlying the world of the senses, and which, therefore, have a causal relation to the latter. *The real world is a world of quantitative characteristics only; its differences are differences of number alone.*

I couldn't get the distinction that was being made between primary and   15
secondary qualities, and I certainly didn't have the background that would enable me to make sense of Burtt's brief historical survey: from "atomist and skeptical schools [to] . . . Campanella." It is clear from the author's italics that the last sentence of the passage is important, so I underlined it, but because Burtt's discussion is built on a rich intellectual history that I didn't know, I was reading words but not understanding text. I was the human incarnation of language-recognition computer programs; able to record the

The declaration is intended to impress upon the signatory the seriousness of the trademark application procedure to ensure that applicants do not claim earlier use dates than those to which they are entitled and do not attempt to "lock up" marks for the purpose of reselling them to others. The applicant or its agent or attorney must then sign the application. If the application is one made by an individual, this individual will sign the document. If the applicant is a corporation or partnership, the application is usually signed by an officer of the corporation or a general partner, respectively. Joint applicants should each sign the application. Applicants not domiciled in the United States must appoint a "domestic representative" in the United States, namely, a party, typically a law firm, who will receive documents and notices affecting the mark.

Although an owner of a trademark may file and prosecute his or her own application for registration of a mark, trademark owners are often represented by attorneys familiar with trademark practice. Any attorney licensed to practice may practice before the PTO, and there is no requirement for any special registration with the PTO. When attorneys represent applicants, the application may contain a power of attorney designating the attorney to represent the applicant regarding all matters related to the mark. A power of attorney is no longer required, however, for an attorney to sign a declaration on behalf of an applicant.

The Principal and Supplemental Registers

The application should designate whether the application seeks registration on the Principal Register or the Supplemental Register. Registration on the **Principal Register** is preferred because it offers a wider scope of protection for a mark. A mark not eligible for registration on the Principal Register, for example, a descriptive mark that has not yet acquired sec-ondary meaning, will be registered on the **Supplemental Register.** Registration on the Supplemental Register is an indication that a mark does not yet distinguish, but ultimately is capable of distinguishing, the applicant's goods or services from those of another. Once the mark has acquired distinctiveness, a new application can be filed seeking registration on the Principal Register. In fact, after five years of substantially continuous and exclusive use of a mark, there is a presumption that it has acquired the necessary distinctiveness to allow for registration on the Principal Register, and the registrant may file a new application for registration of the mark on the Principal Register.

The distinctions between registrations on the Principal Register and Supplemental Register are as follows:

- While a registration on the Principal Register is *prima facie* evidence of the registrant's exclusive right to use of the mark, registration on the Supplemental Register has no such evidentiary effect.
- A registration on the Principal Register is constructive notice of a claim of ownership so as to eliminate a defense of good faith in an infringement suit, but a Supplemental Registration has no such effect.
- While a registration on the Principal Register may become incontestable after five years of registration, a Supplemental Registration may never achieve that status.
- Registration on the Supplemental Register cannot be used to stop importations of infringing goods into the United States.

On the other hand, registration on the Supplemental Register does afford some protections:

- An action for infringement of the mark can be brought in federal court.

dictionary meanings of individual words but unable to generate any meaning out of them.

"What," I asked in class, "are primary and secondary qualities? I don't get it." And here Don Johnson was very good. "The answer," he said, "can be found in the passage itself. I'll go back through it with you. Let's start with primary and secondary qualities. If some qualities are primary and others secondary, which do you think would be most important?"

"Primary?"

"Right. Primary qualities. Whatever they are. Now let's turn to Kepler, since Kepler's the subject of this passage. What is it that's more important to Kepler?"

I pause and say tentatively, "Math." Another student speaks up, reading from the book: "Quantitative characteristics."

"All right. So primary qualities, for Kepler, are mathematical, quantitative. But we still don't know what this primary and secondary opposition really refers to, do we? Look right in the middle of the paragraph. Burtt is comparing mathematical knowledge to the immediate knowledge provided by—what?"   20

My light bulb goes on: "The senses."

"There it is. The primary-secondary opposition is the opposition between knowledge gained by pure mathematical reasoning versus knowledge gained through our five senses."

We worked with *The Metaphysical Foundations of Modern Science* for some time, and I made my way slowly through it. Mr. Johnson was helping me develop an ability to read difficult texts—I was learning how to reread critically, how to tease out definitions and basic arguments. And I was also gaining confidence that if I stayed with material long enough and kept asking questions, I would get it. That assurance proved to be more valuable than any particular body of knowledge I learned that year.

For my second semester, I had to take Philosophy of Man, and it was during that course that Mr. Johnson delivered his second gift. We read Gabriel Marcel and Erich Fromm, learning about phenomenology and social criticism. We considered the human animal from an anthropological as well as philosophical perspective. And we read humanistic psychologist Abraham Maslow's *Toward a Psychology of Being*. Maslow wrote about "the 'will to health,' the urge to grow, the pressure of self-actualization, the quest for one's identity." The book had a profound effect on me. Six months before, Lou Minton's jaw quivered as if to speak the race's deepest sorrow, and through the rest of that summer I could only feel in my legs and chest some fleeting assurance that the world wasn't a thin mask stretched over nothingness. Now I was reading an articulation of that vague, hopeful feeling. Maslow was giving voice to some delicate possibility within me, and I was powerfully drawn to it. Every person is, in part, "'his own project' and makes himself." I had to know more, so I called Mr. Johnson up and asked if I could visit with him. "Sure," he said, and invited me to campus. So one Saturday morning I took a series of early buses and headed west.

Mr. Johnson and the other initiates to the priesthood lived in an old white residence hall on the grassy east edge of campus, and the long walk up Loyola Boulevard was quiet and meditative: Birds were flying tree to tree and a light breeze was coming in off Playa del Rey. I walked up around the gym, back behind Math-Engineering to his quarters, a simple one-story building with those Spanish curves that seem simultaneously thick and weightless. The sun had warmed the stucco. A window by the door was open, and a curtain had fluttered out. I rang the bell and heard steps on a hardwood floor. Mr. Johnson opened the door and stepped out. He was smiling and his eyes were attentive in the light . . . present . . . there. They said, "Come, let's talk."

Dr. Frank Carothers taught what is generally called the sophomore survey, a yearlong sequence of courses that introduces the neophyte English major to the key works in English literary history. Dr. Carothers was tall and robust. He wore thick glasses and a checkered bow tie and his hairline was male Botticelli, picking up somewhere back beyond his brow. As the year progressed, he spread English literary history out in slow time across the board, and I was introduced to people I'd never heard of: William Langland, a medieval acolyte who wrote the dream-vision *Piers Plowman*; the sixteenth-century poet Sir Thomas Wyatt; Elizabethan lyricists with peculiar names like Orlando Gibbons and Tobias Hume (the author of the wondrous suggestion that tobacco "maketh lean the fat men's tumour"); the physician Sir Thomas Browne; the essayist Joseph Addison; the biographer James Boswell; the political philosopher Edmund Burke, whose prose I could not decipher; and poets Romantic and Victorian (Shelley and Rossetti and Algernon Charles Swinburne). Some of the stuff was invitingly strange ("Pallid and pink as the palm of the flag-flower . . ."), some was awfully hard to read, and some was just awful. But Dr. Carothers laid it all out with his reserved passion, drew for us a giant conceptual blueprint onto which we could place other courses, other books. He was precise, thorough, and rigorous. And he started his best work once class was over.

Being a professor was, for Frank Carothers, a profoundly social calling: He enjoyed the classroom, and he seemed to love the more informal contacts with those he taught, those he once taught, and those who stopped by just to get a look at this guy. He stayed in his office until about four each afternoon, leaning back in his old swivel chair, hands clasped behind his head, his bow tie tight against his collar. He had strong opinions, and he'd get irritated if you missed class, and he sometimes gave quirky advice—but there he'd be shaking his head sympathetically as students poured out their troubles. It was pure and primary for Frank Carothers: Teaching allowed him daily to fuse the joy he got from reading literature—poetry especially—with his deep pleasure in human community. What I saw when I was around him—and I hung out in his office from my sophomore year on—was very different from the world I had been creating for myself, a far cry from my withdrawal into an old house trailer with a silent book.

One of Dr. Carothers's achievements was the English Society. The English Society had seventy-eight members, and that made it just about the biggest organization on campus: jocks, literati, C-plus students, frat boys, engineers, mystics, scholars, profligates, bullies, geeks, Republicans—all stood side by side for group pictures. The English Society sponsored poetry readings, lectures, and card games, and best of all, barbecues in the Carotherses' backyard. We would caravan out to Manhattan Beach to be greeted by Betsy, the youngest of the seven Carothers children, and she'd walk us back to her father who, wrapped now in an apron, was poking coals or unscrewing the tops from jugs of red wine.

Vivian Carothers, a delicate, soft-spoken woman, would look after us and serve up trays of cheese and chips and little baked things. Students would knock on the redwood gate all through the late afternoon, more and more finding places for themselves among flowers and elephant ears, patio furniture, and a wizened pine. We would go on way past sunset, talking to Dr. Carothers and to each other about books and sports and currently despised professors, sometimes letting off steam and sometimes learning something new. And Frank Carothers would keep us fed, returning to the big, domed barbecue through the evening to lift the lid and add hamburgers, the smoke rising off the grill and up through the telephone lines stretching like the strings of Shelley's harp over the suburbs of the South Bay.

When I was learning my craft at Jack MacFarland's knee, I continually mis-   30
used words and wrote fragments and run-on sentences and had trouble making my pronouns agree with whatever it was that preceded them. I also produced sentences like these:

> Some of these modern-day Ramses are inherent of their wealth, others are self-made.

> An exhibition of will on the part of the protagonist enables him to accomplish a subjective good (which is an element of tragedy, namely: the protagonist does not fully realize the objective wrong that he is doing. He feels objectively justified if not completely right.)

I was struggling to express increasingly complex ideas, and I couldn't get the language straight: Words, as in my second sentence on tragedy, piled up like cars in a serial wreck. I was encountering a new language—the language of the academy—and was trying to find my way around in it. I have some more examples, written during my first year and a half at Loyola. There was inflated vocabulary:

> I conjectured that he was the same individual who had arrested my attention earlier.

> In his famed speech, "The American Scholar," Ralph Waldo Emerson posed several problems that are particularly germane to the position of the young author.

There were clichés and mixed and awkward metaphors:

> In 1517, when Luther nailed his 95 theses to the door of Wittenburg Cathedral, he unknowingly started a snowball rolling that was to grow to tremendous reprocussions.

And there was academic melodrama:

> The vast realm of the cosmos or the depths of a man's soul hold questions that reason flounders upon, but which can be probed by the peculiar private insight of the seer.

Pop grammarians and unhappy English teachers get a little strange around sentences like these. But such sentences can be seen as marking a stage in linguistic growth. Appropriating a style and making it your own is difficult, and you'll miss the mark a thousand times along the way. The botched performances, though, are part of it all, and developing writers will grow through them if they are able to write for people who care about language, people who are willing to sit with them and help them as they struggle to write about difficult things. That is what Ted Erlandson did for me.

Dr. Erlandson was one of the people who agreed to teach me and my Mercy High companions a seminar—a close, intensive course that would substitute for a larger, standard offering like Introduction to Prose Literature. He was tall and lanky and had a long reddish brown beard and lectured in a voice that was basso and happy. He was a strong lecturer and possessed the best memory for fictional detail I'd ever witnessed. And he cared about prose. The teachers I had during my last three years at Loyola assigned a tremendous amount of writing. But it was Ted Erlandson who got in there with his pencil and worked on my style. He would sit me down next to him at his big desk, sweep books and pencils across the scratched veneer, and go back over the sentences he wanted me to revise.

He always began by reading the sentence out loud: "Camus ascented to a richer vision of life that was to characterize the entirety of his work." Then he would fiddle with the sentence, talking and looking up at me intermittently to comment or ask questions: "'Ascent'. That sounds like 'assent', I know, but look it up, Mike." He'd wait while I fluttered the dictionary. "Now, 'the entirety of his work' . . . try this instead: 'his entire work.' Let's read it.

'Camus assented to a richer vision of life that would characterize his entire work.' Sounds better, doesn't it?"

And another sentence. "'Irregardless of the disastrous ending of *Bread and Wine*, it must be seen as an affirmative work.' 'Irregardless' . . . people use it all the time, but 'regardless' will do just fine. Now, I think this next part sounds a little awkward; listen: 'Regardless of the disastrous ending of *Bread and Wine*, it . . .' Hear that? Let's try removing the 'of' and the 'it': 'Regardless of the disastrous ending, *Bread and Wine* must be seen as an affirmative work.' Hmmm. Better, I think."

And so it would go. He rarely used grammatical terms, and he never got 35 technical. He dealt with specific bits of language: "Try this here" or "Here's another way to say it." He worked as a craftsman works, with particulars, and he shuttled back and forth continually between print and voice, making me breathe my prose, making me hear the language I'd generated in silence. Perhaps he was more directive than some would like, but, to be truthful, direction was what I needed. I was easily frustrated, and it didn't take a lot to make me doubt myself. When teachers would write "no" or "awkward" or "rewrite" alongside the sentences I had worked so hard to produce, I would be peeved and disappointed. "Well, what the hell *do* they want?" I'd grumble to no one in particular. So Ted Erlandson's linguistic parenting felt just right: a modeling of grace until it all slowly, slowly began to work itself into the way I shaped language.

When Father Albertson lectured, he would stand pretty much in one spot slightly to the left or right of center in front of us. He tended to hold his notes or a play or a critical study in both hands, releasing one to emphasize a point with a simple gesture. He was tall and thin, and his voice was soft and tended toward monotone. When he spoke, he looked very serious, but when one of us responded with any kind of intelligence, a little smile would come over his face. Jack MacFarland had told me that it was Clint Albertson's Shakespeare course that would knock my socks off.

For each play we covered, Father Albertson distributed a five- to ten-page list of questions to ask ourselves as we read. These study questions were of three general types.

The first type was broad and speculative and was meant to spark reflection on major characters and key events. Here's a teaser on *Hamlet*:

> Would you look among the portrait-paintings by Raphael, or Rembrandt, or Van Gogh, or El Greco, or Rouault for an ideal representation of Hamlet? Which painting by which of these men do you think most closely resembles your idea of what Hamlet should look like?

The second type focused on the details of the play itself and were very specific. Here are two of the thirty-eight he wrote for *As You Like It*:

ACT I, SCENE 2
How is Rosalind distinguished from Celia in this scene? How do you explain the discrepancy between the Folio version of lines 284–287 and Act I, scene 3, line 117?

ACT II, SCENES 4–6:
It has been said these scenes take us definitely out of the world of reality into a world of dream. What would you say are the steps of the process by which Shakespeare brings about this illusion?

The third kind of question required us to work with some historical or critical study. This is an example from the worksheet on *Romeo and Juliet*:

Read the first chapter of C. S. Lewis's *Allegory of Love*, "Courtly Love." What would you say about Shakespeare's concept of love in relation to what Lewis presents as the traditional contradictory concepts in medieval literature of "romantic love" vs. "marriage."

Father Albertson had placed over 150 books on the reserve shelf in the library, and they ranged from intellectual history to literary criticism to handbooks on theater production. I had used a few such "secondary sources" to quote in my own writing since my days with Jack MacFarland, but this was the first time a teacher had so thoroughly woven them into a course. Father Albertson would cite them during lectures as naturally as though he were recalling a discussion he had overheard. He would add his own opinions and, since he expected us to form opinions, would ask us for ours.

I realize that this kind of thing—the close, line-by-line examination, the citing of critical opinion—has given rise to endless parodies of the academy: repressed schoolmen clucking along in the land of lost language. It certainly can be that way. But with Clint Albertson, all the learning furthered my comprehension of the play. His questions forced me to think carefully about Shakespeare's choice of words, about the crafting of a scene, about the connections between language and performance. I had to read very, very closely, leaning over the thin Formica desk in the trailer, my head cupped in my hands with my two index fingers in my ears to blot out the noise from the alley behind me. There were times when no matter how hard I tried, I wouldn't get it. I'd close the book, feeling stupid to my bones, and go find John. Over then to the liquor store, out into the night. The next day I would visit Father Albertson and tell him I was lost, ask him why this stuff was so damned hard. He'd listen and ask me to tell him why it made me so angry. I'd sputter some more, and then he'd draw me to the difficult passage, slowly opening the language up, helping me comprehend a distant, stylized literature, taking it apart, touching it.

I would then return to a classroom where a historically rich conversation 40 was in progress. Other readers of Shakespeare—from Samuel Johnson to the contemporary literary critic Wylie Sypher—were given voice by Father Albertson, and we were encouraged to enter the dialogue, to consider, to take issue, to be seated amid all that potentially intimidating shoptalk. We were shown how to summarize an opinion, argue with it, weave it into our own interpretations. Nothing is more exclusive than the academic club: Its language is highbrow, it has fancy badges, and it worships tradition. It limits itself to a few participants who prefer to talk to each other. What Father Albertson did was bring us inside the circle, nudging us out into the chatter, always just behind us, whispering to try this step, then this one, encouraging us to feel the moves for ourselves.

Those four men collectively gave me the best sort of liberal education, the kind longed for in the stream of blue-ribbon reports on the humanities that now cross my desk. I developed the ability to read closely, to persevere in the face of uncertainty and ask questions of what I was reading—not with downcast eyes, but freely, aloud, realizing there is no such thing as an open book. My teachers modeled critical inquiry and linguistic precision and grace, and they provided various cognitive maps for philosophy and history and literature. They encouraged me to make connections and to enter into conversations—present and past—to see what talking a particular kind of talk would enable me to do with a thorny philosophical problem or a difficult literary text. And it was all alive. It transpired in backyards and on doorsteps and inside offices as well as in the classroom. I could smell their tobacco and see the nicks left by their razors. They liked books and ideas, and they liked to talk about them in ways that fostered growth rather than established dominance. They lived their knowledge. And maybe because of that their knowledge grew in me in ways that led back out to the world. I was developing a set of tools with which to shape a life.

Working with the Text

1. Mike Rose makes his argument by telling a story based on two pivotal events—the intervention of a mentor and a death in the family—that dramatically change his experience of getting a university education. In a short essay, explore how these two events worked together to bring Rose into a pursuit of knowledge.

2. Why does Rose use narrative to make his argument? What does storytelling lend to his argument that other forms of writing could not? Mark the passages in which Rose interprets the story for the reader—explains to the reader what the settings and events meant to him. Reread the essay, skipping over the interpretive passages. What other meanings might a reader give to the events? In a

short essay, reflect on the roots of Rose's argument and why it emerged as a combination of storytelling and meaning telling.

3. Rose opens the essay asserting, "It is an unfortunate fact of our psychic lives that the images that surround us as we grow up—no matter how much we may scorn them later—give shape to our deepest needs and longings." He then presents images of the homecoming queen and her princesses. Why does he introduce the essay with these images? Beginning with these images, write a short essay tracing the "deepest needs and longings" that eventually lead Rose into an academic life.

4. Through each of the mentors Rose describes, he learned particular approaches to entering the academic community. List the mentors and identify what each of them brought to Rose's undergraduate experience. Reread the final paragraph of the essay. Write a short response essay comparing Rose's experience—or select elements of his experience—to your own. Where there are differences, analyze why those differences might exist.

5. Describing his efforts to understand difficult material, Rose writes, "There were times when no matter how hard I tried, I wouldn't get it. I'd close the book, feeling stupid to my bones, and go find John. Over then to the liquor store, out into the night" (par. 39). As you reread the essay, note Rose's emotional responses to the obstacles he faced. In a short essay, reflect on those responses and the behaviors that came out of them. What was he feeling? Why?

From Text to Field

1. Write an essay in which you invent a mentor for yourself. In what specific ways would this mentor contribute to your university learning experience? How would this mentor fulfill roles that are currently missing from your university experience?

2. Does the fact that you know Rose's reputation as a teacher and scholar color your sense of his narrative? His story has a happy ending. Consider other people from similar backgrounds who don't make it. Write a response to Rose's essay in which you address the factors that lead to other than happy endings. To what extent can those factors be changed to increase the chances of success? To what extent do those factors inevitably—or most often—lead to failure?

3. Find passages in the essay that describe ways Rose's mentors taught him to read and write like an academic. Using those passages as prompts, write an essay that describes and analyzes your own academic reading or writing process. What elements of your process have advanced your ability to enter

into the academic conversation? In what ways does your process fall short of what you would like to be able to do? What would you like to learn to make your process more effective?

4. Rose describes his early attempts to write academically as "words . . . piled up like cars in a serial wreck" (par. 30). Have you ever felt that way about your academic writing? Write a paragraph in which you try to reproduce the language of a field you would like to enter or a course you are required to take. Follow the paragraph with an analysis of why the language is difficult. Is the vocabulary unfamiliar or obscure? Is the sentence structure difficult to master? Every field or discipline has hidden intellectual moves and strategies that express the field's distinctive way of thinking and making arguments. Are those moves and strategies difficult to enter into?

5. In this essay, Rose describes only those mentors who were his teachers. In an essay, reflect on whether peers can serve as mentors. Analyze the role of upperclassmen in orientation, advisement, or study settings, such as a writing center. Consider the influence of other students whose behavior you simply observe for clues on language, attitudes, and other moves expected of students on your campus.

6. Loyola, the university Rose attended as an undergraduate, is a Catholic university. In an essay, reflect on the differences in mentoring offered by a state university versus a religious university dedicated to the larger spiritual well-being of students. What might be the advantages of each institution? What might be the disadvantages?

Disliking Books at an Early Age

Gerald Graff

Gerald Graff has enjoyed a long and distinguished career studying and teaching literature, in spite of the fact that he feared and avoided books well into his undergraduate years as an English major. It was debate among the literary critics, not the literature itself, that gradually drew him in. He remembers in particular *The Adventures of Huckleberry Finn:* He made no connection with Huck's adventures until critical debate over the ending gave him a reason to think about the text. This undergraduate experience informed his career to such an extent that he recently coedited an edition of *Huckleberry Finn* focused on the literary debates that have surrounded it for several decades.

Graff believes his early aversion to reading has given him special insight as a teacher. "[M]any of the students I teach," writes Graff, "seem to have grown up as the same sort of nonintellectual, nonbookish person I was. . . . I like to think it is an advantage for a teacher to know what it feels like to grow up being indifferent to literature and intimidated by criticism and what it feels like to overcome a resistance to talking like an intellectual."

"Disliking Books at an Early Age" is an excerpt from *Beyond the Culture Wars,* which won the American Book Award in 1993. A second excerpt, "Other Voices, Other Rooms," appears on page 163. Gerald Graff is professor of English and dean of curriculum and instruction in the College of Liberal Arts and Sciences at the University of Illinois at Chicago. His most recent book is titled *Clueless in Academe: How Schooling Obscures the Life of the Mind* (2005).

I like to think I have a certain advantage as a teacher of literature because when I was growing up I disliked and feared books. My youthful aversion to books showed a fine impartiality, extending across the whole spectrum of literature, history, philosophy, science, and what by then (the late 1940s) had

- The registration will be on file with the PTO and can be cited by the PTO against another's subsequent application to register a confusingly similar mark.
- The registration will be located through standard searches of PTO records, thus possibly deterring others from using or applying for a similar mark.
- The registrant is entitled to use the registration symbol ®.

FILING THE APPLICATION, DOCKETING CRITICAL DATES, AND INITIAL ROLE OF THE UNITED STATES PATENT AND TRADEMARK OFFICE

Filing the Application

The application must be filed with the PTO within a reasonable time after it has been signed by the applicant, generally within one year after signature. The application must be accompanied by a filing fee in the amount of $335 for each class of goods and/or services. As an alternative to including a check for the filing fee, some applicants establish **deposit accounts** with the PTO and deposit a certain amount of money (at least $1,000) into an account against which fees can be drawn. Alternatively, the PTO accepts payment of fees by credit card. Trademark fees are set forth at the PTO web site at http://www.uspto.gov. (See Exhibit 4–4 for a schedule of PTO filing fees.)

The application can be filed in person at the PTO or can be mailed using either first-class or express mail of the U.S. Postal Service. The official address for many communications sent to the PTO is Commissioner for Trademarks, 2900 Crystal Drive, Arlington, VA 22202-3513, and this address should be used on most mail sent to the PTO, including applications. Because the PTO is in the process of moving its offices,

Application for registration, per class	$335
Filing an amendment to allege use, per class	$100
Filing a statement of use, per class	$100
Filing a request for extension of time to file a statement of use, per class	$150
Application for renewal, per class	$400
Additional fee for late renewal or late section 8 affidavit, per class	$100
Issuing a new certificate of registration	$100
Filing an amendment or correction to registration certificate	$100
Filing section 8 affidavit of use of mark, per class	$100
Filing section 15 affidavit to achieve incontestability, per class	$200
Petition for cancellation, per class	$300
Notice of opposition, per class	$300
Dividing an application, per each new application (file wrapper) created	$100
Certified copy of registered mark	$15
Copy of trademark file wrapper	$50
Recording a trademark assignment (for first mark)	$40
For subsequent marks in the same document	$25 each

EXHIBIT 4–4
Schedule of
PTO Filing Fees
(Trademark Matters)

come to be called social studies. But had I been forced to choose, I would have singled out literature and history as the reading I disliked most. Science at least had some discernible practical use, and you could have fun solving the problems in the textbooks with their clear-cut answers. Literature and history had no apparent application to my experience, and any boy in my school who had cultivated them—I can't recall one who did—would have marked himself as a sissy.

As a middle-class Jew growing up in an ethnically mixed Chicago neighborhood, I was already in danger of being beaten up daily by rougher working-class boys. Becoming a bookworm would have only given them a decisive reason for beating me up. Reading and studying were more permissible for girls, but they, too, had to be careful not to get too intellectual, lest they acquire the stigma of being "stuck up."

In *Lives on the Boundary*, a remarkable autobiography of the making of an English teacher, Mike Rose describes how the "pain and confusion" of his working-class youth made "school and knowledge" seem a saving alternative. Rose writes of feeling "freed, as if I were untying fetters," by his encounters with certain college teachers, who helped him recognize that "an engagement with ideas could foster competence and lead me out into the world."[1] Coming at things from my middle-class perspective, however, I took for granted a freedom that school, knowledge, and engagement with ideas seemed only to threaten.

My father, a literate man, was frustrated by my refusal to read anything besides comic books, sports magazines, and the John R. Tunis and Clair Bee sports novels. I recall his once confining me to my room until I finished a book on the voyages of Magellan, but try as I might, I could do no better than stare bleakly at the pages. I could not, as we would later say, "relate to" Magellan or to any of the other books my father brought home—detective stories, tales of war and heroism, adventure stories with adolescent heroes (the *Hardy Boys, Hans Brinker,* or *The Silver Skates*), stories of scientific discovery (Paul de Kruif's *Microbe Hunters*), books on current events. Nothing worked.

It was understood, however, that boys of my background would go to college and that once there we would get serious and buckle down. For some, "getting serious" meant prelaw, premed, or a major in business to prepare for taking over the family business. My family did not own a business, and law and medicine did not interest me, so I drifted by default into the nebulous but conveniently noncommittal territory of the liberal arts. I majored in English.

At this point the fear of being beaten up if I were caught having anything to do with books was replaced by the fear of flunking out of college if I did not learn to deal with them. But though I dutifully did my homework and made good grades (first at the University of Illinois, Chicago branch, then at the University of Chicago, from which I graduated in 1959), I continued to

find "serious" reading painfully difficult and alien. My most vivid recollec-
tions of college reading are of assigned classics I failed to finish: *The Iliad* (in
the Richmond Lattimore translation); *The Autobiography of Benvenuto
Cellini*, a major disappointment after the paperback jacket's promise of "a
lusty classic of Renaissance ribaldry"; E. M. Forster's *Passage to India*, sixty
agonizing pages of which I managed to slog through before giving up. Even
Hemingway, Steinbeck, and Fitzgerald, whose contemporary world was said
to be "close to my own experience," left me cold. I saw little there that did
resemble my experience.

Even when I had done the assigned reading, I was often tongue-tied and
embarrassed when called on. What was unclear to me was what I was supposed to *say* about literary works, and why. Had I been born a decade or two
earlier, I might have come to college with the rudiments of a literate vocabulary for talking about culture that some people
older than I acquired through family, high school, or   **Getting into immediate con-**
church. As it was, "cultured" phrases seemed effete   **tact with the text was for me**
and sterile to me. When I was able to produce the   **a curiously triangular business.**
kind of talk that was required in class, the intellectu-
alism of it came out sounding stilted and hollow in my mouth. If *Cliffs Notes*
and other such crib sheets for the distressed had yet come into existence,
with their ready-to-copy summaries of widely taught literary works, I would
have been an excellent customer. (As it was, I did avail myself of the primitive version then in existence called *Masterplots.*)

What first made literature, history, and other intellectual pursuits seem
attractive to me was exposure to critical debates. There was no single conversion experience, but a gradual transformation over several years, extending into my first teaching positions, at the University of New Mexico and
then Northwestern University. But one of the first sparks I remember was a
controversy over *The Adventures of Huckleberry Finn* that arose in a course
during my junior year in college. On first attempt, Twain's novel was just
another assigned classic that I was too bored to finish. I could see little connection between my Chicago upbringing and Huck's pre–Civil War adventures with a runaway slave on a raft up the Mississippi.

My interest was aroused, however, when our instructor mentioned that
the critics had disagreed over the merits of the last part of the novel. He
quoted Ernest Hemingway's remark that "if you read [the novel] you must
stop where the nigger Jim is stolen by the boys. This is the real end. The rest
is cheating." According to this school of thought, the remainder of the book
trivializes the quest for Jim's freedom that has motivated the story up to that
point. This happens first when Jim becomes an object of Tom Sawyer's slap-
stick humor, then when it is revealed that unbeknownst to Huck, the reader,
and himself, Jim has already been freed by his benevolent owner, so that the

risk we have assumed Jim and Huck to be under all along has been really no risk at all.

Like the critics, our class divided over the question: Did Twain's ending vitiate the book's profound critique of racism, as Hemingway's charge of cheating implied? Cheating in my experience up to then was something students did, an unthinkable act for a famous author. It was a revelation to me that famous authors were capable not only of mistakes but of ones that even lowly undergraduates might be able to point out. When I chose to write my term paper on the dispute over the ending, my instructor suggested I look at several critics on the opposing sides, T. S. Eliot and Lionel Trilling, who defended the ending, and Leo Marx, who sided with Hemingway.

Reading the critics was like picking up where the class discussion had left off, and I gained confidence from recognizing that my classmates and I had had thoughts that, however stumbling our expression of them, were not too far from the thoughts of famous published critics. I went back to the novel again and to my surprise found myself rereading it with an excitement I had never felt before with a serious book. Having the controversy over the ending in mind, I now had some issues *to watch out for* as I read, issues that reshaped the way I read the earlier chapters as well as the later ones and focused my attention. And having issues to watch out for made it possible not only to concentrate, as I had not been able to do earlier, but to put myself in the text—to read with a sense of personal engagement that I had not felt before. Reading the novel with the voices of the critics running through my mind, I found myself thinking of things that I might say about what I was reading, things that may have belonged partly to the critics but also now belonged to me. It was as if having a stock of things to look for and to say about a literary work had somehow made it possible for me to read one.

One of the critics had argued that what was at issue in the debate over *Huckleberry Finn* was not just the novel's value but its cultural significance: If *Huckleberry Finn* was contradictory or confused in its attitude toward race, then what did that say about the culture that had received the novel as one of its representative cultural documents and had made Twain a folk hero? This critic had also made the intriguing observation—I found out only later it was a critical commonplace at that time—that judgments about the novel's aesthetic value could not be separated from judgments about its moral substance. I recall taking in both this critic's arguments and the cadence of the phrases in which they were couched; perhaps it would not be so bad after all to become the sort of person who talked about "cultural contradictions" and the "inseparability of form and content." Perhaps even mere literary-critical talk could give you a certain power in the real world. As the possibility dawned on me that reading and intellectual discussion might actually have something to do with my real life, I became less embarrassed about using the intellectual formulas.

The Standard Story

It was through exposure to such critical reading and discussion over a period of time that I came to catch the literary bug, eventually choosing the vocation of teaching. This was not the way it is supposed to happen. In the standard story of academic vocation that we like to tell ourselves, the germ is first planted by an early experience of literature itself. The future teacher is initially inspired by some primary experience of a great book and only subsequently acquires the secondary, derivative skills of critical discussion. A teacher may be involved in instilling this inspiration, but a teacher who seemingly effaces himself or herself before the text. Any premature or excessive acquaintance with secondary critical discourse, and certainly with its sectarian debates, is thought to be a corrupting danger, causing one to lose touch with the primary passion for literature.

This, as we have seen, is the charge leveled against the current generation of literature teachers, who are said to have become so obsessed with sophisticated critical theories that they have lost the passion they once had for literature itself. They have been seduced by professionalism, drawn away from a healthy absorption in literature to the sickly fascination with analysis and theory and to the selfish advancement of their careers. This hostility to recent theory would not be so powerful, however, if it were not overlaid on a set of older resentments which long predate the rise of deconstruction and poststructuralism, resentments at literature's having become an academic "field" to begin with. Today's attacks on literary theory are often really attacks on literary criticism, or at least on criticism of the intensely analytic kind that academics practice, which has always been suspected of coming between readers (and students) and the primary experience of literature itself. This resentment is rooted in anxieties about the increasing self-consciousness of modern life, which often leaves us feeling that we are never quite living but only endlessly talking about it, too often in some abstract professional vocabulary. The anxieties are expressed in our romantic literary tradition, which protests against urban forms of sophistication that, it is believed, cause us to lose touch with the innocence of childhood and with our creative impulses.

To those who have never reconciled themselves to the academicization of literature, the seeming overdevelopment of academic criticism with its obtrusive methodology and its endless disputes among interpretations and theories seems a betrayal not just of literature and the common reader but of the professor's own original passion for literature. In a recent letter to an intellectual journal one writer suggests that we should be concerned less about the often-lamented common reader whom academic critics have deserted than about "the souls of the academics and literati themselves, who, as a result of social and professional pressures, have lost touch with the inner impulses that drew them to the world of books in the first place."[2] What this writer cannot imagine is that someone might enter academic literary study because he actually *likes* thinking and talking in an analytical or theoretical way about books and that such a person might see his acceptance of "professional pressures" not as a betrayal of the "inner impulses" that drew him "to the world of books in the first place" but as a way to fulfill those impulses.

The standard story ascribes innocence to the primary experience of literature and sees the secondary experience of professional criticism as corrupting. In my case, however, things had evidently worked the other way around: I had to be corrupted first in order to experience innocence. It was only when I was introduced to a critical debate about *Huckleberry Finn* that my helplessness in the face of the novel abated and I could experience a personal reaction to it. Getting into immediate contact with the text was for me a curiously triangular business; I could not do it directly but needed a conversation of other readers to give me the issues and terms that made it possible to respond.

As I think back on it now, it was as if the critical conversation I needed had up to then been withheld from me, on the ground that it could only interfere with my direct access to literature itself. The assumption was that leaving me alone with literary texts themselves, uncontaminated by the interpretations and theories of professional critics, would enable me to get on the closest possible terms with those texts. But being alone with the texts only left me feeling bored and helpless, since I had no language with which to make them mine. On the one hand, I was being asked to speak a foreign language—literary criticism—while on the other hand, I was being protected from that language, presumably for my own safety.

The moral I draw from this experience is that our ability to read well depends more than we think on our ability to *talk well* about what we read. Our assumptions about what is "primary" and "secondary" in the reading process blind us to what actually goes on. Many literate people learned certain ways of talking about books so long ago that they have forgotten they ever had to learn them. These people therefore fail to understand the reading problems of the struggling students who have still not acquired a critical vocabulary.

How typical my case was is hard to say, but many of the students I teach seem to have grown up as the same sort of nonintellectual, nonbookish person I was, and they seem to view literature with some of the same aversions, fears, and anxieties. That is why I like to think it is an advantage for a teacher to know what it feels like to grow up being indifferent to literature and intimidated by criticism and what it feels like to overcome a resistance to talking like an intellectual.

Notes

1. Mike Rose, *Lives on the Boundary* (New York: Free Press, 1989), pp. 46–47.
2. John Toren, letter, *New Republic* 201, no. 9 (August 28, 1989): 6, 41.

Working with the Text

1. As a professor of English at a prominent university, Gerald Graff confesses that when he was growing up, he "disliked and feared books." Throughout the essay, he continues to draw his argument from personal experience. In a short essay, distill his argument and reflect on why he would choose personal experience as the basis for the assertions he makes. Who is his audience? Why is he making this argument? Why is his personal experience significant?

2. In moving through his argument, Graff relates the reasons behind his resistance to reading as well as the reasons behind his "gradual transformation" into an intellectual and a literary critic. Make two lists of those reasons: one for his resistance and another for his transformation. Based on those lists, write a short essay analyzing the relationship between his resistance and his transformation. Why was reading hard for him? How did he respond to it? In what ways did his university experience meet his resistance and transform it?

3. Graff advocates debate as a point of entering into demanding texts with excitement. Given his assertions on debate, how do you think he conducts his own classroom? Referring to the specific approaches, experiences, and ways of thinking he describes, write a short essay in which you imagine the progression of activities in one of his courses. What role would secondary sources play? What would the relationship between class discussion and writing be? What would you learn?

From Text to Field

1. In this essay, Graff describes texts he was supposed to like, but didn't. He also describes "serious" reading that excited him and the approaches to reading that made this possible. In an autobiographical essay, analyze your own relationship to the reading you do in your university studies. What kinds of reading do you resist? Why? What form does your resistance take? What kinds of reading are exciting for you? Why? What happens to create the excitement? What activities or experiences have made reading that was once hard for you easier and more compelling?

2. Graff describes "the standard story of academic vocation" for literature professors, in which "the germ is first planted by an early experience of literature itself" (par. 13). In Graff's own story, he resisted literature for years but

was gradually drawn into the profession by critical debates over the texts. Graff's observations suggest contrasting ways of entering into any new area of inquiry and choosing to pursue it as a profession or an area of specialization. Consider an area of inquiry or specialization you have been required to enter or have chosen to pursue. Did you enter in a way similar to Graff's "standard story," by being exposed to primary texts or materials? Or did you enter as Graff prefers, by being drawn into the current debates? Write an essay in which you reflect on your own experience and describe the path you would prefer to take in mastering the subject matter. Which approach has been or would be most productive for you? Can you imagine a different approach that would be more useful and compelling to you?

3. In key passages, Graff emphasizes the importance of discussion in learning to write about and engage the debates associated with any discipline. Why does he think talking is critical? What is gained that cannot be gained by reading and writing alone? Write an essay from personal experience in which you analyze the contribution class discussion, study groups, or face-to-face conferences with a teacher have made—or not made—to your academic development. In what ways has discussion helped you learn the critical language of a specialty area? In what ways might the requirement to enter into discussion hamper your progress?

4. Have you taken college courses you think would have been more compelling if you had had the opportunity to learn the material through engaging in debate? Have any of your courses given you such an opportunity? Choose one course from your own experience to analyze in light of Graff's argument for critical debate as a way of learning. For a course that offered little or no debate, write an essay that describes how the material was presented and imagine ways that differing points of view might have been introduced to enliven the material. For a course that drew upon differing points of view as a means for exploring the material, describe how this was accomplished.

Dancing with Professors: The Trouble with Academic Prose

Patricia Nelson Limerick

In 1987, at her own request, Patricia Nelson Limerick, professor of history at the University of Colorado at Boulder and chair of the board of the Center of the American West, was named University Fool. Each year on April 1, she tours the campus to remind people to stop taking themselves so seriously.

Limerick's widely circulated article, "Dancing with Professors: The Trouble with Academic Prose," was first published in 1993 in a nonacademic publication—the *New York Times Book Review.* An academic insider, she bases her argument on the observation (borrowed from a classics professor) that "'professors are the ones nobody wanted to dance with in high school."' The article is an ultimately serious plea for academics to write in such a way that nonspecialists as well as specialists can engage in open discussion, bridging scholarly research with public concerns.

Limerick demonstrated how this could be done in her 1987 revisionist history of the West, *The Legacy of Conquest: The Unbroken Past of the American West* (1987). The book attracted a wide readership among general audiences at the same time it challenged academics inside and outside of history departments to see the West through a new lens. Her books have established her as one of the principal architects of the New Western History, with special interests in the ethnic and environmental aspects of that history.

Among Limerick's numerous accomplishments, she was named a MacArthur Fellow in 1995 and served on the board of advisors for the eight-part PBS series *The West.* Her most recent book is *Something in the Soil: Legacies and Reckonings in the New West* (2001).

In ordinary life, when a listener cannot understand what someone has said, this is the usual exchange:

> *Listener:* I cannot understand what you are saying.
> *Speaker:* Let me try to say it more clearly.

But in scholarly writing in the late twentieth century, other rules apply. This is the implicit exchange:

> *Reader:* I cannot understand what you are saying.
> *Academic Writer:* Too bad. The problem is that you are an unsophisticated and untrained reader. If you were smarter, you would understand me.

The exchange remains implicit, because no one wants to say: "This doesn't make any sense," for fear that the response, "It would, if you were smarter," might actually be true.

While we waste our time fighting over ideological conformity in the scholarly world, horrible writing remains a far more important problem. For all their differences, most right-wing scholars and most left-wing scholars share a common allegiance to a cult of obscurity. Left, right, and center all hide behind the idea that unintelligible prose indicates a sophisticated mind. The politically correct and the politically incorrect come together in the violence they commit against the English language.

University presses have certainly filled their quota every year, in dreary monographs, tangled paragraphs, and impenetrable sentences. But trade publishers have also violated the trust of innocent and hopeful readers. As a prime example of unprovoked assaults on innocent words, consider the verbal behavior of Allan Bloom in *The Closing of the American Mind* published by a large mainstream press. Here is a sample:

> If openness means to "go with the flow," it is necessarily an accommodation to the present. That present is so closed to doubt about so many things impeding the progress of its principles that unqualified openness to it would mean forgetting the despised alternatives to it, knowledge of which makes us aware of what is doubtful in it.

Is there a reader so full of blind courage as to claim to know what this sentence means? Remember, the book in which this remark appeared was a lamentation over the failings of today's students, a call to arms to return to tradition and standards in education. And yet, in twenty years of paper grading, I do not recall many sentences that asked, so pathetically, to be put out of their misery.

Jump to the opposite side of the political spectrum from Allan Bloom, and literary grace makes no noticeable gains. Contemplate this breathless, indefatigable sentence from the geographer Allan Pred, and Mr. Pred and Bloom seem, if only in literary style, to be soul mates:

If what is at stake is an understanding of geographical and historical variations in the sexual division of productive and reproductive labor, of contemporary local and regional variations in female wage labor and women's
work outside the formal economy, of on-the-ground variations in the everyday content of women's lives, inside and outside of their families, then it
must be recognized that, at some nontrivial level, none of the corporal
practices associated with these variations can be severed from spatially and
temporally specific linguistic practices, from languages that not only
enable the conveyance of instructions, commands, role depictions, and
operating rules, but that also regulate and control, that normalize and spell
out the limits of the permissible through the conveyance of disapproval,
ridicule, and reproach.

In this example, 124 words, along with many ideas, find themselves 5
crammed into one sentence. In their company, one starts to get panicky.
"Throw open the windows; bring in the oxygen tanks!" one wants to shout.
"These words and ideas are nearly suffocated. Get them air!" And yet the
condition of this desperately packed and crowded sentence is a perfectly
familiar one to readers of academic writing, readers who have simply learned
to suppress the panic.

Everyone knows that today's college students cannot write, but few seem
willing to admit that the professors who denounce them are not doing much
better. The problem is so blatant there are signs that students are catching
on. In my American history survey course last semester, I presented a few
writing rules that I intended to enforce inflexibly. The students looked more
and more peevish; they looked as if they were about to run down the hall,
find a telephone, place an urgent call, and demand that someone from the
ACLU rush up to campus to sue me for interfering with their First
Amendment rights to compose unintelligible, misshapen sentences.

Finally one aggrieved student raised her hand and said, "You are telling
us not to write long, dull sentences, but most of our assigned reading is full
of long, dull sentences."

As this student was beginning to recognize, when professors undertake to
appraise and improve student writing, the blind are leading the blind. It is,
in truth, difficult to persuade students to write well when they find so few
good examples in their assigned reading.

The current social and political context for higher education makes this
whole issue pressing. In Colorado, as in most states, the legislators are convinced that the university is neglecting students and wasting state resources
on pointless research. Under those circumstances, the miserable writing
habits of professors pose a direct and concrete danger to higher education.
Rather than going to the state legislature, proudly presenting stacks of the
faculty's compelling and engaging publications, you end up hoping that the

check the PTO web site for current mailing addresses. Documents mailed to the PTO should include a certificate of mailing, verifying the date the correspondence was placed in the U.S. mail. When the PTO receives the application, it will perform a cursory review to ensure that the minimum required elements of the application (and the filing fee) are present. The mailroom will then stamp the application with a serial or filing number that will accompany the application throughout the entire application process. The serial number is critical because the PTO responds to inquiries only if a serial number is known. At present, all applications begin with the two-digit number 76, although the series code is "78" for applications filed electronically, using TEAS.

Most applicants include either a duplicate copy of the application with a self-addressed stamped envelope or a postcard or "come-back card," requesting that the PTO place a label on the duplicate application or the postcard with the date of filing and application filing number so the applicant can verify filing. Otherwise, the PTO may take several weeks to send the applicant the official filing receipt verifying filing of the application.

The filing date of the application is critical because it initiates various time limits. For example, applicants have a duty to inquire about the status of an application if they do not hear from the PTO within one year of any filing. Thus, the filing date should be calendared or docketed so that you can ensure the PTO has provided you with the official filing receipt within one year of the filing date. Similarly, if the application is filed based on an applicant's intent to use the mark in the future, the filing date constitutes **constructive use** of the mark. For example, if an intent-to-use application is filed on June 1, 2003, and the mark is ultimately registered, the date for determining priority between conflicting parties is June 1, 2003, even though the mark may not have been actually used until December 1, 2003, and may not have achieved registration until July 1, 2004. Finally, if an applicant wishes to file an application for the mark in a foreign country that is a member of the Paris Convention (discussed in Chapter 8), it has six months from the filing date within which to do so and thereby claim the date of the filing in the United States.

Docketing Critical Dates

Many law firms and offices that do a significant amount of trademark work have sophisticated computer programs that automatically docket critical dates. Such systems will automatically flag a file and provide notification that no action has been taken on an application in nearly twelve months so the applicant may investigate the problem. Nevertheless, most firms (and some malpractice carriers) also require that trademark practitioners maintain their own dockets, whether by means of an independent computerized system or a simple tickler file composed of index cards and divided into monthly categories, to serve as reminders of needed action in the coming months. The very nature of trademark work is deadline-sensitive. Failure to take certain actions on a timely basis may result in abandonment of a mark or application unless the delay was unintentional. Therefore, the utmost care must be taken to protect a client's interests. Develop a docketing system that works effectively and maintain it diligently. Failure to do so may be malpractice.

Initial Role of the United States Patent and Trademark Office: The File Wrapper and the Official Filing Receipt

When the PTO receives an application, it creates a threefold legal-size file, called a **file wrapper,** to hold the papers related to the application. The file wrapper is the official PTO lawmakers stay out of the library and stay away, especially, from the periodical room, with its piles of academic journals. The habits of academic writers lend powerful support to the impression that research is a waste of the writers' time and of the public's money.

Why do so many professors write bad prose?   10

Ten years ago, I heard a classics professor say the single most important thing—in my opinion—that anyone has said about professors: "We must remember," he declared, "that professors are the ones nobody wanted to dance with in high school."

This is an insight that lights up the universe—or at least the university. It is a proposition that every entering freshman should be told, and it is certainly a proposition that helps to explain the problem of academic writing. What one sees in professors, repeatedly, is exactly the manner that anyone would adopt after a couple of sad evenings sidelined under the crepe-paper streamers in the gym, sitting on a folding chair while everyone else danced. Dignity, for professors, perches precariously on how well they can convey this message: "I am immersed in some very important thoughts, which unsophisticated people could not even begin to understand. Thus, I would not want to dance, even if one of you unsophisticated people were to ask me."

Think of this, then, the next time you look at an unintelligible academic text. "I would not want the attention of a wide reading audience, even if a wide audience were to ask for me." Isn't that exactly what the pompous and pedantic tone of the classically academic writer conveys?

Professors are often shy, timid, and even fearful people, and under those circumstances, dull, difficult prose can function as a kind of protective camouflage. When you write typical academic prose, it is nearly impossible to make a strong, clear statement. The benefit here is that no one can attack your position, say you are wrong or even raise questions about the accuracy of what you have said, if they cannot tell what you have said. In those terms, awful, indecipherable prose is its own form of armor, protecting the fragile, sensitive thoughts of timid souls.

The best texts for helping us understand the academic world are, of   15 course, Lewis Carroll's *Alice's Adventures in Wonderland* and *Through the Looking Glass.* Just as devotees of Carroll would expect, he has provided us with the best analogy for understanding the origin and function of bad academic writing. Tweedledee and Tweedledum have quite a heated argument over a rattle. They become so angry that they decide to fight. But before they fight, they go off to gather various devices of padding and protection: "bolsters, blankets, hearthrugs, tablecloths, dish covers, and coal scuttles." Then, with Alice's help in tying and fastening, they transform these household items into armor. Alice is not impressed: "'Really, they'll be more like bundles of old clothes than anything else, by the time they're ready!' she said to herself, as she arranged a bolster round the neck of Tweedledee, 'to keep his head from being cut off, as he said.'" Why this precaution? Because, Tweedledee explains, "'it's one of the most serious things that can possibly happen to one in a battle—to get one's head cut off.'"

Here, in the brothers' anxieties and fears, we have an exact analogy for the problems of academic writing. The next time you look at a classically professorial sentence—long, tangled, obscure, jargonized, polysyllabic—think of Tweedledum and Tweedledee dressed for battle, and see if those timid little thoughts, concealed under layers of clauses and phrases, do not remind you of those agitated but cautious brothers, arrayed in their bolsters, blankets, dish covers, and coal scuttles. The motive, too, is similar. Tweedledum and Tweedledee were in terror of being hurt, and so they padded themselves so thoroughly that they could not be hurt; nor, for that matter, could they move. A properly dreary, inert sentence has exactly the same benefit; it protects its writer from sharp disagreement, while it also protects him from movement.

Why choose camouflage and insulation over clarity and directness? Tweedledee, of course, spoke for everyone, academic or not, when he confessed his fear. It is indeed, as he said, "'one of the most serious things that can possibly happen to one in a battle—to get one's head cut off.'" "Under those circumstances, logic says: Tie the bolster around the neck, and add a protective hearthrug or two. Pack in another qualifying clause or two. Hide behind the passive-voice verb. Preface any assertion with a phrase like "it could be argued" or "a case could be made." Protecting one's neck does seem to be the way to keep one's head from being cut off.

Graduate school implants in many people the belief that there are terrible penalties to be paid for writing clearly, especially writing clearly in ways that challenge established thinking in the field. And yet, in academic warfare (and I speak as a veteran), your head and your neck are rarely in serious danger. You can remove the bolster and the hearthrug. Your opponents will try to whack at you, but they seldom, if ever, land a blow—in large part because they are themselves so wrapped in protective camouflage and insulation that they lose both mobility and accuracy.

So we have a widespread pattern of professors protecting themselves from injury by wrapping their ideas in dull prose, and yet the danger they try to fend off is not a genuine danger. Express yourself clearly, and it is unlikely that either your head—or, more important, your tenure—will be cut off.

How, then, do we save professors from themselves? Fearful people are not made courageous by scolding; they need to be coaxed and encouraged. But how do we do that, especially when this particular form of fearfulness masks itself as pomposity, aloofness, and an assumed air of superiority?

Fortunately, we have available the world's most important and illuminating story on the difficulty of persuading people to break out of habits of timidity, caution, and unnecessary fear. I borrow this story from Larry McMurtry, one of my rivals in the interpreting of the American West, though I am putting this story to a use that Mr. McMurtry did not intend.

In a collection of his essays, *In a Narrow Grave*, Mr. McMurtry wrote about the weird process of watching his book *Horseman, Pass By* being turned into the movie *Hud*. He arrived in the Texas Panhandle a week or two after filming had started, and he was particularly anxious to learn how the buzzard scene had gone. In that scene, Paul Newman was supposed to ride up and discover a dead cow, look up at a tree branch lined with buzzards and, in his distress over the loss of the cow, fire his gun at one of the buzzards. At that moment, all of the other buzzards were supposed to fly away into the blue Panhandle sky.

But when Mr. McMurtry asked people how the buzzard scene had gone, all he got, he said, were "stricken looks."

The first problem, it turned out, had to do with the quality of the available local buzzards—who proved to be an excessively scruffy group. So more appealing, more photogenic buzzards had to be flown in from some distance and at considerable expense.

But then came the second problem: how to keep the buzzards sitting on   25 the tree branch until it was time for their cue to fly.

That seemed easy. Wire their feet to the branch, and then, after Paul Newman fires his shot, pull the wire, releasing their feet, thus allowing them to take off. But, as Mr. McMurtry said in an important and memorable phrase, the filmmakers had not reckoned with the "mentality of buzzards." With their feet wired, the buzzards did not have enough mobility to fly. But they did have enough mobility to pitch forward.

So that's what they did: With their feet wired, they tried to fly, pitched forward and hung upside down from the dead branch, with their wings flapping.

I had the good fortune a couple of years ago to meet a woman who had been an extra for this movie, and she added a detail that Mr. McMurtry left out of his essay: Namely, the buzzard circulatory system does not work upside down, and so, after a moment or two of flapping, the buzzards passed out.

Twelve buzzards hanging upside down from a tree branch: This was not what Hollywood wanted from the West, but that's what Hollywood had produced.

And then we get to the second stage of buzzard psychology. After six or   30 seven episodes of pitching forward, passing out, being revived, being replaced on the branch, and pitching forward again, the buzzards gave up. Now, when you pulled the wire and released their feet, they sat there, saying in clear, non-verbal terms: "We tried that before. It did not work. We are not going to try it again." Now the filmmakers had to fly in a high-powered animal trainer to restore buzzard self-esteem. It was all a big mess; Larry McMurtry got a wonderful story out of it; and we, in turn, get the best possible parable of the workings of habit and timidity.

How does the parable apply? In any and all disciplines, you go to graduate school to have your feet wired to the branch. There is nothing inherently wrong with that: Scholars should have some common ground, share some background assumptions, hold some similar habits of mind. This gives you, quite literally, your footing. And yet, in the process of getting your feet wired, you have some awkward moments, and the intellectual equivalent of pitching forward and hanging upside down. That experience—especially if you do it in a public place like a graduate seminar—provides no pleasure. One or two rounds of that humiliation and the world begins to seem like a very treacherous place. Under those circumstances, it does indeed seem to be the choice of wisdom to sit quietly on the branch, to sit without even the thought of flying, since even the thought might be enough to tilt the balance and set off another round of flapping, fainting, and embarrassment.

Professors are the ones nobody wanted to dance with in high school.

Yet when scholars get out of graduate school and get PhDs, and, even more important, when scholars get tenure, the wire is truly pulled. Their feet are free. They can fly wherever and whenever they like. Yet by then the second stage of buzzard psychology has taken hold, and they refuse to fly. The wire is pulled, and yet the buzzards sit there, hunched and grumpy. If they teach in a university with a graduate program, they actively instruct young buzzards in the necessity of keeping their youthful feet on the branch.

This is a very well-established pattern, and it is the ruination of scholarly activity in the modern world. Many professors who teach graduate students think that one of their principal duties is to train the students in the conventions of academic writing.

I do not believe that professors enforce a standard of dull writing on graduate students in order to be cruel. They demand dreariness because they think that dreariness is in the students' best interests. Professors believe that a dull writing style is an academic survival skill because they think that is what editors want, both editors of academic journals and editors of university presses. What we have here is a chain of misinformation and misunderstanding, where everyone thinks that the other guy is the one who demands dull, impersonal prose.

Let me say again what is at stake here: Universities and colleges are currently embattled, distrusted by the public and state funding institutions. As distressing as this situation is, it provides the perfect setting and the perfect timing for declaring an end to scholarly publication as a series of guarded conversations between professors.

35

The redemption of the university, especially in terms of the public's appraisal of the value of research and publication, requires all the writers who have something they want to publish to ask themselves the question: Does this have to be a closed communication, shutting out all but specialists willing to fight their way through thickets of jargon? Or can this be an open communication, engaging specialists with new information and new thinking, but also offering an invitation to nonspecialists to learn from this study, to grasp its importance and, by extension, to find concrete reasons to see value in the work of the university?

This is a country desperately in need of wisdom, and of clearly reasoned conviction and vision. And that, at the bedrock, is the reason behind this campaign to save professors from themselves and to detoxify academic prose. The context is a bit different, but the statement that Willy Loman made to his sons in *Death of a Salesman* keeps coming to mind: "The woods are burning, boys, the woods are burning." In a society confronted by a faltering economy, racial and ethnic conflicts, and environmental disasters, "the woods are burning," and since we so urgently need everyone's contribution in putting some of those fires out, there is no reason to indulge professorial vanity or timidity.

Ego is, of course, the key obstacle here. As badly as most of them write, professors are nonetheless proud and sensitive writers, resistant to criticism. But even the most desperate cases can be redeemed and persuaded to think of writing as a challenging craft, not as existential trauma. A few years ago, I began to look at carpenters and other artisans as the emotional model for writers. A carpenter, let us say, makes a door for a cabinet. If the door does not hang straight, the carpenter does not say, "I will not change that door; it is an expression of my individuality; who cares if it will not close?" Instead, the carpenter removes the door and works it until it fits. That attitude, applied to writing, could be our salvation. If we thought more like carpenters, academic writers could find a route out of the trap of ego and vanity. Escaped from that trap, we could simply work on successive drafts until what we have to say is clear.

Colleges and universities are filled with knowledgeable, thoughtful people who have been effectively silenced by an awful writing style, a style with its flaws concealed behind a smoke screen of sophistication and professionalism. A coalition of academic writers, graduate advisers, journal editors, university press editors, and trade publishers can seize this moment—*and pull the wire*. The buzzards *can* be set free—free to leave that dead tree branch, free to regain their confidence, free to soar.

Working with the Text

1. The key passage in Patricia Nelson Limerick's essay characterizes academic prose by quoting a classics professor: "'We must remember . . . that professors are the ones nobody wanted to dance with in high school'" (par. 11). The first part of the title of the essay is "Dancing with Professors." How do the quotation and the title work together to identify the problem posed by academic writing? In a short essay, tease out the meaning of this double use of the dance metaphor. Who is dancing with professors? How does the dance proceed? Why? In what ways does the dance influence what happens within the university?

2. As you reread the essay, note Limerick's own writing style, especially her use of extended metaphor and humor. Why does Limerick use this style in making her argument? Write a short essay that analyzes the general relationship between Limerick's use of language and the argument she is making. As an alternative essay, choose one of the extended metaphors and study the details Limerick includes in it. Write a short essay in which you analyze the effect of each of the details Limerick selects. Why does she include that detail? How does the detail contribute to her argument?

3. Limerick asserts that the "habits of academic writers lend powerful support to the impression that research is a waste of the writers' time and of the public's money" (par. 9). As you reread the essay, mark other passages where Limerick addresses "the trouble with academic prose" from the point of view of the public. In a short essay, analyze Limerick's concern. Exactly what problem does she think poor academic writing causes for the public? What kind of academic writing does she advocate, and why does she think it will address this problem?

From Text to Field

1. In the first part of her essay, Limerick asserts that while "today's college students cannot write . . . the professors who denounce them are not doing much better" (par. 6). She quotes a passage from a book published by a prominent academic and denounces it by claiming that "in twenty years of paper grading, I do not recall many sentences that asked, so pathetically, to be put out of their misery" (par. 3). In a short essay, respond to these and similar passages in Limerick's essay. Consider your own encounters with academic writing or with the language used in another field that has high expectations for those who enter it.

2. Choose a passage from a reading in your discipline or in a course you are taking that exemplifies the kind of academic writing Limerick describes. Write an essay in which you first critique the writing and then translate the passage into the kind of direct, lively prose Limerick recommends.

3. Have you ever used language—in the form of either writing or speaking—as armor, padding, or a weapon to protect yourself? In an essay, analyze the situation that prompted you to use language in this way. What demands of the situation and responses on your part drew you into this use of language? What kind of language did you use, and how did you use it? How effective was it in protecting you? What effect did it have on the dynamics of the situation?

4. Some university professors require students to eliminate *I* from their academic writing. Other professors invite students to include themselves in their writing. In an essay, explore the effects of writing yourself out of versus writing yourself into a piece of academic writing. Within an academic field or discipline, what are the disciplinary politics of self-disclosure? When and why is self-disclosure used or not used?

Between the Drafts

Nancy Sommers

In this essay, "Between the Drafts," Nancy Sommers realizes the deeply personal engagement with "authority" that underlies a writer's ability to accomplish "real revision"—a clearer vision of what the "self" has to say.

Nancy Sommers recalls growing up with parents who had escaped Nazi Germany but had passed on to their children a deference to authority that negated personal experience: "I guess it never occurred to them to reflect or to make connections between generations of German children . . . being instructed from early childhood to honor and defer to the parental authority of the state, and the Nazis' easy rise to power." As Sommers works to understand the stalemate she has reached in revising her own writing, she learns neither to defer to nor to escape authority but rather to find her voice by engaging in "a conversation with all the voices I embody."

Nancy Sommers is the Sosland Director of Writing at Harvard University, where she directs the Expository Writing Program, the Harvard Writing Project, and the Harvard Study of Undergraduate Writing. She recently completed a longitudinal study in which she followed the Harvard class of 2001 through their college years to understand the role writing plays in undergraduate education. She has coauthored or coedited four textbooks, authored numerous articles on the practice and theory of teaching writing, and published a number of personal essays. Throughout her career, Sommers has been particularly fascinated with the process of revision, a fascination that stems from always believing that a new vision is possible and from a commitment to explore how a writer's life and written work can come together in fruitful and unexpected ways. "Between the Drafts" won the 1993 Braddock Award, granted by the Conference on College Composition and Communication (CCCC), for the best article of the year published in its journal, *College Composition and Communication.*

I cannot think of my childhood without hearing voices, deep, heavily-accented, instructive German voices.

I hear the voice of my father reading to me from *Struvelpater*, the German children's tale about a messy boy who refuses to cut his hair or his fingernails. Struvelpater's hair grows so long that birds nest in it, and his fingernails grow so long that his hands become useless. He fares better, though, than the other characters in the book who don't listen to their parents. Augustus, for instance, refuses to eat his soup for four days, becomes as thin as a thread, and on the fifth day he is dead. Fidgety Philip tilts his dinner chair like a rocking horse until his chair falls backwards; the hot food falls on top of him and suffocates him under the weight of the table cloth. The worst story by far for me is that of Conrad, an incorrigible thumb-sucker, who couldn't stop sucking his thumb and whose mother warned him that a great, long, red-legged scissor-man would—and, yes, did—snip both his thumbs off.

As a child, I hated these horrid stories with their clear moral lessons, exhorting me to listen to my parents: Do the right thing, they said; obey authority, or else catastrophic things—dissipation, suffocation, loss of thumbs—will follow. It never occurred to me as a child to wonder why my parents, who had escaped Nazi Germany in 1939, were so deferential to authority, so beholden to sanctioned sources of power. I guess it never occurred to them to reflect or to make any connections between generations of German children reading *Struvelpater*, being instructed from early childhood to honor and defer to the parental authority of the state, and the Nazis' easy rise to power.

When I hear my mother's voice, it is usually reading to me from some kind of guidebook showing me how different *They*, the Americans, were from us, the German Jews of Terre Haute. My parents never left home without their passports; we had roots somewhere else. When we traveled westward every summer from our home in Indiana, our bible was the AAA tour guide, giving us the officially sanctioned version of America. We attempted to "see" America from the windows of our 1958 two-tone green Oldsmobile. We were literally the tourists from Terre Haute, those whom Walker Percy describes in "The Loss of the Creature," people who could never experience the Grand Canyon because it had already been formulated for us by picture postcards, tourist folders, guidebooks, and the words *Grand Canyon*.

Percy suggests that tourists never see the progressive movement of depths, 5 patterns, colors, and shadows of the Grand Canyon, but rather measure their satisfaction by the degree to which the canyon conforms to the expectations in their minds. My mother's AAA guidebook directed us, told us what to see, how to see it, and how long it should take us to see it. We never stopped anywhere serendipitously, never lingered, never attempted to know a place.

As I look now at the black-and-white photographs of our trips, seeing myself in ponytail and pedal pushers, I am struck by how many of the photos were taken against the car or, at least, with the car close enough to be included in the photograph. I am not sure we really saw the Grand Canyon or the Painted Desert or the Petrified Forest except from the security of a parking lot. We were traveling on a self-imposed visa that kept us close to our parked car; we lacked the freedom of our own authority and stuck close to each other and to the book itself.

My parents' belief that there was a right and a wrong way to do everything extended to the way they decided to teach us German. Wanting us to learn the correct way, not trusting their own native voices, they bought language-learning records with an officially sanctioned voice of an expert language teacher; never mind that they spoke fluent German.

It is 1959; I am eight years old. We sit in the olive-drab living room with the drapes closed so the neighbors won't see in. What the neighbors would have seen strikes me now as a scene out of a *Saturday Night Live* skit about the Coneheads. The children and their parental-unit sitting in stiff, good-for-your-posture chairs that my brother and I call the electric chairs. Those chairs are at odd angles to each other so we all face the fireplace; we don't look at each other. I guess my parents never considered pulling the chairs around, facing each other, so we could just talk in German. My father's investment was in the best 1959 technology he could find; he was proud of the time and money he had spent, so that we could be instructed in the right way. I can still see him there in that room removing the record from its purple package, placing it on the hi-fi:

Guten Tag.
Wie geht es Dir?
Wie geht es Werner/Helmut/Dieter?
Werner ist heute krank.
Oh, das tut mir Leid.
Gute Besserung.°

We are disconnected voices worrying over the health of Werner, Dieter, and Helmut, foreign characters, names, who have no place in our own family. We go on and on for an eternity with that dialogue until my brother passes gas, or commits some other unspeakable offense, something that sets my father's German sensibility on edge, and he finally says, "We will continue another time." He releases us back into another life, where we speak English, forgetting for yet another week about the health of Werner, Helmut, or Dieter.

Good morning. How are you? How is Werner/Helmut/Dieter? Werner is sick today. Oh, that's too bad. Get well.

file, and it contains the drawing, specimen, and all communications with the PTO. TEAS applications are assembled in an e-commerce law office that prints submissions and creates a file wrapper.

Within four to eight weeks after an application is filed, the PTO will mail the applicant a document called the **Official Filing Receipt.** The official filing receipt will confirm the filing date of the application, provide a serial number, and confirm all details of the application, including dates of first use, basis for filing, applicant's name and address, the goods or services offered under the mark, and the international class. Because the official filing receipt reflects what the PTO believes to be the pertinent details of the application, it should be carefully scrutinized for correctness. If there are any errors, even minor spelling mistakes, the applicant should immediately inform the PTO in writing. Failure to notify the PTO of some discrepancy may result in the certificate of registration including the erroneous information. Once the official filing receipt is received, the docketing system should be updated to ensure that additional action is taken on the application within six months thereafter.

For electronically filed documents, the PTO immediately issues a confirmation of the filing by e-mail. No paper filing receipt is generated.

THE EXAMINATION PROCESS

Examination Procedure

After the PTO issues the official filing receipt, the application is assigned for review to an examining attorney, typically new attorneys employed by the PTO. Many move into private practice after a few years with the PTO. Examining attorneys are assigned to "law offices" within the PTO, each of which has responsibility for certain types of applications.

For example, all applications relating to computer programs may be assigned to Law Office 106, while all applications dealing with business services may be assigned to Law Office 114. Concentrating similar applications in a given law office allows examining attorneys to become expert with certain types of applications, thereby facilitating the registration process. It is the function of an examining attorney to review the application, search the PTO files to determine if the mark applied for is confusingly similar to another, make a determination on whether the mark is registrable, and ultimately either refuse registration of the mark or approve it for publication. Examination is the least predictable stage of the prosecution process. Applications by the same party for identical or similar marks, called **companion applications,** will be handled by the same examining attorney. Conversely, applications by different parties for conflicting marks, called **conflicting applications,** are not handled by the same examining attorney, although the actions of the examining attorneys should be consistent.

Office Actions and Refusals to Register Marks

Approximately six months after the application is filed, the examining attorney assigned to the application will issue a "first action" or **Office Action** regarding the application if there are any defects in the application. If there are no defects, the PTO will approve the application for publication in the *Official Gazette*. The office action is a written communication sent by the examining attorney to the applicant (or, more likely, to the applicant's attorney) that states that the mark has been refused registration and explains why registration has been refused. All office actions must be responded to within six months to avoid abandonment of the application. To monitor pending applications, call the PTO status line or Trademark Status

I thought I had the issue of authority all settled in my mind when I was in   10
college. My favorite T-shirt, the one I took the greatest pleasure in wearing,
was one with the bold words *Question Authority* inscribed across my chest. It
seemed that easy. As we said then, either you were part of the problem or you
were part of the solution; either you deferred to authority or you resisted it by
questioning. Twenty years later, it doesn't seem that simple. I am beginning
to get a better sense of my legacy, beginning to see just how complicated and
how far-reaching is this business of authority. It extends into my life and
touches my students' lives, reminding me again and again of the delicate
relationship between language and authority.

In 1989, thirty years after my German lessons at home, I'm having dinner
with my daughters in an Italian restaurant. The waiter is flirting with eight-
year-old Rachel, telling her she has the most beautiful name, that she is *una
ragazza bellissima.* Intoxicated with this affectionate attention, she turns to
me passionately and says, "Oh, Momma, Momma, can't we learn Italian?" I,
too, for the moment am caught up in the brio of my daughter's passion. I say,
"Yes, yes, we must learn Italian." We rush to our favorite bookstore where we
find Italian language-learning tapes packaged in thirty-, sixty-, and ninety-day
lessons, and in our modesty buy the promise of fluent Italian in thirty lessons.
Driving home together, we put the tape in our car tape player, and begin lesson number 1:

> Buon giorno.
> Come stai?
> Come stai Monica?°

As we wind our way home, our Italian lessons quickly move beyond prelim-
inaries. We stop worrying over the health of Monica, and suddenly we are in
the midst of a dialogue about Signor Fellini who lives at 21 Broadway Street.
We cannot follow the dialogue. Rachel, in great despair, betrayed by the
promise of being a beautiful girl with a beautiful name speaking Italian in
thirty lessons, begins to scream at me: "This isn't the way to learn a language.
This isn't language at all. These are just words and sentences; this isn't about
us; we don't live at 21 Broadway Street."

And I am back home in Indiana, hearing the disembodied voices of my
family, teaching a language out of the context of life.

In 1987, I gave a talk at CCCC entitled "New Directions for Researching
Revision." At the time, I liked the talk very much because it gave me an
opportunity to illustrate how revision, once a subject as interesting to our

---

Good morning. How are you? How is Monica?

profession as an autopsy, had received new body and soul, almost celebrity status, in our time. Yet as interesting as revision had become, it seemed to me that our pedagogies and research methods were resting on some shaky, unquestioned assumptions.

I had begun to see how students often sabotage their own best interests when they revise, searching for errors and assuming, like the eighteenth-century theory of words parodied in *Gulliver's Travels*, that words are a load of things to be carried around and exchanged. It seemed to me that despite all those multiple drafts, all the peer workshops that we were encouraging, we had left unexamined the most important fact of all: Revision does not always guarantee improvement; successive drafts do not always lead to a clearer vision. You can't just change the words around and get the ideas right.

Here I am four years later, looking back on that abandoned talk, thinking   15 of myself as a student writer, and seeing that successive drafts have not led me to a clearer vision. I have been under the influence of a voice other than my own.

I live by the lyrical dream of change, of being made anew, always believing that a new vision is possible. I have been gripped, probably obsessed, with the subject of revision since graduate school. I have spent hundreds of hours studying manuscripts, looking for clues in the drafts of professional and student writers, looking for the figure in the carpet. The pleasures of this kind of literary detective work, this literary voyeurism, are the peeps behind the scenes, the glimpses of the process revealed in all its nakedness, of what Edgar Allan Poe called "the elaborate and vacillating crudities of thought, the true purposes seized only at the last moment, the cautious selections and rejections, the painful erasures."

My decision to study revision was not an innocent choice. It is deeply satisfying to believe that we are not locked into our original statements, that we might start and stop, erase, use the delete key in life, and be saved from the roughness of our early drafts. Words can be retracted; souls can be reincarnated. Such beliefs have informed my study of revision, and yet, in my own writing, I have always treated revising as an academic subject, not a personal one. Every time I have written about revision, I have set out to argue a thesis, present my research, accumulate my footnotes. By treating revision as an academic subject, by suggesting that I could learn something only by studying the drafts of other experienced writers, I kept myself clean and distant from any kind of scrutiny. No Struvelpater was I; no birds could nest in my hair; I kept my thumbs intact. I have been the bloodless academic creating taxonomies, creating a hierarchy of student writers and experienced writers, and never asking myself how I was being displaced from my own work. I never asked, "What does my absence *signify?*"

In that unrevised talk from CCCC, I had let Wayne Booth replace my father. Here are my words:

> Revision presents a unique opportunity to study what writers know. By studying writers' revisions we can learn how writers locate themselves within a discourse tradition by developing a persona—a fictionalized self. Creating a persona involves placing the self in a textual community, seeing oneself within a discourse, and positing a self that shares or antagonizes the beliefs that a community of readers shares. As Wayne Booth has written, "Every speaker makes a self with every word uttered. Even the most sincere statement implies a self that is at best a radical selection from many possible roles. No one comes on in exactly the same way with parents, teachers, classmates, lovers, and IRS inspectors."

What strikes me now, in this paragraph from my own talk, is that fictionalized self I invented, that anemic researcher, who set herself apart from her most passionate convictions. In that paragraph, I am a distant, imponderable, impersonal voice—inaccessible, humorless, and disguised like the packaged voice of Signor Fellini giving lessons as if absolutely nothing depends on my work. I speak in an inherited academic voice; it isn't mine.

I simply wasn't there for my own talk. Just as my father hid behind his language-learning records and my mother behind her guidebooks, I disguised myself behind the authority of "the researcher," attempting to bring in the weighty authority of Wayne Booth to justify my own statements, never gazing inward, never trusting my own authority as a writer.

Looking back on that talk, I know how deeply I was under the influence   20 of a way of seeing: Foucault's "Discourse on Language," Barthes's *S/Z*, Scholes's *Textual Power*, and Bartholomae's "Inventing the University" had become my tourist guides. I was so much under their influence that I remember standing in a parking lot of a supermarket, holding two heavy bags of groceries, talking with a colleague who was telling me about his teaching. Without any reference, except to locate my own authority somewhere else, I felt compelled to suggest to him that he read Foucault. My daughter Alexandra, waiting impatiently for me, eating chocolate while pounding on the hood of the car with her new black patent-leather party shoes, spoke with her own authority. She reminded me that I, too, had bumped on cars, eaten Hershey Bars, worn party shoes without straps, never read Foucault, and knew, nevertheless, what to say on most occasions.

One of my colleagues put a telling cartoon on the wall of our Xerox room. It reads "Breakfast Theory: A morning methodology." The cartoon describes two new cereals: Foucault Flakes and Post-Modern Toasties. The slogan for Foucault Flakes reads: "It's French so it must be good for you. A breakfast commodity so complex that you need a theoretical apparatus to digest it. You don't want to eat it; you'll just want to read it. Breakfast as text." And

Post-Modern Toasties: "More than just a cereal, it's a commentary on the nature of cerealness, cerealism, and the theory of cerealtivity. Free decoding ring inside."

I had swallowed the whole flake, undigested, as my morning methodology, but, alas, I never found the decoding ring. I was lost in the box. Or, to use the metaphor of revision, I was stuck in a way of seeing: reproducing the thoughts of others, using them as my guides, letting the post-structuralist vocabulary give authority to my text.

Successive drafts of my own talk did not lead to a clearer vision because it simply was not my vision. I, like so many of my students, was reproducing acceptable truths, imitating the gestures and rituals of the academy, not having confidence enough in my own ideas, nor trusting the native language I had learned. I had surrendered my own authority to someone else, to those other authorial voices.

Three years later, I am still wondering: Where does revision come from? Or, as I think about it now, what happens **I must bring a voice** between the drafts? Something has to happen or else we are **of my own.** struck doing mop and broom work, the janitorial work of polishing, cleaning, and fixing what is and always has been. What happens between drafts seems to be one of the great secrets of our profession.

Between drafts, I take lots of showers, hot showers, talking to myself as I 25 watch the water play against the gestures of my hands. In the shower, I get lost in the steam. There I stand without my badges of authority. I begin an imagined conversation with my colleague, the one whom I told in the parking lot of the grocery store, "Oh, but you must read Foucault." I revise our conversation. This time I listen.

I understand why he showed so much disdain when I began to pay homage to Foucault. He had his own sources aplenty that nourished him. Yet he hadn't felt the need to speak through his sources or interject their names into our conversation. His teaching stories and experiences are his own; they give him the authority to speak.

As I get lost in the steam, I listen to his stories, and I begin to tell him mine. I tell him about my father not trusting his native voice to teach me German, about my mother not trusting her own eyes and reading to us from guidebooks, about my own claustrophobia in not being able to revise a talk about revision, about being drowned out by a chorus of authorial voices. And I surprise myself. I say, Yes, these stories of mine provide powerful evidence; they belong to me; I can use them to say what I must about revision.

I begin at last to have a conversation with all the voices I embody, and I wonder why so many issues are posed as either/or propositions. Either I suck my thumb *or* the great long-legged scissor-man will cut it off. Either

I cook two chickens *or* my guests will go away hungry. Either I accept authority *or* I question it. Either I have babies and be in service of the species *or* I write books and be in service of the academy. Either I be personal *or* I be academic.

These either/or ways of seeing exclude life and real revision by pushing us to safe positions, to what is known. They are safe positions that exclude each other and don't allow for any ambiguity, uncertainty. Only when I suspend myself between either *and* or can I move away from conventional boundaries and begin to see shapes and shadows and contours—ambiguity, uncertainty, and discontinuity, moments when the seams of life just don't want to hold; days when I wake up to find, once again, that I don't have enough bread for the children's sandwiches or that there are no shoelaces for their gym shoes. My life is full of uncertainty; negotiating that uncertainty day to day gives me authority.

Maybe this is a woman's journey, maybe not. Maybe it is just my own, but   30 the journey between home and work, between being personal and being authoritative, between the drafts of my life, is a journey of learning how to be both personal and authoritative, both scholarly *and* reflective. It is a journey that leads me to embrace the experiences of my life, and gives me the insight to transform these experiences into evidence. I begin to see discontinuous moments as sources of strength and knowledge. When my writing and my life actually come together, the safe positions of either/or will no longer pacify me, no longer contain me and hem me in.

In that unrevised talk, I had actually misused my sources. What they were saying to me, if I had listened, was pretty simple: Don't follow us, don't reproduce what we have produced, don't live life from secondary sources like us, don't disappear. I hear Bob Scholes's and David Bartholomae's voices telling me to answer them, to speak back to them, to use them and make them anew. In a word, they say: Revise me. The language lesson starts to make sense, finally: By confronting these authorial voices, I find the power to understand and gain access to my own ideas. Against all the voices I embody—the voices heard, read, whispered to me from off-stage—I must bring a voice of my own. I must enter the dialogue on my own authority, knowing that other voices have enabled mine, but no longer can I subordinate mine to theirs.

The voices I embody encourage me to show up as a writer and to bring the courage of my own authority into my classroom. I have also learned about the dangers of submission from observing the struggles of my own students. When they write about their lives, they write with confidence. As soon as they begin to turn their attention toward outside sources, they too lose confidence, defer to the voice of the academy, and write in the voice of Everystudent to an audience they think of as Everyteacher. They disguise themselves in the weighty, imponderable voice of acquired authority: "In today's society," for instance, or "Since the beginning of civilization mankind has . . ." Or, as one student wrote about authority itself, "In attempting to investigate the origins of authority of the group, we must first decide exactly what we mean by authority."

In my workshops with teachers, the issue of authority, or deciding exactly what we mean by authority, always seems to be at the center of many heated conversations. Some colleagues are convinced that our writing programs should be about teaching academic writing. They see such programs as the welcome wagon of the academy, the Holiday Inn where students lodge as they take holy orders. Some colleagues fear that if we don't control what students learn, don't teach them to write as scholars write, we aren't doing our job and some great red-legged scissor-man will cut off our thumbs. Again it is one of those either/or propositions: Either we teach students to write academic essays or we teach them to write personal essays—and then who knows what might happen? The world might become uncontrollable: Students might start writing about their grandmother's death in an essay for a sociology course. Or even worse, something more uncontrollable, they might just write essays and publish them in professional journals claiming the authority to tell stories about their families and their colleagues. The uncontrollable world of ambiguity and uncertainty opens up, my colleagues imagine, as soon as the academic embraces the personal.

But, of course, our students are not empty vessels waiting to be filled with authorial intent. Given the opportunity to speak their own authority as writers, given a turn in the conversation, students can claim their stories as primary source material and transform their experiences into evidence. They might, if given enough encouragement, be empowered not to serve the academy and accommodate it, not to write in the persona of Everystudent, but rather to write essays that will change the academy. When we create opportunities for something to happen between the drafts, when we create writing exercises that allow students to work with sources of their own that can complicate and enrich their primary sources, they will find new ways to write scholarly essays that are exploratory, thoughtful, and reflective.

I want my students to know what writers know—to know something no 35 researchers could ever find out no matter how many times they pin my students to the table, no matter how many protocols they tape. I want my students to know how to bring their life and their writing together.

Sometimes when I cook a chicken and my children scuffle over the one wishbone, I wish I had listened to my grandmother and cooked two. Usually, the child who gets the short end of the wishbone dissolves into tears of frustration and failure. Interjecting my own authority as the earth mother from central casting, I try to make their life better by asking: On whose authority is it that the short end can't get her wish? Why can't both of you, the long and the short ends, get your wishes?

My children, on cue, as if they too were brought in from central casting, roll their eyes as children are supposed to do when their mothers attempt to impose a way of seeing. They won't let me control the situation by interpreting it for them. My interpretation serves my needs, temporarily, for sibling compromise and resolution. They don't buy my story because they know something about the sheer thrill of the pull that they are not going to let *me* deny *them*. They will have to revise my self-serving story about compromise, just as they will have to revise the other stories I tell them. Between the drafts, as they get outside my authority, they too will have to question, and begin to see for themselves their own complicated legacy, their own trail of authority.

It *is* in the thrill of the pull between someone else's authority and our own, between submission and independence that we must discover how to define ourselves. In the uncertainty of that struggle, we have a chance of finding the voice of our own authority. Finding it, we can speak convincingly . . . at long last.

Working with the Text

1. In her essay, Nancy Sommers explores the interplay between authority and the self in moving from one draft to another during the process of writing. She writes, "It *is* in the thrill of the pull between someone else's authority and our own, between submission and independence that we must discover how to define ourselves" (par. 38). In a short essay, analyze her conception of this interplay.

2. From the beginning of the essay to the end, Sommers moves from a limiting experience of authority to a freeing experience of authority. Write a short essay that explores and articulates this movement. How does she think authority can be limiting? How does she think it can be freeing? What happened to move her out of one concept of authority into another?

3. Analyzing Sommers's essay requires you to engage and respond to her ideas and experiences. In responding to her ideas and experiences, you are positioning her as an authority. Consider Sommers's descriptions of engaging authority as she works to come to her conclusions. In a short essay, reflect on how you are using her as an authority in the process of coming to your own conclusions about her ideas.

From Text to Field

1. Sommers opens her essay with an extensive description of experiences she had growing up that influenced her approach to writing and revision. Reread, in particular, her description of the German language lessons and the role of parental authority in determining how those lessons were carried out. Reflect on the authority figures inside and outside your family who have influenced you intellectually or personally. Such influences can be both enabling and disabling; we often both honor and distance ourselves from them. In an essay, explore how you write and revise and how these authority figures have influenced the way you approach the process. In what ways have they enabled you? In what ways have they disabled you? What is your concept and experience of authority, and how does it influence the way you write? How and to what extent do you bring your own experience and perspectives into your writing?

2. Although Sommers offers a conceptual framework for revision in this essay, she doesn't provide specific descriptions of how revision might take place. In an essay, analyze your approach to revision in writing courses you are taking or have taken. Do you merely "fix" errors in the text? Do you rethink or re-envision the argument itself? Do you set aside a draft for a period of time before you revise it? If so, why? What happens in the interim? How effective is your revision process? What do you want to continue doing? What do you want to change? Consider Sommers's description of an unsuccessful revision of her own: "Successive drafts . . . did not lead to a clearer vision because it simply was not my vision" (par. 23).

3. As Sommers was growing up, her family's vacations were dictated by the AAA guidebook. She describes her family as "people who could never experience the Grand Canyon because it had already been formulated for us by picture postcards, tourist folders, guidebooks, and the words *Grand Canyon*" (par. 4). Reflect on the ways in which authority, in the form of an authoritative text, influenced their manner of seeing. Consider your own experience of being guided by an authoritative text, such as a travel guide, movie or music reviews, sports commentators, or the program for a museum exhibit. Choose one such text that guided or influenced you. Write an essay in which you reflect on your ability to break away from the authority of the text to form your own perspective. To what extent did you form your own experience? What happened to break you away from the text? Look up the word *dissonance*. Does it apply to the experience you're describing?

4. "Between drafts," Sommers says, "I take lots of showers. . . . I get lost in the steam. There I stand without my badges of authority" (par. 25). In the shower,

she can speak freely in her imagination about her own stories and her struggle to revise. The essay indicates that while she searches for the revision that eludes her, she is free to give the process whatever amount of time it requires. Reflect on this process given the demands of your college or university's institutional structure. In other words, to what extent does the university calendar, course timelines, and pace of an assignment facilitate or undermine revision? Why does that structure make it difficult for teachers and students to approach revision the way Sommers suggests? Conversely, what is it about deadlines and the intense focus on a task that can be enabling, even necessary, to the creative process at times?

INTO THE FIELD: Options for Writing Projects

1. A Gallery of Office Doors

Think of the door to a professor's office as a threshold, as a place where contact with students is encouraged, discouraged, or regulated. The office door, and the surrounding wall space, may also have an array of verbal and visual texts: cartoons, pictures, posters, and announcements. For your fieldwork, develop a project in which you study the office doors of several professors, with a special focus on what this space (and its accompanying texts) communicates to students. You may wish to study several doors in one department or doors in several departments. What does the door say about the professor and his or her character or ethos? Likewise, what does the door tell you about the department or discipline? In what ways might a professor overcome or handle the constraints of the space he or she is occupying (remember, not every office is ideal or to a professor's liking)? Consider interviewing some of the professors whose doors you have studied. Based on your research, develop an essay or a report that describes what you found, draws some inferences or conclusions, and then supports those inferences based on the doors and texts you have studied (and, if possible, the professors you have interviewed).

2. Professors on the Web

Many professors maintain a Web page, which you can often access through a link from their department's Web page. For this field project, study several faculty Web pages in one department (ideally, the department that is or might become your major) or compare faculty Web pages across two or more departments. Pay attention to how the professors present themselves and whom they see as the potential audience(s) of their site. As you review several sites, consider how you might categorize them and what criteria you might use to do so. Are there several basic kinds or genres of faculty Web sites? What kind of access to the professors do these sites encourage, if any? If the sites offer any personal information about the professor, what function might such information have, and what relationship does the personal have to the professional? If you know or have taken classes with the professor, how does the Web site compare to the character or ethos that the professor projects in the classroom or in his or her office? How might students make better use of a faculty member's Web presence?

3. Professors in the Press

As you might expect, most if not all of your professors lead an active life as writers and scholars. Yet not all of their work is destined for obscure academic journals. Some of them may write books or magazine articles for a larger

Line (703/305-8747), a recorded information system that provides updates on the progress and status of applications and registrations, or check the new Trademark Applications and Registration Retrieval database (TARR) on the PTO's web site.

Curing Informalities and Technical Defects in the Application.   In many instances, the application may contain deficiencies that must be corrected before the application may be approved. For example, the applicant's name may be identified as "Lee Inc.," in the application itself and yet be signed by an officer on behalf of "Lee Co." The state of incorporation may need to be specified for a corporate applicant. The identification of goods or services may lack specificity, and the examining attorney may require clarification to the identification. In many instances, the office action suggests that the applicant telephone the examining attorney to resolve the issue (within the six-month period for response) and often suggests a remedy for the defect. The applicant and the examining attorney are often able to resolve the issue in such a telephone communication. Thereafter, the examining attorney will issue an **Examiner's Amendment** setting forth the agreed-upon correction or clarification, thereby eliminating the need for the applicant to file a formal written response to the office action. The application will proceed to publication after the examiner's amendment has corrected any technical informality in the application. The PTO encourages such telephonic communications because they expedite the application process.

Substantive Refusals.   In many instances, the refusal to register is not due to some minor or technical error in the application that can be readily corrected but is due to a more significant or substantive defect or due to a statutory provision that would preclude registration. In these cases, the examining attorney will set forth the reason the mark has been refused reg-

istration. The applicant will then have six months to respond in writing to the office action and present arguments supporting registration. Some of the more common substantive or statutory refusals to register are as follows:

- the mark is immoral or scandalous;
- the mark is deceptive;
- the mark disparages a person or a national institution or displays the flag or insignia of a nation;
- the mark displays a portrait of a living person without his or her consent;
- the mark is primarily merely a surname;
- the mark is geographically deceptively misdescriptive;
- the mark is merely descriptive; or
- the mark is confusingly similar to another registered or applied-for mark at the PTO.

Applicants who receive an office action refusing registration on one of these grounds generally submit written arguments to persuade the examining attorney to allow the mark for registration. Case law and other evidence may be cited. For example, if the mark is refused on the basis that it is primarily merely a surname, the applicant may submit telephone book evidence to show the name is so rare that consumers who encounter the mark would not perceive it to be primarily a surname. If a person's consent is needed, the applicant should secure it.

Refusals on the Basis of Descriptiveness. One of the most serious refusals occurs when the examining attorney refuses registration on the basis that the mark is merely descriptive and is thus barred under 15 U.S.C. § 1052(e)(1). The applicant will then submit a response to the office action arguing that the mark is not descriptive. Common arguments asserted by the applicant are as follows:

audience, pen an occasional column in the local newspaper, or even host a local public radio show. For this fieldwork project, explore the work of one or more of your professors who have ventured beyond academic publishing. To find out who might have done so on your campus, contact your professors directly, query a department secretary, or check in with your college or university's public relations office. Your project may involve an analysis of the published material, with an eye to the strategies they have used to meet the needs of the more public audience.

Alternatively, interview a faculty member on your campus who writes well and frequently for the public. Write a profile of the faculty member that describes this aspect of his or her career. In what publications does his or her work most frequently appear? Who is the audience? What are the issues or topics? From what point of view are they presented? Why does this faculty member write for the public? What does he or she hope to accomplish through this work? Look for reviews of or responses to his or her work; how is it regarded? What are the rewards and the risks of writing beyond one's immediate community?

As a third option, write an essay in which you argue for the role you think academic research and writing should play in your university education and in the world outside the university. What types of research are valuable, and in what ways? How do you think that research should be conveyed to students and to the public? (As part of your inquiry, you may wish to see if your campus has a program that encourages undergraduates to collaborate with faculty on some form of research activity.)

4. Finding a Dance at the Mixer

Opportunities to meet with faculty on your campus may seem restricted to class time itself or to office hours. Both venues can seem intimidating. For your field project, investigate what opportunities exist on your campus for faculty and students to get to know one another more informally. In other words, how might you be able to interact with faculty outside of a more formal classroom structure? And why might you want to? In the spirit of the title for this unit—"Dancing with Professors"—consider how you might go about finding a dance at the mixer. Explore the opportunities offered through dorm programs, advisement, student groups, and receptions at various campus-sponsored events. If you find that such opportunities are rare, you may wish to propose how—and why—your campus might want to develop better ways for students to meet with faculty.

5. Assessing Orientation

Among your very first exposures to college life and learning is surely the orientation you went to on your campus. Whether orientation lasts only for several hours or extends over several days, this program can offer a wealth of information about how to get off to a successful start in college. For your field project, assess what your orientation program offered to you and what messages (subtle or not so subtle) were sent. Did you notice any contradictions between what was said and what life on campus is like? In retrospect, what would you have liked to have heard that was never discussed? Consider writing a letter to the director of orientation, or submitting a more formal proposal, in which you note the program's successes, air your concerns, and propose improvements that might better meet students' needs and the needs of the campus.

6. First Generations

Going to college can represent a major change in your life, all the more so if you or someone you know is the first generation of the family to attend college. This field project offers an opportunity (through a personal essay or a brief memoir) to explore the thoughts of a first-generation college student and their continuing relevance today. This project may well start at home, perhaps with an older relative who was the first in the family to go to college, perhaps with a good friend, perhaps even with yourself. Ask what it meant/means to go to college, and what obstacles and fears presented themselves. Who were the mentors who stood by, supporting this person (or you) on this new journey? What remains relevant and fresh about this tale, even though years may separate that person's experience from your own? What remains universal? Remember that each of us, in our own way, is (or has been) a first-generation student.

7. Campus Outreach

Entering the college conversation can be difficult for anyone but all the more so if members of the community tend not to see your campus as part of their lives. This field project offers you a chance to explore and assess one of several outreach programs your campus may have. These programs may involve students in area schools (K–12) or students and families of underrepresented minorities. The focus of these programs may involve academics but also may involve the arts, sports, or a variety of other public programs. (A good first contact might be the office of community relations on your campus.) How has your campus articulated the goals of a particular outreach program, and how might such a program make a difference, both for the community and for your campus? In turn, why might such a program encounter difficulties or be misperceived? What steps has the program taken to prevent any misunderstanding and to capitalize on existing goodwill? What kind of program would you like to have participated in, and why?

8. Service Learning

Joining the conversation in and about college often entails that we find a way to connect our academic and personal commitments. One means can be through what is known as "service learning"—an approach to learning that moves the student outside of the traditional classroom to perform and then reflect on service in and for the community. This fieldwork project encourages you to think about the broader possibilities of fieldwork in your college or university. (For some initial information, you may wish to contact the administrator or faculty member who is coordinating service learning on your campus.) Consider how a college course you have taken might have been improved or fruitfully augmented if it called on service learning. Did you have a high school course that called on service learning in some fashion? What possibilities are there for a writing course to incorporate service learning into its assignments and activities? What special challenges, misunderstandings, and risks might be associated with service learning, both for students and for faculty? As you discover more about service learning opportunities on your campus, nominate one course that would benefit from such an approach, and develop a proposal that captures the rationale for your nomination. Be sure to consider counterarguments or skeptical questions that may arise.

9. Teaching and Learning the Debates

Gerald Graff discusses the importance of learning about a field not through facts and information but through the debates that occur within that field. Write an essay in which you capture one or two critical key terms that define a field, a community, or an area of specialty you belong to or are just now entering. What is expressed or implied by those terms? In other words, what does the field consider to be important? What is, or isn't, debatable? How might such a debate prove to be a good introduction to the field? Why might such a debate prove to be an inadequate or a misleading introduction?

10. Revision Across the Curriculum

The work of revising a written draft may seem the special province of a writing course, with the rest of the university operating in a "first-draft" universe. Yet a good many courses in other fields may encourage or require you to submit drafts that you then revise or continue to develop. For this fieldwork project, consider courses you have taken, or are now taking, that either encouraged a helpful attitude toward revision or failed to do so when it might have been useful. You also may wish to poll members of your writing class about their experiences in other courses regarding the emphasis (or lack of emphasis) on revision. How was this attitude communicated: on the syllabus or in the professor's own words? Do you think this attitude had more to do with the professor's teaching style and inclinations, or might it reflect a more general attitude toward revision in that discipline? What do you think accounts for the activity of revision being more or less invisible in some fields? You may wish to frame your project as a close reading of one course, as a study of disciplinary attitudes and assumptions about revision, or as a proposal that the design for a particular course be changed to better incorporate revision.

11. Authority: How Have You Been "Author"-ized to Write?

Different disciplines construct and use authority in different ways. Consider the writing you do for a course that is not explicitly a writing course, in a field outside of English or the humanities. Write an essay in which you analyze what counts as authoritative in that class or field, and how you are expected to gain and use authority in your own writing. In other words, as a student in that course or in that discipline, what are the ways in which you have been "author"-ized to write? How have you managed to negotiate the connection between personal authority and external authority in that class or field? This project can take one of several directions. You may wish to write a personal essay about the tensions you have experienced between writing yourself into a text and writing yourself out of a text. Alternatively, you may wish to examine several representative scholarly articles in that field for clues about its attitudes toward and use of authority.

2

Inventing the University

CONSTRUCTING CLASSROOMS

Tu/Th, 9:30–10:45. Hellems Hall, Room 230.

Although the day and time, building name, and room number may be different, you know through years of schooling that these are the coordinates, in time and space, for an academic classroom. Whatever department may be offering the class, the classroom itself possesses a familiarity that cuts across subject matter, even teaching styles. When you enter the door of your classroom, you know the space. You recognize this world both from your long acquaintance with classrooms and from the sediment of teaching practices and learning behaviors that have formed in that space.

Classrooms, it turns out, are recognizable because they are conventional or typical. We know them because they are "types." They are recurrent spaces—spaces in which we happen to be (again and again) and spaces in which things happen (again and again). What happens are rhetorical actions and language practices that are themselves recognizable. You know the moves as well as anybody: teacher talk, and student talk, and how that talk is orchestrated through questions and answers and discussion. You know the classroom as if it were a stage. Even though the particular classroom "script" may change from course to course and teacher to teacher, you do know that there is a script. Even the physical moves are blocked out on stage in advance: You know who enters, when, and how, and what positions they assume. Classrooms are places, but they also put us all, teacher and student, in our places. The time and space of the classroom project a world of relationships and norms—a world of its own.

All of us would like to reinvent that world, to reinvent classrooms that more ideally match our aspirations for the best possible learning environment. And, indeed, classrooms are changing. Classrooms are becoming networked to other spaces, whether through technology or through curricular models like service learning that take students out into the community. Classrooms are likewise becoming more student centered and more collaborative. Even so, we recognize these innovations for what they are precisely because we remember, somewhere deep down in our bones and in our collective social memory, the archetype of the classroom.

As much as we remember, we would also like to forget. When we enter the door of our classroom on the first day of the new term, we invoke a fiction that we all, teacher and student alike, maintain to some degree: the fiction of the fresh classroom. We are eager to put any bad experiences behind us and to anticipate better ones. Through that classroom door lies a new territory and a new period of time. This fiction is an enabling fiction, for in forgetting the prior histories of classrooms (histories that are at once personal and institutional) we are all disposed to teach and learn afresh.

Whether you are just beginning your studies in college or have several college terms behind you, it is important to reflect on the time/space that is the classroom. Forget as we might, we'll try to listen to what classrooms whisper in our ears. In the process, we'll recognize what is conventional—yes, oh so conventional—about classrooms. We will surely become aware of what may be right or wrong in any given classroom and why we may wish to reinvent some classrooms. But by looking *at* classrooms, not just *through* them to the subject matter taught, we can also clear a space for the fresh, opportune moments that we all prize in our learning and teaching—moments when magic does happen, even in settings that might seem conventional. This unit helps us realize that classrooms are always invented, always constructed, always saturated with both memory and possibility.

The five readings included in this unit help us reflect on classrooms from several perspectives. They alert us that classrooms are by no means neutral sites, the mere givens of a college education. Classrooms are where time thickens, where space becomes charged.

Sharon Rubin asks that we take a second look at the course syllabus before filing it away in our notebooks. Syllabi should ideally help explain and create the model classroom that a course might envision, but more often than not syllabi fail to become a meeting place between professor, student, and course.

Alexander Calandra turns his attention to the conventional answers that are expected in many classrooms, answers that often turn students off to learning. He recounts the story of a student who turns the table on his professors, offering unexpected answers that are nevertheless correct.

Gerald Graff broadens the discussion by noting the failure of classrooms to connect with one another. Unless each classroom takes into account other voices in other classrooms, he fears a loss of both coherence and community.

Another perspective on community is offered by bell hooks, who explores how language in the classroom can be a tool for both oppression and resistance. Classrooms are worlds created by words. And as we seek to heal ourselves and each other, we need new words and the new worlds those words might create.

For Charles Bazerman, the classroom is something that is constructed, shaped through the perspectives of teachers, students, and the institution. In asking the question "Where is the classroom?" he prompts us to question the notion that classrooms exist apart from students, teachers, and institutions. Classrooms, it turns out, are not neutral or empty sites; they are charged with and created through our experiences in them.

Reflecting on Prior Knowledge

1. In a journal entry, recall a prior classroom in which you felt discouraged as a learner. Likewise, recall a moment that excited you, a moment that captured what is best about classrooms and learning in classrooms. What might account for these experiences? Is there something about classrooms that might create the conditions for both of your experiences?

2. In classrooms, you are asked to assume positions that are not just intellectual but also physical and spatial, even discursive (in the sense that classrooms position when and how you speak and write). How do classrooms position you? How would you like to position yourself?

3. When you enter the college classroom, you bring with you years of experience, from classroom after classroom, from elementary school through high school. What kind of mind-set might you bring, and how might that influence your view of your current classrooms? What mind-sets might instructors have developed over the years? What role do you think you might have in shaping—and reshaping—classrooms?

4. In your experience, what marks a room as being a classroom? Use concrete examples to begin to fashion a list of objects, spatial arrangements, and architectural details. What relationships and norms do these various elements help create?

5. Enter a classroom at night or during the day when it is not being used. Settle yourself in a seat, and pause to let your mind relax. Imagine the classroom whispering in your ear. What would you hear if the walls could speak? After a few minutes, move around the room and then to the front of the classroom. What difference does perspective make as you continue to listen to those whispers? Why do you think classrooms carry such powerful social memories?

- The applicant may argue that the mark is not descriptive but is rather suggestive and therefore entitled to registration. To support such an assertion, the applicant may cite marks in case law that have been found to be suggestive and analogize them to the mark at issue. The applicant may also conduct a search of PTO records to locate other similar marks that were allowed to proceed to registration. The PTO, however, is not bound by its past actions and may characterize the earlier allowed marks as mistakes that it need not repeat.
- The applicant may argue that the cases cited by the examining attorney in support of the refusal to register are inapplicable and attempt to distinguish the present situation from that presented in the case law relied upon by the examining attorney.
- If the mark has been in commerce for five years, there is a presumption that it has acquired distinctiveness. In such a case, the PTO will allow the applicant to claim distinctiveness under 15 U.S.C. § 1052(f) and the mark can proceed to registration. The wording for a claim of acquired distinctiveness is as follows:

> The mark has become distinctive of Applicant's goods [or services] through the Applicant's substantially exclusive and continuous use in commerce for at least the five years immediately before the date of this statement.

- If the mark has not acquired distinctiveness through continuous use for five years, the applicant may attempt to introduce evidence to show the mark has acquired distinctiveness or secondary meaning through its significant use, sales, and advertising such that con-

sumers associate the mark with applicant. The applicant typically submits evidence consisting of sales and advertising data, survey evidence, and declarations from customers and consumers who confirm they are familiar with the mark and recognize the applicant as the source of the goods offered under the mark.

If none of these arguments are successful, the applicant may be allowed to amend the application to seek registration on the Supplemental Register *if* use of the mark has begun. Applications based solely on intent to use cannot be transferred to the Supplemental Register until after the applicant has shown actual use of the mark, because registration of U.S.-based trademarks is dependent on use in commerce.

If only a portion of the mark is descriptive or generic, that portion may be *disclaimed*. The purpose of a **disclaimer** is to allow registration of a mark that includes nonregistrable matter. For example, in the mark BOLERO TASTY COFFEE (used in connection with coffee), the words *tasty coffee* would likely have to be disclaimed because they merely describe something about the goods offered under the mark. A disclaimer is an acknowledgment by an applicant that he or she does not claim exclusive rights in the matter disclaimed (in this case, the wording *tasty coffee*), apart from the mark as a whole. Disclaimers preserve the rights of other businesses to use needed terms such as *tasty* and *coffee*. Some marks, called **composite marks,** consist of both wording and design elements. If the wording in a composite mark is descriptive or generic, the applicant may have to disclaim exclusive rights to all of the wording, leaving the applicant with exclusive rights only to the design component. An applicant may not disclaim an entire mark.

A disclaimer does not affect one's common law rights; neither does it mean that the mark as a whole is not protectable. In the hypothetical, use by another company of VOLERO TASTY

Professors, Students, and the Syllabus

Sharon Rubin

When Sharon Rubin was assistant dean for undergraduate studies at the University of Maryland, she reviewed dozens of syllabi as part of the process of approving general-education courses. She learned that for most courses, the syllabus presented an incomplete, often confusing, picture of what students could expect. From this evidence she came to the conclusion that "the inadequate syllabus is a symptom of a larger problem—the lack of communication between teachers and students" (par. 8).

"Professors, Students, and the Syllabus" proposes a "place of meeting," sought by students and faculty alike. For Rubin, the answers to the questions a syllabus should address add up to the message that teachers want their students to master the material.

After her assistant deanship at the University of Maryland, Rubin became dean of liberal arts at Salisbury University, part of the University of Maryland system. She continued her work as an administrator at Ramapo College of New Jersey, where she served as the vice president for academic affairs. At Ramapo College, she returned to teaching and is currently professor of American studies in the School of American and International Studies.

For the past two years I've been sitting in on the meetings of a committee charged with approving courses for the University of Maryland's general-education program. Very often the committee members leave those meetings mystified and exasperated. It's not that the courses proposed are inadequate; it's just that the syllabi submitted with the proposals are so often virtually impossible to decode.

I've listened while a faculty member from a related discipline has tried to guess what a syllabus might possibly mean. I've seen carefully worded letters from the dean requesting clarification—and then looked on as the committee has tried to relate a three-page response to the original syllabus. The committee has even developed a new cover sheet for all proposals, which requests detailed information about objectives and asks for samples of test questions and paper assignments. Yet sufficiently informative syllabi are still so rare that when one appears it elicits audible sighs of relief around the conference table.

The syllabi our committee gets are not much different from the ones I've picked up at conferences or seen attached to grant proposals. In other words, I don't believe the problem is local or idiosyncratic; rather, it seems to be basic to the teaching endeavor. We keep forgetting that what we know— about our disciplines, about our goals, about our teaching methods—is not known (or agreed upon) by everyone. We seem to assume that our colleagues and our students will intuitively be able to reconstruct the creature we see in our mind's eye from the few bones we give them in the syllabus.

The worst syllabi seem to fall into one of two categories.

The "listers" merely specify which books or chapters will be read during   5 which weeks, without a hint about the principles behind the selection. The most puzzling of this type assign chapters in the textbooks in an order considerably different from the order intended by the authors. At best, such modification gives students the impression that the teacher is improving on the original organization for some as yet unrevealed purpose, at worst, it gives students the idea that one order is no less logical or coherent than another, and that all parts are interchangeable and equally valid.

The "scolders" give brief descriptions of content and lengthy sets of instruction detailing what will happen if a student comes in late or leaves early, hands in a paper after the deadline, misses an exam, fails to follow the rules for margins and double-spacing, does not participate in class discussion. The scolders often sound more like lawyers than professors. Undoubtedly the syllabus as legal document has evolved because so often students demand that their teachers provide a set of rules, probably to give the students something concrete to cling to as they struggle with the content of the course. If even sophisticated scholars fall into the trap of equating quantitative data with significance, it's not surprising that students mistake the rules for the meaning.

Here are some questions our committee often finds unanswered even in wonderful syllabi for wonderful courses:

- Why should a student want to take this course? How does it make a difference as part of the discipline? How does it fit into the general-education program?

- What are the objectives of the course? Where does it lead, intellectually and practically? Students should be able to find out what they will know by the end of the course, and also what they will be able to do better afterward than before. Is the purpose of the course to increase their problem-solving abilities, improve their communication skills, sharpen their understanding of moral ambiguities, allow them to translate knowledge from one context to another? Why are the objectives important, and how will different parts of the course help students accomplish those objectives?
- What are the prerequisites? Students should be given some idea about what they should already know and what skills they should already have before taking the course, so they can realistically assess their readiness. Will they be expected to know how to compare and contrast, to analyze and synthesize, or will they be taught those skills during the course?
- Why do the parts of the course come in the order they do? Most syllabi note the order in which topics will be discussed, but make no attempt to explain the way the professor has chosen to organize the course. Sections of the syllabus are usually titled, but only infrequently are questions provided for students to help them put the reading assignments and homework into context.
- Will the course be primarily lectures, discussions, or group work? When a percentage of the grade is for "class participation," what does the professor expect from the students—regular attendance? questions? answers to questions? Will the students be given alternative ways to achieve success in the class, based on different learning styles?
- What is the purpose of the assignments? Students are frequently told how much an assignment will "count" and how many pages long it must be, but they are rarely given any idea about what it will demand of them or what the goal is. Will students be required to describe, discuss, analyze, provide evidence, criticize, defend, compare, apply? To what end? If students are expected to present a project before the class, are the criteria for an excellent presentation made clear?
- What will the tests test?—memory? understanding? ability to synthesize? To present evidence logically? To apply knowledge in a new context?
- Why have the books been chosen? What is their relative importance in the course and in the discipline? Is the emphasis in the course on primary or secondary materials and why?

"Well," you may say, "the syllabus isn't the course—everything will be made clear as the semester progresses." Or, "I can't ask my overworked secretary to type a twelve-page syllabus." Or, "Students are interested only in the numbers—of books, of pages to read, of written assignments, of questions on the exam." Or, "A syllabus with all that information is too static—it doesn't allow me the flexibility to be creative on the spur of the moment." Maybe those are relevant objections—and maybe they are excuses for badly thought-out, hurriedly patched-together efforts. Whatever the rationale, I believe that the inadequate syllabus is a symptom of a larger problem—the lack of communication between teachers and students.

Most of the latest reports on undergraduate education have in common the criticism that faculty members and the students no longer seem to be connecting. Our students do not **What we know is not known** seem to be involved in learning, they say. We seem to **(or agreed upon) by everyone.** have lost the ability to create a shared community of values; we have substituted diversity for coherence and cannot find our way back to integrating principles. However, these reports all seem to ignore a very real wish among students and faculty members to find a place of meeting.

In 1982–83, Lee Knefelkamp of the University of Maryland asked 217 fac- 10 ulty members at eight colleges what they worried about most the first day of class. Their three most common concerns were, "Will the students get involved?" "Will they like me?" "Will the class work well as a class?"

When 157 students at those institutions responded to the same question, their three most common concerns were, "Will I be able to do the work?" "Will I like the professor?" "Will I get along with my classmates?"

The notion of relationship between teachers and students and material to be learned is clear in the answers from both groups. However, when the faculty members were asked what they thought students worried about the first day of class, they responded, "Will I get a good grade?" "Will the work be hard?" "Will the class be interesting?" When the students were asked what they thought teachers worried about, they generally couldn't answer the question at all.

The survey showed that there was a real desire on the part of both students and teacher for connectedness, but neither group realized that the other shared that desire. If the participants on both sides don't understand how to develop their relationship, learning will be diminished.

The syllabus is a small place to start bringing students and faculty members back together, of course, and its improvement is not the revolutionary gesture that curriculum reform seems to be. But if students could be persuaded that we are really interested in their understanding the material we offer, that we support their efforts to master it, and that we take their intellectual struggles seriously, they might respond by becoming more involved in our courses, by trying to live up to our expectations, and by appreciating our concern.

Then the real work of learning can begin. 15

Working with the Text

1. Sharon Rubin provides a list of questions that often go unanswered on even well-constructed syllabi. At the end of her essay, she asserts that "if students could be persuaded that we are really interested in their understanding the material we offer, that we support their efforts to master it, and that we take their intellectual struggles seriously, they might respond by becoming more involved in our courses, by trying to live up to our expectations. . . ." (par. 14). In a short essay, explore the connections between her list of questions and her closing assertion. In what ways might a syllabus that answers those questions persuade students that the teacher is interested in helping them master the course material?

2. Commenting on the survey conducted by the University of Maryland, Rubin interprets the findings as showing "that there was a real desire on the part of both students and teacher for connectedness, but neither group realized that the other shared that desire" (par. 13). As evidence, Rubin quotes survey responses from both students and teachers. Write a brief essay analyzing how these answers to the survey support Rubin's interpretation. What can you infer from these answers about the desire for connectedness on the part of both teachers and students? How do the answers indicate that neither group recognized that the desire for connectedness was mutual?

3. Rubin's essay presents evidence that teachers actively resist producing the kind of syllabus she recommends. Based on Rubin's evidence, write a brief essay analyzing how teachers show their resistance and why they might resist. Drawing on your own experience, as well as on Rubin's text, indicate whether or not you agree with Rubin's assessment. Why or why not?

From Text to Field

1. In her essay, Rubin makes a number of assertions about how students read and interpret syllabi. Do any of her assertions reflect your own experience with course syllabi? In a personal essay, analyze yourself as a syllabus reader. How do you read a syllabus? What are you looking for? What do you expect (or want) a syllabus to tell you? To what extent do you look to the syllabus to define the course for you? In addition to the time the teacher spends in class going over the syllabus, do you read it on your own? Do you refer back to it later in the term? If not, why not? If so, for what kind of information?

2. In her description of "scolders," Rubin asserts, "Undoubtedly the syllabus as legal document has evolved because so often students demand that their teachers provide a set of rules, probably to give the students something concrete to cling to as they struggle with the content of the course" (par. 6). Do

you agree with her assertion? What does she mean by the phrase, "something concrete to cling to as they struggle with the content of the course"? How does she define "the rules" of a course? In a brief essay, explore your own attitude toward knowing the rules, as defined by Rubin. Do you demand that teachers provide a set of rules? Do you "cling" to rules as a means for controlling your "struggle with the content of the course"?

3. Review the student responses Rubin quotes from the University of Maryland survey. Do the "first day" worries of these students reflect your own early worries about a course? Write an essay in which you re-create yourself or imagine yourself on the first day of a particular class. What are you thinking and feeling? Where do you look for clues to address your worries about the course? Whether or not you have ever experienced it, imagine that the teacher passes out a syllabus that addresses your worries. What does the syllabus provide to do this?

4. Choose a syllabus from one course—your writing course, another course you are taking or have taken, a course you will take or would take if you could—to analyze in terms of Rubin's essay, in particular the "unanswered" questions from syllabi she has reviewed. Write a brief essay in which you use the syllabus to analyze the course. What is the purpose of the course? What are its objectives? How does it fit into your course of study and your personal development? What are the teacher's values and research interests? What can you tell about the teacher's personality and approach to teaching?

Angels on a Pin:
The Barometer Story

Alexander Calandra

A professor emeritus of physics at Washington University in St. Louis, Alexander Calandra first published the story of the student and the barometer problem in his 1961 textbook, *The Teaching of Elementary Science and Mathematics*. Since then, this parable of playful, creative, even defiant thinking has reappeared several times in various incarnations, one featuring the Nobel Prize–winning Neils Bohr as the young protagonist.

The final paragraph of the *Saturday Review* version (1968) says that the student is reacting to the "*Sputnik*-panicked classrooms of America." *Sputnik 1,* launched by the Soviets in 1957 as the earth's first artificial satellite, sent the United States scrambling to overcome the Soviet Union in the space race. The failure of the United States to beat the Soviets into space was blamed in part on a lax educational system. The National Defense Education Act (NDEA), passed in 1958, poured federal dollars into reforming math and science education from elementary- through graduate-school levels. Although the nation's top scientists urged reforms that encouraged students to think creatively, efforts to bring rigor to the classroom often focused on teaching the *right* methodologies to get the *right* answers.

Born in New York in 1911, Calandra received his PhD from New York University in 1935. Prior to teaching at Washington University, Calandra taught at Brooklyn College, where he had received his undergraduate degree, as well as at the University of Chicago. Concurrently with his professorship at Washington University, he served as chair of the science department at Webster College in St. Louis, starting in 1969. His reputation as an outstanding lecturer who used humor in his teaching is reflected in the barometer story.

In 1979, the American Association of Physics Teachers awarded Calandra the Millikan Medal for "notable and creative contributions to the teaching of physics." He retired in 1981 and passed away in March 2006.

Some time ago, I received a call from a colleague who asked if I would be the referee on the grading of an examination question. He was about to give a student a zero for his answer to a physics question, while the student claimed he should receive a perfect score and would if the system were not set up against the student. The instructor and the student agreed to submit this to an impartial arbiter, and I was selected.

I went to my colleague's office and read the examination question: "Show how it is possible to determine the height of a tall building with the aid of a barometer."

The student had answered: "Take the barometer to the top of the building, attach a long rope to it, lower the barometer to the street, and then bring it up, measuring the length of the rope. The length of the rope is the height of the building."

I pointed out that the student really had a strong case for full credit, since he had answered the question completely and correctly. On the other hand, if full credit were given, it could well contribute to a high grade for the student in his physics course. A high grade is supposed to certify competence in physics, but the answer did not confirm this. I suggested that the student have another try at answering the question. I was not surprised that my colleague agreed, but I was surprised that the student did.

I gave the student six minutes to answer the question, with the warning that his answer should show some knowledge of physics. At the end of five minutes, he had not written anything. I asked if he wished to give up, but he said no. He had many answers to this problem; he was just thinking of the best one. I excused myself for interrupting him, and asked him to please go on. In the next minute, he dashed off his answer, which read:

The student claimed he should receive a perfect score.

"Take the barometer to the top of the building and lean over the edge of the roof. Drop the barometer, timing its fall with a stopwatch. Then, using the formula $S = \frac{1}{2} at^2$, calculate the height of the building."

At this point, I asked my colleague if *he* would give up. He conceded, and I gave the student almost full credit.

In leaving my colleague's office, I recalled that the student had said he had other answers to the problem, so I asked him what they were. "Oh, yes," said the student. "There are many ways of getting the height of a tall building with the aid of a barometer. For example, you could take the barometer out on a sunny day and measure the height of the barometer, the length of its shadow, and the length of the shadow of the building, and by the use of a simple proportion, determine the height of the building."

"Fine," I said. "And the others?"

"Yes," said the student. "There is a very basic measurement method that you will like. In this method, you take the barometer and begin to walk up the stairs. As you climb the stairs, you mark off the length of the barometer along the wall. You then count the number of marks, and this will give you the height of the building in barometer units. A very direct method.   10

"Of course, if you want a more sophisticated method, you can tie the barometer to the end of a string, swing it as a pendulum, and determine the value of 'g' at the street level and at the top of the building. From the difference between the two values of 'g,' the height of the building can, in principle, be calculated."

Finally, he concluded, there are many other ways of solving the problem. "Probably the best," he said, "is to take the barometer to the basement and knock on the superintendent's door. When the superintendent answers, you speak to him as follows: 'Mr. Superintendent, here I have a fine barometer. If you will tell me the height of this building, I will give you this barometer.' "

At this point, I asked the student if he really did not know the conventional answer to this question. He admitted that he did, but said that he was fed up with high school and college instructors trying to teach him how to think, to use the "scientific method," and to explore the deep inner logic of the subject in a pedantic way, as is often done in the new mathematics, rather than teaching him the structure of the subject. With this in mind, he decided to revive scholasticism as an academic lark to challenge the *Sputnik*-panicked classrooms of America.

Working with the Text

1. In Alexander Calandra's essay, the student gives a number of alternative answers to a physics question that has a "conventional answer." (Given this problem, physics students would be expected to calculate the altitude from measurements of the barometric pressure at the top and at the bottom of the building.) As you reread the essay, note the logic behind each of the answers. In a brief essay, analyze the author's intention in using the number and kinds of answers that he assigns to the student. Beyond demonstrating that the conventional answer is not necessarily the only answer, what is Calandra trying to point out? What is the effect of this particular accumulation of alternative

answers on the tone and attitude of the piece? Why would Calandra choose such an effect? Note in particular that the student says that "probably the best" answer is to offer the barometer to the building superintendent.

2. The narrator of the piece, who calls himself the "impartial arbiter," gives the student "almost full credit" for one of his answers, after saying at the outset that the student "had a strong case for full credit" (par. 4). In a brief essay, reflect on how *credit* is used in the story. How is credit significant to the meaning of the story? What factors determine how much credit is given? Do you agree with the arbiter's decision? Why or why not?

3. The first part of the selection title, "Angels on a Pin," refers to an intricate and protracted argument among medieval scholars and clerics over how many angels could stand on the head of a pin. Why would Calandra choose this as the title for his story? Write a brief essay in which you explore the connections between the title and the meaning of the story. In what ways is the title consistent with the meaning of the story? In what ways might the title be a contradiction of the more specific points of the story?

4. In the final paragraph of the story, the student says he is "fed up" with being taught to think in a "pedantic way." Look up the word *pedantic.* Reflecting on what the student does in the rest of the story, write a brief essay in which you analyze what he means by thinking in a "pedantic way." Through the student's behaviors and answers, what argument do you think Calandra is making about science and math instruction?

From Text to Field

1. Calandra uses humor to question the emphasis educators tend to place on "the right answer." Write an essay using a form of humor, such as parody or satire, to send up an aspect of education that you have personally found to be questionable (or ridiculous or absurd). Using "Angels on a Pin" as a model, be aware of how your comic details pinpoint and critique the questionable elements of the aspect of education you have chosen to address.

2. Calandra's story implies that the physics professor expects his students to use particular methods to show their "competence in physics." Taking a position counter to the story, write an essay in which you speculate on the reasons teachers in certain fields might expect you to use certain methods to find "conventional" answers. In what ways might an emphasis on "conventional answers" support, or undermine, the values of the discipline.

3. "Angels on a Pin" was published in 1961 in a book by Calandra, entitled *The Teaching of Elementary Science and Mathematics,* and again in 1968 in the *Saturday Review.* Based on the title of the 1961 book, who do you think was

COFFEE could likely be enjoined on the basis of confusing similarity; however, a mark such as SUNRISE TASTY COFFEE would likely be allowable, inasmuch as the marks can be distinguished on the basis of their nondescriptive components.

The proper wording for a disclaimer is as follows:

> No claim is made to the exclusive right to use "tasty coffee" apart from the mark as shown.

(See Exhibit 4–2 for examples of disclaimers.)

Refusals on the Basis of Confusing Similarity. In addition to refusing to register a mark on the basis that it is merely descriptive, another substantive or statutory ground for refusal to register is that the mark applied for so resembles a mark registered or applied for with the PTO that, when used in connection with the goods or services of the applicant, it would be likely to cause confusion, mistake, or to deceive consumers. 15 U.S.C. § 1052(d).

In determining whether a mark applied for is confusingly similar to a prior registered or applied-for mark, a variety of factors, identified in *In re E. I. du Pont de Nemours & Co.,* 476 F.2d 1357 (C.C.P.A. 1973), are considered:

- the similarity of the marks in their entireties in regard to appearance, sound, connotation, and commercial impression;
- the similarity and nature of the goods or services offered under the respective marks;
- the similarity of the channels of trade in which the goods or services are offered, for example, whether the goods or services offered under the mark are offered through retail or wholesale channels of trade;
- the buyers to whom sales are made, and the conditions of such sales, for example,

whether purchases are made on impulse or after due care and deliberation;
- the fame of the prior mark (sales, advertising, length of use, and so forth);
- the number and nature of similar marks in use on similar goods or services; and
- the nature and extent of actual confusion.

The goods or services need not be identical for confusion to be found, as long as they are related in some manner. Thus, MARTIN'S for bread was held likely to be confused with MARTIN'S for cheese on the basis the marks were used in connection with related food products. *In re Martin's Famous Pastry Shoppe, Inc.,* 748 F.2d 1565 (Fed. Cir. 1984). If the item is purchased by consumers on "impulse," such as an inexpensive beverage, confusion will be more likely than if the item is expensive, is purchased by sophisticated consumers, and is purchased only after great thought and care. The PTO does not use a mechanical approach in determining whether confusion is likely to occur; rather, an examination is made of all the factors. If there is any doubt about whether there is a likelihood of confusion, doubt will be resolved against the newcomer. Additional information relating to likelihood of confusion analysis is found in Chapter 6 in the discussion of trademark infringement. (See Exhibit 4–5 for a comparison of some marks alleged to be confusingly similar.)

An applicant whose mark is rejected on the basis of confusing similarity will attempt to overcome the refusal to register by citing case law and analogizing cases in which confusion was not found, submitting evidence showing that the goods are not in the same channels of trade and that they are offered to different or sophisticated purchasers, and by submitting copies of other registered marks that have been allowed to coexist.

Alternatively, the applicant may contact the owner of the cited mark and seek a license the intended audience for the book? The *Saturday Review* was a popular weekly magazine for many decades before it ceased publication in 1973. Who do you think was the intended audience for that publication? Write an essay in which you analyze why a story published for the audience of the 1961 book would be republished in 1968 for the audience of the *Saturday Review*.

4. Calandra's story captures a student's rebellion against "the conventional answer." In a personal essay, reflect on your own stance on conventional answers. Do you tend to pursue the conventional answer, or do you look for alternative methods and answers? Might there be value in knowing the conventional answer? In your course work, why do you approach answering questions the way that you do? What would you change about your approach? What about your approach do you value and intend to keep? What effect do you anticipate your approach will have on who you are as a person and as a professional?

Other Voices, Other Rooms

Gerald Graff

A professor at the University of Illinois at Chicago, Gerald Graff has made a career of seeking coherence through controversy. His hotly debated book, *Literature against Itself: Literary Ideas in Modern Society* (1979), argues against trends in literary criticism that have driven academic research for some years. "Other Voices, Other Rooms" is taken from *Beyond the Culture Wars: How Teaching the Conflicts Can Revitalize American Education* (1992), which challenges institutional structures and ideological stances that discourage dialogue within the academy. *Beyond the Culture Wars* won the American Book Award in 1993.

From his vantage point as a teacher of undergraduates, Graff views the curriculum, especially the general-education curriculum, as disjointed and confusing. The "cognitive dissonance" undergraduates experience could be the source of a deeper, more coherent education, Graff believes, if the intellectual and cultural debates that drive academic research were brought into the classroom. "Contrast," says Graff, "is fundamental to understanding, for no subject, idea, or text is an island." Although such contrasts can sometimes be brought into the classroom by exceptional teachers, Graff is convinced that the surer source is an institutional atmosphere and structure that encourages dialogue among scholars.

For Graff the goal is not consensus, but the kind of coherence that is won through genuine and explicit conversation: "One of the oddest things about the university is that it calls itself a community of scholars yet organizes its curriculum in a way that conceals the links of the community from those who are not already aware of them."

An undergraduate tells of an art history course in which the instructor observed one day, "As we now know, the idea that knowledge can be objective is a positivist myth that has been exploded by postmodern thought." It so happens the student is concurrently enrolled in a political science course in which the instructor speaks confidently about the objectivity of his discipline as if it had not been "exploded" at all. What do you do? the student is asked. "What else can I do?" he says. "I trash objectivity in art history, and I presuppose it in political science."

A second undergraduate describes a history teacher who makes a point of stressing the superiority of Western culture in developing the ideas of freedom, democracy, and free-market capitalism that the rest of the world is now rushing to imitate. She also has a literature teacher who describes such claims of Western supremacy as an example of the hegemonic ideology by which the United States arrogates the right to police the world. When asked which course she prefers, she replies, "Well, I'm getting an A in both."

To some of us these days, the moral of these stories would be that students have become cynical relativists who care less about convictions than about grades and careers. In fact, if anything is surprising, it is that more students do not behave in this cynical fashion, for the established curriculum encourages it. The disjunction of the curriculum is a far more powerful source of relativism than any doctrine preached by the faculty.

One of the oddest things about the university is that it calls itself a community of scholars yet organizes its curriculum in a way that conceals the links of the community from those who are not already aware of them. The courses being given at any moment on a campus represent any number of rich potential conversations within and across the disciplines. But since students experience these conversations only as a series of monologues, the conversations become actual only for the minority who can reconstruct them on their own. No self-respecting educator would deliberately design a system guaranteed to keep students dependent on the whim of the individual instructor. Yet this is precisely the effect of a curriculum composed of courses that are not in dialogue with one another.

Ships in the Night

The problem deepens when teachers are further apart. A student today can go from a course in which the universality of Western culture is taken for granted (and therefore not articulated) to a course in which it is taken for granted (and therefore not articulated) that such claims of universality are fallacious and deceptive. True, for the best students the resulting cognitive dissonance is no great problem. The chance to try on a variety of clashing ideas, to see what they feel like, is one of the most exciting opportunities an education can provide; it can be especially rewarding for students who come to the university with already developed skills at summarizing and weighing arguments and synthesizing conflicting positions on their own.

Many students, however, become confused or indifferent and react as the above two students did by giving their teachers whatever they seem to want even though it is contradictory.

Then, too, when their teachers' conflicting perspectives do not enter into a common discussion, students may not even be able to infer what is wanted. Like everyone else, teachers tend to betray their crucial assumptions as much in what they do *not* say, what they take to go without saying, as in what they say explicitly. To students who are not at home in the academic intellectual community, the significance of these silences and exclusions is likely to be intimidating, if it does not elude them entirely.

Furthermore, in an academic environment in which there is increasingly less unspoken common ground, it may not even be clear to students that their teachers are in conflict, for different words may be used by several teachers for the same concepts or the same words for different concepts. If students do not know that "positivism" has in some quarters become a derogatory buzzword for any belief in objectivity, they may not become aware that the art history and political science teachers in the above example are in disagreement. A student who goes from one humanist who speaks of "traditional moral themes" to another who speaks of "patriarchal discursive practices" may not become aware that the two teachers are actually referring to the same thing. Students in such cases are being exposed to some of the major cultural debates of their time, but in a way that makes it difficult to recognize them *as* debates.

Note, too, that the instructors in these situations are protected by the insularity of their classrooms, which makes it unnecessary, if not impossible, for them to confront the challenges to their assumptions that would be represented by their colleagues. Professors do not expect such immunity from peer criticism when they publish their work or appear at professional conferences. It is only in the classroom that such immunity is taken for granted as if it were a form of academic freedom. Since students enjoy no such protection, one can hardly blame them if they, too, protect themselves by compartmentalizing the contradictions to which they are exposed, as my first student did when he became an objectivist in one course and an antiobjectivist in the other.

I recall a semester late in college when I took a course in modern poetry taught by a New Critic, a follower of T. S. Eliot, and a course in seventeenth-century English literature taught by an older scholar who resented Eliot and the New Critics, who had attacked John Milton for his grandiloquence and lack of irony. Three days a week between ten and eleven I listened with dutiful respect to the New Critic's theories of irony and paradox, and between eleven and twelve I listened with dutiful respect to the argument that these New Critical theories had no application whatsoever to Milton, Dryden, and their contemporaries. What was really odd, however, is that I hardly focused at the time on the fact that my two teachers were in disagreement.

Was I just ridiculously slow to comprehend the critical issues that were at stake? Perhaps so, but since no one was asking me to think about the relationship between the two courses, I did not. If my teachers disagreed, this was their business—a professional dispute that did not concern me. Each course was challenging enough on its own terms, and to have raised the question of how they related would have only risked needlessly multiplying difficulties for myself. Then, too, for me to ask my teachers about their differences might have seemed impertinent and ill-mannered—who was I to impugn their authority? Only later did it dawn on me that studying different centuries and clashing theories without having them brought together had made things much *harder* since it removed the element of contrast.

Contrast is fundamental to understanding, for no subject, idea, or text is an island. In order to become intelligible "in itself," it needs to be seen in its relation to other subjects, ideas, and texts. When this

The university conceals the links of the community.

relation of interdependence is obscured because different courses do not communicate, subjects, ideas, and texts become harder to comprehend, if not unintelligible. We think we are making things simpler for students by abstracting periods, texts, and authors from their relationships with other periods, texts, and authors so that we can study them closely in a purified space. But the very act of isolating an object from its contrasting background and relations makes it hard to grasp. Since we cannot talk about everything all at once, subjects do have to be distinguished and to that extent isolated from one another. But this isolation does not have to preclude connections and relations. It is hard to grasp the modernity of modern literature unless one can compare it with something that is not modern.

That is why teachers in modern periods need nonmodernists (and vice versa) in order to make their subjects intelligible to their students, just as teachers who defend the culture of the West need the teachers who criticize it (and vice versa). Without the criticisms, after all, there would be no need to defend the West to begin with. Insofar as neither a defense nor a critique of tradition makes sense apart from the dialogue these positions are engaged in, a curriculum which removes that dialogue from view defeats the goals of traditionalists and revisionists alike. It is true that fundamental conflicts like these may turn out to be nonnegotiable. But no one knows this in advance, and even if a dispute proves to be nonnegotiable, to learn that this is the case is not worthless.

I noted earlier that among the factors that make academic culture more confusing today than in the past is not only that there is more controversy but that there is even controversy about what can legitimately be considered controversial. Traditionalists are often angry that there should even *be* a debate over the canon, while revisionists are often angry that there should even be a debate over "political correctness," or the relevance of ideology and politics to their subjects. A recent feminist critic says she finds it "astonishing" that it still needs repeating at this late date that "the perspective assumed to be 'universal' which has dominated knowledge . . . has actually been male and culture-bound."[1] Since the feminist argument, however, is that we still fail to see how culture-bound our thinking is, it is hard to see why this critic should be astonished that she still needs to make the point. Another political critic writes that "we are perhaps already weary of the avalanche of papers, books, and conferences entitled 'The Politics of X,' and we have recently begun to question that most hallowed of all political slogans on the left, 'everything is political.' "[2] Yet the idea of politics that this critic and her audience are already "weary of" is one that most people have not yet encountered and might well find incomprehensible. The "advanced" academic and the layperson (or the traditional academic) are so far apart that what is already old news to one has not yet become intelligible to the other.

Imagine how this affects students who, at the moment they are negotiating the difficult transition from the lay culture to the academic culture, must also negotiate the unpredictable and unfathomable discrepancies between academic departments and factions. When there is no correlation of the different discourses to which students are exposed, it becomes especially difficult for them to infer which assumptions are safe and which are likely to be challenged. The problem is that knowledge of what is and is not considered potentially or legitimately controversial cannot be learned a priori; you cannot get it out of E. D. Hirsch's *Dictionary of Cultural Literacy*. Such knowledge comes only through interaction with a community, and that interaction is precisely what is prevented by a disconnected system of courses. Then, too, assumptions about what is and is not potentially controversial tend to change from one moment to the next and one subcommunity to the next, and they are changing at a faster rate today than in the past.

Thomas S. Kuhn in *The Structure of Scientific Revolutions* describes   15 moments of crisis or "paradigm shift" in the sciences, when "a law that cannot even be demonstrated to one group of scientists may . . . seem intuitively obvious to another."[3] The fate of Kuhn's own book is an interesting case in point. Even as his sociological account of scientific paradigm change has been treated as virtual holy writ by many literary theorists (for a while it seemed almost obligatory to begin every book or essay with a respectful bow to Kuhn), his work has often been ignored or dismissed by scientists and philosophers of science, who accuse him of subverting the concept of objective truth in reducing scientific discovery to "mob psychology." As the controversy over Kuhn has revealed, both the literati and the scientists have remained largely walled up within their clashing assumptions about objectivity, the smugness of which might have been punctured had these parties been forced to argue with each other in their teaching. This mutual smugness has persisted in the sniper fire that continues to be exchanged over the concept of objectivity and the extent to which knowledge is independent of the social situation of the knower; revisionists sneer at the concept and traditionalists sneer at the very idea of questioning it.

The question neither group seems to ask is what it must be like to be a student caught in the crossfire between these conflicting views of objectivity, each one prone to present itself as "intuitively obvious" and uncontroversial. A rhetoric scholar, Gregory Colomb, has studied the disorientation experienced by a bright high school graduate who, after doing well in a humanities course as a freshman at the University of Chicago, tried to apply her mastery to a social science course, only to come up with a grade of C.[4] Imagine trying to write an academic paper when you sense that almost anything you say can be used against you and that the intellectual moves that got you an A in existentialist philosophy may get you a C minus and a dirty look in Skinnerian behaviorism.

Consider the fact that the passive voice that is so standard in sociology writing ("it will be contended in this paper . . .") has been perennially rebuked in English courses.[5] Or consider something so apparently trivial as the convention of using the present tense to describe actions in literature and philosophy and the past tense to describe them in history. Plato *says* things in literary and philosophical accounts while in historical accounts he *said* them. Experienced writers become so accustomed to such tense shifting that it seems a simple matter, but it reflects deep-rooted and potentially controversial differences between disciplines. Presumably, Plato speaks in the present in literary and philosophical contexts because ideas there are considered timeless; only when we move over to history does it start to matter that the writer is dead.[6] We English teachers write "tense shift" in the margin when student writers betray uncertainty about this convention, but how do we expect them to "get" it when they pass from the very different time zones of history and philosophy / English with no engagement of the underlying issues?

One of the most frequent comments teachers make on student papers is "What's your evidence?" But nobody would ever finish a piece of writing if it were necessary to supply evidence for everything being said, so in order to write, one must acquire a sense of which statements have to be supported by evidence (or further argument) and which ones a writer can get away with because they are already taken for granted by the imagined audience. What happens, then, when a writer has no way of knowing whether an assumption that he or she got away with with audience A will also be conceded by audience B? It is no wonder that students protect themselves from the insecurity of such a situation by "psyching out" each course as it comes—and then forgetting about it as soon as possible after the final exam in order to clear their minds for the seemingly unrelated demands of the next set of courses.

It is only ideas and reasoning processes but the recall of basic information as well that figure to be impaired by disjunctive curricular organization. To use the jargon of information theory, an information system that is experienced as an unrelated series of signals will be weak in the kind of redundancy that is needed for information to be retained. Faced with a curriculum overloaded with data and weak in redundancy, students may find it difficult to know which items of information they are supposed to remember. Then, too, a student may be exposed to the same information in several courses while failing to recognize it as "the same," since it is contextualized differently in each course. When students fail to identify a cultural literacy item on a test, the problem may be not that they don't know the information but that they don't know they know it; they may have learned it in a context whose relevance to the test question they don't recognize. What is learned seems so specific to a particular course that it is difficult for students to see its application beyond.

The critic Kenneth Burke once compared the intellectual life of a culture to a parlor in which different guests are forever dropping in and out. As the standard curriculum represents the intellectual life, however, there is no parlor; the hosts congregate in separate rooms with their acolytes and keep their differences and agreements to themselves. Making one's way through the standard curriculum is rather like trying to comprehend a phone conversation by listening at only one end.[7] You can manage it up to a point, but this is hardly the ideal way to do it. 20

To venture a final comparison, it is as if you were to try to learn the game of baseball by being shown a series of rooms in which you see each component of the game separately: pitchers going through their windups in one room; hitters swinging their bats in the next; then infielders, outfielders, umpires, fans, field announcers, ticket scalpers, broadcasters, hot-dog vendors, and so on. You see them all in their different roles, but since you see them separately you get no clear idea of what the game actually looks like or why the players do what they do. No doubt you would come away with a very imperfect understanding of baseball under these conditions. Yet it does not seem far-fetched to compare these circumstances with the ones students face when they are exposed to a series of disparate courses, subjects, and perspectives and expected not only to infer the rules of the academic-intellectual game but to play it competently themselves.

Notes

1. Gayle Green, "The Myth of Neutrality, Again?" in *Shakespeare Left and Right,* ed. Ivo Kamps (New York: Routledge, 1991), p. 24.
2. Diana Fuss, *Essentially Speaking: Feminism, Nature and Difference* (New York: Routledge, 1989), p. 105.
3. Thomas S. Kuhn, *The Structure of Scientific Revolutions,* 2d ed. (Chicago: University of Chicago Press, 1970), p. 150.
4. Gregory Colomb, *Disciplinary "Secrets" and the Apprentice Writer: The Lessons for Critical Thinking* (Upper Montclair, N.J.: Montclair State College, Institute for Critical Thinking, 1988), pp. 2–3.
5. For this point I am indebted to an unpublished talk by Susan Lowry.
6. I am indebted for this point to Susan H. McLeod, "Writing across the Curriculum: An Introduction," forthcoming in *Writing across the Curriculum: A Guide to Developing Programs,* eds. McLeod and Margot Soven (Newberry Park, Calif.: Sage, 1992).
7. I adapt an observation made in a somewhat different context by Mary Louise Pratt, "Humanities for the Future: Reflections on the Western Culture Debate at Stanford," in *Politics of Liberal Education* (Durham: Duke University Press, 1992), p. 19.

Working with the Text

1. In this selection from *Beyond the Culture Wars,* Gerald Graff describes what he considers to be the student experience of the undergraduate curriculum in most American colleges and universities. As you reread Graff's argument, note the specific ways he characterizes the undergraduate experience. In a brief essay, develop a portrait of the student Graff is describing. What does the student encounter? How does the student respond? Consider the terms Graff uses. For instance, what does he mean by "cognitive dissonance" (par. 5)? What connection does he say that dissonance has to the tendency of students to "psych out" (par. 18) a course? What does he think "psyching out" a course involves?

2. Graff weaves examples and personal reminiscence into his discussion of how isolated the individual classroom is on college campuses. What effect do these examples have on Graff's credibility? Do the examples and stories help elicit belief in Graff's argument?

3. Graff titles a section in the excerpt presented here with the phrase "Ships in the Night." Explain the idiomatic expression that Graff is using here. In what ways is the title appropriate as a metaphor for the argument that Graff presents?

4. When discussing how difficult students find it to know what their professors expect, Graff observes: "Like everyone else, teachers tend to betray their crucial assumptions as much in what they do *not* say, what they take to go

without saying, as in what they say explicitly. To students who are not at home in the academic intellectual community, the significance of these silences and exclusions is likely to be intimidating, if it does not elude them entirely" (par. 6). Drawing on examples from your own attempts to figure out those expectations, write a brief explanation of what Graff means by his statement.

From Text to Field

1. Graff, in a part of this selection not reprinted here, asserts that "students have trouble making sense of the disparate and clashing materials with which the curriculum bombards them". Has this been your experience? Write an essay in which you reflect on your ability to "make sense" of the materials you have encountered in your undergraduate education. Have you found the materials to be "disparate and clashing"? Do you see them as separate units of knowledge? Do you play them off of each other or try to reconcile them? Do they seem coherent or fragmented to you?

2. The curriculum Graff describes is commonly found in undergraduate general-education requirements. Examine the requirements for your institution, and consider the general-education courses you have already taken. In an essay, analyze the effectiveness of your general-education curriculum. What is the rationale for that curriculum? In what ways does the curriculum—the rationale, the approach, the courses and their sequence—seem sound to you? In what ways does the curriculum seem questionable?

3. Throughout the selection, Graff refers to the academic debate over Western culture and the debate over objectivity, which are in many ways interrelated. What aspects of these debates have you encountered in your own education or in reading and discussion outside an educational setting? In a personal essay, reflect on those encounters, including your reading of Graff's references to the academic debate. Based on what you know so far, what is your position on the debate over Western culture, objectivity, or both? In what ways do you think they are significant? Over time, how has your position been reinforced or changed? What questions do the debates raise for you?

4. Given Graff's interest in dialogue among courses and among the materials or readings taught in those courses, offer a proposal in which you rethink the design of a course, or of a set of courses, so that the dialogue that Graff has in mind can occur.

Mark #1	Mark #2	Result
CONFIRM (for medical-related goods)	CONFIRMCELLS (for blood reagents)	Confusingly similar due to related goods
LAREDO (for land vehicles)	LAREDO (for pneumatic tires)	Confusingly similar due to related goods
LITTLE PLUMBER (for liquid drain opener)	LITTLE PLUMBER (for advertising services)	Not confusingly similar because goods/services not related
BIGGS (for grocery and general merchandise store)	BIGGS (& DESIGN) (for furniture)	Confusingly similar due to related goods
GOLDEN GRIDDLE PANCAKE HOUSE (with "Golden Griddle" disclaimed) for restaurant services	GOLDEN GRIDDLE (for table syrup)	Confusingly similar due to related goods
CAREER IMAGE (STYLIZED) (for women's clothing and store services)	CREST CAREER IMAGES (for uniforms)	Confusingly similar due to related goods
TMM (for computer software)	TMS (for computer software)	Confusingly similar due to similarity in appearance
COBBLER'S OUTLET (for shoes)	CALIFORNIA COBBLERS (STYLIZED) (for shoes)	Not confusingly similar due to weakness of common element "COBBLERS"
BEST JEWELRY (& DESIGN) (for jewelry store services)	JEWELERS' BEST (for jewelry)	Not confusingly similar because marks create different commercial impression
TRUCOOL (for synthetic coolant)	TURCOOL (for cutting oil)	Confusingly similar due to similarity in appearance

EXHIBIT 4–5
Comparison of Marks Alleged to Be Confusingly Similar and Action Taken by PTO and Courts

to use the mark or seek its consent to coexistence and registration. The applicant may need to pay the prior user some amount of money to secure the consent. Although the PTO is not bound to accept such a coexistence or consent agreement, generally the PTO does so, believing that the owners of marks are in the best position to evaluate whether conflicts might exist and that if they believe no confusion would result from coexistence of the marks, the PTO should affirm their decision. See Chapter 6 for further discussion of consent agreements.

If there is a conflicting mark in a pending application, action on the application with the later filing date will be suspended until the mark in the conflicting application with the earlier filing date is either registered (in which case the later-filed application will be refused) or abandoned (in which case, the later-filed application can proceed to registration).

Teaching New Worlds/ New Words

bell hooks

In her call for classrooms that encourage students to use the language they "know most intimately," bell hooks takes us back to the violence and oppression that gave birth to black English. Hooks describes how Africans who were brought to America as slaves were forced to replace their own languages with standard English, which they in turn "remade" into a tool of resistance.

As a descendant of slaves who grew up speaking the Southern black vernacular of Kentucky, hooks began to challenge the repressiveness of standard English by drawing the vernacular into her classroom, professional writing, and social life. She believes that through listening to each other's first language, "we may disrupt that cultural imperialism that suggests one is worthy of being heard only if one speaks in standard English."

Gloria Watkins writes under the pseudonym bell hooks, her grandmother's name, using the lowercase to draw attention away from her own authorship and to the unheard voices that drive her explorations of identity and culture. A professor at City College in New York, she has taught at Yale University and Oberlin College. As an educator, a writer, and a speaker, she is one of the most provocative and important voices of her generation of intellectuals. "Teaching New Worlds/New Words" first appeared as a chapter in hooks's book *Teaching to Transgress: Education as the Practice of Freedom* (1994).

Like desire, language disrupts, refuses to be contained within boundaries. It speaks itself against our will, in words and thoughts that intrude, even violate the most private spaces of mind and body. It was in my first year of college that I read Adrienne Rich's poem, "The Burning of Paper Instead of

Children." That poem, speaking against domination, against racism and class oppression, attempts to illustrate graphically that stopping the political persecution and torture of living beings is a more vital issue than censorship, than burning books. One line of this poem that moved and disturbed something within me: "This is the oppressor's language yet I need it to talk to you." I've never forgotten it. Perhaps I could not have forgotten it even if I tried to erase it from memory. Words impose themselves, take root in our memory against our will. The words of this poem begat a life in my memory that I could not abort or change.

When I find myself thinking about language now, these words are there, as if they were always waiting to challenge and assist me. I find myself silently speaking them over and over again with the intensity of a chant. They startle me, shaking me into an awareness of the link between languages and domination. Initially, I resist the idea of the "oppressor's language," certain that this construct has the potential to disempower those of us who are just learning to speak, who are just learning to claim language as a place where we make ourselves subject. *This is the oppressor's language yet I need it to talk to you.* Adrienne Rich's words. Then, when I first read these words, and now, they make me think of standard English, of learning to speak against black vernacular, against the ruptured and broken speech of a dispossessed and displaced people. Standard English is not the speech of exile. It is the language of conquest and domination; in the United States, it is the mask which hides the loss of so many tongues, all those sounds of diverse, native communities we will never hear, the speech of the Gullah, Yiddish, and so many other unremembered tongues.

Reflecting on Adrienne Rich's words, I know that it is not the English language that hurts me, but what the oppressors do with it, how they shape it to become a territory that limits and defines, how they make it a weapon that can shame, humiliate, colonize. Gloria Anzaldúa reminds us of this pain in *Borderlands/La Frontera* when she asserts, "So, if you want to really hurt me, talk badly about my language." We have so little knowledge of how displaced, enslaved, or free Africans who came or were brought against their will to the United States felt about the loss of language, about learning English. Only as a woman did I begin to think about these black people in relation to language, to think about their trauma as they were compelled to witness their language rendered meaningless with a colonizing European culture, where voices deemed foreign could not be spoken, were outlawed tongues, renegade speech. When I realize how long it has taken for white Americans to acknowledge diverse languages of Native Americans, to accept that the speech their ancestral colonizers declared was merely grunts and gibberish was indeed *language*, it is difficult not to hear in standard English always the sound of slaughter and conquest. I think now of the grief of displaced "homeless" Africans, forced to inhabit a world where they saw folks like themselves, inhabiting the same skin, the same condition, but who had no shared language to talk with one another, who needed "the oppressor's language." *"This is the oppressor's language yet I need it to talk to you."* When I imagine the terror of Africans on board slave ships, on auction blocks, inhabiting the unfamiliar architecture of plantations, I consider that this terror extended beyond fear of punishment, that it resided also in the anguish of hearing a language they could not comprehend. The very sound of English had to terrify. I think of black people meeting one another in a space away from the diverse cultures and languages that distinguished them from one another, compelled by circumstance to find ways to speak with one another in a "new world" where blackness or the darkness of one's skin and not language would become the space of bonding. How to remember, to reinvoke this terror. How to describe what it must have been like for Africans whose deepest bonds were historically forged in the place of shared speech to be transported abruptly to a world where the very sound of one's mother tongue had no meaning.

I imagine them hearing spoken English as the oppressor's language, yet I imagine them also realizing that this language would need to be possessed, taken, claimed as a space of resistance. I imagine that the moment they realized the oppressor's language, seized and spoken by the tongues of the colonized, could be a space of bonding was joyous. For in that recognition was the understanding that intimacy could be restored, that a culture of resistance could be formed that would make recovery from the trauma of enslavement possible. I imagine, then, Africans first hearing English as "the oppressor's language" and then re-hearing it as a potential site of resistance. Learning English, learning to speak the alien tongue, was one way enslaved Africans began to reclaim their personal power within a context of domination. Possessing a shared language, black folks could find again a way to make community, and a means to create the political solidarity necessary to resist.

Needing the oppressor's language to speak with one another they nevertheless also reinvented, remade that language so that it would speak beyond the boundaries of conquest and domination. In the mouths of black Africans in the so-called New World, English was altered, transformed, and became a different speech. Enslaved black people took broken bits of English and made of them a counterlanguage. They put together their words in such a way that the colonizer had to rethink the meaning of the English language. Though it has become common in contemporary culture to talk about the messages of resistance that emerged in the music created by slaves, particularly spirituals, less is said about the grammatical construction of sentences in these songs. Often, the English used in the song reflected the broken, ruptured world of the slave. When the slaves sang "nobody knows de trouble I see—" their use of the word "nobody" adds a richer meaning than if they had used the phrase "no one," for it was the slave's *body* that was the concrete site of suffering. And even as emancipated black people sang spirituals, they did not change the language, the sentence structure, of our ancestors. For in the incorrect usage of words, in the incorrect placement of words, was a spirit of rebellion that claimed language as a site of resistance. Using English in a way that ruptured standard usage and meaning, so that white folks could often not understand black speech, made English into more than the oppressor's language.

An unbroken connection exists between the broken English of the displaced, enslaved African and the diverse black vernacular speech black folks use today. In both cases, the rupture of standard English enabled and enables rebellion and resistance. By transforming the oppressor's language, making a culture of resistance, black people created an intimate speech that could say far more than was permissible within the boundaries of standard English. The power of this speech is not simply that it enables resistance to white supremacy, but that it also forges a space for alternative cultural production and alternative epistemologies— different ways of thinking and knowing that were crucial to creating a counterhegemonic worldview. It is absolutely essential that the revolutionary power of black vernacular speech not be lost in contemporary culture. That power resides in the capacity of black vernacular to intervene on the boundaries and limitation of standard English.

Words impose themselves, take root in our memory against our will.

In contemporary black popular culture, rap music has become one of the spaces where black vernacular speech is used in a manner that invites dominant mainstream culture to listen—to hear—and, to some extent, be transformed. However, one of the risks of this attempt at cultural translation is that it will trivialize black vernacular speech. When young white kids imitate this speech in ways that suggest it is the speech of those who are stupid or who are only interested in entertaining or being funny, then the subversive power of speech is undermined. In academic circles, both in the sphere of teaching and that of writing, there has been little effort made to utilize black vernacular—or, for that matter, any language other than standard English. When I asked an ethnically diverse group of students in a course I was teaching on black women writers why we only hear standard English spoken in the classroom, they were momentarily rendered speechless. Though many of them were individuals for whom standard English was a second or third language, it had simply never occurred to them that it was possible to say something in another language, in another way. No wonder, then, that we continue to think "This is the oppressor's language yet I need it to talk to you."

I have realized that I was in danger of losing my relationship to black vernacular speech because I too rarely use it in the predominantly white settings that I am most often in, both professionally and socially. And so I have begun to work at integrating into a variety of settings the particular Southern black vernacular speech I grew up hearing and speaking. It has been hardest to integrate black vernacular in writing, particularly for academic journals. When I first began to incorporate black vernacular in critical essays, editors would send the work back to me in standard English. Using the vernacular means that translation into standard English may be needed if one wishes to reach a more inclusive audience. In the classroom setting, I encourage students to use their first language and translate it so they do not feel that seeking higher education will necessarily estrange them from that language and culture they know most intimately. Not surprisingly, when students in my Black Women Writers class began to speak using diverse language and speech, white students often complained. This seemed to be particularly the case with black vernacular. It was particularly disturbing to the white students because they could hear the words that were said but could not comprehend their meaning. Pedagogically, I encouraged them to think of the moment of not understanding what someone says as a space to learn. Such a space provides not only the opportunity to listen without "mastery," without owning or possessing speech through interpretation, but also the experience of hearing non-English words. These lessons seem particularly crucial in a multicultural society that remains white supremacist, that uses standard English as a weapon to silence and censor. June Jordan reminds us of this in *On Call* when she declares:

> I am talking about majority problems of language in a democratic state, problems of a currency that someone has stolen and hidden away and then homogenized into an official "English" language that can only express non-events involving nobody responsible, or lies. If we lived in a democratic state our language would have to hurtle, fly, curse, and sing, in all the common American names, all the undeniable and representative participating voices of everybody here. We would not tolerate the language of the powerful and, thereby, lose all respect for words, per se. We would make our language conform to the truth of our many selves and we would make our language lead us into the equality of power that a democratic state must represent.

That the students in the course on black women writers were repressing all longing to speak in tongues other than standard English without seeing this repression as political was an indication of the way we act unconsciously, in complicity with a culture of domination.

Recent discussions of diversity and multiculturalism tend to downplay or 10 ignore the question of language. Critical feminist writings focused on issues of difference and voice have made important theoretical interventions, calling for a recognition of the primacy of voices that are often silenced, censored, or marginalized. This call for the acknowledgment and celebration of diverse voices, and consequently of diverse language and speech, necessarily disrupts the primacy of standard English. When advocates of feminism first spoke about the desire for diverse participation in women's movement, there was no discussion of language. It was simply assumed that standard English would remain the primary vehicle for the transmission of feminist thought. Now that the audience for feminist writing and speaking has become more diverse, it is evident that we must change conventional ways of thinking about language, creating spaces where diverse voices can speak in words other than English or in broken, vernacular speech. This means that at a lecture or even in a written work there will be fragments of speech that may or may not be accessible to every individual. Shifting how we think about language and how we use it necessarily alters how we know what we know. At a lecture where I might use Southern black vernacular, the particular patois of my region, or where I might use very abstract thought in conjunction with plain speech, responding to a diverse audience, I suggest that we do not necessarily need to hear and know what is stated in its entirety, that we do not need to "master" or conquer the narrative as a whole, that we may know in fragments. I suggest that we may learn from spaces of silence as well as spaces of speech, that in the patient act of listening to another tongue we may subvert that culture of capitalist frenzy and consumption that demands all desire must be satisfied immediately, or we may disrupt that cultural imperialism that suggests one is worthy of being heard only if one speaks in standard English.

Adrienne Rich concludes her poem with this statement:

> I am composing on the typewriter late at night, thinking of today. How well we all spoke. A language is a map of our failures. Frederick Douglass wrote an English purer than Milton's. People suffer highly in poverty. There are methods but we do not use them. Joan, who could not read, spoke some peasant form of French. Some of the sufferings are: It is hard to tell the truth; this is America; I cannot touch you now. In America we have only the present tense. I am in danger. You are in danger. The burning of a book arouses no sensation in me. I know it hurts to burn. There are flames of napalm in Cantonsville, Maryland. I know it hurts to burn. The typewriter is overheated, my mouth is burning, I cannot touch you and this is the oppressor's language.

To recognize that we touch one another in language seems particularly difficult in a society that would have us believe that there is no dignity in the experience of passion, that to feel deeply is to be inferior, for within the dualism of Western metaphysical thought, ideas are always more important than language. To heal the splitting of mind and body, we marginalized and oppressed people attempt to recover ourselves and our experiences in language. We seek to make a place for the intimacy. Unable to find such a place in standard English, we create the ruptured, broken, unruly speech of the vernacular. When I need to say words that do more than simply mirror or address the dominant reality, I speak black vernacular. There, in that location, we make English do what we want it to do. We take the oppressor's language and turn it against itself. We make our words a counterhegemonic speech, liberating ourselves in language.

Working with the Text

1. "Teaching New Worlds/New Words" is a meditation on a line from an Adrienne Rich poem: "This is the oppressor's language yet I need it to talk to you." Write a short essay in which you reflect on hooks's interpretation of this line. Why does bell hooks believe that the speakers of standard English are "oppressors"? Who needs to use the oppressor's language, and why? How do they use it?

2. In her description of ways slaves restructured standard English to reflect their own experience, hooks points out that "it was the slave's *body* that was the concrete site of suffering" (par. 5). As you reread the essay, imagine what is happening to and inside of the bodies of Africans as they are brought to a strange land where their language is nullified. Consider the senses—especially hearing—and the sensations of emotion as well as the effects of physical force. In a brief essay, reflect on the relationship between language and the body for people who find themselves in what hooks calls "this terror." As an alternative to a reflective essay, you might write a short narrative or descriptive essay in which you re-create a scene—using people, places, and actions—to make concrete the experience of either being threatened by a dominant language or using that language as a tool of resistance.

3. Reread hooks's description of her classroom, imagining yourself in it. Write a brief essay that analyzes hooks's approach from your perspective as a student. What, exactly, would she be asking you to do? How would you respond? How might you use your own language—a language other than the English typically spoken in the undergraduate classroom? How would you react to other students using a language you didn't understand?

From Text to Field

1. As hooks moves from the origins of black English to the current "power of this speech," she insists that it is "absolutely essential that the revolutionary power

of black vernacular speech not be lost in contemporary culture" (par. 6). Write an essay that explores the current relationship between black vernacular speech and mainstream culture. Consider ways in which black English has been appropriated by or adopted by that culture. In what ways does black English influence mainstream culture? Does it wield power or provoke resistance? Does it get "lost in contemporary culture"?

2. In commenting on rap music, hooks warns that "one of the risks of this attempt at cultural translation is that it will trivialize black vernacular speech" (par. 7). As you reread this passage, think about this "risk" in terms of the larger concerns that drive the essay. In a brief essay, explore and respond to her concerns about rap music. What actions and attitudes is she referring to? Do you agree with her point of view? How do you respond to rappers and rap music, especially the words? What kinds of attitudes toward rap music and black rappers have you encountered in other people?

3. Although Ebonics—a term for African American language or black English vernacular—has been recognized by language scholars as a legitimate language or dialect, its use, especially in the public school system, remains controversial. If you have not directly encountered this controversy in the schools you have attended, you have probably heard the public debate. Similar debates surround any form of bilingual education. In light of hooks's argument, write an essay in which you argue for or against drawing on languages other than standard English in either the public school or undergraduate classroom. If you have encountered this in your own school system, you may wish to incorporate that experience.

4. Near the end of the essay, hooks makes the following appeal: "I suggest that we may learn from spaces of silence as well as spaces of speech, that in the patient act of listening to another tongue we may subvert that culture of capitalist frenzy and consumption that demands all desire must be satisfied immediately, or we may disrupt that cultural imperialism that suggests one is worthy of being heard only if one speaks in standard English" (par. 10). Write an essay in which you translate this passage into more concrete terms by interpreting her meaning, responding to that meaning, and offering a course of action. What actions, attitudes, and experiences is she calling into question? What, more specifically, is she asking her audience to do? Do you agree with her? If so, how would you carry out her vision? If not, what counter or alternative vision would you offer, and to what end?

5. In her closing paragraph, hooks claims that "[t]o heal the splitting of mind and body, we marginalized and oppressed people attempt to recover ourselves and our experiences in language" (par. 12). Consider the extent to which you have felt "marginalized" or "oppressed," even in a limited way or

in an isolated incident, as an outsider whose sense of self was somehow lost, diminished, or silenced. Write an essay in which you explore the use of language to "recover" yourself. Consider how hooks uses language in her essay to capture the lived experience of people whose experiences were discounted or hidden.

Where Is the Classroom?

Charles Bazerman

We tend to think of "genre" as a form of writing, such as a business proposal, a newspaper editorial, or a novel or poem. Yet the outer or surface form of language only begins to explain the power of genre in language and in our lives. Classrooms, you may be surprised to learn, can also be thought of as genres. Charles Bazerman, along with other rhetoricians, conceives of genre in light of an "activity system"—ways of acting and using language that are based on the challenges or demands of a recurrent situation. Such activities can then often become regularized and controlled by institutions. As you know through your own experience, classrooms as situations occur again and again, and the language practices that go on inside of classrooms have themselves become conventional and typified. With this "activity theory" in mind, we can begin to appreciate Bazerman's claim that "the classroom is always invented, always constructed, always a matter of genre." Classrooms are themselves genres in that they represent typified rhetorical actions in a recurrent situation. The shape of the classroom also emerges from the genres we bring into it, genres that capture institutional and departmental expectations as well as the experience and perspectives of teachers and students.

As professor of English and education at the University of California, Santa Barbara, Bazerman has gained prominence through his work in rhetoric, especially the rhetoric of science and technology. His book *Shaping Written Knowledge: The Genre and Activity of the Experimental Article in Science* (1988) won wide recognition, including awards from the American Medical Writers' Association and the National Council of Teachers of English. His textbooks include *Involved: Writing for College, Writing for Yourself* (1997) and *The Informed Writer* (1995), now in its fifth edition. His recent book, *The Languages of Edison's Light* (1999), examines the rhetorical and representational work that made Edison's incandescent light a social reality.

chance. There have been cases in which students approached their advisors and they appeared to be very nice and interested in their ideas. But later the students were upset when they found out that their advisors did not really have the intention or capacity to help, or in fact exploited their work or even stole their ideas. The advisors might have different points of view, including different ethical standards for both parties' expectations and conduct. But for the students, that is certainly bad luck, in part, because of the responsibility they had to take on themselves.

Where to find your committee members

The selection of the members for your thesis/dissertation committee may start with choosing the readers for your comprehensive or other research papers. Generally speaking, the criteria discussed above for choosing your advisor also apply to the selection of your committee members. Nevertheless, there is an important difference between an advisor and a committee member. No matter how fastidious your advisor could be, she has a stake in your success. Being your advisor she worries no less than you about the quality of your work. Pass or fail, you are her student. An ordinary member on your thesis/dissertation committee, on the other side, may function merely as a gatekeeper following certain criteria in his mind.

The selection of your committee members should be done in consultation with your advisor. If you know some faculty members and/or have established some working relationship with them (e.g., having worked with them on your comprehensive papers), you can put down their names as candidates. Most likely, your advisor will make important suggestions since he usually knows more about the suitable candidate than you do. You and your advisor are also supposed to be aware of the official rules governing the formation of the thesis/dissertation committee. University regulations usually require a minimum number of committee members and specify their minimum qualifications. In addition to faculty members from your own department, an external examiner may also be required. He could come from another department or even another institution.

Your prior working relationship with faculty members is valuable since it provides the opportunity to find your prospective committee members. Especially, your work with the readers of your research or comprehensive papers is a unique experience for you to test their competence, interest, and suitability

Responses to Office Actions.   An applicant has six months to respond to an office action. Failure to respond within the appropriate time period will result in abandonment of the application unless the delay was unintentional.

As soon as an office action is received, its response date should be docketed. The client should then be informed in writing of the basis for the PTO's refusal to register the mark. The law firm typically recommends a course of action and provides an estimate of the costs and fees the client can expect to incur in responding to the office action along with some assessment of the likelihood of success. The IP professional should continue to monitor the matter to ensure the client provides appropriate and timely instructions so the law firm can respond to the office action.

In some instances, a second office action may be issued after the applicant's response to the initial office action. Ultimately, the application will either proceed to the next step (publication) or will be subject to a "Final Refusal." Once a final refusal has been issued, the applicant's only recourse is to comply with the examining attorney's requirements, request reconsideration by bringing new matter before the examining attorney, or appeal the refusal to the Trademark Trial and Appeal Board (TTAB). Adverse decisions of the TTAB are reviewable by the U.S. Court of Appeals for the Federal Circuit and then by the U.S. Supreme Court if it decides to take the case. The Federal Circuit can set aside PTO findings only when the findings are arbitrary, capricious, an abuse of discretion, or unsupported by substantial evidence. *Dickinson v. Zurko,* 527 U.S. 150 (1999). Alternatively, the applicant can initiate an action in federal district court where the issues will be determined *de novo* (literally, "anew").

Generally, an appeal may be taken to the TTAB for any final decision of an examining attorney. An appeal is taken by filing a notice of appeal and by paying the appeal fee of $100 (per class) within six months of the mailing date of the action the party wishes to appeal.

An applicant who wishes to contest a refusal based on substance (such as a rejection of an application because the mark is merely descriptive) should file an appeal to the TTAB. If, however, the only issue in dispute is a question regarding the applicant's compliance with a technical provision of trademark rules, the applicant should file a petition to the Director rather than appeal.

For example, if a trademark application is refused on the basis that the mark is confusingly similar to that of another, an appeal should be taken to the TTAB. If a question arises as to whether PTO practice permits an applicant to correct a typographical error, a petition to the Director should be filed.

POSTEXAMINATION PROCEDURE

Publication in the *Official Gazette*

Assuming the applicant responds satisfactorily to the office action, the examining attorney will approve the mark for publication in the *Official Gazette* (sometimes called the OG; see Exhibit 4–6). The mark as applied for (wording, design, or some combination thereof) will be reproduced as the applicant set it forth in the drawing page together with an identification of the owner, the filing date, the goods or services offered under the mark, and the filing date and serial number of the application. The purpose of publication is to afford interested parties the opportunity to review the mark and oppose its registration, generally on the basis that the mark is confusingly similar to another mark. Opposition actions are discussed in Chapter 6.

A notice of opposition (or request for extension of time to oppose) must be filed with the

Whatever subject we teach, it is easy—too easy—to imagine that the classroom is simply the place where we transmit our subject to students. So then the job of the teacher—who is already presumed competent in the subject— is to figure out how to package and present the information to the students and how to structure assignments and activities so that students gain mastery of the subject matter and skills rapidly and deeply. All the rest of the universe, in which this moment hangs suspended, as the Earth in Milton's cosmos, is taken as a given not to be troubled over—unless one were a social critic who saw in the classroom the consequences and/or reproduction of those inequities, irrationalities, or cruelties that haunt our entire socioeconomic-political arrangements.

Even with the great experimentation in the teaching of writing during the last two decades, the givenness of the classroom is still taken for granted. Much of the work in our field has been to make explicit and consensually validated those aspects of the writing competence which we as literate people know as a practical matter, and to add to that new practical insights. Other parts of the professional work have been to develop and test new methods and materials for transmitting that competence. On the other hand, our insights into the competence and into ways of reorganizing the classroom in order to share that competence with students, very early upset our traditional notions of what can or should happen in this standard modular unit of the classroom. The centrality to writing of the students' processes, motives, and messages removed the teacher from the lectern and handed important aspects of authority over to the students—no matter which of the many varieties of writing pedagogy one pursued.

Once this first move in the disruption of the traditional classroom order was taken, it was not surprising (in the usual hyperbole of social movements) that many took this as a fully radical commitment. The traditional classroom, which we had to readjust for our needs, became the oppressor of all education and individual growth. We wanted to reinvent the university on our model. And some very useful achievements have indeed been gained on this front, although overall they have been much more modest (and much more integrated into the continuing practices of other disciplines) than our field's visionary gleam had hoped for.

Whatever effects process and empowerment pedagogies have had on the classroom, what we have learned about writing should make us consider more fundamentally the social-psychological-political-intellectual location of the classroom. We have always known that writing was a social act, but in recent years we have begun to examine more energetically the implications of that for anatomizing the social location, dynamics, and activity of each instance of writing. We have started to see how the classroom is a particular scene of writing—neither an innately natural nor an innately artificial scene;

neither necessarily an oppressive nor necessarily a liberating scene; just a scene of writing. The classroom is not even one particular fixed scene, but many scenes—the scenes as we make them from our own particular circumstances and desires. Each of those scenes sets in motion expectancies of role and behavior as well as possibilities for statement and action. Each of those scenes suggest genres of communication, genres of ways of being in that setting.

So the issue is no longer what is right or wrong in the classroom so that it   5 must therefore be reinvented, but rather that the classroom is always invented, always constructed, always a matter of genre; therefore, no matter what choices we make, we are always better off to be aware of the materials out of which it is constructed and the spaces for communication created in the design. Then we can know our options, possibilities, and responsibilities as well as the compelling forces that we may be foolish to resist. Architecture must know its landscapes, even if it wants to call attention to its own difference.

The writing classroom is a complex forum. First it is encased in institutional beliefs that we will put students in proper shape for other teachers and will preserve the school from damaging embarrassment as we send our products out into the world. These imperatives are realized in requirements that mandate our courses and bring students unwillingly, but usually compliantly, into our domain. These beliefs are the source of our budget and our jobs, as much as we may rebel against an implied crudeness of understanding of writing that seems mandated by the bureaucracy and finances of public educational institutions. These institutional dynamics are realized through genres of testing and standards, curriculum guidelines and goals, policies and record keeping. There are genres that flow from the surrounding institutions into the classroom to regulate it; there are genres within the classroom that carry out the mandate of the regulation; and there are genres that flow out from the classroom that represent the work and competence of teacher and student, thereby holding them accountable to institutional expectations.

It is our choice whether these definitions of the classroom and the genres which act out these definitions are wholeheartedly accepted, wholeheartedly resisted, compromised with, or sublated into some fuller understanding of our tasks. Whichever choice we make we must consider the prices and responsibilities of our institutional places. Classrooms and hours and available (or unavailable) equipment are perhaps the most concrete manifestation of institutional shaping of the classroom, but we must also keep in mind such union issues as pay, workload, and status that shape the teacher's professional role, commitment, and life circumstances—all of which define limits to the teacher's involvement in the classroom and institution. All these concrete architectural features of the educational landscape are in turn influenced by institutional evaluation of the results of the classroom activity, as revealed in the genres of reporting and accountability that represent the results of the classroom to the wider world.

The institutional framework is given a constraining interpretation by the department's definition in the sequence, levels, and goals of courses, perhaps reinforced by syllabi, textbook lists, and departmental exams as well as by its hiring and course assignment policies. Departments create their own regulatory and coordinating genres. They then enact within various degrees of freedom, enforcement, and evasion the lives defined by those documents and utterances. Individual teachers comprise the department and have some say in setting the constraints, but the political process usually makes the result quite different from any one teacher's direct perception of what the class ought to be. On the other hand, teachers of various seniority and/or independence of spirit can expand the bounds of these departmental interpretations as far as local administrative oversight or negligence allows. Nonetheless, concerns for our own students' ability to proceed smoothly through the departmental offerings and the university maze, as well as a spirit of cooperation with our colleagues in the educational enterprise, may rein in our individual gallops after our own perceived ideal forms.

The next level, the one most professional discussions are aimed at, is the teacher's imaginative construct of the meaning of the course, which the teacher then realizes in a structure of relationships, activities, and materials that create the opportunities for the students' experience in the course. The teacher's construction of what is appropriate to the course also frames the teacher's response to the students' responses to the classroom. Given the usual definition of our professional task as increasing students' competence in written language, one would at first imagine that the teacher's imaginative construct would be built on that goal. However, accepting that definition in itself implies cooperation with various perceived social structures, and may become a point of contention for a number of teachers. Further, there may be a great range of ideas as to what comprises competence in written language and how one attains it.

The classroom is always invented, always constructed.

Most curriculum debates center on such issues as whether competence consists of mastery of the code, particular styles of personal communication, familiarity with self-discovery or other inventional procedures, self-conscious use of revision and editing procedures, rhetorical awareness of audience, or familiarity with selected genres. This professional debate carried out in the genres of professional journals, personal credos, and coffee-room discussion itself provides a frame for each teacher's conceptualizing of the classroom. How the teacher then conceives the classroom will influence the genres within which the teacher communicates to the students, the genres of materials and readings the teacher will bring into the classroom, and the written and spoken genres the teacher will elicit and welcome from the students.

The teacher's role in defining the dynamic of the classroom is realized not just through intellectual commitments and conscious choices, but also through the personal history that shapes the personality and competences and attitudes of the person who walks in front of the classroom. The teacher's history of participation in different situations and developing skill in and affinity towards those genres through which that participation is realized, prepares and predisposes the teacher to act in ways that have already proved personally successful. What competences the teacher has most to offer, what interactional skills the teacher can draw on, what habitual persona and behavior and reactional styles the teacher enacts—these all produce classroom environments and events almost beyond the control of conscious thought, although they may all be open to reflection and change.

Then there are the students' definitions of the situation and of themselves within the situation. Their understanding of where they are headed, where they are coming from, and how much they may bring their historical selves and desires into the classroom shape what the students make of the classroom and of the demands and opportunities presented to them by the teacher. Who do they perceive themselves to be and what are their prior experiences of writing? In what specific ways is the learning of writing rewarding or aversive to them? What are their motivations for being in college and how do these motives translate into their writing attitude in the classroom? What futures do they imagine for themselves and what college curricula stand between them and their goals? Where does writing enter into their actual academic and career goals as well as their imagined paths? How do they perceive teachers and or classmates as potential audiences for their communications? What subjects are compelling for them to communicate about and what are alienating? What underlying needs do they have which may be channeled through their writing? Many other psychological, social, economic, industrial, experiential, behavioral, self-presentational, and even spiritual issues enter into what these complex individuals bring with them into the classroom, what they expect of writing, and how they respond to the curious communicative world the classroom offers them. From the perspective of genre, the students' histories provide the genres that they carry with them into the classroom, their perception of how those forms of communicative participation may or may not be revealed in the classroom and with what encoding and transformation, and how they respond to the generic expectations the teacher builds into the dynamics of the classroom.

It is within the students, of course, that the learning occurs, but it is within the teacher, who sits at the juncture of forces above and below and sideways, that the learning situations are framed. It is in the intersection of all the forces that the classroom occurs. Teachers may try to simplify radically the forces through one or another pedagogical theory or commitment, very often some formal textualized reduction, requiring student enactment of well-defined genres, clearly distinct from the genres that come from outside the classroom. Students will often play along with reductionist strategies of classroom organization because of their own priorities and habits in dealing with bureaucratic institutions. Some simply want to get along institutionally and have learned how. Others perceive that learning grammar or spelling or the five-paragraph essay will serve them well. Others, however, may get lost because the reduction eliminates some important element that might link them more closely into the dynamics of written communication. In some cases formal textualized reduction is a useful and valid and successful thing to do.

On the other hand, teachers may attempt to bring a wider array of forces to play, even though every class is necessarily a reduction—an elimination of unrealized alternatives and underlying dynamics not attended to. Teachers can attempt to let in more of the students' past, future, current reality, or imaginative and emotional privacies. Teachers can look more to institutional and social forms that surround the students' lives and in which they participate; classroom work may be built around the genres of the workplace, journalism, the media, or political participation. Teachers may make much of the dyadic relationship between teacher/student, author/audience, master/apprentice, calling upon both the students' prior experience and interior life; intimate genres of journal, dialogue, personal narrative, and contemplation are given prominence. Or the teacher may constitute the entire class as a sociocommunitive microcosm, perhaps relying on genres of argument, suggesting either seminar room or public debate. Or the teacher may seek to place the students in direct contact with larger networks of communication, writing articles for the local newspaper, proposals for the reformation of campus life, or reports for their current employers.

Since writing is no single thing, but is the textual realization of a wide range of human interactions, one cannot say a priori that any particular path is the one proper path to writing, or that any particular genre ought to be practiced in the writing class. Writing will occur in a great variety of situations. The teacher has wide authority to attempt to select and rearrange the various forces around the classroom to create the character of the particular forum that the class will become, but then the classroom becomes the result of the forces that come to play within the forum. Thus the determination of how to teach writing is a matter of social-ethical choice, but the actual events of the classroom and the learning are dynamic products of interaction beyond any individual's control.

As I mentally review the many writing courses I have taught, the framework I have just proposed helps me make sense of the eclecticism which not   15 only makes every class session a heterogeneous experience, but accounts for the great differences in the ways in which I have approached one course or group of students versus another course or group. Through a seat-of-the-pants estimate of the needs and possibilities and goals of each circumstance, I have located each course differently, enacting my teaching in different genres, bringing in different genres for student consideration, and presenting through assignment genres, differing communicative opportunities and challenges for students to realize their presence in the classroom forum. Within the complex multidimensional matrix of writing, I have tried to find different placements for the classroom, so that the unfolding drama of each term will take us all in the classroom to places we are satisfied with. Each term is a strange interactional journey, which my choices may frame—with bad choices leading to sterile landscapes and more fortunate choices tapping into important and vital communicative dynamics for this class at this time. But once the dynamics begin to unfold, the best I can do is watch where they are taking us, so that I can improvise most appropriately and creatively to allow these dynamics to fulfill themselves. Only then will the deepest and most useful practice of writing emerge.

Working with the Text

1. The term *genre* is key to Charles Bazerman's analysis of the writing classroom. In a brief essay, analyze how Bazerman uses the notion of genre to answer the question, "Where is the classroom?" In what ways is the classroom recurrent as a situation? What typified actions result from that recurrent situation? How are those actions influenced by the histories of classroom writing that teachers and students bring with them? In what ways is the title that Bazerman chose for the essay a tip-off that the classroom is not just one physical spot?

2. Within Bazerman's framework, the teacher "sits at the juncture" of the forces that determine the "learning situations" for students (par. 12). Within this framework, students themselves bring many of those forces into play. Write an essay in which you use Bazerman's framework to explore what he would consider to be a productive relationship between student and teacher. How is this relationship affected by the ways in which you as a student sit at the juncture of different forces, including not only the teacher but also your parents, the institution, and the world of work beyond the university?

3. Institutional or departmental forces that influence the structure of a writing course are often invisible to students. In a brief essay, reflect on the institutional/departmental forces that are beyond a teacher's control. Study those forces, as noted by Bazerman, and, from your own experience, consider what effect they might have on the shape and nature of the course.

From Text to Field

1. Select any one of the forces noted by Bazerman, and write a brief essay in which you imagine in greater detail the effect it might have on the course and classroom teaching.

2. Starting with the sentence "Then there are the students' definitions of the situation and of themselves within the situation" (par. 11), Bazerman devotes an extensive paragraph to the factors students contribute to the shaping of a writing course. Based on the statements and questions in this paragraph—up to the sentence that ends, "how they respond to the curious communicative world the classroom offers them"—write a personal essay in which you provide a profile of yourself as a writing student.

3. In his discussion of the forces students bring with them, Bazerman notes, "From the perspective of genre, the students' histories provide the genres that they carry with them into the classroom . . ." (par. 11). In an essay, identify the genres you carry into the classroom and analyze how those genres influence your expectations for a writing course. What elements from your histories in other classrooms—assignments, kinds of writing produced, approaches to learning, the relationships among students and teacher—do you expect to find in the writing classroom? What genres of writing do you bring from your personal life? How do they affect how you respond to the genres required in a classroom? What genres do you expect to be required of you in the workplace after college, and how do those expectations shape what you are looking for in a writing course?

4. In the paragraph that begins, "On the other hand, teachers may attempt to bring a wider array of forces to play" (par. 13), Bazerman suggests the range of choices left to the teacher in structuring a writing course. Using this paragraph as a prompt, construct your ideal writing course. Explain the reasoning behind your choices.

5. Based on the syllabus, your knowledge of your college's or university's writing requirement, and your experience in the classroom so far, write an essay in which you analyze your writing course. What specific forces have shaped which elements of the course? What choices has the teacher made, and why? What constraints must the teacher work with?

6. Bazerman's essay is written for other teachers. Write a companion piece addressed to other students just entering the university that translates Bazerman's argument into terms that will help them understand and enter into the undergraduate classroom.

INTO THE FIELD: Options for Writing Projects

1. What's in a Syllabus?

Sharon Rubin regards the course syllabus as an important vehicle for conveying the substance of the course to students. A number of the authors in Chapter 2, in particular Charles Bazerman, discuss the wide range of values and perspectives that teachers bring into the university classroom. To explore what a syllabus might be able to tell you about the values and perspectives of a course, write an analysis based on one of the following options.

- Choose a particular syllabus, or a set of syllabi, from your own or other recent university courses. Imagine you are a researcher from another planet who has stumbled upon this syllabus. Develop a description of this alien academic culture based on your interpretation of the syllabus. What inferences can you make about what is taught and why? How does a syllabus construct not just the course but also an image of its students? How does a syllabus position a student with respect to the course material, the professor, and peers?
- Identify a course that is taught by different professors within the same department or is shared and taught by different departments. Assuming that they do not use one required generic syllabus, contrast how the course is taught on the basis of the syllabus produced by each professor. What can you infer about the values and perspectives of each teacher? How does each teacher regard students and the learning process?
- Through a department secretary or a professor who has been in the department for a number of years, find a syllabus or syllabi from earlier decades. For example, for an American history or introduction to psychology course, compare syllabi from the 1950s, the 1970s, and today. What texts and other materials were included? What modes of learning—such as lectures, discussion, research papers, field projects—were being used? What were the primary texts? What were the secondary, critical texts? How was learning tested and evaluated? Based on the evidence, what can you infer about trends in interpretation or theory and/or in attitudes toward teaching?

2. Angels on a Pin

The fact that Alexander Calandra's barometer story has been so widely circulated for several decades indicates that his critique of teaching continues to strike an important chord. To understand Calandra's critique more fully, do some detective work, keeping in mind that he won a prestigious teaching award from the American Association of Physics Teachers. Research the teaching methods mentioned in the final paragraph of "Angels on a Pin"—the "scientific method," the "new mathematics," and scholasticism. Find out more about the medieval argument over how many angels could stand on the head of a pin. What educational philosophies might lie behind Calandra's dislike of "pedantry"? What do these external sources add to your understanding of Calandra's critique of teaching? What approach does he advocate instead? As part of your analysis, you might consider why the final paragraph was added to the version published for a more general audience.

3. Technology and the Teaching of Science

Alexander Calandra's critique of science education was made just as the space race of the 1960s was heating up, a time when technologies such as the computer and the Internet had yet to have an impact on the classroom. Given the growing use of new technologies in science education, such as computer simulations and interactive computer software, does Calandra's critique of science education still hold? Draw on your own experience in college science classes or in science classes in senior high school. One option for this project would be to write an update of Calandra's essay for the new millennium. Another option would be to explore what developments have occurred in science education in the last few years and to consider whether they would meet with Calandra's approval.

4. The General-Education Curriculum

Gerald Graff complains that in the typical undergraduate curriculum, courses have little connection to one another. In other words, the college curriculum is often an à la carte menu or a cafeteria. The criticism might apply most directly to the set of general education requirements that most colleges and universities expect students to fulfill during their first years of higher education. Familiarize yourself with the "gen.-ed." requirements on your campus, and with documents (catalogs, Web sites, advisement materials) that might explain or justify those requirements. Write an essay in which you identify and explore the educational assumptions and philosophy that might lie behind those requirements. Ask your instructor or advisor if the general-education requirements have changed on your campus during the last several decades. If so, what controversies or shifts in educational philosophy might have prompted the change? Likewise, ask whether your campus is currently rethinking its requirements. If so, what problems or dissatisfactions seem to be motivating the discussion, and what educational vision lies behind any proposed changes?

5. Curricular Linkages

In an effort to forge connections between otherwise discrete courses and educational experiences, many colleges and universities have instituted programs that seek to build links between both courses and the students who take them. Explore what programs your campus has in place, choose one, and evaluate its effectiveness in creating more cohesion both in the curriculum and in students' educational experience.

Here are just some of the kinds of programs that might be present on your campus. You may be able to uncover interesting programs not mentioned that also try to create linkages between otherwise separate course experiences.

- programs that link a set of courses or a group of students together so that a group of students take courses together
- residential academic programs, which offer courses in or through the dorms in ways that connect academics with residential life
- honors programs that might offer a curricular program and a sense of community that might link students' efforts in various courses
- bridge programs that seek to help minority or first-generation students adjust to what might be an unfamiliar academic culture
- programs that ask all entering students to read the same book over the summer, which might then inform discussion in a variety of classes
- freshman seminars that offer small-class experiences, often on interdisciplinary topics

6. Ebonics and Students' Right to Their Own Language

In her essay, bell hooks refers to the thwarted "longing to speak in tongues other than standard English" as "repression," repression that is "political." Her argument brings the past into the present. Today, the politics of language is a critical issue in the American educational system, from elementary schools through undergraduate and graduate education. Two professional organizations have taken strong stances on this issue, the National Council of Teachers of English (NCTE) and the Conference on College Composition and Communication (CCCC). Check the following Web sites to review their positions:

- "Statement on Ebonics," NCTE Positions and Guidelines, http://www.ncte .org/about/over/positions/level/gen/107644.htm
- "Students' Right to Their Own Language," CCCC Position Statements, http://www.ncte.org/about/over/positions/category/div/114918.htm

Drawing on these two position statements, choose one of the following projects.

- Based on your own background or research into an Ebonics or a bilingual program you identify, describe a program that successfully embodies the principles of the CCCC and the NCTE. Conversely, describe a program that falls short of those principles. As part of your description, analyze how the elements of the program work. What are the results for students? What is the perspective of the teachers and the administration? How does the public view the program?

OG Publication Data

Serial Number of Application

Filing Date

Applicant

Reproduction of Mark

Goods for which Mark was Applied for

JANUARY 7, 1997   U.S. PATENT AND TRADEMARK OFFICE   TM 25

CLASS 9—ELECTRICAL AND SCIENTIFIC APPARATUS
   FOR COMPUTER SOFTWARE FOR DELIVERING INFORMATION OVER NETWORKS BETWEEN SUBSCRIBER'S AND PUBLISHERS (U.S. CLS. 21, 23, 26, 36 AND 38). FIRST USE 4-11-1996; IN COMMERCE 4-11-1996.

CLASS 42—MISCELLANEOUS SERVICES
   FOR PROVIDING INFORMATION IN A WIDE VARIETY OF FIELDS VIA A GLOBAL COMPUTER INFORMATION NETWORK (U.S. CLS. 100 AND 101). FIRST USE 4-11-1996; IN COMMERCE 4-11-1996.

———

SN 75-095,046. MISSION CONTROL, CHICAGO, IL. FILED 4-26-1996.

CLASS 18—LEATHER GOODS
   FOR FANNY PACKS (U.S. CLS. 1, 2, 3, 22 AND 41). FIRST USE 8-0-1995; IN COMMERCE 8-0-1995.

CLASS 28—TOYS AND SPORTING GOODS
   FOR PLUSH TOYS (U.S. CLS. 22, 23, 38 AND 50). FIRST USE 5-0-1994; IN COMMERCE 5-0-1994.

———

SN 75-096,830. BC INTERNATIONAL COSMETIC & IMAGE SERVICES, INC., WILMINGTON, DE. FILED 4-30-1996.

ALL CLEAR

CLASS 3—COSMETICS AND CLEANING PREPARATIONS
   FOR SKIN CLEANSER, SKIN TONER, SKIN MOISTURIZER AND FACIAL SCRUB (U.S. CLS. 1, 4, 6, 50, 51 AND 52).

CLASS 5—PHARMACEUTICALS
   FOR ACNE CREAM AND ACNE CLEANSER (U.S. CLS. 6, 18, 44, 46, 51 AND 52).

SN 75-098,277. FONG & MALLETT, SANTA CRUZ, CA. FILED 5-3-1996.

ZÏXÏ

CLASS 14—JEWELRY
   FOR JEWELRY (U.S. CLS. 2, 27, 28 AND 50). FIRST USE 2-15-1995; IN COMMERCE 6-15-1995.

CLASS 20—FURNITURE AND ARTICLES NOT OTHERWISE CLASSIFIED
   FOR PICTURE FRAMES AND FURNITURE (U.S. CLS. 2, 13, 22, 25, 32 AND 50). FIRST USE 2-15-1995; IN COMMERCE 6-15-1995.

———

SN 75-099,407. CONWAY, PERVIS ORVIN, WESTCHESTER, IL. FILED 5-6-1996.

CLASS 25—CLOTHING
   FOR CLOTHING, NAMELY, SWEATSHIRTS, SWEATPANTS, T-SHIRTS, TROUSERS, BLOUSES, SWEATERS, SHORTS, COATS, CAPS, SHOES AND SOCKS (U.S. CLS. 22 AND 39).

CLASS 28—TOYS AND SPORTING GOODS
   FOR PROTECTIVE BODY GEAR FOR INLINE SKATERS, NAMELY, KNEE PADS, ELBOW PADS, WRIST SUPPORTS, PROTECTIVE GLOVES; ILLUMINATED IN-LINE SKATE WHEELS, ROLLERSKATE BOOTS, AND HOCKEY STICKS (U.S. CLS. 22, 23, 38 AND 50).

———

SN 75-100,175. TEXAS UTILITIES ELECTRIC COMPANY, DALLAS, TX. FILED 5-7-1996.

TU ELECTRIC

NO CLAIM IS MADE TO THE EXCLUSIVE RIGHT TO USE "ELECTRIC", APART FROM THE MARK AS SHOWN.

EXHIBIT 4–6
Official Gazette

- The NCTE "Statement on Ebonics" notes that "[n]ews media reports and commentaries regarding the recent Ebonics controversy have been, for the most part, incomplete, uninformed, and in some cases, purposefully distorted." Identify reports and commentaries in the mass media that reflect negatively on the use of Ebonics in the public school system. Compare the media reports to the analysis you find through professional organizations such as NCTE or CCCC. If possible, interview an expert on Ebonics or on bilingual education. What are the differences between the perspectives of the media and the language and education professionals? How do you account for those differences?

- As you think through the position statements, note your own questions about the uses of languages other than "standard English" in educational programs. Pursue answers to your key questions through research or interviews. Consider your own experience. On the basis of your reading of the professional position statements as well as your research and experience, write a position statement or a persuasive essay in which you argue for or against the use of languages other than "standard English." As an alternative writing project, develop your own recommendations for how those languages can be most effectively used in educational programs.

7. Classroom Spaces

This project asks you to consider classrooms closely, in very concrete terms. Choose a classroom in which you have a course, or several classrooms in which you have courses from different disciplines. Write a report in which you attend closely to the connection between classroom spaces and teaching.

Here are some questions to get you started: How is the classroom designed? How are the seats located, and what kind of interaction or rearrangement do the seats permit? How is "power" situated in the classroom? What are the material conditions of the classroom (blackboard, AV equipment, computer and Internet access), and how are they employed (or not employed)?

Using these questions as a point of departure, what does a particular classroom space imply about the teaching and learning that occurs there? What role, if any, does technology have in that classroom space, and in what ways does it support (or interfere with) the teaching and learning that occurs in that space? How would you reinvent the classroom space to better suit the objectives of the course? How might a classroom space reflect the particular goals or culture of a discipline? If your campus has remodeled or renovated classrooms recently, what advances or changes do you see over older or more traditional classrooms? Apart from newer chairs and better lighting, has there really been much change from older classrooms?

8. Writing the Writing Classroom

This project asks you to develop a set of "field notes" that you can then use to analyze how your writing classroom is constructed (both physically and through discourse). A good place to start is to attend closely to what happens in your writing class. How is space deployed and used? How do you interact with your teacher and with your peers? How is writing produced and consumed in and for the classroom? Based on these and a host of similar questions, develop an essay that "writes" the writing classroom. How and why does the writing classroom differ from other classrooms? How does the use of physical space, texts, conversation, and personal interaction contribute to that difference? Might there be the occasional incongruity or contradiction between the goals for the course and its institutional setting?

9. The Alternative Classroom

Although traditional classrooms continue to exert enormous influence on how you and others think of your college education, a number of alternatives to and extensions of that traditional classroom have now come into play. This project encourages you to explore an alternative classroom, if you have experienced one, and to consider what influence the traditional and the alternative classroom might have on each other. Does the traditional classroom continue to influence even the most alternative classes? And in what ways might an alternative classroom initiate new ways of thinking about traditional classrooms? In what ways do "traditional" and "alternative" classrooms presuppose one another?

The following is a modest and very incomplete list of alternative classroom experiences that you might find on your own campus.

- online classes
- distance education courses (televised)
- hybrid classes (some time spent online, some time spent in traditional classrooms)
- wired classrooms that extend the reach and resources of the traditional blackboard-and-chalk classroom
- fieldwork classes
- studio classes
- service-learning classes that use service as a means for reflection and learning

To this list one might also wish to add more traditional alternatives to the regular classroom, such as "recitation sections" attached to large lecture courses and "labs" that often accompany courses in the sciences.

Choose one such alternative classroom with which you are familiar, and explore the continuing shadow that is cast by traditional classrooms. Likewise, consider the many ways in which both teacher and learner have to refashion themselves in these new classroom environments. What might make these new environments more interesting, fun, challenging, or frustrating?

10. Discourse in the Classroom

When we think about how classrooms are constructed, we might first think of bricks and mortar, seats and blackboards. But classrooms are also constructed, perhaps most fundamentally constructed, through language. This project has you look at classrooms through the lens of discourse.

Your materials for this project can be found in the very concrete (and sometimes seemingly ordinary) uses of language in a particular classroom. It could be your very own writing classroom or any classes you are currently taking. Think about the texts you read and the texts you write. Think about the conversations and discussions you have in class and about what kind of turn taking occurs in those discussions. Think about who holds the floor and who might be silent (or silenced). What literacy practices and behaviors are in play—everything from the use of overheads and PowerPoint to your own note taking. In other words, think about the class period itself as a kind of text.

Based on your fieldwork over several class periods, write an essay about discourse in the classroom. You'll want to look beyond the immediate and obvious use of language (what is said about the subject matter) and focus on how things are said and how discourse is used in the classroom. In what ways is the classroom, and the course itself, a function of its language? What connection might there be between that language and your own or between that language and the language of a particular discipline or area of study? Are there instances in which the discourse of the classroom presents contradictions? In what ways is your college education not just about information on certain academic subjects but also about how to use language in the academy?

WRITING THE UNIVERSITY

As you enter the university and settle into the work of the academic term, it comes as little surprise that there is plenty of writing done there. You are writing several essays or term papers for some of your courses and surely more in a writing course. Even those courses that do not require much writing in a formal sense will still expect you to write for exams and short assignments, to take notes, and to use writing in a wide range of what are called literacy practices or literate behaviors. So pervasive is writing at the university that we often use it as a measure to describe our lives: I have three papers to write in the next two weeks.

Faculty, as you might imagine, also find their lives saturated with writing. Apart from research activities that find their way into books and articles, administrative activities of one kind or another are carried out through e-mail, memos, and reports. So central is writing to a faculty member's life that the phrase "publish or perish" has become cliché. Yet we might tweak that phrase just a bit. It need not refer exclusively to a faculty member's fate come time for tenure and promotion. It also reminds us that, unless committed to the page, the best of ideas, about research or about the college or university itself, can also disappear. Writing does more than happen at a college or university. Writing is a way of sustaining the institution itself.

The title for this unit hints at this central role for writing. Every day, faculty and, yes, students themselves are writing the university. True, the influence of any one piece of writing cannot be detected, and change at the university often seems glacial in its pace. But through our words, we create—and change—the place.

Because writing, both as process and as product, shapes the essential nature of a college or university, it is hardly surprising that words provide the gate of entry to this community. As you enter the classroom, you surely are trying to write and speak in ways that identify you as a college student. Writing marks us—indicating whether we have become the experts we hope to be or the novices that all of us, in one respect or another, will surely remain. How and what we read, and how we use language in our teaching and learning, also speak volumes about how we conceive of our college or university experience. Far from being the solid, ivy-covered entities we might assume they are, colleges and universities are in some sense continually up for grabs. In our writing and reading, we always return to the question "What are universities for?"

The six readings in this unit help us reflect on the many different ways that we write the university. No immutable text with a fixed meaning, the university is always being inscribed, just as it is being read in different ways.

C. H. Knoblauch reminds us that *literacy* is a complex term, implying much more than a set of objective skills. Indeed, the various meanings of the term are driven by the ideological dispositions of those who advocate one kind of literacy or another.

David Bartholomae writes of the challenges of the first-year college student, for whom writing and language necessarily become a way of demonstrating—or carrying off the bluff—that you do in fact fit in.

Joseph Williams and Gregory G. Colomb reflect on the differences between novice and expert writing. How do we move from one to the other? They take issue with the usual metaphor, often described as an upward curve of "growth," and suggest as an alternative that we think in terms of a different metaphor—that of the outsider entering a new community.

Katha Pollitt reframes the debate about which books should be required reading and thus part of the "canon" of great works that are thought to define our education. Instead of asking "what books we want others to read," she prefers to ask "why we read books ourselves."

Distrustful of an education that simply deposits or banks information in our heads, Paulo Freire proposes a different sort of educational process, a problem-posing process, and along with it a different relationship between teacher and student.

Behind these readings lies that tough but inevitable question, "What are universities for?" Louis Menand tackles that question head-on, prompting us to explore the relationship between universities and our larger society.

Reflecting on Prior Knowledge

1. The writing and reading you did in high school and the writing and reading you now do in college carry with them certain assumptions about why literacy is important. What values or purposes lie behind your literate activities?

2. In a journal entry, recall a time when you were new to an activity but were not entirely sure of its rules or processes. How did you feel, and how did you try to learn that activity and fit in with those who did it often?

3. All of us are, to some degree or another, experts at some things and sheer novices at others. Reflect on what kind of expertise does or doesn't transfer

from one activity or domain to another. Working with a partner, draw up a list of characteristics that distinguish experts from novices.

4. The terms *required* and *enjoyable* seem to be poles apart when it comes to the books we read. In a journal entry, reflect on why this is the case. What are the agendas or reasons that distinguish the two kinds of reading? When and why might you have enjoyed required reading?

5. Although it may be tempting to assume that all teachers "dispense" knowledge that students then "store," surely you have had one or two teachers who broke that stereotype. Why was your relationship different with that teacher, and how did teaching and learning take place?

6. Working in a group, develop a list of why you and others have decided to go to college. Are there items on that list that might become more or less important under certain conditions or to various groups of people? Would this be the same list that your parents or someone of their generation might have drawn up?

Literacy and the Politics of Education

C. H. Knoblauch

Students are often not aware that their education has been shaped by heated debates over the definition of *literacy*. What does it mean to be literate? How do we identify and teach those who are considered to be illiterate? Since C. H. Knoblauch published "Literacy and the Politics of Education" in 1990, in a collection of papers from the Modern Language Association's 1988 Right to Literacy Conference, educators as well as those being educated have increasingly challenged the politics of literacy in terms of the questions Knoblauch raised. With any given approach to literacy, whose values, interests, position, or power will be preserved or promoted, and at whose expense?

A frequent contributor to academic journals and conferences, Knoblauch has taught at Brown University, Columbia University, New York University, and the State University of New York at Albany. His books include *Functional Writing* (1978), *The Process of Writing: Discovery and Control* (1982) with A. D. Van Nostrand, and *Critical Teaching and the Idea of Literacy* (1993) with Lil Brannon. Knoblauch and Brannon are most widely known for *Rhetorical Traditions and the Teaching of Writing* (1984), which served for many as a standard text for graduate studies in the teaching of writing.

Literacy is one of those mischievous concepts, like virtuousness and craftsmanship, that appear to denote capacities but that actually convey value judgments. It is rightly viewed, Linda Brodkey has noted, "as a social trope" and its sundry definitions "as cultural Rorschachs" (47). The labels *literate* and *illiterate* almost always imply more than a degree or deficiency of skill. They are, grossly or subtly, sociocultural judgments laden with approbation, disapproval, or pity about the character and place, the worthiness and prospects, of persons and groups. A revealing exercise would be to catalog the definitions of literacy that lie explicit or implicit in the pages of this collection, definitions that motivate judgments, political no less than scholarly, about which people belong in literate and illiterate categories; the numbers in each group; why and in what ways literacy is important; what should be done for or about those who are not literate or are less literate than others; and who has the power to say so. It would be quickly apparent that there is no uniformity of view, since the values that surround reading and writing abilities differ from argument to argument. Instead, there are competing views, responsive to the agendas of those who characterize the ideal. Invariably, definitions of literacy are also rationalizations of its importance. Furthermore, they are invariably offered by the literate, constituting, therefore, implicit rationalizations of the importance of literate people, who are powerful (the reasoning goes) because they are literate and, as such, deserving of power.

The concept of literacy is embedded, then, in the ideological dispositions of those who use the concept, those who profit from it, and those who have the standing and motivation to enforce it as a social requirement. It is obviously not a cultural value in all times and places; when Sequoya brought his syllabic writing system to the Cherokee, their first inclination was to put him to death for dabbling in an evil magic. The majority of the world's languages have lacked alphabets, though they have nonetheless articulated rich oral traditions in societies that have also produced many other varieties of cultural achievement. To be sure, there is ready agreement, at least among the literate, about the necessity of literacy in the so-called modern world; this agreement is reinforced by explanations that typically imply a more developed mode of existence among literate people. I. J. Gelb has written, for instance: "As language distinguishes man from animal, so writing distinguishes civilized man from barbarian," going on to point out that "an illiterate person cannot expect to participate successfully in human progress, and what is true of individuals is also true of any group of individuals, social strata, or ethnic units" (221–22). This argument offers a common and pernicious half-truth, representing the importance of literacy, which is unquestionable, in absolutist and ethnocentric terms.

However, if literacy today is perceived as a compelling value, the reason lies not in such self-interested justifications but in its continuing association with forms of social reality that depend on its primacy. During the Middle Ages, clerks were trained to read and write so that they could keep accounts for landowners, merchants, and government officials. Bureaucratic documentation was not conceived so that people could acquire literacy. Christian missionaries in nineteenth-century Africa spread literacy so that people could read the Bible; they did not teach the Bible so that the illiterate could become readers and writers. There is no question that literacy is necessary to survival and success in the contemporary world—a world where the literate claim authority to set the terms of survival and success, a world that reading and writing abilities have significantly shaped in the first place. But it is important to regard that necessity in the context of political conditions that account for it, or else we sacrifice the humanizing understanding that life can be otherwise than the way we happen to know it and that people who are measured positively by the yardstick of literacy enjoy their privileges because of their power to choose and apply that instrument on their own behalf, not because of their point of development or other innate worthiness. Possessing that understanding, educators in particular but other citizens as well may advance their agendas for literacy with somewhat less likelihood of being blinded by the light of their own benevolence to the imperial designs that may lurk in the midst of their compassion.

In the United States today, several arguments about the nature and importance of literacy vie for power in political and educational life. Sketching the more popular arguments may remind us of the extent to which definitions of the concept incorporate the social agendas of the definers, serving the needs of the nonliterate only through the mediation of someone's vision of the way the world should be. Literacy never stands alone in these perspectives as a neutral denoting of skills; it is always literacy for something—for professional competence in a technological world, for civic responsibility and the preservation of heritage, for personal growth and self-fulfillment, for social and political change. The struggle of any one definition to dominate the others entails no merely casual or arbitrary choice of values, nor does it allow for a conflating of alternatives in some grand compromise or list of cumulative benefits. At stake are fundamentally different perceptions of social reality; the nature of language and discourse; the importance of culture, history, and tradition; the functions of schools, as well as other commitments, few of which are regarded as negotiable. At the same time, since no definition achieves transcendent authority, their dialectical interaction offers a context of choices within which continually changing educational and other social policies find their justification. The process of choosing is visible every day, for better and worse, in legislative assemblies, television talk shows, newspaper editorials, and classrooms throughout the country.

The most familiar literacy argument comes from the functionalist perspective, with its appealingly pragmatic emphasis on readying people for the necessities of daily life—writing checks, reading sets of instructions— as well as for the professional tasks of a complex technological society. Language abilities in this view are often represented by the metaphors of information theory: Language is a code that enables the sending of messages and the processing of information. The concern of a functionalist perspective is the efficient transmission of useful messages in a value-neutral medium. Basic-skill and technical-writing programs in schools, many on-the-job training programs in business and industry, and the training programs of the United States military—all typically find their rationalization in the argument for functional literacy, in each case presuming that the ultimate value of language lies in its utilitarian capacity to pass information back and forth for economic or other material gain.

The functionalist argument has the advantage of tying literacy to concrete needs, appearing to promise socioeconomic benefit to anyone who can achieve the appropriate minimal competency. But it has a more hidden advantage as well, at least from the standpoint of those whose literacy is more than minimal: It safeguards the socioeconomic status quo. Whatever the rhetoric of its advocates concerning the "self-determined objectives" (Hunter and Harman 7) of people seeking to acquire skills, functionalism serves the world as it is, inviting outsiders to enter that world on the terms of its insiders by fitting themselves to roles that they are superficially free to choose but that have been prepared as a range of acceptable alternatives.

Literacy is one of those mischievous concepts that appear to denote capacities but that actually convey value judgments.

Soldiers will know how to repair an MX missile by reading the field manual but will not question the use of such weapons because of their reading of anti-militarist philosophers; clerks will be able to fill out and file their order forms but will not therefore be qualified for positions in higher management. Functionalist arguments presume that a given social order is right simply because it exists, and their advocates are content to recommend the training of persons to take narrowly beneficial places in that society. The rhetoric of technological progressivism is often leavened with a mixture of fear and patriotism (as in *A Nation at Risk*) in order to defend a social program that maintains managerial classes—whose members are always more than just functionally literate—in their customary places while outfitting workers with the minimal reading and writing skills needed for usefulness to the modern information economy.

Cultural literacy offers another common argument about the importance of reading and writing, one frequently mounted by traditionalist educators but sustained in populist versions as well, especially among people who feel insecure about their own standing and their future prospects when confronted by the volatile mix of ethnic heritages and socioeconomic interests that make up contemporary American life. The argument for cultural literacy moves beyond a mechanist conception of basic skills and toward an affirmation of supposedly stable and timeless cultural values inscribed in the verbal

TTAB within thirty days of publication of the mark in the *Official Gazette*. By law, extensions of up to 120 days from the date of publication may be granted; however, if both parties agree, additional extensions are usually granted by the PTO in order to allow the parties to work out their difficulties. Once again, docketing of dates is critical. A law firm not only should docket the date of its own clients' applications (so it can confirm that no one has opposed the clients' marks and, thus, the marks will proceed to registration), but also should review the *Official Gazette* to search for marks that may conflict with clients' marks and then notify the clients so they can have the opportunity to oppose other applications.

Because thousands of marks are published in the *Official Gazette* each week, it is virtually impossible for a firm with an active trademark practice to devote the effort needed to reading each week's *Official Gazette*. Most law firms suggest their clients authorize one of the professional search firms (identified in Chapter 3) to conduct a **watch service** to review the *Official Gazette* and notify the firm of potential conflicts on a timely basis so the law firm can then inform the client that a conflicting mark may need to be opposed. Watch services can also monitor all applications filed at the PTO after a client's application so immediate action can be taken against a conflicting mark. The cost of the watch services is approximately $300 per year per mark, although costs can be higher if several international classes need to be watched or if the mark includes unique design features. The five most recent issues of the *Official Gazette* are available online at the PTO's web site.

Intent-to-Use Applications and Statements of Use

If the application was based upon the applicant's actual use of the mark in commerce, the **actual use application** will proceed to registration after the publication period (assuming a notice of opposition is not filed). If the application was based on the applicant's intent to use the mark in commerce in the future, the mark cannot proceed to registration until actual use has been shown.

Thus, for intent-to-use (ITU) applications, after publication (and no opposition), the PTO will issue a **Notice of Allowance,** notifying the applicant that the ITU application has been allowed, and granting the applicant six months (which may be extended for five additional six-month periods, up to a total of three years) within which to commence use of the mark and submit a statement and specimen verifying such use and the dates of first use. For example, if an ITU application has been published for opposition (with no one filing an opposition), and a notice of allowance is issued on June 1, 2003, the applicant will have until December 1, 2003, to file its **Statement of Use** (together with a specimen). If use is not commenced by December 1, 2003, the applicant may request an additional six-month period by alleging that it continues to have a bona fide intent to use the mark. Additional six-month extensions may be granted if the applicant alleges its continued good faith intent to use the mark and shows good cause for the extension, namely, ongoing efforts to make use of the mark in commerce, such as stating the additional time is needed to conduct market research and promotional activities.

Note that the first request for extension of time is granted automatically; subsequent extensions must show good cause why the extension should be granted. If no statement of use is submitted by June 1, 2006, the application will be deemed abandoned (unless the delay was unintentional). Filing fees of $100 are required for a statement of use and $150 for each request for extension of time to file a statement of use for each class of goods/services memory—in particular, the canonical literature of Western European society. Its reasoning is that true literacy entails more than technical proficiency, a minimal ability to make one's way in the world; that literacy also includes an awareness of cultural heritage, a capacity for higher-order thinking, even some aesthetic discernment—faculties not automatically available to the encoders and decoders of the functionalist perspective. Language is no mere tool in this view but is, rather, a repository of cultural values and to that extent a source of social cohesion. To guard the vitality of the language, the advocates of cultural literacy say, citizens must learn to speak and write decorously, as well as functionally, and must also read great books, where the culture is enshrined. In some popular versions of cultural literacy, English is regarded as the only truly American language and is, therefore, the appropriate medium of commerce and government. The economic self-interest that pervades the functionalist perspective frequently gives way here to jingoistic protectionism; cultural literacy advocates presume that the salvation of some set of favored cultural norms or language practices lies necessarily in the marginalizing or even extinction of others.

The argument for cultural literacy often presents itself within a myth of the fall from grace: Language and, by extension, culture once enjoyed an Edenlike existence but are currently degenerating because of internal decay and sundry forces of barbarism. People no longer read, write, or think with the strength of insight of which they were once capable. They no longer remember and, therefore, no longer venerate. The age of high culture has passed; minds and characters have been weakened by television or rock music or the 1960s. The reasons vary, but the message is clear: Unless heritage is protected, the former purity of language reconstituted, the past life of art and philosophy retrieved, we risk imminent cultural decay. However extravagant such predictions appear to unbelievers, there is no mistaking the melancholy energy of contemporary proponents of cultural literacy or, if we are to judge from the recent best-seller lists, the number of solemn citizens— anxious perhaps about recent influxes of Mexicans, Vietnamese, and other aliens—who take their warnings to heart.

Arguments for cultural and functional literacy plainly dominate the American imagination at the moment and for obvious reasons. They articulate the needs, hopes, anxieties, and frustrations of the conservative temper. They reveal in different ways the means of using an ideal of literacy to preserve and advance the world as it is, a world in which the interests of traditionally privileged groups dominate the interests of the traditionally less privileged. Schools reflect such conservatism to the extent that they view themselves as agencies for preserving established institutions and values, not to mention the hierarchical requirements of the American economy. But still other arguments, if not quite so popular, reflect the priorities and the agendas of liberal and even radical ideologies struggling to project their altered visions of social reality, seeking their own power over others under the banner of literacy. The liberal argument, for instance, emphasizes literacy for personal growth, finding voice in the process-writing movement in American high schools or in the various practices of personalized learning. The liberal argument has been successful, up to a point, in schools because it borrows from long-hallowed American myths of expressive freedom and boundless individual opportunity, romantic values to which schools are obliged to pay at least lip service even when otherwise promoting more authoritarian curricula.

The assumption of a literacy-for-personal-growth argument is that language 10 expresses the power of the individual imagination, so that nurturing a person's reading and writing abilities enables the development of that power, thereby promoting the progress of society through the progress of the individual learner. The political agenda behind this liberalism tends to be educational and other social change; its concern for personal learning draws attention to school practices that supposedly thwart the needs of individual students or that disenfranchise some groups of students in the interest of maintaining the values of the status quo. The kinds of change that the personal-growth argument recommends are, on the whole, socially tolerable because they are moderate in character: Let students read enjoyable novels, instead of basal reader selections; let young women and young Hispanics find images of themselves in schoolwork, not just images of white males. Using the rhetoric of moral sincerity, the personal-growth argument speaks compassionately on behalf of the disadvantaged. Meanwhile, it avoids, for the most part, the suggestion of any fundamental restructuring of institutions, believing that the essential generosity and fair-mindedness of American citizens will accommodate some liberalization of outmoded curricula and an improved quality of life for the less privileged as long as fundamental political and economic interests are not jeopardized. Frequently, Americans do hear such appeals, though always in the context of an implicit agreement that nothing important is going to change. Accordingly, advocates of expressive writing, personalized reading programs, whole-language curricula, and open classrooms have been permitted to carry out their educational programs, with politicians and school officials quick to realize the ultimate gain in administrative control that comes from allowing such modest symbols of self-determination to release built-up pressures of dissatisfaction.

A fourth argument, substantially to the left of the personal-growth advocates, is one for what Henry Giroux, among others, calls critical literacy (226). Critical literacy is a radical perspective whose adherents, notably Paulo Freire, have been influential primarily in the third world, especially Latin America. Strongly influenced by Marxist philosophical premises, critical literacy is not a welcome perspective in this country, and it finds voice currently in only a few academic enclaves, where it exists more as a facsimile of oppositional culture than as a practice, and in an even smaller number of community-based literacy projects, which are typically concerned with adult learners. Its agenda is to identify reading and writing abilities with a critical consciousness of the social conditions in which people find themselves, recognizing the extent to which language practices objectify and rationalize these conditions and the extent to which people with authority to name the world dominate others whose voices they have been able to suppress. Literacy, therefore, constitutes a means to power, a way to seek political enfranchisement—not with the naive expectation that merely being literate is sufficient to change the distribution of prerogatives but with the belief that the ability to speak alone enables entrance to the arena in which power is contested. At stake, from this point of view, is, in principle, the eventual reconstituting of the class structure of American life, specifically a change of those capitalist economic practices that assist the dominance of particular groups.

For that reason, if for no other, such a view of literacy will remain suspect as a theoretical enterprise and will be considered dangerous, perhaps to the point of illegality, in proportion to its American adherents' attempts to implement it practically in schools and elsewhere. The scholarly Right has signaled this institutional hostility in aggressive attacks on Jonathan Kozol's *Illiterate America*, the most popular American rendering of critical-literacy arguments, for its supposedly inaccurate statistics about illiteracy and in calculatedly patronizing Kozol's enthusiasm for radical change. Meanwhile, although critical literacy is trendy in some academic circles, those who commend it also draw their wages from the capitalist economy it is designed to challenge. Whether its advocates will take Kozol's risks in bringing so volatile a practice into community schools is open to doubt. Whether something important would change if they did take the risks is also doubtful. Whether, if successful, they would still approve a world in which their own privileges were withheld may be more doubtful still. In any case, one can hardly imagine NCTE° or the MLA,° let alone the Department of Education, formally sanctioning such a fundamental assault on their own institutional perquisites.

Definitions of literacy could be multiplied far beyond these popular arguments. But enumerating others would only belabor my point, which is that no definition tells, with ontological or objective reliability, what literacy is; definitions only tell what some person or group—motivated by political

---

NCTE: National Council of Teachers of English.

MLA: Modern Language Association.

commitments—wants or needs literacy to be. What makes any such perspective powerful is the ability of its adherents to make it invisible or, at least, transparent—a window on the world, revealing simple and stable truths—so that the only problem still needing to be addressed is one of implementation: how best to make the world—other people—conform to that prevailing vision. At the same time, what makes any ideology visible as such and, therefore, properly limited in its power to compel unconscious assent is critical scrutiny, the only safeguard people have if they are to be free of the designs of others. To the extent that literacy advocates of one stripe or another remain unconscious of or too comfortable with those designs, their offerings of skills constitute a form of colonizing, a benign but no less mischievous paternalism that rationalizes the control of others by representing it as a means of liberation. To the extent that the nonliterate allow themselves to be objects of someone else's "kindness," they will find no power in literacy, however it is defined, but only altered terms of dispossession. When, for instance, the memberships of U.S. English and English First, totaling around half a million citizens, argue for compulsory English, they may well intend the enfranchisement of those whose lack of English-language abilities has depressed their economic opportunities. But they also intend the extinction of cultural values inscribed in languages other than their own and held to be worthwhile by people different from themselves. In this or any other position on literacy, its advocates, no less than its intended beneficiaries, need to hear—for all our sakes—a critique of whatever assumptions and beliefs are fueling their passionate benevolence.

Works Cited

Brodkey, Linda. "Tropics of Literacy." *Journal of Education* 168 (1986):47–54.

Commission on Excellence in Education. *A Nation at Risk: The Imperative for Educational Reform.* Washington: GPO, 1983.

Gelb, I. J. *A Study of Writing.* Chicago: U of Chicago P, 1963.

Giroux, Henry A. *Theory and Resistance in Education: A Pedagogy for the Opposition.* South Hadley: Bergin, 1983.

Hunter, Carman St. John, and David Harman. *Adult Literacy in the United States.* New York: McGraw, 1979.

Kozol, Jonathan. *Illiterate America.* New York: Anchor, 1985.

Working with the Text

1. Offer a summary of the four types of literacy that C. H. Knoblauch examines, and place them on a spectrum from most conservative to most liberal. Can you think of a fifth type of literacy? If so, where might it fall on the spectrum you have laid out?

2. According to Knoblauch, all positions on literacy must be examined in order to expose the social and cultural agendas of those who promote them. Among the positions he examines, the liberal and the critical literacy arguments both challenge the status quo by centering on the identity of the student, but they still have competing agendas. To explore the significance of differences in positions on literacy, write a brief essay in which you analyze and compare the liberal and critical literacy agendas. How is *literacy* defined? How might it be achieved? Who would benefit? What, exactly, would the benefit be? Why does Knoblauch consider critical literacy to be more radical and threatening than the liberal idea of literacy for personal growth?

3. The values behind functional and cultural literacy still drive curriculum for both public school and higher education. In a brief essay, respond to Knoblauch's charge that these two approaches to literacy "preserve and advance the world as it is, a world in which the interests of traditionally privileged groups dominate the interests of the traditionally less privileged" (par. 9).

4. In effect, Knoblauch urges anyone who has a stake in literacy—which includes all of us—to enter into "a critique of whatever assumptions and beliefs" are driving any given position on literacy. Choose one literacy argument from the essay or from your own experience as a student. With Knoblauch's argument in mind, write a brief critique of that position. What perspective do you represent? Are you an "advocate" or one of "its intended beneficiaries"? What interests you or concerns you about this position on literacy? What "assumptions and beliefs" do you want to expose or promote, and why?

From Text to Field

1. Although some educational institutions are committed to one approach to literacy, most institutions incorporate more than one into their curriculum. Drawing on Knoblauch's descriptions as well as your own awareness of the objectives of your schools, write an essay in which you describe the position or positions on literacy behind your high school and undergraduate education. Does a particular teacher or teaching technique embody the aims and agendas of that approach to literacy?

2. Students often object to or challenge the approaches to literacy they encounter in school. In an essay, describe the literacy or combination of literacies you want for yourself. What do you want to learn through your formal education? Why? How can the literacy you envision for yourself be promoted or furthered outside of formal education?

3. Knoblauch delineates positions on literacy that in many ways are mutually exclusive. If the values and interests behind different literacies compete to the

extent that Knoblauch suggests, how should educational institutions arrive at a definition of literacy? In an essay, propose a process for deciding. Who would be involved in the process? What steps would be taken? Upon what basis would the final decision be made? What allows most institutions to avoid defining literacy in an explicit way?

Inventing the University

David Bartholomae

In the university classroom, you may feel as if you are expected to sound like an expert when you write. Through years of experience as a writing teacher, David Bartholomae has come to recognize that the missteps of inexperienced writers are the result of their efforts to speak authoritatively in a new and foreign language. As a writer new to the material, you must "invent the university," meaning you must not only make your way into new terminology, but you must also move step by step into unfamiliar, specialized ways of thinking, arguing, and establishing authority. Bartholomae suggests that the heart of the problem—and the challenge for teachers—is that students may not be equipped to imagine and conform to the goals of a reader who is an expert.

As professor and chair of the English department at the University of Pittsburgh, David Bartholomae has written widely on composition theory and instruction. A former chair of the Conference on College Composition and Communication, Bartholomae is currently coeditor of the Pittsburgh Series on Composition, Literacy, and Culture. His collection *Writing on the Margins: Essays on Composition and Teaching* (2005) won the Shaughnessey Award from the Modern Language Association. The essay "Inventing the University" first appeared in *When a Writer Can't Write* (1985), edited by Mike Rose. The excerpt from "Inventing the University" that follows is the first of four sections in that essay.

Education may well be, as of right, the instrument whereby every
individual, in a society like our own, can gain access to any kind of
discourse. But we well know that in its distribution, in what it permits and in what it prevents, it follows the well-trodden battle-lines
of social conflict. Every educational system is a political means of
maintaining or of modifying the appropriation of discourse, with the
knowledge and the powers it carries with it.

— FOUCAULT, *The Discourse on Language*

. . . the text is the form of the social relationships made visible, palpable, material.

— BERNSTEIN, *Codes, Modalities and the
Process of Cultural Reproduction: A Model*

Every time a student sits down to write for us, he has to invent the university
for the occasion—invent the university, that is, or a branch of it, like history
or anthropology or economics or English. The student has to learn to speak
our language, to speak as we do, to try on the peculiar ways of knowing,
selecting, evaluating, reporting, concluding, and arguing that define the discourse of our community. Or perhaps I should say the *various* discourses of
our community, since it is in the nature of a liberal-arts education that a student, after the first year or two, must learn to try on a variety of voices and
interpretive schemes—to write, for example, as a literary critic one day and
as an experimental psychologist the next; to work within fields where the
rules governing the presentation of examples or the development of an argument are both distinct and, even to a professional mysterious.

The student has to appropriate (or be appropriated by) a specialized discourse, and he has to do this as though he were easily and comfortably one
with his audience, as though he were a member of the academy or a historian or an anthropologist or an economist; he has to invent the university by assembling and mimicking its language while finding some compromise between idiosyncracy, a personal history, on the one hand, and
the requirements of convention, the history of a discipline, on the other.
He must learn to speak our language. Or he must dare to speak it or to
carry off the bluff, since speaking and writing will most certainly be
required long before the skill is "learned." And this, understandably, causes
problems.

Let me look quickly at an example. Here is an essay written by a college
freshman.

In the past time I thought that an incident was creative was when I had to
make a clay model of the earth, but not of the classical or your everyday
model of the earth which consists of the two cores, the mantle and the
crust. I thought of these things in a dimension of which it would be

unique, but easy to comprehend. Of course, your materials to work with were basic and limited at the same time, but thought help to put this limit into a right attitude or frame of mind to work with the clay.

In the beginning of the clay model, I had to research and learn the different dimensions of the earth (in magnitude, quantity, state of matter, etc.). After this, I learned how to put this into the clay and come up with something different than any other person in my class at the time. In my opinion, color coordination and shape was the key to my creativity of the clay model of the earth.

Creativity is the venture of the mind at work with the mechanics relay to the limbs from the cranium, which stores and triggers this action. It can be a burst of energy released at a precise time a thought is being transmitted. This can cause a frenzy of the human body, but it depends on the characteristics of the individual and how they can relay the message clearly enough through mechanics of the body to us as an observer. Then we must determine if it is creative or a learned process varied by the individuals thought process. Creativity is indeed a tool which has to exist, or our world will not succeed into the future and progress like it should.

I am continually impressed by the patience and goodwill of our students. This student was writing a placement essay during freshman orientation. (The problem set to him was: "Describe a time when you did something you felt to be creative. Then, on the basis of the incident you have described, go on to draw some general conclusions about 'creativity.'") He knew that university faculty would be reading and evaluating his essay, and so he wrote for them.

In some ways it is a remarkable performance. He is trying on the discourse 5 even though he doesn't have the knowledge that would make the discourse more than a routine, a set of conventional rituals and gestures. And he is doing this, I think, even though he *knows* he doesn't have the knowledge that would make the discourse more than a routine. He defines himself as a researcher working systematically, and not as a kid in a high school class: "I thought of these things in a dimension of . . ."; "I had to research and learn the different dimensions of the earth (in magnitude, quantity, state of matter, etc.)." He moves quickly into a specialized language (his approximation of our jargon) and draws both a general, textbook-like conclusion—"Creativity is the venture of the mind at work . . ."—and a resounding peroration—"Creativity is indeed a tool which has to exist, or our world will not succeed into the future and progress like it should." The writer has even picked up the rhythm of our prose with that last "indeed" and with the qualifications and the parenthetical expressions of the opening paragraphs. And through it all he speaks with an impressive air of authority.

> **Every time a student sits down to write for us, he has to invent the university for the occasion.**

There is an elaborate but, I will argue, a necessary and enabling fiction at work here as the student dramatizes his experience in a "setting"—the setting required by the discourse—where he can speak to us as a companion, a fellow researcher. As I read the essay, there is only one moment when the fiction is broken, when we are addressed differently. The student says, "Of course, your materials to work with were basic and limited at the same time, but thought help to put this limit into a right attitude or frame of mind to work with the clay." At this point, I think, we become students and he the teacher giving us a lesson (as in, "You take your pencil in your right hand and put your paper in front of you"). This is, however, one of the most characteristic slips of basic writers. (I use the term *basic writers* to refer to university students traditionally placed in remedial composition courses.) It is very hard for them to take on the role—the voice, the persona—of an authority whose authority is rooted in scholarship, analysis, or research. They slip, then, into a more immediately available and realizable voice of authority, the voice of a teacher giving a lesson or the voice of a parent lecturing at the dinner table. They offer advice or homilies rather than "academic" conclusions. There is a similar break in the final paragraph, where the conclusion that pushes for a definition ("Creativity is the venture of the mind at work with the mechanics relay to the limbs from the cranium") is replaced by a conclusion that speaks in the voice of an elder ("Creativity is indeed a tool which has to exist, or our world will not succeed into the future and progress like it should").

It is not uncommon, then, to find such breaks in the concluding sections of essays written by basic writers. Here is the concluding section of an essay written by a student about his work as a mechanic. He had been asked to generalize about work after reviewing an on-the-job experience or incident that "stuck in his mind" as somehow significant.

> How could two repairmen miss a leak? Lack of pride? No incentive? Lazy? I don't know.

At this point the writer is in a perfect position to speculate, to move from the problem to an analysis of the problem. Here is how the paragraph continues, however (and notice the change in pronoun reference).

> From this point on, I take *my* time, do it right, and don't let customers get under *your* skin. If they have a complaint, tell them to call your boss and he'll be more than glad to handle it. Most important, worry about yourself, and keep a clear eye on everyone, for there's always someone trying to take advantage of you, anytime and anyplace. (Emphasis added)

We get neither a technical discussion nor an "academic" discussion but a Lesson on Life.[1] This is the language he uses to address the general question, "How could two repairmen miss a leak?" The other brand of conclusion, the more academic one, would have required him to speak of his experience in covered by the application. (See Appendix D, Form 2, Statement of Use, and Form 3, Request for Additional Extension of Time to File Statement of Use.)

The statement of use verifies that the mark is in use in commerce, specifies the date of first use, and is accompanied by a specimen (label, packaging, and so forth for goods or promotional material for services) showing actual use of the mark. If the application was a combined application (for example, for pens in I.C. 16 and clothing in I.C. 25), and the applicant can only show use in regard to goods in one class, the application can be divided, by filing a formal **Request to Divide,** with one class proceeding to registration and one lagging behind in a separate application.

If use of a mark was actually commenced during the application process of an ITU application, the applicant may file an amendment to its original application (called an **Amendment to Allege Use**) alleging that use has occurred and providing a specimen showing such use. The only significant difference between an amendment to allege use and a statement of use is the time of filing. The amendment to allege use may be filed during the initial examination phase, while the statement of use is not filed until after the PTO issues a notice of allowance. An amendment to allege use filed after the examining attorney approves the application for publication will be rejected. The period within which the amendment to allege use cannot be filed is called the **blackout period.**

Statements of use and amendments to allege use can be filed electronically through TEAS, with a digitized image of the required specimen. Once a mark that is the subject of an ITU application achieves registration, the filing date of the application is deemed to be the date upon which the owner first used the mark. This "constructive use" date is important to the trademark owner because it will allow the owner to defeat an intervening user who may

have actually used the mark before the ITU owner but after the ITU owner's application filing date. For example, using our case study, assume the following dates for an application by Watson for EXPLORE for entertainment services, namely, a new amusement park attraction:

- Intent to use application filed by Watson for EXPLORE on February 1, 2002.
- Actual use by Smith Co. for EXPLORER for amusement park attraction on June 1, 2002.
- Use-based application filed by Smith Co. for EXPLORER on July 1, 2002.
- Notice of allowance issued for EXPLORE on February 1, 2003.
- Statement of use filed by Watson for EXPLORE on May 1, 2003, alleging actual use began on April 15, 2003.
- Registration issues for EXPLORE on August 1, 2003.

Given these dates, EXPLORE has priority over EXPLORER because once EXPLORE achieved registration, it was as if Watson had actually used the mark on the date it filed its application, namely, February 1, 2002, a date prior to June 1, 2002, the date of Smith's actual first use of EXPLORER. See Exhibit 4–7 for timeline and Exhibit 4–8 for application checklist.

Abandonment and Revival of Applications

Trademark applications are deemed abandoned by the PTO if a timely response is not made to an office action or to a notice of allowance, and the PTO will issue a formal notice of abandonment to the applicant. The PTO, however, allows for revival of abandoned applications if a petition to revive is filed within two months of the mailing date of the notice of abandonment. The applicant's petition must state that the delay in responding to the office action or notice of allowance was unintentional.

our terms; it would, that is, have required a special vocabulary, a special system of presentation, and an interpretive scheme (or a set of commonplaces) he could have used to identify and talk about the mystery of human error. The writer certainly had access to the range of acceptable commonplaces for such an explanation: "lack of pride," "no incentive," "lazy." Each commonplace would dictate its own set of phrases, examples, and conclusions; and we, his teachers, would know how to write out each argument, just as we know how to write out more specialized arguments of our own. A "commonplace," then, is a culturally or institutionally authorized concept or statement that carries with it its own necessary elaboration. We all use commonplaces to orient ourselves in the world; they provide points of reference and a set of "prearticulated" explanations that are readily available to organize and interpret experience. The phrase "lack of pride" carries with it its own account of the repairman's error, just as at another point in time a reference to "original sin" would have provided an explanation, or just as in certain university classrooms a reference to "alienation" would enable writers to continue and complete the discussion. While there is a way in which these terms are interchangeable, they are not all permissible: A student in a composition class would most likely be turned away from a discussion of original sin. Commonplaces are the "controlling ideas" of our composition textbooks, textbooks that not only insist on a set form for expository writing but a set view of public life.[2]

When the writer says, "I don't know," then, he is not saying that he has nothing to say. He is saying that he is not in a position to carry on this discussion. And so we are addressed as apprentices rather than as teachers or scholars. In order to speak as a person of status or privilege, the writer can either speak to us in our terms—in the privileged language of university discourse—or, in default (or in defiance) of that, he can speak to us as though we were children, offering us the wisdom of experience.

I think it is possible to say that the language of the "Clay Model" paper has come *through* the writer and not from the writer. The writer has located himself (more precisely, he has located the self that is represented by the "I" on the page) in a context that is finally beyond him, not his own and not available to his immediate procedures for inventing and arranging text. I would not, that is, call this essay an example of "writer-based" prose. I would not say that it is egocentric or that it represents the "interior monologue or a writer thinking and talking to himself" (Flower, 1981, p. 63). It is, rather, the record of a writer who has lost himself in the discourse of his readers. There is a context beyond the intended reader that is not the world but a way of talking about the world, a way of talking that determines the use of examples, the possible conclusions, acceptable commonplaces, and key words for an essay on the construction of a clay model of the earth. This writer has entered the discourse without successfully approximating it.

Linda Flower (1981) has argued that the difficulty inexperienced writers 10 have with writing can be understood as a difficulty in negotiating the transition between "writer-based" and "reader-based" prose. Expert writers, in other words, can better imagine how a reader will respond to a text and can transform or restructure what they have to say around a goal shared with a reader. Teaching students to revise for readers, then, will better prepare them to write initially with a reader in mind. The success of this pedagogy depends on the degree to which a writer can imagine and conform to a reader's goals. The difficulty of this act of imagination and the burden of such conformity are so much at the heart of the problem that a teacher must pause and take stock before offering revision as a solution. A student like the one who wrote the "Clay Model" paper is not so much trapped in a private language as he is shut out from one of the privileged languages of public life, a language he is aware of but cannot control.

Notes

1. David Olson (1981) has made a similar observation about school-related problems of language learning in younger children. Here is his conclusion: "Hence, depending upon whether children assumed language was primarily suitable for making assertions and conjectures or primarily for making direct or indirect commands, they will either find school texts easy or difficult" (p. 107).

2. For Aristotle, there were both general and specific commonplaces. A speaker, says Aristotle, has a "stock of arguments to which he may turn for a particular need."

> If he knows the *topoi* (regions, places, lines, or argument)—and a skilled speaker will know them—he will know where to find what he wants for a special case. The general topics, or *common*places, are regions containing arguments that are common to all branches of knowledge.. . . But there are also special topics (regions, places, *loci*) in which one looks for arguments appertaining to particular branches of knowledge, special sciences, such as ethics or politics. (1932, pp. 154–55)

And, he says, "the topics or places, then, may be indifferently thought of as in the science that is concerned, or in the mind of the speaker." But the question of location is "indifferent" *only* if the mind of the speaker is in line with set opinion, general assumption. For the speaker (or writer) who is not situated so comfortably in the privileged public realm, this is indeed not an indifferent matter at all. If he does not have the commonplace at hand, he will not, in Aristotle's terms, know where to go at all.

References

Aristotle. (1932). *The Rhetoric of Aristotle* (L. Cooper, Trans.). Englewood Cliffs, NJ: Prentice-Hall.

Flower, L. S. (1981). Revising writer-based prose. *Journal of Basic Writing* 3, 62–74.

Olson, D. R. (1981). Writing: The divorce of the author from the text. In B. M. Kroll and R. J. Vann (Eds.), *Exploring speaking-writing relationships: Connections and contrasts.* Urbana, IL: National Council of Teachers of English.

Working with the Text

1. Although universities have been in existence for many centuries, the language of the university, its way of proceeding, is not a given. The purposes and structures of universities must themselves be invented and reinvented. David Bartholomae asserts that students, too, must "invent the university" as they enter this community, drawing on their own growing problem-solving skills. As you reread the essay, note the particular processes this involves for the student. Based on your understanding of these processes, write a short essay in which you analyze Bartholomae's use of the word *invent* to describe what the student has to do. Why would he use the term *invent*, rather than simply *learn* (a term he also uses)? Why is "assembling and mimicking [the university's] language" a matter of invention? What exactly is the student inventing?

2. In analyzing the "Clay Model" paper, Bartholomae decides that the paper "has come *through* the writer and not *from* the writer" (par. 9). Drawing on Bartholomae's argument, write a brief statement in which you explore what he means by this.

3. Bartholomae argues that students "invent the university by assembling and mimicking its language" (par. 2). Reflect on your own writing process or on a specific writing assignment that was especially challenging or difficult. As you reread the essay, highlight terms that seem to be the specialized language of Bartholomae's field. Write a brief essay in which you analyze your own writing process or the specific assignment, by mimicking Bartholomae's analysis of "Clay Model."

From Text to Field

1. Reread the passage in which Bartholomae discusses the use of "commonplaces" as a set of "'prearticulated' explanations that are readily available to organize and interpret experience" (par. 7). Choose a commonplace from a language that you use comfortably, such as a term used in a particular field, specialty, or working community. Write an essay in which you explain to an outsider how the commonplace is used and in what ways it offers a culturally or institutionally authorized means to orient us in that world.

2. As a student, in what ways have you "invented the university"? Focus on a particular class or on a discipline or field you have begun to enter. Using Bartholomae's selection as a prompt, write an essay in which you describe and reflect on the process you used to invent for yourself that segment of the university.

3. In the closing paragraph of this section of Bartholomae's essay, he challenges writing teachers to "pause and take stock" of the difficulty students face in imagining an audience for their academic writing (par. 10). In an essay, discuss the challenges you face as you try to imagine the audience that you write for in a particular class (perhaps even your writing class) or in a discipline or field you plan to enter.

4. Bartholomae's essay has been criticized in some quarters as expecting students to mimic already institutionalized ways of writing. What are the creative opportunities, but also the considerable risks, of college writing that does not seek to invent (yet again) the university? Draw on your own experiences of negotiating this tension—a tension between adhering to yet departing from existing norms or expectations.

Two Metaphors for Learning
and The Novice Writer

Joseph Williams and
Gregory G. Colomb

How often have you felt like a novice, able to manage only the simplest, most concrete thinking in a new subject area? How often have you admired the complex, abstract, articulate thinking of an expert? It might encourage you to know that studies have shown that even experts tend to think and write at the novice level once they leave their area of expertise. In light of these studies, Joseph Williams and Gregory G. Colomb propose that we think of learning to write in a particular field not as an upward curve of growth but in terms of a novice trying to join a community of experts, a metaphor that leaves room for acquiring the "extensive, structured knowledge" necessary for expert writing.

Williams and Colomb collaborate frequently on books and essays that explore style, argument, research, and the teaching of writing. With Wayne Booth, they have produced *The Craft of Research* (2003) and *The Craft of Argument* (2003). Joseph Williams is well known for his book *Style: Ten Lessons in Clarity and Grace* (2005). Williams is professor of English, the humanities, and linguistics in the Department of English Language and Literature at the University of Chicago. Gregory G. Colomb is professor of English at the University of Virginia.

Two Metaphors for Learning

PROGRESS AS LINEAR MOVEMENT. Metaphors influence not only how we think about experience, but how we deal with it. We speak of anger, for example, with images of liquids boiling inside sealed containers: "I was so boiling mad that I blew my lid. After I let off steam, though, I felt better" (Johnson, 1987). Had circumstances been different, our culture might have adopted the

216

metaphor of the machine: "I was so racing mad that I was already running too high for my specs, so I knew I had to lower my rpms or burn out my bearings. After I cooled the system down, I operated better." Under our presiding metaphorical frame, we often encourage—or at least condone—the expression of anger because we consider its "release" therapeutic; under another metaphorical system, we might consider the expression of anger damaging because it could lead to systemic breakdown.

The metaphors we use to describe learning, particularly skills such as reading, writing, and thinking, are metaphors of natural development and growth. When we develop normally, we grow "up." As we grow "up," we also "progress" left to right along a time scale (controlled by the tacit metaphor of reaching a "goal"). So we visually graph development from low to high and progress from a starting point on the lower left to a goal on the upper right. We picture normal growth as a curve (or stair step, if we think growth has stages), from lower left to higher right. We typically combine this growth metaphor with construction metaphors: We have to "lay a solid foundation" and then "reinforce" what we learn so that we both "maintain" what we have learned and "build" on it toward mastery.

These metaphors of linear development and building up come so naturally to us that we become particularly receptive to theories of learning expressible through them. So it is not surprising that administrators and teachers, particularly those who teach "generic" skills such as reading, writing, and thinking, should be attracted to the work of developmentalists such as Jean Piaget (Inhelder and Piaget, 1958), William Perry (1968), Lawrence Kohlberg (1984), and others whose models of development would seem to impose order on the more puzzling patterns of student behavior.

For Piaget, developing children move from concrete operational thinking to formal operational thinking, not smoothly, but in ways that let us account for their early cognitive limitations not by IQ or diligence, but by a qualitative structure of mind. Young children are not yet able to manipulate the abstractions derived from sets of sets; they are not able to juggle multiple hypotheticals, think probabilistically, etc. To put it crudely, younger children are incapable of thinking abstractly, a cognitive constraint Piagetians explain not by intelligence or cultural background, but by genetic epistemology.

Perry found a roughly similar pattern of development in the social/academic ₅ development of Harvard undergraduates: In their academic careers, students often appeared in his office at a stage he calls "dualistic"—the stage at which students simply want to know who the authorities are and what they know. When students "progress," they move to what he called the "multiple/relative" stage, that stage where students believe that since there are no final authorities and no final answers, then "everyone's opinion must be equally good." Perry claimed that the dualist stage regularly precedes the multiple/relative stage, and that these are followed by stages in which the student is increasingly able to handle ambiguities, to appreciate the legitimacy of different conclusions drawn from different premises, to understand the importance of the process of reasoning as opposed to its outcome, etc.

Kohlberg laid out a sequence of moral reasoning that begins at the stage of preconventional moral reasoning involving immediate, concrete approval and disapproval; then moves up to conventional moral reasoning governed by socially established values and peer pressure; and culminates in postconventional moral reasoning, that stage where the mature moral reasoner comes to recognize that local systems in particular societies rest not on rules that govern, but on universal moral principles that guide. Again, this is movement from the concrete to the abstract.

All three of these models describe a pattern of cognitive growth that begins with the immediate, concrete, rule-governed here and now, and that develops to more abstract, hypothetical forms of reasoning guided by principles. To be sure, these models differ profoundly, in ways our reductive description ignores. But to put it in a way that is not deceptively reductive, they describe a movement from relatively "lower-level" concreteness to relatively "higher-order" abstraction.

Like all models that reflect tacit metaphors, however, these models have consequences. One is that "regression" is bad. A student who does not continue to perform at a level "reached" earlier has "fallen back" to a "lower" level of performance. And whoever taught the student at that "lower level"— teaching writing is a paradigm case—did not do the job right. The student failed to learn the "bas(e)ics."

It is a metaphoric scheme that motivates us to abuse those who taught our students before they reach us. In the case of writing, teachers of first-year college students criticize the high schools; teachers of upperclass students criticize teachers of first-year composition; teachers in professional and graduate schools criticize the colleges; and professional organizations such as law firms and businesses criticize the whole educational system. A skill such as writing, the story goes, should follow a model of steady, linear development from lower-left to upper-right. When our students do not write as we expect, we feel empowered by our metaphors to decide that our predecessors must have failed to raise them to the level we think they should have achieved. A related consequence is that entire curricula are constructed to "raise" the student to achieve objectifiable levels of performance. If students are identifiably dualists when they enter the system, they should be measurably closer to being multiple relativists at the end of the first semester. That kind of thinking produces a system of testing that reductively categorizes students according to their cognitive/moral/social/academic development.

But the most problematical consequences come when we rely on these   10
linear models to make policy decisions about education. Such decisions may
be costly, because evidence suggests that these models may not entirely com-
port with reality. The evidence comes from three directions. First, some
reports increasingly suggest that children who test at the concrete operational
level of thinking can be induced to behave in ways that characterize formal
operational thinking (Bryant, 1983). By manipulating the form of the test
and particularly the kind of knowledge that the child controls about the
materials of the test, one can "move" a concrete-operational-thinking child
to a formal operational level of thinking.

A second line of evidence comes from an opposite direction. A number of
researchers have asserted that up to half of first-year college students are still
concrete operational thinkers, this long after Piaget's model would have had
them move "up" to formal operational thinking (Dunlop and Fazio, 1976;
Tomlinson-Keasey, 1972). And when the American Accounting Association
studied a group of upper-class and graduate students, up to half were judged
to be either concrete operational thinkers or in transition from concrete to
formal operational thinking (Shute, 1979). Is it plausible that large numbers
of graduate students think in ways generically similar to ten-year-olds?
Possible, perhaps, but put together these two lines of evidence—young
children can be taught to think in formal operational terms, and graduate
students can seem to think in concrete operational terms—and a more
likely hypothesis suggests itself. Perhaps what counts in "higher-level" cognitive processing is not only those abstract and generic operations, but also
knowledge, experience, control over specific content (see Glaser, 1984).
"Concrete" behavior may in fact indicate thin categories of knowledge, not
some intrinsic quality of mind.

This hypothesis is encouraged by a third line of evidence emerging from
research into expert versus novice thinking. Most of the research into this
matter involves what is called in cognitive psychology "well-structured" problems, problems that have a single right answer and a relatively clear-cut algorithm for getting there (Larkin, McDermott, Simon, and Simon, 1980; Chi,
Feltovitch, and Glaser, 1981). Experts and novices solve well-structured
problems in different ways. Most relevant is that novices (not "lower-level"
thinkers, please note) are characterized by relatively concrete thinking, while
experts tend to be characterized by more abstract thinking. For example, a
novice problem solver in physics might look at a problem containing a picture of a spring and assume that the problem belongs to the category of
"spring problems" and begin to think about what she knows about springs.
The expert looks at the problem and categorizes the problem not on the basis
of its most concrete, physically present feature, but by the abstract character
of its intellectual content.

Still more interesting is the line of research into "ill-formed" problems, problems for which there is no obviously "correct" answer, much less obviously correct algorithms for a solution. Voss and others (1985) put the following problem to four groups of subjects: If you were in charge, how would you solve the problems of agriculture in the Soviet Union? The problem solvers were grouped as follows:

1. Novice/low-knowledge: students taking a first course in Soviet affairs
2. Novice/high-knowledge: graduate students in Soviet affairs
3. Expert/low-knowledge: senior chemistry professors
4. Expert/high-knowledge: senior faculty in Soviet affairs

The high-knowledge experts differed from the novices in three ways: (a) the high-knowledge experts spent more time decomposing the problem, defining the problem space, explaining why the problem was complex; (b) where the novices would propose solutions at a relatively concrete level—more fertilizer, better roads, better farm machinery, etc.—the high-knowledge experts began at a "higher," more abstract level—with the system, infrastructure, or history; (c) the novices constructed relatively shorter chains of arguments, moving from point to point without developing any one of them extensively. However, once the high-knowledge experts introduced a topic, they stayed with it, developing a chain of reasoning based on that argument.

The most salient outcome is that of the low-knowledge experts, the chemistry professors. They behaved in ways similar to the low-knowledge novices. This outcome suggests that while there may be some generic quality of expert thinking that characterizes all experts *in their field*, its deployment is crucially linked both to the amount of knowledge one controls about the matter in question, and to the complexity of the structure of that knowledge. Confronting a problem in an unfamiliar area, experts in an alien field seem to behave in ways similar to generic novices.

It seems, then, that extensive, structured knowledge counts for much in good thinking. Some suggest everything. Indeed, it may count for much in development in general. If formal thinking can be induced in a young child by providing substantial experience with the problem materials, if a dualist becomes a relativist once he or she accumulates multiple points of view and sees that all of them are at best intrinsically tentative, if a preconventional moral reasoner becomes a conventional reasoner when that person becomes part of a larger community and understands the shared and therefore abstract values of the community, then the notion of intellectual growth as biological or cognitive epistemology with its own teleology becomes an open question. And so does the model of learning represented by linear movement on a steady or staggered lower-left, upper-right curve.

PROGRESS AS JOINING THE COMMUNITY. Another—and perhaps more productive—metaphor for growth is the equally familiar one of an "outsider" trying to "get into" a community, a metaphor that models the movement of a learner situated outside a bounded field, who then "enters" the field and so "joins" the community by acting like its members. (This metaphor does not place any single community at the upper right of the chart as an ultimate goal.) To join a disciplinary community is, in part, to master a body of knowledge. But that knowledge does not exist "out there," independent of those who control it, just waiting to be acquired. Knowledge belongs to groups of people who have some shared stake in exploring, preserving, and expanding it. The outsider must acquire knowledge from insiders, usually through some form of an apprenticeship. Perhaps we should not, but we draw institutional boundaries around knowledge by locating it in communities defined by experts and by those novices who are trying to learn what experts know. We call those communities by different names—subjects, fields, areas, majors, departments, disciplines. They often overlap, and they consist of subcommunities that also overlap. That these names cut up the pie so differently only reflects the unruliness of communities.

Whatever we call these fields and however we define them, the knowledge they bound is colored by the values, conventions, and styles of the communities that make that knowledge the object of their interest. While the novice is committed to mastering the knowledge that the community thinks is important, the novice is equally committed to acquiring the *ways* of thinking that characterize that community, the tone of voice that identifies one member to another, the required silences whose violation instantly identifies the outsider. However true it is that Shakespeare is a famous writer who wrote many plays, it is usually inappropriate for those trying to join the ranks of literary experts to express that sentiment, either in writing or in speech.

We want to use this metaphor to redescribe the concrete operational thinker or the dualist or the preconventional moral reasoner as a novice standing outside a knowledge community. Of course, our metaphor has its own consequences, particularly in regard to the central interest of this volume—projects that seek to extend writing "across the curriculum." But we believe that the consequences of our description do more justice to—and do more to help—the novice learner.

The Novice Writer

Those new to a knowledge community often exhibit some characteristic patterns of learning behavior, patterns that teachers can learn to anticipate. First, we should expect from novices behavior that is relatively "concrete" (*not* "lower-level"). A moment of reflection suggests why. Abstraction is at

EXHIBIT 4–7
Timeline for
ITU Application

2/1/02	6/1/02	7/1/02	2/1/03	5/1/03	8/1/03
ITU application filed by Watson for EXPLORE	Actual use by Smith of EXPLORER	Smith files application for EXPLORER	PTO issues notice of allowance for EXPLORE	Watson files statement of use for EXPLORE alleging date of first use of 4/15/03	Registration issues for EXPLORE. Watson has priority due to date of constructive use of 2/1/02

EXHIBIT 4–8
Trademark Application
Checklist

Application Checklist

An application for trademark registration must include the following:

- written application with the following elements:
    - applicant's name;
    - applicant's legal entity (individual, corporation, and so forth) and identification of country of which applicant is citizen or country or state of incorporation;
    - applicant's address;
    - basis for use of mark, namely, a statement that applicant has used the mark (and, if so, dates of first use and first use in commerce) or statement that applicant has bona fide intent to use the mark in the future;
    - identification of goods and services offered under the mark; and
    - identification of international class (if known by applicant)
- declaration by applicant
- one specimen for each international class
- drawing page
- appropriate filing fee

Generally, it is not necessary to explain the circumstances that cause the unintentional delay.

An application can also be expressly abandoned, as when the applicant simply decides it does not wish to pursue registration.

REGISTRATION

For a use-based application, a registration will issue about twelve weeks after publication in the *Official Gazette* if no notice of opposition is filed to the application. For an ITU application, registration will occur after publication in least partially based on the number and variety of instances of a category. By definition, a novice's knowledge is simultaneously very thin and relatively unstructured, with categories defined by as few as a single instance. The student of architecture who knows only classical forms has a very thin category of "architectural style." From the point of view of someone who also knows romanesque, gothic, baroque, modern, etc., that less knowledgeable student's problem-solving behavior would seem concrete operational indeed.

In regard to writing, we can predict a number of "concrete," "immature" forms of behavior: mapping the particular (concrete) language of the assignment into the opening paragraph of the paper; mapping any hint of organization in the assignment onto the paper itself; close-

The novice is committed to acquiring the *ways* of thinking that characterize that community.

ly following the sequence of events or topics in an assigned text; and in particular, summarizing rather than analyzing. Novices will tend to say those things that are ordinarily left unsaid by insiders, things that can be left unsaid just because they are shared. Novices will also seize on those features of the "voice" that seem most markedly to characterize the discourse of the field. In a field as stylistically marked as the law, for example, new students typically seize on the *heretofore*'s and *whereas*'s because they are among the most concretely obvious signals of legal language, the language of the tribe.

Second, this "concrete" behavior may be compounded by a predictable deterioration of performance in skills mastered earlier. Someone trying to enter a new community of discourse must bring under control a new body of knowledge, new ways of thinking, new ways of writing and speaking. So it is entirely predictable that some skills already mastered will deteriorate, often by default reliance on the most concrete forms of behavior.

Concrete, novice behavior appears in those aspects of writing that depend on the ability to analyze and synthesize. Here the consequences can be especially damaging because this failing is so often perceived as a sign that the learner cannot think. Because it is so important to our pedagogy, we will examine this behavior at more length and at three different levels: (1) professional school writing, (2) advanced upper-class undergraduate writing, and (3) first-year undergraduate writing. (We might have included professional writing by new attorneys.)

We begin with the mixed professional/academic setting of law school because we want to emphasize that "novice" behavior is not limited to the young and untalented—the effort to join a discourse community invites it even at very high levels of professional writing. Nor are inappropriate judgments of novice behavior limited to teachers of the young: Even at "higher" levels, learners write in ways that can by the old, linear metaphor be described as "low-level," "immature," "unskilled," etc., but that we prefer to describe as the predictable response of the novice, independent of any level of development.

WRITING BY FIRST-YEAR LAW STUDENTS. Most schools of law require a first-year   25
legal-writing course, but most of those courses do not teach legal writing. They teach research, citation forms, some aspects of legal thinking. This is especially so at the most selective law schools. They understandably assume that students who had A− and B+ averages in college are not merely competent, but proficient writers. And yet in their first weeks and months of law school, many of those writers display the very forms of behavior that characterize writers in their first year of college.

Let us describe a paper given to us by a legal-writing instructor as an example of the work of a student who had not learned how to write well, a paper written by a law student in his fourth week. . . . This student attends one of the country's most selective law schools, has graduated from a prestigious college near the top of his class, and has produced laudatory letters of recommendation, high LSAT scores, and an articulate application essay. The assignment was to analyze how a jurist used precedent while deciding whether a person can be convicted of second-degree murder if that person was coerced into participating in a crime in which another participant commits murder in the first degree.

The faculty person teaching in the legal-writing program was led by a linear conception of development to decide that this writer had never learned to write well. But the essay paradigmatically illustrates the behavior of a novice trying to deal with a new field. First, it precisely tracks the sequence of the jurist's text rather than abstracting from the text the principles of law that the jurist followed. Second, each of the student's middle, supposedly analytical paragraphs (see excerpts) corresponds to one section of the decision and precisely tracks the sequence of its section. It is not surprising, therefore, that the instructor considered this "mere summary." Third, although the conclusion begins to address the abstractions that the jurist considered, it merely lists them in the order in which they appeared in the original text and in the essay. Finally and most importantly, the middle, analytical paragraphs do not (with a few exceptions) specifically state the key analytical terms of the conclusion, terms first announced only at the end of the paper, where the writer seemed to discover them.

Like so many novice performances, this paper replicates the act of discovery. The writer structured the paper on the narrative of his thinking, discovering the abstract terms of analysis only at the end, where he summarizes them in a list. On the one hand, this might be treated merely as an example of "writer-based prose" (Flower, 1979). But "writer-based prose" is not necessarily a sign of generic "novice writer," as Flower seemed at that time to suggest. It may reflect the concrete behavior of a very experienced writer who is a novice in the field.

The signs of concrete, novice behavior are also evident in the style of that essay. This peculiarly awkward sentence presents the jurist's thinking in the writer's own words:

> The final step in Lord Morris's **preparation** to introduce the precedents is his **consideration** of the idea of **conviction** despite the **presence** of duress and then immediate **pardon** for that crime as an unnecessary step which is in fact injurious for it creates the stigma of the criminal on a potentially blameless (or at least not criminal) individual.

Pervasive nominalization characterizes bad legal writing in particular and bad academic writing in general. But as we noted above, it also characterizes a kind of stylistic breakdown typical of mature writers trying to wrestle with difficult concepts. The student might have written

> Before he **introduces** the precedents, Lord Morris **considers** a final issue: If a court first **convicts** a defendant who acted under duress and then immediately **pardons** that defendant, has the court taken an unnecessary step, a step that may even injure the defendant by stigmatizing him as criminal when he may be blameless?

This is a complex "if-then" question, involving two conditionals ("if a court convicts . . . and then pardons"), one of which contains an embedded conditional ("a defendant who acted under duress"), followed by a conclusion ("taken an unnecessary step") that itself becomes a cause ("may even injure the defendant") of a complex consequence ("by stigmatizing him as criminal when he may be blameless"). It is not surprising that a novice in legal reasoning should suffer a stylistic breakdown in the face of complex conditions and consequences. But note that his confused tangle of nominalizations is akin to an equally ponderous but professionally deliberate legal style:

> Because the individualized assessment of the appropriateness of the death penalty is a moral inquiry into the culpability of the defendant, and not an emotional response to the mitigating evidence, I agree with the Court that an instruction informing the jury that they "must not be swayed by mere sentiment, conjecture, sympathy, passion, prejudice, public opinion or public feeling" does not by itself violate the Eighth and Fourteenth Amendments to the United States Constitution. (Sandra Day O'Connor, concurring, *California v. Albert Greenwood Brown, Jr.*)

As turgid as this is, it is not the turgidity of a novice unfamiliar with legal thinking. One of the great ironies of modern prose is that the turgid professional, most deeply socialized into the language of a profession, and the awkward novice can seem to have so much in common.

A related, though less turgid novice response is to concretize in the text too much of the writer's thinking process. In the following example, a new law student as academically distinguished as the previous one tries to adopt the voice of a judge. But in doing so he uses metadiscourse to raise to a level of textual concreteness the machinery of thinking and reasoning—"the main point supporting my point of view," etc.—that experts usually suppress. At the same time, this student raises to the same level of textual concreteness certain substantive matters that any expert would leave unsaid, such as the obvious assertion that a plaintiff must produce evidence against a defendant. (In this passage, we have boldfaced the metadiscourse and italicized the statements that anyone socialized into the world of the law would be unlikely to make.)

> **It is my opinion that** *the ruling of the lower court concerning the case of* Haslem v. Lockwood **should be upheld, thereby denying** *the appeal of the plaintiff.* **The main point supporting my point of view** *on this case* **con-cerns** *the tenet of our court system which holds that in order to win his case, the plaintiff must prove that he was somehow wronged by the defendant. The burden of proof rests on the plaintiff. He must show enough evidence to convince the court that he is in the right.* **However, in this case, I do not believe that** *the plaintiff has satisfied this requirement. In order to prove that the defendant owes him recompense for the six loads of manure,* he must first show that he was the legal owner of those loads, and then show that the defendant removed the manure for his own use [the paper goes on for several more paragraphs].

A more professional (i.e., socialized, i.e., "expert") version would be, "Plaintiff has failed to show that he was the legal owner of the loads and that the defendant removed the manure for his own use. The court affirms *Haslem v. Lockwood.*"

In both cases, the instructors took these as examples of bad writing and unskilled writers. In our terms, they are examples of novices trying to express themselves in a field that largely baffles them, and displaying the signs of novice behavior—concreteness, saying what can be left unsaid, and occasional breakdowns in stylistic performance in the direction of the most visible and concrete features of the "voice" that characterizes the prose of a field.

These examples illustrate forms of writing familiar to every teacher of freshman composition: summary rather than analysis, thinking out loud, a conclusion discovered at the end, evident stylistic infelicity, etc. In neither case could we assert that the writers were in some general sense immature or unintelligent. And yet they display the generic shortcomings of novice, "concrete" writers.

WRITING BY UPPER-CLASS STUDENTS. As they move into a discipline, undergraduates face many of the conceptual difficulties faced by new professional students. The next example comes from a paper by a third-year student taking a course in Western civilization, a good student who had written excellent papers in his first-year humanities course, but who had had no preparation in historical thinking. By the concluding paragraph of his paper, he at last reached a point worth making:

> The Popes, Urban II and Gregory VII, used the concept of the Crusades as a means to achieve a form of unity important to them during their pontificate. During Urban's pontificate, he could establish his authority, fight the devil (Muslims), and control fighting amongst the Europeans and direct those energies elsewhere. Gregory VII wishes to achieve unification between the Roman Church and the Greek Orthodox Church. . . . Therefore the Crusade was not just a fight against the Muslims to recapture the Holy Land and to save God's faith, but it was an effort to save the Church and Europe from the dissensions which were tearing it apart.

This paper was given a C+ because it was considered "disorganized," "largely summary," etc. Why? Because all of the first five and most of the next five paragraphs offered only a close summary of the assigned texts, so that the central concept of the conclusion—the Crusades achieving Christian unity—did not begin to emerge until about the tenth paragraph. The introduction was wholly summary and pointless:

> During the eleventh through thirteenth centuries, the Roman Catholic Church initiated several Crusades against the Muslims in the Holy Lands. The Pope would usually instigate and call for armament and support for this endeavor. Pope Urban II started the first Crusade in 1096. His predecessor, Gregory VII, had also petitioned to get support for a crusade in 1074 but did not succeed in launching his Crusade. There are written statements from these Popes concerning the Crusades. Pope Urban II in "Speech at the Council of Clermont" in the year 1095 calls for a Crusade and Pope Gregory VII in a Letter to King Henry IV during the year 1074 also proposes a Crusade.

This is the writing of a student gripped by novice concreteness. Since he does not control the information from the sources well enough to hold it whole in his mind as he thinks through its implications, he predictably summarizes the source, closely following the structure of its text. Once the material is concretized in the form of a linear summary, he is able to draw from it some inferences that qualify as analysis.

WRITING BY FIRST-YEAR STUDENTS. By this point it is almost redundant to offer 35 a typical first-year student paper that might illustrate these same features. Let us briefly look at one from a student with a VSAT well over 600. He was in his third week of college and writing about two speeches in Thucydides' history of the Peloponnesian war, a subject wholly strange to him. This was the assignment:

In the second chapter of his history, Thucydides presents two speakers asking Athens for help against the other. As we know Thucydides wrote these speeches to represent what "probably would have been said." Compare and contrast the way Thucydides had the Corcyrans and Corinthians rhetorically appeal to the Athenians in different ways.

And here are some indicative excerpts from the paper:

A Comparison of the Corcyran and Corinthian Speeches

The Corcyran and Corinthian speeches in Thucydides's *The Peloponnesian War* differ in several ways. The most important way that the two speeches differ is in the particular appeals each side gives to support its arguments. I will first discuss the Corcyran speech and then the Corinthian speech in order to show what we can learn from these differences.

The Corcyrans first apologize. . . . Then they give three reasons why the Athenians should help them and join in an alliance. They say that . . . Then they predict that . . . They say that . . . Finally, they emphasize that . . .

The Corinthians start out by attacking the Corcyrans. . . .

The Athenians decide to join with the Corcyrans against the Corinthians because they are sure that there is going to be a war between them soon and that they would have a good ally with the Corcyrans. The speeches are different in that the Corcyrans had the better argument because they understood the Athenians better than the Corinthians since the Athenians were very practical and self-interested at this time. Therefore, the Corcyran speech was a more clever appeal.

We need not dwell on the obvious here: Like the novice problem solver who thinks that a concrete picture of a spring in the problem statement means the problem is a spring-type problem, the student here takes the concrete language of the problem statement—the assignment—and maps it directly into the opening paragraph. The writer takes the sequence of the speeches from the assignment and from the text. In each section, he marches through each speech in summary fashion, at the end discovering his conclusion. While the style of the paper is competent, the organization and thought reflect the student's "concrete" thinking, which is to say, his inexperience in thinking about matters of this kind.

In three cases (new law student, upper-class student new to a field, new college student) we see the same generic pattern—the tyranny of the concrete and the breakdown of control over skills mastered earlier. If our narrative is plausible, the upward curve of growth is at best misleading. While there must certainly be development of some kind, it is not the kind of development that can be graphed like height and weight. A metaphor more insightful and useful than the upward curve is that of the outsider trying to get in, that of the novice trying to join a community of experts, an experience that happens to our best students many times over.

References

Bryant, Peter. "Piaget's Struggle and the Struggle about Piaget." In *Jean Piaget: An Interdisciplinary Critique*, edited by Sohan Modgil, Celia Modgil, and Geoffrey Brown. London: Routledge & Kegan Paul, 1983.

Chi, M. P. Feltovitch, and R. Glaser. "Categorization and Representation of Physics Problems by Experts and Novices." *Cognitive Science* 5 (1981): 121–52.

Colomb, Gregory G., and Joseph M. Williams. "Perceiving Structure in Professional Prose." In *Writing in Non-Academic Settings* edited by Lee Odell and Dixie Goswami. New York: Guilford, 1986.

Colomb, Gregory G., and Mark Turner. "Computers, Literary Theory, and Theory of Meaning." In *Critical Projections: The Future of Literary Theory*, edited by Ralph Cohen. London: Methuen, 1988.

Dunlop, D., and F. Fazio. "Piagetian Theory and Abstract Preferences of College Science Students." *Journal of College Science Teaching* (May 1976): 297–300.

Flower, Linda. "Writer Based Prose: A Cognitive Basis for Problems in Writing." *College English* 41 (September 1979), 19–37.

Glaser, Robert. "Education and Thinking: The Role of Knowledge." *American Psychologist* 39 (1984): 93–104.

Inhelder, B., and Jean Piaget. *The Growth of Logical Thinking from Childhood to Adolescence.* New York: Basic Books, 1958.

Johnson, Mark. *The Body in the Mind: The Bodily Basis of Meaning, Reasoning and Imagination.* Chicago: University of Chicago Press, 1987.

Kohlberg, Lawrence. *The Psychology of Moral Development.* Vol. 2. New York: Harper & Row, 1984.

Larkin, J., J. McDermott, D. Simon, and H. Simon. "Expert and Novice Performance in Solving Physics Problems." *Science* 208 (1980): 1, 335–42.

Perry, William G., Jr. *Forms of Intellectual and Ethical Development in the College Years.* New York: Holt, Rinehart & Winston, 1968.

Shute, George E. *Accounting Students and Abstract Reasoning: An Exploratory Study.* Sarasota, FL: American Accounting Association, 1979.

Tomlinson-Keasey, C. "Formal Operations in Females Aged 11 to 54 Years of Age." *Developmental Psychologist* 6 (1972): 364.

Toulmin, Stephen, R. Rieke, and A. Janik. *An Introduction to Reasoning.* New York: Macmillan, 1979.

Voss, James, T. Green, T. Post, and B. Penner. "Problem-solving Skill in the Social Sciences." *The Psychology of Learning and Motivation* 17 (1985): 165–213.

Working with the Text

1. Joseph Williams and Gregory G. Colomb use the term *novice* rather than *lower-level thinker* to designate writers who have not yet mastered the language and the structured knowledge of a given learning community. As a salient example, Williams and Colomb point to the chemistry professor who has as much trouble handling a question about Soviet agriculture as do undergraduate students. Review this example (pars. 13–15). Why is it central to the case the authors are making?

2. Williams and Colomb develop their hypothesis by focusing on the "concrete" behaviors (par. 21) of novice writers. In a brief essay, identify those behaviors and reflect on why a novice writer would exhibit them. Draw on your own prior or current experience as a novice writer.

3. Williams and Colomb assert that the metaphor of an outsider trying to join a community is "more insightful and useful" (par. 37) than the metaphor of growth that is more commonly used to describe the process of learning to write. In what ways is the growth metaphor misleading? What does the outsider metaphor contribute to our understanding of the novice writer's situation that the growth metaphor does not? Write an essay in which you imagine the effect of each metaphor on a novice writer in one particular setting. What would the writer be expected to do? How would the teacher respond to the writer's work? What would the writer be thinking and feeling?

From Text to Field

1. In questioning the linear "growth" metaphor, Williams and Colomb voice their concern that "the most problematical consequences come when we rely on these linear models to make policy decisions about education" (par. 10). Consider your own experience in and knowledge of the American education system, from elementary schools through college and on to professional or graduate schools. Write an essay in which you suggest changes to the system, or to one level of the system, that would help it shift from the metaphor of linear growth to the metaphor of an outsider trying to join a community.

2. Williams and Colomb point out that within communities—defined by subjects, fields, departments, disciplines—"the knowledge they bound is colored by the values, conventions, and styles of the communities that make that knowledge the object of their interest" (par. 18). In an essay, analyze the values and styles that color the knowledge of a community you have entered, or are entering, or a community you have observed as an outsider. This community can be academic, civic, professional, or involve any area of expertise, such as music, sports, use of the Internet, or skateboarding.

3. Reflect on your experience as a novice writer. Do you recognize in yourself any of the behaviors that Williams and Colomb describe? In what respects might the metaphors of growth or entering a community apply to your experiences? In a personal essay, reflect on your own learning process as a novice writing for a "knowledge" community. What do you find discouraging—or comforting—in your experiences and in the metaphors used to describe them?

Why We Read: Canon to the Right of Me

Katha Pollitt

> Katha Pollitt takes on the continuing debate over the literary canon—
> the list of books we are expected to read to be considered educated.
> At issue is not only the value of a book but also, more importantly, the
> criteria and perspectives that drive the judgment of value. *Why* should
> we read certain books? To what end? If books are to teach us about
> our culture—itself a debatable assumption—as members of a highly
> diverse culture we have to ask, whose culture? For Pollitt, the debate
> leads to the question of why we read the books we have chosen for
> ourselves and those that have been chosen for us.
>
> Pollitt's perspective is informed by her education at Harvard
> University and the Columbia School of the Arts, as well as her experi-
> ence teaching poetry at Barnard College and at the 92nd Street Y in
> New York City. As a widely published poet, she has received several
> grants, fellowships, and awards. As an essayist, Pollitt has won wide
> recognition for the incisiveness and wit of her social criticism. She has
> been contributing to the *Nation* since 1980 and has written essays for
> a number of high-profile publications, including the *New Yorker*, the
> *Atlantic*, the *New York Times*, *Harper's*, the *New Republic*, *Mother
> Jones*, and *Ms*. She has also been a guest on national television and
> radio programs. Her essays have been collected in *Reasonable
> Creatures: Essays on Women and Feminism* (1994) and, most recently, in
> *Subject to Debate: Sense and Dissents on Women, Politics, and Culture*
> (2001). "Why We Read: Canon to the Right of Me. . ." won the National
> Magazine award for essays and criticism.

For the past couple of years we've all been witness to a furious debate about
the literary canon. What books should be assigned to students? What books
should critics discuss? What books should the rest of us read, and who are

"we" anyway? Like everyone else, I've given these questions some thought, and when an invitation came my way, I leaped to produce my own manifesto. But to my surprise, when I sat down to write—in order to discover, as E. M. Forster once said, what I really think—I found that I agreed with all sides in the debate at once.

Take the conservatives. Now, this rather dour collection of scholars and diatribists—Allan Bloom, Hilton Kramer, John Silber, and so on—are not a particularly appealing group of people. They are arrogant, they are rude, they are gloomy, they do not suffer fools gladly, and everywhere they look, fools are what they see. All good reasons not to elect them to public office, as the voters of Massachusetts recently decided. But what is so terrible, really, about what they are saying? I too believe that some books are more profound, more complex, more essential to an understanding of our culture than others; I too am appalled to think of students graduating from college not having read Homer, Plato, Virgil, Milton, Tolstoy—all writers, dead white Western men though they be, whose works have meant a great deal to me. As a teacher of literature and of writing, I too have seen at firsthand how ill-educated many students are, and how little aware they are of this important fact about themselves. Last year I taught a graduate seminar in the writing of poetry. None of my students had read more than a smattering of poems by anyone, male or female, published more than ten years ago. Robert Lowell was as far outside their frame of reference as Alexander Pope. When I gently suggested to one student that it might benefit her to read some poetry if she planned to spend her life writing it, she told me that yes, she knew she should read more but when she encountered a really good poem it only made her depressed. That contemporary writing has a history which it profits us to know in some depth, that we ourselves were not born yesterday, seems too obvious even to argue.

But ah, say the liberals, the canon exalted by the conservatives is itself an artifact of history. Sure, some books are more rewarding than others, but why can't we change our minds about which books those are? The canon itself was not always as we know it today: Until the 1920s, *Moby-Dick* was shelved with the boys' adventure stories. If T. S. Eliot could single-handedly dethrone the Romantic poets in favor of the neglected Metaphysicals and place John Webster alongside Shakespeare, why can't we dip into the sea of stories and fish out Edith Wharton or Virginia Woolf? And this position too makes a great deal of sense to me. After all, alongside the many good reasons for a book to end up on the required-reading shelf are some rather suspect reasons for its exclusion: because it was written by a woman and therefore presumed to be too slight; because it was written by a black person and therefore presumed to be too unsophisticated or to reflect too special a case. By all means, say the liberals, let's have great books and a shared culture. But let's the *Official Gazette,* notice of allowance of mark, and submission of the statement of use and requisite specimen. The application process for use-based applications can take twelve to eighteen months or longer, and the process for ITU applications can take from eighteen to forty-two months, or longer.

Eventually, however, the PTO will issue a **Certificate of Registration** for the mark. The term of the registration is presently ten years from the date the mark is registered (for registration issued before November 16, 1989, the term is twenty years). The certificate will include all of the pertinent information about the mark and the owner and will set forth a registration number and a registration date. The mark as applied for will be reproduced. The law firm should carefully review the certificate and request a correction of any errors. Once the mark is registered, the owner (now called the **registrant**) can use any of the following registration notices in connection with the mark (assume the mark is EXPLORE):

- EXPLORE Registered in U.S. Patent and Trademark Office;
- EXPLORE Reg. U.S. Pat. & Tm. Off.; or
- EXPLORE® (the letter *R* enclosed in a circle is the most common notice).

The federal registration symbol or language cannot be used with a mark unless it has been registered with the PTO. Until that time, trademark owners and applicants often use the designation "TM" (for trademark) or "SM" (for service mark) placed alongside the mark to notify others the owner claims rights in the mark. A registrant is not required to use any registration notice; however, in an infringement suit based on the mark, no monetary damages can be recovered by the registrant unless the defendant had actual notice of the registration. Using the registration notice provides such actual

notice such that the registrant can later recover damages for infringement of the mark.

Once the law firm receives the certificate of registration, it will forward the certificate to the client along with pertinent information about monitoring the mark, using the registration notice, and pertinent dates to maintain the mark. Once again, the law firm must be certain to docket the critical dates to avoid abandonment of the registration. For example, between the fifth and sixth years after registration, and within the year before the end of every ten-year period after the registration date, the registrant must file a continued use affidavit with the PTO verifying the mark is still in use or the registration will be canceled (to clear the PTO files of **deadwood** and allow unused marks to be used by others). Additionally, the registration must be renewed at the end of each ten-year period following the registration date. The affidavit of continuing use and renewal document can be filed electronically through TEAS with a digitized image of the required specimen.

See Exhibit 4–9 for Certificate of Registration and Exhibit 4–10 for a trademark prosecution flowchart that shows each step of the prosecution process.

THE UNITED STATES PATENT AND TRADEMARK OFFICE'S MONITORING SYSTEM

The PTO maintains an automated telephone system called the Trademark Status Line that allows applicants and interested persons to check the status of an application or registration. After the welcoming message, you will be instructed to enter an application number or registration number. You will be given recorded status updates and information relating to the application or registration. Five requests may be entered per call. The status make sure that all the different kinds of greatness are represented and that the culture we share reflects the true range of human experience.

If we leave the broadening of the canon up to the conservatives, this will never happen, because to them change only means defeat. Look at the recent fuss over the latest edition of the Great Books series published by Encyclopedia Britannica, headed by that old snake-oil salesman Mortimer Adler. Four women have now been added to the series: Virginia Woolf, Willa Cather, Jane Austen, and George Eliot. That's nice, I suppose, but really! Jane Austen has been a certified Great Writer for a hundred years! Lionel Trilling said so! There's something truly absurd about the conservatives earnestly sitting in judgment on the illustrious dead, as though up in Writers' Heaven Jane and George and Willa and Virginia were breathlessly waiting to hear if they'd finally made it into the club, while Henry Fielding, newly dropped from the list, howls in outer darkness and the Brontës, presumably, stamp their feet in frustration and hope for better luck in twenty years, when *Jane Eyre* and *Wuthering Heights* will suddenly turn out to have qualities of greatness never before detected in their pages. It's like Poets' Corner at Manhattan's Cathedral of St. John the Divine, where mortal men—and a woman or two—of letters actually vote on which immortals to honor with a plaque, a process no doubt complete with electoral campaigns, compromise candidates, and all the rest of the underside of the literary life. "No, I'm sorry, I just can't vote for Whitman. I'm a Washington Irving man myself."

Well, a liberal is not a very exciting thing to be, as *Nation* readers know,   5 and so we have the radicals, who attack the concepts of "greatness," "shared," "culture" and "lists." (I'm overlooking here the ultraradicals, who attack the "privileging" of "texts," as they insist on calling books, and think one might as well spend one's college years deconstructing *Leave It to Beaver*.) Who is to say, ask the radicals, what is a great book? What's so terrific about complexity, ambiguity, historical centrality, and high seriousness? If *The Color Purple*, say, gets students thinking about their own experience, maybe they ought to read it and forget about —— and here you can fill in the name of whatever classic work you yourself found dry and tedious and never got around to finishing. For the radicals the notion of a shared culture is a lie, because it means presenting as universally meaningful and politically neutral books that reflect the interests and experiences and values of privileged white men at the expense of those of others—women, blacks, Latinos, Asians, the working class, whoever. Why not scrap the one-list-for-everyone idea and let people connect with books that are written by people like themselves about people like themselves? It will be a more accurate reflection of a multifaceted and conflict-ridden society, and will do wonders for everyone's self-esteem, except, of course, living white men—but they have too much self-esteem already.

Now, I have to say that I dislike the radicals' vision intensely. How foolish to argue that Chekhov has nothing to say to a black woman—or, for that matter, myself—merely because he is Russian, long dead, a man. The notion that one reads to increase one's self-esteem sounds to me like more snake oil. Literature is not an aerobics class or a session at the therapist's. But then I think of myself as a child, leafing through anthologies of poetry for the names of

Why is everyone so hot under the collar about what to put on the required-reading shelf?

women. I never would have admitted that I needed a role model, even if that awful term had existed back in the prehistory of which I speak, but why was I so excited to find a female name, even when, as was often the case, it was attached to a poem of no interest to me whatsoever? Anna Laetitia Barbauld, author of "Life! I know not what thou art / But know that thou and I must part!"; Lady Anne Lindsay, writer of languid ballads in incomprehensible Scots dialect; and the other minor female poets included by chivalrous Sir Arthur Quiller-Couch in the old *Oxford Book of English Verse*: I have to admit it, just by their presence in that august volume they did something for me. And although it had nothing to do with reading or writing, it was an important thing they did.

Now, what are we to make of this spluttering debate, in which charges of imperialism are met by equally passionate accusations of vandalism, in which each side hates the others, and yet each one seems to have its share of reason? Perhaps what we have here is one of those debates in which the opposing sides, unbeknownst to themselves, share a myopia that will turn out to be the most telling feature of the whole discussion: a debate, for instance, like that of our Founding Fathers over the nature of the franchise. Think of all the energy and passion spent pondering the question of property qualifications or direct versus legislative elections while all along, unmentioned and unimagined, was the fact—to us so central—that women and slaves were never considered for any kind of vote.

Something is being overlooked: the state of reading, and books, and literature in our country at this time. Why, ask yourself, is everyone so hot under the collar about what to put on the required-reading shelf? It is because while we have been arguing so fiercely about which books make the best medicine, the patient has been slipping deeper and deeper into a coma.

Let us imagine a country in which reading is a popular voluntary activity. There, parents read books for their own edification and pleasure, and are seen by their children at this silent and mysterious pastime. These parents also read to their children, give them books for presents, talk to them about books and underwrite, with their taxes, a public library system that is open all day, every day. In school—where an attractive library is invariably to be found—the children study certain books together but also have an active reading life of their own. Years later it may even be hard for them to remember if they read *Jane Eyre* at home and Judy Blume in class, or the other way around. In college young people continue to be assigned certain books, but far more important are the books they discover for themselves—browsing in the library, in bookstores, on the shelves of friends, one book leading to another, back and forth in history and across languages and cultures. After graduation they continue to read, and in the fullness of time produce a new generation of readers. Oh happy land! I wish we all lived there.

In that other country of real readers—voluntary, active, self-determined   10 readers—a debate like the current one over the canon would not be taking place. Or if it did, it would be as a kind of parlor game: What books would *you* take to a desert island? Everyone would know that the top-ten list was merely a tiny fraction of the books one would read in a lifetime. It would not seem racist or sexist or hopelessly hidebound to put Hawthorne on the syllabus and not Toni Morrison. It would be more like putting oatmeal and hot noodles on the breakfast menu—a choice part arbitrary, part a nod to the national past, part, dare one say it, a kind of reverse affirmative action: School might frankly be the place where one read the books that are a little off-putting, that have gone a little cold, that you might pass over because they do not address, in reader-friendly contemporary fashion, the issues most immediately at stake in modern life, but that, with a little study, turn out to have a great deal to say. Being on the list wouldn't mean so much. It might even add to a writer's cachet *not* to be on the list, to be in one way or another too heady, too daring, too exciting to be ground up into institutional fodder for teenagers. Generations of high school kids have been turned off to George Eliot by being forced to read *Silas Marner* at a tender age. One can imagine a whole new readership for her if grown-ups were left to approach *Middlemarch* and *Daniel Deronda* with open minds, at their leisure.

Of course, they rarely do. In America today the assumption underlying the canon debate is that the books on the list are the only books that are going to be read, and if the list is dropped no books are going to be read. Becoming a textbook is a book's only chance; all sides take that for granted. And so all agree not to mention certain things that they themselves, as highly educated people and, one assumes, devoted readers, know perfectly well. For example, that if you read only twenty-five, or fifty, or a hundred books, you can't understand them, however well chosen they are. And that if you don't have an independent reading life—and very few students do—you won't *like* reading the books on the list and will forget them the minute you finish them. And that books have, or should have, lives beyond the syllabus—thus, the totally misguided attempt to put current literature in the classroom. How strange to think that people need professorial help to read John Updike or Alice Walker, writers people actually do read for fun. But all sides agree, if it isn't taught, it doesn't count.

Let's look at the canon question from another angle. Instead of asking what books we want others to read, let's ask why we read books ourselves. I think the canon debaters are being a little disingenuous here, are suppressing, in the interest of their own agendas, their personal experience of reading. Sure, we read to understand our American culture and history, and we also read to recover neglected masterpieces, and to learn more about the accomplishments of our subgroup and thereby, as I've admitted about myself, increase our self-esteem. But what about reading for the aesthetic pleasures of language, form, image? What about reading to learn something new, to have a vicarious adventure, to follow the workings of an interesting, if possibly skewed, narrow and ill-tempered mind? What about reading for the story? For an expanded sense of sheer human variety? There are a thousand reasons why a book might have a claim on our time and attention other than its canonization. I once infuriated an acquaintance by asserting that Trollope, although in many ways a lesser writer than Dickens, possessed some wonderful qualities Dickens lacked: a more realistic view of women, a more skeptical view of good intentions, a subtler sense of humor, a drier vision of life which I myself found congenial. You'd think I'd advocated throwing Dickens out and replacing him with a toaster. Because Dickens is a certified Great Writer, and Trollope is not.

Am I saying anything different from what Randall Jarrell said in his great 1953 essay "The Age of Criticism"? Not really, so I'll quote him. Speaking of the literary gatherings of the era, Jarrell wrote:

> If, at such parties, you wanted to talk about *Ulysses* or *The Castle* or *The Brothers Karamazov* or *The Great Gatsby* or Graham Greene's last novel—Important books—you were at the right place. (Though you weren't so well off if you wanted to talk about *Remembrance of Things Past*. Important, but too long.) But if you wanted to talk about Turgenev's novelettes, or *The House of the Dead*, or *Lavengro*, or *Life on the Mississippi*, or *The Old Wives' Tale*, or *The Golovlyov Family*, or Cunningham-Grahame's stories, or Saint-Simon's memoirs, or *Lost Illusions*, or *The Beggar's Opera*, or *Eugen Onegin*, or *Little Dorrit*, or the *Burnt Njal Saga*, or *Persuasion*, or *The Inspector-General*, or *Oblomov*, or *Peer Gynt*, or *Far from the Madding Crowd*, or *Out of Africa*, or the *Parallel Lives*, or *A Dreary Story*, or *Debits and Credits*, or *Arabia Deserta*, or *Elective Affinities*, or *Schweik*, or—any of a thousand good or interesting but Unimportant books, you couldn't expect a very ready knowledge or sympathy from most of the readers there. They had looked at the big sights, the current sights, hard, with guides and glasses; and those walks in the

country, over unfrequented or thrice-familiar territory, all alone—those walks from which most of the joy and good of reading come—were walks that they hadn't gone on very often.

I suspect that most canon debaters have taken those solitary rambles, if only out of boredom—how many times, after all, can you reread the *Aeneid*, or *Mrs. Dalloway*, or *Cotton Comes to Harlem* (to pick one book from each column)? But those walks don't count, because of another assumption all sides hold in common, which is that the purpose of reading is none of the many varied and delicious satisfactions I've mentioned; it's medicinal. The chief end of reading is to produce a desirable kind of person and a desirable kind of society. A respectful, high-minded citizen of a unified society for the conservatives, an up-to-date and flexible sort for the liberals, a subgroup-identified, robustly confident one for the radicals. How pragmatic, how moralistic, how American! The culture debaters turn out to share a secret suspicion of culture itself, as well as the antipornographer's belief that there is a simple, one-to-one correlation between books and behavior. Read the conservatives' list and produce a nation of sexists and racists—or a nation of philosopher kings. Read the liberals' list and produce a nation of spineless relativists—or a nation of open-minded world citizens. Read the radicals' list and produce a nation of psychobabblers and ancestor-worshipers—or a nation of stalwart proud-to-be-me pluralists.

But is there any list of a few dozen books that can have such a magical effect, for good or for ill? Of course not. It's like arguing that a perfectly nutritional breakfast cereal is enough food for the whole day. And so the canon debate is really an argument about what books to cram down the resistant throats of a resentful captive populace of students; and the trick is never to mention the fact that, in such circumstances, one book is as good, or as bad, as another. Because, as the debaters know from their own experience as readers, books are not pills that produce health when ingested in measured doses. Books do not shape character in any simple way—if, indeed, they do so at all—or the most literate would be the most virtuous instead of just the ordinary run of humanity with larger vocabularies. Books cannot mold a common national purpose when, in fact, people are honestly divided about what kind of country they want—and are divided, moreover, for very good and practical reasons, as they always have been.

For these burly and energetic purposes, books are all but useless. The way books affect us is an altogether more subtle, delicate, wayward, and individual, not to say private, affair. And that reading is being made to bear such an inappropriate and simplistic burden speaks to the poverty both of culture and of frank political discussion in our time.

15

On his deathbed, Dr. Johnson° — once canonical, now more admired than read — is supposed to have said to a friend who was energetically rearranging his bedclothes, "Thank you, this will do all that a pillow can do." One might say that the canon debaters are all asking of their handful of chosen books that they do a great deal more than any handful of books can do.

Working with the Text

1. Katha Pollitt is known for her skill and style as an essayist. As you reread the essay, notice the structure of her argument. Write a brief analysis of her strategy. Why does she start with characterizing the debate? What does her summary, and the particular points she makes within it, allow her to do in the rest of the essay? In what ways has she succeeded in reframing the debate?

2. Pollitt makes the assumption that reading contributes to an understanding of our culture. Write a brief essay in which you analyze and elaborate on her view of the relationship between books and culture. What does it mean to understand culture? Whose culture is, or should be, at issue, and why? What role do books play in either entering into or challenging culture? What about our culture does Pollitt think our reading should reflect?

3. Pollitt's position on the canon debate is reflected in the tone of her writing. In a brief essay, describe the tone she uses and explore the effect it creates. What attitude does it project? How does it contribute to her argument? The article, adapted from Pollitt's participation in a panel discussion for the Columbia University Center for American Culture Studies, was published in the *Nation*. From the article, infer the intended audience. Why would she choose this tone for a panel discussion on culture studies? Why would the *Nation* choose to publish the article?

From Text to Field

1. Pollitt writes, "School might frankly be the place where one read the books that are a little off-putting, that have gone a little cold, that you might pass over because they do not address, in reader-friendly contemporary fashion, the issues most immediately at stake in modern life, but that, with a little study, turn out to have a great deal to say" (par. 10). Does this capture your experience of assigned reading in school? Using this passage as a guide, write

---

Dr. Johnson: Samuel Johnson (1709–1789), are of England's greatest literary figures who worked as a poet, essayist, biographer, and lexicographer.

a personal essay in which you reflect on your response to literature that is required reading. How do you respond to the reading itself? What is your attitude toward the fact that it is considered to be an essential or required part of your education? As an alternative, write a personal essay that re-creates your experience with one particular book that was required reading.

2. The debate over the canon leads Pollitt to consider the reasons we read. In an essay, explore your own reasons for reading or for not reading. What do you read voluntarily? What draws you to that kind of reading? What role does reading play in your life? If you don't read willingly, why don't you?

3. Consider the reading list for one of the literature classes you have taken or are taking, in either high school or college. Based on the reading list as well as the syllabus, lectures, discussions, and other materials for the course, write an essay in which you analyze your teacher's implicit position on the debate over the canon. What criteria does your teacher use for selecting required reading? What does the teacher regard as the purpose for reading? How does the teacher view the relationship between books and understanding our culture?

4. Pollitt does not address other media—such as television, film, and the Internet—that reflect or influence our culture. Write an essay in which you explore the ways in which these other media have affected how we read. You may choose to write a personal essay about the effect certain media have had on your reading, a cultural critique that analyzes contemporary attitudes and behaviors, or a combination of both.

The "Banking" Concept of Education

Paulo Freire

Most of us have had learning experiences driven by what Paulo Freire calls the "banking" concept of education—the teacher, as the authority, "deposits" knowledge into students. Freire (pronounced "Fr-air-ah") believes that learning should instead be driven by inquiry involving dialogue between teachers and students, in which teachers become students and students become teachers. To submit to the "banking" concept, says Freire, is to capitulate to those in power, who control learning in order to maintain the status quo. Freire proposes displacing "banking" with "problem-posing" education, a process of seeing reality in terms of our relationship to the world. It is through this process that students are liberated, by "becoming more fully human."

Freire's approach to education was deeply influenced by his work with adults living in the impoverished urban and rural areas of Brazil. A native of Brazil, Freire was drawn to education after university studies in law, philosophy, and the psychology of language. In addition to reading extensively in education, he absorbed the writings of Marx as well as Catholic intellectuals. Working through government and university organizations, he developed a "pedagogy of the oppressed," for the purpose of giving marginalized people the power to shape their own lives. His approach encouraged political action during a time when competing reform movements in Brazil challenged those in positions of military and economic power. The effectiveness, and consequent threat, of Freire's work led to his exile from Brazil after a 1964 military coup.

Exile gave Freire the opportunity to continue developing and spreading the practice of his pedagogy, first in Chile, then as a teacher and fellow at Harvard University, and eventually through the World Council of Churches in Geneva, Switzerland. After sixteen years in exile, Freire returned to Brazil as a faculty member at the University of São Paulo. In his capacity as minister of education for the city of São Paulo, he later led in the reform of Brazil's schools.

Worldwide, Freire is regarded as one of the central figures in educational philosophy and practice. His books include *Education as the Practice of Freedom* (1967); *Pedagogy of the Oppressed* (1970), the source of the following selection; *Education for Critical Consciousness* (1973); and *The Politics of Education* (1985). Freire died in 1997 at the age of seventy-five.

A careful analysis of the teacher-student relationship at any level, inside or outside the school, reveals its fundamentally *narrative* character. This relationship involves a narrating Subject (the teacher) and patient, listening objects (the students). The contents, whether values or empirical dimensions of reality, tend in the process of being narrated to become lifeless and petrified. Education is suffering from narration sickness.

The teacher talks about reality as if it were motionless, static, compartmentalized, and predictable. Or else he expounds on a topic completely alien to the existential experience of the students. His task is to "fill" the students with the contents of his narration—contents which are detached from reality, disconnected from the totality that engendered them and could give them significance. Words are emptied of their concreteness and become a hollow, alienated, and alienating verbosity.

The outstanding characteristic of this narrative education, then, is the sonority of words, not their transforming power. "Four times four is sixteen; the capital of Pará is Belém." The student records, memorizes, and repeats these phrases without perceiving what four times four really means, or realizing the true significance of "capital" in the affirmation "the capital of Pará is Belém," that is, what Belém means for Pará and what Pará means for Brazil.

Narration (with the teacher as narrator) leads the students to memorize mechanically the narrated content. Worse yet, it turns them into "containers," into "receptacles" to be "filled" by the teacher. The more completely she fills the receptacles, the better a teacher she is. The more meekly the receptacles permit themselves to be filled, the better students they are.

Education thus becomes an act of depositing, in which the students are 5 the depositories and the teacher is the depositor. Instead of communicating, the teacher issues communiqués and makes deposits which the students patiently receive, memorize, and repeat. This is the "banking" concept of education, in which the scope of action allowed to the students extends only as far as receiving, filing, and storing the deposits. They do, it is true, have the opportunity to become collectors or catalogers of the things they store. But in the last analysis, it is the people themselves who are filed away through the lack of creativity, transformation, and knowledge in this (at best) misguided system. For apart from inquiry, apart from the praxis, individuals cannot be truly human. Knowledge emerges only through invention and reinvention, through the restless, impatient, continuing, hopeful inquiry human beings pursue in the world, with the world, and with each other.

In the banking concept of education, knowledge is a gift bestowed by those who consider themselves knowledgeable upon those whom they consider to know nothing. Projecting an absolute ignorance onto others, a characteristic of the ideology of oppression, negates education and knowledge as processes of inquiry. The teacher presents himself to his students as their necessary opposite; by considering their ignorance absolute, he justifies his own existence. The students, alienated like the slave in the Hegelian dialectic,° accept their ignorance as justifying the teacher's existence — but, unlike the slave, they never discover that they educate the teacher.

The raison d'être° of libertarian education, on the other hand, lies in its drive towards reconciliation. Education must begin with the solution of the teacher-student contradiction, by reconciling the poles of the contradiction so that both are simultaneously teachers *and* students.

This solution is not (nor can it be) found in the banking concept. On the contrary, banking education maintains and even stimulates the contradiction through the following attitudes and practices, which mirror oppressive society as a whole:

a. the teacher teaches and the students are taught;
b. the teacher knows everything and the students know nothing;
c. the teacher thinks and the students are thought about;
d. the teacher talks and the students listen — meekly;
e. the teacher disciplines and the students are disciplined;
f. the teacher chooses and enforces his choice, and the students comply;
g. the teacher acts and the students have the illusion of acting through the action of the teacher;
h. the teacher chooses the program content, and the students (who were not consulted) adapt to it;
i. the teacher confuses the authority of knowledge with his or her own professional authority, which she and he sets in opposition to the freedom of the students;
j. the teacher is the Subject of the learning process, while the pupils are mere objects.

Hegelian dialectic: The dynamic model of nature and mind offered by German philosopher Georg Wilhelm Friedrich Hegel (1770–1831), where a thesis comes into tension with an antithesis leading to new or further synthesis).
raison d'être: Reason for being.

EXHIBIT 4–9
Trademark Registration Certificate

The United States of America

CERTIFICATE OF REGISTRATION
PRINCIPAL REGISTER

The Mark shown in this certificate has been registered in the United States Patent and Trademark Office to the named registrant.

The records of the United States Patent and Trademark Office show that an application for registration of the Mark shown in this Certificate was filed in the Office; that the application was examined and determined to be in compliance with the requirements of the law and with the regulations prescribed by the Director of the United States Patent and Trademark Office; and that the Applicant is entitled to registration of the Mark under the Trademark Act of 1946, as Amended.

A copy of the Mark and pertinent data from the application are part of this certificate.

This registration shall remain in force for TEN (10) years, unless terminated earlier as provided by law, and subject to compliance with the provisions of Section 8 of the Trademark Act of 1946, as Amended.

Nicholas P. Godici

Acting Director of the United States Patent and Trademark Office

---

Int. Cl.: 35

Prior U.S. Cls.: 100, 101, and 102

United States Patent and Trademark Office

Reg. No. 2,502,926
Registered Oct. 30, 2001

SERVICE MARK
PRINCIPAL REGISTER

GROWTH ARCHITECTURE

SCHULER, ANDREW J. (UNITED STATES CITI-
ZEN)
6300 STEVENSON AVE., SUITE 916
ALEXANDRIA, VA 22304

FOR: BUSINESS MANAGEMENT CONSULTING
SERVICES, IN CLASS 35 (U.S. CLS. 100, 101 AND 102).

FIRST USE 8-1-2000; IN COMMERCE 8-1-2000.

SN 75-857,060, FILED 11-24-1999.

GEOFFREY FOSDICK, EXAMINING ATTORNEY

It is not surprising that the banking concept of education regards men as adaptable, manageable beings. The more students work at storing the deposits entrusted to them, the less they develop the critical consciousness which would result from their intervention in the world as transformers of that world. The more completely they accept the passive role imposed on them, the more they tend simply to adapt to the world as it is and to the fragmented view of reality deposited in them.

The capability of banking education to minimize or annul the students' creative power and to stimulate their credulity serves the interests of the oppressors, who care neither to have the world revealed nor to see it transformed. The oppressors use their "humanitarianism" to preserve a profitable situation. Thus they react almost instinctively against any experiment in education which stimulates the critical faculties and is not content with a partial view of reality but always seeks out the ties which link one point to another and one problem to another.

Indeed, the interests of the oppressors lie in "changing the consciousness of the oppressed, not the situation which oppresses them"[1] for the more the oppressed can be led to adapt to that situation, the more easily they can be dominated. To achieve this end, the oppressors use the banking concept of education in conjunction with a paternalistic social action apparatus, within which the oppressed receive the euphemistic title of "welfare recipients." They are treated as individual cases, as marginal persons who deviate from the general configuration of a "good, organized, and just" society. The oppressed are regarded as the pathology of the healthy society, which must therefore adjust these "incompetent and lazy" folk to its own patterns by changing their mentality. These marginals need to be "integrated," "incorporated" into the healthy society that they have "forsaken."

The truth is, however, that the oppressed are not "marginals," are not people living "outside" society. They have always been "inside"—inside the structure which made them "beings for others." The solution is not to "integrate" them into the structure of oppression, but to transform that structure so that they can become "beings for themselves." Such transformation, of course, would undermine the oppressors' purposes; hence their utilization of the banking concept of education to avoid the threat of student *conscientização.*°

The banking approach to adult education, for example, will never propose to students that they critically consider reality. It will deal instead with such vital questions as whether Roger gave green grass to the goat, and insist upon the importance of learning that, on the contrary, Roger gave green

---

conscientização: The ability to perceive social, political, and economic contradictions, and to act against the oppressive elements of reality.

grass to the rabbit. The "humanism" of the banking approach masks the effort to turn women and men into automatons—the very negation of their ontological vocation to be more fully human.

Those who use the banking approach, knowingly or unknowingly (for there are innumerable well-intentioned bank-clerk teachers who do not realize that they are serving only to dehumanize), fail to perceive that the deposits themselves contain contradictions about reality. But, sooner or later, these contradictions may lead formerly passive students to turn against their domestication and the attempt to domesticate reality. They may discover through existential experience that their present way of life is irreconcilable with their vocation to become fully human. They may perceive through their relations with reality that reality is really a *process*, undergoing constant transformation. If men and women are searchers and their ontological vocation is humanization, sooner or later they may perceive the contradiction in which banking education seeks to maintain them, and then engage themselves in the struggle for their liberation.

But the humanist, revolutionary educator cannot wait for this possibility to materialize. From the outset, her efforts must coincide with those of the students to engage in critical thinking and the quest for mutual humanization. His efforts must be imbued with a profound trust in people and their creative power. To achieve this, they must be partners of the students in their relations with them.

The banking concept does not admit to such partnership—and necessarily so. To resolve the teacher-student contradiction, to exchange the role of depositor, prescriber, domesticator, for the role of student among students would be to undermine the power of oppression and serve the cause of liberation.

Implicit in the banking concept is the assumption of a dichotomy between human beings and the world: a person is merely *in* the world, not *with* the world or with others; the individual is spectator, not re-creator. In this view, the person is not a conscious being (*corpo consciente*); he or she is rather the possessor of *a* consciousness: an empty "mind" passively open to the reception of deposits of reality from the world outside. For example, my desk, my books, my coffee cup, all the objects before me—as bits of the world which surrounds me—would be "inside" me, exactly as I am inside my study right now. This view makes no distinction between being accessible to consciousness and entering consciousness. The distinction, however, is essential: The objects which surround me are simply accessible to my consciousness, not located within it. I am aware of them, but they are not inside me.

It follows logically from the banking notion of consciousness that the educator's role is to regulate the way the world "enters into" the students. The teacher's task is to organize a process which already occurs spontaneously, to "fill" the students by making deposits of information which he or she considers to constitute true knowledge.[2] And since people "receive" the world as passive entities, education should make them more passive still, and adapt them to the world. The educated individual is the adapted person, because she or he is better "fit" for the world. Translated into practice, this concept is well suited to the purposes of the oppressors, whose tranquility rests on how well people fit the world the oppressors have created, and how little they question it.

The more completely the majority adapt to the purposes which the dominant minority prescribe for them (thereby depriving them of the right to their own purposes), the more easily the minority can continue to prescribe. The theory and practice of banking education serve this end quite efficiently. Verbalistic lessons, reading requirements,[3] the methods for evaluating "knowledge," the distance between the teacher and the taught, the criteria for promotion: Everything in this ready-to-wear approach serves to obviate thinking.

The bank-clerk educator does not realize that there is no true security in his hypertrophied role, that one must seek to live *with* others in solidarity. One cannot impose oneself, nor even merely, coexist with one's students. Solidarity requires true communication, and the concept by which such an educator is guided fears and proscribes communication.

Yet only through communication can human life hold meaning. The teacher's thinking is authenticated only by the authenticity of the students' thinking. The teacher cannot think for her students, nor can she impose her thought on them. Authentic thinking, thinking that is concerned about *reality*, does not take place in ivory-tower isolation, but only in communication. If it is true that thought has meaning only when generated by action upon the world, the subordination of students to teachers becomes impossible.

Because banking education begins with a false understanding of men and women as objects, it cannot promote the development of what Fromm calls "biophily," but instead produces its opposite: "necrophily."

> While life is characterized by growth in a structured, functional manner, the necrophilous person loves all that does not grow, all that is mechanical. The necrophilous person is driven by the desire to transform the organic into the inorganic, to approach life mechanically, as if all living persons were things. . . . Memory, rather than experience; having, rather than being, is what counts. The necrophilous person can relate to an object—a flower or a person—only if he possesses it; hence a threat to his possession is a threat to himself; if he loses possession he loses contact with the world. . . . He loves control, and in the act of controlling he kills life.[4]

Oppression—overwhelming control—is necrophilic; it is nourished by love of death, not life. The banking concept of education, which serves the interests of oppression, is also necrophilic. Based on a mechanistic, static, naturalistic, spatialized view of consciousness, it transforms students into receiving objects. It attempts to control thinking and action, leads women and men to adjust to the world, and inhibits their creative power.

When their efforts to act responsibly are frustrated, when they find themselves unable to use their faculties, people suffer. "This suffering due to impotence is rooted in the very fact that the human equilibrium has been disturbed."[5] But the inability to act which causes people's anguish also causes them to reject their impotence, by attempting

> . . . to restore [their] capacity to act. But can [they], and how? One way is to submit to and identify with a person or group having power. By this symbolic participation in another person's life, [men have] the illusion of acting, when in reality [they] only submit to and become part of those who act.[6]

Populist manifestations perhaps best exemplify this type of behavior by the oppressed, who, by identifying with charismatic leaders, come to feel that they themselves are active and effective. The rebellion they express as they emerge in the historical process is motivated by that desire to act effectively. The dominant elites consider the remedy to be more domination and repression, carried out in the name of freedom, order, and social peace (that is, the peace of the elites). Thus they can condemn—logically, from their point of view—"the violence of a strike by workers and [can] call upon the state in the same breath to use violence in putting down the strike."[7]

Education as the exercise of domination stimulates the credulity of students, with the ideological intent (often not perceived by educators) of indoctrinating them to adapt to the world of oppression. This accusation is not made in the naive hope that the dominant elites will thereby simply abandon the practice. Its objective is to call the attention of true humanists to the fact that they cannot use banking educational methods in the pursuit of liberation, for they would only negate that very pursuit. Nor may a revolutionary society inherit these methods from an oppressor society. The revolutionary society which practices banking education is either misguided or mistrusting of people. In either event, it is threatened by the specter of reaction.

Unfortunately, those who espouse the cause of liberation are themselves surrounded and influenced by the climate which generates the banking concept, and often do not perceive its true significance or its dehumanizing power. Paradoxically, then, they utilize this same instrument of alienation in what they consider an effort to liberate. Indeed, some "revolutionaries" brand as "innocents," "dreamers," or even "reactionaries" those who would challenge this educational practice. But one does not liberate people by alienating them. Authentic liberation—the process of humanization—is not another deposit to be made in men. Liberation is a praxis: the action and reflection of men and women upon their world in order to transform it. Those truly committed to the cause of liberation can accept neither the mechanistic concept of consciousness as an empty vessel to be filled, nor the use of banking methods of domination (propaganda, slogans—deposits) in the name of liberation.

Those truly committed to liberation must reject the banking concept in its entirety, adopting instead a concept of women and men as conscious beings, and consciousness as consciousness intent upon the world. They must abandon the educational goal of deposit-making and replace it with the posing of the problems of human beings in their rela-

Education is suffering from tions with the world. "Problem-posing" education,
narration sickness. responding to the essence of consciousness—*intentionality*—rejects communiqués and embodies communications. It epitomizes the special characteristic of consciousness: being *conscious of*, not only as intent on objects but as turned in upon itself in a Jasperian° "split"—consciousness as consciousness *of* consciousness.

Liberating education consists in acts of cognition, not transferrals of information. It is a learning situation in which the cognizable object (far from being the end of the cognitive act) intermediates the cognitive actors—teacher on the one hand and students on the other. Accordingly, the practice of problem-posing education entails at the outset that the teacher-student contradiction be resolved. Dialogical relations—indispensable to the capacity of cognitive actors to cooperate in perceiving the same cognizable object—are otherwise impossible.

Indeed, problem-posing education, which breaks with the vertical patterns 30 characteristic of banking education, can fulfill its function as the practice of freedom only if it can overcome the above contradiction. Through dialogue, the teacher-of-the-students and the students-of-the-teacher cease to exist and a new term emerges: teacher-student with students-teachers. The teacher is no longer merely the-one-who-teaches, but one who is himself taught in dialogue with the students, who in turn while being taught also teach. They become jointly responsible for a process in which all grow. In this process, arguments based on "authority" are no longer valid; in order to function, authority must be *on the side of* freedom, not *against* it. Here, no one teaches another, nor is anyone self-taught. People teach each other, mediated by the world, by the cognizable objects which in banking education are "owned" by the teacher.

The banking concept (with its tendency to dichotomize everything) distinguishes two stages in the action of the educator. During the first, he

---

Jasperian: Karl Jaspers (1883–1969), a German psychiatrist and philosopher who had a strong influence on modern theology, psychiatry, and philosophy.

cognizes a cognizable object while he prepares his lessons in his study or his laboratory; during the second, he expounds to his students about that object. The students are not called upon to know, but to memorize the contents narrated by the teacher. Nor do the students practice any act of cognition, since the object towards which that act should be directed is the property of the teacher rather than a medium evoking the critical reflection of both teacher and students. Hence in the name of the "preservation of culture and knowledge" we have a system which achieves neither true knowledge nor true culture.

The problem-posing method does not dichotomize the activity of the teacher-student: She is not "cognitive" at one point and "narrative" at another. She is always "cognitive," whether preparing a project or engaging in dialogue with the students. He does not regard cognizable objects as his private property, but as the object of reflection by himself and the students. In this way, the problem-posing educator constantly re-forms his reflections in the reflection of the students. The students—longer docile listeners—are now critical coinvestigators in dialogue with the teacher. The teacher presents the material to the students for their consideration, and reconsiders her earlier considerations as the students express their own. The role of the problem-posing educator is to create, together with the students, the conditions under which knowledge at the level of the *doxa* is superseded by true knowledge, at the level of the *logos*.

Whereas banking education anesthetizes and inhibits creative power, problem-posing education involves a constant unveiling of reality. The former attempts to maintain the *submersion* of consciousness; the latter strives for the *emergence* of consciousness and *critical intervention* in reality.

Students, as they are increasingly posed with problems relating to themselves in the world and with the world, will feel increasingly challenged and obliged to respond to that challenge. Because they apprehend the challenge as interrelated to other problems within a total context, not as a theoretical question, the resulting comprehension tends to be increasingly critical and thus constantly less alienated. Their response to the challenge evokes new challenges, followed by new understandings; and gradually the students come to regard themselves as committed.

Education as the practice of freedom—as opposed to education as the ³⁵ practice of domination—denies that man is abstract, isolated, independent, and unattached to the world; it also denies that the world exists as a reality apart from people. Authentic reflection considers neither abstract man nor the world without people, but people in their relations with the world. In these relations consciousness and world are simultaneous: Consciousness neither precedes the world nor follows it.

> La conscience et le monde sont donnés d'un même coup: extérieur par essence à la conscience, le monde est, par essence relatif à elle.[8]

In one of our culture circles in Chile, the group was discussing (based on a codification) the anthropological concept of culture. In the midst of the discussion, a peasant who by banking standards was completely ignorant said: "Now I see that without man there is no world." When the educator responded: "Let's say, for the sake of argument, that all the men on earth were to die, but that the earth itself remained, together with trees, birds, animals, rivers, seas, the stars . . . wouldn't all this be a world?" "Oh no," the peasant replied emphatically. "There would be no one to say: 'This is a world.'"

The peasant wished to express the idea that there would be lacking the consciousness of the world which necessarily implies the world of consciousness. *I* cannot exist without a *non-I*. In turn, the *not-I* depends on that existence. The world which brings consciousness into existence becomes the world *of* that consciousness. Hence, the previously cited affirmation of Sartre: "*La conscience et le monde sont donnés d'un même coup.*"

As women and men, simultaneously reflecting on themselves and on the world, increase the scope of their perception, they begin to direct their observations towards previously inconspicuous phenomena:

> In perception properly so-called, as an explicit awareness [*Gewahren*], I am turned towards the object, to the paper, for instance. I apprehend it as being this here and now. The apprehension is a singling out, every object having a background in experience. Around and about the paper lie books, pencils, inkwell, and so forth, and these in a certain sense are also "perceived," perceptually there, in the "field of intuition"; but whilst I was turned towards the paper there was no turning in their direction, nor any apprehending of them, not even in a secondary sense. They appeared and yet were not singled out, were not posited on their own account. Every perception of a thing has such a zone of background intuitions or background awareness, if "intuiting" already includes the state of being turned towards, and this also is a "conscious experience," or more briefly a "consciousness of" all indeed that in point of fact lies in the co-perceived objective background.[9]

That which had existed objectively but had not been perceived in its deeper implications (if indeed it was perceived at all) begins to "stand out," assuming the character of a problem and therefore of challenge. Thus, men and women begin to single out elements from their "background awarenesses" and to reflect upon them. These elements are now objects of their consideration, and, as such, objects of their action and cognition.

In problem-posing education, people develop their power to perceive critically *the way they exist* in the world *with which* and *in which* they find themselves; they come to see the world not as a static reality, but as a reality in process, in transformation. Although the dialectical relations of women and men with the world exist independently of how these relations are perceived (or whether or not they are perceived at all), it is also true that the form of action they adopt is to a large extent a function of how they perceive themselves in the world. Hence, the teacher-student and the students-teachers reflect simultaneously on themselves and the world without dichotomizing this reflection from action, and thus establish an authentic form of thought and action.

Once again, the two educational concepts and practices under analysis come into conflict. Banking education (for obvious reasons) attempts, by mythicizing reality, to conceal certain facts which explain the way human beings exist in the world; problem-posing education sets itself the task of demythologizing. Banking education resists dialogue; problem-posing education regards dialogue as indispensable to the act of cognition which unveils reality. Banking education treats students as objects of assistance; problem-posing education makes them critical thinkers. Banking education inhibits creativity and domesticates (although it cannot completely destroy) the *intentionality* of consciousness by isolating consciousness from the world, thereby denying people their ontological and historical vocation of becoming more fully human. Problem-posing education bases itself on creativity and stimulates true reflection and action upon reality; thereby responding to the vocation of persons as beings who are authentic only when engaged in inquiry and creative transformation. In sum: Banking theory and practice, as immobilizing and fixating forces, fail to acknowledge men and women as historical beings; problem-posing theory and practice take the people's historicity as their starting point.

Problem-posing education affirms men and women as beings in the process of *becoming*—as unfinished, uncompleted beings in and with a likewise unfinished reality. Indeed, in contrast to other animals who are unfinished, but not historical, people know themselves to be unfinished; they are aware of their incompletion. In this incompletion and this awareness lie the very roots of education as an exclusively human manifestation. The unfinished character of human beings and the transformational character of reality necessitate that education be an ongoing activity.

Education is thus constantly remade in the praxis. In order to *be*, it must *become*. Its "duration" (in the Bergsonian° meaning of the word) is found in the interplay of the opposites *permanence* and *change*. The banking method emphasizes permanence and becomes reactionary; problem-posing education—which accepts neither a "well-behaved" present nor a predetermined future—roots itself in the dynamic present and becomes revolutionary.

Bergsonian: Henri-Louis Bergson (1859–1941), a French philosopher influential in the first half of the twentieth century.

Problem-posing education is revolutionary futurity. Hence, it is prophetic (and, as such, hopeful). Hence, it corresponds to the historical nature of humankind. Hence, it affirms women and men as beings who transcend themselves, who move forward and look ahead, for whom immobility represents a fatal threat, for whom looking at the past must only be a means of understanding more clearly what and who they are so that they can more wisely build the future. Hence, it identifies with the movement which engages people as beings aware of their incompletion—a historical movement which has its point of departure, its Subjects and its objective.

The point of departure of the movement lies in the people themselves. But since people do not exist apart from the world, apart from reality, the movement must begin with the human-world relationship. Accordingly, the point of departure must always be with men and women in the "here and now," which constitutes the situation within which they are submerged, from which they emerge, and in which they intervene. Only by starting from this situation—which determines their perception of it—can they begin to move. To do this authentically they must perceive their state not as fated and unalterable, but merely as limiting—and therefore challenging.

Whereas the banking method directly or indirectly reinforces men's fatalistic perception of their situation, the problem-posing method presents this very situation to them as a problem. As the situation becomes the object of their cognition, the naive or magical perception which produced their fatalism gives way to perception which is able to perceive itself even as it perceives reality, and can thus be critically objective about that reality.

A deepened consciousness of their situation leads people to apprehend   45
that situation as a historical reality susceptible of transformation. Resignation gives way to the drive for transformation and inquiry, over which men feel themselves to be in control. If people, as historical beings necessarily engaged with other people in a movement of inquiry, did not control that movement, it would be (and is) a violation of their humanity. Any situation in which some individuals prevent others from engaging in the process of inquiry is one of violence. The means used are not important; to alienate human beings from their own decision-making is to change them into objects.

This movement of inquiry must be directed towards humanization—the people's historical vocation. The pursuit of full humanity, however, cannot be carried out in isolation or individualism, but only in fellowship and solidarity; therefore it cannot unfold in the antagonistic relations between oppressors and oppressed. No one can be authentically human while he prevents others from being so. Attempting *to be more* human, individualistically, leads to *having more*, egotistically, a form of dehumanization. Not that it is not fundamental *to have* in order *to be* human. Precisely because it *is* necessary, some men's *having* must not be allowed to constitute an obstacle to others' *having*, must not consolidate the power of the former to crush the latter.

Problem-posing education, as a humanist and liberating praxis, posits as fundamental that the people subjected to domination must fight for their emancipation. To that end, it enables teachers and students to become Subjects of the educational process by overcoming authoritarianism and an alienating intellectualism; it also enables people to overcome their false perception of reality. The world—no longer something to be described with deceptive words—becomes the object of that transforming action by men and women which results in their humanization.

Problem-posing education does not and cannot serve the interests of the oppressor. No oppressive order could permit the oppressed to begin to question: Why? While only a revolutionary society can carry out this education in systematic terms, the revolutionary leaders need not take full power before they can employ the method. In the revolutionary process, the leaders cannot utilize the banking method as an interim measure, justified on grounds of expediency, with the intention of *later* behaving in a genuinely revolutionary fashion. They must be revolutionary—that is to say, dialogical—from the outset.

Notes

1. Simone de Beauvoir, *La pensée de droite, aujourd'hui* (Paris); ST, *El pensamiento político de la derecha* (Buenos Aires, 1963), p. 34.

2. This concept corresponds to what Sartre calls the "digestive" or "nutritive" concept of education, in which knowledge is "fed" by the teacher to the students to "fill them out." See Jean-Paul Sartre, "Une idée fundamentale de la phénomenologie de Husserl: L'intentionalité," *Situations* I (Paris, 1947).

3. For example, some professors specify in their reading lists that a book should be read from pages 10 to 15—and do this to "help" their students!

4. Eric Fromm, *The Heart of Man* (New York, 1966), p. 41.

5. Ibid., p. 31.

6. Ibid.

7. Reinhold Niebuhr, *Moral Man and Immoral Society* (New York, 1960), p. 130.

8. Sartre, op. cit., p. 32. [The passage is obscure but could be read as "Consciousness and the world are given simultaneously: The outside world as it enters consciousness is relative to our ways of perceiving it."—Editor's note]

9. Edmund Husserl, *Ideas—General Introduction to Pure Phenomenology* (London, 1969), pp. 105–06.

Working with the Text

1. Paulo Freire opens his argument with a description of what he calls the "banking" concept of education, in which "the students are the depositories and the

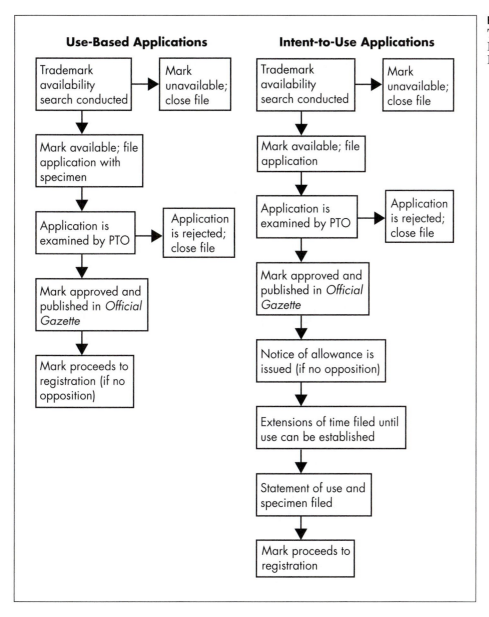

EXHIBIT 4-10
Trademark
Prosecution
Flowchart

line is an invaluable tool, allowing parties to track applications and to receive information and critical dates. Many IP practitioners routinely call the status line and take notes on the progress of an application so they will be ready to respond if a client has questions about an application. The status line number is (703) 305-8747. Alternatively, the PTO web site offers a new method of monitoring the status of applications and registrations. This new system, called Trademark Applications and Retrieval (TARR), at http://www.uspto.gov allows checking of an unlimited number of applications and registrations.

teacher is the depositor" (par. 5). He uses related metaphors to describe students as "containers" or "receptacles" to be "filled" by the teacher. Write a brief essay in which you use specific examples from your own education to illustrate your understanding of what Freire means by the "banking" concept.

2. As you reread the essay, think about the ways in which Freire constructs his image of the student. In a brief essay, compare the student who is a "container" to the student who is a "problem-poser." What is their relationship to the teacher? How do they gather knowledge? Who do they become as the result of how they are educated?

3. Freire argues that the "capability of banking education to minimize or annul the students' creative power and to stimulate their credulity serves the interests of the oppressors, who care neither to have the world revealed nor to see it transformed" (par. 10). Based on what Freire sees as the effects of both banking education and problem-posing education, write a brief essay that teases out the meaning of this assertion. In what ways does banking education minimize creative power and stimulate credulity? In what ways does problem-posing education reveal and transform the world?

From Text to Field

1. In his description of problem-posing education, Freire emphasizes communication, intentionality, action, and becoming fully human. Identify passages in which he is most specific about what teachers and students do in the problem-posing process. In an essay, recall a time when you experienced some aspect of the process Freire describes. As you re-create the experience, capture not only what was said and done but also your awareness that you were seeing something new, making connections to what Freire calls your own "situation" or being moved to action. Alternatively, have you ever been in a class that seemed to be based on processes similar to Freire's problem-posing method but that did not challenge you to a commitment to learning and exploring? In an essay, describe the experience, using Freire's selection to help you analyze what was missing or what was not working.

2. Students will not necessarily, or will not always, respond to problem-posing education in the ways Freire describes. In a short essay, analyze why a student might prefer banking education or might sometimes find it more useful. Consider, in those cases, whether the student risks becoming the "adapted man" Freire warns against. Might the role or value of problem-posing education differ according to the discipline or the subject studied? Might there be a place for the "banking" concept in our educational system? Why or why not?

3. In describing the "problem-posing method," Freire says that "[t]he teacher presents the material to the students for their consideration, and reconsiders his earlier considerations as the students express their own" (par. 33). In Freire's sense of the word, "consider" his essay from the vantage point of your own experience and knowledge. In a letter, or in an imagined dramatic dialogue with Freire, respond to one of his concepts or assertions. Based on your understanding of his method, pose a problem that invites a response from him. Keep in mind that you, the student, are also the teacher, and that Freire, the teacher, is also the student.

What Are Universities For?

Louis Menand

Why are you pursuing a college education? What do universities regard as their mission? What does the American public expect higher education to contribute to the making of individuals as well as citizens? Louis Menand's question—"What are universities for?"— emerged as a national issue in 1987, when Allan Bloom, a professor of social thought at the University of Chicago, published the best-selling *The Closing of the American Mind.* Widely read outside as well as inside the academy, Bloom's book is an indictment of what he regards as the abandonment of Western culture—with principle, tradition, and depth of soul being displaced by relativism and the politicization of the humanities. Menand contends that Bloom's assessment, along with the debate it sparked, misses the mark because it fails to consider how students actually regard their college education and how, in historical and social terms, the university has become "too many things to too many people." In Menand's view, the university must face its limitations as a social force and "restrict itself to the business of imparting some knowledge to the people who need it."

Menand brings to the debate his own teaching experience at Princeton, Columbia, and the University of Virginia. He is currently professor of English at the Graduate Center of the City University of New York. A prolific and highly respected social critic, Menand is a contributing editor for the *New York Review of Books* and a staff writer at the *New Yorker.* He most recently published *The Metaphysical Club* (2001), a study of the rise of American pragmatism that explores the cultural contexts that shaped the work of William James, John Dewey, and others. Highly regarded, this book has won many awards, among them the Pulitzer Prize.

Several times in the last few years I have taught a course called Introduction to Poetry. The class was always overenrolled; I usually spent the beginning of the first few meetings turning students away. Its popularity had nothing to do with me—I was one of many instructors, teaching one of many sections, and all the sections were overenrolled. Introduction to Poetry was popular because it happened to satisfy three requirements: It was a prerequisite for English department courses; it could be used as the final installment in a sequence of composition courses all students had to take; and, as a "humanities" elective, it satisfied a college-wide distribution requirement.

There are 18,000 students at my school, which is one campus of a public university. Most of them are pursuing careers in fields remote from literature; many know English only as a second language. These students approach a course on poetry with the same sense of dread with which most English majors might approach an advanced course in statistics. Other students, though, are eager to take an English course—not because they hope to acquire an appreciation of poetry, but because they believe it will enhance their communications skills and help them get into law school. And there are a few students who want to become English majors because English literature is their primary academic interest.

All of these types of students have turned up in every section of Introduction to Poetry, so I found myself trying to teach some of my students how to write a grammatical sentence, to introduce others to the academic study of literature, and to give the rest of them—though most were essentially unacquainted with serious literary culture—exposure to the best that has been thought and said in the world. For the majority of the students, of course (as they were not shy about making me aware), the principal object was to secure the passing grade needed to fulfill whatever requirement happened to apply in their case. You could walk away from a session of Introduction to Poetry feeling that whatever the current public debate over the university was about—"political correctness," deconstruction, "multiculturalism," the canon—what you had just spent the last hour or so doing had very little to do with it. Ideology was about as remote a presence in an Introduction to Poetry classroom as leather bindings.

In all the uproar over the academy—which entered the mainstream of public debate in 1987 with Allan Bloom's best-selling *The Closing of the American Mind*, and which has produced, more recently, Roger Kimball's *Tenured Radicals*, Dinesh D'Souza's *Illiberal Education* (also a best seller), cover stories in almost every news and opinion magazine of note, and even some observations in a commencement address last spring by President Bush—no one has bothered to ask what practical effect the so-called politicization of the humanities has actually had on the undergraduate mind. Seventy-four percent of the nation's freshman class last year described themselves, in a poll conducted by the American Council on Education, as politically middle-of-the-road or conservative. When they were asked why they chose to attend college, the most popular answer, picked by 78 percent, was to "get a better job" followed by to "make more money" (73 percent). Asked to name an objective they considered "essential or very important," 74 percent chose "being very well-off financially"; second place went to "raising a family," named by 70 percent (an answer almost equally popular among male and female students).

There is no evidence I know of to suggest that in four years spent trying to win the grades and recommendations needed for jobs or for admission to graduate or professional school, these students become radicalized, or are in any way deflected from the social mainstream, by the few humanities courses they are required to take. Students enrolled in Introduction to Poetry would learn just as much about poetry from a professor who thought Milton was a sexist as they would from one who didn't—which is to say, in either case, that they would have had to read and talk for a few hours about a writer of whom they would otherwise remain essentially ignorant. The professor's political slant, if it can be ferreted out, makes a difference to most students only insofar as it might determine the kind of questions likely to turn up on an exam. The effect the course might have on those students' good opinion of Milton—or of any other poet they are likely to be required to read—is a microscopic influence, rapidly diminishing to zero as college recedes behind them, on their ultimate sense of things.

The educational ethos is different at a selective, residential, private college. There students are likely to be better primed to become personally engaged with the course material; they are also likely to feel the loss of income higher education represents less acutely, which enables them to enter into the spirit of their instruction with their eyes a little less fixed on the bottom line. Students at elite colleges identify much more strongly with their professors: They want to argue the nuances and to pick up the insights. But in the end the practical impact is much the same. Anyone who has taught literature at such a school knows the phenomenon: The brightest students happily learn the most advanced styles of contemporary critical theory, with all of their radical political implications, and then they apply, with equal good cheer, to business school. Whatever subversiveness they have ingested has mostly served to give them a kind of superior intellectual sophistication that they are right to feel is not in the least bit incompatible with professional success on Wall Street or Madison Avenue.

Academic thought may have been heading left in the last ten years or so, in other words, but college students themselves have been heading straight into the mainstream. Even comfortably middle-class students feel an economic imperative almost unknown to middle-class students of twenty years ago. When I was a freshman, in 1969, I didn't have a thought in my head about how I was eventually going to support myself. I suppose I imagined that I would just hitchhike around the country with my guitar (which I didn't know how to play) reciting my poetry (which I didn't know how to write).

In the 1990s, though, young people in the middle class are perfectly alive to the fact that they go to college because they have to; young people not in the middle class continue to go to college for the reason they always have, which is to get into the middle class. It seems to me that there is every good reason to challenge these students for a semester or two to think with a little balanced skepticism about the conventional wisdom of the society they are so anxious to join. But whether they're being taught skepticism or not, literature classes are the last places students are likely to be getting their values. Madonna has done more to affect the way young people think about sexuality than all the academic gender theorists put together. Perhaps D'Souza should write a book about her.

It's easier, of course, to attack Catharine Stimpson, the former dean of graduate school at Rutgers and former president of the Modern Language Association, who has become one of the point persons in the defense of new academic trends. Stimpson doesn't appear on MTV, so there isn't a tidal wave of popular sentiment to overcome before one can take her to task. But the lack of a mass following ought to be a clue to the extent of Stimpson's, or any other academic's, real influence on the culture at large. A group of literature professors calling themselves Teachers for a Democratic Culture has come together this fall to launch a counteroffensive against the attack on "political correctness." I suspect that it's a little late in the day for a counteroffensive: The center on this issue has already been grabbed. But one of the arguments this new group wants to make is that the whole situation has been exaggerated. I think it's a just complaint.

It isn't hard to guess the motives behind the controversy in its present melo- 10 dramatic mode. It is always tempting to blame bad conditions on bad ideas, and it must seem to conservatives that since liberal and leftist thinking has been driven out of nearly every other part of American life, the pitiful remnant of left-wing ideology that has taken refuge in university literature departments must be the reason social problems so disobligingly persist. It is the good fortune of conservatives that this is a view that meets exactly the belief of some of the professors being attacked, which is that they are in possession of the one ground—the humanities curriculum of American colleges—on which real social change might be accomplished. The American media, for their rather inflammatory part, are always happy to find an occasion not to appear too liberal, and the excesses of "political correctness" are the perfect thing to get noisily to the right of. The whole controversy is marvelously apt in a country that no longer shows any interest in publicly funded social programs; for whichever political faction wins control of the undergraduate reading list, no taxpayer dollars will have been spent.

This doesn't mean that there's not a crisis. But the issue is not whether (in the words of some of the demonstrators against Stanford's core curriculum a few years ago) Western culture's got to go. Western culture, whether it's in good odor at the Modern Language Association these days or not, we're stuck with. The real issue concerns the role of higher education in American life. Too many people are fighting over how much T. S. Eliot versus how much Alice Walker young minds ought to be exposed to, and not enough people are asking why undergraduate English courses should be bearing the load of this debate in the first place. What is it we are expecting colleges to do that makes the particular mix of the reading lists in literature courses seem to spell the difference between—well, between culture and anarchy?

Matthew Arnold is, indeed, the name most frequently associated with the traditional idea of liberal arts education that the new wave of "politicization" in the academy is supposed to be wrecking. But the liberal arts component of higher education belongs to what is in some ways the least salient of the university's social functions. In fact, the Arnoldian program of using humanistic studies as a means of moral instruction, far from being the most venerable of the university's activities, entered the modern university almost as an afterthought.

The modern university in America is defined by two features, both of which date from the late nineteenth century: the existence of an elective curriculum for undergraduates and the existence of a graduate school, which trains the people who teach the undergraduates. The elective system was not designed to disseminate culture. When Charles William Eliot instituted the first elective system, at Harvard in 1883, his idea was to allow college students to "track" themselves in the direction of their future careers—not to acquire a common culture, but to specialize according to individual needs. Eliot believed that college ought to play a vocational role, to serve a frankly utilitarian function. His faith in the real-world utility of academic studies was great enough, in fact, to allow him, in 1901, to praise the assembled scholars of the Modern Language Association, virtually all of whom were philologists, by telling them that their work enjoyed "a vital connection with the industrial and commercial activities of the day."

At the same time, Eliot saw the need to provide specialists to train college students, and in 1890 he established the Harvard Graduate School of Arts and Sciences, modeled on the first research institution in the country, Johns Hopkins (founded in 1876). The principal function of the graduate school is the production of teachers, whom it certifies with the doctoral degree, to staff the modern college; but it also produces scholarly research, and the research ideal is expressly nonutilitarian. The researcher cannot be influenced by what the world will find profitable: The goal is knowledge for its own sake, without regard for "the industrial and commercial activities of the day."

So there was already in the modern university, as Eliot and the other ₁₅
late-nineteenth-century pioneers of higher education helped to create it, a
contradiction between what professors do, which is to follow their research
interests, and what their students do, which is to prepare for careers outside
the academy—to pursue "education for experience," as Eliot called it.
There is no reason, of course, as William James complained in 1903 in an
essay called "The Ph.D. Octopus," why the possession of a doctorate,
earned by scholarship, should serve as a credential for teaching undergraduates; yet these separate functions were made to complement each
other, and by the end of the nineteenth century the ideals of research and
of vocational training had achieved such an ascendancy in American universities that a reaction against them occurred on behalf of what was called,
by many of its champions, "liberal culture." This reaction is the origin of
the idea that college is the place of future social leaders to be exposed to,
in Arnold's phrase, "the study of perfection." The liberal arts "tradition"
that the new scholarship is accused of trashing, in other words, is not even
a century old.

The "true aim of culture," wrote Hiram Corson, the chairman of the
Cornell English department and a proponent of "liberal culture," in 1894, is
"to induce soul states or conditions, soul attitudes, to attune the inward
forces to the idealized forms of nature and of human life produced by art,
and not to make the head a cockloft for storing away the trumpery of barren
knowledge." This ideal is both anti-utilitarian and antiresearch, and the reaction on its behalf was successful enough to lead, in 1909, to Eliot's replace-
ment as president of Harvard by A. Lawrence Lowell—a member of the faculty who, many years before, had opposed the institution of the elective system. Thus emerged the third mission of the modern academy: the liberalization, through exposure to art, literature, and philosophy, of the undergraduate mind.

Although no school was ever purely one type or another, universities
before 1910 could be distinguished according to their leading educational
ideals: Harvard was utilitarian, for example; Johns Hopkins, Clark, and
Chicago were research institutions. Schools like Princeton and Yale tended
to resist both these trends. But after 1910 (as Laurence Veysey explains in *The
Emergence of the American University*) there was a shift. Educators stopped
arguing about ideals; the various versions of what properly constituted higher
education were no longer regarded as conflicting. The university learned to
accommodate divergent views of its purpose, and the goal of the people who
administered universities became not the defense of an educational philosophy but the prosperity of the institution. And the prosperity of the institution
depended on its being, to as great an extent as it found possible, all things to
all people.

This is how a pedagogical portmanteau like Introduction to Poetry could come into being—a single course on a specific subject expected to serve, all at the same time, a utilitarian function (by training students how to read and write), a research function (by preparing future English majors for the scholarly study of literature), and a liberal arts function (by exposing students to the leavening influence of high culture).

Even at schools where there is no actual Introduction to Poetry course, the overall effect of the undergraduate curriculum is the same. Students in the humanities are expected to major in a field—French, say, or religion—that will provide them with a lot of knowledge most of which will be useful only in the unlikely event they decide to enter graduate school and become professors themselves. At the same time, they are required to fulfill "distribution" requirements designed to expose them to smatterings of learning in every major area—with the vague idea that this contributes to something approximating genuine well-roundedness, and thus serves a "liberalizing" function. And there is the expectation, now almost universal, that beyond college lies professional school, for which some practical training will be useful.

It's possible to argue that these three educational functions—scholarly, vocational, and liberalizing—are only three ways of looking at the same thing, which is the exposure to knowledge. For higher

The university is unequipped to deal with conflicts that cannot be treated simply as conflicts of ideas.

education in any field certainly can serve, simultaneously, all three purposes: pure speculation, practical application, and general enlightenment. Even so, there needs to be a consensus that these benefits are worth pursuing, and that the traditional structure of the university provides the best means of doing so, in order for the system to work effectively. Three recent developments, none of them having to do explicitly with politics—illiberal or not—seem to me to have undermined this consensus.

The first is the major demographic change in the undergraduate population over the last twenty years, a change that reflects both a significant increase in the proportion of people who attend college (from 1970 to 1988, the percentage of Americans who had completed four years of college doubled) and a significant increase on most campuses in the proportion of students who are not white or not male. This means that the average college class is not the relatively homogeneous group, culturally and socioeconomically speaking, it once was: The level of preparation among students differs more widely, and their interests and assumptions differ as well.

Since the whole idea of liberal arts education is to use literature and philosophy as a way of learning how to value one's interests and assumptions, it is (or it ought to be) obviously absurd to insist that books that served this function when the audience was predominantly made up of young middle-class

20

white men can serve the same function now that the audience is more diverse. When Columbia College admitted women for the first time, in 1983, it was suddenly realized by the faculty that the reading list for Humanities A, the famous great books course required of all students, had never included a book by a woman. Though for years it had been advertised as representing the best that the educated person needed to know, the list was changed: Sappho and Jane Austen became great writers. It took some fancy rhetoric to explain why this adjustment didn't amount to a confession that "the great books" is really just a grand name for "the books that will expose students to ideas we want them at the moment to be talking about." And that is part of the problem; for since so much has been emotionally (and, I think, mistakenly) invested in the traditional great books curriculum, changes can't happen without resentment and reaction.

The second development putting pressure on traditional educational ideals is the spread of critical theory as a kind of interdisciplinary currency in university humanities departments. For contemporary critical theory—in particular post-structuralist theories, emphasizing the indeterminacy of meaning, and ideological theories, emphasizing the social construction of values—rejects precisely the belief on which the professional apparatus of the university (graduate exams, dissertation defenses, tenure review, publication in refereed journals, and so forth) depends: the belief that the pursuit of knowledge is a disinterested activity whose results can be evaluated objectively by other trained specialists in one's field. "What's really going on" in the production of knowledge is now regarded, by these new theoretical lights, as not a disinterested enterprise at all but an effort to make the views of a particular class of people prevail.

This rejection of the positivistic model of knowledge production has helped to turn the system of professional rewards, always an arena for academic politics, into an arena for real-world politics as well. Critical theorists whose work attacks the traditional premises of scholarship are invited into humanities departments for the good marketing reason that their work is where the action is today: Every graduate program wants a prominent profile. But the system whose principles those professors teach one another to regard with skepticism remains, except that it has been thoroughly corrupted. It is now regarded as legitimate by some professors to argue that the absence of a political intention or multicultural focus in another professor's work constitutes a prima facie disqualification for professional advancement. And why not, if all scholarship is at bottom political anyway?

Finally, there has been a change in the role of college in the preparation   25 of young people for careers outside the academy. Although the number of bachelor's degrees awarded each year has been increasing steadily—by 28 percent between 1970 and 1989—the number of professional degrees has

TRIVIA

- The public initiates more than 1 million queries per month through TESS (the online trademark search system).
- Mattel Inc. applied for 5,501 trademarks in 1999.
- Elvis Presley Enterprises, Inc. (the successor to the estate of Elvis Presley) owns more than 100 trademark applications and registrations, including registrations for HEART-BREAK HOTEL for toys and BLUE SUEDE SHOES for key chains and shot glasses.
- In early 2001, the Federal Circuit held that a hair care company's mark TREVIVE was likely to cause confusion with Alberto-Culver's trademark TRESEMME® used for hair care products for more than forty years.

CHAPTER SUMMARY

After searching and clearance of a mark for availability, an application should be filed with the PTO for registration of the mark. If the mark has actually been used in interstate commerce, the application should be accompanied by a specimen showing how the mark is actually used.

The application will be carefully reviewed by an examining attorney to determine if it meets the statutory requirements and whether any marks similar to the proposed mark have been registered or applied for in the same or related industries. The examining attorney's objections are enumerated in an office action. An applicant has six months to respond to an office action. The process continues until either the application is finally refused or it is allowed for publication in the *Official Gazette,* a weekly government publication. Individuals who believe they may be injured by the proposed registration have a statutory period within which to oppose registration of the mark. If no opposition is filed, the mark will proceed to registration.

If the applicant has not yet engaged in actual use of the mark, the procedure is essentially the same. The application will be reviewed by an examining attorney, who will approve it, publish it for opposition in the *Official Gazette,* and issue a notice of allowance. The applicant will then have six months to begin use of the mark in commerce and file a statement of use verifying such use with an actual specimen attached. Extensions of time may be granted. After review of the statement of use and specimen, the mark will be registered. Registration is a complex and lengthy process even if there are only minimal problems.

CASE ILLUSTRATION—USE IN COMMERCE

Case: *Zazu Designs v. L'Oreal, S.A.,* 979 F.2d 499 (1992)

Facts: Zazu used the mark ZAZU for salon services only in a suburb of Chicago. After conducting a search, L'Oreal applied for federal registration for ZAZU for hair care products. Zazu alleged infringement.

been increasing at a much greater rate. The material value of a BA is a function of supply: The greater the number of people who have one, the less a BA is worth in the marketplace. Particularly for students interested in "being very well-off financially" (74 percent, according to the American Council of Education survey), it has now become imperative not to stop with the BA but to proceed to professional school; and the number of MBAs awarded between 1970 and 1989 therefore increased by 239 percent, the number of MDs by 88 percent, the number of law degrees by 143 percent. Increases in advanced degrees in architecture, engineering, and a number of other nonacademic professional fields were similarly dramatic.

This wave of professionalism has transformed the experience of college. The academic demands on undergraduates are in a sense now more real, since good grades are essential for getting over the hurdle to the next degree program; but the content is somehow less real, since most students now perceive that the education that matters to them will take place after college is finished. This helps to explain the phenomenon of the undergraduate whiz in Foucauldian analysis who goes merrily on to a career in corporate finance.

These various challenges to the established design of higher education present difficulties that have little to do with politics. Perhaps the university will find a way to muddle through them, but muddling alone is not likely to be very effective. For it is not only a philosophical idea about education that is being thrown into doubt by these recent developments. It is also the institutional structure of the university itself.

I happen to think, for example—and without putting any political valuation on the judgment—that contemporary theoretical skepticism about the positivistic nature of "knowledge" in fields like literature is perfectly justified. It is absurd to treat literary criticism as a species of scientific inquiry; the professional system of rewards in the humanistic disciplines is essentially bogus and leads mostly to intellectual conformity, predictable "demonstrations" of theoretical points, and a panicky desire to please one's elders and superiors. But what university is about to tear down the bureaucratic system of professional advancement in the humanities? How would departments administer themselves without the fiction that they were engaged in the production of real knowledge about real specialities?

Similarly, the undergraduate major seems to me an institution that is at best pedagogically inefficient (why should students going on to law school have to pass a course of what amounts to preprofessional training for graduate school in English or some other academic discipline?) and at worst a contributor to the perpetuation of a fundamentally arbitrary definition of knowledge. The modern academic discipline is only as old as the modern university: Before the 1800s, no one imagined that history, political science, economics, anthropology, and sociology constituted distant areas of study, each with its own theoretical and methodological traditions. Nor was it imagined by most people that "literature" was a discriminable area of human endeavor that must be talked about exclusively in literary-critical (as opposed to sociological or ethical or theological) terms.

But these distinctions have become institutionalized in the form of aca- 30 demic departments; the people who work in those departments have professionalized themselves to keep out "unqualified" practitioners; and the professions run the fields, monopolizing both instruction and scholarship. It seems to me that a college student today might want, in four years, to acquire knowledge about American culture, about American politics and law, and about capitalism. What a student who bothers to seek out knowledge in these areas is likely to get are courses introducing him or her to the academic specialities of American studies, political science, and economics. Though there is no reason why every undergraduate should not receive it, a practical introduction to the law or to business must usually wait until law school or business school, since that is where the specialists are. Because there are no instructors who are not certified members of an academic discipline, there is very little genuinely general education going on in American colleges.

These problems are severe enough, but they don't explain completely why the university is in such a bad way right now. Questions about educational philosophy must eventually have educational answers; the contemporary university, though, has reached beyond the purview of education, and it has thereby become entangled in problems it lacks the means to resolve. Universities can decide the things people ought to know, and they can decide how those things should be taught. But universities cannot arbitrate disputes about democracy and social justice, or govern the manner in which people relate socially to one another, or police attitudes; and that is what they are being asked to do today.

To some extent this overreaching is the fault of the society as a whole, which is happy to turn over to educators problems it lacks the will (and, it believes, the means) to address politically. It is easier to integrate a reading list, or even a dormitory, than it is to integrate a suburban neighborhood. But to some extent it is the consequence of the university's own indiscriminate appetite, whose history begins in the 1960s.

The contention that the current problems in the academy are the natural outcome of sixties radicalism is common to many of the recent attacks on higher education—it can be found in Bloom's, Kimball's, and D'Souza's books. I think the claim is basically false, and that (as Camille Paglia argued in a long diatribe on the subject last spring in the journal *Arion*) the humorless ethos of the politically correct humanities department could not be more antithetical to the spirit of the 1960s. Even the most callow radicalism of that era has nothing to do with the sort of doctrinaire political attitudes critics of the contemporary academy complain about. Are the people who are so eager to censor "fighting words" on campus today the same people who went around in 1968 calling anyone wearing a uniform or a necktie a "pig"? If they are the same people, they've left their radicalism behind.

There is one thing, however, that the present situation does owe to the 1960s, and that is the belief that the university is a miniature reproduction of the society as a whole. That idea dominates, for example, the Port Huron Statement, the manifesto of the New Left drafted by Tom Hayden and endorsed by the Students for a Democratic Society in 1962. But it is not only a leftist idea; for the postwar university has always been eager to incorporate every new intellectual and cultural development that has come its way.

The university is, in fact, expressly designed to do this: It can accommo- 35 date almost any interest by creating a new course, a new program, a new studies center. It has managed, for instance, to institutionalize activities like painting and creative writing, not traditionally thought to require academic preparation, by devising MFA programs—which, in turn, provide a place on university faculties for practicing painters and writers. When new scholarly movements emerged—Third World Studies, Women's Studies—the university was quick to establish research centers and institutes to house them. Degrees are now offered in almost everything. There are few intellectual activities left that do not have an academic incarnation.

The problems begin when this process of absorption extends beyond the intellectual realm. In the late 1960s, serious attention began to be paid by university administrators to the quality of campus life. This, too, was in part a response to student protest: Everyone agreed, for example, that one of the lessons of the crisis that led to the shutdown of Columbia in 1968 was that the college had to become less like a corporation and more like a community. But it was also natural that, as higher education became accessible to (and desired by) a greater variety of people in the postwar boom years, the university would evolve in this direction of its own accord.

This development of the university as a social microcosm has been guided in most places by the view (which originated with the students themselves) that there should be available within the walls of the academy the full range of experiences available (or ideally available) outside. The initial breakthrough was a purely middle-class phenomenon: the liberalization of parietal restrictions. (In the late 1960s, to give an idea of the magnitude of the change that has taken place, a student at Barnard, a sophisticated school in a sophisticated city, was expelled for sharing an apartment with her boyfriend *off campus*.) The eventual abandonment of regulations governing relations between the sexes was followed by the sexual integration of many traditionally single-sex schools (Princeton, Yale, Dartmouth, Vassar), and by the recruitment of ethnic minorities in the interest (among other things) of social diversity on campus.

This enormous and successful engulfment of intellectual and social variety, coming on top of the shocks to the system's *academic* identity, is what has given the university its present headache. The university has become, at last, too many things to too many people. It now reproduces all the conflicts of the culture at large; but it reproduces them, as it were, in vitro. For unlike the society it simulates, the university is unequipped, both administratively and philosophically, to deal with conflicts that cannot be treated simply as conflicts of ideas. It has the machinery needed to arbitrate the sorts of disagreements that arise naturally in the pursuit of the university's traditional educational goals; but it is not designed to arbitrate among antagonistic interest groups, or to discover ways of correcting inequities and attitudes that persist in the society as a whole.

The reason is that the university is required, by its accommodationist philosophy, to give equal protection to every idea and point of view anyone chooses to express. This is, of course, an indispensable principle of intellectual freedom. But when the issue is political, when it involves the distribution of power, accommodationism fails. For power is a zero-sum game. In the real world, interest groups vie against one another for resources in the knowledge that one group gains by taking from other groups. Political and legal institutions exist to mediate these struggles.

In the university, though, no one has ever needed to cede ground to someone else, since conflict has always been avoided by expanding the playing field. But this strategy doesn't work when the stakes are not simply intellectual. As long as the activities of the Gay Student Alliance and the Bible Study Group remain merely academic, they can coexist. Once those groups become versions of their real-world counterparts — once they become actively political — there is no way to keep both of them happy. But who in the university wants to have to choose between them? In the nonacademic world, pluralism means a continual struggle over the distribution of a single pie. In the academic world (and the Democratic Party), it means trying to give every group a pie of its own. 40

Yet somehow it is expected that, once they are relocated to a campus, differences that have proved intractable elsewhere will be overcome, both in the classroom and in the student union. This insistence, on the part of academics and nonacademics alike, on making higher education the site for political and social disputes of all types, and on regarding the improvement of social relations and the mediation of political differences as one of higher education's proper functions, has produced ridiculous distortions. Thus we have a debate, for example, in which the economic rights of women are argued about in terms of reading lists for introductory literature courses — as though devoting fewer class hours to male authors might be counted a blow against discrimination in the workplace. And outside the classroom, in the dorms and the dean's office, the university has managed to become a laboratory for the study and cure of social problems like date rape.

There are as well the notorious speech codes and disciplinary procedures aimed at enforcing campus "civility." These are mostly the results of hasty attempts to jury-rig disciplinary systems whose need had not been felt until it became commonly assumed that how students addressed one another was a matter college administrators ought to be concerned about. That the president of the university should have become the leading figure and spokesperson in the incident in which a Brown undergraduate was expelled for drunkenly shouting insults at no one in particular is an indication not only that the university doesn't know how seriously it is supposed to be taking these sorts of "problems" but that it has no appropriate administrative apparatus for dealing with them either.

And there is, to take a final example, the notion—much less prevalent than the critics of political correctness claim, but present nonetheless—that the undergraduate curriculum should include courses whose purpose is, in effect, to cheerlead for civil and sexual rights. There is no doubt that many civil and sexual rights remain to be secured in this country; there is no doubt that scandalous inequities persist unattended to. But English professors are not experts on these matters. They are taught how to identify tropes, not how to eliminate racist attitudes. To turn their courses into classes on (say) Post-Colonial Literature with the idea of addressing with some degree of insight the problem of ethnocentrism is to ask someone equipped to catch butterflies to trap an elephant.

This is done, usually, by pretending the butterfly is an elephant—by loading up a poem with so much ideological baggage that it can pass for an instrument of oppression. Poems won't bear the weight; most works of literature are designed to deflect exactly this kind of attention and to confute efforts to assign them specific political force. If literature is taught honestly from an ideological perspective—if what a book seems to say about the relations of power among people is made the focus of classroom discussion—students are just being led around the mulberry bush. It's not that the spirit of great literature is being dishonored, for literature can surely be talked about ideologically; it's that a false impression is being created among students that unhappiness whose amelioration lies in real-world political actions is being meaningfully addressed by classroom debates about the representation of the Other in the work of Herman Melville.

Professors should not be regarded as the people in possession of the "cor- ⁴⁵ rect" views on subjects of public concern. But the idea that they ought to be has become an illusion shared by academics and their critics alike. When George Will wrote last spring in *Newsweek* that the task faced by Secretary of Defense Dick Cheney was less urgent than the one confronting his wife, Lynne, who is the director of the National Endowment for the Humanities, he sounded clearly the note of hysteria that has come to dominate debate about higher education in America. Mrs. Cheney, Will suggested, "is secretary of domestic defense. The foreign adversaries her husband, Dick, must keep at bay are less dangerous, in the long run, than the domestic forces with which she must deal. Those forces are fighting against the conservation of the common culture that is the nation's social cement."

This is witch-hunt talk; but it repeats an error found in less partisan writing as well, which is that the care of "the common culture" is the responsibility of college professors. Professors are people trained to *study* culture, not to *conserve* it (whatever that would mean). Their purview is limited by the kind of work, always highly specialized and narrowly defined, professionals in their disciplines have traditionally done. It is no favor to these people to regard them as the guardians of our culture or as experts on ministering to its self-inflicted wounds. Nor is it a favor to the culture to hand it over to academics for its nourishment and protection.

Social and political controversies have swamped the academy for two reasons: because universities, unwilling to define their mission in specific terms and eager to accommodate everything that comes along, could not find a rationale for keeping those controversies at bay; and because there has been so little serious intellectual debate in the rest of American society in the last ten years. There have been no real ideas argued in American politics, for instance, since Ronald Reagan showed that ideas were overrated. And intellectual journalism has become dominated by position-taking—the point-counterpoint syndrome, which permits just two points of view to every prepackaged "issue."

It is almost certain that one of the effects of the public scrutiny of what professors do will be to turn the academy into another bastion of intellectual predictability. I'm not sure that hasn't happened already. But if not, the only way to prevent it is for the university to renounce the role of model community and arbiter of social disputes that it has assumed, to ignore the impulse to regulate attitudes and expressions that are the epiphenomena of problems far outside the college walls, to stop trying to set up academic housing for every intellectual and political interest group that comes along, and to restrict itself to the business of imparting some knowledge to the people who need it.

Working with the Text

1. Louis Menand's essay addresses what he considers to be a crisis in university education. In his argument, he assumes his audience has a certain amount of familiarity with the debate, a familiarity you might not share. As you reread the essay, what can you infer about the nature of the crisis? Based on your reading of Menand's argument, write a brief essay in which you provide a snapshot or distillation of the crisis to an audience of your peers—students with a level of familiarity similar to yours. What prompted the debate? What are the key issues? What is at stake, for university students as well as for American culture?

2. According to Menand, one of the recent developments that have undermined reaching consensus on university education has been "the major demographic change in the undergraduate population over the last twenty years" (par. 21). Choose one specific aspect of demographic change (socioeconomic status, access to education, gender, ethnic diversity, etc.) to analyze this assertion in more detail, adding your own observations and reasoning to Menand's. For example, how would such a shift in demographics influence codes of conduct or the attempt to "discover ways of correcting inequities and attitudes that persist in the society as a whole" (par. 38) or the trend toward more students going on to professional schools?

3. In the final sentence, Menand answers the question he poses in the essay's title by asserting that the university must "restrict itself to the business of imparting some knowledge to the people who need it." In a brief essay, respond to this assertion by first analyzing what Menand means by "some knowledge" and "the people who need it." According to Menand, who needs to know what? Why do they "need" to know it? Do you agree with him? Why or why not? Is Menand's assertion realistic or desirable? What might universities or citizens lose if Menand were to have his way?

4. In large part, Menand argues for what universities should be by arguing against what he believes they have become. As you reread the essay, note Menand's objections to particular roles now taken on by universities. In a brief essay, address one of those objections. Do you agree with him? Why or why not?

From Text to Field

1. As a point of departure for his argument, Menand notes the results of a poll conducted by the American Council on Education that asked students why they chose to attend college. Menand also describes student attitudes that he has encountered as an educator. With these and other passages in mind, write a personal essay that reveals your own reasons for pursuing an undergraduate degree. What "knowledge" do you think you "need," and to what end? Do you

expect certain courses to have a lasting influence or "a microscopic influence, rapidly diminishing to zero as college recedes" on your "ultimate sense of things" (par. 5)?

2. Menand criticizes "the notion . . . that the undergraduate curriculum should include courses whose purpose is, in effect, to cheerlead for civil and sexual rights" (par. 43). In a brief essay, analyze a course you are taking or have taken that has or seems to have cheerleading for rights as one of its purposes. What form does the advocacy for civil and sexual rights take? How large a part of the course is it? Is the advocacy effective? Do you think this is a legitimate purpose for a course? How realistic is it to avoid advocacy of any kind?

3. Commenting on where students get their values, Menand says, "Madonna has done more to affect the way young people think about sexuality than all the academic gender theorists put together" (par. 8). In a personal essay that reflects on your own values or in a cultural critique that examines the values of your peers or a particular group of your peers, identify the sources—outside of your family—of those values. Be specific about personalities, ideas, the medium (such as music, film, discussion groups, lectures, books), and style. What engages and moves you? How do values take root? What authority do the sources carry? As an alternative essay, reflect on one source—one artist, author, teacher, or group—that has been especially powerful in shaping your values or those of your peers.

INTO THE FIELD: Options for Writing Projects

1. Agendas for Literacy

From elementary, high school, and college courses to community programs for recent immigrants and nonnative speakers, your community is the site for various literacy efforts. Choose one program—academic or community based—and examine how this program approaches its interest in literacy. What is its explicit or implied mission statement? How might various pedagogical tools (books, materials, etc.) reflect a choice in how literacy is defined? Does the funding source for the program suggest an interest in one approach over another? How does the program define the needs of its target audience? What other stakeholders are involved in the program's efforts?

Drawing on your research and fieldwork, write a profile of the literacy program that reflects how it situates its definitions of *literacy* among other contending definitions.

2. Writing the Writing Requirement

Based on interviews and available documents such as your college catalog or Web pages, analyze the writing program or writing requirement in your institution. What are its stated purposes? How is it structured, and why? What course options are available? What is the rationale behind the range (or lack of range) of options, and what assumptions about student growth and learning lie behind their sequencing? Based on your analysis, develop a flyer or pamphlet for incoming students in which you speak as one student to another, acting as a peer advisor, about what to expect from and how to navigate the writing program and the writing classroom. Use a style that will readily appeal to other students. Feel free to use humor as you try to help these new students feel comfortable in this new course.

3. Exploring Your Writing Archive

Unearth examples of your writing from some years ago. Look to your parents as (unofficial) archivists, for they often keep copies of your work from elementary or middle school, even high school. As you reflect on your writing from years past, consider what struggles or challenges you had as a writer at that time. What virtues or strengths do you see in your old writing that you would like to regain, if at a more sophisticated level? Based on your close reading of a sample or two, choose one of the following for your writing project:

- Offer an analysis of your writing and how it reflects your attempts to succeed at a task that is now quite familiar to you but was at the time new and foreign. What distinguishes your writing as that of a novice? As you look back at that writing and compare it to your current work, what specific details might help you explain your development as a writer?

- Offer a memoir of yourself as a writer, using the writing you have chosen as its centerpiece or touchstone. How does this seemingly isolated and discrete piece of writing provide a window on your life, both then and now?

4. Reviewing the Transition to College-Level Learning

Locate several books, articles and book chapters, or pamphlets that were written as guides to making the transition into college-level learning. To what extent does the material reflect learning theories as discussed in the readings by Williams and Colomb and by Freire? What alternatives to those theories does the material present, if only implicitly? Feel free to draw on other learning theorists. (You might, for example, be interested in exploring the work of William Perry and his scheme of multiple stages of intellectual development.) Write an analysis or a review of the guide material you have found in light of your reading and your own experience. You may wish to interview classmates or work together as an editorial or review team. How helpful are such guides? To what extent can they prepare you well for the transition to college-level learning? How valid are generalizations about "college-level learning"? What might make those generalizations difficult to offer?

5. The Expert as Novice

Have you ever found yourself in a situation where your expertise in one area offered little help as you moved to a slightly different area? Write an extended personal narrative using one of the options offered below.

- Choose an area in which you clearly have some expertise (such as music, sports, or art), and then reflect on the challenges you might face when trying your hand in a related area or activity at which you are a novice. Why might you easily become frustrated? What might happen—to your learning process, self-image, or confidence—when processes that are second nature in your field of expertise become conscious, concrete, rule-governed, and step by step in the new activity?
- By senior year in high school, you had become an expert in the system of secondary education. Now, as an undergraduate, you are more of a novice. Reflect on what has—and hasn't—changed for you. As you encounter college-level learning and knowledge making, how have your thinking and study habits changed in terms of your ability to master the subject matter, articulate questions, and solve the problems that are posed? Has anything other than the level or amount of knowledge changed? In what ways have expectations changed? Has anyone ever made explicit what those new expectations are? If not, why not?

Holding: Zazu did not have sufficient sales to establish nationwide trademark rights. The Lanham Act allows only trademarks "used in commerce" to be registered. This use requirement is "neither a glitch . . . nor a historical relic." The law requiring use prevents entrepreneurs from reserving marks in order to make their rivals' marketing more costly. Zazu had no product sales until months after L'Oreal had embarked on its nationwide campaign to launch its products. Zazu's few sales did not secure it rights against the world.

CASE STUDY AND ACTIVITIES

Case Study.   Watson has operated a well-known gift and souvenir shop called Treasure Palace at its amusement park for several years. The shop offers a variety of harmonicas, mugs, and shot glasses that display the mark KINGDOM RAPIDS RUN, which is also the name of Watson's new water tube ride. Within the next year or two, Watson also intends to build a new roller coaster called SAFARI EXPLORER. Watson recently filed a trademark application for TREASURE PALACE. The first office action issued by the PTO has stated that the mark is merely descriptive of gift store services. Watson intends to file applications for KINGDOM RAPIDS RUN and SAFARI EXPLORER.

Activities.   You may need to access the PTO web site (http://www.uspto.gov) or the Trademark Manual of Examining Practice (TMEP) to answer some of these questions.
- Describe the arguments Watson should advance in its response to the office action issued rejecting TREASURE PALACE.
- Draft an identification of goods and services for the goods and services offered under KINGDOM RAPIDS RUN (and identify the international classes applicable to the mark), identify the filing fee Watson will need to pay in connection with the application(s), and describe any potential challenges the PTO may raise to registration of the mark.
- Describe the type of application that Watson would file for SAFARI EXPLORER, and draft the identification of services and identify the international class applicable to the mark.

ROLE OF PARALEGAL

Paralegals typically have significant responsibility in the prosecution stage of a trademark application. In many law offices, primary responsibility may be assigned to paralegals, with attorney involvement limited to supervising and advising the paralegal and providing advice to the client on suggested strategies to overcome refusals to register. Among the many tasks IP professionals assume responsibility for are the following:

- gathering information from clients to assist in preparing applications;
- preparing the trademark application;
- reviewing specimen that supports use of a mark for consistency and proper display of mark;
- filing the application and confirming same to client;

6. Reading Fashions and Curricular Politics

When you enroll in a course for just one term, your sense of the syllabus can easily become limited to those few weeks during which you are engaged with the material. But beyond the artificial boundaries of any one term, courses and their reading lists evolve, often in response to reading fashions, the latest pedagogical trend, or curricular politics. Each of the options listed below can help you place your current work in a broader perspective.

- Find one particular course that has been part of the curriculum on your campus for twenty years or more. Based on a review of reading lists and syllabi, catalog course descriptions, and interviews with those faculty or department secretaries who carry around with them some "institutional memory," compare the course in the past to the course as it is currently taught. What inferences can you make about the changes? What hasn't changed?
- Every department has an array of required and elective courses. Choosing one department, consult the current edition of your college catalog for course descriptions and compare it to a catalog from twenty or forty or eighty years ago. (Your campus library or library archive should have a complete run of catalogs from the founding of your institution.) Which new courses have been added, which have disappeared, and which simply seem to endure? What might these changes tell you about which books are being read, and for what purposes? How has the department evolved over time? What might those changes tell you about the evolving mission of the department or your college or about the pressures and expectations that society might place on your institution?
- Propose a new course or a new reading list for an existing course. (Most campuses have a required form for such proposals, and you might find it interesting to try your hand at filling it out.) What decisions did you encounter in proposing that new course or reading list? How would you justify your choices? What are the prevailing interests and concerns of faculty and administrators who would have to approve your proposal?

7. Public Reading Habits

When Katha Pollitt turns her attention to required-reading lists and the currently accepted canon of "Important Books," she urges us not to forget why we read books ourselves. In that spirit, and using her essay as an invitation, check out the reading habits of your community as reflected by your local public library and bookstores. What's hot, and what is in demand? What local interests, concerns, or preferences might be reflected in library circulation statistics or bookstore sales figures? How might your community compare to others in your state or with more national indicators, such as the best-seller lists compiled by the *New York Times* and other publications? You may find it very helpful to interview a local librarian or library administrator.

Alternatively, you may wish to explore one of several national book clubs, such as Oprah Winfrey's. Such clubs have a long history in our society, and some communities even have local chapters. What do their reading lists look like, and how have they changed over the years? What influence might such clubs have in guiding the reading tastes of the public (or in confirming existing tastes)? What special satisfactions or enjoyments might be found in being a member of such a club?

8. What's Off the List: Reading Lists and Censorship

Our preoccupation with required-reading lists and the changing fortunes of various writers may hide from view the darker side of reading lists: Some books are not "on the list" because they have been censored by one of several local or national groups or because the threat of such censorship is very real. You may be surprised to learn that a number of well-known books—both classic and contemporary—have been the subjects of censorship campaigns, among them *The Adventures of Huckleberry Finn* by Mark Twain, *The Diary of a Young Girl* by Anne Frank, *The Catcher in the Rye* by J. D. Salinger, *Nineteen Eighty-four* by George Orwell, and the several books in the Harry Potter series. For your fieldwork project, consider one of the options below. You may find the following Web site to be a helpful point of departure for your fieldwork: http://www.ncte.org/about/over/positions/category/cens. This Web site has links to other national and international organizations concerned with censorship issues.

- Choose a book you know well that has been the subject of censorship battles. After you become familiar with the concerns that prompted calls for censorship, draw on your knowledge of the book to write an essay that evaluates the censorship debate and places it in historical context or the context of prevailing community attitudes.
- Contact the middle school or high school that you attended and interview an English teacher or the principal. Does he or she know of censorship issues that your school is currently experiencing or has experienced in the recent past? Contribute to that debate from the perspective of a former student who has now gone on to college. Alternatively, explore what selection procedures your middle school or high school has in place when determining what books will be read in the classroom. Do those procedures seem adequate or fair?

9. From Banking to Problem-Posing

Describe a course that you have taken that used what Paulo Freire refers to as the "banking concept" of education, and propose specific changes that would permit the course to emphasize to a greater degree a "problem-posing" approach. Focus in some detail on an activity, assignment, or other concrete aspect of the course. What are some of the challenges that both teachers and students might face in seeking to implement a problem-solving approach? What responsibilities do students have in making such an approach successful? Do certain kinds of courses, topics, or activities lend themselves more than others to this kind of reworking? What might be the risks in such a reworking, and what might be lost that you think is of value?

Alternatively, choose one of the many other readings in this book and write a teaching guide that would suggest how to work with that selection in a Freirian manner. How would you orchestrate the discussion, and what might you emphasize? What kind of writing assignment would suit a Freirian approach, and how might a Freirian-inspired instructor comment on that essay? Do you think students would respond positively to your approach? If not, why? What adjustments would your teaching and writing suggestions require of both teachers and students? Can you anticipate ways in which your suggestions might not work as you intend them to?

10. The Banking System

When reading Paulo Freire it is tempting to connect what he says to particular teachers or courses you have had. Yet for the banking approach to education to have such a strong grip on our society, more must be involved than just stories about particular people or courses, be they good or bad. This fieldwork project has you look beyond the particulars to the larger system of education that tends to reinforce the banking approach. What institutional practices support the banking concept? Referring to your secondary education or to your current experiences in college, discuss particular institutional practices and what influence they have. Those practices might include assessment and testing, transcripts and credit hours, the use of textbooks, prerequisites and the sequencing of courses, and the role of credentials. What positive role might some of these institutional practices have? Could a Freirian-inspired approach to education do without such institutional practices, or how might it change them?

11. Menand Comes to Campus

Louis Menand asserts that "universities cannot arbitrate disputes about democracy and social justice, or govern the manner in which people relate socially to one another, or police attitudes; and that is what they are being asked to do today" (par. 31). Identify a policy, practice, or program in your institution that Menand might say is aimed at taking on this kind of responsibility. Write an analysis of that policy, practice, or program. Why was it instituted? What debates surrounded its establishment? Who are its advocates and critics, and what are their positions? How effective is it in accomplishing its purpose? What is your view of its validity as a function of your particular institution?

12. A 1960s Retrospective

In discussing the changing role of higher education in our society, Louis Menand points to the 1960s and early 1970s as a watershed, a turning point in how universities conceived of their social and educational mission and in how society viewed universities. Here are two options for fieldwork projects that invite you to revisit that era.

- Interview one person, or ideally several people, who went to college during the 1960s and early 1970s. What was their firsthand experience? What do they remember of the incidents and developments discussed by Menand? What did they see as the purpose of their own university education? How do they describe their experience of being on a college campus during those years? If possible, include the perspective of someone who taught on a university level during those years. Offer the results of your interviews as a brief oral history or memoir.
- Explore the history of your college or university during the '60s and early '70s. In the context of broader historical events, what specific changes occurred on campus during that time or, if later, may be attributed to the new attitudes that this period fostered? In short, what is the legacy of this period on your campus? Was this period a watershed for your institution? For this fieldwork project, consider interviews with older faculty, back issues of campus newspapers, and published histories of your college or university (in print or online). You may wish to offer the results of your fieldwork as one chapter in such a history.

13. Student Attitudes and Educational Plans

How you "write the university" depends in good measure on your attitudes and educational plans. According to Louis Menand, these attitudes and plans have a profound effect on the changing role of colleges and universities in our society. With your classmates, you might explore why you and others are attending college and what your attitudes might be on a range of educational and career issues. How do your own attitudes square with Menand's portrayal of them?

To lend some national context to your discussions, you may wish to consult the Web site of the Higher Education Research Institute (HERI) at the UCLA Graduate School of Education and Information Studies (GSEIS): http:// www.gseis.ucla.edu/heri/heri.html. For some forty years, the institute has conducted a comprehensive assessment survey of the attitudes and education plans of entering college students. For recent results and survey instruments, consult http://www.gseis.ucla.edu/heri/cirp.html. More recently, the institute has begun to survey students about their experiences during freshman year. Results of the latest "Your First College Year" survey can be found at http://www.gseis.ucla.edu/heri/yfcy/. To what extent do you see your attitudes and plans captured in these surveys? Do you feel that your campus reflects these national results, or is your college community distinctive in one or more respects?

14. The Educational Mission of Your Campus

When Louis Menand speaks of the relationship between colleges and society and tries to answer the question "What are universities for?" he speaks in the most generic ways about higher education. Yet as you may know, there are important differences between fields of study and between types of institutions (public and private, community colleges, regional four-year institutions, flagship state institutions, elite or marquee institutions, etc.). Drawing on the characteristics of your own institution, offer a response to Menand that takes into account the kind of college or university you attend or the kind of degree program in which you are enrolled.

Alternatively, offer an analysis of your institution's mission statement and what it might suggest about the particular relationship with society that your campus seeks to foster. Typically, such mission statements can be found in the catalog or on your college or university Web site. You may find it helpful to compare your school's mission statement with those of similar institutions ("peers," as it were) and with institutions that are quite different. Keep in mind that such mission statements are lofty expressions of an ideal or a goal. To what extent does your college or university follow through on that statement? Consider offering suggestions for refining or revising that mission statement and a rationale for making those suggestions.

3

Persuading Each Other

FRAMES OF REFERENCE

So much information, so little time. If you view your role as a student in the university as something akin to a sponge, soaking up facts, you can easily become overwhelmed and bewildered. Some college courses, alas, encourage that approach, with tests that put a premium on sheer recall of facts. And yet, just because tests may have familiarized you with a binge-regurgitate-forget cycle, the process is no less overwhelming. After all, there is no end to information, and all of it seems to make sense, at least on its own terms.

The key to orienting yourself when you are knee-deep in information is to ask what those "terms" are. As you have already noted, or will quickly learn, debates in the university often hinge on the propensity to define or—what is more often the case—work with terms that come laden with hidden assumptions and unexamined baggage. Understanding and evaluating what the terms of the discussion are can help you make sense of the academic and civic conversations that swirl around you, conversations to which you are now contributing.

Yet our impulse to define, or more broadly, our need to call on or accept any number of terms, can also blind us. We see things in certain ways and forget that other perspectives are possible or are already in play. Kenneth Burke, one of the most prominent and interesting rhetoricians and philosophers of language in the twentieth century, put it this way: "Even if any given terminology is a reflection of reality, by its very nature as a terminology it must be a selection of reality; and to this extent it must function also as a deflection of reality." Our terms function as the glasses on our noses, filtering, shaping, and coloring what and how we see. Terms offer a frame of reference, all too often unacknowledged and unexamined. Indeed, we would do well to think of terms as "filters," which let certain glimpses of the world appear but also withhold others. Kenneth Burke himself termed the screens—"terministic screens."

In much of your university work, it becomes tempting to think that you are working with reality, or at least reflections of reality. For this reason, Burke offers a healthy reminder that the terms we use can also select and deflect reality. But Burke even pushes his case further: "Not only does the nature of our terms affect the nature of our observations, in the sense that the terms direct the attention to one field rather than to another. Also many of the 'observations' are but implications of the particular terminology in terms of which the observations are made." What we see depends on what and how we name. To a writer, someone who trades in words and terms, this conundrum becomes both important and fascinating.

The several readings in this chapter ask us to take a step back from our studies, from the information we use and consume, to ask broader questions about the frames of reference that orient our work. Collectively, the readings help us ask how it is that (to quote Burke once again) "one's terms jump to conclusions." Theodore Roszak cautions us not to become too enamored with data, lest we forget that *the mind thinks with ideas, not with information.* Christopher Lasch challenges us to rethink the relationship between information and public debate. Playing off of our usual associations of science with facts and test tubes, George Orwell also urges us to think of science as a "rational, skeptical, experimental habit of mind." Roger Schank invites us to consider how underlying explanation patterns, or "story skeletons" as he calls them, influence how we perceive and interpret events, and even shape our memory and identity. George Lakoff and Mark Johnson round out the readings by exploring how we not only use metaphors to express what we think but also that those metaphors actually shape our thinking.

Reflecting on Prior Knowledge

1. In a journal entry, recall your experiences with what might be called "information overload." How do you respond to this overload? Does acquiring more information help you think? At what point does additional information make thinking more difficult, and why?

2. Reflect on your experiences with debate. How did you use and search for information? What new information, or the need for information, became evident in the process of debate?

3. In many of your prior courses, whether in college or in high school, you were working on two fronts at once: learning the material in the course ("what" is covered in that field of study) even as you were learning the methods of working in that field ("how" things are done in that field). Working in a small group of your peers, discuss the competing demands of learning both content and method.

4. Consider a scenario drawn from your own experience in which different people knew the same basic facts of a situation, yet developed very different stories to explain that situation to themselves and to others. In a journal entry,

examine how the stories we tell reflect our purposes and our audiences. How might those stories also affect how we recall past events or interpret future events?

5. Working as a team, develop a list of everyday phrases and expressions that we use to communicate, often unconsciously, larger ways of thinking. For example, "time is money" and "living on borrowed time" might suggest ways in which our culture thinks about time and about assigning value. Why do you suppose common, everyday expressions are often our best window on these otherwise hidden or unexamined ways of thinking?

for the role of a thesis/dissertation committee member.

How to work with your advisor and your committee

Even though you have selected your advisor and your committee with great care, it is unlikely there exists a perfect match between what you need and what they can provide. Now, you must know how to work with your advisor and your committee since if any problem arises, you are the one who will be most affected. You should take the initiative to build a satisfactory relationship by seeking advice and showing your improvement and progress. If you would not like to bother your advisor and your committee members, you should not expect them to bother you. After all, it is your thesis/dissertation project. It is desirable for you to derive your own time line and provide them with regular progress reports.

Your advisor, whom you are likely to choose as your committee chair, has the closest working relationship with you, especially if you have been her research assistant for some time. If you also have some prior contacts with the other committee members, you are at a vantage to start your new round of interaction with them. They are there to help you with encouragement for creative thinking, professional judgment to avoid mistakes, additional information, and a referential framework as to what is an acceptable thesis/dissertation. If you run into bad luck, you might have included someone who would regard this committee duty mainly as a reportable work load and may not be very helpful to you. In such a case you will still have to get along with this person and show your respect to her for the time she spent with you anyway. Trying to improve the existing work relationship could be more remedial and timesaving than simply requesting a change of your thesis/dissertation committee.

If your thesis/dissertation is a continuation of the comprehensive or research papers you previously wrote, it is good for you to have the readers on your committee who were satisfied with those papers. Different faculty members have different tastes. Your ideas will not necessarily be appreciated by every faculty member. And you do not want your work to become a subject of debate, even if the debate is purely scientific, because you can hardly afford its consequence as a student. The best way to test the academic market is to put forth such an idea in your paper(s), or in the draft of your thesis/dissertation proposal, to see whether or not your readers buy it. If not, then save the idea and argue for it when you can stand on your own feet (i.e., after you graduate). In any case, the

ROLE OF PARALEGAL (cont'd)

- reviewing the official filing receipt;
- reviewing office actions and reporting same to client;
- performing research for responses to office actions;
- assisting in preparing responses to office actions;
- reviewing the *Official Gazette* to ensure client's mark is accurately reproduced;
- reviewing notice of allowance for ITU applications;
- preparing statement of use and gathering specimen for ITU applications;
- reviewing certificate of registration for accuracy;
- assisting in reporting registration to client;
- docketing all critical dates throughout the prosecution process; and
- monitoring the progress of the application.

INTERNET RESOURCES

PTO web site:	http://www.uspto.gov
Trademark Manual of Examining Practice (TMEP):	http://www.uspto.gov/web/offices/tac/tmep/index.html
Acceptable Identification of Goods and Services Manual:	http://www.uspto.gov (access the PTO web site and select Trademarks. Under Manuals and Publications, select this manual for thousands of examples of goods and services and their classifications, from "abacuses" to "zwieback")
TEAS information and forms:	http://www.uspto.gov/teas/index.html
Official Gazette:	http://www.uspto.gov (access PTO web site and select Trademarks. Under Manuals and Publications, select *Official Gazette* for online access to last five issues of the *Official Gazette*)
General trademark information:	http://www.ll.georgetown.edu; http://www.findlaw.com; and http://www.ipmall.fplc.edu (intellectual property resource web site offered by Pierce Law School)

Of Ideas and Data

Theodore Roszak

The proliferation of information made possible by computer technology can lead us to believe that more facts will result in better ideas. Theodore Roszak contends that technology enthusiasts—especially those who stand to gain from it—actively promote this stance, one that he insists is both intellectually and morally damaging.

The following essay is an excerpt from Roszak's book *The Cult of Information: The Folklore of Computers and the True Art of Thinking* (1986), which examines our fascination with information and the distortions such a fascination can bring to our pursuit of ideas. He writes, "Is our capacity to think creatively being undermined by the very 'information' that is supposed to help us? Is information processing being confused with science or even beginning to replace thought? And are we in danger of blurring the distinction between what machines do when they process information and what minds do when they think?" From Roszak's perspective, if we undermine the deepest ways the human mind works, we will lose the source of our greatest ideas, from scientific theory to moral concepts such as justice.

A professor of history and director of the Ecopsychology Institute of California State University, Hayward, Roszak has gained national recognition as a social commentator. His 1969 book, *The Making of a Counterculture: Reflections on the Technocratic Society and Its Youthful Opposition,* is regarded as a key commentary on the 1960s. His writings include fiction, *The Memoirs of Elizabeth Frankenstein* (1995), as well as nonfiction, such as *Ecopsychology: Restoring the Earth, Healing the Mind* (1995), and *Where the Wasteland Ends* (1995). He has received a Guggenheim Fellowship and has been nominated twice for the National Book Award.

Ideas Come First

In raising these questions about the place of the computer in our schools, it is not my purpose to question the value of information in and of itself. For better or worse, our technological civilization needs its data the way the Romans needed their roads and the Egyptians of the Old Kingdom needed the Nile flood. To a significant degree, I share that need. As a writer and teacher, I must be part of the 5 to 10 percent of our society which has a steady professional appetite for reliable, up-to-date information. I have long since learned to value the services of a good reference library equipped with a well-connected computer.

Nor do I want to deny that the computer is a superior means of storing and retrieving data. There is nothing sacred about the typed or printed page when it comes to keeping records; if there is a faster way to find facts and manipulate them, we are lucky to have it. Just as the computer displaced the slide rule as a calculating device, it has every right to oust the archive, the filing cabinet, the reference book, if it can prove itself cheaper and more efficient.

But I do want to insist that information, even when it moves at the speed of light, is no more than it has ever been: discrete little bundles of fact, sometimes useful, sometimes trivial, and never the substance of thought. I offer this modest, common-sense notion of information in deliberate contradiction to the computer enthusiasts and information theorists who have suggested far more extravagant definitions. In the course of this chapter . . . , as this critique unfolds, it will be my purpose to challenge these ambitious efforts to extend the meaning of information to nearly global proportions. That project, I believe, can only end by distorting the natural order of intellectual priorities. And insofar as educators acquiesce in that distortion and agree to invest more of their limited resources in information technology, they may be undermining their students' ability to think significantly.

That is the great mischief done by the data merchants, the futurologists, and those in the schools who believe that computer literacy is the educational wave of the future: They lose sight of the paramount truth that *the mind thinks with ideas, not with information*. Information may helpfully illustrate or decorate an idea; it may, where it works under the guidance of a contrasting idea, help to call other ideas into question. But information does not create ideas; by itself it does not validate or invalidate them. An idea can only be generated, revised, or unseated by another idea. A culture survives by the power, plasticity, and fertility of its ideas. Ideas come first, because ideas define, contain, and eventually produce information. The principal task of education, therefore, is to teach young minds how to deal with ideas: how to evaluate them, extend them, adapt them to new uses. This can be done with the use of very little information, perhaps none at all. It certainly does not require data processing machinery of any kind. An excess of information may actually crowd out ideas, leaving the mind (young minds especially) distracted by sterile, disconnected facts, lost among shapeless heaps of data.

It may help at this point to take some time for fundamentals.   5

The relationship of ideas to information is what we call a *generalization*. Generalizing might be seen as the basic action of intelligence; it takes two forms. *First*, when confronted with a vast shapeless welter of facts (whether in the form of personal perceptions or secondhand reports), the mind seeks for a sensible, connecting pattern. *Second*, when confronted with very few facts, the mind seeks to create a pattern by enlarging upon the little it has and pointing it in the direction of a conclusion. The result in either case is some general statement which is not in the particulars, but has been imposed upon them by the imagination. Perhaps, after more facts are gathered, the pattern falls apart or yields to another, more convincing possibility. Learning to let go of an inadequate idea in favor of a better one is part of a good education in ideas.

Generalizations may take place at many levels. At the lowest level, they are formulated among many densely packed and obvious facts. These are cautious generalizations, perhaps even approaching the dull certainty of a truism. At another level, where the information grows thinner and more scattered, the facts less sharp and certain, we have riskier generalizations which take on the nature of a guess or hunch. In science, where hunches must be given formal rigor, this is where we find theories and hypotheses about the physical world, ideas that are on trial, awaiting more evidence to strengthen, modify, or subvert them. This is also the level at which we find the sort of hazardous generalizations we may regard as either brilliant insights or reckless prejudices, depending upon our critical response: sweeping statements perhaps asserted as unassailable truths, but based upon very few instances.

Generalizations exist, then, along a spectrum of information that stretches from abundance to near absence. As we pass along that spectrum, moving away from a secure surplus of facts, ideas tend to grow more unstable, therefore more daring, therefore more controversial. When I observe that women have been the homemakers and child minders in human society, I make a safe but uninteresting generalization that embraces a great many data about social systems past and present. But suppose I go on to say, "And whenever women leave the home and forsake their primary function as housewives, morals decline and society crumbles." Now I may be hard pressed to give more than a few questionable examples of the conclusion I offer. It is a risky generalization, a weak idea.

In Rorschach psychological testing, the subject is presented with a meaningless arrangement of blots or marks on a page. There may be many marks or there may be few, but in either case they suggest no sensible image. Then, after one has gazed at them for a while, the marks may suddenly take on a form which becomes absolutely clear. But where is this image? Not in the marks, obviously. The eye, searching for a sensible pattern, has projected it into the material; it has imposed a meaning upon the meaningless. Similarly in Gestalt psychology, one may be confronted with a specially contrived perceptual image: an ambiguous arrangement of marks which seems at first to be one thing but then shifts to become another. Which is the "true" image? The eye is free to choose between them, for they are both truly there. In both cases — the Rorschach blots and the Gestalt figure—the pattern is in the eye of the beholder; the sensory material simply elicits it. The relationship of ideas to facts is much like this. The facts are the scattered, possibly ambiguous marks; the mind orders them one way or another by conforming them to a pattern of its own invention. *Ideas are integrating patterns* which satisfy the mind when it asks the question, What does this mean? What is this all about?

Information is never the substance of thought.

But, of course, an answer that satisfies me may not satisfy you. We may see   10
different patterns in the same collection of facts. And then we disagree and seek to persuade one another that one or the other of these patterns is superior, meaning that it does more justice to the facts at hand. The argument may focus on this fact or that, so that we will seem to be disagreeing about particular facts — as to whether they really *are* facts, or as to their relative importance. But even then, we are probably disagreeing about ideas. For as I shall suggest further on, facts are themselves the creations of ideas.

Those who would grant information a high intellectual priority often like to assume that facts, all by themselves, can jar and unseat ideas. But that is rarely the case, except perhaps in certain turbulent periods when the general idea of "being skeptical" and "questioning authority" is in the air and attaches itself to any dissenting, new item that comes along. Otherwise, in the absence of a well-formulated, intellectually attractive, new idea, it is remarkable how much in the way of dissonance and contradiction a dominant idea can absorb. There are classic cases of this even in the sciences. The Ptolemaic cosmology° that prevailed in ancient times and during the Middle Ages had been compromised by countless contradictory observations over many generations. Still, it was an internally coherent, intellectually pleasing idea; therefore, keen minds stood by the familiar old system. Where there seemed to be any conflict, they simply adjusted and elaborated the idea, or

---

Ptolemaic cosmology: A geocentric view of the universe formulated by the Greek-speaking geographer and astronomer Claudius Ptolemaeus (90–168 A.D.) that was widely accepted until it was superseded by the heliocentric solar system of Copernicus.

restructured the observations in order to make them fit. If observations could not be made to fit, they might be allowed to stand along the cultural sidelines as curiosities, exceptions, freaks of nature. It was not until a highly imaginative constellation of ideas about celestial and terrestrial dynamics, replete with new concepts of gravitation, inertia, momentum, and matter, was created that the old system was retired. Through the eighteenth and nineteenth centuries, similar strategies of adjustment were used to save other inherited scientific ideas in the fields of chemistry, geology, and biology. None of these gave way until whole new paradigms were invented to replace them, sometimes with relatively few facts initially to support them. The minds that clung to the old concepts were not necessarily being stubborn or benighted; they simply needed a better idea to take hold of.

No Ideas, No Information

From the viewpoint of the strict, doctrinaire empiricism which lingers on in the cult of information, the facts speak for themselves. Accumulate enough of them, and they will conveniently take the shape of knowledge. But how do we recognize a fact when we see one? Presumably, a fact is not a mental figment or an illusion; it is some small, compact particle of truth. But to collect such particles in the first place, we have to know what to look for. There has to be the idea of a fact.

The empiricists were right to believe that facts and ideas are significantly connected, but they inverted the relationship. *Ideas create information,* not the other way around. Every fact grows from an idea; it is the answer to a question we could not ask in the first place if an idea had not been invented which isolated some portion of the world, made it important, focused our attention, and stimulated inquiry.

Sometimes an idea becomes so commonplace, so much a part of the cultural consensus, that it sinks out of awareness, becoming an invisible thread in the fabric of thought. Then we ask and answer questions, collecting information without reflecting upon the underlying idea that makes this possible. The idea becomes as subliminal as the grammar that governs our language each time we speak.

Take an example. The time of day, the date. These are among the simplest, least ambiguous facts. We may be right or wrong about them, but we know they are subject to a straightforward true or false decision. It is either 2:15 PM in our time zone, or it is not. It is either March 10, or it is not. This is information at its most irreducible level.

Yet behind these simple facts, there lies an immensely rich idea: the idea of time as a regular and cyclical rhythm of the cosmos. Somewhere in the distant past, a human mind invented this elegant concept, perhaps out of some rhapsodic or poetic contemplation of the bewilderingly congested universe. That mind decided the seemingly shapeless flow of time can be ordered in circles, the circles can be divided into equal intervals, the intervals can be counted. From this insight, imposed by the imagination on the flux of experience, we derive the clock and the calendar, the minutes, days, months, seasons we can now deal with as simple facts.

Most of our master ideas about nature and human nature, logic and value eventually become so nearly subliminal that we rarely reflect upon them as human inventions, artifacts of the mind. We take them for granted as part of the cultural heritage. We live off the top of these ideas, harvesting facts from their surface. Similarly, historical facts exist as the outcroppings of buried interpretive or mythic insights which make sense of, give order to the jumbled folk memory of the past. We pick up a reference book or log on to a data base and ask for some simple information. When was the Declaration of Independence signed and who signed it? Facts. But behind those facts there lies a major cultural paradigm. We date the past (not all societies do) because we inherit a Judeo-Christian view of the world which tells us that the world was created in time and that it is getting somewhere in the process of history. We commemorate the names of people who "made history" because (along other lines) we inherit a dynamic, human-centered vision of life which convinces us that the efforts of people are important, and this leads us to believe that worthwhile things can be accomplished by human action.

When we ask for such simple points of historical information, all this stands behind the facts we get back as an answer. We ask and we answer the questions within encompassing ideas about history which have become as familiar to us as the air we breathe. But they are nonetheless human creations, each capable of being questioned, doubted, altered. The dramatic turning points in culture happen at just that point—where new idea rises up against old idea and judgment must be made.

What happens, then, when we blur the distinction between ideas and information and teach children that information processing is the basis of thought? Or when we set about building an "information economy" which spends more and more of its resources accumulating and processing facts? For one thing, we bury even deeper the substructures of ideas on which information stands, placing them further from critical reflection. For example, we begin to pay more attention to "economic indicators"—which are always convenient, simple-looking numbers—than to the assumptions about work, wealth, and well-being which underlie economic policy. Indeed, our orthodox economic science is awash in a flood of statistical figments that serve mainly to obfuscate basic questions of value, purpose, and justice. What contribution has the computer made to this situation? It has raised the flood level, pouring out misleading and distracting information from every government agency and corporate boardroom. But even more ironically, the hard focus on information which the computer encourages must in time have the effect of crowding out new ideas, which are the intellectual source that generates facts.

In the long run, no ideas, no information.   20

Working with the Text

1. Theodore Roszak wrote this essay out of concern that the amount and speed of information available through computers could distort our view of the relationship between facts and ideas. In a brief essay, explore his concern. What misguided frame of reference does he think we're developing? How does he think we might come to regard information, in the form of facts? What damage does he think this attitude toward information might do to our ability to work with ideas?

2. Roszak's central argument is that "*the mind thinks with ideas, not with information*" (par. 4). Write a short essay in which you respond to his argument by analyzing his description of how the mind works. What does he mean by the assertion, "Ideas come first, because ideas define, contain, and eventually produce information" (par. 4)? Exactly how does Roszak think ideas emerge? What role does he think information plays? Do you agree with him? How do you think ideas emerge? Based on your own experience and observations, what role do you think information plays?

3. Roszak questions our assumptions about the origin of facts themselves, asserting that "Every fact grows from an idea; it is the answer to a question we could not ask in the first place if an idea had not been invented which isolated some portion of the world, made it important, focused our attention, and stimulated inquiry" (par. 13). As you reread the essay, think through the examples he gives of "the substructures of ideas" which serve as the foundation for information we accept as fact—the day and date or certain historical facts. Write a brief essay in which you explore Roszak's idea by proposing and then analyzing another example, one not mentioned in the text. Offer an analysis of the hidden idea behind that fact, in much the same fashion that Roszak might.

From Text to Field

1. A large part of pursuing a college education is learning that, as Roszak says, facts are "human creations, each capable of being questioned, doubted, altered . . . new idea rises up against old idea and judgment must be made" (par. 18). With Roszak's essay in mind, write about your own experience of a new idea

rising up against an old idea in a way that challenged you to either rethink or reaffirm a belief or a point of view.

2. Roszak asks, "What happens, then, when we blur the distinction between ideas and information and teach children that information processing is the basis of thought?" (par. 19). His argument is based on the assumption that computer literacy in the schools is promoting just that. Were you taught, directly or implicitly, that "information processing is the basis of thought"? In a personal essay, describe the approach to computer literacy that you developed in the course of your elementary and secondary education. What kind of information did you learn to gather? What were you asked to do with it? How were you taught to regard computer-based research? What attitudes and assumptions about sources available through the Internet did you develop on your own?

3. As you consider Roszak's description of how ideas and thinking emerge, reflect on your own processes of thinking and developing ideas. How do new ideas or new understandings of ideas emerge for you? Write a description of your thought process, either tracing the way it tends to work in general or recalling a specific experience developing an idea as you were learning new material. Do you, or did you, experience "generalization," as Roszak describes it? Do you recognize what Roszak is describing when he states, "*Ideas are integrating patterns* which satisfy the mind when it asks the question, What does this mean? What is this all about?" (par. 9). Can you say that for you, "*the mind thinks with ideas, not with information*"? Or does information seem to come before ideas in your thought process? If so, why might that seem to be the case?

4. If you have an interest in computer science, you may wish to consider to what extent Roszak's views still hold true or might be modified, given current work in the area of artificial intelligence.

The Lost Art of Political Argument

Christopher Lasch

Although we are less likely to believe that the American press actually achieves objectivity than we were a few decades ago, we still tend to hold it up as an ideal. American historian Christopher Lasch not only dismisses any remaining faith we might have in the objectivity of the press, but he also debunks the ideal itself. He contends that the press should be a forum for open and heated political debate, which he believes is the only course to true democracy. In Lasch's view, we are informed citizens, not when we accumulate information passively and arbitrarily, but when we seek information for deciding a specific, immediate course of action. For Lasch, argument is the vehicle for finding sound information: "We do not know what we need to know until we ask the right questions, and we can identify the right questions only by subjecting our own ideas about the world to the test of public controversy."

A historian at the University of Rochester, Lasch gained respect across the political spectrum as a deeply informed and relentless critic of contemporary American culture. In books published between 1962 and 1995, he challenged what he considered to be ineffective as well as spiritually and morally shallow attempts—particularly by liberals, progressives, and materialists—to shape American society. His influential 1979 book, *The Culture of Narcissism*, was a best seller. The range of his critique is reflected in the titles of other books: *The American Liberals and the Russian Revolution* (1962), *The New Radicalism in America* (1965), *The Minimal Self* (1984), and *The True and Only Heaven: Progress and Its Critics* (1991). The selection offered here was first published as part of the essay "Journalism, Publicity, and the Lost Art of Political Argument" in the *Gannett Center Journal* (Spring 1990) and excerpted shortly thereafter in the September 1990 edition of *Harper's Magazine*. Christopher Lasch died in 1994.

Let us begin with a simple proposition: What democracy requires is public debate, not information. Of course it needs information too, but the kind of information it needs can be generated only by vigorous popular debate. We do not know what we need to know until we ask the right questions, and we can identify the right questions only by subjecting our own ideas about the world to the test of public controversy. Information, usually seen as the precondition of debate, is better understood as its by-product. When we get into arguments that focus and fully engage our attention, we become avid seekers of relevant information. Otherwise, we take in information passively—if we take it in at all.

From these considerations it follows that the job of the press is to encourage debate, not to supply the public with information. But as things now stand the press generates information in abundance, and nobody pays any attention. It is no secret that the public knows less about public affairs than it used to know. Millions of Americans cannot begin to tell you what is in the Bill of Rights, what Congress does, what the Constitution says about the powers of the presidency, how the party system emerged or how it operates. Ignorance of public affairs is commonly attributed to the failure of the public schools, and only secondarily to the failure of the press to inform. But since the public no longer participates in debates on national issues, it has no reason to be better informed. When debate becomes a lost art, information makes no impression.

Let us ask why debate has become a lost art. The answer may surprise: Debate began to decline around the turn of the century, when the press became more "responsible," more professional, more conscious of its civic obligations. In the early nineteenth century the press was fiercely partisan. Until the middle of the century papers were often financed by political parties. Even when they became more independent of parties they did not embrace the ideal of objectivity or neutrality. In 1841 Horace Greeley launched his *New York Tribune* with the announcement that it would be a "journal removed alike from servile partisanship on the one hand and from gagged, mincing neutrality on the other." Strong-minded editors like Greeley, James Gordon Bennett, E. L. Godkin, and Samuel Bowles did not attempt to conceal their own views or to impose a strict separation of news and editorial content. Their papers were journals of opinion in which the reader expected to find a definite point of view, together with unrelenting criticism of opposing points of view.

It is no accident that journalism of this kind flourished during the period from 1830 to 1900, when popular participation in politics was at its height. Eighty percent of the eligible voters typically went to the polls in presidential elections. (After 1900 the percentage began to decline sharply.) Torchlight

DISCUSSION QUESTIONS

1. Would an identification of "toys" in a trademark application be acceptable? Discuss.
2. Describe the type of specimen that would support use of the following marks:

   PLAYROOM   (for child care center services)
   CIRCLES   (for bracelets and necklaces)
   AQUARIUM   (for restaurant services)

3. If an application for INTEGRA COMPUTER SERVICES (for computer consulting services) is refused registration on the basis that the mark is merely descriptive, how should the applicant respond?
4. Assume a notice of allowance is issued on July 1, 2003, for a mark that is the subject of an ITU application. Discuss the deadlines applicable to the mark to ensure the application is not abandoned.
5. Assume the owner of the registered mark AVALON BAY PERFUME (for perfume) disclaimed "Perfume." A later user applies for the mark AVALAR BAY PERFUME (for perfume). Discuss whether the marks are confusingly similar.
6. The mark LE CHAT was registered for clothing on July 1, 2003. What actions must be taken after registration to maintain the registration? Give all appropriate dates.
7. Assume the mark KELLY KELLY is published in the *Official Gazette* on June 10. When should a notice of opposition be filed if one intends to oppose the registration of this mark?

parades, mass rallies, and gladiatorial contests of oratory made nineteenth-century politics an object of consuming popular interest.

In the midst of such politics, nineteenth-century journalism served as an   5
extension of the town meeting. It created a public forum in which the issues of the day were hotly debated. Newspapers not only reported political controversies but participated in them, drawing in their readers as well. And print culture rested on the remnants of an oral tradition: Printed language was still shaped by the rhythms and requirements of the spoken word, in particular by the conventions of verbal argumentation. Print served to create a larger forum for the spoken word, not yet to displace or reshape it.

The "best men," as they liked to think of themselves, were never altogether happy with this state of affairs, and by the 1870s and 1880s their low opinion of politics had come to be widely shared by the educated classes. The scandals of the Gilded Age° gave party politics a bad name. Genteel reformers — "mugwumps," to their enemies — demanded a professionalization of politics, designed to free the civil service from party control and to replace political appointees with trained experts.

The drive to clean up politics gained momentum in the Progressive Era. Under the leadership of Theodore Roosevelt, Woodrow Wilson, Robert La Follette, and William Jennings Bryan, the Progressives preached efficiency, "good government," "bipartisanship," and the "scientific management" of public affairs, and declared war on "bossism." These reformers had little use for public debate. Most political questions were too complex, in their view, to be submitted to popular judgment. They liked to contrast the scientific expert with the orator — the latter a useless windbag whose rantings only confused the public mind.

What democracy requires is public debate, not information.

Professionalism in politics meant professionalism in journalism. The connection between the two was spelled out by Walter Lippmann in the twenties, in a series of books that provided a founding charter for modern journalism — an elaborate rationale for a journalism guided by the new idea of professional objectivity. Lippmann held up standards by which the press is still judged.

In Lippmann's view, democracy did not require that people literally govern themselves. Questions of substance should be decided by knowledgeable administrators whose access to reliable information immunized them against

---

Gilded Age: A term first coined by Mark Twain to characterize the difference between a gilded and a golden age. It refers to a time of economic excess, materialism, and political corruption in the 1870s and 1880s.

the emotional "symbols" and "stereotypes" that dominated public debate. The public, according to Lippmann, was incompetent to govern itself and did not even care to do so.

At one time this may not have been the case, but now, in the "wide and   10 unpredictable environment" of the modern world, the old ideal of citizenship was obsolete. A complex industrial society required a government carried on by officials who would necessarily be guided — since any form of direct democracy was now impossible — by either public opinion or expert knowledge. Public opinion was unreliable because it could be united only by an appeal to slogans and "symbolic pictures." Lippmann's distrust of public opinion rested on the epistemological distinction between truth and mere opinion. Truth, as he conceived it, grew out of disinterested scientific inquiry; everything else was ideology. Public debate was at best a disagreeable necessity. Ideally, it would not take place at all; decisions would be based on scientific "standards of measurement" alone.

The role of the press, as Lippmann saw it, was to circulate information, not to encourage argument. The relationship between information and argument was antagonistic, not complementary. He did not take the position that argumentation was a necessary outcome of reliable information; on the contrary, his point was that information precluded argument, made argument unnecessary. Arguments were what took place in the absence of reliable information.

Lippmann had forgotten what he learned (or should have learned) from William James and John Dewey,° that our search for reliable information is itself guided by the questions that arise during arguments about a given course of action. It is only by subjecting our preferences and projects to the test of debate that we come to understand what we know and what we still need to learn. Until we have to defend our opinions in public, they remain opinions in Lippmann's pejorative sense — half-formed convictions based on random impressions and unexamined assumptions. It is the act of articulating and defending our views that lifts them out of the category of "opinions," gives them shape and definition, and makes it possible for others to recognize them as a description of their own experience as well. In short, we come to know our own minds only by explaining ourselves to others.

The attempt to bring others around to our own point of view carries the risk, of course, that we may adopt their point of view instead. We have to enter imaginatively into our opponents' arguments, if only for the purpose of refuting them, and we may end up being persuaded by those we sought to

---

William James and John Dewey: Philosopher and psychologist William James (1842–1910) argued that the question or problem being considered should determine the "truth" of the theory or approach being used. John Dewey (1859–1952) embraced this philosophy, "pragmatism," to reform American education in ways that incorporate experiential learning.

persuade. Argument is risky and unpredictable — and therefore educational. Most of us tend to think of it (as Lippmann thought of it) as a clash of rival dogmas, a shouting match in which neither side gives any ground. But arguments are not won by shouting down opponents. They are won by changing opponents' minds.

If we insist on argument as the essence of education, we will defend democracy not as the most efficient but as the most educational form of government — one that extends the circle of debate as widely as possible and thus forces all citizens to articulate their views, to put their views at risk, and to cultivate the virtues of eloquence, clarity of thought and expression, and sound judgment. From this point of view, the press has the potential to serve as the equivalent of the town meeting.

This is what Dewey argued, in effect — though not, unfortunately, very   15 clearly — in *The Public and Its Problems* (1927), a book written in reply to Lippmann's disparaging studies of public opinion. Lippmann's distinction between truth and information rested on a "spectator theory of knowledge," as James W. Carey explains in his recently published book, *Communication as Culture.* As Lippmann understood these matters, knowledge is what we get when an observer, preferably a scientifically trained observer, provides us with a copy of reality that we can all recognize. Dewey, on the other hand, knew that even scientists argue among themselves. He held that the knowledge needed by any community — whether it is a community of scientific inquirers or a political community — emerges only from "dialogue" and "direct give and take."

It is significant, as Carey points out, that Dewey's analysis of communication stressed the ear rather than the eye. "Conversation," Dewey wrote, "has a vital import lacking in the fixed and frozen words of written speech. . . . The connections of the ear with vital and outgoing thought and emotion are immensely closer and more varied than those of the eye. Vision is spectator; hearing is a participator."

The proper role of the press is to extend the scope of debate by supplementing the spoken word with the written word. The written word is indeed a poor substitute for the spoken word; nevertheless, it can serve as an acceptable substitute as long as written speech takes spoken speech (and not, say, mathematics) as its model. According to Lippmann, the press was unreliable because it could never give us accurate representations of reality, only "symbolic pictures" and stereotypes. Dewey's analysis implied a more penetrating line of criticism. As Carey puts it, "The press, by seeing its role as that of informing the public, abandons its role as an agency for carrying on the conversation of our culture." Having embraced Lippmann's ideal of objectivity, the press no longer serves to cultivate "certain vital habits" in the community — "the ability to follow an argument, grasp the point of view of another, expand the boundaries of understanding, debate the alternative purposes that might be pursued."

The rise of the advertising and public-relations industries, side by side, helps to explain why the press abdicated its most important function — enlarging the public forum — at the same time that it became more "responsible." A responsible press, as opposed to a partisan or opinionated one, attracted the kind of readers advertisers were eager to reach: well-heeled readers, most of whom probably thought of themselves as independent voters. These readers wanted to be assured that they were reading all the news that was fit to print, not an editor's idiosyncratic and no doubt biased view of things. Responsibility came to be equated with the avoidance of controversy because advertisers were willing to pay for it. Some advertisers were also willing to pay for sensationalism, though on the whole they preferred a respectable reader-ship to sheer numbers. What they clearly did not prefer was "opinion" — not because they were impressed with Lippmann's philosophical arguments but because opinionated reporting did not guarantee the right audience. No doubt they also hoped that an aura of objectivity, the hallmark of responsible jour-nalism, would rub off on the advertisements that surrounded increasingly slen-der columns of print.

In a curious historical twist, advertising, publicity, and other forms of com-mercial persuasion themselves came to be disguised as information and, eventually, to substitute for open debate. "Hidden persuaders" (as Vance Packard called them) replaced the old-time editors, essayists, and orators who made no secret of their partisanship. And information and publicity became increasingly indistinguishable. Today, most of the "news" in our newspapers consists of items churned out by press agencies and public-relations offices and then regurgitated intact by the "objective" organs of journalism.

The decline of the partisan press and the rise of a new type of journalism 20 professing rigorous standards of objectivity do not assure a steady supply of usable information. Unless information is generated by sustained public debate, most of it will be irrelevant at best, misleading and manipulative at worst. Increasingly, information is generated by those who wish to promote something or someone — a product, a cause, a political candidate or office-holder — without either arguing their case on its merits or explicitly adver-tising it as self-interested material. Much of the press, in its eagerness to inform the public, has become a conduit for the equivalent of junk mail. When words are used merely as instruments of publicity or propaganda, they lose their power to persuade. Soon they cease to mean anything at all. People lose the capacity to use language precisely and expressively, or even to dis-tinguish one word from another. The spoken word models itself on the writ-ten word instead of the other way around, and ordinary speech begins to sound like the clotted jargon we see in print. Ordinary speech begins to sound like "information"—a disaster from which the English language may never recover.

Working with the Text

1. Christopher Lasch bases his insistence that the press serve as a forum for public debate on an analysis of key developments in the history of American journalism. In a brief essay, reflect on his reasons for using history to build his argument. Why are these particular historical developments relevant to our current expectations of the press? What do these developments tell us about the relationship between American journalism and democracy?

2. For Lasch, American journalism began to depart from its critical role in public debate in the Progressive Era, when the "'scientific management' of public affairs" became the order of the day. According to Lasch, the press became an instrument of the Progressives under the influence of writer Walter Lippmann, who held the view that the public "was incompetent to govern itself and did not even care to do so" (par. 9). As you reread the essay, study the reasoning behind the views of the Progressives and Lippmann, as well as Lasch's challenge to their positions on professionalism and objectivity. In a brief essay, take a position on whether the public is competent to govern itself and wishes to do so. Do you agree or disagree with the Progressives, Lippmann, or Lasch? Why?

3. Lasch takes exception to Lippmann's view that the "role of the press . . . was to circulate information, not to encourage argument" (par. 11). Lasch counters this view with that of William James and John Dewey, who claimed, according to Lasch, that "our search for reliable information is itself guided by the questions that arise during arguments about a given course of action" (par. 12). In a brief essay, reflect on what the position of James and Dewey would mean for journalism. What would the press have to do to support or promote our "search for reliable information"?

4. In the closing paragraph of the essay, Lasch warns, "When words are used merely as instruments of publicity or propaganda, they lose their power to persuade. Soon they cease to mean anything at all." In light of your own observations and experience as well as Lasch's argument, review the final paragraph to think through the deterioration he describes. In a brief essay, analyze his claim, starting with the first sentence. Why would the "decline of the partisan press and the rise of a new type of journalism professing rigorous standards of objectivity" lead people to "lose the capacity to use language precisely and expressively, or even to distinguish one word from another"?

From Text to Field

1. Lasch claims that political argument has become a lost art largely because the American press long ago relinquished its role in public debate. With Lasch's argument in mind, write an essay in which you present your view of the state of public debate in terms of its political influence and of the current role of the press in promoting that debate. Do you think political argument has become a lost art? Why or why not?

2. In concurring with the views of William James and John Dewey, Lasch insists that "it is only by subjecting our preferences and projects to the test of debate that we come to understand what we know and what we still need to learn" (par. 12). Write an essay in which you describe and reflect on your own experience of this.

3. Lasch argues that the public has long confused "commercial persuasion" with objective journalism. In a small discussion group, review Lasch's claim and brainstorm examples of types of journalism or specific press coverage that demonstrate this confusion. Write an essay in which you analyze one or more of the examples identified by your discussion group. Why do readers tend to accept your example(s) as objective journalism? Why do you think it is actually "commercial persuasion"?

4. In the spirit of a rebuttal to Lasch, identify a form of journalism that you think may well create a forum for public debate. What are the features of this form? How does it promote participation and debate? Are there any gatekeepers to this forum? How might technology create and shape this forum?

What Is Science?

George Orwell

"What Is Science?" was published in 1945 in the *Tribune,* a British socialist weekly, in the wake of World War II and the first use of the atomic bomb. The fact that scientists had developed weaponry of unprecedented power threw science into a new kind of spotlight, one that prompted horror as well as respect.

The power of nations, however it was derived, had long been a concern for Eric Arthur Blair, who wrote under the pen name George Orwell. A British citizen born in India and educated in England, he gained his first insight into political and social power as a middle-class student trying to find his way in the prestigious preparatory and secondary schools designed to groom upper-class children. Instead of pursuing a university education, Orwell took a position as a policeman in the Burma branch of the Indian Imperial Police, an experience that prompted him to write, "When the white man turns tyrant it is his own freedom that he destroys. He wears a mask, and his face grows to fit it."

Orwell's career as a writer, soldier, and political activist was marked by independence of thought in an era of mass political movements that spanned capitalism, socialism, communism, and fascism. His aim was economic and social justice, and although he identified most strongly with socialism, he was unsparing in his criticism of any ideology or movement that limited personal freedom or undermined family life. His two most enduring novels—*Animal Farm* (1945) and *Nineteen Eighty-four* (1949)—still stand as landmark critiques of the abuse of power. His essay "Politics and the English Language" is an often-anthologized discussion about how language can be misused in "defense of the indefensible."

Orwell's body of work includes seven novels and seventeen books of nonfiction, a number of which are collections of his essays. In 1950, he died of tuberculosis at the age of forty-six. Orwell's obituary, written by V. S. Pritchett, a prominent writer who was his contemporary, named Orwell "the wintry conscience of a generation."

In last week's *Tribune*, there was an interesting letter from Mr. J. Stewart Cook, in which he suggested that the best way of avoiding the danger of a "scientific hierarchy" would be to see to it that every member of the general public was, as far as possible, scientifically educated. At the same time, scientists should be brought out of their isolation and encouraged to take a greater part in politics and administration.

As a general statement, I think most of us would agree with this, but I notice that, as usual, Mr. Cook does not define science, and merely implies in passing that it means certain exact sciences whose experiments can be made under laboratory conditions. Thus, adult education tends "to neglect scientific studies in favor of literary, economic, and social subjects," economics and sociology not being regarded as branches of science, apparently. This point is of great importance. For the word *science* is at present used in at least two meanings, and the whole question of scientific education is obscured by the current tendency to dodge from one meaning to the other.

Science is generally taken as meaning either (a) the exact sciences, such as chemistry, physics, etc., or (b) a method of thought which obtains verifiable results by reasoning logically from observed fact.

If you ask any scientist, or indeed almost any educated person, "What is science?" you are likely to get an answer approximating to (b). In everyday life, however, both in speaking and in writing, when people say "science" they mean (a). Science means something that happens in a laboratory: the very word calls up a picture of graphs, test-tubes, balances, Bunsen burners, microscopes. A biologist, an astronomer, perhaps a psychologist or a mathematician, is described as a "man of science": No one would think of applying this term to a statesman, a poet, a journalist, or even a philosopher. And those who tell us that the young must be scientifically educated mean, almost invariably, that they should be taught more about radioactivity, or the stars, or the physiology of their own bodies, rather than that they should be taught to think more exactly.

This confusion of meaning, which is partly deliberate, has in it a great 5 danger. Implied in the demand for more scientific education is the claim that if one has been scientifically trained one's approach to *all* subjects will be more intelligent than if one had had no such training. A scientist's political opinions, it is assumed, his opinions on sociological questions, on morals, on philosophy, perhaps even on the arts, will be more valuable than those of a layman. The world, in other words, would be a better place if the scientists were in control of it. But a "scientist," as we have just seen, means in practice a specialist in one of the exact sciences. It follows that a chemist or a physicist, as such, is politically more intelligent than a poet or a lawyer, as such. And, in fact, there are already millions of people who do believe this.

But is it really true that a "scientist," in this narrower sense, is any likelier than other people to approach nonscientific problems in an objective way? There is not much reason for thinking so. Take one simple test — the ability to withstand nationalism. It is often loosely said that "Science is international," but in practice the scientific workers of all countries line up behind their own governments with fewer scruples than are felt by the writers and the artists. The German scientific community, as a whole, made no resistance to Hitler. Hitler may have ruined the long-term prospects of German science, but there were still plenty of gifted men to do the necessary research on such things as synthetic oil, jet planes, rocket projectiles, and the atomic bomb. Without them the German war machine could never have been built up.

The word *science* is at present used in at least two meanings.

On the other hand, what happened to German literature when the Nazis came to power? I believe no exhaustive lists have been published, but I imagine that the number of German scientists — Jews apart — who voluntarily exiled themselves or were persecuted by the regime was much smaller than the number of writers and journalists. More sinister than this, a number of German scientists swallowed the monstrosity of "racial science." You can find some of the statements to which they set their names in Professor Brady's *The Spirit and Structure of German Fascism.*

But, in slightly different forms, it is the same picture everywhere. In England, a large proportion of our leading scientists accept the structure of capitalist society, as can be seen from the comparative freedom with which they are given knighthoods, baronetcies, and even peerages. Since Tennyson, no English writer worth reading — one might, perhaps, make an exception of Sir Max Beerbohm — has been given a title. And those English scientists who do not simply accept the status quo are frequently Communists, which means that, however intellectually scrupulous they may be in their own line of work, they are ready to be uncritical and even dishonest on certain subjects. The fact is that a mere training in one or more of the exact sciences, even combined with very high gifts, is no guarantee of a humane or sceptical outlook. The physicists of half a dozen great nations, all feverishly and secretly working away at the atomic bomb, are a demonstration of this.

But does all this mean that the general public should *not* be more scientifically educated? On the contrary! All it means is that scientific education for the masses will do little good, and probably a lot of harm, if it simply boils down to more physics, more chemistry, more biology, etc., to the detriment of literature and history. Its probable effect on the average human being would be to narrow the range of his thoughts and make him more than ever contemptuous of such knowledge as he did not possess: And his political reactions would probably be somewhat less intelligent than those of an illiterate peasant who retained a few historical memories and a fairly sound aesthetic sense.

Clearly, scientific education ought to mean the implanting of a rational, 10 sceptical, experimental habit of mind. It ought to mean acquiring a *method* — a method that can be used on any problem that one meets — and not simply piling up a lot of facts. Put it in those words, and the apologist of scientific education will usually agree. Press him further, ask him to particularize, and somehow it always turns out that scientific education means more attention to the exact sciences, in other words — more *facts*. The idea that science means a way of looking at the world, and not simply a body of knowledge, is in practice strongly resisted. I think sheer professional jealousy is part of the reason for this. For if science is simply a method or an attitude, so that anyone whose thought-processes are sufficiently rational can in some sense be described as a scientist — what then becomes of the enormous prestige now enjoyed by the chemist, the physicist, etc., and his claim to be somehow wiser than the rest of us?

A hundred years ago, Charles Kingsley described science as "making nasty smells in a laboratory." A year or two ago a young industrial chemist informed me, smugly, that he "could not see what was the use of poetry." So the pendulum swings to and fro, but it does not seem to me that one attitude is any better than the other. At the moment, science is on the upgrade, and so we hear, quite rightly, the claim that the masses should be scientifically educated: We do not hear, as we ought, the counterclaim that the scientists themselves would benefit by a little education. Just before writing this, I saw in an American magazine the statement that a number of British and American physicists refused from the start to do research on the atomic bomb, well knowing what use would be made of it. Here you have a group of sane men in the middle of a world of lunatics. And though no names were published, I think it would be a safe guess that all of them were people with some kind of general cultural background, some acquaintance with history or literature or the arts — in short, people whose interests were not, in the current sense of the word, purely scientific.

Working with the Text

1. In this essay, written in 1945, George Orwell contends that "the demand for more scientific education" implies that the world "would be a better place if the scientists were in control of it" (par. 5). He questions this assumption by examining the two different ways he believes his readers use the term *science*. In a brief essay, analyze his use of these two definitions of science. What does he conclude about the connection between scientific thinking and a better world? How do the two differing definitions of *science* contribute to his argument?

Postregistration Procedures, Trademark Maintenance, and Transfer of Rights to Marks

CHAPTER OVERVIEW

The Lanham Act imposes various requirements on registrants after registration of marks to ensure that only marks in use remain on the registers. Thus, registrants must file an affidavit between years five and six after registration and in the year before the end of each successive ten-year period after registration to allege continued use of the mark and file an application for renewal within one year before the end of the initial registration term and every ten years thereafter. Failure to file the appropriate documents will result in cancellation of the registration for a mark.

Rights to marks can be lost by other means as well, primarily when the mark becomes generic or when the mark is abandoned by

2. Orwell distinguishes between experiments themselves and an "experimental habit of mind" (par. 10). To further describe that habit of mind, Orwell speaks of acquiring a "method" (par. 10). In a brief essay, explore what Orwell means by the term *method*.

3. Orwell asserts that "a mere training in one or more of the exact sciences, even combined with very high gifts, is no guarantee of a humane or sceptical outlook" (par. 8). As evidence, he cites not only the behavior of scientists in Nazi Germany but also the affiliations of scientists in England and "half a dozen great nations" (par. 8). In a brief essay, analyze Orwell's critique of the thinking exhibited by these scientists. How does Orwell view the relationship between science and public policy?

4. Orwell warns against "more physics, more chemistry, more biology, etc., to the detriment of literature and history" (par. 9). Concluding his essay, he makes the "safe guess" that physicists who refused to do research on the atomic bomb "were people with some kind of general cultural background, some acquaintance with history or literature or the arts" (par. 11). With the entire selection in mind (note especially his remark about writers and journalists in Nazi Germany) and drawing on your own understanding of history, literature, and the arts, write a brief essay in which you reflect on Orwell's view of these areas of study. Why does Orwell believe that the arts and the humanities, as opposed to "exact science," contribute to our ability to see the world humanely? How does the historical context of the essay — just after the end of World War II and after the dropping of the atomic bomb — color his view of what it means to be humane?

From Text to Field

1. Orwell observes that for his contemporaries "scientific education means more attention to the exact sciences, in other words — more *facts*. The idea that science means a way of looking at the world, and not simply a body of knowledge, is in practice strongly resisted" (par. 10). Has this been your experience of science education? Using Orwell's two definitions of *science*, write a personal essay in which you describe the progression of your scientific education and the purposes you understood to be behind it. Was it an accumulation of facts or practice in a certain way of thinking? What effect has science had on your own habits of mind?

2. History, literature, and art as well as math and science are standard fare in the American elementary and secondary curriculum. Orwell would urge educators to pursue this combination of subjects for the purpose of instilling "a humane or sceptical outlook" (par. 8). Write an essay in which you reflect on the extent

to which your schooling has made you more skeptical—more willing to pose questions — or more humane. How have your studies in the arts and the humanities influenced your view of the world? How have your studies in math and science influenced your view? What relationship, if any, have you found between being skeptical and being humane?

3. Orwell's essay was written in the context of British society and in the aftermath of World War II, when advanced weaponry as well as the atomic bomb drew new attention and concern to the practice of science. Since then, we have seen science and technology move rapidly into new territory. In an essay, update and revise Orwell's argument to address a contemporary American context. Analyze what you consider to be the American view of science and scientists and their relation to the arts and humanities and to public policy. In what ways has science become part of our lives? How do we regard scientists and scientific advances? Do you think our view is healthy?

Story Skeletons and Story-Fitting

Roger C. Schank

"We are," as Roger C. Schank reminds us, "the stories we tell." And yet storytelling is hardly straightforward, a simple matter of recounting events.

According to Schank, the stories we tell follow—and may perhaps be determined by—basic patterns for explaining events to ourselves and to others. Stories, in short, provide a hidden set of lenses or filters that cause us to understand and relay the same facts or events in very different ways. Roger Schank suggests that our stories follow certain explanation patterns by uncovering what he calls the "skeleton stories" that underlie the particulars of our immediate story. We "enter a storytelling situation," says Schank, "wanting to tell a certain kind of story and only then worry about whether the facts fit onto the bones of the skeleton." What's more, as we repeat these stories and use the same skeletons for new stories, we influence what we remember, how we perceive, and even how we see ourselves.

The example that Schank uses to explore these ideas has to do with an international incident in 1988: A civilian Iranian airliner was shot down by a United States Navy warship while on patrol in the Persian Gulf. The incident resulted in the loss of 290 passengers and crew, and heightened tensions throughout the Middle East. Schank draws on published statements by various world leaders to reveal the story skeletons in play. Far from a commentary on a now distant historical event, Roger Schank's discussion draws our attention to the frames of reference that always guide how we interpret our world. We don't so much tell stories as fit them into underlying explanatory patterns.

Roger Schank is a leading researcher in artificial intelligence, learning theory, cognitive science, and the construction of virtual learning environments. He served as distinguished professor at Carnegie Mellon University, founded the Institute for Learning Sciences at Northwestern University, and directed Yale University's Artificial

Intelligence Project. His most recent contributions have been in the area of education, where he has explored the role of technology in learning. The selection offered here is from his book *Tell Me a Story: A New Look at Real and Artificial Memory* (1990).

SOME SKELETON STORIES

If we construct our own version of truth by reliance upon skeleton stories, two people can know exactly the same facts but construct a story that relays those facts in very different ways. Because they are using different story skeletons, their perspectives will vary. For example, a United States Navy warship shot down an Iranian airliner carrying 290 passengers on July 3, 1988. Let's look at some different stories that were constructed to explain this event. All the stories that follow are excerpts from various *New York Times* reports in the days following this incident:

> Mr. Reagan smiled and waved at tourists as he returned to the White House. But in speaking to reporters he remarked on what he had previously called "a terrible human tragedy. I won't minimize the tragedy," Mr. Reagan said. "We all know it was a tragedy. But we're talking about an incident in which a plane on radar was observed coming in the direction of a ship in combat and the plane began lowering its altitude. And so, I think it was an understandable accident to shoot and think that they were under attack from that plane," he said.

In this quotation from Ronald Reagan, the use of skeletons to create stories can be easily seen. Mr. Reagan has chosen a common skeleton: *understandable tragedy*. The skeleton looks something like this:

> Actor pursues justifiable goal.
> Actor selects reasonable plan to achieve goal.
> Plan involves selection of correct action.
> Action taken has unintended and unanticipated result.
> Result turns out to be undesirable.
> Innocent people are hurt by result.

In essence, what Mr. Reagan has done is to select this skeleton and to interpret the events of the shooting down of the airplane in terms of that skeleton. Had he been asked to tell the story of what happened, he would simply have had to fill in each line above with the actual event that matches it. As it is, he merely had to recognize that that skeleton was applicable and to use the phrases "terrible human tragedy" and "understandable accident," which are well-known referents to that skeleton.

Now let's look at some other comments on the event:

After expressing "profound regret" about the attack, Mrs. Thatcher said: "We understand that in the course of an engagement following an Iranian attack on the U.S. force, warnings were given to an unidentified aircraft. We fully accept the right of forces engaged in such hostilities to defend themselves."

Mrs. Thatcher has used a much more specific skeleton, namely the *justi- 5 fiability of self-defense*. This skeleton proceeds as follows:

> First actor pursues unjustifiable goal.
> First actor selects plan.
> Plan has intention of negative effect on second actor.
> Second actor is justified in selecting goal.
> Second actor selects justifiable plan.
> Plan causes action to take place which harms first actor.

Let's look at the other side of the political spectrum now:

Libya's official press agency called the downing "a horrible massacre perpetrated by the United States." It said the attack was "new proof of state terrorism practiced by the American administration" and it called Washington "insolent" for insisting that the decision to down the plane was an appropriate defensive measure.

Here, two different skeletons are invoked. The first is *state terrorism* and the second is *insolence*. The insolence skeleton is an amusing one to invoke, but we shall ignore it and concentrate on the terrorism skeleton:

> Actor chooses high-level goal.
> Country blocks high-level goal.
> Actor chooses secondary goal to harm citizens of country.
> Actor endangers or actually harms citizens of country.
> Actor expects blockage of high-level goal by country to go away.

"State terrorism" supposedly means that the actor is a country too. But "state terrorism" is not exactly a well-known story skeleton for an American. In fact, Arab leaders refer to this skeleton quite often and we can figure what it must mean and why Arab leaders used it to justify their own actions. Other people's story skeletons, ones that we have not heard before, are usually best understood by analogy to skeletons we already know.

Notice that the events under discussion fit as easily into the state terrorism skeleton as into the above two skeletons. The art of skeleton selection is exactly that—an art. No real objective reality exists here. One can see and tell about events in any way that one wants to. In each case, certain aspects of the story being transmitted are enhanced and certain elements are left out altogether.

The real problem in using skeletons this way is that the storytellers usually believe what they themselves are saying. Authors construct their own reality by finding the events that fit the skeleton convenient for them to believe. They enter a storytelling situation wanting to tell a certain kind of story and only then worrying about whether the facts fit onto the bones of the skeleton that they have previously chosen. This method has almost comic qualities to it when various interpretations of an event are so clearly interpretations independent of the event itself. For example, consider the following comment:

> A newspaper in Bahrain, *Akhbar Al Khalij*, said, "No doubt yesterday's painful tragedy was the result of Iran's insistence in continuing the Iran-Iraq war. The United States as a great power does not lack moral courage in admitting the mistake. This will help contain the effects of the incident."

The remarks above refer to two skeletons: the *justifiable bad effects of war*   10 *on the aggressor* and *moral courage*. Both of these skeletons could have been used to describe nearly any event in the Middle East that the newspaper wanted to comment upon.

The use of new events as fodder for invoking old skeletons is the stuff of which international political rhetoric is made. In the *Times* of the same period, we have another reference to how Reagan commented on a similar situation some years back:

> President Reagan, in a speech after the Korean plane was shot down after straying over Soviet airspace above Sakhalin Island, said: "Make no mistake about it, this attack was not just against ourselves or the Republic of Korea. This was the Soviet Union against the world and the moral precepts which guide human relations among people everywhere.
>
> "It was an act of barbarism," Mr. Reagan went on, "born of a society which wantonly disregards individual rights and the value of human life and seeks constantly to expand and dominate other nations."

While the Americans used the *barbarism* skeleton, where the Koreans were the victim and the Russians the actor, to describe the shooting down of the Korean airliner, the Russians, in describing the Korean Airlines attack, used the *military aggressor* skeleton, where the Koreans were the actor and the Russians the victim. This same discrepancy occurred in the Russian statement about the Iranian airliner:

> The Tass statement said the attack Sunday was the inevitable result of the extensive American military presence in the Persian Gulf.
>
> "The tragedy, responsibility for which is wholly with the American command, has been far from accidental," the agency said. "It has been, in effect, a direct corollary of United States actions over the past year to increase its military presence in the gulf."

It added: "The Soviet Union has repeatedly warned at different forums that the path of military actions cannot lead to a normalized situation. If the warnings had been heeded, the July 3 tragedy would not have occurred."

International politicians are not alone in telling stories by selecting their favorite skeletons and fitting the event to the skeletons. The candidates for president [in the 1988 race] also had something to say:

> Mr. Jackson said there was "no evidence that the U.S. ship was under attack by that plane." But he added, "The issue is not just failed technology, but failed and vague policy for the region." Mr. Jackson argued that the United States should not be in the gulf unilaterally, but as part of a United Nations peacekeeping effort that would have as its prime goal a negotiated settlement of the Iran-Iraq war.
>
> At a Fourth of July address at the Charlestown Navy Yard in Boston today, Mr. Dukakis described the incident as a "terrible accident," adding: "Clearly we have the right to defend our forces against imminent threats. And apparently, the shooting down of the airliner occurred over what appears to have been an unprovoked attack against our forces."

For Mr. Jackson, the appropriate skeletons were *bad technology causes errors*, and *vague policy causes problems*. Mr. Dukakis, on the other hand, looked suspiciously like Mr. Reagan, indicating that he was already acting presidential. Mr. Jackson had already realized that he was not going to be president at this point, but he was still campaigning to be taken seriously. Therefore, he was still raising issues. The Iran incident reminded him of two of his favorite issues, so he chose to see the Iranian airplane event in terms of those issues.

Last, we should look at the Iranian point of view. They, too, have their favorite skeletons in terms of which they can look at this event. First, let us look at the remarks of an exiled Iranian official:

> "It must be clear that much of the policies in Iran today are dictated by the internal struggle for power," said Abolhassan Bani-Sadr, the first president of Iran. Mr. Bani-Sadr, who spoke in an interview, lives in exile in Paris and opposes the current regime.
>
> "In that sense," Mr. Bani-Sadr said, "this American act of aggression will increase pressure to steer away from conciliatory policies in favor of radicals inside Iran who want to crush all talk of compromise. I am sure the trend now will be toward more mobilization for more war, although it will get nowhere."

Mr. Bani-Sadr was trying to predict the future rather than retell an old story. Nevertheless, he still relied upon a skeleton to create his new story. The skeleton he chose was *fanatics find fuel to add to fire*. Now look at a comment from inside Iran:

> Hojatolislam Rafsanjani, who is the commander of Iran's armed forces, warned today against a hasty response to the American action. In a speech

reported by the Teheran radio, he told Parliament, "We should let this crime be known to everyone in the world and be discussed and studied."

The Speaker, who has emerged as Iran's most powerful figure after Ayatollah Khomeini, went on to say that the Americans might "want a clumsy move somewhere in the world so that they can take the propaganda pressure off America and transfer it somewhere else."

Hojatolislam Rafsanjani added that Iran retains the right of taking revenge, but that "the timing is up to us, not America." He called the downing of the airliner "an unprecedented disaster in contemporary history" and said it should be used by Iran to "expose the nature of America," statements indicating that for now the Speaker favors a measured response.

Here again, we have a story about the future. Two skeletons are invoked as possible candidates for the basis of this story. One, *force opponents into bad move*, refers to the intentions of the United States as seen by the Iranians and is really a part of a continuing story of conflict between the two countries. The second, *avoid revenge to show up opponent*, is more or less the other side of the same coin. In both cases, we have a kind of conscious admission by Mr. Rafsanjani that the real question is which story skeleton will be followed in the creation of the next set of events. The only problem with this assertion is that Mr. Rafsanjani naively seems to assume that some audience is waiting to see the next act in the play. A more accurate assumption is that, no matter what happens next, all the viewers of the play will retell the story according to skeletons that they have already selected; i.e., they will probably not be moved to reinterpret any new event in terms of some skeleton that they do not already have in mind.

Skeletons and Memory

Story skeletons can have an important effect on memory. Since we see the world according to the stories we tell, when we tell a story in a given way, we will be likely to remember the facts in terms of the story we have told. This effect on memory has an interesting offshoot. When we select a particular skeleton because we have no real choice from a political point of view, we, most likely, will begin to believe the story we find ourselves telling. Consider the following statement, for example:

Iran Air's senior Airbus instructor, Captain Ali Mahdaviani, ruled out the possibility of pilot error in the tragedy. He said it was possible that the airliner's captain, Mohsen Rezaian, failed to respond to signals from the American cruiser *Vincennes* because at that stage in the flight he was busy receiving air controller instructions off two radios and from four control towers, Bandar Abbas, Teheran, Dubai, and Qeshon Island in the gulf.

He insisted that the airliner would not have been outside the flight corridor and certainly would not have been descending, as early Pentagon reports said. He attributed the incident to a panicky reaction from the American cruiser, but did concede that the decision to fire the two surface-to-air missiles was made in difficult circumstances. "I think the decision to shoot down the plane was taken in very nervous conditions," he said.

And now consider an opposing statement:

"We have in this briefing all the facts that were made available to the captain when he made his decision," said Senator John Warner, a Virginia Republican and former Navy Secretary. "We are all of the same view, that he acted properly and professionally."

Senator Sam Nunn, the Georgia Democrat who is the chairman of the Armed Services Committee, agreed. "I find nothing to second-guess him on, based on his information," Mr. Nunn said.

He was quick to add, however, that the information that Captain Will C. Rogers 3rd, the commanding officer of the *Vincennes*, was working with might be contradicted by information on the computer tapes, which are believed to have recorded every action taken by the ship's operators, every bit of data picked up by its sensors, and every communication heard in the region during the encounter.

"It is an entirely different matter to second-guess a decision that had to be made in three or four minutes, to second-guess it over a two-week period," Mr. Nunn said, referring to the deadline for Navy investigators looking into the events.

Each of these statements is what might have been expected from the peo- 20 ple who made them. Yet how were the memories of the spokesmen affected by the stories they told? In some sense, they told stories that they had to tell. Neither of these spokesmen was necessarily one hundred percent sure that the pilot and/or the captain weren't somewhat wrong in what they did. Situations are rarely that black-and-white. But having made a statement to support his man, each spokesman probably believed more in his man after defending him.

We choose to see the world according to a view that we find convenient.

One issue in story understanding, then, is to determine which story skeleton is the right one to choose. Moreover, this issue is important in storytelling and, therefore, in memory as well. We can see an event in so many different ways that we must understand how we decide which story skeleton is applicable. In politics, this decision is easy. Russians or Iranians don't have to debate about which skeleton to choose. Rather, they make choices on the basis of political positions adopted before any story is heard. But for individuals who must decide how to look at a given situation, the possibilities are much larger.

One of the oddities of story-based understanding is that people have difficulty making decisions if they know that they will have trouble constructing a coherent story to explain their decision. In a sense, people tell stories to themselves to see whether they are comfortable enough with telling them for a while. You need to believe your own story in order to tell it effectively. Thus, decision making often depends upon story construction.

A storyteller might be more accurately described as a story-fitter. Telling stories of our own lives, especially ones with high emotional impact, means attempting to fit events to a story that has already been told, a well-known story that others will easily understand. Story-fitting, then, is a kind of deceptive process, one that creates stories that are not always exactly true, that lie by omission. These lies, however, are not necessarily intentional.

A true story could be told but would take much more time. So time, in many ways, is the villain here. Your listener doesn't have hours to listen to your story, so you create a short version that looks more standard, that fits a well-known story skeleton. The problem with this solution, as we have seen, is that the teller himself begins to believe his story. In short, storytelling is a very powerful process. We remember our own stories. Stories replace the memory of events that actually took place. So when people tell the kinds of stories we have seen [here], they usually believe them.

Married couples often comment on a sequence from the Woody Allen 25 movie *Annie Hall.* The sequence involves two scenes, where first the female lead and then the male lead discuss their sex life as a couple with their respective therapists. The woman complains that her boyfriend wants to have sex all the time — two or three times a week. The man complains that they almost never have sex together — only two or three times a week.

This movie scene expresses the essence of story construction. We take the facts and we interpret them in such a way as to create a story. In order to facilitate communication and to allow easy conversation, we use standard story skeletons that we share as a culture. The choice, however, of which skeleton to use is, in essence, a political choice. We choose to see the world according to a view that we find convenient, and we communicate by adopting standard points of view. The stories we tell communicate this view both to others and to ourselves. In the end, we become shaped by the skeletons we use.

Which of the *Annie Hall* characters is right? This question is, of course, absurd. Both characters are right, as are all the politicians quoted earlier. The skeletons we use indicate our point of view. Storytelling causes us to adopt a point of view. With this adoption comes a kind of self-definition, however. We are the stories we tell. We not only express our vision of the world, we also shape our memory by the stories we tell. As we come to rely upon certain skeletons to express what has happened to us, we become incapable of seeing the world in any other way. The skeletons we use cause specific episodes to conform to one another. The more a given skeleton is used, the nonuse. Trademark owners often institute trademark use and compliance policies to ensure marks are not lost through genericide or abandonment.

Because a trademark is a form of property, it can be transferred or assigned to another if the goodwill symbolized the mark is assigned with it. Similarly, a mark may be licensed to another party to use, as long as the trademark owner controls the nature and quality of the goods or services offered by the licensee.

THE AFFIDAVIT OF CONTINUED USE

Background

Although a registration is valid for ten years, between years five and six after a registration is issued, and in the year before the end of each ten-year period after registration, the registrant is required to file an **Affidavit** (or *Declaration*) **of Continued Use** with the PTO, verifying that the mark is still in use in commerce in connection with the goods or services identified in the registration. Failure to submit the affidavit of use, called a "section 8 affidavit," within the appropriate deadline (or within a six-month grace period) will lead to cancellation of the registration. Requiring registrants to notify the PTO that marks are still in use allows the PTO to clear its files of deadwood, making unused marks available for others. Nevertheless, the mark may still be used by its owner who will continue to have common law rights to the mark even though the federal registration for the mark has been canceled.

If the registration covers goods or services in several classes, the registrant must verify that the mark is in use in connection with all of the goods or services. If the mark is in use with regard to some items, but not for others, the registrant must indicate such. The registration will be canceled as to any goods for which the mark is not in use. The PTO filing fee is $100 per class of goods or services. Filing during the grace period results in additional fees of $100 (per class). The PTO prefers that the document be filed electronically through TEAS.

Changes in Ownership of the Mark

The section 8 affidavit must be filed by the owner of the registration. Often, marks are transferred or assigned to other new owners who fail to notify the PTO of the change in ownership. Although the section 8 affidavit is filed by the new owner, PTO records may continue to reflect the original registrant. In such cases, the section 8 affidavit is refused until the appropriate changes are made to the PTO records showing proper continuity of title, called the **chain of title,** to the party now filing the section 8 affidavit. Even a change in the state of incorporation is a change of legal entity. Thus, if a Virginia corporation dissolves its status in Virginia so it can become a Delaware corporation, unless the PTO has received formal notification of such change, as well as documentary evidence, such as certified copies of the Delaware incorporation documents, a section 8 affidavit will not be accepted.

Changes in the Mark

When filing the affidavit, the owner must attach a specimen showing the mark as it is presently used for each class of goods or services identified in the registration. Thus, if the mark is used in connection with coffee creamer in I.C. 29 and coffee in I.C. 30, a specimen (generally labels, tags, packaging materials, or containers) for each class must be provided. If the mark as presently used differs from the mark as registered, the PTO must determine whether the change is material. If the change is determined to be a material alteration, the section 8 affidavit will be refused.

Because trademarks evolve over time (for example, consider the periodic updating of the more the stories it helps to form begin to cohere in memory. Consequently, we develop consistent, and rather inflexible, points of view.

Working with the Text

1. Review the various comments made by world leaders in response to the downing of the Iranian airliner, and compare the "skeleton stories" or explanation patterns that underlie each of those comments. In what ways do the various skeleton stories serve the purpose of its teller and the audience being addressed?

2. Roger Schank suggests that the stories we'd like to tell trump the events that the stories are based on: "Authors construct their own reality by finding the events that fit the skeleton convenient for them to believe" (par. 9). As you review the various stories told by world leaders, consider what are the facts that each has foregrounded and emphasized, and what are the facts that each has downplayed or avoided altogether. What argument do you think Schank is advancing, if only implicitly, about truth, reality, memory, and language?

3. Given Schank's discussion about how our stories or explanations adhere to underlying patterns that draw on predetermined beliefs, it is only fair to ask whether there might be a story skeleton or explanation pattern at work in Schank's own account. If so, what might that story skeleton be?

4. At the end of the selection excerpted here, Schank states that "we are the stories we tell." Write a brief essay that explores what you think Schank means by that statement. In particular, what is the connection between narrative or storytelling on the one hand, and belief, memory, and identity on the other?

From Text to Field

1. Many explanation patterns or "story skeletons" are predictable; they literally offer a stock of commonplaces to which writers and speakers turn, and which audiences have come to expect. The following situations invoke story skeletons around which more detailed explanations can be fashioned. For each, list the basic explanation patterns that writers would likely turn to when justifying decisions. Clarify who your audience might be: friend, parents, or professor. Compare your list with those developed by your classmates.

> Changing your major from business to English
> Taking a year off between high school and college
> Attending college out of state, far away from home
> Joining the Peace Corps

Choosing a small college rather than a large university

Joining a fraternity or sorority

2. Schank states that "the use of new events as fodder for invoking old skeletons is the stuff of which international political rhetoric is made." We might add that the same often holds true for domestic politics as well. Choose a particular issue or event that is likely to preoccupy the news media for several days. What explanation patterns or story skeletons are being invoked by various political parties or groups, and how are those skeletons linked to prior explanation patterns and belief systems or ideologies? In what ways might story skeletons both express and help create or maintain these belief systems?

3. Although seemingly far removed from high-profile international events like the downing of the Iranian airliner, events on your own campus are also explained and understood in light of certain patterns or story skeletons. Examine a recent issue or event on your campus in light of Schank's discussion of story skeletons and story-fitting. The issue might be a scandal in the athletic department, controversy surrounding a particular campus policy, concerns about student life, or tensions between the campus and the city. How is the situation explained by various stakeholders — students, faculty, administration, city residents — using their own particular stock of story skeletons?

Concepts We Live By

George Lakoff and Mark Johnson

A linguist and a philosopher joined forces to produce *Metaphors We Live By*, which introduced a theory of metaphor based on the deep structure of thought and behavior. George Lakoff and Mark Johnson saw metaphor not as a literary device or a matter of mere words but rather as evidence for a "conceptual system" that determines how we think, which in turn drives how we act. *Metaphors We Live By*, published in 1980, continues to influence the work of scholars in fields ranging from cognitive science to literary theory. "Concepts We Live By" is the book's first chapter.

George Lakoff—the linguist—is a professor at the University of California at Berkeley. He has taught at Harvard University and the University of Michigan and has worked with the Center for Advanced Study in the Behavioral Sciences at Stanford University. He continues to research metaphor in the context of human conceptual systems, with a special interest in metaphors for time, events, causation, emotions, morality, the self, and politics. His work in cognitive linguistics includes the neural theory of language. Among his publications are *Women, Fire and Dangerous Things* (1987), *More Than Cool Reason: A Field Guide to Poetic Metaphor* (1989), and *Moral Politics* (2nd ed., 2004).

The philosopher, Mark Johnson, is a professor at the University of Oregon. His current research, an extension of his earlier study of metaphor, focuses on the question of how structures of meaning grow out of bodily experience. His books include *Philosophical Perspectives on Metaphor* (2nd ed., 1981), *The Body in the Mind* (1987), and *Moral Imagination: Implications of Cognitive Science for Ethics* (1993).

In 1999, Lakoff and Johnson published another collaborative effort, *Philosophy in the Flesh: The Embodied Mind and Its Challenge to Western Thought.*

Metaphor is for most people a device of the poetic imagination and the rhetorical flourish—a matter of extraordinary rather than ordinary language. Moreover, metaphor is typically viewed as characteristic of language alone, a matter of words rather than thought or action. For this reason, most people think they can get along perfectly well without metaphor. We have found, on the contrary, that metaphor is pervasive in everyday life, not just in language but in thought and action. Our ordinary conceptual system, in terms of which we both think and act, is fundamentally metaphorical in nature.

The concepts that govern our thought are not just matters of the intellect. They also govern our everyday functioning, down to the most mundane details. Our concepts structure what we perceive, how we get around in the world, and how we relate to other people. Our conceptual system thus plays a central role in defining our everyday realities. If we are right in suggesting that our conceptual system is largely metaphorical, then the way we think, what we experience, and what we do every day is very much a matter of metaphor.

But our conceptual system is not something we are normally aware of. In most of the little things we do every day, we simply think and act more or less automatically along certain lines. Just what these lines are is by no means obvious. One way to find out is by looking at language. Since communication is based on the same conceptual system that we use in thinking and acting, language is an important source of evidence for what that system is like.

Primarily on the basis of linguistic evidence, we have found that most of our ordinary conceptual system is metaphorical in nature. And we have found a way to begin to identify in detail just what the metaphors are that structure how we perceive, how we think, and what we do.

To give some idea of what it could mean for a concept to be metaphorical   5 and for such a concept to structure an everyday activity, let us start with the concept ARGUMENT and the conceptual metaphor ARGUMENT IS WAR. This metaphor is reflected in our everyday language by a wide variety of expressions:

ARGUMENT IS WAR

Your claims are *indefensible.*
He *attacked every weak point* in my argument.
His criticisms were *right on target.*
I *demolished* his argument.
I've never *won* an argument with him.
You disagree? Okay, *shoot!*
If you use that *strategy,* he'll *wipe you out.*
He *shot down* all of my arguments.

It is important to see that we don't just *talk* about arguments in terms of war. We can actually win or lose arguments. We see the person we are arguing with as an opponent. We attack his positions and we defend our own. We gain and lose ground. We plan and use strategies. If we find a position indefensible, we can abandon it and take a new line of attack. Many of the things we *do* in arguing are partially structured by the concept of war. Though there is no physical battle, there is a verbal battle, and the structure of an argument — attack, defense, counterattack, etc. — reflects this. It is in this sense that the ARGUMENT IS WAR metaphor is one that we live by in this culture; it structures the actions we perform in arguing.

Try to imagine a culture where arguments are not viewed in terms of war, where no one wins or loses, where there is no sense of attacking or defending, gaining or losing ground. Imagine a culture where an argument is viewed as a dance, the participants are seen as performers, and the goal is to perform in a balanced and aesthetically pleasing way. In such a culture, people would view arguments differently, experience them differently, carry them out differently, and talk about them differently. But *we* would probably not view them as arguing at all: They would simply be doing something different. It would seem strange even to call what they were doing "arguing." Perhaps the most neutral way of describing this difference between their culture and ours would be to say that we have a discourse form structured in terms of battle and they have one structured in terms of dance.

Our ordinary conceptual system, in terms of which we both think and act, is fundamentally metaphorical in nature.

This is an example of what it means for a metaphorical concept, namely, ARGUMENT IS WAR, to structure (at least in part) what we do and how we understand what we are doing when we argue. *The essence of metaphor is understanding and experiencing one kind of thing in terms of another.* It is not that arguments are a subspecies of war. Arguments and wars are different kinds of things — verbal discourse and armed conflict — and the actions performed are different kinds of actions. But ARGUMENT is partially structured, understood, performed, and talked about in terms of WAR. The concept is metaphorically structured, the activity is metaphorically structured, and, consequently, the language is metaphorically structured.

Moreover, this is the *ordinary* way of having an argument and talking about one. The normal way for us to talk about attacking a position is to use the words "attack a position." Our conventional ways of talking about arguments presuppose a metaphor we are hardly ever conscious of. The metaphor is not merely in the words we use — it is in our very concept of an argument. The language of argument is not poetic, fanciful, or rhetorical; it is literal. We talk about arguments that way because we conceive of them that way — and we act according to the way we conceive of things.

The most important claim we have made so far is that metaphor is not just a matter of language, that is, of mere words. We shall argue that, on the contrary, human *thought processes* are largely metaphorical. This is what we mean when we say that the human conceptual system is metaphorically structured and defined. Metaphors as linguistic expressions are possible precisely because there are metaphors in a person's conceptual system. Therefore, whenever . . . we speak of metaphors, such as ARGUMENT IS WAR, it should be understood that *metaphor* means *metaphorical concept*.

Working with the Text

1. In the opening paragraph of their book, George Lakoff and Mark Johnson establish a concept of metaphor that they consider to be more accurate than the typical usage of the term:

   . . . metaphor is typically viewed as characteristic of language alone, a matter of words rather than thought or action. . . . We have found, on the contrary, that metaphor is pervasive in everyday life, not just in language but in thought and action.

   Write a brief essay in which you analyze the authors' conception of the difference between regarding metaphor as words and recognizing metaphor as thought or action. Why is establishing this difference important to their argument? Why did they choose to open with this contrast, instead of simply presenting their concept of metaphor?

2. In developing their argument, Lakoff and Johnson state, "Our concepts structure what we perceive, how we get around in the world, and how we relate to other people." As you reread the essay, look closely at the war metaphors we use for argument, as well as the dance metaphors the authors imagine another culture using for argument. In a brief essay, expand on Lakoff and Johnson's insight. If we conceptualize argument as war, what does that say about "what we perceive" and "how we relate to other people" (par. 2)? What would the dance metaphor for argument suggest about the culture that used it?

3. To underscore its importance to their argument, the authors italicize the statement, *"The essence of metaphor is understanding and experiencing one kind of thing in terms of another"* (par. 8). Think through the paragraph in which it appears. In a brief essay, explore the significance of this statement. What questions does it raise about human behavior? Why do the authors include this point in the opening chapter of their book? What does it suggest about the direction their argument will take?

From Text to Field

1. Lakoff and Johnson close their first chapter of their book by noting, "Metaphors as linguistic expressions are possible precisely because there are metaphors in a person's conceptual system" (par. 10). Reflect on your own use of the "argument is war" metaphor or on any other commonly used metaphor that illustrates the authors' thesis. Write an essay in which you suggest the origin of this metaphor. Do you think it is entirely socially conditioned? If so, how might it have been introduced? Is it somehow innate? Why did this particular metaphor, rather than another, take hold?

2. To illustrate their thesis, the authors list a number of expressions we use within the "argument is war" metaphor (par. 5). Using this list as a model, produce a similar list for the imaginary culture that uses dance as their metaphor for argument. As an alternative, choose another metaphor (such as music or barn raising or kneading bread) that suggests argument to you. To choose a metaphor, you might begin by reflecting on what argument is for you (if it's not war) or what you would prefer it to be.

3. Once the authors introduce the difference between metaphor as words and metaphor as thought and action, they move into illustrating the central assertion of their book, which is that "human *thought processes* are largely metaphorical" (par. 10). *Metaphors We Live By* is frequently used as a source in undergraduate courses. Taking the position of a reviewer writing for a student publication, explain the central assertion to an undergraduate audience who hasn't yet read any portion of the book. What does it mean for thought processes—not just thoughts themselves—to be metaphorical? Do you agree with the authors' conception? How important do you think this concept is to someone pursuing a college education? How might it help anyone understand daily life?

INTO THE FIELD: Options for Writing Projects

1. From Data Back to Ideas

One threat of the "information economy," according to Theodore Roszak, is that "we bury even deeper the substructures of ideas on which information stands, placing them further from critical reflection. For example," he says, "we begin to pay more attention to 'economic indicators'— which are always convenient, simple-looking numbers — than to the assumptions about work, wealth, and well-being which underlie economic policy" (par. 19). To explore the validity of Roszak's concern, consider one of the following two options for your fieldwork:

- Become familiar with the economic indicators that are most commonly used in the mass media. Through interviews with experts, if possible, as well as your own reading of the mass media and other observations, identify what you consider to be the American assumptions about "work, wealth, and well-being" that drive our economic policy. Taking on the role of a social commentator, write a critique of the relationship between the information conveyed by economic indicators and the values you think should drive economic policy.
- As an alternative, choose another social concern (e.g., marriage, low-wage jobs, home ownership and homelessness, capital punishment) that tends to be defined by statistics or other "facts" that you think camouflage or distort the underlying ideas and issues. What "substructure of ideas" do the statistics tend to remove from critical reflection?

2. Public Debate and the Information It Requires

This field project invites you to examine in some detail one current public debate in light of Christopher Lasch's essay. Your purpose in this project is not to take a side in the debate but rather to examine what assumptions the debate makes about information and the deliberative process. How does the debate you are considering involve information and misinformation? How might the debate encourage more access to or better use of information? Given the debate you are exploring, are appeals to objectivity helpful or would a more engaged or partisan approach yield better information and a more satisfying outcome? What assumptions do you see operating concerning the very nature of debate or deliberation?

3. The Rationale for Science in General Education

George Orwell suggests that two rival definitions of science tend to complicate our discussion about science education. For this field project, consider how implicit definitions of science have shaped your educational experience. Here are some specific options:

- Contact the school district or districts where you attended elementary and secondary school for documents and possible interviews. What definitions of *science* are at work in the elementary and secondary curriculum—as suggested either by its stated objectives or its progression over several grade levels?
- At your college or university, find documents and, if possible, conduct interviews that help you understand how your institution articulates the science curriculum for general education and for one of the specializations (biology, chemistry, physics, etc.). Based on the evidence, analyze and argue for or against the American approach to science education. Start by creating a "blueprint" of what educators have intended your exposure to science to accomplish. What are the key objectives? To what extent are those objectives met?
- What are the stages of science education, and how do they build on each other? In what ways do elementary, secondary, undergraduate general education, and specialized science education differ from each other? What is your view of this approach? In what ways would you change it?

4. Content and Method

George Orwell observes that "scientific education ought to mean the implanting of a rational, sceptical, experimental habit of mind. It ought to mean acquiring a *method*—a method that can be used on any problem that one meets—and not simply piling up a lot of facts" (par. 10). For your fieldwork, explore Orwell's observation in one of the following two ways:

- What frame of reference does one or more of your courses this term seem to have? Does the course stress covering content and "piling up a lot of facts" or does it help you to acquire a method? Why might some courses succeed in doing both?
- Apply Orwell's insight to your prospective major. Review courses and major requirements in your chosen department in light of this distinction between coverage and method. What kind of balance does your department strike between coverage of content and the practice of method?

5. Story Skeletons in the Classroom

Roger Schank discusses story skeletons and story-fitting in light of international politics. Yet story skeletons or explanation patterns are at work in everyday settings as well. One such setting is the college classroom. This field project invites you to explore the explanation patterns that are invoked in the day-to-day interactions between faculty and students.

These interactions might have to do with assignments, course policies, office hours, and the like. Pay attention to both the story skeletons used by your professor and the story skeletons that lie behind student comments and questions. You may also wish to consider the story skeletons that lie behind how your professor treats the actual topics being taught. That is, in introducing new material or summarizing the relevance of material you have just covered, your professor may invoke a story skeleton appropriate for that pedagogical situation or teaching moment.

What do the use of these story skeletons by both faculty and students reveal about your classrooms? Can tensions in the classroom be traced to the use of different story skeletons by students and faculty? Does the presence of story skeletons make the classroom seem rather conventional, a genre of its own, or does the background presence of these story skeletons help highlight moments when faculty or students depart from expected roles and patterns?

6. Academic Research and the Logic of Storytelling

It is easy to assume that academic research is far removed from storytelling. Yet storytelling often plays a role in research articles, especially as authors position their own work in light of previous publications. Read some academic articles in a field of interest to you (one you know a bit about, or one that might be your prospective major). You might focus on the introduction to the article, in which prior research is often summarized. Does the way the research is reported tend to follow the logic of storytelling? Are there heroes and villains, so to speak? Are there protagonists and antagonists? What sets the story in motion? Is there conflict or misunderstanding or a faulty assumption? To what extent is this storytelling logic fairly clear, or hidden? What are the explanation patterns or story skeletons that might underlie how the author tells the particulars of his or her story? For example, is the story skeleton behind the article one of "filling a gap in the research" or is it "new data prompts us to review our assumptions"?

7. "Argument Is War"—across the University

Argument is integral to university studies and is typically the focus of college-level writing courses. Indeed, some might refer to the university as a "house of argument." For your fieldwork, consider one of the following two options:

- Recall your experience with argumentative writing, in this or other university writing courses you have taken. Consider ways in which the "argument is war" metaphor is at work in the argumentative writing you do or have done for such a course. Write an essay in which you reflect on the extent to which the war metaphor has helped or hindered your ability to write an effective argument.

BETTY CROCKER® portrait mark and the TACO BELL bell design), alterations in marks are common. The PTO will review the original mark as registered and compare it with the current specimen; if they are substantially the same, the affidavit will be accepted. A material alteration will result in a refusal on the basis that the mark currently in use is a new mark and that the registered mark is no longer in use. Generally, a mere pluralization in wording or a slight change in nonessential background design may be acceptable. Thus, if wording in a mark appears in a different typeface or script, it will likely be accepted. The addition of wording or design elements, however, will likely result in a refusal, requiring the registrant to file a new application and begin the registration process anew.

If the PTO agrees that a change is not material and accepts the section 8 affidavit, the registrant will usually be encouraged to amend the registration so it conforms to the mark as presently used.

If the registered mark is not in use in commerce, the owner may provide facts to the PTO showing that nonuse is excusable due to special circumstances rather than any intent to abandon the mark and must state the date use of the mark stopped and when it is expected to resume. Merely stating that the applicant does not intend to abandon the mark is not sufficient. Additionally, reduced demand for the product or service does not excuse nonuse; ordinary economic or social conditions that result in nonuse of the mark cannot be excused, because these are exactly the types of marks the PTO wants to eliminate. On the other hand, if there is some governmental regulation that precludes the owner from using the mark (for example, a trade embargo against the sale of insecticides or certain chemicals), nonuse would be acceptable. Similarly, if the mark is temporarily not being used because of sale of a business, plant retooling (and production is

scheduled to resume at some point), fire, illness, or other catastrophe, the nonuse might be excused. As soon as the external cause passes, the owner must resume use within a reasonable amount of time. Finally, if sales of a product are sporadic because the product is so expensive that few sales are customary in the particular industry, such is excusable nonuse.

THE AFFIDAVIT OF INCONTESTABILITY

Section 15 of the Trademark Act permits owners of registrations on the Principal Register to file affidavits whereby the right to use the registered marks for the goods or services set forth in the affidavit becomes **incontestable.** A section 15 affidavit, also called an **Affidavit of Incontestability,** may not be filed until the mark has been in continuous use in commerce for at least five consecutive years. Thus, the section 15 affidavit is often combined with the first section 8 affidavit in one submission to the PTO. The filing fee for the section 15 affidavit is $200 per class of goods or services identified in the registration. The PTO prefers that the owner file the document electronically through TEAS.

The benefit to filing a section 15 affidavit is that it significantly reduces the challenges that may be made to a mark. Generally, a mark that is incontestable cannot be attacked unless it has become generic, has been abandoned, is functional, or was procured by fraud. Thus, incontestability precludes challenges to a mark on the basis that it is descriptive or that it is confusingly similar to a mark owned by a prior user.

In addition to verifying that the mark has been in continuous use for the five-year period, the section 15 affidavit must state that there has been no final decision adverse to the registrant's claim of ownership of the mark, or to the registrant's right to register the mark, or to keep the mark on the Principal Register. The

- Consider to what extent various disciplines have slightly different expectations about what constitutes argument. Identify a metaphor that is widely used in your prospective discipline or field. Write an essay in which you analyze it according to the theory of metaphor proposed by George Lakoff and Mark Johnson. You might find such a metaphor by reviewing the texts and materials used in your courses, by listening to experts in the field and reading their publications, or by interviewing one or more of your professors. What does this metaphor say about your field and how its members construct their sense of the world?

8. Other Metaphors We Live By

Choose an everyday activity or behavior, other than argument, that is governed by a metaphor widely used in our culture. For ideas, set aside a day for being aware of what you do (eating, going to class, driving, working, socializing) and what you observe (the news, television, other people around you). The media can be a good source for cultural metaphor. Using George Lakoff and Mark Johnson's argument, analyze your metaphor as a basis for thought and action and as an example of "understanding and experiencing one kind of thing in terms of another."

ARGUING IN COMMUNITIES

This unit explores the proposition that arguments have habitats. The very notion might seem strange if we think of arguments only in abstract, logical terms, as specimens to be dissected. Arguments are conversations that take place in communities — and thus are inherently social. Arguments are situated, touching on and drawing their strength from our problems, desires, needs, and agendas. When we argue or deliberate, we do so *with* others, *within* a community. When we advance a claim, it is more than a claim that something is so; it is a claim on the belief of our audience, our community.

The word *community* comes from the Latin for "common" or "shared." Communities develop and maintain themselves through the activities and interests we share and through the ways our lives intersect with each other. That very intersection also helps us understand how communities overlap, how we live simultaneously in several communities. Communities have internal tensions and disagreements, and where they overlap with other communities these tensions can become more apparent. College is no different. The arguments made in classes and on campus are shaped by that habitat and by the more particular habitats of departments and disciplines.

Communities sustain themselves through language, an important link apparent in words themselves: *communication* coming from the same Latin root as *community*. This relationship is nowhere more important than in university communities, where language use (and its accompanying behaviors and rituals) becomes especially prominent. You may have come to college thinking you were going to study biology or sociology. But a lot of what you end up studying is how biologists and sociologists speak about their work. Little wonder, for you are initiated into communities in good part through the language you learn. Likewise, language can be a barrier or gatekeeping device to restrict people from communities. Communities can facilitate communication, but they can also erect barriers to communication and thus fragment the university community as much as draw it together.

This unit invites you to explore the habitats of argument in college and university settings. We can speak of these habitats as "discourse communities."

In some respects, these discourse communities can easily remain invisible — that is, until we are identified as the outsider by not having mastered the appropriate linguistic "secret handshake."

The several readings in this unit can help demystify this link between language and community in your own college experience. David Russell questions whether there really is such a thing as one "academic community" or whether there are many smaller communities. In other words, is college but a Tower of Babel, with many languages making mutual comprehension difficult, if not impossible? Wayne C. Booth isn't nearly so ready to concede the point. His essay helps identify how it is that we can understand as much as we do when we talk to people in other fields.

The language games and rituals that define discourse communities in college are perhaps best exposed through parody. And here there is no finer example than Horace Miner's now-classic send-up of cultural anthropology, "Body Ritual among the Nacirema."

Why is it that initiation into an academic discipline has much in common with initiation into some secret cult? Robin Tolmach Lakoff helps reveal the mysteries behind such initiation rites and why the elders of any academic tribe prefer that newcomers not be told too much. As you might imagine, it all has to do with mystique and power.

Discourse communities are often mapped and divided into particular groups or areas, like the sciences, social sciences, and humanities. In the final selection Jared Diamond has us take a second look at those distinctions and cautions us not to trust them. What seems less rigorous, even intuitive, may in fact turn out to be more complex than we think.

Reflecting on Prior Knowledge

1. Develop an inventory of the various communities, on campus and off, of which you are a part. Include not only geographically specific communities but also social, intellectual, recreational, political, and religious ones. How are these communities formed and supported through the use of language — often a language specific to that community? Describe some of the distinct communities to which you belong. What common bonds hold these communities together? Where is there agreement and disagreement? Do you act or use language differently in one community than in another? After you have developed some initial responses, meet in teams to compare them.

2. In one way or another, all of us have had to convince a group to accept us as a member. We work to gain acceptance in groups ranging from a circle of friends to larger communities based on social, recreational, political, professional, religious, or cultural interests. Recall two different situations in which

you worked to gain acceptance. In a journal entry, describe what you said and did, noting the different approaches required by each situation or group.

3. Nearly all communities have a "secret handshake"—not necessarily an actual handshake but some way (often through language) by which insiders recognize each other and by which the outsider is immediately identified as such. In a journal entry, recall the secret "language" handshakes you were privy to in high school and college, and some of the handshakes—and communities—that were not available to you.

4. Working in teams, develop a list of traits that characterize your college as a language community—a group with common purposes that uses language in particular ways. Share your work with the class. Next, consider the ways in which your current or prospective major is likewise a language community, one that might differ from the language community of other majors. How much overlap is there between these various communities?

5. In a journal entry, explore the ways in which the obligation to "make an argument" (something very different from just "having an argument") encourages us to think strategically about conversations in a community, about finding community-based reasons, and about objections to a position that stem from that community. To what extent do most real, situated deliberations involve the problems, needs, and interests of a community?

Academic Discourse: Community or Communities?

David R. Russell

Students in university writing programs are often unaware that their course work has grown out of heated, ongoing debates about how writing should be taught. David R. Russell became a key voice in the debates with the publication of *Writing in the Academic Disciplines, 1870–1990* (1991), which explores the historical context for understanding why teaching writing on the university level presents so many challenges. In the following excerpt from his book, Russell identifies what he considers to be one of the core challenges, tying it to particular developments in the emergence of the modern university.

In Russell's view, the shift from the traditional liberal-arts education provided before 1870 to the modern focus on professional preparation fragmented the academic community, a development that complicated the task of initiating students into a "discourse community." Instead of working with a uniform approach to academic and professional writing, students — and their writing teachers — now contend with "competing discourse communities," each requiring a specialized approach to communication.

Through his research, Russell has become a central figure in the development of "writing across the curriculum" or "communication across the curriculum," a teaching approach that seeks to use writing as a tool for learning, even as it addresses the diverse composing and speaking demands of specialized academic and professional fields. Among Russell's current interests are genre theory and how various kinds of writing grow out of systems of activity in which authors and readers find themselves.

Russell, a professor of English at Iowa State University, teaches in the PhD program in rhetoric and professional communication in addition to teaching undergraduate courses in writing and rhetoric.

A prolific writer and frequent speaker, Russell also collaborates on program development and has edited several collections of essays on writing and writing instruction.

The complex origins of mass education in America made it difficult for academia to view learning to write as an initiation into a discourse community, a process of gradually coming to use language in a certain way to become accepted, "literate," or, as is often the case in modern American higher education, credentialed in some profession. Before the advent of the modern university in the 1870s, academia was indeed a single discourse community. Institutions of higher learning built an intellectual and social community by selecting students primarily on the basis of social class (less than 1 percent of the population was admitted), which guaranteed linguistic homogeneity, and by initiating them intellectually through a series of highly language-dependent methods—the traditional recitation, disputation, debate, and oral examination of the old liberal curriculum. Equally important, most students shared common values (Christian, often sectarian) with their teachers (primarily ministers). They pursued a uniform course of study and were then duly welcomed as full members of the nation's governing elite.[1]

The modern university changed all that. It provided the specialized knowledge that drove the new urban-industrial economy and a new class of specialized *professionals* (the term came into use during the period) who managed that economy, with its secular rationale and complex bureaucratic organization — what Burton J. Bledstein has aptly called "the culture of professionalism." Beginning with the land-grant colleges of the late nineteenth century and continuing with the rise of the modern university on the German model, the academic discourse community became fragmented. Numbers swelled, with enrollments tripling as a percentage of the population between 1900 and 1925 alone. Students from previously excluded social groups were admitted, destroying linguistic homogeneity. The new elective curriculum was introduced to prepare students for a host of emerging professional careers in the new industrial society. The elective curriculum compartmentalized knowledge and broke one relatively stable academic discourse community into many fluctuating ones. And the active, personal, language-dependent instructional methods of the old curriculum were replaced by passive, rather impersonal methods borrowed from Germany or, later, from scientific management: lecture, objective testing, and the like. Ultimately, the professional faculty who replaced the gentlemen scholars and divines of the old curriculum came to see secondary and undergraduate education as only one of several competing responsibilities (along with graduate teaching, research, and professional service). And the teaching of writing—initiating the neophytes into a discourse community—suffered accordingly.

Because it is tempting to recall academia's very different past and hope for a very different future, the term *academic community* has powerful spiritual and political connotations, but today academia is a *discourse* community only in a context so broad as to have little meaning in terms of shared linguistic forms, either for the advancement of knowledge (which now goes on in disciplinary communities and subcommunities) or for the initiation of new members (who are initiated into a specific community's discourse). Thus, to speak of the academic community as if its members shared a single set of linguistic conventions and traditions of inquiry is to make a categorical mistake. In the aggregate of all the tightly knit, turf-conscious disciplines and departments, each of its own discourse community, the modern university consists. Many have wished it otherwise.

The term *academic community* has powerful spiritual and political connotations.

Despite these profound changes, American educators have continued to think of the academic community as holding out a single compositional norm, which would speak intelligently about the multiform new knowledge to a "general reader." In their complaints about student writing, academics hark back nostalgically to a golden age of academic community where Johnny could both read and write the "plain English" that purists enshrine. But that golden age never existed in the modern university (and writing per se was not valued or even evaluated in the old college). As Daniel P. and Lauren B. Resnick have observed, "There is little to go back to in terms of pedagogical method, curriculum, or school organization. The old tried and true approaches, which nostalgia today prompts us to believe might solve current problems, were designed neither to achieve the literacy standards sought today nor to assure successful literacy for everyone . . . there is no simple past to which we can return."[2] Though academia held onto a generalized ideal of an academic community sharing a single advanced literacy, there was never any consensus in the modern university about the nature of that community or its language. Academic discourse, like academia itself, continued its drive toward increasing specialization. The university became an aggregate of competing discourse communities; it was not a single community. But the myth of a single academic discourse community—and a golden age of student writing—endured.

American academia today (and for the last hundred years or so) is a community primarily in a broad institutional sense, a collection of people going about a vast enterprise, in much the same way that we speak of the "business community" as a sector of national life. The academic disciplines are in one sense united through their common missions: teaching, research, and service. But disciplines have been so diverse, so independent, and so bound up with professional communities outside academia that they require no common language or even shared values and methods within the university in order to pursue those missions. Those genres and conventions of writing that are shared by all academic disciplines are also shared by professional communities outside academia. And within academia, the conventions (and beyond them the assumptions and methodologies) of the various disciplines are characterized more by their differences than by their similarities. The various disciplines have grown to constitute the modern university through accretion, as Gerald Graff has forcefully argued, and through their relevance to concerns in the wider society, not through their logical relation to each other — so much so that "interdisciplinary" study is always a notable (and often suspect) exception.[3] Indeed, an academic is likely to have more linguistic common ground with a fellow professional in the corporate sector than with another academic in an unrelated field, except in regard to purely institutional matters (governance, academic freedom, teaching loads, etc.). As a leading sociologist of higher education, Burton Clark, puts it, academia is made up of "small worlds, different worlds."[4]

Notes

1. See Halloran, "Rhetoric" 249–56.
2. Daniel P. Resnick and Lauren B. Resnick, "The Nature of Literacy: An Historical Exploration," *Harvard Educational Review* 47 (1977): 385, qtd. in Rose 355. On the increasing and proliferating standards of literacy, see also Dell H. Hymes, "Foreword," in Wagner xi–xvii.
3. Gerald Graff, *Professing Literature* (Chicago: U of Chicago P, 1987) 6–15. See also theoretical discussions in *Interdisciplinary Relationships in the Social Sciences*, ed. Muzafer Sherif and Carolyn W. Sherif (Chicago: Aldine, 1969); and Stanley Fish, "Being Interdisciplinary Is So Very Hard To Do," *Profession* (1989): 15–22.
4. See Clark, *Academic Life* esp. chap. 5.

Works Cited

Clark, Burton R. *The Academic Life: Small Worlds, Different Worlds.* Princeton: Carnegie Foundation for the Advancement of Teaching, 1987.
Halloran, S. Michael. "Rhetoric in the American College Curriculum: The Decline of Public Discourse." *Pre/Text* 3 (1982): 245–69.
Rose, Mike. "The Language of Exclusion: Writing Instruction at the University." *College English* 47 (1985): 341–59.
Wagner, Daniel A., ed. *The Future of Literacy in a Changing World.* Oxford: Pergamon, 1987.

Working with the Text

1. In order to explore problems in the teaching and use of writing in various fields, David Russell analyzes changes in university education that took place after the 1870s. As you reread the essay, note the concerns he raises— explicitly or implicitly — as he examines particular historical developments. In a brief essay, analyze how he uses history to make his argument. Why is the historical dimension important to how he sees the current challenges facing teachers and students of writing within the university? What particular changes does he consider to be significant? What specific difficulties did those changes create?

2. Russell is recognized internationally for his work in writing across the curriculum, which involves teaching writing within the context of particular academic disciplines and using writing as a means to learn disciplinary material. When you reread this excerpt from his book, note his use of *community* and *discourse community* — terms that are central to current research on the teaching of writing. Based on this excerpt, write a brief essay in which you analyze his position on how writing should be taught on a university level. What can you infer about his position from the problem he poses in this essay? What can you infer from what he says about communities and discourse communities? Why are discourse communities important to teaching and learning and, more particularly, to your success as a writer?

3. Russell summarizes the shift from "the old liberal curriculum" to "the modern university" by pointing out that "the active, personal, language-dependent instructional methods of the old curriculum were replaced by passive, rather impersonal methods borrowed from Germany or, later, from scientific management: lecture, objective testing, and the like" (par. 2). Drawing on your own experience in the classroom (in all of your courses, not just writing courses), reflect on what constitutes active and passive learning. Based on Russell's argument, write a brief essay in which you analyze how the shift from active to passive teaching methods affected where and how writing is taught and the role of writing assignments in various disciplines. Look for passages, in addition to the one quoted above, that might directly or indirectly indicate Russell's view on the effects of this shift.

From Text to Field

1. At the end of this excerpt from Russell's book, he quotes Burton Clark's observation that academia is made up of "small worlds, different worlds" (par. 5). Given your own experience on campus, what different worlds can you identify? Consider both academic and nonacademic "worlds" as you think about this

question. What makes these worlds distinct? Are there any intersections between them? Are these worlds shaped and maintained by their use of language? In what ways are these small and different worlds on campus different from the various communities you belong to off campus, or might they have some commonalities? Write an essay in which you introduce one such small world on campus and reflect on your entry into that world.

2. Review Russell's essay to focus on what he has to say about "the culture of professionalism" (par. 2) and the effect it has had on the university system of education, particularly on the teaching of writing. Write an essay in which you take a position on the relationship between higher education and the professions and how you think that relationship should influence the teaching of writing. To what extent should higher education be focused on preparing students for the professions? What other purposes, if any, are there for pursuing a college education? What are the reasons behind your stance? Given what you think should be the goals of higher education, how should writing be taught?

3. This unit also includes an excerpt from an influential essay by Wayne C. Booth, "The Idea of a *University* — as Seen by a Rhetorician" (p. 332). Booth describes what he sees as the common rhetoric — shared language, values, and thinking processes—sed to communicate across highly specialized disciplines. Russell's argument implies that there is no single approach to writing that could prepare students to write within all of the academic or professional communities they might encounter. Do you agree with Booth or with Russell? Is there some common form of communication that cuts across specialized fields? Write an essay in which you respond to Russell's argument by drawing on your own experience with writing and writing courses.

affidavit must also state that there is no proceeding involving these rights pending in the PTO or any court.

No registrant is required to file a section 15 affidavit; however, for obvious reasons, if the mark has been in continuous use for at least five years and satisfies the other conditions, a registrant should be strongly encouraged to do so to immunize the mark from various challenges. Only marks registered on the Principal Register (not the Supplemental Register) may become incontestable under section 15. (See Appendix D, Form 4, for a combined affidavit under sections 8 and 15.)

RENEWAL OF REGISTRATIONS

Any trademark registration issued after the Trademark Law Revision Act (namely, November 16, 1989) has a duration of ten years. Before that date, registrations were valid for twenty years. Within one year before expiration of each pertinent period, the registrant must renew the registration or it will be automatically canceled (although common law rights to the mark may still exist if the mark is in use). The new **renewal** period for all marks is ten years. Although the application for renewal (often called a "section 9 renewal application") must be filed within a one-year period before each expiration date, there is a grace period of six months following the expiration of a registration during which an application for renewal may be filed. For example, for a registration issued November 1, 2003, the first application for renewal can be filed as early as November 1, 2012, and as late as November 1, 2013, before entering the six-month grace period. The filing fee for an application for renewal is $400 per class of goods or services. Filing during the grace period results in additional fees of $100 per class. The section 8 affidavit required every ten years can be combined

with the renewal application in a single document filed every ten years. The form for the combined filing is available through TEAS. (See Appendix D, Form 5.)

The requirements previously discussed for section 8 affidavits (filed between years five and six after registration and every ten years after registration) and applications for renewal are somewhat similar:

- the document should be filed by the owner of the mark. If the owner identified for the application for renewal is different from the one identified in the registration itself, renewal will issue in the name of the party who is shown as owner in the original registration; and
- if the renewal application lists only some of the goods/services in the registration, it will be presumed that the renewal is sought for only the goods/services listed (and the goods/services omitted from the renewal application will be omitted from the registration).

No specimen is required and there is no requirement of showing that any nonuse is due to special circumstances that excuse nonuse, generally because a specimen or showing of excusable nonuse are covered by section 8 affidavits of continuing use, usually filed at the same time and in the same document as the renewal application under section 9. (See Appendix D, Form 5, Application for Renewal of Trademark Registration Combined with Declaration of Use under section 8 of Lanham Act.) (See Exhibit 5–1 for chart showing due dates for postregistration documents.)

DOCKETING REQUIREMENTS

As discussed, certain actions must be taken to maintain a trademark or service mark registration. Failure to take the appropriate action

The Idea of a *University* — as Seen by a Rhetorician

Wayne C. Booth

In 1987, Wayne C. Booth, a professor at the University of Chicago, was asked to address his colleagues as part of an annual lecture series dedicated to helping academic specialists understand each other's areas of research. Booth opened his address by questioning the ambitious goal of the annual lectures and coming to the conclusion that academics are "a pack of ignoramuses."

> [E]ven if we could create a university inhabited solely by geniuses, geniuses who, unlike most actual geniuses, were full of an infinite good-will toward, and determination to understand, one another's disciplines . . . we would find that under modern conditions of inquiry, conditions that we have no hope of changing fundamentally, none of them could come to an understanding of more than a fraction of what the others would take to be real knowledge.

In the spirit of the lecture series, Booth continued the address by examining the problem of understanding each other's work through the lens of his expertise in rhetoric. The excerpt that follows presents his solution — a recognition that academics use what he considers to be several valid forms of rhetoric to inform judgments they would otherwise be too "ignorant" to make. Through rhetoric, Booth explores the means for mutual understanding that might help a *uni*versity from splintering into a *multi*versity.

At the time this lecture was written, Booth was a Distinguished Service Professor at the University of Chicago. After retiring in 1992 at the age of seventy-one, he was the George M. Pullman Professor Emeritus of English and continued to be active as a researcher, writer, and lecturer. Booth died in 2005. The first of several landmark books he wrote, *The Rhetoric of Fiction,* published in 1961, is considered essential to the study of narrative theory and technique. *A Rhetoric of*

Irony (1974) explores how authors and readers participate in the complex interchange of ironic communication. *Modern Dogma and the Rhetoric of Assent* (1974) explores how speakers are able to change listeners' minds and when and why listeners should change their minds. More recently, Booth published several collections of his essays and lectures. Through the breadth and importance of his writings—ranging from literary criticism and rhetorical studies to examinations of pluralism and ethics—Booth has become a major influence both in and beyond his field.

I assume that many of you have long since wanted to protest against my picture. We all know that the islands are not in fact totally isolated, that somehow we have managed to invent communication systems. Though it may be true that on each island we speak a language not fully intelligible on any other, and though it may be true that some of the islands conduct active warfare against some of the others, and though some islands are in a state of civil war, the fact is that somehow we do manage to talk with one another and come to judgments that we are convinced are not *entirely* capricious. We write interdepartmental and even interdivisional memos, we indite letters of recommendation at breakneck speed and in appalling numbers, purporting to appraise the quality of colleagues whose work we don't know beans about. We appraise other scholars according to what we take to be high standards, even when we ourselves cannot state literally what the standards are. We pass judgment upon students in "related fields" and one another whenever promotion is at stake, and we seem not to suffer intolerable anxiety about our decisions. Even more shocking, in view of the plight I have described, we ask our deans and provosts and presidents to approve our judgments, and even grant the right to reverse them, implying that somehow *somebody* can be competent to judge work in *all* fields. Finally, we busy ourselves with a great deal of what we call "interdisciplinary work": degree-granting committees like Ideas and Methods, imperialistic fields like geography, anthropology, English, and rhetoric, conferences and workshops galore. None of us really thinks that *all* of these operations are totally fraudulent. We act *as if* our discussions and conferences and tenure decisions make *real* sense. Do they?

How do we actually work, as we run those of our affairs that depend on some kind of understanding different from the one I have applied so far? Do we work, as some say, only according to blind trust of friends and mistrust of enemies? Do we work according to guesses only? Are we, as some would claim, simply servants of money and power? In what sense, if any, do we employ a kind of reasoning and proof—knowledge and genuine understanding under any definition — that we might point to without shame?

After my informants of the past months have confessed their ignorance, I have asked them to tell me how they in fact operate when judging colleagues whose work they do not understand. All of them have said something like this — though never in this precise language: "We are by no means fraudulent, because we have available certain rational resources that your definition of understanding leaves out. We have learned to make use of our knowledge [one professor even called it 'wisdom'] about character and how to appraise character witnesses; we have learned how to read the signs of quality even in the fields where we cannot follow the proofs. We have learned how to determine whether a referee is trustworthy, and we have learned something about how to judge the quality of a candidate's thinking, just by the way he or she writes and speaks." They have not gone on to say, though I wish we could have shared this language: "You see, what all this means is that we are experienced both as practitioners and students of — rhetoric."

When I press them further with the question, "Do you make mistakes with this kind of thinking?" the answer is always "Yes, sometimes." But nobody I've talked with has claimed that the process depends on a trust that is utterly blind, totally a matter of nonrational power grabs or logrolling or back-scratching or moneygrubbing. Everyone, absolutely everyone, has played into this rhetorician's hands by claiming to employ a kind of thought that is not identical with what we do when proving conclusions in our frontline inquiry — and yet a kind that is still genuine thought.

Of course nobody has claimed that we offer our rhetorical proofs to each other and test them as well as we ought; indeed my main point today is that we could all employ them better, and thus improve our quality as a *university*, *if* we all studied how such peculiar yet rational persuasion works. But even in our fallen condition, even as we in our imperfection now operate, we do not perform our personal and administrative judgments on indefensible, nonscholarly grounds; we perform those judgments on grounds that are considered nonscholarly only by those who think that all knowledge is of the kind yielded by frontline specialties, only by those who embrace uncritically the criterion for understanding, and thus of knowledge, with which I began. If knowledge is confined to what experts discover at the front line, and if understanding is confined to participation in full dialogue at the front line, then we operate ourselves without *knowing* what we do and without *understanding* each other. If we know and understand only what we can *prove* — with empirical observation, or with statistics, or with rigorous logical deduction — we will never *know* whether a colleague is worth listening to or promoting, unless we ourselves can follow his or her proofs, in detail, and then replicate them. All else is dubious, all else is guesswork, all else is blind faith.

But one thing we all know is that we know more than that criterion implies. Though unable to tell for ourselves whether the new mathematical proof is indeed new and indeed a proof, we learn how to consider, with the eye of nonspecialists, both the rhetoric of scholarship that we cannot hope fully to understand, and the rhetoric offered us *about* the scholar, the arguments offered by those who give us some reason to trust or mistrust their judgment as specialists.

We all thus implicitly aspire to mastery in three kinds of rhetoric, leading to three kinds of understanding, not just one. There are, first, the many and diverse rhetorics peculiar to each of our various front lines. Here each small group of experts relies on what Aristotle calls *special topics* of persuasion, the often tacit convictions that are shared by all within a discipline and that are therefore available in constructing arguments within the field: The assumption, say, that photographs of bubble chambers and their interpretations can somehow be relied on; or the conventional agreements about how to deal with normal curves and chi-squares, about the proper use of graphs, about what makes a **All three of these rhetorics** sound equation, or about how to do a sensitive report **are of course highly fallible.** of poetic scansion or a convincing analysis of sonata form in a symphony. Though these assumptions shift over time, we can at any given time rely on them without argument in their support, as we construct our arguments to our peers. I'll risk offending some of you by dubbing this frontline stuff and its workings "rhetoric-1." If calling it "hard proof" will make you happier, feel free, but I know that few specialists will want to claim that they or their successors will find themselves fifty years from now relying on the same tacit assumptions, leading to the same conclusions, that they share today.

A second kind that I call "general rhetoric," or "rhetoric-2," is what we share with members of every functioning organization or society—businesses, governments, clubs, families: the whole range of plausible or probable beliefs and modes of proof that make the world go round. Think of it as what even the most rigorous of scientists must rely on when testifying before a government committee. Here we rely on the *common*, or general topics: "More of any good thing is better than less of it—usually"; "It's wrong to lie, at least to friends and colleagues"; "Loyalty matters"; "Actions that usually produce bad consequences should be avoided." Obviously many of these are included in everyone's notion of "common sense": what *makes* sense in any argument.

Though the common topics are indispensable in every domain, they are especially prominent in our running of the university whenever we must appraise character. We all have a little storehouse of beliefs about character that we have to rely on, more or less efficiently, whenever we read a letter of recommendation, or predict the future behavior of a colleague in order to grant or deny tenure. Such common topics, "commonplaces," crop up in all public debate. "It is probable that someone who failed to carry through on her previous research plan will fail in this one; turn her down." "Ah, yes, but she was deep in the anguish of a divorce then, and she's changed a lot. I say give her the grant." "Well, but her strongest supporter is Professor Smiler, who has usually been wrong in his predictions that young colleagues are late bloomers. Why should we believe him in this case?" Or: "The truth is that Louise and Harry used to live together, and they had an angry breakup. I think — though we must say nothing of it in public — that we cannot trust his negative judgment on her scholarly ability."

Rhetoric-2 is thus the set of resources available in the functioning of all organizations, not just of universities. Arbitragers and government officers function or fail to function, depending on whether the trust they yield to their CEOs and marine sergeants and colonels is justified. We in the university similarly succeed to the degree that our trust is granted when it should be, withheld when it should not be. The case with which rhetoric-2 can be abused accounts largely for why rhetoric has always had, and probably always *will* have, a bad press. Philosophers and moralists have often wished that it would just go away — but of course they express the wish for a purer world in the only language available to any of us when we press our wishes on the world: rhetorical argument.

There is, thirdly, a kind of rhetoric that is neither as special as the first nor as general as the second, a rhetoric relying on shared topics that are proper or special only to those within a university, but to all within that university, not to any one special group. We have no name for this peculiar stuff that we all to some degree share, but call it "the rhetoric of inquiry," or of "intellectual engagement"; "academy-rhetoric," or "rhetoric-3." We learn how to judge whether the arguments in fields beyond our full competence *somehow* track, whether the style of presentation *somehow* accords with standards we recognize. We learn to sense whether a colleague, even in a quite remote field, *seems* to have mastered the tricks of the trade — not just the trade of this or that kind of economist or philosopher, but the tricks of this whole trade, the trade of learning and teaching for the sake of learning and teaching. One often hears, in the Quadrangle Club, not just the contemptuous comments I have mentioned about fools and knaves but comments like this: "What a mind that man has." "What a pleasure to argue with that woman — she never misses a stroke." "He always seems to have just the right analogy to make his point." "Have you noticed how you always come away from a conversation with him having to think through the problem in a different way?"

All three of these rhetorics are of course highly fallible. Even our many versions of rhetoric-1 are notoriously unstable, as I have already implied, shifting in threatening ways from decade to decade and field to field. But the second and third rhetorics are much more obviously fallible, indeed staggeringly so. Tough-minded appraisal of characters and witnesses through close reading of letters of recommendation and reader's reports, close listening during telephone calls and hallway conversations, careful appraisal of past records of performance—these are all dangerously unreliable, partly because charlatans can so easily mimic the proper use of the topics. If this were not so, we would not have so many successful frauds in every field. The Piltdown hoaxers, the Cyril Burts, the Darsees,° the unqualified but practicing surgeons, the undiploma-ed lawyers—all the hoaxers of our world succeed as they do because they have mastered the surface conventions of all three rhetorics and through that mastery have collected or forged references testifying to high quality. We read about so many successes in this burgeoning field of pseudoscientific conning that we are in danger of forgetting the solid and indispensable base of merely probable inferences on which it rests. The breakdowns in the system result from, and depend on, a process—the practice of producing sound conclusions from rhetorical proofs—that by its very necessities opens the door to frauds. But this is not to say that we, their dupes, could not protect ourselves better if we would study rhetoric as hard as we study lab techniques, say, or formal logic.

Again and again I have been told by my informants that "it's not really very hard to tell competent work from incompetent, even if you know nothing about the details and cannot replicate the argument or experiment." And when I then ask, "How do you *do* that?" I am told—never in this language—that "I do it using rhetorics-2 and -3—not the appraisal of frontline proofs but the careful judgment of both 'general rhetoric' and 'academy rhetoric.' One editor told me, "Even when I know little or nothing about a special field, I can tell just by the opening paragraphs whether a would-be contributor is at least competent." What does that mean, if not that he claims to judge the author's skill in rhetorical conventions shared with other fields: skill in saying what needs saying and in not saying what should not be said; skill in implying a scholarly ethos appropriate to the subject; skill in avoiding moves that give away the novice; and so on. Though the practice and appraisal of

---

The Piltdown hoaxers . . . the Darsees: The Piltdown hoax was an infamous case in which faked remains of an unknown form of early man were planted near Piltdown, England. Cyril Burt was a British psychologist accused of scientific fraud. John Darsee was a medical researcher found to have fabricated data for his research publications.

such skills is chancy, if we ruled them out we could not operate for a day without disaster. Most of our journals would have to be scrapped, most of our grants and awards would have to be eliminated, and the university would have to surrender to total balkanization or even tribal warfare, becoming not a *uni*versity at all but a multiversity, a mere collection of research institutes warring for funds.

Working with the Text

1. Because Wayne C. Booth explores the inner workings of the university from his point of view as a rhetorician, his argument centers on the term *rhetoric.* As you reread the selection, consider how he uses the term. In a brief essay, define the term as Booth uses it in the context of his argument. What actions or mental processes does rhetoric involve? Why and how is it used? What connection does it have to understanding and judgment?

2. Booth presents rhetoric-2 as a "general rhetoric" that "we share with members of every functioning organization or society — businesses, governments, clubs, families: the whole range of plausible or probable beliefs and modes of proof that make the world go round" (par. 8). Study Booth's examples of these "commonplaces." In a brief response, add your own examples and explain why you think they are what Booth describes as "'common sense': what *makes* sense in any argument" (par. 8).

3. By Booth's definition, rhetoric-1 (the basic knowledge, assumptions, and principles of a particular academic specialization) and rhetoric-3 (shared topics and modes of inquiry within a community that spans diverse specializations) grow out of different kinds of specialized knowledge and experience. Write a brief essay in which you analyze the differences in specialization required by these two rhetorics. For instance, what is the difference between the "tacit convictions" of rhetoric-1 and the "intellectual engagement" of rhetoric-3?

4. According to Booth, all of us share in rhetoric-2, which is based on "common sense" — the principles, values, and ways of reasoning that "we share with members of every functioning organization or society" (par. 8). For Booth, this kind of rhetoric makes particular demands on trust. Reread the definition of rhetoric-2 as well as the passage in which Booth points out its fallibility. Write a brief essay in which you reflect on the role that trust plays in the reliability of rhetoric-2.

From Text to Field

1. Inside or outside of an educational setting, all of us have pursued interests or specializations that involve making judgments about our work or the work of other people. As part of this process, we have developed what Booth calls "the often tacit convictions that are shared by all" (par. 7) within a specialized area. Choose an area in which you have developed a certain amount of expertise, an area in which you talk about quality or performance with other people who share your interest. Using the examples Booth provides under the definition of rhetoric-1 as prompts, develop a guide to the "tacit convictions" you share with members of your group or area of expertise.

2. Booth introduces the three kinds of rhetoric to other academics in order to identify the "rational resources" they already use to understand each other and to challenge them to learn to use those resources more effectively. To help yourself absorb Booth's insights, study the three kinds of rhetoric from your point of view as a student. Although students do not yet have the knowledge and experience that academics bring to judgments of each other's work, students do have "rational resources" that they use to judge the quality of their teachers. In the form of a brochure or a brief guide for students entering the university, challenge them to improve their judgments by applying the three kinds of rhetoric. Your task will be to translate Booth's description of each kind of rhetoric into terms other students would readily understand when evaluating their professors as teachers.

3. In this excerpt from his talk, Booth is arguing for what he considers to be a valid approach for judging the performance of people whose work we do not have the expertise to understand. Consider his argument as it applies to situations both inside and outside of academic communities. Reflect on how his approach might affect you, if you were an expert being judged by nonexperts or a nonexpert being called upon to judge an expert. Write an essay in which you respond to Booth's argument, calling upon experiences in which you were either the judge or the judged.

4. Booth appears to be more optimistic than David Russell regarding the possibility of understanding one another's work in different disciplines. After reading the selection by Russell in this unit, write an essay in which you assess Booth's response to the fragmentation of community that Russell identifies. Draw on your experiences that seem to confirm or question the views of these two authors.

Body Ritual among the Nacirema

Horace Miner

This classic essay was first published in *American Anthropologist* in 1956. Since then, it has been widely read, making frequent appearances in anthologies and on reading lists developed for undergraduate courses in anthropology, sociology, and the humanities.

"Body Ritual among the Nacirema" offers writing students a rich source for exploring form and style. Based on the language and methodology of anthropologists conducting fieldwork, the essay demonstrates how a discipline constructs (and potentially limits) meaning through specialized terms, frames of reference, and forms of inquiry. It reveals both the power and pitfalls of working within a well-developed construct.

Horace Miner studied archaeology in Paris and Munich before working in anthropology as a museum curator at the University of Kentucky, as a graduate student at the University of Chicago, and as a professor of anthropology and sociology at the University of Michigan. He is known primarily for his study of the Nacirema, which grew out of an interest in using anthropological techniques to examine modern communities. Miner died in 1993, at the age of eighty-one.

The anthropologist has become so familiar with the diversity of ways in which different peoples behave in similar situations that he is not apt to be surprised by even the most exotic customs. In fact, if all of the logically possible combinations of behavior have not been found somewhere in the world, he is apt to suspect that they must be present in some yet undescribed tribe. This point has, in fact, been expressed with respect to clan organization by Murdock (1949: 71). In this light, the magical beliefs and practices of the Nacirema present such unusual aspects that it seems desirable to describe them as an example of the extremes to which human behavior can go.

Professor Linton first brought the ritual of the Nacirema to the attention of anthropologists twenty years ago (1936: 326), but the culture of this people is still very poorly understood. They are a North American group living in the territory between the Canadian Cree, the Yaqui and Tarahumare of Mexico, and the Carib and Arawak of the Antilles. Little is known of their origin, although tradition states that they came from the east. According to Nacirema mythology, their nation was originated by a culture hero, Notgnihsaw, who is otherwise known for two great feats of strength— the throwing of a piece of wampum across the river Pa-To-Mac and the chopping down of a cherry tree in which the Spirit of Truth resided.

Nacirema culture is characterized by a highly developed market economy which has evolved in a rich natural habitat. While much of the people's time is devoted to economic pursuits, a large part of these labors and a considerable portion of the day are spent in ritual activity. The focus of this activity is the human body, the appearance and health of which loom as a dominant concern in the ethos of the people. While such a concern is certainly not unusual, its ceremonial aspects and associated philosophy are unique.

The fundamental belief underlying the whole system appears to be that the human body is ugly and that its natural tendency is to debility and disease. Incarcerated in such a body, man's only hope is to avert these characteristics through the use of the powerful influences of ritual and ceremony. Every household has one or more shrines devoted to this purpose. The more powerful individuals in the society have several shrines in their houses and, in fact, the opulence of a house is often referred to in terms of the number of such ritual centers it possesses. Most houses are of wattle and daub construction, but the shrine rooms of the more wealthy are walled with stone. Poorer families imitate the rich by applying pottery plaques to their shrine walls.

While each family has at least one such shrine, the rituals associated with 5 it are not family ceremonies but are private and secret. The rites are normally only discussed with children, and then only during the period when they are being initiated into these mysteries. I was able, however, to establish sufficient rapport with the natives to examine these shrines and to have the rituals described to me.

The focal point of the shrine is a box or chest which is built into the wall. In this chest are kept the many charms and magical potions without which no native believes he could live. These preparations are secured from a variety of specialized practitioners. The most powerful of these are the medicine men, whose assistance must be rewarded with substantial gifts. However, the medicine men do not provide the curative potions for their clients, but decide what the ingredients should be and then write them down in an ancient and secret language. This writing is understood only by the

EXHIBIT 5–1
Dates for
Maintenance
of Trademarks

Document	Statutory Requirement	Due Date for EXPLORE® (registered 6/01/03)	Grace Period	Specimen Needed
Section 8 Affidavit of Continued Use	Due between fifth and sixth year after registration and within the year before the end of every ten-year period	Due between 6/01/08 and 6/01/09; due between 6/01/12 and 6/01/13 (and every ten years thereafter)	Yes (six-month grace period)	One specimen needed
Section 15 Affidavit of Incontestability	Filing is optional; affidavit may be filed only after mark is in use in commerce for at least five consecutive years (for any five-year period)	May be filed at any time after 6/01/08	No grace period is needed because section 15 affidavit can be filed at any time after five years of consecutive use	No
Section 9 Application for Renewal	Must be filed within one year before ten-year anniversary of registration and every ten years thereafter	Renewal can be filed between 6/01/12 and 6/01/03 and every ten years thereafter	Yes (six-month grace period)	No (specimen not required because section 9 renewal application is usually filed with section 8 affidavit, which is accompanied by specimen)

in a timely fashion will result in cancellation of a registration. Although an owner can petition the director to review refusals of section 8 affidavits and applications for renewal, such refusals are seldom reversed, and the decision of the director is final (unless the registrant appeals to the appropriate court within two months). The registration will then be canceled.

Because cancellation is such an extreme result, the utmost care must be given to docketing critical dates. While many IP professionals maintain their own docketing systems, others use the services of one of the professional search firms (identified in Chapter 3) to docket these critical dates. Because ownership of companies is in flux, marks evolve, and contact between the law firm and the registrant may have been intermittent in the years following registration, trademark maintenance (namely, handling affidavits of use under section 8, affimedicine men and the herbalists who, for another gift, provide the required charm.

The charm is not disposed of after it has served its purpose, but is placed in the charm-box of the household shrine. As these magical materials are specific for certain ills, and the real or imagined maladies of the people are many, the charm-box is usually full to overflowing. The magical packets are so numerous that people forget what their purposes were and fear to use them again. While the natives are very vague on this point, we can only assume that the idea in retaining all the old magical materials is that their presence in the charm-box, before which the body rituals are conducted, will in some way protect the worshipper.

Beneath the charm-box is a small font. Each day every member of the family, in succession, enters the shrine room, bows his head before the charm-box, mingles different sorts of holy water in the font, and proceeds with a brief rite of ablution. The holy waters are secured from the Water Temple of the community, where the priests conduct elaborate ceremonies to make the liquid ritually pure.

In the hierarchy of magical practitioners, and below the medicine men in prestige, are specialists whose designation is best translated "holy-mouth-men." The Nacirema have an almost pathological horror of and fascination with the mouth, the condition of which is believed to have a supernatural influence on all social relationships. Were it not for the rituals of the mouth, they believe that their teeth would fall out, their gums bleed, their jaws shrink, their friends desert them, and their lovers reject them. They also believe that a strong relationship exists between oral and moral characteristics. For example, there is a ritual ablution of the mouth for children which is supposed to improve their moral fiber.

The daily body ritual performed by everyone includes a mouth-rite. 10 Despite the fact that these people are so punctilious

The magical beliefs and about care of the mouth, this rite involves a practice
practices of the Nacirema which strikes the uninitiated stranger as revolting. It
present ... unusual aspects. was reported to me that the ritual consists of inserting a small bundle of hog hairs into the mouth, along with certain magical powders, and then moving the bundle in a highly formalized series of gestures.

In addition to the private mouth-rite, the people seek out a holy-mouth-man once or twice a year. These practitioners have an impressive set of paraphernalia, consisting of a variety of augers, awls, probes, and prods. The use of these objects in the exorcism of the evils of the mouth involves almost unbelievable ritual torture of the client. The holy-mouth-man opens the client's mouth and, using the above mentioned tools, enlarges any holes which decay may have created in the teeth. Magical materials are put into these holes. If there are no naturally occurring holes in the teeth, large sections of one or more teeth are gouged out so that the supernatural substance can be applied. In the client's view, the purpose of these ministrations is to arrest decay and to draw friends. The extremely sacred and traditional character of the rite is evident in the fact that the natives return to the holy-mouth-men year after year, despite the fact that their teeth continue to decay.

It is to be hoped that, when a thorough study of the Nacirema is made, there will be careful inquiry into the personality structures of these people. One has but to watch the gleam in the eye of a holy-mouth-man, as he jabs an awl into an exposed nerve, to suspect that a certain amount of sadism is involved. If this can be established, a very interesting pattern emerges, for most of the population shows definite masochistic tendencies. It was to these that Professor Linton referred in discussing a distinctive part of the daily body ritual which is performed only by men. This part of the rite involves scraping and lacerating the surface of the face with a sharp instrument. Special women's rites are performed only four times during each lunar month, but what they lack in frequency is made up in barbarity. As part of this ceremony, women bake their heads in small ovens for about an hour. The theoretically interesting point is that what seems to be a preponderantly masochistic people have developed sadistic specialists.

The medicine men have an imposing temple, or *latipso*, in every community of any size. The more elaborate ceremonies required to treat very sick patients can only be performed at this temple. These ceremonies involve not only the thaumaturge° but a permanent group of vestal maidens who move sedately about the temple chambers in distinctive costume and headdress.

The *latipso* ceremonies are so harsh that it is phenomenal that a fair proportion of the really sick natives who enter the temple ever recover. Small children whose indoctrination is still incomplete have been known to resist attempts to take them to the temple because "that is where you go to die." Despite this fact, sick adults are not only willing but eager to undergo the protracted ritual purification, if they can afford to do so. No matter how ill the supplicant or how grave the emergency, the guardians of many temples will not admit a client if he cannot give a rich gift to the custodian. Even after one has gained admission and survived the ceremonies, the guardians will not permit the neophyte to leave until he makes still another gift.

The supplicant entering the Temple is first stripped of all his or her   15 clothes. In every-day life the Nacirema avoids exposure of his body and its natural functions. Bathing and excretory acts are performed only in the secrecy of the household shrine, where they are ritualized as part of the body-rites. Psychological shock results from the fact that body secrecy is suddenly

---

thaumaturge: A worker of marvels or miracles.

lost upon entry into the *latipso*. A man, whose own wife has never seen him in an excretory act, suddenly finds himself naked and assisted by a vestal maiden while he performs his natural functions into a sacred vessel. This sort of ceremonial treatment is necessitated by the fact that the excreta are used by a diviner to ascertain the course and nature of the client's sickness. Female clients, on the other hand, find their naked bodies are subjected to the scrutiny, manipulation, and prodding of the medicine man.

Few supplicants in the temple are well enough to do anything but lie on their hard beds. The daily ceremonies, like the rites of the holy-mouth-men, involve discomfort and torture. With ritual precision, the vestals awaken their miserable charges each dawn and roll them about on their beds of pain while performing ablutions, in the formal movements of which the maidens are highly trained. At other times they insert magic wands in the supplicant's mouth or force him to eat substances which are supposed to be healing. From time to time the medicine men come to their clients and jab magically treated needles into their flesh. The fact that these temple ceremonies may not cure, and may even kill the neophyte, in no way decreases the people's faith in the medicine men.

There remains one other kind of practitioner, known as a "listener." This witch-doctor has the power to exorcise the devils that lodge in the heads of people who have been bewitched. The Nacirema believe that parents bewitch their own children. Mothers are particularly suspected of putting a curse on children while teaching them the secret body rituals. The counter-magic of the witch-doctor is unusual in its lack of ritual. The patient simply tells the "listener" all his troubles and fears, beginning with the earliest difficulties he can remember. The memory displayed by the Nacirema in these exorcism sessions is truly remarkable. It is not uncommon for the patient to bemoan the rejection he felt upon being weaned as a babe, and a few individuals even see their troubles going back to the traumatic effects of their own birth.

In conclusion, mention must be made of certain practices which have their base in native esthetics but which depend upon the pervasive aversion to the natural body and its functions. There are ritual fasts to make fat people thin and ceremonial feasts to make thin people fat. Still other rites are used to make women's breasts larger if they are small, and smaller if they are large. General dissatisfaction with breast shape is symbolized in the fact that the ideal form is virtually outside the range of human variation. A few women afflicted with almost inhuman hypermammary development are so idolized that they make a handsome living by simply going from village to village and permitting the natives to stare at them for a fee.

Reference has already been made to the fact that excretory functions are ritualized, routinized, and relegated to secrecy. Natural reproductive functions are similarly distorted. Intercourse is taboo as a topic and scheduled as an act. Efforts are made to avoid pregnancy by the use of magical materials or by limiting intercourse to certain phases of the moon. Conception is actually very infrequent. When pregnant, women dress so as to hide their condition. Parturition takes place in secret, without friends or relatives to assist, and the majority of women do not nurse their infants.

Our review of the ritual life of the Nacirema has certainly shown them to   20
be magic-ridden people. It is hard to understand how they have managed to exist so long under the burdens which they have imposed upon themselves. But even such exotic customs as these take on real meaning when they are viewed with the insight provided by Malinowski when he wrote (1948: 70):

> Looking from far and above, from our high places of safety in the developed civilization, it is easy to see all the crudity and irrelevance of magic. But without its power and guidance early man could not have mastered his practical difficulties as he has done, nor could man have advanced to the higher stages of civilization.

References Cited

Linton, Ralph. (1936). *The Study of Man*. New York: D. Appleton Century Co.
Malinowski, Bronislaw. (1948). *Magic, Science, and Religion*. Glencoe: The Free Press.
Murdock, George P. (1949). *Social Structure*. New York: The Macmillan Co.

Working with the Text

1. "Body Ritual among the Nacirema" is frequently assigned in introductory anthropology and sociology courses to explore the basic methods and ways of thinking used in those fields. The fact that the essay is a parody only serves to underscore how professional language is used to construct meaning. As you reread Horace Miner's essay, highlight words and phrases that suggest how anthropologists and sociologists gather and interpret data. In a brief essay, analyze Miner's use (and parody) of the professional language. What is the anthropologist's vantage point? What is the anthropologist looking for? How does he or she collect and interpret data? Study the references to other anthropologists. What professional categories and concepts does the narrator use? Where in the research process is there a risk of misinterpretation?

2. The essay is written to make you think by making you laugh. Note the particular places in the essay that make you smile or laugh. Choose five or six of those passages. In a series of journal entries, explain what you found funny about each passage and what you learned from your response. What mental images did the passage conjure up? What does your response reveal about

your attitudes as well as those of the Nacirema and the anthropologist? What new insights did you gain?

3. In his anthropologist's report on the Nacirema, Miner sends up Americans at the same time he is sending up anthropologists. Write a brief essay in which you respond to Miner's view of how Americans regard their bodies. What is his view? What data does he use to support it? Do you agree with his interpretation of the data? Why or why not?

From Text to Field

1. Remember that Miner's essay was published in *American Anthropologist* in 1956. Review the specific "data" Miner uses to demonstrate an American obsession with the human body. Entering into a persona similar to Miner's anthropologist, write a "report" in which you update "Body Ritual among the Nacirema." Revisit the culture as it functions now and interpret the data you gather. What are the current body-related practices? In what ways is the cult of the human body the same as it was in the 1956 report? In what ways has it changed over the last half century? Does the current data confirm the 1956 analysis or have you arrived at a somewhat different interpretation?

2. The persona and methods of Miner's anthropologist can be applied to any aspect of human culture. Choose a set of practices—other than those examined by Miner—to interpret in your own anthropological "study." You might choose a different aspect of American culture, or you might examine the culture of another country where you have lived or traveled. You might choose an American subculture, such as residents of a geographical region or a group with a distinctive identity. Your own family or hometown could constitute a culture worth studying. For your "study," write either a parody or a serious analysis. Whichever approach you adopt, base your interpretation on solid data and accurate observation. Think of yourself as an anthropologist entering into uncharted territory and a foreign, exotic culture.

3. An effective way to learn new methods and ways of thinking is to send them up in a parody. To experiment with your own parody, choose one form of communication between teachers and students, either written or spoken, that is used in a field or discipline you are just beginning to study. You could write a parody of the very questions you are reading right now. Other possibilities include lab reports, the course syllabus, the objective or short-answer tests in one of your science classes, or faculty Web pages. Use Miner's essay as a model for identifying ways to mimic and exaggerate terms, structures, concepts, and attitudes.

The Grooves of Academe

Robin Tolmach Lakoff

What we now know as the university was first called "the groves of academe" by the ancient Roman poet Horace, who wrote in his *Epistles*, "seek for truth in the groves of academe." The phrase evokes images of strolling among the trees, cultivating the mind through study and debate. To capture the current realities of academic survival, Robin Lakoff changes "groves" to "grooves," suggesting "moves" that are part of being "in the groove." She surely also has in mind being "in a rut."

At the center of her argument is a belief that the mission of the university is the pursuit of truth and knowledge. Her question is this: If our mission is truth and knowledge, and if language, discourse, and communication are the means for pursuing that mission (which she believes they are), why is academic discourse so marked by obscure language and rituals of silence? Why don't departments and professors simply tell students directly how they might succeed? Instead, they presume that students will figure out the mysteries of initiation into the field all on their own.

Lakoff gained an insider's view of academia as a PhD candidate at Harvard University and as a professor of pragmatics and sociolinguistics at the University of California, Berkeley. Her insights are informed by her research into the relationships among language, identity, and power. These concerns are reflected in the titles of her books, among them *Language and Women's Place* (1975), *Face Value: The Politics of Beauty* (1984), *When Talk Is Not Cheap* (1985), and *Talking Power: The Politics of Language in Our Lives* (1990). *The Language War* (2000) examines the interplay between language and politics in the media treatment of high-profile events such as the murder trial of O. J. Simpson and the impeachment of President Clinton. "The Grooves of Academe" is an excerpt from *Talking Power*.

My department is at it again.

Every five years or so we go through it, only to undo our work, like Penelope,° with perfect regularity some five years later. We are fighting about revamping the department's graduate program: how many courses, and which, and in what order, are to be required for the PhD. It always turns out to be a long-drawn-out process, entailing almost as much internecine acrimony as our all-time favorite fighting issue — hiring of new colleagues. And the real conflicts, the things that fill a simple process with dissension, are never brought out into the light of day: They remain covert, while we debate superficialities.

The Curriculum Committee (and academics do love committees, almost as much as we love subcommittees! they allow us to postpone the inevitable moment of climax, the decision) has proposed a new course, to be required of all graduate students in their first semester of residence, for one unit (most courses are three or four), meeting for one and a half hours, once a week — a very small commitment.

Ordinarily, such small fish don't attract a great deal of discussion, pro or con. We reserve our verbal ammunition for the bigger stuff. But the proposed course is largely concerned with the underpinnings of the field, its ineffable mystique. It would cover, for instance, how to get articles published; how to write abstracts; where to look for bibliography; which journals are geared toward which subfields; the professional interests of the various faculty members of the department.

And more, and worse: how power is allocated in the field of linguistics; 5 who has it, why, and how to get it. And why linguists are such a contentious group, why we can't listen to one another across theoretical boundaries, why scholarly arguments too often turn into personal vendettas.

Everyone agrees that, to receive a PhD in linguistics from the University of California at Berkeley, a student must demonstrate knowledge in a variety of topics: sounds and sound-systems; word-formation and lexical semantics; syntax and sentence-level semantics; processes of historical change; methodology of various types; the claims of competing theories; and, of course, much much more. All this is the explicit and overt knowledge of the field, our public culture, as it were — what we transmit openly to the young and expect them to demonstrate proof of mastering. But that knowledge alone, however broad and deep, does not a competent professional linguist make.

Penelope: The wife of Odysseus, who held suitors at bay throughout his twenty-year absence during the Trojan War. She promised to wed when she finished weaving a burial shroud, which she wove by day and unraveled by night.

To be one, you not only have to know facts, theories, and methods, you have to know how to be a linguist, how to play by the rules. You have to know how to cite sources and which sources to cite; how to talk and how to write, in terms of style; how to talk and how to write, in terms of which questions may legitimately be raised and which (apparently equally attractive) may not, and what constitutes an "answer." You have to know something about the history of the field, which in turn explains the politics of the field: who likes who and who hates who, who invites contributions from who in the volume who is editing, who is not invited (though working in the same area) and why. You must master the forms, in terms of length, topic, and style: the *abstract*, the *paper* (or *article*), the *monograph*, the *book*, in writing; the *talk*, the *job talk*, the *lecture*, the *panel contribution*, among oral forms. These requirements exist in all academic fields, but each field does them differently and values them differently. In determining tenurability, some departments rank a single book higher than several articles with about the same number of pages; others, the reverse. It's useful to know these things — in fact, often vital for survival in an increasingly competitive business. But no one will tell you this — certainly not spontaneously. Some students know how to pick up a lot of underground stuff by judicious looking and listening; others are sophisticated and brash enough to frame the questions and insist on answers from diffident mentors. But many are not, and it takes them years of agonizing in pretenure positions before they understand — too often, too late.

We would be scandalized at a department that refused to tell its students about sentence-construction or typological differences among languages. But we are, some of us, equally scandalized at a proposal to provide the second kind of information openly to all, in the guise of formal course work. When the Curriculum Committee had submitted its lengthy proposal, the first and bitterest fight erupted over this peripheral one-unit course: whether, as "nonintellectual subject matter" it should be taught at all.

We are, in fact, fighting about something much bigger than a proposed Linguistics-200 requirement, but no one says so: that would be vulgar. We are fighting about mystique. We are elders in the tribal sweathouse, discussing the rites of initiation the next generation is to undergo. We went through them once, that's how we achieved our present esteemed status. They must, too, in their turn. We all agree on that, and we also agree pretty much that there are certain explicit skills the youth must know before they are deemed ready to take their place in adult society. But someone has raised an unheard-of question: Should they be told the secrets — what happens during the ordeal, what is done and why it is done? It would make it easier for them; the suffering (which we all agree is essential) would make sense; it would be coherent, all the fasting, mutilation, deprivation. Why not enlighten them?

But the oldest of the elders demurs indignantly. Don't we understand *any-*   10
thing? The whole point is in the mystery. The very senselessness gives the
experience a special meaning, a curious depth, makes tribal membership of
greater value. If they have to figure it out themselves, by vague hints and
overheard whispers, through trial and error, with pain and suffering, they will
prize full membership, when it is conferred, all the more. The elders of the
tribe must keep its mysteries holy.

Any anthropologically sophisticated Westerner can understand that reasoning in a primitive tribe. But it's a little disconcerting to encounter ourselves at it — ourselves, not only sophisticated Westerners, but intellectuals to
boot and, more, intellectuals in an institution which claims as its territory the
pursuit of knowledge by reason alone. Mystique has a place, but it is not the
stuff of which scholarship is made. But reason alone cannot explain the pas-
sions of the argument over Linguistics 200.

Like any other institution, the university has a complex mission, only
some of which is supposed to be overtly visible, even to insiders. Therefore,
its power relations are complex, and its communications — to outsiders, and
to and among its members — are more often than not obscure and ambiguous. In fact, the discourse of academe seems (and not only to noninitiates)
especially designed for incomprehensibility. This is demonstrably true. But
many of its ambiguities and eccentricities are intentional and intrinsic to the
institution, not (as sometimes argued) mere side effects of the university's
main communicative purpose.

Truth in Language: Mission Impossible?

Every institution has a public mission, its reason for being, generally
couched in benign and even lofty language. The mission of psychotherapy is
change or *understanding;* of the law, *justice;* of the military, *protection* or
defense; of government, *order.* In this semantic of noble purpose, we can
define the university's mission as the production of *truth,* or *knowledge,* a virtuous enterprise if ever there was one. Unlike the others, it would seem to
have no dark side, no hidden risk to anyone. There would seem to be nothing to hide or dissemble.

But for all its virtuousness, the university is an institution, like the others. As
such, it must ensure its own survival and the enhancement of the status of itself
and its members. It must appear to the outside world, and to its own personnel,
as benevolent and useful: It must have something the outside world needs
enough to pay for, to support the institution and guarantee its survival. It must
be awesome, to convince others of its value; and more, it must seem *good.*

This is a lot to ask of anyone, individual or institution. It is hard to require   15
both love and respect, to retain power and yet radiate benevolence, to get

from outsiders scarce resources against strong competition — even more for an institution whose product is abstract, often inscrutable, of no immediate use. We can see why we have to support the government and the military (well, some of us can, some of the time); if we are in pain, we can justify giving money to the medical or psychotherapeutic establishments; if we are legally entangled, we appreciate the necessity of supporting the representatives of the law. But the university has to persuade society that knowledge per se is worthy of support.

Institutions, then, like individuals, have interests at stake; they must compete for resources. But at the same time, to succeed in getting their needs met, they must convince others of their benevolence and disinterestedness. We know what individuals do in such a quandary: They lie. Institutions are no different. Unless the lies become too outrageous or harmful, we mostly accept them. Watergate was intolerable, but Iran-Contragate was within bounds. We know Freud lied, or at least engaged in self-deception, about "infantile seduction," but psychoanalysis retains society's respect. The university, as an institution, can be expected to lie to protect its power and authority.

Cases are not hard to come by. For example, universities are known to reinvent their history when convenient. In 1964, the University of California at Berkeley was shaken by the Free Speech Movement. Popular among students, it was anathema to the administration and many of the faculty, who did everything they could to stamp it out **We are fighting about** and remove its ringleaders from influence. But life **mystique.** goes on, times change, and what was once a dire threat to institutional business as usual is seen nostalgically, twenty years later, as the shot heard' round the world, the opening statement of the sixties. It was *important*, it was *historic*, it put the university on the cultural map.

Therefore, in 1984, it seemed appropriate to the university administration — heirs to the men who had called armed deputies in to their rescue — to celebrate the twentieth anniversary of the Free Speech Movement with a plethora of university-sponsored activities stressing the movement's historic role and the university's participation therein. There were speeches by the powerful and influential, publications, retrospective photography shows, colloquia, everything that can be trotted out to say, This was history and we were a part of it — we made it happen. Lost in the hoopla is the fact that the university was involved, all right — against its will and as a force in opposition. The administration never (that I am aware of) said in so many words: We supported the FSM. But the inviting of celebrities, the holding of public festivities, said as much and, by saying it implicitly, said it more potently, as the message could not easily be contradicted. Nowadays we see the willful distortion of history as evil when it is done by a government or the media. Should it be viewed any differently as an act of the benevolent university?

davits of incontestability under section 15, and applications for renewal under section 9) can be difficult and time-consuming.

LOSS OF TRADEMARK RIGHTS

While registrations can be canceled due to failure to file appropriate documents with the PTO, as discussed earlier, rights to marks can also be forfeited due to **abandonment** of marks, failure to protect marks, or improper assignment or licensing of the mark.

The Lanham Act (15 U.S.C. § 1127) provides that a mark will be deemed to be abandoned when either of the following occurs:

- the mark has become a generic name; or
- use of the mark has been discontinued with intent not to resume use. Nonuse for three consecutive years is *prima facie* evidence of abandonment.

Genericide

As discussed in Chapter 2, a mark can become generic (referred to as **genericide**) when consumers begin to call the product or service offered under the mark by the mark. Examples of once-valid marks that have become generic terms are *aspirin, yo-yo, cellophane, thermos,* and *escalator.* Once a mark becomes generic, it may be used by anyone. XEROX Corporation has always been worried that its famous mark would become generic due to consumers' misuse of the mark in saying, "I'm going to make a xerox of this document." XEROX Corporation has therefore expended substantial amounts of money in attempting to ensure consumers use the mark correctly by consistently saying in advertising copy, "XEROX® brand copiers are . . ." Similarly, Kimberly-Clark's promotional materials always refer to "KLEENEX® brand tissues" to ensure the mark does not become generic through consumers saying, "I need a kleenex."

Similarly, while ROLLERBLADE® is a registered trademark for in-line skates, it is in danger of becoming generic due to consumer misuse, as in "Let's go rollerblading" or "I need a new pair of rollerblades." Such use of a trademark as if it is the actual name for the product can cause a loss of trademark rights. Thus, while owners of marks want consumers to know and recognize their marks, the danger of a mark becoming too popular is that it can be misused, leading to genericide.

Abandonment by Nonuse

The more common means by which a mark becomes abandoned is through nonuse. One of the most famous trademark doctrines is "Use it or lose it." Mere cessation of use is insufficient; the nonuse must be coupled with an intent not to resume use for abandonment to occur. There is a presumption that a mark has been abandoned if it has not been used for three years. Once a party can demonstrate such nonuse for three years, the trademark owner has the burden of rebutting the presumption of abandonment by proving that mark has not been abandoned (either by producing evidence of actual use during the relevant period or intent to resume use).

In determining whether abandonment due to nonuse has occurred, courts have concluded that "intent to resume use" means an intent to resume use within the reasonably foreseeable future. In one famous case, CBS stopped using the AMOS AND ANDY mark due to civil rights objections. When a third party began using the mark twenty years later, CBS sued for infringement, arguing that it intended to resume use of the mark when social policies permitted. The court held the mark had been abandoned because CBS did not have an intent to use the mark in the reasonably foreseeable future. *Silverman v. CBS Inc.,* 870 F.2d 40 (2d Cir. 1989).

The trademark owner need not use the mark everywhere in the United States; use

In fact, it's more troubling. Since it is an institution, it might seem unfair to hold the university to a standard of truthfulness higher than we demand of others. But there is a reason we must. The success of an institution is linked to its efficacy in turning out a well-functioning product. Any institution-internal uncertainty about that product, any hesitation or self-contradiction in the institution, will vitiate the product and, ultimately, eviscerate the institution itself. It may live on (institutions are survivors), but its influence will be much diminished.

Imagine if the military proved unable to protect the people, or if a government allowed rioting to go on unchecked. Those institutions would become objects of ridicule, and be either overthrown or ineffectual, because they were not fulfilling their mission, not producing the goods that they were created and supported in order to produce. Even a partial falling off, a single instance of failure of mission, will weaken an institution's legitimacy, though it probably takes either an egregious example or repeated lesser abuses to actually bring it down. [20]

To catch any institution in a lie is disconcerting, but seldom deeply damaging. The member who lied may be punished, and the institution close over the injury, essentially untouched. Its mission is not compromised. But the mission of the university *is* truth, or knowledge: So when the university lies, it is precisely as if the government dissolved in chaos. To lie is to contravene the mission of the university directly. Therefore, when the university lies (or rather, is lied for by its representatives), it necessarily contributes in a serious way to its loss of legitimacy as an institution.

Unlike other institutions, then, the university has discourse of a particular sort as its mission and its sole product. Some institutions use language just peripherally: The military gets its job done via the giving of orders; but it is weapons that actually do the job, and the job is not intrinsically communicative in nature. The courts and psychotherapy are somewhat different, in that they use particular forms of language specifically to create specific real-world situations; the choice of language influences their result, so that communicative efficacy is crucial for their members, more than in less linguistically oriented institutions.

But the university alone trades only in language, discourse, communication. The university's only acts are speech acts, in Austin's sense.° Truth and knowledge are linguistic entities, existing only through and in language. Only for the university is language an end in itself. Therefore (one might

---

speech acts . . . in Austin's sense: A concept in linguistics and the philosophy of language developed by J. L. Austin, the speech act describes how, when we use language to say something, we also *do* something — as when a minister says "I pronounce you husband and wife." Common examples of speech acts include voicing a request, giving an order, or making a promise.

argue) the members of the university ought to be especially skillful communicators, since that is all they have to offer, and that is solely how they achieve their effects.

Well, but. . . .

Surely the members of the university community produce a lot of lan- 25
guage, in a lot of forms, oral and written, public and private, formal and informal. But by any stylistic standards, the university's prose is inelegant. Indeed, some would call it abysmal—turgid, pompous, inflated, impenetrable, closing off understanding rather than furthering it. The conventional view is that this is a by-product of our mission. We are here to educate and inform not to entertain. Therefore there is no need for the product to be delightful, amusing, or pleasurable. But "no need" does not begin to express the prevailing attitude toward stylistic amenity. Those who write relatively accessibly are often the recipients of barely veiled hostility, in the form of scholarly disdain: "Just a popular piece." The idea is, if more than three people can understand it, it can't be worth much. In fact, the distress clarity arouses is oddly reminiscent of the discomfiture, at the faculty meeting described earlier at the breaching of the mystique. It's not that there's no need to be intelligible. It's that there is a need not to. Our power, our authority, is intertwined with our ability to maintain secrets even as we seem to dispense them. We write and speak, but we do not communicate. That is our art.

Horizontal Communication

The university and its members must speak with many voices to fit their many functions—no easy task. First, the university as an institution communicates with the outside world, to show that it is doing a valuable job well. Most universities have public-relations offices to send out items to the media on the accomplishments of the university and its members: awards won, public works performed, research completed. It arranges interviews with the media—if a reporter needs a semanticist in a hurry, it will provide one. The university also puts out informational pamphlets: how to apply for admission, the availability of financial aid, and so on. There are publications produced by and about the university intended for the outside world, often alumni, to solicit financial contributions. In all of these contacts, the university presents itself as "the University," a faceless monolith rather than the assortment of diverse interests that it is.

Individuals within the university sometimes communicate, in their identities as university personnel, with the world at large or at least nonacademic institutions. They carry from the university, as part of the presuppositions underlying their discourse, the intellectual legitimacy that comes of being a member of that community: Expertise is implicitly, if not always legitimately, transferable. In these roles, members consult for industry and government, serve on the panels of government and private granting agencies, serve as expert witnesses in the courtroom. In these roles almost uniquely, professors are addressed and referred to as "Professor" and "Doctor." Within the university, these titles are dispensed with; their use is a mark of naivete, outsidership (and so is mostly reserved for undergraduates, who are neither members nor even potential members).

More often, and more significantly, members of the university community, especially faculty, communicate as individuals to individuals. Faculty status brings with it membership in several constituencies. First, one is a member of a discipline, a relatively egalitarian relationship. At the same time, one is a member of a department, entailing some hierarchical distinctions; and of one's university's cross-disciplinary community, entailing status distinctions of a different kind. A linguist keeps in contact with other linguists, through publication, professional society meetings, and other conferences, as well as letters and visits. We exchange letters of recommendation for our students and junior colleagues; we review one another's grant applications and submissions for publication.

Within disciplines, we develop special languages. Like any linguistic code, these play two roles. Toward the outside world, they are elitist: We know, you cannot understand, you may not enter. But for insiders they are a secret handshake. When I encounter my profession's terms of art in a piece of writing or a talk, I am obscurely comforted: I am at home among friends. True, "ethnomethodology" and "equi-noun-phrase deletion" are not the friends everyone would choose, but when I find them, I know I am welcome. An article submitted for publication in a professional journal may contain useful and significant information; but if it has been submitted (as occasionally happens) by someone outside the field who does not know the communicative conventions, the reviewer will immediately sense that something is amiss from the absence of the secret wink. In all probability the paper will be rejected. It isn't just that we are being snobbish (we are, of course); but over time we become attuned to our special form of discourse, and literally become unable to understand anything labeled "linguistics" that is not expressed as "linguistics" is supposed to be. The form must match the context, or understanding fails.

A significant part of a graduate student's education consists of learning this 30 language. Part of becoming worthy of the PhD, the certificate of membership, is the demonstration that one knows and can use the language.

There are recognizable power ploys in academic discourse, often lost on outsiders. In intradisciplinary prose, the footnote is wielded as cavemen wielded clubs, a blunt but effective weapon. The footnote (nowadays, to save printing expenses, more often the end note) says: I know everything about this topic. I could go on forever. Maybe I will. In any case, don't think you can overwhelm me with obscure information. I said it first, here. I control the scholarship, I've read everything, *this is my turf.* The conscientious reader of academic prose must break concentration to read the footnote, another secret signal between writer and reader: We are serious professionals. This communication is not for entertainment. It is *supposed* to be obnoxious.[1]

How to Write Like a Professor

The written style of the university, too, has its own separate formats, each justified by function. This is especially true of intradisciplinary scholarly writing. A significant part of a student's training involves learning these procedures, learning how to sound right as well as how to make valid contributions. I spoke earlier of the relation between the traditional convoluted style of academia and the academic's need for signals of solidarity and acceptance by peers. But turgidity does not come naturally. It must be acquired by slow degrees. Deviation in any direction is punishable.

Neophytes must learn both correct surface form and deeper matters of style and content. They must, first and most obviously, learn how to juggle the technical terminology of their field: the secret handshake par excellence. They must learn what each special term means, who introduced it, and therefore its political significance. (While *scenario, frame,* and *schema* may, in discourse semantics and pragmatics, be mutually interchangeable, students who study with the scholars responsible for each term will use that term rather than the others in their own writing.) They will learn what ideas justify the postulation of special terminology: how revolutionary, how important they must be. They will read enough of the literature to know, when they have thought of an idea, whether a term already exists for it, to avoid duplication. They will also learn that creating a term, and offering it to the world, is an act of power best left to the established members of the field. It takes some gall for graduate students to propose terms for their own ideas; for an undergraduate to attempt this borders on the treasonable. And of course, to propose a term when one already exists exposes one to ridicule; and to misuse someone else's terminology, worse.

Undergraduates (and beginning graduate students) are not encouraged to play the same game as their betters. It does not become an undergraduate to sound like a professor. Moreover, since the undergraduate does not

---

[1]See what I mean? [Lakoff's note].

have sufficient experience or knowledge, the attempt is apt to be risible. As students progress through graduate school, they are expected to acquire academic style, a little in course papers, more in qualifying papers. But the usage must grow gradually, sparingly, avoiding the appearance of presumptuousness, the accusations of usurpation of territory that belongs to the elders. The pinnacle is reached with the dissertation, wherein a student demonstrates worthiness to become a full-fledged member of the society, having passed all the ordeals the elders have to provide. The dissertation shows not only that the student has mastered the knowledge of the field and its methods; not only that the student has something original to add to that store of knowledge; but that the student knows the rules, knows how to behave like a member of the culture. So the dissertation must be couched in the finest and most etiolated of academese, redolent of footnotes, stylistically impenetrable, bristling with jargon. Only thus can proper deportment be demonstrated.

Indeed, never again is it expected to this extent. For the next several years, 35 through the assistant professorship and until tenure, caution is recommended: Style should be academic, though a little relaxation is permissible. The dissertation showed one could take direction: Now one must show an ability to be on one's own. Tenure decisions involve the assessment of "collegiality": practically speaking, that means, Do nothing that might offend the thinnest-skinned colleague. Only after the granting of tenure is it safe to abandon the style for something snappier; and even then, obloquy is a probable outcome. But tenure smiles at obloquy.

If academic style were merely the result of carelessness or unconcern for the graces, it would increase as its user advanced in the field, in a straight upward direction; and if undergraduates were capable of using the style, it would be deemed an unmixed sign of competence, not a little off-color. But we find instead the parabolic curve . . . [in Fig. 1], which suggests that the style is connected to notions of privilege and power. You are *allowed* to use academese when you have convinced the elders that you are a serious apprentice, no longer an outsider (who is not allowed knowledge of the mysteries). You *must* use academese to prove your worthiness of acceptance and your ability to submit to discipline. You *may* abandon academese, wholly or more likely in part, when you are the gatekeeper and need no longer worry about being excluded from the society.

Over the course of an academic career, writing gradually becomes more overtly territorial, assumes more power for its producer, by achieving more length and broader topical scope. Undergraduate and early graduate course papers are unseemly if they exceed twenty pages or so. They deal with small and concrete topics: no total solutions, no metatheoretical debate. Later, through qualifying papers and other predissertation work, length increases to

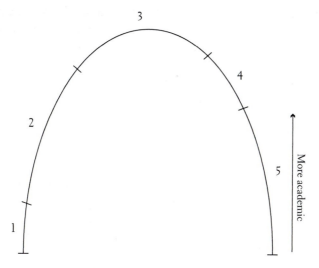

1. Undergraduates and beginning graduate students
2. Advanced graduate students
3. Students writing dissertations
4. Nontenured faculty
5. Tenured faculty

Figure 1. Privilege and Power in Academia

a maximum of fifty to one hundred pages, and topics become more abstract, more cutting-edge, and of broader scope, as the student demonstrates the desire to achieve full maturity and the ability to understand what the territorial battles are about. The dissertation stakes a claim. The writer takes a theoretical stance, either adapting a mentor's theory or inventing a modest theoretical innovation; applies it to a fairly broad swath of language; and tests it against the best that the field has to offer, engaging in conflict with established members of the group (but always respectfully). A dissertation is longer, too, around three hundred pages. Much more than that, though, or too grandiose a proposal, marks the writer as hubristic. The assistant professor is allowed a larger swath of territory. But because of the pressure to publish, the tendency is to stick to only mildly controversial topics that can be handled in a relatively short space, in a relatively short time. Later, with tenure, the sky's the limit—on length, breadth, and self-assurance, as well as interpersonal obnoxiousness.

The discourse style of academia turns out not to be solely a by-product of the knowledge factory. It is also the language of a society with complex and covert power and territorial assumptions, often in conflict with its express mission. As an institution, the university is relatively but not totally benign. As a society it is hierarchical and authoritarian, yet necessarily egalitarian and collaborative in its creation of a product. That it does so often produce products of value, that it protects its members from evaluation by the crass standards of the outside, make it an unusually benevolent institution. But that fact should not blind observers to its shortcomings, or cause them to overlook the ways in which those who have power in the university, as in any other institution, misuse it and abuse its weaker members.

Work Cited

Austin, J. L. *How To Do Things with Words*. Oxford: Clarendon Press, 1962.

Working with the Text

1. At the center of Robin Tolmach Lakoff's argument is the question of "mystique," especially as it relates to power. As you note Lakoff's use of the word, try to imagine how mystique plays itself out, from the point of view of those who are entering into the ritual as well as those who are creating it. Write an essay in which you analyze Lakoff's insight into the inner workings of academic mystique. What is that mystique? How is it created? How do initiates acquire mystique? What do those who create it hope to accomplish? What might be gained in the process, and what might be lost?

2. At one point Lakoff notes that "the university alone trades only in language, discourse, communication" (par. 23). What does Lakoff mean by that statement? Why might this place special responsibility on universities and pose special difficulties and hardships for students?

3. While acknowledging that the university is "an unusually benevolent institution" (par. 38) in producing products of value and in protecting its members from uninformed outsiders, Lakoff warns that observers must not "overlook the ways in which those who have power in the university . . . misuse it and abuse its weaker members" (par. 38). With this in mind, write a brief essay in which you elaborate on Lakoff's view of the contradiction between the university's pursuit of truth and knowledge and the questionable treatment of "its weaker members." Why would abuse of its weaker members call the university's mission into question? How might such abuse undermine the university's effectiveness in producing valuable products?

4. To illustrate how language and power play out in academia, Lakoff presents a figure of a parabolic curve that traces the uses of academic language over the course of a professor's career. Although Lakoff is addressing other academics, her insights could prove useful to undergraduates who are trying to understand how to work with their professors. Taking the position of a student helping to orient incoming students, offer an analysis of Lakoff's curve, with the

purpose of explaining why academics behave the way they do. Why do they use the language they use? What professional pressures might they be bringing into the classroom? How might these factors affect their teaching style, materials, and evaluation of student work?

From Text to Field

1. It is common for groups of people who share expertise, skill, or artistry to seek mystique in order to increase the power of their identity. Choose a group or shared identity you have either entered or observed that seeks to create mystique, along the lines described by Lakoff. The mystique might be sought through language, silence and secrecy, or ritual. The ritual might be formal (such as an initiation ceremony) or informal (a sequence of actions or words, whether part of the group's activity or part of the process of bringing in new members). In an essay, describe how the mystique surrounding this group identity is created. Include your perspective on whether these efforts actually increase the power of the identity. If you are part of the group you are describing, how does the mystique affect your image of yourself? If you are an outsider or observer, what is your attitude toward the group's mystique?

2. Lakoff claims that undergraduates are not encouraged to use academic style in their writing. Commenting wryly on the attitude of professors, Lakoff says, "It does not become an undergraduate to sound like a professor" (par. 34). Write a personal essay in which you reflect on your experience with academic language. Approach the essay as if you were writing your own "Grooves of Academe," from the point of view of an undergraduate. What is your response to the academic language that you encounter? To what extent do you try to use it? Do you think professors expect you to use it? Do you think they discourage you from using it? What kind of "game" do you feel you are expected to play to prove yourself as a student?

3. The mission of the university, according to Lakoff, is "the production of *truth,* or *knowledge*" (par. 13). Is this the mission you see for the university? As you reread the essay, take note of the high standards of truth Lakoff expects of an academic institution. Do you hold your college or university to the same high standards? Write an essay in which you set forth the mission of the university from your point of view as a student. What is the purpose of the university? What do you expect it to produce? What values should it embody? In what ways do you expect it to preserve its integrity as an institution? How are these purposes advanced or undermined by the language employed by the university?

Soft Sciences Are Often Harder than Hard Sciences

Jared Diamond

Why should we be concerned about "a dogfight among intellectuals," one in which a mathematician succeeds in blocking a highly regarded political scientist from membership in the National Academy of Sciences (NAS)? Jared Diamond, a member of the NAS, sees a threat in store for all of us if experts in the hard sciences continue to be ignorant of the rather different challenges in the so-called soft sciences, which include sociology, political science, and areas of psychology, as well as other fields. Diamond is convinced that soft science requires researchers to work harder to develop the controls necessary for testing their hypotheses. From Diamond's perspective, respect for their work — especially as it addresses human behavior — is critical to the survival of the human race.

A professor of physiology at the University of California, Los Angeles, School of Medicine, Diamond has pursued research that spans the hard and soft sciences. In 1999, he was awarded the National Medal of Science for his uncommon ability to write about important scientific issues for the public and for his groundbreaking research in applying Darwinian theory to the fields of human history, physiology, ecology, and conservation biology. Diamond's public writings include regular contributions to both *Nature* and *Discover* magazines. One of his major conservation efforts was to design a comprehensive nature-reserve system for Indonesian New Guinea. He is widely known for his Pulitzer Prize–winning book, *Guns, Germs, and Steel: The Fates of Human Societies* (1997), which examines 13,000 years of human development and behavior. Diamond's most recent book is *Collapse: How Societies Choose to Fail or Succeed* (2005).

In addition to his NAS membership, Diamond has been elected to the American Academy of Arts and Sciences and the American

Philosophical Society. He has also received the MacArthur Foundation Fellowship, known as the "genius grant."

The following essay was originally published in 1987, as an opinion piece in *Discover.*

The overall correlation between frustration and instability [in 62 countries of the world] was 0.50.

— SAMUEL HUNTINGTON, professor of government, Harvard

This is utter nonsense. How does Huntington measure things like social frustration? Does he have a social-frustration meter? I object to the academy's certifying as science what are merely political opinions.

— SERGE LANG, professor of mathematics, Yale

What does it say about Lang's scientific standards that he would base his case on twenty-year-old gossip? . . . a bizarre vendetta . . . a madman . . .

— Other scholars, commenting on Lang's attack

For those who love to watch a dogfight among intellectuals supposedly above such things, it's been a fine dogfight, well publicized in *Time* and elsewhere. In one corner, political scientist and coauthor of *The Crisis of Democracy,* Samuel Huntington. In the other corner, mathematician and author of *Diophantine Approximation on Abelian Varieties with Complex Multiplication,* Serge Lang. The issue: whether Huntington should be admitted, over Lang's opposition, to an academy of which Lang is a member. The score after two rounds: Lang 2, Huntington 0, with Huntington still out.

Lang *vs.* Huntington might seem like just another silly blood-letting in the back alleys of academia, hardly worth anyone's attention. But this particular dogfight is an important one. Beneath the name calling, it has to do with a central question in science: Do the so-called soft sciences, like political science and psychology, really constitute science at all, and do they deserve to stand beside "hard sciences," like chemistry and physics?

The arena is the normally dignified and secretive National Academy of Sciences (NAS), an honor society of more than 1,500 leading American scientists drawn from almost every discipline. NAS's annual election of about sixty new members begins long before each year's spring meeting, with a multistage evaluation of every prospective candidate by members expert in the candidate's field. Challenges of candidates by the membership assembled at the annual meeting are rare, because candidates have already been so thoroughly scrutinized by the appropriate experts. In my eight years in NAS, I can recall only a couple of challenges before the Lang-Huntington episode, and not a word about those battles appeared in the press.

anywhere is usually sufficient. However, trademark owners cannot make sporadic and token sales merely for the purpose of reserving rights in a mark. Moreover, minor activities will not suffice. Press releases and other similar announcements by a company that it is discontinuing a product line associated with a mark likely show an intent not to resume use from which abandonment will be inferred.

A trademark owner challenged with an allegation that his or her mark has been abandoned through nonuse may attempt to show special circumstances that would justify nonuse. These special circumstances are similar to those that excuse nonuse when a registrant files a section 8 affidavit. For example, a labor strike that results in inability to ship products or government regulation precluding importation or shipping of goods bearing the mark will usually excuse nonuse. Similarly, the sale of few products bearing the mark when the products are extremely expensive may excuse nonuse. However, mere economic conditions that make selling the product or service unprofitable do not excuse nonuse.

It is possible that the mark has been so changed by the owner over time that the original mark has become abandoned. As discussed, minor changes will not result in loss of rights, but a material alteration in the mark may result in abandonment of the original mark. For protection, owners should register each version of a mark.

Marks can also be expressly abandoned, such as when a trademark owner cancels or surrenders his or her registration, perhaps as a result of a settlement agreement with another.

Abandonment causes a loss of common law rights as well as rights under the Lanham Act. Resumption of use by the owner after abandonment does not revive the mark but merely establishes a new use date for the new mark. On the other hand, if an applicant inadvertently abandons an application (perhaps because the applicant failed to timely respond to an office action) or a registration (because the registrant forgot to renew the registration), but continues to use a mark, rights to the mark continue and the owner retains common law rights from its date of first use and can reapply for trademark registration.

TRADEMARK USE AND COMPLIANCE POLICIES

Because misuse of a mark by allowing it to become generic or alteration of a mark can cause loss of rights, trademark owners should initiate compliance policies to ensure use of marks is proper. Failure to monitor and actively police a mark may result in abandonment of all rights to the mark. A **trademark compliance policy** will help to ensure that a company's marks continue to enjoy protection both under the Lanham Act and at common law.

Following are some guidelines for proper trademark usage:

- A trademark should be displayed prominently in comparison with its surroundings and should clearly stand out on a label, advertisement, in text, and so forth. Thus, many owners capitalize their marks, display them in some prominent style or larger-than-average typeface, place them in quotation marks, or use distinctive lettering, colors, or the word *brand* after the mark, as in "VASELINE® brand petroleum jelly" to remind consumers that VASELINE is the brand name of or trademark for a certain product from a certain source and not the name of the product itself.
- Marks should be used in connection with the appropriate goods and services. Companies that have numerous similar marks for similar products and services must exercise care that a mark does not become abandoned because it is no

At first glance, Huntington's nomination in 1986 seemed a very unlikely one to be challenged. His credentials were impressive: president of the American Political Science Association; holder of a named professorship at Harvard; author of many widely read books, of which one, *American Politics: The Promise of Disharmony*, got an award from the Association of American Publishers as the best book in the social and behavioral sciences in 1981; and many other distinctions. His studies of developing countries, American politics, and civilian-military relationships received the highest marks from social and political scientists inside and outside NAS. Backers of Huntington's candidacy included NAS members whose qualifications to judge him were beyond question, like Nobel Prize–winning computer scientist and psychologist Herbert Simon.

If Huntington seemed unlikely to be challenged, Lang was an even more   5 unlikely person to do the challenging. He had been elected to the academy only a year before, and his own specialty of pure mathematics was as remote as possible from Huntington's specialty of comparative political development. However, as *Science* magazine described it, Lang had previously assumed for himself "the role of a sheriff of scholarship, leading a posse of academics on a hunt for error," especially in the political and social sciences. Disturbed by what he saw as the use of "pseudomathematics" by Huntington, Lang sent all NAS members several thick mailings attacking Huntington, enclosing photocopies of letters describing what scholar A said in response to scholar B's attack on scholar C, and asking members for money to help pay the postage and copying bills. Under NAS rules, a candidate challenged at an annual meeting is dropped unless his candidacy is sustained by two-thirds of the members present and voting. After bitter debates at both the 1986 and 1987 meetings, Huntington failed to achieve the necessary two-thirds support.

Much impassioned verbiage has to be stripped away from this debate to discern the underlying issue. Regrettably, a good deal of the verbiage had to do with politics. Huntington had done several things that are now anathema in U.S. academia: He received CIA support for some research; he did a study for the State Department in 1967 on political stability in South Vietnam; and he's said to have been an early supporter of the Vietnam War. None of this should have affected his candidacy. Election to NAS is supposed to be based solely on scholarly qualifications; political views are irrelevant. American academics are virtually unanimous in rushing to defend academic freedom whenever a university president or an outsider criticizes a scholar because of his politics. Lang vehemently denied that his opposition was motivated by Huntington's politics. Despite all those things, the question of Huntington's role with respect to Vietnam arose repeatedly in the NAS debates. Evidently, academic freedom means that outsiders can't raise the issue of a scholar's politics but other scholars can.

It's all the more surprising that Huntington's consulting for the CIA and other government agencies was an issue, when one recalls why NAS exists. Congress established the academy in 1863 to act as official adviser to the U.S. government on questions of science and technology. NAS in turn established the National Research Council (NRC), and NAS and NRC committees continue to provide reports about a wide range of matters, from nutrition to future army materials. As is clear from any day's newspaper, our government desperately needs professionally competent advice, particularly about unstable countries, which are one of Huntington's specialties. So Huntington's willingness to do exactly what NAS was founded to do — advise the government — was held against him by some NAS members. How much of a role his politics played in each member's vote will never be known, but I find it unfortunate that they played any role at all.

I accept, however, that a more decisive issue in the debates involved perceptions of the soft sciences — e.g., Lang's perception that Huntington used pseudomathematics. To understand the terms soft and hard science, just ask any educated person what science is. The answer you get will probably involve several stereotypes: Science is something done in a laboratory, possibly by people wearing white coats and holding test tubes; it involves making measurements with instruments, accurate to several decimal places; and it involves controlled, repeatable experiments in which you keep everything fixed except for one or a few things that you allow to vary. Areas of science that often conform well to these stereotypes include much of chemistry, physics, and molecular biology. These areas are given the flattering name of hard science, because they use the firm evidence that controlled experiments and highly accurate measurements can provide.

We often view hard science as the only type of science. But science (from the Latin *scientia*—knowledge) is something much more general, which isn't defined by decimal places and controlled experiments. It means the enterprise of explaining and predicting—gaining knowledge of—natural phenomena, by continually testing one's theories against empirical evidence. The world is full of phenomena that are intellectually challenging and important to understand, but that can't be measured to several decimal places in labs. They constitute much of ecology, evolution, and animal behavior; much of psychology and human behavior; and all the phenomena of human societies, including cultural anthropology, economics, history, and government.

These soft sciences, as they're pejoratively termed, are more difficult to 10 study, for obvious reasons. A lion hunt or revolution in the third world doesn't fit inside a test tube. You can't start it and stop it whenever you choose. You can't control all the variables; perhaps you can't control *any* variable. You may even find it hard to decide what a variable is. You can still use empirical tests to gain knowledge, but the types of tests used in the hard sciences must be modified. Such differences between the hard and soft sciences are regularly misunderstood by hard scientists, who tend to scorn soft sciences and reserve special contempt for the social sciences. Indeed, it was only in the early 1970s that NAS, confronted with the need to offer the government competent advice about social problems, began to admit social scientists at all. Huntington had the misfortune to become a touchstone of this widespread misunderstanding and contempt.

While I know neither Lang nor Huntington, the broader debate over soft versus hard science is one that has long fascinated me, because I'm among the minority of scientists who work in both areas. I began my career at the hard pole of chemistry and physics, then took my PhD in membrane physiology, at the hard end of biology. Today I divide my time equally between physiology and ecology, which lies at the soft end of biology. My wife, Marie Cohen, works in yet a softer field, clinical psychology. Hence I find myself forced every day to confront the differences between hard and soft science. Although I don't agree with some of Lang's conclusions, I feel he has correctly identified a key problem in soft science when he asks, "How does Huntington measure things like social frustration? Does he have a social-frustration meter?" Indeed, unless one has thought seriously about research in the social sciences, the idea that anyone could measure social frustration seems completely absurd.

The issue that Lang raises is central to any science, hard or soft. It may be termed the problem of how to "operationalize" a concept. (Normally I hate such neologistic jargon, but it's a suitable term in this case.) **We often view hard science** To compare evidence with theory requires that you **as the only type of science.** measure the ingredients of your theory. For ingredients like weight or speed it's clear what to measure, but what would you measure if you wanted to understand political instability? Somehow, you would have to design a series of actual operations that yield a suitable measurement—i.e., you must operationalize the ingredients of theory.

Scientists do this all the time, whether or not they think about it. I shall illustrate operationalizing with four examples from my and Marie's research, progressing from hard science to softer science.

Let's start with mathematics, often described as the queen of the sciences. I'd guess that mathematics arose long ago when two cave women couldn't operationalize their intuitive concept of "many." One cave woman said, "Let's pick this tree over here, because it has many bananas." The other cave woman argued, "No, let's pick that tree over there, because it has more bananas." Without a number system to operationalize their concept of "many," the two cave women could never prove to each other which tree offered better pickings.

There are still tribes today with number systems too rudimentary to settle the argument. For example, some Gimi villagers with whom I worked in

New Guinea have only two root numbers, *iya* = 1 and *rarido* = 2, which they combine to operationalize somewhat larger numbers: 4 = *rarido-rarido*, 7 = *rarido-rarido-rarido-iya*, etc. You can imagine what it would be like to hear two Gimi women arguing about whether to climb a tree with 27 bananas or one with 18 bananas.

Now let's move to chemistry, less queenly and more difficult to operationalize than mathematics but still a hard science. Ancient philosophers speculated about the ingredients of matter, but not until the eighteenth century did the first modern chemists figure out how to measure these ingredients. Analytical chemistry now proceeds by identifying some property of a substance of interest, or of a related substance into which the first can be converted. The property must be one that can be measured, like weight, or the light the substance absorbs, or the amount of neutralizing agent it consumes.

For example, when my colleagues and I were studying the physiology of hummingbirds, we knew that the little guys liked to drink sweet nectar, but we would have argued indefinitely about how sweet sweet was if we hadn't operationalized the concept by measuring sugar concentrations. The method we used was to treat a glucose solution with an enzyme that liberates hydrogen peroxide, which reacts (with the help of another enzyme) with another substance called dianisidine to make it turn brown, whereupon we measured the brown color's intensity with an instrument called a spectrophotometer. A pointer's deflection on the spectrophotometer dial let us read off a number that provided an operational definition of sweet. Chemists use that sort of indirect reasoning all the time, without anyone considering it absurd.

My next-to-last example is from ecology, one of the softer of the biological sciences, and certainly more difficult to operationalize than chemistry. As a bird watcher, I'm accustomed to finding more species of birds in a rain forest than in a marsh. I suspect intuitively that this has something to do with a marsh being a simply structured habitat, while a rain forest has a complex structure that includes shrubs, lianas, trees of all heights, and crowns of big trees. More complexity means more niches for different types of birds. But how do I operationalize the idea of habitat complexity, so that I can measure it and test my intuition?

Obviously, nothing I do will yield as exact an answer as in the case where I read sugar concentrations off a spectrophotometer dial. However, a pretty good approximation was devised by one of my teachers, the ecologist Robert MacArthur, who measured how far a board at a certain height above the ground had to be moved in a random direction away from an observer standing in the forest (or marsh) before it became half obscured by the foliage. That distance is inversely proportional to the density of the foliage at that height. By repeating the measurement at different heights. MacArthur could calculate how the foliage was distributed over various heights.

In a marsh all the foliage is concentrated within a few feet of the ground, 20 whereas in a rain forest it's spread fairly equally from the ground to the canopy. Thus the intuitive idea of habitat complexity is operationalized as what's called a foliage height diversity index, a single number. MacArthur's simple operationalization of these foliage differences among habitats, which at first seemed to resist having a number put on them, proved to explain a big part of the habitats' differences in numbers of bird species. It was a significant advance in ecology.

For the last example let's take one of the softest sciences, one that physicists love to deride: clinical psychology. Marie works with cancer patients and their families. Anyone with personal experience of cancer knows the terror that a diagnosis of cancer brings. Some doctors are more frank with their patients than others, and doctors appear to withhold more information from some patients than from others. Why?

Marie guessed that these differences might be related to differences in doctors' attitudes toward things like death, cancer, and medical treatment. But how on earth was she to operationalize and measure such attitudes, convert them to numbers, and test her guesses? I can imagine Lang sneering "Does she have a cancer-attitude meter?"

Part of Marie's solution was to use a questionnaire that other scientists had developed by extracting statements from sources like tape-recorded doctors' meetings and then asking other doctors to express their degree of agreement with each statement. It turned out that each doctor's responses tended to cluster in several groups, in such a way that his responses to one statement in a cluster were correlated with his responses to other statements in the same cluster. One cluster proved to consist of expressions of attitudes toward death, a second cluster consisted of expressions of attitudes toward treatment and diagnosis, and a third cluster consisted of statements about patients' ability to cope with cancer. The responses were then employed to define attitude scales, which were further validated in other ways, like testing the scales on doctors at different stages in their careers (hence likely to have different attitudes). By thus operationalizing doctors' attitudes, Marie discovered (among other things) that doctors most convinced about the value of early diagnosis and aggressive treatment of cancer are the ones most likely to be frank with their patients.

In short, all scientists, from mathematicians to social scientists, have to solve the task of operationalizing their intuitive concepts. The book by Huntington that provoked Lang's wrath discussed such operationalized concepts as economic well-being, political instability, and social and economic modernization. Physicists have to resort to very indirect (albeit accurate) operationalizing in order to "measure" electrons. But the task of operationalizing is inevitably more difficult and less exact in the soft sciences, because there are so many uncontrolled variables. In the four examples I've given, number of bananas and concentration of sugar can be measured to more decimal places than can habitat complexity and attitudes toward cancer.

Unfortunately, operationalizing lends itself to ridicule in the social sciences, because the concepts being studied tend to be familiar ones that all of us fancy we're experts on. Anybody, scientist or no, feels entitled to spout forth on politics or psychology, and to heap scorn on what scholars in those fields write. In contrast, consider the opening sentences of Lang's paper *Diophantine Approximation on Abelian Varieties with Complex Multiplication:* "Let A be an abelian variety defined over a number field K. We suppose that A is embedded in projective space. Let A_K be the group of points on A rational over K." How many people feel entitled to ridicule these statements while touting their own opinions about abelian varieties?

No political scientist at NAS has challenged a mathematical candidate by asking "How does he measure things like 'many'? Does he have a many-meter?" Such questions would bring gales of laughter over the questioner's utter ignorance of mathematics. It seems to me that Lang's question "How does Huntington measure things like social frustration?" betrays an equal ignorance of how the social sciences make measurements.

The ingrained labels "soft science" and "hard science" could be replaced by hard (i.e., difficult) science and easy science, respectively. Ecology and psychology and the social sciences are much more difficult and, to some of us, intellectually more challenging than mathematics and chemistry. Even if NAS were just an honorary society, the intellectual challenge of the soft sciences would by itself make them central to NAS.

But NAS is more than an honorary society; it's a conduit for advice to our government. As to the relative importance of soft and hard science for humanity's future, there can be no comparison. It matters little whether we progress with understanding the diophantine approximation. Our survival depends on whether we progress with understanding how people behave, why some societies become frustrated, whether their governments tend to become unstable, and how political leaders make decisions like whether to press a red button. Our National Academy of Sciences will cut itself out of intellectually challenging areas of science, and out of the areas where NAS can provide the most needed scientific advice, if it continues to judge social scientists from a posture of ignorance.

Working with the Text

1. In addressing the controversy over whether to admit political scientist Samuel Huntington into the National Academy of Sciences (NAS), Jared Diamond, a member of the NAS, makes a point of explaining the origin and purposes of

the academy. As you reread the essay, note what Diamond chooses to say about the NAS. In a brief essay, analyze how he uses this information to make his case. Why does he include these particular points? How do they contribute to his argument?

2. Although Diamond is arguing an issue that can only be decided by members of the National Academy of Sciences (NAS), the essay was originally published as an opinion piece in *Discover*, a magazine primarily written for laypeople who have an interest in current scientific research. A regular contributor to *Discover*, Diamond chose to discuss this issue in its pages. Why would a physiology professor at UCLA Medical School and a member of the NAS choose to argue this issue publicly in *Discover*? What might he hope to accomplish? Why would *Discover* choose to publish it? Why might the audience of *Discover* read it? In a brief essay, reflect on the reasons for publishing this particular essay in this particular periodical.

3. The title of the essay captures Diamond's central assertion, which is that "soft sciences are often harder than hard sciences." He centers his argument around his own use of the term *operationalize*. Write a brief essay in which you examine the reasoning and structure of his argument by analyzing his use of this term. What does he mean by *operationalize*? Why would he choose the concept of "operationalizing" to argue this particular issue with an audience of scientists as well as of laypeople who have an interest in science? How does the sequencing of his examples contribute to his argument?

From Text to Field

1. "Soft Sciences Are Often Harder than Hard Sciences" ran as an opinion piece in *Discover* magazine, which is written for a lay audience. From your point of view as a student and layperson, write a response to Diamond's argument, as if you were submitting it to *Discover* for possible publication. Do you agree with his view of soft and hard sciences? Do you support Huntington or Lang in the controversy over admitting Huntington into the National Academy of Sciences? Take a position on at least one of the issues in Diamond's opinion piece, and present your reasons in essay form. Think in terms of what is at stake for you — as a student, a taxpayer, or someone with a special interest in the state of scientific research. If you plan to enter into a scientific field, consider addressing the issue from the perspective of someone who is looking into a professional future.

2. In our own reading as well as through our education system, all of us have been exposed to both soft and hard sciences. In a personal essay, compare your encounters with soft and hard science. You might choose to address them

broadly, drawing on examples from several books or courses, or you might choose to compare two books or two courses, one concerned with soft science and the other with hard science. How did these encounters compare in terms of difficulty—the amount of effort needed to understand and work with the material? Reflect on Diamond's assertion that "[o]ur survival depends on whether we progress with understanding how people behave" (par. 28)—in other words, our understanding of soft science. How does what you learned from soft science and from hard science compare in terms of preparing you to live in the "real world"?

3. Diamond points out that "all scientists, from mathematicians to social scientists, have to solve the task of operationalizing their intuitive concepts" (par. 24). Whether or not we are scientists, all of us have formed intuitive concepts based on observation and experience. In the course of our education, all of us have also been asked to think scientifically, in subjects ranging from psychology to chemistry or physics. Review Diamond's definition of *operationalizing* as well as his examples of intuitive concepts. Brainstorm for intuitive ideas of your own — theories based on human behavior or physical phenomena you have observed. In an essay, present your intuitive concept; then formulate ways in which you could operationalize that concept in order to test it.

INTO THE FIELD: Options for Writing Projects

1. Exploring Discourse Communities

According to David Russell's argument in "Academic Discourse: Community or Communities?" every discipline and profession creates and maintains its own discourse community. Here are two options for exploring discourse communities based on your interests and on your experience on campus:

- Through interviews and research, explore the discourse community of the discipline or field you are entering or considering, either as a major or as a profession. Analyze written documents that have been produced by members of that discourse community. What forms of writing does the community produce, for what purposes and what audiences, and how are those forms of writing related to concrete activities? What knowledge and critical-thinking skills are required? Develop a guide that might orient newcomers like yourself to this discourse community.

- Based on your own experience, write an essay in which you analyze the differences between the discourse in two fields, such as art history and political science. Pay special attention to the ways in which students experience the two discourse communities in terms of the classes taken, assignments completed, and assumptions present in the language of the field. Be sure to keep field notes about your experience, and draw, if possible, on interviews with students in both classes and with the instructors who teach them.

2. Academic Communities — Many or One?

As the essays by David Russell and Wayne C. Booth make clear, there is some discussion about whether the academic community is in fact one community or multiple communities. Clearly, the situation varies somewhat from campus to campus, as much depends on the size, mission of, and distinctive culture of the institution in question. This field project encourages you to particularize the various arguments about discourse communities to your campus. At least two options suggest themselves:

- Through interviews, Web sites, and informational materials, analyze what is being done in your institution to create dialogue among diverse discourse communities. These discourse communities may be academic in nature or they may involve student groups, or both. What are the goals of that dialogue? What mechanisms are used to encourage campus and disciplinary dialogue? How effective are they?

- Because the work of a writing program typically cuts across a number of discourse communities, such programs offer an interesting starting place to reflect on assumptions about discourse communities on your campus.

Given the general philosophy of the writing program, and its particular course offerings and course descriptions, analyze what you believe to be its assumptions about academic discourse. Where does the writing program on your campus lie on a spectrum that extends, at one end, from the notion that there is one generalized academic discourse to the other extreme, that writing can only be taught well when geared to writing in any one particular discipline? If you are studying at a four-year institution, how does curricular level affect the program's assumptions? That is, how different are the assumptions between first-year courses and courses taught for juniors and seniors? Through interviews, informational materials, and the published work of writing teachers in your institution, analyze how your writing program addresses the problem of multiple academic discourse communities.

3. The Rhetorics of Understanding Each Other's Fields

Although Wayne C. Booth is addressing his academic colleagues in his essay "The Idea of a *University*," the three kinds of rhetoric he describes can be found in other organizations, groups, and professions. Select a field of endeavor — such as music, athletics, or finance — that has a distinct identity and purpose but that also encompasses a number of areas of further specialization. You may choose a field in which you have experience or one that you are interested in exploring. Develop a project in which you investigate and describe how the three kinds of rhetoric would be applied in that field and its several areas of specialization. Write an essay in which you explore what permits — and prevents —understanding of each other's work in that field. Does the field you have chosen have its own "rhetoric-1" with its own "special topics"? Is there an equivalent, outside of the academy, for Booth's "rhetoric-3," which seems to be an important intermediary between very particular field-specific rhetorics and a much more generalized civic rhetoric available to all?

4. Parody of Your Own Discipline

Horace Miner could produce a parody such as "Body Ritual among the Nacirema" because, as a practicing anthropologist, he understood how the arguments in his field are structured. For a field or discipline you are entering or considering, locate two or three examples of the written arguments used among the experts. Identify the "moves" used in the arguments — how the central assertion is introduced, the kinds of language and common terminology that are used, the structure and progression of the argument, the evidence and reasoning. In the spirit of Horace Miner's send-up of cultural anthropology, write a parody of that form of argument in your chosen field, based on what you have learned so far about the discipline.

longer used in correlation with the product or service for which it was registered. For marks used in connection with goods, the mark should be placed on the goods or on labels attached to the goods or packaging for the goods.

- Appropriate designations and notices should be used to inform the public that trademark rights are claimed in the mark. The federal registration symbol ® is most often used for registered marks while the initials "TM" or "SM" are often used in connection with marks that are not yet registered. The symbols are generally placed to the right of and slightly above (or below) the mark, such as in "CAMPBELL'S® condensed cream of chicken soup." The symbol should be large enough to be easily spotted but need not be obtrusive. If a mark is repeated several times in an advertisement or brochure, the symbol can be displayed with the first or most prominent use of the mark. Alternatively, the mark can be displayed with an asterisk. A corresponding footnote at the bottom of the page can provide the information that the mark is a registered trademark owned by the company.

- Marks should be used consistently. The addition of words or symbols to a mark may lead to the conclusion that the company has abandoned its original mark and is now using some nonregistered form of the mark.

- The owner of the mark should be identified. For example, a notice may state "SOUTHRISE® is a federally registered trademark of Hutchins Associates, Inc."

- The mark should not be used in the plural form or possessive form, such as "Excedrins are great pain relievers" or "Shout's spot-removing power is improved." Such uses may result in the mark becoming generic.

- Marks should be used as adjectives rather than nouns to ensure the mark does not become generic. The mark should not be used to refer to the general type of a product or service or to the owner. Use of a mark as a noun, rather than an adjective, suggests that the mark is the generic name for a product or service rather than a unique trademark for a particular product or service of a particular company. To avoid genericide, follow each use of a mark with the generic name for the product identified, as in "ROLLERBLADE® in-line skates" or "KLEENEX® tissues." Using such a term after the mark (or using the word *brand* as in "BAND-AID® brand adhesive strips") makes a mark an adjective rather than a noun.

Correct: SOUTHRISE® juices are refreshing.
            SOUTHRISE® cranberry juice is the juiciest.

Incorrect: SOUTHRISE® refreshes you.
            SOUTHRISE® is a sparkling beverage.
            SOUTHRISE® contains real cranberries.

Famous marks such as COKE® and FORD® are exceptions to this rule, and their owners do not always follow the noun-adjective rule. For example, advertising copy may read, "Have you driven a Ford lately?" This copy would be using the mark as a noun rather than an adjective. Other than these extraordinary cases, marks should always be used as adjectives rather than nouns.

To ensure that trademark use is proper and consistent, many companies use trademark handbooks and provide detailed information sheets to their employees, advertisers,

5. Parody of College Experience

Parody can represent an effective way to pursue an argument not by direct means, but by indirection. Horace Miner takes this approach when he examines the American obsession with bodies. By adopting the persona of an anthropologist, he is able to render the ordinary aspects of our lives as foreign and strange and thus make his point more effectively than might a straightforward argument.

For this field project, develop your own parody of one aspect of college or campus life. Using Miner's essay as a general model, offer an anthropologist's reflections on that one aspect. Among the many topics ripe for parody are the college admissions process, dorm life, sports, classroom behavior, and fraternities and sororities. Be sure your humor is grounded in close observation and extended reflection.

6. College 101

Robin Tolmach Lakoff opens her account of academic mystique, power, and privilege by describing the deliberations of a curriculum committee about a one-credit graduate course that would help students understand the "secret handshake" of their field. For your field project, consider what debates and arguments might surround the establishment of a similar course for first-year college students. Let's call it "College 101"—a course that would help orient new students to college academic life, such as how to study or how to use the library. Consider whether the need for such a course and reservations about offering it parallel the various arguments described by Lakoff regarding the graduate course. Depending on the situation on your campus, this project could take one of several forms:

- If your campus does not have such a course, you may wish to propose one. Consider using actual course-proposal forms employed by the curriculum committee on your campus. Alternatively, you may wish to offer a rationale for why such a course may not be appropriate for academic credit.
- If your campus does in fact offer such a course, evaluate its usefulness and the rationale for continuing or not continuing it. What controversies might have surrounded the course when it was first proposed?

7. Mapping and Divding the Disciplines: Hard, Soft, and in Between

As Jared Diamond makes clear in his essay, various academic fields take their places along a spectrum, from hard science (chemistry) to soft science (sociology), to the softer still (English, let's say). The point of Diamond's essay is to encourage us to rethink those categories. This field project has you venture forth on your campus to see how and in what way these distinctions matter to faculty and students.

In part as an administrative convenience, some universities divide departments in a large college like "Arts and Sciences" into science, social science, and arts and humanities divisions. Explore the rationale for which departments have found their way into which divisions. On your campus, is history in the humanities division or in the social-science division? Is psychology or geography in the science division or the social-science division? Anthropology is one rather eclectic discipline whose several subdisciplines can lay claim to belonging in any one of three areas. To support your inquiry, read departmental descriptions in the catalog and interview faculty in a department that interests you. Do you find tensions within certain fields? For example, do you find some faculty in the social sciences less than enthusiastic about the growing emphasis on "quantification" in their disciplines? Do these administrative divisions erect barriers to work between departments?

Your own course work can reflect these same divisions and struggles. For example, consider how your campus's general-education course requirements are carved up. If you need to take a certain number of credit hours in the social sciences, which departments offer which courses that satisfy that requirement? Is the rationale for that selection always clear? Do you find that categorizing fields in this way supports or hinders your broad education? How might such categorization hinder interdisciplinary work? Can you think of new or emerging fields that cut across the more traditional map of the disciplines?

4

Engagements

COLLABORATIONS

If asked to picture, in your mind, the image of a writer at work, you might easily conjure up a solitary figure working at a desk or sitting alone in front of a computer. Such an image is not entirely wrong so much as it is incomplete. Who among us hasn't spent some time (perhaps a good deal of time) working on a writing project while sitting alone at the keyboard? But such an image tends to discount just how collaborative the writing process is in many settings. Writing — and for that matter reading — is a social activity.

Our received image of the writer has its roots in the romantic notion of genius. The inspired individual, prompted by a creative muse, works alone in a dimly lit and poorly heated garret and finds from within the emotion and imagination to express great ideas. Oh, yes, did I mention that the writer is hungry and poor or that threadbare fingerless gloves keep this author's hands warm enough to allow for writing? And for good measure, we might throw in a romantic twist — perhaps a love that has been lost or a love that remains unrequited. You get the picture. Or rather, we've gotten this picture for some two hundred years. What's more, the image also suggests that good ideas come only to the creative, renegade mind and that those ideas are owned and capitalized on by the individual.

This romantic image of the writer is far removed from the realities of writing in most organizations and professional settings. We write when prompted by problems that affect not only ourselves but others as well. We discuss ideas with others, and those ideas evolve, often in a messy and unpredictable way. We produce drafts, often with others or at least aided by others. And we share those drafts with colleagues and friends, who help us anticipate the needs and interests of readers who will themselves respond to our words.

Even in the university setting, writing is far more social and collaborative than it often seems to be. Appearances can be deceiving. On one level, all that you may hear is the shuffle of paper as you silently hand in your essays and as they are later handed back. What's hidden is the din of voices just beyond the page or the tug and pull of ideas as they rub up against each other. Writing classes make such collaborative dynamics more visible and immediate. Peers not only help to shape the writing through feedback in workshops, but they also serve as readers who help the author orient the prose to the audience it must serve.

The Russian theorist of discourse Mikhail Bakhtin has observed that "language . . . lies on the borderline between oneself and the other. The word in language is half someone else's." Writing, too, is half someone else's, both in the collaboration that inevitably accompanies its creation, and in the presence and role of the reader, who collaborates in its reception.

This unit offers several voices that extend and enrich our notion of writing as a collaborative and social act — an act performed, not in the garret by that solitary creative genius, but in the marketplace and on the street, where ideas trade amidst a din of voices. By listening to the marginalia in books, Michael Parker helps us hear the voices that occur in the tug and pull of reading. Books, as it turns out, beckon us to talk back. Lisa Ede and Andrea Lunsford share the dynamics behind their several collaborative writing projects, encouraging us to rethink how we ourselves can be enriched by collaborations, through the written word, with other minds and hearts. Kenneth A. Bruffee explores how, through collaboration, we can learn from our knowledgeable peers. Highlighting the social processes by which we compose knowledge, Bruffee reminds us that "learning occurs among persons rather than between a person and things." Malcolm Gladwell offers the provocative notion that smart people may well be overrated, noting that organizations — and more generally collaborative activities — can make people smart. Thomas S. Kuhn likewise questions our preoccupation with the solitary, creative individual. As much as we may prize creative, divergent thinking, new advances in science and in other fields rest on our ability to work together to produce the convergent thinking out of which new insights emerge.

Reflecting on Prior Knowledge

1. In a journal entry, reflect on an experience in which you collaborated with other people in an activity that you normally pursue alone. What made this experience different, more valuable, or more difficult?

2. Working in groups, develop an inventory of various daily activities that require or invite collaboration or shared participation. Highlight those activities in which collaboration seems especially important or in which you feel enriched by the collaborative experience. Feel free to range widely, drawing on your nonacademic and personal lives.

3. Working in groups, develop a list of various factors that are essential to productive and enjoyable collaborative work, especially in writing. For example, you may find that your list includes such factors as trust, equal standing and equitable roles, ability to reflect on the collaboration, flexibility, and so on. Be

sure to brainstorm about factors that may not be immediately obvious. Draw on your own collaborative experiences, both positive and negative.

4. Although we may first think of collaboration as involving a group of people who share the same time and space, many activities can be highly collaborative even if the people participating do not occupy the same time and space. Develop and share a list of such activities. For example, writing letters and reading books seem to be highly private endeavors, yet clearly they have us talking to or engaging with others. In a journal entry, reflect on what makes these activities instances of collaboration.

5. In a small group, brainstorm a list of qualities that you think make a job candidate attractive to a potential employer. Be prepared to share your list with the entire class.

6. In a journal entry, reflect on the degree to which your prior educational experiences were private and highly individual or shared and essentially collaborative. In what ways are both dimensions important, although perhaps in different ways and for different purposes?

7. Americans have been known to have a penchant for individualism and divergent thinking, prizing creativity above nearly all other virtues. Working first in groups, develop a list of reasons why consensus is not only essential to some degree, but also highly productive. Drawing on the work of your group, in a journal entry reflect on the discussion you have had, integrating into your writing your personal experiences.

Talking Back to Books:
In Defense of Marginalia

Michael Parker

Michael Parker based his first novel, *Hello Down There* (1993), on the image of a hand reaching through a window to snatch the bag of morphine Parker's father regularly delivered from the drugstore. Parker wrote the novel to find out, through his own imagination, who the man might be.

The imagination that draws the writer Parker into seeing an entire life in one mysterious gesture also draws the reader Parker into engaging the marginal notes written in used books, as if he were in a running conversation with "a well-created fictional character." Whether marginalia suggests a student studying for a test, an armchair critic, or a reader with an attitude, Parker is fascinated by this urge to talk back to books, to record some form of personal conversation with the author.

Hello Down There was named a New York Times Notable Book. Parker has also published *The Geographical Cure* (1994), a collection of stories and novellas and winner of the 1994 Sir Walter Raleigh Award, and *Towns without Rivers* (2001), a novel. His latest novel is *If You Want Me to Stay* (2005). His fiction and nonfiction have appeared in journals such as the *Georgia Review, Idaho Review, Carolina Quarterly,* and the *Washington Post.* In 1996, *Granta Magazine* cited Parker as one of the best American fiction writers under forty, and in 2002 "Off Island," a story originally published in *Five Points,* won a Pushcart Award.

Michael Parker is a professor of English at the University of North Carolina–Greensboro, where he teaches graduate and undergraduate classes in fiction writing and contemporary literature.

If like me you spend hours foraging amongst the dank aisles of used bookstores because you can rarely afford the price of a trade paperback, and live

380

in a place where the book business is cornered by chain stores whose selection reflects that week's best-seller list topped off with cat calendars and audio tapes of techno-thrillers; if like me you have happened upon treasures — Charles Olson's monograph of Melville, a battered but lovable copy of Frank O'Connor's *The Lonely Voice*, *Wide Sargasso Sea* in hardback — in stores which, to the untrained eye seem stocked with the usual excess of John O'Hara potboilers and Richard Henry Dana's *Two Years Before the Mast*; if after such finds you, like me, become convinced that more treasures lay hidden beneath the dust of disintegrating copies of *Ragtime*, then you have almost certainly brought home a book which contains in its margins the scribble-scribble of previous owners.

Marginalia comes with the territory, and it comes in categories. In my years of collecting second-hand books, I have identified three such categories. The first is peculiar but not exclusive to college towns and usually applies to books listed on syllabi. This type is meant to summarize; it reduces the subtleties of language and idea into a few words — one is preferable — which will help the student study for the test. Flipping through the *Aeneid* in the bookstore outside of Lynchburg, Virginia, I found the following written next to the line, "the news I heard was true, your death was I its cause?" "Aenas feels real sorry for what he had done to Dido." A few pages later, scrawled alongside the line "From under the tomb a gliding snake, seven huge circles, seven rolling coils," I found the penciled equation "Snake = Evil." A math major? Knocking out that liberal arts requirement? As for the idea, I've heard it somewhere before, though it always helps to write these things down.

Some marginalia is intentionally comic, but laughs are usually derived at the previous owner's expense. In keeping with the synoptic nature of note taking, student marginalia strives to hook the most literal developments of action, plot, or idea, and throw back all indigestible abstractions. Irony is rarely a keeper. Leafing through a copy of *Ulysses*, I read the following lines. "Watering cart: to provoke the rain. On earth as it is in heaven." The last line was underscored, the word "religious" clogging the margin. Somehow I doubt this line was meant to suggest that Leopold Bloom regularly attended Sunday school.

Of course marginalia is a harried act; astute, beautifully written commentary is not the objective. Although for years I seem to have blocked this fact from my mind, it turns out I was fairly active as a student marginaliast myself, and am guilty of some god-awful examples, some of which I discovered recently while leafing through an old copy of *King Lear*. I can only surmise that I was writing a paper — long forgotten and better that way — discussing the use of clothing as a metaphor in the play, for my copy is filled with examples which make the following seem smart. "Through tattered clothes small vices do appear; Robes feedback from your readers will spur you to further look into the issue, gather more information, rethink your ideas, and better prepare yourself for eventually publishing them.

In a sense, your proposal is an academic contract between you and your thesis/ dissertation committee. Once the committee members approve it, they grant you the right to proceed with the plan as laid out. To get your research ideas accepted and thesis/dissertation plan approved by your committee, your performance in your oral examination (the defense of your proposal) is extremely important. If you do a very good job, your final defense of your thesis/dissertation may not be needed. You should carefully prepare for your presentation so that it can be done beautifully within the time allowed. You must get your main ideas across to the audience, and the feedback from your committee members is very important. You should avoid overwhelming your committee members with too much detail, and address their interests by highlighting the information that particularly appeals to them. Some of your committee members may not have read through your proposal. You should be prepared to answer all kinds of questions regarding your thesis/dissertation research.

An important and sometimes sensitive aspect of your relationship with your advisor and/or committee members is the kind of colleagueship. For example, if you work as a team member on your advisor's research project and your thesis/dissertation is part of it, your research interest and your advisor's are closely tied together. Your advisor may spend a lot of time on your writing and give you a lot of ideas in constructing the research and the report. Even if it is no problem for you to write the thesis/dissertation, there might be some problem in publishing it, especially if it can be considered a case of work for hire or having a coauthorship not clearly defined. In fact, to coauthor some articles for publication with your advisor and/or committee members would perfectly sum up your experience in this important period of your life. Not all students and their advisors, however, are able to attain this ideal. We will further discuss this topic in chapter fourteen.

EXHIBIT 5–2
Trademark
Usage Guide

Guideline	Trademark Do	Trademark Don't
Display mark prominently.	EXPLORE®; **EXPLORE**®	Explore
Use mark as registered and use in consistent manner.	EXPLORE®	Ex-plore; Exploring; Explorer; Exploreride
Use trademark registration notice.	EXPLORE®	EXPLORE
Identify owner of mark.	EXPLORE® is a registered trademark of Watson Inc.	Explore
Do not use mark in plural form.	EXPLORE® roller coaster is a wild ride.	Explores offer a wild ride.
Do not use in possessive form.	EXPLORE® roller coaster is the ride of a lifetime.	Explore's ride will leave you breathless.
Use mark as an adjective rather than a noun.	EXPLORE® roller coaster is a thrill. The EXPLORE® attraction will amaze you.	Explore thrills you. Explore amazes you with its dips and rolls.

suppliers, vendors, and licensees to instruct them in proper use of trademarks. When marks comprise color or design components rather than mere wording, companies usually supply advertising "slicks" as well so users can faithfully reproduce the mark. Many companies designate a responsible person to regulate use of the company's marks and verify compliance with guidelines and policies regarding use of the marks.

(See Exhibit 5–2 for a chart showing examples of trademark usage.)

TRADEMARK POLICING AND MAINTENANCE

In addition to ensuring that marks are used properly to avoid genericide or abandonment,

trademark owners should initiate active policing and maintenance procedures to avoid infringement of their marks. The classic trademark rule is "Police it or lose it." Among the steps trademark owners should take to protect their marks from infringement are the following:

- Critical dates for required actions with the PTO should be docketed to ensure marks, applications, and registrations are not inadvertently abandoned and then used by others.
- Owners should subscribe to watching or tracking services to monitor marks for potential infringement. Professional service companies will review a number of trademark resources, including applications filed at the PTO, the *Official Gazette,* state trademark registers, Internet domain names, and common law sources. Worldwide watching

and furred gowns hide all," says Lear in Act IV. Ever alert, I underscored the word "clothes" and wrote in the margin the word "clothes."

A step up from student marginalia is the more serious scribbling of arm-   5
chair (or for all I know, endowed-chair) critics. Since I have spent most of the past fifteen years in college towns, the timbre of marginalia found in my library tends to reflect the academy in all its various triumphs and failings. This type could qualify as annotation but for its slightly onanistic quality. In an early Saul Bellow novel I found these words in near indecipherable script on the inside flyleaf. "The meaning of the fact is Bellow's enduring concern. Is there a moral debt to be paid and by what means can it be paid? More than that, when is the debt actually discharged? . . . An early example of the advantages made available to morality through several decades of naturalis-tic fiction." Though I've long been curious as to what advantages naturalis-tic fiction availed to morality, I've never actually bothered to read the novel, its central themes (the meaning of the fact? the debt actually discharged?) having been summed up so nicely for me on the front flyleaf.

Marginalia does not make for speed-read or skim, which is only one of the reasons why detractors despise it in all forms. They say it distracts. They say it defaces books and that it is a moronic habit, the product of an inferior mind. They equate it with counting on fingers, with lips forming syllables while reading.

A retrograde strain in my sensibility leads me to defend most things in danger of extinction, and it seems to me that marginalia has suffered a falling off. I know how fashionable it has become to blame

The marginaliast . . . shapes everything from the quality of prose to the attention
indirectly your understand- span of readers on the advent of word processors, yet it
ing of the idea at hand. is a fact that these days many books are written entire-
ly on screens; the scars and sutures of cross out and transposition evaporate at the touch of a key. Writers no longer care to see where they've been; the rich and decodeable battlefield upon which ideas take shape is no longer of interest. (It is no longer even a physical entity.) Something subliminal may be alerting readers: If the writer no longer both-ers with us, why the hell should you, says margin to reader. Pens are capped and put away.

As for the third and final category, it can include both the student and the learned, and is defined more by attitude than intelligence or intent. My favorite example involves a bit of background. Back in 1982 I bought a copy of Schopenhauer's *The Art of Literature* from a used bookstore in Chapel Hill. Having just read *A Long Day's Journey into Night* and been struck by the scene in which Tyrone senior, admonishing Edwin for his literary tastes, consigns Schopenhauer (along with Voltaire, Rousseau, Neitzsche, and Ibsen) to a scrap heap of atheists, fools, and madmen, I was eager to try the great father of pessimism. Any writer one's father warns against is worth checking out, I reasoned. I must have flipped through the book before purchasing it and the few margin scrawls I noticed did not bother me, since they were only asking sixty-five cents.

On the first page of the first essay, I encountered the first of what would turn out to be numerous color fields of golfer's-slacks yellow which had somehow escaped my notice. (Underscoring does not to my mind qualify as marginalia unless it is accompanied by written commentary — a paltry distinction but a necessary one. Actually, I detest underscoring, and especially if rendered in day-glo lemon or lime.)

I was put off by the lurid highlight, yet I pushed on, intrigued by Schopenhauer's own attitude, the gleamings of recalcitrance which stood out amongst stock opinions on writing and writers. In his essay on style I encountered my first flourish of veritable marginalia. My predecessor had underscored the following line — "a man's style shows the formal nature of all his thoughts — the formal nature which can never change, be the subject or the character of his thoughts what it may . . ." — and written alongside, "No! No! No! How wrong!" Rather than irksome grammatical tic, these exclamation points seemed lightning bolts of vehemence. Already, on page 13, I understood Schopenhauer to be a formidable man to cross, and wasn't sure I'd venture to do so even considering the fact that he has been dead these 130 years. I began to feel that I was in the middle of something, and that something promised to be lively.

The next skirmish was a quiet one. "To find where the point lies is the problem of style, and the business of the critical faculty; for a word too much always defeats its purpose. This is what Voltaire means when he says that *the adjective is the enemy of the substantive.* [translator's italics] "But V. was one of greatest adjective abusers," responds my guide. It had been a while since I'd read *Candide,* but I seemed then to remember it as a bit of a pileup. I was impressed that my guide recognized the contradiction, even more impressed that he was on an initial basis with yet another of Tyrone senior's "atheists, fools, and madmen."

I came to Schopenhauer's chapter on the study of Latin, prepared for a berating, since I failed to learn even the simplest roots of the language despite the fact that my mother once earned her living by teaching it. I wasn't disappointed: Schopenhauer had unsheathed the exclamation points by the second paragraph. "If it should really come to this" [the abolition of Latin as the universal language of learned men] "then farewell, humanity! Farewell, noble taste and high thinking! The age of barbarism will return, in spite of railways, telegraphs, and balloons." I was ready to put in a call to the nearest classics department when my guide resurfaced. "Is it language or ideas that are important? Is the author insecure because he has spent time to learn the language and others have not? Does he feel thwarted?"

My guess is that only by expressions of joie de vivre did the granddaddy of gloom and doom feel thwarted, and the idea that Schopenhauer's bellicosity arises from insecurity strikes me now as pop psychology at its most tepid. Yet at the time I was searching for an ally, someone to help me rationalize my laziness and assert that erudition was possible without fluency in Latin and that, railways, telegraphs, and balloons notwithstanding, we are not all barbarians in this barbaric age.

Advantage: marginaliast.

The equanimity of my guide's last few exchanges was not to last, and   15 bullet-spray of departure was provoked by, to my mind, the most innocuous comment in the entire treatise. Discussing the practice of anonymity in literature and journalism, Schopenhauer suggests, rather mildly for him, that "every article should be accompanied by the name of its author; and the editor should be made strictly responsible for the accuracy of the signature." "You screaming socialist!" rants my guide in chicken scratch which suggests the surge of his blood pressure. "And how would you put this in motion? No doubt by government regulations. You idiot, don't you see what you are doing?"

While it is true that literary criticism is not Schopenhauer's forte (he is much better, I have since learned, in decrying the cracking of whips as "a genuine assassin of thought"), the man had a right to say what he thought without being labeled a socialist. Filled with doubt about my once trustworthy trailblazer, I scoured the book for clues. The only trace was rubber-stamped boldly across the front flyleaf: THE BOOK RACK, Trade 2 For 1; WINSTON-SALEM, N.C.

I checked the publication date: 1960, or years before the thaw of the Cold War. Though I had no idea when the book was bought, read, or written in, it seemed easy to blame my guide's outburst on the spirit of the times. With only a little less enthusiasm I plugged ahead. My guide was silent throughout the whole of Schopenhauer's essay on Reputation, which did not shy away from referring to the overwhelming idiocy of the masses as well as most writers, and in general was as in-your-face as any of the preceding essays. Did he agree? Did he not care much about literary reputations? Did he not even bother to read it? Though it is impossible to feel lost in an essay of Schopenhauer's—and anticipation of what mordant thing he'll say next spurs you onward—I felt a little disoriented, as if I was venturing out into a foreign city for the first time without an interpreter. Every time I turned the page I did a quick scan of the margin for signs of another conflagration.

And finally I found one: one word, in the manner of that first category, the student intent on extracting the essence, on summing up for later study. I did not allow myself to read the word. I entered slowly the underscored passage as if wading into frigid waters, giving myself time to become accustomed to the waves of sentences, savoring each for meaning and mood before they receded. Schopenhauer was complaining of the intellectual vacuity of the human race. "If anyone wishes for entertainment, such as will prevent him feeling solitary even when he is alone, let me recommend the company of dogs, whose moral and intellectual qualities may almost afford delight and gratification."

My fearless guide had circled "dogs," drawn a line out to the margin and in a primitive hand printed the word "SPIKE."

Well, now. What to think? I felt confident enough, after having gone 20 through the book with this person, to assume that he did not have a dog named Spike. His response showed a certain spunk — by dredging up one of the most generic of dog names and offering it unelaborated, in such stick-figure hand, he called attention to Schopenhauer's intellectual snobbishness with a certain subtle flair. Yet finally it seemed more desperate than humorous; it showed resignation, a flagging. I felt cheated. This is after all the screaming socialist you're up against, I felt like writing in the margin. Screaming socialists, like toddlers and students in survey courses, are not much on irony.

That the outcome was less than pyrotechnic has become over the years beside the point. Now, any time I come across mention of Schopenhauer I think of my experience with his *Art of Literature,* of how it was enlivened by the efforts of my ardent guide. His comments made the strident tone of the treatise even more strident, and more memorable. Personally I have nothing against socialists or even those socialists who scream, but the point is that it's not necessary to agree or disagree with this third stripe of marginaliast; like a well-created fictional character, their presence shapes indirectly your understanding of the idea at hand.

My purpose here is not to encourage the defacement of books or to suggest everyone should take pen to margin. Marginalia is not for everyone, though it tends to be practiced by all types of readers and thinkers. I would merely like to offer a gentle rebuff to those readers who see margins as sacrosanct, a demilitarized zone; to whom margins, with their white blanketed space, whisper "Don't tread on me." The marginaliast's is an art of accumulation, of yeas and nays accrued. When they say something stupid, you can choose to ignore or trounce. When they say something smart, something which mirrors your own incisive opinion, you pay attention. Yes, you say, I was just thinking the same thing myself. Only I got there first.

Working with the Text

1. Although Michael Parker's essay emphasizes the relationship between the writer and the reader of marginalia, the first phrase in his title is "Talking Back to Books." As you reread the essay, consider this phrase as it applies to both the marginaliast and the reader of marginalia. Write a brief essay in which you

reflect on what Parker means by "talking back to books." What does talking back to books involve, for both the marginaliast and the reader of marginalia? What can be gained by it?

2. As a practiced reader of the markings in used books, Parker has identified three categories of marginalia. He describes these categories primarily by offering examples. For his first category of marginalia, usually written by college students, he notes that it is "meant to summarize" (par. 2). For the other two categories, he provides no comparable definition. Based on analysis of the examples Parker offers, write a brief essay in which you define each category of marginalia. What kinds of comments do the marginaliasts make? What purposes do the comments serve? As you define the first category, think beyond Parker's note that it is "meant to summarize" by analyzing what the marginaliast is trying to capture and why.

3. In a paragraph that almost functions as an aside, Parker blames the invisible corrections made possible by word processors for what he views as a "falling off" of marginalia. Parker charges, "Something subliminal may be alerting readers: If the writer no longer bothers with us, why the hell should you, says margin to reader" (par. 7). As you reread the essay, consider this charge in light of Parker's larger argument in favor of marginalia. With Parker's phrase "says margin to reader" in mind, write a brief essay from the point of view of the margin. What relationship does the margin have to the writer? What changes when the writer replaces handwritten corrections with electronic ones? How might this change the relationship between the margin and the reader as well as the reader and the author of the text?

4. Parker devotes most of his essay to describing the marginalia he encountered in a used copy of Schopenhauer's *The Art of Literature*. At the end of the essay, Parker describes the effects of such an encounter: "[I]t's not necessary to agree or disagree with this third stripe of marginaliast; like a well-created fictional character, their presence shapes indirectly your understanding of the idea at hand" (par. 21). Write a brief essay in which you analyze the relationship that developed between Parker and the marginaliast. What does Parker's description of the encounter tell you about the personality of the "fictional character" that emerged from the marginalia? What does the encounter tell you about Parker himself? In what ways did the marginaliast shape Parker's understanding of Schopenhauer?

From Text to Field

1. Parker wrote "Talking Back to Books: In Defense of Marginalia" because he is well aware of what the detractors say: "They say it distracts. They say it defaces books and that it is a moronic habit, the product of an inferior mind" (par. 6).

In what respects is Parker's essay not just about talking back but is itself a response, or as the title suggests, a "defense"? Join this exchange. Write a short personal essay in which you describe your own response when you encounter marginalia. Do you welcome it or resent it? How does it affect your reading of the text? What kinds of thoughts do you have of the person who wrote it?

2. Behind the "well-created fictional character" that Parker finds in marginalia is a real person who talks back to books. When we write marginalia, we might not be conscious of the "fictional character" we may be creating for someone who reads it. In a short personal essay, analyze your own use of marginalia. If you are a marginaliast, what do you write and for what purpose? In what ways are you talking back to the book? What "character" or representation of yourself do you think you might be creating? If you never write in books, why not? If someone bought a used book of yours that has no marks in it, how might the new owner interpret this? Are there other characteristics of your used book — folded-down page corners, battered cover, food stains — that might provide some hint of who you are, as a person and as a reader? Are there other ways, outside of marking in a book, in which you talk back to it?

3. Parker's essay indicates that he is very conscious of his interaction with the marginalia. To practice this level of awareness, locate a used book that has a fair amount of marginalia. Write an analysis of that marginalia, which you have never before read or haven't read closely. Which of Parker's categories does it represent? What purpose did it seem to serve for the marginaliast? What does the marginaliast seem to be saying to the book? What "fictional character" is created by the marginalia? How did it influence your reading of the passage?

4. Work in pairs or small groups to analyze each other's marginalia. Each person might choose a short reading (perhaps one from this book) to "talk back to" in marginal notes. Then give the marked-up reading to a peer to analyze in light of the marginalia. Alternatively, the group might write marginal notes on Parker's essay to exchange and discuss as a way of interpreting the essay together.

Why Write . . . Together?

Lisa Ede and Andrea Lunsford

When Lisa Ede and Andrea Lunsford—professors of writing and rhet-oric—cowrote "Why Write . . . Together?" (1983), they had already col-laborated on two other articles. At the time, they acknowledged that their different styles, as both people and writers, created difficulties they didn't encounter when each of them wrote alone. Yet over the twenty years since their first round of collaborations, they have con-tinued to work together on articles, books, conference presentations, and talks on campuses across the country.

Collaborative writing itself became a scholarly interest for both Ede and Lunsford, to the extent that they are considered to be among the foremost experts in the study and practice of collaboration, in professional as well as in academic writing. They were among the first in their field to recognize that university students are taught to write almost exclusively as individuals, even though most move into profes-sions that require a substantial amount of coauthorship. As promoters of collaborative writing, Ede and Lunsford explore the situations in which two (or more) heads are better than one.

Lisa Ede is professor of English and director of the Center for Writing and Learning at Oregon State University. Andrea Lunsford taught at the University of British Columbia and then was for many years professor of English at Ohio State University. She is currently professor of English and director of the Program for Writing and Rhetoric at Stanford University. Among Ede and Lunsford's many col-laborative projects, the most notable in this context is their detailed study of joint authorship in academic and professional worlds, *Singular Texts, Plural Authors: Perspectives on Collaborative Writing* (1990). The article presented here offers Lunsford and Ede's early — and prescient—thoughts on the role of collaboration; it was published in the January 1983 issue of *Rhetoric Review*.

It was 10:00 PM. We had just spent another twelve-hour day working on our paper. Lisa was settling into a chair with a hot toddy. Andrea was shoving off for a shower. We were grumpy, tired, full of self-pity; this was the third day we had worked at such a pace. Only one day remained before Lisa had to begin the eight-hour trek from Andrea's home in Vancouver to her own in Corvallis. We had to finish a draft of the paper, our first joint writing project, the next day.

All at once — we both remember it this way — Lisa sat upright and announced: "Andrea takes a shower every night; Lisa takes one every morning." Since the meaning of this toddy-stimulated statement was hardly self-evident, Lisa went on to explain that suddenly the significance of all our differences, of which this was just one example, seemed clear. How could two such opposite people ever hope to write a paper — together?

Warming to the silliness of the topic, we began to list all the ways we differ. Andrea showers every night; Lisa, every morning. Andrea drinks only iced tea, even at breakfast; Lisa drinks only the hottest of hot tea. Andrea hates milk and most dairy products; they form a staple of Lisa's diet. Andrea always wears her hair pulled back; Lisa gets a headache from even the thought of a single barrette. Andrea is a meticulous housekeeper; Lisa, so-so at best.

As the list of opposites grew, we felt a giddy sense of relief. No wonder the past few days had been so trying. Two such contrary, often downright cantankerous, people should have *expected* trouble. The struggle began to make sense: not just our personalities but our composing processes and, to a lesser degree, our styles, differed radically. After all, didn't Lisa love dashes, sprinkling them liberally through her prose, while Andrea seldom used them? Andrea preferred long paragraphs; Lisa's were usually shorter. Lisa wrote at a desk or (in a pinch) at a table; Andrea worked sitting cross-legged on the floor or on the bed. Andrea was a sprinter; she liked to write a draft straight through, as quickly as possible, revising and typing later. Lisa worked more slowly, dividing a paper into small sections, revising and typing as she went.

We decided that night that if we ever did complete our joint essay, we would someday explore the mystery — or the madness — of coauthorship. Since that time, we have coauthored two other articles and have several joint projects in mind. Thus, while we continue individual research efforts, our status as sometime coauthors seems assured. Somehow, despite the difficulties, we not only manage to write essays together, but actually like doing so. And, as we have worked together, the question that arose that night — how can two people with different interests, personalities, habits, and composing processes together write one essay? — has expanded into many questions. This article is a brief anecdotal response to some of those questions. In it, we wish to sketch the outlines of the process of coauthorship as we have come to understand it, to set forth the advantages and disadvantages we encountered, and to pose a series of questions which we hope will be explored in future research.

In our experience, coauthorship has meant the two of us creating one text — together. We discovered and thought through ideas together, talked through almost every section and draft of the papers together, and often wrote drafts by talking and then recording directly. Such is not always the case. Indeed, our use of the term is probably atypical. More typically, no doubt, two authors contribute separate sections, which are then put together. Only at that point do the coauthors revise the whole text, and even in revising authors may work separately. In this way, people can coauthor articles without ever being together or doing any writing together. This second form of coauthorship may best describe the kind of academic writing done by, say, a professor and a student, or the kind done by many researchers in science. It may also describe coauthorship in much professional and business writing. Yet a third concept covered by the blanket term *coauthorship* is that of group writing. It is not unusual, especially in business, for a number of people to contribute to a single text. The head of the writing division for an international mining corporation recently told us that as many as fifteen people contribute sections to their annual report. Subsequently, four or five of those people come together to revise the entire report, which generally goes through a dozen drafts.

We believe that important distinctions exist among these types of coauthorship and, indeed, that other types of coauthorship can be identified. Since our experience has been primarily of the first type, however — that of conceiving, drafting, and revising a text together — we will concentrate on that concept and will use the term *coauthorship* in this essay to refer to this type of writing together.

We are also here referring only to academic writing. The essays we have coauthored have all been addressed to those in our field, readers of *College Composition and Communication, College English,* and rhetoric journals. In that sense, we have gone into each project with a clear sense of audience, medium of publication, and purpose (although we could, of course, easily misjudge our audience or medium or alter our purposes). As with much academic writing, we began by working within only our own time constraints. But as so often is the case, this internal control soon gave way to external pressures. An invitation to speak at a conference was accepted; an article was solicited for a journal or committed to a book — and suddenly the external pressure to write on demand appeared. In this important regard, that of writing on demand, much academic writing may be closer to professional writing than we usually consider it to be. But in other ways, the genres vary markedly. As writers of an article for *Rhetoric Review,* for instance, we have a different kind of control over shape and substance than we would if we were writing an annual report for a mining company. As with the various types of coauthorship, we think these generic distinctions are important ones that need to be explored. While we hope to pursue these questions in the future, we are speaking here not of business or professional writing, but only of the academic genre with which we are all so familiar.

So what is this process of coauthoring an academic paper? We've drawn boxes and arrows, spirals and loops, but will offer no schematized representation of the process we have experienced. If you can imagine the words *talk* . . . *write* . . . *talk* . . . *read* . . . *talk* . . . *write* . . . *talk* . . . *read* . . . written in a large looping spiral — that comes closest to a description of the process as we know it. We wish especially to emphasize the frequency and proportion of *talking* in this process.

As we noted earlier, each of our projects grew out of a particular rhetori   10 cal situation: We were constrained by a broad topic and by a medium of publication and an audience. Within those guidelines, our first and longest talks occurred. These early talks were characterized by a lot of foolishness (Why not claim that the concept of audience simply doesn't exist? or, How about writing a dialogue between Aristotle and Wittgenstein?), fantasy (What if we could visit Kenneth Burke for a month?), and unfocused rambling (Where do you suppose we've put our notes on those ten articles? What do you think is the best reading for *krisis*?)° In our first project, these talks helped us sound the depths of our topic and, most importantly, discover the enormity of what we did not know. Intensive periods of reading and research followed, as did more and more talking, trading of notes, and posing of yet more unanswered questions. All told, this first coauthored essay took us six months, during which we met four times for two- to four-day writing sessions. These sessions were pressure-filled, frustrating — and very exciting. For one of them, we met half-way between our homes, in Seattle, and worked for two-and-a-half days in a hotel room, distracted only by the person trying unsuccessfully to "tidy up" around the stacks of books, articles, and drafts, and by our husbands, who insisted on reporting on all the fun they were having while we worked. We estimate writing and talking time in these sessions to be almost equal, with more time given to writing in the last session and more to talk in the earlier ones. At the end of each session the process of talk . . . write . . . talk . . . read . . . talk . . . write . . . talk . . . read . . . left us tired but exhilarated. And in each case the process produced a draft, one we could take back home, work

---

krisis: A classical Greek term etymologically related to the verb *krinō,* "to pull apart or separate." The word *krisis* means an agreed-upon choice or judgment. Lunsford and Ede's choice of *krisis* as an example is interesting in that the coauthors themselves must make a choice or judgment about their reading of the term.

is also available for marks used internationally. Early notification of potential conflicts allows an owner to take aggressive action to protect a mark. The companies identified in Chapter 3 (Thomson & Thomson, CCH Corsearch, and so forth) perform these watching services at varying rates. The most comprehensive watch of all resources previously described might cost more than $1,000 per year per mark per class. However, for a company like McDonald's Corporation that has spent years and substantial amounts of money in building goodwill in its marks, such as its GOLDEN ARCHES® mark, such a sum represents a very reasonable investment. Some trademark owners conduct an annual intellectual property "audit" to review the status of their intellectual property and detect potential infringing uses (see Chapter 24). More limited watches, such as one only of new applications filed at the PTO, might cost approximately $165 per year per mark.

- Company employees should be asked to be alert to competing uses in the marketplace. Trade publications, business press, and marketing materials of competitors should be monitored to ensure that marks that may be confusingly similar to the company's marks are not being used.
- Trademark owners should review Internet uses to locate infringing marks or misuses of a mark. Policing the Internet is a double-edged sword, however; while a few simple keystrokes may reveal numerous uses, the trademark owner then runs the risk that ignoring infringers will lead to a loss of trademark rights. Some companies with famous marks use a team to review

Internet uses and then send e-mails explaining their trademark rights and asking the user to stop use of the owner's mark. If such a strategy is not successful, a more serious **cease and desist letter** is sent (see discussion later in this chapter).

USE OF MARKS OWNED BY THIRD PARTIES

Parties often use their competitors' marks in promotional materials comparing and contrasting the respective goods or services of the parties. A trademark owner does not have an absolute right to prohibit any and all uses of its trademarks. A **collateral use** of another party's marks may be acceptable in some circumstances. For example, it is not trademark infringement for a party to inform consumers truthfully that its products will "fit with" the trademark product of another. Thus, a seller of sponges was able to advertise that its sponges fit as replacements in the "O-CEDAR® 76 mop." Many parents are familiar with the announcements that certain blocks "work with LEGOS®."

Statements that one's products are "superior to" or "better than" another's, however, may be actionable as false advertising if the statement is untrue. Courts tend to examine language in advertising to ensure there is no misleading use, product disparagement, or confusion caused to the public. To reduce confusion, a party should always place the registration symbol ® next to another party's registered mark and provide the announcement, "XYZ® is a federally registered trademark owned by XYZ Corp." This will help ensure that consumers are not confused about the source and origin of goods or services offered under the respective marks. The law of unfair competition is discussed in Chapter 23.

on, and talk about in our frequent phone calls. We have kept every draft, all our notes, and some protocols from each of our projects, but we do not wish to turn this into a full-blown case study of our admitted idiosyncrasies. Rather, we wish to turn to a brief discussion of how coauthoring altered our individual writing processes.

Most noticeable, as we have mentioned, was the much larger proportion of talking together about our research and writing. Papers written singly have never been completely silent affairs; we talk to others

We would . . . explore the mystery — or the madness — of coauthorship.

about our work or ask colleagues to read and discuss essays or drafts with us. But never had either of us (both prodigious talkers to begin with) ever talked so much or for so long while writing a paper. This talking, in fact, seemed to be a necessary part of coauthoring, one that made our writing more productive and efficient. Nor is this result surprising. Our "talks," after all, gave us the constant benefits of dialectic, the traditional counterpart of rhetoric.

Coauthorship effected a second, less pleasurable change in our ordinary writing processes. All academic writers are accustomed to the pressure of deadlines, but in single authorship these deadlines are more or less manageable. Coauthorship presented us with completely rigid time-schedules and hence with more pressure than either of us was used to working under: If we had only two-and-a-half days to work together, then we had to come up with a text at that very time. Or else.

We also noted shifts in our usual revision strategies. In the first place, neither of us was accustomed to having *talk* serve as the basis for a majority of the revisions we made. When writing alone, writers usually revise while or after reading. We found also that our individual revising strategies differed substantially: Lisa generally revises and types each section as it is drafted; Andrea favors long periods of staring into space during which she composes various alternative drafts in her head before beginning a long burst of writing. Editing strategies were equally affected. In the coauthored articles, we found ourselves attending much more closely to quotation format and footnote citations in our early drafts than we would ordinarily have done. We were concerned to get the citations exactly right, since our resources were split up between us and our two libraries. Going back to find a missing source would be much more difficult than usual.

These changes in revision strategies reflect, we believe, a change in the rhetorical situations coauthors work within; they must cooperate and collaborate at every turn. Coauthorship, then, demands flexibility and compromise, traits single writers can often eschew. For us, this changed situation meant giving up some of our cherished stylistic tics — like Lisa's dashes — or a favored revision strategy.

The spirit of cooperation and compromise necessary to coauthorship 15 helped us identify two additional ways in which our customary experience with writing was changed. As of this writing, we feel less ego involvement with the pieces we have coauthored than those we have written alone. Hence, we have a greater distance from the work. At this point, we cannot report whether coauthorship gives us more — or less — confidence in the written product. But the questions of confidence and of ego-involvement raise a number of issues, some of which we will address in the concluding section of this essay. Most importantly, we found that coauthoring led us to alter our normal problem-solving styles. In spite of the tendency to work on writing and revising a paper one small section at a time, Lisa's basic approach to problems is broad and synthetic; she ordinarily begins by casting a very wide net. Andrea, on the other hand, approaches problems analytically, narrowing and drawing out implications, searching for closure almost at once. Working as coauthors identified this difference in approach for us, and led us to balance the two styles continually against one another. As a result, one often felt we were circling endlessly, spinning our wheels, while the other alternatively felt we were roaring hell-bent toward our conclusion.

Such changes obviously require significant accommodation and compromise, which can be seen as either advantages or disadvantages of coauthorship. Had we not finally decided on the former, we would not be writing this now. Many others, in similar situations and with similar interests, might choose differently. Indeed, some time in the future our own circumstances or any of a number of other internal or external changes could prompt us to decide that the advantages of coauthorship no longer outweigh the disadvantages. Coauthorship, as we have pointed out, makes the whole process of writing more difficult in some ways. (Perhaps our worst moment occurred one afternoon in Seattle when Lisa revised the mid section of our first project three times — requiring Andrea to change the following pages, which she was working on at the time, substantially every time.) Those problems were offset for us, however, by the stimulation of working with someone who shares the same interests. Even more important to us was the strong sense that in some writing situations we were more likely to achieve a better understanding, generate potentially richer and fresher ideas, and develop a stronger overall argument than we might have done working alone. (We specify "some writing situations" to emphasize that we chose the projects on which we collaborated carefully and for a number of particular reasons; as we have noted, we continued to work on independent research efforts during this period.)

We felt, in short, a kind of synergism when we worked together. This synergism, the sense that by combining our efforts we could in some instances achieve more together than alone, carried us through some difficult times.

But other factors also played a role. Although we knew before we began writing together that we differed in our composing habits and stylistic preferences, we each shared a respect for the other's abilities. Also, each of us knew the other was a person on whom we could count, once committed, to complete a project no matter how much or how violently we differed. Finally, we *wanted* to work together, both because we are friends (who now can deduct the expenses for all the trips we would have taken anyway) and because we feel that collaboration and collegiality are ideals much discussed but little practiced in academic life.

Although we have gone into some detail about our relationship as coauthors, we have by no means given a full accounting of the ups and downs, ins and outs, arguments and counter-arguments involved in working together. (For a while we planned to include process footnotes such as [1]"Believe it or not, Andrea put this dash in here"; or [7]"At this point, Lisa *begged* to be able to type what we had written.") We hope in future research to investigate further the concepts and kinds of coauthorship and the implications coauthoring may hold for our field. In the meantime, we would very much like to hear from other coauthors about their experiences writing with others. Because Andrea lives in the land of lost mail, please write to Lisa. We hope shortly to begin a more formal gathering of data about coauthoring in various disciplines and professions. Even this brief exploration, however, has raised a number of questions which we believe need to be addressed.

(1) What specific features distinguish the processes of co- or group-authoring from those of single authorship? Are these features the same for the three types of coauthorship described above? Can these features of process be linked to any features of the resulting products? In short, how can we best *define* coauthorship?

(2) Is there a limit to how many people can write together? Are projects [20] such as the *Oxford English Dictionary*, Bible, *Short Title Catalogue*, elaborate computer programs, encyclopedias — all often involving more than 100 authors — examples of coauthorship? That is to say, what are the parameters of coauthorship?

(3) In what ways, if any, does co- or group-authorship affect the way we view the traditional rhetor-audience relationship?

(4) How does technology affect the processes of coauthoring? In our experience, writing together would have been much more difficult and much slower without the telephone, xerox, and self-correcting typewriter. Had we each had word processors at home and a computer link, what other differences might we have noted?

(5) What epistemological implications does coauthorship hold for traditional notions of creativity and originality? Our own strong sense that two

may create ideas that neither would have reached alone argues for the value of dialectic as invention.

(6) How might the ethics of coauthorship be examined and defined? We spoke earlier of noting less ego involvement in our coauthored pieces. Perhaps this factor is related to our sense of shared responsibility: If we are wrong, at least we are wrong together. But in cases of group authorship, where does the responsibility lie? Who stands behind the words of a report written by fifteen people? As group authorship becomes more and more the norm in some genres, such questions gather urgency.

(7) Is the emphasis on or weight of various cognitive and rhetorical strategies different when coauthoring than when writing alone? As we noted, many of our customary revision strategies were altered by the process of coauthorship, and the rhetorical situation, which demanded collaboration and compromise, strongly affected our usual processes.

(8) Finally, we were led to think most seriously of the pedagogical implications of coauthorship. What do we know as a discipline about the advantages or disadvantages of having students participate in co- or group-writing? If advantages do exist, don't they in some ways contradict our profession's traditional insistence on students' working alone? And perhaps most importantly, do we have ways to teach students to adjust readily to co- or group-writing tasks?

Although this whimsical report of our experiences as coauthors is severely limited, perhaps serving best to raise questions, the issue of co- and group-authorship in general is not of limited or peripheral significance. As a rule, writers in the humanities have tended to ignore coauthorship, both in writing and in teaching, while colleagues in the sciences and the professions have long used it as a major mode. In view of this anomaly, the images of the lonely writer in a garret, or students hunched against the solitary ordeal of writing proficiency examinations, seem particularly inappropriate. We are, after all, most often responsible for teaching those who go into science and the professions how to write. And when we consider that these students are going into jobs already making use of rapidly developing computer technology, which holds such potential significance for coauthoring, the question for both writers and teachers may be not "Why write together?" but "Why NOT write together?"

Working with the Text

1. For the purposes of the article, Lisa Ede and Andrea Lunsford define *coauthorship* as "conceiving, drafting, and revising a text together" (par. 7). Although the collaborative process they describe is for writing within the field of humanities for an academic audience, many of the elements in their process could be

used by undergraduates coauthoring projects for humanities courses. Based on the article, write directions to be used by pairs of undergraduate writers preparing to coauthor a research project for a history, English, or other humanities class. How should they choose their project partner? What process or work sequence do you recommend? What options do they have for dividing and sharing the work? What attitudes and work habits do they need to bring to the process to make it work? Throughout, focus on the range of options that collaboration can present.

2. For Ede and Lunsford, one of the most essential features of collaboration is talking. "This talking, in fact, seemed to be a necessary part of coauthoring, one that made our writing more productive and efficient" (par. 11). In a brief essay, analyze what they mean by this claim. Why do they start with talking instead of with writing? In what ways does talking move their process forward? What do they accomplish through talking that they wouldn't accomplish through simply revising each other's writing? What work dynamic does talking produce for them?

3. In 2000, Ede and Lunsford were invited to present at a Modern Language Association forum on "Creative Collaboration: Alternatives to the Adversarial Academy." In "Why Write . . . Together?"—written seventeen years earlier—the authors stated that they work together in part "because we feel that collaboration and collegiality are ideals much discussed but little practiced in academic life" (par. 17). Based on evidence from the article, write a brief essay in which you reflect on what you have witnessed of the supposed adversarial dynamics of academic life, where "collaboration and collegiality" are "little practiced." Regard the article as the description of a process that is a distinct alternative to common practice among academics, especially in the humanities. What might cause such an adversarial atmosphere? What form might the conflict take? What might collaboration produce that cannot be accomplished by taking adversarial positions? Why is collaboration far more common in the sciences and more widespread in professional and workplace environments?

From Text to Field

1. Although "Why Write . . . Together?" describes collaboration in academic writing within the humanities, many elements in the process experienced by the authors can be found in any form of collaboration. Write an essay in which you reflect on a collaborative effort of your own that involved processes or dynamics similar to those described by Ede and Lunsford. You might have been involved in a collaborative effort such as a group project in a class, a music or drama production, a sport, a volunteer activity, or an activity for an organization.

How did the process unfold? What were the work dynamics among the group members? How was it different from pursuing the same activity as an individual? Did you consider it to be a success? Why or why not?

2. In a group of two or three students, cowrite a response to one of the questions in the "Working with the Text" section. Think of coauthorship as defined by Ede and Lunsford: "conceiving, drafting, and revising a text together" (par. 7). After you have completed your text, discuss your process with your cowriters. Review the article for ways to reflect on your process. What steps did you take? What difficulties did you encounter? How was working together on the text different from working alone? To what extent did you experience the "synergism" described by the authors? Be prepared to describe your process to the rest of the class.

3. Whether or not you have experience in collaborative writing, you probably have an opinion about whether or not you would pursue it, if given the choice. Write an essay in which you analyze your attitude toward coauthorship. In what situations, if any, would you choose to write collaboratively? If you would never choose to collaborate, why not? If you would choose to collaborate in certain situations, why do you think those situations would lend themselves to coauthoring? What conditions would have to exist for you to have confidence that the process would succeed?

4. Ede and Lunsford wrote "Why Write . . . Together?" before they had researched the collaborative process extensively. The questions at the end of the article, based on their early experience of working together, were a starting place for their later research. In a group of two or three, choose one of those questions. Based on the combined experience and judgment of the group members, collaboratively write an essay that offers an initial answer to the question. For each assertion you make, explain why you have come to that conclusion, using reasoning as well as evidence from your personal experience and observation.

The Art of Collaborative Learning: Making the Most of Knowledgeable Peers

Kenneth A. Bruffee

Most students pursue higher education as preparation for work in the "real world." As Kenneth A. Bruffee observes, the fact that the real world works primarily through collaboration has prompted teachers in colleges and universities to explore collaborative learning as a means for preparing students for professional life — and academic success. Studies indicate that not only do students learn the art of collaboration, they gain knowledge and judgment more quickly and effectively.

According to Bruffee, professional collaboration and collaborative learning work because knowledge itself is the result of our ongoing work with each other. In terms used by the social constructionists who have influenced Bruffee's thinking, knowledge is "socially constructed." For Bruffee, knowledge as a social construct means that "learning occurs among persons rather than between a person and things." This calls into question the authority we have traditionally assigned to some kinds of knowledge as being entirely objective and absolute and has us rethink the authority we traditionally grant to the teachers who convey that knowledge. Drawing on research in teaching and learning, Bruffee subscribes to the notion that learning "does not involve people's assimilation of knowledge, it involves people's assimilation into communities of knowledgeable peers" (par. 24).

Collaborative learning has been an area of specialization for Bruffee throughout his academic career. In addition to publishing articles and books — including *Collaborative Learning: Higher Education, Interdependence, and the Authority of Knowledge* (2nd ed., 1990) — he has led colloquia on collaborative learning, liberal education, and the authority of knowledge at a number of prominent colleges and universities. Bruffee is professor of English and director of the Scholars Program and the Honors Academy at Brooklyn College, City University of New York.

The essay reprinted here was originally published in 1987 in *Change*, a bimonthly magazine that focuses on contemporary issues in higher education. It was subsequently reprinted in 1994 in a special retrospective issue of *Change*. The author has kindly included a short bibliography that notes recent work on collaborative learning.

Late last spring, a colleague of mine at a university out West — I'll call him Jim — wrote and asked if I would read a manuscript of his. He felt he was finally ready for someone to take a close look at it.

Jim's an old friend. I dashed off a note saying of course I'd read it, with pleasure. At the beginning of June, which luckily for both of us was right at the end of exams, I got a weighty package in the mail — 279 pages plus notes. I read it, scribbled clouds of barely decipherable marginal notes, and drafted a six-page letter to Jim congratulating him on first-rate work, suggesting a few changes and mentioning one or two issues he might think through a bit further.

He phoned to thank me when he got the letter and asked some questions. We then spent an hour or so discussing these questions and supporting AT&T in the manner to which it has become accustomed.

Before the snow blows, I expect I shall see some of Jim's manuscript again. I doubt that he needs another reading, but I'm happy to do it if he wants me to. I learned a lot reading his book. We both learned something talking out the few stickier points in it. Anyway, I owe him one. He did the same for me five years ago, when I was thrashing about in the terminal throes of the book I was finishing. His name appeared prominently on my acknowledgments page; I suppose mine will appear prominently on his.

The experience I have just described is familiar to most readers of 5 *Change*. To enjoy such an experience, you don't have to write a book. All you have to do is work with an intelligent, compatible committee on an interesting grant proposal or a new development plan for your college. You know how it can go. Joe gets an idea and sketches it out in a couple of pages. Mary says, hey, wait a minute — that makes me think of . . . . Then Fred says, but look, if we change this or add that. . . . In the end everyone, with a little help from his and her friends, exceeds what anyone could possibly have learned or accomplished alone.

If I'm right that this kind of experience is familiar, then no one reading this article is a stranger to collaborative learning, however strange the term may be. Jim and I are peers. When Jim asked me to read his work and I agreed, we became an autonomous collaborative learning group of two with the task of revising and developing the written product of one of its members.

The term "collaborative learning" has become increasingly familiar today because it is applied not only to voluntary associations such as my work with Jim, but also to teaching that tries to imitate that experience in college and university classrooms. Teachers of writing at institutions throughout the country are discovering that teaching students in a variety of ways to work productively on their writing demonstrably improves students' work.

And it is not just writing teachers who are interested. Clark Bouton and Russell Y. Clark's useful book, *Learning in Groups,* reports on the way collaborative learning is being applied in subjects from business management to medicine to math. And there is at least one physics lab manual in the country (at Montana State University) that presents an extended rationale of collaborative learning on its front cover.

Perhaps more to the point for some of us, at least one trenchant article exists that explains collaborative learning for the benefit of faculty and administrators who find themselves evaluating teachers. Harvey S. Wiener's "Collaborative Learning in the Classroom: A Guide to Evaluation" (*College English* 48) suggests ways to tell when teachers are using collaborative learning most effectively. It is also, therefore, a useful guide to, effective use of collaborative learning for teachers.

Admittedly, there is not much research to date on the effects of collaborative learning in college and university education. But recent work on its effect in primary and secondary schools is relevant. Surveys of research by David Johnson (*Psychological Bulletin* 89) and by Shlomo Sharan (*Review of Educational Research* 50) tend to support the experience of college and university instructors who have used collaborative learning. Students learn better through noncompetitive collaborative group work than in classrooms that are highly individualized and competitive. Robert E. Slavin's *Cooperative Learning* reports similar results.

Interest in collaborative learning in colleges and schools is motivated in part by these results. It is motivated also by the observation that the rest of the world now works collaboratively almost as a universal principle. Japanese "Theory-Z" quality circles on the factory floor aside, there is hardly a bank, legal firm, or industrial management team that strives — much less dares — to proceed in the old-fashioned individualistic manner. Physicians are increasingly collaborative, too, although they prefer to call it "consultation." At Harvard Medical School, 25 percent of each entering class currently studies in collaborative groups, bypassing systematic lecture courses almost entirely.

Interest in collaborative learning is motivated also by recent challenges to our understanding of what knowledge is. This challenge is being felt throughout the academic disciplines. That is, collaborative learning is related to the social constructionist views promulgated by, among others, the philosopher Richard Rorty (*Philosophy and the Mirror of Nature*) and the anthropologist Clifford Geertz. These writers say (as Geertz puts it in his recent book, *Local Knowledge*) that "the way we think now" differs in essential ways from the way we thought in the past. Social constructionists tend to assume that knowledge is a social construct and that, as the historian of science Thomas Kuhn has put it, all knowledge, including scientific knowledge, "is intrinsically the common property of a group or else nothing at all." (See Bruffee, "Social Construction, Language, and the Authority of Knowledge: A Bibliographical Essay," *College English*, vol. 48, December 1986, pp. 773–90.)

Collaborative learning is related to these conceptual changes by virtue of the fact that it assumes learning occurs among persons rather than between a person and things. It even turns out that some teachers who are using collaborative learning have found that social constructionist assumptions enhance their understanding of what they are trying to do and give them a better chance of doing it well.

So, although the term *collaborative learning* may be unfamiliar for some, collaborative learning itself is not new. Our understanding of its importance to higher education began in the late 1950s with Theodore Newcomb's work on peer-group influence among college students (*College Peer Groups, The American College*, ed. Nevitt Sanford) and with M. L. J. Abercrombie's research on educating medical students at University Hospital, University of London. Newcomb demonstrated that peer-group influence is a powerful but wasted resource in higher education. Abercrombie's book, *The Anatomy of Judgment*, showed medical students learning the key element in successful medical practice, diagnosis — that is, medical judgment — more quickly and accurately when they worked collaboratively in small groups than when they worked individually.

Abercrombie began her important study by observing the scene that most 15 of us think is typical of medical education: the group of medical students with a teaching physician gathered around a ward bed to diagnose a patient. Then she made a slight but crucial change in the way that such a scene is usually played out. Instead of asking each individual medical student in the group to diagnose the patient on his or her own, Abercrombie asked the whole group to examine the patient together, discuss the case as a group, and arrive at a consensus — a single diagnosis agreed to by all.

When she did this, what she found was that students who learned diagnosis collaboratively in this way acquired better medical judgment faster than individual students working alone.

With the exception of small, recently instituted experimental programs at the medical schools of the University of New Mexico and Harvard University,

TRANSFER OF OWNERSHIP OR RIGHTS IN TRADEMARKS

Assignment of Marks

A trademark or service mark may be transferred or assigned to another *if* the goodwill symbolized by the mark is assigned with it. TMEP 501.06 provides that partial assignments are permissible. Thus, a sole owner may assign 50 percent of his or her interest in a mark to another. The more common approach is an assignment or transfer of all of one's rights in a mark to another.

Because a mark is used to identify the source of goods and services, rather than existing as an independent object of property, it is inseparable from the goodwill of the business to which it applies. Thus, an arrangement by which a mark is assigned without the business goodwill that the mark symbolizes, called an **assignment in gross,** is ineffective to transfer trademark rights, and the new owner who begins using the mark cannot claim the original owner's use date for purposes of establishing priority in the mark. The new owner, the "assignee," will establish its own first use date upon using the mark. Thus, valuable trademark rights could be lost if a third party begins using a mark *after* the assignor's original use date but *before* the date of an assignment in gross to the assignee. This third party would have priority over the assignee and could prevent use of a confusingly similar mark by the assignee. To prevent such a situation, the parties should enter into a written **assignment** agreement that recites that the mark is being transferred together with the goodwill of the portion of the business associated with the mark. A recitation that goodwill is transferred with the mark is usually sufficient to ensure the assignee can capture or retain the original date of first use. Assignments of marks in which federal rights are claimed must be in writing (15 U.S.C. § 1060(a)).

The transfer of common law rights to a mark does not require a written agreement. If the assignment is oral, its existence may be proven by clear and uncontradicted testimony. However, while an oral agreement to transfer a common law mark is valid, a written agreement lends certainty and should always be used. Moreover, the assignment document should recite that the mark and the goodwill symbolized by the mark are being transferred to ensure there is no loss of trademark rights. The assignment document itself is a relatively simple agreement (see Exhibit 5–3).

An entire business need not be transferred with a mark. A trademark owner may assign a mark used in connection with specific goods or services and retain other marks used in connection with other goods or services. If all of the assets of a business are sold, however, it is assumed that all marks and their goodwill pass with the other assets, even if they are not specifically mentioned in the sales documents.

In many cases, owners prepare written assignments on a later date to reflect an assignment that actually occurred earlier. For example, if Watson Inc. transferred or assigned its mark TAYLOR TIGER to another party but the parties neglected to prepare the actual assignment document at the time of transfer, Watson would prepare a document reflecting such an event. Called a **Nunc Pro Tunc Assignment** (literally, "now for then"), the document merely recites that the assignment occurred on an earlier date but reflects an earlier transfer or assignment.

If the mark assigned has been registered or is the subject of a pending use-based application at the PTO, the assignment must be in writing and should be filed or "recorded" with the PTO. Although there is no requirement that the assignment be recorded to be effective, **recordation** is a relatively simple procedure that affords several advantages:

Abercrombie's conclusion has had little impact as yet on medical school faculties anywhere, in Britain or America. But when I read the book in 1972, a dozen years or so after it was published, her conclusion had an immediate and, I believe, positive impact on my thinking about university instruction and, eventually, on the role I see myself in as a classroom instructor.

The aspect of Abercrombie's book that I found most illuminating was her evidence that learning diagnostic judgment is not an individual process but a social one. Learning judgment, she saw, patently occurs on an axis drawn not between individuals and things, but among people. But in making this observation, she had to acknowledge that there is something wrong with our normal cognitive assumptions about the nature of knowledge. Cognitive assumptions, she says, disregard "the biological fact that [the human being] . . . is a social animal." "How [do] human relationships," that is, relations among persons, she asked, "influence the receipt of information about apparently nonpersonal events?"

In trying to answer this question, Abercrombie makes the brilliant observation that, in general, people learn judgment best in groups; she infers from this observation that we learn judgment well in groups because we tend to talk each other out of our unshared biases and presuppositions. And in passing, she drops an invaluable hint: The social process of learning judgment that she has observed seems to have something to do with language and with "interpretation."

These three principles underlie the practice of collaborative learning. 20 One thing that college and university instructors most hope to do through collaborative learning is increase their students' ability to exercise judgment within the teacher's field of expertise, whatever that field is.

But there is today another thing that instructors hope to do through collaborative learning. They hope to raise their students' level of social maturity as exercised in their intellectual lives. In doing so, instructors are trying to prepare their students for the "real world." They are preparing them to enter law, medicine, architecture, banking, engineering, research science — any field, in fact, that depends on effective interdependence and consultation for excellence.

This discovery that excellent undergraduate education also depends on effective interdependence and consultation awaited the work of William Perry. Perry's book, *Forms of Intellectual and Ethical Development in the College Years*, has made an indelible impression on the thinking of many college and university instructors, but not in every instance for the right reason. Like Abercrombie, Perry makes cognitive assumptions about the nature of knowledge, and most readers to date have found his developmental "scheme" of greatest interest.

Yet Perry himself is not entirely comfortable with the cognitive assumptions underlying his scheme. He has read Thomas Kuhn's *The Structure of Scientific Revolutions,* and he acknowledges that our current view that "knowledge is contextual and relative" is only the most recent phase in a tendency toward the assimilation of cultural diversity that needs for its fulfillment "a new social mind."

As a result, again like Abercrombie, Perry implies that the central educational issues today hinge on social relations, not on cognitive ones: relations among persons, not relations between persons and things. Learning as we must understand it today, he concludes, does not involve people's assimilation of knowledge, it involves people's assimilation into communities of knowledgeable peers. Liberal education today must be regarded as a process of leaving one community of knowledgeable peers and joining another.

Perry's discomfort with this conclusion when it comes to educational practice, however, suggests that he himself may never have quite recognized the full implications of his study. He denies that the creating of communities of knowledgeable peers among students is a legitimate part of rationally and consciously organized university education. He prefers to rely on "spontaneity" to organize knowledge communities among students. He politely dismisses as unprofessional attempts to foster communities among students by using "particular procedures or rituals." Students must independently manage their "identification with the college community" as they go about "divorcing themselves" from the communities they have left behind.

Fortunately, Perry quotes liberally from his raw material—statements made by a sizable number of informants among the Harvard College undergraduate body. And these undergraduates are not at all as ambivalent as Perry seems to be about regarding learning as a social process. Many of them see their undergraduate education quite explicitly as a difficult, perhaps even treacherous passage from one homogeneous community—the one they came from — to another homogeneous community — the college community of their student peers.

> Collaborative learning . . . assumes learning occurs among persons rather than between a person and things.

This "marrying into" the new community of students at college is clearly, as the students describe it, an informal, autonomous variety of collaborative learning that challenges students to define their individuality not as starkly and lonesomely independent, but as interdependent members of their new undergraduate community.

The more formal varieties of collaborative learning organized by instructors in classrooms imitate this informal type. And they imitate the "real world" interdependence and consultation that goes on in much business and professional work, including the work my friend Jim and I did together on his book and mine. In classroom collaborative learning, typically, students organized by the teacher into small groups discuss a topic proposed by the teacher with the purpose of arriving at consensus, much as Abercrombie's medical students practiced diagnosis on patients chosen by the teaching physician. Or students may edit each other's writing, or tutor each other, or develop and carry through assigned (or group-designed and teacher-approved) projects together.

But this classroom work, however collaborative, differs in striking ways from autonomous, "real world" interdependence. Classroom collaborative learning is inevitably no more than semiautonomous, because students don't usually organize their own groups or choose their own tasks, as Jim and I did. In most cases, teachers design and structure students' work for maximum learning as part of a course of study. And teachers evaluate the work when it is completed, comparing it with professional standards and the work other students have done, both currently and in the past.

Now, to be accurate to a fault, of course, Jim and I were not an absolutely 30 autonomous group either, any more than any interdependent consultative professional work is. Like most independently organized groups — such as political clubs, golf foursomes, and sand-lot baseball teams — he and I organized our working group on our own initiative for our own purposes, but we played the game, so to speak, by a set of rules we held in common with many other such groups.

The mores, conventions, values, and goals of our professional organization (in our case, the Modern Language Association), of that motley class of human beings called "university faculty," of promotion and tenure committees whose values are probably similar at Jim's college and mine, and so on — these large institutional communities determine to some extent what Jim and I did and said, how we did it and said it, and in point of fact, that we were doing it and saying it at all. Institutional motives and constraints always apply when people prepare themselves to take a hand in what is going on in the prevailing economic, legal, and educational world.

Formed within the immediate confines of a college's institutional structure, however, working groups in a collaborative learning classroom are clearly semiautonomous. Like the New York Yankees, a Boy Scout troop, or the United States Supreme Court, their collaboration is organized by a larger institutional community and with its sanction. Group members abide by the conventions, mores, values, and goals of that institution. The autonomy of classroom groups derives from the fact that once the tasks are set and the groups organized, instructors step back, leaving peers to work in groups or pairs to organize, govern, and pace their work by themselves and to negotiate its outcome.

That this partial autonomy is the key to the impact of collaborative learning is evident when we compare semiautonomous work with work that is entirely nonautonomous. The work of nonautonomous groups cannot reasonably be called collaborative learning at all. Like life in a Trappist monastery or an army platoon, in which activity is rigorously controlled, classroom group work is nonautonomous whenever instructors do not step back from the groups of working students, but rather "sit in" on them or "hover," predetermining the outcome of the work and maintaining the students' direct dependency on the teacher's presence, resources, and expertise.

Degree of autonomy is the key to collaborative learning because the issue that collaborative learning addresses is the way authority is distributed and experienced in college and university classrooms. It would be disingenuous to evade the fact that collaborative learning challenges our traditional view of the instructor's authority in a classroom and the way that authority is exercised.

This issue is much too complex to go into here. But perhaps we can get a provocative glimpse of the possible rewards that might accrue from pursuing it further if we take a brief look at the nature and source of the authority of knowledge in any autonomous working group. Return for a moment to my friend Jim and me at work together on his manuscript. What was the source of the authority exercised in that work? Where was it placed and how did it get there? Not to put too fine a point on it, where did I get the authority to comment on his writing? 35

The answer, of course, is that Jim and I together generated the authority in our group of two. And to occur at all in this way, that generation of authority required certain conditions. For starters, we like each other. We have read each other's stuff. We respect each other's intelligence. We have similar interests. We have worked together professionally in other circumstances. In short, we were *willing* to collaborate.

It was under these conditions that *Jim granted me* authority over his work by asking me to read it. The authority of my knowledge with regard to his manuscript originated primarily with him. I mean "primarily" here in the strongest possible sense. My authority began with his request, and the principal claim to the validity of my authority resulted from that request.

Furthermore, and equally important, when I responded positively, *I agreed to take on and assert* authority relative to him and his work. In that sense, the authority of my knowledge with regard to his manuscript originated primarily not only with his granting me the authority, but also with my accepting it, both, of course, in a context of friendliness and good grace.

Willingness to grant authority, willingness to take on and exercise authority, and a context of friendliness and good grace are the three ingredients essential to successful autonomous collaboration. If any of these three is missing or flags, collaboration fails. These three ingredients are essential also to successful semiautonomous collaboration, such as classroom collaborative learning.

But when instructors use semiautonomous groups in classes, the stark reality is that willingness to grant authority, willingness to take it on and exercise it, and a context of friendliness and good grace are severely compromised. Classroom authority does not necessarily begin — as Jim's and mine began — with the participants' (that is, the students') willing consent to grant authority and exercise it. In a classroom, authority still begins in most cases with the representative or agent of the institution, the instructor. Furthermore, except in highly unusual classrooms, most students start the semester as relative strangers. They do not begin, as Jim and I did, as friends. It is not surprising that, as a result, in many classrooms students may at first be wary and not overly eager to collaborate.

That is, collaborative learning has to begin in most cases with an attempt to *reacculturate* students. Given most students' almost exclusively traditional experience of classroom authority, they have to learn, sometimes against considerable resistance, to grant authority to a peer ("What right has he got to . . . ?"), instead of the teacher. And students have to learn to take on the authority granted by a peer ("What right have I got to . . . ?"), and to exercise that authority responsibly and helpfully in the interest of a peer.

Skillfully organized, collaborative learning can itself reacculturate students in this way. Once the task is set and the groups organized, collaborative learning places students working in groups on their own to interpret the task and invent or adapt a language and means to get the work done. When the instructor is absent, the chain of hierarchical institutional authority is for the moment broken. Students are free to revert to the collaborative peership that they are quite used to exercising in other kinds of extracurricular activities from which faculty are usually absent.

Of course, students do not always exercise effective collaborative peership in classrooms, especially at first, because they have all so thoroughly internalized our long-prevailing academic prohibitions against it. And it need hardly be added that nonautonomous groups, in which the instructor insists on remaining in direct authority even after the task is set and the groups organized, cannot reacculturate students in these ways, because the chain of hierarchical institutional authority is never broken.

Because we usually identify the authority of knowledge in a classroom with the instructor's authority, the brief hiatus in the hierarchical chain of authority in the classroom that is at the heart of collaborative learning in the long run also challenges, willy-nilly, our traditional view of the nature and source of the knowledge itself. Collaborative learning tends, that is, to take its toll on the cognitive understanding of knowledge that most of us assume unquestioningly. Teachers and students alike may find themselves asking the sorts of questions Abercrombie asked. How can knowledge gained through a social process have a source that is not itself also social?

This is another aspect of collaborative learning too complex to go into 45
here. But raising it momentarily gives us a hint about why collaborative learning may empower students to work more successfully beyond the confines of college or university classrooms. Collaborative learning calls on levels of ingenuity and inventiveness that many students never knew they had. And it teaches effective interdependence in an increasingly collaborative world that today requires greater flexibility and adaptability to change than ever before.

Bibliography

Brown, John Seely, and Paul Duguid. *The Social Life of Information*. Boston: Harvard Business School Press, 2000.

Bruffee, Kenneth A. *A Short Course in Writing: Composition, Collaborative Learning, and Constructive Reading*. 5th ed. New York: Pearson Longman, 2006.

Cohen, Elizabeth G. *Designing Groupwork: Strategies for the Heterogeneous Classroom*. 2nd ed. New York: Teachers College, Columbia University Press, 1994.

Farrell, Michael P. *Collaborative Circles: Friendship Dynamics and Creative Work*. Chicago: University of Chicago Press, 2001.

Mazur, Eric. *Peer Instruction: A User's Manual*. Upper Saddle River, NJ: Prentice Hall, 1997.

Working with the Text

1. According to Kenneth A. Bruffee, his approach to collaborative learning assumes that "learning occurs among persons rather than between a person and things" (par. 13). Write a brief essay in which you reflect on this rather pithy statement, analyzing Bruffee's view of what knowledge is and how we acquire it. Point to examples in Bruffee's essay, and in your own experience, that might support this view.

2. Throughout the article, Bruffee is concerned not with the passive acquisition of knowledge but with "judgment." In a brief essay, explore what Bruffee means by judgment. Why might collaborative learning and assimilation into a community of knowledgeable peers be essential for the cultivation of judgment?

3. Bruffee champions collaborative learning as an approach that reflects the "real world" more accurately than traditional classroom teaching methods. Choose one or more of his examples of collaborative learning in various professional and work settings. In a brief essay, describe in more detail how you think collaborative learning would play itself out in a given setting. To prompt ideas on

ways collaborative learning might be used in a setting, refer to Bruffee's more general descriptions of how the process works.

From Text to Field

1. Forms of collaborative learning have now been used in elementary, secondary, and university classrooms for a number of years. Based on Bruffee's descriptions of collaborative learning, recall how it was used in one of your classrooms. In a personal essay, describe the experience, reflecting on how you responded to the approach and how it affected your learning process. If your experience with collaborative learning was positive, explore in some detail why that was the case. Do your reasons support or extend Bruffee's analysis? If your experience was less than positive (and, if so, you are not alone), explore why it did not support your learning process.

2. It is now widely accepted that students have different styles of learning. To what extent is collaborative learning one of several styles, or might it serve as a basis for all learning styles? When might some students not be well served by learning in groups? Are there learning tasks or disciplines in which collaborative learning is either particularly appropriate or, on occasion, inappropriate?

3. Bruffee observes that college and university teachers use collaborative learning for a number of reasons: to "increase their students' ability to exercise judgment within the teacher's field of expertise," to "raise their students' level of social maturity as exercised in their intellectual lives," and to prepare them to enter any field "that depends on effective interdependence and consultation for excellence" (pars. 20–21). In an essay, reflect on the extent to which collaborative learning as Bruffee describes it would prepare you for professional work in a field you are interested in entering or exploring. In what ways would collaborative learning help you enter that field? In what ways do you think other learning methods might be more effective? Be as specific as you can about the kinds of knowledge and skill required by the field.

4. In the latter part of the article, Bruffee raises issues that he says are too complex to address in the context of the article. One is the issue of classroom authority: "collaborative learning challenges our traditional view of the instructor's authority in a classroom and the way that authority is exercised" (par. 34). He raises this issue in the course of discussing the effects of different levels of autonomy for students doing group work. Another issue is the source of knowledge itself: "How can knowledge gained through a social process have a source that is not itself also social?" (par. 44). As you reread the article, consider these issues in light of your own experience and reasoning. Write an essay on one of these two questions, fleshing out views that Bruffee only touches on.

The Talent Myth:
Are Smart People Overrated?

Malcolm Gladwell

Business cultures are often influenced by, if not created by, the latest and hottest management theory. Malcolm Gladwell examines what he calls "the new orthodoxy of American management," which claims that competitiveness in today's economy hinges on hiring highly talented people and giving them free rein. Through the first half of 2001, one of the most enthusiastic — and, by most accounts, wildly successful — proponents of "the talent mind-set" was the corporate giant Enron. By 2002, Enron, along with its prestigious auditor, Arthur Andersen, were in shambles and its investment bankers were under investigation. Gladwell poses the question, "What if Enron failed not in spite of its talent mind-set but because of it?" We tend to think that smart people make organizations smart; Gladwell asks us to consider that an effective organization may well make people smart. In other words, the right kind of collaboration can trump individual talent.

Malcolm Gladwell has been a staff writer for the *New Yorker* since 1996 and wrote for the *Washington Post* from 1987 to 1996. The subtitles for his articles reflect his fascination with the many faces of our culture, from "The paradoxes of intelligence reform," "Big business and the myth of the lone investor," and "How far can airline safety go?" to "How caffeine created the modern world," "What does *Saturday Night Live* have in common with German philosophy?" and "The disposable diaper and the meaning of progress."

Building on his success at the *New Yorker,* Gladwell has recently published two well-received books. *The Tipping Point: How Little Things Can Make a Big Difference* (2002) explores the notion that ideas, products, messages, and behaviors can spread in much the same way that viruses do. That is, when even a few people start behaving differently, their preferences and ideas can spread outward until a "tipping point" is reached, one that can change the world. Drawing on research from a wide range of fields, *Blink: The Power of Thinking without Thinking* (2005) explores our "adaptive unconscious" that enables us to make snap — and often very perceptive and correct — judgments. The essay reprinted here was first published in the July 22, 2002, issue of the *New Yorker*.

Five years ago, several executives at McKinsey & Company, America's largest and most prestigious management-consulting firm, launched what they called the War for Talent. Thousands of questionnaires were sent to managers across the country. Eighteen companies were singled out for special attention, and the consultants spent up to three days at each firm, interviewing everyone from the CEO down to the human-resources staff. McKinsey wanted to document how the top-performing companies in America differed from other firms in the way they handle matters like hiring and promotion. But, as the consultants sifted through the piles of reports and questionnaires and interview transcripts, they grew convinced that the difference between winners and losers was more profound than they had realized. "We looked at one another and suddenly the light bulb blinked on," the three consultants who headed the project — Ed Michaels, Helen Handfield-Jones, and Beth Axelrod — write in their new book, also called *The War for Talent*. The very best companies, they concluded, had leaders who were obsessed with the talent issue. They recruited ceaselessly, finding and hiring as many top performers as possible. They singled out and segregated their stars, rewarding them disproportionately, and pushing them into ever more senior positions. "Bet on the natural athletes, the ones with the strongest intrinsic skills," the authors approvingly quote one senior General Electric executive as saying. "Don't be afraid to promote stars without specifically relevant experience, seemingly over their heads." Success in the modern economy, according to Michaels, Handfield-Jones, and Axelrod, requires "the talent mind-set": the "deep-seated belief that having better talent at all levels is how you outperform your competitors."

This "talent mind-set" is the new orthodoxy of American management. It is the intellectual justification for why such a high premium is placed on degrees from first-tier business schools, and why the compensation packages for top executives have become so lavish. In the modern corporation, the system is considered only as strong as its stars, and, in the past few years, this message has been preached by consultants and management gurus all over the world. None, however, have spread the word quite so ardently as McKinsey, and, of all its clients, one firm took the talent mind-set closest to heart. It was a company where McKinsey conducted twenty separate projects, where McKinsey's billings topped ten million dollars a year, where a McKinsey director regularly attended board meetings, and where the CEO himself was a former McKinsey partner. The company, of course, was Enron.

The Enron scandal is now almost a year old. The reputations of Jeffrey Skilling and Kenneth Lay, the company's two top executives, have been destroyed. Arthur Andersen, Enron's auditor, has been driven out of business, and now investigators have turned their attention to Enron's investment bankers. The one Enron partner that has escaped largely unscathed is McKinsey, which is odd, given that it essentially created the blueprint for the Enron culture. Enron was the ultimate "talent" company. When Skilling started the corporate division known as Enron Capital and Trade, in 1990, he "decided to bring in a steady stream of the very best college and MBA graduates he could find to stock the company with talent," Michaels, Handfield-Jones, and Axelrod tell us. During the nineties, Enron was bringing in 250 newly minted MBAs a year. "We had these things called Super Saturdays," one former Enron manager recalls. "I'd interview some of these guys who were fresh out of Harvard, and these kids could blow me out of the water. They knew things I'd never heard of." Once at Enron, the top performers were rewarded inordinately, and promoted without regard for seniority or experience. Enron was a star system. "The only thing that differentiates Enron from our competitors is our people, our talent," Lay, Enron's former chairman and CEO, told the McKinsey consultants when they came to the company's headquarters, in Houston. Or, as another senior Enron executive put it to Richard Foster, a McKinsey partner who celebrated Enron in his 2001 book, *Creative Destruction*, "We hire very smart people and we pay them more than they think they are worth."

The management of Enron, in other words, did exactly what the consultants at McKinsey said that companies ought to do in order to succeed in the modern economy. It hired and rewarded the very best and the very brightest—and it is now in bankruptcy. The reasons for its collapse are complex, needless to say. But what if Enron failed not in spite of its talent mind-set but because of it? What if smart people are overrated?

At the heart of the McKinsey vision is a process that the War for Talent advo- 5 cates refer to as "differentiation and affirmation." Employers, they argue, need to sit down once or twice a year and hold a "candid, probing, no-holds-barred debate about each individual," sorting employees into A, B, and C groups. The As must be challenged and disproportionately rewarded. The Bs need to be encouraged and affirmed. The Cs need to shape up or be shipped out. Enron followed this advice almost to the letter, setting up internal Performance Review Committees. The members got together twice a year,

- it clarifies the records of the PTO and affords notice to all of the identity of the owner of the mark;
- it allows the new owner to commence and defend actions at the PTO in its name;
- it ensures that documents and notices issued by the PTO will be sent to and will identify the correct owner;
- it simplifies postregistration procedures inasmuch as section 8 affidavits will be rejected unless their identification of the trademark owner is consistent with the PTO records; and

- it provides public notice of the fact of the assignment such that later purchasers of the mark are bound by it.

Although common law marks, registered marks, and marks that are the subject of pending use-based applications can be assigned, marks that are the subject of intent-to-use (ITU) applications cannot be assigned prior to filing an amendment to allege use or a statement of use with the PTO verifying that the mark is in use in commerce, unless the mark is being assigned to a successor of the business of the applicant to which the mark pertains and the

EXHIBIT 5–3
Assignment
of Trademark

WHEREAS, Hollis & Sanders Co., a corporation organized under the laws of the State of California, located and doing business at 890 Second Avenue, San Diego, CA 92117 ("Assignor"), is the owner of U.S. Trademark Registration No. 1,908,457 for the mark BLAST RIDER issued December 14, 1996, for entertainment services in I.C. 41 in the United States (the "Mark"); and

WHEREAS, Watson Inc., a corporation organized under the laws of the State of Delaware, located and doing business at 885 Third Avenue, 24th Floor, New York, NY 10022 ("Assignee"), desires to acquire all of Assignor's rights in and to the Mark and the goodwill symbolized thereby;

NOW, THEREFORE, for good and valuable consideration, the receipt and sufficiency of which are hereby acknowledged, Assignor hereby sells, assigns, transfers, and conveys to Assignee all of its right, title, and interest in and to the Mark, together with the goodwill of the business associated with the Mark, the same to be held and enjoyed by Assignee, its successors, assigns, and other legal representatives.

Assignor further assigns to Assignee all right to sue for and receive all damages accruing from past infringements of the Mark herein assigned.

Assignor represents it is the legal owner of all right, title, and interest in and to the Mark and has the right to assign the Mark and that there are no pending legal proceedings involving the Mark.

This Assignment shall be binding upon the parties, their successors and/or assigns, and all others acting by, through, with, or under their direction, and all those in privity therewith.

Assignee agrees to cooperate with Assignor and take any further action and execute any documents required to effect the purposes of this Assignment.

Hollis & Sanders Co.   Watson Inc.

By: _____   By: _____

Title: _____   Title: _____

Date: _____   Date: _____

and graded each person in their section on ten separate criteria, using a scale of one to five. The process was called "rank and yank." Those graded at the top of their unit received bonuses two-thirds higher than those in the next 30 percent; those who ranked at the bottom received no bonuses and no extra stock options — and in some cases were pushed out.

How should that ranking be done? Unfortunately, the McKinsey consultants spend very little time discussing the matter. One possibility is simply to hire and reward the smartest people. But the link between, say, IQ and job performance is distinctly underwhelming. On a scale where 0.1 or below means virtually no correlation and 0.7 or above implies a strong correlation (your height, for example, has a 0.7 correlation with your parents' height), the correlation between IQ and occupational success is between 0.2 and 0.3. "What IQ doesn't pick up is effectiveness at common-sense sorts of things, especially working with people," Richard Wagner, a psychologist at Florida State University, says. "In terms of how we evaluate schooling, everything is about working by yourself. If you work with someone else, it's called cheating. Once you get out in the real world, everything you do involves working with other people."

Wagner and Robert Sternberg, a psychologist at Yale University, have developed tests of this practical component, which they call "tacit knowledge." Tacit knowledge involves things like knowing how to manage yourself and others, and how to navigate complicated social situations. Here is a question from one of their tests:

> You have just been promoted to head of an important department in your organization. The previous head has been transferred to an equivalent position in a less important department. Your understanding of the reason for the move is that the performance of the department as a whole has been mediocre. There have not been any glaring deficiencies, just a perception of the department as so-so rather than very good. Your charge is to shape up the department. Results are expected quickly. Rate the quality of the following strategies for succeeding at your new position.
>
> a. Always delegate to the most junior person who can be trusted with the task.
> b. Give your superiors frequent progress reports.
> c. Announce a major reorganization of the department that includes getting rid of whomever you believe to be "dead wood."
> d. Concentrate more on your people than on the tasks to be done.
> e. Make people feel completely responsible for their work.

Wagner finds that how well people do on a test like this predicts how well they will do in the workplace: good managers pick (b) and (e); bad managers tend to pick (c). Yet there's no clear connection between such tacit knowledge and other forms of knowledge and experience. The process of assessing ability in the workplace is a lot messier than it appears.

An employer really wants to assess not potential but performance. Yet that's just as tricky. In *The War for Talent*, the authors talk about how the Royal Air Force used the A, B, and C ranking system for its pilots during the Battle of Britain. But ranking fighter pilots — for whom there are a limited and relatively objective set of performance criteria (enemy kills, for example, and the ability to get their formations safely home) — is a lot easier than assessing how the manager of a new unit is doing at, say, marketing or business development. And whom do you ask to rate the manager's performance? Studies show that there is very little correlation between how someone's peers rate him and how his boss rates him. The only rigorous way to assess performance, according to human-resources specialists, is to use criteria that are as specific as possible. Managers are supposed to take detailed notes on their employees throughout the year, in order to remove subjective personal reactions from the process of assessment. You can grade someone's performance only if you *know* their performance. And, in the freewheeling culture of Enron, this was all but impossible. People deemed "talented" were constantly being pushed into new jobs and given new challenges. Annual turnover from promotions was close to 20 percent. Lynda Clemmons, the so-called weather babe who started Enron's weather derivatives business, jumped, in seven quick years, from trader to associate to manager to director and, finally, to head of her own business unit. How do you evaluate someone's performance in a system where no one is in a job long enough to allow such evaluation?

The answer is that you end up doing performance evaluations that aren't 10 based on performance. Among the many glowing books about Enron written before its fall was the best seller *Leading the Revolution*, by the management consultant Gary Hamel, which tells the story of Lou Pai, who launched Enron's power-trading business. Pai's group began with a disaster: It lost tens of millions of dollars trying to sell electricity to residential consumers in newly deregulated markets. The problem, Hamel explains, is that the markets weren't truly deregulated: "The states that were opening their markets to competition were still setting rules designed to give their traditional utilities big advantages." It doesn't seem to have occurred to anyone that Pai ought to have looked into those rules more carefully before risking millions of dollars. He was promptly given the chance to build the commercial electricity-outsourcing business, where he ran up several more years of heavy losses before cashing out of Enron last year with $270 million. Because Pai had "talent," he was given new opportunities, and when he failed at those new opportunities he was given still more opportunities . . . because he had "talent." "At Enron, failure — even of the type that ends up on the front page of the *Wall Street Journal* — doesn't necessarily sink a career," Hamel writes, as if that were a good thing. Presumably, companies that want to encourage risk taking must be willing to tolerate mistakes. Yet if talent is defined as something separate from an employee's actual performance, what use is it, exactly?

What the War for Talent amounts to is an argument for indulging A employees, for fawning over them. "You need to do everything you can to keep them engaged and satisfied — even delighted," Michaels, Handfield-Jones, and Axelrod write. "Find out what they would most like to be doing, and shape their career and responsibilities in that direction. Solve any issues that might be pushing them out the door, such as a boss that frustrates them or travel demands that burden them." No company was better at this than Enron. In one oft-told story, Louise Kitchin, a twenty-nine-year-old gas trader in Europe, became convinced that the company ought to develop an online-trading business. She told her boss, and she began working in her spare time on the project, until she had 250 people throughout Enron helping her. After six months, Skilling was finally informed. "I was never asked for any capital," Skilling said later. "I was never asked for any people. They had already purchased the servers. They had already started ripping apart the building. They had started legal reviews in twenty-two countries by the time I heard about it." It was, Skilling went on approvingly, "exactly the kind of behavior that will continue to drive this company forward."

Kitchin's qualification for running EnronOnline, it should be pointed out, was not that she was good at it. It was that she wanted to do it, and Enron was a place where stars did whatever they wanted. "Fluid movement is absolutely necessary in our company. And the type of people we hire enforces that," Skilling told the team from McKinsey. "Not only does this system help the excitement level for each manager, it shapes Enron's business in the direction that its managers find most exciting." Here is Skilling again: "If lots of [employees] are flocking to a new business unit, that's a good sign that the opportunity is a good one. . . . If a business unit can't attract people very easily, that's a good sign that it's a business Enron shouldn't be in." You might expect a CEO to say that if a business unit can't attract *customers* very easily that's a good sign it's a business the company shouldn't be in. A company's business is supposed to be shaped in the direction that its managers find most *profitable*. But at Enron the needs of the customers and the shareholders were secondary to the needs of its stars.

A dozen years ago, the psychologists Robert Hogan, Robert Raskin, and Dan Fazzini wrote a brilliant essay called "The Dark Side of Charisma." It argued that flawed managers fall into three types. One is the High Likability Floater, who rises effortlessly in an organization because he never takes any difficult decisions or makes any enemies. Another is the Homme de Ressentiment, who seethes below the surface and plots against his enemies.

The most interesting of the three is the Narcissist, whose energy and self-confidence and charm lead him inexorably up the corporate ladder. Narcissists are terrible managers. They resist accepting suggestions, thinking it will make them appear weak, and they don't believe that others have anything useful to tell them. "Narcissists are biased to take more credit for success than is legitimate," Hogan and his coauthors write, and "biased to avoid acknowledging responsibility for their failures and shortcomings for the same reasons that they claim more success than is their due." Moreover:

> Narcissists typically make judgments with greater confidence than other people . . . and, because their judgments are rendered with such conviction, other people tend to believe them and the narcissists become disproportionately more influential in group situations. Finally, because of their self-confidence and strong need for recognition, narcissists tend to "self-nominate"; consequently, when a leadership gap appears in a group or organization, the narcissists rush to fill it.

Tyco Corporation and WorldCom were the Greedy Corporations: They were purely interested in short-term financial gain. Enron was the Narcissistic Corporation—a company that took more credit for success than was legitimate, that did not acknowledge responsibility for its failures, that shrewdly sold the rest of us on its genius, and that substituted self-nomination for disciplined management. At one point in *Leading the Revolution*, Hamel tracks down a senior Enron executive, and what he breathlessly recounts—the braggadocio, the self-satisfaction—could be an epitaph for the talent mind-set:

> "You cannot control the atoms within a nuclear fusion reaction," said Ken Rice when he was head of Enron Capital and Trade Resources (ECT), America's largest marketer of natural gas and largest buyer and seller of electricity. Adorned in a black T-shirt, blue jeans, and cowboy boots, Rice drew a box on an office whiteboard that pictured his business unit as a nuclear reactor. Little circles in the box represented its "contract originators," the gunslingers charged with doing deals and creating new businesses. Attached to each circle was an arrow. In Rice's diagram the arrows were pointing in all different directions. "We allow people to go in whichever direction that they want to go."

The distinction between the Greedy Corporation and the Narcissistic   15 Corporation matters, because the way we conceive our attainments helps determine how we behave. Carol Dweck, a psychologist at Columbia University, has found that people generally hold one of two fairly firm beliefs about their intelligence: They consider it either a fixed trait or something that is malleable and can be developed over time. Five years ago, Dweck did a study at the University of Hong Kong, where all classes are conducted in

English. She and her colleagues approached a large group of social-sciences students, told them their English-proficiency scores, and asked them if they wanted to take a course to improve their language skills. One would expect all those who scored poorly to sign up for the remedial course. The University of Hong Kong is a demanding institution, and it is hard to do well in the social sciences without strong English skills. Curiously, however, only the ones who believed in malleable intelligence expressed interest in the class. The students who believed that their intelligence was a fixed trait were so concerned about appearing to be deficient that they preferred to stay home. "Students who hold a fixed view of their intelligence care so much about looking smart that they act dumb," Dweck writes, "for what could be dumber than giving up a chance to learn something that is essential for your own success?"

In a similar experiment, Dweck gave a class of preadolescent students a test filled with challenging problems. After they were finished, one group was praised for its effort and another group was praised for its intelligence. Those praised for their intelligence were reluctant to tackle difficult tasks, and their performance on subsequent tests soon began to suffer.

The talent myth assumes that people make organizations smart.

Then Dweck asked the children to write a letter to students at another school, describing their experience in the study. She discovered something remarkable: 40 percent of those students who were praised for their intelligence lied about how they had scored on the test, adjusting their grade upward. They weren't naturally deceptive people, and they weren't any less intelligent or self-confident than anyone else. They simply did what people do when they are immersed in an environment that celebrates them solely for their innate "talent." They begin to define themselves by that description, and when times get tough and that self-image is threatened they have difficulty with the consequences. They will not take the remedial course. They will not stand up to investors and the public and admit that they were wrong. They'd sooner lie.

The broader failing of McKinsey and its acolytes at Enron is their assumption that an organization's intelligence is simply a function of the intelligence of its employees. They believe in stars, because they don't believe in systems. In a way, that's understandable, because our lives are so obviously enriched by individual brilliance. Groups don't write great novels, and a committee didn't come up with the theory of relativity. But companies work by different rules. They don't just create; they execute and compete and coordinate the efforts of many different people, and the organizations that are most successful at that task are the ones where the system *is* the star.

There is a wonderful example of this in the story of the so-called Eastern Pearl Harbor, of the Second World War. During the first nine months of 1942, the United States Navy suffered a catastrophe. German U-boats, operating just off the Atlantic coast and in the Caribbean, were sinking our merchant ships almost at will. U-boat captains marvelled at their good fortune. "Before this sea of light, against this footlight glare of a carefree new world were passing the silhouettes of ships recognizable in every detail and sharp as the outlines in a sales catalog," one U-boat commander wrote. "All we had to do was press the button."

What made this such a puzzle is that, on the other side of the Atlantic, the British had much less trouble defending their ships against U-boat attacks. The British, furthermore, eagerly passed on to the Americans everything they knew about sonar and depth-charge throwers and the construction of destroyers. And still the Germans managed to paralyze America's coastal zones.

You can imagine what the consultants at McKinsey would have concluded: They would have said that the navy did not have a talent mind-set, that President Roosevelt needed to recruit and promote top performers into key positions in the Atlantic command. In fact, he had already done that. At the beginning of the war, he had pushed out the solid and unspectacular admiral Harold R. Stark as chief of naval operations and replaced him with the legendary Ernest Joseph King. "He was a supreme realist with the arrogance of genius," Ladislas Farago writes in *The Tenth Fleet*, a history of the navy's U-boat battles in the Second World War. "He had unbounded faith in himself, in his vast knowledge of naval matters, and in the soundness of his ideas. Unlike Stark, who tolerated incompetence all around him, King had no patience with fools."

The navy had plenty of talent at the top, in other words. What it didn't have was the right kind of organization. As Eliot A. Cohen, a scholar of military strategy at Johns Hopkins, writes in his brilliant book *Military Misfortunes in the Atlantic*:

> To wage the antisubmarine war well, analysts had to bring together fragments of information, direction-finding fixes, visual sightings, decrypts, and the "flaming datum" of a U-boat attack — for use by a commander to coordinate the efforts of warships, aircraft, and convoy commanders. Such synthesis had to occur in near "real time" — within hours, even minutes in some cases.

The British excelled at the task because they had a centralized operational system. The controllers moved the British ships around the Atlantic like chess pieces, in order to outsmart U-boat "wolf packs." By contrast, Admiral King believed strongly in a decentralized management structure: He held that managers should never tell their subordinates "'how' as well as what to 'do.'" In today's jargon, we would say he was a believer in "loose-tight" management, of the kind celebrated by the McKinsey consultants

Thomas J. Peters and Robert H. Waterman in their 1982 best seller, *In Search of Excellence.* But "loose-tight" doesn't help you find U-boats. Throughout most of 1942, the navy kept trying to act smart by relying on technical know-how, and stubbornly refused to take operational lessons from the British. The navy also lacked the organizational structure necessary to apply the technical knowledge it did have to the field. Only when the navy set up the Tenth Fleet — a single unit to coordinate all antisubmarine warfare in the Atlantic — did the situation change. In the year and a half before the Tenth Fleet was formed, in May of 1943, the navy sank thirty-six U-boats. In the six months afterward, it sank seventy-five. "The creation of the Tenth Fleet did *not* bring more talented individuals into the field of ASW" — antisubmarine warfare — "than had previous organizations," Cohen writes. "What Tenth Fleet did allow, by virtue of its organization and mandate, was for these individuals to become far more effective than previously." The talent myth assumes that people make organizations smart. More often than not, it's the other way around.

There is ample evidence of this principle among America's most successful companies. Southwest Airlines hires very few MBAs, pays its managers modestly, and gives raises according to seniority, not "rank and yank." Yet it is by far the most successful of all United States airlines, because it has created a vastly more efficient organization than its competitors have. At Southwest, the time it takes to get a plane that has just landed ready for takeoff — a key index of productivity — is, on average, twenty minutes, and requires a ground crew of four, and two people at the gate. (At United Airlines, by contrast, turnaround time is closer to thirty-five minutes, and requires a ground crew of twelve and three agents at the gate.)

In the case of the giant retailer Wal-Mart, one of the most critical periods in its history came in 1976, when Sam Walton "unretired," pushing out his handpicked successor, Ron Mayer. Mayer was just over forty. He was ambitious. He was charismatic. He was, in the words of one Walton biographer, "the boy-genius financial officer." But Walton was convinced that Mayer was, as people at McKinsey would say, "differentiating and affirming" in the corporate suite, in defiance of Wal-Mart's inclusive culture. Mayer left, and Wal-Mart survived. After all, Wal-Mart is an organization, not an all-star team. Walton brought in David Glass, late of the army and Southern Missouri State University, as CEO; the company is now ranked No. 1 on the Fortune 500 list.

Procter & Gamble doesn't have a star system, either. How could it? [25] Would the top MBA graduates of Harvard and Stanford move to Cincinnati to work on detergent when they could make three times as much reinventing the world in Houston? Procter & Gamble isn't glamorous. Its CEO is a lifer—a former navy officer who began his corporate career as an assistant brand manager for Joy dishwashing liquid—and, if Procter & Gamble's best played Enron's best at Trivial Pursuit, no doubt the team from Houston would win handily. But Procter & Gamble has dominated the consumer-products field for close to a century, because it has a carefully conceived managerial system, and a rigorous marketing methodology that has allowed it to win battles for brands like Crest and Tide decade after decade. In Procter & Gamble's navy, Admiral Stark would have stayed. But a cross-divisional management committee would have set the Tenth Fleet in place before the war ever started.

Among the most damning facts about Enron, in the end, was something its managers were proudest of. They had what, in McKinsey terminology, is called an "open market" for hiring. In the open-market system — McKinsey's assault on the very idea of a fixed organization—anyone could apply for any job that he or she wanted, and no manager was allowed to hold anyone back. Poaching was encouraged. When an Enron executive named Kevin Hannon started the company's global broadband unit, he launched what he called Project Quick Hire. A hundred top performers from around the company were invited to the Houston Hyatt to hear Hannon give his pitch. Recruiting booths were set up outside the meeting room. "Hannon had his fifty top performers for the broadband unit by the end of the week," Michaels, Handfield-Jones, and Axelrod write, "and his peers had fifty holes to fill." Nobody, not even the consultants who were paid to think about the Enron culture, seemed worried that those fifty holes might disrupt the functioning of the affected departments, that stability in a firm's existing businesses might be a good thing, that the self-fulfillment of Enron's star employees might possibly be in conflict with the best interests of the firm as a whole.

These are the sort of concerns that management consultants ought to raise. But Enron's management consultant was McKinsey, and McKinsey was as much a prisoner of the talent myth as its clients were. In 1998, Enron hired ten Wharton MBAs; that same year, McKinsey hired forty. In 1999, Enron hired twelve from Wharton; McKinsey hired sixty-one. The consultants at McKinsey were preaching at Enron what they believed about themselves. "When we would hire them, it wouldn't just be for a week," one former Enron manager recalls, of the brilliant young men and women from McKinsey who wandered the hallways at the company's headquarters. "It would be for two to four months. They were always around." They were there looking for people who had the talent to think outside the box. It never occurred to them that, if everyone had to think outside the box, maybe it was the box that needed fixing.

Working with the Text

1. At a pivotal point in his argument, Malcolm Gladwell claims that "The talent myth assumes that people make organizations smart. More often than not, it's the other way around" (par. 22). In light of Gladwell's contrast between failed "talent" ventures and successful "systems," write a brief essay in which you analyze his claim. What does Gladwell mean by *smart*? How is it possible for talented people to fail to make an organization smart? How can systems within organizations make people smart?

2. Gladwell points out that the management consulting firm McKinsey & Company "escaped largely unscathed . . . which is odd, given that it essentially created the blueprint for the Enron culture" (par. 3). In a brief essay, reflect on the differences between McKinsey and Enron that made it possible for McKinsey to continue working in the "talent mind-set." What did the "talent" at Enron do? What does the "talent" at McKinsey do? Why might the differences in their job descriptions create differences in how long they could think and work "outside the box"?

3. McKinsey advocates a process called "differentiation and affirmation" that drives a talent-centered work culture. Review this process, as well as how the "A, B, and C ranking system" was applied by the Royal Air Force in World War II. Based on your own observation and experience as well as Gladwell's critique, write a brief essay in which you argue for or against using such systems in the workplace.

4. To show how Enron applied the "talent mind-set," Gladwell tells the stories of a few of Enron's "stars." As you reread the article, review these stories in light of Gladwell's critique of the "talent myth." In a brief essay, provide a profile Enron might have used in hiring new staff. How do you think Enron defined *talent*? What signs or measures of talent do you think they were seeking?

From Text to Field

1. In his critique of the "talent myth," Gladwell touches on a number of approaches to management. Drawing on Gladwell's analysis as well as your own experience and observations, write an essay in which you advocate a management theory of your own.

2. In questioning the value of IQ scores to predict work performance, Gladwell notes the conclusion of Florida State University psychologist Richard Wagner: "In terms of how we evaluate schooling, everything is about working by yourself. If you work with someone else, it's called cheating. Once you get out in the real world, everything you do involves working with other people" (par. 6).

While students do spend a significant amount of time doing individual work, they also gain experience in working with groups—and being evaluated as a group—not only in the classroom but also in extracurricular activities. In a personal essay, reflect on the differences you have experienced between performing as an individual and performing as a member of a group. What skills do you use in each situation? Which skills are essential to performing well in each situation?

3. To illustrate the differences in skill required for performing individually and in groups, Gladwell includes a question from a test of "tacit knowledge," developed by psychologists Richard Wagner of Florida State University and Robert Sternberg of Yale University (par. 7). Based on your own responses to the question, write an essay in which you analyze your "tacit knowledge." Why would "good managers" pick *b* and *e*? Why would "bad managers" pick *c*? Which strategies would you choose, and why? What do your responses suggest about how you would perform as a manager? What strengths and weaknesses do your preferences in strategy suggest?

4. Gladwell notes three types of "flawed managers" identified by psychologists Robert Hogan, Robert Raskin, and Dan Fazzini: the High Likability Floater, the Homme de Ressentiment, and the Narcissist. Based on the definitions of each type, write a character sketch of someone you know or have known who is either already one of these types or who you predict will become one of these types of flawed manager.

business is ongoing and existing (15 U.S.C. § 1060). The purpose of the prohibition against assignment of marks not yet in use is to prevent the sale or trafficking of ITU applications. Additionally, permitting assignment of an application before a mark is used would conflict with the principle that a mark may be validly assigned only with some of the business or goodwill attached to use of the mark. There can be no goodwill attached to a mark that has not been used. An assignment of an ITU application prior to the filing of the verified statement of use is not only invalid but voids the underlying trademark application or any resulting registration.

Recording documents at the PTO requires that a party file a specific PTO cover sheet or form (Form 1594, Recordation Form Cover Sheet; see Exhibit 5–4), identifying the conveying and receiving parties, the marks affected by the transfer, and a correspondent to whom the PTO can send notices. The fees for recording are $40 for the first mark being assigned and $25 for each subsequent mark identified in the form. Form 1594 is also used to inform the PTO that a mark has been acquired by a party through a merger (as when a corporation that owns a mark is acquired by another corporation) or in the event the trademark owner changes its name or state of incorporation.

Licensing of Marks

A party may allow another party to use a mark and yet retain ownership rights in the mark. Such a form of limited transfer is called a **license.** Some of the most common license arrangements occur in franchising. For example, McDonald's Corporation will grant a franchise to a party to open a McDonald's restaurant in a certain territory. In connection with the franchise, McDonald's will grant the party a license to use McDonald's marks on the cups, packaging, signs, and in advertising. McDonald's continues to own the marks; it has merely granted a license to its franchisee to use its marks for certain specific purposes.

The licensor will lose its rights to the mark, however, if it does not control the nature and quality of the goods or services offered by the licensee under the mark. Thus, license agreements must include "quality control" provisions whereby the licensor protects the mark by ensuring the goods and services offered under it by the licensee are consistent with those offered by the licensor. Failure of the licensor to exercise quality control will result in a **naked license** and a loss of the licensor's rights in the mark. Failure to monitor the goods and services offered under the license may result in abandonment of the mark and may preclude or estop the trademark owner/licensor from challenging use of the mark by the licensee during the period of unsupervised use. License agreements should therefore allow the licensor to conduct periodic inspection of the licensee's facilities and its use of the mark. The licensor may require the licensee to submit samples of how the mark is being applied to the goods or how it is used in advertising or may require testing of products offered under the mark. Such measures ensure that the licensee's products and services are of the same level of quality that consumers have come to associate with the licensor's mark. Failure to control and supervise the mark by the owner so as to ensure quality and consistency in the goods or services offered under the mark leads to public deception inasmuch as the function of a mark is to identify the source of goods or services. Thus, a naked license (one without quality control provisions) results in loss of trademark rights.

In one famous example, for years a well-known trademark lawyer, Julius R. Lunsford Jr., traveled the country going to bars and restaurants to order COCA-COLA drinks to determine if the establishments were actually serving COCA-COLA. Lunsford would secretly

The Essential Tension: Tradition and Innovation in Scientific Research

Thomas S. Kuhn

In 1959, the Third University of Utah Research Conference on the Identification of Scientific Talent invited Thomas S. Kuhn to address the issue of cultivating creative thinking in science students. The conference sought to encourage "divergent thinking"—the "flexibility and open-mindedness" to depart from conventional methods and theories. Somewhat to the surprise of conference participants, Kuhn made the case for "convergent thinking"—training in and commitment to accepted methods and theories—as the necessary precursor to the divergent thinking that produces scientific revolutions or any progress in the development of science. His study of the history of science helped him formulate the concept of "paradigms" and had convinced him that the very best scientists are capable of sustaining the "essential tension" between working rigorously within a paradigm and recognizing the evidence that will overturn that paradigm.

Kuhn's theory of scientific progress challenged assumptions about development and change, not only within the sciences but also in disciplines ranging from economics and sociology to history, philosophy, and the arts. Kuhn's most widely known and influential book is *The Structure of Scientific Revolutions* (1962), which examines the making and changing of knowledge in scientific communities. Required reading in a number of disciplines and now translated into some sixteen languages, this book explores how scientific knowledge is based not on objective reality alone but also on the contingent judgment of specific communities of knowers.

Shortly after earning his PhD in physics, Kuhn changed his focus to the history of science, which he taught first at Harvard University, then at the University of California at Berkeley, Princeton University, and the Massachusetts Institute of Technology (MIT). He held honorary degrees from institutions such as the University of Chicago, Columbia University, and the University of Athens. In 1982, he was awarded the George Sarton Medal in the History of Science. Thomas Kuhn died in 1996.

I am grateful for the invitation to participate in this important conference, and I interpret it as evidence that students of creativity themselves possess the sensitivity to divergent approaches that they seek to identify in others. But I am not altogether sanguine about the outcome of your experiment with me. As most of you already know, I am no psychologist, but rather an ex-physicist now working in the history of science. Probably my concern is no less with creativity than your own, but my goals, my techniques, and my sources of evidence are so very different from yours that I am far from sure how much we do, or even *should*, have to say to each other. These reservations imply no apology: Rather they hint at my central thesis. In the sciences, as I shall suggest below, it is often better to do one's best with the tools at hand than to pause for contemplation of divergent approaches.

If a person of my background and interests has anything relevant to suggest to this conference, it will not be about your central concerns, the creative personality and its early identification. But implicit in the numerous working papers distributed to participants in this conference is an image of the scientific process and of the scientist; that image almost certainly conditions many of the experiments you try as well as the conclusions you draw; and about it the physicist-historian may well have something to say. I shall restrict my attention to one aspect of this image—an aspect epitomized as follows in one of the working papers: The basic scientist "must lack prejudice to a degree where he can look at the most 'self-evident' facts or concepts without necessarily accepting them, and, conversely, allow his imagination to play with the most unlikely possibilities" (Selye, 1959). In the more technical language supplied by other working papers (Getzels and Jackson), this aspect of the image recurs as an emphasis upon "divergent thinking, . . . the freedom to go off in different directions, . . . rejecting the old solution and striking out in some new direction."

I do not at all doubt that this description of "divergent thinking" and the concomitant search for those able to do it are entirely proper. Some divergence characterizes all scientific work, and gigantic divergences lie at the core of the most significant episodes in scientific development. But both my own experience in scientific research and my reading of the history of sciences lead me to wonder whether flexibility and open-mindedness have not been too exclusively emphasized as the characteristics requisite for basic research. I shall therefore suggest below that something like "convergent thinking" is just as essential to scientific advance as is divergent. Since these two modes of thought are inevitably in conflict, it will follow that the ability to support a tension that can occasionally become almost unbearable is one of the prime requisites for the very best sort of scientific research.

I am elsewhere studying these points more historically, with emphasis on the importance to scientific development of "revolutions."[1] These are episodes — exemplified in their most extreme and readily recognized form by the advent of Copernicanism, Darwinism, or Einsteinianism — in which a scientific community abandons one time-honored way of regarding the world and of pursuing science in favor of some other, usually incompatible, approach to its discipline. I have argued in the draft that the historian constantly encounters many far smaller but structurally similar revolutionary episodes and that they are central to scientific advance. Contrary to a prevalent impression, most new discoveries and theories in the sciences are not merely additions to the existing stockpile of scientific knowledge. To assimilate them the scientist must usually rearrange the intellectual and manipulative equipment he has previously relied upon, discarding some elements of his prior belief and practice while finding new significances in and new relationships between many others. Because the old must be revalued and reordered when assimilating the new, discovery and invention in the sciences are usually intrinsically revolutionary. Therefore, they do demand just that flexibility and open-mindedness that characterize, or indeed define, the divergent thinker. Let us henceforth take for granted the need for these characteristics. Unless many scientists possessed them to a marked degree, there would be no scientific revolutions and very little scientific advance.

Yet flexibility is not enough, and what remains is not obviously compatible with it. Drawing from various fragments of a project still in progress, I must now emphasize that revolutions are but one of two complementary aspects of scientific advance. Almost none of the research undertaken by even the greatest scientists is designed to be revolutionary, and very little of it has any such effect. On the contrary, normal research, even the best of it, is a highly convergent activity based firmly upon a settled consensus acquired from scientific education and reinforced by subsequent life in the profession. Typically, to be sure, this convergent or consensus-bound research ultimately results in revolution. Then, traditional techniques and beliefs are abandoned and replaced by new ones. But revolutionary shifts of a scientific tradition are relatively rare, and extended periods of convergent research are the necessary preliminary to them. As I shall indicate below, only investigations firmly rooted in the contemporary scientific tradition are likely to break that tradition and give rise to a new one. That is why I speak of an "essential tension" implicit in scientific research. To do his job the scientist must undertake a complex set of intellectual and manipulative commitments. Yet his claim to fame, if he has the talent and good luck to gain one, may finally rest upon his ability to abandon this net of commitments in favor of another of his own invention. Very often the successful scientist must simultaneously display the characteristics of the traditionalist and of the iconoclast.[2]

The multiple historical examples upon which any full documentation of these points must depend are prohibited by the time limitations of the conference. But another approach will introduce you to at least part of what I have in mind — an examination of the nature of education in the natural sciences. One of the working papers for this conference (Getzels and Jackson) quotes Guilford's very apt description of scientific education as follows: "[It] has emphasized abilities in the areas of convergent thinking and evaluation, often at the expense of development in the area of divergent thinking. We have attempted to teach students how to arrive at 'correct' answers that our civilization has taught us are correct. . . . Outside the arts [and I should include most of the social sciences] we have generally discouraged the development of divergent-thinking abilities, unintentionally." That characterization seems to me eminently just, but I wonder whether it is equally just to deplore the product that results. Without defending plain bad teaching, and granting that in this country the trend to convergent thinking in all education may have proceeded entirely too far, we may nevertheless recognize that a rigorous training in convergent thought has been intrinsic to the sciences almost from their origin. I suggest that they could not have achieved their present state or status without it.

Let me try briefly to epitomize the nature of education in the natural sciences, ignoring the many significant yet minor differences between the various sciences and between the approaches of different educational institutions. The single most striking feature of this education is that, to an extent totally unknown in other creative fields, it is conducted entirely through textbooks. Typically, undergraduate *and* graduate students of chemistry, physics, astronomy, geology, or biology acquire the substance of their fields from books written especially for students. Until they are ready, or very nearly ready, to commence work on their own dissertations, they are neither asked to attempt trial research projects nor exposed to the immediate products of research done by others, that is, to the professional communications that scientists write for each other. There are no collections of "readings" in the natural sciences. Nor are science students encouraged to read the historical classics of their fields — works in which they might discover other ways of regarding the problems discussed in their textbooks, but in which they would also meet problems, concepts, and standards of solution that their future professions have long since discarded and replaced.

In contrast, the various textbooks that the student does encounter display different subject matters, rather than, as in many of the social sciences, exemplifying different approaches to a single problem field. Even books that compete for adoption in a single course differ mainly in level and in pedagogic detail, not in substance or conceptual structure. Last, but most important of all, is the characteristic technique of textbook presentation. Except in their occasional introductions, science textbooks do not describe the sorts of problems that the professional may be asked to solve and the variety of techniques available for their solution. Rather, these books exhibit concrete problem solutions that the profession has come to accept as paradigms, and they then ask the student, either with a pencil and paper or in the laboratory, to solve for himself problems very closely related in both method and substance to those through which the textbook or the accompanying lecture has led him. Nothing could be better calculated to produce "mental sets" or *Einstellungen*. Only in their most elementary courses do other academic fields offer as much as a partial parallel.

Even the most faintly liberal educational theory must view this pedagogic technique as anathema. Students, we would all agree, must begin by learning a good deal of what is already known, but we also insist that education give them vastly more. They must, we say, learn to recognize and evaluate problems to which no unequivocal solution has yet been given; they must be supplied with an arsenal of techniques for approaching these future problems; and they must learn to judge the relevance of these techniques and to evaluate the possibly partial solutions which they can provide. In many respects these attitudes toward education seem to me entirely right, and yet we must recognize two things about them. First, education in the natural sciences seems to have been totally unaffected by their existence. It remains a dogmatic initiation in a preestablished tradition that the student is not equipped to evaluate. Second, at least in the period when it was followed by a term in an apprenticeship relation, this technique of exclusive exposure to a rigid tradition has been immensely productive of the most consequential sorts of innovations.

I shall shortly inquire about the pattern of scientific practice that grows out 10 of this educational initiation and will then attempt to say why that pattern proves quite so successful. But first, a historical excursion will reinforce what has just been said and prepare the way for what is to follow. I should like to suggest that the various fields of natural science have not always been characterized by rigid education in exclusive paradigms, but that each of them acquired something like that technique at precisely the point when the field began to make rapid and systematic progress. If one asks about the origin of our contemporary knowledge of chemical composition, of earthquakes, of biological reproduction, of motion through space, or of any other subject matter known to the natural sciences, one immediately encounters a characteristic pattern that I shall here illustrate with a single example.

Today, physics textbooks tell us that light exhibits some properties of a wave and some of a particle: Both textbook problems and research problems are designed accordingly. But both this view and these textbooks are products of an early twentieth-century revolution. (One characteristic of scientific revolutions is that they call for the rewriting of science textbooks.) For more than half a century before 1900, the books employed in scientific education had been equally unequivocal in stating that light was wave motion. Under those circumstances scientists worked on somewhat different problems and often embraced rather different sorts of solutions to them. The nineteenth-century textbook tradition does not, however, mark the beginning of our subject matter. Throughout the eighteenth century and into the early nineteenth, Newton's *Opticks* and the other books from which men learned science taught almost all students that light was particles, and research guided by this tradition was again different from that which succeeded it. Ignoring a variety of subsidiary changes within these three successive traditions, we may therefore say that our views derive historically from Newton's views by way of two revolutions in optical thought, each of which replaced one tradition of convergent research with another. If we make appropriate allowances for changes in the locus and materials of scientific education, we may say that each of these three traditions was embodied in the sort of education by exposure to unequivocal paradigms that I briefly epitomized above. Since Newton, education and research in physical optics have normally been highly convergent.

The history of theories of light does not, however, begin with Newton. If we ask about knowledge in the field before his time, we encounter a significantly different pattern — a pattern still familiar in the arts and in some social sciences, but one which has largely disappeared in the natural sciences. From remote antiquity until the end of the seventeenth century there was no single set of paradigms for the study of physical optics. Instead, many men advanced a large number of different views about the nature of light. Some of these views found few adherents, but a number of them gave rise to continuing schools of optical thought. Although the historian can note the emergence of new points of view as well as changes in the relative popularity of older ones, there was never anything resembling consensus. As a result, a new man entering the field was inevitably exposed to a variety of conflicting viewpoints: He was forced to examine the evidence for each, and there always was good evidence. The fact that he made a choice and conducted himself accordingly could not entirely prevent his awareness of other possibilities. This earlier mode of education was obviously more suited to produce a scientist without prejudice,

> **The successful scientist must simultaneously display the characteristics of the traditionalist and of the iconoclast.**

alert to novel phenomena, and flexible in his approach to his field. On the other hand, one can scarcely escape the impression that, during the period characterized by this more liberal educational practice, physical optics made very little progress.[3]

The preconsensus (we might here call it the divergent) phase in the development of physical optics is, I believe, duplicated in the history of all other scientific specialties, excepting only those that were born by the subdivision and recombination of preexisting disciplines. In some fields, like mathematics and astronomy, the first firm consensus is prehistoric. In others, like dynamics, geometric optics, and parts of physiology, the paradigms that produced a first consensus date from classical antiquity. Most other natural sciences, though their problems were often discussed in antiquity, did not achieve a first consensus until after the Renaissance. In physical optics, as we have seen, the first firm consensus dates only from the end of the seventeenth century; in electricity, chemistry, and the study of heat, it dates from the eighteenth; while in geology and the nontaxonomic parts of biology no very real consensus developed until after the first third of the nineteenth century. This century appears to be characterized by the emergence of a first consensus in parts of a few of the social sciences.

In all the fields named above, important work was done before the achievement of the maturity produced by consensus. Neither the nature nor the timing of the first consensus in these fields can be understood without a careful examination of both the intellectual and the manipulative techniques developed before the existence of unique paradigms. But the transition to maturity is not less significant because individuals practiced science before it occurred. On the contrary, history strongly suggests that, though one can practice science — as one does philosophy or art or political science — without a firm consensus, this more flexible practice will not produce the pattern of rapid consequential scientific advance to which recent centuries have accustomed us. In that pattern, development occurs from one consensus to another, and alternate approaches are not ordinarily in competition. Except under quite special conditions, the practitioner of a mature science does not pause to examine divergent modes of explanation or experimentation.

I shall shortly ask how this can be so — how a firm orientation toward an 15 apparently unique tradition can be compatible with the practice of the disciplines most noted for the persistent production of novel ideas and techniques. But it will help first to ask what the education that so successfully transmits such a tradition leaves to be done. What can a scientist working within a deeply rooted tradition and little trained in the perception of significant alternatives hope to do in his professional career? Once again limits of time force me to drastic simplification, but the following remarks will at least suggest a position that I am sure can be documented in detail.

In pure or basic science — that somewhat ephemeral category of research undertaken by men whose most immediate goal is to increase understanding rather than control of nature — the characteristic problems are almost always repetitions, with minor modifications, of problems that have been undertaken and partially resolved before. For example, much of the research undertaken within a scientific tradition is an attempt to adjust existing theory or existing observation in order to bring the two into closer and closer agreement. The constant examination of atomic and molecular spectra during the years since the birth of wave mechanics, together with the design of theoretical approximations for the prediction of complex spectra, provides one important instance of this typical sort of work. Another was provided by the remarks about the eighteenth-century development of Newtonian dynamics in the paper on measurement supplied to you in advance of the conference.[4] The attempt to make existing theory and observation conform more closely is not, of course, the only standard sort of research problem in the basic sciences. The development of chemical thermodynamics or the continuing attempts to unravel organic structure illustrate another type — the extension of existing theory to areas that it is expected to cover but in which it has never before been tried. In addition, to mention a third common sort of research problem, many scientists constantly collect the concrete data (e.g., atomic weights, nuclear moments) required for the application and extension of existing theory.

These are normal research projects in the basic sciences, and they illustrate the sorts of work on which all scientists, even the greatest, spend most of their professional lives and on which many spend all. Clearly their pursuit is neither intended nor likely to produce fundamental discoveries or revolutionary changes in scientific theory. Only if the validity of the contemporary scientific tradition is assumed do these problems make much theoretical or any practical sense. The man who suspected the existence of a totally new type of phenomenon or who had basic doubts about the validity of existing theory would not think problems so closely modeled on textbook paradigms worth undertaking. It follows that the man who does undertake a problem of this sort — and that means all scientists at most times — aims to elucidate the scientific tradition in which he was raised rather than to change it. Furthermore, the fascination of his work lies in the difficulties of elucidation rather than in any surprises that the work is likely to produce. Under normal conditions the research scientist is not an innovator but a solver of puzzles, and the puzzles upon which he concentrates are just those which he believes can be both stated and solved within the existing scientific tradition.

Yet — and this is the point — the ultimate effect of this tradition-bound work has invariably been to change the tradition. Again and again the continuing attempt to elucidate a currently received tradition has at last produced one of those shifts in fundamental theory, in problem field, and in scientific standards to which I previously referred as scientific revolutions. At least for the scientific community as a whole, work within a well-defined and deeply ingrained tradition seems more productive of tradition-shattering novelties than work in which no similarly convergent standards are involved. How can this be so? I think it is because no other sort of work is nearly so well suited to isolate for continuing and concentrated attention those loci of trouble or causes of crisis upon whose recognition the most fundamental advances in basic science depend.

As I have indicated in the first of my working papers, new theories and, to an increasing extent, novel discoveries in the mature sciences are not born de novo. On the contrary, they emerge from old theories and within a matrix of old beliefs about the phenomena that the world does *and does not* contain. Ordinarily such novelties are far too esoteric and recondite to be noted by the man without a great deal of scientific training. And even the man with considerable training can seldom afford simply to go out and look for them, let us say by exploring those areas in which existing data and theory have failed to produce understanding. Even in a mature science there are always far too many such areas, areas in which no existing paradigms seem obviously to apply and for whose exploration few tools and standards are available. More likely than not the scientist who ventured into them, relying merely upon his receptivity to new phenomena and his flexibility to new patterns of organization, would get nowhere at all. He would rather return his science to its preconsensus or natural history phase.

Instead, the practitioner of a mature science, from the beginning of his   20 doctoral research, continues to work in the regions for which the paradigms derived from his education and from the research of his contemporaries seem adequate. He tries, that is, to elucidate topographical detail on a map whose main outlines are available in advance, and he hopes — if he is wise enough to recognize the nature of his field — that he will some day undertake a problem in which the anticipated does *not* occur, a problem that goes wrong in ways suggestive of a fundamental weakness in the paradigm itself. In the mature sciences the prelude to much discovery and to all novel theory is not ignorance, but the recognition that something has gone wrong with existing knowledge and beliefs.

What I have said so far may indicate that it is sufficient for the productive scientist to adopt existing theory as a lightly held tentative hypothesis, employ it faute de mieux in order to get a start in his research, and then abandon it as soon as it leads him to a trouble spot, a point at which something has gone wrong. But though the ability to recognize trouble when confronted by it is surely a requisite for scientific advance, trouble must not be too easily recognized. The scientist requires a thoroughgoing commitment to the tradition with which, if he is fully successful, he will break. In part this commitment is demanded by the nature of the problems the scientist normally undertakes. These, as we have seen, are usually esoteric puzzles whose challenge lies less in the information disclosed by their solutions (all but its details are often known in advance) than in the difficulties of technique to be surmounted in providing any solution at all. Problems of this sort are undertaken only by men assured that there is a solution which ingenuity can disclose, and only current theory could possibly provide assurance of that sort. That theory alone gives meaning to most of the problems of normal research. To doubt it is often to doubt that the complex technical puzzles which constitute normal research have any solutions at all. Who, for example, would have developed the elaborate mathematical techniques required for the study of the effects of interplanetary attractions upon basic Keplerian orbits if he had not assumed that Newtonian dynamics, applied to the planets then known, would explain the last details of astronomical observation? But without that assurance, how would Neptune have been discovered and the list of planets changed?

In addition, there are pressing practical reasons for commitment. Every research problem confronts the scientist with anomalies whose sources he cannot quite identify. His theories and observations never quite agree; successive observations never yield quite the same results; his experiments have both theoretical and phenomenological by-products which it would take another research project to unravel. Each of these anomalies or incompletely understood phenomena could conceivably be the clue to a fundamental innovation in scientific theory or technique, but the man who pauses to examine them one by one never completes his first project. Reports of effective research repeatedly imply that all but the most striking and central discrepancies could be taken care of by current theory if only there were time to take them on. The men who make these reports find most discrepancies trivial or uninteresting, an evaluation that they can ordinarily base only upon their faith in current theory. Without that faith their work would be wasteful of time and talent.

Besides, lack of commitment too often results in the scientist's undertaking problems that he has little chance of solving. Pursuit of an anomaly is fruitful only if the anomaly is more than nontrivial. Having discovered it, the scientist's first efforts and those of his profession are to do what nuclear physicists are now doing. They strive to generalize the anomaly, to discover other and more revealing manifestations of the same effect, to give it structure by examining its complex interrelationships with phenomena they still feel they understand. Very few anomalies are susceptible to this sort of treatment. To be so they must be in explicit and unequivocal conflict with some structurally central tenet of current scientific belief. Therefore, their recognition

EXHIBIT 5–4
PTO
Recordation
Cover Sheet

Form **PTO-1594**
(Rev. 10/02)
OMB No. 0651-0027 (exp. 6/30/2005)

**RECORDATION FORM COVER SHEET
TRADEMARKS ONLY**

U.S. DEPARTMENT OF COMMERCE
U.S. Patent and Trademark Office

Tab settings ⇨ ⇨ ⇨   ▼   ▼   ▼   ▼   ▼   ▼   ▼

To the Honorable Commissioner of Patents and Trademarks: Please record the attached original documents or copy thereof.

1. Name of conveying party(ies):	2. Name and address of receiving party(ies)
	Name:_____
	Internal Address:_____
☐ Individual(s) ☐ Association	Street Address:_____
☐ General Partnership ☐ Limited Partnership	City:_____State:_____Zip:_____
☐ Corporation-State	☐ Individual(s) citizenship_____
☐ Other _____	☐ Association_____
	☐ General Partnership_____
Additional name(s) of conveying party(ies) attached? ☐ Yes ☐ No	☐ Limited Partnership _____

3. Nature of conveyance:	☐ Corporation-State_____
☐ Assignment ☐ Merger	☐ Other _____
☐ Security Agreement ☐ Change of Name	If assignee is not domiciled in the United States, a domestic representative designation is attached: ☐ Yes ☐ No
☐ Other_____	(Designations must be a separate document from assignment)
Execution Date:_____	Additional name(s) & address(es) attached? ☐ Yes ☐ No

4. Application number(s) or registration number(s):	
A. Trademark Application No.(s)	B. Trademark Registration No.(s)

Additional number(s) attached   ☐ Yes ☐ No

5. Name and address of party to whom correspondence concerning document should be mailed:	6. Total number of applications and registrations involved: .... [____]
Name:_____	
Internal Address:_____	7. Total fee (37 CFR 3.41)...................$_____
_____	☐ Enclosed
_____	☐ Authorized to be charged to deposit account
Street Address:_____	8. Deposit account number:
_____	
_____	_____
City:_____ State:_____ Zip:_____	(Attach duplicate copy of this page if paying by deposit account)

DO NOT USE THIS SPACE

9. Statement and signature.
To the best of my knowledge and belief, the foregoing information is true and correct and any attached copy is a true copy of the original document.

_____   _____   _____
Name of Person Signing   Signature   Date

Total number of pages including cover sheet, attachments, and document: [____]

**Mail documents to be recorded with required cover sheet information to:
Commissioner of Patent & Trademarks, Box Assignments
Washington, D.C. 20231**

and evaluation once again depend upon a firm commitment to the contemporary scientific tradition.

This central role of an elaborate and often esoteric tradition is what I have principally had in mind when speaking of the essential tension in scientific research. I do not doubt that the scientist must be, at least potentially, an innovator, that he must possess mental flexibility, and that he must be prepared to recognize troubles where they exist. That much of the popular stereotype is surely correct, and it is important accordingly to search for indices of the corresponding personality characteristics. But what is no part of our stereotype and what appears to need careful integration with it is the other face of this same coin. We are, I think, more likely fully to exploit our potential scientific talent if we recognize the extent to which the basic scientist must also be a firm traditionalist, or, if I am using your vocabulary at all correctly, a convergent thinker. Most important of all, we must seek to understand how these two superficially discordant modes of problem solving can be reconciled both within the individual and within the group.

Everything said above needs both elaboration and documentation. Very likely some of it will change in the process. This paper is a report on work in progress. But, though I insist that much of it is tentative and all of it incomplete, I still hope that the paper has indicated why an educational system best described as an initiation into an unequivocal tradition should be thoroughly compatible with successful scientific work. And I hope, in addition, to have made plausible the historical thesis that no part of science has progressed very far or very rapidly before this convergent education and correspondingly convergent normal practice became possible. Finally, though it is beyond my competence to derive personality correlates from this view of scientific development, I hope to have made meaningful the view that the productive scientist must be a traditionalist who enjoys playing intricate games by preestablished rules in order to be a successful innovator who discovers new rules and new pieces with which to play them.

As first planned, my paper was to have ended at this point. But work on it, against the background supplied by the working papers distributed to conference participants, has suggested the need for a postscript. Let me therefore briefly try to eliminate a likely ground of misunderstanding and simultaneously suggest a problem that urgently needs a great deal of investigation.

Everything said above was intended to apply strictly only to basic science, an enterprise whose practitioners have ordinarily been relatively free to choose their own problems. Characteristically, as I have indicated, these problems have been selected in areas where paradigms were clearly applicable but where exciting puzzles remained about how to apply them and how to make nature conform to the results of the application. Clearly the inventor and

applied scientist are not generally free to choose puzzles of this sort. The problems among which they may choose are likely to be largely determined by
social, economic, or military circumstances external to the sciences. Often
the decision to seek a cure for a virulent disease, a new source of household
illumination, or an alloy able to withstand the intense heat of rocket engines
must be made with little reference to the state of the relevant science. It is, I
think, by no means clear that the personality characteristics requisite for pre-
eminence in this more immediately practical sort of work are altogether the
same as those required for a great achievement in basic science. History indicates that only a few individuals, most of whom worked in readily demarcated
areas, have achieved eminence in both.

I am by no means clear where this suggestion leads us. The troublesome
distinctions between basic research, applied research, and invention need far
more investigation. Nevertheless, it seems likely, for example, that the
applied scientist, to whose problems no scientific paradigm need be fully relevant, may profit by a far broader and less rigid education than that to which
the pure scientist has characteristically been exposed. Certainly there are
many episodes in the history of technology in which lack of more than the
most rudimentary scientific education has proved to be an immense help.
This group scarcely needs to be reminded that Edison's electric light was produced in the face of unanimous scientific opinion that the arc light could not
be "subdivided," and there are many other episodes of this sort.

This must not suggest, however, that mere differences in education will
transform the applied scientist into a basic scientist or vice versa. One could
at least argue that Edison's personality, ideal for the inventor and perhaps also
for the "oddball" in applied science, barred him from fundamental achievements in the basic sciences. He himself expressed great scorn for scientists and
thought of them as wooly-headed people to be hired when needed. But this
did not prevent his occasionally arriving at the most sweeping and irresponsi-
ble scientific theories of his own. (The pattern recurs in the early history of
electrical technology: Both Tesla and Gramme advanced absurd cosmic
schemes that they thought deserved to replace the current scientific knowledge of their day.) Episodes like this reinforce an impression that the personality requisites of the pure scientist and of the inventor may be quite different,
perhaps with those of the applied scientist lying somewhere between.[5]

Is there a further conclusion to be drawn from all this? One speculative
thought forces itself upon me. If I read the working papers correctly, they suggest that most of you are really in search of the *inventive* personality, a sort of
person who does emphasize divergent thinking but whom the United States
has already produced in abundance. In the process you may be ignoring certain of the essential requisites of the basic scientist, a rather different sort of
person, to whose ranks America's contributions have as yet been notoriously

sparse. Since most of you are, in fact, Americans, this correlation may not be entirely coincidental.

Notes

1. *The Structure of Scientific Revolutions* (Chicago, 1962).

2. Strictly speaking, it is the professional group rather than the individual scientist that must display both these characteristics simultaneously. In a fuller account of the ground covered in this paper that distinction between individual and group characteristics would be basic. Here I can only note that, though recognition of the distinction weakens the conflict or tension referred to above, it does not eliminate it. Within the group some individuals may be more traditionalistic, others more iconoclastic, and their contributions may differ accordingly. Yet education, institutional norms, and the nature of the job to be done will inevitably combine to insure that all group members will, to a greater or lesser extent, be pulled in both directions.

3. The history of physical optics before Newton has recently been well described by Vasco Ronchi in *Histoire de la lumière*, trans. J. Taton (Paris, 1956). His account does justice to the element I elaborate too little above. Many fundamental contributions to physical optics were made in the two millennia before Newton's work. Consensus is not prerequisite to a sort of progress in the natural sciences, any more than it is to progress in the social sciences or the arts. It is, however, prerequisite to the sort of progress that we now generally refer to when distinguishing the natural sciences from the arts and from most social sciences.

4. A revised version appeared in *Isis* 52 (1961): 161–93.

5. For the attitude of scientists toward the technical possibility of the incandescent light see Francis A. Jones, *Thomas Alva Edison* (New York, 1908), pp. 99–100, and Harold C. Passer, *The Electrical Manufacturers, 1875–1900* (Cambridge, Mass., 1953), pp. 82–83. For Edison's attitude toward scientists see Passer, ibid., pp. 180–81. For a sample of Edison's theorizing in realms otherwise subject to scientific treatments see Dagobert D. Runes, ed., *The Diary and Sundry Observations of Thomas Alva Edison* (New York, 1948), pp. 205–44, passim.

Working with the Text

1. Note that Thomas S. Kuhn speaks at some length early in his talk about his audience, the topic of the conference, and the interests and agendas of his listeners. Why and in what ways does Kuhn's awareness of his audience shape his remarks? How do these early comments give us clues about Kuhn's "rhetorical situation"?

2. Kuhn's talk turns on several key terms: *convergent, divergent, paradigm,* and *anomaly.* In a brief essay, clarify what these words mean and why they give us insight into scientific knowledge and innovation.

3. Early in his talk, Kuhn refers to two fairly common terms — *tradition* and *innovation* — and then proceeds to translate them into a pair of terms: *convergent* and *divergent.* What does Kuhn gain by this shift in terms? What

unhelpful assumptions or baggage might have come with the terms *tradition* and *innovation*?

4. In making a case for the importance of convergent thinking, Kuhn states that for much of a career, a scientist "aims to elucidate the scientific tradition in which he was raised rather than to change it" (par. 17). As you reread the essay, consider what is involved in "elucidating" a tradition. Based on your own experience in the science classroom as well as on Kuhn's argument, write a brief essay in which you interpret what Kuhn means by this statement. How does the scientist do this? What does it contribute to the development of science? Under what circumstances does this lead to change?

From Text to Field

1. Recalling Kuhn's definition of the term *paradigm*, consider what paradigms we use today in areas beyond basic science. How do these paradigms influence what we think and how we act?

2. Reflect on a time when, as part of a group, you experienced "rapid progress" as a result of "consensus," in the sense that Kuhn uses those terms. What was the consensus? How was it formed? What was the catalyst for "rapid progress"? What form did it take? What was the effect of the progress on the earlier consensus? In other words, how did the experience of progress change what you or the group had earlier held as a value or an assumption? Why might collaboration be especially important, even (or perhaps especially) for the divergent thinker?

3. Although Kuhn's theory has been applied to a number of other disciplines, in this early essay he makes a sharp distinction between the practice of science and the practice of other disciplines: "[H]istory strongly suggests that, though one can practice science—as one does philosophy or art or political science—without a firm consensus, this more flexible practice will not produce the pattern of rapid consequential scientific advance to which recent centuries have accustomed us" (par. 14). Write an essay in which you respond to Kuhn's assertion that consensus plays a more critical role in the progress of science than in the progress of other fields. If "firm consensus" is more critical to scientific advancement, why is this the case? How do the applied sciences, such as engineering, which often emphasize invention or innovation, fit into this tension between convergent and divergent thinking? Can philosophy or art or political science be practiced without firm consensus? What role does consensus play in these disciplines? Does the lack of firm consensus in these disciplines mean that they have advanced less rapidly than science? Why or why not?

INTO THE FIELD: Options for Writing Projects

1. Talking Back and Listening: Reading Revealed

It is easy, if not tempting, to construe reading as a passive process. Yet Michael Parker's essay alerts us to the tensions and back talk that are possible, and perhaps even desirable, in the process of reading. Reading thus becomes highly collaborative, hardly the one-way street it might seem to be.

This field project asks you to reflect on the process of reading the written page and responding to it. The marginalia that Parker discusses are only one aspect of this larger process. Often in college, you are asked to attend to the content that is on the page. Here we'll try something different, inviting you to attend to the reading process itself. You may wish to address some of the following issues in your field project:

- Explore ways of talking back that go beyond or are different from the physical marginalia in actual books. What role might a "double-entry notebook" have, one in which you record quotes in one column and your responses in another? Do you engage in unrecorded dialogues or debates with an author? What options for talking back are offered or encouraged in your various classes?
- When might it be okay, or even preferable, to listen attentively to the author, rather than responding right away? In what ways do different kinds of texts in different disciplines change the dynamic of your reading process?
- How do the various purposes for and types of reading (skimming, test preparation, critical reading, etc.) influence your reading habits? Have you become habituated to one kind of reading? How do you shift gears? How has nonacademic pleasure reading influenced your approach to reading in college?
- Reading is in one sense a very private affair. In what ways and for what purposes might reading groups play an especially valuable role?
- How have technology and online resources changed your role as a reader? Do you find it enjoyable or annoying to read "on the screen"? Does the availability of online texts and resources affect your willingness to engage hard-copy texts and books?
- How do you handle the rhythms of reading during a longer project? When is sympathetic reading, or "reading with the grain," particularly useful? And when is it important to become skeptical and read "against the grain"?

For this project, be sure to attend carefully to your reading process. Consider keeping a journal or log in which you record your habits as a reader.

2. Collaborative Constructions

When you enter a classroom, you enter an arena that is already, to some degree, constructed for you and that even structures, to some degree, your identity. Different styles of teaching and particular classroom settings encourage you to adopt a particular role as a student in that class. This field project invites you to reflect on how your role as a student and as a reader is guided and on how your interaction and collaboration with other students is constructed. You may reflect on any of your college classes, including your writing class. Here are several options for you to pursue:

- Consider the manner in which texts and textbooks construct your role as a reader. In what ways is your response to the readings guided? How are you expected to behave as a reader? And how are you expected to collaborate with fellow students in the process of learning course material?
- The physical classroom setting can go a long way in determining what options you and your instructor have for collaborative activities. Think about the material conditions that either encourage or inhibit collaboration: Can chairs and tables be moved? Can you arrange the room in ways that depart from the usual lecture configuration (rows of chairs, with the professor up front)? Does the use of technology encourage or undermine potential collaboration?
- What indications can you glean from the syllabus about the role of collaboration in your classroom? How or to what extent is collaboration with fellow classmates part of the normal rhythm of classroom activities? In what ways might tradition and the history of teaching in that discipline affect how collaboration is or isn't enacted in your classroom?

3. Group Work: An Insider's Perspective

Lisa Ede and Andrea Lunsford offer in their essay a detailed analysis of their own collaborative process. This field project invites you to contribute an analysis of your own experience in collaborative writing or in a group project, whether it occurred in college or in high school. Offer a detailed account of your experience, an evaluation of its success or failure, and recommendations about how the experience might be improved in the future. Remember, a collaborative experience doesn't have to be completely successful and enjoyable for you to derive benefit and insight from it. Here are some issues you may wish to address:

- How and by whom is your role determined in the collaborative undertaking? What latitude do you have to negotiate your roles?
- What guidance has your instructor offered in advance about the dynamics of collaborative work? Are you thrown together in a group and expected to discover

effective means for collaboration? Or has the collaboration been charted out in advance, with particular expectations about roles and procedures?

- How has the collaborative nature of your work affected assessment? Will individual contributions to the collaborative project be taken into account (and should they)? In what ways were individual contributions and responsibilities unevenly distributed? Can such responsibilities always be fairly divided?

- Occasionally you will find in your midst a "slacker," someone who doesn't shoulder his or her responsibilities as a group member or collaborative partner. How have you or other members of your group handled the situation? To what extent, if any, is the instructor expected to intervene?

- Some conscientious students find themselves in a situation such that they carry more than their fair share of the burden in a collaborative undertaking. If you have found yourself in that situation, how have you handled it? To what extent has that extra burden on you shaped your perception about the nature and value of collaborative work?

4. Niches for Collaboration

Our desire and need for social interaction in the process of education is so strong that collaborative activities may take place even when they are not explicitly sanctioned or authorized. Indeed, collaboration often thrives in those niches where it becomes self-organizing and not in some sense "official." This field project invites you to explore collaboration in your courses and on your campus that occurs "under the radar." Your job is to go "undercover," seek out collaborative work that occurs outside of formal classroom time, and analyze what role it plays in student learning and in the development of a learning community.

Here are some tips on where to find these collaborative niches and on what questions you might pose:

- What ways do students in a course find to interact with each other outside of the classroom? What kinds of conversations occur before and after class? Do students trade phone numbers, or is there a class e-mail list? Do some students form study groups on their own initiative?

- What kinds of collaboration occur in the dorms or in off-campus housing? In what ways is collaboration different, or richer, when conducted in pajamas over a bowl of popcorn?

- What are some of the different venues for collaboration? Does collaboration take place in the library, the computer lab, the campus or dorm cafeteria, the nearby coffeehouse, the rec center, online?

- Do any of your courses encourage collaboration outside of class? In what ways could or does your campus facilitate collaboration outside of class?

- What are the barriers to or fears concerning collaboration? To what extent does the specter of plagiarism or cheating haunt collaborative work?

- Why might the social dimension of collaboration — getting to know each other as fellow students and as friends — play an important part in the success of academic purposes for collaboration?
- What would you change — on campus or in a particular course — to encourage collaboration?

5. Workplace Collaborations

Investigate and report on the role of collaborative activities, especially as they pertain to writing, in the profession you have chosen for yourself. If you currently have a job, even part-time, you may wish to explore collaboration in that workplace. Your investigations can include "ethnographic field notes" (close observations of ongoing daily activities), an analysis of typical documents, and interviews. The following tips and questions might help you launch your exploration:

- Find a company or an organization in your community that offers a local resource for your investigations into your future profession.
- Conduct an "environmental scan" of the profession, or an organization in that profession, to determine where and how collaboration might take place. How does collaboration figure into the daily work of people in that organization?
- You may wish to focus on the life cycle of a major project in that organization. How does collaboration enter into the development of the project and its final presentation in written form? What is the interplay of writing and speaking, and virtual and physical meetings, as modes through which collaboration takes place?
- Who "owns" the material? What is the role of "boilerplate" or generic prewritten material? What issues of intellectual property or plagiarism arise in the writing activities of this profession or organization?
- In what ways does the "culture" of the organization or profession encourage collaborative work? What rewards or incentives support collaborative work?
- How does collaboration in this profession or workplace differ from collaboration on campus and in classrooms?
- If you are in a major that is in some sense preprofessional (business, engineering, nursing, etc.), to what extent does your present academic training help prepare you for the collaborative environment that is part of the workplace reality you will face in the future?

6. Collaboration in Your Academic Discipline

This field project invites you to explore attitudes toward collaboration in your academic major. You may find that these attitudes vary considerably, depending on whether your major is in the humanities, the social sciences, or the sciences.

A good barometer of these attitudes can be found in how professors in your field carry out and publish their work. Choose the top three academic journals in your field (an instructor in your major or a reference librarian can help you identify those journals). Scan the tables of contents of those journals from one year to determine how many of the articles are coauthored or have multiple authors. You may wish to compare notes with other classmates who are majoring in different fields. What does your inventory suggest about collaboration in your field?

You may wish to augment your study by conducting several interviews with professors or by scanning faculty Web sites. What can you gather about the role of collaboration in the development and funding of research in your field? How do faculty interact with their colleagues— on campus or across the country—as they carry on their professional activities?

A further resource in your fieldwork may initially strike you as somewhat odd: the acknowledgments section in the prefatory material of published work, especially books. Yes, you'll find loving tributes to the supportive spouse, apologies to the children who have lost time with the parent, and perhaps even mention of the household pet. But beyond these more personal expressions of gratitude are debts to colleagues and reviewers. An author's acknowledgment of these personal and intellectual debts can give you a good behind-the-scenes look at collaboration in your field.

7. An Insider's Guide to the Collaborative Classroom

Throughout his article, Kenneth A. Bruffee argues for particular characteristics of collaborative learning that his research and teaching experience have convinced him will lead to the most effective classroom practice. From the point of a student, write instructions for college-level teachers who are planning to experiment with collaborative learning in their classrooms. Draw from your experience as a student as well as from Bruffee's argument. In your instructions, include suggestions for introducing collaborative learning to students, setting up work groups, determining how and to what extent the teacher will interact with the groups, and evaluating group work.

As an alternative project, draw on your experience as well as Bruffee's argument to compose a manual or pamphlet for incoming freshmen to prepare them for what Bruffee describes as the process of "assimilation into communities of knowledgeable peers." Given your own experience on campus, how might you be able to help incoming students find their way into learning communities or discover ways of collaborating with one another? Address why entry into such collaborative communities can benefit their personal and academic lives, what the process involves, how they should regard it, and how they can make it work for them.

8. The Talent Myth—On Campus and Beyond

Malcolm Gladwell challenges our received notions about the importance of talent and asks us to reconsider just how important collaboration in organizations may be. This field project invites you to consider his proposition in light of organizations you know well. One such organization is your college or university itself. Another organization may be a current or prior workplace. Here are three project options for your consideration:

- Explore what Gladwell terms "the talent myth" in light of your own classes and course work. To what extent do your professors look for native individual talent, or do they also prize collaborative skills? Are you just waiting for a professor to come up to you and say, "You've got talent, kid!" or are you concerned that your skills in collaboration and group work may hide the talent you feel you possess? As you work your way through college and prepare for professional life, do you believe the talent expected of you in college and the talent expected of you in the workplace are different? As a student, how do you deal with this discrepancy or negotiate the difference?

- Your campus is a complex organization. This field project invites you to consider how it handles "individual talent." Chances are, you'll find some tensions around that question. In many respects, individual talent is prized in university settings, with some professors acting as if they were free agents. Nevertheless, research labs and whole departments—indeed the campus itself—need to function well as groups. Through interviews with faculty and staff, consider the climate on your campus or in your major department with regard to the role of individual talent in an organization.

- A third option for this field project invites you to consider an organization for which you have worked. Through interviews with coworkers and with owners and managers, assess the respective roles of individual talent and organizational collaboration. How well does Gladwell's argument apply to that particular work setting? What influence does the type of work the company performs have in your assessment? How does seniority or the level of employment factor into your assessment?

9. Handling the Tension: Received Wisdom and New Ideas

Thomas S. Kuhn presented his talk on "The Essential Tension" to suggest that it is not enough to encourage creative, divergent thinking in its own right. Divergent thinking needs to be grounded in and held in tension with convergent thinking—thinking that honors the traditions, practices, and received wisdom of a field.

Although Kuhn speaks of this "essential tension" in light of advanced scientific research, that tension can also exist in your own studies as an undergraduate.

retain a sample of the beverage and have it tested by company chemists. If necessary, Coca-Cola Co. would then prosecute the establishments for unfair competition.

The license may grant the licensee exclusive rights to use the mark. Alternatively, the licensor may limit the licensee's rights by allowing the licensee to use the mark only in specific geographic areas or may allow others to use the mark. Similarly, the licensor may retain rights to use the mark itself. The license agreement should specify whether the license is an **exclusive** or **nonexclusive license,** indicate whether use is restricted to any specific goods or services, or to any geographic territory, and must include adequate quality control provisions. Most license agreements also recite that the licensee acquires no ownership rights in the mark and cannot challenge the licensor's rights to the mark. A one-time fee may be paid by the licensee for the privilege of using the mark, or the licensee may make periodic royalty payments to the licensor based upon sales of the products. For example, the licensee may be required to pay the licensor 4 percent of its net profits arising out of its use of the mark as **royalties** or to achieve certain levels of sales. On occasion, a trademark owner may assign the entire mark to a party who then "licenses back" to the original owner the right to use the mark for some purpose. Some adversarial proceedings between trademark claimants are resolved by such licensing arrangements. Although a license can be recorded with the PTO (using Form 1594), there is no requirement of recording, and most parties in the United States do not do so, believing the license is a private agreement of which the public need not be informed. Moreover, license agreements do not involve a change of ownership or affect the chain of title to a mark. In most foreign countries, however, as discussed in Chapter 8, there is usually a statutory duty to record a license agreement with the appropriate governing body.

The dates relating to trademark licenses should be docketed or calendared so that the license is terminated or renewed at the appropriate time.

(See Exhibit 5–5 for a sample trademark license agreement.)

Trademarks as Collateral

Trademark owners may use their marks as collateral to secure their promise to perform some obligation. For example, a trademark owner may wish to borrow $400,000 from a bank. The bank may insist that certain property be pledged as collateral so that in the event of a default by the owner, the bank can seize the assets pledged. Trademarks can be used as such collateral. Typically, the parties enter into an agreement called a **security agreement** that contains the terms and conditions of their arrangement. The security agreement will identify the marks being pledged as collateral. The security agreement is typically recorded at the PTO (using Form 1618A) to afford notice to the public that the marks are subject to the security interest. When the trademark owner satisfies its obligations, the security interest is released, again by using Form 1618A. During the existence of the security agreement, the owner retains all rights in the mark. Granting a security interest in a trademark is not a transfer of any present rights in a mark. It allows a party to seize the marks (and then exercise all rights of ownership) only in the event of a default by the owner in regard to some promise or obligation. Because the grant of a security interest is conditional (because it has no effect unless there is a default), a trademark that is the subject of an ITU application can be used as collateral.

On the one hand, you are expected to master concepts and techniques that have long been established by others. Yet on the other hand, you are also expected to offer (in some fields more than in others) your own fresh insights and new ideas. This "essential tension" can become an "essential quandary" and can lead to more than a few headaches. How can you be expected to learn, master, and demonstrate knowledge of received wisdom and also offer serious, new ideas?

This field project provides an opportunity to explore and understand that tension in your own course of study. Because the tension presents itself differently in different areas of study, place your own experience in one of several ways:

- If you are intending to major in the sciences, write an introduction, from your perspective as a student, to the "essential tension" in scientific work for undergraduates considering a career in that field. How does the ratio of convergent and divergent thinking appear during the undergraduate years? How might the emphasis on convergent thinking explain a whole range of undergraduate experiences, from the lecture style of teaching, to the replication of classic experiments in the lab, to the role of science textbooks?

- If you are intending to major in the humanities, write an explanation of this "essential tension" for undergraduates who may be a bit puzzled or threatened by the demand that they offer fresh, original ideas. Given the classes you have taken or are now taking, how do you handle this tension? Why might the ratio of convergent to divergent thinking differ in the humanities? To what extent is there a commonly agreed-upon set of theories, practices, and techniques in any of the humanities fields? As you try to offer new, fresh ideas, how do you establish your authority as someone who knows the received wisdom in that field?

- If you are planning to major in one of the "applied" fields, such as engineering, business, or studio arts, write an introduction to the "essential tension" as it presents itself in your field. In what ways does the tension between convergent and divergent thinking present itself a bit differently in applied fields? In what ways does the need to be "inventive" or to apply knowledge in very specific, concrete circumstances present different challenges from those experienced by majors in the sciences or the humanities?

For this field project, draw on your experience in the classroom or with particular assignments. Use this project as an opportunity to explore how the "essential tension" between convergent and divergent thinking might apply to a field or area of expertise you are familiar with or would like to pursue.

10. Textbooks, Convergence, and Collaboration

Early in his lecture on "The Essential Tension," Thomas S. Kuhn points to textbooks in the sciences as offering a revealing glimpse of convergent thinking in action. Not only do students immerse themselves in textbooks until well into their graduate education, those textbooks themselves provide a distillation of agreed-upon knowledge. In this sense, divergent thinking and textbooks can hardly be thought to go together. Nevertheless, not all fields are quite as insistent on convergent thinking as the sciences, and the role of textbooks in non-scientific fields departs from what Kuhn had in mind.

This field project invites you to examine textbooks and other classroom instructional materials as a way of gaining insight into how they establish and pass on a discipline's particular approach to the tension between convergent and divergent thinking. Consider the varied purposes of textbooks in different disciplines and how those textbooks are deployed in different ways in the classroom. Although some textbooks might be thought of as providing definitive knowledge, others may be thought of as providing resources for engagement with course materials. As you conduct your fieldwork, pay special attention to new kinds of classroom materials, often electronic in nature. How do new advances in software, such as individualized diagnostic testing, interactive tutorials, or customized applications, affect your assessment of textbooks and teaching materials in your field?

You may also want to take your field project in a slightly different direction by examining the relationship between textbooks and collaborative learning. In what ways do the textbooks you use in your various classes support or hinder collaboration? In what ways might an emphasis on convergent thinking lead, oddly enough, to some fairly private learning experiences? On the other hand, why might some very collaborative group learning activities lead to some very divergent insights or outcomes?

BORDER CROSSINGS

Borders mark boundaries. They demarcate what lies on our side of the world, what is ours or near and familiar to us, even as they mark off what lies beyond us and, thus, what we count as foreign and strange. Borders separate zones of comfort and arenas of influence. Through the borders we encounter — or erect — we find ourselves at home or abroad.

Geopolitical borders, those boundaries that separate countries, are only one of many kinds of borders. There are others, and those with the most influence tend not to be marked with a fence or appear on maps. Given the many borders we encounter and sometimes cross in our daily lives and inter-actions with each other, we live simultaneously in many lands, even as many realms lie beyond our ken.

Day in and day out, we come upon many opportunities to cross borders. But college offers a special opportunity to do so. In ways that are more explic-it and insistent, college asks us to cross borders we may not have contem-plated and, thus, to cross into lands — intellectual and cultural — that we owe it to ourselves to know. With each border crossing, we hear and learn new voices and come to discover new resources and depth in our own.

This unit invites you to cross borders by offering you a chance to reflect on how words, language, and verbal representations operate in those social spaces where cultures meet. In these borderlands, we come to be more aware of the implicit rules that govern our conversations and how various games are played. We likewise are given opportunities we might not otherwise have to reflect on how we represent other cultures and how those representations offer a sometimes unflattering portrait of ourselves. We learn about borders with an eye to how power is often unequally distributed and to the role of conflict even within seemingly coherent communities. And we learn above all about many voices and the challenges we face in trying to find, if not our own voice, at least those several voices that speak authentically to our own experiences and the needs of others.

The three readings included in this unit provide both invitations and provocations. What they share is an interest in the life of words at the various borders we encounter. Nancy Masterson Sakamoto offers a glimpse of the unspoken rules that govern conversations in different cultures. Learning the language — any language, even academese — is not enough, nor is it even sufficient to know, in some abstract sense, what the rules are. We need to learn how to play the conversational game in any particular culture. Inviting us with her as she tours and reflects on several museums, Jane Tompkins has us look behind the exhibit cases to ponder how we represent other cultures and how our museums represent us. Her essay has the unsettling effect of having us wonder which side of the exhibit case we are on. By coining the term *contact zone*, Mary Louise Pratt gives us the means to interpret and enter those "social spaces where cultures meet, clash, and grapple with each other." The social spaces she considers include the baseball-card world of preteens, the Spanish conquest of the Andean peoples, and a controversial new course at Stanford University.

Reflecting on Prior Knowledge

1. Most of us have experienced awkward moments when speaking to people from other cultures. The difficulties we—and surely they—experienced cannot always be attributed to weak vocabulary or an imperfect mastery of verb tenses. Working in groups, develop a set of reasons why conversations may be hard to carry on between peoples of difficult cultures. What do we assume about our conversations that may not always be shared by others?

2. In a journal entry, recall a visit to a museum where the lives and histories of other cultures were represented. What did you expect from the museum? What would you imagine the response to be from a member of that culture? In what ways might museums offer insights not just into different cultures, but also into your own?

3. Recall an experience when, as a member of a group, you met, clashed, or grappled with a group that had more power or influence. In a journal entry, reflect on that encounter and on the role of language in that encounter. What rhetorical and linguistic resources did you—and they—have at hand?

4. In some respects, entering the college or university community is like trying to enter a different (and seemingly odd or exotic) culture. Working in groups, consider what challenges you have encountered while trying to pass yourself off as a native. In what ways do you continue to straddle several cultures or communities?

5. While tackling writing assignments in college, you encounter a good many voices as you read and research. In a journal entry, reflect on how you handle these voices and how you decide which voice you will adopt in your own writing.

Conversational Ballgames

Nancy Masterson Sakamoto

She knew the right Japanese words and phrases, but Nancy Masterson Sakamoto couldn't enter a conversation with her husband's Japanese family and friends without unsettling them. She taught English to Japanese students but couldn't get them to converse like English speakers. She decided to find out why and discovered two very different conversational ballgames.

"Conversational Ballgames" was first published in 1982 in *Polite Fictions: Why Japanese and Americans Seem Rude to Each Other,* which Sakamoto coauthored with a Japanese colleague, Reiko Naotsuka. The essay has since been widely anthologized, recognized in particular for the game analogies that capture the complex use of language in social settings marked by the meeting of different cultures. In an increasingly multicultural society, and as travel permits us to cross cultural borders ever more frequently, her brief essay stands as a welcome reminder that we need to be aware of the implicit rules of our own culture, even as we strive to learn the different rules that govern other cultures. We might also bear in mind that college can be its own rather odd culture, and learning how to play the academic ballgame, in conversation and in writing, may seem every bit as difficult as learning how to interact in a foreign language.

Born in Los Angeles, Nancy Masterson Sakamoto straddled two cultures in her professional and personal life. Living in Japan with her Japanese husband, she was for many years a teacher of English and a teacher trainer. Coauthor of *Mutual Understanding of Different Cultures* (1981), Sakamoto served as professor of American Studies at Shitennoji Gakuen University and at Hawaii Institute, as well as at the University of Hawaii.

After I was married and had lived in Japan for a while, my Japanese gradually improved to the point where I could take part in simple conversations with my husband and his friends and family. And I began to notice that often, when I joined in, the others would look startled, and the conversational topic would come to a halt. After this happened several times, it became clear to me that I was doing something wrong. But for a long time, I didn't know what it was.

Finally, after listening carefully to many Japanese conversations, I discovered what my problem was. Even though I was speaking Japanese, I was handling the conversation in a Western way.

Japanese-style conversations develop quite differently from Western-style conversations. And the difference isn't only in the languages. I realized that just as I kept trying to hold Western-style conversations even when I was speaking Japanese, so my English students kept trying to hold Japanese-style conversations even when they were speaking English. We were unconsciously playing entirely different conversational ballgames.

A Western-style conversation between two people is like a game of tennis. If I introduce a topic, a conversational ball, I expect you to hit it back. If you agree with me, I don't expect you simply to agree and do nothing more. I expect you to add something — a reason for agreeing, another example, or an elaboration to carry the idea further. But I don't expect you always to agree. I am just as happy if you question me, or challenge me, or completely disagree with me. Whether you agree or disagree, your response will return the ball to me.

And then it is my turn again. I don't serve a new ball from my original 5
starting line. I hit your ball back again from where it has bounced. I carry your idea further, or answer your questions or objections, or challenge or question you. And so the ball goes back and forth, with each of us doing our best to give it a new twist, an original spin, or a powerful smash.

And the more vigorous the action, the more interesting and exciting the game. Of course, if one of us gets angry, it spoils the conversation, just as it spoils a tennis game. But getting excited is not at all the same as getting angry. After all, we are not trying to hit each other. We are trying to hit the ball. So long as we attack only each other's opinions, and do not attack each other personally, we don't expect anyone to get hurt. A good conversation is supposed to be interesting and exciting.

If there are more than two people in the conversation, then it is like doubles in tennis, or like volleyball. There's no waiting in line. Whoever is nearest and quickest hits the ball, and if you step back, someone else will hit it. No one stops the game to give you a turn. You're responsible for taking your own turn.

But whether it's two players or a group, everyone does his best to keep the ball going, and no one person has the ball for very long.

A Japanese-style conversation, however, is not at all like tennis or volley-ball. It's like bowling. You wait for your turn. And you always know your place in line. It depends on such things as whether you are older or younger, a close friend or a relative stranger to the previous speaker, in a senior or junior position, and so on.

When your turn comes, you step up to the starting line with your bowling ball, and carefully bowl it. Everyone else stands back and watches politely, murmuring encouragement. Everyone waits until the ball has reached the end of the alley, and watches to see if it knocks down all the pins, or only some of them, or none of them. There is a pause, while everyone registers your score.

Then, after everyone is sure that you have completely finished your turn, the next person in line steps up to the same starting line, with a different ball. He doesn't return your ball, **Everyone is trying to bowl** and he does not begin from where your ball stopped. **with a volleyball.** There is no back and forth at all. All the balls run par-allel. And there is always a suitable pause between turns. There is no rush, no excitement, no scramble for the ball.

No wonder everyone looked startled when I took part in Japanese conver-sations. I paid no attention to whose turn it was, and kept snatching the ball halfway down the alley and throwing it back at the bowler. Of course the con-versation died. I was playing the wrong game.

This explains why it is almost impossible to get a Western-style conversa-tion or discussion going with English students in Japan. I used to think that the problem was their lack of English language ability. But I finally came to realize that the biggest problem is that they, too, are playing the wrong game.

Whenever I serve a volleyball, everyone just stands back and watches it fall, with occasional murmurs of encouragement. No one hits it back. Everyone waits until I call on someone to take a turn. And when that person speaks, he doesn't hit my ball back. He serves a new ball. Again, everyone just watches it fall.

So I call on someone else. This person does not refer to what the previous speaker has said. He also serves a new ball. Nobody seems to have paid any attention to what anyone else has said. Everyone begins again from the same starting line, and all the balls run parallel. There is never any back and forth. Everyone is trying to bowl with a volleyball.

And if I try a simpler conversation, with only two of us, then the other per-son tries to bowl with my tennis ball. No wonder foreign English teachers in Japan get discouraged.

Now that you know about the difference in the conversational ballgames, you may think that all your troubles are over. But if you have been trained all your life to play one game, it is no simple matter to switch to another, even if you know the rules. Knowing the rules is not at all the same thing as playing the game.

Even now, during a conversation in Japanese I will notice a startled reaction, and belatedly realize that once again I have rudely interrupted by instinctively trying to hit back the other person's bowling ball. It is no easier for me to "just listen" during a conversation, than it is for my Japanese students to "just relax" when speaking with foreigners. Now I can truly sympathize with how hard they must find it to try to carry on a Western-style conversation.

If I have not yet learned to do conversational bowling in Japanese, at least I have figured out one thing that puzzled me for a long time. After his first trip to America, my husband complained that Americans asked him so many questions and made him talk so much at the dinner table that he never had a chance to eat. When I asked him why he couldn't talk and eat at the same time, he said that Japanese do not customarily think that dinner, especially on fairly formal occasions, is a suitable time for extended conversation.

Since Westerners think that conversation is an indispensable part of dining,   20
and indeed would consider it impolite not to converse with one's dinner partner, I found this Japanese custom rather strange. Still, I could accept it as a cultural difference even though I didn't really understand it. But when my husband added, in explanation, that Japanese consider it extremely rude to talk with one's mouth full, I got confused. Talking with one's mouth full is certainly not an American custom. We think it very rude, too. Yet we still manage to talk a lot and eat at the same time. How do we do it?

For a long time, I couldn't explain it, and it bothered me. But after I discovered the conversational ballgames, I finally found the answer. Of course! In a Western-style conversation, you hit the ball, and while someone else is hitting it back, you take a bite, chew, and swallow. Then you hit the ball again, and then eat some more. The more people there are in the conversation, the more chances you have to eat. But even with only two of you talking, you still have plenty of chances to eat.

Maybe that's why polite conversation at the dinner table has never been a traditional part of Japanese etiquette. Your turn to talk would last so long without interruption that you'd never get a chance to eat.

Working with the Text

1. Nancy Masterson Sakamoto uses sports analogies to capture the differences between Western and Japanese conversations. While her article is primarily descriptive, she is pinpointing behaviors that suggest deep cultural differences in the *purpose* of conversation. In a brief essay, analyze the purpose of each style of conversation. From the analogies, what can you infer about how each

culture views relationships? In what ways does each culture expect conversation to define or advance relationships? What cultural values do you think are at play?

2. Sakamoto gained insight into these "conversational ballgames" through her attempts as a Westerner to converse with Japanese people and as an English teacher to engage her Japanese students in conversation. With her essay as a guide, use conversation to explore the difficulties she faced. With a group of other students in the class, imagine that you are preparing for a cultural-exchange trip to Japan. Choose a topic that will give you a substantial amount of conversational material. First, converse in your usual style. After ending the conversation, discuss the extent to which you used the Western "tennis" style described by Sakamoto. Using the same topic, try to converse in the Japanese "bowling" style she describes. Discuss the difficulties as well as any new avenues created by the style. Consider why it might be difficult to mimic the tacit or deeply ingrained conversational rules of a different culture. Individually, reflect on your experience in a brief essay.

3. As we encounter other cultures, we tend to judge, reject, or borrow what is unfamiliar or intriguing to us; at the same time, we come to see our own culture in a new light. As you reread Sakamoto's essay, be aware of your own response to the cultural differences she describes. In a brief essay, note what you consider to be the advantages and disadvantages of each conversational style in building personal relationships and in making decisions in professional situations.

4. Sakamoto frequently uses analogies to support her analysis. An analogy offers an extended comparison between two ideas, objects, or processes, for the purpose of explaining something unfamiliar or foreign by referring to something more familiar. What analogies does Sakamoto use in this brief essay, and do they serve her purpose?

From Text to Field

1. Although cultural differences come in many forms, Sakamoto focuses on conversation, the point of personal contact. Most of us have met someone whose first language is not English, or we have learned a new spoken language. Many of us have traveled abroad. In an essay, recall an experience of conversing with someone whose first language was not English. You might have spoken together in English or in the other person's first language. With Sakamoto's essay as an example, use analogies to explore the differences in conversational style. Find sports analogies other than tennis or bowling, or look for analogies in other fields, such as music, dance, or some form of craftsmanship.

2. Personal interaction with people from other cultures can change our perception of their culture, making it more understandable or more mysterious, more

EXHIBIT 5–5
Trademark License
Agreement

This Trademark License Agreement (the "Agreement") is entered into and is effective as of this _____ day of _____ , 20_____ , by and between Watson Inc., a Delaware corporation with its principal offices at 885 Third Avenue, 24th Floor, New York, NY 10022 ("Licensor") and _____ , a _____ corporation with its principal offices at _____ ("Licensee").

WHEREAS, Licensor is the owner of the trademark ADVENTURE RIVER (the "Mark") and U.S. Registration No. 1,789,746 therefor for children's books in I.C. 16, toys in I.C. 28, and a variety of houseware items in I.C. 21, all as specified in the registration and Licensor has the right to license use of the Mark to others;

WHEREAS, Licensor is desirous of licensing and Licensee is desirous of obtaining a license to use the Mark in connection with its business;

NOW, THEREFORE, in consideration of the above, and for other good and valuable consideration, the receipt and sufficiency of which are hereby acknowledged, the parties agree as follows:

1. GRANT OF LICENSE AND LICENSE FEE

Licensor grants to Licensee an exclusive, nontransferable, worldwide license to use the Mark in its name in connection with the goods covered by the registration of the Mark.

Upon execution of this Agreement, Licensee shall pay Licensor the sum of _____ Dollars ($_____) as consideration for the grant of license to use Licensor's Mark as described herein.

2. TERM OF LICENSE

Unless sooner terminated as provided in Section 8 hereof, the grant, as specified in Section 1, shall continue for a period of three (3) years from the date of this Agreement. This Agreement may be renewed for additional terms of three (3) years by mutual written agreement of the parties, which agreement may specify a license fee greater than the license fee provided in Section 1, not less than six (6) months prior to the expiration of the initial or any renewal term of this Agreement. Upon expiration of this Agreement:

    a. All rights of the Licensee to the Mark shall terminate and the Licensee shall have no further rights with respect thereto;

    b. Licensee shall not offer any goods in connection with the Mark or any confusingly similar mark and shall cease all use of the Mark or any confusingly similar mark; and

    c. Licensee shall cease any activity that suggests that it has any right to the Mark or that it has any association with the Licensor.

3. OWNERSHIP OF MARK

Licensee acknowledges the ownership of the Mark in Licensor, agrees that it will do nothing inconsistent with such ownership and that all use of the Mark by Licensee shall inure to the benefit of and be on behalf of Licensor, and agrees to assist Licensor in recording this Agreement with any appropriate domestic or foreign government authorities. Licensee agrees that nothing in this Agreement shall give Licensee any right, title, or interest in the Mark other than the right to use the Mark in accordance with this Agreement, and Licensee agrees that it will not challenge the title of Licensor to the Mark or challenge the validity of this Agreement.

(continues)

attractive or more suspicious. In a brief essay, reflect on such an encounter of your own. How did you regard the culture before the encounter? How did your perception of the culture change? What was it about the personal interaction that created the change?

3. Even those who share English as a first language can confuse, unnerve, or offend each other with their different conversational styles. Conversations with your parents probably work under very different rules than talks with your friends. You may be disoriented by the conversation style of a roommate from another part of the country or from another race, ethnic group, or economic level. Approaching a college professor may require a style you never had to know in approaching a high school teacher. Membership in a new group might involve learning not only a new vocabulary but also a new game for initiating or entering conversations. Identify a situation that required or is requiring you to learn or teach a new game for conversing with someone who speaks English as a first language. Write a short guide in which you describe the two clashing styles and advise the reader on how to adjust to the new game.

4. In her analysis of conversational rules, Sakamoto focuses in large part on how we "take turns" in conversation and on continuity or changes in topic. Yet there are many other cultural rules that inform our conversations. These include how physical space and gesture guide our interactions. Write a brief essay in which you reflect on the role of such things as personal space, gesture, and eye contact. Alternatively, you may wish to pay close attention to certain key moments in the course of a conversation, such as greetings or introductions and leave-takings.

5. As you take courses in different departments on campus, you may find that members of particular disciplines, each with their own kind of "culture," have distinctive ways of carrying on conversations, whether spoken or in print. Choose a discipline you are interested in, perhaps your prospective major, and try to articulate what might be the conversation rules that govern how the academic game is played in that field.

A Visit to the Museum

Jane Tompkins

Jane Tompkins is aware of her surroundings. As a teacher, author, lecturer, and workshop leader, she brings a holistic perspective to issues of teaching and learning in higher education. For her, this includes attention to the physical environment. Tompkins has also made a career of seeing into the self, not only in terms of cultivating individual identity, but also in terms of understanding other selves. In addition to literary theory, her work has spanned personal criticism, the opening of the American canon, popular culture, and women's writing.

In "A Visit to the Museum," first published in the *Georgia Review,* Tompkins's interests merge. Identity, self-examination, education, and the physical elements of culture come into play as she questions the American fascination with Indians. She touches on a range of issues that have to do with how we represent other cultures — and ourselves. How can non-Indians know Native Americans? How can museums reveal them? What, in the first place, should museums be about?

Tompkins was for many years professor of English at Duke University. She is currently professor of English and education at the University of Illinois at Chicago. In addition to books on reader-response criticism and the cultural work of American fiction, Tompkins has authored the widely acclaimed *A Life in School: What a Teacher Learned* (1996) and *West of Everything: The Inner Life of Westerns* (1992).

On impulse, during a recent trip across the country, I turned off the interstate at Oklahoma City to follow the signs to the National Cowboy Hall of Fame. I had taken to visiting museums lately, not only because I was interested in their contents, but also because I wanted to see how the contents had been selected, with what aim and what results. I knew that anthropologists and cultural historians had been writing about the politics of museums, and I shared their concerns, but I was interested too in the kinds of experience one has in a museum: The feelings and thoughts they arouse, the physical sensations they provide. I had started to reflect, in particular, on how museums devoted to the American West educated people to see the country's past in a certain way.

As befits a museum that celebrates the grandeur of the West, everything in the National Cowboy Hall of Fame is on a large scale. A long colonnade leads to the broad entranceway; the lobby is open and inviting. An attractive older woman greeted me after I had paid admission, handed me a brochure, and asked if I had any questions. All this opulence and graciousness made me feel well launched, if a little guilty. I had gone in prepared to analyze and find fault (a previous experience at a Western museum had alerted me to the bloodthirsty, conquistador character of some commemorations of the West), but the generosity and sophistication of this environment disarmed me almost completely. So what if the paintings showed stereotyped Indian chiefs and idealized cowboys; so what if the Indian art was displayed as if it were in an apartment featured by *Architectural Digest*; I was lulled by the soothing colors, the luminous spaces, the hushed admiration of the visitors, and the excellent air-conditioning. Even the enormous hall devoted to busts of the museum's donors wasn't enough to mar the experience.

Exiting along the stone path that curves across a pond dotted by fountains, I found it impossible to cavil. It no longer mattered if a hundred pictures of rodeo stars, shown next to a hundred saddles and a hundred lassos, had been boring (never mind that it celebrated an American tradition of cruelty to animals). The museum itself had been beautiful, comfortable, and serene. I had enjoyed looking at the contemporary paintings; the portraits of western movie stars were a particular treat for me — and so was the John Wayne alcove, which offered a video full of wonderful clips from his films and a display of his collection of Chinese art and Western Americana. The hour had been a pleasure — exactly right as a respite from the long, hot drive between Amarillo and Tulsa.

This benign episode made me wonder. If I, a professional critic blooded for the kill, had come away from the Cowboy Hall of Fame grateful for the pleasant interlude, maybe museum-going wasn't the serious business I had long considered it. Maybe it was more like going to the ballpark and eating a hot dog than attending a lecture or reading a book. Maybe, on the model of TV news programs like *60 Minutes* and *20/20*, it was information as entertainment. The product was no longer "culture" in the standard sense but a total experience — gorgeous gift shop, great snack bar, fantastic lighting, terrific videos — all of these making up the package. I had to admit that I liked visiting a really luxurious rest room, browsing through expensive art books, looking at some curious paintings, and listening to the splash of fountains. Under these conditions, questions of cultural indoctrination — of racism, male-worship, and ethnocentrism — just couldn't get any purchase in my brain. I felt refreshed.

In the history of my experiences with museums this one was uncharacter- 5 istically mild. I have an indelible memory of the children's lunchroom in the Museum of Natural History in New York: the little, olive-drab lockers where we deposited our brown paper bags reeking of bananas and mayonnaise, cheese, and oranges and bologna. The huge dinosaurs made of bones, the great canoe filled with terrifying warriors, the dioramas of Indians in their villages — these are among the most vivid impressions of my childhood. From a later period, I remember the Museum of the Works of the Duomo in Florence — an austere, light-filled space, all stone and air — with its Donatello statues of the prophets, radiating moral purpose.

These and other museums became for me touchstones, summarizing eras of experience, my cultural capital, homes away from home. I had a love affair once with the De Young Museum in Golden Gate Park in San Francisco. Its jade collection and fierce Chinese bronzes drew me again and again; it was a temple where I came to worship something I now cannot describe. Museums always seemed to me to hold the key to higher realms. They stood for knowledge, skill, treasure, and ungraspable values, things for which a person ought to strive. They were like secular churches where people could come to reverence what they loved— baseball, Thomas Jefferson, the French Impressionists — and their teaching had been influential in my life.

What museums didn't say, however, turned out to be more important than what they did. For I have recently learned that museums can teach one much amiss. Their power to distort history and to frustrate learning, as well as to inspire emulation, was brought home to me a few months ago when, on a sunny December afternoon, I made a visit to the Museum of the American Indian in New York.

After a half-hour delay on the 7th Avenue subway, I emerged blinking into the sunlight of Spanish Harlem, feeling unsure of myself. Should I be frightened? Everything looked seedy, normal, and unthreatening. Instead of feeling I was in a war zone, which was what people had led me to expect, it was more like having left the capital for the provinces. No downtown bustle and importance here, just old people pulling grocery carts. I made my way across Broadway to the sidewalk at 155th Street, the old-fashioned kind made of hexagonal pieces of stone, to where the museum stands. It occupies the left wing of a large gray building that surrounds three sides of a disused courtyard, most of which is shut off from the public by an iron fence. The whole thing looked as if it had been built a hundred years ago and then forgotten. And inside, the Museum of the American Indian also has the air of a place that hasn't changed in a long time. It's the lighting that contributes to this impression most. A dim light spreads itself evenly over everything, giving all the spaces and the objects in them an indescribable tinge of sickly yellow-gray, the color of old train-station lavatories and ancient public-school buildings.

For here, indeed, is the museum of one's childhood. Here were cases crammed with unfamiliar objects, glutting the eye and mind before one had even begun to look. The burden of so many things made me desperate for information, anything to stay mentally afloat. But in the Museum of the American Indian, aids to reflection are few. There's a mimeographed pamphlet available in the bookshop whose title sums up the situation nicely: "On Your Own with Great North American Indians." The information the museum does provide comes on placards, hand-lettered, a little shakily, in a vaguely gothic script, conveying an impression of old age all by themselves. The first one I read, propped in the corner of an overstuffed case, had two misspelled words, "enviornment" and "develope." Maybe it's just that I've been an English teacher all my life, but those misspelled words — and the thought of generations of schoolchildren reading them — filled me with despair and foreboding. These mistakes, along with the studied penmanship, prepared me for the prose, which had the character of labored student compositions: monotonous sentence structure, everything in the passive voice, no concrete details.

After a while, still reading to get my bearings, I began to notice a certain   10 turn these descriptions took. It often seemed that the clothing or decorative style or implement under discussion wasn't, in some subtle way, all that it could have been. What the case contained would be secondary to, or less important than, or not so brilliant as what had been produced by some other tribe, or in some other period, or at some different location. It was as if whoever had been responsible for the descriptions was unconsciously sabotaging an already doomed operation, unable to help himself. I felt rage mounting in me, and frustration. Why couldn't these objects have been displayed better, with imagination and flair, not to mention adequate lighting? Why couldn't the museum have provided lively, engaging accounts of the life these objects stood for? Why, for heaven's sake, couldn't they even get the *spelling* right? Why did they (whoever "they" were) have to be so *negative* about the things they had? And why, after all, was it the remains of the American Indians that were being treated in this shabby way? I had seen, two days before, Sienese paintings at the Metropolitan Museum of Art treated as holy treasures, magnificently offered for our veneration. Why were fourteenth-century Italians so much more important to us than the inhabitants of our own continent?

The sense of failure hit me strongest when I heard a metallic voice emanating from behind some cases on the first floor. Wending my way back I discovered the Indian Museum's excuse for a video: a box with some colored slides of Indian artifacts that changed every few seconds, while a voiceover recited facts about the museum. These, too, were tinged by the air of defeat. The museum displayed 11,000 items; *however,* these were only a fraction of the one million items it owned, which were stored in a warehouse in the Bronx. The man who had amassed the collection, George Gustav Heye, had established the museum early in the century; *however,* the opening was delayed by World War I. Why include this fact in a two-minute description?

There were other depressing features: On the walls of the dark stairwell hung small hand-colored pictures of, I think, Indian costumes: it was hard to tell because they were unidentified. Stylistically flat, amateurishly mounted, brightly colored, they seemed more appropriate for a kindergarten than for a major collection. As I stood on the landing, deciding whether to look at the exhibit of contemporary Indian painting on my left, I heard someone urinating, long and heavy. I was standing outside the men's room. When I reflected on why I'd never had this experience before — hearing what I was hearing while staring into a roomful of paintings — I realized it was because in most museums the rest rooms are located at some distance from the exhibits.

Leaving the second floor, I went up to the third where, in a special exhibit of artifacts from Central America, the museum seemed to be putting its best foot forward. Here, what my colleague Marianna Torgovnick calls "the jewelry-store method" of display had been adopted with a vengeance. Small cases with dark interiors housed a small number of items, **Museums can teach one much amiss.** spotlit from unexpected angles. Each case was visually stunning, a striking composition in light and shade. But most of the objects were lit only on one side or not illuminated at all, and this, coupled with the scarcity of information, made it hard to know what you were looking at and harder to remember what you had seen.

By this time I was so aggravated I couldn't look at anything without getting angry. I realized that if I were going to get something out of this visit I would have to change my frame of mind. I would have to stop imagining the way it should have been — lustrous marble, elegant spaces, brilliant illumination, sophisticated aids to comprehension — and start looking for what *was* there. So, determined to get what I had come for, some experience or insight to treasure, I went back downstairs and began to look at the cases again, carefully, state by state — Oklahoma, Nebraska, Kentucky. And little by little I began to notice that what was in them was much richer, more varied, and more beautiful than any collection of American Indian artifacts I had ever seen.

There was statuary: I hadn't known that North American Indians made statues, if you except the totem carvings of the Northwest. Yet here were

15

wooden figures of men and women, squat, square, austere, enigmatic, and powerful as any African carvings I had ever seen. There was an incredible variety of clothing, of different styles, in different materials, intricately and beautifully decorated. There were gorgeous cloaks, vests, leggings, shawls, headdresses, slippers, boots. Explosions of jewelry, amulets, necklaces, arm bands, leg bands. Every kind of implement, bowls, baskets, sieves, carving tools, weapons, pipes, cooking utensils, blankets, toys, carrying bags, dolls, masks, fetishes, drawings. And all of it made from so many kinds of skins, furs, hides, bones, teeth, claws, horns, stones, woods, clays, and grasses.

One reads about the intense spiritual lives of the North American Indians, but their physical existence, it is always implied, was nasty, brutish, and short. The display cases in the Museum of the American Indian contradict these notions. What came through to me in a way it never had before was the richness of the material lives of these peoples, the reality of the Indians' contact with things. Things they had held in their hands, things they had protected and adorned their bodies with, things they had used, things they had simply seen. The beauty, stylistic coherence, workmanship, and utility of the objects in each case, and the way they fit together into a kind of whole made me think, involuntarily, the word *culture*. I knew of course that North American Indians had a culture, or rather, individual cultures. All "peoples" had "cultures," no matter how technologically unlike our culture theirs may have been. I had known this, but until now, I had known it only as a piety of cultural relativism, not as an immediate experience. *That* was what the Museum of the American Indian gave me. The immediate visual and tactile experience, the sensory evidence, abundant, amassed, incontrovertible, of the textural life-world of Native American people.

But this was not just an impression of material shapes. For as the objects of a given tribe reflected those of others stylistically, the labor that went into them, the knowledge and skill, the time and care, the consistency with which motifs were repeated, and the talismanic power that certain objects obviously possessed, combined to hint at what must have been the density and force of the cultural stories that gave the objects meaning. And yet their stillness now, cheek by cheek with one another, under glass where they had lain for so many years, was the stillness of death. Testaments of life, of the vibrancy, cohesion, and viability of a particular way of life, now they were testaments of extinction.

It was odd. Something about the way the objects were displayed — too many, too close together, not really explained, in depressing surroundings — or something in the objects themselves, or something in me, allowed them to speak in a way they had never spoken to me before. I didn't know what to feel. The objects had given me a glimpse of an independent life, glorious and untouchable, an integrity of action and being that had existed once in

Oklahoma, in Kentucky, and perhaps existed somewhere still, on another plane, like music. That was cause for celebration. But at the same time and all around me was evidence of failure — whose failure was hard to say — the museum's failure to honor what it possessed, the failure of the society that had produced Spanish Harlem, the failure of the nation that had destroyed the civilizations whose remnants it now half-heartedly preserved?

Museums are halls of fame, meant to honor those whose works they preserve, not to superintend their slide into oblivion. In our culture — and who, exactly, were "we"? — honor meant space, light, opulence, being up-to-date; it meant pride of place, prominence, visibility. The Museum of the American Indian had been accorded none of these. The feelings of secondariness and disappointment I had felt creeping into even the most impersonal information did not come out of nowhere: They were a response to neglect. I felt neglected myself as I stood there, and at the same time, responsible. I looked at the meager offerings of the gift shop and went home.

Three days later I came back to learn more about the museum (it was my 20 last day in New York), and to verify some of the observations I had made. It was Friday of the week after Christmas and New York was full of tourists; I had twice fought my way through crowds at the Met. But the Indian Museum seemed even more deserted than it had before. It was only early afternoon, and a weekday, but on reaching the entrance I found a pair of great brass doors — depicting, in bas-relief, scenes from American Indian life — swung tightly shut. There was no sign telling when the Museum would be open or when it would be closed, only the doors, and from their surface, staring back at me, indecipherable, some patches of brilliant white graffiti.

I wasn't surprised. The day before I had imagined the museum staff working in crowded back rooms, ill lit, with old oak desks (or if you were lower in the pecking order, old metal ones), ancient filing cabinets, partitions made of wood or pebbled glass, linoleum floors, and vintage watercoolers. The people who staffed the museum, I thought as I stood by the closed doors, probably didn't want to work. They were too demoralized. They would jump at a holiday, I thought. But of course this couldn't be the real reason the museum was closed. The real reason, as someone suggested later, was probably that there wasn't enough money to keep it open. Not enough to pay the heat and electricity. Still, it came to the same thing: No one had cared enough.

There was a certain logic in this. The main traditions of this country grow out of Europe. The masters of fourteenth-century Sienese painting currently being honored at the Met had been Christian and urban, they had spoken an Indo-European language, they had the alphabet, the printing press, gunpowder, the stirrup; their institutions, their technology, their worldviews were the grandfathers of ours. Some of their kinsmen would "discover" this continent a century or so later. Culturally, they were more "American" than the Iroquois and the Chippewa, so it made sense that we should honor their works.

But there was another logic which spoke more plainly still. The line that led from the European "discovery" of the continent led also to the near extinction of Native Americans and to the massive destruction of animals, even of entire species. It led to cancer, unbreathable air, dead lakes, dying forests, toxic-waste dumps, chemical disasters, and the possible annihilation of all living creatures through nuclear war. There was a connection, I thought, between these dusty trophies and the dying continent. Whatever ferocities the Indian peoples might have practiced, their traditions had a reverence for the whole web of creation that could have served us as a model for understanding the planet we inhabited, that could have helped us to live less destructively.

Books I had read about the native peoples of North America — *Black Elk Speaks*, Paula Gunn Allen's *The Sacred Hoop*, Calvin Martin's *Keepers of the Game*, Anthony F. C. Wallace's *The Death and Rebirth of the Seneca*, James Axtell's *The European and the Indian*, Vine Deloria's *God Is Red* — these books and others had taught me that Indians did not behave as if the human species were infinitely more important and valuable than all other species, or even more important than plants and stones, rivers and mountains. A person could become a wolf or an owl without loss of status. The instrumental relationship people of "our" culture have to the material world, treating nonhuman existents as if they had no value except their utility for us, allowed for a dazzling manipulation of the external environment. But the price seemed to be a loss of mutuality. If you treat a person as a slave, naturally that person will hate you. If you treat things as if they have no intrinsic worth, they will turn against you, too.

I had scarcely any right to these speculations, knowing so little about Indian cultures. But I couldn't help thinking that the neglect of their treasures, and what that neglect stood for in terms of our ignorance, was correlated with the dungeon of the subway I had ridden, the trash I had seen on Broadway, and the graffiti glaring back from the doors. The subway that had gotten me to the museum and the airplane that had brought me to New York and that I was about to board again in a few hours belonged to the same machinery that had made these items into relics. I saw that, being a creature of modern technology, my coming to the museum on a subway, reading some placards, and then going home in an airplane guaranteed that I would never know what the objects in the museum meant in any thoroughgoing, tangible sense. And it occurred to me that the way to find out about them would not be to read more books about Indians.

Studying had its place, but studying was what *we* did — collecting, in the process, so many dry bones. (I subsequently learned that there were tens of thousands of Indian skeletons being held in American museums for purposes of "study.") Studying was part of the machinery, which is to say, of the instrumentalism that destroyed the environment that had made Indian life possible. Study was what had motivated collections such as this. Later on, I read about the controversy surrounding the Museum of the American Indian— where it should be housed, who should control it, who should pay, how much — and discovered that the founder, George Gustav Heye, had cared nothing for the public, nothing for what Native Americans themselves felt about his disposition of their treasures, but only for "solving the great mystery of the origin of the prehistoric races of the Western Hemisphere." I wanted to distance myself from this way of relating to the objects in the cases, I wanted to see the world as the people who made the objects saw it, I wanted to get into their bodies and feel what they had felt, and I saw that to do this, it would be necessary to live differently.

What would have to happen was this: A rattle in one of the cases would have to begin to shake, a headdress start to tremble, an amulet to levitate and hurtle through the glass and into my hand. I would have to walk onto a reservation somewhere and start living without books or TV. I would have to get to the other plane. It didn't matter that the Museum of the American Indian was on 155th Street instead of further downtown. It didn't matter that the lighting was dim. A better address and glitzier surroundings wouldn't have made the difference, as far as learning was concerned. In fact, the opulent, high pressure, visually exciting, marble-and-mirrors display I'd imagined as an alternative to the museum's dinginess might have been the worst thing of all. Such an exhibition would have sent me home satisfied, having created the illusion of "being there." The dim light and dull paint let me know I wasn't anywhere but in an underfunded, dispirited, bureaucratic institution. Maybe that was why the objects spoke. It was the contrast that had allowed them to appear.

So my visit was a success after all. The museum had done its work. I had received my instruction.

Or so I thought — until I sent this description of my museum visit to my friend Annette Kolodny, who had recently become Dean of Humanities at the University of Arizona in Tucson. Her reply was hard to take, like some good medicines that in the end will make you better. For though deeply appreciative of the essay, she begged me to consider the following:

> . . . The awakening you describe . . . leaves you open to charges of "romanticizing" the Indian yourself. For example: Except for a small enclave of rabid traditionalists on a very few reservations, you would have great difficulty "walking onto a reservation somewhere and starting to live without books or TV." TV is ubiquitous on the reservations. Books less so.

EXHIBIT 5–5
Trademark License
Agreement
(continued)

4. QUALITY CONTROL STANDARDS AND MAINTENANCE

a. Licensee agrees that the nature and quality of all goods offered or sold by Licensee in connection with the Mark shall be of high quality, manufactured free from defects and in full compliance with all laws, and of such style and appearance to be adequately suited to their exploitation to the best advantage and enhancement of the Mark and consistent with the quality control standards established by Licensor.

b. At reasonable times during the term of this Agreement, Licensor may request Licensee to submit samples of any advertising or promotional materials and specimens of all uses of the Mark. If any such materials fail to meet with Licensor's approval, Licensee shall cease using such disapproved materials or items until such times that it modifies such materials and items and receives approval in writing from the Licensor of such materials and items, as modified.

c. Licensor shall have the right to review the Licensee's use of the Mark and Licensee's business operations at any reasonable time and upon reasonable notice. Upon notice of defects given by Licensor, Licensee shall cure such defects in the use of the Mark or the goods offered thereunder. In the event that Licensee does not take reasonable steps to cure such defects within thirty (30) days after notification by Licensor, Licensor shall have the right to require that Licensee remove the Mark from any products or materials or, at the sole discretion of Licensor, to terminate this Agreement.

d. Licensee shall operate its business in a manner that reflects favorably at all times on the Mark.

5. FORM OF USE

Licensee agrees to use the Mark only in the form and manner and with appropriate legends and notices as prescribed herein and from time to time by Licensor and not to use any other trademark or service mark in combination with the Mark without prior written approval of Licensor.

6. PROPRIETARY RIGHTS AND GOODWILL

a. Licensee acknowledges that the Mark is owned by Licensor, which has the sole and exclusive right to license the Mark. The parties intend that Licensee shall use the Mark only under the terms and conditions of this Agreement. Licensor has the sole and exclusive right to deal with the U.S. Patent and Trademark Office in connection with the Mark, and Licensee will perform any acts reasonably required by Licensor in connection with same. All costs associated with maintenance of the Mark shall be borne by Licensor.

b. Licensee shall use all reasonable precautions and take all necessary steps to prevent the Mark from being acquired or duplicated or used by unauthorized persons. Licensee shall take appropriate action, by instructions, agreements, or otherwise, with any persons permitted access to the Mark to ensure that Licensee satisfies its obligations under this Agreement.

c. Any goodwill arising out of Licensee's use of the Mark shall inure solely and exclusively to the benefit of Licensor, and Licensee shall have no rights therein or claims thereto. Licensee acknowledges that this Agreement does not confer any goodwill or other interest in or to the Mark except the right to use the same in accordance with the terms hereof.

7. INFRINGEMENT BY THIRD PARTIES

Licensee agrees to notify Licensor of any unauthorized use of the Mark by others promptly as it comes to Licensee's attention. Licensor shall have the sole right and discretion to bring infringement or unfair competition proceedings involving the Mark.

The essay also has an insistently nostalgic tone which assumes the "vanishing Red Man" motif. In fact, Native Americans continue to have and practice a viable, meaningful culture; some of the native people I have come to know here would bridle at your suggestion that all is vanished; or that the adaptations made to the modern world (and to white conquest) are somehow inauthentic. For many native people, the white tendency nowadays to sing the praises of the Indian as having lived in harmony with nature is a species of white self-delusion. Whites make the Indian the new pastoral locus; but whites don't do a damned thing to help reverse the appalling statistics of infant mortality or TB on the reservations. What I'm saying, Jane, is that you need to monitor the essay to make certain you're not inadvertently singing another hymn to some version of the Noble Savage (in harmony with nature, freed of the constraints of modern society, unfettered by the complications of technology, etc.). The rugs now being woven by Navajo, Hopi, etc. — but which don't sell to the tourists — show reservation scenes, representationally, with broken-down cars behind a shack, in the front yard of a hogan, and various animals scattered around. Tourists don't buy these rugs, of course, because the rugs are true; and we still want our Indians living in some kind of pure rural splendor. No place in the image for abandoned cars.

I love what you're trying to do and say in that essay. Just try to read it as a Pascua Yaqui living on a reservation in the middle of Tucson, where whites repeatedly come to "watch" the seasonal dances but never stay to help teach the children or provide medicine for the ill. And imagine the Yaqui's seething resentment of those whites who believe that, because they attend the public dances, they "know" or "understand" or have experienced something authentic about Yaqui culture. And also imagine the rage of some other native person who *knows* that contained within the walls of that museum are precious religious artifacts belonging to the tribe, indeed, without which the tribe can no longer prosper. That Indian doesn't want a better museum to display the artifacts; s/he wants the thing(s) returned to the tribe!

Everything Annette had said rang true. I knew that white people like me used Indian culture as a way of dreaming about what their own culture couldn't give them while ignoring the present realities of Native American life, behaving as if there weren't any Indians any more or as if those who survived were somehow less real than those who had lived in the seventeenth century. I had even written, in an essay published three years ago: "The relationship most non-Indians have to the people who first populated this continent . . . [is] characterized by narcissistic fantasies of freedom and adventure, of a life lived closer to nature and to spirit than the life we lead now. . . . The American Indian Movement in the early seventies couldn't get people to pay attention to what was happening to Indians who were alive in the present, so powerful was this country's infatuation with people who wore loincloths, lived in tepees, and roamed the plains and forests long ago." Knowing this, why had I fallen into the trap? For it was true that I had been "romanticizing" for my own purposes.

It was worse than that. I had recently read an entire book manuscript by Marianna Torgovnick, *Gone Primitive*, about the way modern anthropologists, art critics, novelists, psychologists, explorers, and ordinary citizens use primitive peoples as the site for elaborating their dreams — of power, sexual conquest, racial superiority, belonging. How had I forgotten all this? And finally: Was my dream of another life — away from TV and airplanes and worry over spelling mistakes — just an ignorant fantasy? Or did it represent some legitimate impulse to deepen and intensify my contact with the world, to get closer to reality, and to myself?

I don't have an answer to such questions, but they, in turn, raise others that are worth considering. It is one thing to think and write in the abstract about the politics of museums. It is another to make a visit: to take the subway uptown on Christmas vacation, or to turn off the highway on a cross-country trip and walk into a real place, have real sensations, react to spaces, lighting, information (or the lack thereof); to see actual objects — feathers, bones, paintings; and then to browse in a gift shop, have a cup of coffee, sit down to rest your feet.

Something about the immediacy of the experience makes museum-going not the purely intellectual encounter it becomes when one is writing professional criticism about it. The real-life context of a visit—time pressures, physical needs, the desire to be lifted out of oneself momentarily—push other considerations aside. In the event, one tries to get some enjoyment out of what is there, and to learn something from it, no matter how inadequately presented or overproduced the exhibits may be. For one does feel educated, however minimally, by the information that typically accompanies a Native American artifact displayed in a glass case; one learns what it was made from and how, what it was used for, and by what kind of person. The trouble is, the placards never say how, and by what right, this particular object got to the museum, who took it away from whom, under what circumstances, and for what reason. Museum information provides a kind of false contextualization. One learns more than enough about decorative styles and methods of production, but nothing about the historical and political conditions that put the objects there — nothing that would interrupt one's dream of another life.

Could there be an Indian museum that represented the totality of Native American experience to which people would want to come on their vacations? Should such a museum provoke utopian desires as well as a sense of tragedy and the need for present help?

I once visited a small museum in Cherokee, North Carolina — the "Cyclorama" — that was controlled by Indians themselves. It was modest: a few dioramas that told the story of the Trail of Tears, a few artifacts exhibited so that you could really see how they had been used, and a sound-and-light show (made of practically nothing) that dramatized the Cherokees' loss of territory and the diminution of their numbers over the years.

The visit took little more than a half hour (my husband was waiting for me   35 in the parking lot). Everything in the place looked homemade and more than a little worn. But this museum had achieved its purpose fully: It had taught me some things about the Cherokee Nation in a straightforward and consistently interesting way. Whoever had put it together had brought to it two elements that most such enterprises lack: a sense of what works and what doesn't when it comes to educating the public — and the Cherokee point of view.

I learned recently that museum curators are beginning to respond to critiques of their policies and practices. Stanford University and the University of Minnesota are returning their entire collections to local tribes, and the Smithsonian itself has agreed to return burial artifacts and skeletal remains, on request, to contemporary tribes that can prove with "reasonable certainty" that the objects in question belong to them. Signs, perhaps, that museums of the future may be differently conceived and organized. I hope so. The Cherokee museum suggests to me that what will be needed, however, is not a great deal of money, nor a great deal of space, nor a lot of high-tech video equipment, nor even hundreds of objects to put on display, but rather — in the case of Indian museums — the Native American perspective and some good pedagogical sense.

One month ago, it was announced that the long and bitter controversy over where to house the extensive collection of the Museum of the American Indian had at long last been resolved, and that, ironically, it was to be given the last available space on the Mall in Washington. At one time, I would have been overjoyed at the news. Now, I am not so sure.

Working with the Text

1. As you read "A Visit to the Museum," it quickly becomes apparent that the focus of the essay is on the Museum of the American Indian. Why, then, does Jane Tompkins open the essay with an account of her visit to the Cowboy Hall of Fame? What rhetorical purpose does this opening have? In what ways might it provide historical and cultural context for the entire essay?

2. As a cultural critic, Tompkins examines the effects of specific, concrete elements of American culture. To draw the reader into her response to the National Cowboy Hall of Fame and the Museum of the American Indian,

Tompkins uses sensory detail—color, shape, light, movement—to describe the exhibits and their surroundings. Review the essay, focusing on just the sensory detail. Imagine yourself in both museums. Using Tompkins's essay as a model, write your reflections on the significance and meaning of the design of each museum.

3. The structure of this essay is built on successive stages, each of which marks a change in thinking. What changes of mind does Tompkins record? Why has she adopted this structure as a rhetorical strategy?

4. Tompkins's critique of the Museum of the American Indian takes an unexpected turn when she sends the description of her visit to her colleague Annette Kolodny, the dean of humanities at the University of Arizona. Kolodny tells her that "[t]he awakening you describe . . . leaves you open to charges of 'romanticizing' the Indian yourself" (par. 29). Consider Tompkins's view of Indian culture in the description she sent to Kolodny, Kolodny's critique of the description, and Tompkins's reflections on Kolodny's critique. Does the succession of reflections and critiques invalidate—or enrich—prior views? What does Tompkins achieve by including the critique of her essay? Write an essay in which you respond to their views of Indian culture and how non-Indians have represented it, as if Tompkins had sent the entire essay to you to critique.

From Text to Field

1. Work with a group of students in your class to design or plan the elements of a museum of Native American culture. Include a rationale for the design or plan. What should the purpose of a museum be? How should Native American culture be represented? Who should be involved in the planning process? Why? If visitors to your museum are to achieve a more informed understanding of American Indian culture, what should they do besides visit museums?

2. Since the publication of Tompkins's essay, the National Museum of the American Indian (part of the Smithsonian Institution) has opened a new facility on the National Mall in Washington, D.C. Based on Web sites ‹nmai.si.edu›, published reviews of the new space, or perhaps a personal visit, offer a comparison of the two museums. How does the new museum fare, given the concerns that Tompkins offers in her essay?

3. Recall a visit to a particular museum, or head off to visit a museum, notebook in hand. It could be a museum representing another culture, another time in history, natural history, science, or some specialized field. Write an autobiographical essay in which you reflect on and perhaps critique the museum. What did the surroundings and exhibits suggest about the attitude of the exhibitors toward their subject? What current cultural attitudes were reflected in the surroundings? In what ways did it educate you or influence your perception of the

culture, history, or field represented in the museum? In what ways might the museum romanticize its subject or inaccurately position the objects it has on display in cultural terms?

4. Tompkins's essay raises questions about the non-Indian view of Native Americans. Write an essay in which you reflect on your own view. What image do you have of Native Americans? What is your perspective on their place in our cultural history? What are the sources—in popular culture and in your own childhood—of these images and perspectives?

5. Write a plan for a museum representing a culture or field of specialty you know well. The possibilities range from an ethnic group or a time in history to an area of expertise such as music, sports, or science. What would you display? How would you display it? What kind of building would you house it in? What image and purpose would determine its design?

Arts of the Contact Zone

Mary Louise Pratt

In the early seventeenth century, after the fall of the Inca Empire to the Spanish, an Andean sends a thousand pages, written in a mix of his native language and Spanish, to King Philip III of Spain—an attempt to reveal the effects of conquest on the Andean people. In the early 1980s, an American schoolboy hands in an essay, full of misspellings, that proposes an "inventchin"—"a shot that would put every thing you learn at school in your brain." Later that decade, students at Stanford University confront their own and each other's identities in a course that explores "multiple cultural histories." All of them have entered the "contact zone."

Mary Louise Pratt developed the concept of "contact zones" as a way of examining interactions between people from clashing cultures. Pratt offers this term as a way to refer to "social spaces where cultures meet, clash, and grapple with each other, often in contexts of highly asymmetrical relations of power." She found that when the people of one culture are subordinated, they wield particular "arts" to challenge the image imposed on them by those in power.

As a scholar in Spanish and Portuguese as well as comparative literature, Mary Louise Pratt brings both historical and multicultural perspectives to her writing and teaching. A professor at Stanford University, Pratt works in areas that span Latin American women's studies, literature, and cultural theory; postcolonial criticism and theory; discourse and ideology; and travel literature. Her books include *Toward a Speech Act Theory of Literary Discourse* (1977); *Linguistics for Students of Literature* (coauthored with Elizabeth Closs Traugott, 1980); *Amor Brujo: The Images and Culture of Love in the Andes* (1990); and *Imperial Eyes: Travel Writing and Transculturation* (1992).

> "Arts of the Contact Zone" was first delivered as a keynote address at the second Modern Language Association Literacy Conference, held in Pittsburgh in 1990.

Whenever the subject of literacy comes up, what often pops first into my mind is a conversation I overheard eight years ago between my son Sam and his best friend, Willie, aged six and seven, respectively: "Why don't you trade me Many Trails for Carl Yats . . . Yesits . . . Ya-strum-scrum." "That's not how you say it, dummy, it's Carl Yes . . . Yes . . . oh, I don't know." Sam and Willie had just discovered baseball cards. Many Trails was their decoding, with the help of first-grade English phonics, of the name Manny Trillo. The name they were quite rightly stumped on was Carl Yastremski. That was the first time I remembered seeing them put their incipient literacy to their own use, and I was of course thrilled.

Sam and Willie learned a lot about phonics that year by trying to decipher surnames on baseball cards, and a lot about cities, states, heights, weights, places of birth, stages of life. In the years that followed, I watched Sam apply his arithmetic skills to working out batting averages and subtracting retirement years from rookie years; I watched him develop senses of patterning and order by arranging and rearranging his cards for hours on end, and aesthetic judgment by comparing different photos, different series, layouts, and color schemes. American geography and history took shape in his mind through baseball cards. Much of his social life revolved around trading them, and he learned about exchange, fairness, trust, the importance of processes as opposed to results, what it means to get cheated, taken advantage of, even robbed. Baseball cards were the medium of his economic life too. Nowhere better to learn the power and arbitrariness of money, the absolute divorce between use value and exchange value, notions of long- and short-term investment, the possibility of personal values that are independent of market values.

Baseball cards meant baseball card shows, where there was much to be learned about adult worlds as well. And baseball cards opened the door to baseball books, shelves and shelves of encyclopedias, magazines, histories, biographies, novels, books of jokes, anecdotes, cartoons, even poems. Sam learned the history of American racism and the struggle against it through baseball; he saw the Depression and two world wars from behind home plate. He learned the meaning of commodified labor, what it means for one's body and talents to be owned and dispensed by another. He knows something about Japan, Taiwan, Cuba, and Central America and how men and boys do things there. Through the history and experience of baseball stadiums he thought about architecture, light, wind, topography, meteorology, the dynamics of public space. He learned the meaning of expertise, of knowing about something well enough that you can start a conversation with a stranger and feel sure of holding your own. Even with an adult— especially with an adult. Throughout his preadolescent years, baseball history was Sam's luminous point of contact with grown-ups, his lifeline to caring. And, of course, all this time he was also playing baseball, struggling his way through the stages of the local Little League system, lucky enough to be a pretty good player, loving the game and coming to know deeply his strengths and weaknesses.

Literacy began for Sam with the newly pronounceable names on the picture cards and brought him what has been easily the broadest, most varied, most enduring, and most integrated experience of his thirteen-year life. Like many parents, I was delighted to see schooling give Sam the tools with which to find and open all these doors. At the same time I found it unforgivable that schooling itself gave him nothing remotely as meaningful to do, let alone anything that would actually take him beyond the referential, masculinist ethos of baseball and its lore.

However, I was not invited here to speak as a parent, nor as an expert on literacy. I was asked to speak as an MLA [Modern Language Association] member working in the elite academy. In that capacity my contribution is undoubtedly supposed to be abstract, irrelevant, and anchored outside the real world. I wouldn't dream of disappointing anyone. I propose immediately to head back several centuries to a text that has a few points in common with baseball cards and raises thoughts about what Tony Sarmiento, in his comments to the conference, called new visions of literacy. In 1908 a Peruvianist named Richard Pietschmann was exploring in the Danish Royal Archive in Copenhagen and came across a manuscript. It was dated in the city of Cuzco in Peru, in the year 1613, some forty years after the final fall of the Inca Empire to the Spanish and signed with an unmistakably Andean indigenous name: Felipe Guaman Poma de Ayala. Written in a mixture of Quechua and ungrammatical, expressive Spanish, the manuscript was a letter addressed by an unknown but apparently literate Andean to King Philip III of Spain. What stunned Pietschmann was that the letter was twelve hundred pages long. There were almost eight hundred pages of written text and four hundred of captioned line drawings. It was titled *The First New Chronicle and Good Government*. No one knew (or knows) how the manuscript got to the library in Copenhagen or how long it had been there. No one, it appeared, had ever bothered to read it or figured out how. Quechua was not thought of as a written language in 1908, nor Andean culture as a literate culture.

Pietschmann prepared a paper on his find, which he presented in London in 1912, a year after the rediscovery of Machu Picchu by Hiram

Bingham. Reception, by an international congress of Americanists, was apparently confused. It took twenty-five years for a facsimile edition of the work to appear in Paris. It was not till the late 1970s, as positivist reading habits gave way to interpretive studies and colonial elitisms to postcolonial pluralisms, that Western scholars found ways of reading Guaman Poma's *New Chronicle and Good Government* as the extraordinary intercultural tour de force that it was. The letter got there, only 350 years too late, a miracle and a terrible tragedy.

I propose to say a few more words about this erstwhile unreadable text, in order to lay out some thoughts about writing and literacy in what I like to call the *contact zones.* I use this term to refer to social spaces where cultures meet, clash, and grapple with each other, often in contexts of highly asymmetrical relations of power, such as colonialism, slavery, or their aftermaths as they are lived out in many parts of the world today. Eventually I will use the term to reconsider the models of community that many of us rely on in teaching and theorizing and that are under challenge today. But first a little more about Guaman Poma's giant letter to Philip III.

Insofar as anything is known about him at all, Guaman Poma exemplified the sociocultural complexities produced by conquest and empire. He was an indigenous Andean who claimed noble Inca descent and who had adopted (at least in some sense) Christianity. He may have worked in the Spanish colonial administration as an interpreter, scribe, or assistant to a Spanish tax collector — as a mediator, in short. He says he learned to write from his half brother, a mestizo whose Spanish father had given him access to religious education.

Guaman Poma's letter to the king is written in two languages (Spanish and Quechua) and two parts. The first is called the *Nueva corónica,* "New Chronicle." The title is important. The chronicle of course was the main writing apparatus through which the Spanish presented their American conquests to themselves. It constituted one of the main official discourses. In writing a "new chronicle," Guaman Poma took over the official Spanish genre for his own ends. Those ends were, roughly, to construct a new picture of the world, a picture of a Christian world with Andean rather than European peoples at the center of it — Cuzco, not Jerusalem. In the *New Chronicle* Guaman Poma begins by rewriting the Christian history of the world from Adam and Eve (Fig. 1), incorporating the Amerindians into it as offspring of one of the sons of Noah. He identifies five ages of Christian history that he links in parallel with the five ages of canonical Andean history — separate but equal trajectories that diverge with Noah and reintersect not with Columbus but with Saint Bartholomew, claimed to have preceded Columbus in the Americas. In a couple of hundred pages, Guaman Poma constructs a veritable encyclopedia of Inca and pre-Inca history, customs, laws, social forms, public offices, and dynastic leaders. The depictions resemble European manners and customs description, but also reproduce the meticulous detail with which knowledge in Inca society was stored on *quipus°* and in the oral memories of elders.

Guaman Poma's *New Chronicle* is an instance of what I have proposed to   10
call an *autoethnographic* text, by which I mean a text in which people undertake to describe themselves in ways that engage with representations others have made of them. Thus if ethnographic texts are those in which European metropolitan subjects represent to themselves their others (usually their conquered others), autoethnographic texts are representations that the so-defined others construct *in response to* or in dialogue with those texts. Autoethnographic texts are not, then, what are usually thought of as autochthonous forms of expression or self-representation (as the Andean *quipus* were). Rather they involve a selective collaboration with and appropriation of idioms of the metropolis or the conqueror. These are merged or infiltrated to varying degrees with indigenous idioms to create self-representations intended to intervene in metropolitan modes of understanding. Autoethnographic works are often addressed to both metropolitan audiences and the speaker's own community. Their reception is thus highly indeterminate. Such texts often constitute a marginalized group's point of entry into the dominant circuits of print culture. It is interesting to think, for example, of American slave autobiography in its autoethnographic dimensions, which in some respects distinguish it from Euramerican autobiographical tradition. The concept might help explain why some of the earliest published writing by Chicanas took the form of folkloric manners and customs sketches written in English and published in English-language newspapers or folklore magazines (see Treviño). Autoethnographic representation often involves concrete collaborations between people, as between literate ex-slaves and abolitionist intellectuals, or between Guaman Poma and the Inca elders who were his informants. Often, as in Guaman Poma, it involves more than one language. In recent decades autoethnography, critique, and resistance have reconnected with writing in a contemporary creation of the contact zone, the *testimonio*.

Guaman Poma's *New Chronicle* ends with a revisionist account of the Spanish conquest, which, he argues, should have been a peaceful encounter of equals with the potential for benefiting both, but for the mindless greed of the Spanish. He parodies Spanish history. Following contact with the Incas,

---

quipus: Recording devices consisting of colored threads with numeric and other values encoded by knots, used chiefly by administrators in the Inca Empire. Some quipus have up to 2,000 strands.

EXHIBIT 5–5
Trademark License
Agreement
(continued)

8. DEFAULT AND TERMINATION

Licensee shall be deemed to be in default and Licensor may, at its option, terminate this Agreement and all rights granted hereunder, without affording Licensee any opportunity to cure the default, effective immediately upon receipt of notice by Licensee, upon the occurrence of any of the following events:

    a. If Licensee ceases to do business or otherwise forfeits the right to do or transact business in any jurisdiction where its business offices are located.

    b. If a threat or danger to public health or safety results from the management and operation of Licensee's business conducted in connection with the Mark.

    c. If Licensee is convicted of a crime of moral turpitude or similar felony or is convicted of any other crime or is the subject of any civil action that Licensor reasonably believes is likely to have an adverse effect on the Mark, the goodwill associated therewith, or Licensor's interest therein.

    d. If Licensee purports to transfer any rights or obligations under this Agreement to any third party without Licensor's prior written consent.

    e. If Licensee fails to maintain any of the quality control standards prescribed by Licensor in this Agreement or otherwise in writing.

    f. If Licensee engages in any business or markets any service or product under a name or mark which, in Licensor's opinion, is confusingly similar to the Mark.

9. MISCELLANEOUS

    a. This Agreement shall be construed in accordance with the law of the State of New York.

    b. Licensee shall not assign, sublicense, encumber, or otherwise transfer its rights and obligations under this Agreement without the prior written consent of Licensor.

    c. This Agreement contains the entire agreement between the parties with respect to licensing of the Mark. It supersedes and cancels any prior oral or written understandings or negotiations and may not be modified in any respect except in writing signed by both parties.

    d. The terms of this Agreement shall be severable such that if any term hereof is held to be illegal, invalid, or unenforceable, such holding shall not affect the validity of any of the other provisions of the Agreement, unless the severing of such term would defeat the purpose of this Agreement.

    e. The failure of any party to exercise any right or option given to it by or to insist upon strict adherence to the terms of this Agreement shall not constitute a waiver of any terms or conditions herein with respect to any other or subsequent breach.

    f. Any notice, payment, or statement required by this Agreement shall be either personally delivered or sent by registered or certified mail, postage prepaid, to the addresses indicated above and shall be effective when placed in the U.S. mail, properly addressed and containing the proper postage.

    g. This Agreement shall be binding on and shall inure to the benefit of the parties to this Agreement and their successors and assigns, if any.

IN WITNESS WHEREOF, the parties hereto have caused this License Agreement to be executed as of the date provided herein.

LICENSEE   LICENSOR

By: _____   By: _____

Name: _____   Name: _____

Title: _____   Title: _____

Figure 1. Adam and Eve.

he writes, "In all Castille, there was a great commotion. All day and at night in their dreams the Spaniards were saying, 'Yndias, yndias, oro, plata, oro, plata del Piru'" ("Indies, Indies, gold, silver, gold, silver from Peru") (Fig. 2). The Spanish, he writes, brought nothing of value to share with the Andeans, nothing "but armor and guns con la codicia de oro, plata oro y plata, yndias, a las Yndias, Piru" ("with the lust for gold, silver, gold and silver, Indies, the Indies, Peru") (372). I quote these words as an example of a conquered subject using the conqueror's language to construct a parodic, oppositional representation of the conqueror's own speech. Guaman Poma mirrors back to the Spanish (in their language, which is alien to him) an image of themselves that they often suppress and will therefore surely recognize. Such are the dynamics of language, writing, and representation in contact zones.

The second half of the epistle continues the critique. It is titled *Buen gobierno y justicia*, "Good Government and Justice," and combines a description of colonial society in the Andean region with a passionate denunciation of Spanish exploitation and abuse. (These, at the time he was writing, were

Figure 2. Conquista. Meeting of Spaniard and Inca. The Inca says in Quechua, "You eat this gold?" Spaniard replies in Spanish, "We eat this gold."

decimating the population of the Andes at a genocidal rate. In fact, the potential loss of the labor force became a main cause for reform of the system.) Guaman Poma's most implacable hostility is invoked by the clergy, followed by the dreaded *corregidores*, or colonial overseers (Fig. 3). He also praises good works, Christian habits, and just men where he finds them, and offers at length his views as to what constitutes "good government and justice." The Indies, he argues, should be administered through a collaboration of Inca and Spanish elites. The epistle ends with an imaginary question-and-answer session in which, in a reversal of hierarchy, the king is depicted asking Guaman Poma questions about how to reform the empire — a dialogue imagined across the many lines that divide the Andean scribe from the imperial monarch, and in which the subordinated subject single-handedly gives himself authority in the colonizer's language and verbal repertoire. In a way, it worked — this extraordinary text did get written — but in a way it did not, for the letter never reached its addressee.

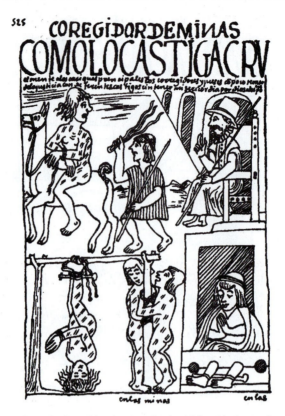

Figure 3. Corregidor de minas. Catalog of Spanish abuses of indigenous labor force.

To grasp the import of Guaman Poma's project, one needs to keep in mind that the Incas had no system of writing. Their huge empire is said to be the only known instance of a full-blown bureaucratic state society built and administered without writing. Guaman Poma constructs his text by appropriating and adapting pieces of the representational repertoire of the invaders. He does not simply imitate or reproduce it; he selects and adapts it along Andean lines to express (bilingually, mind you) Andean interests and aspirations. Ethnographers have used the term *transculturation* to describe processes whereby members of subordinated or marginal groups select and invent from materials transmitted by a dominant or metropolitan culture. The term, originally coined by Cuban sociologist Fernando Ortiz in the 1940s, aimed to replace overly reductive concepts of acculturation and assimilation used to characterize culture under conquest. While subordinate peoples do not usually control what emanates from the dominant culture, they do determine to varying extents what gets absorbed into their own and what it gets used for. Transculturation, like autoethnography, is a phenomenon of the contact zone.

As scholars have realized only relatively recently, the transcultural character of Guaman Poma's text is intricately apparent in its visual as well as its written component. The genre of the four hundred line drawings is European — there seems to have been no tradition of representational drawing among the Incas — but in their execution they deploy specifically Andean systems of spatial symbolism that express Andean values and aspirations.[1]

In figure 1, for instance, Adam is depicted on the left-hand side below the sun, while Eve is on the right-hand side below the moon, and slightly lower than Adam. The two are divided by the diagonal of Adam's digging stick. In Andean spatial symbolism, the diagonal descending from the sun marks the basic line of power and authority dividing upper from lower, male from female, dominant from subordinate. In figure 2, the Inca appears in the same position as Adam, with the Spaniard opposite, and the two at the same height. In figure 3, depicting Spanish abuses of power, the symbolic pattern is reversed. The Spaniard is in a high position indicating dominance, but on the "wrong" (right-hand) side. The diagonals of his lance and that of the servant doing the flogging mark out a line of illegitimate, though real, power. The Andean figures continue to occupy the left-hand side of the picture, but clearly as victims. Guaman Poma wrote that the Spanish conquest had produced *"un mundo al reves,"* "a world in reverse."

In sum, Guaman Poma's text is truly a product of the contact zone. If one thinks of cultures, or literatures, as discrete, coherently structured, monolingual edifices, Guaman Poma's text, and indeed any autoethnographic work, appears anomalous or chaotic — as it apparently did to the European scholars Pietschmann spoke to in 1912. If one does not think of cultures this way, then Guaman Poma's text is simply heterogeneous, as the Andean region was itself and remains today. Such a text is heterogeneous on the reception end as well as the production end: It will read very differently to people in different positions in the contact zone. Because it deploys European and Andean systems of meaning making, the letter necessarily means differently to bilingual Spanish-Quechua speakers and to monolingual speakers in either language; the drawings mean differently to monocultural readers, Spanish or Andean, and to bicultural readers responding to the Andean symbolic structures embodied in European genres.

In the Andes in the early 1600s there existed a literate public with considerable intercultural competence and degrees of bilingualism. Unfortunately, such a community did not exist in the Spanish court with which Guaman Poma was trying to make contact. It is interesting to note that in the same year Guaman Poma sent off his letter, a text by another Peruvian was adopted in official circles in Spain as the canonical Christian mediation between the Spanish conquest and Inca history. It was another huge encyclopedic work, titled the *Royal Commentaries of the Incas*, written, tellingly, by a mestizo, Inca Garcilaso de la Vega. Like the mestizo half brother who taught Guaman Poma to read and write, Inca Garcilaso was the son of an Inca princess and a Spanish official, and had lived in Spain since he was seventeen. Though he too spoke Quechua, his book is written in eloquent, standard Spanish, without illustrations. While Guaman Poma's life's work sat somewhere unread, the *Royal Commentaries* was edited and re-edited in Spain and the New World, a mediation that coded the Andean past and present in ways thought unthreatening to colonial hierarchy.[2] The textual hierarchy persists; the *Royal Commentaries* today remains a staple item on PhD reading lists in Spanish, while the *New Chronicle and Good Government*, despite the ready availability of several fine editions, is not. However, though Guaman Poma's text did not reach its destination, the transcultural currents of expression it exemplifies continued to evolve in the Andes, as they still do, less in writing than in storytelling, ritual, song, dance-drama, painting and sculpture, dress, textile art, forms of governance, religious belief, and many other vernacular art forms. All express the effects of long-term contact and intractable, unequal conflict.

Autoethnography, transculturation, critique, collaboration, bilingualism, mediation, parody, denunciation, imaginary dialogue, vernacular expression — these are some of the literate arts of the contact zone. Miscomprehension, incomprehension, dead letters, unread masterpieces, absolute heterogeneity of meaning — these are some of the perils of writing in the contact zone. They all live among us today in the transnationalized metropolis of the United States and are becoming more widely visible, more pressing, and, like Guaman Poma's text, more decipherable to those who once would have ignored them in defense of a stable, centered sense of knowledge and reality.

Contact and Community

The idea of the contact zone is intended in part to contrast with ideas of community that underlie much of the thinking about language, communication, and culture that gets done in the academy. A couple of years ago, thinking about the linguistic theories I knew, I tried to make sense of a utopian quality that often seemed to characterize social analyses of language by the academy. Languages were seen as living in "speech communities," and these tended to be theorized as discrete, self-defined, coherent entities, held together by a homogeneous competence or grammar shared identically and equally among all the members. This abstract idea of the speech community seemed to reflect, among other things, the utopian way modern nations conceive of themselves as what Benedict Anderson calls "imagined communities."[3] In a book of that title, Anderson observes that with the possible exception of what he calls "primordial villages," human communities exist as *imagined* entities in which people "will never know most of their fellow-members, meet them or even hear of them, yet in the mind of each lives the image of their communion." "Communities are distinguished," he goes on to say, "not by their falsity/genuineness, but by *the style in which they are imagined*" (15; emphasis mine). Anderson proposes three features that characterize the style in which the modern nation is imagined. First, it is imagined as *limited*, by "finite, if elastic, boundaries"; second, it is imagined as *sovereign*; and, third, it is imagined as *fraternal*, "a deep, horizontal comradeship" for which millions of people are prepared "not so much to kill as willingly to die" (15). As the image suggests, the nation-community is embodied metonymically in the finite, sovereign, fraternal figure of the citizen-soldier.

Anderson argues that European bourgeoisies were distinguished by their ability to "achieve solidarity on an essentially imagined basis" (74) on a scale far greater than that of elites of other times and places. Writing and literacy play a central role in this argument. Anderson maintains, as have others, that the main instrument that made bourgeois nation-building projects possible was print capitalism. The commercial circulation of books in the various European vernaculars, he argues, was what first created the invisible networks that would eventually constitute the literate elites and those they ruled as nations. (Estimates are that 180 million books were put into circulation in Europe between the years 1500 and 1600 alone.)

Now obviously this style of imagining of modern nations, as Anderson describes it, is strongly utopian, embodying values like equality, fraternity, liberty, which the societies often profess but systematically fail to realize. The prototype of the modern nation as imagined community was, it seemed to me, mirrored in ways people thought about language and the speech community. Many commentators have pointed out how modern views of language as code and competence assume a unified and homogeneous social world in which language exists as a shared patrimony—as a device, precisely, for imagining community. An image of a universally shared literacy is also part of the picture. The prototypical manifestation of language is generally taken to be the speech of individual adult native speakers face-to-face (as in Saussure's famous diagram) in monolingual, even monodialectal situations— in short, the most homogeneous case linguistically and socially. The same goes for written communication. Now one could certainly imagine a theory that assumed different things — that argued, for instance, that the most revealing speech situation for understanding language was one involving a gathering of people each of whom spoke two languages and understood a third and held only one language in common with any of the others. It depends on what workings of language you want to see or want to see first, on what you choose to define as normative.

In keeping with autonomous, fraternal models of community, analyses of language use commonly assume that principles of cooperation and shared understanding are normally in effect. Descriptions of interactions between people in conversation, classrooms, medical and **Social spaces where cultures** bureaucratic settings, readily take it for granted that **meet, clash, and grapple with** the situation is governed by a single set of rules or **each other.** norms shared by all participants. The analysis focuses then on how those rules produce or fail to produce an orderly, coherent exchange. Models involving games and moves are often used to describe interactions. Despite whatever conflicts or systematic social differences might be in play, it is assumed that all participants are engaged in the same game and that the game is the same for all players. Often it is. But of course it often is not, as, for example, when speakers are from different classes or cultures, or one party is exercising authority and another is submitting to it or questioning it. Last year one of my children moved to a new elementary school that had more open classrooms and more flexible curricula than the conventional school he started out in. A few days into the term, we asked him what it was like at the new school. "Well," he said, "they're a lot nicer, and they have a lot less rules. But know *why* they're nicer?" "Why?" I asked. "So you'll obey all the rules they don't have," he replied. This is a very coherent analysis with considerable elegance and explanatory power, but probably not the one his teacher would have given.

When linguistic (or literate) interaction is described in terms of orderliness, games, moves, or scripts, usually only legitimate moves are actually named as part of the system, where legitimacy is defined from the point of view of the party in authority — regardless of what other parties might see themselves as doing. Teacher-pupil language, for example, tends to be described almost entirely from the point of view of the teacher and teaching, not from the point of view of pupils and pupiling (the word doesn't even exist, though the thing certainly does). If a classroom is analyzed as a social world unified and homogenized with respect to the teacher, whatever students do other than what the teacher specifies is invisible or anomalous to the analysis. This can be true in practice as well. On several occasions my fourth grader, the one busy obeying all the rules they didn't have, was given writing assignments that took the form of answering a series of questions to build up a paragraph. These questions often asked him to identify with the interests of those in power over him — parents, teachers, doctors, public authorities. He invariably sought ways to resist or subvert these assignments. One assignment, for instance, called for imagining "a helpful invention." The students were asked to write single-sentence responses to the following questions:

> What kind of invention would help you?
> How would it help you?
> Why would you need it?
> What would it look like?
> Would other people be able to use it also?
> What would be an invention to help your teacher?
> What would be an invention to help your parents?

Manuel's reply read as follows:

A grate adventchin

> Some inventchins are GRATE!!!!!!!!!!! My inventchin would be a shot that would put every thing you learn at school in your brain. It would help me by letting me graduate right now!! I would need it because it would let me play with my friends, go on vacachin and, do fun a lot more. It would look like a regular shot. Ather peaple would use to. This inventchin would help my teacher parents get away from a lot of work. I think a shot like this would be GRATE!

Despite the spelling, the assignment received the usual star to indicate the task had been fulfilled in an acceptable way. No recognition was available, however, of the humor, the attempt to be critical or contestatory, to parody the structures of authority. On that score, Manuel's luck was only slightly better than Guaman Poma's. What is the place of unsolicited oppositional discourse, parody, resistance, critique in the imagined classroom community? Are teachers supposed to feel that their teaching has been most successful when they have eliminated such things and unified the social world, probably in their own image? Who wins when we do that? Who loses?

Such questions may be hypothetical, because in the United States in the 1990s, many teachers find themselves less and less able to do that even if they want to. The composition of the national collectivity is changing and so are the styles, as Anderson put it, in which it is being imagined. In the 1980s in many nation-states, imagined national syntheses that had retained hegemonic force began to dissolve. Internal social groups with histories and lifeways different from the official ones began insisting on those histories and lifeways *as part of their citizenship,* as the very mode of their membership in the national collectivity. In their dialogues with dominant institutions, many groups began asserting a rhetoric of belonging that made demands beyond those of representation and basic rights granted from above. In universities we started to hear, "I don't just want you to let me be here, I want to belong here; this institution should belong to me as much as it does to anyone else."

Institutions have responded with, among other things, rhetorics of diversity and multiculturalism whose import at this moment is up for grabs across the ideological spectrum.

These shifts are being lived out by everyone working in education today,   25 and everyone is challenged by them in one way or another. Those of us committed to educational democracy are particularly challenged as that notion finds itself besieged on the public agenda. Many of those who govern us display, openly, their interest in a quiescent, ignorant, manipulable electorate. Even as an ideal, the concept of an enlightened citizenry seems to have disappeared from the national imagination. A couple of years ago the university where I work went through an intense and wrenching debate over a narrowly defined Western-culture requirement that had been instituted there in 1980. It kept boiling down to a debate over the ideas of national patrimony, cultural citizenship, and imagined community. In the end, the requirement was transformed into a much more broadly defined course called Cultures, Ideas, Values.[4] In the context of the change, a new course was designed that centered on the Americas and the multiple cultural histories (including European ones) that have intersected here. As you can imagine, the course attracted a very diverse student body. The classroom functioned not like a homogeneous community or a horizontal alliance but like a contact zone. Every single text we read stood in specific historical relationships to the students in the class, but the range and variety of historical relationships in play were enormous. Everybody had a stake in nearly everything we read, but the range and kind of stakes varied widely.

It was the most exciting teaching we had ever done, and also the hardest. We were struck, for example, at how anomalous the formal lecture became in a contact zone (who can forget Atahuallpa throwing down the Bible because it would not speak to him?). The lecturer's traditional (imagined) task — unifying the world in the class's eyes by means of a monologue that rings equally coherent, revealing, and true for all, forging an ad hoc community, homogeneous with respect to one's own words — this task became not only impossible but anomalous and unimaginable. Instead, one had to work in the knowledge that whatever one said was going to be systematically received in radically heterogeneous ways that we were neither able nor entitled to prescribe.

The very nature of the course put ideas and identities on the line. All the students in the class had the experience, for example, of hearing their culture discussed and objectified in ways that horrified them; all the students saw their roots traced back to legacies of both glory and shame; all the students experienced face-to-face the ignorance and incomprehension, and occasionally the hostility, of others. In the absence of community values and the hope of synthesis, it was easy to forget the positives; the fact, for instance, that kinds of marginalization once taken for granted were gone. Virtually every student was having the experience of seeing the world described with him or her in it. Along with rage, incomprehension, and pain, there were exhilarating moments of wonder and revelation, mutual understanding, and new wisdom — the joys of the contact zone. The sufferings and revelations were, at different moments to be sure, experienced by every student. No one was excluded, and no one was safe.

The fact that no one was safe made all of us involved in the course appreciate the importance of what we came to call "safe houses." We used the term to refer to social and intellectual spaces where groups can constitute themselves as horizontal, homogeneous, sovereign communities with high degrees of trust, shared understandings, temporary protection from legacies of oppression. This is why, as we realized, multicultural curricula should not seek to replace ethnic or women's studies, for example. Where there are legacies of subordination, groups need places for healing and mutual recognition, safe houses in which to construct shared understandings, knowledges, claims on the world that they can then bring into the contact zone.

Meanwhile, our job in the Americas course remains to figure out how to make that crossroads the best site for learning that it can be. We are looking for the pedagogical arts of the contact zone. These will include, we are sure, exercises in storytelling and in identifying with the ideas, interests, histories, and attitudes of others; experiments in transculturation and collaborative work and in the arts of critique, parody, and comparison (including unseemly comparisons between elite and vernacular cultural forms); the redemption of the oral; ways for people to engage with suppressed aspects of history (including their own histories), ways to move *into and out of* rhetorics of authenticity; ground rules for communication across lines of difference and hierarchy that go beyond politeness but maintain mutual respect; a systematic approach to the all-important concept of *cultural mediation*. These arts were in play in every room at the extraordinary Pittsburgh conference on literacy. I learned a lot about them there, and I am thankful.

Works Cited

Adorno, Rolena. *Guaman Poma de Ayala: Writing and Resistance in Colonial Peru.* Austin: U of Texas P, 1986.

Anderson, Benedict. *Imagined Communities: Reflections on the Origins and Spread of Nationalism.* London: Verso, 1984.

Garcilaso de la Vega, El Inca. *Royal Commentaries of the Incas.* 1613. Austin: U of Texas P, 1966.

CHAPTER FIVE

Establishing Your Research Questions

Your research project usually begins with the requirement of establishing your research questions. This is a very challenging task for many of us. Should you ever experience a kind of faltering or indecision, do not feel bad. Searching for prospective research topics and narrowing down to specific questions take time. Sometimes you just have to wait for the sort of brainstorm, while thinking about your topic, since establishing your research questions could be a very creative process. And making the final decision might be even harder since this often demands knowledge, understanding, foresight, and courage. You are advised to start thinking about your research project as soon as you work on your study plan. Keep your eyes open with your coursework, and your progressive study in selected areas will give you a good introduction to various research topics. Your review of the literature through the course readings will give you the kind of experience and comparison needed for assessing the research possibilities and specifying the research questions. By starting early, you can afford the time to go back and forth between different research questions while expanding to different subjects. The transitional time leading to your thesis/dissertation could be reduced accordingly and considerably.

Selecting a research topic

If you are an undergraduate student starting to think about a research project for your honors thesis, you may or may not already have a specific research interest. For graduate students, especially for doctoral students, many possess some

TRIVIA

- Words that were once valid trademarks but have become genericized include *corn flakes, dry ice, kerosene, linoleum, nylon, shredded wheat,* and *trampoline.*
- Someone registers a trademark every five minutes.
- In 1772 George Washington asked to use his name as a trademark for flour.

CHAPTER SUMMARY

Merely obtaining a federal trademark registration does not guarantee an owner unlimited and perpetual rights to a mark. Because rights to a mark stem from use (rather than mere registration), the Lanham Act imposes certain requirements on registrants to ensure that only active marks remain on the PTO rolls.

Thus, a registration will be canceled unless, between the fifth and sixth year after registration, and in the year before the end of each ten-year period after registration, the owner files a section 8 affidavit with the PTO alleging its continued use of the mark and submitting a specimen showing the mark as presently used.

If the mark is registered on the Principal Register, has been in continuous use for five years, and has not been the subject of any adverse action, the owner may file a section 15 affidavit and thereby obtain incontestability status for the mark, severely limiting the grounds upon which attacks on the mark may be made.

At the end of the registration period, and every ten years thereafter, an application for renewal must be filed to maintain the registration in force.

In addition to losing rights to federal registration, a trademark owner can lose rights to the mark if it becomes generic or if it is abandoned with intent not to resume use. Nonuse for three years creates a presumption of abandonment.

To ensure rights to marks are maintained, many trademark owners develop compliance policies that set forth guidelines for proper use and display of the mark. Additionally, many owners monitor use of marks in the marketplace to detect potentially infringing marks.

Finally, rights to marks can be lost by acts that cause the mark to lose significance, such as by an assignment of a mark that does not include its goodwill or a license of a mark without quality control provisions to ensure that a licensee's use will be consistent with the standards of quality the public has come to expect of a mark. Trademarks can be used as collateral to secure a party's obligation to perform a promise. In the event of a party's default, the marks are then seized by the secured party, who is usually a lender of money.

Guaman Poma de Ayala, Felipe. *El primer nueva corónica y buen gobierno.*
Manuscript. Ed. John Murra and Rolena Adorno. Mexico: Siglo XXI, 1980.
Pratt, Mary Louise. "Linguistic Utopias." *The Linguistics of Writing.* Ed. Nigel
Fabb et al. Manchester: Manchester UP, 1987. 48–66.
Treviño, Gloria. "Cultural Ambivalence in Early Chicano Prose Fiction." Diss.
Stanford U, 1985.

Notes

1. For an introduction in English to these and other aspects of Guaman Poma's work, see Rolena Adorno. Adorno and Mercedes Lopez-Baralt pioneered the study of Andean symbolic systems in Guaman Poma.

2. It is far from clear that the *Royal Commentaries* was as benign as the Spanish seemed to assume. The book certainly played a role in maintaining the identity and aspirations of indigenous elites in the Andes. In the mid-eighteenth century, a new edition of the *Royal Commentaries* was suppressed by Spanish authorities because its preface included a prophecy by Sir Walter Raleigh that the English would invade Peru and restore the Inca monarchy.

3. The discussion of community here is summarized from my essay "Linguistic Utopias."

4. For information about this program and the contents of courses taught in it, write Program in Cultures, Ideas, Values (CIV), Stanford Univ., Stanford, CA 94305.

Working with the Text

1. Mary Louise Pratt's essay may at first seem to bring together at least three seemingly unrelated subjects: her son's interest in baseball cards, a seventeenth-century Peruvian text, and a new course at Stanford University. Yet with these diverse subjects, Pratt draws on her research, classroom experience, and personal life to question our assumptions about language and community. In a brief essay, explain Pratt's concept of a "contact zone" by identifying and analyzing the common thread that runs through the stories of the early seventeenth-century Andean writer Guaman Poma; students in Stanford University's Cultures, Ideas, and Values course; and Pratt's son.

2. In the context of defining the contact zone, Pratt introduces the term *autoethnographic* text — a text in which subordinated people "undertake to describe themselves in ways that engage with representations others have made of them" (par. 10). The "others" in her definition are people who dominate culture or have conquered another people. Review Pratt's descriptions of autoethnographic texts. Drawing on the concepts and examples she presents, write a brief essay in which you introduce autoethnography to your peers or to another group as a means for resisting authority or asserting identity.

3. Two key terms in Pratt's essay — *culture and community* — are often thought of in broad, positive, even warm and fuzzy ways. One of the many virtues of

Pratt's essay is that she encourages us to look for the tensions and ambiguities in these two terms. In a brief essay, reflect on Pratt's use of these terms. What received or traditional definitions are implied in her essay? In what ways does her term *contact zone* help us rethink these terms?

From Text to Field

1. When Pratt introduces her concept of contact zones, she presents them as places of conflict, "social spaces where cultures meet, clash, and grapple with each other, often in contexts of highly asymmetrical relations of power" (par. 7). When she applies the term to the classes in culture she teaches, she also refers to "exhilarating moments of wonder and revelation, mutual under-standing, and new wisdom—the joys of the contact zone" (par. 27). In a per-sonal essay, reflect on your experience within one or more contact zones. Was the contact zone primarily a place of conflict and domination? Did it produce mutual understanding? Were both conflict and understanding parts of the experience?

2. In discussing Benedict Anderson's concept of "imagined communities," Pratt describes the "nation-building" made possible through the "commercial circu-lation of books in the various European vernaculars," starting in the fifteenth and sixteenth century (par. 20). Based on Pratt's definition of "imagined com-munities," write an essay in which you identify media—especially commercial media—that promote nation-building or the development of imagined com-munities today. How do media bring people into an imagined community? What images or identities do the media create? How accurate do you think the images or identities are? In what ways might such communities be, to use Pratt's term, "linguistic utopias"?

3. In the final paragraph of Pratt's essay, she notes, "We are looking for the peda-gogical arts of the contact zone" (par. 29). Drawing on the extensive list she provides, consider your own educational experiences in college. Do any of your courses or professors draw on "the pedagogical arts of the contact zone"? If so, in what ways and with what effectiveness? If not, in what ways could a particular course be reimagined so that it might draw on such arts?

4. In Pratt's view, teachers—especially those in higher education—can no longer assume that they are in a position to deliver knowledge that "rings equally coherent, revealing, and true for all" (par. 26). According to Pratt, movements that emerged in and after the 1980s began questioning the supposed homo-geneity in American education:

> In their dialogues with dominant institutions, many groups began assert-ing a rhetoric of belonging that made demands beyond those of repre-sentation and basic rights granted from above. In universities we started

to hear, "I don't just want you to let me be here, I want to belong here; this institution should belong to me as much as it does to anyone else." (par. 24)

In an essay, interpret this passage by providing examples from your own observation, experience, and awareness of the role of contact zones and conflict in communities and community building.

INTO THE FIELD: Options for Writing Projects

1. Conversation Partners

Nancy Masterson Sakamoto gleaned her insights into conversation patterns as they differ across cultures not from theory or cloistered research but from her daily interactions with Japanese friends, neighbors, and students. This field project invites you to extend and amplify Sakamoto's thoughts on cross-cultural conversation by joining such a conversation yourself with a foreign student on campus.

Most colleges and universities offer what is sometimes called a "conversation partners" program for foreign students on campus or for students for whom English is a second language. Such programs are often sponsored by an office of international education or by an English as a second language (ESL) program, typically housed in English or linguistics departments. A "conversation partners" program matches American students with foreign students so that they might meet about one hour per week to converse. Apart from helping the nonnative speaker develop fluency in English, you'll find yourself amply rewarded by learning about a foreign culture and gaining a new perspective on American culture. You'll be introduced to a potential new friend and to the foreign student's circle of friends.

This field project invites you to reflect on the conversational patterns you see occurring with your partner and on the delights and challenges of cross-cultural understanding. Your essay might focus as much on your own changing attitudes as on the foreign student's background. As you both cross borders to find common ground and mutual interests, how does your conversation grow and evolve? In what ways are you now able to see American culture through a new set of eyes?

2. Sharing Tables: The Cultures of Food

In the final section of Nancy Masterson Sakamoto's essay, she turns to the connection between conversation and eating food. Little wonder. Cuisine offers a wonderfully rich opportunity to explore foreign cultures and the regional cultures in our own country. Sharing a table with others sparks conviviality and conversation in ways not otherwise possible. Share food and drink, and you share an experience that connects you with people in ways that can sometimes transcend cultural barriers.

This field project invites you to share your table with others and in the process explore how cuisine can further cultural awareness. Here are just some of the many directions you might pursue:

- Share a charged memory from childhood that turns on a particular food dish or on the role of food in a special celebration or event.

- Investigate regional or ethnic cookbooks, cookbooks or recipes that have been handed down in your family, or old cookbooks that are themselves historical documents.
- Explore the role of food in civic events — be it the pie-baking contest at the local county fair or the large urban food festival.
- Reflect on the role of food in campus activities — be it in student organizations or in departmental events. Ask why the first law of drumming up attendance at meetings — "feed them and they will come" — has more to it than just the natural instinct for free munchies.
- Hold a potluck in your writing class, perhaps at a special evening meeting. You might use this event either as a kick-off for food-related projects or as a culminating event during which you and your classmates read from your essays. Think of your words, and those of others, as tasty morsels.
- Analyze the ways in which students share — or don't share — tables in your dorm or campus cafeteria. How does ethnic or cultural difference reflect itself in the cafeteria setting? In what ways does the cafeteria promote or undermine interactions among students and the ability to cultivate new friendships?
- Explore the underworld of student cooking in your dorm. It may not be entirely legal or sanctioned, but if experience rings true, students try to escape from the institutionalized world of the food service — be it through hotplates, microwaves, toaster ovens, or popcorn poppers.

3. **Touring the Campus or Local Museum**

The visits that Jane Tompkins made to the Cowboy Hall of Fame and the Museum of the American Indian might inspire you to explore museums and galleries on your campus or in your community. Armed with Tompkins's insights about the problems of representing others — and yourself — you are now in a position to cast a more critical eye on the various installations or exhibits that you will see. Here are just some of the places your museum tour might take you:

- Many campuses will have a heritage center that showcases the history of your college or university, often focusing on the accomplishments of alumni and the prowess of sports teams. In what ways does your campus represent itself to others? Who is the intended or anticipated audience, and what are their expectations and assumptions? What presence might academics have in the exhibits? If sports have a prominent place in the exhibits, what might that tell you about how our culture constructs the college experience or about the role of sports in your institution's sense of itself?
- Your campus or community may also have a natural history museum or a fine-arts gallery, with permanent collections and visiting exhibits. What

issues of cultural representation might arise in these venues? How do such exhibits project an image of the college or university for the community and the state? Consider interviewing the curators of the shows, seeking their views on the role of the museum and the often difficult issues of representation that can arise in exhibits.

- Your campus library and even some departments may present more modest exhibits, which can nevertheless offer fascinating case studies about how we represent others and how we represent ourselves.

- Consider planning (and even mounting) a modest exhibit about writing and writing instruction on your campus. What might you present in a hallway exhibit case or on the wall-mounted bulletin board? What is difficult to represent about the writing process? Who is your audience, and what expectations or attitudes might they carry with them to your exhibit? Considering that most exhibits are veiled arguments of one kind or another, what message or argument would you want to present? What is the role of text, graphic devices, and visual arguments in exhibit design? How do you plan to implement them?

4. Representations of Other Cultures in Popular Media

Although Jane Tompkins focuses on museums as important sites through which to study cultural representation, museums are by no means the only such sites, nor are they the most influential. This field project invites you to explore other sites where cultures are represented. Popular media, such as film and television, offer rich resources for such a study.

In addition to studying depictions of foreign cultures (e.g., the Disney film *Aladdin*), you might also wish to consider any one of many marginalized groups in American culture. In what ways does popular media stereotype such groups or cultures? What opportunities or risks might a film (or some other form of popular media) take to more genuinely address the challenges of cultural representation?

Your field project might take the form of an academic analysis or of a more popular journalistic piece, such as a review.

5. Contact Zones in Your Core Curriculum

As a teacher and scholar whose work challenges dominant cultures, Mary Louise Pratt brought her interest in contact zones to her involvement in broadening the Western-culture course requirement at Stanford University to include "multiple cultural histories." Reread her description of the dynamics of the new course so that you might consider discussions of curriculum on your own campus. This field project invites you to evaluate the core or general-education curriculum on your campus in light of the discussions in Pratt's essay and on the Stanford campus. Address the questions of how history and culture should be taught to undergraduates and what bearing Pratt's discussion of "contact zones" might have on those questions. Depending on the state of discussions on your campus, your field project could take one of several forms:

- If your campus does not have a required course or set of courses in the area of history and culture, argue for or against adopting the approach suggested by Pratt. Given the particular culture on your campus and the history of curricular discussions, what specific arguments on either side of the issue appear to be most relevant? Make a point of interviewing faculty for their views on the issue. Depending on your stance and on the audience you wish to address, your project might take the form of an essay, a substantive letter to an administrator, an opinion piece in the campus newspaper, or even a formal course proposal (using the required forms).
- If your institution already requires a course that comes close to meeting the spirit of Pratt's suggestion, offer an assessment of the course, with recommendations for retaining, improving, or transforming it. What concerns or controversies accompanied the proposal for the course, and to what degree do those same concerns and controversies still exist? Your project might take the form of an essay or a substantive letter to the faculty member who administers the course.
- Even if your campus does not have a course that meets the spirit of Pratt's discussion and there is little likelihood of such a course coming into existence, there are surely several courses already "on the books" that might lend themselves to some of her suggestions. What innovative "pedagogical arts of the contact zone" might be introduced into existing courses? Focus on one or two courses you have taken or are currently taking which might benefit from those pedagogical arts. You might find interviews with faculty currently teaching those courses to be especially helpful.

6. The Composition Classroom as Contact Zone

Because writing courses are usually taught in small classes, it may be tempting to assume that the sense of community that develops in the classroom over the course of a term is entirely unproblematic. After all, the instructor and students get to know each other in ways that are not possible in most courses, and they are working on some of the most intimate and revealing concerns — one's own writing and its inevitable link to one's identity. It would be hard to imagine a classroom community coming out of a composition course that did not emerge stronger, more cooperative, and more homogeneous — a discrete, self-defined, and coherent speech community. Yet for all of the positive ways in which a composition classroom can come together, it may still be far from the idealized or utopian speech community that we might imagine. Indeed, the classroom may resemble the sort of "contact zone" that Mary Louise Pratt discusses.

This field project invites you to attend closely to your composition classroom. Your goal is not to criticize per se but rather to speak frankly about the tensions and differences that can sometimes intersect in this contact zone. Composition classrooms emerge stronger when they acknowledge these issues and make productive use of them through what Pratt calls innovative "pedagogical arts of the contact zone." Your essay should contribute to an honest and healthy classroom.

Drawing on Pratt's definition of a "contact zone" early in her essay, and attending closely to her discussion of "contact and community" later in the piece, develop a set of questions you want to address in the context of your own composition classroom. In addition to uncovering some of the characteristics that may make the classroom a contact zone, you should also address the "pedagogical arts" that are being used or that could be used to make productive use of those characteristics. Remember that for all of the "rage, incomprehension, and pain" that can occur in a contact zone, Pratt also stresses "exhilarating moments of wonder and revelation, mutual understanding, and new wisdom — the joys of the contact zone."

7. Mapping and Crossing Borders on Campus

When judged by the map you held in your hands during your first days on campus, your college or university may seem to be one undifferentiated (if sometimes vast) territory. The borders that you see may divide your campus from the nearby town, but once on campus you may see little in the way of internal boundaries — at first. After only a few weeks, you were surely far more aware of the different territories or regions on campus and the subtle barriers between them.

This field project invites you to map and discuss the internal borders on your campus. You'll want to note the tensions that may exist and how those tensions can take shape in concrete ways — often physical or geographic. In addition to describing those existing tensions, you may want to inquire into their causes and propose ways in which various members of your campus community can cross those borders.

A good place to start your investigation is to look for contact zones, for those "seams" in what is otherwise the large fabric of your campus. You may find those seams (paraphrasing Mary Louise Pratt) in the social spaces where campus cultures meet and rub up against each other. Look to interactions between students and faculty, faculty and staff, administration and faculty, administration and parents, or between various student groups themselves.

You may also wish to explore what might be thought of as "disciplinary geographies" on your campus. Are the science departments clustered in one area? Are the professional schools (such as engineering, business, and law) located at the far end of campus? What of the boundaries between academic areas and dorm areas or between dorms and "fraternity or sorority row"? Who has the new buildings, and who is housed in the old? Where is the writing program located? (Chances are it is in a basement or in a "temporary building.") What key geographic landmarks seem to have a leading role in orienting people on campus? Is it the student union, the main administration building, or some tower or other landmark? In addition to your essay, you may wish to craft an interpretive map of campus, much as those early explorers developed when they were charting new territories.

8. The Freshman Year as a Borderland Experience

As you enter college, you must straddle the community from which you came and the new community of college. In the process, you must find a way of dealing with the voices of your home and heritage, even as you develop an academic voice. This field project encourages you to explore your experience in college as you find yourself at the borders between different cultures and their voices. In many respects the first year of college can be especially challenging — and rewarding — because of experiences "at the border."

In addition to taking a close look at your experiences, place them in a larger context by talking to other students, your resident advisor, and people on campus who are involved in the first-year experience. You may also wish to consult the growing research literature on experiences during the first year of college. As you plan and draft your essay, ask yourself how you wish to present yourself, and with what voice or voices. Use this essay as an opportunity to reflect on — or even experiment with — different voices.

5

(En)gendering Knowledge

CASE ILLUSTRATION—GENERICIDE

Case: *Kellogg Co. v. Nat. Biscuit Co.,* 305 U.S. 111 (1938)

Facts: The National Biscuit Company (National) sued Kellogg to enjoin the sale of breakfast food known as "shredded wheat," which National had marketed for more than thirty years.

Holding: The term *shredded wheat* is generic. One party has no exclusive right to use the term *shredded wheat* as a trademark for that is the generic name of the article and is the term by which the biscuit is generally known to the public. If a term is generic, a party has no exclusive right to use it. To establish trademark rights, a party must show that the primary significance of a term in the minds of the consuming public is not the product but the producer.

CASE STUDY AND ACTIVITIES

Case Study.   Watson has obtained trademark registrations for a number of its amusement park attractions, including its roller coaster ride DYNAMITE® (the trademark for which was registered on October 10, 2003) and toys and other goods offered at the park. It recently purchased all of the assets of a company that operated a water park whose main attraction was a water ride called LUMBERJACK RIVER, the trademark for which was registered to the defunct company. Two significant problems Watson has recently encountered are a trade embargo in Southeast Asia that has prevented it from importing its popular stuffed animal GIGGLY LAMB® (the trademark for which was registered exactly five and one-half years ago) from Southeast Asia and decreasing sales of PINKIE PIGGIE®, its once popular stuffed toy.

Activities

1. Give all dates relating to maintenance for the DYNAMITE® trademark.
2. What activities should be undertaken with regard to LUMBERJACK RIVER?
3. Watson would like to file the section 8 affidavit of continuing use for GIGGLY LAMB®. What difficulties might it encounter?
4. Watson has found a company that has expressed interest in trying to market the PINKIE PIGGIE® animal; however, Watson believes that it eventually may be able to stimulate sales of PINKIE PIGGIE® itself. What type of arrangement should Watson consider with the other company?

ROLE OF PARALEGAL

Paralegals play a significant role in trademark maintenance. Some law firms with large trademark practices maintain separate departments for trademark prosecution and

SPEAKING OF GENDER

As a topic of casual conversation or academic interest, we may sometimes "speak of gender." The subject has grown in interest, and sometimes controversy, over the years. The women's movement has evolved, and some might even speak of past or present "gender wars." Indeed, our very notion of gender has grown more complex as we recognize how difficult it may be to make easy distinctions about what is male or female. Yet more may be at stake than simply the many things we may say or write "about" men and women. This chapter explores the notion that speaking and writing are themselves gendered. Gender can be voiced and silenced as well. That is, gender is more than one of many topics of conversation; it also influences our conversation and, no matter what the subject, our use of language to learn, know, and communicate. As we speak here of gender, we may find that speaking is itself gendered.

History teaches us that our speaking has always been gendered, but the prevalence of male power — patriarchal ideologies and institutions — made that gender influence all but invisible. Indeed, *feminist* originally meant the same thing as *feminine* — "of the female" and remained so through much of the nineteenth century. In the mid-to-late nineteenth century, the meaning of *feminist* began to shift, with efforts to improve the status of women lending the term what some saw as negative connotations.

In the nineteenth century, women who worked on behalf of other reform movements — agitating against slavery, alcohol abuse, and prostitution — prompted debate about whether women should even exercise a public voice in such matters. When activists worked more directly on behalf of women's rights, that debate only grew in intensity. Women had to struggle for a voice because they asserted their concerns publicly, beyond the home and the domestic realm, and in ways that were seen as selfish, even uppity. In a word, they were unwomanly.

Struggling to win a voice only raised a related question: how that voice might be found credible. Gender is an influential factor in rhetoric, as it is in personal identity. So much of the speaker's ethos or character and his or her persuasiveness are tied to the extent to which that individual embodies community values. With many rhetorical strategies — such as rational deliberation, refutation, and debate — linked to what were often perceived as masculine qualities, women needed to choose between or balance two options. They could adopt those traditional strategies or find a credible voice of their own, developing a feminist rhetoric built on qualities such as egalitarian cooperation and connection to the personal and the experiential. These rhetorical choices mirror a larger question: Should feminist arguments be based on equality or on sexual and gender difference? Both options continue to offer rhetorical resources in contemporary debates.

What has become clear in the last few years is that questions of gender speak to the very ways we use language to learn, know, and communicate. Our knowledge of gender has contributed to an awareness of the ways in which we engender knowledge.

The four essays in this unit offer complementary perspectives on speaking and writing as gendered activities. Well known for her research on the role of gender in workplace and in personal conversations, Deborah Tannen offers an essay on how male and female students use language differently in the classroom. Aware that verbal put-downs can offer salient examples of gender in language, Beverly Gross explores the history and current use of the word *bitch*, finding that what men fear most in women is power. Hermione Lee takes up the issue of power in language more directly as she questions the value of both utopian and confrontational uses of language in feminist discourse. For Lee, we find power in language by embracing its potential—a potential to transform not just the world but ourselves as well. Barbara Smith cautions us to consider ways in which some issues of gender and sexual orientation can be silenced. Drawing attention to the ways in which various kinds of oppression are intertwined, she notes that homophobia is rarely brought up, for it seems to be the one *ism* that progressive people still tolerate.

Reflecting on Prior Knowledge

1. In all the hours you have spent in classrooms, you have observed the ways in which students—including you—conduct themselves during class discussions. In a journal entry, reflect on whether you have noticed differences between the ways male and female students participate in discussions. If you have noticed differences, what are the primary ones? Why do you think these differences exist? If, in your experience, differences in classroom behavior do not fall along gender lines, what do you think does cause differences? In what ways, if any, is your own class participation influenced by gender?

2. Humans have a long history of pointing out differences in the ways females and males use language. We often talk about female and male ways of carrying on a conversation or about differences in the books and movies that tend to attract significantly more of one gender or the other. In preparation for a

class discussion, write down what you consider to be the typically female *and* typically male version of one of the following: conversations (make a point of listening to real ones before you start writing), types or titles of books, or types or titles of movies. When you share your notes in class, discuss the reasons for any differences you have observed, as well as the attitudes females and males might have toward the conversation or book or movie preferences of the opposite gender.

3. Stereotypes abound when it comes to gender, and they often come into play most clearly when someone offers a verbal put-down. In gender-segregated groups, develop a list of ways—or specific words—that are used when putting down men and putting down women. Share your group's lists with the entire class. In a follow-up journal entry, reflect on the role of language in gender identity and gender conflict.

4. Personal power is a common theme in American culture—in music, the mass media, popular writing, and academic writing. In a journal entry, reflect on your own power. In what ways do you express or experience it? Who challenges or tries to suppress it? How might it be suppressed, either through language or action?

5. In a journal entry, describe the man who had the greatest influence on how you regard men or the woman who had the greatest influence on how you regard women. What personal attributes led to your choice? Are those attributes usually shared by the same gender?

How Male and Female Students Use Language Differently

Deborah Tannen

As a linguist and writer, Deborah Tannen has encouraged millions of her readers to improve their relationships by becoming more aware of how they talk. Her insights transformed her own approach to teaching, as a result of her work on the international best seller *You Just Don't Understand: Women and Men in Conversation* (1990). As a professor, she discovered that differences in male and female conversational styles find their way into the classroom. As she notes in the following essay on gender in classroom conversations, published in the *Chronicle of Higher Education* in 1991, "treating people the same is not equal treatment if they are not the same."

University professor and professor of linguistics in the Department of Linguistics at Georgetown University, Tannen conducts research in the areas of sociolinguistics and discourse analysis and is widely known for her ability to speak to both academic and lay audiences. A prolific writer of numerous articles and nineteen books, Tannen has also held positions at Princeton and Stanford universities, lectured throughout the world, and appeared on programs ranging from CBS, ABC, and CNN news broadcasts to *The Oprah Winfrey Show* and *Larry King Live*.

Her 1994 book, *Talking from 9 to 5: Women and Men at Work*, was a *New York Times* business best seller and served as the basis for a training video. Her 1998 book, *The Argument Culture*, criticizes our tendency to resort to debate instead of dialogue. In 2001, she received the Books for a Better Life Award for *I Only Say This Because I Love You: Talking to Your Parents, Partner, Sibs, and Kids When You're All Adults* (2001).

When I researched and wrote my latest book, *You Just Don't Understand: Women and Men in Conversation,* the furthest thing from my mind was reevaluating my teaching strategies. But that has been one of the direct benefits of having written the book.

The primary focus of my linguistic research always has been the language of everyday conversation. One facet of this is conversational style: how different regional, ethnic, and class backgrounds, as well as age and gender, result in different ways of using language to communicate. *You Just Don't Understand* is about the conversational styles of women and men. As I gained more insight into typically male and female ways of using language, I began to suspect some of the causes of the troubling facts that women who go to single-sex schools do better in later life, and that when young women sit next to young men in classrooms, the males talk more. This is not to say that all men talk in class, nor that no women do. It is simply that a greater percentage of discussion time is taken by men's voices.

The research of sociologists and anthropologists such as Janet Lever, Marjorie Harness Goodwin, and Donna Eder has shown that girls and boys learn to use language differently in their sex-separate peer groups. Typically, a girl has a best friend with whom she sits and talks, frequently telling secrets. It's the telling of secrets, the fact and the way that they talk to each other, that makes them best friends. For boys, activities are central: Their best friends are the ones they do things with. Boys also tend to play in larger groups that are hierarchical. High-status boys give orders and push low-status boys around. So boys are expected to use language to seize center stage: by exhibiting their skill, displaying their knowledge, and challenging and resisting challenges.

These patterns have stunning implications for classroom interaction. Most faculty members assume that participating in class discussion is a necessary part of successful performance. Yet speaking in a classroom is more congenial to boys' language experience than to girls', since it entails putting oneself forward in front of a large group of people, many of whom are strangers and at least one of whom is sure to judge speakers' knowledge and intelligence by their verbal display.

Another aspect of many classrooms that makes them more hospitable to 5 most men than to most women is the use of debatelike formats as a learning tool. Our educational system, as Walter Ong argues persuasively in his book *Fighting for Life* (Cornell University Press, 1981), is fundamentally male in that the pursuit of knowledge is believed to be achieved by ritual opposition: public display followed by argument and challenge. Father Ong demonstrates that ritual opposition — what he calls "adversativeness" or "agonism" — is fundamental to the way most males approach almost any activity. (Consider, for example, the little boy who shows he likes a little girl by pulling her braids and shoving her.) But ritual opposition is antithetical to the way most females learn and like to interact. It is not that females don't fight, but that they don't fight for fun. They don't *ritualize* opposition.

Anthropologists working in widely disparate parts of the world have found contrasting verbal rituals for women and men. Women in completely unrelated cultures (for example, Greece and Bali) engage in ritual laments: spontaneously produced rhyming couplets that express their pain, for example, over the loss of loved ones. Men do not take part in laments. They have their own, very different verbal ritual: a contest, a war of words in which they vie with each other to devise clever insults.

When discussing these phenomena with a colleague, I commented that I see these two styles in American conversation: Many women bond by talking about troubles, and many men bond by exchanging playful insults and put-downs, and other sorts of verbal sparring. He exclaimed: "I never thought of this, but that's the way I teach: I have students read an article, and then I invite them to tear it apart. After we've torn it to shreds, we talk about how to build a better model."

This contrasts sharply with the way I teach: I open the discussion of readings by asking, "What did you find useful in this? What can we use in our own theory building and our own methods?" I note what I see as weaknesses in the author's approach, but I also point out that the writer's discipline and purposes might be different from ours. Finally, I offer personal anecdotes illustrating the phenomena under discussion and praise students' anecdotes as well as their critical acumen.

These different teaching styles must make our classrooms wildly different places and hospitable to different students. Male students are more likely to be comfortable attacking the readings and might find the inclusion of personal anecdotes irrelevant and "soft." Women are more likely to resist discussion they perceive as hostile, and, indeed, it is women in my classes who are most likely to offer personal anecdotes.

A colleague who read my book commented that he had always taken for 10 granted that the best way to deal with students' comments is to challenge them; this, he felt it was self-evident, sharpens their minds and helps them develop debating skills. But he had noticed that women were relatively silent in his classes, so he decided to try beginning discussion with relatively open-ended questions and letting comments go unchallenged. He found, to his amazement and satisfaction, that more women began to speak up.

Though some of the women in his class clearly liked this better, perhaps some of the men liked it less. One young man in my class wrote in a questionnaire about a history professor who gave students questions to think about and called on people to answer them: "He would then play devil's advocate . . . i.e., he debated us. . . . That class *really* sharpened me intellectually. . . . We as students do need to know how to defend ourselves." This young man valued the experience of being attacked and challenged publicly. Many, if not most, women would shrink from such "challenge," experiencing it as public humiliation.

A professor at Hamilton College told me of a young man who was upset because he felt his class presentation had been a failure. The professor was puzzled because he had observed that class members had listened attentively and agreed with the student's observations. It turned out that it was this very agreement that the student interpreted as failure: since no one had engaged his ideas by arguing with him, he felt they had found them unworthy of attention.

One monolithic classroom-participation structure is not equal opportunity.

So one reason men speak in class more than women is that many of them find the "public" classroom setting more conducive to speaking, whereas most women are more comfortable speaking in private to a small group of people they know well. A second reason is that men are more likely to be comfortable with the debatelike form that discussion may take. Yet another reason is the different attitudes toward speaking in class that typify women and men.

Students who speak frequently in class, many of whom are men, assume that it is their job to think of contributions and try to get the floor to express them. But many women monitor their participation not only to get the floor but to avoid getting it. Women students in my class tell me that if they have spoken up once or twice, they hold back for the rest of the class because they don't want to dominate. If they have spoken a lot one week, they will remain silent the next. These different ethics of participation are, of course, unstated, so those who speak freely assume that those who remain silent have nothing to say, and those who are reining themselves in assume that the big talkers are selfish and hoggish.

When I looked around my classes, I could see these differing ethics and   15 habits at work. For example, my graduate class in analyzing conversation had twenty students, eleven women and nine men. Of the men, four were foreign students: two Japanese, one Chinese, and one Syrian. With the exception of the three Asian men, all the men spoke in class at least occasionally. The biggest talker in the class was a woman, but there were also five women who never spoke at all, only one of whom was Japanese. I decided to try something different.

I broke the class into small groups to discuss the issues raised in the readings and to analyze their own conversational transcripts. I devised three ways of dividing the students into groups: one by the degree program they were in, one by gender, and one by conversational style, as closely as I could guess it. This meant that when the class was grouped according to conversational style, I put Asian students together, fast talkers together, and quiet students together. The class split into groups six times during the semester, so they met in each grouping twice. I told students to regard the groups as examples of interactional data and to note the different ways they participated in the different groups. Toward the end of the term, I gave them a questionnaire asking about their class and group participation.

I could see plainly from my observation of the groups at work that women who never opened their mouths in class were talking away in the small groups. In fact, the Japanese woman commented that she found it particularly hard to contribute to the all-woman group she was in because "I was overwhelmed by how talkative the female students were in the female-only group." This is particularly revealing because it highlights that the same person who can be "oppressed" into silence in one context can become the talkative "oppressor" in another. No one's conversational style is absolute; everyone's style changes in response to the context and others' styles.

Some of the students (seven) said they preferred the same-gender groups; others preferred the same-style groups. In answer to the question "Would you have liked to speak in class more than you did?" six of the seven who said yes were women; the one man was Japanese. Most startlingly, this response did not come only from quiet women; it came from women who had indicated they had spoken in class never, rarely, sometimes, and often. Of the eleven students who said the amount they had spoken was fine, seven were men. Of the four women who checked "fine," two added qualifications indicating it wasn't completely fine: One wrote in "maybe more," and one wrote, "I have an urge to participate but often feel I should have something more interesting/relevant/wonderful/intelligent to say!!"

I counted my experiment a success. Everyone in the class found the small groups interesting, and no one indicated he or she would have preferred that the class not break into groups. Perhaps most instructive, however, was the fact that the experience of breaking into groups, and of talking about participation in class, raised everyone's awareness about classroom participation. After we had talked about it, some of the quietest women in the class made a few voluntary contributions, though sometimes I had to ensure their participation by interrupting the students who were exuberantly speaking out.

Americans are often proud that they discount the significance of cultural differences: "We are all individuals," many people boast. Ignoring such issues as gender and ethnicity becomes a source of pride: "I treat everyone the same." But treating people the same is not equal treatment if they are not the same.   20

The classroom is a different environment for those who feel comfortable putting themselves forward in a group than it is for those who find the prospect of doing so chastening, or even terrifying. When a professor asks, "Are there any questions?" students who can formulate statements the fastest have the greatest opportunity to respond. Those who need significant time to do so have not really been given a chance at all, since by the time they are ready to speak, someone else has the floor.

In a class where some students speak out without raising hands, those who feel they must raise their hands and wait to be recognized do not have equal opportunity to speak. Telling them to feel free to jump in will not make them feel free; one's sense of timing, of one's rights and obligations in a classroom, are automatic, learned over years of interaction. They may be changed over time, with motivation and effort, but they cannot be changed on the spot. And everyone assumes his or her own way is best. When I asked my students how the class could be changed to make it easier for them to speak more, the most talkative woman said she would prefer it if no one had to raise hands, and a foreign student said he wished people would raise their hands and wait to be recognized.

My experience in this class has convinced me that small-group interaction should be part of any class that is not a small seminar. I also am convinced that having the students become observers of their own interaction is a crucial part of their education. Talking about ways of talking in class makes students aware that their ways of talking affect other students, that the motivations they impute to others may not truly reflect others' motives, and that the behaviors they assume to be self-evidently right are not universal norms.

The goal of complete equal opportunity in class may not be attainable, but realizing that one monolithic classroom-participation structure is not equal opportunity is itself a powerful motivation to find more-diverse methods to serve diverse students — and every classroom is diverse.

Working with the Text

1. Deborah Tannen bases her approach to stimulating classroom discussions on what she describes as "typically male and female ways of using language." As you reread the article, consider her claims for how males and females learn to converse and how these disparate conversational styles affect their behavior in the classroom. In light of your own experience, write a brief essay in which you agree or disagree with Tannen's characterization of male and female styles of participation in class discussions.

2. Whether or not you agree with Tannen that styles of class participation are typically "male" or "female," you probably recognize the behaviors she

ROLE OF PARALEGAL (cont'd)

maintenance, with IP professionals taking an active role in every aspect of both. Among the activities participated in are the following:

- docketing dates for the section 8 affidavits of use and the section 9 applications for renewal;
- corresponding with (and often locating) clients to notify them that their registrations will be canceled unless the section 8 affidavit or the renewal application is filed;
- ensuring the chain of title is continuous so that the party who files the postregistration documents with the PTO is "of record" with the PTO as the owner of the mark and recording changes in ownership of the marks, if required;
- comparing a specimen of the mark as presently used with that in the original registration to ensure a material alteration has not occurred that would preclude the filing of a section 8 affidavit;
- conducting due diligence to determine whether a mark has been in such continuous use that the owner can file a section 15 affidavit to obtain incontestable status of its mark;
- preparing, filing, and monitoring sections 8 and 15 affidavits and applications for renewal;
- communicating PTO action on affidavits and renewal applications to clients and docketing new date for renewal;
- docketing the fifth anniversary after registration of a mark on the Supplemental Register so a new application can be filed for registration on the Principal Register (due to the presumption that after five years of exclusive and continuous use of a mark, it has acquired distinctiveness);
- assisting clients in drafting trademark compliance policies;
- assisting clients in conducting monitoring of marks to detect possible infringing uses;
- reviewing clients' advertising copy and other materials to ensure display and use of marks is proper and that there is no misuse of another party's marks;
- drafting assignments and licenses;
- docketing dates for renewals and expiration of license agreements; and
- recording assignments, mergers, changes of name, and security interests with the PTO.

INTERNET RESOURCES

PTO web site: http://www.uspto.gov (offers form for recordation cover sheet for assignment of trademarks) describes. Based on Tannen's descriptions as well as your own experience, write a brief essay in which you analyze the strengths and weaknesses of each style. In what contexts and for what purposes might each style be especially effective?

3. Based on observations of her students, Tannen claims that there is an unspoken "ethics of participation" behind decisions to speak or remain silent in class, which can result in misinterpretations of someone else's motives: "[T]hose who speak freely assume that those who remain silent have nothing to say, and those who are reining themselves in assume that the big talkers are selfish and hoggish" (par. 14). Drawing on Tannen's descriptions of typically male and female conversational styles, write a brief essay in which you analyze these conflicting ethical viewpoints. What is the reasoning behind them? Why would the reasoning be a matter of ethics?

4. In small groups, discuss your response to Tannen's description of how females and males develop their use of language or their conversational styles. Do you agree with her? Why or why not? As you discuss, observe your group's style of interaction, especially in terms of Tannen's argument. Write a brief essay analyzing the group's interaction, to share and discuss with the entire class.

From Text to Field

1. As you review Tannen's essay, reflect on your own style of participating in class discussion. In a personal essay, analyze your style. In what ways would Tannen regard your style as "female"? In what ways would she consider it "male"? Why do you participate in this way? What do you consider to be your "ethics of participation"? Describe any approaches you use that Tannen does not address in her essay.

2. Draw on Tannen's essay to analyze how you developed your particular conversational style. In what ways does it fit within or depart from Tannen's analysis of how females and males learn to use language? Looking back over your schooling, do any particular moments, classes, or teachers stand out in ways that you think may have shaped your current conversational style? In what ways has the development of your conversational style paralleled your growing sense of an "ethics of participation"?

3. Tannen's descriptions of typically male and female classroom behavior include teachers as well as students. Review her anecdotes comparing her own teaching style to the styles of male colleagues. In a personal essay, reflect on your experience working with female and male teachers. Did they use the typically female and male styles described by Tannen? What styles

did they use other than those Tannen describes? What style or styles were more hospitable to you, in terms of your ability to learn as well as to contribute to class discussions?

4. Based on Tannen's argument as well as your experience in the classroom, write an essay as if you were a teacher, articulating a teaching style or philosophy that you think would create the best learning environment for both female and male students. How would you approach classroom discussions? Why would you use this approach?

Bitch

Beverly Gross

Slang can provide some of the most powerful expressions of how men and women regard each other and themselves. Both abuse and endearment take the form of slang. As straightforward as the words can sound, they often camouflage or skew the meaning behind the emotion. Beverly Gross began exploring how the word *bitch* is used after a student in her course on Women Writers and Literary Tradition asked why critics so often referred to twentieth-century novelist Mary McCarthy as a "bitch." Why McCarthy? What did they mean?

Gross reaches back to the eighteenth century to trace the history of the word's meaning, from "the female of the dog" and "a lewd or sensual woman" through the nineteenth century, to "a malicious, unpleasant, selfish woman . . . who stops at nothing to reach her goal" in the twentieth century. Why this progression? And why, according to Gross, are there no equivalent terms for men?

An engaging meditation on language and gender, Gross's essay "Bitch" was published in 1994 in *Salmagundi,* a quarterly magazine devoted to the humanities and social sciences that publishes poetry, fiction, critical essays, and social analysis. A professor of English, Gross has taught at Northwestern University, Vassar College, and Queens College of the City University of New York. She is the coeditor of *The Shapes of Fiction: Open and Closed* (1970) and served as literary editor for *Nation* (1969–1970) and fiction editor for the *Chicago Review* (1962–1964). Her work has appeared in journals such as the *Antioch Review* and the *South Atlantic Quarterly.*

We were discussing Mary McCarthy's *The Group* in a course called Women Writers and Literary Tradition. McCarthy's biographer Carol Gelderman, I told the class, had been intrigued by how often critics called Mary McCarthy a bitch. I read a few citations. "Her novels are crammed with cerebration and bitchiness" (John Aldridge). "Her approach to writing [is] reflective of the modern American bitch" (Paul Schlueter). Why McCarthy? a student asked. Her unrelenting standards, I ventured, her tough-minded critical estimates — there was no self-censoring, appeasing Angel in the House of Mary McCarthy's brain. Her combativeness (her marital battles with Edmund Wilson became the stuff of academic legend). Maybe there were other factors. But the discussion opened up to the more inclusive issue of the word *bitch* itself. What effect does that appellation have on women? What effect might it have had on McCarthy? No one ever called Edmund Wilson a bitch. Do we excuse, even pay respect when a man is critical, combative, assertive? What is the male equivalent of the word bitch, I asked the class.

"Boss," said Sabrina Sims.

This was an evening class at a branch of the City University of New York. Most of the students are older adults trying to fit a college education into otherwise busy lives. Most of them have full-time jobs during the day. Sabrina Sims works on Wall Street, is a single mother raising a ten-year-old daughter, is black, and had to take an Incomplete in the course because she underwent a kidney transplant in December.

Her answer gave us all a good laugh. I haven't been able to get it out of my mind. I've been thinking about *bitch*, watching how it is used by writers and in conversation, and have explored its lexical history. "A name of reproach for a woman" is how Doctor Johnson's Dictionary dealt with the word in the eighteenth century, as though anticipating the great adaptability of this particular execration, a class of words that tends toward early obsolescence. Not *bitch*, however, which has been around for a millennium, outlasting a succession of definitions. Its longevity is perhaps attributable to its satisfying misogyny. Its meaning matters less than its power to denounce and subjugate. Francis Grose in *A Classical Dictionary of the Vulgar Tongue* (1785) considered *bitch* "the most offensive appellation that can be given to an English woman, even more provoking than that of whore." He offered as evidence "a low London woman's reply on being called a bitch" in the late-eighteenth century: "I may be a whore but can't be a bitch!" The meaning of *bitch* has changed over the centuries but it remains the word that comes immediately to the tongue, still "the most offensive appellation" the English language provides to hurl at a woman.

The *Oxford English Dictionary* records two main meanings for the noun 5 *bitch* up through the nineteenth century.

1. The female of the dog
2. Applied opprobriously to a woman; strictly a lewd or sensual woman. Not now in decent use.

It was not until the twentieth century that *bitch* acquired its opprobrious application in realms irrespective of sensuality. The Supplement to the *OED* (1972) adds:

2a: "In mod. use, esp. a malicious or treacherous woman."

Every current desk dictionary supplies some such meaning:

A spiteful, ill-tempered woman [*World Book Dictionary*]
A malicious, unpleasant, selfish woman, esp. one who stops at nothing to reach her goal. [*Random House Dictionary*]

But malice and treachery only begin to tell the story. The informal questionnaire that I administered to my students and a number of acquaintances elicited ample demonstration of the slippery adaptability of bitch as it might be used these days:

a conceited person, a snob
a self-absorbed woman
a complainer
a competitive woman
a woman who is annoying, pushy, possibly underhanded (in short, a man in a woman's body)
someone rich, thin, and free!

"A word used by men who are threatened by women" was one astute response. Threat lurks everywhere: for women the threat is in being called a bitch. "Someone whiny, threatening, crabby, pestering" is what one woman offered as her definition. "Everything I try hard not to be," she added, "though it seeps through." I offer as a preliminary conclusion that *bitch* means to men whatever they find threatening in a woman and it means to women whatever they particularly dislike about themselves. In either case the word functions as a misogynistic club. I will add that the woman who defined *bitch* as everything she tries hard not to be when asked to free associate about the word came up immediately with "mother." That woman happens to be my sister. We share the same mother, who was often whiny and crabby, though I would never have applied the word *bitch* to her, but then again, I don't consider whiny, crabby and pestering to be prominent among my own numerous flaws.

Dictionaries of slang are informative sources, in touch as they are with nascent language and the emotive coloration of words, especially words of abuse. A relatively restrained definition is offered by the only female lexicographer I consulted for whom *bitch* is "a nasty woman" or "a difficult task" (Anita Pearl, *Dictionary of Popular Slang*). The delineations of *bitch* by the male lexicographers abound with such cascading hostility that the compilers sometimes

10

seem to be reveling in their task. For example, Howard Wentworth and Stuart Berg Flexner in *Dictionary of American Slang*:

> A woman, usu., but not necessarily, a mean, selfish, malicious, deceiving, cruel, or promiscuous woman.

Eugene E. Landy's *The Underground Dictionary* (1971) offers:

> 1. Female who is mean, selfish, cruel, malicious, deceiving. a.k.a. cunt.
> 2. Female. See Female.

I looked up the entry for *Female* (Landy, by the way, provides no parallel entry for *Male*):

> beaver, bird, bitch, broad, bush, cat, chick, crack, cunt, douche, fish, fox, frail, garbage can, heffer, pussy, quail, ruca, scag, snatch, stallion, slave, sweet meat, tail, trick, tuna. See GIRLFRIEND; WIFE.

Richard A. Spear's *Slang and Euphemism* comments on the derivative adjective:

> bitchy 1. pertaining to a mood wherein one complains incessantly about anything. Although this applies to men or women, it is usually associated with women, especially when they are menstruating. Cf. DOG DAYS

Robert L. Chapman's definition in *Thesaurus of American Slang* starts off like a feminist analysis:

> bitch. 1 n. A woman one dislikes or disapproves of.

Followed, however, by a sobering string of synonyms: "broad, cunt, witch."

And then this most interesting note:

> Female equivalents of the contemptuous terms for men, listed in this book under *asshole*, are relatively rare. Contempt for females, in slang, stresses their putative sexual promiscuity and weakness rather than their moral vileness and general odiousness. Some terms under *asshole*, though, are increasingly used of women.

"See ball-buster." Chapman suggests under his second definition for *bitch* ("anything arduous or very disagreeable"). I looked up "ball-buster":

> n. Someone who saps or destroys masculinity.
> ball-whacker
> bitch
> nut-cruncher.

Some*thing* has become some*one*. The ball-buster is not a disagreeable thing but a disagreeable (disagreeing?) person. A female person. "A woman one dis- likes or disapproves of." For someone so sensitive to the nuances of hostility and verbal put-down, Chapman certainly takes a circuitous route to get to the underlying idea that no other dictionary even touches: *Bitch* means ball-buster.

What one learns from the dictionaries: there is no classifiable thing as a bitch, only a label produced by the act of name-calling. The person named is almost always a female. The name-calling refers to alleged faults of ill-temper, selfishness, malice, cruelty, spite, all of them faults in the realm of interpersonal relating — women's faults: It is hard to think of a put-down word encompassing these faults in a man. *Bastard* and even *son of a bitch* have bigger fish to fry. And an asshole is an asshole in and of himself. A bitch is a woman who makes the name-caller feel uncomfortable. Presumably that name-caller is a man whose ideas about how a woman should behave toward him are being violated.

What men primarily fear and despise in women is power.

"Women," wrote Virginia Woolf, "have served all these centuries as looking-glasses possessing the magic and delicious power of reflecting the figure of man at twice its natural size." The woman who withholds that mirror is a bitch. Bitchiness is the perversion of womanly sweetness, compliance, pleasantness, ego-building. (Male ego-building, of course, though that is a virtual tautology; women have egos but who builds them?) If a woman is not building ego she is busting balls.

Ball-buster? The word is a nice synecdoche (like asshole) with great powers of revelation. A ball-buster, one gathers, is a demanding bitch who insists on overexertion from a man to satisfy her sexual or material voraciousness. "The bitch is probably his wife." But balls also bust when a disagreeable woman undermines a guy's ego and "saps or destroys masculinity." The bitch could be his wife, but also his boss, Gloria Steinem, the woman at the post office, the woman who spurns his advances. The familiar Freudian delineation of the male-female nexus depicts male sexuality as requiring the admiration, submission, and subordination of the female. The ultimate threat of (and to) the back-talking woman is male impotence.

Bitch, the curse and concept, exists to insure male potency and female submissiveness. Men have deployed it to defend their power by attacking and neutralizing the upstart. *Bitch* is admonitory, like *whore,* like *dyke.* Borrowing something from both words, *bitch* is one of those verbal missiles with the power of shackling women's actions and impulses.

The metamorphosis of *bitch* from the context of sexuality (a carnal woman, a promiscuous woman) to temperament (an angry woman, a malicious woman) to power (a domineering woman, a competitive woman) is a touchstone to the changing position of women through this century. As women have become more liberated, individually and collectively, the word has taken on connotations of aggressive, hostile, selfish. In the old days a bitch was a harlot; nowadays she is likely to be a woman who won't put out.

Female sensuality, even carnality, even infidelity, have been supplanted as what men primarily fear and despise in women. Judging by the contemporary colorations of the word *bitch*, what men primarily fear and despise in women is power.

Some anecdotes:

1. Barbara Bush's name-calling of Geraldine Ferraro during the 1984 presidential election: "I can't say it but it rhymes with 'rich.'"

How ladylike of the future First Lady to avoid uttering the unmentionable. The slur did its dirty work, particularly among those voters disturbed by the sudden elevation of a woman to such unprecedented political heights. In what possible sense did Barbara Bush mean that Geraldine Ferraro is a bitch? A loose woman? Hardly. A nasty woman? Not likely. A pushy woman? Almost certainly. The unspoken syllable was offered as a response to Ferraro's lofty ambitions, potential power, possibly her widespread support among feminists. Imagine a woman seeking to be vice president instead of vice husband.

The ascription of bitchery seems to have nothing to do with Ferraro's bearing and behavior. Certainly not the Ferraro who wrote about the event in her autobiography:

Barbara Bush realized what a gaffe she had made. . . .

"I just want to apologize to you for what I said," she told me over the phone while I was in the middle of another debate rehearsal. "I certainly didn't mean anything by it."

"Don't worry about it," I said to her. "We all say things at times we don't mean. It's all right."

"Oh," she said breathlessly. "You're such a lady."

All I could think of when I hung up was: Thank God for my convent school training.

2. Lady Ashley at the end of *The Sun Also Rises:* "It makes one feel rather 25 good, deciding not to be a bitch." The context here is something like this: A bitch is a woman who ruins young heroic bullfighters. A woman who is propelled by her sexual drive, desires, and vanity. The fascination of Brett Ashley is that she lives and loves like a man: Her sexuality is unrepressed and she doesn't care much for monogamy. (Literary critics until the 1960s commonly called her a nymphomaniac.) She turns her male admirers into women— Mike becomes a self-destructive alcoholic, Robert a moony romantic, Pedro a sacrificial virgin, and Jake a frustrated eunuch. At her entrance in the novel she is surrounded by an entourage of twittering fairies. Lady Ashley is a bitch not because she is nasty, bossy, or ill-tempered (she has lovely manners and a terrific personality). And perhaps not even because of her freewheeling, strident sexuality. She is a bitch because she overturns the male/female nexus. What could be a more threatening infraction in a Hemingway novel?

2a. Speaking of Hemingway: After his falling out with Gertrude Stein who had made unflattering comments about his writing in *The Autobiography of Alice B. Toklas*, Hemingway dropped her off a copy of his newly published *Death in the Afternoon* with the handwritten inscription, "A bitch is a bitch is a bitch."

[Q.] Why was Gertrude Stein a bitch?

[A.] For no longer admiring Hemingway. A bitch is a woman who criticizes.

3. "Ladies and gentlemen. I don't believe Mrs. Helmsley is charged in the indictment with being a tough bitch" is how her defense lawyer Gerald A. Feffer addressed the jury in Leona Helmsley's trial for tax fraud and extortion. He acknowledged that she was "sometimes rude and abrasive," and that she "may have overcompensated for being a woman in a hard-edged men's business world." Recognizing the difficulty of defending what the New York *Post* called "the woman that everyone loves to hate," his tactic was to preempt the prosecution by getting there first with "tough bitch." He lost.

4. *Esquire* awarded a Dubious Achievement of 1990 to Victor Kiam, owner of the New England Patriots football team, for saying "he could never have called Boston *Herald* reporter Lisa Olson 'a classic bitch' because he doesn't use the word *classic*." Some background on what had been one of that year's most discussed controversies: Olson aroused the ire of the Patriots for showing up in their locker room with the male reporters after a game. Members of the Patriots, as *Esquire* states, surrounded her, "thrusting their genitals in her face and daring her to touch them."

Why is Lisa Olson a bitch? For invading the male domain of sports reportage and the male territory of the locker room? For telling the world, instead of swallowing her degradation, pain, and anger? The club owner's use of "bitch" seems meant to conjure up the lurking idea of castrating female. Seen in that light the Patriots' act of "thrusting their genitals in her face" transforms an act of loutishness into a position of innocent vulnerability.

5. Bumper sticker observed on back of pickup truck: 30

> Impeach Jane Fonda, American Traitor Bitch

The bumper sticker seemed relatively new and fresh. I observed it a full two decades after Jane Fonda's journey to North Vietnam which is the event that surely inspired this call to impeachment (from what? aerobics class?). *Bitch* here is an expletive. It originates in and sustains anger. Calling Jane Fonda a "traitor" sounds a bit dated in the 1990s, but adding "bitch" gives the accusation timelessness and does the job of rekindling old indignation.

6. Claude Brown's account in *Manchild in the Promised Land* of how he learned about women from a street-smart older friend:

> Johnny was always telling us about bitches. To Johnny, every chick was a bitch. Even mothers were bitches. Of course there were some nice bitches,

but they were still bitches. And a man had to be a dog in order to handle a bitch.

Johnny said once, "If a bitch ever tells you she's only got a penny to buy the baby some milk, take it. You take it, 'cause she's gon git some more. Bitches can always git some money." He really knew about bitches. Cats would say, "I saw your sister today, and she is a fine bitch." Nobody was offended by it. That's just the way things were. It was easy to see all women as bitches.

Bitch in black male street parlance seems closer to its original meaning of a female breeder—not a nasty woman and not a powerful woman, but the biological bearer of litters. The word is likely to be used in courting as well as in anger by males seeking the sexual favor of a female, and a black female addressed as bitch by an admirer is expected to feel not insulted but honored by the attention. (*Bitch* signifies something different when black women use it competitively about other black women.) But even as an endearment, from male to female, there is no mistaking the lurking contempt.

A *Dictionary of Afro-American Slang* compiled by Clarence Major (under the imprint of the leftist International Publishers) provides only that *bitch* in black parlance is "a mean, flaunting homosexual," entirely omitting any reference to its rampant use in black street language as the substitute word for woman. A puzzling omission. Perhaps the word is so taken for granted that its primary meaning is not even recognized as black vernacular.

Bitch, mama, motherfucker—how frequently motherhood figures in street language. Mothers are the object of insults when playing the dozens. The ubiquitous motherfucker simultaneously strikes out at one's immediate foe as well as the sanctity of motherhood. Mama, which Clarence Major defines as "a pretty black girl," is an endearment that a man might address to a sexy contemporary. "Hey mama" is tinged with a certain sweetness. "Hey bitch" has more of an edge, more likely to be addressed to a woman the man no longer needs to sweet-talk. It is hard to think of white males coming on by evoking motherhood or of white women going for it. A white male addressing a woman as bitch is not likely to be expecting a sexual reward. She will be a bitch behind her back and after the relationship is over or didn't happen.

The widespread use of *bitch* by black men talking to black women, its currency in courting, and its routine acceptance by women are suggestive of some powerful alienation in male-female relations and in black self-identity. Although there may be the possibility of ironic inversion, as in calling a loved one nigger, a black man calling a loved one bitch is expressing contempt for the object of his desire with the gratuitous fillip of associative contempt for the woman who gave him life. Bitch, like motherfucker, bespeaks something threatening to the male sense of himself, a furious counter to emasculation in a world where, as the young Claude Brown figured out, mothers have all

Trademark Manual of Examining
  Practice (TMEP):   http://www.uspto.gov/web/offices/tac/tmep/index.html
                                    (offers information on trademark maintenance and
                                    assignments)

Forms for assignments: http://www.allaboutforms.com and
                                    http://www.siccode.com/forms.php3

Guide to proper trademark use: http://www.inta.org/info/faqsU.htm#2

General information: http://www.ll.georgetown.edu and
                                    http://www.ipmall.fplc.edu

DISCUSSION QUESTIONS

1. What is the latest possible date to file a section 8 affidavit of continuing use for a mark registered on July 14, 2003?

2. The display of a registered mark has gradually changed over the years from PRECAR-IUM® to PRE-CARIUM. Discuss whether this is such a material alteration in the mark that a section 8 affidavit of continuing use for the mark would be rejected.

3. The mark LIBERTY FLIGHT® is used in connection with the sale of luxury private airplanes, sold primarily to chief executives of Fortune 500 companies. Only three planes have been sold in the past five years, and last year there were no sales at all. Discuss whether this situation constitutes excusable nonuse so that the owner of the mark could file a section 8 affidavit of continuing use.

4. At the time of filing a section 15 affidavit of incontestability for the mark SALON REMORE®, there is a pending infringement action relating to the mark. What effect will the litigation have on the registrant?

5. Describe whether the following uses of marks are advisable and what danger there may be, if any, in any of these uses:
     PILLSBURY® biscuits are the best.
     Grab a SWIFFER and get busy!
     CARNATION® brand milk is smooth and creamy.
     Try a GODIVA—you won't be disappointed.

6. The owner of the trademark GODIVA® for chocolates will license use of the mark to a candy store in Dallas. What types of quality control provisions should a license agreement include?

For additional resources, go to www.westlegalstudies.com.

the power. It is not hard to see that the problem of black men is much more with white racism than it is with black women. Whatever the cause, however, the language sure doesn't benefit the women. Here is still one more saddening instance of the victim finding someone even more hapless to take things out on. (Does this process explain why Clarence Major's only reference for *bitch* is to the "mean, flaunting homosexual"?)

7. "Do you enjoy playing that role of castrating bitch" is a question put to Madonna by an interviewer for the *Advocate*. Madonna's answer: "I enjoy expressing myself. . . ."

A response to another question about the public's reaction to her movie *Truth or Dare*: "They already think I'm a cunt bitch, they already think I'm Attila the Hun. They already compare me to Adolf Hitler and Saddam Hussein."

Bitch has lost its power to muzzle Madonna. Unlike other female celebrities who have cringed from accusations of bitchiness (Joan Rivers, Imelda Marcos, Margaret Thatcher, Nancy Reagan), Madonna has made her fortune by exploiting criticism. Her career has skyrocketed with the media's charges of obscenity and sacrilege; she seems to embrace the *bitch* label with the same eager opportunism.

"I enjoy expressing myself" is not merely the explanation for why Madonna gets called bitch; "I enjoy expressing myself" is the key to defusing the power of *bitch* to fetter and subdue. Madonna has appropriated the word and turned the intended insult to her advantage. This act of appropriation, I predict, will embolden others with what consequences and effects it is impossible to foresee.

Working with the Text

1. Beverly Gross devotes the first half of her essay to exploring dictionary meanings of the word *bitch*, starting with Doctor Johnson's Dictionary in the eighteenth century: "A name of reproach for a woman." In a brief essay, analyze her use of these evolving dictionary definitions. What do the definitions tell us about the dictionary compilers and the eras in which they lived? What does this history tell us about how we use the word today? How does the history of the word contribute to Gross's argument? How would you summarize her argument?

2. In addition to studying dictionaries, Gross conducted an informal survey of her students and friends to explore contemporary meanings of *bitch*. She lists the following responses:

   a conceited person, a snob
   a self-absorbed woman

a complainer

a competitive woman

a woman who is annoying, pushy, possibly underhanded (in short, a man in a woman's body)

someone rich, thin, and free!

In a brief essay, reflect on how all of these meanings could come from the same word. What is the relationship among the meanings? What does this range of meaning suggest about current ideas of what it is to be a woman — both in terms of what we think women should be and what we think they actually are?

3. One of Gross's central claims is that there is no "put-down word" for men comparable to *bitch* for women. As you reread the essay, reflect not only on the contemporary meanings of the word but also on the effect Gross argues the word is intended to have on the woman being called a bitch. In particular, consider Gross's assertion that "*Bastard* and even *son of a bitch* have bigger fish to fry. And an asshole is an asshole in and of himself. A bitch is a woman who makes the name-caller feel uncomfortable" (par. 16). Write a brief essay in which you analyze put-downs used for men, comparing the effect they are intended to have on men to the effect *bitch* is intended to have on women. Do you agree with Gross that there is no comparable name for men? Why or why not? To what extent does *boss*, proposed by one of Gross's students, offer a comparable put-down?

4. Gross comes to the conclusion that "what men primarily fear and despise in women is power" (par. 20). Drawing on your experience as well as Gross's argument, write a brief essay in which you respond to this assertion. To what extent do you agree with Gross's conclusion? What is the basis for your position?

From Text to Field

1. The crux of Gross's argument is that the word *bitch* reflects a long history of misogyny — the hatred of women. Women, as well as men, can be misogynists. Based on your experience and knowledge of history, literature, psychology, and other relevant fields of study, write an essay in which you reflect on whether there has been a comparable history of hatred of men. If you think there has been such a history, what is the male equivalent of the word *misogyny?* If you cannot identify such a word, what term would you invent? What attitudes toward men are represented by the existing term or the term you would invent? If you think there has not been a history of some form of hating men, why do you think that has been the case? How does your knowledge of the women's movement fit into your view of this history?

2. To illustrate contemporary uses of *bitch*, Gross presents several anecdotes. Using the anecdotes and her commentary as a model, write an essay in which you present one or more anecdotes from your own experience or knowledge of celebrities or public figures. What circumstances surrounded the woman being called a bitch? What did the name-caller mean by the word? What is your view of the woman and the situation? How does gender figure into the use of the term? If a man is called a bitch, is it emasculating? Have you ever been called a "bitch"?

3. Toward the end of her essay, Gross notes an apparent exception to her analysis: the use of *bitch* in black male street parlance as a term of endearment. How does Gross integrate this example into her overall analysis? In what ways does the example serve her general argument about the fear of power—and powerlessness? Drawing on this example in the essay, consider other instances in which gendered terms, or other highly charged terms, have distinctive meanings within particular communities.

4. Gross uses Madonna to signal what may be a shift in our culture's take on bitches. Make a list of celebrities or public figures you think have used their designation as a bitch to their advantage. Discuss your list in a small group. On the basis of your discussion, write an essay in which you analyze either the actions of one of the "bitches" or what you see as a shift in how the term is being regarded and used.

Power: Women and the Word

Hermione Lee

We use the word *power* so often that its meaning becomes fragmented or blurred. Hermione Lee recognizes how susceptible *power* is to the context in which it is used. What is it? Who is wielding it? Who is gaining it and who is losing it? As Lee enters into the debate among feminists over the sources and uses of power, she examines in particular the feminist concern over the power of words themselves. If, as feminists claim, power is gained in large part through language, how can women use words to gain power?

In this essay, Lee reviews and critiques two very different approaches to "making over the language": a utopian impulse to reinvent the language for feminism and a confrontational impulse that turns the language of power against men. Lee finds both approaches to be problematic. Her essay was first published in *The State of the Language* (1980), edited by Leonard Michaels and Christopher Ricks, a collection of essays on the English language as a sensitive register of our ideas, feelings, politics, and manners.

As a biographer and critic, Lee has gained an international reputation among both academic and lay audiences for her keen analysis of writers. Her work includes books on Elizabeth Bowen, Phillip Roth, Willa Cather, and Virginia Woolf. *Virginia Woolf: A Biography* (1996) won an award from the British Academy and was a best seller in England as well as a *New York Times Book Review* Editor's Choice and a National Book Critics Circle Award finalist. Currently, she is writing a biography of Edith Wharton.

In England, where she is widely known as a broadcaster and commentator on the arts, Lee is the Goldsmiths' Professor of English Literature and fellow of New College, Oxford. In the United States, she has been a visiting fellow at Princeton University, Yale University, and the University of Indiana at Bloomington.

Power. Meanings: the ability to do something, to effect, to act upon. A faculty of body or mind. A force. Political or national strength. Authority or dominion over. Legal authority. A ruler, a state, a prerogative, a celestial body or influence. A body of armed men. The rate at which electrical energy is fed into a system. A measure of magnification. A large amount. Nuclear energy. Power drill, power house, power plant, power politics, black power, power of attorney. Examples: from kings, fathers, patriarchs, princes, bishops, armies, lawyers. (Exceptional cases: the daughter of Jove, Cleopatra.) Quotations: Absolute power corrupts absolutely, thine is the Kingdom, the Power and the Glory, happy men that have the power to die, the balance of power, Him the Almighty Power hurl'd headlong flaming, He that hath power to hurt and will do none, the awful shadow of some unseen power. Etymology: from Middle English *poër*, Old French *poer, poeir, pouoir. Pouoir* goes forward into Modern French *pouvoir*, and backwards to *podere*, from late vulgar Latin *potere*, from Latin *posse*, to be able. The present participle of *posse, potentem*, provides *potentia*, and hence Old French *potence*. Meaning: power, ability, strength, sexual power (male). From this comes *potency*, also potent, potentate, potential, and potentiality.[1]

No wonder, with this pedigree, that the word *power*, derived from the same root as *potency*, is used more often than any other word in feminist discourse to stand for male supremacy. That supremacy is frequently identified as linguistic: Naming is power. The word *power* belongs to those who are in power. It follows that the feminist use of the word is extremely ambivalent. *Power* names something which is resented and feared, but which is also desired and aspired to. It is a revealing word in current feminist discourse because it can take opposite meanings. Other key words do not require a context for their value to be expressed. *Creative*, or *pleasure*, or *freedom* is likely to mean well; *rape*, or *humiliation*, is bound to be bad. *Power* is bad when it is identified with male supremacy and the oppression of women, as in Andrea Dworkin's "it is through intercourse that men express and maintain their power and dominance over women," or Kate Millett's "both the courtly and the romantic versions of love are 'grants' which the male concedes out of his total power."[2] *Power* is good when it is identified with female creativity and potential.

In the good sense it is frequently associated with the use of language, as when Adrienne Rich asks women to consider "language as transforming power," or Mary Daly plays with language to release "the complex creative power" of women, or Toril Moi describes Kate Millett's rhetoric as "a powerful fist in the solar plexus of patriarchy."[3] A word that can mean both well and ill is a manipulable word. Adrienne Rich, in an essay called "Power and Danger," gives a feminist history of the word as used against women:

> Powerless, women have been seduced into confusing love with false power— the "power" of mother-love, the "power" of gentle influence, the "power" of nonviolence, the "power" of the meek who are to inherit the earth.[4]

Rich's scorn of a rhetoric which pretends that powerlessness can be a form of power is directed, of course, at male (and especially Christian) rhetoric. But strategic manipulations of the word are not a male prerogative. In the uses to which it is put in current feminist writing, two ways of making over the language can be discerned, the one utopian, the other confrontational. Both are intensely problematic.

If the language is to be reinvented for feminism, the word *power* presents a crucial challenge — and invitation. Can it be transformed, or must it be rejected? Any rewriting of women's history, as in this neutrally informative passage, has to center on the word:

> An understanding of the interdependence of the spheres reveals that women have wielded more power than has been apparent, and that aspects of women's lives which appear to be restrictive may actually be enabling. Women's history is concerned to see women, not as victims of oppression, as passive spectators of the drama of history, but as having an influence and a history of their own. . . . Historians of women broaden their conception of power to include subtler forms — informal, invisible, collective — recognizing that "the location of power" is "a tricky business."[5]

Here the word changes its value through a historical reinterpretation which makes powerlessness, after all, into a form of power. This would presumably not suit Adrienne Rich, who argues in "Power and Danger" that this is what women have always been told, and much good it has done us. Rich requires more than historical reconsideration. Like Virginia Woolf in *A Room of One's Own*, inviting women writers to make use of the special knowledge they have inherited from their mothers' history of exclusion and silence, Rich wants a history of powerlessness to issue in a distinctive language (essentially a language of poetry) which will

Strategic manipulations of the word [*power*] are not a male prerogative.

express "that instinct for true power, not domination, which poets like Barrett Browning, Dickinson, H.D., were asserting in their own very different ways and voices."[6] Rich's phrasing shows what a tricky business it is to give a utopian meaning to the word *power*. *Power* still has to go with *asserting* (though *asserting* is an inaccurate description of what Emily Dickinson and H.D. were doing). Yet *asserting* is contrasted, in a shaky opposition, with *domination*. And *power* itself has to be qualified by *true*, in order to distinguish it from the bad old "false power" (that is, powerlessness) offered to women by the male oppressors. We are presented, then, somewhat awkwardly, with a utopian idea of a language of "true power" which will assert but not dominate. What could such a language actually be?

Feminist revisions of language in the last decade, powerfully influenced   5
by Julia Kristeva's critique of Freud and Lacan, have insisted on a female language as the expression of *what has been repressed* in the male sentence.

Mary Jacobus defines *écriture féminine* as that which is "located in the gaps, the absences, the unsayable or unrepresentable of discourse and representation."[7] Female language is identified, in such now-legendary texts as Hélène Cixous's "Le Rire de la Méduse" (1975) and Luce Irigaray's "Ce sexe qui n'en est pas un" (1977), as a playful revealing of what has been hidden. Language as an eruption of female sexuality, or *jouissance*, can be a potent alternative discourse. This discourse is indebted to Kristeva's theory that the pre-Oedipal phase of childhood, in intimate connection with the mother, which precedes the "entry into signification and the symbolic order," can persist in "oral and instinctual aspects of language which punctuate, evade, or disrupt the symbolic order — in prosody, intonation, puns, verbal slips, even silences."[8] For Irigaray, this means that "woman would find herself on the side of everything in language that is multiple, duplicitous, unreliable"; her language is "a deranging power."[9]

Utopian polemicists for a female language repeatedly oppose its "deranging power" to the established power systems within which it must operate. So woman must be, and speak, "that which is neither power nor structure."[10] How can this be put into practice? Recommendations vary from the use of myth and fable, diaries and notebooks, gaps on the page, poetical prose and domestic imagery, to, at the most inept, "the vocabulary of menstruation, reproduction, or craft work."[11] More specific linguistic programs call for women to coin neologisms, break grammatical rules, and defamiliarize taken-for-granted parts of speech.

If this fabricated language is to express "that which is neither power nor structure," it has to be identified with negatives: amorphousness, evasiveness, splits, darkness, and depth. Here, for instance, a conscientious Americanized version of *écriture féminine* uses strategies of syntactical blurring, fragmentation, exclamation, rhythmic patterns, and an alternative vocabulary to ridicule the culture's mythical respect for male linguistic power:

> But that male body, how IT dominates the culture, the environment, the language. Since 3,000 BC in Sumeria, Tiamat's monsters again and again, and every myth an effort to keep the sun rising. Save the sun, everybody, from the watery deeps, the dark underneath it must go—Into— Every night into such dangers, such soft inchoate darkness, what will become of it, will it rise again will it will it rise again? The language of criticism: "lean, dry, terse, powerful, strong, spare, linear, focused, explosive," — god forbid it should be "limp"!! But — "soft, moist, blurred, padded, irregular, going around in circles," and other descriptions of *our* bodies — the very *abyss* of aesthetic judgment, danger, the wasteland for artists! That limp dick — an entire civilization based on it, help the sun rise, watch out for the dark underground, focus focus focus, keep it high, let it soar, let it transcend, let it aspire to Godhead ——.[12]

This kind of programmatic writing consigns women and their language, all over again (as they have traditionally been consigned by inspired "phallocentric" writers such as Yeats, Whitman, and Lawrence) to the realms of "inchoate darkness," the unconscious, mothering, hysteria, and babble. It is a version of female "powers" which has been emphatically challenged, very often as part of a debate between the Gallic school of psychoanalytical and linguistic feminists, and the Anglo-American school of Marxist/socialist/"materialist" feminists. The latter criticize the essentialist identification of the feminine with "absence, silence, incoherence, even madness" as "a mistaken strategy" which "abandons territory which can and ought to be defended against masculine imperialism: coherence, rationality, articulateness."[13]

A more socialized, functional attempt at fabricating a female language is currently being made by the American feminist theologian Mary Daly. In *Gyn/Ecology: The Metaethics of Radical Feminism* (1978) and *Pure Lust: Elemental Feminist Philosophy* (1984) she makes determined efforts at "wrenching back some word power."[14] The phrase refers to her title, *Gyn/Ecology*, which Daly says is meant to draw attention to the pollution spread by patriarchal myth and language. Daly's split words and coinages (dis-membering and re-membering, a-maze, man/ipulate, O-Zone, Hagocracy, the/rapist, Nag-Gnostics) belong to a self-conscious process of reeducating the users of the language by "targeting/humiliating the right objects."

> Gynocentric writing means risking. Since the language and style of patriarchal writing simply cannot contain or carry the energy of women's exorcism and ecstasy, in this book I invent, dis-cover, re-member. At times I make up words (such as *gynaesthesia* for women's synaesthesia). Often I unmask deceptive words by dividing them and employing alternate meanings for prefixes (for example, *re-cover* actually says "cover again"). I also unmask their hidden reversals, often by using less known or "obsolete" meanings (for example, *glamour* as used to name a witch's power). Sometimes I simply invite the reader to listen to words in a different way (for example, *de-light*). When I play with words I do this attentively, deeply, paying attention to etymology, to varied dimensions of meaning, to deep Background meanings and subliminal associations.[15]

Daly subverts the word *power* by pluralizing it, proposing an opposition between "Elemental Powers of Be-ing" (female, naturally) and "patriarchal power." The strategy perfectly sums up the utopian feminist desire to reclaim all the "established" meanings of power (potency, control, activity, authority) and change their value:

> Women who are unveiling the Archimage, Realizing active potency, are unleashing Archaic powers. To be actively potent is to Realize/release that

which is most Dreadful to the impotent priests, the prurient patriarchs —
our participation in Be-ing. . . . It is predictable that priestly predators will
attempt to use fear-filled women as powers holding down Elemental
female powers.[16]

Daly's self-conscious, artificial wordplay, bent on reminding us that language is a construct which can therefore be de- and re-constructed according to different laws, is liable to disbelief or ridicule. Why? Partly because her
educative intention — to alert readers to the covert or suppressed potential in
their language and to make moribund usages or weakened meanings come
back to life — can look too much like willfulness or whimsicality. (Daly's passion for puns and coy alliterative pairings, and her solemnity about her own
playfulness, don't help.) But the problem is not just one of manner. This
extreme example of a utopian project to manufacture an alternative language
differs from comparable attempts of dialect or minority-language speakers to
free themselves from the superimposition of a dominant culture's "standard"
language.[17] The aim of such groups is to *write what they speak*: to challenge
the power of a mainstream, colonial literary tradition by the force of an oral
tradition. But no one speaks, or has ever spoken, a distinctive, alternative
female language. If it is to come into being, it must be an entirely fabricated,
artificial, written invention.

The danger — the "risking" — of a utopian, alternative female language   10
expressive of "woman's powers" is that it will be felt to fall short of, or evade,
the real world's balance of power. In which case, feminists have to find another
way of making their words potent.

The confrontational mode of female language mimics or mirrors the
enemy's use of the word *power*. Kristeva, in a section called "The terror of
power or the power of terrorism" in *Women's Time* (1979), analyzes the tendency of women struggling against the "power structure" to "make of the second sex a counter-society," "a counter-power which necessarily generates . . .
its essence as a simulacrum of the combated society or of power." This coun-
tersociety is as violent, as paranoid, and as power-hungry, as the system it
opposes. Hence, according to this argument, the large number of women in
terrorist groups.[18]

Monique Wittig demonstrates a linguistic version of terrorist "counter-
power," explaining her use, in *Les Guérillères*, of the pronoun *elles*:

> To succeed textually, I needed to adopt some very draconian measures,
> such as to eliminate . . . *he* or *they-he*. I had to provide a shock for the reader
> entering a text in which *elles* by its unique presence constitutes an assault,
> yes, even for female readers. . . . The adoption of a pronoun as my subject
> matter dictated the form of the book. Although the theme of the text was
> total war, led by *elles* on *ils*, in order for this new person to take effect,

two-thirds of the text had to be totally inhabited, haunted, by *elles.* Word by word, *elles* establishes itself as a sovereign subject [and] also imposed an epic form, where it is not only the complete subject of the world but its conqueror.[19]

Draconian measures, eliminate, shock, assault, dictated, total war, sovereign subject, imposed, epic, conqueror: The language of power is being not transformed, but turned against the enemy with a vengeance.

The most offensive of these counteroffensives is that of the American polemicist Andrea Dworkin, frequently referred to as a "powerful" voice in the women's movement, whose argument is that the sex act is an act of terrorism against women. There are no exceptions to this rule, since the world according to Dworkin is a constructed male-dominated system of social institutions, sexual practices, and economic relations in which women are silenced, exploited, and damaged. There is ("thus") an essential connection between the foul end — what Dworkin calls "the real shit" — of sexual relations (pornography, rape, wife-battering, incest, prostitution) and the sanctioned end (marriage, love, "so-called" normal intercourse). As much in the legal as in the illegal sphere, "intercourse is political dominance; power as power or power as pleasure." The conspiracy to believe that women like to be hurt is universal. Just as the law allows for unspeakable abuses of women in pornography, so it gives "protective legitimacy" to the ownership of women by men. *Ergo,* "marriage is a legal license to rape," "fucking is the means by which the male colonializes the female":

> Women are a degraded and terrorized people. Women are degraded and terrorized by men. Rape is terrorism. Wife-beating is terrorism. Medical butchering is terrorism. Sexual abuse in its hundred million forms is terrorism. . . . Women are an occupied people. . . . This fascist ideology of female inferiority is the preeminent ideology on this planet.

Dworkin thinks of, and uses, language as a weapon: "dirty words" and "antifeminist epithets" are the equivalent of physical attacks. "Women live defensively, not just against rape but against the language of the rapist." She provides the clearest and most extreme example in the feminist belief in language as power, since, in her argument, "power determines the meaning of language." It is, noticeably, her most used word, as in "Intercourse consistently expresses illegitimate power, unjust power, wrongful power."[20]

Dworkin's weapons, like those of Kristeva's "counter-society," are simulacrums of the enemy's. So her strategies—generalizations, diktats, exhortations—are those of dictatorship. The objects of her attack are, frequently, horrifyingly convincing. But her totalitarian refusal to allow exceptions ("Men love death"; "Women have to pretend to like men to survive"; "Relationships called love are based on exploitation") makes a desolating language which

CHAPTER 6

Inter Partes Proceedings, Infringement, and Dilution

CHAPTER OVERVIEW

Disputes often arise between parties regarding use and ownership of marks. Some proceedings occur at the PTO, and others may be initiated in federal court. There are four categories of actions involving disputes over trademark rights: inter partes proceedings, trademark infringement cases, actions alleging dilution, and actions alleging unfair competition.

Inter partes (literally, "between parties") proceedings fall into four categories: oppositions, cancellations, interferences, and concurrent use proceedings. All of these matters are adjudicated by the Trademark Trial and Appeal Board (TTAB).

A person who believes a mark is being used so as to create a likelihood of confusion in the marketplace with his or her registered mark may initiate an action for trademark infringement under the Lanham Act. Infringement actions are brought in federal court.

The Federal Trademark Dilution Act protects famous marks by prohibiting uses that are not confusingly similar under conventional trademark analysis but may nonetheless dilute the strength of or tarnish another's rights in a mark.

Finally, the Lanham Act provides broad sweeping protection for nearly all forms of unfair competition, including false advertising and infringement of trade dress, which protection is available to those who do not own a registered mark.

can only imitate what it opposes. In this language, the meaning of *power* cannot be transformed.

Must it be so? Toril Moi (arguing with Irigaray over the word *power*) writes   15 these heartening words:

> Women's relationship to power is not exclusively one of victimization. Feminism is not simply about rejecting power, but about transforming the existing power structures — and, in the process, transforming the very *concept* of power itself.[21]

How is the "very *concept*" of power to be transformed? We go back to the beginning again. There are no conclusions, only arguments. But it may be that through the arguments themselves, transformation begins to occur, and *power* takes on its most promising and least hurtful meaning, that of *potential.*

Notes

1. *Oxford English Dictionary, Collins English Dictionary, Oxford Dictionary of Quotations.*

2. Andrea Dworkin, *Right-Wing Women* (New York, 1983), p. 83; Kate Millett, *Sexual Politics* (1969; London, 1977), p. 37.

3. Adrienne Rich, *On Lies, Secrets, and Silences* (New York, 1979; London, 1980, p. 247); Mary Daly, *Gyn/Ecology: The Metaethics of Radical Feminism* (Boston, 1978; London, 1979), p. 79; Toril Moi, *Sexual/Textual Politics* (London, 1985), p. 26.

4. Rich, *On Lies, Secrets, and Silences,* p. 254.

5. Gayle Greene and Coppélia Kahn, eds., *Making a Difference: Feminist Literary Criticism* (London, 1985), p. 17.

6. Rich, *On Lies, Secrets, and Silences,* p. 257.

7. Mary Jacobus, *Reading Woman: Essays in Feminist Criticism* (New York and London, 1986), p. 109.

8. *Reading Woman,* p. 148.

9. *Reading Woman,* p. 65.

10. Josette Féral, "Antigone or *The Irony of the Tribe,*" *Diacritics* 8 (1978): II, quoted by Elizabeth Meese, *Crossing the Double-Cross* (Chapel Hill, 1986), p. 112.

11. Maggie Humm, *Feminist Criticism* (Brighton, 1986), p. 8.

12. Frances Jaffer and Rachel Blau du Plessis, "For the Etruscans: The Debate over a Female Aesthetic," in *Feminist Literary Theory: A Reader,* ed. Mary Eagleton (Oxford, 1986), p. 228.

13. Terry Lovell, "Writing Like a Woman," in *Feminist Literary Theory,* p. 85.

14. Daly, *Gyn/Ecology,* p. 9.

15. Daly, *Gyn/Ecology,* p. 24.

16. Mary Daly, *Pure Lust: Elemental Feminist Philosophy* (London, 1984), pp. 188–89.

17. See the essays on "Identities," especially those by Geneva Smitherman and Monroe K. Spears, in *The State of the Language,* ed. Leonard Michaels and Christopher Ricks (Berkeley and Los Angeles, 1980).

18. Julia Kristeva, "Women's Time" (1979), trans. Alice Jardine and Harry Blake, in *The Kristeva Reader*, ed. Toril Moi (Oxford, 1986), pp. 201–3.

19. Monique Wittig, "The Mark of Gender," in *The Poetics of Gender*, ed. Nancy K. Miller (New York, 1986), p. 70.

20. Andrea Dworkin, *Intercourse* (1987; London, 1988), p. 197; *Letters from a War Zone* (London, 1988), p. 200; *Right-Wing Women*, p. 202; *Intercourse*, p. 201; *Right-Wing Women*, p. 84.

21. Toril Moi, *Sexual/Textual Politics*, p. 148.

Working with the Text

1. Hermione Lee's argument works from a central tenet of feminist thought: "Naming is power" (par. 2). She bases her analysis on the recognition that feminists "have insisted on a female language as the expression of *what has been repressed* in the male sentence" (par. 5). As you reread the essay, look for indications of what feminists might mean by these assertions. Drawing inferences from Lee's argument for an effective "female language," write a brief essay in which you analyze the source of her concern. What problem is she addressing? Why would the claim that naming "is power" lead to the need for a different language? What has been repressed?

2. After analyzing "utopian" and "confrontational" attempts to develop a distinctively female language, Lee concludes, "There are no conclusions, only arguments. But it may be that through the arguments themselves, transformation begins to occur, and *power* takes on its most promising and least hurtful meaning, that of *potential*" (par. 15). As an introduction to undergraduates who are not familiar with Lee's essay or with feminist arguments for a female language, distill the three approaches—utopian, confrontational, and power as potential—and translate them into terms you think your peers would understand.

3. As she builds her argument, Lee quotes from another source in almost every paragraph. In a brief essay, consider her reasons for incorporating so much material from the work of other writers. How does she use the sources? Who are they? What do they contribute to her argument? Why would Lee approach her argument in this way?

4. Lee concludes her essay with the following statement: "There are no conclusions, only arguments. But it may be that through the arguments themselves, transformation begins to occur, and *power* takes on its most promising and least hurtful meaning, that of *potential*." Write a brief essay in which you explain Lee's concluding statement. Does power as potential represent a distinct third alternative to the utopian and confrontational approaches she criticizes? Or does Lee believe that power as potential can only be realized

or developed by engaging—even criticizing—the utopian and confrontational approaches? Does Lee believe that those two approaches, even if misguided, are nevertheless important for us to consider if we are to discover in language the potential for transformation?

From Text to Field

1. Lee opens and closes her essay by offering her own concept of power. Although her argument draws on concepts of power developed by other writers, Lee's analysis of their thinking reveals her own perspective. In a personal essay, explore your concept of the male and female forms of power Lee examines. What is the power relationship between women and men? Who has power, and in what forms? What does it mean to have personal power? What does it mean to be empowered? In the spirit of the power in language that Lee advocates, focus on using your own voice, the language and tone that express who you are.

2. A central theme in feminist writing is an indictment of the ways in which the "dominant male culture" silences women. As you review Lee's essay, infer from her argument as well as the arguments of her sources how they think this silencing takes place. Write an essay in which you reflect on your experience of women being silenced by men or by a culture dominated by men. What does it mean to be silenced? As a woman, do you feel silenced? As a man, do you find that a male-dominated culture could silence women? Have you observed women being silenced? In what ways? Based on your own experience, do you think the feminist argument is valid?

3. Feminists argue that men suppress women because they fear the unleashing of female power. In an essay, argue for or against this view. As you develop your argument, consider the source of your perspective: what you have been taught, your own experience and observation, images from the media or from other forms of American culture, or other sources you identify. Do you think these sources are valid? Why or why not?

4. The writers Lee cites in developing her argument make a number of provocative claims. In an essay, reflect on your response to one of these writers. Which source would you want to read in full? Why? What attracts or provokes you? In what ways do you agree or disagree with the writer's claims, as Lee quotes or summarizes them in her essay? What in the writer's claims would you want to explore further?

Homophobia: Why Bring It Up?

Barbara Smith

Over the last decades, Barbara Smith's ideas, courage, and spirit have inspired social justice work. Smith is a black feminist writer and activist who has been at the forefront of discussions about race, gender, and sexuality. She consistently underscores the connections among ostensibly separate patterns of discrimination.

Smith cofounded the groundbreaking Combahee River Collective, a black feminist organizing group that became famous for its 1977 statement confronting racism in the gay movement and homophobia in the black community. Also in 1977, Smith wrote the influential essay "Toward a Black Feminist Criticism," which called for literary studies to directly address race and gender politics. She is cofounder and publisher of Kitchen Table: Women of Color Press, which has brought to wide attention a series of books and collected essays on race and gender.

Smith has written, coauthored, and coedited a number of books, among them *All the Women Are White, All the Blacks Are Men, but Some of Us Are Brave: Black Women's Studies* (1982), *Home Girls: A Black Feminist Anthology* (1983), and more recently *The Truth That Never Hurts: Writings on Race, Gender, and Freedom* (1998), a collection of her essays. Her articles and essays have appeared in a wide variety of publications, among them the *Nation* and the *New York Times Book Review*. Smith has lectured and served as writer in residence at numerous colleges and universities.

Originally published in 1990 in the *Interracial Books for Children Bulletin,* the essay included here takes as its occasion the brutal police beating of patrons at Blues, a gay, black, working-class bar. The widespread reluctance of newspapers to cover this incident and of civil rights groups to call for a response becomes for Smith further confirmation that homophobia is the one "ism" that otherwise progressive people tolerate.

In 1977 the Combahee River Collective, a Black feminist organization in Boston of which I was a member, wrote:

> The most general statement of our politics at the present time would be that we are actively committed to struggling against racial, sexual, hetero-sexual, and class oppression and see as our particular task the development of integrated analysis and practice based upon the fact that the major sys-tems of oppression are interlocking. . . . We . . . often find it difficult to sep-arate race from class from sex oppression because in our lives they are most often experienced simultaneously.[1]

Despite the logic and clarity of third world women's analysis of the simul-taneity of oppression, people of all colors, progressive ones included, seem peculiarly reluctant to grasp these basic truths, especially when it comes to incorporating an active resistance to homophobia into their everyday lives. Homophobia is usually the last oppression to be mentioned, the last to be taken seriously, the last to go. But it is extremely serious, sometimes to the point of being fatal.

Consider that on the night of September 29, 1982, 20–30 New York City policemen rushed without warning into Blues, a Times Square bar. They harassed and severely beat the patrons, vandalized the premises, emptied the cash register, and left without making a single arrest. What motivated such brutal behavior? The answer is simple. The cops were inspired by three cher-ished tenets of our society: racism, classism, and homophobia: The bar's clientele is Black, working class, and gay. As the police cracked heads, they yelled racist and homophobic epithets familiar to every schoolchild. The attackers' hatred of both the queer and the colored, far from making them exceptional, put them squarely in the mainstream. If their actions were more extreme than most, their attitudes certainly were not.

The Blues bar happens to be across the street from the offices of the *New York Times*. The white, upper-middle-class, presumably heterosexual staff of the nation's premier newspaper regularly calls in complaints about the bar to the police. Not surprisingly, none of the New York daily papers, including the *Times*, bothered to report the incident. A coalition of third world and white lesbians and gay men organized a large protest demonstration soon after the attack occurred. Both moderate and militant civil rights and antiracist organizations were notably absent, and they have yet to express public outrage about a verifiable incident of police brutality, undoubtedly because the Black people involved were not straight.

Intertwining "Isms"

What happened at Blues perfectly illustrates the ways in which the major ⁵ "isms" *including* homophobia are intimately and violently intertwined. As a

Black woman, a lesbian, a feminist, and an activist, I have little difficulty seeing how the systems of oppression interconnect, if for no other reason than
that their meanings so frequently affect my life. During the 1970s and 1980s
political lesbians of color have often been the most
astute about the necessity for developing understand- **Homophobia is usually the**
ings of the connections between oppressions. They **last oppression to be men-**
have also opposed the building of hierarchies and chal- **tioned. . . .**
lenged the "easy way out" of choosing a "primary
oppression" and downplaying those messy inconsistencies that occur whenever race, sex, class, and sexual identity actually mix. Ironically, for the forces
on the right, hating lesbians and gay men, people of color, Jews, and women
go hand in hand. *They* make connections between oppressions in the most
negative ways with horrifying results. Supposedly progressive people, on the
other hand, who oppose oppression on every other level, balk at acknowledging the societally sanctioned abuse of lesbians and gay men as a serious
problem. Their tacit attitude is "Homophobia, why bring it up?"

There are numerous reasons for otherwise sensitive people's reluctance to
confront homophobia in themselves and others. A major one is that people
are generally threatened about issues of sexuality, and for some the mere existence of homosexuals calls their sexuality/heterosexuality into question.
Unlike many other oppressed groups, homosexuals are not a group whose
identity is clear from birth. Through the process of coming out, a person
might indeed acquire this identity at any point in life. One way to protect
one's heterosexual credentials and privilege is to put down lesbians and gay
men at every turn, to make as large a gulf as possible between "we" and "they."

There are several misconceptions and attitudes which I find particularly
destructive because of the way they work to isolate the concerns of lesbians
and gay men:

1. Lesbian and gay male oppression is not as serious as other oppressions.
   It is not a political matter, but a private concern. The life-destroying
   impact of lost jobs, children, friendships, and family; the demoralizing
   toll of living in constant fear of being discovered by the wrong person
   which pervades all lesbians and gay men's lives whether closeted or out;
   and the actual physical violence and deaths that gay men and lesbians
   suffer at the hands of homophobes can be, if one subscribes to this myth,
   completely ignored.
2. "Gay" means gay white men with large discretionary incomes, period.
   Perceiving gay people in this way allows one to ignore that some of us
   are women *and* people of color *and* working class *and* poor *and* disabled
   and old. Thinking narrowly of gay people as white, middle class, and
   male, which is just what the establishment media want people to think,
   undermines consciousness of how identities and issues overlap. It is

essential, however, in making connections between homophobia and other oppressions, not to fall prey to the distorted reasoning that the justification for taking homophobia seriously is that it affects some groups who are "verifiably" oppressed, for example, people of color, women, or disabled people. Homophobia is in and of itself a verifiable oppression and in a heterosexist system, all nonheterosexuals are viewed as "deviants" and are oppressed.

3. Homosexuality is a white problem or even a "white disease." This attitude is much too prevalent among people of color. Individuals who are militantly opposed to racism in all its forms still find lesbianism and male homosexuality something to snicker about or, worse, to despise. Homophobic people of color are oppressive not just to white people, but to members of their own groups—at least 10 percent of their own groups.

4. Expressions of homophobia are legitimate and acceptable in contexts where other kinds of verbalized bigotry would be prohibited. Put-downs and jokes about "dykes" and "faggots" can be made without the slightest criticism in circles where "nigger" and "chink" jokes, for instance, would bring instant censure or even ostracism. One night of television viewing indicates how very acceptable public expressions of homophobia are.

How can such deeply entrenched attitudes and behavior be confronted and changed? Certainly gay and lesbian/feminist activism has made significant inroads since the late 1960s, both in the public sphere and upon the awareness of individuals. These movements have served a highly educational function, but they have not had nearly enough impact upon the educational system itself. Curriculum that focuses in a positive way upon issues of sexual identity, sexuality, and sexism is still rare, particularly in primary and secondary grades. Yet schools are virtual cauldrons of homophobic sentiment, as witnessed by everything from the graffiti in the bathrooms and the put-downs yelled on the playground, to the heterosexist bias of most texts and the firing of teachers on no other basis than that they are not heterosexual.

In the current political climate schools are constantly under hostile scrutiny from well-organized conservative forces. More than a little courage is required to challenge students' negative attitudes about what it means to be homosexual, female, third world, etc., but these attitudes *must* be challenged if pervasive taken-for-granted homophobia is ever to cease. I have found both in teaching and in speaking to a wide variety of audiences that making connections between oppressions is an excellent way to introduce the subjects of lesbian and gay male identity and homophobia, because it offers people a frame of reference to build upon. This is especially true if efforts have already been made in the classroom to teach about racism and sexism. It is factually inaccurate and strategically mistaken to present gay materials as if all gay people were white and male. Fortunately, there is an increasing body of work available, usually written by third world feminists, that provides an integrated approach to the intersection of a multiplicity of identities and issues.

Perhaps some readers are still wondering, "Homophobia, why bring it up?" One reason to bring it up is that at least 10 percent of your students will be or already are lesbians and gay males. Ten percent of your colleagues are as well. Homophobia may well be the last oppression to go, but it will go. It will go a lot faster if people who are opposed to *every* form of subjugation work in coalition to make it happen.

Note

1. The Combahee River Collective, "A Black Feminist Statement," in *All the Women Are White, All the Blacks Are Men, but Some of Us Are Brave: Black Women's Studies*, pp. 13, 16 (The Feminist Press), 1982.

Working with the Text

1. Barbara Smith describes the incident at the Blues bar early in her essay. Why did she include the details of a particular incident? Why did she place it where she did in the essay? Why is the location of the bar, in Times Square, especially relevant to Smith's point?

2. Smith notes that "[u]nlike many other oppressed groups, homosexuals are not a group whose identity is clear from birth" (par. 6). In what ways is this observation important as Smith comments on the intertwining of "isms"?

3. Smith titles her essay with a question. Offer a succinct summary of her response. In what ways does her title speak to the "silencing" of homophobia and its connection to other forms of oppression?

From Text to Field

1. Smith observes that "schools are virtual cauldrons of homophobic sentiment" (par. 8). Describe and reflect on incidents or experiences in your education that confirm or respond to Smith's characterization. Why does Smith focus on schools and schooling in her essay?

2. Smith notes four specific misconceptions or attitudes that she finds particularly destructive. Focusing on any one of the four, offer detailed, concrete instances of that misconception or attitude. Why is it destructive? Might there be a fifth misconception or attitude that merits inclusion in Smith's list? If so, what is it and why should it be included?

3. Either in your library or on the Internet, locate a copy of or an excerpt from the statement produced by the Combahee River Collective in 1977. What in the document might be tied to the history of its day? What endures and continues to be relevant? If you were to update this statement or offer one of your own, given more contemporary concerns, what would you focus on?

INTO THE FIELD: Options for Writing Projects

1. Logging the Classroom Conversation

The conversations you have in your college classrooms surely vary by subject matter, and their dynamics are constrained by the size of the class. A small seminar in the humanities will permit and encourage different conversational styles than a larger class in the sciences. Yet even within the same general context, conversational styles and patterns can vary, depending on the professor, the teaching philosophy employed, the gender composition of the class, and even the time of day.

This field project invites you to offer a fine-grained analysis of the conversational styles employed in one of your classes. Drawing on Deborah Tannen's discussion (p. 781) of gender in conversation and her own close observation of conversation in one of her classes, record in your notebook or diary the give-and-take of classroom talk. You may opt to choose your writing class for this study, in which case you may want to focus on the relationship between talk and the writing or revision process. You may also choose to work undercover in one of your other classes. (Whichever site you choose, be sure to respect the privacy of your classmates. For example, you may simply wish to identify speakers by number, rather than by name.)

As you log the conversation during one or several class periods, here are just a few of the many questions you may wish to consider: Who initiates the conversation? Who asks questions? How long do speakers hold the floor? Who speaks, and just as importantly, who doesn't tend to speak? How is turn taking handled? To what extent are there interruptions or overlaps in speaking? Are different styles of conversation evident based on the genders involved? How prevalent are challenges and counterarguments in the conversation? Are other speakers acknowledged or referred to, and if so how? How are shifts in topic handled? To what degree does the instructor orchestrate the conversation and its outcome? Does the physical environment of the classroom (e.g., how seats are arranged) have an effect on the conversation? To what extent do shadow conversations (e.g., whispered asides) occur during the primary conversation? Do you discern an educational philosophy or pedagogical approach that informs how and why the instructor has called upon conversation in this course?

As you offer your analysis, based on these observations, do you believe that "talking about ways of talking" has helped you understand the course and its classroom dynamics in a new or deeper way? Based on your analysis, what recommendations might you have for the instructor, the students, or both?

531

INTER PARTES PROCEEDINGS

Inter partes proceedings are those involving disputes between parties regarding rights, use, and ownership of marks. These actions are heard before the TTAB, a department of the PTO. Generally, the Federal Rules of Civil Procedure govern these proceedings, making the proceedings substantially similar to actions brought in federal courts. There are four types of inter partes proceedings: oppositions, cancellations, interferences, and concurrent use proceedings.

Oppositions

Timing Requirements. An **opposition** is a proceeding initiated by a person who believes that he or she would be damaged by registration of a mark on the Principal Register. Oppositions may not be initiated against marks sought to be registered on the Supplemental Register—those marks may be objected to by way of cancellation proceedings, discussed later. The document initiating the proceeding is called a **Notice of Opposition.** The time for initiating an opposition is triggered by the publication of a mark in the *Official Gazette.* Publication occurs after the examining attorney at the PTO has approved the mark and is intended to provide notice to the public of the pending application so interested persons can oppose the registration.

A notice of opposition must be filed within thirty days after publication of the mark in the *Official Gazette* or, if an extension of time has been granted, within the extended time period. If additional time to oppose is desired, the potential opposer should prepare and file (in triplicate) a written request for extension of time to oppose before the initial thirty days expires. A thirty-day extension will be granted by the TTAB upon request, without any necessity of showing cause why the extension is needed. However, subsequent extensions must be for good cause and, unless the applicant consents, the TTAB will not grant extensions aggregating more than 120 days from the date of publication. Typically, alleging that the potential opposer needs additional time to investigate whether the applied-for mark may conflict with his or her mark is sufficient to demonstrate good cause.

For example, if EXPLORE is published in the *Official Gazette* on March 1, 2003, either a notice of opposition or a request for extension of time must be filed by March 31, 2003. Extensions of time may be granted by the TTAB until June 29, 2003 (120 days from publication). Additional extensions will be granted only if the applicant for EXPLORE consents. The PTO is fairly liberal in approving extensions, believing that parties should always be given the opportunity to work out disagreements between themselves, much as courts prefer litigants to reach settlement rather than going to trial. There is no fee required for filing a request for extension of time to oppose. (See Appendix D, Form 6, for a sample form for request for extension of time to oppose.)

Notice of Opposition. If the parties themselves cannot reach some resolution, an opposition proceeding will be initiated by the filing (in triplicate) of a notice of opposition. The Lanham Act requires only that the notice of opposition set forth a "short and plain statement" of the reasons why the opposer believes it will be damaged by registration of the mark and the grounds for opposition. When the TTAB receives the notice of opposition, it forwards it to the applicant for response, much as a defendant in a civil action is provided with a copy of a complaint so the defendant may answer its allegations. The filing fee for a notice of opposition is $300 per class of goods/services identified in the application. (See Appendix D, Form 7, for a notice of opposition.)

Even if the parties ultimately reach resolution of the matter, the filing of a notice of

2. Gender, Conversation, and Group Dynamics

Small groups for discussion or other activities, often formed within a larger group setting, prove interesting test subjects by which to explore the role of gender in group dynamics. Some courses, such as your writing class, may make frequent use of small groups for peer feedback. Other courses may also use group work on occasion, and more than a few courses call for group or collaborative projects. Small groups, such as informal study groups, may also form outside of class and its more structured academic setting. Although academic discussion may be the overt purpose for the work of these groups, the dynamics that shape the group and its conversations are influenced by gender and conversational style. This field project invites you to explore the dynamics at work in a group in which you participate.

Many of the questions you may wish to ask about small groups parallel those in question 1 above that pertain to classroom conversation. Here are a few additional questions, many of which take into account the special dynamics of small groups. How does your group regulate itself? How is consensus achieved? If there seems to be a leader in the group, what kind of leadership style does he or she seem to present? How are roles assumed or assigned? How does the group encourage or respond to its less active members? How are conflicts or disagreements handled? What conversational style seems to predominate in your interactions with each other? What role does "off-task" conversation (e.g., what you did on Saturday night) have in developing trust and group solidarity? How do group members assume and grant authority and responsibility? Do gender and gender roles have a discernible effect on the group's dynamics?

As an alternative to this field project, you may wish to focus on a group outside of an explicitly academic setting, such as a group in your residence halls, a student group active on campus, or a group of citizens that is active in your community.

3. The Ethics of Conversational Participation

In her essay "How Male and Female Students Use Language Differently" (p. 496), Deborah Tannen briefly refers to what she terms an "ethics of participation" that can guide our role in conversations. This field project encourages you to flesh out what those ethics might be, either in your own life or in a particular classroom setting.

- In a substantive essay, explore your ethics for participation in conversation. How did you acquire those ethics? What educational or other experiences had a formative influence on those ethics? How do you see your ethics playing themselves out in real conversational contexts that often present dilemmas that cannot be addressed in easy ways? Have your participatory ethics conflicted with those of people who hold different ethics? How do such ethics vary given different contexts and perhaps different cultural backgrounds? How do your ethics of participation relate to your educational goals and to your views on learning and teaching? What influence do you think gender and gender roles might have on your ethics of participation?

- Explore the ethics of participation that are at work in a particular class you are taking. In what ways has your instructor articulated a conversational ethics for the class? How might that ethic be rooted in an education philosophy or a distinctive teaching style? To what extent might the ethics of participation or the class's conversational style be influenced by unspoken "rules" in that academic discipline or by a certain disciplinary "culture"? How does that ethic play itself out in actual classroom conversation? What learning outcomes seem to follow from or are posited by that ethic? Do you detect any dissonance or disconnect between the announced conversational ethic and the ethic as practiced in the classroom? What role does conversation, and its ethical and educational underpinnings, have in your attitude toward the class and toward your own learning? What place does conversation have in your distinctive learning style and gender role?

4. Academic Put-Downs: Language, Gender, and Power

In her meditation on the effect of calling someone a "bitch," Beverly Gross (p. 504) explores the intersection of language, gender, and power. This field project invites you to extend her investigation of "put-downs" by focusing on a distinctive type, as practiced in college classrooms and labs and during professors' office hours.

Your college or university campus would seem to be above the sort of street talk that Gross encounters when she explores the purposes toward which the appellation *bitch* is put. After all, isn't college supposed to be about tweed jackets and sherry hours, polite and learned conversation, and the life of the mind? Isn't college all about getting beyond high school behaviors? Although academic conversation is generally more polite, it can also be as ruthless and hurtful as conversations in other contexts. Indeed, part of what makes it so ruthless is that it masks itself with polite subtlety.

This field project is your opportunity to exact a measure of equally polite revenge. Surely all of us have been subjected to the hurtful academic put-down more than a few times. Sometimes the put-down comes from the instructor, but often it comes from a fellow classmate. It can take the form of exposing ignorance of something you supposedly should have known or of denigrating your abilities in a particular area. It might involve gender, as when a science or an engineering professor questions the interest or ability of a female student or when a male student feels put down in a women's studies class. Or the put-down might involve, as it often does, hierarchy and differences in power. (By the way, professors have raised academic put-downs to a high art by practicing among themselves.)

You might find it convenient and effective to organize the essay that comes out of this field project in the following way.

- First, describe the conversation or interaction in which the put-down occurred, including context that will help the reader of your essay understand the encounter.
- Next, analyze the details of the encounter. Here you might offer insights into the language strategies employed and what response, if any, you made. Why and in what ways do academic put-downs trade on people's facility (or lack of facility) with language and texts? How might gender and power have come into play? You also may wish to reflect on what response you would have liked to have made, given your current perspective on the situation.
- For the final section of your essay, generalize and extend your analysis. In what ways does the encounter you discuss reflect on academic culture (and its neuroses) or on the challenges you face when studying or majoring in a particular field?

5. Gender, in a Word

As identified and discussed by Beverly Gross (p. 504), the word *bitch* is certainly a term that captures many of the gender issues of our time. Yet that one word is by no means the only barometer of current or past attitudes. This field project encourages you to explore other words that might help us trace and understand our evolving discussions on gender.

How might you choose a particular word or term? Class discussion or brainstorming in small groups can provide a rich list of candidates. Dictionaries of slang, some of which Gross cites, are also good sources for terms that carry gender implications. Although terms of a sexual nature may be the first to spring to mind, don't overlook a whole host of terms that speak more generally of a male-oriented culture. The essay by Hermione Lee (p. 515), for example, turns to the word *power* to capture key issues — and problems — in feminist discourse.

You may find it highly instructive to review the etymology, or historical development, of your chosen word, as do both Gross and Lee. The *Oxford English Dictionary*, often referred to by its acronym *OED*, is the authoritative source on such matters. Your college library will have the multivolume print copy but may have online access to this reference work as well. Use other, more specialized dictionaries, such as dictionaries of slang, to supplement your work with the *OED*.

Once you have a solid grounding in the history of the word and a sense of its range of meanings, work collaboratively with others in your class to offer anecdotal evidence of its use and an analysis of how that particular term might offer insight into issues of gender.

6. Bathroom Graffiti: Tracing Gendered Conversation

Academic discussion of gender politics can often obscure the reality and influence that gendered conversation can have in our lives. One site where that conversation can be observed is the bathroom stall, a realm that is public in one sense, but also private and uncensored. Graffiti, and graffiti on graffiti, often reveal, in the most intimate ways, our obsession and fears about sexuality and gender orientation, our concerns about personal and group identity, and our worries about fitting in or standing out.

This field project invites you to explore a site that is in some sense taboo: graffiti in bathroom stalls and graffiti in other areas of campus. Your task is to observe the inscriptions not so much in their own terms, but as part of a conversation. Graffiti are written to mark or tag a site but also to make a statement and initiate a conversation. And those conversations may vary considerably between men and women.

This project calls for collaboration and a division of roles. Working in coed pairs or teams, divide up the field research so that men and women visit their respective bathrooms and other graffitied sites and then share notes with other members of the team. Working in this fashion, your team can gather and record data and then interpret and analyze it in ways that highlight differences in bathroom discourse. The goal throughout is to understand how issues of gender and sexuality are expressed in sites that are at once public yet also uncensored. (Caution: This project is not an invitation to add to graffiti. Moreover, because of the often explicit nature of graffiti texts, the project demands that all members of the team exercise good taste and discretion.)

Here are just a few questions to get you started: Based on the data that your team has gathered, do you see differences in the graffiti? Are men more competitive, with issues of power and performance often emerging as central? Do women express more cooperation and solidarity? How are members of the opposite sex portrayed? How do multiple responses to an initial item of graffiti suggest different ways in which conversation might unfold? Do graffiti vary according to location (the library, the dorm, the student center)? What do the graffiti tell us about our obsessions, desires, and fears?

7. Bias in Language

Because language is such a powerful instrument in the creation and reflection of our identities, the presence of bias in language has become a growing concern. Such bias can involve gender and has prompted greater awareness about how we might write in more gender-neutral or nonsexist ways. Bias also involves issues of race, ethnicity, and disability. This field project invites you to explore such bias and our responses to it.

For a brief but well-done introduction to bias in language, you should consult the Web site of the American Psychological Association (APA). This organization has developed the APA style manual for authors working in the social sciences, which offers an excellent introduction to the role of bias and to practical editorial remedies for addressing bias in language ‹apastyle.org›.

Your work can take one of several directions, depending on your interests and on the field site you wish to explore:

- You may wish to focus on one aspect of bias. Among the most common are gender bias, bias in race and ethnicity, and bias regarding disability.
- You should focus your work in one domain or field site, such as bias in the media or bias in the classroom.
- You may find it helpful to focus on one or more concrete instances of bias, as a way of grounding your work.
- In the course of your fieldwork, you might find it quite helpful to interview people who have experienced bias or those who have sought—as writers, teachers or community activists—to address and correct such bias.

Throughout, you may wish to consider whether bias in language is a reflection of the biases we have or whether it might also create or perpetuate those biases.

8. Gender Equity and Support on Your Campus

Your campus offers a compelling and multifaceted site in which to see issues of gender being played out. This field project offers several options for exploring gender equity and gender support on your campus, with respect to either students or faculty. Here are some avenues you may wish to pursue:

- Does your campus offer support for students majoring in a field in which women are underrepresented (engineering or some of the sciences, for example)? If so, how effective are those programs? If not, might such a program be helpful?
- What effect has Title IX (gender equity in sports) had on your campus? What steps did your campus take to come into compliance with Title IX? What problems might still persist for your campus to come into full compliance?
- What programs might your campus have for so-called nontraditional students, many of whom may be women with families? What issues for non-traditional students remain unaddressed on your campus?
- Are women faculty (especially in male-dominated fields) present in sufficient numbers? Are there special programs for the recruitment and retention of

women faculty? Do women faculty have their own support group? Are there discussions on your campus about salary inequities between male and female faculty?

As you inventory the state of discussion about gender or about programs that address gender issues on your campus, focus on one particular issue or problem as the nexus for further exploration.

9. Same-Sex Colleges

Early in her essay on how male and female students use language differently, Deborah Tannen (p. 496) offers a passing comment on the possible value of single-sex or same-sex schools and colleges. This field project offers you an opportunity to explore in far more detail the rationale for such institutions and how these institutions present themselves to prospective students and parents. Web sites for each college, and their comments on institutional mission and history, offer a valuable resource.

Although several elite East-coast colleges for women may immediately come to mind (among them Smith, Mount Holyoke, Wellesley, and Bryn Mawr), there are some seventy women's colleges in the United States. Consult the Women's College Coalition for a list of member institutions <womenscolleges.org>. Although many prominent men's colleges started accepting women students in the 1970s and are now fully coeducational (among them Amherst and Wesleyan), there remain a handful of men's colleges. For representative instances, you may wish to consult the Web sites of Hampden-Sydney College, Morehouse College, and Wabash College. Debates about single-sex or coed housing facilities may replicate some aspects of this larger debate.

As you explore the rationale for same-sex institutions, pay special attention to the role of language and of a common community. You may wish to compare the rationale to that of attending a religiously affiliated institution or historically black college or university.

As you explore this world of single-sex colleges and universities, reflect on the role that gender played in your decision about where to go to college. Although the vast majority of students have chosen to attend coeducational institutions, what role did a range of gender-related issues have in your decision? To what extent do gender-related issues have a role in your decision to major in a particular field?

10. Bringing up Homophobia

As we speak of gender and sexual orientation, it is important to note what is silent or silenced. In her essay, Barbara Smith (p. 525) makes the case that homophobia remains the one "ism" (among such concerns as racism or sexism) that otherwise progressive people will tolerate.

Drawing on one particular site, such as your campus or your hometown, explore the extent to which homophobia is silent or silenced. To what extent are the concerns of the queer community (e.g., gays, lesbians, bisexuals) given voice? How does that particular community respond to other concerns of social justice, such as racism or sexism? Develop a substantive essay in which you particularize and test Smith's observations, given one local community.

MINDING GENDER

Our minds are in many respects a theater of memory. Rarely if ever do we encounter something or someone in fresh, unencumbered ways. Those encounters are invariably filtered through the images we carry in our minds. This is especially true of experiences concerning or influenced by gender.

Our "images in mind" about gender roles and expectations, about what it means to be a man or a woman, filter and help construct our experience. Yet those very images in mind can also be — and indeed should be — the subject of reflection and self-awareness. If we remain unaware of those images, we know little about their influence and know even less about the alternative images we might develop for ourselves over time. This unit considers those images, looking *at* them rather than through them.

Most of us will clearly grant that our "images in mind" about gender shape our personal lives and identities and, what is more, our social interactions. Our parents and our family life surely have enormous influence on how we think of ourselves. That influence can start at the earliest of ages and continues, in various forms, throughout our adolescent and adult lives. The advice we receive about being a boy or a girl, or a man or woman, shapes our self-image and, in turn, the advice we give to others. Sometimes that advice will prompt us to challenge expected gender roles and refashion or experiment with received identities.

It only follows that the very personal images we carry in our minds shape our social interactions. How we behave in social and public settings — in the classroom and the dorm, in the workplace and on the street — is in good measure shaped by the images that we see in our theater of the mind. Indeed, that internal theater guides how we perceive the advantages and liabilities of both genders and influences how we might respond to the so-called gender wars of the last decades. Yet even as we begin to appreciate the social expression of our internal images, we also find that social conventions of behavior have likewise had a hand in shaping them. Social roles and constraints become internalized and help form our sense of who we are.

If the gender images we carry in our minds shape our personal lives and social interactions, they can likewise influence endeavors that may seem far more objective and impersonal. Scientific research lies at the far end of that spectrum, yet here too the influence of gender may be more telling than we might think. We presume that such research is untainted from bias, yet the history of science teaches us that bias—here, gender bias—can at times influence the conclusions drawn from data and the data themselves. The same can hold true for the ways in which scientific research is communicated. The language we employ and the metaphors we call upon can carry hidden freight and unexamined implications. Our "images in mind" regarding gender—our assumptions and dispositions—can profoundly influence the supposedly impartial observation of phenomena. Even scientific work, it seems, remains rooted in human culture.

The four essays in this unit offer different yet complementary perspectives on the theater of the mind—one in which images of gender hold surprising sway. Caribbean-born author Jamaica Kincaid explores in her short, evocative story "Girl" how images of being a girl and a woman are shaped by culture and are passed on from mother to daughter. Scott Russell Sanders likewise places the issue of gender identity in social and interpersonal contexts as he traces the role of men back to "the men we carry in our minds." The eminent scientist and science writer Stephen Jay Gould offers an excursion into the history of science devoted to brain size and intelligence. In the process, he reminds us that research interests and scientific conclusions can remain rooted in human culture and gender assumptions. Emily Martin explores the ways in which dominant or accepted metaphors about male-female roles make their way into serious scientific study and helps us appreciate that cultural assumptions can shape how scientists interpret and describe what they observe.

Reflecting on Prior Knowledge

1. The "images in mind" that we hold regarding gender affect how and what we know. In a journal entry, reflect on the origins or sources of what you know about gender. When, where, and from whom did you learn about gender— about being a boy or girl, man or woman? Have recent experiences reinforced or challenged your "images in mind"?

2. Cultural critics and political commentators have on occasion talked about the "gender wars." Implied by this term, to be sure, are the struggles faced by women as they work toward equality and equity. Yet the term also points to the challenges experienced by men as they adapt to evolving expectations and roles. Above all, the term suggests that these struggles and challenges have pitted woman against man. In a journal entry, or through a classroom activity where you pair up with another student, reflect on the term *gender wars*. Does

the term capture your experience or the experiences of your mother or father? What, if anything, might be misleading about the term? If you have struggled, in what ways, and how might those ways be misunderstood by others?

3. All of us have misjudged matters, and this can often be the case when it comes to gender and sexual orientation. Not only might we misjudge others, but we might also misjudge ourselves. In a journal entry, reflect on an image you held in mind about yourself or others that needed or invited correction or further consideration. How or why might your confidence in certain assumptions be misplaced? What have you learned or how have you grown through that experience and others like it?

4. The stories we tell, and the accounts we give of our world, often reflect in their very language and metaphors the gendered perspectives that we carry with us. In a journal entry, or perhaps in a brief story, offer two or more versions of a conversation, an encounter, or an event, each one guided by a different sense of gender and sexual identity. Think of this invitation as an opportunity to create your own *Rashomon* based on issues of gender—*Rashomon* (1950) being a famous movie by Japanese filmmaker Akira Kurosawa in which different versions of the same event are told by several individuals.

opposition or even a request for extension of time to oppose seriously delays the application process. Thus, IP professionals should use the Trademark Status line or TARR, the PTO's online status reporting system, to monitor applications to determine if such documents have been filed and alert clients of such an impediment to registration.

Grounds for Opposition. In brief, an opposer wishes to prevent registration of a mark. The most common reason a person might believe he or she will be damaged if the mark applied for proceeds to registration is that the mark is confusingly similar to the opposer's mark. Opposers are not, however, limited to asserting confusing similarity as a basis for opposition. The opposer is only required to state why he or she believes registration of the mark in question would result in damage. Thus, oppositions can also be initiated on the basis of descriptiveness or that the mark is a surname, contains immoral or disparaging matter, has been abandoned, dilutes another's trademark, and so forth. Nevertheless, the vast majority of oppositions allege that the mark in an application should be refused because it is likely to cause confusion with the opposer's mark. In one novel case, in 1999 the Federal Circuit held that an individual was entitled to come before the TTAB to oppose registration of the trademarks O. J. SIMPSON, O.J., and THE JUICE on the grounds that the marks disparaged his values, were scandalous because they would attempt to justify violence against women, and that others in the public shared his views. *Ritchie v. Simpson*, 170 F.3d 1092 (Fed. Cir. 1999). The court held that the opposer had asserted a reasonable belief of damage and thus had standing to oppose registration of the marks. A strongly worded dissent expressed concern that the ruling would open the PTO up to oppositions or cancellations from any member of the public who found a mark to be offensive. The applications were eventually abandoned by the applicant.

Nature of Proceeding.   As soon as either a notice of opposition or a request for extension of time to oppose is filed, the examining attorney at the PTO relinquishes the file to the TTAB, which will handle the matter until its conclusion. Opposition proceedings are somewhat like trials. The notice (and a duplicate copy) of opposition (equivalent to a complaint) is filed, and a copy is forwarded to the applicant; within thirty days the applicant will file a response to the notice of opposition (equivalent to an answer); a discovery schedule will be issued by the TTAB and will occur by way of interrogatories, depositions, and the like; briefs are filed by each party; and the TTAB will render a decision. However, the entire opposition proceeding is done by filing of documents with the PTO; no trial or oral presentations of evidence occur, unless the parties request to present oral argument. The schedule in an opposition is faster than that for most trials and the issue is narrow: Should the mark be allowed to register? Damages are not awarded, and the opposer cannot force the applicant to stop using the mark. A successful opposition merely results in denial of registration of a mark in a pending application.

Just as most civil cases do not go to trial and conclude by voluntary settlement, opposition proceedings are overwhelmingly concluded by voluntary agreements. Generally, the opposer and the applicant enter into a written **consent agreement** (called a Consent to Use Agreement) whereby they agree on the scope and nature of each party's use of its mark, submit the agreement to the TTAB, and then ask for dismissal of the opposition proceeding. The consent to use agreement is the equivalent of a settlement agreement in a civil action. Until relatively recently, the PTO accorded such agreements little weight; however, since the decision in *In re Four Seasons Hotels Ltd.*, 987 F.2d 1565 (Fed. Cir. 1993), such agreements have been given great weight in determining whether confusion is likely to result from coex-

Girl

Jamaica Kincaid

Born Elaine Potter Richardson in 1949, Jamaica Kincaid adopted this pen name when she began writing for the *New Yorker* magazine, becoming a regular contributor for nearly twenty years (1976–1995) with her "Talk of the Town" column. But behind this name change lies a quest for self and a journey from home.

Kincaid was born in St. John's, Antigua, which was then a British colony in the Caribbean. Her mother's family members were landed peasants and her father a carpenter and cabinetmaker. Precocious and an early reader, Jamaica fled her island home and family at seventeen. Arriving in New York, she worked as an au pair and a receptionist, studied photography, and attended college before her writing caught the attention of editors at the *New Yorker.* She now lives in Vermont with her husband, son, and daughter.

Kincaid's experience as an exile and her troubled relationship with her mother inform much of her writing. Her tight, lyrical prose captures the conflicted emotions of that mother-daughter relationship and of her connection to, yet distance from, her homeland. In addition to her magazine writing, Kincaid has published many books, among them *Annie John* (1985), her story of growing up and leaving home; *A Small Place* (1988), an angry account of colonization; *Lucy* (1990), the story of an au pair in a family whose happiness unravels; and *Autobiography of My Mother* (1994).

"Girl" was first published in the *New Yorker* and then anthologized in Kincaid's collection of stories *At the Bottom of the River* (2000), which focuses on the childhood and coming of age of a Caribbean girl.

Wash the white clothes on Monday and put them on the stone heap; wash the color clothes on Tuesday and put them on the clothesline to dry; don't walk barehead in the hot sun; cook pumpkin fritters in very hot sweet oil; soak your little cloths right after you take them off; when buying cotton to make yourself a nice blouse, be sure that it doesn't have gum on it, because that way it won't hold up well after a wash; soak salt fish overnight before you cook it; is it true that you sing benna in Sunday school?; always eat your food in such a way that it won't turn someone else's stomach; on Sundays try to walk like a lady and not like the slut you are so bent on becoming; don't sing benna in Sunday school; you mustn't speak to wharf-rat boys, not even to give directions; don't eat fruits on the street — flies will follow you; *but I don't sing benna on Sundays at all and never in Sunday school*; this is how to sew on a button; this is how to make a buttonhole for the button you have just sewed on; this is how to hem a dress when you see the hem coming down and so to prevent yourself from looking like the slut I know you are so bent on becoming; this is how you iron your father's khaki shirt so that it doesn't have a crease; this is how you iron your father's khaki pants so that they don't have a crease; this is how you grow okra — far from the house, because okra tree harbors red ants; when you are growing dasheen, make sure it gets plenty of water or else it makes your throat itch when you are eating it; this is how you sweep a corner; this is how you sweep a whole house; this is how you sweep a yard; **This way they won't recognize immediately the slut I have warned you against becoming.** this is how you smile to someone you don't like too much; this is how you smile to someone you don't like at all; this is how you smile to someone you like completely; this is how you set a table for tea; this is how you set a table for dinner; this is how you set a table for dinner with an important guest; this is how you set a table for lunch; this is how you set a table for breakfast; this is how to behave in the presence of men who don't know you very well, and this way they won't recognize immediately the slut I have warned you against becoming; be sure to wash every day, even if it is with your own spit; don't squat down to play marbles — you are not a boy, you know; don't pick people's flowers — you might catch something; don't throw stones at blackbirds, because it might not be a blackbird at all; this is how to make a bread pudding; this is how to make doukona; this is how to make pepper pot; this is how to make a good medicine for a cold; this is how to make a good medicine to throw away a child before it even becomes a child; this is how to catch a fish; this is how to throw back a fish you don't like, and that way something bad won't fall on you; this is how to bully a man; this is how a man bullies you; this is how to love a man, and if this doesn't work there are other ways, and if they don't work don't feel too bad about giving up; this is how to spit up in the air if you feel like it, and this is how to move quick so that it doesn't fall on you; this is how to make ends meet; always squeeze bread to make sure it's fresh; *but what if the baker won't let me feel* *the bread?*; you mean to say that after all you are really going to be the kind of woman who the baker won't let near the bread?

Working with the Text

1. The two italicized lines in the story clarify that there are two speakers involved in this encounter. Who is the main speaker, and who is speaking in italics? How would you describe the interaction between the two speakers?

2. Jamaica Kincaid's story is cast as one very long sentence. Why do you think she made this choice? What effect does this form have on you, and how might it underscore the point she wishes to make or the effect she wishes to create?

3. How would you describe this "girl," and what attitude does the speaker have about her? What can you discern about the attitude of the girl? What identity does the speaker encourage her to adopt?

From Text to Field

1. Study the advice given to the "girl" for what it implies about the cultural context in which she is growing up. What can you infer about Antigua's society? How valuable or effective might the advice be as the girl comes to terms with the island's traditional social hierarchies?

2. In offering a cascade of advice—presumably parental advice—this brief lyrical story places you, the reader, in a familiar position. You too have received a cascade of advice about what to do and how to act. Using Kincaid's story as a loose model, write your own version, titled "Boy" or "Girl," in which you capture the kind of advice you have been offered, given your own cultural and historical context.

3. Writers are used to receiving—and giving—advice. Write your own version of Kincaid's story in which you portray someone giving advice to a young writer. The speaker could be a teacher or a fellow student. What advice about writing might matter to the speaker, and what would the reader or listener wish to hear? What role might grammatical correctness or certain conventions in writing play in the advice? How might the advice capture the complex relationships between the writing process and the final product of that process? What connection might the advice forge between the demands of writing for an audience and the concerns about the writer's own identity?

The Men We Carry in Our Minds

Scott Russell Sanders

Scott Russell Sanders is a widely published author of essays, short stories, novels, and children's books. He has won numerous awards for his writing, and his essays have been selected four times for inclusion in the annual *Best American Essays*. His writings are frequently reprinted in anthologies, including *The Norton Reader* and *The Art of the Essay*. He has received fellowships from institutions such as the National Endowment for the Arts and the Guggenheim Foundation. With a PhD from Cambridge University, Sanders is a professor of English at Indiana University, where he has won that institution's highest teaching award and has earned the rank of distinguished professor.

These are not the credentials usually expected of someone who grew up in what Sanders calls "the back roads of Tennessee and Ohio." A scholarship to Brown University gave him opportunities that few of his childhood friends ever even imagined for themselves.

Although education enabled Sanders to become a distinguished writer, his life and writing are haunted by the world he grew up in. In the following essay, "The Men We Carry in Our Minds," Sanders reveals memories that set him apart from men who, as many women insist, carry the guilt for "having kept all the joys and privileges of the earth for themselves."

"The Men We Carry in Our Minds," originally published in *Milkweed Chronicle* (1984), was included in Sanders's essay collection *Paradise of Bombs* (1987), which won the Associated Writing Programs Award in Creative Nonfiction in 1987. Sanders's collections of essays also include *Secrets of the Universe: Scenes from the Journey Home* (1991), *Writing from the Center* (1995), *Hunting for Hope: A Father's Journey* (1998), and *The Force of Spirit* (2000).

"This must be a hard time for women," I say to my friend Anneke. "They have so many paths to choose from, and so many voices calling them."

"I think it's a lot harder for men," she replies.

"How do you figure that?"

"The women I know feel excited, innocent, like crusaders in a just cause. The men I know are eaten up with guilt."

We are sitting at the kitchen table drinking sassafras tea, our hands 5 wrapped around the mugs because this April morning is cool and drizzly. "Like a Dutch morning," Anneke told me earlier. She is Dutch herself, a writer and midwife and peacemaker, with the round face and sad eyes of a woman in a Vermeer painting who might be waiting for the rain to stop, for a door to open. She leans over to sniff a sprig of lilac, pale lavender, that rises from a vase of cobalt blue.

"Women feel such pressure to be everything, do everything," I say. "Career, kids, art, politics. Have their babies and get back to the office a week later. It's as if they're trying to overcome a million years' worth of evolution in one lifetime."

"But we help one another. We don't try to lumber on alone, like so many wounded grizzly bears, the way men do." Anneke sips her tea. I gave her the mug with owls on it, for wisdom. "And we have this deep-down sense that we're in the *right*—we've been held back, passed over, used—while men feel they're in the wrong. Men are the ones who've been discredited, who have to search their souls."

I search my soul. I discover guilty feelings aplenty—toward the poor, the Vietnamese, Native Americans, the whales, an endless list of debts—a guilt in each case that is as bright and unambiguous as a neon sign. But toward women I feel something more confused, a snarl of shame, envy, wary tenderness, and amazement. This muddle troubles me. To hide my unease I say, "You're right, it's tough being a man these days."

"Don't laugh." Anneke frowns at me, mournful-eyed, through the sassafras steam. "I wouldn't be a man for anything. It's much easier being the victim. All the victim has to do is break free. The persecutor has to live with his past."

How deep is that past? I find myself wondering after Anneke has left. How 10 much of an inheritance do I have to throw off? Is it just the beliefs I breathed in as a child? Do I have to scour memory back through father and grandfather? Through St. Paul? Beyond Stonehenge and into the twilit caves? I'm convinced the past we must contend with is deeper even than speech. When I think back on my childhood, on how I learned to see men and women, I have a sense of ancient, dizzying depths. The back roads of Tennessee and Ohio where I grew up were probably closer, in their sexual patterns, to the campsites of Stone Age hunters than to the genderless cities of the future into which we are rushing.

The first men, besides my father, I remember seeing were black convicts and white guards, in the cottonfield across the road from our farm on the outskirts of Memphis. I must have been three or four. The prisoners wore dingy gray-and-black zebra suits, heavy as canvas, sodden with sweat. Hatless, stooped, they chopped weeds in the fierce heat, row after row, breathing the acrid dust of boll-weevil poison. The overseers wore dazzling white shirts and broad shadowy hats. The oiled barrels of their shotguns flashed in the sunlight. Their faces in memory are utterly blank. Of course those men, white and black, have become for me an emblem of racial hatred. But they have also come to stand for the twin poles of my early vision of manhood—the brute toiling animal and the boss.

When I was a boy, the men I knew labored with their bodies. They were marginal farmers, just scraping by, or welders, steelworkers, carpenters; they swept floors, dug ditches, mined coal, or drove trucks, their forearms ropy with muscle; they trained horses, stoked furnaces, built tires, stood on assembly lines wrestling parts onto cars and refrigerators. They got up before light, worked all day long whatever the weather, and when they came home at night they looked as though somebody had been whipping them. In the evenings and on weekends they worked on their own places, tilling gardens that were lumpy with clay, fixing broken-down cars, hammering on houses that were always too drafty, too leaky, too small.

The bodies of the men I knew were twisted and maimed in ways visible and invisible. The nails of their hands were black and split, the hands tattooed with scars. Some had lost fingers. Heavy lifting had given many of them finicky backs and guts weak from hernias. Racing against conveyor belts had given them ulcers. Their ankles and knees ached from years of standing on concrete. Anyone who had worked for long around machines was hard of hearing. They squinted, and the skin of their faces was creased like the leather of old work gloves. There were times, studying them, when I dreaded growing up. Most of them coughed, from dust or cigarettes, and most of them drank cheap wine or whiskey, so their eyes looked bloodshot and bruised. The fathers of my friends always seemed older than the mothers. Men wore out sooner. Only women lived into old age.

I was baffled. What privileges? What joys?

As a boy I also knew another sort of men, who did not sweat and break down like mules. They were soldiers, and so far as I could tell they scarcely worked at all. During my early school years we lived on a military base, an arsenal in Ohio, and every day I saw GIs in the guardshacks, on the stoops of barracks, at the wheels of olive drab Chevrolets. The chief fact of their lives was boredom. Long after I left the arsenal I came to recognize the sour smell the soldiers gave off as that of souls in limbo. They were all waiting—for wars, for transfers, for leaves, for promotions, for the end of their hitch—like so many braves waiting for the hunt to begin. Unlike the warriors of older tribes, however, they would have no say about when the battle would start or how it would be waged. Their waiting was broken only when they practiced for war. They fired guns at targets, drove tanks across the churned-up fields of the military reservation, set off bombs in the wrecks of old fighter planes. I knew this was all play. But I also felt certain that when the hour for killing arrived, they would kill. When the real shooting started, many of them would die. This was what soldiers were *for*, just as a hammer was for driving nails.

Warriors and toilers: Those seemed, in my boyhood vision, to be the chief destinies for men. They weren't the only destinies, as I learned from having a few male teachers, from reading books, and from watching television. But the men on television—the politicians, the astronauts, the generals, the savvy lawyers, the philosophical doctors, the bosses who gave orders to both soldiers and laborers—seemed as remote and unreal to me as the figures in tapestries. I could no more imagine growing up to become one of these cool, potent creatures than I could imagine becoming a prince.

A nearer and more hopeful example was that of my father, who had escaped from a red-dirt farm to a tire factory, and from the assembly line to the front office. Eventually he dressed in a white shirt and tie. He carried himself as if he had been born to work with his mind. But his body, remembering the earlier years of slogging work, began to give out on him in his fifties, and it quit on him entirely before he turned sixty-five. Even such a partial escape from man's fate as he had accomplished did not seem possible for most of the boys I knew. They joined the army, stood in line for jobs in the smoky plants, helped build highways. They were bound to work as their fathers had worked, killing themselves or preparing to kill others.

A scholarship enabled me not only to attend college, a rare enough feat in my circle, but even to study in a university meant for the children of the rich. Here I met for the first time young men who had assumed from birth that they would lead lives of comfort and power. And for the first time I met women who told me that men were guilty of having kept all the joys and privileges of the earth for themselves. I was baffled. What privileges? What joys? I thought about the maimed, dismal lives of most of the men back home. What had they stolen from their wives and daughters? The right to go five days a week, twelve months a year, for thirty or forty years to a steel mill or a coal mine? The right to drop bombs and die in war? The right to feel every leak in the roof, every gap in the fence, every cough in the engine, as a wound they must mend? The right to feel, when the lay-off comes or the plant shuts down, not only afraid but ashamed?

I was slow to understand the deep grievances of women. This was because, as a boy, I had envied them. Before college, the only people I had ever known who were interested in art or music or literature, the only ones who read books, the only ones who ever seemed to enjoy a sense of ease and grace were the mothers and daughters. Like the menfolk, they fretted about money, they scrimped and made-do. But, when the pay stopped coming in, they were not the ones who had failed. Nor did they have to go to war, and that seemed to me a blessed fact. By comparison with the narrow, ironclad days of fathers, there was an expansiveness, I thought, in the days of mothers. They went to see neighbors, to shop in town, to run errands at school, at the library, at church. No doubt, had I looked harder at their lives, I would have envied them less. It was not my fate to become a woman, so it was easier for me to see the graces. Few of them held jobs outside the home, and those who did filled thankless roles as clerks and waitresses. I didn't see, then, what a prison a house could be, since houses seemed to me brighter, handsomer places than any factory. I did not realize — because such things were never spoken of — how often women suffered from men's bullying. I did learn about the wretchedness of abandoned wives, single mothers, widows; but I also learned about the wretchedness of lone men. Even then I could see how exhausting it was for a mother to cater all day to the needs of young children. But if I had been asked, as a boy, to choose between tending a baby and tending a machine, I think I would have chosen the baby. (Having now tended both, I know I would choose the baby.)

So I was baffled when the women at college accused me and my sex of having cornered the world's pleasures. I think something like my bafflement has been felt by other boys (and by girls as well) who grew up in dirt-poor farm country, in mining country, in black ghettos, in Hispanic barrios, in the shadows of factories, in third world nations — any place where the fate of men is as grim and bleak as the fate of women. Toilers and warriors. I realize now how ancient these identities are, how deep the tug they exert on men, the undertow of a thousand generations. The miseries I saw, as a boy, in the lives of nearly all men I continue to see in the lives of many — the body-breaking toil, the tedium, the call to be tough, the humiliating powerlessness, the battle for a living and for territory.

When the women I met at college thought about the joys and privileges 20 of men, they did not carry in their minds the sort of men I had known in my childhood. They thought of their fathers, who were bankers, physicians, architects, stockbrokers, the big wheels of the big cities. These fathers rode the train to work or drove cars that cost more than any of my childhood houses. They were attended from morning to night by female helpers, wives and nurses and secretaries. They were never laid off, never short of cash at month's end, never lined up for welfare. These fathers made decisions that mattered. They ran the world.

The daughters of such men wanted to share in this power, this glory. So did I. They yearned for a say over their future, for jobs worthy of their abilities, for the right to live at peace, unmolested, whole. Yes, I thought, yes yes. The difference between me and these daughters was that they saw me, because of my sex, as destined from birth to become like their fathers, and therefore as an enemy to their desires. But I knew better. I wasn't an enemy, in fact or in feeling. I was an ally. If I had known, then, how to tell them so, would they have believed me? Would they now?

Working with the Text

1. In the story that opens the essay, Scott Russell Sanders's friend Anneke tells him, "The men I know are eaten up with guilt" (par. 4). In the soul-searching this comment prompts for Sanders, he finds that instead of guilt toward women he feels "something more confused, a snarl of shame, envy, wary tenderness, and amazement" (par. 8). With the title in mind, reread the essay for insight into the difference between the guilt felt by the men Anneke knows and the more confused emotions felt by Sanders. In a brief essay, reflect on this difference. Given the men in their minds, why might Anneke's friends feel guilty, while Sanders feels other emotions?

2. Sanders's descriptions of men tend to focus on their bodies and their jobs. Write a brief essay in which you reflect on the role these descriptions play in Sanders's exploration of "the joys and privileges of men" (par. 20). Why does Sanders introduce men in terms of their jobs? Why does he place so much emphasis on their bodies? What effects do these aspects of men's lives have on his own identity? What effect does this identity have on the women who live with and around men, and on the men's attitudes toward these women?

3. Sanders confronts one of the most significant social issues of our time—the roles and competing rights of men and women—by drawing on his personal experience. While the essay centers on the men—and women—in his own mind, his title refers to the men in *our* minds. In a brief essay, analyze the significance of this approach to his argument. Why would Sanders search for the people in his own mind to address a social issue? Why would he shift the emphasis, in his title, to include the minds of his readers? In what ways does basing the essay on personal experience strengthen the argument? In what ways does it weaken the argument?

4. Sanders closes the essay by claiming that he was an ally, not an enemy, to the women he knew in college who regarded men as "an enemy to their desires." He asks, "If I had known, then, how to tell them so, would they have believed me? Would they now?" (par. 21). In a brief essay, answer this question from your

point of view. Do you believe that Sanders is an ally of women? In what ways do you think he truly identifies with them? In what ways do you think he fails to speak to their concerns? As an alternative assignment, write a brief essay in which you reflect on Sanders's reasons for ending the essay with these questions. Why would he doubt that women would believe him?

From Text to Field

1. When Sanders went to college, he found that his peers regarded the roles and identities of men and women very differently than he did because they had grown up in very different worlds. In a personal essay, respond to Sanders's story by telling your own. Who are the men in your mind? How do they regard and treat the women in your mind? How does your story of men and women compare to the story of someone you have met who grew up in different circumstances? What bearing do you think these differences have on your view of the roles and identities of men and women?

2. Sanders's friend Anneke believes that men feel guilty toward women. Sanders says that he feels "shame, envy, wary tenderness, and amazement" (par. 8), but not guilt. Write an essay in which you explore your beliefs and feelings about how men regard women. If you are a man, what feelings do you have toward women? Why? How do you think women regard you? If you are a woman, how do you think men regard you? Why? How do you feel about the attitude you believe men have toward you?

3. As Sanders searches for the roots of his feelings toward women, he asks, "How much of an inheritance do I have to throw off?" (par. 10). As he draws the essay to a close, he observes, "I realize now how ancient these identities are, how deep the tug they exert on men, the undertow of a thousand generations" (par. 19). Although he points out that the history of "toilers and warriors" is ancient, he makes only general references to that history. In an essay, draw on your knowledge and awareness of history to seek out the roots of your view of men. What ancient roles do the men in your mind play? What were the origins of these roles, and how have they developed over time? Think of the essay as a brief history, driven by your own interpretations and commentary.

istence of marks. While the PTO or TTAB can always refuse such an agreement on the basis that the public interest is not served thereby, *Four Seasons* makes it clear that if those parties who have the greatest interest in reducing confusion agree that confusion is unlikely, their decision should be respected by the PTO. If an agreement is reached, the applicant's file wrapper will be returned to the PTO for further processing, namely, registration (if the application was use-based) or allowance (if the application was based on the applicant's intent to use the mark). (See Appendix D, Form 8, for a consent to use agreement.)

Cancellations

As discussed, an opposition can be initiated only within a very limited time period. In fact, if no action is taken within thirty days of publication of the mark in the *Official Gazette,* an opposition proceeding may not be instituted. Because reading the *Official Gazette* and filing a timely notice of opposition can be extremely difficult, the Lanham Act recognizes that additional opportunity to object to registration of a mark should be afforded to those who might be injured by it. Thus, **cancellation** proceedings may be initiated after a mark is registered. The primary difference between oppositions and cancellations relates to their timing: oppositions must be initiated before registration of a mark, while cancellations are initiated after registration. Additionally, cancellation actions are the only appropriate challenge to marks registered on the Supplemental Register.

Timing Requirements. Any person who believes that he or she will be damaged by the continued existence of a registration (whether on the Principal or Supplemental Register) may petition to cancel the registration. If the mark is registered on the Supplemental Register, a **Petition to Cancel** can be filed at any time. If the mark is on the Principal Register, the petition to cancel must be filed within five years of the registration date if the grounds are those that would have justified denial of registration to begin with (such as descriptiveness, that the mark is confusingly similar to that owned by another, and so forth).

After five years, the Lanham Act narrows the grounds for cancellation and the registration may be canceled only if certain grounds are proven, typically that the mark has become generic, the registration was obtained through fraud, the mark is functional, or the mark has become abandoned through nonuse.

The Petition to Cancel.   The petition to cancel must set forth a "short and plain statement" of the reasons for the petitioner's belief that he or she will be damaged by continued registration of the mark, state the grounds for cancellation, and identify the owner of the registration so a copy of the petition can be forwarded to the owner. The filing fee for a petition to cancel is $300 per class of goods or services covered by the registration, and a duplicate copy must be forwarded to the TTAB so it can be forwarded to the owner of the registration.

Grounds for Petition to Cancel.   Just as with notices of opposition, petitions to cancel must be brought by one who believes he or she will be damaged by registration of the mark. Similar to the allowance of an opposition to the various O. J. Simpson marks described above, the rules relating to those who may petition to cancel a registration appear to have been relaxed in recent years. For example, in *Harjo v. ProFootball Inc.*, 30 U.S.P.Q.2d 1828 (T.T.A.B. 1994), it was held that Native Americans had the right to petition to cancel various registered trademarks relating to the Washington Redskins football team on the basis that the marks were disparaging to them as Native Americans. On appeal, the decision was reversed on procedural grounds. Thus, at present, there is no determination whether the marks disparage Native Americans.

Women's Brains

Stephen Jay Gould

Late in the nineteenth century, scientists went to great lengths to determine whether women's brains were smaller than the brains of men. Interpretations of the early data claimed that women's brains were significantly smaller. Later data, corrected for factors that influence brain size, indicated that the difference in size was significantly less than earlier thought, or that there was no difference, or that women's brains were actually larger.

In the following essay, Stephen Jay Gould examines the data not only for accuracy but also for the social significance that can be found in the range of interpretations. As a prominent evolutionary theorist and writer — internationally recognized by lay audiences as well as academics — Gould influenced both scientific inquiry and public opinion. He spoke out against biological determinism and often emphasized in his writings that while scientists pursue objective data, their research interests and scientific conclusions are invariably rooted in human culture.

"Women's Brains" was originally published in a collection of essays, *The Panda's Thumb: More Reflections in Natural History* (1980), which won a National Book Award and an American Library Association Notable Book citation. A version of the essay appeared in *The Mismeasure of Man* (1981)— a winner of awards from the National Book Critics Circle and the American Educational Research Association as well as a nominee for the American Book Award in science — which challenged scientific attempts, through IQ testing, to develop objective measures of human intelligence.

When Gould died in 2002 at the age of sixty, he was professor of zoology at Harvard University. He was among the first to receive the MacArthur Foundation Prize Fellowship, informally known as the "genius grant." Throughout his career, he received awards and widespread praise for his engaged and engaging writing as well as for his scientific achievement.

In the prelude to *Middlemarch*, George Eliot lamented the unfulfilled lives of talented women:

> Some have felt that these blundering lives are due to the inconvenient indefiniteness with which the Supreme Power has fashioned the natures of women: If there were one level of feminine incompetence as strict as the ability to count three and no more, the social lot of women might be treated with scientific certitude.

Eliot goes on to discount the idea of innate limitation, but while she wrote in 1872, the leaders of European anthropometry were trying to measure "with scientific certitude" the inferiority of women. Anthropometry, or measurement of the human body, is not so fashionable a field these days, but it dominated the human sciences for much of the nineteenth century and remained popular until intelligence testing replaced skull measurement as a favored device for making invidious comparisons among races, classes, and sexes. Craniometry, or measurement of the skull, commanded the most attention and respect. Its unquestioned leader, Paul Broca (1824–80), professor of clinical surgery at the Faculty of Medicine in Paris, gathered a school of disciples and imitators around himself. Their work, so meticulous and apparently irrefutable, exerted great influence and won high esteem as a jewel of nineteenth-century science.

Broca's work seemed particularly invulnerable to refutation. Had he not measured with the most scrupulous care and accuracy? (Indeed, he had. I have the greatest respect for Broca's meticulous procedure. His numbers are sound. But science is an inferential exercise, not a catalog of facts. Numbers, by themselves, specify nothing. All depends upon what you do with them.) Broca depicted himself as an apostle of objectivity, a man who bowed before facts and cast aside superstition and sentimentality. He declared that "there is no faith, however respectable, no interest, however legitimate, which must not accommodate itself to the progress of human knowledge and bend before truth." Women, like it or not, had smaller brains than men and, therefore, could not equal them in intelligence. This fact, Broca argued, may reinforce a common prejudice in male society, but it is also a scientific truth. L. Manouvrier, a black sheep in Broca's fold, rejected the inferiority of women and wrote with feeling about the burden imposed upon them by Broca's numbers:

> Women displayed their talents and their diplomas. They also invoked philosophical authorities. But they were opposed by *numbers* unknown to Condorcet or to John Stuart Mill. These numbers fell upon poor women like a sledge hammer, and they were accompanied by commentaries and sarcasms more ferocious than the most misogynist imprecations of certain church fathers. The theologians had asked if women had a soul. Several

centuries later, some scientists were ready to refuse them a human intelligence.

Broca's argument rested upon two sets of data: the larger brains of men in modern societies, and a supposed increase in male superiority through time. His most extensive data came from autopsies performed personally in four Parisian hospitals. For 292 male brains, he calculated an average weight of 1,325 grams; 140 female brains averaged 1,144 grams for a difference of 181 grams, or 14 percent of the male weight. Broca understood, of course, that part of this difference could be attributed to the greater height of males. Yet he made no attempt to measure the effect of size alone and actually stated that it cannot account for the entire difference because we know, a priori, that women are not as intelligent as men (a premise that the data were supposed to test, not rest upon):

> We might ask if the small size of the female brain depends exclusively upon the small size of her body. Tiedemann has proposed this explanation. But we must not forget that women are, on the average, a little less intelligent than men, a difference which we should not exaggerate but which is, nonetheless, real. We are therefore permitted to suppose that the relatively small size of the female brain depends in part upon her physical inferiority and in part upon her intellectual inferiority.

In 1873, the year after Eliot published *Middlemarch*, Broca measured the ⁵ cranial capacities of prehistoric skulls from L'Homme Mort cave. Here he found a difference of only 99.5 cubic centimeters between males and females, while modern populations range from 129.5 to 220.7. Topinard, Broca's chief disciple, explained the increasing discrepancy through time as a result of differing evolutionary pressures upon dominant men and passive women:

> The man who fights for two or more in the struggle for existence, who has all the responsibility and the cares of tomorrow, who is constantly active in combating the environment and human rivals, needs more brain than the woman whom he must protect and nourish, the sedentary woman, lacking any interior occupations, whose role is to raise children, love, and be passive.

In 1879, Gustave Le Bon, chief misogynist of Broca's school, used these data to publish what must be the most vicious attack upon women in modern scientific literature (no one can top Aristotle). I do not claim his views were representative of Broca's school, but they were published in France's most respected anthropological journal. Le Bon concluded:

> In the most intelligent races, as among the Parisians, there are a large number of women whose brains are closer in size to those of gorillas than to the

most developed male brains. This inferiority is so obvious that no one can contest it for a moment; only its degree is worth discussion. All psychologists who have studied the intelligence of women, as well as poets and novelists, recognize today that they represent the most inferior forms of human evolution and that they are closer to children and savages than to an adult, civilized man. They excel in fickleness, inconstancy, absence of thought and logic, and incapacity to reason. Without doubt there exist some distinguished women, very superior to the average man, but they are as exceptional as the birth of any monstrosity, as, for example, of a gorilla with two heads; consequently, we may neglect them entirely.

Nor did Le Bon shrink from the social implications of his views. He was horrified by the proposal of some American reformers to grant women higher education on the same basis as men:

A desire to give them the same education, and, as a consequence, to propose the same goals for them, is a dangerous chimera. . . . The day when, misunderstanding the inferior occupations which nature has given her, women leave the home and take part in our battles; on this day a social revolution will begin, and everything that maintains the sacred ties of the family will disappear.

Sound familiar?[1]

I have reexamined Broca's data, the basis for all this derivative pronouncement, and I find his numbers sound but his interpretation ill-founded, to say the least. The data supporting his claim for increased difference through time can be easily dismissed. Broca based his contention on the samples from L'Homme Mort alone — only seven male and six female skulls in all. Never have so little data yielded such far ranging conclusions.

In 1888, Topinard published Broca's more extensive data on the Parisian hospitals. Since Broca recorded height and age as well as brain size, we may use modern statistics to remove their effect. Brain weight decreases with age, and Broca's women were, on average, considerably older than his men. Brain weight increases with height, and his average man was almost half a foot taller than his average woman. I used multiple regression, a technique that allowed me to assess simultaneously the influence of height and age upon brain size. In an analysis of the data for women, I found that, at average male height and age, a woman's brain would weigh 1,212 grams. Correction for height and age reduces Broca's measured difference of 181 grams by more than a third, to 113 grams.

---

[1]When I wrote this essay, I assumed that Le Bon was a marginal, if colorful, figure. I have since learned that he was a leading scientist, one of the founders of social psychology, and best known for a seminal study on crowd behavior, still cited today (*La psychologie des foules*, 1895), and for his work on unconscious motivation.

556   CHAPTER 5 (En)gendering Knowledge

I don't know what to make of this remaining difference because I cannot   10
assess other factors known to influence brain size in a major way. Cause of
death has an important effect: degenerative disease often entails a substantial
diminution of brain size. (This effect is separate from the decrease attributed
to age alone.) Eugene Schreider, also working with Broca's data, found that
men killed in accidents had brains weighing, on average, 60 grams more
than men dying of infectious diseases. The best modern data I can find (from
American hospitals) records a full 100-gram difference between death by
degenerative arteriosclerosis and by violence or accident. Since so many of
Broca's subjects were very elderly women, we may assume that lengthy
degenerative disease was more common among them than among the men.

More importantly, modern students of brain size still have not agreed on
a proper measure for eliminating the powerful effect of body size. Height is
partly adequate, but men and women of the same height do not share the
same body build. Weight is even worse than height, because most of its variation reflects nutrition rather than intrinsic size — fat versus skinny exerts little influence upon the brain. Manouvrier took up this subject in the 1880s
and argued that muscular mass and force should be used. He tried to measure this elusive property in various ways and found a marked difference in
favor of men, even in men and women of the same height. When he corrected for what he called "sexual mass," women actually came out slightly
ahead in brain size.

Thus, the corrected 113-gram difference is surely too large; the true figure
is probably close to zero and may as well favor women as men. And 113
grams, by the way, is exactly the average difference
Women, like it or not, had between a 5 foot 4 inch and a 6 foot 4 inch male in
smaller brains than men. Broca's data. We would not (especially us short folks)
want to ascribe greater intelligence to tall men. In
short, who knows what to do with Broca's data? They certainly don't permit
any confident claim that men have bigger brains than women.

To appreciate the social role of Broca and his school, we must recognize
that his statements about the brains of women do not reflect an isolated prejudice toward a single disadvantaged group. They must be weighed in the
context of a general theory that supported contemporary social distinctions
as biologically ordained. Women, blacks, and poor people suffered the same
disparagement, but women bore the brunt of Broca's argument because he
had easier access to data on women's brains. Women were singularly deni-
grated but they also stood as surrogates for other disenfranchised groups. As
one of Broca's disciples wrote in 1881: "Men of the black races have a brain
scarcely heavier than that of white women." This juxtaposition extended
into many other realms of anthropological argument, particularly to claims
that, anatomically and emotionally, both women and blacks were like white

children — and that white children, by the theory of recapitulation, represented an ancestral (primitive) adult stage of human evolution. I do not regard as empty rhetoric the claim that women's battles are for all of us.

Maria Montessori did not confine her activities to educational reform for young children. She lectured on anthropology for several years at the University of Rome, and wrote an influential book entitled *Pedagogical Anthropology* (English edition, 1913). Montessori was no egalitarian. She supported most of Broca's work and the theory of innate criminality proposed by her compatriot Cesare Lombroso. She measured the circumference of children's heads in her schools and inferred that the best prospects had bigger brains. But she had no use for Broca's conclusions about women. She discussed Manouvrier's work at length and made much of his tentative claim that women, after proper correction of the data, had slightly larger brains than men. Women, she concluded, were intellectually superior, but men had prevailed heretofore by dint of physical force. Since technology has abolished force as an instrument of power, the era of women may soon be upon us: "In such an epoch there will really be superior human beings, there will really be men strong in morality and in sentiment. Perhaps in this way the reign of women is approaching, when the enigma of her anthropological superiority will be deciphered. Woman was always the custodian of human sentiment, morality, and honor."

This represents one possible antidote to "scientific" claims for the constitu-   15
tional inferiority of certain groups. One may affirm the validity of biological distinctions but argue that the data have been misinterpreted by prejudiced men with a stake in the outcome, and that disadvantaged groups are truly superior. In recent years, Elaine Morgan has followed this strategy in her *Descent of Woman*, a speculative reconstruction of human prehistory from the woman's point of view — and as farcical as more famous tall tales by and for men.

I prefer another strategy. Montessori and Morgan followed Broca's philosophy to reach a more congenial conclusion. I would rather label the whole enterprise of setting a biological value upon groups for what it is: irrelevant and highly injurious. George Eliot well appreciated the special tragedy that biological labeling imposed upon members of disadvantaged groups. She expressed it for people like herself—women of extraordinary talent. I would apply it more widely—not only to those whose dreams are flouted but also to those who never realize that they may dream— but I cannot match her prose. In conclusion, then, the rest of Eliot's prelude to *Middlemarch*:

> The limits of variation are really much wider than anyone would imagine from the sameness of women's coiffure and the favorite love stories in prose and verse. Here and there a cygnet is reared uneasily among the ducklings in the brown pond, and never finds the living stream in fellowship with its own oary-footed kind. Here and there is born a Saint Theresa, foundress of

nothing, whose loving heartbeats and sobs after an unattained goodness tremble off and are dispersed among hindrances instead of centering in some long-recognizable deed.

Working with the Text

1. Stephen Jay Gould opens and closes the essay with quotations from the prelude to *Middlemarch*, a novel published in 1872 by George Eliot, the pen name for novelist Mary Ann Evans. Gould also notes that the craniometry scientist Paul Broca gathered data from prehistoric skulls in the year after Eliot published *Middlemarch*. The novel is set in a small English country town in the 1830s and explores the prevailing morals and conventions of that time. As you reread the essay, look for connections between Gould's argument and his references to *Middlemarch*. In a brief essay, analyze Gould's reasons for including these references. Even if you have not read the novel, you can infer its central theme from the prelude excerpts. Consider not only the plight of the protagonist implied in these excerpts but also the fact that Evans took the pen name of a man.

2. The scientists whose data Gould examines published their findings a century before he wrote the essay. Write a brief essay in which you explore whether and in what way the work of these scientists might hold significance today. If the findings have been largely discredited, why does Gould pay attention to that work? What can we learn from Gould about the role of social attitude in the interpretation of supposedly objective data?

3. Gould devotes most of the essay to analyzing how data on brain size was gathered, interpreted, and corrected for factors influencing brain size, only to come to the conclusion that "the whole enterprise of setting a biological value upon groups" is "irrelevant and highly injurious" (par. 16). In a brief essay, analyze the progression of Gould's argument. Why would he work to determine the validity of this series of scientific developments in order to dismiss scientific inquiry into biological factors in intelligence as "irrelevant"? Consider, in particular, the attention he gives to "corrected" data. In what way does Gould's essay offer an intriguing look at our obsession with numbers and quantification, especially when it comes to discussions about intelligence?

4. Gould's essay on nineteenth-century studies of brain size was incorporated into a book, *The Mismeasure of Man*, in which Gould challenges IQ testing. Drawing on "Women's Brains," write an essay in which you analyze Gould's reasons for believing that "setting a biological value upon groups" is "highly injurious" (par. 16). In what ways does Gould's essay raise larger questions about

intelligence (What do we mean by "smart"?) and objective assessment (How do we "measure" it?)?

From Text to Field

1. Gould captures the perspective of nineteenth-century scientists by quoting directly from their writings. Choose one or more of the following passages: "The man who fights for two or more in the struggle for existence . . ." (Topinard, par. 5), "In the most intelligent races, as among the Parisians . . ." (Gustave Le Bon, par. 6), or "A desire to give them the same education . . ." (Le Bon, par. 7). In an essay, write a response to the passage or passages, as if you were writing directly to the scientist Gould is quoting.

2. Relatively recent efforts by feminists and by scientists sympathetic to women have generated a number of approaches to comparing the characteristics and abilities of men and women. Each of us holds a personal view of the differences, or lack of difference, between the sexes. In a personal essay, present your view of gender identity. You may find it helpful to focus your essay on a specific trait. Is that trait biologically based or socially determined? From your perspective, does that trait suggest one way that one gender is superior to the other? Look beyond commonly discussed general traits (e.g., physical strength) to uncover more specific, and perhaps telling, concerns. Select a specific point of comparison that can be addressed well within the length of an essay.

3. In the essay, Gould points out, "To appreciate the social role of Broca and his school, we must recognize that his statements about the brains of women do not reflect an isolated prejudice toward a single disadvantaged group" (par. 13). He ends the same paragraph with the assertion, "I do not regard as empty rhetoric the claim that women's battles are for all of us." After reflecting on the entire paragraph, write an essay in which you interpret the final sentence in terms of your own education, observations, and experience. In what ways have you seen that "women's battles are for all of us"?

4. To most twenty-first-century ears, the nineteenth-century studies of brain size and comparisons between women and gorillas or children are outrageous, even comic. Many of us would agree with Gould that "setting a biological value upon groups" is "irrelevant." As a send-up of nineteenth-century attitudes (many of which still influence us), write a parody of the scientific pursuits of that era in which you claim—in our century—the superiority or inferiority of one gender based on a biological or physical characteristic (other than brain size) that you consider to be irrelevant.

The Egg and the Sperm: How Science Has Constructed a Romance Based on Stereotypical Male-Female Roles

Emily Martin

We tend to view science as being objective, driven by impartial observation of phenomena and interpretation of data. When Emily Martin studies scientific practices through the lens of an anthropologist, she sees the cultural assumptions that influence how scientists interpret and describe what they observe. In the essay that follows, she scrutinizes biological research on one of the deepest, most enduring mysteries of human existence—the relationship between egg and sperm. How much of what scientists see is biological phenomena, and how much is romance?

"The Egg and the Sperm," originally published in *Signs: Journal of Women in Culture and Society* in 1991, has been widely reprinted in journals and anthologies throughout the United States and abroad. The essay is drawn from research presented in Martin's influential 1987 book, *The Woman in the Body: A Cultural Analysis of Reproduction*, which was published in a second edition (1992) as well as a third (2001).

Martin is a professor of anthropology at New York University. In addition to gender and science, Martin's research interests include medicine, money and other measures of value, and the ethnography of work. Her published works often interpret culture in terms of how the human body—especially a woman's body—is regarded and described.

The theory of the human body is always a part of a world-picture. . . . The theory of the human body is always a part of a *fantasy*.
— JAMES HILLMAN, *The Myth of Analysis*[1]

As an anthropologist, I am intrigued by the possibility that culture shapes how biological scientists describe what they discover about the natural world. If this were so, we would be learning about more than the natural world in high school biology class; we would be learning about cultural beliefs and practices as if they were part of nature. In the course of my research I realized that the picture of egg and sperm drawn in popular as well as scientific accounts of reproductive biology relies on stereotypes central to our cultural definitions of male and female. The stereotypes imply not only that female biological processes are less worthy than their male counterparts but also that women are less worthy than men. Part of my goal in writing this article is to shine a bright light on the gender stereotypes hidden within the scientific language of biology. Exposed in such a light, I hope they will lose much of their power to harm us.

Egg and Sperm: A Scientific Fairy Tale

At a fundamental level, all major scientific textbooks depict male and female reproductive organs as systems for the production of valuable substances, such as eggs and sperm.[2] In the case of women, the monthly cycle is described as being designed to produce eggs and prepare a suitable place for them to be fertilized and grown — all to the end of making babies. But the enthusiasm ends there. By extolling the female cycle as a productive enterprise, menstruation must necessarily be viewed as a failure. Medical texts describe menstruation as the "debris" of the uterine lining, the result of necrosis, or death of tissue. The descriptions imply that a system has gone awry, making products of no use, not to specification, unsalable, wasted, scrap. An illustration in a widely used medical text shows menstruation as a chaotic disintegration of form, complementing the many texts that describe it as "ceasing," "dying," "losing," "denuding," "expelling."[3]

Male reproductive physiology is evaluated quite differently. One of the texts that sees menstruation as failed production employs a sort of breathless prose when it describes the maturation of sperm: "The mechanisms which guide the remarkable cellular transformation from spermatid to mature sperm remain uncertain. . . . Perhaps the most amazing characteristic of spermatogenesis is its sheer magnitude: The normal human male may manufacture several hundred million sperm per day."[4] In the classic text *Medical Physiology*, edited by Vernon Mountcastle, the male/female, productive/destructive comparison is more explicit: "Whereas the female *sheds* only a single gamete each month, the seminiferous tubules *produce* hundreds of millions of sperm each day" (emphasis mine).[5] The female author of another text marvels at the length of the microscopic seminiferous tubules, which, if uncoiled and placed end to end, "would span almost

Although a variety of grounds may be asserted in a petition to cancel (the mark comprises a flag of another nation, it is primarily merely a surname, it dilutes the mark of another, it contains immoral or scandalous matter, it includes the name of a living person without consent, or it is disparaging), the most common grounds asserted in a petition to cancel are the ones that must be brought within five years of registration: that the mark is merely descriptive, it is confusingly similar to another mark, or it has become abandoned.

Nature of Proceeding. The proceedings at the TTAB relating to cancellations are nearly identical to those involving oppositions. The petition to cancel will be filed at the TTAB, which will then forward a copy to the registrant. Within thirty days, the registrant will file an answer to the petition (typically denying the grounds asserted in the petition and raising various defenses). Discovery will commence and depositions may be taken, interrogatories served, and documents requested. The TTAB will set dates for submission of written briefs and will review those briefs and render a decision.

As with oppositions, the vast majority of cancellations are settled voluntarily by the parties (who will enter into a trademark settlement agreement that is highly similar to the consent to use agreement shown in Appendix D, Form 8) rather than by TTAB decision. (See Exhibit 6–1 and Appendix D, Form 9, Petition to Cancel Trademark Registration.)

Interferences

If two pending applications conflict or if a pending application conflicts with an existing registration (that is not yet incontestable), the PTO may declare an **interference.** Interferences are rare proceedings and occur only upon a showing of "extraordinary circumstances." Typically, if marks conflict, the parties resolve their differences by way of an opposition (if the potentially conflicting mark is not yet registered) or cancellation (if registration has occurred). Generally, only when an opposition or cancellation proceeding is unavailable to a party or will not adequately protect a party may a party request an interference proceeding. The TTAB will then determine the rights of the parties if they cannot reach a voluntary settlement arrangement.

Concurrent Use Proceedings

If parties use similar marks in different geographical areas, a **concurrent use proceeding** may be initiated. Generally, these parties have used their marks in their respective areas in good faith and without knowledge of the other's existence. In a concurrent use application, a party requests that the registration that will ultimately issue be restricted geographically, so that on its face the registration will state that the owner has the right to use the mark in certain identified states, cities, or regions in the United States. Once the applicant files an application for concurrent use, the matter is referred to the TTAB. In most instances, the concurrent use proceeding is initiated after an application for registration is refused on the basis the mark is confusingly similar to another. The applicant then often approaches the other party in an effort to reach an accord whereby they each agree to use the mark in certain designated geographic markets. The applicant will then amend its original application to seek concurrent use by stating, "The Applicant claims the exclusive right to use the mark in the area comprising [specifying the geographic area]." The TTAB will allow concurrent use only if confusion is not likely to result.

In brief, in a concurrent use proceeding, the parties "carve up" the United States and each agrees to use his or her mark only in a specific geographical area. Concurrent use proceedings are relatively rare.

one-third of a mile!" She writes, "In an adult male these structures produce millions of sperm cells each day." Later she asks, "How is this feat accomplished?"[6] None of these texts expresses such intense enthusiasm for any female processes. It is surely no accident that the "remarkable" process of making sperm involves precisely what, in the medical view, menstruation does not: production of something deemed valuable.[7]

One could argue that menstruation and spermatogenesis are not analogous processes and, therefore, should not be expected to elicit the same kind of response. The proper female analogy to spermatogenesis, biologically, is ovulation. Yet ovulation does not merit enthusiasm in these texts either. Textbook descriptions stress that all of the ovarian follicles containing ova are already present at birth. Far from being *produced*, as sperm are, they merely sit on the shelf, slowly degenerating and aging like overstocked inventory: "At birth, normal human ovaries contain an estimated one million follicles [each], and no new ones appear after birth. Thus, in marked contrast to the male, the newborn female already has all the germ cells she will ever have. Only a few, perhaps 400, are destined to reach full maturity during her active productive life. All the others degenerate at some point in their development so that few, if any, remain by the time she reaches menopause at approximately 50 years of age."[8] Note the "marked contrast" that this description sets up between male and female: the male, who continuously produces fresh germ cells, and the female, who has stockpiled germ cells by birth and is faced with their degeneration.

Nor are the female organs spared such vivid descriptions. One scientist ⁵ writes in a newspaper article that a woman's ovaries become old and worn out from ripening eggs every month, even though the woman herself is still relatively young: "When you look through a laparoscope . . . at an ovary that has been through hundreds of cycles, even in a superbly healthy American female, you see a scarred, battered organ."[9]

To avoid the negative connotations that some people associate with the female reproductive system, scientists could begin to describe male and female processes as homologous. They might credit females with "producing" mature ova one at a time, as they're needed each month, and describe males as having to face problems of degenerating germ cells. This degeneration would occur throughout life among spermatogonia, the undifferentiated germ cells in the testes that are the long-lived, dormant precursors of sperm.

But the texts have an almost dogged insistence on casting female processes in a negative light. The texts celebrate sperm production because it is continuous from puberty to senescence, while they portray egg production as inferior because it is finished at birth. This makes the female seem unproductive, but some texts will also insist that it is she who is wasteful.[10] In a section heading for *Molecular Biology of the Cell*, a best-selling text, we are told that "Oogenesis is wasteful." The text goes on to emphasize that of the seven million oogonia, or egg germ cells, in the female embryo, most degenerate in the ovary. Of those that do go on to become oocytes, or eggs, many also degenerate, so that at birth only two million eggs remain in the ovaries. Degeneration continues throughout a woman's life: By puberty 300,000 eggs remain, and only a few are present by menopause. "During the forty or so years of a woman's reproductive life, only 400 to 500 eggs will have been released," the authors write. "All the rest will have degenerated. It is still a mystery why so many eggs are formed only to die in the ovaries."[11]

The real mystery is why the male's vast production of sperm is not seen as wasteful.[12] Assuming that a man "produces" 100 million (10^8) sperm per day (a conservative estimate) during an average reproductive life of sixty years, he would produce well over two trillion sperm in his lifetime. Assuming that a woman "ripens" one egg per lunar month, or thirteen per year, over the course of her forty-year reproductive life, she would total five hundred eggs in her lifetime. But the word "waste" implies an excess, too much produced. Assuming two or three offspring, for every baby a woman produces, she wastes only around two hundred eggs. For every baby a man produces, he wastes more than one trillion (10^{12}) sperm.

How is it that positive images are denied to the bodies of women? A look at language — in this case, scientific language — provides the first clue. Take the egg and the sperm.[13] It is remarkable how "femininely" the egg behaves and how "masculinely" the sperm.[14] The egg is seen as large and passive.[15] It does not *move* or *journey*, but passively "is transported," "is swept,"[16] or even "drifts"[17] along the fallopian tube. In utter contrast, sperm are small, "streamlined,"[18] and invariably active. They "deliver" their genes to the egg, "activate the developmental program of the egg,"[19] and have a "velocity" that is often remarked upon.[20] Their tails are "strong" and efficiently powered.[21] Together with the forces of ejaculation, they can "propel the semen into the deepest recesses of the vagina."[22] For this they need "energy," "fuel,"[23] so that with a "whiplashlike motion and strong lurches"[24] they can "burrow through the egg coat"[25] and "penetrate" it.[26]

At its extreme, the age-old relationship of the egg and the sperm takes on a royal or religious patina. The egg coat, its protective barrier, is sometimes called its "vestments," a term usually reserved for sacred, religious dress. The egg is said to have a "corona,"[27] a crown, and to be accompanied by "attendant cells."[28] It is holy, set apart and above, the queen to the sperm's king. The egg is also passive, which means it must depend on sperm for rescue. Gerald Schatten and Helen Schatten liken the egg's role to that of Sleeping Beauty: "a dormant bride awaiting her mate's magic kiss, which instills the spirit that brings her to life."[29] Sperm, by contrast, have a "mission,"[30] which is to "move through the female genital tract in quest of the ovum."[31] One popular account has it that the sperm carry out a "perilous journey" into the "warm darkness," where some fall away "exhausted." "Survivors" "assault" the egg, the successful candidates "surrounding the prize."[32] Part of the urgency of this journey, in more scientific terms, is that "once released from the supportive environment of the ovary, an egg will die within hours unless rescued by a sperm."[33] The wording stresses the fragility and dependency of the egg, even though the same text acknowledges elsewhere that sperm also live for only a few hours.[34]

In 1948, in a book remarkable for its early insights into these matters, Ruth Herschberger argued that female reproductive organs are seen as biologically interdependent, while male organs are viewed as autonomous, operating independently and in isolation:

> At present the functional is stressed only in connection with women: It is in them that ovaries, tubes, uterus, and vagina have endless interdependence. In the male, reproduction would seem to involve "organs" only.
>
> Yet the sperm, just as much as the egg, is dependent on a great many related processes. There are secretions which mitigate the urine in the urethra before ejaculation, to protect the sperm. There is the reflex shutting off of the bladder connection, the provision of prostatic secretions, and various types of muscular propulsion. The sperm is no more independent of its milieu than the egg, and yet from a wish that it were, biologists have lent their support to the notion that the human female, beginning with the egg, is congenitally more dependent than the male.[35]

Bringing out another aspect of the sperm's autonomy, an article in the journal *Cell* has the sperm making an "existential decision" to penetrate the egg: "Sperm are cells with a limited behavioral repertoire, one that is directed toward fertilizing eggs. To execute the decision to abandon the haploid state, sperm swim to an egg and there acquire the ability to effect membrane fusion."[36] Is this a corporate manager's version of the sperm's activities — "executing decisions" while fraught with dismay over difficult options that bring with them very high risk?

There is another way that sperm, despite their small size, can be made to loom in importance over the egg. In a collection of scientific papers, an electron micrograph of an enormous egg and tiny sperm is titled "A Portrait of the Sperm."[37] This is a little like showing a photo of a dog and calling it a picture of the fleas. Granted, microscopic sperm are harder to photograph than eggs, which are just large enough to see with the naked eye. But surely the use of the term *portrait*, a word associated with the powerful and wealthy, is significant. Eggs have only micrographs or pictures, not portraits.

One depiction of sperm as weak and timid, instead of strong and powerful — the only such representation in Western civilization, so far as I know — occurs in Woody Allen's movie *Everything You Always Wanted to Know*

About Sex[*] *But Were Afraid to Ask.* Allen, playing the part of an apprehensive sperm inside a man's testicles, is scared of the man's approaching orgasm. He is reluctant to launch himself into the darkness, afraid of contraceptive devices, afraid of winding up on the ceiling if the man masturbates.

The more common picture — egg as damsel in distress, shielded only by   15
her sacred garments; sperm as heroic warrior to the rescue — cannot be proved to be dictated by the biology of these events. While the "facts" of biology may not *always* be constructed in cultural terms, I would argue that in this case they are. The degree of metaphorical content in these descriptions, the extent to which differences between egg and sperm are emphasized, and the parallels between cultural stereotypes of male and female behavior and the character of egg and sperm all point to this conclusion.

New Research, Old Imagery

As new understandings of egg and sperm emerge, textbook gender imagery is being revised. But the new research, far from escaping the stereotypical representations of egg and sperm, simply replicates elements of textbook gender imagery in a different form. The persistence of this imagery calls to mind what Ludwik Fleck termed "the self-contained" nature of scientific thought. As he described it, "the interaction between what is already known, what remains to be learned, and those who are to apprehend it, go to ensure harmony within the system. But at the same time they also preserve the harmony of illusions, which is quite secure within the confines of a given thought style."[38] We need to understand the way in which the cultural content in scientific descriptions changes as biological discoveries unfold, and whether that cultural content is solidly entrenched or easily changed.

In all of the texts quoted above, sperm are described as penetrating the egg, and specific substances on a sperm's head are described as binding to the egg. Recently, this description of events was rewritten in a biophysics lab at Johns Hopkins University — transforming the egg from the passive to the active party.[39]

Prior to this research, it was thought that the zona, the inner vestments of the egg, formed an impenetrable barrier. Sperm overcame the barrier by mechanically burrowing through, thrashing their tails and slowly working their way along. Later research showed that the sperm released digestive enzymes that chemically broke down the zona; thus, scientists presumed that the sperm used mechanical *and* chemical means to get through to the egg.

In this recent investigation, the researchers began to ask questions about the mechanical force of the sperm's tail. (The lab's goal was to develop a contraceptive that worked topically on sperm.) They discovered, to their great surprise, that the forward thrust of sperm is extremely weak, which contradicts the assumption that sperm are forceful penetrators.[40] Rather than thrusting forward, the sperm's head was now seen to move mostly back and forth. The sideways motion of the sperm's tail makes the head move sideways with a force that is ten times stronger than its forward movement. So even if the overall force of the sperm were strong enough to mechanically break the zona, most of its force would be directed sideways rather than forward. In fact, its strongest tendency, by tenfold, is to escape by attempting to pry itself off the egg. Sperm, then, must be exceptionally efficient at *escaping* from any cell surface they contact. And the surface of the egg must be designed to trap the sperm and prevent their escape. Otherwise, few if any sperm would reach the egg.

The researchers at Johns Hopkins concluded that the sperm and egg stick   20
together because of adhesive molecules on the surfaces of each. The egg traps the sperm and adheres to it so tightly that the sperm's head is forced to lie flat against the surface of the zona, a little bit, they told me, "like Br'er Rabbit getting more and more stuck to tar baby the more he wriggles." The trapped sperm continues to wiggle ineffectually side to side. The mechanical force of its tail is so weak that a sperm cannot break even one chemical bond. This is where the digestive enzymes released by the sperm come in. If they start to soften the zona just at the tip of the sperm and the sides remain stuck, then the weak, flailing sperm can get oriented in the right direction and make it through the zona — provided that its bonds to the zona dissolve as it moves in.

Although this new version of the saga of the egg and the sperm broke through cultural expectations, the researchers who made the discovery continued to write papers and abstracts as if the sperm were the active party who attacks, binds, penetrates, and enters the egg. The only difference was that sperm were now seen as performing these actions weakly.[41] Not until August 1987, more than three years after the findings described above, did these researchers reconceptualize the process to give the egg a more active role. They began to describe the zona as an aggressive sperm catcher, covered with adhesive molecules that can capture a sperm with a single bond and clasp it to the zona's surface.[42] In the words of their published account: "The innermost vestment, the *zona pellucida*, is a glyco-protein shell, which captures and tethers the sperm before they penetrate it. . . . The sperm is captured at the initial contact between the sperm tip and the *zona*. . . . Since the thrust [of the sperm] is much smaller than the force needed to break a single affinity bond, the first bond made upon the tip-first meeting of the sperm and *zona* can result in the capture of the sperm."[43]

Experiments in another lab reveal similar patterns of data interpretation. Gerald Schatten and Helen Schatten set out to show that, contrary to conventional wisdom, the "egg is not merely a large, yolk-filled sphere into which the sperm burrows to endow new life. Rather, recent research suggests the almost heretical view that sperm and egg are mutually active partners."[44] This sounds like a departure from the stereotypical textbook view, but further reading reveals Schatten and Schatten's conformity to the aggressive-sperm metaphor. They describe how "the sperm and egg first touch when, from the tip of the sperm's triangular head, a long, thin filament shoots out and harpoons the egg." Then we learn that "remarkably, the harpoon is not so much fired as assembled at great speed, molecule by molecule, from a pool of protein stored in a specialized region called the acrosome. The filament may grow as much as twenty times longer than the sperm head itself before its tip reaches the egg and sticks."[45] Why not call this "making a bridge" or "throwing out a line" rather than firing a harpoon? Harpoons pierce prey and injure or kill them, while this filament only sticks. And why not focus, as the Hopkins lab did, on the stickiness of the egg, rather than the stickiness of the sperm?[46] Later in the article, the Schattens replicate the common view of the sperm's perilous journey into the warm darkness of the vagina, this time for the purpose of explaining its journey into the egg itself: "[The sperm] still has an arduous journey ahead. It must penetrate farther into the egg's huge sphere of cytoplasm and somehow locate the nucleus, so that the two cells' chromosomes can fuse. The sperm dives down into the cytoplasm, its tail beating. But it is soon interrupted by the sudden and swift migration of the egg nucleus, which rushes toward the sperm with a velocity triple that of the movement of chromosomes during cell division, crossing the entire egg in about a minute."[47]

Like Schatten and Schatten and the biophysicists at Johns Hopkins, another researcher has recently made discoveries that seem to point to a more interactive view of the relationship of egg and sperm. This work, which Paul Wassarman conducted on the sperm and eggs of mice, focuses on identifying the specific molecules in the egg coat (the zona pellucida) that are involved in egg-sperm interaction. At first glance, his descriptions seem to fit the model of an egalitarian relationship. Male and female gametes "recognize one another," and "interactions . . . take place between sperm and egg."[48] But the article in *Scientific American* in which those descriptions appear begins with a vignette that presages the dominant motif of their presentation: "It has been more than a century since Hermann Fol, a Swiss zoologist, peered into his microscope and became the first person to see a sperm penetrate an egg, fertilize it, and form the first cell of a new embryo."[49] This portrayal of the sperm as the active party — the one that *penetrates* and *fertilizes* the egg and *produces* the embryo — is not cited as an example of an earlier, now outmoded view. In fact, the author reiterates the point later in the article: "Many sperm can bind to and penetrate the zona pellucida, or outer coat, of an unfertilized mouse egg,

> One clear feminist challenge is to wake up sleeping metaphors in science.

but only one sperm will eventually fuse with the thin plasma membrane surrounding the egg proper (*inner sphere*), fertilizing the egg and giving rise to a new embryo."[50]

The imagery of sperm as aggressor is particularly startling in this case: The main discovery being reported is isolation of a particular molecule *on the egg coat* that plays an important role in fertilization! Wassarman's choice of language sustains the picture. He calls the molecule that has been isolated, ZP3, a "sperm receptor." By allocating the passive, waiting role to the egg, Wassarman can continue to describe the sperm as the actor, the one that makes it all happen: "The basic process begins when many sperm first attach loosely and then bind tenaciously to receptors on the surface of the egg's thick outer coat, the zona pellucida. Each sperm, which has a large number of egg-binding proteins on its surface, binds to many sperm receptors on the egg. More specifically, a site on each of the egg-binding proteins fits a complementary site on a sperm receptor, much as a key fits a lock."[51] With the sperm designated as the "key" and the egg the "lock," it is obvious which one acts and which one is acted upon. Could this imagery not be reversed, letting the sperm (the lock) wait until the egg produces the key? Or could we speak of two halves of a locket matching, and regard the matching itself as the action that initiates the fertilization?

It is as if Wassarman were determined to make the egg the receiving partner. Usually in biological research, the *protein* member of the pair of binding molecules is called the receptor, and physically it has a pocket in it rather like a lock. As the diagrams that illustrate Wassarman's article show, the molecules on the sperm are proteins and have "pockets." The small, mobile molecules that fit into these pockets are called ligands. As shown in the diagrams, ZP3 on the egg is a polymer of "keys"; many small knobs stick out. Typically, molecules on the sperm would be called receptors and molecules on the egg would be called ligands. But Wassarman chose to name ZP3 on the egg the receptor and to create a new term, "the egg-binding protein," for the molecule on the sperm that otherwise would have been called the receptor.[52]

Wassarman does credit the egg coat with having more functions than those of a sperm receptor. While he notes that "the zona pellucida has at times been viewed by investigators as a nuisance, a barrier to sperm and hence an impediment to fertilization," his new research reveals that the egg coat "serves as a sophisticated biological security system that screens incoming sperm, selects only those compatible with fertilization and development, prepares sperm for fusion with the egg and later protects the resulting embryo from polyspermy [a lethal condition caused by fusion of more than one sperm with a single egg]."[53] Although this description gives the egg an active role, that role is drawn in stereotypically feminine terms. The egg *selects* an appropriate mate, *prepares* him for fusion, and then *protects* the resulting offspring from harm. This is courtship and mating behavior as seen through the eyes of a sociobiologist: woman as the hard-to-get prize, who, following union with the chosen one, becomes woman as servant and mother.

And Wassarman does not quit there. In a review article for *Science*, he outlines the "chronology of fertilization."[54] Near the end of the article are two subject headings. One is "Sperm Penetration," in which Wassarman describes how the chemical dissolving of the zona pellucida combines with the "substantial propulsive force generated by sperm." The next heading is "Sperm-Egg Fusion." This section details what happens inside the zona after a sperm "penetrates" it. Sperm "can make contact with, adhere to, and fuse with (that is, fertilize) an egg."[55] Wassarman's word choice, again, is astonishingly skewed in favor of the sperm's activity, for in the next breath he says that sperm *lose* all motility upon fusion with the egg's surface. In mouse and sea urchin eggs, the sperm enters at the *egg's* volition, according to Wassarman's description: "Once fused with egg plasma membrane [the surface of the egg], how does a sperm enter the egg? The surface of both mouse and sea urchin eggs is covered with thousands of plasma membrane-bound projections, called microvilli [tiny "hairs"]. Evidence in sea urchins suggests that, after membrane fusion, a group of elongated microvilli cluster tightly around and interdigitate over the sperm head. As these microvilli are resorbed, the sperm is drawn into the egg. Therefore, sperm motility, which ceases at the time of fusion in both sea urchins and mice, is not required for sperm entry."[56] The section called "Sperm Penetration" more logically would be followed by a section called "The Egg Envelops," rather than "Sperm-Egg Fusion." This would give a parallel—and more accurate— sense that both the egg and the sperm initiate action.

Another way that Wassarman makes less of the egg's activity is by describing components of the egg but referring to the sperm as a whole entity. Deborah Gordon has described such an approach as "atomism" ("the part is independent of and primordial to the whole") and identified it as one of the "tenacious assumptions" of Western science and medicine.[57] Wassarman employs atomism to his advantage. When he refers to processes going on within sperm, he consistently returns to descriptions that remind us from whence these activities came: They are part of sperm that penetrate an egg or generate propulsive force. When he refers to processes going on within eggs, he stops there. As a result, any active role he grants them appears to be assigned to the parts of the egg, and not to the egg itself. In the quote above, it is the microvilli that actively cluster around the sperm. In another example, "the driving force for engulfment of a fused sperm comes from a region of cytoplasm just beneath an egg's plasma membrane."[58]

Social Implications: Thinking Beyond

All three of these revisionist accounts of egg and sperm cannot seem to escape the hierarchical imagery of older accounts. Even though each new account gives the egg a larger and more active role, taken together they bring into play another cultural stereotype: woman as a dangerous and aggressive threat. In the Johns Hopkins lab's revised model, the egg ends up as the female aggressor who "captures and tethers" the sperm with her sticky zona, rather like a spider lying in wait in her web.[59] The Schatten lab has the egg's nucleus "interrupt" the sperm's dive with a "sudden and swift" rush by which she "clasps the sperm and guides its nucleus to the center."[60] Wassarman's description of the surface of the egg "covered with thousands of plasma membrane-bound projections, called microvilli" that reach out and clasp the sperm adds to the spiderlike imagery.[61]

These images grant the egg an active role but at the cost of appearing dis-   30
turbingly aggressive. Images of woman as dangerous and aggressive, the femme fatale who victimizes men, are widespread in Western literature and culture.[62] More specific is the connection of spider imagery with the idea of an engulfing, devouring mother.[63] New data did not lead scientists to eliminate gender stereotypes in their descriptions of egg and sperm. Instead, scientists simply began to describe egg and sperm in different, but no less damaging, terms.

Can we envision a less stereotypical view? Biology itself provides another model that could be applied to the egg and the sperm. The cybernetic model — with its feedback loops, flexible adaptation to change, coordination of the parts within a whole, evolution over time, and changing response to the environment — is common in genetics, endocrinology, and ecology and has a growing influence in medicine in general.[64] This model has the potential to shift our imagery from the negative, in which the female reproductive system is castigated both for not producing eggs after birth and for producing (and thus wasting) too many eggs overall, to something more positive. The female reproductive system could be seen as responding to the environment (pregnancy or menopause), adjusting to monthly changes (menstruation), and flexibly changing from reproductivity after puberty to nonreproductivity later in life. The sperm and egg's interaction could also be described in cybernetic terms. J. F. Hartman's research in reproductive biology demonstrated fifteen years ago that if an egg is killed by being pricked with a needle, live sperm cannot get through the zona.[65] Clearly, this evidence shows that the egg and sperm *do* interact on more mutual terms, making biology's refusal to portray them that way all the more disturbing.

We would do well to be aware, however, that cybernetic imagery is hardly neutral. In the past, cybernetic models have played an important part in the imposition of social control. These models inherently provide a way of thinking about a "field" of interacting components. Once the field can be seen, it can become the object of new forms of knowledge, which in turn can allow new forms of social control to be exerted over the components of the field. During the 1950s, for example, medicine began to recognize the psychosocial *environment* of the patient: the patient's family and its psychodynamics. Professions such as social work began to focus on this new environment, and the resulting knowledge became one way to further control the patient. Patients began to be seen not as isolated, individual bodies, but as psychosocial entities located in an "ecological" system: Management of "the patient's psychology was a new entrée to patient control."[66]

The models that biologists use to describe their data can have important social effects. During the nineteenth century, the social and natural sciences strongly influenced each other: The social ideas of Malthus about how to avoid the natural increase of the poor inspired Darwin's *Origin of Species*.[67] Once the *Origin* stood as a description of the natural world, complete with competition and market struggles, it could be reimported into social science as social Darwinism, in order to justify the social order of the time. What we are seeing now is similar: the importation of cultural ideas about passive females and heroic males into the "personalities" of gametes. This amounts to the "implanting of social imagery on representations of nature so as to lay a firm basis for reimporting exactly that same imagery as natural explanations of social phenomena."[68]

Further research would show us exactly what social effects are being wrought from the biological imagery of egg and sperm. At the very least, the imagery keeps alive some of the hoariest old stereotypes about weak damsels in distress and their strong male rescuers. That these stereotypes are now being written in at the level of the *cell* constitutes a powerful move to make them seem so natural as to be beyond alteration.

The stereotypical imagery might also encourage people to imagine that ³⁵ what results from the interaction of egg and sperm — a fertilized egg — is the result of deliberate "human" action at the cellular level. Whatever the intentions of the human couple, in this microscopic "culture" a cellular "bride" (or femme fatale) and a cellular "groom" (her victim) make a cellular baby. Rosalind Petchesky points out that through visual representations such as sonograms, we are given "*images* of younger and younger, and tinier and tinier, fetuses being 'saved.'" This leads to "the point of visibility being 'pushed back' *indefinitely*."[69] Endowing egg and sperm with intentional action, a key aspect of personhood in our culture, lays the foundation for the point of viability being pushed back to the moment of fertilization. This will likely lead to greater acceptance of technological developments and new

EXHIBIT 6-1
PTO Form
for Petition
to Cancel
Trademark
Registration

Suggested Format for Petition to Cancel

This is a suggested format for preparing a Petition to Cancel a trademark registration. This document is not meant to be used as a form to be filled in and returned to the Board. Rather, it is a suggested format, which shows how the petition should be set up. Petitioners may follow this format in preparing their own petition but need not copy those portions of the suggested format which are not relevant.

IN THE UNITED STATES PATENT AND TRADEMARK OFFICE
BEFORE THE TRADEMARK TRIAL AND APPEAL BOARD

In the matter of trademark Registration No................................

For the mark...

Date registered..............................

(Name of petitioner)

v.

(Name of registrant)

PETITION TO CANCEL

State petitioner's name, address, and entity information as follows:[1]

(Name of individual as petitioner, and business trade name, if any;
Business address)
_____

OR   (Name of partnership as petitioner; Names of partners;
Business address of partnership)
_____

OR   (Name of corporation as petitioner; State or country of incorporation;
Business address of corporation)
_____

To the best of petitioner's knowledge, the name and address of the current owner of the registration are _____*(provide if known)*_____

The above-identified petitioner believes that it/he/she will be damaged by the above-identified registration, and hereby petitions to cancel the same.[2]

The grounds for cancellation are as follows:
[Please set forth, in separately numbered paragraphs,
the allegations of petitioner's standing and grounds for cancellation][3]

By ____Signature[4]____   Date _____
(Identification of person signing)[5]

OMB No. 0651-0040 (Exp. 5/31/04)

Appeals from TTAB Decisions

If a party is dissatisfied with the decision of the TTAB in an opposition, cancellation, interference, or concurrent use proceeding, an appeal may be taken to the Court of Appeals for the Federal Circuit (CAFC), located in Washington, DC. The Federal Circuit can set aside PTO findings only when the findings are arbitrary, capricious, an abuse of discretion, or unsupported by forms of scrutiny and manipulation, for the benefit of these inner "persons": court-ordered restrictions on a pregnant woman's activities in order to protect her fetus, fetal surgery, amniocentesis, and rescinding of abortion rights, to name but a few examples.[70]

Even if we succeed in substituting more egalitarian, interactive metaphors to describe the activities of egg and sperm, and manage to avoid the pitfalls of cybernetic models, we would still be guilty of endowing cellular entities with personhood. More crucial, then, than what *kinds* of personalities we bestow on cells is the very fact that we are doing it at all. This process could ultimately have the most disturbing social consequences.

One clear feminist challenge is to wake up sleeping metaphors in science, particularly those involved in descriptions of the egg and the sperm. Although the literary convention is to call such metaphors "dead," they are not so much dead as sleeping, hidden within the scientific content of texts — and all the more powerful for it.[71] Waking up such metaphors, by becoming aware of when we are projecting cultural imagery onto what we study, will improve our ability to investigate and understand nature. Waking up such metaphors, by becoming aware of their implications, will rob them of their power to naturalize our social conventions about gender.

Notes

Portions of this article were presented as the 1987 Becker Lecture, Cornell University. I am grateful for the many suggestions and ideas I received on this occasion. For especially pertinent help with my arguments and data I thank Richard Cone, Kevin Whaley, Sharon Stephens, Barbara Duden, Susanne Kuechler, Lorna Rhodes, and Scott Gilbert. The article was strengthened and clarified by the comments of the anonymous *Signs* reviewers as well as the superb editorial skills of Amy Gage.

1. James Hillman, *The Myth of Analysis* (Evanston, Ill.: Northwestern University Press, 1972), 220.

2. The textbooks I consulted are the main ones used in classes for undergraduate premedical students or medical students (or those held on reserve in the library for these classes) during the past few years at Johns Hopkins University. These texts are widely used at other universities in the country as well.

3. Arthur C. Guyton, *Physiology of the Human Body*, 6th ed. (Philadelphia: Saunders College Publishing, 1984), 624.

4. Arthur J. Vander, James H. Sherman, and Dorothy S. Luciano, *Human Physiology: The Mechanisms of Body Function*, 3d ed. (New York: McGraw Hill, 1980), 483–84.

5. Vernon B. Mountcastle, *Medical Physiology*, 14th ed. (London: Mosby, 1980), 2:1624.

6. Eldra Pearl Solomon, *Human Anatomy and Physiology* (New York: CBS College Publishing, 1983), 678.

7. For elaboration, see Emily Martin, *The Woman in the Body: A Cultural Analysis of Reproduction* (Boston: Beacon, 1987), 27–53.

8. Vander, Sherman, and Luciano, 568.

9. Melvin Konner, "Childbearing and Age," *New York Times Magazine* (December 27, 1987), 22–23, esp. 22.

10. I have found but one exception to the opinion that the female is wasteful: "Smallpox being the nasty disease it is, one might expect nature to have designed antibody molecules with combining sites that specifically recognize the epitopes on smallpox virus. Nature differs from technology, however: It thinks nothing of wastefulness. (For example, rather than improving the chance that a spermatozoon will meet an egg cell, nature finds it easier to produce millions of spermatozoa.)" (Niels Kaj Jerne, "The Immune System," *Scientific American* 229, no. 1 [July 1973]: 53). Thanks to a *Signs* reviewer for bringing this reference to my attention.

11. Bruce Alberts et al., *Molecular Biology of the Cell* (New York: Garland, 1983), 795.

12. In her essay "Have Only Men Evolved?" (in *Discovering Reality: Feminist Perspectives on Epistemology, Metaphysics, Methodology, and Philosophy of Science,* ed. Sandra Harding and Merrill B. Hintikka [Dordrecht: Reidel, 1983], 45–69, esp. 60–61), Ruth Hubbard points out that sociobiologists have said the female invests more energy than the male in the production of her large gametes, claiming that this explains why the female provides parental care. Hubbard questions whether it "really takes more 'energy' to generate the one or relatively few eggs than the large excess of sperms required to achieve fertilization." For further critique of how the greater size of eggs is interpreted in sociobiology, see Donna Haraway, "Investment Strategies for the Evolving Portfolio of Primate Females," in *Body/Politics*, ed. Mary Jacobus, Evelyn Fox Keller, and Sally Shuttleworth (New York: Routledge, 1990), 155–56.

13. The sources I used for this article provide compelling information on interactions among sperm. Lack of space prevents me from taking up this theme here, but the elements include competition, hierarchy, and sacrifice. For a newspaper report, see Malcolm W. Browne, "Some Thoughts on Self Sacrifice," *New York Times* (July 5, 1988), C6. For a literary rendition, see John Barth, "Night-Sea Journey," in his *Lost in the Funhouse* (Garden City, NY: Doubleday, 1968), 3–13.

14. See Carol Delaney, "The Meaning of Paternity and the Virgin Birth Debate," *Man* 21, no. 3 (September 1986): 494–513. She discusses the difference between this scientific view that women contribute genetic material to the fetus and the claim of long-standing Western folk theories that the origin and identity of the fetus comes from the male, as in the metaphor of planting a seed in soil.

15. For a suggested direct link between human behavior and purportedly passive eggs and active sperm, see Erik H. Erikson, "Inner and Outer Space: Reflections on Womanhood," *Daedalus* 93, no. 2 (Spring 1964): 582–606, esp. 591.

16. Guyton (n. 3 above), 619; and Mountcastle (n. 5 above), 1609.

17. Jonathan Miller and David Pelham, *The Facts of Life* (New York: Viking Penguin, 1984), 5.

18. Alberts et al., 796.

19. Ibid., 796.

20. See, e.g., William F. Ganong, *Review of Medical Physiology*, 7th ed. (Los Altos, Calif. Lange Medical Publications, 1975), 322.

21. Alberts et al. (n. 11 above), 796.

22. Guyton, 615.

23. Solomon (n. 6 above), 683.

24. Vander, Sherman, and Luciano (n. 4 above), 4th ed. (1985), 580.

25. Alberts et al., 796.

26. All biology texts quoted above use the word *penetrate.*

27. Solomon, 700.

28. A. Beldecos et al., "The Importance of Feminist Critique for Contemporary Cell Biology," *Hypatia* 3, no. 1 (Spring 1988): 61–76.

29. Gerald Schatten and Helen Schatten, "The Energetic Egg," *Medical World News* 23 (January 23, 1984): 51–53, esp. 51.

30. Alberts et al., 796.

31. Guyton (n. 3 above), 613.

32. Miller and Pelham (n. 17 above), 7.

33. Alberts et al. (n. 11 above), 804.

34. Ibid., 801.

35. Ruth Herschberger, *Adam's Rib* (New York: Pelligrini & Cudaby, 1948), esp. 84. I am indebted to Ruth Hubbard for telling me about Herschberger's work, although at a point when this paper was already in draft form.

36. Bennett M. Shapiro. "The Existential Decision of a Sperm," *Cell* 49, no. 3 (May 1987): 293–94, esp. 293.

37. Lennart Nilsson, "A Portrait of the Sperm," in *The Functional Anatomy of the Spermatozoan,* ed. Bjorn A. Afzelius (New York: Pergamon, 1975), 79–82.

38. Ludwik Fleck, *Genesis and Development of a Scientific Fact,* ed. Thaddeus J. Trenn and Robert K. Merton (Chicago: University of Chicago Press, 1979), 38.

39. Jay M. Baltz carried out the research I describe when he was a graduate student in the Thomas C. Jenkins Department of Biophysics at Johns Hopkins University.

40. Far less is known about the physiology of sperm than comparable female substances, which some feminists claim is no accident. Greater scientific scrutiny of female reproduction has long enabled the burden of birth control to be placed on women. In this case, the researchers' discovery did not depend on development of any new technology. The experiments made use of glass pipettes, a manometer, and a simple microscope, all of which have been available for more than one hundred years.

41. Jay Baltz and Richard A. Cone, "What Force Is Needed to Tether a Sperm?" (abstract for Society for the Study of Reproduction, 1985), and "Flagellar Torque on the Head Determines the Force Needed to Tether a Sperm" (abstract for Biophysical Society, 1986).

42. Jay M. Baltz, David F. Katz, and Richard A. Cone, "The Mechanics of the Sperm-Egg Interaction at the Zona Pellucida," *Biophysical Journal* 54, no. 4 (October 1988): 643–54. Lab members were somewhat familiar with work on metaphors in the biology of female reproduction. Richard Cone, who runs the lab, is my husband, and he talked with them about my earlier research on the subject from time to time. Even though my current research focuses on biological imagery and I heard about the lab's work from my husband every day, I myself did not recognize the role of imagery in the sperm research until many weeks after the period of research and writing I describe. Therefore, I assume that any awareness the lab members may have had about how underlying metaphor might be guiding this particular research was fairly inchoate.

43. Ibid., 643, 650.

44. Schatten and Schatten (n. 29 above), 51.

45. Ibid., 52.

46. Surprisingly, in an article intended for a general audience, the authors do not point out that these are sea urchin sperm and note that human sperm do not shoot out filaments at all.

47. Schatten and Schatten, 53.

48. Paul M. Wassarman, "Fertilization in Mammals," *Scientific American* 259, no. 6 (December 1988): 78–84, esp. 78, 84.

49. Ibid., 78.

50. Ibid., 79.

51. Ibid., 78.

52. Since receptor molecules are relatively *immotile* and the ligands that bind to them relatively *motile*, one might imagine the egg being called the receptor and the sperm the ligand. But the molecules in question on egg and sperm are immotile molecules. It is the sperm as a *cell* that has motility, and the egg as a cell that has relative immotility.

53. Wassarman, 78–79.

54. Paul M. Wassarman, "The Biology and Chemistry of Fertilization," *Science* 235, no. 4788 (January 30, 1987): 553–60, esp. 554.

55. Ibid., 557.

56. Ibid., 557–58. This finding throws into question Schatten and Schatten's description (n. 29 above) of the sperm, its tail beating, diving down into the egg.

57. Deborah R. Gordon, "Tenacious Assumptions in Western Medicine," in *Biomedicine Examined*, ed. Margaret Lock and Deborah Gordon (Dordrecht: Kluwer, 1988), 19–56, esp. 26.

58. Wassarman, "The Biology and Chemistry of Fertilization," 558.

59. Baltz, Katz, and Cone (n. 42 above), 643, 650.

60. Schatten and Schatten, 53.

61. Wassarman, "The Biology and Chemistry of Fertilization," 557.

62. Mary Ellman, *Thinking about Women* (New York: Harcourt Brace Jovanovich, 1968), 140; Nina Auerbach, *Woman and the Demon* (Cambridge, Mass.: Harvard University Press, 1982), esp. 186.

63. Kenneth Alan Adams, "Arachnophobia: Love American Style," *Journal of Psychoanalytic Anthropology* 4, no. 2 (1981): 157–97.

64. William Ray Arney and Bernard Bergen, *Medicine and the Management of Living* (Chicago: University of Chicago Press, 1984).

65. J. F. Hartman, R. B. Gwatkin, and C. F. Hutchison, "Early Contact Interactions between Mammalian Gametes *In Vitro*," *Proceedings of the National Academy of Sciences* (U.S.) 69, no. 10 (1972): 2767–69.

66. Arney and Bergen, 68.

67. Ruth Hubbard, "Have Only Men Evolved?" (n. 12 above), 51–52.

68. David Harvey, personal communication, November 1989.

69. Rosalind Petchesky, "Fetal Images: The Power of Visual Culture in the Politics of Reproduction," *Feminist Studies* 13, no. 2 (Summer 1987): 263–92, esp. 272.

70. Rita Arditti, Renate Klein, and Shelley Minden, *Test-Tube Women* (London: Pandora, 1984); Ellen Goodman, "Whose Right to Life?" *Baltimore Sun* (November 17, 1987); Tamar Lewin, "Courts Acting to Force Care of the Unborn," *New York*

Times (November 23, 1987), A1 and B10; Susan Irwin and Brigitte Jordan, "Knowledge, Practice, and Power: Court Ordered Cesarean Sections," *Medical Anthropology Quarterly* 1, no. 3 (September 1987): 319–34.

71. Thanks to Elizabeth Fee and David Spain, who in February 1989 and April 1989, respectively, made points related to this.

Working with the Text

1. On a first reading of Emily Martin's essay, it is possible to become overwhelmed by the various scientific descriptions of reproductive processes. To help you discern the argumentative strategy at work in the essay, take a step back from the details of the text to consider the overall shape and structure of the article. Where does Martin start? How does she move through her evidence? Consider the role of subheadings in guiding the reader. Why does Martin start with the fairy tale and only then consider more recent research? Does that new research still bear traces of the fairy tale? In a brief essay, describe the strategy behind the organization of the article.

2. Martin's essay focuses on the metaphorical language scientists use to describe the phenomena they are observing. She notes in particular the verbs and verb forms that create metaphorical images. As you reread the essay, highlight descriptions of scientific observation that seem to you to be objective data, free of metaphor. In a brief essay, create a summary of the research that conveys the progression of what you consider to be the objective findings, omitting images and metaphors that depict the egg and the sperm as adult women and men or other creatures or objects. Exchange your essay with one or more of your classmates. Mark any language in your classmates' essays that seems to carry images or metaphors. Discuss your findings with the class. Were you able to omit metaphorical language? If so, what language did you use instead? How did you choose it? If not, what images and metaphors crept into your writing without you realizing it?

3. Although gender stereotypes can be found in virtually every discipline or profession, Martin focuses on those perpetuated by scientists, particularly those who publish textbooks. Write a brief essay in which you explore Martin's reasons for pursuing this line of inquiry. Why is she concerned about gender stereotypes in reproductive research? What influence does she seem to think science and medicine have on our culture? What is the significance of finding so many gender stereotypes in textbooks?

From Text to Field

1. Martin opens the essay by announcing, "As an anthropologist, I am intrigued by the possibility that culture shapes how biological scientists describe what they discover about the natural world" (par. 1). The presumption behind Martin's comment is that the realm of science is based exclusively on objective fact and that scientists should remain untouched by matters of culture and language. Based on Martin's insights as well as your understanding of how scientists—and human beings—work and think, write an essay in which you reflect further on why and how scientists are influenced by culture and by language.

2. In her opening paragraph, as Martin raises the possibility that scientists are influenced by the culture they live in, she points out, "If this were so, we would be learning about more than the natural world in high school biology class; we would be learning about cultural beliefs and practices as if they were part of nature." In high school, you were required to take one or more science courses, very likely a biology course. In a personal essay, reflect on the extent to which the science you learned was influenced by images and assumptions from American or even world culture. Did you receive them as if they were "part of nature"? Consider, in particular, whether changes in social attitudes toward gender and ethnicity were reflected in how science was presented to you.

3. Martin moves through her critique of gender stereotyping to the conclusion that projecting human behavior onto the egg and sperm is ill conceived and dangerous. As she brings her argument to a close, she asserts, "More crucial, then, than what *kinds* of personalities we bestow on cells is the very fact that we are doing it at all" (par. 36). In an essay, respond to this premise. If the biological relationship between the egg and sperm determines whether and how a new human being is created, do you think that it is unreasonable to treat that relationship as a reflection of—or a precursor to—stereotypically male and female characteristics? Why or why not? You might consider why Martin argues that recent biological research shows a more mutual relationship between the sperm and egg than is reflected in the language that traditionally describes it. Why does Martin only then turn to the argument that assigning any personality at all is highly questionable?

INTO THE FIELD: Options for Writing Projects

1. Family Ties: A Memoir

The "images in mind" that we have of gender—our own and that of others—can have their origins in our parents and in the parenting we received. In our mother or father we find embodied our first memories of gender roles and the source of influence and advice on our own roles. We also find in their roles confirmation of, or perhaps resistance to, broader social conventions about gender. The effect of our parents lingers on, long after we become more independent. The essays by Jamaica Kincaid (p. 542) and Scott Russell Sanders (p. 545) both address that effect.

This field project invites you to recall, honor, or resist the profound gender influences that family ties exert. Drawing on your own lived experience, and perhaps on some readings (both in and beyond this collection), write a memoir on gender identities, and through that memoir reflect on the images those gender identities have left in your mind. A memoir does more than simply tell a story from the past. It also reflects on that story, unraveling what it means in light of current self-knowledge. Whereas stories unfold and move forward, a memoir provides a retrospective glance, a chance to make sense of an incident given further experience. The term literally means "memory," and thus memoir has as much to do with an image in the mind as with any actual event.

You may find that focusing on one particular episode may afford a greater chance for reflection than an attempt to tell the "whole story." Moreover, because of the premium placed on reflection in a memoir, feel free to draw in other sources and material as you make sense of your experience. You will also find yourself shuttling back and forth between an experience you recall and your present reflections on its meaning and relevance.

As an alternative field project, you may wish to focus your memoir on the role of a friend or mentor who, through their own embodied experience, influenced your gender identity.

2. A Word of Advice

When you arrived as a new student on campus, you were surely inundated with advice of all sorts—from parents, from school administrators, from residence-hall advisors, and from fellow students. This field project invites you to make sense of that advice and of assumptions about gender identity that lie just behind that advice.

Jamaica Kincaid's "Girl" (p. 542) offers an engaging if somewhat distinctive model for offering advice. Consider imitating Kincaid's piece, but with a focus on the advice offered about going to and arriving at college. Be sure to draw on the distinctive features of your campus and the particularities of your background and cultural context. What does it mean to be a man or woman on your campus? What does it mean to explore gender at a time when you are shaping and reshaping your identity?

Accompany the advice with a separate essay that reflects on that advice and the decisions you made about focus and voice. What roles and identities did you assign to the speaker or narrator of the first piece and to its listener or reader? What was conventional in your advice, and what was perhaps intentionally radical or unexpected? How did you handle the urge to resist or question advice? What did you learn about yourself and your early experiences on campus as you wrote this project?

3. A Dialogue on Gender

Scott Russell Sanders (p. 545) opens his essay on gender in terms of a dialogue between himself and his friend Anneke. Their conversation about men and women, and in turn about envy, shame, guilt, and confusion, becomes the setting in which Sanders then interrogates his own memories and pursues his own reflections. In Sanders's essay on different perspectives, dialogue, or perhaps more accurately the desire for dialogue and trust, becomes the guiding structural device.

For this field project, Sanders's essay offers an invitation to create your own extended dialogue about the complex questions of gender identity. Your dialogue can be explicit, much as the text of a drama assigns different speaking roles, or it can take shape in your prose through your juxtaposition of different perspectives. Likewise, the dialogue can be between a man and a woman, between several men and women, between a group of women or a group of men, or for that matter between the contending voices in one person's head. Your dialogue might also capture *how* men and women might speak of gender.

4. Engendering Knowledge through Play

What we know about the world and what we know about ourselves are often profoundly shaped not just through formal schooling but through informal play. This field project invites you to explore a particular facet of the world of play. Here are just some of the possibilities you may wish to consider:

- Offer a detailed analysis of the informal games that children create during their play. What roles are assumed, and how are rules negotiated? What expectations govern improvised play? In what ways does such play follow or at times resist conventional gender roles?
- Consider in some detail one of the classic toys or games that has shaped gender identities for an entire generation of children. The Barbie and Ken dolls and GI Joe are among the more obvious examples. You may wish to focus on a toy or game that is somewhat less well known, but nevertheless influential.

- Visit a local toy store and consider the ways in which toys and games are marketed. Walk the aisles and note packaging and promotion. Media representations of play, whether on television or on the Internet, might also serve as an engaging focus for your work.
- In recent years, there has been considerable interest in gender-neutral games and toys or in activities that may even actively resist stereotypical gender roles. Evaluate this movement and some representative toys or activities. Alternatively, consider the ways in which the world of play can also be a world of hurt. Offer a close analysis of the ways in which gender identity can be used as a weapon during play.
- Some children's games explicitly call on language as part of the activity. The songs and rhymes sung during jumping rope are but one example. What do those songs say about the game and its cultural context and about the participants themselves?
- Offer a detailed analysis of one toy or game that actively wishes to reshape gender perceptions. Consider, for example, the American Girls Collection americangirl.com/agcn/. It offers a series of dolls from various periods in American history, accompanied by books about the lives of girls in that period. Does that collection have more to do with contemporary perceptions of self than with historical reality, or can it accomplish both ends?

5. Media Constructions of Gender Identity

If contemporary media have a powerful influence on the construction of gender identities, that influence is felt in particular films, television shows, advertisements, and media campaigns. Resisting sweeping generalization, this field project has you study in some detail one specific text or instance of gender construction. In what ways does your particular instance reinforce stereotypical gender identities and our responses to them, or in what ways might your particular instance resist or subvert gender expectations? The results of your field project might take the form of an academic paper, a review in the media or entertainment section of a newspaper or magazine, or perhaps a series of pages in a critic's notebook.

6. Gendered Histories of Your Field

As a student majoring in a particular field, your first preoccupation might be to learn its disciplinary content. Yet that content can be influenced by the field's sense of its own history and the way it may be discovering and reclaiming the role of women in that field. From literature departments to science departments, previously neglected women in the field are now being celebrated as path breakers.

This field project invites you to profile one such leader whose accomplishments are only now being appreciated and to analyze how that person might be affecting your education and your own initiation into your field. You may wish to consult a professor in your major or an instructor in one of your courses for suggestions on which figure might be an appropriate choice to study. A search in your campus library can also uncover rich resources. Conduct a Library of Congress subject-heading search for "Women in [your field]." To locate helpful compilations of resources in reference books, do a word search using the search string "women and biography and encyclopedia" or "women and biography and dictionary." But even as you unearth biographical information, bear in mind that this field project should go well beyond recounting a life. Your focus should be on assessing the impact of that figure on your own education in your major.

7. Gendering the Curriculum and the Classroom

Our collective conversations on gender over the last several decades have had an impact on the curricula you now study and on the classrooms in which you now learn. This field project invites you to explore what that impact has been in your major or in a field that holds some interest for you.

Historical perspective on your curriculum may help highlight the changes that have occurred. Consider engaging in a bit of archival work by consulting your college's course catalog from forty or even eighty years ago (contact a reference librarian to help you locate these resources). By comparing those historical documents with today's curriculum, you will find that in many fields new courses have appeared, as have whole new subfields, such as women's literature in the English department or gender studies in the sociology department. In fact, whole new majors or departments might have appeared, such as women's studies.

If your field leaves little explicit room for gender in the curriculum (such as in an engineering or a science major), consider the ways that your field has considered gender in the teaching and learning of its subject or in its efforts to attract women professors and students. You may also wish to consider how traditionally female-gendered fields, such as nursing, are now attracting males.

8. Gender and Campus Climate

This field project invites you to take the temperature, so to speak, of your campus with regard to its attitudes toward gender. What climate does your campus offer for heterosexual women and men and the queer communities (gay, lesbian, bisexual)? What tensions or controversial concerns might be a subject of campus conversation? In what ways might your campus reflect broader social conventions, or in what ways might your campus actively seek to question some of those conventions? To explore these and other questions, you may find it helpful to contact one of several campus groups concerned working experience in one or a few areas. Yet more often than not, the students would find themselves in need of clarifying or redefining their research interests. After finishing all their course requirements, some students might still feel at a loss in their search of a suitable research topic. In the worst case, they would eventually drop out because they could no longer afford struggling in such seemingly endless work. It is exhausting indeed to write one paper after another before finding the time to think about a thesis/dissertation project.

Even if you are pressed for time or have started late for some reason, it is not recommended that you choose a topic for which you have no or little preparation. It is critical to observe and follow your time line. And it would be very helpful to base your thesis/dissertation on your previous work, including the papers you have successfully written for various purposes.

If you are planning well ahead, whether to expand on your previous interest or to dig into a new field is a matter of your choice. Should you know what you are doing is what you want and there is enough room for your future development, you could further your interest by asking new questions about your old topic. If you need to make a change (due to new funding possibilities, sociopolitical significance, academic orientation, etc.), you may have to spend time reading, rethinking, and working hard to make new topics open up for you.

The selection of a research topic for your thesis/dissertation is not so easy as thinking immediately about a subject that appears interesting to you. Since your thesis/dissertation research project is so important to you career, you should link it to your goals as directly as possible. For instance, if you intend to tie your future with a profession that has a strong emphasis on practical issues, you should think about whether or not a theoretical work for your thesis/dissertation would be well received when you present it to your prospective employers.

An important characteristic of a good subject for your research topic is its potential for bringing in some research funding, sooner or later. In a sense, this practical consideration outweighs a general talk about its sociopolitical significance. The society influences and directs your research interest to what it regards as important through its funding mechanism. Even if you do not want to invest in writing for a grant at this time, you may need to carefully evaluate the relationship between your direction and the major interests of the "society" as represented by various public and private agencies.

Your research topic may also be influenced by your current employment. If you are working with someone on something, what you do for your thesis/dissertation could be taken as an addition to or an integral part of a collaborative project.

substantial evidence. *Dickinson v. Zurko,* 527 U.S. 150 (1999). Thereafter, an appeal may be taken to the United States Supreme Court if the Court, in its discretion, decides to hear the appeal. As an alternative to appealing to CAFC, the party may institute a civil action in the federal district court that will determine the issues *de novo,* meaning that it can determine the issues anew and new evidence may be presented.

INFRINGEMENT OF TRADEMARKS

Introduction

Section 32 of the Lanham Act (15 U.S.C. § 1114) provides that the owner of a federally registered trademark may bring a civil action in federal court against any person who uses, without the registrant's consent, a mark that is likely to cause confusion with the registrant's mark. Such an action is for "trademark infringement." To prevail on a trademark infringement claim, a mark's owner must prove two things: That its mark has priority and that the infringer's mark is likely to cause confusion.

The central inquiry in an **infringement** action is whether there is a likelihood that an appreciable number of ordinarily prudent purchasers are likely to be misled or confused about the source, affiliation, or sponsorship of goods or services. If consumers, upon encountering the defendant's goods or services, would believe they are produced by or somehow affiliated with a plaintiff's goods or services, the defendant's mark infringes the plaintiff's.

The standard for determining whether there is a likelihood of confusion is the same as that used in the application process when an examining attorney refuses registration of a mark on the basis that it is likely to be confused with that of another prior mark. The standard is also identical to that used in opposition and cancellation proceedings when a party alleges

registration of another mark should be denied or canceled because the mark is likely to be confused with that of the opposer or petitioner.

In the typical infringement action, a prior user alleges that a subsequent user is causing confusion in the marketplace by using a confusingly similar mark. In essence, the later or junior user is attempting to get a "free ride" on the reputation and renown of the senior user by adopting a similar mark. In some instances, however, the second user may become so well-known and famous that it dwarfs the prior user and allegedly causes consumers to believe that the prior user's goods come from the subsequent user. The prior owner can then initiate an infringement action for "reverse confusion." Generally, reverse confusion occurs when the later user is a large, powerful company that uses its economic power to saturate the market with advertising, thereby causing confusion. (See Appendix D, Form 10, Complaint for Trademark Infringement.)

Standard for Determining Likelihood of Confusion

Various courts in various circuits have enumerated tests for determining whether one mark is likely to be confused with another. Generally, no one factor is determinative; courts examine the totality of circumstances in attempting to determine whether infringement has occurred. In general, pursuant to *E.I. du Pont de Nemours & Co.,* 476 F.2d 1357 (C.C.P.A. 1973), the following factors are considered by courts in determining whether trademark infringement exists:

- the similarity of the marks in regard to appearance, sound, connotation, and commercial impression;
- the similarity of the goods or services offered under the marks;
- the similarity in the channels of trade in which the goods or services are offered;

with gender issues or to interview a professor or staff member who has taken a leading role in campus discussions.

Based on your fieldwork, consider writing a proposal for action on behalf of a campus group or writing a profile of your campus with respect to gender climate for a magazine or college guidebook.

As an alternative, you may wish to delve into the history of your college or university to explore how questions of gender might have influenced it. For example, an episode in the early history of the University of Colorado at Boulder captures just how strong conventional gender roles were. When Mary Rippon was invited to join the faculty in 1878, she became one of the first female professors at any public university in the country. Popular and esteemed both on campus and in the community, she nevertheless led a very secret and separate life. She married one of her students and had a daughter, yet she hid her family life for decades for fear of losing her job. Only well after her death did her private life emerge. Consider writing a profile of an influential figure in the history of your campus, analyzing how that figure either embodied gender norms of the time or successfully challenged them.

9. Science and Gender/Cultural/Political Bias

It is both easy and convenient to work under the assumption that the sciences are immune to the sorts of bias that can affect other disciplines. But if the essays by Stephen Jay Gould (p. 552) and Emily Martin (p. 560) are any indication, such biases can indeed influence fields that most would consider to be data driven and objective. This field project invites you to consider such bias by engaging in one of three kinds of fieldwork:

- Report on and consider the implications of a current or historical case of bias in science that involved one of the following factors: race, nationality, age, sexual orientation, religion, values and beliefs, political leanings, and vested interests and financial support.
- One way to learn how to recognize and understand bias in scientific studies is to propose a fraudulent or biased study yourself. Think of this field project as a kind of explicit satire. Write a proposal for a fictional scientific study in which you consciously embed an element of bias, whether it is in data collection or in the hidden assumptions that guide your work. Consider how you can nevertheless give your study the veneer of respectability so that others may not immediately recognize how bias operates in your work. Analyze how the bias in your study might affect the results of your work and its reception.
- One particular kind of bias has to do with political leanings and their effect on the funding, use, and dissemination of scientific studies and the role of

those studies in setting public policy. For this field project, choose one scientific concern (e.g., water quality) that you are already interested in. Your task is to analyze how and to what extent political interests may have a role in how hard science is used to craft public policy. Although it may be tempting to disparage the influence of political groups with whom you disagree, do not discount the influence of groups you are sympathetic to. For an initial orientation to possible scientific issues you might focus on, consult Web sites hosted by organizations that track the role of science in public affairs. One such organization is the Union of Concerned Scientists ucsusa.org/.

10. Gender, Intelligence, and Intellectual Development

The "images in mind" that we carry with us about gender can easily influence how we regard intelligence and intellectual development. This field project offers you three different avenues for exploring the influence of gender in your learning environment.

- If you are interested in or majoring in a field that has traditionally been dominated by one gender (e.g., engineering, nursing), explore the influence of gender bias and stereotyping on teaching and learning in that field. You may wish to contact or interview someone in a support group, organization, or office that seeks to help students overcome those barriers, such as a group supporting women in engineering.

- In your precollegiate educational experiences, did you find that one gender was favored or discriminated against, perhaps in one particular sphere of activity (e.g., sports, reading, math)? Offer an educational memoir that reflects on the challenges of growing up as a boy or a girl in your school system and how you may have had to challenge assumptions about your intellectual development and interests.

- Many parents, teachers, and students hold that girls or boys may be better at something or learn that thing more easily or more quickly (at least at the outset). Drawing on educational and psychological research, consider to what extent there may or may not be any truth to such claims. Given what you have learned, how would you improve learning environments or teaching techniques? How might your own learning have been affected by such perceptions or improved by the changes you suggest?

6

Learning Technology

VIRTUAL COMMUNITIES

Technology has a powerful grip on our society. That grip extends well beyond the various electronic gizmos that may capture our immediate attention. Technologies represent ways of designing our world, of lending one kind of order, among many possible orders, to our endeavors and our relationships. Thus, even as we focus our attention on mastering the use of the latest gizmo, that gizmo can be thought of as "using" us. For all of our focus on "learning technology," on knowing how to work something, we too easily forget that technology also influences how we learn about and encounter the world.

This chapter explores this second, less obvious meaning: Technologies are ways of learning, of mastering and being mastered. It may be tempting to think of technology as an ally, or even as a boon, but it is also a contested site of social and educational struggle. In these pages, we set aside our habitual concern with becoming competent users of technology, as we consider how technology shapes us and how we can become more conscious of and savvy about that technology.

This unit focuses on how communities, because of digital technologies such as the Internet, now have a virtual dimension to them. Some communities may be almost entirely virtual. We no longer need to be together physically in order to think of ourselves as a community. Our colleagues can be across the ocean, not just down the hall. With the advent of online education, students taking the same course you are may be hundreds of miles away. Thus, by loosening the strictures of space and time, technology is reworking our relations with each other. Although we tend to think of virtual communities as offering new communities or additional kinds of communities, one of the strongest influences that technology has is to augment and expand those local communities that already have a place in our lives.

Of the local communities that have a place in your life, perhaps the most pervasive and influential is school. Certainly, your experiences from kindergarten through twelfth grade were as much about the community you were a part of as what you learned from books in that community. New technologies offer the prospect of decoupling learning from the traditional community of the school. Yet even as we may celebrate and take advantage of that possibility, we also become more aware of the value of physical community in the learning process.

The learning process occurs, then, not just *through* technology but also *about* technology. Given the latest developments in cyberspace, literacy (traditionally, the ability to read and write) has itself acquired a new dimension. No longer is it sufficient to be computer literate — that is, to know how to work computers. We must now be literate about computers, in the broadest sense. We must know how computers work to shape our lives and how we can shape our own lives through technology more consciously.

One key aspect of our new literacy about cyberspace is our willingness to question the assumption that new technologies arrive unencumbered with old baggage. Even though the latest technologies may push the envelope of what we think is possible, trailing behind them are issues — questions of gender and communication style, for example — that endure, no matter what the technology. If we are to take a self-reflective and activist approach to "learning technologies" (in the double meaning of that phrase), we need to assess not only the new prospects that technology opens up but also the enduring questions that technology continues to have us ask.

The three readings in this unit invite you to explore how technology is asking us to learn afresh about community, learning, literacy, and gender. Each of the readings takes up a particular challenge.

Nancy Hass explores how Facebook.com is more than a benign tool for social networking; it raises concerns that shed light on "the changing nature of public and private identity." Media critic Neil Postman challenges the utopian dream that technology can deliver education anytime and anywhere, reminding us that there are reasons why gathering together in a classroom is still valid. Challenging the notion that computer-mediated communication is more gender neutral and democratic, Susan Herring reminds us that new technologies can carry with them familiar baggage. Together, these three readings emphasize that our success in dealing with all that is new in technology might best be measured by how we deal, through that technology, with issues that are all too familiar.

Reflecting on Prior Knowledge

1. All of us live in communities or find ourselves, more accurately, in a variety of overlapping communities. But not all communities are now built and maintained exclusively through face-to-face contact in a geographically specific place. Some communities have virtual or electronic components, and some even exist largely, if not solely, as virtual entities with no physical location. In a journal entry, explore your acquaintance with virtual communities. What might draw you to them? What qualities might you miss in such communities?

2. Describe a project for school or college that was based on extensive use of the computer and that was either a very effective or very disappointing learning experience. How did you use the computer for the project? In what ways did technology contribute to or obstruct the process?

3. In a journal entry, reflect on what you think computer technology contributes, or could contribute, to education. How do you think it should be used? In what ways might such technology be misused? Used well, how does it enhance learning?

4. Recall school or college projects based on research. Some you may have conducted primarily through books, while others may have employed some form of computer technology. In a journal entry, compare the effectiveness of the approaches. What, if any, differences did you find in the type and quality of material? In your sense of discovery? In the level of thinking you were prompted to do? In the quality of your writing?

5. Working in small groups and drawing on your own experience, discuss whether communication using computer technology can help us overcome gender differences or whether such technology only heightens or perpetuates those differences.

6. In a journal entry, recall an experience in which something you were trying to communicate was misconstrued or ignored. What were you trying to convey? How was it received and interpreted? Why do you think your audience responded in this way?

In Your Facebook.com

Nancy Hass

How many times have you logged on to Facebook during the last week? Or during the last 24 hours? If national statistics are any indication, three-quarters of Facebook users log on every day, and average users check their sites six times a day. Popular on college campuses, the site is among the top ten most visited on the Internet.

What accounts for Facebook's popularity, and what can Facebook tell us about how college students present themselves, or at any rate about how they would like to be seen? For Nancy Hass, writing in the *New York Times* on January 8, 2006, Facebook sheds light on the "changing nature of public and private identity." Hass acknowledges the powerful potential of Facebook as a community-building tool, a tool that draws on current interest in social networks. Yet Hass also notes the concerns that have developed amid Facebook's growing popularity. Questions about privacy and propriety abound, even as many students relish the role-playing opportunities and social connections that Facebook offers. As Facebook continues to evolve, and students accommodate their own use of the site to the particulars of their situation and interests, this much remains clear: Facebook has become far more than a digital version of the old hard copy facebooks that were meant as a way for students to get to know each other. Facebook has implicated itself into the very fabric of college life.

Nancy Hass is a freelance journalist living in the New York area. She teaches journalism at New York University and has written on culture, education, fashion, and the media for such publications as the *New York Times, New York Magazine, Elle, Newsweek,* and *The Economist*.

As far as Kyle Stoneman is concerned, the campus police were the ones who started the Facebook wars. "We were just being, well, college students, and they used it against us," says Mr. Stoneman, a senior at George Washington

University in Washington. He is convinced that the campus security force got wind of a party he and some buddies were planning last year by monitoring Facebook.com, the phenomenally popular college networking site. The officers waited till the shindig was in full swing, Mr. Stoneman grouses, then shut it down on discovering underage drinking.

Mr. Stoneman and his friends decided to fight back. Their weapon of choice? Facebook, of course.

Once again they used the site, which is visited by more than 80 percent of the student body, to chat up a beer blast. But this time, when the campus police showed up, they found 40 students and a table of cake and cookies, all decorated with the word *beer*. "We even set up a cake-pong table," a twist on the beer-pong drinking game, he says. "The look on the faces of the cops was priceless." As the coup de grâce, he posted photographs of the party on Facebook, including a portrait of one nonplussed officer.

A university spokesman, Tracy Schario, insists that noise complaints, not nosing around Facebook, led the police to both parties. But, she says, "it's sort of an inevitability that if a party is talked about on the site, word of it will reach the enforcement people, who then have no choice but to investigate." In fact, two campus police officers and the chief's assistant are among the fourteen thousand Facebook members at George Washington.

The stunt could be read as a sign that Facebook has become more than a   5 way for young people to stay in touch. Started in 2004 by Harvard students who wanted to animate the black-and-white thumbnail photos of freshman directories, the site is the ninth most visited on the Internet, according to Nielsen/Net Ratings, and is used by nearly five million college students. Facebook is available at most of the country's four-year colleges, and many two-year colleges, too.

Because of its popularity, though, the site has become a flashpoint for debates about free speech, privacy, and whether the Internet should be a tool for surveillance. It has also raised concerns from parents, administrators, and even students about online "addiction." "There are people on this campus who are totally obsessed with it, who check their profile five, six, twenty times a day," says Ingrid Gallagher, a sophomore at the University of Michigan. "But I think that more and more people are realizing that it also has a dark side."

Her estimates are not far off. Nearly three-quarters of Facebook users sign on at least once every twenty-four hours, and the average users sign on six times a day, says Chris Hughes, a spokesman for the site.

Using it is simple: Students create online profiles, which they can stock with personal details like sexual preferences, favorite movies, and phone contact numbers, with links to photo albums and diaries. The details listed are by no means reliable; it's common, under "personal relationships," to list a

- the conditions under which sales are made, namely, whether the purchases are made on impulse or after careful consideration by sophisticated purchasers;
- the strength or fame of the prior mark;
- whether there has been any actual confusion;
- the number and nature of similar marks on similar goods; and
- the length of time during which there has been concurrent use with no confusion.

Other courts consider the defendant's intent in adopting the mark when testing for likelihood of confusion.

Sight, Sound, Meaning, and Connotation. With dissimilar marks, there is little likelihood of confusion. The more similar marks are, the more likely it is that confusion will occur. The single most important factor in determining likelihood of confusion is the similarity of the marks. Generally, marks are compared in their entireties rather than on the basis of a side-by-side comparison or a dissection of their respective elements inasmuch as courts cannot assume consumers would have the opportunity to make a side-by-side comparison when making a purchase. Some general rules have emerged:

- Marks may be confusingly similar in appearance notwithstanding the addition, deletion, or substitution of letters. Thus, TRUCOOL for synthetic coolant was held likely to be confused with TUR-COOL for cutting oil. *In re Lamson Oil Co.,* 6 U.S.P.Q.2d 1041 (T.T.A.B. 1987).
- Similarity may occur due to sound or pronunciation. For example, BONAMINE was held confusingly similar to DRAMAMINE when both were used for medical goods. *G.D. Searle & Co. v. Charles Pfizer & Co.,* 265 F.2d 835 (7th Cir. 1959).
- Similarity in meaning may result in a finding of confusion. Thus, AQUA-CARE

(STYLIZED) was held likely to be confused with WATERCARE when both were used for water conditioning products. *Watercare Corp. v. Midwesco Enterprise Inc.,* 171 U.S.P.Q. 696 (T.T.A.B. 1971). Similarly, BUENOS DIAS for soap was held likely to be confused with GOOD MORNING for shaving cream, *In re American Safety Razor Co.,* 2 U.S.P.Q.2d 1459 (T.T.A.B. 1987), and CYCLONE and TORNADO were held confusingly similar for wire fencing because their connotations were the same.

- If the marks include compound words, some courts consider whether there is a dominant portion of the mark and give less weight to common or descriptive elements. Thus, there was no likelihood of confusion between SOLVENTOL and SOLVITE. *Solventol Chemical Prods. v. Langfield,* 134 F.2d 899 (6th Cir. 1943). Because the descriptive prefixes *solvent* and *sol* are so commonly used, the court held that the remaining portions of the marks were distinguishable.
- When marks comprise both words and designs, greater weight is sometimes given to the wording, which would be used by consumers in requesting the goods or services.
- If an owner has a famous mark or a "family" of marks that has achieved public recognition, such as the family of "Mc" marks owned by McDonald's, the mark may be more likely to be infringed. Courts have held that marks with extensive public recognition and renown deserve more protection than obscure or weak marks. Thus, due to the strong association by the public of the "Mc" prefix with McDonald's, many attempted uses of a mark including "Mc" have been found to infringe McDonald's marks. For

spouse as a joke (as does Mr. Stoneman). Like most networking sites, Facebook enables users to compile lists of friends whose names and photos are displayed, and to post public comments on other people's profiles.

One of the most attractive features to many students is that they can track down friends from high school at other colleges. Users can also join or form groups with names that run from the prosaic ("Campus Republicans") to the prurient ("We Need to Have Sex in Widener Before We Graduate") and the dadaesque ("I Am Fond of Biscuits and Scones"). Unlike general networking sites like Friendster and myspace.com, which let anyone join, Facebook and xuqa.com, which was started last year by a student at Williams, are confined to the insular world of the campus, which Internet experts say is the key to their success. Last fall, Facebook opened a parallel site for high school students. To sign up, a high school student has to be referred by a college student who is a Facebook user.

Facebook's charms are obvious even to administrators. "It's a fantastic tool   10
for building community," says Anita Farrington-

Facebook illuminates the Brathwaite, assistant dean for freshmen at New York
changing nature of public University. "In a school like ours that doesn't have an
and private identity. enclosed campus, it really gives people a way to find
each other and connect." Harvard's president,
Lawrence H. Summers, gave kudos to Facebook in the opening lines of his address to freshmen in September, saying he had been browsing the site to get to know everyone.

But concerns have flourished with Facebook's popularity. Despite safeguards placed on access —only those with valid university e-mail addresses, ending in *edu*, can register as users, and students can bar specific people from viewing their profiles— administrators and parents worry about cyberstalking.

Robin Raskin, a technology consultant whose three children are in college and use Facebook, says students should be cautious about putting personal information on the site. "There's something about all that ivy climbing up those walls that makes kids feel they're safe, but anybody can get in there who wants to," Ms. Raskin says.

It's not just parents who are uneasy.

"Every girl I know has had some sort of weird experience," says Shanna Andus, a freshman at the University of California, Berkeley. "Someone gets on a 'friend list' of one of your friends and starts to contact you. They met you at a party or checked out your picture online or went to high school with someone you barely know. It's just a little creepy."

Some colleges have taken action: In October, the University of New   15
Mexico banned access to Facebook on its campus system, citing numerous concerns, including student privacy. Campus officials say they will restore

the service for this semester. Mr. Hughes, the Facebook spokesman, says that when the site could not be accessed via the university's networks, half the users continued to sign on through outside networks.

Mr. Hughes defends the site's privacy safeguards, insisting that it rarely receives reports of stalking or other harassment, and that complaints usually require only a readjustment of a user's privacy settings and a warning message sent to the person accused of inappropriate behavior.

But parents and administrators have another worry: that potential employers are wangling themselves e-mail addresses ending with *edu*—perhaps someone in the office was given one by his alma mater or has signed up for an extension course at a college with Facebook access—so that they can vet job applicants. Administrators at both NYU and Brandeis say on-campus employers use the site for just that purpose. Aware that many students post pictures and descriptions of their X-rated, booze-soaked exploits, administrators at Tufts and Texas Christian University began offering seminars in Facebook propriety last year.

Students themselves seem split on the issue of Facebook exposure: Some are outraged that their youthful indiscretions may be used against them; others seem resigned to privacy being a fantasy in the age of the Internet. In a case that was reported in the *Boston Globe* last year and that many students cite as a cautionary tale, a Brandeis student included her "appreciation of the festive greens" in her profile, a not-so-subtle allusion to marijuana that got to her parents and became the buzz at her grandmother's retirement home.

"The way I look at it is that in the future with the growing nature of information transparency, having embarrassing pictures out there will be the norm," says Mr. Stoneman, a political communications major who has a job lined up with a consulting firm that specializes in online campaign fundraising. "Sure, five years down the line it might hurt me, but ten or fifteen years, I don't think it will matter."

But, as Mr. Stoneman's beer party hoax suggests, he and his peers may not 20 be as sanguine about how some colleges are using Facebook to police the student body or at least influence it. As part of freshman orientation at Rollins College in Florida, student coordinators will create Facebook groups for campus organizations like the Rollins Outdoor Club.

"We cannot deny the impact of Facebook, but we believe that it's the responsibility of the institution to find ways to create the most positive communities," says Roger Casey, dean of faculty. "These communities can be positive or negative."

Other colleges are even more aggressive. A student at Fisher College in Boston was expelled last year for his online criticism of a campus security officer. Officials at the University of California, Santa Barbara, said they would discipline students living on campus who posted information or photographs on their profiles that involved illegal activity like underage drinking. At North Carolina State, residential advisers, the upperclassmen who oversee dorm life, wrote up fifteen students seen consuming alcohol in photos on Facebook; it caused an uproar and resulted in a town-hall-style meeting.

Campus officials are not the only ones trawling for miscreants: The Secret Service investigated a student at the University of Oklahoma who posted a comment on Facebook about assassinating the president.

Ms. Farrington-Brathwaite acknowledges that the privacy issues presented by Facebook create challenges for administrators, even at liberal institutions like NYU, which she says has not used the site to patrol student behavior. While several hundred professors and deans across the country have added their own profiles as a way to reach out to students—a development that, arguably, has lowered Facebook's cool quotient—she does not plan to do so. "I wouldn't want to come upon something that I felt was inappropriate," she says, "so I just choose not to get involved."

But Ms. Farrington-Brathwaite encourages resident advisers to come to   25 her if they spot a Facebook cry for help, like an allusion to suicide. NYU has experienced a spate of student suicides in recent years. "Still, it's a difficult balancing act, preserving student privacy and freedom, yet not sticking our head in the sand," she says.

With the abundance of groups that treat almost everything with irreverence, Facebook has also inflamed racial conflicts. At Indiana University and the University of Virginia, two Facebook groups recently caused fracases by poking fun at Asian students, who make up a large part of their student bodies. Students created dueling groups, and Asian organizations made the conflict a cause célèbre.

Mr. Hughes says the site does not censor content but tries to deal directly with offensive or inflammatory postings if there are complaints. At both campuses, students removed the groups of their own accord after administrators brought complaints to their attention. "We see Facebook as a land mine," says Daisy Rodriguez, assistant dean of students at the University of Virginia, "but we understand we have no authority over it. So our policy is to meet with students who may post things that people find offensive and talk about the issues and consequences. Then we hope for the best."

Mr. Stoneman of George Washington considers such an attitude enlightened—and realistic. "Facebook is part of an evolving dialogue," he says. "One of the things that's most fascinating about it is how it illuminates the changing nature of public and private identity. This is new ground on every level. What people in positions of power have to realize is that people my age have a completely different attitude about what is fair game."

Working with the Text

1. Nancy Hass opens her article on Facebook.com with a four-paragraph story about an incident at George Washington University. What is the function of that story as the opening to the article? How does the story open up a range of issues that Hass explores regarding Facebook?

2. In an article that is otherwise preoccupied with the issues and conflicts that Facebook.com has opened up on college campuses, Hass quotes an administrator as saying that Facebook offers "a fantastic tool for building community" (par. 10). Drawing on the article, and your own acquaintance with Facebook, explain this reference to community building. What are social networks, and how can a virtual tool like Facebook help establish and maintain them?

3. Hass notes that some universities are now offering seminars in Facebook propriety. What is meant by the term *propriety*? What is or isn't proper in an environment like Facebook? Can propriety be seen as a general or universal standard, or can it only be judged in light of a specific situation or context? Can something that is improper in some circumstances be proper or acceptable in others? What bearing does the digital or virtual environment of Facebook have on the question of propriety?

4. Hass concludes her article with a quote that Facebook "illuminates the changing nature of public and private identity." Explain the quote more fully. Why might this quote be a fitting conclusion to the article and the various issues that it discusses?

From Text to Field

1. Drawing on the article by Hass and your own experience with Facebook.com, assess Facebook as a tool for community building. How do real and artificial or virtual communities coexist, or do they sometimes conflict or work at cross purposes? How does the "group" function work on Facebook, and what role does it have in the formation and maintenance of groups? What are the possibilities and limits of community building through Facebook?

2. Given the frequency with which Facebook users are reported to log on to their site, or the sites of friends (often multiple times each day), discuss the attraction of Facebook, and possible "addiction" to Facebook. As you interview users that you know, also be sure to interview those who do not use Facebook or who only log on sporadically.

3. How does Facebook encourage you to define "friendship"? Among the functions available on a Facebook site is the opportunity to ask to be someone's friend, or to accept others as your friend. Facebook also allows you to "poke"

someone else on Facebook. How do Facebook users treat or perceive these functions? Does Facebook further friendships in a social network, or does it trivialize friendship?

4. Given the popularity of Facebook as students' preferred means of contact and interaction, it is perhaps understandable that professors are interested in tapping this resource for their teaching and their communication with students. How do you and other students feel about this use of Facebook? Do you welcome it? Or do you feel it intrudes on and changes the nature of Facebook communications?

5. Nearly every user of Facebook has his or her own Facebook "story," some notable consequence of using the site, whether positive or negative. What is your story? Does your story support some of the points made in the article by Hass, or does your story offer a different perspective?

Virtual Students, Digital Classroom

Neil Postman

Will technology eventually replace schools? Will access to the Internet as well as other computer-based sources of information transform our attitudes toward knowledge? What will we want to learn, and how will high-tech learning influence the ways we think? In the following article from the *Nation*, adapted from his 1996 book, *The End of Education: Redefining the Value of School*, Neil Postman addresses these questions, observing that the deeper issue about all of our technologies is "not how to use them but how they use *us*."

As an educator internationally recognized for his writings on the media, Postman was especially concerned about the effects of technology on learning and civic life. His own classroom experience as well as his research convinced him that teachers and school environments contribute to our social and psychological health in ways that can never be duplicated by any form of technology. Postman warned that we too easily idolize technology, embracing its allure and convenience without reflecting on what its real goals and long-term effects might be.

A prolific writer who attracted a wide readership by fearlessly debunking fashionable trends, Postman authored nearly twenty books. He is perhaps best known for his 1985 book, *Amusing Ourselves to Death: Public Discourse in the Age of Show Business*, in which he criticizes the television industry for treating the world's most serious issues as entertainment. Postman was also particularly troubled by how the media shaped children's lives, a concern expressed in *The Disappearance of Childhood* (1982). Other notable books include *Teaching as a Subversive Activity* (1969, with Charles Weingartner), *Technopoly: The Surrender of Culture to Technology* (1992), and *Building a Bridge to the 18th Century: How the Past Can Improve Our*

Future (1999). A member of the *Nation's* editorial board, Postman published articles in periodicals ranging from the *New York Times Magazine,* the *Atlantic,* and *Harper's* to *Time* magazine and the *Harvard Education Review.*

A faculty member at New York University for forty-four years, Postman founded its program in media ecology and was for many years chair of the Department of Culture and Communication. His interest in education extended to his own classroom, where his work was honored with several teaching awards. Postman died in October 2003.

If one has a trusting relationship with one's students (let us say, graduate students), it is not altogether gauche to ask them if they believe in God (with a capital G). I have done this three or four times and most students say they do. Their answer is preliminary to the next question: If someone you love were desperately ill, and you had to choose between praying to God for his or her recovery or administering an antibiotic (as prescribed by a competent physician), which would you choose?

Most say the question is silly since the alternatives are not mutually exclusive. Of course. But suppose they were — which would you choose? God helps those who help themselves, some say in choosing the antibiotic, therefore getting the best of two possible belief systems. But if pushed to the wall (e.g., God does not always help those who help themselves; God helps those who pray and who believe), most choose the antibiotic, after noting that the question is asinine and proves nothing. Of course, the question was not asked, in the first place, to prove anything but to begin a discussion of the nature of belief. And I do not fail to inform the students, by the way, that there has recently emerged evidence of a "scientific" nature that when sick people are prayed for they do better than those who aren't.

As the discussion proceeds, important distinctions are made among the different meanings of "belief," but at some point it becomes far from asinine to speak of the god of Technology — in the sense that people believe technology works, that they rely on it, that it makes promises, that they are bereft when denied access to it, that they are delighted when they are in its presence, that for most people it works in mysterious ways, that they condemn people who speak against it, that they stand in awe of it, and that, in the "born again" mode, they will alter their lifestyles, their schedules, their habits and their relationships to accommodate it. If this be not a form of religious belief, what is?

In all strands of American cultural life, you can find so many examples of technological adoration that it is possible to write a book about it. And I would if it had not already been done so well. But nowhere do you find more enthusiasm for the god of Technology than among educators. In fact, there are those, like Lewis Perelman, who argue (for example, in his book, *School's Out*) that modern information technologies have rendered schools entirely irrelevant since there is now much more information available outside the classroom than inside it. This is by no means considered an outlandish idea. Dr. Diane Ravitch, former Assistant Secretary of Education, envisions, with considerable relish, the challenge that technology presents to the tradition that "children (and adults) should be educated in a specific place, for a certain number of hours, and a certain number of days during the week and year." In other words, that children should be educated in school. Imagining the possibilities of an information superhighway offering perhaps a thousand channels, Dr. Ravitch assures us that:

> in this new world of pedagogical plenty, children and adults will be able to dial up a program on their home television to learn whatever they want to know, at their own convenience. If Little Eva cannot sleep, she can learn algebra instead. At her home-learning station, she will tune in to a series of interesting problems that are presented in an interactive medium, much like video games. . . .
>
> Young John may decide that he wants to learn the history of modern Japan, which he can do by dialing up the greatest authorities and teachers on the subject, who will not only use dazzling graphs and illustrations, but will narrate a historical video that excites his curiosity and imagination.

In this vision there is, it seems to me, a confident and typical sense of ⁵ unreality. Little Eva can't sleep, so she decides to learn a little algebra? Where does Little Eva come from? Mars? If not, it is more likely she will tune in to a good movie. Young John decides that he wants to learn the history of modern Japan? How did young John come to this point? How is it that he never visited a library up to now? Or is it that he, too, couldn't sleep and decided that a little modern Japanese history was just what he needed?

What Ravitch is talking about here is not a new technology but a new species of child, one who, in any case, no one has seen up to now. Of course, new technologies do make new kinds of people, which leads to a second objection to Ravitch's conception of the future. There is a kind of forthright determinism about the imagined world described in it. The technology is here or will be; we must use it because it is there; we will become the kind of people the technology requires us to be, and whether we like it or not, we will remake our institutions to accommodate technology. All of this must happen because it is good for us, but in any case, we have no choice. This point of view is present in very nearly every statement about the future relationship of learning to technology. And, as in Ravitch's scenario, there is always a cheery, gee-whiz tone to the prophecies. Here is one produced by the National Academy of Sciences, written by Hugh McIntosh.

School for children of the information age will be vastly different than it was for mom and dad.

Interested in biology? Design your own life forms with computer simulation.

Having trouble with a science project? Teleconference about it with a research scientist.

Bored with the real world? Go into a virtual physics lab and rewrite the laws of gravity.

These are the kinds of hands-on learning experiences schools could be providing right now. The technologies that make them possible are already here, and today's youngsters, regardless of economic status, know how to use them. They spend hours with them every week—not in the classroom, but in their own homes and in video-game centers at every shopping mall.

It is always interesting to attend to the examples of learning, and the motivations that ignite them, in the songs of love that technophiles perform for us. It is, for example, not easy to imagine research scientists all over the world teleconferencing with thousands of students who are having difficulty with their science projects. I can't help thinking that most research scientists would put a stop to this rather quickly. But I find it especially revealing that in the scenario above we have an example of a technological solution to a psychological problem that would seem to be exceedingly serious. We are presented with a student who is "bored with the real world." What does it mean to say someone is bored with the real world, especially one so young? Can a journey into virtual reality cure such a problem? And if it can, will our troubled youngster want to return to the real world? Confronted with a student who is bored with the real world, I don't think we can solve the problem so easily by making available a virtual-reality physics lab.

The role that new technology should play in schools or anywhere else is something that needs to be discussed without the hyperactive fantasies of cheerleaders. In particular, the computer and its associated technologies are awesome additions to a culture, and are quite capable of altering the psychic, not to mention the sleeping, habits of our young. But like all important technologies of the past, they are Faustian bargains,° giving and taking away, sometimes in equal measure, sometimes more in one way than the other. It is strange—indeed, shocking — that with the twenty-first century so close, we can still talk of new technologies as if they were unmixed blessings— gifts, as it were, from the gods. Don't we all know what the combustion engine has done for us and against us? What television is doing for us and against us? At the very least, what we need to discuss about Little Eva, Young John, and McIntosh's trio is what they will lose, and what we will lose, if they enter a

---

Faustian bargains: Faust is the protagonist of a popular German folktale that concerns his pact with the devil.

world in which computer technology is their chief source of motivation, authority, and, apparently, psychological sustenance. Will they become, as Joseph Weizenbaum warns, more impressed by calculation than human judgment? Will speed of response become, more than ever, a defining quality of intelligence? If, indeed, the idea of a school will be dramatically altered, what kinds of learning will be neglected, perhaps made impossible? Is virtual reality a new form of therapy? If it is, what are its dangers?

These are serious matters, and they need to be discussed by those who know something about children from the planet Earth, and whose vision of children's needs, and the needs of society, go beyond thinking of school mainly as a place for the convenient distribution of information. Schools are not now and have never been largely about getting information to children. That has been on the schools' agenda, of course, but has always been way down on the list. For technological utopians, the computer vaults information access to the top. This reshuffling of priorities comes at a most inopportune time. The goal of giving people greater access to more information faster, more conveniently and in more diverse forms was the main technological thrust of the nineteenth century. Some folks haven't noticed it but that problem was largely solved, so that for almost a hundred years there has been more information available to the young outside the school than inside. That fact did not make the schools obsolete, nor does it now make them obsolete. Yes, it is true that Little Eva, the insomniac from Mars, could turn on an algebra lesson, thanks to the computer, in the wee hours of the morning. She could also, if she wished, read a book or magazine, watch television, turn on the radio or listen to music. All of this she could have done before the computer. The computer does not solve any problem she has but does exacerbate one. For Little Eva's problem is not how to get access to a well-structured algebra lesson but what to do with all the information available to her during the day, as well as during sleepless nights. Perhaps this is why she couldn't sleep in the first place. Little Eva, like the rest of us, is overwhelmed by information. She lives in a culture that has 260,000 billboards, 17,000 newspapers, 12,000 periodicals, 27,000 video outlets for renting tapes, 400 million television sets, and well over 500 million radios, not including those in automobiles. There are 40,000 new book titles published every year, and each day 41 million photographs are taken. And thanks to the computer, more than 60 billion pieces of advertising junk come into our mailboxes every year. Everything from telegraphy and photography in the nineteenth century to the silicon chip in the twentieth has amplified the din of information intruding on Little Eva's consciousness. From millions of sources all over the globe, through every possible channel and medium—

Nowhere do you find more enthusiasm for the god of Technology than among the educator.

example, McPRETZEL was held to infringe McDonald's family of "Mc" marks. *J & J Snack Foods Corp. v. McDonald's Corp.,* 932 F.2d 1460 (Fed. Cir. 1991).

Similarity of Goods or Services.   Generally, the more similar the goods or services are that are offered under the marks, the less similar the marks need be for confusion to be found, and vice versa. The goods or services need not be identical; confusion may be found if they are related in some manner in that they serve the same purpose, relate to the same activities, or are likely to be encountered by the same types of purchasers. Thus, LAREDO for vehicles was held likely to be confused with LAREDO for tires because both relate to vehicles, *In re Jeep Corp.,* 222 U.S.P.Q. 333 (T.T.A.B. 1984), while LEXUS for vehicles was allowed to register over LEXIS for computer-assisted legal research services (because the goods are unrelated).

In a recently filed case, Kellogg Company sued Exxon Corporation for trademark infringement, alleging that the energy company's tiger character is likely to be confused with Kellogg's "Tony the Tiger" character used to promote food products. Although the two characters had peacefully coexisted for more than thirty years, when Exxon began selling food products at its gasoline/convenience outlets, Kellogg sued for infringement. At the time of writing this text, the litigation is still ongoing.

This type of infringement is often referred to as **progressive encroachment,** meaning that a once permissible use gradually becomes an infringing use. Some departure in business practices or use of the mark has changed a once acceptable use into an infringement. For example, for several years the World Wildlife Fund allowed World Wrestling Federation Entertainment to use the initials WWF for certain purposes. After a period of time, the wrestling group, through extensive television and Internet exposure, began such widespread use of WWF and departure from the parties' original agreement that infringement occurred. After an adverse decision in London, the wrestling group agreed to cease use of WWF and refer to itself as WWE.

In many instances, in infringement lawsuits, when the plaintiff is accused of an undue delay in protecting its mark (the defense of laches, discussed below), the plaintiff responds by alleging progressive encroachment, namely, that it had no duty to initiate an action until the defendant's use moved from the permissible realm to a squarely competitive use.

Courts also consider that parties may extend their product lines at some future time. Thus, the mark THE PALM for pasta would likely be refused on the basis of confusing similarity to THE PALM®, already registered for restaurant services, because restaurants often sell their food products, and consumers, upon encountering THE PALM for pasta, might believe it was associated with the restaurant of the same name.

Channels of Trade.   In determining likelihood of confusion, courts consider to what extent the parties' respective goods or services are distributed through the same trade channels and advertised in the same media. Thus, if products offered under one mark are marketed to wholesalers while those under the other mark are marketed to retailers, there may be little likelihood of confusion because the goods are offered to different classes of purchasers. For example, no likelihood of confusion was found where one party sold computer services under the mark E.D.S. while the other sold power supplies and battery chargers under EDS. Although the marks were nearly identical and both parties sold in the medical field, the plaintiff sold its E.D.S. data processing services to medical insurers while the defendant sold its EDS batteries to makers of medical equipment. Because purchases would be made by different persons in different departments, coexistence of light waves, air waves, ticker tape, computer banks, telephone wires, television cables, satellites, and printing presses — information pours in. Behind it in every imaginable form of storage—on paper, on video, on audiotape, on disks, film, and silicon chips—is an even greater volume of information waiting to be retrieved. In the face of this we might ask, What can schools do for Little Eva besides making still more information available? If there is nothing, then new technologies will indeed make schools obsolete. But in fact, there is plenty.

One thing that comes to mind is that schools can provide her with a seri- 10
ous form of technology education. Something quite different from instruction in using computers to process information, which, it strikes me, is a trivial thing to do, for two reasons. In the first place, approximately 35 million people have already learned how to use computers without the benefit of school instruction. If the schools do nothing, most of the population will know how to use computers in the next ten years, just as most of the population learns how to drive a car without school instruction. In the second place, what we needed to know about cars — as we need to know about computers, television, and other important technologies — is not how to use them but how they use *us*. In the case of cars, what we needed to think about in the early twentieth century was not how to drive them but what they would do to our air, our landscape, our social relations, our family life, and our cities. Suppose in 1946 we had started to address similar questions about television: What will be its effects on our political institutions, our psychic habits, our children, our religious conceptions, our economy? Would we be better positioned today to control TV's massive assault on American culture? I am talking here about making technology itself an object of inquiry so that Little Eva and Young John are more interested in asking questions about the computer than getting answers from it.

I am not arguing against using computers in school. I am arguing against our sleepwalking attitudes toward it, against allowing it to distract us from important things, against making a god of it. This is what Theodore Roszak warned against in *The Cult of Information*: "Like all cults," he wrote, "this one also has the intention of enlisting mindless allegiance and acquiescence. People who have no clear idea of what they mean by information or why they should want so much of it are nonetheless prepared to believe that we live in an information age, which makes every computer around us what the relics of the True Cross were in the age of faith: emblems of salvation." To this, I would add the sage observation of Alan Kay of Apple Computer. Kay is widely associated with the invention of the personal computer, and certainly has an interest in schools using them. Nonetheless, he has repeatedly said that any problems the schools cannot solve without computers, they cannot solve with them. What are some of those problems? There is, for example, the traditional task of teaching children how to behave in groups. One might even say that schools have never been essentially about individualized learning. It is true, of course, that groups do not learn, individuals do. But the idea of a school is that individuals must learn in a setting in which individual needs are subordinated to group interests. Unlike other media of mass communication, which celebrate individual response and are experienced in private, the class-room is intended to tame the ego, to connect the individual with others, to demonstrate the value and necessity of group cohesion. At present, most sce-narios describing the uses of computers have children solving problems alone; Little Eva, Young John, and the others are doing just that. The pres-ence of other children may, indeed, be an annoyance.

Like the printing press before it, the computer has a powerful bias toward amplifying personal autonomy and individual problem solving. That is why educators must guard against computer technology's undermining some of the important reasons for having the young assemble (to quote Ravitch) "in a specific place, for a certain number of hours, and a certain number of days during the week and year."

Although Ravitch is not exactly against what she calls "state schools," she imagines them as something of a relic of a pretechnological age. She believes that the new technologies will offer all children equal access to information. Conjuring up a hypothetical Little Mary who is presumably from a poorer home than Little Eva, Ravitch imagines that Mary will have the same opportunities as Eva "to learn any subject, and to learn it from the same master teachers as children in the richest neighborhood." For all of its liberalizing spirit, this scenario makes some important omissions. One is that though new technologies may be a solution to the learning of "subjects," they work against the learning of what are called "social values," including an understanding of democratic processes. If one reads the first chapter of Robert Fulghum's *All I Really Need to Know I Learned in Kindergarten*, one will find an elegant summary of a few things Ravitch's scenario has left out. They include learning the following lessons: Share everything, play fair, don't hit people, put things back where you found them, clean up your own mess, wash your hands before you eat, and, of course, flush. The only thing wrong with Fulghum's book is that no one has learned all these things at kindergarten's end. We have ample evidence that it takes many years of teaching these values in school before they have been accepted and inter-nalized. That is why it won't do for children to learn in "settings of their own choosing." That is also why schools require children to be in a certain place at a certain time and to follow certain rules, like raising their hands when they wish to speak, not talking when others are talking, not chewing gum, not leaving until the bell rings, exhibiting patience toward slower learners, etc. This process is called making civilized people. The god of Technology does not appear interested in this function of schools. At least, it does not come up much when technology's virtues are enumerated.

The god of Technology may also have a trick or two up its sleeve about something else. It is often asserted that new technologies will equalize learning opportunities for the rich and poor. It is devoutly to be wished for, but I doubt it will happen. In the first place, it is generally understood by those who have studied the history of technology that technological change always produces winners and losers. There are many reasons for this, among them economic differences. Even in the case of the automobile, which is a commodity most people can buy (although not all), there are wide differences between the rich and poor in the quality of what is available to them. It would be quite astonishing if computer technology equalized all learning opportunities, irrespective of economic differences. One may be delighted that Little Eva's parents could afford the technology and software to make it possible for her to learn algebra at midnight. But Little Mary's parents may not be able to, may not even know such things are available. And if we say that the school could make the technology available to Little Mary (at least during the day), there may be something else Little Mary is lacking.

It turns out, for example, that Little Mary may be having sleepless nights ¹⁵ as frequently as Little Eva but not because she wants to get a leg up on her algebra. Maybe because she doesn't know who her father is, or, if she does, where he is. Maybe we can understand why McIntosh's kid is bored with the real world. Or is the child confused about it? Or terrified? Are there educators who seriously believe that these problems can be addressed by new technologies?

I do not say, of course, that schools can solve the problems of poverty, alienation, and family disintegration, but schools can *respond* to them. And they can do this because there are people in them, because these people are concerned with more than algebra lessons or modern Japanese history, and because these people can identify not only one's level of competence in math but one's level of rage and confusion and depression. I am talking here about children as they really come to us, not children who are invented to show us how computers may enrich their lives. Of course, I suppose it is possible that there are children who, waking at night, want to study algebra or who are so interested in their world that they yearn to know about Japan. If there be such children, and one hopes there are, they do not require expensive computers to satisfy their hunger for learning. They are on their way, with or without computers. Unless, of course, they do not care about others or have no friends, or little respect for democracy or are filled with suspicion about those who are not like them. When we have machines that know how to do something about these problems, that is the time to rid ourselves of the expensive burden of schools or to reduce the function of teachers to "coaches" in the uses of machines (as Ravitch envisions). Until then, we must be more modest about this god of Technology and certainly not pin our hopes on it.

We must also, I suppose, be empathetic toward those who search with good intentions for technological panaceas. I am a teacher myself and know how hard it is to contribute to the making of a civilized person. Can we blame those who want to find an easy way, through the agency of technology? Perhaps not. After all, it is an old quest. As early as 1918, H. L. Mencken° (although completely devoid of empathy) wrote, "There is no sure-cure so idiotic that some superintendent of schools will not swallow it. The aim seems to be to reduce the whole teaching process to a sort of automatic reaction, to discover some master formula that will not only take the place of competence and resourcefulness in the teacher but that will also create an artificial receptivity in the child."

Mencken was not necessarily speaking of technological panaceas but he may well have been. In the early 1920s a teacher wrote the following poem:

Mr. Edison says
That the radio will supplant the teacher.
Already one may learn languages by means of Victrola records.
The moving picture will visualize
What the radio fails to get across.
Teachers will be relegated to the backwoods,
With fire-horses,
And long-haired women;
Or, perhaps shown in museums.
Education will become a matter
Of pressing the button.
Perhaps I can get a position at the switchboard.

I do not go as far back as the radio and Victrola, but I am old enough to remember when 16-millimeter film was to be the sure-cure. Then closed-circuit television. Then 8-millimeter film. Then teacher-proof textbooks. Now computers.

I know a false god when I see one.   20

Working with the Text

1. In arguing for his view of education, Neil Postman pits what he considers to be the limitations of technology against the "process" of "making civilized people." In a brief essay, argue for or against Postman's stance. Do you agree with

---

H. L. Mencken: Henry Louis Mencken (1880–1956) was a journalist, satirist, and social critic often regarded as one of the most influential writers in the early twentieth century.

his assessment of technology-based learning? Do you think schools do, or should, focus on the kinds of socialization he promotes? Why or why not?

2. Postman opens his essay by asserting that in our culture technology has become a god. He refers to the godlike nature of technology throughout the essay, ending with the assertion, "I know a false god when I see one" (par. 20). Review the first four paragraphs of the essay. In a small group, debate the questions Postman poses to his students. Drawing on your debate, write a brief essay in which you reflect on Postman's use of *god* in making his argument. How does it contribute to the argument? Why does he place so much emphasis on it? Do you agree that we treat technology as a god?

3. When Postman asserts that what we need to know about technologies is "not how to use them but how they use *us*" (par. 10), he is referring to cars and television as well as computers. Throughout the essay, he draws on history to make his argument. In a brief essay, analyze his comparisons of computers to earlier technologies. What characteristics does Postman claim that the technologies have in common? What does he want us to learn from our culture's attitudes toward earlier technologies? What does he mean by the phrase, "how they use *us*"?

From Text to Field

1. In his essay, Postman examines technology-based education through the lenses of educators and administrators. In a personal essay, examine your experience of and relationship to technology as a tool for learning. Possible approaches to your essay include the following:

   - Compare how you have used technology for completing school assignments to how you have used it for pursuing subject matter you have chosen for yourself.
   - Compare your experience of learning through technology to learning through traditional teaching methods.
   - Compare your use of technology in a school setting to your use of it outside of school.

2. Throughout the essay, Postman challenges the descriptions of "Little Eva" and "Young John" envisioned by Dr. Diane Ravitch, former assistant secretary of education. When Little Eva cannot sleep, she goes to her computer to learn algebra. Young John takes it upon himself to learn the history of modern Japan by "dialing up the greatest authorities and teachers on the subject" (par. 4). Based on your observations of real school-age people — and awareness of your own behaviors — write your own "Little Eva" or "Young John" scenario.

3. Postman claims that "[s]chools are not now and have never been largely about getting information to children" (par. 9). With Postman's analysis of schools in mind, write a personal essay in which you explore what your own experience of school has been "largely about."

4. Referring to the fictional characters Little Eva and Young John in the scenarios posed by proponents of technology-based learning, Postman insists that "[a]t the very least, what we need to discuss . . . is what they will lose, and what we will lose, if they enter a world in which computer technology is their chief source of motivation, authority, and, apparently, psychological sustenance" (par. 8). In a small group, discuss this question. Based on your discussion, develop a brief presentation for the entire class in which you postulate "what we will lose" or in which, rebutting Postman, you clarify what we will gain that offsets such losses.

Bringing Familiar Baggage to the New Frontier: Gender Differences in Computer-Mediated Communication

Susan Herring

When network technology ushered in online discussion groups, enthusiasts regarded computer-mediated communication (CMC) as highly democratic. The claim was that everyone could participate as equals, without regard to social standing, race, or gender. Susan Herring was among the first to observe that gender differences in styles of CMC actually tended to extend the gender inequalities found off-line. Based on online surveys as well as her study of a number of computer-mediated discussion lists, Herring concluded that differences in communication style were driven by differences in values. She found that males and females typically held conflicting views of what constitutes a productive online discussion.

Herring is a professor of information science and linguistics at Indiana University, where she is a fellow at the Center for Social Informatics and at the Center for Research on Learning and Technology. Her recent research has focused on media and technology and their influence on the evolution of language, with an emphasis on issues related to gender. Among her numerous publications are *Computer-Mediated Conversation* (2004) and *Computer-Mediated ommunication: Linguistic, Social, and Cross-Cultural Perspectives* (1996). She has also edited several special issues of leading journals, the most recent being *The Multilingual Internet: Language, Culture, and Communication in Instant Messaging, E-mail, and Chat*, a special 2003 issue of the *Journal of Computer-Mediated*

Communication. Herring's essay was originally delivered as a speech in June 1994 at a meeting of the American Library Association, as part of a panel entitled "Making the Net*Work*."

Introduction

Although research on computer-mediated communication (CMC) dates back to the early days of computer network technology in the 1970s, researchers have only recently begun to take the gender of users into account.[1] This is perhaps not surprising considering that men have traditionally dominated the technology and have comprised the majority of users of computer networks since their inception, but the result is that most of what has been written about CMC incorporates a very one-sided perspective. However, recent research has been uncovering some eye-opening differences in the ways men and women interact "online," and it is these differences that I will address here.

My basic claim has two parts: first, that women and men have recognizably different styles in posting electronic messages to the Internet, contrary to claims that CMC neutralizes distinctions of gender, and second, that women and men have different communication ethics — that is, they value different kinds of online interactions as appropriate and desirable. I illustrate these differences — and some of the problems that arise because of them — with specific reference to the phenomenon of "flaming."

Background

Since 1991 I've been lurking (or what I prefer to call "carrying out ethnographic observation") on various computer-mediated discussion lists, downloading electronic conversations and analyzing the communicative behaviors of participants. I became interested in gender shortly after subscribing to my first discussion list, LINGUIST-L, an academic forum for professional linguists. Within the first month after I began receiving messages, a conflict arose on the list (what I would later learn to call a "flame war") in which the two major theoretical camps within the field became polarized around an issue of central interest. My curiosity was piqued by the fact that very few women were contributing to this important professional event; they seemed to be sitting on the sidelines while men were airing their opinions and getting all the attention. In an attempt to understand the women's silence, I made up an anonymous survey which I sent to LINGUIST-L asking subscribers what they thought of the discussion and, if they hadn't contributed, why not.

Initial Observations

The number one reason given by both men and women for not contributing to the LINGUIST discussion was "intimidation" — as one respondent commented, participants were "ripping each other's lungs out." Interestingly, however, men and women responded differently to feeling intimidated. Men seemed to accept such behavior as a normal feature of academic life, making comments to the effect that "Actually, the barbs and arrows were entertaining, because of course they weren't aimed at me." In contrast, many women responded with profound aversion. As one woman put it: "That is precisely the kind of human interaction I committedly avoid. . . . I am dismayed that human beings treat each other this way. It makes the world a dangerous place to be. I dislike such people and I want to give them WIDE berth."

When I analyzed the messages in the thread itself, another gender difference emerged, this time relating to the linguistic structure and rhetoric of the messages. A daunting 68 percent of the messages posted by men made use of an adversarial style in which the poster distanced himself from, criticized, and/or ridiculed other participants, often while promoting his own importance. The few women who participated in the discussion, in contrast, displayed features of attenuation—hedging, apologizing, asking questions rather than making assertions—and a personal orientation, revealing thoughts and feelings and interacting with and supporting others.

It wasn't long before I was noticing a similar pattern in other discussions and on other lists. Wherever I went on mixed-sex lists, men seemed to be doing most of the talking and attracting most of the attention to themselves, although not all lists were as adversarial as LINGUIST. I started to hear stories about and witness men taking over and dominating discussions even of women-centered topics on women-centered lists.[2] In contrast, on the few occasions when I observed women attempting to gain an equal hearing on male-dominated lists, they were ignored, trivialized, or criticized by men for their tone or the inappropriateness of their topic.[3] It wasn't until I started looking at lists devoted to women's issues, and to traditionally "feminized" disciplines such as women's studies, teaching English as a second language, and librarianship, that I found women holding forth in an amount consistent with their numerical presence on the list. I also found different interactional norms: little or no flaming, and cooperative, polite exchanges.

Different Styles

As a result of these findings, I propose that women and men have different characteristic online styles. By characteristic styles, I do not mean that all or even the majority of users of each sex exhibit the behaviors of each style, but rather that the styles are recognizably—even stereotypically—gendered. The male style is characterized by adversariality: put-downs, strong, often contentious assertions, lengthy and/or frequent postings, self-promotion, and sarcasm. Below are two examples, one from an academic list (LINGUIST) and the other from a nonacademic list (POLITICS).[4]

1. [Jean Linguiste's] proposals towards a more transparent morphology in French are exactly what he calls them: a farce. Nobody could ever take them seriously — unless we want to look as well at pairs such as *pe`re - me`re*, *coq - poule* and defigure the French language in the process.

[strong assertions ("exactly," "nobody"), put-downs ("JL's proposals are a farce"; implied: "JL wants to defigure the French language")]

2. >yes, they did . . . This is why we must be allowed to remain armed
. . .
>who is going to help us if our government becomes a tyranny?
>no one will.

oh yes we *must* remain armed. anyone see day one last night abt charlestown where everyone/s so scared of informing on murderers the cops have given up? where the reply to any offense is a public killing? knowing you/re not gonna be caught cause everyone/s to afraid to be a witness?

yeah, right, twerp.

> — [RON) "THE WISE"—

what a joke.

[sarcasm, name calling, personal insults]

The second example would be characterized as a "flame" by most readers because of its personally offensive nature.

Less exclusively male-gendered but still characteristic of male postings is an authoritative, self-confident stance whereby men are more likely than women to represent themselves as experts, e.g., in answering queries for information. The following example is from NOTIS-L.

3. The NUGM Planning meeting was canceled before all of this came up. It has nothing to do with it. The plans were simply proceeding along so well that there was no need to hold the meeting. That is my understanding from talking to NOTIS staff just last week.

[authoritative tone, strong assertions ("nothing," "simply," "just")]

The female-gendered style, in contrast, has two aspects which typically co-occur: supportiveness and attenuation. "Supportiveness" is characterized by expressions of appreciation, thanking, and community-building activities that make other participants feel accepted and welcome. "Attenuation" includes hedging and expressing doubt, apologizing, asking questions, and contributing the marks was unlikely to cause confusion. *Electronic Design & Sales Inc. v. Electronic Data Systems Corp.,* 954 F.2d 713 (Fed. Cir. 1992).

Consumer Care and Sophistication. In determining trademark infringement, everything hinges on whether there is a likelihood of confusion in the mind of an appreciable number of reasonably prudent buyers. The price level of the goods or services is an important factor in determining the amount of care the buyer will use. If the goods or services are relatively expensive, more care is taken and buyers are less likely to be confused. Thus, purchasers of inexpensive items such as snack foods and sodas, which are purchased on impulse, do not give much care to such purchases and are more likely to be confused by items that bear similar marks. If the goods are expensive, however, the discriminating purchaser does not purchase casually or on impulse but only after thoughtful consideration. Thus, confusion is less likely than where the goods are inexpensive.

Strength of Marks. "Strong" marks are afforded greater protection than weak marks. Thus, marks that are coined, fanciful, or arbitrary are given greater weight than marks that are suggestive, descriptive, or generic. MUCKY DUCK (& DESIGN) for mustard was held confusingly similar to MUCKY DUCK for restaurant services primarily because MUCKY DUCK was viewed as a unique and memorable mark. *In re Mucky Duck Mustard Co.,* 6 U.S.P.Q.2d 1467 (T.T.A.B. 1988). Thus, the marks EXXON® and XEROX® are given a broad scope of protection inasmuch as these coined or made-up marks had no meaning before their owners built up or developed goodwill in them. Nevertheless, even weak marks are entitled to protection against similar marks for closely related goods or services.

Actual Confusion. Actual confusion is not required to support a case for trademark infringement; the standard is likelihood of con-

fusion. It is unnecessary to show actual confusion to establish likelihood of confusion. However, plaintiffs who can demonstrate that some significant level of actual confusion has already occurred in the marketplace generally prevail in trademark infringement cases. Conversely, if the marks have coexisted for a number of years with no confusion, such is strongly suggestive that confusion is not likely.

Plaintiffs establish actual confusion in two ways: through testimony by consumers who have been confused about the products and by survey evidence. In the first instance, a party's initial knowledge that a competing mark is in the marketplace and is causing confusion may come about through complaint letters from consumers, misdirected orders, or inquiries and e-mail and telephone calls sent to the wrong party. If, however, evidence shows that only a few purchasers were confused, such supports a finding that confusion may be unlikely. For example, when determining that SCOTT® (for paper products) and SCOTT'S LIQUID GOLD® (for furniture polish) were unlikely to be confused, the court noted that only nineteen misdirected letters had been received even though some 50 million cans of the furniture polish had been sold during the relevant period. *Scott Paper Co. v. Scott's Liquid Gold,* 589 F.2d 1225 (3d Cir. 1978).

A plaintiff may also demonstrate actual confusion by survey evidence, namely, surveys conducted by experts to determine whether confusion of consumers is likely. However, flaws in survey methodology, the types of questions asked, and the failure to survey the proper universe of purchasers may dilute the impact of a survey.

Existence of Other Similar Marks. If numerous other marks that are similar to the alleged infringer's mark coexist with the plaintiff's mark, this may be evidence that confusion is unlikely. Defendants thus often conduct comprehensive searches to demonstrate that the ideas in the form of suggestions. The following examples from a nonacademic list (WOMEN) and an academic list (TESL-L) illustrate each aspect:

4. >[AILEEN],
   >
   >I just wanted to let you know that I have really enjoyed all
   >your posts about Women's herstory. They have been
   >extremely informative and I've learned alot about the
   >women's movement. Thank you!
   >
   >— [ERIKA]

   DITTO!!!! They are wonderful!

   Did anyone else catch the first part of a Century of Women? I really enjoyed it. Of course, I didn't agree with everything they said. . . . but it was really informative.
   [ROBERTA]~~~~~~~~~~~~~~~~~~~~~~~~~~~~~~~~~~~~

   [appreciates, thanks, agrees, appeals to group]

5 [. . .] I hope this makes sense. This is kind of what I had in mind when I realized I couldn't give a real definitive answer. Of course, maybe I'm just getting into the nuances of the language when it would be easier to just give the simple answer. Any response?

   [hedges, expresses doubt, appeals to group]

The female style takes into consideration what the sociologist Erving [10] Goffman called the "face" wants of the addressee — specifically, the desire of the addressee to feel ratified and liked (e.g., by expressions of appreciation) and her desire not to be imposed upon (e.g., by absolute assertions that don't allow for alternative views). The male style, in contrast, confronts and threatens the addressee's "face" in the process of engaging him in agonistic debate.

Although these styles represent in some sense the extremes of gendered behavior, they have symbolic significance above and beyond their frequency of use. For example, other users regularly infer the gender of message posters on the basis of features of these styles, especially when the self-identified gender of a poster is open to question. Consider the following cases, the first involving a male posting as a female, the second a suspected female posting as a male:

i. A male subscriber on SWIP-L (Society for Women in Philosophy list) posted a message disagreeing with the general consensus that discourse on SWIP-L should be nonagonistic, commenting, "There's nothing like a healthy denunciation by one's colleagues every once in a while to get one's blood flowing, and spur one to greater subtlety and exactness of thought." He signed his message with a female pseudonym, however, causing another (female) subscriber to comment later, "I must confess to looking for the name of the male who wrote the posting that [Suzi] sent originally and was surprised to find a female name at the end of it." The female subscriber had (accurately) inferred that anyone actively advocating "denunciation by one's colleagues" was probably male.

ii. At a time when one male subscriber had been posting frequent messages to the WOMEN list, another subscriber professing to be a man posted a message inquiring what the list's policy was towards men participating on the list, admitting, "I sometimes feel guilty for taking up bandwidth." The message, in addition to showing consideration for the concerns of others on the list, was very attenuated in style and explicitly appreciative of the list: "I really enjoy this list (actually, it's the best one I'm on)." This prompted another (female) subscriber to respond, "Now that you've posed the question . . . how's one to know you're not a woman posing this question as a man?" Her suspicion indicates that on some level she recognized that anyone posting a message expressing appreciation and consideration for the desires of others was likely to be female.

The existence of gendered styles has important implications, needless to say, for popular claims that CMC is anonymous, "gender blind," and hence inherently democratic. If our online communicative style reveals our gender, then gender differences, along with their social consequences, are likely to persist on computer-mediated networks.[5]

Entire lists can be gendered in their style as well. It is tacitly expected that members of the nondominant gender will adapt their posting style in the direction of the style of the dominant gender. Thus men on women's special interest lists tend to attenuate their assertions and shorten their messages, and women, especially on male-dominated lists such as LINGUIST and PAGLIA-L, can be contentious and adversarial. Arguably, they must adapt in order to participate appropriately in keeping with the norms of the local list culture. Most members of the nondominant gender on any given list, however, end up style mixing, that is, taking on some attributes of the dominant style while preserving features of their native style— for example, with men often preserving a critical stance and women a supportive one at the macromessage level. This suggests that gendered communication styles are deeply rooted— not surprising, since they are learned early in life — and that some features are more resistant to conscious reflection and modification than others.

Different Communication Ethics

The second part of this essay concerns the value systems that underlie and are used to rationalize communicative behavior on the Net. In particular, I focus on the phenomenon of flaming, which has been variously defined as "the expression of strong negative emotion," use of "derogatory, obscene, or inappropriate language," and "personal insults." A popular explanation advanced by CMC researchers[6] is that flaming is a by-product of the medium itself — the decontextualized and anonymous nature of CMC leads to "disinhibition in users and a tendency to forget that there is an actual human being at the receiving end of one's emotional outbursts. However, until recently CMC research has largely overlooked gender as a possible influence on behavior, and the simple fact of the matter is that it is virtually only men who flame. If the medium makes men more likely to flame, it should have a similar effect on women, yet if anything the opposite appears to be the case. An adequate explanation of flaming must therefore take gender into account.

Women and men constitute different discourse communities in cyberspace.

Why do men flame? The explanation, I suggest, is that women and men have different communication ethics, and flaming is compatible with male ethical ideals. I stumbled upon this realization recently as a result of a survey I conducted on politeness on the Internet. I originally hypothesized that the differences in the extremes of male and female behavior online — in particular, the tendency for women to be considerate of the "face" needs of others while men threaten others' "face" — could be explained if it turned out that women and men have different notions of what constitutes appropriate behavior. In other words, as a woman I might think adversarial behavior is rude, but men who behave adversarially might think otherwise. Conversely, men might be put off by the supportive and attenuated behaviors of women.

In the survey, I asked subscribers from eight Internet discussion lists to rank their like or dislike for 30 different online behaviors, including "flaming," "expressing thanks and appreciation," and "overly tentative messages," on a scale of 1 (like) to 5 (dislike). The survey also asked several open-ended questions, including most importantly: "What behaviors bother you most on the Net?"

My initial hypothesis turned out to be both correct and incorrect. It was incorrect in that I found no support whatsoever for the idea that men's and women's value systems are somehow reversed. Both men and women said they liked expressions of appreciation (avg. score of 2), were neutral about tentative messages (avg. about 3), and disliked flaming (although women expressed a stronger dislike than men, giving it a score of 4.3 as compared with only 3.9 for men). This makes male flaming behavior all the more puzzling. Should we conclude, then, that men who flame are deliberately trying to be rude?

The answers to the open-ended questions suggest a different explanation. These answers reveal a gender contrast in values that involves politeness but cannot be described in terms of politeness alone. It seems women place a high value on consideration for the wants and needs of others, as expressed in the following comment by a female Net user:

> If we take responsibility for developing our own sensitivities to others and controlling our actions to minimize damage—we will each be doing [good deeds] for the whole world constantly.

Men, in contrast, assign greater value to freedom from censorship (many advocate absolute free speech), forthright and open expression, and agonistic debate as a means to advance the pursuit of knowledge. Historically, the value on absolute freedom of speech reflects the civil libertarian leanings of the computing professionals who originally designed the Net and have contributed much of the utopian discourse surrounding it; the value on agonistic debate is rooted in the Western (male) philosophical tradition.

These ideals are stirringly evoked in the following quote from R. Hauben (1993) praising the virtues of the Usenet system, on which 95 percent of the contributors are estimated to be male:

> The achievement of Usenet News demonstrates the importance of facilitating the development of uncensored speech and communication—there is debate and discussion — one person influences another — people build on each other's strengths and interests, differences, etc.

One might think that uncensored speech if abused could cause problems, but M. Hauben (1993) explains that there is a democratic way of handling this eventuality:

> When people feel someone is abusing the nature of Usenet News, they let the offender know through e-mail. In this manner . . . people fight to keep it a resource that is helpful to society as a whole.

In daily life on the Internet, however, the ideal of "people fight[ing] to keep [the Net] a resource that is helpful to society as a whole" often translates into violent action. Consider, for example, the response of a male survey respondent to the question: "What behaviors bother you most on the Net?" (typos are in the original):

> As much as I am irritated by [incompetent posters], I don't want imposed rules. I would prefer to "out" such a person and let some public minded citizen fire bomb his house to imposing rules on the Net. Letter bombing a annoying individual's feed is usually preferable to building a formal heirarchy of Net cops.

Another Net vigilante responds graphically as follows:

> I'd have to say commercial shit. Whenever someone advertises some damn get-rich-quick scheme and plasters it all over the Net by crossposting it to

every newsgroup, I reach for my "gatling gun mailer crasher" and fire away at the source address.

These responses not only evoke an ideal of freedom from external author- 20 ity, they provide an explicit justification for flaming — as a form of self-appointed regulation of the social order, a rough-and-ready form of justice on the virtual frontier. Thus a framework of values is constructed within which flaming and other aggressive behaviors can be interpreted in a favorable (even prosocial) light. This is not to say that all or even most men who flame have the good of Net society at heart, but rather that the behavior is in principle justifiable for men (and hence tolerable) in ways that it is not for most women.

Netiquette

Further evidence that flaming is tolerated and justified within a system of male values comes from the content of written rules of network etiquette, or "netiquette," such as are available on many public FTP sites and in introductory messages to new members of some discussion lists. I analyzed the content of netiquette rules from six lists, along with those found in the guidelines for Usenet and in the print publication *Towards an Ethics and Etiquette for Electronic Mail*, by Norman Shapiro and Robert Anderson (1985). What do netiquette rules have to say about flaming?

The answer is: remarkably little, given that it is one of the most visible and frequently complained about "negatives" cited about the Internet. One might even say there is a striking *lack* of proscription against flaming, except on a few women-owned and women-oriented lists. And in the rare instances where flaming is mentioned, it is implicitly authorized. Thus the guidelines for new subscribers to the POLITICS list prohibit "flames of a personal nature," and Shapiro and Anderson advise, "Do not insult or criticize third parties without giving them a chance to respond." While on the surface appearing to oppose flaming, these statements in fact implicitly authorize "flames other than of a personal nature" (for example, of someone's ideas or values) and "insulting or criticizing third parties" (provided you give them a chance to respond!). Normative statements such as these are compatible with male values and male adversarial style; the intimidating rhetoric on LINGUIST and many other lists is not a violation of Net etiquette according to these rules.[7] Yet these are behaviors that female survey respondents say intimidate them and drive them away from lists and newsgroups. Can the Internet community afford to tolerate behaviors that intimidate and silence women? This is a question that urgently needs to be raised and discussed Net wide.

Conclusions

To sum up, I have argued that women and men constitute different discourse communities in cyberspace — different cultures, if you will — with differing communicative norms and practices. However, these cultures are not "separate but equal," as recent popular writing on gender differences in communication has claimed. Rather, the norms and practices of masculine Net culture, codified in netiquette rules, conflict with those of the female culture in ways that render cyberspace — or at least many "neighborhoods" in cyberspace — inhospitable to women. The result is an imbalance whereby men control a disproportionate share of the communication that takes place via computer networks.

This imbalance must be redressed if computer-mediated communication is ever to live up to its much-touted democratic potential. Fortunately, there are ways in which women can promote their concerns and influence the discourse of the Net;[8] I will mention three here. First and foremost is to participate, for example in women-centered lists. Such lists provide supportive fora for women online and are frequently models of cooperative discourse whose norms can spread if subscribers participate in other lists as well. But separatism has its disadvantages, among them the risk of ghettoization. Women must not let themselves be driven by flame throwers away from mainstream, mixed-sex fora, but rather should also actively seek to gain influence there, individually and collectively, especially in fora where metadiscourse about the Net itself takes place.

The second way to promote women's interests Netwide is to educate online communities about the rhetorical strategies used in intimidating others, and to call people on their behavior and its consequences when they use such strategies.[9] This is already happening on some women-centered lists such as WMST-L and SWIP-L — aware of the tendency for a single man or group of men to dominate discussions, female subscribers call attention to this behavior as soon as they realize it is happening; interestingly, it is happening less and less often on these lists. Group awareness is a powerful force for change, and it can be raised in mixed-sex fora as well.

Finally, women need to contribute in any way they can to the process that leads to the encoding of netiquette rules. They need to instigate and participate persuasively in discussions about what constitutes appropriate and inappropriate behavior online — seeking to define in concrete terms what constitutes "flaming," for instance, since women and men are likely to have different ideas about this. They must be alert to opportunities (or make their own opportunities) to write out guidelines for suggested list protocol (or modifications to list protocol if guidelines already exist) and post them for discussion. No greater power exists than the power to define values, and the structure of the

Internet— especially now, while it is still evolving and seeking its ultimate definition —provides a unique opportunity for individual users to influence the normative process.

Indeed, it may be vital that we do so if women's online communication styles are to be valued along with those of men, and if we are to insure women the right to settle on the virtual frontier on their own — rather than on male-defined —terms.

Notes

This essay was originally delivered as a speech to the American Library Association as part of a panel entitled "Making the Net*Work*: Is there a Z39.50 in gender communication?", Miami, June 27, 1994. Copyright rests with the author.

1. A notable exception to this generalization is the work of Sherry Turkle in the 1980s on how women and men relate to computers.

2. For an extreme example of this phenomenon that took place on the soc.feminism Usenet newsgroup, see Sutton (1994).

3. Herring, Johnson, and DiBenedetto (1992, in press).

4. All names mentioned in the messages are pseudonyms.

5. This problem is discussed in Herring (1993a).

6. For example, Kiesler et al. (1984), Kim and Raja (1990), and Shapiro and Anderson (1985).

7. The discussion of politeness and communication ethics here is an abbreviated version of that presented in Herring (In press a, In press b).

8. For other practical suggestions on how to promote gender equality in networking, see Kramarae and Taylor (1993).

9. Cases where this was done, both successfully and unsuccessfully, are described in Herring, Johnson & DiBenedetto (In press).

References

Hauben, Michael. 1993. "The social forces behind the development of Usenet News." Electronic document. (FTP weber.ucsd.edu, directory/pub/usenet.hist)

Hauben, Ronda. 1993. "The evolution of Usenet News: The poor man's ARPANET." Electronic document. (FTP weber.ucsd.edu, directory/pub/usenet.hist)

Herring, Susan. 1992. "Gender and participation in computer-mediated linguistic discourse." Washington, DC: ERIC Clearinghouse on Languages and Linguistics, document no. ED345552.

Herring, Susan. 1993a. "Gender and democracy in computer-mediated communication." *Electronic Journal of Communication* 3(2), special issue on Computer-Mediated Communication, T. Benson, ed. Reprinted in R. Kling (ed.), *Computerization and Controversy*, 2nd ed. New York: Academic (In press).

Herring, Susan. 1993b. "Men's language: A study of the discourse of the Linguist list." In A. Crochetihre, J. -C. Boulanger, and C. Ouellon (eds.), *Les Langues Menacies: Actes du XVe Congres International des Linguistes*, Vol. 3. Quebec: Les Presses de l'Université Laval, 347–350.

Herring, Susan. In press a. "Politeness in computer culture: Why women thank and men flame." In M. Bucholtz, A. Liang, and L. Sutton (eds.), *Communicating In, Through, and Across Cultures: Proceedings of the Third Berkeley Women and Language Conference.* Berkeley Women and Language Group.

Herring, Susan. In press b. "Posting in a different voice: Gender and ethics in computer-mediated communication." In C. Ess (ed.), *Philosophical Perspectives on Computer-Mediated Communication.* Albany: SUNY Press.

Herring, Susan. In press c. "Two variants of an electronic message schema." In S. Herring (ed.), *Computer-Mediated Communication: Linguistic, social, and cross-cultural perspectives.* Amsterdam/Philadelphia: John Benjamins.

Herring, Susan, Deborah Johnson, and Tamra DiBenedetto. 1992. "Participation in electronic discourse in a 'feminist' field." In M. Bucholtz, K. Hall, and B. Moonwomon, eds., *Locating Power: Proceedings of the Second Berkeley Women and Language Conference.* Berkeley Women and Language Group.

Herring, Susan, Deborah Johnson, and Tamra DiBenedetto. In press d. "'This discussion is going too far!' Male resistance to female participation on the Internet." In M. Bucholtz and K. Hall, eds., *Gender Articulated: Language and the Socially-Constructed Self.* New York: Routledge.

Kiesler, Sara, Jane Seigel, and Timothy W. McGuire. 1984. "Social psychological aspects of computer-mediated communication." *American Psychologist,* 39, 1123–34.

Kim, Min-Sun, and Narayan S. Raja. 1990. "Verbal aggression and self-disclosure on computer bulletin boards." ERIC document (ED334620).

Kramarae, Cheris, and H. Jeanie Taylor. 1993. "Women and men on electronic networks: A conversation or a monologue?" In Taylor, Kramarae, and Ebben, eds., *Women, Information Technology and Scholarship,* 52–61. Urbana, IL: Center for Advanced Study.

Rheingold, Howard. 1993. *The Virtual Community: Homesteading on the Electronic Frontier.* Reading, MA: Addison-Wesley.

Seabrook, John. 1994. "My first flame." *The New Yorker,* June 6, 1994, 70–79.

Shapiro, Norman Z., and Robert H. Anderson. 1985. *Toward an Ethics and Etiquette for Electronic Mail.* The Rand Corporation.

Sutton, Laurel. 1994. "Using USENET: Gender, power, and silencing in electronic discourse." *Proceedings of the 20th Annual Meeting of the Berkeley Linguistics Society* (BLS-20). Berkeley: Berkeley Linguistics Society, Inc.

Turkle, Sherry. 1984. *The Second Self: Computers and the Human Spirit.* London: Granada.

Working with the Text

1. In the "Conclusions" section of her article, Susan Herring implies that the female style of computer-mediated communication (CMC) is preferable to the male style. Write a brief essay in which you analyze her position, arguing for or against it. What characteristics of the female style does she value? What characteristics of the male style does she think should be changed? Why? Do you agree with her? Why or why not?

2. Herring calls into question what she refers to as the "popular claims that CMC is anonymous, 'gender blind,' and hence inherently democratic" (par. 11). Based on your inferences from, as well as direct assertions in, the essay, analyze her argument. What about CMC does she consider to be undemocratic? What does her position on equality in communication reveal about her values?
3. To examine male and female styles in CMC, Herring analyzes messages she has found on online discussion lists. To test the currency of her analysis, find an online discussion list. Based on Herring's descriptions of gender differences in CMC, analyze the messages, using her examples as models. Develop your analysis into a brief paper. Prepare to share your findings with the entire class.

From Text to Field

1. By the time you enter college, many of you have participated in online discussions or chat rooms. With Herring's analysis of gender styles in mind, write a personal essay in which you describe your experience with computer-mediated communication (CMC). Have you noticed or have you yourself used some of the discourse features that Herring mentions in her article? If you have not participated in an online discussion, interview someone who has, first explaining Herring's arguments as a point of reference.
2. Review Herring's "Netiquette" section as well as her "Conclusions," where she discusses the need for protocols (etiquette and behavior guidelines) for computer-mediated communication. In a small group, draft a list protocol for a discussion group, then post it for discussion by sending it via e-mail or other electronic means to one other small group from the class. Individually, write a list protocol based on those online discussions. How would such a protocol differ from a protocol for effective in-class discussions? What makes communication that is not face-to-face more challenging to understand, maintain, and regulate?
3. After arguing that male styles of computer-mediated communication can exclude women, Herring raises the question, "Can the Internet community afford to tolerate behaviors that intimidate and silence women?" (par. 22). With Herring's descriptions of gender styles in mind, write an essay in which you answer this question from your own perspective.
4. In calling upon women to "promote their concerns and influence the discourse of the Net," Herring observes that "[no] greater power exists than the power to define values" (par. 26). In an essay, apply this statement to a situation from your own experience involving communication—online or off-line—in which you were either subject to someone else's values regarding acceptable styles of communication or able to participate in defining those values.

INTO THE FIELD: Options for Writing Projects

1. Facebook Culture on Your Campus

Although Facebook is widely used at colleges and universities across the country, each institution has what might be called its own "Facebook culture." For this field project, describe and assess the Facebook culture on your campus. Has that culture evolved over time, perhaps in response to concerns or incidents? What administrative policies (if any) are in place, and how does the administration view Facebook? Feel free to draw on national discussions about Facebook, but be sure to ground your assessment in the specifics of Facebook use on your particular campus.

2. Local Community Networks

When we consider community building through virtual means, we might easily think of worldwide communities or far-flung, but like-minded, people brought together by technology. But technology can also extend and augment the bond of local communities that already have some face-to-face social networking in place. This project invites you to explore one particular local community network. Such a network can function as part of local government; a civic or public interest group; a school or other local educational institution; a religious, arts, or recreational group; or most any other kind of citizen-based community information system.

For your own fieldwork, choose an online civic network that is functioning in your hometown or in the town where you now go to college, ideally a network in which you are already involved or in which you might have an interest. Your task is to evaluate the effectiveness of this online network in fostering stronger community.

You may wish to consider how such a network contributes to the presence of a public space for that group, how it might encourage discussion and deliberation in ways not possible by face-to-face meetings alone, and how such a civic network both relies on and contributes to social capital (that is, the trust and reciprocity needed to maintain community). How does the civic network you have chosen encourage deliberation on shared issues, expand participation, and develop local culture, pride, and community ownership? You may also wish to analyze why a particular civic network may fall short of those goals, despite the best of intentions.

As you conduct your fieldwork, you may wish to do more than navigate and analyze a Web site or electronic discussion list. Consider interviewing some of the key leaders in that civic network to learn more about the history of the group, its mission, and its reasons for developing an online presence of its members. You may even wish to query members on that very network about

621

field is crowded and that numerous other marks all coexist with the plaintiff's mark. For example, in Arizona, marks including the term *Desert* are common, and the owner of a restaurant operating under the mark DESERT SUN might have a difficult time persuading a court that a bar called the DESERT STAR infringes his or her mark. When numerous similar marks coexist, consumers often become adept in distinguishing those marks from each other. Thus, even the slight differences between DESERT STAR and DESERT SUN may be sufficient to obviate confusion when numerous "Desert" marks coexist. In fact, in *Sun Banks of Florida, Inc. v. Sun Federal Savings & Loan Ass'n*, 651 F.2d 311 (5th Cir. 1981), the court gave special weight to the fact that twenty-five competing financial institutions used the word *sun* in their titles and that more than 4,400 businesses in Florida used the term, thus making it weak in that locality.

Coexistence of Marks with No Confusion. If the allegedly infringing mark has coexisted with the plaintiff's mark for a period of time and there is no evidence of confusion in the marketplace, courts often find that confusion is unlikely. For example, when STEAMEX DELUXE 15 XL coexisted with Oreck's XL mark for seventeen months with no instances of confusion, the court held there was no infringement. *Oreck Corp. v. U.S. Floor Systems, Inc.*, 803 F.2d 166 (5th Cir. 1986).

Intent of Alleged Infringer. Proving an alleged infringer's intent or lack of good faith is not required to sustain an action for trademark infringement. However, if a party adopts a confusingly similar mark with the intent of reaping the benefits of the prior user's goodwill, such tends to weigh in favor of confusing similarity; the infringer would not have willingly adopted a similar mark unless he or she intended to trade off another's established reputation and divert customers.

When the alleged infringer had actual knowledge of the plaintiff's mark or had a prior business relationship with the plaintiff, such tends to suggest an intent to cause confusion. On the other hand, conducting a comprehensive search and relying on advice of counsel tend to rebut any inference of an intent to cause confusion. In fact, in *Frehling Enterprises, Inc. v. International Select Group, Inc.*, 192 F.3d 1330 (11th Cir. 1999), *cert. denied,* 531 U.S. 944 (2000), the court held that failure to conduct a trademark search was "intentional blindness" and evidence of improper intent. Further, the court held that if it can be shown that a defendant adopted a plaintiff's mark with the intention of deriving a benefit from the plaintiff's business reputation, *this fact alone* might be enough to justify the inference that there is confusing similarity.

(See Exhibit 6–2, Anatomy of an Infringement Case.)

Defenses to Infringement

There are a variety of defenses that may be raised by one accused of trademark infringement. They include the following:

- the defendant may assert that an *abandonment* of plaintiff's rights in the mark has occurred through nonuse prior to the time the defendant began using the mark or through a naked license;
- the defendant may allege that the plaintiff's mark has become *generic* and is thus undeserving of exclusive appropriation by the plaintiff; thus, for example, because the word *bundt* has been held to be generic for a certain type of ring cake, anyone can use this word without fear of infringement;
- a defense may be raised that the mark is *merely descriptive* and that it has not acquired secondary meaning, and, thus, it is undeserving of protection;

its effectiveness and its role in their lives and the life of their community. This project may have the added bonus of encouraging you to become more active in one or more networks in your community.

3. Bowling Alone

This field project is by no means reserved just for bowling aficionados. Rather, this project asks you to consider how technology might be strengthening or weakening the bonds that hold us together. In other words, does technology really provide any kind of social "glue"?

In a 1995 article "Bowling Alone," and in a subsequent book by the same title, Robert D. Putnam claims that for the last twenty or thirty years civic engagement has been declining and with it "social capital." Putnam notes that while bowling itself has grown in popularity, participation in organized bowling leagues has fallen dramatically. Putnam uses this observation as the touchstone for a broader argument: We have become increasingly disconnected from family and friends, from neighbors and local communities, and from our democratic structures. The stock of our social capital — those qualities that make our connections with each other possible — has dramatically declined. Putnam himself notes that the jury is still out on the role of technology. Will the Internet reinforce existing social networks (much as the telephone has done), or will it substitute for them, in virtual and all too often solitary ways?

For this field project, draw on your experience as you assess the current state of civic engagement and social capital. Does your experience differ from the experiences of your parents and your grandparents? What do you do alone? What role do groups and social ties have in your life? Do you find yourself living alone even as you live next to others? Do minority groups experience a heightened degree of isolation and, consequently, appreciate even more opportunities to associate with members of their group? To what extent does college life mirror the trends that Putnam discerns, or is the college environment a special case? Given these general questions, what is the effect of technology on your responses?

As you pursue your fieldwork, consider focusing on one kind of activity or one specific group or opportunity for association. Or, you may wish to focus on college life itself, where dorms, classes, and the local party scene might offer a certain kind of "glue" yet also hide or mask an underlying social isolation. What role does technology play on your campus in overcoming that isolation or contributing to it?

4. Building Campus Community on the Net

It may be tempting to assume that a college campus offers a ready-made community. But like all communities, the one on your campus requires ongoing maintenance and attention if it is to stay vibrant and avoid the fragmentation and dissention that can so easily occur. But even as we cling to the representations of community that we find in college brochures and public-relations materials, we also sense that communities are never quite as homogeneous as they might appear. Most college campuses offer multiple communities, each overlapping to some degree. Tension among these communities is a given and may in fact be healthy and normal. In short, even as we might speak of "the campus community," the real nature of that community may be far more divided and contentious than we would like to admit.

In an effort to foster community and greater cohesion on campus, administrators, faculty, and student leaders often turn to technology. E-mail, Web sites, and other forms of electronic communication are seen as new vehicles for creating and maintaining civic, social, and intellectual communities on campus. To facilitate such interaction some colleges have launched so-called Web portals, which offer ways for students and others to receive and communicate information, often in a very customized fashion.

This field project invites you to explore and assess the role of technology in building community on your campus. This issue is a broad one, so be sure to focus your efforts on one dimension or case study. Here are just a few examples:

- Evaluate the effectiveness of campus e-mail messages in building community.
- What role does your campus Web site or Web portal play in fostering community?
- Does your major's department use technology to make you feel invited into that disciplinary community?
- What role did (or could) technology play in helping you join and feel welcome in the campus community, especially during the period from acceptance through your first semester?
- How do student groups make use of technology to organize themselves? Could a particular group make more effective use of technology?
- How might a particular dorm or housing unit use technology to support face-to-face contact?
- Does technology minimize or exaggerate real or potential conflicts within campus communities?

Depending on your focus or issue and the audience involved, your project could take the form of a personal essay, an analytic or argumentative report, or a proposal for action.

5. Seat Time

When Neil Postman (p. 597) defends the idea that students should be educated in school, he is responding to the prospect that technology might liberate us from an educational tradition that roots instruction in time and place. Your own educational career, in school and now in college, was surely shaped by the notion that you should be educated in a certain place or classroom, for a certain number of hours. So pervasive is this thinking that much of education is planned, budgeted, and assessed in terms of one metric: the student credit hour, which itself is a measure of how much time you spend in a seat taking a particular course. In so many ways, education is reduced to "seat time."

This field project invites you to explore how technology is asking us to reassess "seat time." There are good reasons why technology might liberate us from seat time, for it facilitates such approaches as self-paced learning and distance education. Yet, even as we avail ourselves of technology, face-to-face meeting and, yes, seat time, may prove valuable in ways that we might easily underestimate. As you weigh these positions, you may find it helpful to focus your efforts around one case or instance of technology at work in education. Here are just a few of the many ways that you might ground your work:

- Is there a class you have taken in which seat time was not used productively and in which technology might have been an effective tool to release you from the constraints of time and place? Assess the course and the teaching style, and consider the prospect of technology as a tool for teaching and learning.
- Conversely, is there a class you have taken in which seat time was enormously valuable and technology, even if used, would not have dissuaded you from attending and actively participating? Assess the course and the teaching style, and consider the value of gathering as a class in one place at the same time.
- Have you encountered an experience in which educational technology was used either successfully or poorly in an effort to transcend seat time, as in an online course? Where did the success or failure lie, and what lessons might you have taken away from the experience?
- Writing instruction can and has benefited enormously from recent technologies, which have prompted the development of new teaching methods and fresh ways for delivering courses. Even so, contact with fellow writers and your audience, even face-to-face contact, remains particularly valuable. As a writer and as a student in a writing course, how do you weigh both the value of traditional seat time and the prospects of new technologies?

6. Digital Classrooms . . . and Those Who Are in Them

When Neil Postman (p. 597) discusses the promises of the digital classroom (false promises, he would add), he also focuses attention on the kind of student such technology presumes, or may well create. These twin interests are captured in the title of his essay: "Virtual Students, Digital Classroom."

This field project encourages you to examine not just the technology you experience in the classroom but also the ways in which the uses of that technology construct roles and identities for both students and faculty. For the site of your fieldwork, choose one particular course in which classroom technology or the use of technology in assignments had an important presence. Here are some questions you may wish to consider:

- What does the technology assume about you and your teacher, in terms of your roles, responsibilities, and learning or teaching styles?
- In what ways does the technology bring out or encourage capacities and talents that might otherwise have remained dormant?
- In what ways might that technology construct roles and identities for you and others that you find uncomfortable or unproductive?
- What recommendations do you have—for the instructor and for fellow students—about how best to maximize the advantages of the technology and minimize its negative or unfortunate consequences?
- If the course you have chosen is a writing course, what role did the technology play in constructing you as a writer or as a particular kind of writer? In what ways did the technology help or hinder you in constructing a sense of your audience?

To answer these and other questions, you will need to look beyond the sheer use of technology and inquire into the ways that technology uses us, instructor and student alike.

You can present your findings either through a personal essay about your experiences in the course, a report about teaching and learning in digital classrooms, or a set of recommendations to the instructor or the department chair. Consider how your writing and analysis will need to change as you accommodate a particular audience or pursue a specific purpose.

7. Cyber Assumptions

This field project asks you to uncover, analyze, and respond to the assumptions that your college makes about what it expects of its entering students when it comes to computer knowledge relevant to the classroom. Although some of this information can be found in admissions and orientation materials, much of your work will involve close analysis of those expectations as they play out in specific courses, online tutorials, and computer labs. Much of your fieldwork may involve, not texts, but conversations and interviews.

Because this topic offers several different paths of inquiry, you may wish to select from the following incomplete list of options:

- Are the assumptions the college has about your cyberliteracy largely correct, or have they misjudged you or other students (either by assuming too much or too little)? Do these assumptions become visible only when they prove to be inaccurate? What should your college assume about the computer skills and cyberawareness of its entering students?

- What does your college assume about your access to computers and the Internet? Are those assumptions accurate? Have you ever found yourself on the wrong side of the "digital divide," not having the equipment or access that teachers or other students assumed that you did? How did this digital divide affect your performance, your attitudes, and your sense of self?

- Does your college offer a computer-skills course or an introduction to college life or an introduction to the library that seeks to establish some baseline competence with information technology? If so, was that course helpful or unnecessary? If not, would such a course prove useful?

- When considering computer literacy, there is a strong tendency to focus on discrete computer skills and slight the need for a critical, self-reflective awareness of the social and ethical dimensions of computer technology. Do you find this to be the case on your campus or in a particular course?

8. Internet Activism

Not only has the Internet added new dimensions to how we think of building community, it has also changed the face of civic and political activism. These changes are certainly visible on the national political scene, yet important lessons can also be learned from the local scene.

This field project invites you to study a specific instance of Internet activism on campus or in your community. Whether the issue involves a campus issue, a matter of local politics, a concern in the local schools, or a focused special-interest cause, your project should analyze how the technology involved made an impact on that particular instance of advocacy. Among many possible aspects, you may wish to address how the issue was brought to the Internet, what role that speed and reach played in mobilizing members or interested parties, what impact the Internet presence had on the audience being lobbied, what Internet response was elicited from those disagreeing with the campaign, and what relationship that one instance of Internet activism had to the group's overall activities and mission. The questions you ask will be specific to the instance of Internet activism you are studying. In some cases, a preexisting group may have used the Internet for activist purposes; in other instances, a loose coalition of people might have formed and then dissolved, only coming together to address one pressing concern. You may also wish to offer recommendations on how the Internet activism might have been improved or how certain errors or missteps might have been avoided.

To study an instance of Internet activism, you will need to have access to the conversation, of course. But beyond the conversation itself, you might find it productive to interview key players in this instance of Internet activism, and ask them for their reflections on how that medium influenced their strategies and purposes.

9. Chats, Blogs, and IM

Susan Herring's analysis of gender differences in computer-mediated communication (p. 608) is based on data drawn from e-mail-based academic listserv discussion groups in the early and mid-1990s. Even as the "familiar baggage of gender differences" remains recognizable a decade or more later, the new technological frontier that Herring explores continues to expand. Widely available today are forms of computer-mediated communication—chat rooms, blogs, and instant messaging—that were only beginning to catch on when Herring wrote her article.

This field project invites you to explore one or more of the issues raised by Herring—gender styles, identity, communication ethics, and language change—in technological arenas not discussed by Herring. Chat rooms, with their online, real-time conversation and with their opportunities to play with identity, offer an engaging environment for analysis. Blogs — sorts of hybrid diary and guide sites that are both personal and public—have likewise emerged as a new form of electronic communication that deserves closer analysis. Likewise, instant messaging heightens the speed of exchanges and has introduced new shorthand into our language. In addition to examining your own use of such technology, pay attention, as does Herring, to the actual language and conversational dynamics. Close analysis of concrete examples can launch you into engaging fieldwork more effectively than sticking to broad generalizations can.

Feel free to explore technologies or applications not listed here. Who knows what lies over the horizon? Your fieldwork is important in that it will address the need to assess the use of the latest technologies in light of perennial issues.

10. Computer-Mediated Communication in the Writing Class

As computer technologies and electronic communication become ever more central to writing courses, their use and effectiveness should become the concern not just of instructors and researchers but also of students of writing themselves. This field project offers a chance to reflect on the impact of technology in your writing class and in writing instruction on your campus.

Given the many possible directions this project could take, you will find it useful to focus on one particular issue or concern. Here are just a few possibilities:

- What role does or could computer-mediated communication play in collaboration or jointly authored projects?

- What impact does computer technology have for peer editing and the revision process?
- What are the opportunities — and the pitfalls — of using computers as you develop your information literacy or research skills?
- What new opportunities for publication and dissemination do computers offer?
- How do computers affect the communication between teacher and student, and among students themselves?

MINDING THE MACHINE

As we learn to use and maximize the potential of computers and other digital tools, our focus is surely on the instrumental: how to get the software or hardware to work, and how to minimize our own errors. If something goes wrong, we tend to blame ourselves, confessing our general clumsiness with technology. This unit invites you to look beyond our efforts to use machines well. More is at stake, as the unit title "Minding the Machine" suggests.

In addition to working the machine, we must understand how the machine works to influence our larger lives, even our minds. What role do digital tools play in shaping society and personal relations? How do these tools mold daily behaviors and activities? To answer these and other questions, we must do more than use the machine; we must become aware of its reach and its capacity for using us. In short, we must "mind the machine."

One further reason why we should be mindful of the reach and influence of digital tools is that those tools affect our thinking and learning. Not only do we sometimes ascribe intelligence to the machines, but those machines also both assist and shape our own intelligence. Here we discover a further meaning in the title of this unit. We are "minding the machine" in the sense that these tools have a mind (or so it sometimes seems) and work to influence our own.

Given the wordplay in the unit title, we will explore several areas in which we are "minding the machine." The first concerns education. Computers and other tools are shaping the face of learning, from preschool to college. Computers, the World Wide Web, and other digital tools open up new opportunities for accessing information and for simulating and testing our ideas. The networked computer becomes an extension of our own networked mind. It becomes a tool for thinking, not just a tool to be used when we think.

One key aspect of these tools is their ability to link one application or Web site to another. Such links have a powerful influence on how we organize and navigate the world of knowledge. Whereas our knowledge was at one time logical, linear, and hierarchical, the tools now invite us to operate in a different fashion: knowledge appears associative, lateral, and wildly democratic. With a mere click, we can access most anything, and most anyone can try to claim our attention and elicit our belief. Learning tools that capitalize on this technology do more than provide information; they shape the very way we learn.

Because our new digital tools provide ways of integrating images with text, the way we make arguments has become visual, not just verbal. For evidence, we need look no further than the latest presentation software, such as PowerPoint. With its animations and its array of bulleted lists, PowerPoint lends clarity, force, and even an air of cockiness and certainty to the most complex arguments. Yet so pervasive has this tool become that we must ask whether PowerPoint now has a role in shaping how we argue. In presenting what's on our minds, it may also have a role in shaping them.

New technologies for writing may not only be shaping our minds but also our collective sense of identity. As print makes way for digital media, we find that we are becoming a network culture. This transformation is challenging everything from our assumptions about cultural unity to the ways in which we think about intellectual property.

The three readings in this unit pick up on these themes as they challenge us to reflect on how we "mind our machines." Sven Birkerts cautions us that the very tools we find so helpful and powerful may have effects beyond our imagining. They might influence how we organize and navigate the world of knowledge, and even how we attend to and learn from artifacts and texts. The next reading takes up a particular software tool that has become especially pervasive in our culture: PowerPoint. Here, Ian Parker explores how and why the software tool was developed, and its possible effect on how we present— and shape— our thoughts. Says one of its developers: "Oh Lord, what have we done?" For Jay David Bolter it is but one small step from arguing that writing and writing technologies shape our mind to arguing that such technologies also write our culture. Bolter explores the late age of print, where print technologies vie with new digital media, creating cultural tensions that we experience in our daily lives.

Reflecting on Prior Knowledge

1. All of us entered the digital age not in one dramatic moment but in a series of small steps, chiefly as we learned our way around computers. Meet in groups of two or three and discuss how you first became acquainted with digital tools for writing and researching. What are children, at home or in school, learning about reading, accessing, and writing texts in a digital age? What is common and different in your experiences? How are your experiences different from what your parents learned about texts? Write an account of your childhood exposure to these tools or describe how today's children are likely to encounter the digital age.

2. As we navigate and read digital texts and Web sites, it is commonplace to find a host of links to other sites and resources. But even as we become adept at clicking on those links, we may not pause to consider how they affect our thinking and learning. In a journal entry, reflect on your use of hyperlinks. What kind of learning does a hypertext link make possible? What kind of intellectual navigation and exploration does it privilege, and what kind does it discourage?

3. Imagine the following scenario: You enter a meeting room or a lecture hall and discover that the next hour will be dominated by a PowerPoint presentation. In a journal entry that you can then share with your class, give voice to what goes through your mind as people take their seats and the lights are dimmed. What prior experiences with PowerPoint have you had—either constructing or listening to presentations—and how have those experiences influenced your attitudes toward this presentation software?

4. Growing up in the early twenty-first century, you are a product of what is becoming a "network culture." Meet in small groups and discuss what it means to be or to have been a network kid. What kind of culture—and cultural conflicts—have new digital tools produced? How has this network culture influenced your relationship to the world and your relationships with each other? Record your comments and observations—both positive and negative—so that you can report back to the class as a whole.

EXHIBIT 6–2
Anatomy of an
Infringement Case

Case: *Phat Fashions, L.L.C. v. Phat Game Athletic Apparel, Inc.,* No. CIV. S-01-1771 (E.D. Cal. 2002).

Background: In 1992, Russell Simmons, the cofounder of Def Jam Records, founded Phat Fashions, a manufacturer and distributor of urban and athletic apparel offered under the registered mark PHAT FARM® and other marks, including PHAT® and BABY PHAT®. In 1998, defendants began to sell athletic apparel and accessories bearing the mark PHAT or PHAT GAME. Defendants filed a trademark application to register PHAT GAME, and plaintiff brought an action for trademark infringement, unfair competition, and dilution.

Marks: Plaintiff's Marks: **PHAT FARM® and PHAT®**
         Defendants' Mark: **PHAT GAME**

Analysis: After stating that to prove trademark infringement a plaintiff must show he or she has a valid, protectable trademark and that the defendant's mark created a likelihood of confusion, the court analyzed the various infringement factors as follows:

Factor	Court Analysis	Court Conclusion
Strength of the Mark	The plaintiff's PHAT mark was arbitrary and thus strong and was well known by the purchasing public.	First factor weighs heavily in plaintiff's favor.
Similarity of Marks	First word (*phat*) in each mark is dominant feature and consumers would conclude that the word *phat* in defendants' mark refers to plaintiff.	Second factor weighs in plaintiff's favor.
Similarity of Goods	Marks are both used on identical goods (namely, wearing apparel).	Third factor weighs in plaintiff's favor.
Channels of Trade	Goods are sold for similar prices and there is similarity in marketing channels used for distribution.	This factor weighs in plaintiff's favor.
Purchaser Care	Both parties market to young people, and prices for many goods are under $30. These young consumers are often not careful purchasers, especially when prices are low.	Because of youth of defendants' market and relatively low prices, this factor weighs in plaintiff's favor.

(continues)

Perseus Unbound

Sven Birkerts

In 1992, Perseus 1.0, an interactive database published on CD-ROM and videodisc, became the hottest new resource for the study of ancient Greek culture. The impressive capacity and flexibility of Perseus accelerated the ongoing debate over the use of computer technology in education. "Perseus Unbound" is an excerpt from Sven Birkerts's 1994 book, *The Gutenberg Elegies: The Fate of Reading in an Electronic Age*. Referring to Johann Gutenberg, the German printer often credited with inventing movable type and thereby spawning the widespread availability of books, *Elegies* questions the wisdom of indiscriminately replacing print media with high-speed access to a limitless reservoir of information. A now-classic discussion about computers in the late age of print, *Elegies* continues to provoke consideration and debate well after its publication.

The Gutenberg Elegies continues to draw Birkerts, a writer specializing in literature and culture, into a debate that intensifies as technology makes further inroads into not only education, but also into the information gathering and thinking habits of the entire culture. In addition to books and collections of essays on literary subjects ranging from Tolstoy to twentieth-century literature, Birkerts has written articles for publications such as the *New York Times Sunday Book Review*, the *New Republic, Esquire, Atlantic Monthly,* and *Village Voice*. He was awarded the Citation for Excellence in Reviewing by the National Book Critics Circle and has received Guggenheim and Lila Wallace fellowships. Birkerts has taught writing and literature at Harvard University, Emerson College, and Amherst College, and is currently a lecturer at Mount Holyoke College and a member of the core faculty of the Bennington Writing Seminars.

Like it or not, interactive video technologies have muscled their way into the formerly textbound precincts of education. The videodisc has mated with the microcomputer to produce a juggernaut: a flexible and encompassing teaching tool that threatens to overwhelm the linearity of print with an array of option-rich multimedia packages. And although we are only in the early stages of implementation — institutions are by nature conservative — an educational revolution seems inevitable.

Several years ago in *Harvard Magazine*, writer Craig Lambert sampled some of the innovative ways in which these technologies have already been applied at Harvard. Interactive video programs at the Law School allow students to view simulated police busts or actual courtroom procedures. With a tap of a digit they can freeze images, call up case citations, and quickly zero-in on the relevant fine points of precedent. Medical simulations, offering the immediacy of video images and instant access to the mountains of data necessary for diagnostic assessment, can have the student all but performing surgery. And language classes now allow the learner to make an end run around tedious drill repetitions and engage in protoconversations with video partners.

The hot news in the classics world, meanwhile, is Perseus 1.0, an interactive database developed and edited by Harvard associate professor Gregory Crane. Published on CD-ROM and videodisc, the program holds, according to its publicists, "the equivalent of twenty-five volumes of ancient Greek literature by ten authors (one million Greek words), roughly four thousand glosses in the online classical encyclopedia, and a 35,000-word online Greek lexicon." Also included are an enormous photographic database (six thousand images), a short video with narration, and "hundreds of descriptions and drawings of art and archeological objects." The package is affordable, too: Perseus software can be purchased for about $350. Plugged in, the student can call up a text, read it side by side with its translation, and analyze any word using the Liddell-Scott lexicon; he can read a thumbnail sketch on any mythic figure cited in the text, or call up images from an atlas, or zoom in on color Landsat photos;° he can even study a particular vase through innumerable angles of vantage. The dusty library stacks have never looked dustier.

Although skepticism abounds, most of it is institutional, bound up with established procedures and the proprietorship of scholarly bailiwicks. But there are grounds for other, more philosophic sorts of debate, and we can expect to see flare-ups of controversy for some time to come. For more than any other development in recent memory, these interactive technologies throw into relief the fundamental questions about knowledge and learning.

Landsat photos: Photographs of earth from satellites; the Landsat program has satellites in orbit that survey the earth's natural resources and monitor ecological changes.

Not only what are its ends, but what are its means? And how might the means be changing the ends?

From the threshold, I think, we need to distinguish between kinds of knowledge and kinds of study. Pertinent here is German philosopher Wilhelm Dilthey's distinction between the natural sciences (*Naturwissenschaften*), which seek to explain physical events by subsuming them under causal laws, and the so-called sciences of culture (*Geisteswissenschaften*), which can only understand events in terms of the intentions and meanings that individuals attach to them.

To the former, it would seem, belong the areas of study more hospitable to the new video and computer procedures. Expanded databases and interactive programs can be viewed as tools, pure and simple. They give access to more information, foster cross-referentiality, and by reducing time and labor allow for greater focus on the essentials of a problem. Indeed, any discipline where knowledge is sought for its application rather than for itself could only profit from the implementation of these technologies. To the natural sciences one might add the fields of language study and law.

But there is a danger with these sexy new options — and the rapture with which believers speak warrants the adjective — that we will simply assume that their uses and potentials extend across the educational spectrum into realms where different kinds of knowledge, and hence learning, are at issue. The realms, that is, of *Geisteswissenschaften*, which have at their center the humanities.

In the humanities, knowledge is a means, yes, but it is a means less to instrumental application than to something more nebulous: understanding. We study history or literature or classics in order to compose and refine a narrative, or a set of narratives about what the human **Here are a few reservations** world used to be like, about how the world came to be **worth pondering.** as it is, and about what we have been — and are — like as psychological or spiritual creatures. The data — the facts, connections, the texts themselves — matter insofar as they help us to deepen and extend that narrative. In these disciplines the *process* of study may be as vital to the understanding as are the materials studied.

Given the great excitement generated by Perseus, it is easy to imagine that in the near future a whole range of innovative electronic-based learning packages will be available and, in many places, in use. These will surely include the manifold variations on the electronic book. Special new software texts are already being developed to bring us into the world of, say, Shakespeare, not only glossing the literature, but bathing the user in multimedia supplements. The would-be historian will step into an environment rich in choices, be they visual detailing, explanatory graphs, or suggested connections and sideroads. And so on. Moreover, once the price is right, who will be the curmudgeons who would deny their students access to the state of the art?

Being a curmudgeon is a dirty job, but somebody has to do it. Someone   10
has to hoist the warning flags and raise some issues that the fast-track prose-
lytizers might overlook. Here are a few reservations worth pondering.

1. Knowledge, certainly in the humanities, is not a straightforward matter
of access, of conquest via the ingestion of data. Part of any essential understanding of the world is that it is opaque, obdurate. To me, Wittgenstein's°
famous axiom, "The world is everything that is the case," translates into a
recognition of otherness. The past is as much about the disappearance of
things through time as it is about the recovery of traces and the reconstruction of vistas. Say what you will about books, they not only mark the backward trail, but they also encode this sense of obstacle, of otherness. The look
of the printed page changes as we regress in time; under the orthographic
changes are the changes in the language itself. Old-style textual research may
feel like an unnecessarily slow burrowing, but it is itself an instruction: It
confirms that time is a force as implacable as gravity.

Yet the multimedia packages would master this gravity. For opacity they
substitute transparency, promoting the illusion of access. All that has been
said, known, and done will yield to the dance of the fingertips on the terminal keys. Space becomes hyperspace, and time, hypertime (*hyper-* being
the fashionable new prefix that invokes the nonlinear and nonsequential
"space" made possible by computer technologies). One gathers the data of
otherness, but through a medium which seems to level the feel — the
truth — of that otherness. The field of knowledge is rendered as a lateral
and synchronic enterprise susceptible to collage, not as a depth phenomenon. And if our media restructure our perceptions, as McLuhan° and others have argued, then we may start producing generations who know a
great deal of "information" about the past but who have no purchase on
pastness itself.

Described in this way, the effects of interactive programs on users sound
a good deal like the symptoms of postmodernism. And indeed, this recent
cultural aesthetic, distinguished by its flat, bright, and often affectless assemblages of materials may be a consequence of a larger transformation of sensibility by information-processing technologies. After all, our arts do tend to
mirror who we are and anticipate what we might be becoming. Changes of
this magnitude are of course systemic, and their direction is not easily dictated. Whether the postmodern "vision" can be endorsed as a pedagogic plat-
form, however, is another question.

Wittgenstein's: Ludwig Wittgensten (1889–1951), an Austrian philosopher interested in language,
thought, the mind, and reality.
McLuhan: Herbert Marshall McLuhan (1911–1980), a Canadian communication theorist and one
of the pioneers in the study of media ecology.

2. Humanistic knowledge, as I suggested earlier, differs from the more instrumental kinds of knowledge in that it ultimately seeks to fashion a comprehensible narrative. It is, in other words, about the creation and expansion of meaningful contexts. Interactive media technologies are, at least in one sense, anticontextual. They open the field to new widths, constantly expanding relevance and reference, and they equip their user with a powerful grazing tool. One moves at great rates across subject terrains, crossing borders that were once closely guarded. The multimedia approach tends ineluctably to multidisciplinarianism. The positive effect, of course, is the creation of new levels of connection and integration; more and more variables are brought into the equation.

But the danger should be obvious: The horizon, the limit that gave defi-   15
nition to the parts of the narrative, will disappear. The equation itself will become nonsensical through the accumulation of variables. The context will widen until it becomes, in effect, everything. On the model of Chaos science, wherein the butterfly flapping its wings in China is seen to affect the weather system over Oklahoma, all data will impinge upon all other data. The technology may be able to handle it, but will the user? Will our narratives—historical, literary, classical—be able to withstand the data explosion? If they cannot, then what will be the new face of understanding? Or will the knowledge of the world become, perforce, a map as large and intricate as the world itself?

3. We might question, too, whether there is not in learning as in physical science a principle of energy conservation. Does a gain in one area depend upon a loss in another? My guess would be that every lateral attainment is purchased with a sacrifice of depth. The student may, through a program on Shakespeare, learn an immense amount about Elizabethan politics, the construction of the Globe theater, the origins of certain plays in the writings of Plutarch, the etymology of key terms, and so on, but will this dazzled student find the concentration, the will, to live with the often burred and prickly language of the plays themselves? The play's the thing —but will it be? Wouldn't the sustained exposure to a souped-up cognitive collage not begin to affect the attention span, the ability if not willingness to sit with one text for extended periods, butting up against its cruxes, trying to excavate meaning from the original rhythms and syntax? The gurus of interaction love to say that the student learns best by doing, but let's not forget that *reading* a work is also a kind of doing.

4. As a final reservation, what about the long-term cognitive effects of these new processes of data absorption? Isn't it possible that more may be less, and that the neural networks have one speed for taking in—a speed that

can be increased—and quite another rate for retention? Again, it may be that our technologies will exceed us. They will make it not only possible but irresistible to consume data at what must strike people of the book as very high rates. But what then? What will happen as our neural systems, evolved through millennia to certain capacities, modify themselves to hold ever-expanding loads? Will we simply become smarter, able to hold and process more? Or do we have to reckon with some other gain/loss formula? One possible cognitive response—call it the "SAT cram-course model"—might be an expansion of the short-term memory banks and a correlative atrophying of long-term memory.

But here our technology may well assume a new role. Once it dawns on us, as it must, that our software will hold all the information we need at ready access, we may very well let it. That is, we may choose to become the technicians of our auxiliary brains, mastering not the information but the retrieval and referencing functions. At a certain point, then, we could become the evolutionary opposites of our forebears, who, lacking external technology, committed everything to memory. If this were to happen, what would be the status of knowing, of being educated? The leader of the electronic tribe would not be the person who knew most, but the one who could execute the broadest range of technical functions. What, I hesitate to ask, would become of the already antiquated notion of wisdom?

I recently watched a public television special on the history of the computer. One of the many experts and enthusiasts interviewed took up the knowledge question. He explained how the formerly two-dimensional process of book-based learning is rapidly becoming three-dimensional. The day will come, he opined, when interactive and virtual technologies will allow us to more or less dispense with our reliance on the sequence-based print paradigm. Whatever the object of our study, our equipment will be able to get us there directly: inside the volcano or the violin-maker's studio, right up on the stage. I was enthralled, but I shuddered, too, for it struck me that when our technologies are all in place—when all databases have been refined and integrated—that will be the day when we stop living in the old hard world and take up residence in some bright new hyperworld, a kind of Disneyland of information. I have to wonder if this is what Perseus and its kindred programs might not be edging us toward. That program got its name, we learn from the brochure, from the Greek mythological hero Perseus, who was the explorer of the limits of the known world. I confess that I can't think of Perseus without also thinking of Icarus, heedless son of Daedalus, who allowed his wings to carry him over the invisible line that was inscribed across the skyway.

Working with the Text

1. In the course of his essay, Sven Birkerts draws important distinctions between knowledge and understanding. What is the relationship between these two terms? What role does information have in each?

2. In "Perseus Unbound," Birkerts's concern over how "the means" might "be changing the ends" centers on his view that "[i]n the humanities, knowledge is a means, yes, but it is a means less to instrumental application than to something more nebulous: understanding" (par. 8). As you reread the essay, infer his definition of "understanding" from his critique of the effects, or potential effects, of replacing books with technology. Write a brief essay in which you analyze Birkerts's concept of "understanding." What does it require? What can prevent it?

3. According to Birkerts, humanistic knowledge is "about the creation and expansion of meaningful contexts" (par. 14). His concern over access to proliferating amounts of information is that "[t]he context will widen until it becomes, in effect, everything" (par. 15). Review Birkerts's argument about context, in the second of his four reservations. Using examples from your own education and reading, write a brief essay in which you reflect on his argument. What does he mean by a "meaningful context," and why does he think it is essential? Do you consider a context of "everything" to be counter to an understanding of humanistic knowledge? Why or why not?

4. In the closing paragraph of "Perseus Unbound," Birkerts claims that "when our technologies are all in place — when all databases have been refined and integrated — that will be the day when we stop living in the old hard world and take up residence in some bright new hyperworld, a kind of Disneyland of information." In a brief essay, argue for or against Birkerts's position. Do you think technology will eventually entice us to "stop living in the old hard world"? Do you think our technologies create, or will create, "a Disneyland of information"?

From Text to Field

1. Birkerts raises the possibility that if the "field of knowledge is rendered as a lateral and synchronic enterprise susceptible to collage, not as a depth phenomenon . . . we may start producing generations who know a great deal of 'information' about the past but who have no purchase on pastness itself" (par. 12). Review the passage in which Birkert discusses this concern (the first of his four reservations). In a personal essay, reflect on your understanding of "pastness." Do you have a sense of "otherness"? If so, how does this sense color

the way you regard people, cultures, and events of the past? How do you experience the passage of time that precedes you by decades, centuries, millennia, millions or billions of years? How have books or primary documents and artifacts influenced this sense? How has computer-generated material influenced it?

2. Birkerts charges that information technologies may be responsible for tuning our sensibilities into the "flat, bright, and often affectless assemblages of materials" that he thinks characterize our culture and "mirror who we are and anticipate what we might be becoming" (par. 13). In an essay, present your own critique of the sensibility that dominates our culture. How would you characterize it? What do you think drives it? What does it say about "who we are" and "what we might be becoming"?

3. Birkerts's third reservation about information technology is that in pursuing breadth of knowledge, we will sacrifice depth. Drawing on your experience using information technology as well as on Birkerts's argument, write an essay in which you address the breadth versus depth issue from your point of view. How has this tension played itself out in one of your courses or in the college curriculum you are now studying?

4. In his fourth and final "reservation," Birkerts questions "the long-term cognitive effects of these new processes of data absorption" (par. 17). With Birkerts's discussion in mind, offer your own prediction of what the "long-term cognitive effects" might be. Consider answering one or both of the following questions posed by Birkerts:

- "What will happen as our neural systems, evolved through millennia to certain capacities, modify themselves to hold ever-expanding loads?" (par. 17)
- "[W]hat would be the status of knowing, of being educated? The leader of the electronic tribe would not be the person who knew most, but the one who could execute the broadest range of technical functions. What, I hesitate to ask, would become of the already antiquated notion of wisdom?" (par. 18)

Absolute PowerPoint: Can a Software Package Edit Our Thoughts?

Ian Parker

Producing and viewing PowerPoint presentations can be such a relief— difficult concepts seem comprehensible, complicated processes fall into a logical sequence, and mazes of information find form. In his 2001 article for the *New Yorker*, Ian Parker calls all of this ease and apparent clarity into question. What is PowerPoint doing to the way we think? Tracing the history of its development, Parker examines the needs and vulnerabilities that inspired, and still drive, PowerPoint and what its design helps us to avoid.

A staff writer for the *New Yorker*, Parker bases his critique on discussions with the originators and developers of PowerPoint technology as well as professionals and academics who have both used it and analyzed its influence on how we think and communicate. Since its publication, "Absolute PowerPoint" has been widely read as a source of commentary and debate in arenas ranging from business and technology to communication theory and cultural criticism. Parker's article is also frequently found on the syllabi of undergraduate and graduate courses in universities across the country.

Before there were presentations, there were conversations, which were a little like presentations but used fewer bullet points, and no one had to dim the lights. A woman we can call Sarah Wyndham, a defense-industry consultant living in Alexandria, Virginia, recently began to feel that her two daughters weren't listening when she asked them to clean their bedrooms and do their chores. So, one morning, she sat down at her computer, opened Microsoft's PowerPoint program, and typed:

FAMILY MATTERS

An approach for positive change to the Wyndham family team

On a new page, she wrote:

- Lack of organization leads to confusion and frustration among all family members.
- Disorganization is detrimental to grades and to your social life.
- Disorganization leads to inefficiencies that impact the entire family.

Instead of pleading for domestic harmony, Sarah Wyndham was pitching for it. Soon she had eighteen pages of large type, supplemented by a color photograph of a generic happy family riding bicycles, and, on the final page, a drawing of a key—the key to success. The briefing was given only once, last fall. The experience was so upsetting to her children that the threat of a second showing was enough to make one of the Wyndham girls burst into tears.

PowerPoint, which can be found on 250 million computers around the world, is software you impose on other people. It allows you to arrange text and graphics in a series of pages, which you can project, slide by slide, from a laptop computer onto a screen, or print as a booklet (as Sarah Wyndham did). The usual metaphor for everyday software is the tool, but that doesn't seem to be right here. PowerPoint is more like a suit of clothes, or a car, or plastic surgery. You take it out with you. You are judged by it—you insist on being judged by it. It is by definition a social instrument, turning middle managers into bullet-point dandies.

But PowerPoint also has a private, interior influence. It edits ideas. It is, 5 almost surreptitiously, a business manual as well as a business suit, with an opinion — an oddly pedantic, prescriptive opinion— about the way we should think. It helps you make a case, but it also makes its own case: about how to organize information, how much information to organize, how to look at the world. One feature of this is the AutoContent Wizard, which supplies templates— "Managing Organizational Change" or "Communicating Bad News," say— that are so close to finished presentations you barely need to do more than add your company logo. The "Motivating a Team" template, for example, includes a slide headed "Conduct a Creative Thinking Session":

- Ask: In what ways can we . . . ?
  —Assess the situation. Get the facts.
  —Generate possible solutions with green light, nonjudgmental thinking.
  —Select the best solution.

The final injunction is "Have an inspirational close."

It's easy to avoid these extreme templates — many people do — as well as embellishments like clip art, animations, and sound effects. But it's hard to

EXHIBIT 6–2
Anatomy of an
Infringement Case
(continued)

Intent of Defendants	Defendants knew of plaintiff's marks and had conducted some research and trademark searches. Thus, defendants deliberately adopted their mark to obtain a business advantage.	This factor weighs heavily in plaintiff's favor.
Holding:	Defendants have infringed plaintiff's trademarks and have engaged in unfair competition. Defendants were ordered to cease using PHAT GAME, disable their Internet web site (http://www.phatgame.com), and transfer their domain name to the plaintiff.	

- the defendant might assert that the plaintiff's registration was procured by *fraud,* is thus invalid, and cannot support an action for infringement;
- the accused infringer might assert **estoppel,** that is, that the plaintiff is *estopped* or precluded from asserting trademark infringement because it led the defendant to believe that it could use the mark (for example, by allowing numerous other similar uses to go unchallenged);
- the defendant might assert **acquiescence,** a defense that alleges that conduct on the plaintiff's part amounted to an assurance to the defendant-infringer that plaintiff would not assert its trademark rights against the defendant;
- the defendant might assert that the plaintiff has **unclean hands** and has committed such a serious wrongful act (such as wrongfully using a trademark notice when it had no right to do so) that relief should not be awarded to it;
- the defendant might assert **laches,** namely, that the plaintiff delayed an unreasonable amount of time to bring the action and this delay has prejudiced the defendant (who, during the period of delay, expended significant time and money in promoting the mark and thus should be allowed to continue using the mark);
- the defendant may allege the mark is *functional* and thus unprotectable;
- the defendant might allege that its use is a mere *parody* and is protected by the First Amendment; and/or
- the defendant may assert that its use was a **fair use,** meaning that it did not use the plaintiff's name or mark as a trademark but merely to describe its goods in a general fashion.

One of the more interesting modern defenses is a free speech defense. Recently, artist Tom Forsythe was sued by Mattel Inc. (owner of the famous BARBIE® mark) for posing BARBIE dolls in inappropriate positions, such as mooning the camera. Forsythe prevailed in a suit by Mattel on the basis that his work was legitimate social commentary protected under the First Amendment and was not a commercial use of Mattel's mark.

Monitoring and policing for misuse of trademarks is critical because a failure to assert an infringement claim promptly might give rise to successful defenses based on acquiescence or laches. As discussed in Chapter 5, shake off AutoContent's spirit: Even the most easygoing PowerPoint template insists on a heading followed by bullet points, so that the user is shepherded toward a staccato, summarizing frame of mind, of the kind parodied, for example, in a PowerPoint Gettysburg Address posted on the Internet: "Dedicate portion of field — fitting!"

Because PowerPoint can be an impressive antidote to fear — converting public-speaking dread into moviemaking pleasure — there seems to be no great impulse to fight this influence, as you might fight the unrelenting animated paperclip in Microsoft Word. Rather, PowerPoint's restraints seem to be soothing — so much so that where Microsoft has not written rules, businesses write them for themselves. A leading U.S. computer manufacturer has distributed guidelines to its employees about PowerPoint presentations, insisting on something it calls the "Rule of Seven": "Seven (7) bullets or lines per page, seven (7) words per line."

Today, after Microsoft's decade of dizzying growth, there are great tracts of corporate America where to appear at a meeting without PowerPoint would be unwelcome and vaguely pretentious, like wearing no shoes. In darkened rooms at industrial plants and ad agencies, at sales pitches and conferences, this is how people are communicating: no paragraphs, no pronouns — the world condensed into a few upbeat slides, with seven or so words on a line, seven or so lines on a slide. And now it's happening during sermons and university lectures and family arguments, too. A New Jersey PowerPoint user recently wrote in an online discussion, "Last week I caught myself planning out (in my head) the slides I would need to explain to my wife why we couldn't afford a vacation this year." Somehow, a piece of software designed, fifteen years ago, to meet a simple business need has become a way of organizing thought at kindergarten show-and-tells. "Oh, Lord," one of the early developers said to me. "What have we done?"

Forty years ago, a workplace meeting was a discussion with your immediate 10 colleagues. Engineers would meet with other engineers and talk in the language of engineering. A manager might make an appearance — acting as an interpreter, a bridge to the rest of the company — but no one from the marketing or production or sales department would be there. Somebody might have gone to the trouble of cranking out mimeographs — that would be the person with purple fingers.

But the structure of American industry changed in the 1960s and '70s. Clifford Nass, who teaches in the Department of Communication at Stanford, says, "Companies weren't discovering things in the laboratory and then trying to convince consumers to buy them. They were discovering — or creating — consumer demand, figuring out what they can convince consumers they need, then going to the laboratory and saying, 'Build this!'

People were saying, 'We can create demand. Even if demand doesn't exist, we know how to market this.' SpaghettiOs is the great example. The guy came up with the jingle first: 'The neat round spaghetti you can eat with a spoon.' And he said, 'Hey! Make spaghetti in the shape of small circles!'"

As Jerry Porras, a professor of organizational behavior and change at Stanford Graduate School of Business, says, "When technologists no longer just drove the product out but the customer sucked it out, then you had to know what the customer wanted, and that meant a lot more interaction inside the company." There are new conversations: Can we make this? How do we sell this if we make it? Can we do it in blue?

America began to go to more meetings. By the early 1980s, when the story of PowerPoint starts, employees had to find ways to talk to colleagues from other departments, colleagues who spoke a different language, brought together by SpaghettiOs and by the simple fact that technology was generating more information. There was more to know and, as the notion of a job for life eroded, more reason to know it.

In this environment, visual aids were bound to thrive. In 1975, 50,000 overhead projectors were sold in America. By 1985, that figure had increased to more than 120,000. Overheads, which were developed in the mid-forties for use by the police, and were then widely used in bowling alleys and schools, did not fully enter business life until the mid-seventies, when a transparency film that could survive the heat of a photocopier became available. Now anything on a sheet of paper could be transferred to an overhead slide. Overheads were cheaper than the popular alternative, the 35-mm. slide (which needed graphics professionals), and they were easier to use. But they restricted you to your typewriter's font—rather, your secretary's typewriter's font—or your skill with **PowerPoint also has a pri-** Letraset and a felt-tipped pen. A businessman couldn't **vate, interior influence.** generate a handsome, professional-looking font in his own office.

In 1980, though, it was clear that a future of widespread personal com- 15 puters—and laser printers and screens that showed the very thing you were about to print—was tantalizingly close. In the Mountain View, California, laboratory of Bell-Northern Research, computer-research scientists had set up a great mainframe computer, a graphics workstation, a phototypesetter, and the earliest Canon laser printer, which was the size of a bathtub and took six men to carry into the building—together, a cumbersome approximation of what would later fit on a coffee table and cost a thousand dollars. With much trial and error, and jogging from one room to another, you could use this collection of machines as a kind of word processor.

Whitfield Diffie had access to this equipment. A mathematician, a former peacenik, and an enemy of exclusive government control of encryption systems, Diffie had secured a place for himself in computing legend in 1976, when he and a colleague, Martin Hellman, announced the discovery of a new method of protecting secrets electronically — public-key cryptography. At Bell-Northern, Diffie was researching the security of telephone systems. In 1981, preparing to give a presentation with 35-mm. slides, he wrote a little program, tinkering with some graphics software designed by a BNR colleague, that allowed you to draw a black frame on a piece of paper. Diffie expanded it so that the page could show a number of frames, and text inside each frame, with space for commentary around them. In other words, he produced a storyboard — a slide show on paper — that could be sent to the designers who made up the slides, and that would also serve as a script for his lecture. (At this stage, he wasn't photocopying what he had produced to make overhead transparencies, although scientists in other facilities were doing that.) With a few days' effort, Diffie had pointed the way to PowerPoint.

Diffie has long gray hair and likes to wear fine English suits. Today, he works for Sun Microsystems, as an internal consultant on encryption matters. I recently had lunch with him in Palo Alto, and for the first time he publicly acknowledged his presence at the birth of PowerPoint. It was an odd piece of news: As if Lenin° had invented the stapler. Yes, he said, PowerPoint was "based on" his work at BNR. This is not of great consequence to Diffie, whose reputation in his own field is so high that he is one of the few computer scientists to receive erotically charged fan mail. He said he was "mildly miffed" to have made no money from the PowerPoint connection, but he has no interest in beginning a feud with an old friend. "Bob was the one who had the vision to understand how important it was to the world," he said. "And I didn't."

Bob is Bob Gaskins, the man who has to take final responsibility for the drawn blinds of high-rise offices around the world and the bullet points dashing across computer screens inside. His account of PowerPoint's parentage does not exactly match Diffie's, but he readily accepts his former colleague as "my inspiration." In the late 1970s and early '80s, Gaskins was BNR's head of computer-science research. A former Berkeley PhD student, he had a family background in industrial photographic supplies and grew up around overhead projectors and inks and gels. In 1982, he returned from a six-month overseas business trip and, with a vivid sense of the future impact of the Apple Macintosh and of Microsoft's Windows (both of which were in development), he wrote a list of fifty commercial possibilities — Arabic typesetting, menus, signs. And then he looked around his own laboratory and realized what had happened while he was away: Following Diffie's lead, his colleagues were trying to make overheads to pitch their projects for funding, despite the

---

Lenin: Vladimir Ilych Lenin (1870–1924), a Communist revolutionary in Russia.

difficulties of using the equipment. (What you saw was not at all what you got.) "Our mainframe was buckling under the load," Gaskins says.

He now had his idea: a graphics program that would work with Windows and the Macintosh, and that would put together, and edit, a string of single pages, or "slides." In 1984, he left BNR, joined an ailing Silicon Valley software firm, Forethought, in exchange for a sizable share of the company, and hired a software developer, Dennis Austin. They began work on a program called Presenter. After a trademark problem, and an epiphany Gaskins had in the shower, Presenter became PowerPoint.

Gaskins is a precise, bookish man who lives with his wife in a meticulously restored and furnished nineteenth-century house in the Fillmore district of San Francisco. He has recently discovered an interest in antique concertinas. When I visited him, he was persuaded to play a tune, and he gave me a copy of a forthcoming paper he had cowritten: "A Wheatstone Twelve-Sided 'Edeophone' Concertina with Pre-MacCann Chromatic Duet Fingering." Gaskins is skeptical about the product that PowerPoint has become — AutoContent and animated fades between slides — but he is devoted to the simpler thing that it was, and he led me through a well-preserved archive of PowerPoint memorabilia, including the souvenir program for the PowerPoint reunion party, in 1997, which had a quiz filled with in-jokes about font size and programming languages. He also found an old business plan from 1984. One phrase — the only one in italics — read, "Allows the content-originator to control the presentation." For Gaskins, that had always been the point: to get rid of the intermediaries— graphic designers — and never mind the consequences. Whenever colleagues sought to restrict the design possibilities of the program (to make a design disaster less likely), Gaskins would overrule them, quoting Thoreau: "I came into this world, not chiefly to make this a good place to live in, but to live in it, be it good or bad."

PowerPoint 1.0 went on sale in April 1987 — available only for the Macintosh, and only in black-and-white. It generated text-and-graphics pages that a photocopier could turn into overhead transparencies. (This was before laptop computers and portable projectors made PowerPoint a tool for live electronic presentations. Gaskins thinks he may have been the first person to use the program in the modern way, in a Paris hotel in 1992 — which is like being the first person ever to tap a microphone and say, "Can you hear me at the back?") The Macintosh market was small and specialized, but within this market PowerPoint — the first product of its kind — was a hit. "I can't describe how wonderful it was," Gaskins says. "When we demonstrated at trade shows, we were mobbed." Shortly after the launch, Forethought accepted an acquisition offer of fourteen million dollars from Microsoft. Microsoft paid cash and allowed Bob Gaskins and his colleagues to remain partly self-governing in Silicon Valley, far from the Microsoft campus, in Redmond, Washington. Microsoft soon regretted the terms of the deal; PowerPoint workers became known for a troublesome independence of spirit (and for rewarding themselves, now and then, with beautifully staged parties — caviar, string quartets, Renaissance-period fancy dress).

PowerPoint had been created, in part, as a response to the new corporate world of interdepartmental communication. Those involved with the program now experienced the phenomenon at first hand. In 1990, the first PowerPoint for Windows was launched, alongside Windows 3.0. And PowerPoint quickly became what Gaskins calls "a cog in the great machine." The PowerPoint programmers were forced to make unwelcome changes, partly because in 1990 Word, Excel, and PowerPoint began to be integrated into Microsoft Office — a strategy that would eventually make PowerPoint invincible — and partly in response to market research. AutoContent was added in the mid-nineties, when Microsoft learned that some would-be presenters were uncomfortable with a blank PowerPoint page — it was hard to get started. "We said, 'What we need is some automatic content!'" a former Microsoft developer recalls, laughing. "'Punch the button and you'll have a presentation.'" The idea, he thought, was "crazy." And the name was meant as a joke. But Microsoft took the idea and kept the name — a rare example of a product named in outright mockery of its target customers.

Gaskins left PowerPoint in 1992, and many of his colleagues followed soon after. Now rich from Microsoft stock, and beginning the concertina-collecting phase of their careers, they watched as their old product made its way into the heart of American business culture. By 1993, PowerPoint had a majority share of the presentation market. In 1995, the average user created four and a half presentations a month. Three years later, the monthly average was nine. PowerPoint began to appear in cartoon strips and everyday conversation. A few years ago, Bob Gaskins was at a presentations-heavy conference in Britain. The organizer brought the proceedings to a sudden stop, saying, "I've just been told that the inventor of PowerPoint is in the audience — will he please identify himself so we can recognize his contribution to the advancement of science?" Gaskins stood up. The audience laughed and applauded.

Cathleen Belleville, a former graphic designer who worked at PowerPoint as a product planner from 1989 to 1995, was amazed to see a clip-art series she had created become modern business icons. The images were androgynous silhouette stick figures (she called them Screen Beans), modeled on a former college roommate: a little figure clicking its heels; another with an inspirational light bulb above its head. One Screen Bean, the patron saint of PowerPoint — a figure that stands beneath a question mark, scratching its head in puzzlement — is so popular that a lawyer at a New York firm who has seen many PowerPoint presentations claims never to have seen one without the head-scratcher. Belleville herself has seen her Beans all over the world, reprinted on baseball caps, blown up fifteen feet high in a Hamburg bank. "I told my mom, 'You know, my artwork is in danger of being more famous than the *Mona Lisa.*'" Above the counter in a laundromat on Third Avenue in New York, a sign explains that no responsibility can be taken for deliveries to doorman buildings. And there, next to the words, is the famous puzzled figure. It is hard to understand the puzzlement. Doorman? Delivery? But perhaps this is simply how a modern poster clears its throat: Belleville has created the international sign for *sign.*

According to Microsoft estimates, at least thirty million PowerPoint presentations are made every day. The program has about 95 percent of the presentations-software market. And so perhaps it was inevitable that it would migrate out of business and into other areas of our lives. I recently spoke to Sew Meng Chung, a Malaysian research engineer living in Singapore who got married in 1999. He told me that, as his guests took their seats for a wedding party in the Goodwood Park Hotel, they were treated to a PowerPoint presentation: 130 photographs — one fading into the next every four or five seconds, to musical accompaniment. "They were baby photos, and courtship photos, and photos taken with our friends and family," he told me.

I also spoke to Terry Taylor, who runs a Web site called eBibleTeacher.com, which supplies materials for churches that use electronic visual aids. "Jesus was a storyteller, and he gave graphic images," Taylor said. "He would say, 'Consider the lilies of the field, how they grow,' and all indications are that there were lilies in the field when he was talking, you know. He used illustrations." Taylor estimates that 15 percent of American churches now have video projectors, and many use PowerPoint regularly for announcements, for song lyrics, and to accompany preaching. (Taylor has seen more than one sermon featuring the head-scratching figure.) Visitors to Taylor's site can download photographs of locations in the Holy Land, as well as complete PowerPoint sermons—for example, "Making Your Marriage Great":

- Find out what you are doing to harm your marriage and heal it.
- Financial irresponsibility
- Temper
- Pornography
- Substance abuse
- You name it!

When PowerPoint is used to flash hymn lyrics, or make a quick pitch to a new client, or produce an eye-catching laundromat poster, it's easy to understand the enthusiasm of, say, Tony Kurz, the vice president for sales and marketing of a New York–based Internet company, who told me, "I love PowerPoint. It's a brilliant application. I can take you through at exactly the pace I want to take you." There are probably worse ways to transmit fifty or a hundred words of text, or information that is mainly visual—ways that involve more droning, more drifting. And PowerPoint demands at least some rudimentary preparation: A PowerPoint presenter is, by definition, not thinking about his or her material for the very first time. Steven Pinker, the author of *The Language Instinct* and a psychology professor at the Massachusetts Institute of Technology, says that PowerPoint can give visual shape to an argument. "Language is a linear medium: one damn word after another," he says. "But ideas are multidimensional. . . . When properly employed, PowerPoint makes the logical structure of an argument more transparent. Two channels sending the same information are better than one."

Still, it's hard to be perfectly comfortable with a product whose developers occasionally find themselves trying to suppress its use. Jolene Rocchio, who is a product planner for Microsoft Office (and is upbeat about PowerPoint in general), told me that, at a recent meeting of a nonprofit organization in San Francisco, she argued *against* a speaker's using PowerPoint at a future conference. "I said, 'I think we just need her to get up and speak.'" On an earlier occasion, Rocchio said, the same speaker had tried to use PowerPoint and the projector didn't work, "and everybody was, like, cheering. They just wanted to hear this woman speak, and they wanted it to be from her heart. And the PowerPoint almost alienated her audience."

This is the most common complaint about PowerPoint. Instead of human contact, we are given human display. "I think that we as a people have become unaccustomed to having real conversations with each other, where we actually give and take to arrive at a new answer. We present to each other, instead of discussing," Cathy Belleville says. Tad Simons, the editor of the magazine *Presentations* (whose second-grade son used PowerPoint for show-and-tell), is familiar with the sin of triple delivery, where precisely the same text is seen on the screen, spoken aloud, and printed on the handout in front of you (the "leave-behind," as it is known in some circles). "The thing that makes my heart sing is when somebody presses the 'B' button and the screen goes black and you can actually talk to the person," Simons told me.

In 1997, Sun Microsystems' chairman and CEO, Scott McNealy, 30 "banned" PowerPoint (a ban widely disregarded by his staff). The move might have been driven, in part, by Sun's public-relations needs as a Microsoft rival, but, according to McNealy, there were genuine productivity issues. "Why did we ban it? Let me put it this way: If I want to tell my forty thousand employees to attack, the word *attack* in ASCII is forty-eight bits. As a Microsoft Word document, it's 90,112 bits. Put that same word in a PowerPoint slide and it becomes 458,048 bits. That's a pig through the python when you try to send it over the Net." McNealy's concern is shared by the American military. Enormously elaborate PowerPoint files (generated by presentation obsessives — so-called PowerPoint Rangers) were said to be clogging up the military's bandwidth. Last year, to the delight of many under his command, General Henry H. Shelton, the chairman of the Joint Chiefs of Staff, issued an order to U.S. bases around the world insisting on simpler presentations.

PowerPoint was developed to give public speakers control over design decisions. But it's possible that those speakers should be making other, more important decisions. "In the past, I think we had an inefficient system, where executives passed all of their work to secretaries," Cathy Belleville says. "But now we've got highly paid people sitting there formatting slides — spending hours formatting slides — because it's more fun to do that than concentrate on what you're going to say. It would be much more efficient to off-load that work onto someone who could do it in a tenth of the time, and be paid less. Millions of executives around the world are sitting there going, 'Arial? Times Roman? Twenty-four point? Eighteen point?'"

In the glow of a PowerPoint show, the world is condensed, simplified, and smoothed over — yet bright and hyperreal — like the cityscape background in a PlayStation motor race. PowerPoint is strangely adept at disguising the fragile foundations of a proposal, the emptiness of a business plan; usually, the audience is respectfully still (only venture capitalists dare to dictate the pace of someone else's slide show), and, with the visual distraction of a dancing pie chart, a speaker can quickly move past the laughable flaw in his argument. If anyone notices, it's too late — the narrative presses on.

Last year, three researchers at Arizona State University, including Robert Cialdini, a professor of psychology and the author of "Influence: Science and Practice," conducted an experiment in which they presented three groups of volunteers with information about Andrew, a fictional high-school student under consideration for a university football scholarship. One group was given Andrew's football statistics typed on a piece of paper. The second group was shown bar graphs. Those in the third group were given a PowerPoint presentation, in which animated bar graphs grew before their eyes.

Given Andrew's record, what kind of prospect was he? According to Cialdini, when Andrew was PowerPointed, viewers saw him as a greater potential asset to the football team. The first group rated Andrew four and a half on a scale of one to seven; the second rated him five; and the PowerPoint group rated him six. PowerPoint gave him power. The experiment was repeated, with three groups of sports fans that were accustomed to digesting sports statistics; this time, the first two groups gave Andrew the same rating. But the group that saw the PowerPoint presentation still couldn't resist it.

Again, Andrew got a six. PowerPoint seems to be a way for organizations to turn expensive, expert decision makers into novice decision makers. "It's frightening," Cialdini says. He always preferred to use slides when he spoke to business groups, but one high-tech company recently hinted that his authority suffered as a result. "They said, 'You know what, Bob? You've got to get into PowerPoint, otherwise people aren't going to respond.' So I made the transfer."

Clifford Nass has an office overlooking the Oval lawn at Stanford, a university ₃₅ where the use of PowerPoint is so widespread that to refrain from using it is sometimes seen as a mark of seniority and privilege, like egg on one's tie. Nass once worked for Intel, and then got a PhD in sociology, and now he writes about and lectures on the ways people think about computers. But, before embarking on any of that, Professor Nass was a professional magician — Cliff Conjure — so he has some confidence in his abilities as a public performer.

According to Nass, who now gives PowerPoint lectures because his students asked him to, PowerPoint "lifts the floor" of public speaking: A lecture is less likely to be poor if the speaker is using the program. "What PowerPoint does is very efficiently deliver content," Nass told me. "What students gain is a lot more information—not just facts but rules, ways of thinking, examples."

At the same time, PowerPoint "lowers the ceiling," Nass says. "What you miss is the process. The classes I remember most, the professors I remember most, were the ones where you could watch how they thought. You don't remember what they said, the details. It was 'What an elegant way to wrap around a problem!' PowerPoint takes that away. PowerPoint gives you the outcome, but it removes the process."

"What I miss is, when I used to lecture without PowerPoint, every now and then I'd get a cool idea," he went on. "I remember once it just hit me. I'm lecturing, and all of a sudden I go, 'God! *The Wizard of Oz*! The scene at the end of *The Wizard of Oz*!'" Nass, telling this story, was almost shouting. (The lecture, he later explained, was about definitions of "the human" applied to computers.) "I just went for it — twenty-five minutes. And to this day students who were in that class remember it. That couldn't happen now: 'Where the hell is the slide?'"

PowerPoint could lead us to believe that information is *all* there is. According to Nass, PowerPoint empowers the provider of simple content (and that was the task Bob Gaskins originally set for it), but it risks squeezing out the provider of process — that is to say, the rhetorician, the storyteller, the poet, the person whose thoughts cannot be arranged in the shape of an AutoContent slide. "I hate to admit this," Nass said, "but I actually removed a book from my syllabus last year because I couldn't figure out how to PowerPoint it. It's a lovely book called *Interface Culture*, by Steven Johnson, but it's very discursive; the charm of it is the throwaways. When I read this book, I thought, My head's filled with ideas, and now I've got to write out exactly what those ideas are, and — they're not neat." He couldn't get the book into bullet points; every time he put something down, he realized that it wasn't quite right. Eventually, he abandoned the attempt, and, instead of a lecture, he gave his students a recommendation. He told them it was a good book, urged them to read it, and moved on to the next bullet point.

Working with the Text

1. Based on interviews with designers as well as critics and users of PowerPoint, Ian Parker observes that "[i]n the glow of a PowerPoint show, the world is condensed, simplified, and smoothed over — yet bright and hyperreal — like the cityscape background in a PlayStation motor race" (par. 32). Parker shares the view of one of his sources, Clifford Nass of the Department of Communication at Stanford University, that "PowerPoint empowers the provider of simple content . . . , but it risks squeezing out the provider of process . . . whose thoughts cannot be arranged in the shape of an AutoContent slide" (par. 39). Drawing on your experience with PowerPoint as well as on Parker's argument, write a brief essay in which you argue for or against his critique of PowerPoint and its effects on how we think.

2. Parker devotes part of his article to describing the impetus behind the development of PowerPoint, when advancements in technology coincided with a time when "America began to go to more meetings" (par. 13). As you reread the article, note the developments in the American business environment that created the need for more meetings. In a brief essay, analyze this development, explaining to a group of peers why it would give rise to the demands PowerPoint was designed to meet.

3. According to Parker, a sign of PowerPoint's influence over the "restraints" and "rules" of business presentations is "the 'Rule of Seven': 'Seven (7) bullets or lines per page, seven (7) words per line,'" rules created by a "leading U.S. computer manufacturer" that are now widely used in the business world (par. 8). In a small group, explore Parker's concerns by using the "Rule of Seven" to develop a PowerPoint presentation that captures his argument. At the end of the presentation, describe and discuss your experience with the "Rule" with the entire class. Did you find, as Parker suggests, that the rules were "soothing"? Were they confining? How did they influence the ways in which you thought about the article?

policing trademarks has become more complicated due to the thousands of misuses that can appear on the Internet. Simply enter "Jell-O" on any search engine and you will be presented with hundreds of misuses of Kraft's registered trademark. Because trademark owners must vigorously enforce their marks or they risk loss of trademark rights, the Internet presents special problems for trademark owners. A number of companies have hired agencies to scour the Internet for misuses of their marks and then send e-mail requests asking the user to cease use of the registered mark. (See Exhibit 6–3.)

Trademark owners should thus maintain a consistent level of enforcement and protection for their marks; however, the need for active enforcement should be balanced by the reality that it may be impossible to detect and stop all infringing uses, especially insignificant and minor uses of the mark. Some experts suggest using an initial warning letter, informing the user of the owner's rights and stating that the trademark owner will continue to monitor the user to ensure infringement does not occur. In any event, courts seem to be recognizing this dilemma, and at least one judge has remarked that a trademark owner is not bound to "take on" more than one infringer at a time.

Remedies for Infringement

A plaintiff who is successful in proving trademark infringement might obtain a variety of remedies, including the following:

- an **injunction** preventing the defendant from further use of the confusingly similar mark, ordering an infringer to disable an offending web site, or ordering the defendant to print a notice (called a *disclaimer*) on its goods that it

EXHIBIT 6–3
Case Study: Food Fight

In 1968 the Kern family registered the trademark DERBY-PIE® for their chocolate and walnut pie first served in their restaurant in Kentucky. Since then, the family has challenged a variety of users of its registered mark, including church cookbooks, *Bon Appetit* magazine, and the *Washington Post* newspaper, all of which published recipes for "Derby Pie." In fact, the family has hired an individual to scour the Internet to find offending uses of its mark. The users are then sent an e-mail request to cease using the registered trademark. If the misuse persists, the family has often sued, instituting about thirty lawsuits over the years to protect the mark, including a lawsuit against the Public Broadcasting Service, which featured actress Annie Potts baking her grandmother's "Derby Pie" on a televised broadcast. Thus, there's only one DERBY-PIE®. Everyone else is baking chocolate nut pie.

Similarly, Unilever has hired an agency to review the Internet to find infringing uses of its marks POPSICLE®, CREAMSICLE®, and FUDGSICLE®, and Pillsbury has a registration for BAKE-OFF® and will not allow other baking contests to use the name. Finally, your recipes can call for "hot sauce" or "chocolate chips" but not TABASCO® or TOLL HOUSE® morsels.

4. Review Parker's description of the Arizona State University experiment that asked subjects to assess the scholarship prospects of a fictional high school athlete named Andrew. Note the outcome of both phases of the experiment, as well as Parker's assertion that "PowerPoint seems to be a way for organizations to turn expensive, expert decision makers into novice decision makers" (par. 34). In a brief essay, analyze Parker's assertion. What does his assertion mean? How did he draw such a conclusion from the results of the experiment? Why did he end his account of this experiment with the story told by one of the researchers, Robert Cialdini, in which Cialdini was advised by representatives from a high-tech company to "'get into PowerPoint, otherwise people aren't going to respond'" (par. 34)?

From Text to Field

1. The use of PowerPoint has become so widespread that most of us have viewed, and even produced, a PowerPoint presentation. With Parker's critique in mind, write a personal essay in which you reflect on your experience of viewing or using PowerPoint. In what ways did it aid or constrain you? In what ways did it clarify or distort the content of the presentation or the process of your thinking?

2. In his critique of what he considers to be the limitations of PowerPoint, Parker makes a distinction between conveying simple content and capturing complex thought processes. Based on Parker's descriptions and your own experience of PowerPoint in the classroom or in other settings — such as religious organizations, athletic organizations, or clubs—write an essay in which you identify the kinds of rhetorical or communication situations in which you think PowerPoint would or would not work. Where and why would it be effective? Where and why would it be ineffective?

3. Parker points out that Bob Gaskins, the primary creator of PowerPoint, pressed for a design that "'Allows the content-originator to control the presentation.'" In spite of Gaskins's early efforts, PowerPoint became, according to Parker, a highly structured "antidote to fear." Drawing on your observations and knowledge of human behavior, as well as Parker's argument, write an essay in which you analyze the reasons for this course of development. Why would users prefer constraints rather than creative freedom?

4. Imagine that you are part of a marketing group proposing PowerPoint enhancements to Microsoft's software designers. Based on Parker's critique as well as your experience, what capabilities would you add to the program? What current capabilities would you consider changing or deleting altogether? Working with a small group, brainstorm the possibilities and agree on a brief proposal.

As a group, use PowerPoint to develop a presentation of your proposal to give to the class. To gain insight into Parker's contrast between simple content and complex process, try to incorporate both into your presentation. Be prepared to discuss your experience with the class.

Writing Culture

Jay David Bolter

As most of us focus on learning to work with rapidly evolving computer technologies, Jay David Bolter and his colleagues are asking how those technologies are shaping our minds and our cultures. For Bolter, the questions are as much historical and philosophical as they are social and cultural. How do electronic technologies of writing define cultural relationships? What are the differences between a print culture and a network culture, and what are the issues as we transition from one to the other? How are questions of intellectual property serving as barometers of this transition? Is cultural unity and stability possible—or even desirable—in the chaotic distributed system that is the new network culture? How will new technologies of writing shape culture, and how will that culture in turn shape writing?

"Writing Culture" is the final chapter in Bolter's 2001 book, *Writing Space: Computers, Hypertext, and the Remediation of Print* (an updated and revised second edition of his widely read and debated 1991 book, *Writing Space: The Computer, Hypertext, and the History of Writing*). The new edition reflects Bolter's current interest in "remediation," which he describes as "the ways in which new digital media refashion or 'remediate' older visual and verbal forms."

Bolter's education spans the study of Greek, computer science, and the classics. He is Wesley Professor of New Media in the School of Literature, Communications, and Culture at the Georgia Institute of Technology, where he also serves as director of the Center for New Media Research and Education. His primary interest is the computer as a new medium for verbal and visual communication. Other publications include *Turing's Man: Western Culture in the Computer Age* (1984), *Remediation: Understanding New Media* (1999, coauthored with Richard Grusin), and *Windows and Mirrors: Electronic Art, Design, and the Myth of Transparency* (2003, coauthored with Diane Gromala), along with numerous articles on reading, writing, and visualization in computer environments.

The Network Culture

Just as we can claim to write our minds, we can also claim to write the culture in which we live. And just as we have used print technology in the past, so we are now turning to electronic technologies of writing to define our cultural relationships both metaphorically and operationally. If, as Sherry Turkle (1995) and others have argued, electronic communication corresponds to a postmodern sense of self, it may also correspond to a postmodern definition of affiliation and community. We exploit the World Wide Web, e-mail, and chat rooms to facilitate a culture of temporary allegiances and changing cultural positions — to fashion our "network culture." The Internet and particularly the Web become for us a metaphor for the ways in which we function in our various communities by sending out dozens of links to sites of interest or contestation. We compile hot lists or bookmarks that indicate which groups we choose to belong to at any given moment, and we can erase these lists as easily as we create them.

It is a truism that American culture encourages individualism and therefore breaks with the European traditions of many of its immigrants. In the 1980s, before the explosion of interest in the Internet, the authors of *Habits of the Heart* saw contemporary, though not perhaps postmodern, individualism as the culmination of this historical process:

> [T]he colonists [to America] brought with them ideas of social obligation and group formation that disposed them to re-create in America structures of family, church, and polity that could continue . . . the texture of older European society. Only gradually did it become clear that every social obligation was vulnerable, every tie between individuals fragile. Only gradually did what we have called ontological individualism, the idea that the individual is the only firm reality, become widespread (Bellah, Madsen, Sullivan, Sundler, & Tipton, 1985, p. 276).

But if individuals become indeed "the only firm reality," this does not mean that American individuals would no longer form groups. Americans may well form more groups than ever, because they feel so much freer to associate and break off their associations as they please. Individuals now regularly join and quit jobs, neighborhoods, clubs, political parties and action committees, and even churches several times in their lives. These affiliations are all seen as voluntary, and they are usually horizontal rather than vertical. The network is displacing the hierarchy. The culture of interconnections both reflects and is reflected in our new technology of writing, so that, with all these transitions, the making and breaking of social links, people are beginning to function as elements in a hypertextual network of affiliations.

Electronic communication is increasingly the medium through which we form and maintain our affiliations. E-mail, chat rooms, and the World Wide Web have become sites for highly mediated versions of community. These new technologies join earlier ones that have promoted visions and versions of community: television, radio, and film as well as print. However, if our culture has chosen to exploit these earlier technologies largely for their ability to unify and homogenize cultural difference, we seem today to prefer to deploy electronic technologies in other ways, as interactive applications that allow individuals to talk back and talk to each other.

There is nothing inevitable about the construction of our network culture. 5 We could have chosen to exploit computers to reinforce traditional notions of community — perhaps by strengthening communication channels for existing institutional structures. What we have come to valorize in electronic communication, however, is largely the capacity to promote multiplicity, heterogeneity, and immediate, if temporary, connections. The popular writer Fred Rheingold argued in *Virtual Community* (1994) that news groups and bulletin boards could both reconstitute local communities and forge new groups from those who share common interests but are separated in space. He pointed to thousands or millions of users who have shared the vision of the virtual community since the prototype of such a community, the WELL, was formed in the San Francisco Bay area in the 1980s:

> People in virtual communities use words on screens to exchange pleasantries and argue, engage in intellectual discourse, conduct commerce, exchange knowledge, share emotional support, make plans, brainstorm, gossip, feud, fall in love, find friends and lose them . . . To the millions who have been drawn into it, the richness and vitality of computer-linked cultures is attractive, even addictive. There is no such thing as a single, monolithic, online subculture; it's more like an ecosystem of subcultures, some frivolous, some serious (p. 3).

Clearly what Rheingold values is the diversity that finds expression in these virtual environments, a diversity that is for him ultimately liberating on a political as well as personal level:

> The technology that makes virtual communities possible has the potential to bring enormous leverage to ordinary citizens at relatively little cost — intellectual leverage, social leverage, commercial leverage, and most important political leverage. But the technology will not in itself fulfill that potential; this latent technical power must be used intelligently and deliberately by an informed population. More people must learn about that leverage and learn to use it, while we still have the freedom to do so, if it is to live up to its potential (pp. 4–5).

For those, like Rheingold, who see the Internet and Web as enabling new forms of community or democratic empowerment, there remains the key problem that the technology is not universally available. Although it is called the "World Wide Web," this global hypertext system is largely limited to North America, Europe, Israel, and the developed countries of the Far East. As it continues to expand, the Web will likely remain limited to the middle and upper classes in the third world as elsewhere, so that the virtual communities that the Web and Internet mediate will remain exclusive as well. To say that these virtual communities will be exclusive, however, is not to say that they will be elite in the traditional sense. In developed countries, millions of users find on the Web expressions of their popular culture (from fan sites for film stars or country music divas to sites on weight loss or astrology) as well as their commodity culture (in online marketing and sales sites offering everything from books and CD-ROMs to fine wines or used cars). Traditional high culture is also represented, but has no special claim to the user's attention.

Cultural Unity

One consequence of this networking of culture is in fact the abandonment of the ideal of high culture (literature, music, the fine arts) as a unifying force. If there is no single culture, but only a network of interest groups, then there can be no single favored literature or music. Nor is there a single standard of grammar or diction in writing. Elizabeth Eisenstein (1979) has argued that printing was used to promote cultural unification during the centuries when the modern nation-states were being formed. "Typography arrested linguistic drift, enriched as well as standardized vernaculars, and paved the way for the more deliberate purification and codification of all major European languages" (vol. 1, p. 117). Today we are exploiting electronic writing to oppose standardization and unification as well as hierarchy. The World Wide Web is a famously chaotic distributed system, in which individuals or their organizations are free to create new pages and sites and to add them to the global hypertext without the approval or even the knowledge of any central authority. The Web offers as a paradigm a writing system that changes to suit its audiences of reader-writers rather than expecting that audience to conform to some predetermined authority or standard.

As we rewrite our culture into a vast hypertext, each of us as readers becomes free to choose to explore one subnetwork or as many as she wishes. It is no longer convincing to say that one subject is more important than another. Today even highly educated readers, humanists as well as scientists and social scientists, may know only one or a few areas well. Such ignorance of any shared textual tradition is in part the result of the specialization of the sciences that has been proceeding since the seventeenth century. But even the humanities are now utterly fragmented, so that a student of postcolonial literature may know very little about Renaissance poetry or ancient epic. The Web itself with its millions of pages is far too large and disorganized for any individual to encompass it, and the Web is still small in comparison with the verbal and visual information stored in a large research library, where the materials are much better organized but vastly beyond the scale of an individual reader.

Through the last decades there has remained some uneasiness about this situation: hence the traditionalist's plea for a canon of great authors, his call somehow to reestablish a core of textual knowledge that everyone must possess. But the specialization in the sciences and the humanities and social sciences has gone far too far to be recalled. The academic world, like the rest of our culture, is now defined by its numerous "special interest groups." Although all the groups are interconnected — some grew out of others, and each sends out runners (links) into other camps — nevertheless, an overarching unification is no longer even the goal. In *After Virtue*, published in 1981, just prior to the advent of electronic writing, Alasdair MacIntyre was already complaining about the fragmented state of moral philosophy and drew the following analogy (MacIntyre, 1981). Imagine an environmental catastrophe that causes human society to turn against modern science. Scientists are persecuted, and science texts are torn up or destroyed. Then imagine a later generation trying to reassemble these fragments ("half-chapters from books, single pages from articles, not always fully legible because torn and charred") into a single system. The result would be a mish-mash of incoherent theories and misunderstood facts. Of course, this disaster has not happened to modern science, but it is, according to MacIntyre, exactly what happened to the great systems of moral philosophy (pp. 2–3). For MacIntyre, the disaster was the Enlightenment. MacIntyre's analogy can be extended beyond moral philosophy to almost all humanistic fields today: Each is an incomplete and disorganized hypertext that no one knows how to read in its entirety.

To call this fragmentation a disaster, however, is to assume that unity is an achievable and desirable goal. In fact, the fragmentation of our textual world is only a problem when judged by the standards of print technology, which expects the humanities, including metaphysics and ethics, to be relatively stable and hierarchically organized. Postmodern culture values instead the heterogeneity and spontaneity of shifting positions — the ability to form small groups that fit local circumstances. Ironically, the global hypertext of the World Wide Web affords small groups just such an opportunity: groups with interests in dead languages, in local or national political problems, in any imaginable disease can each have Web sites. The tiniest

10

political organization or interest group can afford to purchase space on a Web server somewhere in the world and to make that space available to its members. Hypertextual publication can and does accommodate all the mutually incomprehensible languages that the academic and political worlds now speak. Within the hypertextual libraries that are now being assembled, individual communities can retreat into their subnetworks and operate with as much or as little connection to each other as they desire.

On the World Wide Web, as elsewhere, the distinction between high culture and popular culture has all but vanished. If one click of the mouse will take a Web surfer to Project Gutenberg, a textual repository of the "classics" (www.gutenberg.net September 6, 1999), another click will take her to sites for current Hollywood movies or popular music on CD or to ostensibly marginal sites for body art or homeopathy. The ease and equality of access to all the various forms of cultural representation (including pornography) appall traditionalists, who want to see a hierarchy that reinforces the distinction between respectable literature and forbidden images. On the Web, however, none of the familiar indications of quality apply. A site on body piercing may be far better designed than the ASCII° format of Shakespeare's plays available through Project Gutenberg. An unwillingness to distinguish between high art and popular entertainment has long been a feature of American culture, and we have chosen to confirm and accelerate this trend in the Web and other new media forms.

The Remediation of Culture

Electronic forms of communication give us the opportunity to redefine cultural ideals inherited from printed genres and forms. We have been discussing one such redefinition: the breakdown of the distinction between elite and popular literature (and art in general). This breakdown was not determined or predetermined by our shift to electronic communications. It is rather that our network culture, which rejects such hierarchical distinctions, finds in the Internet and the Web media that it can shape to express its preference for popular forms. More generally, our network culture is construing new media as radical forces that disrupt the traditions of print.

For hundreds of years, we had associated with print an ideal of stability: Print was supposed to preserve and promote a stable, authoritative, and yet vital literate culture, in which tradition and innovation were in balance and in which verbal representations were of a higher order than visual. This is the ideal espoused in the late age of print by cultural traditionalists or political

---

ASCII: The acronym for American Standard Code for Information Interchange, a coding system based on the English alphabet that represents text in computer and digital devices.

conservatives from Sven Birkerts (1994) and Mark Slouka (1995) to William Bennett (1984). Just as there are many cultural constructions for electronic writing, however, there have also been many constructions for print. At various historical moments, print technology could in fact have been used to radicalize culture. The most obvious example would be the publication of printed tracts by Reformation theologians and polemicists (Eisenstein, 1979, pp. 303–450). Historian Carla Hesse (1996) has explored another historical moment, pointing out that Condorcet° and other Enlightenment thinkers also saw printed newspapers and periodicals as instruments of revolution:

> The best way to spread knowledge, according to Condorcet, was through authorless and open-ended texts, circulating freely between all citizens: He imagined the periodical press supported through the mechanism of subscription rather than through the institution of royalties to authors or monopolies to publishers. Indeed, what Condorcet conceived of as an ideally transparent mode of exchange through the deregulation of print publishing looks a lot like a mechanical version of the Internet (p. 24).

Although in the past print could be construed as radical, this is not its role today, according to either the critics of or the enthusiasts for electronic writing. In the late age of print, electronic technology defines itself as remediation, and print technology defines itself as resisting that remediation. Some enthusiasts for electronic writing still believe that it can radicalize our culture by providing that transparency that Condorcet ascribed to print publication. For these enthusiasts, the goal of perfect or authentic communication has not changed; they are simply pursuing the goal with new technological means. For them, electronic writing in chat rooms or by e-mail is more diverse and democratic, because unlike print, electronic writing can be published without the intervention of authorities (publishers and editors) who will decide on its commercial or intellectual value and therefore enforce cultural norms and biases. The traditionalists, too, still believe in authentic communication, but authenticity for them is defined differently. They favor their construction of print, with its traditions, its hierarchies, and its unidirectional form of communication. For them the authenticity of print derives from the privileged nature of the dialogue it fosters—a dialogue in which the author is necessarily dominant. As Laura Miller put it, in terms almost of sexual domination, readers in print crave "the intimacy to be had in allowing a beloved author's voice into the sanctums of

People are beginning to function as elements in a hypertextual network of affiliations.

15

°*Condorcet:* Marie Jean Antoine Nicolas Caritat, marquis de Condorcet (1743–1794), a French philosopher, mathematician, and political scientist whose writings embody the ideals of the Enlightenment and rationalism.

our minds" (NY *Times*, 1998, p. 43). For Miller this "intimacy" is what constitutes an authentic reading experience.

To what extent do the technologies determine these different qualities that our culture is assigning? It seems clear that communication on the Internet could have evolved differently. Instead of diversity and distribution, communications systems on the Internet could have been designed to emphasize uniformity and central control. Computer systems after all can easily produce identical copies of data and establish and monitor the hierarchical control of information. In the 1980s, however, the Internet matured through the efforts of dedicated computer specialists, mostly graduate students and faculty in universities. They constructed a technology that was congenial to their culture, in which individual autonomy was highly prized. That the World Wide Web grew out of that same culture explains its distributed architecture, lack of security, and use of the hypertext model of associative linking. We can easily imagine a World Wide Web protocol in which all sites had to be registered and validated by a central authority, but that protocol would have contradicted the ethos of the Internet community at the time. By the time the Web had become a cultural phenomenon and attracted the attention of the corporate and government bureaucracies, it was too late to change its architecture radically. Control issues continue to be raised: for example, the questions of censoring pornography on the Web and of protecting intellectual property (or the economic interests of the entertainment industry). These questions are often met with the answer that the technology itself will defeat almost any method of censorship and that any means of protecting intellectual property must be evaluated in terms of what the technology, as constructed, will permit. The hierarchies of previous information technologies do not seem to be easily grafted onto the network technologies of today.

Theorists in the humanities and social sciences would, however, argue that hierarchies based on gender, race, and economic advantage remain strong in our culture. The late age of print is like late capitalism in this respect. It is a well-known irony that global capitalism is flourishing at the very time when it is being condemned by theorists to senescence. Similarly, in the late age of print, books and other printed materials are more abundant than ever: Laser printers and copying machines are largely responsible. Once again, the term "late" does not mean that print technology is necessarily about to disappear: It may continue to survive and even prosper for an undetermined future. The term refers instead to the relationship of print technology to our literate culture. The printed book is no longer the only or necessarily the most important space in which we locate our texts and images. For all our communicative purposes, print is now measured over against digital technology, and the ideal of perfect communication that our culture associated with print is under constant challenge.

is not affiliated with the plaintiff (for example, in one recent case, the publisher of *Polo* magazine was ordered to issue a disclaimer stating, "not affiliated with Polo Ralph Lauren," to avoid consumer confusion);

• *monetary damages* to compensate the plaintiff for the damage it has suffered, including actual damages due to lost sales and injury to its reputation and goodwill (which damages may be trebled, if necessary to compensate the plaintiff), and an accounting of the profits earned by defendant (however, no profits and no damages may be recovered unless the defendant had actual knowledge of the trademark registration—thus, a registrant should always use the registration symbol ® to afford such notice);

• *seizure* or *destruction* of the infringing articles and related marketing materials; and/or

• *costs* of the action, including attorneys' fees and actual expenditures.

Courts have noted that injunctive relief is the "remedy of choice" for infringement because stopping the infringing use is usually the trademark owner's primary goal. If an infringing use is for a similar good or service, a broad injunction is especially appropriate. As to monetary relief, the largest trademark verdict to date is $143 million awarded against Pfizer Inc. for use of the mark TROVAN® registered to another, although the case was reversed on appeal. *Trovan Ltd. v. Pfizer Inc.*, No. CV-98-0094 (C.D. Cal. 2000).

Resolving an Infringement Dispute

Because an infringement action, like any civil action, is expensive and time-consuming, parties often try to resolve trademark disputes between themselves before or during the pendency of litigation. Typically, a party who believes its mark is being infringed will send a cease and desist letter (see Exhibit 6–4) to the alleged infringer, notifying the infringer of its rights to the mark and demanding that the infringer cease any further use of the confusingly similar mark. Even if the cease and desist letter does not achieve the goal of convincing the infringer to stop use of the mark, it puts the infringer on notice of the prospective plaintiff's rights and thus serves to cut off any defense of good faith or lack of knowledge of the existence of the prior mark the infringer may later attempt to assert. Moreover, as discussed above, informing another of a registration allows one to recover damages for infringement. Investigation should be conducted before sending a threatening letter to ensure the alleged infringer is the junior user. Otherwise, the alleged infringer may turn the tables on the sender of the letter.

The accused infringer typically responds to the cease and desist letter by denying its allegations, asserting various defenses, or suggesting a compromise. A compromise might be reached by the parties agreeing to use their marks only in certain geographic areas. The accused infringer might agree to place a prominent notice on its goods that it is not affiliated in any way with the prior user (although called a *disclaimer,* this notice is different from the disclaimer used in the prosecution process when an applicant disclaims or agrees it has no exclusive rights in a descriptive term in a mark). The parties might agree that the defendant should modify its mark in some way or gradually phase out use of the infringing mark. They may enter into a monetary arrangement whereby the infringer pays a sum of money to the senior user to license the mark. One party may acquire the other's mark by outright purchase. One party might agree to assign its interest in the mark to the other who then permits or licenses the original assignor to use the mark. They may agree to have an arbitrator resolve the dispute rather than going to federal court.

That ideal is deeply ingrained, however, and may not be easily over-turned. The recent history of intellectual property shows us how tenacious the standard can be. The modern legal concepts of intellectual property and the ownership of ideas and their expression grew up in the eighteenth century and have developed since that time in the context of print technology (see Woodmansee & Jaszi, 1994). Many of these concepts fit comfortably into our current world of print, but do not seem to make sense for new media forms. In print, the words and images are determined once and for all in the process of publication, so that the expression of an idea fixed in words and images can be copyrighted. In the electronic writing space, as we have seen, words and images are not necessarily fixed; instead, they are called forth through the interaction of the author(s), the computer system, and the readers. Electronic documents can also be copied and altered with remarkable ease. On the World Wide Web, for example, every time a reader visits a page, she is in fact making a copy of that page, with all its images, in her computer. Although she cannot modify the page at its source (on the server), she can always save and even revise the version that she has captured on her machine.

If technologies really determined cultural values, then the notion of copyright would already have been severely curtailed, if not abolished, at least for electronic publication. Hypertext certainly seems to suggest a different economic and social model (e.g., Samuelson & Glushko, 1991). And it could be argued that popular notions of intellectual property are in fact changing: People use copying machines, VCRs, and computer storage to make the copies that they require without much concern for legal propriety. Nevertheless, powerful economic forces (of late capitalism) are seeking to extend the notion of ownership of verbal and especially audiovisual materials throughout the realm of electronic media. They are seeking to set even stricter limits on the rights of readers and viewers to make fair use of copyrighted materials (Samuelson, 1997). Tyanna Herrington sees an ideological struggle around the question of intellectual property — a struggle between those who want to use electronic technologies to distribute information and entertainment for what they see as social benefit and those who want to insure economic gain for the (corporate) owners of information and entertainment. Rather than acknowledging that the notion of intellectual property is socially constructed, economic interests, with the help of the government, are insisting that electronic text, graphics, audio, and video are all property in a strict sense, sanctioned by a long legal tradition (see Herrington, forthcoming). Instead of withering in the electronic age, the notion of intellectual property seems to be strengthening and extending itself into new domains.

Our late age of print is characterized by such struggles, as economically 20 dominant groups and forces attempt to define the new technology to their advantage, usually by extending definitions appropriate to earlier technologies that they already dominate. Notions of intellectual property are extrapolated from those appropriate to print and the music and film industries. Entertainment giants have been trying to "converge" new media around the model of commercial, broadcast television. Electronic commerce on the Internet has focused on reestablishing familiar genres and services: newspapers and magazines, bookstores, auctions, pornography, and so on. On the other hand, other constructions of new media are working subtly against the extension of older models of economic and cultural control. Our culture continues to find in these new forms, particularly in the Internet and on the World Wide Web, qualities of decentralization, local autonomy, and flexibility. It is for this reason that politicians from across the spectrum, at least in the United States, speak of the democratic and educational potential of the Internet: They are simply developing a rhetoric to which their constituents respond.

Thus, the reforming or remediating potential of the new writing space has probably not been exhausted. It would be foolish to doubt the power that entrenched hierarchies will bring to bear in forcing new media technologies into traditional formal, legal, and economic structures. Nevertheless, it seems likely that these traditional structures will be changed even as they attempt to assimilate new media. For example, those in the television and computer industry who are trying to promote Web television must find something to distinguish their product from pure broadcast television. So they are envisioning ways in which the Web could serve as an information resource for traditional television programs. They imagine a viewer watching a sporting event on television, having a question, and then using her browser to access a database of sports information while the television broadcast proceeds. As unimaginative as this scenario is, it nevertheless defines a changed relationship between the viewer and the viewing space. It presents an opening for the viewer to intervene in the flow of traditional television and suggests, however timidly, a myriad of other possibilities, other ways to arrange the act of communication.

It seems likely that our heterogeneous culture will choose to explore many of these possibilities — revised relationships between the media that we have known and the new media in which we are rediscovering the familiar. The future of text as a remediator of culture is uncertain, even if text (as hypertext) continues to serve a variety of functions in cyberspace. Textual forms such as e-mail, chat facilities, and even MOOs° remain popular precisely because of their role in defining electronic community. Teachers and scholars continue to promote these electronic textual forms as refashioners of the traditional

----

MOOs: An online system where multiple users are connected simultaneously.

sense of community that was (and is) mediated by face-to-face meetings and conventional mail. E-mail and chat facilities still provide most users with their best means of "talking back" in cyberspace. Although millions of World Wide Web participants now have the skills and opportunity to create their own Web sites combining graphics and text, a far larger number of the hundreds of millions of Internet users can still only be consumers of Web sites and other multimedia forms. That far larger number, however, can be producers as well as consumers of verbal e-mail. In other words, multimedia remains a somewhat privileged mode of communication within the already privileged world of the Internet.

This situation may change. Even for users at home, it is becoming easier to generate as well as receive multimedia. When most users gain fast access to the Internet and have the software and hardware needed for audiovisual communication, will they continue to type e-mail messages? Will they not seek to recapture the immediacy of phone and face-to-face conversation through real-time, video and audio conferencing over the Internet? Will they not look to other audiovisual media (television, film, and radio) as defining the authenticity of communication that they wish to capture and refashion in new media? Will written verbal communication come to be regarded as an ancillary form, to be used when microphones or cameras fail or when the Internet connection is degraded?

It is fair to wonder whether the late age of print may also become the late age of prose itself.

References

Bellah, R. N., Madsen, R., Sullivan, W. M., Swidler, A., & Tipton, S. M. (1985). *Habits of the heart: Individualism and commitment in American life.* Berkeley: University of California Press.

Bennett, W. J. (1984). *To reclaim a legacy: A report on the humanities in higher education.* Washington, DC: National Endowment for the Humanities.

Birkerts, S. (1994). *The Gutenberg elegies: The fate of reading in an electronic age.* Boston: Faber and Faber.

Eisenstein, E. (1979). *The printing press as an agent of change: Communications and cultural transformations in early-modern Europe (Vols. 1–2).* Cambridge: Cambridge University Press.

Herrington, T. K. (forthcoming). *Controlling voices: Dissonance at the intersection of intellectual property, the Internet, and humanistic studies.* Carbondale, IL: Southern Illinois University Press.

Hesse, C. (1996). Books in time. In Geoffrey Nunberg (Ed.), *The future of the book* (pp. 21–36). Berkeley: University of California Press.

MacIntyre, A. (1981). *After virtue: A study in moral theory.* Notre Dame, IN: University of Notre Dame Press.

Miller, L. (1998, March 15). *www.claptrap.com.* In *New York Times Book Review,* p. 43.

Rheingold, H. (1994). *The virtual community: Homesteading the electronic frontier.* New York: HarperCollins.

Samuelson, P. (1997, May). The never-ending struggle for balance. *Communications of the ACM 40(5):* 17–21.

Samuelson, P., & Glushko, R. J. (1991). Intellectual property rights for digital library and hypertext publishing systems: An analysis of Xanadu. In *Hypertext '91 Proceedings* (pp. 39–50). New York: ACM.

Slouka, M. (1995). *War of the worlds: Cyberspace and the high-tech assault on reality.* New York: Basic Books.

Turkle, S. (1995). *Life on the screen: Identity in the age of the Internet.* New York: Simon & Schuster.

Woodmansee, M., & Jaszi, P. (Eds.). (1994). *The construction of authorship: Textual appropriation in law and literature.* Durham, NC: Duke University.

Working with the Text

1. Jay David Bolter writes near the middle of his essay: "In the late age of print, electronic technology defines itself as remediation, and print technology defines itself as resisting that remediation" (par. 15). This observation contains two terms — *late age of print* and *remediation* — that are central to Bolter's view of how new technologies are "writing" cultural change. Reread the selection with these two terms in mind, and then in a brief essay, analyze what Bolter means by both terms. In what ways are these terms central to Bolter's argument?

2. Even as new media undermine the dominance of print media, disputes about intellectual property have become ever more contentious. In a brief essay, explain why. Why has the "remediation" of culture made intellectual property a pressing and high profile issue?

3. Bolter concludes his essay with a provocative statement: "It is fair to wonder whether the late age of print may also become the late age of prose itself." Bearing in mind Bolter's understanding of the term *late age*, write a brief essay in which you first explain and interpret this comment and then agree or disagree with it. Does Bolter mean all prose, or does he mean prose as defined or esteemed given particular values or qualities?

From Text to Field

1. Early in his essay, Bolter writes: "We exploit the World Wide Web, e-mail, and chat rooms to facilitate a culture of temporary allegiances and changing cultural positions — to fashion our 'network culture'" (par. 1). After comparing notes and observations in a small group, write an essay in which you describe

your own "network culture" or your attitude to the network culture you see around you. To what degree have you been influenced by the network culture you experience around you? How—and why—might you shift allegiances and positions? How or why might you resist such shifting?

2. Some see the fragmentation of our cultural world as disastrous. Bolter responds by asking whether cultural unity "is an achievable and desirable goal" (par. 11). Bolter continues by observing that "the fragmentation of our textual world is only a problem when judged by the standards of print technology, which expects the humanities, including metaphysics and ethics, to be relatively stable and hierarchically organized" (par. 11). In an essay, characterize the state of the textual world in which you live and study. Is it fragmented or relatively stable? What view of the textual world does your major discipline present? Do the courses you take reflect the fragmentation, or do they provide a narrative of stability and continuity?

3. Bolter asserts that "on the World Wide Web, as elsewhere, the distinction between high culture and popular culture has all but vanished" (par. 9). Can the same be said for your curriculum or for a particular course? In an essay, reflect on the tensions between and competing demands of high and popular culture. Has an interest in popular culture now become chic and an accepted part of, if not high culture, then the academic study of culture? What have we gained — and lost — through the softening of the distinction between high and popular culture?

INTO THE FIELD: Options for Writing Projects

1. Reviewing a Hypertext or Multimedia Teaching Tool

Sven Birkerts's detailed discussion of the Perseus hypertext teaching tool on CD-ROM and how it affects learning (p. 632) offers the inspiration for this field project. Such teaching tools are becoming ever more commonplace, and the chances that you have or will encounter such a tool in your college courses increase each year. Your task is to evaluate a particular learning tool and its integration into a college course and, based on that evaluation, to offer recommendations regarding its future use or next edition. Bearing in mind Birkerts's reservations about such tools in certain kinds of courses, do you find that this tool enhances learning? Why might the tool be more or less effective than it seems at first? Does the tool suit certain learning styles but not others?

The audience for this project could be either the professor of the course you are taking or have taken, the department chair in which the course is offered, the publisher of the teaching tool, or educators in that discipline. Given the possible audiences, your project could take shape as a substantive letter, a report, or a published review.

One approach to this project is to work in teams of two or three. Even if you haven't used such a learning tool before or if you are not in the course or major where this tool is being used, your perspectives and feedback remain important. Indeed, you may be in a position to ask questions in ways not possible for someone closer to the field or to the particular tool. In addition to test driving the tool and analyzing its features, consider interviewing other students who have used the tool.

2. Imagining a Digital Teaching Tool

This field project calls on your sense of the possible. It asks you to envision the application of new technology in a course you are taking or have taken recently. The course may already call on some technology as a teaching or learning tool or it may not currently use any technology at all. In either case, your task is to propose a new tool that will expand the teaching and learning in useful and productive ways.

As you consider this opportunity, you will need to draw on your knowledge of what tools may be currently available and on your imaginative sense of what tools might yet be developed. The tool may involve the content of the course or may facilitate teaching, learning, and classroom collaboration in some way. Even as you explore a new world of technology, you will also need to pay close attention to the objectives of the course and what learning outcomes are desired. After all, what you are looking for is a tool that will enhance the course, not a tool that will create an altogether different course. You might find it useful to bear in mind Sven Birkerts's discussion (p. 632) about different kinds of knowledge (natural sciences and the sciences of culture) and the different kinds of learning involved in each.

As you develop your proposal, consider what needs, problems, or missed opportunities prompt you to offer your suggestion. After explaining the tool and its capabilities, offer a detailed rationale for its use in the course, given the course objectives. As you do so, be sure to acknowledge and respond to potential questions or reservations about your proposed tool.

3. Touching the Past

Given the glitz of new digital technologies in education, Sven Birkerts (p. 632) observes that "the dusty library stacks have never looked dustier" (par. 3). Yet for Birkerts, as for many who study and teach in the humanities, books, primary documents, and artifacts allow us a "recognition of otherness" (par. 11), a tangible sense of the course of time and the particularities of context. This sort of "depth perception" made possible through the humanities cannot be easily won through computer technologies that are largely lateral and synchronous.

This field project celebrates the pleasures of dust. It honors the old and the particular. Drawing on your major and your interests, this project begins by asking you to select an old book, magazine, or artifact. There are any number of opportunities for you to engage the past in ways that are concrete and tangible. Here are just a few possibilities:

- Visit the rare-book collection in your college library.
- Uncover old back issues of magazines (for example, *National Geographic, Life, Saturday Evening Post*) from the 1920s, 1930s, or 1940s.
- Spend time in the "heritage center" on your campus, where campus history is celebrated or archived.
- Familiarize yourself with the historical society in your local community.

Given these opportunities, what can you learn from the materiality or physical presence of these texts, documents, or artifacts that might be lost if you had simply seen them on a computer screen? What becomes tangible as you look at worn pages or encounter a time and place far removed from your own? In what ways is the "pastness" of earlier ages preserved by a print culture or by the preservation of actual artifacts, not just their digital representations? What does it mean to touch, feel, or witness in what is otherwise becoming a "virtual" age?

This field project can be developed as a substantial reflective essay or as a substantive proposal to incorporate the sort of fieldwork you have experienced into a particular course.

4. PowerPoint on PowerPoint

Having sat through more than a few PowerPoint presentations, you are most likely in a position to offer some comments on the software tool and a few suggestions as to its effective use. But instead of just enthusing or grousing out loud, or even writing a traditional essay on the tool, this field project offers the following challenge: Develop and offer a PowerPoint presentation about the benefits and possible drawbacks of using it.

The field project encourages some detailed reflection, and a good deal of self-awareness on your part, because it asks you to use the very tool on which you are commenting. Do not focus your talk on the nuts-and-bolts "how-to" issues of using the software; focus instead on evaluating the effectiveness of the tool and on some of its specific features. Here are a few questions to get you started:

- Given the various options and special effects available to you (e.g., color, sound, font and type size, animation, clip art), what are their potential contributions — and drawbacks — to a presentation? How can these features focus attention on the substance of a presentation, rather than proving to be a distraction?
- For what kinds of presentations is PowerPoint most well suited? Are there presentations whose purpose or goals do not match up well with PowerPoint? Where does your own presentation for this field project fit along this spectrum? Do some presentations have purposes or goals that would only be undermined by the use of PowerPoint?
- How can various kinds of audiences take in and use a PowerPoint presentation? How do you anticipate your current audience to use and respond to your presentation? In what ways might the use of PowerPoint constrain or limit its response?
- In many settings, the slides of a PowerPoint presentation, whether in electronic or hard copy form, become the official "document of record." That is, the presentation is often not about another document; it is the document itself. What are the advantages and disadvantages of such a practice? Does such a practice trade efficiency for complexity and nuance?
- What are appropriate strategies for connecting the text as it appears on your slides with your own verbal comments? What are the problems of reading verbatim off of the slides or of departing too far from them?

As you discuss the use of PowerPoint, you should both model best practices and illustrate common mistakes.

Because the presentation of your field project before a live audience can raise important issues or prompt new insights, follow up on your presentation with a revision of your work or, better yet, with a reflective essay in which you comment on the challenges and rewards of the project.

5. PowerPoint in the Classroom

Ian Parker's discussion of Microsoft's PowerPoint presentation software (p. 640) reminds us just how ubiquitous this tool has become. Having long dominated corporate boardrooms, PowerPoint has more recently made its appearance in the college lecture hall. There's a good chance that one or more of your professors use PowerPoint in your college courses. Your friends or roommates will likewise have a range of experiences about the use of PowerPoint in the classroom.

This field project invites you to evaluate and make recommendations regarding the use of PowerPoint in college classrooms. Here are just a few of the questions you might want to consider:

- In what type of class does the professor use PowerPoint? Is it a large class (more than two hundred students) or a moderately sized class (around fifty students)? What kind of delivery or teaching method is employed (lecture, lab, discussion, seminar, or some mixed model)? How do the capabilities of PowerPoint match the teaching and classroom environment?
- What discipline or subject matter is being taught? Is PowerPoint better suited for certain disciplines but not for others? Why?
- How is PowerPoint deployed and used in the actual teaching of the course? What relationship do the PowerPoint presentations have to the textbook and to the professor's own words and remarks? Does the professor read from the slides verbatim, or does the professor comment on them, perhaps ranging widely from what appears on the screen? What do the slides capture or fail to capture in the course?
- Are the PowerPoint slides available for printing or downloading from a Web site? If so, what effect does this have on attendance in the course? Does the presence of PowerPoint increase or diminish involvement or participation in the course?
- What role do the PowerPoint presentations have in testing and grading? What kinds of strategic decisions do you make regarding the material covered in the presentations as you study and learn?

Because you may have more than one class using PowerPoint, or you may be working collaboratively with others on this field project, you will likely have a range of classroom applications to study.

This field project draws together several avenues for research and study. In addition to familiarizing yourself with PowerPoint, you should take careful notes on the day-in, day-out use of PowerPoint in classroom teaching. You also might query or informally survey students about their responses to the use of PowerPoint in a particular classroom. Also consider interviewing the professor about his or her goals in using PowerPoint and how the tool might contribute to teaching and learning.

Your project might take shape as a substantive letter to the professor or department chair or a report to one of several offices on campus (they might go by names such as the Center for Teaching Excellence, the Office for Undergraduate Education, or the Office for Information and Technology Services).

6. Intellectual Property in the Digital Age

Because modern concepts of intellectual property developed in the context of print technology, the challenge to that technology by digital media has given issues of intellectual property fresh urgency. This field project invites you to explore some of those issues, based on your experience with print and digital media. Here are two possible ways in which you might focus your efforts:

- In the late age of print, print technologies and digital technologies coexist and compete. As a college student, you are likely submitting much of your work and writing in traditional ways, by turning in a hard copy of your writing that looks little different from something turned in decades ago. Yet your writing and research processes are shaped by digital technologies, with word-processing software and access to the Internet profoundly influencing how you write and how you use and reference the vast sea of texts that you navigate. This option for your field project has you reflect on how you use and produce text in college and on the advice and warnings you receive. What is your intellectual property, and how do you—or your fellow students —use the property of others?
- New multimedia technologies—and the ease of accessing and copying work circulated with those technologies—have given rise to everyday digital practices that can run counter to formal legal requirements regarding the use of those works. Witness, for example, the widespread practice of downloading and circulating music. This option for your field project has you explore intellectual property and everyday digital behavior. Are the two totally at odds, or have you and your friends negotiated informal rules and expectations about what is or isn't appropriate? How has life on a college campus influenced your everyday behaviors or your understanding of intellectual property? What new technologies or commercial options might help reduce conflicts in the future? How has your college campus treated the tension between intellectual property and everyday digital practice?

EXHIBIT 6–4
Cease and Desist
Letter

June 24, 2003

Mr. Michael Taylor
InterSys Products, Inc.
2957 Fifth Avenue
New York, NY

   Re: Trademark BENSON BEAR
       U.S. Reg. No. 1,423,293

Dear Mr. Taylor:

   Watson Inc. ("Watson") is the owner of U.S. Trademark Registration No. 1,423,293 for the mark BENSON BEAR used by Watson since 1988 in connection with its well-known stuffed plush animal toy. A copy of Watson's registration certificate for BENSON BEAR is enclosed. This trademark is a valuable asset of Watson, which has expended a great deal of time and effort in establishing and maintaining consumer recognition of the mark.

   Watson recently became aware that InterSys Products, Inc. ("InterSys") is using the mark BENSON BEAR in connection with stuffed toys. Your use of the mark BENSON BEAR is likely to cause confusion, mistake, or deception of the purchasing public and the trade as to the source and origin of the goods offered under the respective marks, thereby causing damage and irreparable injury to Watson and diminishing the valuable goodwill associated with Watson's mark. Consequently, InterSys's conduct is an infringement and violation of Watson's proprietary rights in its mark, unfair competition, false advertising, and false designation of origin under applicable state laws and the U.S. Trademark Act.

   Watson therefore demands that InterSys immediately cease and desist from using the mark BENSON BEAR or any other mark confusingly similar to Watson's mark and cease and desist from marketing, selling, or distributing any goods or materials bearing the mark of any confusingly similar name or mark.

   Because this matter is of significant importance to Watson, we request that you respond within ten days of the date of this letter to confirm your intention to cease and desist from any further use of BENSON BEAR or any other mark confusingly similar to any of Watson's marks. If we do not receive a satisfactory response within this time period, we will consider all available remedies under state and federal law, including requesting injunctive relief and the recovery of damages for trademark infringement, which damages may be trebled by a court, and attorneys' fees and costs incurred by Watson in protecting its mark.

   We sincerely desire a quick and amicable resolution to this matter. Therefore, we look forward to your timely reply.

                        Sincerely,

                        _____

Typically, the arrangement between the parties is set forth in a written agreement, usually called a "Trademark Settlement Agreement." (See Appendix D, Form 11, for a sample trademark settlement agreement.)

Trademark Infringement Litigation

If the dispute cannot be resolved, the plaintiff will file an action for infringement in federal district court. The action will be governed by

7. Portraits in Technology: Beyond Enthusiasts and Traditionalists

When we speak of our attitudes toward technology, it is common to express them in almost stereotypical terms. Indeed, we are fond of turning those attitudes into personalities. On the one hand, we have "the enthusiasts," who embrace new technologies and are often seen as hip and forward looking. On the other hand, we have "the traditionalists," who seem conservative and backward looking and may openly disdain technology. These traditionalists might even be referred to as "Luddites," after the bands of textile laborers who rioted in the early nineteenth century to protest how technology had changed their social and economic lives. Whatever the attitude, we are prone to attach a face to it.

This field project invites you to draw a more complex portrait, one that avoids caricature and stereotype and seeks out the mixed attitudes and reactions that most of us have about technology. For your portrait in words, you may profile either a professor or an instructor teaching on campus, a staff member working on campus, or one of your classmates.

As with any portrait or profile, your work becomes interesting insofar as you attend to detail, become aware of unexpected contradictions, and develop both a sympathetic and a discerning eye. You'll need to discover and represent the daily habits of technology use, not the recycled clichés that might be given about technology. How does the person you are profiling actually handle technology, and what might be the sources of that person's attitudes? As you look closely and write with sympathetic attention to detail, you will find a portrait emerging that avoids the extremes of "the enthusiast" and "the traditionalist."

8. University Libraries in the Late Age of Print

In the transition from the age of print to the digital age, no place on campus has felt the change quite as acutely as has your campus library. After all, libraries were developed in an age when their mission was to collect and store information in the form of manuscripts, books, and periodicals. Libraries were repositories, and the more they held, the better they were deemed to be. But the digital revolution is changing all of that. The focus is now moving to delivering materials rather than just collecting them, and that delivery can occur electronically to spaces far removed from the library itself.

These changes have raised the question of whether libraries — in their old incarnation—are even necessary anymore. Why have a library on campus when it seems that the computer in your dorm room or home can bring you a wealth of information? Clearly, we do need libraries; in the late age of print, digital offerings will by no means replace print materials entirely. Even so, libraries have been going through an identity crisis and are reassessing their roles on campus and in your education.

Given these developments, libraries on more than a few campuses are now presenting themselves as intellectual gathering places—idea cafés, as it were—

where the focus is on collaborative learning and on accessing and exchanging information, not on collecting and hoarding it. Libraries, with their hushed atmospheres, used to be places for hermits, for solitary academic experiences. Now more than a few libraries are reinventing themselves to invite students to partake in a social academic experience. Rooms for group collaboration—and even cafés—are now finding their way into library floor plans.

This field project invites you to join this reassessment of the academic library. Your ethnographic site will be your own campus library. You can frame your project either as a profile of how your library is navigating the challenges it faces in the late age of print or as a proposal for change and action.

Among the questions you may wish to ask: What does the floor plan, or any recent additions or renovations, tell you about the changing function of the library? How has the library's Web presence changed the habits and expectations of students and faculty? To what extent is your library a social gathering place or a place for collaborative work? How has the library modified its plans over time regarding the acquisition of materials? What strategic plans might the library have for the future? As you consider these questions, interview fellow students as well as librarians. Spend time in your library, and explore its physical—and virtual—spaces.

9. Writing Culture—and the Culture of Writing

Jay David Bolter (p. 654) concludes "Writing Culture" by offering the following comment: "It is fair to wonder whether the late age of print may also become the late age of prose itself."

This field project invites you to reflect on Bolter's remark. If technology helps write the culture in which we live how have digital tools changed, in turn, the culture of writing? As a student in a writing class, offer your insight on the "culture of writing" as you see it from your vantage point. What are you learning about, and how are you implementing, the new tools available to you? What promise might a writing class offer in the late age of print, and what burdens might it be under? How do you see writing treated, and practiced, in other courses on campus? If your campus has a writing center that offers student consultations, what role is accorded to technology and what stance, if only implicit, is taken toward digital tools? What are your day-to-day literacy behaviors, and how might they reflect the mixture of print and digital technologies? Is there a gap between your literacy behaviors and the formal writing class in which you participate? If so, is that gap a place for productive learning—or could it be?

This field project is an opportunity for you to assess your place, as a writer and as a college student, in the late age of print.

7

Seeing and Believing

MIND'S EYE

When we repeat, mindlessly perhaps, the cliché "seeing is believing," we are merely expressing a far more fundamental assumption that the world is "out there," ready to be perceived—and believed. And what we perceive, so this assumption goes, has nothing to do with our minds. There's much in our daily experience that, at first blush, would seem to confirm this assumption. Whether we are observing fall foliage or spring buds, artwork or photographs, we all too easily believe that what we see is what is there. Seeing is simply recording the external world; what we seek needs no composing of our own. Or so it seems.

This unit explores the connection between seeing and believing from the perspective of what the "mind's eye" contributes to our vision. Nature itself, and writing about nature, can be good starting points to question our naive assumptions about what it means to see. Close observation rarely happens by itself. To see nature, we must intervene, verbalizing what and how we perceive so that we might see all the more clearly. Yet the mind's eye in the process of observing nature can also play tricks on us, for we carry with us expectations about what we might find and how the natural world should look. Surprise and serendipity remain essential, and it turns out that we can do much to cultivate in ourselves a degree of watchfulness and readiness, a receptivity of mind.

If the natural world we see is forged as much from our responsiveness to it and readiness for it as from nature itself, the manner in which we see and respond to art offers a similar lesson. Consider crafted art objects. What we see and how we evaluate what we see are grounded in our response to art. We share in the creation, just as we appreciate art not so much for its imitation of nature as for its imitation of creation itself.

Photographs, the camera's supposedly neutral capture of the world around us, offer further cues on our role in shaping what we see. We often turn to photographs in the naive hope that they provide unbiased documentary evidence. But a cultural-studies focus on how we use photos, and how photos use us, suggests that seeing is a rather complicated act, tied not only to issues of belief but also to the role of images as a cultural commodity.

As our naive faith in what we see becomes less certain—whether it is nature, art, or photos—work in art history and the psychology of perception can teach us much about the role of culturally determined frames of reference in how we view the world.

These and related issues are explored in the four readings included here, which together help us explore the role of "the mind's eye" in what we see. Annie Dillard's essay "Seeing," from her Pulitzer Prize–winning book *Pilgrim at Tinker Creek*, invites us to see nature through the act of verbalization and written expression and to discover how such writing can send us back to nature with our eyes more open to its wonder. Using a small white wood-carved bird as his immediate example, John Berger reflects on how we respond to art and to nature and finds that the role of our own response is as telling as what we respond to. Photography, and commodified images that spring from photos, go far in defining, in cultural terms, how we see. Susan Sontag's classic essay on photography, "In Plato's Cave," explores how our culture uses photos and how photographic images shape our culture. The art historian E. H. Gombrich explores our desire for truth and accuracy in the ways in which we depict our world, yet he finds that what we draw or illustrate depends on stereotypes and schemas that help us understand the unfamiliar in terms of the already known.

Reflecting on Prior Knowledge

1. In a journal entry, recall a time when you were fascinated by observing something closely, be it in nature or in a lab. What kind of focus or concentration was required, and what kinds of insight or fruit did your sustained attention yield? What aided you in the process of close observation? Did you call upon deliberate and organized observation or general watchfulness and receptivity, or a combination of both?

2. What do you see when you look at a hand-crafted art object? If you have been astonished or pleased by that object, why was that the case? Does your response to images of nature, or to nature itself, parallel in any way your response to crafted art objects? What do you find pleasing or beautiful? In a journal entry that draws on your experience, respond to these questions about "aesthetic response."

3. Working in groups, share your early experiences with taking photos and being photographed. What do you find enjoyable or annoying about such experiences? As you share your thoughts, develop a catalog of the various reasons you or others take and circulate photos, and then share your catalog with the whole class.

4. All of us are forced to understand and explain the unfamiliar in terms of the familiar, the unknown in terms of what we already know. In a journal entry, explore one episode that captures this process. To what extent was your prior experience a useful frame of reference, and when and how might it have gotten in the way of understanding something new?

Seeing

Annie Dillard

We often segregate the senses from each other and from our mental
and verbal worlds: Touching is touching; seeing is, well, seeing. We
accord our senses a naive self-evidence. Annie Dillard looks more
closely, more openly, and finds that "[s]eeing is of course very much a
matter of verbalization."

Dillard started her writing life as a poet and spent some fifteen
years composing poetry before she discovered the possibilities of seeing the world in and through nonfiction prose. Her essay on seeing is
drawn from *Pilgrim at Tinker Creek,* which won the Pulitzer Prize for
general nonfiction in 1974, when she was only twenty-nine years old.
After nearly dying from pneumonia, Dillard began keeping a regular
diary during her year-long stay in a cabin on the banks of Tinker Creek
in Virginia's Roanoke Valley. Her lengthy entries would later form the
basis of *Pilgrim at Tinker Creek.* A record of her observations and
reflections on the natural world, the book is also a philosophical
exploration.

Born Meta Annie Doak in Pittsburgh, Dillard received a BA and an
MA from Hollins College. A keen observer throughout her life, Dillard
has published two books of poems, *Tickets for a Prayer Wheel* (1974)
and *Mornings like This: Found Poems* (1995). Her other publications
include *Teaching a Stone to Talk* (1982), a collection of essays; *Living by
Fiction* (1982), a book of theory; *An American Childhood* (1987), a memoir; and *The Living* (1992), a novel about pioneers on Puget Sound. In
The Writing Life (1989), Dillard explores her life as a writer. She has
taught at several universities, among them Wesleyan, and at a number
of writers' workshops.

Seeing is of course very much a matter of verbalization. Unless I call my
attention to what passes before my eyes, I simply won't see it. It is, as

Ruskin° says, "not merely unnoticed, but in the full, clear sense of the word, unseen." My eyes alone can't solve analogy tests using figures, the ones which show, with increasing elaborations, a big square, then a small square in a big square, then a big triangle, and expect me to find a small triangle in a big triangle. I have to say the words, describe what I'm seeing. If Tinker Mountain erupted, I'd be likely to notice. But if I want to notice the lesser cataclysms of valley life, I have to maintain in my head a running description of the present. It's not that I'm observant; it's just that I talk too much. Otherwise, especially in a strange place, I'll never know what's happening. Like a blind man at the ball game, I need a radio.

When I see this way I analyze and pry. I hurl over logs and roll away stones; I study the bank a square foot at a time, probing and tilting my head. Some days when a mist covers the mountains, when the muskrats won't show and the microscope's mirror shatters, I want to climb up the blank blue dome as a man would storm the inside of a circus tent, wildly, dangling, and with a steel knife claw a rent in the top, peep, and, if I must, fall.

But there is another kind of seeing that involves a letting go. When I see this way I sway transfixed and emptied. The difference between the two ways of seeing is the difference between walking with and without a camera. When I walk with a camera I walk from shot to shot, reading the light on a calibrated meter. When I walk without a camera, my own shutter opens, and the moment's light prints on my own silver gut. When I see this second way I am above all an unscrupulous observer.

It was sunny one evening last summer at Tinker Creek; the sun was low in the sky, upstream. I was sitting on the sycamore log bridge with the sunset at my back, watching the shiners the size of minnows who were feeding over the muddy sand in skittery schools. Again and again, one fish, then another, turned for a split second across the current and flash! the sun shot out from its silver side. I couldn't watch for it. It was always just happening somewhere else, and it drew my vision just as it disappeared: flash, like a sudden dazzle of the thinnest blade, a sparking over a dun and olive ground at chance intervals from every direction. Then I noticed white specks, some sort of pale petals, small, floating from under my feet on the creek's surface, very slow and steady. So I blurred my eyes and gazed towards the brim of my hat and saw a new world. I saw the pale white circles roll up, roll up, like the world's turning, mute and perfect, and I saw the linear flashes, gleaming silver, like stars being born at random down a rolling scroll of time. Something broke and something opened. I filled up like a new wineskin. I breathed an air like

---

Ruskin: John Ruskin (1819–1900), an English author, art critic, and social critic.

light; I saw a light like water. I was the lip of a fountain the creek filled forever; I was ether, the leaf in the zephyr; I was flesh-flake, feather, bone.

When I see this way I see truly. As Thoreau says, I return to my senses. I am the man who watches the baseball game in silence in an empty stadium. I see the game purely; I'm abstracted and dazed. When it's all over and the white-suited players lope off the green field to their shadowed dugouts, I leap to my feet; I cheer and cheer.

But I can't go out and try to see this way. I'll fail, I'll go mad. All I can do is try to gag the commentator, to hush the noise of useless interior babble that keeps me from seeing just as **The secret of seeing is, then,** surely as a newspaper dangled before my eyes. The **the pearl of great price.** effort is really a discipline requiring a lifetime of dedicated struggle; it marks the literature of saints and monks of every order East and West, under every rule and no rule, discalced and shod. The world's spiritual geniuses seem to discover universally that the mind's muddy river, this ceaseless flow of trivia and trash, cannot be dammed, and that trying to dam it is a waste of effort that might lead to madness. Instead you must allow the muddy river to flow unheeded in the dim channels of consciousness; you raise your sights; you look along it, mildly, acknowledging its presence without interest and gazing beyond it into the realm of the real where subjects and objects act and rest purely, without utterance. "Launch into the deep," says Jacques Ellul,° "and you shall see."

The secret of seeing is, then, the pearl of great price. If I thought he could teach me to find it and keep it forever I would stagger barefoot across a hundred deserts after any lunatic at all. But although the pearl may be found, it may not be sought. The literature of illumination reveals this above all: Although it comes to those who wait for it, it is always, even to the most practiced and adept, a gift and a total surprise. I return from one walk knowing where the killdeer nests in the field by the creek and the hour the laurel blooms. I return from the same walk a day later scarcely knowing my own name. Litanies hum in my ears; my tongue flaps in my mouth Ailinon,° alleluia! I cannot cause light; the most I can do is try to put myself in the path of its beam. It is possible, in deep space, to sail on solar wind. Light, be it particle or wave, has force: You rig a giant sail and go. The secret of seeing is to sail on solar wind. Hone and spread your spirit till you yourself are a sail, whetted, translucent, broadside to the merest puff.

Jacques Ellul (1912–1994): A French philosopher, sociologist, and theologian whose key concern was the threat to freedom and faith created by modern technology.

Ailinon: In classical Greek, Ailinon refers to a dirge or cry of grief. By juxtaposing Ailinon with alleluia, Dillard highlights her mixed feelings of loss and exaltation.

Usually you will gain time if that project is in a good shape when you get involved. Yet you may have to face some subtle issues and dealing with them could be energy consuming, especially when your effort is considered as part of your "work for hire." Some journals require authors to get sign-offs from their employers before their contributions get accepted. It is to your advantage to consult your employer beforehand and make your common understanding a contract by taking notes and having them verified by the employer. You are better off if your project is invited or genuinely welcomed by your employer. The ideal situation is one in which your thesis/dissertation itself is taken as your contribution to the project and nothing else is expected. There are actually many such cases in practice. The employers, who are oftentimes the principal investigators (PI's) of various research projects, do hope to see a greater and wider use of their information resources unless they are restricted by some regulations. Student researchers especially are often encouraged to make use of their data sets.

Getting focused

If selecting an interest area and a research topic appears straightforward to you, asking specific and appropriate research questions may turn out not to be. Many people falter at this stage and some quit not because they do not have an area of study or a topic to write about, but because they just could not get to the point where they know exactly what they want. Nor are they confident about the value and the possibility of the answers they would try to seek out.

In practice, there are researchers who sometimes launch their research projects without much specificity. These researchers may justify their design as a necessary scientific exploration in areas that are not covered by previous research. But as a student you are always required to be clear about what you are doing and what you are going to do, for the purpose of education and training. You might also be advised to choose an area where the scientific body of knowledge is sufficiently broad. In any case, you should try to locate and position yourself properly through a thorough literature review.

An effective approach to breaking the deadlock is called "narrowing down," a step-by-step process of specifying and selecting the contents for a particular study. If you are interested in aging, for example, you can choose it as a research topic or a general area of study. However, aging study involves all kinds of the Federal Rules of Civil Procedure relating to federal civil actions generally; these rules set the times for responding to the complaint, matters pertaining to motions and discovery, and any other litigation-related matters. Within one month after the action is commenced (and upon its conclusion), the clerk of the court must provide notice thereof to the Director so notice of the action and its conclusion can be published in the file wrappers relating to the marks.

If the defendant has a cause of action relating to the trademark to assert against the plaintiff, it must be asserted by way of a counterclaim in the litigation so that all disputes between the parties affecting the mark can be resolved at the same time.

A claim may also be made for **contributory infringement** when one party aids another to infringe a party's mark. Thus, assisting in infringement or inducing infringement are also actionable.

After the complaint, answer, and counterclaim have been filed, various motions may be made. Discovery will commence. The plaintiff and defendant will take depositions to obtain testimony of those who may have information about the case (for example, the plaintiff may depose individuals in the defendant's marketing department to determine how the defendant came to adopt its mark); interrogatories may be served on either party to obtain information, such as to inquire about experts either side may intend to call or the existence of documents; and each party may ask the other to produce relevant documents, such as surveys or complaints by consumers indicating confusion.

Ultimately, if the matter cannot be resolved by private agreement, it will proceed to trial. Either party may request a jury trial; otherwise, a judge will render the decision. The decision in the case may be appealed to the United States Court of Appeals for the circuit in which the district court is located. Thereafter, the

matter may be appealed to the United States Supreme Court, if the Court decides, in its discretion, to hear the appeal.

DILUTION OF TRADEMARKS

Introduction

In January 1996, the long-awaited Federal Trademark Dilution Act (15 U.S.C. § 1125) was enacted to provide special protection to "famous" marks when the owners of those marks are unable to establish likelihood of confusion and thus avail themselves of the many avenues afforded to protect marks from confusingly similar uses. Moreover, the Act was intended to bring uniformity to the protection of famous marks, which were previously protected on an inconsistent basis in the various states.

Dilution refers to unauthorized acts that tend to blur the distinctiveness of a famous mark or to tarnish the mark by using it in a disparaging or unsavory way. For example, use of the mark TIFFANY® by a restaurant in Boston was found not to be likely to be confused with TIFFANY for jewelry store services in New York, inasmuch as no reasonable consumer would believe the uses were related or that the restaurant services were sponsored by or originated with Tiffany Jewelers. Nevertheless, use by the restaurant was held to be a dilution of Tiffany Jeweler's famous mark and was enjoined. *Tiffany & Co. v. Boston Club, Inc.,* 231 F. Supp. 836 (D. Mass. 1964).

Another well-known case involved the use of DOGIVA in connection with dog biscuits. Clearly, consumers would not be confused upon encountering the mark and believe that the dog biscuits were related to GODIVA® brand chocolates. However, use of DOGIVA on such a product tended to injure or tarnish the plaintiff's business reputation and was enjoined.

When her doctor took her bandages off and led her into the garden, the girl who was no longer blind saw "the tree with the lights in it." It was for this tree I searched through the peach orchards of summer, in the forests of fall and down winter and spring for years. Then one day I was walking along Tinker Creek thinking of nothing at all and I saw the tree with the lights in it. I saw the backyard cedar where the mourning doves roost charged and transfigured, each cell buzzing with flame. I stood on the grass with the lights in it, grass that was wholly fire, utterly focused and utterly dreamed. It was less like seeing than like being for the first time seen, knocked breathless by a powerful glance. The flood of fire abated, but I'm still spending the power. Gradually the lights went out in the cedar, the colors died, the cells unflamed and disappeared. I was still ringing. I had been my whole life a bell, and never knew it until at that moment I was lifted and struck. I have since only very rarely seen the tree with the lights in it. The vision comes and goes, mostly goes, but I live for it, for the moment when the mountains open and a new light roars in spate through the crack, and the mountains slam.

Working with the Text

1. Annie Dillard speaks of two ways or modes of seeing: a seeing in which we "analyze and pry" and a seeing that requires of us a "letting go." How does Dillard define each mode? How are they related? Might they be mutually dependent? Are there moments in Dillard's essay when she calls on one type of seeing and then the other?

2. Dillard's writing craft relies on both an accumulation of concrete details and on general statements or maxims. Review Dillard's essay to explore how she relates the two levels, the particular and the abstract. How is a cascade of particular observations framed by other passages? How are general statements of truth exemplified or concretized so that they ring true for readers?

3. Dillard speaks of the need "to gag the commentator, to hush the noise of useless interior babble" (par. 6). Why is this so? Nevertheless, Dillard asserts that "[s]eeing is of course very much a matter of verbalization" (par. 1). Explain this apparent contradiction. What is the proper role for words in the process of seeing?

4. At several moments in her essay, Dillard calls upon the language of religious mysticism and spiritual illumination. Why? How does she weave such references into her writing in ways that might make them compelling to readers with a range of religious beliefs?

From Text to Field

1. In a brief essay, try out Dillard's observational and stylistic techniques. After closely analyzing how she shuttles between concrete particulars and more abstract or general statements, try to render this effect yourself. You might think of this as an invitation to imitate Dillard or to write a *pastiche*—a literary, artistic, or musical work that imitates the style of previous work.

2. We are often blinded by preconceptions or assumptions that inhibit our ability to see clearly or freshly. For this reason, Dillard's essay invites us to slow down and become a scrupulous observer. Write a brief essay in which you offer and comment on an instance in which you needed to experience, or in which you benefited from, such close observation. The example may come from your connection to the natural world, or it may come from a realm seemingly far removed from Dillard's Tinker Creek.

3. In some sense, Dillard's essay is less about what she sees and more about the very process of seeing itself. Review Dillard's essay for her suggestions and comments on that process. Write an essay in which you lay out, step by step, what you see as her advice, her recommended method. Then, continue the essay by considering what might be incomplete or misleading about the very method you have abstracted. What does any "recipe" or "algorithm" for seeing succeed or fail to capture? Alternatively, instead of a conventional essay, consider offering your advice in the form of an actual "recipe for seeing." Then annotate or gloss the recipe (perhaps with side bars or hyperlinks) to comment on the shortcomings of that recipe. What are the ingredients for or steps in seeing? Can good observational techniques prepare you to see better? If so, what are the limits of such techniques?

The White Bird

John Berger

The relationship between art and society, between making or seeing and underlying cultural and social conditions, has been at the heart of John Berger's life and work. Born in London in 1926, Berger has led a distinguished and varied career as an essayist, novelist, painter, and art historian. After studies at the Central and Chelsea Schools of Art, he worked as a painter and drawing teacher. Even as he turned his attention to writing, he has continued to paint all of his life.

In 1952, Berger began writing for London's *New Statesman* and quickly became established as an influential art and cultural critic. He has published a number of books and collections of essays on art criticism, including the well-known *Ways of Seeing* (1972), which was turned into a television series by the BBC. He has also written *About Looking* (1980), a collection of essays on culturally and historically influenced interpretation; *Art and Revolution* (1969), on the role of revolutionary art in transforming society; *Keeping a Rendezvous* (1991) and *The Sense of Sight* (1992), two anthologies of essays; and *The Success and Failure of Picasso* (1965), a critical reassessment of the twentieth century's most famous artist. Berger's Marxist orientation and his own artistic background are also ever present in his four novels, among them *G* (1971), a story of migrant workers in Europe, which won the coveted Booker Prize in 1972. Berger has also written three screenplays and four plays.

For the past quarter century, Berger has lived in a small village in the French Jura alps. Fascinated by the artistic traditions and way of life of such mountain communities, he has written about them in both his fiction and nonfiction. Berger's essay "The White Bird," from the collection *The Sense of Sight,* draws on peasant art to explore the relationships among art, nature, and society.

684

From time to time I have been invited by institutions—mostly American—
to speak about aesthetics. On one occasion I considered accepting and I
thought of taking with me a bird made of white wood. But I didn't go. The
problem is that you can't talk about aesthetics without talking about the principle of hope and the existence of evil. During the long winters the peasants
in certain parts of the Haute Savoie° used to make wooden birds to hang in
their kitchens and perhaps also in their chapels. Friends who are travelers
have told me that they have seen similar birds, made according to the same
principle, in certain regions of Czechoslovakia, Russia, and the Baltic countries. The tradition may be more widespread.

The principle of the construction of these birds is simple enough,
although to make a fine bird demands considerable skill. You take two bars
of pine wood, about six inches in length, a little less than one inch in height
and the same in width. You soak them in water so that the wood has the maximum pliability, then you carve them. One piece will be the head and body
with a fan tail, the second piece will represent the wings. The art principally
concerns the making of the wing and tail feathers. The whole block of each
wing is carved according to the silhouette of a single feather. Then the block
is sliced into thirteen thin layers and these are gently opened out, one by one,
to make a fan shape. Likewise for the second wing and for the tail feathers.
The two pieces of wood are joined together to form a cross and the bird is
complete. No glue is used and there is only one nail where the two pieces of
wood cross. Very light, weighing only two or three ounces, the birds are usually hung on a thread from an overhanging mantelpiece or beam so that they
move with the air currents.

It would be absurd to compare one of these birds to a van Gogh self-portrait
or a Rembrandt crucifixion. They are simple, homemade objects, worked
according to a traditional pattern. Yet, by their very simplicity, they allow one
to categorize the qualities which make them pleasing and mysterious to
everyone who sees them.

First there is a figurative representation—one is looking at a bird, more precisely a dove, apparently hanging in midair. Thus, there is a reference to the
surrounding world of nature. Secondly, the choice of subject (a flying bird)
and the context in which it is placed (indoors where live birds are unlikely)
render the object symbolic. This primary symbolism then joins a more general, cultural one. Birds, and doves in particular, have been credited with
symbolic meanings in a very wide variety of cultures.

Thirdly, there is a respect for the material used. The wood has been fash-   5
ioned according to its own qualities of lightness, pliability, and texture. Looking

---

Haute Savoie: A district in southeastern France, near the Alps and bordering on Switzerland and
Italy.

at it, one is surprised by how well wood becomes bird. Fourthly, there is a formal unity and economy. Despite the object's apparent complexity, the grammar of its making is simple, even austere. Its richness is the result of repetitions which are also variations. Fifthly, this man-made object provokes a kind of astonishment: How on earth was it made? I have given rough indications above, but anyone unfamiliar with the technique wants to take the dove in his hands and examine it closely to discover the secret which lies behind its making.

These five qualities, when undifferentiated and perceived as a whole, provoke at least a momentary sense of being before a mystery. One is looking at a piece of wood that has become a bird. One is looking at a bird that is somehow more than a bird. One is looking at something that has been worked with a mysterious skill and a kind of love.

Thus far I have tried to isolate the qualities of the white bird which provoke an aesthetic emotion. (The word *emotion*, although designating a motion of the heart and of the imagination, is somewhat confusing for we are considering an emotion that has little to do with the others we experience, notably because the self here is in a far greater degree of abeyance.) Yet my definitions beg the essential question. They reduce aesthetics to art. They say nothing about the relation between art and nature, art and the world.

Art does not imitate nature, it imitates a creation.

Before a mountain, a desert just after the sun has gone down, or a fruit tree, one can also experience aesthetic emotion. Consequently we are forced to begin again—not this time with a man-made object but with the nature into which we are born.

Urban living has always tended to produce a sentimental view of nature. Nature is thought of as a garden, or a view framed by a window, or as an arena of freedom. Peasants, sailors, nomads have known better. Nature is energy and struggle. It is what exists without any promise. If it can be thought of by man as an arena, a setting, it has to be thought of as one which lends itself as much to evil as to good. Its energy is fearsomely indifferent. The first necessity of life is shelter. Shelter against nature. The first prayer is for protection. The first sign of life is pain. If the Creation was purposeful, its purpose is a hidden one which can only be discovered intangibly within signs, never by the evidence of what happens.

It is within this bleak natural context that beauty is encountered, and the encounter is by its nature sudden and unpredictable. The gale blows itself out, the sea changes from the color of grey shit to aquamarine. Under the fallen boulder of an avalanche a flower grows. Over the shanty town the moon rises. I offer dramatic examples so as to insist upon the bleakness of the context. Reflect upon more everyday examples. However it is encountered, beauty is always an exception, always *in despite of*. This is why it moves us.

It can be argued that the origin of the way we are moved by natural beauty was functional. Flowers are a promise of fertility, a sunset is a reminder of fire and warmth, moonlight makes the night less dark, the bright colors of a bird's plumage are (atavistically even for us) a sexual stimulus. Yet such an argument is too reductionist, I believe. Snow is useless. A butterfly offers us very little.

Of course the range of what a given community finds beautiful in nature will depend upon its means of survival, its economy, its geography. What Eskimos find beautiful is unlikely to be the same as what the Ashanti° found beautiful. Within modern class societies there are complex ideological determinations: We know, for instance, that the British ruling class in the eighteenth century disliked the sight of the sea. Equally, the social use to which an aesthetic emotion may be put changes according to the historical moment: The silhouette of a mountain can represent the home of the dead or a challenge to the initiative of the living. Anthropology, comparative studies of religion, political economy, and Marxism have made all this clear.

Yet there seem to be certain constants which all cultures have found 'beautiful': among them—certain flowers, trees, forms of rock, birds, animals, the moon, running water . . .

One is obliged to acknowledge a coincidence or perhaps a congruence. The evolution of natural forms and the evolution of human perception have coincided to produce the phenomenon of a potential recognition: What *is* and what we can see (and by seeing also feel) sometimes meet at a point of affirmation. This point, this coincidence, is two-faced: What has been seen is recognized and affirmed and, at the same time, the seer is affirmed by what he sees. For a brief moment one finds oneself—without the pretensions of a creator—in the position of God in the first chapter of Genesis . . . And he saw that *it was* good. The aesthetic emotion before nature derives, I believe, from this double affirmation.

Yet we do not live in the first chapter of Genesis. We live—if one follows the biblical sequence of events—after the Fall. In any case, we live in a world of suffering in which evil is rampant, a world whose events do not confirm our Being, a world that has to be resisted. It is in this situation that the aesthetic moment offers hope. That we find a crystal or a poppy beautiful means that we are less alone, that we are more deeply inserted into existence than the course of a single life would lead us to believe. I try to describe as accurately as possible the experience in question; my starting point is phenomenological, not deductive; its form, perceived as such, becomes a message that one receives but cannot translate because, in it, all is instantaneous. 15

Ashanti: A major ethnic group in West Africa; the Ashanti Confederacy was a major state in precolonial Africa, in what is now Ghana.

For an instant, the energy of one's perception becomes inseparable from the energy of the creation.

The aesthetic emotion we feel before a man-made object—such as the white bird with which I started—is a derivative of the emotion we feel before nature. The white bird is an attempt to translate a message received from a real bird. All the languages of art have been developed as an attempt to transform the instantaneous into the permanent. Art supposes that beauty is not an exception—is not *in despite of*—but is the basis for an order.

Several years ago, when considering the historical face of art, I wrote that I judged a work according to whether or not it helped men in the modern world claim their social rights. I hold to that. Art's other, transcendental face raises the question of man's ontological right.

The notion that art is the mirror of nature is one that only appeals in periods of skepticism. Art does not imitate nature, it imitates a creation, sometimes to propose an alternative world, sometimes simply to amplify, to confirm, to make social the brief hope offered by nature. Art is an organized response to what nature allows us to glimpse occasionally. Art sets out to transform the potential recognition into an unceasing one. It proclaims man in the hope of receiving a surer reply . . . the transcendental face of art is always a form of prayer.

The white wooden bird is wafted by the warm air rising from the stove in the kitchen where the neighbors are drinking. Outside, in minus 25°C, the real birds are freezing to death!

Working with the Text

1. At the outset of his essay, John Berger notes that when he has been invited to speak about aesthetics, he has most often declined. "The problem," he says, "is that you can't talk about aesthetics without talking about the principle of hope and the existence of evil" (par. 1). How does this statement hint at the motivation behind Berger's essay and the direction that it will take? As you ponder this question, you might want to consult one or two dictionaries for definitions of *aesthetics*. To what extent is Berger's essay a response to or a corrective for such definitions? By addressing hope and evil, how does Berger enlarge our notion of aesthetics?

2. Roughly halfway through his essay, having already talked about the white bird itself, Berger raises the question of the relation of art to nature and to the world and confesses that "we are forced to begin again" (par. 8). The essay has in this sense two beginnings. How does the structure of the essay underline the argument Berger is making? Why the contrast? The very last paragraph of the essay brings the two parts together, only to highlight the difference

between the crafted white birds and the real birds coping with subzero temperatures. How does Berger's final comment reflect the structure of his argument? Likewise, how does that final comment speak to questions of hope and evil that he raises in the opening paragraph?

3. In the penultimate paragraph of Berger's essay, he addresses the complex relationship between art and nature: "Art does not imitate nature, it imitates a creation, sometimes to propose an alternative world, sometimes simply to amplify, to confirm, to make social the brief hope offered by nature. Art is an organized response to what nature allows us to glimpse occasionally." Write a brief essay in which you explore this statement in light of Berger's essay and its discussion of aesthetic response—both to art and to nature. To what extent does this statement invite us to rethink our views of both art and nature?

From Text to Field

1. Near the opening of the essay, Berger discusses the carved white bird in light of five categories of aesthetic response. To what extent can these five categories apply equally well to other forms of art, most particularly to written texts? How is our aesthetic response in the act of reading similar to or different from response in the act of seeing? Can the five categories of aesthetic response that Berger calls upon be used to inform the act of writing?

2. Berger observes that "the range of what a given community finds beautiful in nature will depend upon its means of survival, its economy, its geography" (par. 12). Although he grants that there seem to be "certain constants which all cultures have found 'beautiful'" (par. 13), Berger accords a large role for cultural factors in our aesthetic response. Choose a given community of your own—where you grew up, where you now live, or where you go to college—and explore why certain features of nature seem important and beautiful to your community. For evidence, consider the ways in which campus architecture draws on its natural setting, public art is framed in your community, or brochures link nature's beauty to the community's history, economy, and future survival.

3. Berger's essay uses as its prime example and test case a miniature carved wooden bird. What other examples or art objects might Berger have chosen? How might different art objects require some shifts in Berger's argument? How might you rewrite Berger's essay by drawing on an art object that you value or that has value in your community?

In Plato's Cave

Susan Sontag

A well-known American essayist, novelist, cultural critic, public intellectual, and controversial activist, Susan Sontag did much to define the intellectual landscape in the final third of the twentieth century.

Finishing high school at age fifteen, Sontag went on to study at the University of Chicago, Harvard University, and St. Anne's College, Oxford University. She wrote four novels and a number of short stories, most notably "The Way We Live Now," which remains a key text on the AIDS epidemic. Yet it was as an essayist and cultural critic that Sontag won lasting fame and notoriety. Sontag consistently sought to challenge conventional thinking and often explored the intersection of "high" and "low" art. Her 1964 essay "Notes on 'Camp'" helped to define the "so bad it's good" concept in popular culture. Shortly thereafter, with the publication of "Against Interpretation," she sought to make the case that response to literature was an intuitive rather than an entirely analytic process. Writing about such matters as fashion, pornography, and other aspects of contemporary culture, Sontag's essays invariably galvanized debate. In the 1970s and 1980s, she turned to examine cultural attitudes about illness and disease, which led to *Illness as Metaphor* (1978) and *AIDS and Its Metaphors* (1988). This concern was rooted in her own battles with cancer, a fight she lost to leukemia in 2004. A controversial activist and human rights advocate, Sontag made trips to North Vietnam and Cuba in the 1960s, China in 1973, and Sarajevo in 1993, and invariably saw immediate events of the day—such as the September 11, 2001, attacks—in cultural, political, and ideological terms.

Sontag's exploration of photography and media remains central to her work as a cultural critic. With her 1977 essay collection, *On Photography,* in which "In Plato's Cave" serves as the opening chapter, Sontag was one of the first to question how our culture uses images and photographs, steering the debate away from the traditional question of whether photography was an art form. Late in her life, she returned to the questions of photography and image production and consumption in her book-length essay *Regarding the Pain of Others* (2002). Here she reexamines photography from a moral perspective and explores how media coverage affects how our culture views conflict.

Humankind lingers unregenerately in Plato's cave, still reveling, its age-old habit, in mere images of the truth. But being educated by photographs is not like being educated by older, more artisanal images. For one thing, there are a great many more images around, claiming our attention. The inventory started in 1839 and since then just about everything has been photographed, or so it seems. This very insatiability of the photographing eye changes the terms of confinement in the cave, our world. In teaching us a new visual code, photographs alter and enlarge our notions of what is worth looking at and what we have a right to observe. They are a grammar and, even more importantly, an ethics of seeing. Finally, the most grandiose result of the photographic enterprise is to give us the sense that we can hold the whole world in our heads—as an anthology of images.

To collect photographs is to collect the world. Movies and television programs light up walls, flicker, and go out; but with still photographs the image is also an object, lightweight, cheap to produce, easy to carry about, accumulate, store. In Godard's *Les Carabiniers* (1963), two sluggish lumpenpeasants are lured into joining the King's Army by the promise that they will be able to loot, rape, kill, or do whatever else they please to the enemy, and get rich. But the suitcase of booty that Michel-Ange and Ulysse triumphantly bring home, years later, to their wives turns out to contain only picture postcards, hundreds of them, of Monuments, Department Stores, Mammals, Wonders of Nature, Methods of Transport, Works of Art, and other classified treasures from around the globe. Godard's gag vividly parodies the equivocal magic of the photographic image. Photographs are perhaps the most mysterious of all the objects that make up, and thicken, the environment we recognize as modern. Photographs really are experience captured, and the camera is the ideal arm of consciousness in its acquisitive mood.

To photograph is to appropriate the thing photographed. It means putting oneself into a certain relation to the world that feels like knowledge—and, therefore, like power. A now notorious first fall into alienation, habituating people to abstract the world into printed words, is supposed to have engendered that surplus of Faustian energy and psychic damage needed to build modern, inorganic societies. But print seems a less treacherous form of leaching out the world, of turning it into a mental object, than photographic images, which now provide most of the knowledge people have about the

Finally, use of a bottle in the shape of that protected by Coca-Cola Company for white bubble gum resembling cocaine was held to tarnish Coca-Cola's well-known and famous marks and was enjoined even though, under traditional likelihood of confusion analysis, there would have been no infringement.

The primary focus of the new Dilution Act is to preserve a trademark owner's property rights and goodwill in its famous mark, which might evaporate if junior users were allowed to use the mark even on unrelated goods. Dilution is generally defined as the lessening of the capacity of a famous mark to identify and distinguish goods and services.

The chief distinction between an infringement claim and a dilution claim is that one can prove dilution without a showing of likelihood of confusion. Moreover, injunctive relief is available once dilution is proved, but monetary damages are awarded only on a showing of willfulness.

To prevail on a dilution claim, a plaintiff must show four things:

1. its mark is famous;
2. the defendant is making a commercial use of its mark in commerce;
3. the defendant's use began after the plaintiff's mark became famous; and
4. the defendant's use of its mark actually dilutes the quality of the plaintiff's mark by diminishing the capacity of the plaintiff's mark to identify and distinguish the plaintiff's goods and services.

The United States Supreme Court's first review of the Federal Trademark Dilution Act occurred in 2003, and many trademark experts believe that owners of famous marks will now have a more difficult time prevailing in dilution cases. In *Moseley v. V Secret Catalogue, Inc.,* 537 U.S. 418 (2003), a case involving the use of the mark VICTOR'S LITTLE SECRET for a sex-toy shop and which was alleged to dilute the famous VICTORIA'S SECRET® marks, the Court stated that owners of famous marks must show *actual* dilution of their marks in the form of at least circumstantial evidence that the marks have lost the capacity to identify and distinguish their goods or services. The Court stated that the mere fact that consumers mentally associate a junior user's mark with a famous mark is not sufficient to establish dilution. The requirement of showing actual dilution through empirical evidence will undoubtedly make winning dilution cases more difficult for owners of famous marks.

Blurring and Tarnishment

Generally, there are two types of unauthorized use that constitute dilution: blurring and tarnishment. **Blurring** is the whittling away of an established trademark's selling power through its unauthorized use upon dissimilar products. Examples might include STARBUCKS PENS, SHELL COFFEE, PEPSI VIDEO, or the use of TIFFANY for restaurant services as described earlier. Such uses would eventually drain away the distinctive power of the original mark even if they did not cause consumer confusion. **Tarnishment** occurs when a mark is linked to products of an inferior quality or when the mark is portrayed in an unwholesome or embarrassing context (such as a poster reading "Enjoy Cocaine" in a script and color identical to that used by Coca-Cola Company or the substitution of an expletive for "Dunkin" in the mark DUNKIN' DONUTS®). Tarnishment is often found when the senior mark is linked to sexual activity, obscenity, or illegal activity. For example, General Electric's mark was found to be tarnished by GENITAL ELECTRIC, and Anheuser-Busch (owner of the famous BUDWEISER beer mark) was able to enjoin the distribution of BUTTWEISER T-shirts.

look of the past and the reach of the present. What is written about a person or an event is frankly an interpretation, as are handmade visual statements, like paintings and drawings. Photographed images do not seem to be statements about the world so much as pieces of it, miniatures of reality that anyone can make or acquire.

Photographs, which fiddle with the scale of the world, themselves get reduced, blown up, cropped, retouched, doctored, tricked out. They age, plagued by the usual ills of paper objects; they disappear; they become valuable, and get bought and sold; they are reproduced. Photographs, which package the world, seem to invite packaging. They are stuck in albums, framed and set on tables, tacked on walls, projected as slides. Newspapers and magazines feature them; cops alphabetize them; museums exhibit them; publishers compile them.

For many decades the book has been the most influential way of arranging (and usually miniaturizing) photographs, thereby guaranteeing them longevity, if not immortality—photographs are fragile objects, easily torn or mislaid—and a wider public. The photograph in a book is, obviously, the image of an image. But since it is, to begin with, a printed, smooth object, a photograph loses much less of its essential quality when reproduced in a book than a painting does. Still, the book is not a wholly satisfactory scheme for putting groups of photographs into general circulation. The sequence in which the photographs are to be looked at is proposed by the order of pages, but nothing holds readers to the recommended order or indicates the amount of time to be spent on each photograph. Chris Markers's film, *Si j'avais quatre dromadaires* (1966), a brilliantly orchestrated meditation on photographs of all sorts and themes, suggests a subtler and more rigorous way of packaging (and enlarging) still photographs. Both the order and the exact time for looking at each photograph are imposed; and there is a gain in visual legibility and emotional impact. But photographs transcribed in a film cease to be collectable objects, as they still are when served up in books.

Photographs furnish evidence. Something we hear about, but doubt, seems proven when we're shown a photograph of it. In one version of its utility, the camera record incriminates. Starting with their use by the Paris police in the murderous roundup of Communards° in June 1871, photographs became a useful tool of modern states in the surveillance and control of their increasingly mobile populations. In another version of its utility, the camera record

---

Communards: Supporters of the short-lived Commune, the socialist movement that briefly ruled Paris during the period immediately following the Franco-Prussian War. In June 1871, French national forces attacked the Communards; in one week some 20,000 Communards were executed, and 7,500 jailed or deported.

justifies. A photograph passes for incontrovertible proof that a given thing happened. The picture may distort; but there is always a presumption that something exists, or did exist, which is like what's in the picture. Whatever the limitations (through amateurism) or pretensions (through artistry) of the individual photographer, a photograph — any photograph — seems to have a more innocent, and therefore more accurate, relation to visible reality than do other mimetic objects. Virtuosi of the noble image like Alfred Stieglitz and Paul Strand, composing mighty, unforgettable photographs decade after decade, still want, first of all, to show something "out there," just like the Polaroid owner for whom photographs are a handy, fast form of note taking, or the shutterbug with a Brownie who takes snapshots as souvenirs of daily life.

While a painting or a prose description can never be other than a narrowly selective interpretation, a photograph can be treated as a narrowly selective transparency. But despite the presumption of veracity that gives all photographs authority, interest, seductiveness, the work that photographers do is no generic exception to the usually shady commerce between art and truth. Even when photographers are most concerned with mirroring reality, they are still haunted by tacit imperatives of taste and conscience. The immensely gifted members of the Farm Security Administration photographic project of the late 1930s (among them Walker Evans, Dorothea Lange, Ben Shahn, Russell Lee) would take dozens of frontal pictures of one of their sharecropper subjects until satisfied that they had gotten just the right look on film—the precise expression on the subject's face that supported their own notions about poverty, light, dignity, texture, exploitation, and geometry. In deciding how a picture should look, in preferring one exposure to another, photographers are always imposing standards on their subjects. Although there is a sense in which the camera does indeed capture reality, not just interpret it, photographs are as much an interpretation of the world as paintings and drawings are. Those occasions when the taking of photographs is relatively undiscriminating, promiscuous, or self-effacing do not lessen the didacticism of the whole enterprise. This very passivity — and ubiquity — of the photographic record is photography's "message," its aggression.

Images which idealize (like most fashion and animal photography) are no less aggressive than work which makes a virtue of plainness (like class pictures, still lifes of the bleaker sort, and mug shots). There is an aggression implicit in every use of the camera. This is as evident in the 1840s and 1850s, photography's glorious first two decades, as in all the succeeding decades, during which technology made possible an ever increasing spread of that mentality which looks at the world as a set of potential photographs. Even for such early masters as David Octavius Hill and Julia Margaret Cameron who used the camera as a means of getting painterly images, the point of taking

Figure 1. Arthur "Weegee" Fellig, *Top Hats—In Trouble*, 1942. Charles Sodokoff and Arthur Webber Use Their Top Hats to Hide Their Faces, January 27, 1942. New York Daily News Photo. (Weegee/ICP/Liaison.)

photographs was a vast departure from the aims of painters. From its start, photography implied the capture of the largest possible number of subjects. Painting never had so imperial a scope. The subsequent industrialization of camera technology only carried out a promise inherent in photography from its very beginning: to democratize all experiences by translating them into images.

That age when taking photographs required a cumbersome and expensive contraption—the toy of the clever, the wealthy, and the obsessed—seems remote indeed from the era of sleek pocket cameras that invite anyone to take pictures. The first cameras, made in France and England in the early 1840s, had only inventors and buffs to operate them. Since there were then no professional photographers, there could not be amateurs either, and taking photographs had no clear social use; it was a gratuitous, that is, an artistic activity, though with few pretensions to being an art. It was only with its industrialization that photography came into its own as art. As industrialization provided social uses for the operations of the photographer, so the reaction against these uses reinforced the self-consciousness of photography-as-art.

Recently, photography has become almost as widely practiced an amuse- 10
ment as sex and dancing—which means that, like every mass art form, photography is not practiced by most people as an art. It is mainly a social rite, a
defense against anxiety, and a tool of power.

Memorializing the achievements of individuals considered as members of
families (as well as of other groups) is the earliest popular use of photography.
For at least a century, the wedding photograph has been as much a part of the
ceremony as the prescribed verbal formulas. Cameras go with family life.
According to a sociological study done in France, most households have a camera, but a household with children is twice as likely to have at least one camera as a household in which there are no children. Not to take pictures of one's
children, particularly when they are small, is a sign of parental indifference,
just as not turning up for one's graduation picture is a gesture of adolescent
rebellion.

Through photographs, each family constructs a portrait-chronicle of itself—
a portable kit of images that bears witness to its connectedness. It hardly matters what activities are photographed so long as photographs get taken and are
cherished. Photography becomes a rite of family life just when, in the industri-
alizing countries of Europe and America, the very institution of the family starts
undergoing radical surgery. As that claustrophobic unit, the nuclear family,
was being carved out of a much larger family aggregate, photography came
along to memorialize, to restate symbolically, the imperiled continuity and
vanishing extendedness of family life. Those ghostly traces, photographs,
supply the token presence of the dispersed relatives. A family's photograph
album is generally about the extended family—and, often, is all that remains
of it.

As photographs give people an imaginary possession of a past that is unreal,
they also help people to take possession of space in which they are insecure.
Thus, photography develops in tandem with one of the most characteristic of
modern activities: tourism. For the first time in history, large numbers of people
regularly travel out of their habitual environments for short periods of time. It
seems positively unnatural to travel for pleasure without taking a camera
along. Photographs will offer indisputable evidence that the trip was made,
that the program was carried out, that fun was had. Photographs document
sequences of consumption carried on outside the view of family, friends,
neighbors. But dependence on the camera, as the device that makes real
what one is experiencing, doesn't fade when people travel more. Taking photographs fills the same need for the cosmopolitans accumulating photograph
trophies of their boat trip up the Albert Nile or their fourteen days in China
as it does for lower-middle-class vacationers taking snapshots of the Eiffel
Tower or Niagara Falls.

A way of certifying experience, taking photographs is also a way of refusing it—by limiting experience to a search for the photogenic, by converting experience into an image, a souvenir. Travel becomes a strategy for accumulating photographs. The very activity of taking pictures is soothing, and assuages general feelings of disorientation that are likely to be exacerbated by travel. Most tourists feel compelled to put the camera between themselves and whatever is remarkable that they encounter. Unsure of other responses, they take a picture. This gives shape to experience: Stop, take a photograph, and move on. The method especially appeals to people handicapped by a ruthless work ethic—Germans, Japanese, and Americans. Using a camera appeases the anxiety which the work driven feel about not working when they are on vacation and supposed to be having fun. They have something to do that is like a friendly imitation of work: They can take pictures.

People robbed of their past seem to make the most fervent picture takers,   15 at home and abroad. Everyone who lives in an industrialized society is obliged gradually to give up the past, but in certain countries, such as the United States and Japan, the break with the past has been particularly traumatic. In the early 1970s, the fable of the brash American tourist of the 1950s and 1960s, rich with dollars and Babbittry,° was replaced by the mystery of the group-minded Japanese tourist, newly released from his island prison by the miracle of overvalued yen, who is generally armed with two cameras, one on each hip.

Photography has become one of the principal devices for experiencing something, for giving an appearance of participation. One full-page ad shows a small group of people standing pressed together, peering out of the photograph, all but one looking stunned, excited, upset. The one who wears a different expression holds a camera to his eye; he seems self-possessed, is almost smiling. While the others are passive, clearly alarmed spectators, having a camera has transformed one person into something active, a voyeur: Only he has mastered the situation. What do these people see? We don't know. And it doesn't matter. It is an Event: something worth seeing—and therefore worth photographing. The ad copy, white letters across the dark lower third of the photograph like news coming over a teletype machine, consists of just six words: ". . . Prague . . . Woodstock . . . Vietnam . . . Sapporo . . . Londonderry . . . LEICA." Crushed hopes, youth antics, colonial wars, and winter sports are alike—are equalized by the camera. Taking photographs has set up a chronic voyeuristic relation to the world which levels the meaning of all events.

Babbittry: Conformity to standards and attitudes of the middle class. The term comes from the character George F. Babbitt in the novel *Babbitt* (1922) by Sinclair Lewis.

A photograph is not just the result of an encounter between an event and a photographer; picture taking is an event in itself, and one with ever more peremptory rights—to interfere with, to invade, or to ignore whatever is going on. Our very sense of situation is now articulated by the camera's interventions. The omnipresence of cameras persuasively suggests that time consists of interesting events, events worth photographing. This, in turn, makes it easy to feel that any event, once underway, and whatever its moral character, should be allowed to complete itself—so that something else can be brought into the world, the photograph. After the event has ended, the picture will still exist, conferring on the event a kind of immortality (and importance) it would never otherwise have enjoyed. While real people are out there killing themselves or other real people, the photographer stays behind his or her camera, creating a tiny element of another world: the image-world that bids to outlast us all.

Photographs are a grammar and, even more importantly, an ethics of seeing.

Photographing is essentially an act of nonintervention. Part of the horror of such memorable coups of contemporary photojournalism as the pictures of a Vietnamese bonze° reaching for the gasoline can, of a Bengali guerrilla in the act of bayoneting a trussed-up collaborator, comes from the awareness of how plausible it has become, in situations where the photographer has the choice between a photograph and a life, to choose the photograph. The person who intervenes cannot record; the person who is recording cannot intervene. Dziga Vertov's great film, *Man with a Movie Camera* (1929), gives the ideal image of the photographer as someone in perpetual movement, someone moving through a panorama of disparate events with such agility and speed that any intervention is out of the question. Hitchcock's *Rear Window* (1954) gives the complementary image: The photographer played by James Stewart has an intensified relation to one event, through his camera, precisely because he has a broken leg and is confined to a wheelchair; being temporarily immobilized prevents him from acting on what he sees, and makes it even more important to take pictures. Even if incompatible with intervention in a physical sense, using a camera is still a form of participation. Although the camera is an observation station, the act of photographing is more than passive observing. Like sexual voyeurism, it is a way of at least tacitly, often explicitly, encouraging whatever is going on to keep on happening. To take a picture is to have an interest in things as they are, in the status quo remaining unchanged (at least for as long as it takes to get a "good" picture), to be in complicity with whatever makes a subject interesting, worth photographing— including, when that is the interest, another person's pain or misfortune.

---

bonze: A Buddhist monk.

"I always thought of photography as a naughty thing to do—that was one of my favorite things about it," Diane Arbus wrote, "and when I first did it I felt very perverse." Being a professional photographer can be thought of as naughty, to use Arbus's pop word, if the photographer seeks out subjects considered to be disreputable, taboo, marginal. But naughty subjects are harder to find these days. And what exactly is the perverse aspect of picture taking? If professional photographers often have sexual fantasies when they are behind the camera, perhaps the perversion lies in the fact that these fantasies are both plausible and so inappropriate. In *Blowup* (1966), Antonioni has the fashion photographer hovering convulsively over Verushka's body with his camera clicking. Naughtiness, indeed! In fact, using a camera is not a very good way of getting at someone sexually. Between photographer and subject, there has to be distance. The camera doesn't rape, or even possess, though it may presume, intrude, trespass, distort, exploit, and, at the farthest reach of metaphor, assassinate—all activities that, unlike the sexual push and shove, can be conducted from a distance, and with some detachment.

Figure 2. James Stewart as L. B. Jeffries in *Rear Window*, directed by Alfred Hitchcock. (© Bettmann/CORBIS.)

There is a much stronger sexual fantasy in Michael Powell's extraordinary   20
movie *Peeping Tom* (1960), which is not about a Peeping Tom but about a
psychopath who kills women with a weapon concealed in his camera, while
photographing them. Not once does he touch his subjects. He doesn't desire
their bodies; he wants their presence in the form of filmed images—those
showing them experiencing their own death—which he screens at home for
his solitary pleasure. The movie assumes connections between impotence
and aggression, professionalized looking and cruelty, which point to the central fantasy connected with the camera. The camera as phallus is, at most, a
flimsy variant of the inescapable metaphor that everyone unself-consciously
employs. However hazy our awareness of this fantasy, it is named without
subtlety whenever we talk about "loading" and "aiming" a camera, about
"shooting" a film.

The old-fashioned camera was clumsier and harder to reload than a
brown Bess musket. The modern camera is trying to be a ray gun. One ad
reads:

> The Yashica Electro-35 GT is the space-age camera your family will love.
> Take beautiful pictures day or night. Automatically. Without any nonsense.
> Just aim, focus, and shoot. The GT's computer brain and electronic shut-
> ter will do the rest.

Like a car, a camera is sold as a predatory weapon—one that's as automated
as possible, ready to spring. Popular taste expects an easy, an invisible technology. Manufacturers reassure their customers that taking pictures demands
no skill or expert knowledge, that the machine is all-knowing, and responds
to the slightest pressure of the will. It's as simple as turning the ignition key
or pulling the trigger.

Like guns and cars, cameras are fantasy machines whose use is addictive.
However, despite the extravagances of ordinary language and advertising,
they are not lethal. In the hyperbole that markets cars like guns, there is at
least this much truth: Except in wartime, cars kill more people than guns
do. The camera/gun does not kill, so the ominous metaphor seems to be all
bluff—like a man's fantasy of having a gun, knife, or tool between his legs.
Still, there is something predatory in the act of taking a picture. To photograph people is to violate them, by seeing them as they never see themselves, by having knowledge of them they can never have; it turns people
into objects that can be symbolically possessed. Just as the camera is a sub-
limation of the gun, to photograph someone is a sublimated murder—a soft
murder, appropriate to a sad, frightened time.

Eventually, people might learn to act out more of their aggressions with
cameras and fewer with guns, with the price being an even more image-
choked world. One situation where people are switching from bullets to film

is the photographic safari that is replacing the gun safari in East Africa. The hunters have Hasselblads instead of Winchesters; instead of looking through a telescopic sight to aim a rifle, they look through a viewfinder to frame a picture. In end-of-the century London, Samuel Butler complained that "there is a photographer in every bush, going about like a roaring lion seeking whom he may devour." The photographer is now charging real beasts, beleaguered and too rare to kill. Guns have metamorphosed into cameras in this earnest comedy, the ecology safari, because nature has ceased to be what it always had been — what people needed protection from. Now nature — tamed, endangered, mortal — needs to be protected from people. When we are afraid, we shoot. But when we are nostalgic, we take pictures.

It is a nostalgic time right now, and photographs actively promote nostalgia. Photography is an elegiac art, a twilight art. Most subjects photographed are, just by virtue of being photographed, touched with pathos. An ugly or grotesque subject may be moving because it has been dignified by the attention of the photographer. A beautiful subject can be the object of rueful feelings, because it has aged or decayed or no longer exists. All photographs are memento mori.° To take a photograph is to participate in another person's (or thing's) mortality, vulnerability, mutability. Precisely by slicing out this moment and freezing it, all photographs testify to time's relentless melt.

Cameras began duplicating the world at that moment when the human 25 landscape started to undergo a vertiginous rate of change: While an untold number of forms of biological and social life are being destroyed in a brief span of time, a device is available to record what is disappearing. The moody, intricately textured Paris of Atget and Brassaï is mostly gone. Like the dead relatives and friends preserved in the family album, whose presence in photographs exorcises some of the anxiety and remorse prompted by their disappearance, so the photographs of neighborhoods now torn down, rural places disfigured and made barren, supply our pocket relation to the past.

A photograph is both a pseudopresence and a token of absence. Like a wood fire in a room, photographs — especially those of people, of distant landscapes and faraway cities, of the vanished past — are incitements to reverie. The sense of the unattainable that can be evoked by photographs feeds directly into the erotic feelings of those for whom desirability is enhanced by distance. The lover's photograph hidden in a married woman's wallet, the poster photograph of a rock star tacked up over an adolescent's bed, the campaign-button image of a politician's face pinned on a voter's coat, the snapshots of a cabdriver's children clipped to the visor — all such talismanic uses of photographs express a feeling both sentimental and implicitly magical: They are attempts to contact or lay claim to another reality.

---

memento mori: A Latin phrase, "remember your death," used to refer to reminders of one's mortality.

Photographs can abet desire in the most direct, utilitarian way — as when someone collects photographs of anonymous examples of the desirable as an aid to masturbation. The matter is more complex when photographs are used to stimulate the moral impulse. Desire has no history — at least, it is experienced in each instance as all foreground, immediacy. It is aroused by archetypes and is, in that sense, abstract. But moral feelings are embedded in history, whose personae are concrete, whose situations are always specific. Thus, almost opposite rules hold true for the use of the photograph to awaken desire and to awaken conscience. The images that mobilize conscience are always linked to a given historical situation. The more general they are, the less likely they are to be effective.

A photograph that brings news of some unsuspected zone of misery cannot make a dent in public opinion unless there is an appropriate context of feeling and attitude. The photographs Mathew Brady and his colleagues took of the horrors of the battlefields did not make people any less keen to go on with the Civil War. The photographs of ill-clad, skeletal prisoners held at Andersonville inflamed Northern public opinion — against the South. (The effect of the Andersonville photographs must have been partly due to the very novelty, at that time, of seeing photographs.) The political understanding that many Americans came to in the 1960s would allow them, looking at the photographs Dorothea Lange took of Nisei on the West Coast being transported to internment camps in 1942, to recognize their subject for what it was — a crime committed by the government against a large group of American citizens. Few people who saw these photographs in the 1940s could have had so unequivocal a reaction; the grounds for such a judgment were covered over by the prowar consensus. Photographs cannot create a moral position, but they can reinforce one — and can help build a nascent one.

Photographs may be more memorable than moving images, because they are a neat slice of time, not a flow. Television is a stream of underselected images, each of which cancels its predecessor. Each still photograph is a privileged moment, turned into a slim object that one can keep and look at again. Photographs like the one that made the front page of most newspapers in the world in 1972 — a naked South Vietnamese child just sprayed by American napalm, running down a highway toward the camera, her arms open, screaming with pain — probably did more to increase the public revulsion against the war than a hundred hours of televised barbarities.

One would like to imagine that the American public would not have been 30 so unanimous in its acquiescence to the Korean War if it had been confronted with photographic evidence of the devastation of Korea, an ecocide and genocide in some respects even more thorough than those inflicted on Vietnam a decade later. But the supposition is trivial. The public did not see such photographs because there was, ideologically, no space for them. No one brought

Federal Remedies for Dilution

The new act provides a remedy for owners of famous marks in federal court. The Federal Trademark Dilution Act (15 U.S.C. § 1125(c)(1)) lists several factors for courts to consider in determining whether a mark is sufficiently famous that it is protectable under the Act, including the duration and extent of use of the mark, duration and extent of advertising and publicity for the mark, the degree of inherent or acquired distinctiveness of the mark, fame of the mark in the parties' respective trading areas, and whether the mark is federally registered. Dilution can occur even if the mark is not famous on a nationwide basis but rather famous only in a niche market. Thus, the mark LAS VEGAS SPORTING NEWS was found to dilute THE SPORTING NEWS although THE SPORTING NEWS was famous only in the niche market of sports periodicals and not to the general public. *Times Mirror Magazine v. Las Vegas Sports News,* 212 F.3d 157 (3d Cir. 2000). An owner who prevails is entitled to injunctive relief, destruction of all diluting goods, and, if willful intent to dilute is shown, actual damages, treble damages, the violator's profits, and costs.

Some types of conduct are exempt from liability, such as fair use of a famous mark in comparative advertising, parody for noncommercial purposes, and news reporting. These uses are protected under the First Amendment.

Many of the newer cases discussing dilution relate to the use of Internet addresses that dilute famous marks. Thus, the address "candyland.com" for sexually explicit goods and services was held to dilute the famous CANDYLAND® mark owned by Hasbro Toys, *Hasbro Inc. v. Entertainment Group Ltd.,* 40 U.S.P.Q.2d 1479 (W.D. Wash. 1996), and the address "adultsrus.com" for sexual paraphernalia was held to dilute the famous TOYS R US® mark owned by Toys "R" Us, Inc. *Toys "R" Us, Inc. v. Akkaouli,* WL 772709 (N.D. Cal. 1996).

RELATED TRADEMARK CLAIMS

Trademark owners often assert additional claims in actions for trademark infringement. For example, in *Phat Fashions* (see Exhibit 6–3), the plaintiff alleged trademark infringement, dilution, and unfair competition, all arising out of the same course of conduct. Thus, there is an array of various causes of action a trademark owner might assert.

Importation of Gray Market Goods

In many instances, U.S. trademark owners grant rights to those in foreign countries to manufacture goods that bear their U.S. trademark. After the goods are distributed in the foreign markets, other parties buy them (often in bulk) and import them back into the United States to resell to others, in competition with the U.S. trademark owner. These goods are called **gray market goods** or **parallel imports.** The law relating to the permissibility of such importation is unsettled, with most courts holding that the import and sale of gray market goods is not infringement, because once a mark owner sells goods bearing its mark, it cannot prevent subsequent owners from reselling the goods if there is no deception or consumer confusion; the goods are physically the same as those sold by the U.S. trademark owner; and the U.S. registrant and the foreign manufacturer are the same or related entities. The situation is analogous to resales in the United States. For example, a consumer who purchases a baby stroller bearing the APRICA® mark can later resell it to another. This doctrine is referred to as the **exhaustion theory** inasmuch as once the first lawful sale is made, the trademark owner's rights are exhausted or extinguished in regard to subsequent sales. Allowing importation of gray market or parallel goods is consistent with the exhaustion theory. As discussed in Chapter 16, recent holdings in the copyright field are also consistent with this theory.

back photographs of daily life in Pyongyang, to show that the enemy had a human face, as Felix Greene and Marc Riboud brought back photographs of Hanoi. Americans did have access to photographs of the suffering of the Vietnamese (many of which came from military sources and were taken with quite a different use in mind) because journalists felt backed in their efforts to obtain those photographs, the event having been defined by a significant number of people as a savage colonialist war. The Korean War was understood differently—as part of the struggle of the free world against the Soviet Union and China—and, given that characterization, photographs of the cruelty of unlimited American firepower would have been irrelevant.

Though an event has come to mean, precisely, something worth photographing, it is still ideology (in the broadest sense) that determines what constitutes an event. There can be no evidence, photographic or otherwise, of an event until the event itself has been named and characterized. And it is never photographic evidence which can construct — more properly, identify — events; the contribution of photography always follows the naming of the event. What determines the possibility of being affected morally by photographs is the existence of a relevant political consciousness. Without a politics, photographs of the slaughter bench of history will most likely be experienced as, simply, unreal or as a demoralizing emotional blow.

The quality of feeling, including moral outrage, that people can muster in response to photographs of the oppressed, the exploited, the starving, and the massacred also depends on the degree of their familiarity with these images. Don McCullin's photographs of emaciated Biafrans° in the early 1970s had less impact for some people than Werner Bischof's photographs of Indian famine victims in the early 1950s because those images had become banal, and the photographs of Tuareg° families dying of starvation in the sub-Sahara that appeared in magazines everywhere in 1973 must have seemed to many like an unbearable replay of a now familiar atrocity exhibition.

Photographs shock insofar as they show something novel. Unfortunately, the ante keeps getting raised — partly through the very proliferation of such images of horror. One's first encounter with the photographic inventory of ultimate horror is a kind of revelation, the prototypically modern revelation: a negative epiphany. For me, it was photographs of Bergen-Belsen and Dachau° which I came across by chance in a bookstore in Santa Monica in July 1945. Nothing I have seen — in photographs or in real life — ever cut me as sharply, deeply, instantaneously. Indeed, it seems plausible to me to

---

Biafrans: People of southeastern Nigeria ravaged by civil war, hunger, and economic collapse.

Tuareg: A nomadic ethnic group, now found chiefly in West Africa, who had been involved for a millennia in trans-Saharan caravan trade.

Bergen-Belsen and Dachau: Two Nazi concentration camps.

divide my life into two parts, before I saw those photographs (I was twelve) and after, though it was several years before I understood fully what they were about. What good was served by seeing them? They were only photographs — of an event I had scarcely heard of and could do nothing to affect, of suffering I could hardly imagine and could do nothing to relieve. When I looked at those photographs, something broke. Some limit had been reached, and not only that of horror; I felt irrevocably grieved, wounded, but a part of my feelings started to tighten; something went dead; something is still crying.

To suffer is one thing; another thing is living with the photographed images of suffering, which does not necessarily strengthen conscience and the ability to be compassionate. It can also corrupt them. Once one has seen such images, one has started down the road of seeing more — and more. Images transfix. Images anesthetize. An event known through photographs certainly becomes more real than it would have been if one had never seen the photographs — think of the Vietnam War. (For a counterexample, think of the Gulag Archipelago,° of which we have no photographs.) But after repeated exposure to images it also becomes less real.

The same law holds for evil as for pornography. The shock of pho- 35 tographed atrocities wears off with repeated viewings, just as the surprise and bemusement felt the first time one sees a pornographic movie wear off after one sees a few more. The sense of taboo which makes us indignant and sorrowful is not much sturdier than the sense of taboo that regulates the definition of what is obscene. And both have been sorely tried in recent years. The vast photographic catalog of misery and injustice throughout the world has given everyone a certain familiarity with atrocity, making the horrible seem more ordinary—making it appear familiar, remote ("it's only a photograph"), inevitable. At the time of the first photographs of the Nazi camps, there was nothing banal about these images. After thirty years, a saturation point may have been reached. In these last decades, "concerned" photography has done at least as much to deaden conscience as to arouse it.

The ethical content of photographs is fragile. With the possible exception of photographs of those horrors, like the Nazi camps, that have gained the status of ethical reference points, most photographs do not keep their emotional charge. A photograph of 1900 that was affecting then because of its subject would, today, be more likely to move us because it is a photograph taken in 1900. The particular qualities and intentions of photographs tend to be swallowed up in the generalized pathos of time past. Aesthetic distance

---

Gulag Archipelago: The chain of Soviet slave labor and concentration camps. "Gulag" itself is the acronym for the Russian term "Chief Administration for Corrective Labor Camps," the camp system that, like the islands of an archipelago, spread out across Siberia.

seems built into the very experience of looking at photographs, if not right away, then certainly with the passage of time. Time eventually positions most photographs, even the most amateurish, at the level of art.

The industrialization of photography permitted its rapid absorption into rational — that is, bureaucratic — ways of running society. No longer toy images, photographs became part of the general furniture of the environment —touchstones and confirmations of that reductive approach to reality which is considered realistic. Photographs were enrolled in the service of important institutions of control, notably the family and the police, as symbolic objects and as pieces of information. Thus, in the bureaucratic cataloging of the world, many important documents are not valid unless they have, affixed to them, a photograph token of the citizen's face.

The "realistic" view of the world compatible with bureaucracy redefines knowledge—as techniques and information. Photographs are valued because they give information. They tell one what there is; they make an inventory. To spies, meteorologists, coroners, archaeologists, and other information professionals, their value is inestimable. But in the situations in which most people use photographs, their value as information is of the same order as fiction. The information that photographs can give starts to seem very important at that moment in cultural history when everyone is thought to have a right to something called news. Photographs were seen as a way of giving information to people who do not take easily to reading. The *Daily News* still calls itself "New York's Picture Newspaper," its bid for populist identity. At the opposite end of the scale, *Le Monde*, a newspaper designed for skilled, well-informed readers, runs no photographs at all. The presumption is that, for such readers, a photograph could only illustrate the analysis contained in an article.

A new sense of the notion of information has been constructed around the photographic image. The photograph is a thin slice of space as well as time. In a world ruled by photographic images, all borders ("framing") seem arbitrary. Anything can be separated, can be made discontinuous, from anything else: All that is necessary is to frame the subject differently. (Conversely, anything can be made adjacent to anything else.) Photography reinforces a nominalist view of social reality as consisting of small units of an apparently infinite number—as the number of photographs that could be taken of anything is unlimited. Through photographs, the world becomes a series of unrelated, freestanding particles; and history, past and present, a set of anecdotes and *faits divers.*° The camera makes reality

---

faits divers: French for "current news."

atomic, manageable, and opaque. It is a view of the world which denies interconnectedness, continuity, but which confers on each moment the character of a mystery. Any photograph has multiple meanings; indeed, to see something in the form of a photograph is to encounter a potential object of fascination. The ultimate wisdom of the photographic image is to say: "There is the surface. Now think—or rather feel, intuit—what is beyond it, what the reality must be like if it looks this way." Photographs, which cannot themselves explain anything, are inexhaustible invitations to deduction, speculation, and fantasy.

Photography implies that we know about the world if we accept it as the camera records it. But this is the opposite of understanding, which starts from *not* accepting the world as it looks. All possibility of understanding is rooted in the ability to say no. Strictly speaking, one never understands anything from a photograph. Of course, photographs fill in blanks in our mental pictures of the present and the past: for example, Jacob Riis's images of New York squalor in the 1880s are sharply instructive to those unaware that urban poverty in late-nineteenth-century America was really that

40

Figure 3. Jacob A. Riis, "Room in tenement flat, 1910," from *How the Other Half Lives*, by Jacob A. Riis. (Jacob A. Riis Collection, Museum of the City of New York.)

Dickensian.° Nevertheless, the camera's rendering of reality must always hide more than it discloses. As Brecht points out, a photograph of the Krupp works° reveals virtually nothing about that organization. In contrast to the amorous relation, which is based on how something looks, understanding is based on how it functions. And functioning takes place in time, and must be explained in time. Only that which narrates can make us understand.

The limit of photographic knowledge of the world is that, while it can goad conscience, it can, finally, never be ethical or political knowledge. The knowledge gained through still photographs will always be some kind of sentimentalism, whether cynical or humanist. It will be a knowledge at bargain prices—a semblance of knowledge, a semblance of wisdom; as the act of taking pictures is a semblance of appropriation, a semblance of rape. The very muteness of what is, hypothetically, comprehensible in photographs is what constitutes their attraction and provocativeness. The omnipresence of photographs has an incalculable effect on our ethical sensibility. By furnishing this already crowded world with a duplicate one of images, photography makes us feel that the world is more available than it really is.

Needing to have reality confirmed and experience enhanced by photographs is an aesthetic consumerism to which everyone is now addicted. Industrial societies turn their citizens into image junkies; it is the most irresistible form of mental pollution. Poignant longings for beauty, for an end to probing below the surface, for a redemption and celebration of the body of the world—all these elements of erotic feeling are affirmed in the pleasure we take in photographs. But other, less liberating feelings are expressed as well. It would not be wrong to speak of people having a *compulsion* to photograph: to turn experience itself into a way of seeing. Ultimately, having an experience becomes identical with taking a photograph of it, and participating in a public event comes more and more to be equivalent to looking at it in photographed form. That most logical of nineteenth-century aesthetes, Mallarmé,° said that everything in the world exists in order to end in a book. Today everything exists to end in a photograph.

Dickensian: A reference to the novels of Charles Dickens (1812–1870) that offered fierce criticisms of poverty and social stratification in nineteenth-century England.

Brecht . . . Krupp works: Bertolt Brecht (1898–1956), a German author, dramatist, and poet known for his social criticism. Krupp works refers to the factories of the Krupp family in Germany that produced steel, armaments, and ammunition.

Mallarmé: Stéphane Mallarmé (1842–1898), a French poet and critic.

Working with the Text

1. Susan Sontag titles this, the first essay in her collection *On Photography*, by alluding to a famous passage in Plato's *Republic*, known as the "Allegory of the Cave." Plato argues that we, like cave dwellers accustomed to the dark, mistake shadows for reality, mere images for truth. Why does Sontag title her essay as she does? What attitudes or arguments in the body of the essay justify the title she gives it?

2. Sontag's essay seems to privilege the provocative statement or insight over sustained, clearly structured argument. Indeed, the essay might on a first reading overwhelm the reader with its range and its densely packed commentary. After you have taken the opportunity for a second or third reading, consider the question of the essay's style and structure. How would you characterize the essay's structure or its progression of argument? How might the style of Sontag's essay suit the subject that she addresses? What connection might there be between Sontag's series of insights or perceptions and photographs themselves?

3. At the beginning of her essay, Sontag asserts, "In teaching us a new visual code, photographs alter and enlarge our notions of what is worth looking at and what we have a right to observe. They are a grammar and, even more importantly, an ethics of seeing" (par. 1). Drawing on the specific positions that Sontag stakes out in her essay, develop a two-page statement of her ethics of seeing. What is won and what is lost as you translate Sontag's essay into such a statement?

From Text to Field

1. Sontag's essay was first published in 1977, some thirty years ago. In the span of a generation, much has changed in how we make, circulate, and read the photographic image. Writing in the twilight of the age of traditional photography, Sontag could hardly have imagined the world of the image today, with the Internet, digital cameras, and even cell phones that take photos. Write an essay in which you revisit Sontag's arguments in light of today's technology. What in Sontag's essay stands the test of time and continues to be relevant, and what might be now outdated?

2. Sontag mentions at one point in the essay that hers is a "sad, frightened time" (par. 22). Indeed, the essay is dark in tone, pessimistic in outlook. Write an essay in which you reflect on that tone or outlook from your vantage point thirty years later. You may find yourself justifying and explaining her

approach or offering an optimist's reply. Do you share Sontag's vision, disagree with her assessment, or find some alternative implications of photography as a technology?

3. The range of Sontag's essay is impressive, as she links photography and its effect on society to such issues as desire, conscience, aggression, and social ritual, among many others. Select one particular issue that Sontag raises, and explore it in some detail, drawing on your own experience with photography and on the role of photography in today's world.

4. Although the range and complexity of Sontag's essay might suggest otherwise, it invites our close consideration of individual photographs. Choose one photo that has enduring relevance in your life; it may be a personal family photo or a photo that captures a memorable or traumatic moment that you have shared with others or even a widely published photo that has special meaning for you. Write a close analysis of the photo, in light of both Sontag's arguments and your assessment of her essay. How and why might you and Sontag see the photo in similar—or different—ways?

Truth and Stereotype

E. H. Gombrich

> The essay that follows is an excerpt from the art history classic *Art and Illusion: A Study in the Psychology of Pictorial Representation.* Published in 1960, the book proposed a groundbreaking theory of art that continues to serve as a springboard for inquiry into stylistic development and change. Based on scientific insights into visual perception, Gombrich's understanding of the psychology of representation suggests that even outside the realm of art, we think in terms of received models: We look at the world, literally and figuratively, through the language and images we have been given.
>
> Gombrich was born in Vienna in 1909 and through his family and his schooling became immersed in both culture and science. An art historian, he was known for pursuing questions that could only be answered through a thorough knowledge of psychology and the history of ideas, as well as the development of styles in art. In addition to producing a number of landmark books, he taught at Oxford, Cambridge, Harvard, and Princeton universities and the University of Washington and served as the director of the Warburg Institute and professor of the History of the Classical Tradition at the University of London. His best-known work, *The Story of Art* (1950; 16th ed., 1995), was translated into twenty-nine languages and was widely read by children as well as adults. E. H. Gombrich remained active until his death in 2001, at the age of ninety-two.

Perhaps the earliest instance of [illustrated reportage] dates back more than three thousand years, to the beginnings of the New Kingdom in Egypt, when the Pharaoh Thutmose included in his picture chronicle of the Syrian campaign a record of plants he had brought back to Egypt (Fig. 1). The inscription, though somewhat mutilated, tells us that Pharaoh pronounces these pictures to be "the truth." Yet botanists have found it hard to agree on what

Figure 1. Limestone relief of botanical garden with plants and animals brought to Egypt from Syria by Thutmose III (1479–1425 BC).

plants may have been meant by these renderings. The schematic shapes are not sufficiently differentiated to allow secure identification.

An even more famous example comes from the period when medieval art was at its height, from the volume of plans and drawings by the Gothic master builder, Villard de Honnecourt, which tells us so much about the practice and outlook of the men who created the French cathedrals. Among the many architectural, religious, and symbolic drawings of striking skill and beauty to be found in this volume, there is a curiously stiff picture of a lion, seen *en face* (Fig. 2). To us, it looks like an ornamental or heraldic image, but Villard's caption tells us that he regarded it in a different light: "*Et sacies bien*," he says, "*qu'il fu contrefais al vif*." "Know well that it is drawn from life." These words obviously had a very different meaning for Villard than they have for us. He can have meant only that he had drawn his schema in the presence of a real lion. How much of his visual observation he allowed to enter into the formula is a different matter.

Once more the broadsheets of popular art show us to what extent this attitude survived the Renaissance. The letterpress of a German woodcut from the sixteenth century informs us that we here see "the exact counterfeit" of a kind of locust that invaded Europe in menacing swarms (Fig. 3). But the zoologist would be rash to infer from this inscription that there existed an entirely different species of creatures that has never been recorded since. The artist had again used a familiar schema, compounded of animals he had learned to portray, and the traditional formula for locusts that he knew from

Figure 2. Villard de Honnecourt, *Lion and Porcupine*, c. 1235, pen and ink.

an apocalypse where the locust plague was illustrated. Perhaps the fact that the German word for a locust is *Heupferd* (hay horse) tempted him to adopt a schema of a horse for the rendering of the insect's prance.

The creation of such a name and the creation of the image have, in fact, much in common. Both proceed by classifying the unfamiliar with the familiar, or more exactly, to remain in the zoological sphere, by creating a sub-species. Since the locust is called a kind of horse it must therefore share some of its distinctive features.

The caption of a Roman print of 1601 (Fig. 4) is as explicit as that of the German woodcut. It claims the engraving represents a giant whale that had been washed ashore near Ancona the same year and "was drawn accurately from nature." ("*Ritratto qui dal naturale appunto.*") The claim would be more trustworthy if there did not exist an earlier print recording a similar "scoop" from the Dutch coast in 1598 (Fig. 5). But surely the Dutch artists of the late sixteenth century, those masters of realism, would be able to portray a whale? Not quite, it seems, for the creature looks suspiciously as if it had ears, and whales with ears, I am assured on higher authority, do not exist. The draftsman probably mistook one of the whale's flippers for an ear and therefore placed it far too close to the eye. He, too, was misled by a familiar schema, the schema of the typical head. To draw an unfamiliar sight presents

Counterfeiting

Trademark **counterfeiting** is a particularly specious type of infringement. A counterfeiter applies the trademark owner's mark to goods or services that do not originate with the owner. Perhaps the best examples of counterfeiting or "black market" activities involve the unauthorized sale of scarves bearing the HERMES® mark, handbags bearing the KATE SPADE® or LOUIS VUITTON® marks, watches bearing the ROLEX® mark, and other high-end or designer items that are sold at flea markets, corner stands, and "on the street." The items sold and which bear the mark are not genuine and are intentionally sold for the express purpose of trading off the owner's established goodwill and reputation.

Universities, athletic teams, and rock bands that own valuable marks often have their marks counterfeited and placed on black market goods, primarily T-shirts, sweatshirts, and jackets. To deter counterfeiters, statutes allow for the immediate impoundment and destruction of the "knockoff" goods; awards of treble damages, actual damages, and attorneys' fees; and criminal penalties. It has been reported that in just the few months prior to the 1996 Atlanta Olympics, $2.5 million worth of infringing merchandise was seized, mostly in the Atlanta area. Similarly, the night of game four of the 2000 baseball World Series, Major League Baseball Properties Inc. assembled a squad of twenty-five in-house investigators and, accompanied by court-ordered marshals and lawyers, served 150 complaints and seized 15,000 T-shirts and other unauthorized apparel from counterfeiters around the stadium. Unfortunately, however, seizing the goods provides little long-term benefit, inasmuch as the counterfeiter simply moves its stall or stand to some other location the next day.

Unfair Competition

Section 43 of the Lanham Act (15 U.S.C. § 1125) provides that any person injured by a false designation of origin or false representation may bring a civil action against the offending party. This statute is often used as a catchall because it is so broadly worded that it prohibits nearly all forms of **unfair competition,** including false advertising and infringement of trade dress. Moreover, a party need not have a registered trademark to invoke its protections. Thus, it affords even broader protection than section 32 of the Lanham Act (15 U.S.C. § 1114), which prohibits infringement of a registered mark. In most instances, parties alleging trademark infringement under section 32 of the Lanham Act also include a cause of action for unfair competition under section 43 (and state consumer protection or unfair competition statutes, if they exist). In fact, in *Phat Fashions,* No. CIV S-01-1771 (E.D. Cal. 2002), the court stated that because the plaintiff had demonstrated infringement, *it followed that* the plaintiff had equally established unfair competition. Unfair competition is fully discussed in Chapter 23.

Customs Regulation

Additional protection is provided to trademark owners through section 42 of the Lanham Act (15 U.S.C. § 1124), which allows owners of registered trademarks to deposit their certificates of registration with the U.S. Customs Service in order to allow Customs to block importation of offending goods. The trademark owner files an application with the Intellectual Property Rights Branch of the U.S. Customs Service in Washington, DC, to have its marks recorded with Customs, deposits one certified copy and five additional copies of its registration certificates with Customs, and pays an application fee of $190 per class. The U.S. Customs will then "post its ports." **Posting of ports** means that Customs will monitor ports of entry into the United States and will seize any unpermitted goods bearing the owner's mark. Criminal sanctions may be imposed on the offending party.

Figure 3. Anonymous, *Locust*, 1556, woodcut.

Figure 4. Anonymous Italian, *Whale Washed Ashore at Ancona*, 1601, engraving.

Figure 5. After Goltzius, *Whale Washed Ashore in Holland*, 1598, engraving.

greater difficulties than is usually realized. And this, I suppose, was also the reason why the Italian preferred to copy the whale from another print. We need not doubt the part of the caption that tells the news from Ancona, but to portray it again "from the life" was not worth the trouble.

In this respect, the fate of exotic creatures in the illustrated books of the last few centuries before the advent of photography is as instructive as it is amusing. When Dürer published his famous wood-cut of a rhinoceros (Fig. 6), he had to rely on sec-ondhand evidence which he filled in from his own imagination, colored, no doubt, by what he had learned of the most famous of exotic beasts, the drag-on with its armored body. Yet it has been shown that **The familiar will always remain the likely starting point for the rendering of the unfamiliar.** this half-invented creature served as a model for all renderings of the rhi-noceros, even in natural-history books, up to the eighteenth century. When, in 1790, James Bruce published a drawing of the beast (Fig. 7) in his *Travels to Discover the Source of the Nile*, he proudly showed that he was aware of this fact:

> The animal represented in this drawing is a native of Tcherkin, near Ras el Feel . . . and this is the first drawing of the rhinoceros with a double horn that has ever yet been presented to the public. The first figure of the Asiatic

Figure 6. Dürer, *Rhinoceros*, 1515, woodcut.

Figure 7. Heath, *Rhinoceros of Africa*, 1789, engraving.

rhinoceros, the species having but one horn, was painted by Albert Durer, from the life. . . . It was wonderfully ill-executed in all its parts, and was the origin of all the monstrous forms under which that animal has been painted, ever since. . . . Several modern philosophers have made amends for this in our days; Mr. Parsons, Mr. Edwards, and the Count de Buffon, have given good figures of it from life; they have indeed some faults, owing chiefly to preconceived prejudices and inattention. . . . This . . . is the first that has been published with two horns, it is designed from the life, and is an African.

If proof were needed that the difference between the medieval draftsman and his eighteenth-century descendant is only one of degree, it could be found here. For the illustration, presented with such flourishes of trumpets, is surely not free from "preconceived prejudices" and the all-pervading memory of Dürer's woodcut. We do not know exactly what species of rhinoceros the artist saw at Ras el Feel, and the comparison of his picture with a photograph taken in Africa (Fig. 8) may not, therefore, be quite fair. But I am told that none of the species known to zoologists corresponds to the engraving claimed to be drawn *al vifl!*°

The story repeats itself whenever a rare specimen is introduced into Europe. Even the elephants that populate the paintings of the sixteenth and seventeenth centuries have been shown to stem from a very few archetypes and to embody all their curious features, despite the fact that information about elephants was not particularly hard to come by.

These examples demonstrate, in somewhat grotesque magnification, a tendency which the student of art has learned to reckon with. The familiar will always remain the likely starting point for the rendering of the unfamiliar; an

Figure 8. African rhinoceros.

---

al vifl: Literally, "from the life"; a drawing based on a live specimen.

existing representation will always exert its spell over the artist even while he strives to record the truth. Thus it was remarked by ancient critics that several famous artists of antiquity had made a strange mistake in the portrayal of horses: They had represented them with eyelashes on the lower lid, a feature which belongs to the human eye but not to that of the horse. A German ophthalmologist who studied the eyes of Dürer's portraits, which to the layman appear to be such triumphs of painstaking accuracy, reports somewhat similar mistakes. Apparently not even Dürer knew what eyes "really look like."

This should not give us cause for surprise, for the greatest of all the visual explorers, Leonardo° himself, has been shown to have made mistakes in his anatomical drawings. Apparently he drew features of the human heart which Galen° made him expect but which he cannot have seen.   10

The study of pathology is meant to increase our understanding of health. The sway of schemata did not prevent the emergence of an art of scientific illustration that sometimes succeeds in packing more correct visual information into the image than even a photograph contains. But the diagrammatic maps of muscles in our illustrated anatomies (Fig. 9) are not "transcripts" of things seen but the work of trained observers who build up the picture of a specimen that has been revealed to them in years of patient study.

Figure 9. Muscles of the neck, from *Gray's Anatomy*.

Leonardo: Leonardo da Vinci (1452–1519), an Italian painter, sculptor, inventor, architect, and anatomist.

Galen (AD 129–200): A Greek physician whose views influenced western medicine.

Now in this sphere of scientific illustration it obviously makes sense to say that Thutmose's artists or Villard himself could not have done what the modern illustrator can do. They lacked the relevant schemata, their starting point was too far removed from their motif, and their style was too rigid to allow a sufficiently supple adjustment. For so much certainly emerges from a study of portrayal in art: You cannot create a faithful image out of nothing. You must have learned the trick if only from other pictures you have seen.

Working with the Text

1. E. H. Gombrich uses the word *schema* to designate the formulas and stereotypes artists bring to their illustrations of observable phenomena such as plants, animals, and human anatomy. As Gombrich points out, "To draw an unfamiliar sight presents greater difficulties than is usually realized" (par. 5). Inferring from Gombrich's argument and using your own insights into human behavior, write a brief essay in which you explore the challenges of artistic representation. Why would artists—even those who could observe the live phenomenon for themselves—use schemas? Where do you think schemas come from?

2. Why do you think Gombrich believes that it is difficult for close, detailed observation to challenge the formulas or schemas with which we are already familiar? Where might the difficulty lie—in our inability to see accurately, in our inability to render faithfully, or both? In what ways is it difficult to escape from the spell that schemas have over us? Why is it natural or helpful to rely on schemas?

3. As this excerpt from Gombrich's *Art and Illusion: A Study in the Psychology of Pictorial Representation* (2nd ed., 1961) draws to a conclusion, he speaks of scientific illustration as offering something more or different from photography:

   > The sway of schemata did not prevent the emergence of an art of scientific illustration that sometimes succeeds in packing more correct visual information into the image than even a photograph contains. But the diagrammatic maps of muscles in our illustrated anatomies are not "transcripts" of things seen but the work of trained observers who build up the picture of a specimen that has been revealed to them in years of patient study.

   Why might the artist, who "packs in" information and "builds up" an image, offer more information to the anatomy student than the photographer?

From Text to Field

1. Gombrich's argument assumes that the illustrators he discusses learned to draw, at least in part, by following certain schemata. In an essay, recall how your art teachers—or one particularly influential art teacher—taught you how

to draw. Did you learn to use what Gombrich would term "schemas"? If so, what were they? If not, how were you taught to render something real? How were you taught to translate three-dimensional phenomena into two-dimensional renderings? What role did observation play? What role did technique play? As a prelude to writing this essay, or as an accompaniment to it, try your hand at drawing—that is, faithfully reproducing—an animal, a flower, or a natural object. What have you learned by trying to draw, now that you have read Gombrich's essay?

2. In the chapter "Truth and Stereotype" from *Art and Illusion*, Gombrich's central assertion is that we look at the world through the language and images we have been given. To explore his assertion on a personal level, choose a stereotype you hold or have held (such as stereotypes of race, gender, or certain professions). Write a personal essay in which you describe your own psychology regarding the stereotype. What are the specific elements of the stereotype? How did you acquire it? What do you think are its origins? How do you regard it? What, in your view, does it omit or distort?

3. You might recall that as Gombrich discusses "illustrated reportage" (par. 1) he pays a good deal of attention to the captions that accompany the illustrations. In an essay, reflect on the several functions that captions have. What work do they perform? Insofar as photojournalism might be thought of as modern illustrated reportage, do Gombrich's insights still apply? What role do captions have as they accompany photographs? Consider using illustrations in your essay.

INTO THE FIELD: Options for Writing Projects

1. Seeing Your Campus Afresh

Although your college campus may seem new and unexplored during your first days as a student, you will soon have settled into a routine. You will frequent some parts of campus so regularly that you will become inured to their local details, their specific characteristics. Sheer habit of walking or biking your regular route will blind you. Other parts of campus may remain as remote and uncharted as ever, a terra incognita even after months or several years as a student.

This field project offers an opportunity to rediscover a small corner of your campus. Through close observation of a particular site and the activities that occur there, develop an essay in which you introduce fellow students and other members of your campus community to a space you all share but of which you may have become unaware. As you choose your particular site, you may want to consider the following options:

- A prominent spot on campus, often heavily trafficked, offers a chance for your readers to rediscover something they may think they already know quite well. Such a site may be layered with a rich history, multiple meanings, and various, sometimes competing, activities.
- A remote or unnoticed site on campus offers a different challenge. Here your job is to bring the site alive for those who don't know it well, or at all, and to suggest its significance. Why should members of the campus community stop and notice this little corner, this patch of ground?
- Buildings define campus geography, and yet we often don't listen well to what the walls of those buildings whisper in our ears. What would a particular building on campus want you to know about its history, about the disciplinary or residential activities that it houses, about those who inhabit its halls?
- Landmarks and memorials offer a further option and may include public art on campus, as well as benches, stones, or other markers that memorialize a teacher or a student. As you uncover the history behind such sites, and the people they honor, you will help your readers see a corner of your campus afresh.

2. Seeing to Write, Writing to See

This field project invites you to explore in some detail the complex relationships between seeing and writing, observing and expressing, envisioning and communicating. It places a premium on close attention to your writing process and the use of apt, detailed examples. Four points of departure may enrich your essay as you uncover these relationships:

- Start with the process of seeing. What is it about seeing that leads to or requires verbalization? Seeing—close observation—is often considered a precursor to writing, yet the process of writing often enables or requires us to see more deeply.
- You should also approach the relationship from the perspective of writing and the writing and revision process. How does revision invite us to see differently? As we write, how do we "envision" a text? How do we write in cues that help readers envision a text (its terrain, its structure, its progression)?
- The relationship between seeing and writing takes on different forms in particular disciplines or fields. How might the dynamic between seeing and writing differ, for example, in anthropology and sociology on the one hand and engineering and architecture on the other hand? How do seeing and writing inform work in your major?
- Even academic texts are becoming, in today's world, far more visual, as they call on not just illustrations but also forms of multimedia. How has the relationship between seeing and writing been influenced by your experience as a multimedia reader?

3. **Aesthetic Response, across the Curriculum**

We tend to think of aesthetic response as something that belongs to art and literature departments and that it has little if any relevance elsewhere on campus. Yes, aesthetic response concerns how we value the beautiful, yet we may unduly limit the range and importance of that response if we think of it in terms of paintings, sculpture, or novels. This field project asks that you consider the role of aesthetic response in fields far removed from art and literature.

To help you unpack that tricky concept "aesthetic response," let's recall that John Berger (p. 684) spoke of the wood carving of the white bird in terms of five categories or qualities that make it both pleasing and mysterious: its reference to or place in the surrounding world; its meaning, significance, or symbolic value; its respect for the material used; its formal unity and economy; and its ability to elicit astonishment at how it was made, its craftsmanship. Drawing on some or all of these qualities, consider whether and in what way aesthetic emotion plays a role across the curriculum. A few examples might prompt you to look further:

- Design, whether in engineering or in architecture and planning, involves more than building functional "things." Design also has an aesthetic dimension. What we build often depends on how users respond; function can, and perhaps must, be in some sense beautiful or pleasing.
- The best research designs in the social and natural sciences are sometimes praised as being "elegant." Is there a research aesthetic? If so, which of Berger's five qualities might be crucial to that aesthetic?

- A well-crafted analysis or argument often involves more than sheer logic and hard evidence. Is there an aesthetic of analysis and argument, one that involves its design or perhaps the author's voice? In what ways does the aesthetic of nonfiction expository prose parallel or depart from the aesthetic of fictional literature?

4. Concerned Photography

When photography is used as a means of activism of one kind or another—ecological or political, for example—we might think of it as "concerned photography." Photos can be used, as Susan Sontag (p. 690) puts it, "to stimulate the moral impulse" (par. 27). Yet she cautions that "[p]hotographs cannot create a moral position, but they can reinforce one—and can help build a nascent one" (par. 28).

This field project invites you to explore "concerned photography" through one particular case study. You might choose to examine the role of images in an environmental appeal or a fund-raising campaign or the function of images in mobilizing response to human rights abuse. Collect primary texts—brochures, Web sites, print advertisements, and the like—so that you can analyze the function of these images in some detail.

Whatever your particular case study, your task is to explore the connection between "seeing" and "believing." How do images elicit belief and spur action? What is the value of shock? And what are the dangers of repetition, repeated exposure, and cliché—in short, the banality of the image?

5. Campus Image Making

The images of college life that you find in admissions brochures and on university Web sites can influence educational and career decisions. Perhaps such images—a class held outside under a tree on a verdant lawn or a female engineering student in a lab—enticed you as well or provided a sense that you might fit in. This field project invites you to look behind the glossy public presentation of your institution to examine the process of campus image making.

The first step is to assemble a set of texts—printed and/or digital—that can serve as your primary documents. As you analyze these documents, you may wish to consider a range of questions:

- How do the images communicate a sense of your college's identity and its institutional mission? You might find it helpful to compare your images with those of similar kinds of institutions (community colleges, large state universities, private liberal arts colleges, religious institutions, and so on).
- Do the images draw on stereotypical features of college life in general, or do they capture something of the local context, the life actually lived on your campus?

TRIVIA

- After objections from Pfizer, Inc., the owner of the mark VIAGRA®, the supplier of NIAGRA (a drink marketed as "Viagra for women") agreed to change the name of the drink.
- In 2001, the maker of the nougat treat offered under the NUTELLA® mark forced the owner of the domain names GNUTELLA.DE and NEWTELLA.DE (used in connection with music) to cease use of the names on the basis that the latter marks infringed the NUTELLA® mark.
- Uncle Milton Industries still owns the trademark ANT FARM®. "Everyone else can call it a 'formicarium,'" says a company spokesperson.

CHAPTER SUMMARY

Disputes over use and ownership of trademarks are common. Such disputes typically fall into one of four categories: inter partes proceedings, infringement actions, actions for dilution, and actions alleging unfair competition.

An inter partes proceeding is one brought before the Trademark Trial and Appeal Board and may be categorized as follows:

- an opposition by a party to registration of a mark;
- a petition to cancel an existing registration of a mark;
- an interference; or
- a concurrent use proceeding whereby parties each agree to use their respective marks in specifically designated geographical areas.

An action for trademark infringement can be brought in federal court if a defendant's use of a mark is likely to cause confusion with a registered mark to an appreciable number of reasonably prudent consumers about the source, origin, affiliation, or sponsorship of goods or services. Courts consider a variety of factors in determining whether there is a likelihood of confusion, including the similarity of the marks, the similarity of the goods/services offered under the marks, the similarity of trade channels, the strength of the senior mark, whether the sale is made on impulse or only after careful deliberation, and whether actual confusion has occurred. A trademark infringement action proceeds much like any trial: a complaint is filed, an answer is filed, motions may be made, discovery occurs, and a trial is held. Relief may include injunctions, monetary damages, and destruction of infringing articles.

An action for dilution may be brought even when another's use of a mark is not likely to cause confusion if another uses a mark in a way that blurs the distinctiveness of a famous mark or tarnishes its reputation and goodwill.

If a mark is not registered, an action for unfair competition may be brought against a party who is using a false designation of origin or is engaged in false advertising. Additional protection is

- How does the making of your campus in images balance two competing demands: the wish to project the institution your campus would like to become and the need to portray the institution as it is?
- Is there truth in advertising? Have you had a class that actually met outside on a lawn? Does the percentage of female engineering students merit the portrayal it received? How does the portrayal of ethnic and racial minorities match the actual climate on campus?

To understand the behind-the-scenes work that leads to campus publications and their use with different audiences, you may find it helpful to interview admissions counselors and the editorial and photographic staff in the campus publications office.

6. Truth, Lies, and Your Life in Images

This field project uses autobiography as an opportunity to analyze the role of images in forging identity. Your source documents for this project include family albums and personal photographs, augmented by your reflection on how you and others take photos. This project can be approached from at least two perspectives:

- Consider how your life has been captured by others in images. What truths, even if unpleasant, have been captured in these photos, and likewise what lies or distortions might be apparent? Your task in this project is not merely to describe photos or assess their truth but rather to use such questions as springboards to an analysis of what has occurred to your representation through the camera's eyes and the eyes of others. For example, what is it about family photos, with their "say cheese" moments, that can be both comforting and distressing, both true and fake?
- Consider how you have captured images of others. With the miniaturization of digital cameras and with cell phones now having photographic capability, one needn't lug around a large single-lens reflex camera, or even a pocket camera. What is the story of your life as an image taker? Has technology changed your photographic habits? In what ways do you consider the truth and lies in the photos you take? Here, too, your focus in this project is not your photo-taking adventures in and of themselves; your task is to use such adventures as an opportunity to consider broader social and cultural attitudes through your own photographic acts.

7. Blindness and Insight

Our culture has organized many of its metaphors around issues of sight. For example, consider the idiomatic expression "seeing eye to eye." Likewise, stereotypes about blindness abound, as in the blind beggar with the tin cup in his hand. This field project invites you to explore and consider the consequences of such metaphors and stereotypes. Because this field project can quickly become complex and take you in different directions, consider how you might focus your efforts.

A good place to begin is to catalog as many of the metaphors or idiomatic expressions about blindness and sight as you can. Ask a classmate or a friend to help you develop such a catalog. You may also wish to interview disability counselors about how such metaphors and expressions are received by those who have issues with their eyesight.

You may also wish to focus your analysis in a particular area, such as film, literature, or cartoons and comic strips. Another option is to examine cultural icons, such as Helen Keller. To what extent do such icons dispel misconceptions about blindness, and to what extent does the very popularity of such icons make it difficult to change perceptions that are by now quite dated?

8. Pictorial Representation

In the excerpt you have read from "Truth and Stereotype" (p. 709), a chapter in *Art and Illusion*, E. H. Gombrich uses illustrated reportage and scientific illustration as examples of the psychology of pictorial representation that he addresses throughout the book. Deepen or extend your reflection on pictorial representation by choosing one of the following two options for fieldwork:

- To further explore the psychology Gombrich describes, conduct interviews or research to find out how artists learn to illustrate. How are they taught to see? How are they taught to translate what they see into a pictorial form? What role does technique play? How might schemas come into play?
- Write an essay in which you apply Gombrich's argument in this excerpt to other forms of art or other periods of art. Or apply the argument to other forms of "pictorial representation," which could range from advertising to the mental images that serve as our stereotypes for people, activities, or events. To support and enrich your analysis, pursue some research and, if possible, conduct interviews regarding the "pictorial representation" you have chosen to discuss.

9. Writing: Schemas and Imitation

The excerpt from E. H. Gombrich's *Art and Illusion* offers insights into the role that schemas play in orienting our perceptions and representations of our world. Although Gombrich confines himself to illustration, writing also involves schemas that guide our composing and reading processes. Moreover, just as pictorial representation relies in good measure on imitation, so too does writing ask us to proceed using forms and styles that we inherit. This fieldwork project invites you to consider the role of underlying schemas and imitation in the writing process through one of several perspectives or issues:

- For many centuries, writing instruction placed heavy emphasis on copying and imitating exemplary texts. What rationale do you see in that form of instruction?
- To what extent might genre—or forms of writing often meant to support certain activities—be a schema in the sense proposed by Gombrich?
- Writing instruction in school and college often proceeds on the basis of preconceived schemas or frameworks, such as the "five paragraph essay." Assess their value and limitations.
- Initiation into an academic field often involves imitating basic kinds of texts and literate behaviors. Consider how an assignment in an introductory course (such as a lab report in physics) can succeed or fail in accomplishing that purpose.

10. Received Vocabularies

Elsewhere in *Art and Illusion*, E. H. Gombrich observes that "the artist, no less than the writer, needs a vocabulary before he can embark on a 'copy' of reality." For your field project, consider the role of "received vocabularies" in an academic discipline, in teaching and learning, or in contemporary cultural and political life. Here is a short, illustrative list of the sort of projects you might pursue:

- Consider a specific field in which one term or concept, as a received "vocabulary," is now under reconsideration or has become a matter of some dispute.
- In what ways might cultural anthropology help us understand the insight offered by the art historian Gombrich: why the "unfamiliar" is inevitably understood, if only at first, through the "familiar."
- Consider how an issue of contemporary interest (gender, for example, or international conflict) is complicated by misunderstandings resulting from a "received vocabulary."

WITNESSING THE IMAGE

We live in a media culture that has saturated our lives with images. Specific purveyors of images—television, Web sites, magazines, consumer commodities themselves—all contribute to this surfeit of the visual. But it is not sheer quantity that poses challenges for us. Images have changed how we witness our world.

Our connection with images has grown more distant even as the images multiply. Chances are, the image we see is not the image we produced or the image we ourselves circulated. What the image depicts is not necessarily grounded in the world we ourselves experience. Images are now produced, circulated, and consumed in an economy of the visual that extends well beyond our experience.

We have long questioned the image—especially the photographic image—in terms of its adequacy. Does the image adequately represent what we know and have experienced, what we ourselves have seen? This question has now become secondary to a larger question about believability. Can we believe images when what we know of the world is chiefly drawn from images themselves? What happens when our acquaintance with the real largely comes by way of the image itself? What happens when we find ourselves increasingly dependent on the image yet ever more uncomprehending about what it shows?

This unit explores these issues—ones that arise as we witness the image. The belief we invest in photos seems natural enough, grounded as it is in our assumption that they capture our world. Photos seem to be the ultimate testimony about our world. And yet, we would do well to ask who is using the photo and to what end. Belief in photos must remain something that we bestow, through individual initiative and acts of conscience. Yet the larger economy of the visual would have us believe that we have already acquiesced to the image. Its very presence makes a claim on our credence.

As images become more pervasive, they have also intertwined themselves with words in ways that challenge centuries of separation between seeing and speaking. Images now speak, and words are tethered to images. In our media culture, showing and telling are no longer easily separated. With the intertwined lives of image and word come new possibilities but also challenges.

Likewise, images and our easy access to them have us question what it means to be a witness and to bear witness. What is our proximity to events, and can we trust the testimony of our eyes and ears, especially when the media function ever more frequently as borrowed eyes and ears? Witnessing has always raised difficult issues about the connections between seeing and saying, experience and language. But in an image-saturated media culture, those issues become pressing.

Our difficulties and fascination with images are nowhere made more apparent than in images that trouble us—images of war and terrorism, images of the fragility of community. Those images themselves tell a tale—about what we care to know and care to hide and about the increasingly global reach of images. As we witness images from halfway around the world, we are also witnessing profound changes in the ways we see and believe.

The four readings in this unit help us raise and explore these issues in ways that connect image and word in their own texts. David Levi Strauss asks us to question the link between photography and believability, for he is worried that belief itself may become the "collateral damage" of our media culture. In his article on "Witnessing" John Durham Peters asks us to reflect on the precarious journey from experience to words, from the seen to the said. That journey is made all the more precarious by a media culture that is happy to witness for us. We close with two essays that deal with specific images that sear into our minds and hearts. H. Bruce Franklin surveys the history of war photography and is troubled by the ways in which war images have slipped into a sanitized virtual reality. Francis A. Beer and G. R. Boynton reflect on images of terrorism in a post–9/11 world. They find that the globalization of terror goes hand in hand with the globalization of the media. The reach and speed of images brings terror into our living rooms. And terrorism itself has found a new stage: image-driven media.

Reflecting on Prior Knowledge

1. We believe in photographic images perhaps even more resolutely than we do other forms of art or texts that capture experience. In a journal, reflect on a photograph that has, for whatever reason, captured your belief. Explore why this has been the case.

2. Our culture has traditionally separated words from pictures. Working in groups, and drawing on your own reading and viewing experience, share ideas on why image and text have led isolated lives. Is this changing? If so, why and to what effect?

3. Images of conflict and war are among the most gruesome we know. They are real, all too real. And yet, images of war can often take on the quality of virtual reality, where they are, if not romanticized, at least sanitized. In a journal entry, recall and describe an image of war or conflict that has made an impression on you. What about it seems real and immediate or eerily distant and removed? How is this image used, and by whom?

4. Experience is fleeting, yet we are sometimes called upon to remember and talk about it after the fact. Have you ever been asked to talk about an event or experience that you witnessed? What was difficult about serving, if only informally, as a witness? Working in groups of two or three, develop a catalog of issues that make witnessing reliable or unreliable and always a challenge.

5. Thanks to the media, many of the images we witness have been circulated widely, often across the globe. Given the speed and reach of today's global media, how have such images affected our ability or willingness to respond to them? Writing individually in a journal or working collectively in a small group, reflect on what place images from across the globe have in your life.

Photography and Belief

David Levi Strauss

An essayist, poet, and art critic living in New York, David Levi Strauss has written provocative essays on the relationships among photography, politics, and culture. He asks his readers to look behind the apparently self-evident nature of photographs and to interrogate their place in our culture, especially in our politics.

After studying at Goddard College, Strauss worked at the Center of Curatorial Studies at Bard College and as a faculty member at the Avery Graduate School of the Arts. He has received several awards, among them a Guggenheim Fellowship. His essays and reviews appear regularly in such journals as *Artforum* and *Aperture* and have been gathered in two collections: *Between Dog and Wolf: Essays on Art and Politics* (1999) and *Between the Eyes: Essays on Photography and Politics* (2003). His essays have also appeared in monographs on such artists as Carolee Schneemann, Leon Golub, Miguel Rio Branco, Alfredo Jaar, Francesca Woodman, and Daniel Martinez.

The essay that follows—"Photography and Belief"—appears in Strauss's collection *Between the Eyes: Essays on Photography and Politics.* Here, as in many of his essays, Strauss writes about the crisis of representation, and asks us to consider the connection between what we see and what we believe. The question is pressing because, in today's world, much of what we know of the real comes by way of images. In this wide-ranging collection, Strauss tackles such subjects as photography and propaganda and the social life of the images of September 11, and he explores photographs as both social documents and as personal revelation.

> They say that pictures don't lie, but that's not really true anymore.
> — Advance promotion line for an interview with Fred Ritchin on National Public Radio, February 7, 1991

> If material conditions need to be redescribed, more painstakingly
> and in novel forms, in order to be reinvested with "believability," then
> we can surely develop the form — and the means of dissemination —
> to do so.
> — MARTHA ROSLER, "Image Simulations, Computer Manipulations:
> Some Ethical Considerations"

"Seeing is believing." It's been that way from the beginning, long before
Messrs. Niépce and Daguerre changed the technology of seeing by inventing photography. But photography materialized seeing in a new way, and significantly changed the relation between seeing and believing. Photography
as mechanical reproduction almost immediately altered the aura of the work
of art, and over the next 150 years photography acquired its own aura — the
aura of believability.

Now the technology of seeing is changing again, with rapid advances in
electronic imaging technologies that allow one to alter or "make up" photographs at will, and some say these new technologies are causing a tremendous crisis of believability in photography. In his book *In Our Own Image:
The Coming Revolution in Photography/How Computer Technology is
Changing Our View of the World*, Fred Ritchin raises a cry of alarm. In the
preface to his book, he states that it was written "in appreciation of the important historical juncture at which we stand, just before the widespread adoption of electronic technology, out of a sense that we must try to take some
responsibility for the future of the immensely popular *and still believable*
medium of photography." (Emphasis added.) The questions raised by the
new imaging technologies were discussed in *Newsweek* (July 30, 1990) under
the title "When Photographs Lie: Advances in 'electronic imaging' are
assaulting the meaning of the picture"; five years before that (July 1985),
Whole Earth Review had declared with dogmatic finality that "the photograph as evidence of anything is dead." Commentators of all kinds say we are
moving into a period in which the boundaries between fact and fiction, real
and artificial, actual and virtual reality are going to become much more operationally porous and movable than they have been in the past.

Most of these speculations about the impact of new imaging technologies
on photography have tended to be strictly materialist (unlike the more hetero-
dox, reality-hacking, *Mondo 2000* hyperspeculations of the burgeoning cyber-
punk subculture), and many are based on a series of severely restricted assumptions about how photographs are actually received and used. If we are to understand the coming changes, we must try harder to understand the present and
evolving complexity of the way we look at, use, and "believe" photographs now.

Is That a Real Photograph or Did You Just Make It Up?

The word *belief* derives from the Anglo-Saxon word *geliefan*, meaning "to hold dear." The Sanskrit root for this word, *Lubh*, means "to desire, love." Belief involves the "assent of the mind to a statement, or to the truth of a fact beyond observation, on the testimony of another, or to a fact or truth on the evidence of consciousness" (*Oxford English Dictionary*). In relation to photography, this assent is influenced, but not exhausted, by the photograph's relation to "objective reality." It is also influenced and determined by its place in the complex web of subjectivities that determines how we negotiate the world.

Reputed Identities

The relation between photography and belief is especially complicated in   5 images having to do with identity, where the effect of a photograph can be decisive. When Burl Ives shows James Dean a photograph he's been holding for years of Dean's father and mother on their wedding day in the film *East of Eden*, Dean looks at it and says, "I *knew* it was true. I knew it." Sometimes,

Figure 1. Found photograph of unknown boy, believed to be the author's brother. For more information, please call 1-800-929-2323 or visit www.aperture.org. Aperture is a not-for-profit public foundation dedicated to promoting photography as an unique form of artistic expression.

the photograph doesn't need to prove anything on its own; it corroborates and confirms what we already know.

Many of us possess certain photographs that accrete believability over time. These may be photographs of family members or loved ones, autobiographical images, or other photographs that come to act as amulets or talismans, triggering certain emotions or states and warding off others. The relation of these photographs to belief is often not bound by their objective veracity. Rupert Jenkins (assistant director at San Francisco Camerawork) told me that when he was a child he picked up a photograph lying in the street and carried it around, telling everyone that this was a picture of his mother. After a while, he came to believe it *was* his mother. I had a similar experience in adolescence with a picture I found somewhere of a boy resembling pictures I had seen of my father as a child. I began to think of this found photograph as a picture of my brother who had died before I was born. In some real way, that photograph did come to represent my brother.

People use photographs to construct identities, investing them with "believability." Of course, advertisers and news-picture editors do the same thing, mimicking the private use of photographs in order to manufacture desire for products and to manufacture public consent. This has caused a great deal of confusion. The first question must always be: Who is using this photograph, and to what end?

Friendly Fire

Increasingly, those who control technology control information, and those who control information manage consent. The Gulf War ushered in a new era of information control and consensus reality in the United States, and this change can be read in the way images were used during the war. Following the successful press blackouts of their invasions of Grenada and Panama, the U.S. military was able to drop a seamless screen around the entire theater of operations in the Gulf from day one. The only images released to the U.S. public were the ones projected onto that screen by military authorities. Since photojournalists were effectively shut out of the area or relegated to tightly controlled Department of Defense pools, few of the images projected onto that screen were conventional documentary photographs. Instead, the images came from electronically manipulated and enhanced tapes; video arcade images of crosshairs floating over targets, ending in delicate puffs of smoke.

As the war progressed, most of the "photographs" printed in newspapers were actually video stills from CNN footage. These strangely attractive images of fireworks against liquid green skies, tightly composed explosions, and handsome talking heads before cold blue mosques were, literally, not to afforded by depositing a certificate of trademark registration with the U.S. Customs Service to prohibit offending goods from entering the United States.

Thus, securing a federal registration for one's mark enhances the level of protection for a trademark owner who may then bring a civil action for infringement of the registered mark and may obtain the assistance of U.S. Customs in blocking offending goods from entry into the United States. Owners of unregistered marks may seek protection under section 43 of the Lanham Act for unfair competition, but the remedies specifically provided for infringement actions and posting of ports are not available to them.

CASE ILLUSTRATION—INFRINGEMENT ANALYSIS

Case: *AMF Inc. v. Sleekcraft Boats,* 599 F.2d 341 (9th Cir. 1979)

Facts: The plaintiff used the mark SLICKCRAFT to market its boats, and the defendant later adopted the mark SLEEKCRAFT to market its boats.

Holding: After analyzing the "confusion factors" (strength of the marks, relatedness of the goods, similarity of the marks, evidence of actual confusion, marketing channels, type of goods and care of purchasing public, defendant's intent, and the likely expansion of product lines), the court concluded the defendant's mark was likely to cause confusion with the plaintiff's mark and therefore infringement was found. Because the parties had both used their marks for more than ten years, the court fashioned a limited injunction and ordered the defendant to use its logo with every display of the word mark SLEEKCRAFT.

CASE STUDY AND ACTIVITIES

Case Study.   In reviewing the *Official Gazette* for August 18, Watson noticed a pending application for PIRATE'S CAVE for an amusement park attraction. One of Watson's popular boat rides at Fantasy Fun Adventure Park is PIRATE'S COVE®. Watson is also planning to build a new ride called BLAST RIDER. In conducting its trademark search, Watson has discovered that while Disney Co. owns a registration for BLAST RIDER®, it appears that the actual ride called BLAST RIDER was dismantled and removed from Disney World four years ago. Watson recently discovered that another company is marketing a stuffed bear, called FLUFFY PUFFY BEAR, that is nearly the same size and has the same appearance as the bear offered under Watson's mark FLUFFY BUFFY BEAR®. Finally, Watson, which offers a well-known line of confections, baked goods, and candies in its General Store under the mark MRS. SWEET®, has found out that a phone sex line is using the name of MISS SWEET, offering "a fun and fantasy adventure in intimacy."

Activities.   Discuss the appropriate actions Watson should take to protect its marks PIRATE'S COVE®, FLUFFY BUFFY BEAR®, and MRS. SWEET®. Finally, if Watson wishes to use BLAST RIDER for a new ride, what should it do with regard to the current registration issued to Disney Co.?

be believed. What was to believe? *This is a direct hit on a munitions dump. This is the air war over Baghdad.* The actual war information in these images was so restricted that questions of believability never really came up. What did come up, over and over, was *deniability.*

In an unusually frank piece titled "The Propaganda War" (subtitled "Amid the bombs, words and pictures carry a payload on the battlefield of public opinion"), the February 25, 1991, issue of *Newsweek* stated:

> Propaganda is a broad approach to persuasion that encompasses several disciplines. So-called public diplomacy — a variation on standard public relations — involves presenting one's position in the best possible light, often on TV. Formal military psychological operations ("psyops") include broadcasting and dropping leaflets over enemy lines. Each of these mind games relies at times on "disinformation" — planting false information so as to confuse and manipulate. *Still, the most persuasive propaganda is that which is both graphic and demonstrably true.*
>
> In theory, reporters in democratic societies work independent of propaganda. In practice they are treated during war as simply more pieces of military hardware to be deployed. While the allies play it straighter than Iraq, much of the information they release has propaganda value, too. No video displays of missed targets, for instance, are ever shown. *The problem for the American press is that the American people seem to like it that way.* (Emphasis added.)

The American public had been well prepared for this type of propaganda war over the last decade. Watching it play across their screens now, they believed it because they wanted to believe it. This was war with a happy face — a "no body count" war in which the public quite clearly communicated to the press: "Don't tell us — we don't want to know. We know what we believe."

Photography materialized seeing in a new way, and significantly changed the relation between seeing and believing.

When former CBS anchor Walter Cronkite, whom the polls once named "the most trusted public figure in America," spoke out against Gulf War censorship, he was quickly given the bum's rush by *CBS News.* In a chilling piece published in that same February 25, 1991, issue of *Newsweek,* Cronkite brought up the analogy of post–World War II Germany, when most Germans claimed ignorance of the Holocaust. "But this claim of ignorance did not absolve them from blame," wrote Cronkite. "They had complacently permitted Hitler to do his dirty business in the dark. They raised little objection, most even applauded when he closed their newspapers and clamped down on free speech. Certainly our leaders are not to be compared with Hitler, but today, because of onerous, unnecessary rules, Americans are not being permitted to see and hear the full story of what their military forces are doing in an action that will reverberate long into the nation's future."

Saddam Hussein's bumbling attempts at electronic propaganda afforded no such shelter of deniability, and were about as effective as were his army and air force. Hussein's propaganda was of the old, premodern type: transparently manipulative, often verifiably untrue, and easily turned to the enemy's advantage. When the videotaped confessions of downed U.S. and British pilots hit the airwaves, they backfired famously. The tortured faces of the pilots, reproduced thousands of times all over the world, along with those of Israeli citizens huddled in sealed rooms in gas masks, immediately became emblematic of Hussein's brutality and recklessness, and made almost any action against him possible.

Even so, the Vietnam-era generals in charge of Desert Storm recognized from the beginning that modern communications technologies make it impossible to wage war in the open. Today, war must be hidden behind an impenetrable propaganda curtain—no images of death and destruction, no fields bloody with carnage, no dismembered corpses; no orphans, or gangrene, or naked napalmed little girls; and no body count. The surprise was how readily, and how completely, the American public acquiesced.

Blindsided by the New World Order

The way that images were manipulated and controlled during the Gulf War makes Ritchin's warnings about the dangers of digital retouching seem almost quaint. That type of manipulation is a very small part of postmodern propaganda, and focusing on it may cause the big picture to become blurred. Take an image that appeared early in the conflict, before war was declared, in a supposedly "liberal" magazine. The cover of the September 3, 1990, issue of the *New Republic* featured a closely cropped, full-face photograph of Saddam Hussein. The image was slightly altered, not by means of advanced electronic imaging techniques, but in the old-fashioned way. The edges of Hussein's broad mustache were simply airbrushed away to create the universally recognizable sign for Adolph Hitler. Just to make sure the effect wasn't too subtle, the word *Furor* (in the headline "Furor in the Gulf") was emblazoned in red across Hussein's forehead, invoking "Der Führer in the Gulf."

Although an article inside by Edward N. Luttwak interrogates the Hitler/Hussein analogy (Iraq in 1990 was *not* Germany in 1935, and George Bush Sr. is *not* Churchill), and suggests that the cover is intended satirically, the effect of the image is unambiguous. Like Bush Sr.'s oft-repeated refrain about "Hitler revisited," the image doesn't need to be accurate to be effective, and arguing its accuracy has little relevance to this effect. Its effectiveness— the only applicable measurement of propaganda—derives from the historical amnesia of most Americans and the perennial desire to reduce the scale and significance of atrocities by attributing them to lone, monstrously evil madmen. The *New Republic's* image contains everything one needs to know about the analogy for it to be effective, and reflects the subtle manipulations of that analogy visually. *Saddam Hussein is Hitler.* What's not to believe?

> All information should be considered false until proven true.
> — Prussian military strategist Karl von Clausewitz

> The more crap you believe in, the better off you are.
> — Faye Dunaway's character to Mickey Rourke's Bukowski,
> in the film Barfly

The aura of believability surrounding photographs is not all that vulnerable to new electronic imaging technologies *in themselves.* But belief itself is vulnerable to the kind of massive propaganda assault and general degradation of information that accompanied (and will certainly follow) the Gulf War. The crisis of belief we are experiencing is much larger than a simple mistrust of photographs. It involves the wholesale, active relinquishing of our public right to know. When the manipulation and control of all forms of public imaging have become this pervasive, this *complete,* it is more than ever necessary to resist, to reassert individual initiative in the production, reception, and use of images, and to find new ways to reinvest images with "believability" — before belief itself becomes part of the collateral damage.

Working with the Text

1. David Levi Strauss opens his essay with three paragraphs before turning to the connections between personal and political belief. What function do those three paragraphs serve? To what extent do they raise issues (such as digital retouching) only to redirect or reframe those issues?

2. Strauss notes near the beginning of his essay that assent or belief "is influenced, but not exhausted, by the photograph's relation to 'objective reality.' It is also influenced and determined by its place in the complex web of subjectivities that determines how we negotiate the world" (par. 4). In light of the arguments made in the rest of the essay, what does Strauss mean by a "complex web of subjectivities"?

3. The terrain explored by Strauss in his essay extends from the family photo to the propaganda photo, from the personal to the political. How does Strauss connect such disparate issues? Does Strauss's discussion of "belief" and an "aura of believability" benefit from this broad spectrum of examples, and if so, in what ways?

4. The final paragraph of Strauss's essay returns to the term *aura of believability* that he raised earlier. What role does this paragraph serve in making explicit the argument Strauss has been advancing throughout the essay? What reasoning lies implicit in his call, at the very end of the essay, for reasserting "individual initiative" and for finding new ways to "reinvest images with 'believability'"?

5. Strauss opens his essay with two epigraphs and prior to the closing paragraph offers another two epigraphs. What function do these quotes have? How do they frame and augment his argument?

From Text to Field

1. Drawing in part on Strauss's essay, write a reflection on a personal photograph that has special meaning for you. In what respect is the photo real, and in what respect is the photo infused with belief? What role does the photo play in how you construct identity—both the identity of the person photographed and your own identity?

2. Drawing on the Gulf War in 1991, Strauss discusses the use of photographs by the government and the military. Offer a brief analysis of your own that draws on a current issue involving photos by the government and the military. Does your example substantiate Strauss's insights, or does your example raise questions or perspectives not fully addressed by him?

3. Strauss's argument turns, in part, on what he sees as the responsibilities of a free press. Drawing on a current news story in which widely circulated images play a central role, discuss how you see the press fulfilling (or abrogating) its role. To what extent do you think the American public is interested in a vigorous free press? Given your news story, what challenges or constraints do the news media encounter? How do you think most readers respond to the circulation of images related to your news story? What are the limits to the readers' willingness to believe?

Witnessing

John Durham Peters

Many of the most important recent debates in the humanities seem to be tied to issues of communication—the anxieties we feel about it, its conundrums and, yes, its breakdowns. John Durham Peters has emerged as a daring, insightful, and elegant voice in the study of how and why we communicate.

Peters is interested in media and cultural history, communication and social theory, and understanding communication in its broad historical, legal, philosophical, religious, and technological contexts. After receiving his BA in English and his MA in speech communication from the University of Utah, Peters pursued his graduate study at Stanford University, where he received his PhD in 1986. He has since been on the faculty of the University of Iowa, where he serves as F. Wendell Miller Distinguished Professor in the Department of Communication Studies.

Peters is best known for his 1999 award-winning book, *Speaking into the Air: A History of the Idea of Communication*. He asks how new media and faster forms of transportation and communication can lead to increasing anxieties about miscommunication and writes to reclaim a sense of authenticity in a media-saturated world. His most recent book is *Courting the Abyss: Free Speech and the Liberal Tradition* (2005), which revisits the tangled history of free speech in light of concerns in a post–9/11 world.

In his 2001 essay on "Witnessing," Peters explores what he considers to be the fragile and complex juncture between "seeing" and "saying," experience and discourse; in so doing, he suggests that witnessing raises enduring issues regarding how we encounter and talk about our world.

Witnessing is a common but rarely examined term in both the professional performance and academic analysis of media events. Media institutions have enthusiastically adopted its rhetoric, especially for nonfiction genres such as news, sports, and documentary. Such titles as *Eyewitness News, See It Now, Live at Five,* or *As It Happens* advertise their program's privileged proximity to events. Media personae such as correspondents and newsreaders can be institutionalized as witnesses. Cameras and microphones are often presented as substitute eyes and ears for audiences who can witness for themselves. Ordinary people can be witnesses *in* media (the vox pop interview, 'tell us how it happened'), *of* media (members of studio audiences), and *via* media (watching history unfold at home in their armchairs). The media claim to provide testimonies for our inspection, thus making us witnesses of the way of the world. As a term of art, witnessing outshines more colorless competitors such as viewing, listening or consuming, reading, interpreting, or decoding, for thinking about the experience of media. What is the significance of this pervasive way of talking?

In this article, I propose to untangle the concept of witnessing in order to illuminate basic problems in media studies. Witnessing is an intricately tangled practice. It raises questions of truth and experience, presence and absence, death and pain, seeing and saying, and the trustworthiness of perception—in short, fundamental questions of communication. The long history of puzzlement and prescription about proper witnessing that developed in oral and print cultures is a rich resource for reflection about some of the ambiguities of audiovisual media. Hoary philosophical issues (such as the epistemological status of the senses) often show up in media practices in surprising ways; in turn, media practices can, if seen in the proper lighting, also clarify old philosophical worries.

An important step in this direction has been taken in John Ellis's *Seeing Things* (2000), whose lucid arguments I wish to extend and nuance. Witnessing, for Ellis, is a distinct mode of perception: "we cannot say we do not know" is its motto. To witness an event is to be responsible in some way to it. The stream of data flowing through the unaided senses already exceeds our explanatory schemata. The present moment supplies enough sensory information to outlast a lifetime of analysis. Audiovisual media, however, are able to catch contingent details of events that would previously have been either imperceptible or lost to memory. A camera can reveal the impact of a bullet in an apple; the tape recorder can fix an off-the-record comment. Such mechanical, "dumb" media seem to present images and sounds as they happened, without the embellishments and blind spots that human perception and memory routinely impose. We thus find ourselves endowed with a much amplified and nuanced record of events, a "superabundance of details" rich with evidentiary value. Though photography, sound-recording, film, and radio have all expanded the realm of sensory evidence, Ellis singles out television in particular. "Separated in space yet united in time, the copresence of the television image was developing a distinct form of witness. Witnessing became a domestic act. . . . Television sealed the twentieth century's fate as the century of witness" (Ellis, 2000: 32). Liveness is a key characteristic of televisual witnessing, including the morally problematic witnessing of violence and carnage. He advances witnessing as a key term for media analysis that, he believes, is freer of ontological baggage than other more commonly used concepts.

For Ellis, in sum, witnessing has to do with complicity; owes much to modern media of inscription; is an attitude cultivated by live television, particularly nonfiction programming; and a valuable resource for media analysis. I would concur with Ellis in everything with the exception that witnessing actually carries weighty baggage, if not ontological, at least historical. Yet this baggage is not only a burden, but also a potential treasure, at least since it makes explicit the pervasive link between witnessing and suffering and shows the degree to which media problems with witnessing are built upon venerable communication problems that are inherent in the witness as a kind of signifying act. The "baggage" has three main interrelated sources: law, theology, and atrocity. In law, the notion of the witness as a privileged source of information for judicial decisions is ancient, and is part of most known legal systems. In theology, the notion of witness, especially as martyr, developed in early Christianity, though it has resonance for other religious traditions as well. The third, most recent, source dates from the Second World War: the witness as a survivor of hell, prototypically but not exclusively the Holocaust or *Shoah*. These three domains endow "witnessing" with its extraordinary moral and cultural force today, since each ties the act of witnessing, in some deep way, to life and death. The procedures of the courtroom, the pain of the martyr, and the cry of the survivor cast light on basic questions such as what it means to watch, to narrate, or to be present at an event. Witnessing, as an amazingly subtle array of practices of securing truth from the facts of our sensitivity to pain and our inevitable death, increases the stakes of our thinking about media events.

Analyzing the Term

As a noun, *witness* is intricate. The term involves all three points of a basic   5
communication triangle: (1) the agent who bears witness, (2) the utterance or text itself, (3) the audience who witnesses. It is thus a strange, but intelligible sentence to say: The witness (speech-act) of the witness (person) was witnessed (by an audience). A witness can also be the performance itself. Thus we speak of a Holocaust survivor's witness against fascism. In African American churches when preachers ask, "Can I get a witness?", they invite

audience affirmation and participation, the witness as a public gesture of faith. In religious contexts, witness can also have a more private meaning as inward conviction of religious truth, which in turn may motivate the activity of "witnessing" (evangelizing). In law, literature, history, and journalism alike, a witness is an observer or source possessing privileged (raw, authentic) proximity to facts. A witness, in sum, can be an actor (one who bears witness), an act (making of a special sort of statement), the semiotic residue of that act (the statement as text), or the inward experience that authorizes the statement (the witnessing of an event).

As a verb, to *witness* has a double aspect. To witness can be a sensory experience—the witnessing of an event with one's own eyes and ears. We are all, constantly, witnesses in this sense simply by virtue of finding ourselves in places and times where things happen. Most of what we witness is insignificant in the larger scheme of things, and vanishes into oblivion. But witnessing is also the discursive act of stating one's experience for the benefit of an audience that was not present at the event and yet must make some kind of judgment about it. Witnesses serve as the surrogate sense organs of the absent. If what we have witnessed is crucial for a judgment, we may be summoned to a formal institutional setting: a court of law, a church, or a television studio. A witness is the paradigm case of a *medium*: the means by which experience is supplied to others who lack the original.

To witness thus has two faces: the passive one of *seeing* and the active one of *saying*. In passive witnessing an accidental audience observes the events of the world; in active witnessing one is a privileged possessor and *producer* of knowledge in an extraordinary, often forensic, setting in which speech and truth are policed in multiple ways. What one has seen authorizes what one says: An active witness first must have been a passive one. Herein lies the fragility of witnessing: the difficult juncture between experience and discourse. The witness is authorized to speak by having been present at an occurrence. A private experience enables a public statement. But the journey from experience (the seen) into words (the said) is precarious. Witnessing presupposes a discrepancy between the ignorance of one person and the knowledge of another: It is an intensification of the problem of communication more generally. It always involves an epistemological gap whose bridging is always fraught with difficulty. No transfusion of consciousness is possible. Words can be exchanged, experiences cannot. Testimony is another's discourse whose universe of reference diverges from one's own. Like somebody else's pain, it always has a twilight status between certainty and doubt. A parent may bear witness to a child that a stove is hot, but getting burnt may be more persuasive. Witnessing is a discourse with a hole in it that awaits filling.

The Unreliability of Witnesses

Witnesses, human or mechanical, are notoriously contradictory and inarticulate. Different people who witness the "same" event can produce remarkably divergent accounts. Though awareness of the poor epistemological quality of witnessing is ancient, twentieth-century social science has explored it in detail. Eyewitness testimony, for instance, has been subject to intense social-psychological scrutiny (e.g., Ross et al., 1994). We now know that errors in identifying people and faces are common, with potentially devastating consequences for justice. In reports by different eyewitnesses, moustaches fly on and off of faces, blondes morph into brunettes and clothes change color like chameleons. Hats have major effects on recognition, because of the role of the hairline in identifying faces. Post-event tampering, both from inside and outside, can also alter testimony. From within, the psychological process of dissonance-reduction has the paradoxical effect of increasing confidence in accuracy of recall even while the memory of the event is fading; from without, testimonies can be shaped by the schematic constraints of narrative structure and altered, perhaps even created, by the way they are probed ("refreshed") by others. Social science methodology has noted the dubious evidentiary status of statements about even one's own attitudes and opinions. From polling, we know about acquiescence effects (the tendency of people to agree), the huge effects of phrasing on reported opinions, and the divergence between front-door and back-door measures (Webb et al., 1981). Fabrication seems inherent in the loose coupling between sentences and the world; witnesses are evidently a fallible transmission and storage medium for sensory experience.

The legal theory of evidence is also a compendium of reflections about the (un)reliability of witnesses. There is a long history of excluding people as incompetent witnesses on various grounds. Non-Christians, convicts, interested parties, spouses, children, the insane, or those standing in a relationship of professional privilege with the defendant have all been considered hindered in truth telling or as possessing special motives to fabrication. As in survey research, the law has an acute awareness about the ways that modes of interrogation (e.g., leading questions) can manufacture, rather than elicit, testimony.

Since the transformation from experience to discourse lies at the heart of   10
communication theory, witnessing entails many of the most fundamental issues in the social life of signs, especially how the raw, apparently private, stuff of sensation can have any input into the public world of intelligible words (also a fundamental question in empiricist philosophy since Locke and Hume°). The forensics of the trial, the pains of the martyr, and the memoirs

---

Locke and Hume: John Locke (1632–1704) and David Hume (1711–1776), philosophers in the empiricist tradition that emphasized the role of experience and the senses.

of the survivor are all attempts to overpower the melancholy fact that direct sensory experience—from the taste of pineapple to the pains of childbirth—vanishes when put into words and remains inaccessible to others except inasmuch as they claim to share similar experiences. Sensation is encircled into privately personal ontologies. Only words are public.

Pain and the Veracity Gap

A variety of answers have been offered to cope with the fallibility of witnessing. Devices to compensate for its inherent dubiousness are ancient. One can vouch for veracity by an oath promising to trade death or pain for truth, a practice that persists in the children's line, "cross my heart and hope to die." One may appeal to ultimate authority: "God is my witness." According to Aristotle,° witnesses in a court of law testify at risk of punishment if they do not tell the truth; he considers dead witnesses more trustworthy, since they cannot be bribed (*Rhetoric*, 1376a). To witness as if you were as dumb and indifferent as the dead is the obvious ideal, since you would be free from interest, interpretation, care, and spin. A signature is a testimony: "in witness hereof . . . ," and like all forms of witnessing, it founders on the reef of forgery. The requirement of swearing on a Bible before testifying in court is yet another device to enforce truth telling, presumably by instilling the specter of eternal consequences. A reminder of the ancient worry about corrupt testimony is the ninth Mosaic commandment forbidding false witness (not the same thing as simple lying).

From the ancient Greeks to "modern" intelligence gathering, the effort to assure the transition from sensation to sentences in testimony has involved torture—a perverse but illuminating fact. As Page duBois (1991) argues, the ancient Greek word for torture, *basanos*, originally meant a touchstone, against which you could rub golden artifacts to test if they were genuine; if so, a bit would rub off and leave a mark. From there, *basanos* came to mean any test of truth or authenticity (e.g., of friendship or fidelity), and eventually moved specifically into torture, which served as an instrument of proof in ancient Athens. In Greek ideology, torture served as a cultural line dividing slaves, who respect only bodily pain, and citizens, who speak the *logos* in freedom. Since slaves supposedly lie compulsively, torture exposes the truth by extinguishing the power to invent. (Here again we see the snobbery about who can be expected to be a truthful witness.) Torture enforces the claim that slaves are ruled by necessity (*anangke*). A slave could not appear in

---

Aristotle (384–322 BCE): Greek philosopher and a student of Plato. In addition to his writings on ethics, metaphysics, and politics, Aristotle has had enormous influence in the development of rhetoric, the art of persuasion.

ROLE OF PARALEGAL

Paralegals are typically involved in a variety of interesting and challenging tasks related to trademark protection, including the following:

- reviewing the *Official Gazette* to locate marks that may need to be opposed or reviewing reports from watching services relating to publication of marks that may need to be opposed;
- docketing relevant dates for filing a notice of opposition, request for time to oppose, or petition to cancel;
- preparing or responding to cease and desist letters;
- preparing notices of opposition, petitions to cancel, complaints for infringement, or responses or answers thereto;
- docketing all relevant dates in opposition, cancellation, and infringement proceedings, such as dates for close of discovery, submission of written briefs, and so forth;
- assisting in the discovery process by drafting interrogatories, reviewing documents produced, summarizing depositions, reviewing surveys, and so forth;
- conducting searches and investigations to determine the number and use of other similar marks;
- drafting consent to use or trademark settlement agreements;
- providing general assistance for infringement trials, such as locating witnesses, organizing exhibits and documents, conducting research, and preparing jury instructions; and
- preparing applications to U.S. Customs to record trademark registrations to block importation of offending goods.

INTERNET RESOURCES

PTO web site:	http://www.uspto.gov (offers basic forms for notices of opposition and petitions to cancel registered marks) Additionally, select Trademarks and then U.S. Trademark Law: Rules of Practice & Federal Statutes for rules relating to inter partes proceedings.
Trademark Manual of Examining Practice (TMEP):	http://www.uspto.gov/web/offices/tac/tmep/index.html (offers information on standards for likelihood of confusion of marks in Chapter 12)
U.S. Customs Service:	http://www.customs.gov (provides information about filing requests with U.S. Customs Service to post ports and prevent importation of infringing goods)

court, but a slave's testimony obtained under torture was admissible as evidence. Even so, there were already doubts about the notion that pain produces truth. Aristotle (*Rhetoric*, 1377a) thought testimony obtained under torture "inartistic" and generally distrusted testimony in any case.

The shift toward the confession as a source of legal proof in thirteenth-century Europe reintroduced judicial torture. It was not understood as a kind of punishment, but, cruel as it may sound, as a kind of data gathering; that innocent people might suffer and even die under interrogation was considered an unfortunate by-product of legal investigation (Langbein, 1977; Peters, 1985). Pain was supposed to be the midwife of authenticity. Judicial torture was an attempt to assure the validity of the confession, a rather nasty way of coping with the veracity gap. In our grisly age, torture is both a method of punishment and of extracting intelligence, a fact signaled in the French term *la question*, which means both torture and interrogation, or the English phrase, "put to the question." Even a polygraph test—a "lie-detector" that circumvents discourse to tap "direct" physiological indicators—shows the retreat to the body as the haven of truth. Deathbed confessions possess special legal status, since the incentive to deceive is thought minimal. As one judge wrote, "they are declarations made in extremity, when the party is at the point of death, and when every hope of this world is gone; when every motive to falsehood has been silenced, and the mind is induced by the most powerful considerations to speak the truth . . ." (Cross, 1974: 472). Here again is the sense that death or pain impel the mind to forego the temptation to embellish.

The bodily basis of testimony is seen in a strange etymological complex. Testimony stems from *testamentum*, covenant (*testis* plus *mentum*). *Testis*, which in Latin means both witness and testicle, itself stems from *tertius*, meaning third (party). In ancient Greek, the word for witness is the word for testicle: *parastatês*, which literally means bystander. In German, *Zeugnis* means testimony, and *zeugen* means to testify as well as to procreate. The explanation of this pervasive and odd system of metaphors is obscure, but one may conjecture that the testicles, as physical bystanders to the act of procreation, were thought witnesses of paternity or virility in Indo-European culture. That knowing firsthand should be associated with the testicles may suggest an ancient preference for the testimony of men over women. This curious web of metaphors, whatever its significance, attests to some deep assumptions about the physicality of witnessing. The body serves as a sort of collateral to justify the loan of our credence. The whole apparatus of trying to assure truthfulness, from torture to martyrdom to courtroom procedure, only testifies of the strange lack at its core. Witnessing is necessary, but not sufficient: If there are no witnesses, there is no trial, but witnesses do not secure a conviction or acquittal. A witness is never conclusive or final despite the most militant attempts of martyrs or torturers to make it so.

Another ancient attempt bodily to bridge the gap between inner convic-   15
tion and outer persuasion is the tradition of Christian martyrology. As Paul
Ricoeur argues (1981: 129):

> The witness is capable of suffering or dying for what he believes. When
> the test of conviction becomes the price of life, the witness changes his
> name; he is called a martyr. But is it a change of name?—*Martus* in Greek
> means "witness." . . . Testimony is both a manifestation and a crisis of
> appearances.

To judge from appearances is the fate of all who have to rely on communication for access to other's experiences. The martyr's death proves nothing
for certain, but demonstrates the limit case of persuasion, the vanishing point
at which proof stops and credence begins. Saints Stephen or Sebastian, or
their secular equivalents, the many political martyrs whose legacies are so
powerful today, may impress bystanders with their composure under the
most gruesome abuses, but their deaths alone will not convince anyone of
the truth of their faith: One needs internal grounds for believing. To bear witness is to put one's body on the line. Within every witness, perhaps, stands a
martyr, the will to corroborate words with something beyond them, pain and
death being the last resorts.

Since the Second World War, new kinds of witnessing have been forged
in the furnace of suffering. The Holocaust has generated deep thinking about
the nature of witnessing (Felman and Laub, 1992). It is striking, by the way,
that Ellis (2000), despite his incisive comments on psychoanalytic working
through of trauma and the complicity of the bystander, hardly mentions the
Holocaust—perhaps because it is too obvious. In any case, from ashes and
hell have emerged witnesses whose task, paradoxically, is to proclaim experiences that cannot be shared and to immortalize events that are uniquely tied
to the mortal bodies of those who went through them. Elie Wiesel, for
instance, has made his career reflecting on the privilege and loneliness of the
survivor. One's responsibility to bear witness, he argues, cannot be delegated:
Testimony is unique to the survivor. It is impossible for the witness to remain
silent; but it is also impossible for the witness to describe the event. The militancy in the survivor's voice owes to the battle against oblivion and indifference. Such militancy is found no less in the martyr, who likewise uses his or
her body as spectacle of pain to convict the conscience of the observer.
Already having cheated death, the survivor seeks to save his or her experiences for others who can never have them.

Specifically, the witness has become a literary genre growing out of the
Second World War. Primo Levi, Anne Frank, Victor Klemperer, Wiesel, to
name a few, have the cultural authority of witnesses of atrocity. As survivors
of events, they in turn bear active witness which we, at one remove, can in

turn witness passively. There is a strange ethical claim in the voice of the victim. Witnessing in this sense suggests a morally justified individual who speaks out against unjust power. Imagine a Nazi who published his memoirs of the war as a "witness" — it might be accepted as an account of experiences, but never as a "witness" in the moral sense: To witness means to be on the right side. Václav Havel, Jacopo Timerman, Rigoberta Menchú, Martin Luther King, Solzhenitsyn, Mandela, Aung San Suu Kyi — those who have languished in jail all stand as witnesses against inhumanity. (*Testimonio* is a recent genre of Latin American writing which records the cry against oppression.) The prison (or prison camp) is the house of witness, a maker of moral authority, just as prison literature has turned out to be one of the great forms of twentieth-century writing. The moral privilege of the captive and martyr is a founding narrative in European civilization, as in the case of both Socrates and Jesus.° Not surprisingly, there has been something of a scramble to capture the prestige of the victim-witness, and media who speak of their role as witnesses are not immune. (A recent book on the making of *Schindler's List* is pretentiously called *Witness*, confusing the film and what the film was about.)

Witnessing places mortal bodies in time. To witness always involves risk, potentially to have your life changed. The Roman poet Ovid bemoaned his banishment to the Black Sea for seeing something in the emperor's court he wasn't supposed to. You can be marked for life by being the witness of an event. The FBI runs the evocatively named "witness protection program" providing personal security and sometimes new identities for those willing to turn state witness. Abraham Zapruder is famous (and his heirs are now rich) for a few seconds of home-movie footage of a presidential parade in Dallas on 22 November 1963. In Graham Greene's *Brighton Rock*, the gangster Pinky marries the only witness to a murder he committed in order to make her, as a wife, an incompetent witness, but of course, as usual in Greene, a sort of redemption occurs via the corruption. That simply seeing can mark your bodily fate is a suggestive way of getting beyond the idea of mere spectatorship.

In sum, the indisputables of pain and death can serve as a resource to persuade others of the truth of one's words of witness. Witnessing is a mode of communication intimately tied to the mortality of both the one who bears witness and the one who in turn witnesses that act. As Jorge Luis Borges° (1964: 243) writes:

Socrates and Jesus: The Greek philosopher Socrates (470–399 BCE) was condemned to death by the court for corrupting the youth of Athens with his philosophy. Likewise Jesus was tried by Pontius Pilot and crucified.

Jorge Luis Borges (1899–1986): Argentine writer considered one of the prominent literary figures of the twentieth century.

Deeds which populate the dimensions of space and which reach their end when someone dies may cause us wonderment, but one thing, or an infinite number of things, dies in every final agony. . . . In time there was a day that extinguished the last eyes to see Christ; the battle of Junin and the love of Helen° died with a man.

Witnessing, as we will see, not only turns on the mortality of the witness, but the contingencies of the event.

Objectivity and the Veracity Gap

A different tradition seeks to secure the validity of statements without the metaphysical and moral conundrums of pain. Very roughly speaking, the effort to put testimony on a sound footing is a project of the Enlightenment, both in the effort to minimize violence and to secure trustworthy knowledge. Indeed, one of the major tasks in the rise of modern science generally, with its need for cumulative observation from many eyes and ears, was to overcome the low repute of testimony. This was first achieved in seventeenth-century England with the creation of a genteel class of scientists, whose shared social status and norms of civility established a basis for trusting each other's reports (Shapin, 1994). As one scholar quips of the epistemology of testimony in early modern English science, gentlemen prefer gentlemen (Lipton, 1998). Without trust in other's statements about sensory experiences, science as we know it would be impossible. Further, the use of scientific instrumentation was motivated in part by the desire to bypass the stains of subjectivity, fallibility, and interest that attach to our sense organs. Scientific instruments such as the microscope or telescope were thought thinglike, and hence credible, in their indifference to human interests. The camera and microphone inherit this tradition of objectivity as passivity.

John Locke exemplifies these transformations. In his *Essay Concerning Human Understanding* (1975: book 4, chs 13–16), Locke inverted the medieval notion of testimony: He maintained it was not the authority of an ancient text (such as scripture) but the report of the senses. Few things, he argues, in human knowledge are demonstrably certain. As social creatures with limited time to gain knowledge of a world in commotion, we rely on the reports of others but must find ways to test their trustworthiness. Among the various standards he offers, key is a hierarchy of testimony determined by the witness's proximity to the event: "any Testimony, the farther off it is from the original Truth, the less force and proof it has" (1975: 663–64). Eyewitness accounts lose truth (but may gain color) as they pass from mouth to mouth:

20

---

the battle of Junin . . . Helen: The battle of Junin (1824) was a pivotal military engagement in the Peruvian War of Independence. Helen refers to Helen of Troy, whose abduction by Paris, a Trojan prince, led to the Trojan War.

> A credible Man vouching his Knowledge of it, is a good proof: But if another equally credible, do witness it from his Report, the Testimony is weaker; and a third that attests the Hear-say of an Hear-say, is yet less considerable. (1975: 664)

Locke notes already the infinite regress in witnessing: To be an active witness requires another to witness your testimony (a passive witness).

Locke reflects the low legal status of hearsay: the reporting of statements made by someone else outside court without the opportunity for cross-examination. Any statement not made in court under oath is of dubious admissibility. Hearsay is quotation, testimony at second-hand. Each sentence is supposed to be funded by direct sensation, and in reporting another's reports, one is a passive witness of an active witness (instead of the reverse), which is dangerously derivative. The low esteem in which hearsay is held signals not only the hierarchy of the senses (the precedence of eyes over ears) but also the working epistemology of the courtroom: The act of linking experience and discourse must be done in a controlled setting in which speech is subject to cross-examination and penalties for perjury are in force. In this the law still maintains respect for death or pain as truth serums. Witness is borne under sanction—whether of pain or death or legal charges and dishonor. One testifies quite literally *sub poena* —under threat of punishment. Witnesses can find themselves bodily compelled to appear in court. It doesn't take a Foucault° to see that today witnessing is policed at its boundaries by an apparatus of pain.

Legal rules prefer a mechanical witness. A witness, for instance, may not offer an opinion (about culpability, for instance) but may only describe the facts of what was seen. The blanker the witness the better. Things, after all, can bear witness—the biblical stone of witness, trophies, or other sorts of material evidence (bloodstains). The ideal human witness would behave like a thing: a mere tablet of recording. The structure of address in testimony should be radically open and public, not varying your story for different audiences. ("Estoppel" is the legal principle that prevents altering testimony previously given.) Since a dumb witness doesn't know what's at stake, there is no motive to lend comfort to one party or the other.

In the preference for the dumb witness lies a distant origin of both scientific and journalistic ideas of objectivity: the observer as a mirror, dull as the microscope to human concerns or consequences. The objective witness is very different from the survivor, whose witness lies in mortal engagement with the story told. The objective witness claims disembodiment and passivity, a

---

Foucault: Michel Foucault (1926–1984), a French philosopher whose writings have had enormous impact on a wide range of scholarly disciplines. Foucault is known for his study of social institutions, among them prisons, as they bear on the relationship between power and knowledge.

cold indifference to the story, offering "just the facts." The hearers have to compose the story for themselves. In one sense, the claim to objectivity is simply passive witnessing idealized, that is, the dream of an unadulterated and public record of events as they "really happened." The cultural authority of mechanical recording lies in the claim to document events without the filter of subjective experience. Since witnesses were supposed to be like machines, machines are also held to be good witnesses. The conventional wisdom about film and photography today, however, is the inescapability of interest in all representation. What most irks the friends of science and reason—Locke's heirs—about this position is not so much the notion that a consensual and objective document of events is impossible, but rather its darker corollary: that pain serves as the default measure of reality and authenticity. We were, they say, supposed to have graduated from all that!

Broadcasting and the Veracity Gap

Distance is a ground of distrust and doubt. We waver about another's testimony because of our distance from the experience they narrate. In the same way, reports from distant personae are more dubious than those from people we know and trust. The communication situation of broadcasting is analogous to that of witnessing: Experiences are mediated to an audience which has no firsthand acquaintance with them. The legitimation of the veracity gap in media followed the same path as in witnessing: using pain and the body as a criterion of truth and truthfulness. The body is authenticity's last refuge in situations of structural doubt. Perhaps the best single thing Walter Cronkite ever did for his reputation of credibility, besides the years of steady service, was to shed an unrehearsed tear on camera when reporting the news of President Kennedy's assassination. In the Gospel of Luke, Christ's disciples "were startled and terrified, and thought that they were seeing a ghost" (Luke 24:37). The resurrected Jesus assures them, "Handle me and see, for a ghost does not have flesh and bones as you see that I have" (Luke 24:39). Modern media—which resurrect and transport phantasms in optical and acoustic channels—both place us in the situation of doubting Thomas and attempt a similar reassurance: Handle me and see (Peters, 1999).

One of the most daring things in media events theory (Dayan and Katz, 1992) is the question: Just when can media be agents of truth or authenticity instead of prevarication and ideology? In other words, can the media sustain the practice of witnessing? The notion that home audiences could be witnesses is one of those apparent category mistakes whose elaboration the media events movement has made its task. It's easy to mock Ronald Reagan for confusing newsreels and his own experience: He claimed to have witnessed the liberation of the concentration camps in the Second World War when he had never left the United States. He believed in false presence: that he had really been there when he had only watched films. But presence-at-a-distance is precisely what witnessing a media event claims to offer. Critical theory has rightly highlighted the veracity gap in mass communication, the hermeneutics° of suspicion, but media-events studies seek the conditions in which the willing suspension of disbelief is justified. In media events, the borrowed eyes and ears of the media become, however tentatively or dangerously, one's own. Death, distance, and distrust are all suspended, for good and evil.

Singularity is key to the communication economics of witnessing. President Clinton came to my hometown, Iowa City, Iowa, for example, in February 1996, on a campaign stop, and spoke in an indoor arena. The whole event was to be televised locally, but the tickets were snapped up within two hours. Why the excitement to attend when one could get a better view on television at home? Because at home you can't be a witness to history. If Clinton were to be shot, or make a major announcement, people could say, "I was there." That would be a witness forever thereafter restricted to 14,000 people (if they are honest), whereas we home viewers, a much larger and potentially infinite group, would only be able to say, "I saw it on television." There's no comparison in the authority or cultural capital of the two statements! Clinton's goal after the speech was to touch as many people as possible, to spread the charisma of the king's body by working the crowd, in the apt idiom of "pressing the flesh." A live witness can shake hands with the great man, receive the torch of contagious magic, in the same way that Clinton shook JFK's hand as a teenager (luckily for him on camera). "Handle me and see" said the man we know mostly as a TV persona.

> **The journey from experience (the seen) into words (the said) is precarious.**

"Being there" matters since it avoids the ontological depreciation of being a copy. The copy, like hearsay, is indefinitely repeatable; the event is singular, and its witnesses are forever irreplaceable in their privileged relation to it. Recordings lose the *hic et nunc*° of the event. The live event is open to unscripted happenings, chance, and gaffes. Accidents are a key part of media events—going off script. That so much of live coverage involves some sort of trauma suggests the draw of the unpredictable and of those occurrences that leave a mark in time. Media events are not always the happy social body celebrating its core values, but also the nasty stuff of degradation and disaster (Carey, 1998; Liebes, 1998).

Presence is fragile and mortal; recordings have durability that survives in multiple times and spaces. Billions of dollars in the entertainment industries

---

hermeneutics: A discipline within philosophy concerned with the study of interpretation.

hic et nunc: A Latin phrase meaning "here and now."

turn on this apparently minute distinction. Why will people pay high prices for music performed in concert whose quality and polish is often better on the CD player at home? Obviously extramusical values shape concertgoing: party, spectacle, noise, dance. Even so, live music is different. A concert is an event, not a record. A homemade bootleg tape is a souvenir, a marker of time and place, but a CD made from the tape is a commodity, even if they are musically identical. In a concert, one's mortal time line on earth is spent. Touch and eye contact with the artist are possible. So is imperfection: In the concert one may hear strains edited out in the studio, and witness the labor of the performing body. What postproduction adds musically (e.g., overdubbing) it subtracts from eventfulness, since those sounds never could have occurred in time as we know it. Recording media can do time-axis manipulation, stopping, slowing, speeding, or reversing time—one reason why audiovisual media, despite aptitude in recording, are dubious witnesses. The body, however, lives only in real time. Singing, dancing, and live performance all engage time's passage. Music can reveal the meaning of, and sometimes even provide a brief escape from, growing older.

Why Liveness?

The love of liveness also relates to the power of real time. If one sees it live, one can claim status as a witness present in time if not in space; if one sees it on tape, one is no longer a witness, but rather the percipient of a transcription. Sports fans, in the case of big games, will remain glued to the television screen, even though they know that any key plays will be shown ad nauseam in the game's afterlife as reportage and video. They must be there *as it happens*. To see the big moment with even a slight delay is to be placed in a derivative role, a hearer of a report rather than a witness of an event. The fan wants to be involved in history (the happening), not historiography (the recording). The few seconds between occurrence and replay open up a metaphysical gulf in the meaning and quality of what is seen. As far as the electromagnetic tracings are concerned, the live event and its instant replay are identical, but in the psychology of the fan, one is history, the other is television. One is a window to the event, the other is its representation. Liveness serves as an assurance of access to truth and authenticity.

The hard-core sports fan sweating the seconds actually offers a profound lesson about the nature of time. Why should liveness matter? It does matter, to the tune of billions of dollars in bids for live rights. Because events only happen in the present. In a word, gambling. As Walter Benjamin° noted, gambling is a phantasmagoria of time. No one knows what the future holds,

---

Walter Benjamin (1892–1940): A German literary critic and philosopher.

and the gambler infuses the present with the diceyness of the future. There is absolutely no point in betting on a game or a race whose outcome is already known. A classic con job, as in the film *The Sting*, is to institute a small time lag in publicizing race results so that punters think they are betting on an uncertain future when in fact they are wagering on an already determined past. A few seconds do matter, and profoundly. The past, in some sense, is safe. The present, in contrast, is catastrophic, subject to radical alterations. In a single second a swerve of the steering wheel or a pull of the trigger can change history forever. Possible futures come into being and vanish with every act. In a brief moment the penalty kick is made or missed, a life conceived or taken. All history culminates in the present moment. Of course, the present is rarely so dramatic, but without a live connection its explosive possibility — its danger— is missing. Nothing quite excites like an event about to take place. In Raymond Williams's° phrase, one waits for a knock on the door. Fortuna, goddess of history and gamblers, reveals her face only in the present. In the past she veils herself as necessity, in the future as probability.

The contrast between the live and the recorded is a structuring principle of broadcasting. It replays the contrast of fact and fiction, so central to modern historiography, a field, like law and theology, whose enterprise rests on the evaluation of sources and documents — testimonies. Though theorists justly remind us of the factuality of fictions and the fictive character of facts, this contrast stubbornly resists total resolution. The division of fact and fiction, so central for historians and sports fans, as well as the structuring principle of media and literary genres, turns on witnessing. An event requires witnesses, a story only needs tellers and listeners. A fiction can be heard or told, but a fact is witnessed. Some kinds of events (baptisms, marriages) legally require witnesses. Testimony assures us—as children often ask about stories—that it really happened.

Historicity (or historical authenticity) has a similar logic to live coverage. If in visiting the Tower of London I am told that a block of wood is the one on which Henry VIII's victims were dispatched, I will act and feel differently than if I learn the block is a replica, even if it is physically identical or equally old. The block hovers in a limbo between reality and fake, its metaphysical status depending on something so slight as a caption. The caption "real" ties it to a tradition of testimony passed across the generations, an accumulation of time that links the block historically to the event. If it has the right label I can ponder edifying lessons about overweening power and look for traces of martyr's blood; I will have to work a lot harder if the caption announces that it's only figurative. Live broadcasting, like objects certified as historical,

---

Raymond Williams (1921–1988): A Welsh novelist and critic whose writing on culture, politics, mass media, and literature were widely influential.

offers the chance to witness, while recorded material stands at one remove as a representation (replica) of events. It takes about a sixth-grade education in our postmodern age to puncture the idea that history is free of representation, so that is not the point. Rather, it is to read small distinctions about what is real in cultural matters, distinctions too often written off as neurosis or fetishism, as insights into structures of history and experience. Between the historical and the verisimilar lies a small but gigantic gap, that of testimony.

Of four basic types of relations to an event, three can sustain the attitude of a witness. To be there, present at the event in space and time is the paradigm case. To be present in time but removed in space is the condition of liveness, simultaneity across space. To be present in space but removed in time is the condition of historical representation: Here is the possibility of a simultaneity across time, a witness that laps the ages. To be absent in both space and time but still have access to an event via its traces is the condition of recording: the profane zone in which the attitude of witnessing is hardest to sustain (see Table 1).

	Presence in Time	Absence in Time
Presence in Space	BEING THERE Assembled Audience e.g., concert, game, theater	HISTORICITY (dead not "live") Serial Mass Audience e.g., shrine, memorial, museum
Absence in Space	LIVE TRANSMISSION Broadcast Audience e.g., radio, TV, webcast	RECORDING Dispersed, private audience Profane, witnessing difficult e.g., book, CD, video

Table 1. Sorts of Witnessing an Event.

Fact and Fiction, Pain and Time

Ultimately, the boundary between fact and fiction is an ethical one before it is an epistemological one: It consists in having respect for the pain of victims, in being tied by simultaneity, however loosely, to someone else's story of how they hurt. We may weep in reading of the slaughter of the innocents by King Herod, but we owe them nothing besides remembrance. "Live" pain is different. Simultaneous suffering forms the horizon of responsibility: Liveness matters for the living. Facts impose moral and political obligations that fictions do not. This is the ancient ethical problem of tragedy: why people take pleasure in sights that would terrify or disgust them in real life. Aristotle's

General information: http://www.ll.georgetown.edu and
                                 http://www.ipmall.fplc.edu

Sample cease and desist letters: http://www.chillingeffects.org (offers sample cease
                                 and desist letters and general information about
                                 trademark infringement)

DISCUSSION QUESTIONS

1. If a mark is published for opposition on January 4 and a party wishes to oppose registration of the mark, when must it do so?

2. If a registration is issued on February 18, 2003, what are the time limits to object to registration of the mark and how would a party go about objecting to the registration?

3. Your client is an author who is writing a book about the collapse of Enron Corp. Throughout the book, your client will be using the mark ENRON. Would Enron Corp. be able to allege that such use of its mark causes dilution? Discuss.

4. Harris Co. is the owner of the registered mark SHOEBITS® for footwear. It has been aware of the use by another party of SHOOBITTS for footwear for the past two years. Harris Co. would like to allege that SHOOBITTS infringes its mark SHOEBITS®. What defenses is the owner of SHOOBITTS likely to assert? What responses might Harris Co. assert?

5. Discuss whether the following uses constitute dilution by blurring or dilution by tarnishment:

   FEDERAL EXPRESS   (for coffee)
   BETTY CROCKER   (for drug paraphernalia)
   JOHNNIE WALKER   (for canes and walking aids)
   BARBIE   (for lewd images on shot glasses)

6. If one party uses a mark west of the Mississippi River and the other uses a somewhat similar mark only in Connecticut and New York, what strategy might be appropriate to allow each to use the mark?

For additional resources, go to www.westlegalstudies.com.

Poetics starts the debate about why we take pleasure in depictions of violence and human suffering. In tragedy, the representation of pain (and pain is definitional for the genre) is not supposed to excite the spectator to humanitarian service but to clarify through representation what is possible in life. The drama offers terror without danger, pity without duty. The awareness of its unreality releases us from moral obligation to the sufferers we behold. Fiction lacks the responsibility or complicity that Ellis makes definitional for witnessing. As David Hume remarked (1987), "It is certain, that the same object of distress, which pleases in a tragedy, were it really set before us, would give the most unfeigned uneasiness." Factual distress calls for our aid, not our appreciation; our duty, not our pleasure. Death is meaningful in fiction: It marks the passage of time, punishes the wicked, gives closure to events. But in fact, death is a blank, completely beyond meaning. "Nothing brings them back, neither love nor hate. They can do nothing to you. They are as nothing" (Conrad, 1921). The contrast of fact and fiction has less to do with different orders of truth than with who is hurting and when. Living people's pain is news; dead people's pain is history.

It is easy to make fun of the obsession to keep up to date with the news. Kierkegaard° suggested that if we treated all news as if it had happened fifty years ago we would sound its true importance. He is right about triviality, but misses what he is so lucid about elsewhere: the present moment as the point of decision. We have to keep up with the world because we are, in some complicated way, responsible to act in it, and we can only act in the present. We feel guilty about hurt people in news, not in fiction films. Pain separates facts from fictions. Facts are witnessed, fictions are narrated. Fictions may indeed inspire us to action, but the beholders' responsibility is diffuse. "Live" coverage of global sorrow is ethically recalcitrant: Because it is fact, we are not protected by the theater's "teleological suspension of the ethical" (Kierkegaard); because it is spatially remote, our duty to action is unclear. We find ourselves in the position of spectators at a drama without the relief of knowing that the suffering is unreal. Hence the "unfeigned uneasiness" (Hume) we face in watching the news. We feel a gruesome fascination for trauma without the exoneration of knowing it is all an experiment in mimesis. We are witnesses without a tribunal.

Finally, the curious thing about witnessing is its retroactive character, the jealousy the present has for the past. The present may be the point of decision, but it is always underinformed about what will come after. Most observers don't know they are witnesses when the event is happening: They are elected after the fact. A vast quantitative difference separates what we experience and what we are summoned to witness. There's a lot more sensation around than

---

Kierkegaard: Soren Kierkegaard (1813–1855), a Danish philosopher and theologian, generally regarded as the first existentialist philosopher.

stories. In testifying we must take responsibility for what we once took little responsibility for. We must report on events, the details of which have assumed as massive an importance as they were once trivial. What time did you catch the bus? What color was the car? What kind of shoes was the defendant wearing? In witnessing we look backwards on events we did not realize we were observing, restoring deleted files from memory. We don't know that what we notice or neglect may be the key to prison and liberty for someone. The present is blind to what the future will value. We didn't notice the butterfly that started the typhoon.°

Hence the notion, found in liberalism, existentialism, and Christian theology alike, that it is the duty of everyone to be vigilant—to be ready to stand as a witness at any time or place. Testifying has the structure of repentance: retroactively caring about what we were once careless of. A later moment revisits an earlier one in which consciousness was not fully awake. The witness's attitude to sensation (radical vigilance) goes together with the future anterior attitude to time (treating the present as if it was being witnessed from the future). To witness is to wish that the record of the past were more whole, and to grasp this lesson now is to live vigilantly, to make the present worthy as we imagine contemplating it from a future point. To cope with our fixity in the present, we can at least be awake. Every act puts one in the witness box, both seeing and saying. In Christian eschatology this attitude is dramatized by the notion of a Last Judgment that calls up the whole history of the world as judge and witness. In Nietzsche's° thought it is the notion of the eternal return, acting in the present so that the action could be eternally repeated (and witnessed) without regret. In everyday civic ideology it is the idea that citizens have a duty to be informed about the events of the day. In a phrase all broadcasters would endorse, and with apologies to Matthew 25:13, the motto of witnessing should be: "Watch, therefore, for you know neither the day nor the hour wherein the event will come."

References

duBois, P. (1991) *Torture and Truth.* London: Routledge.

Borges, J. L. (1964) "The Witness," in *Labyrinths: Selected Stories and Other Writings.* New York: New Directions.

Carey, J. W. (1998) "Political Ritual on Television," In T. Liebes and J. Curran (eds.) *Media, Ritual, and Identity.* London: Routledge.

---

butterfly that started the typhoon: A reference to the butterfly effect, in chaos theory. Small variations in initial conditions can lead to large variations over the long term.

Nietzsche: Friedrich Wilhelm Nietzsche (1844–1900), a German philologist and philosopher whose critiques of culture, religion, and philosophy—although overlooked in his own lifetime—have gained prominence since the mid-twentieth century.

Conrad, J. (1921) *The Secret Agent.* New York: Doubleday.

Cross, R. (1974) *Evidence,* 4th edn. London: Butterworths.

Dayan, D. and E. Katz (1992) *Media Events: The Live Broadcasting of History.* Cambridge, MA: Harvard University Press.

Ellis, J. (2000) *Seeing Things: Television in the Age of Uncertainty.* London: I. B. Tauris.

Felman, S. and D. Laub (1992) *Testimony: Crises of Witnessing in Literature, Psychoanalysis, and History.* New York: Routledge.

Hume, D. (1987) "Of Tragedy," *Essays: Moral, Political, and Literary,* rev. edn. Indianapolis: Liberty Fund.

Langbein, J. H. (1977) *Torture and the Law of Proof: Europe and England in the Ancien Régime.* Chicago, IL: University of Chicago Press.

Liebes, T. (1998) "Television's Disaster Marathons," in T. Liebes and J. Curran (eds.) *Media, Ritual, and Identity.* London: Routledge.

Lipton, P. (1998) "The Epistemology of Testimony," *History and Philosophy of Science* 29(1).

Locke, J. (1975) *An Essay Concerning Human Understanding,* ed. P. H. Nidditch. Oxford: Clarendon Press. (Orig. pub. 1690.)

Peters, E. (1985) *Torture.* New York: Blackwell.

Peters, J. D. (1999) *Speaking into the Air.* Chicago, IL: University of Chicago Press.

Ricoeur, P. (1981) "The Hermeneutics of Testimony," in *Essays in Biblical Interpretation.* London: SPCK.

Ross, D. F., J. D. Read, and M. P. Toglia (1994) *Adult Eyewitness Testimony: Current Trends and Developments.* Cambridge: Cambridge University Press.

Shapin, S. (1994) *A Social History of Truth: Civility and Science in Seventeenth-Century England.* Chicago, IL: University of Chicago Press.

Webb, E. J. et al. (1981) *Nonreactive Measures in the Social Sciences.* Boston, MA: Houghton Mifflin.

Working with the Text

1. John Durham Peters opens his article by referring to prior published work. How does Peters use this reference to frame and set up his own discussion? How does reference to someone else's work help to establish both focus and relevance for Peters's work?

2. Why does Peters consider *witnessing* to be a multifaceted and complex term? What are the several aspects of witnessing that readers must keep in mind as they follow Peters's discussion?

3. Issues of time and place become reoccurring themes in the essay. Track the many ways in which time and place become relevant in Peters's discussion.

4. Although much of Peters's exploration of witnessing takes us back into history, the relevance of the topic is clearly made compelling by technology and new media. How has broadcasting and new media heightened the age-old issues of witnessing? Has new media introduced new issues?

From Text to Field

1. Whether in the home, in school, or in public, you have probably served as a witness on many occasions, if only informally. In other words, you have surely seen or experienced something that you then had to talk about. Describe and then analyze one such occasion in some detail, drawing on Peters's discussion.

2. Peters wrote his article on witnessing just prior to the events of September 11, 2001. Those events, witnessed firsthand by many, became in turn a media event, in that millions more witnessed media images of 9/11. Offer an update of Peters's essay that draws on and incorporates "witnessing 9/11" as a running example. What changes or new insights, if any, do the events of 9/11 suggest for Peters's essay? Do the events and media coverage of 9/11 make the essay, and the problems it addresses, more relevant?

3. Working in teams or small groups, identify an event (such as a political, musical, or sporting event) that some of you might witness firsthand and others through media coverage. Compare your experiences of the event with how others have experienced it. What makes for reliable and unreliable witnessing? Can your witnessing differ from others and still be true or legitimate? Draw on the article by Peters to help you raise issues and refine your responses.

4. Opportunities for witnessing, and for communicating as a witness, grow with advances in technology. Choose one new technology that you believe has a potential impact on witnessing and analyze how the age-old issues of witnessing take on a particular form and salience given that new technology. Cell phones, video phones, and surveillance technology are just some of the many technologies that you may wish to consider.

From Realism to Virtual Reality: Images of America's Wars

H. Bruce Franklin

From a captain in the U.S. Air Force to a Vietnam War protester, from a Melville scholar to a scholar on the literature born in American prisons— such has been the career of H. Bruce Franklin. He won notoriety in 1972 for being the only tenured professor at Stanford University ever to be fired for his political views. Well-documented and researched, his writings (some eighteen books and more than two-hundred journal articles) position Franklin as someone who is both a scholar and an activist.

After completing his undergraduate studies at Amherst College, Franklin joined the air force, rising to the rank of captain. Upon receiving his PhD at Stanford, he joined its faculty as an assistant professor and won acclaim—and tenure—as a scholar of nineteenth-century American literature, with interests in Melville and Hawthorne. Following his dismissal in 1972, and three years of unemployment, he joined Rutgers University, becoming Distinguished Professor of English in 1980. He has also had visiting-teacher appointments at Johns Hopkins, Wesleyan, and Yale universities.

Following his early interest in Melville, Franklin turned to three other areas of research. He wrote *The Victim as Criminal and Artist: Literature from the American Prison* (1978, 1982), a seminal work that argues that prison and slave artists have created a tradition of protest against America as a prison, one that offers a vision of an alternative future. He has also written several books on the literature of the Vietnam War and is known for his pioneering studies of science fiction.

First published in the *Georgia Review* in 1994, "From Realism to Virtual Reality" surveys the role of images of warfare, arguing that as our technology has improved so too has our control over and propagandistic use of images.

The Industrial Revolution was only about one century old when modern technological warfare burst upon the world in the U.S. Civil War. During that century human progress had already been manifested in the continually increasing deadliness and range of weapons, as well as in other potential military benefits of industrial capitalism. But it was the Civil War that actually demonstrated industrialism's ability to produce carnage and devastation on an unprecedented scale, thus foreshadowing a future more and more dominated by what we have come to call *technowar*. For the first time, immense armies had been transported by railroad, coordinated by telegraph, and equipped with an ever-evolving arsenal of mass-produced weapons designed by scientists and engineers. The new machines of war—such as the repeating rifle, the primitive machine gun, the submarine, and the steam-powered, ironclad warship—were being forged by other machines. Industrial organization was essential, therefore, not only in the factories where the technoweapons were manufactured but also on the battlefields and waters where these machines destroyed each other and slaughtered people.

Prior to the Civil War, visual images of America's wars were almost without exception expressions of romanticism and nationalism. Paintings, lithographs, woodcuts, and statues displayed a glorious saga of thrilling American heroism from the Revolution through the Mexican War. Drawing on their imagination, artists could picture action-filled scenes of heroic events, such as Emmanuel Leutze's 1851 painting *Washington Crossing the Delaware*.[1]

Literature, however, was the only art form capable of projecting the action of warfare as temporal flow and movement. Using words as a medium, writers had few limitations on how they chose to paint this action, and their visions had long covered a wide spectrum. One of the Civil War's most distinctively modern images was expressed by Herman Melville in his poem "A Utilitarian View of the Monitor's Fight." Melville sees the triumph of "plain mechanic power" placing war "Where War belongs—/Among the trades and artisans," depriving it of "passion": "all went on by crank, / Pivot, and screw, / And calculations of caloric." Since "warriors / Are now but operatives," he hopes that "War's made / Less grand than Peace."

The most profoundly deglamorizing images of that war, however, were produced not by literature but directly by technology itself. The industrial processes and scientific knowledge that created technowar had also brought forth a new means of perceiving its devastation. Industrial chemicals, manufactured metal plates, lenses, mirrors, bellows, and actuating mechanisms—all were essential to the new art and craft of photography. Thus the Civil War was the first truly modern war—both in how it was fought and in how it was imaged. The romantic images of warfare projected by earlier visual arts were now radically threatened by images of warfare introduced by photography.

Scores of commercial photographers, seeking authenticity and profits, fol- ₅
lowed the Union armies into battle. Although evidently more than a million
photographs of the Civil War were taken, hardly any show actual combat or
other exciting action typical of the earlier paintings.[2] The photographers' need
to stay close to their cumbersome horse-drawn laboratory wagons usually kept
them from the thick of battle, and the collodion wet-plate process, which
demanded long exposures, forced them to focus on scenes of stillness rather
than action. Among all human subjects, those who stayed most perfectly still
for the camera were the dead. Hence Civil War photography, dominated by
images of death, inaugurated a grim, profoundly antiromantic realism.

Perhaps the most widely reproduced photo from the war, Timothy
O'Sullivan's "A Harvest of Death, Gettysburg," contains numerous corpses
of Confederate soldiers, rotting after lying two days in the rain (see Fig. 1).
Stripped of their shoes and with their pockets turned inside out, the bodies
stretch into the distance beyond the central corpse, whose mouth gapes
gruesomely.

The first of such new images of war were displayed for sale to the public
by Mathew Brady at his Broadway gallery in October 1862. Brady entitled his
show "The Dead of Antietam." The *New York Times* responded in an awed
editorial:

Figure 1. "A Harvest of Death, Gettysburg," 1863, photograph by Timothy O'Sullivan, courtesy of
George Eastman House.

The living that throng Broadway care little perhaps for the Dead at Antietam, but we fancy they would jostle less carelessly down the great thoroughfare . . . were a few dripping bodies, fresh from the field, laid along the pavement. . . . .

Mr. Brady has done something to bring home to us the terrible reality and earnestness of war. If he has not brought bodies and laid them in our dooryards and along the streets, he has done something very like it. At the door of his gallery hangs a little placard, "The Dead of Antietam." Crowds of people are constantly going up the stairs; follow them, and you find them bending over photographic views of that fearful battle-field, taken immediately after the action. . . . You will see hushed, reverent groups standing around these weird copies of carnage, bending down to look in the pale faces of the dead, chained by the strange spell that dwells in dead men's eyes.[3]

Oliver Wendell Holmes° went further in explicating the meaning of the exhibition, which gives "some conception of what a repulsive, brutal, sickening, hideous thing it is, this dashing together of two frantic mobs to which we give the name of armies." He continues: "Let him who wishes to know what war is look at this series of illustrations. These wrecks of manhood thrown together in careless heaps or ranged in ghastly rows for burial were alive but yesterday. . . ."[4]

Nevertheless, three decades after the end of the Civil War the surging forces of militarism and imperialism were reimaging the conflict as a glorious episode in America's history. The disgust, shame, guilt, and deep national divisions that had followed this war—just like those a century later that followed the Vietnam War—were being buried under an avalanche of jingoist culture, the equivalent of contemporary Ramboism, even down to the cult of muscularism promulgated by Teddy Roosevelt.

It was in this historical context that Stephen Crane used realism, then flourishing as a literary mode, to assault just such treacherous views of war. Although *The Red Badge of Courage* is generally viewed as the great classic novel of the Civil War, it can be read much more meaningfully as Crane's response to the romantic militarism that was attempting to erase from the nation's memory the horrifying lessons taught by the war's realities.[5] Crane, not subject to the technological limitations of the slow black-and-white photographs that had brought home glimpses of the war's sordid repulsiveness, was able to image the animal frenzy that masqueraded as heroic combat and even to add color and tiny moving details to his pictures of the dead:

Oliver Wendell Holmes (1809–1894): An American physician, writer, and poet, and the father of Oliver Wendell Holmes Jr. (1841–1935), who served in the Civil War and would become a Supreme Court justice.

The corpse was dressed in a uniform that once had been blue but was now faded to a melancholy shade of green. The eyes, staring at the youth, had changed to the dull hue to be seen on the side of a dead fish. The mouth was opened. Its red had changed to an appalling yellow. Over the grey skin of the face ran little ants. One was trundling some sort of a bundle along the upper lip.[6]

Other literary reactions to the new militarism looked even further back- 10
ward to project images of a future dominated by war. Melville's *Billy Budd*, completed in 1891, envisions this triumph of violence in the aftermath of the American Revolution on the (aptly named) British warship HMS *Bellipotent*, where the best of humanity is hanged to death by the logic of war, the common people are turned into automatons "dispersed to the places allotted them when not at the guns," and the final image is of a sterile, life-less, inorganic mass of "smooth white marble."[7]

In *A Connecticut Yankee in King Arthur's Court* (1889), Mark Twain reca-pitulates the development of industrial capitalism and extrapolates its future in a vision of apocalyptic technowar. Hank Morgan and his young disciples have run "secret wires" to dynamite deposits under all their "vast factories, mills, workshops, magazines, etc." and have connected them to a single com-mand button so that nothing can stop them "when we want to blow up our civilization." When Hank does initiate this instantaneous push-button war, "In that explosion all our noble civilization-factories went up in the air and disappeared from the earth." Beyond an electrified fence, the technowarriors have prepared a forty-foot-wide belt of land mines. The first wave of thousands of knights triggers a twentieth-century-style explosion: "As to destruction of life, it was amazing. Moreover, it was beyond estimate. Of course we could not *count* the dead, because they did not exist as individuals, but merely as homogeneous protoplasm, with alloys of iron and buttons."

After Hank and his boys trap the rest of the feudal army inside their elec-tric fence, Hank electrocutes the first batch, a flood is released on the sur-vivors, and the boys man machine guns that "vomit death" into their ranks: "Within ten short minutes after we had opened fire, armed resistance was totally annihilated. . . . Twenty-five thousand men lay dead around us."[8] That number of dead, it is worth noting, matches exactly the total casualties in America's costliest day of war, the battle of Antietam, and thus recalls Brady's exhibition, "The Dead of Antietam." Twain's vision is even more horrific, for the victors themselves are conquered by "the poisonous air bred by those dead thousands." All that remains of this first experiment in industrialized warfare is a desolate landscape pockmarked by craters and covered with unburied, rotting corpses.

Twain's vision of the future implicit in industrial capitalism began to materialize in the First World War, when armies slaughtered each other on an unprecedented scale, sections of Europe were turned into a wasteland, and weapons of mass destruction first seemed capable of actually destroying civilization. Meanwhile, the scientific, engineering, and organizational progress that had produced the modern machine gun, long-range artillery, poison gas, and fleets of submarines and warplanes had also created a new image-making technology that broke through the limits of still photography. Just as the Civil War was the first to be extensively photographed, the "War to End All Wars" was the first to be extensively imaged in motion pictures.[9]

World War I, of course, generated millions of still photographs, many showing scenes at least as ghastly as the corpse-strewn battlefields of the Civil War, and now there was also authentic documentary film of live action. But for various reasons the most influential photographic images from World War I, though realistic in appearance, displayed not reality but fantasy. Filmmakers who wished to record actual combat were severely restricted by the various governments and military authorities. At the same time, powerful forces were making a historic discovery: the tremendous potential of movies for propaganda and for profits. This was the dawn of twentieth-century image making.

In the United States the most important photographic images were 15 movies designed to inflame the nation, first to enter the war and then to support it. Probably the most influential was *The Battle Cry of Peace*, a 1915 smash hit that played a crucial role in rousing the public against Germany by showing realistic scenes of the invasion and devastation of America by a rapacious Germanic army. Once the United States entered the war, the American public got to view an endless series of feature movies, such as *To Hell with the Kaiser; The Kaiser, the Beast of Berlin;* and *The Claws of the Hun*—each outdoing its predecessors in picturing German bestiality. Erich von Stroheim's career began with his portrayal of the archetypal sadistic German officer in films like *The Unbeliever* and *Heart of Humanity*, where in his lust to rape innocent young women he murders anyone who gets in the way—even the crying baby of one intended victim. This genre is surveyed by Larry Wayne Ward, who describes the 1918 Warner Brothers hit *My Four Years in Germany*, which opens with a title card telling the audience they are seeing "Fact Not Fiction":

> After the brutal conquest of Belgium, German troops are shown slaughtering innocent refugees and tormenting prisoners of war. Near the end of the film one of the German officials boasts that "America Won't Fight," a title which dissolves into newsreel footage of President Wilson and marching American soldiers. Soon American troops are seen fighting their way across the European battlefields. As he bayonets another German soldier, a young American doughboy turns to his companions and says, "I promised Dad I'd get six."[10]

New Developments in Trademark Law

CHAPTER OVERVIEW

New issues have arisen in trademark law that were entirely unanticipated just a few years ago. The emergence of the Internet as a tool for electronic communication has resulted in complex intellectual property issues; chief among them are the assignment of Internet domain names and attendant disputes over such domain names. Companies that have invested significant amounts of time and money in their marks have been surprised when they have attempted to use their marks as part of their domain names, only to find the names have been taken by cybersquatters or electronic pirates who register famous domain names in the hopes of ransoming them back to their rightful owners. The issue of domain name assignment and dispute resolution is one that has caused great controversy and cries for reform.

The passage of the Anticybersquatting Consumer Protection Act in 1999 has resulted in far fewer acts of cybersquatting in recent years.

Use of marks on the Internet has also led to various First Amendment issues, especially with regard to the practice of using another party's mark on one's web site as a link to another site. Finally, courts have struggled with the issue whether merely operating a passive web site should expose a party to jurisdiction in all states where the web site can be accessed. Generally, courts have held that passive web sites offering information only should not subject the web site operator to personal jurisdiction in other states.

As use of the Internet continues to increase in ways not yet imagined, intellectual property rights are likely to continue to be affected, requiring courts to be imaginative and flexible in dealing with emerging technologies.

Before the end of World War I, the motion picture had already proved to
be a more effective vehicle for romanticizing and popularizing war than the
antebellum school of heroic painting that had been partly debunked by Civil
War photography. Indeed, the audiences that thronged to *My Four Years in
Germany* frequently burned effigies of the kaiser outside the theaters and in
some cases turned into angry mobs that had to be dispersed by police.

To restore the glamour of preindustrial war, however, it would take more
than glorifying the men fighting on the ground or even the aviators supposedly
dueling like medieval knights high above the battlefield. What was necessary to
reverse Melville's "utilitarian" view of industrial warfare was the romanticizing
of machines of war themselves.

The airplane was potentially an ideal vehicle for this romance. But photographic technology had to develop a bit further to bring home the thrills
generated by destruction from the sky, because it needed to be seen *from* the
sky, not from the ground where its reality was anything but glamorous. The
central figure in America's romance with warplanes (as I have discussed at
length elsewhere[11]) was Billy Mitchell, who also showed America and the
world how to integrate media imagery with technowar.

In 1921, Mitchell staged a historic event by using bombers to sink captured German warships and turning the action into a media bonanza. His
goal was to hit the American public with immediate, nationwide images of
the airplane's triumph over the warship. The audacity of this enterprise in
1921 was remarkable. There were no satellites to relay images, and no television; in fact, the first experimental radio broadcast station had begun operation only in November 1920.

Back in 1919, Mitchell had given the young photographer George   20
Goddard his own laboratory where, with assistance from Eastman Kodak,
Goddard developed high-resolution aerial photo-
graphy. As soon as Mitchell won the opportunity
to bomb the German ships, he put Goddard in
command of a key unit: a team of aerial photographers provided with eighteen airplanes and a diri-
gible. Mitchell's instructions were unambiguous:
"I want newsreels of those sinking ships in every theater in the country,
just as soon as we can get 'em there." This demanded more than mere picture taking. With his flair for public relations, Mitchell explained to
Goddard: "Most of all I need you to handle the newsreel and movie people.
They're temperamental, and we've got to get all we can out of them."[12]
Goddard had to solve unprecedented logistical problems, flying the film
first to Langley Field and thence to Bolling Field for pickup by the newsreel people who would take it to New York for development and national distribution. The sinking of each ship, artfully filmed by relays of

**The generation raised in
video arcades and on
Nintendo could hardly be
more satisfied.**

Goddard's planes, was screened the very next day in big-city theaters across the country.

This spectacular media coup implanted potent images of the warplane in the public mind, and Mitchell himself became an overnight national hero as millions watched the death of great warships on newsreel screens. Mitchell was a prophet. The battleship was doomed. The airplane would rule the world.

America was now much closer to the 1990 media conception of the Gulf War than to Melville's "Utilitarian View of the Monitor's Fight." Melville's vision of technowar as lacking "passion" was becoming antiquated, for what could be more thrilling—even erotic—than aerial war machines? The evidence is strewn throughout modern America: the warplane models assembled by millions of boys and young men during World War II; the thousands of warplane magazines and books filled with glossy photographs that some find as stimulating as those in "men's" magazines; and Hollywood's own warplane romances, such as *Top Gun*—one of the most popular movies of the 1980s—or *Strategic Air Command*, in which Jimmy Stewart's response to his first sight of a B-47 nuclear bomber is, "She's the most beautiful thing I've ever seen in my life."

One of the warplane's great advantages as a vehicle of romance is its distance from its victims. From the aircraft's perspective, even the most grotesque slaughter it inflicts is sufficiently removed so that it can be imaged aesthetically. The aesthetics of aerial bombing in World War II were prefigured in 1937 by Mussolini's son Vittorio, whose ecstasy about his own experience bombing undefended Ethiopian villages was expressed in his image of his victims "bursting out like a rose after I had landed a bomb in the middle of them."[13] These aesthetics were consummated at the end of World War II by the mushroom clouds that rose over Hiroshima and Nagasaki.

Bracketed by these images, the aerial bombing of World War II has been most insightfully explored in *Catch-22* by Joseph Heller, a bombardier with sixty combat missions. The novel envisions the political and cultural triumph of fascism through the very means used to defeat it militarily. The turning point in Heller's work is the annihilation of an insignificant antifascist Italian mountain village, an event which allows fascist forces, embodied by U.S. Air Corps officers, to gain total control.[14] The sole purpose of the American bombing of the village is image making. The novel's General Peckem privately admits that bombing this "tiny undefended village, reducing the whole community to rubble" is "entirely unnecessary," but it will allow him to extend his power over the bombing squadrons. He has convinced them that he will measure their success by "a neat aerial photograph" of their *bomb pattern*—"a term I dreamed up," he confides, that "means nothing." The briefing officer tells the crews:

Colonel Cathcart wants to come out of this mission with a good clean aerial photograph he won't be ashamed to send through channels. Don't forget that General Peckem will be here for the full briefing, and you know how he feels about bomb patterns.[15]

Pictures of bomb patterns were not, of course, the most influential   25
American photographic image making in World War II. The still photos published in *Life* alone could be the subject of several dissertations, and World War II feature movies about strategic bombing have been discussed at length by myself and many others. Indeed, in 1945 one might have wondered how the camera could possibly play a more important role in war.

The answer came in Vietnam, the first war to be televised directly into tens of millions of homes.[16] Television's glimpses of the war's reality were so horrendous and so influential that these images have been scapegoated as one of the main causes of the United States' defeat. Indeed, the Civil War still photographs of corpses seem innocuous when compared to the Vietnam War's on-screen killings, as well as live-action footage of the bulldozing of human carcasses into mass graves, the napalming of children, and the ravaging of villages by American soldiers.

As appalling as these public images were, however, few had meanings as loathsome as the pictures that serve as the central metaphor of Stephen Wright's novel *Meditations in Green*. The hero of the novel has the job that the author had in Vietnam: He works as a photoanalyst in an intelligence unit whose mission is to aid the torture and assassination campaign known as Operation Phoenix, the ecocidal defoliation campaign originally designated Operation Hades, and the genocidal bombing. His official job as "image interpreter" is to scrutinize reconnaissance films to find evidence of life so that it can be eliminated. Not just humans are targets to be erased by bombing; trees themselves become the enemy. Anyone in the unit who has qualms about such genocide and ecocide is defined—in a revealing term—as a "smudge," thus becoming another target for elimination. The perfect image, it is implied, should have nothing left of the human or the natural. From the air, the unit's own base looks like "a concentration camp or a movie lot." The climax of the novel comes when the base is devastated by an enemy attack intercut with scenes from *Night of the Living Dead*, that ghoulish 1968 vision of America which is simultaneously being screened as entertainment.[17]

One of the most influential and enduring single images from the Vietnam War—certainly the most contested—exploded into the consciousness of millions of Americans in February 1968 when they actually watched, within the comfort of their own homes, as the chief of the Saigon national police executed a manacled NLF[18] prisoner. In a perfectly framed sequence, the notorious General Nguyen Ngoc Loan unholsters a snub-nosed revolver and places its muzzle to the prisoner's right temple. The prisoner's head jolts, a sudden spurt of blood gushes straight out of his right temple, and he collapses in death. The next morning, newspaper readers were confronted with AP [Associated Press] photographer Eddie Adams's potent stills of the execution (see Fig. 2). The grim ironies of the scene were accentuated by the cultural significance of the weapon itself: a revolver, a somewhat archaic handgun, symbolic of the American West.

Precisely one decade later this image, with the roles now reversed, was transformed into the dominant metaphor of a Hollywood production presenting a new version of the Vietnam War: *The Deer Hunter.* This lavishly financed movie, which the New York Film Critics' Circle designated the best English-language film of 1978 and which received four Academy Awards, including Best Picture of 1978, succeeded not only in radically reimaging the war but in transforming prisoners of war (POWs) into central symbols of American manhood for the 1980s and 1990s.

The manipulation of familiar images—some already accruing symbolic 30 power—was blatant, though most critics at the time seemed oblivious to it. The basic technique was to take images of the war that had become deeply embedded in America's consciousness and transform them into their opposites. For example, in the film's first scene in Vietnam, a uniformed soldier throws a grenade into an underground village shelter harboring women and children, and then with his automatic rifle mows down a woman and her

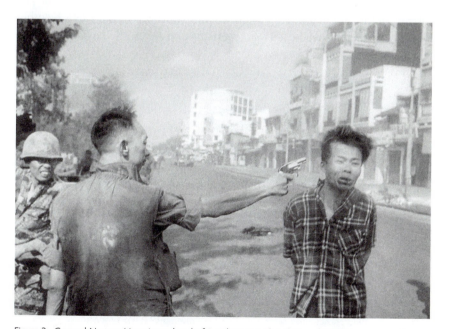

Figure 2. General Nguyen Ngoc Loan, head of South Vietnam's police and intelligence, executing a prisoner.

baby. Although the scene resembles the familiar TV sequence of GIs in Vietnamese villages (as well as *Life*'s photographs of the My Lai massacre), the soldier turns out to be not American but North Vietnamese. In turn he is killed by a lone guerrilla—who is not a Viet Cong but our Special Forces hero, played by Robert DeNiro. Later, when two men plummet from a helicopter, the images replicate a familiar telephotographic sequence showing an NLF prisoner being pushed from a helicopter to make other prisoners talk;[19] but the falling men in the movie are American POWs attempting to escape from their murderous North Vietnamese captors.

The structuring metaphor of the film is the Russian roulette that the sadistic Asian Communists force their prisoners to play. The crucial torture scene consists of sequence after sequence of images replicating and replacing the infamous killing of the NLF prisoner by General Nguyen Ngoc Loan. Prisoner after prisoner is hauled out of the tiger cages (which also serve as a substitute image for the tiger cages of the Saigon government) and then forced by the demonic North Vietnamese officer in charge (who always stands to the prisoner's right, our left) to place a revolver to his own right temple. Then the image is framed to eliminate the connection between the prisoner's body and the arm holding the revolver, thus bringing the image closer to the famous execution image (see Fig. 3). One sequence even replicates the blood spurting out of the victim's right temple.

The Deer Hunter's manipulation of this particular image to reverse the roles of victim and victimizer was used again and again in the 1980s by other vehicles of the militarization of American culture from movies to comic

Figure 3. In *The Deer Hunter* (1978), General Loan's revolver metamorphoses into a North Vietnamese revolver, and his NLF prisoner is replaced by South Vietnamese and U.S. prisoners forced to play Russian roulette.

books. Take, for example, *P.O.W.: The Escape*, an overtly militaristic 1986 POW rescue movie, inspired by *Rambo* and starring David Carradine as superhero. The bestiality of the Asian Communists is here embodied by a North Vietnamese prison-camp commander who executes an American prisoner with a revolver shot to the right temple in a tableau modeled even more precisely than *The Deer Hunter*'s on the original execution of the NLF prisoner in Saigon (see Fig. 4). Then—just in case viewers missed it—this scene is replayed later as the movie's only flashback.

Toward the end of the 1980s, however, the infamous execution got manipulated incredibly further, actually shifting the role of the most heartless shooter (originally a South Vietnamese official) from the Vietnamese Communists to the photographers themselves! For example, the cover story of the November 1988 issue of the popular comic book *The 'Nam* portrays the photojournalists, both still photographers and TV cameramen, as the real enemies because they had placed the image on the "front page of every newspaper in the states!" The cover literally reverses the original image by showing the execution scene from a position behind the participants (Fig. 5). This offers a frontal view of the photographer, whose deadly camera conceals his face and occupies the exact center of the picture. The prisoner appears merely as an arm, shoulder, and sliver of a body on the left. The only face shown belongs to the chief of the security police, who displays the righteous—even heroic—indignation that has led him to carry out this justifiable revenge against the treacherous actions of the "Viet Cong" pictured in the story. The climactic image (Fig. 6) is a full page in which the execution scene appears

Figure 4. *P.O.W.: The Escape* (1986) transforms the South Vietnamese execution of a prisoner into a North Vietnamese prison commander's murder of a U.S. prisoner.

Figure 5. Cover story of the November 1988 issue of *The 'Nam*, glorifying General Nguyen Ngoc Loan and making the photographer into the villain.

as a reflection in the gigantic lens of the camera above the leering mouth of the photographer, from which comes a bubble with his greedy words, "Keep shooting! Just keep shooting!" "Shooting" a picture here has become synonymous with murder and treason. In the next panel, two GIs register their shock—not at the execution, but at a TV cameraman focusing on the dead body:

> "Front page of every newspaper in the states!"
> "Geez . . ."

One can hardly imagine a more complete reversal of the acclaim accorded to Civil War photographers for bringing the reality of war and death home to the American people.

The logic of this comic-book militarism, put into practice for each of America's wars since Vietnam, is inescapable: Photographers must be

Figure 6. *The 'Nam* images the photographer as the shooter—and the camera as the most destructive weapon.

allowed to image for the public only what the military deems suitable. Nonmilitary photographers and all journalists were simply banished from the entire war zone during the 1983 invasion of Grenada. Partly as a result of this treatment, the major media accepted a pool system for the 1989 invasion of Panama—and meekly went along with the military's keeping even these selected journalists confined to a U.S. base throughout most of the conflict. (A European reporter who attempted to report directly from the scene was actually shot to death when the military unit sent to arrest him became involved in "friendly fire" with another group of U.S. soldiers.)

The almost complete absence of photographic images was quite conven- 35 ient for the Grenada and Panama invasions, which were carried out so swiftly and with such minimal military risk that they required no Congressional or public endorsement. And for the first several days after U.S. troops had been dispatched to confront Iraq in August 1990, Secretary of Defense Dick Cheney refused to allow journalists to accompany them. The Pentagon seemed to be operating under the belief that photographic and televised images had helped bring about the U.S. defeat in Vietnam. But for the Gulf War, with its long buildup, its potential for significant casualties, and its intended international and domestic political purposes, *some* effective images proved to be essential.

To control these images, the U.S. government set up pools of selected reporters and photographers, confined them to certain locations, required them to have military escorts when gathering news, established stringent guidelines limiting what could be reported or photographed, and subjected all written copy, photographs, and videotape to strict censorship.[20] Most of those admitted to the pools, it is interesting to note, represented the very newspapers and TV networks that were simultaneously mounting a major campaign to build support for the war. Journalists were forced to depend on military briefings, where they were often fed deliberately falsified information. Immediately after the ground offensive began, all press briefings and pool reports were indefinitely suspended. In a most revealing negation of the achievement of Civil War photography, with its shocking disclosure of the reality of death, the Pentagon banned the press entirely from Dover Air Force Base during the arrival of the bodies of those killed in the war. Responding to an ACLU legal argument that it was attempting to shield the public from disturbing images, the Pentagon replied that it was merely protecting the privacy of grieving relatives.[21]

Although the media were largely denied access to the battlefields, the Gulf War nevertheless gained the reputation of the first "real-time" television war, and the images projected into American homes helped to incite the most passionate war fever since World War II. These screened images ranged from the most traditional to the most innovative modes of picturing America's wars. Even the antiquated icon of the heroic commanding general, missing for about forty years, was given new life. Although hardly as striking a figure as the commander in Leutze's *Washington Crossing the Delaware* or the posed picture of General Douglas MacArthur returning to the Philippines during World War II, a public idol took shape in the corpulent form of General Norman Schwarzkopf in his fatigues, boots, and jaunty cap.

But perhaps the most potent images combined techniques pioneered by Billy Mitchell with General Peckem's quest for aerial photos of perfect bomb patterns, the medium of television, and the technological capabilities of the weapons themselves. After all, since one of the main goals of the warmakers was to create the impression of a "clean" technowar—almost devoid of human suffering and death, conducted with surgical precision by wondrous mechanisms—why not project the war from the point of view of the weapons? And so the most thrilling images were transmitted directly by the laser-guidance systems of missiles and by those brilliant creations, "smart" bombs. Fascinated and excited, tens of millions of Americans stared at their screens, sharing the experience of these missiles and bombs unerringly guided by the wonders of American technology to a target identified by a narrator as

Figure 7. Technowar triumphs in TV sequence of a smart bomb destroying an Iraqi building.

an important military installation. The generation raised in video arcades and
on Nintendo could hardly be more satisfied. The target got closer and closer,
larger and larger (Fig. 7). And then everything ended with the explosion.
There were no bloated human bodies, as in the photographs of the battlefields of Antietam and Gettysburg—and none of the agony of the burned and
wounded glimpsed on television relays from Vietnam. There was just nothing
at all. In this magnificent triumph of technowar, America's images of its wars
had seemingly reached perfection.

Notes

1. See especially Alan Trachtenberg, *Reading American Photographs: Images as
History, Mathew Brady to Walker Evans* (New York: Hill and Wang, 1989), p. 74; and
William A. Frassanito, *Antietam: The Photographic Legacy of America's Bloodiest Day*
(New York: Charles Scribner's Sons, 1978), pp. 27–28.

2. William C. Davis, "Finding the Hidden Images of the Civil War," *Civil War
Times Illustrated*, 21 (1982, #2), 9.

3. "Brady's Photographs: Pictures of the Dead at Antietam," *The New York Times*,
20 October 1862.

4. Oliver Wendell Holmes's "Doings of the Sunbeam," *Atlantic Monthly* (July
1863), p. 12.

5. This concept is developed most effectively by Amy Kaplan in "The Spectacle
of War in Crane's Revision of History," *New Essays on* The Red Badge of Courage,
ed. Lee Clark Mitchell (Cambridge: Cambridge University Press, 1986), pp. 77–108.

6. Stephen Crane, The Red Badge of Courage: *An Episode in the American Civil
War,* ed. Henry Binder (New York: Avon Books, 1983), p. 37.

THE INTERNET

Introduction

Trademark owners throughout the world are struggling with new issues presented by increased electronic communication, primarily that occurring through the Internet. The Internet derives from a network set up in the 1970s by the Department of Defense to connect military and research sites that could continue to communicate even in the event of nuclear attack. In the 1980s, the National Science Foundation expanded on the system, and its first significant users were government agencies and universities. In the early 1990s, however, it became apparent that the system could provide a global communication network, allowing people from all over the world to talk with each other; send written messages (electronic mail or "e-mail"), pictures, and text to each other; and establish web pages (also called home pages) to advertise their wares and provide information to their customers. Thus, the Internet has become a channel of commerce with more than 500 million users worldwide. In the United States alone, retail commerce on the Internet exceeded $45 billion in 2002.

To communicate on the Internet, businesses and individuals are assigned addresses called domain names, for example, "ford.com." To consumers, these domain names function much like a trademark in that they identify a source of goods or services.

Assignment of Domain Names

The rapid explosion of the Internet has presented two novel trademark issues: How should domain names be registered for use on the Internet, and how should disputes over domain names be resolved? As marks are used more frequently on the Internet, trademark owners need

to ensure that their marks continue to serve their key functions of distinguishing an owner's goods and services from those of others and protecting the public from deception and confusion. Moreover, businesses desire domain names that are easy to remember and that relate to their name, products, or services. Owners of famous trademarks, such as Nestlé Co., typically register their primary trademark as their domain name, as in "nestle.com." Additionally, consumers who do not definitely know a company's domain name often merely type in the company name, such as "ibm.com," in the hope of locating the company's site. This method is often successful.

A company's presence on the Internet begins with its address or **domain name.** A domain name not only serves as a locator for a company but also functions as a designation of origin and a symbol of goodwill—a trademark. There are two portions to a domain name: the **generic top-level domain,** which is the portion of the name to the right of a period (such as .gov or .com), and the **secondary level domain,** which is the portion of the name to the left of a period (such as "kraft" in "kraft.com"). Disputes frequently arise between owners of registered marks and owners of domain names who use domain names similar or identical to the registered marks. While several parties might have identical trademarks because their products or services are not confusingly similar (for example, DOVE® for soap can coexist with DOVE® for ice cream), it is not possible for two parties to have identical web addresses. For example, a company might register the mark SHOEBIZ® for its shoes. Another party might adopt the domain name "shoebiz.com." When consumers encounter the domain name, they may go to the site seeking information on the shoe products and instead be presented with information from an entirely unrelated company. Moreover, the owner of the

7. H. Bruce Franklin, "From Empire to Empire: *Billy Budd, Sailor*," in *Herman Melville: Reassessments*, ed. A. Robert Lee (London: Vision Press, 1984), pp. 199–216.

8. Mark Twain, *A Connecticut Yankee in King Arthur's Court*, ed. Bernard L. Stein (Berkeley: University of California Press, 1979), pp. 466–86.

9. During the Spanish-American War, the Edison Company had recorded some motion pictures of the embarking troops but was unable to obtain any battle footage. Later the company re-created battle scenes in a mountain reservation near Edison's headquarters in Essex County, New Jersey. See "Historian Remembers the Maine, Spain-America Conflict," Newark (NJ) *Star Ledger*, 11 February 1992.

10. Larry Wayne Ward, *The Motion Picture Goes to War: The U.S. Government Film Effort during World War I* (Ann Arbor: UMI Research Press, 1985), pp. 55–56.

11. H. Bruce Franklin, *War Stars: The Superweapon and the American Imagination* (New York: Oxford University Press, 1988), chapter 15.

12. Burke Davis, *The Billy Mitchell Affair* (New York: Random House, 1967), p. 16.

13. *Voli sulle ambe* (Florence, 1937), a book Vittorio Mussolini wrote to convince Italian boys they should all try war, "the most beautiful and complete of all sports." Quoted by Denis Mack Smith, *Mussolini's Roman Empire* (New York: Viking, 1976), p. 75.

14. For extended analyses of the significance of this event, see Franklin, *War Stars*, pp. 123–27, and Clinton Burhans Jr., "Spindrift and the Sea: Structural Patterns and Unifying Elements in *Catch-22*," *Twentieth Century Literature*, 19 (1973), 239–50.

15. Joseph Heller, *Catch-22* (New York: Dell, 1962), pp. 334–37.

16. When the Korean War began in mid-1950, there were fewer than ten million television sets in the United States. Americans' principal visual images of that war came from newsreels shown before feature films in movie theaters and from still photos in magazines.

17. Stephen Wright, *Meditations in Green* (New York: Bantam, 1984).

18. The National Liberation Front opposed the government of South Vietnam because it was allied with the North Vietnamese. [Editors' note.]

19. "How Helicopter Dumped a Viet Captive to Death," *Chicago Sun-Times*, 29 November 1969; "Death of a Prisoner," *San Francisco Chronicle*, 29 November 1969.

20. Everette E. Dennis et al., *The Media at War: The Press and the Persian Gulf Conflict* (New York: Gannett Foundation, 1991), pp. 17–18.

21. Dennis, pp. 21–22.

Working with the Text

1. H. Bruce Franklin's essay opens with a discussion of America's Civil War, and it closes with a discussion of the 1991 Gulf War. How does Franklin's treatment of images from the Civil War provide a foundation or point of reference for the rest of the essay? Are you convinced by Franklin's argument that images of the Civil War possess a reality that is largely absent from images of the Gulf War?

2. A key term in Franklin's essay is *technowar*. How does Franklin define and deploy this term? How, and to what end, does Franklin connect the technology of war with the technologies of image production and image circulation?

3. A key distinction for Franklin lies in the opposition between realism and romanticism. How does he discuss these terms? What does he mean by the "romanticizing of the machines of war" (par. 17)? How is aesthetic distance achieved in war photography? Troubling as it may be, is there an aesthetic of war?

4. The title of Franklin's essay points us to a progression from "realism" to "virtual reality." How real is virtual reality? Is virtual reality really born out of an impulse to romanticize and fictionalize?

5. Franklin concludes his essay with a discussion of the televised wars, principally the Vietnam and the Gulf wars. What is it about the medium of television that may change our relation to the image and our perception of war?

From Text to Field

1. Drawing on Franklin's essay, analyze current news broadcasts that show images of war and conflict. Do the images and the press's treatment of them support Franklin's argument, or does the broadcast raise issues not fully explored in Franklin's essay?

2. Franklin makes brief reference to video games in his essay. Drawing on your own experience or the experience of your contemporaries, discuss the relationship between video games and the virtual reality of technowar.

3. Even as he discusses photographic or video images of war, Franklin makes frequent reference to the images of war in novels and feature films. Drawing on Franklin's essay, offer an analysis of a war novel or war movie with which you are familiar. Does your "text" support, complicate, or draw into question Franklin's argument?

4. Although images of America's wars are the explicit focus of Franklin's essay, he does offer the occasional comment on what we don't see or what is censored or withheld from view (caskets arriving at Dover Air Force Base, for example). What place does the un-imaged—and the unimaginable—have in our perceptions of war? How and for what purpose are images "managed"?

Globalizing Terror

Francis A. Beer and
G. R. Boynton

Acts of terrorism and images of those terrorist acts have become, sad to say, part of our contemporary world. The images, even when taken half a world away, strike close to home. Francis A. Beer and G. R. Boynton seek to understand why terrorism, though concrete and local in its immediate consequences, has itself become globalized. They find that such globalization goes hand in hand with the globalization of the media, which has created a new public space—a stage, if you will, on which terrorists themselves have become possible actors.

A political-science professor at the University of Colorado at Boulder, Beer has focused his recent work on the cognitive and rhetorical aspects of politics and international relations. He has published *Peace against War: The Ecology of International Violence* (1981) and *Meanings of War and Peace* (2001) and has edited volumes on *Post-Realism: The Rhetorical Turn in International Relations* (with Robert Hariman, 1996) and *Metaphorical World Politics* (with Christ'l De Landtsheer, 2004).

Boynton is a professor of political science at the University of Iowa, where he pursues research in multimedia politics and communication and cognition. Among other books and articles, he has authored, with John S. Nelson, *Video Rhetorics: Televised Advertising in American Politics* (1997).

Beer and Boynton find that, just as politics and international relations have entered a multimedia domain, so too must scholarship draw on new media. They published their article on "Globalizing Terror" in *Poroi: An Interdisciplinary Journal of Rhetorical Analysis and Invention* (Vol. 2, No. 1, August 2003). As an online journal, *Poroi* afforded the authors a chance to integrate multimedia in their scholarly text, with links to actual video clips of news broadcasts. You can access their full work at inpress.lib.uiowa.edu/poroi/papers/beer030725.html.

In the aftermath of the attack on September 11, 2001, British Prime Minister Tony Blair said, "Never forget how we felt watching the planes fly into those twin towers." There is nothing extraordinary about his statement until you think about what he did not say. He did not say the people of New York City watched. He did not say the people of New York and New Jersey watched. He did not say Americans watched. He was speaking to and for the world, and he said that we watched and felt. The change in the speed of communication over the past fifty years has produced a revolution. For the first time in human history the shot was heard around the world.

Terror has existed through human history, but it has become a critical political issue since 9/11. The political use of terror, terrorism, is the subject of a growing library of work. Amazon lists almost four thousand books for terrorism and terrorists, including five encyclopedias of terrorism. There is also an extensive literature in scholarly journals and the popular press. Among other things, this work describes the psychological profiles of terrorists; the extent to which they are rational or irrational; the political, social, economic, and cultural environments that encourage them; public reactions to terrorism; possible and probable future terrorist scenarios; and strategies for controlling future terrorism (Healy et al. 2002).

The visual media have provided a feast of terrorist coverage, allowing the world to move from reading about terrorism to, as the prime minister said, watch it — in real time and in replay. The globalization of terror is something new. It goes hand in hand with the globalization of the media. The creation of new media technology has created a public space in which political actors may perform: Terrorists are some of the actors who can now play on a global stage (see Norris, Just, and Kern 2003; Greenberg and Thompson 2002; Hachten and Scotton 2002; Nacos 2002; Nelson and Boynton 1997; Alali and Byrd 1994; Livingston 1994).

We trace this change. We began in 1998 and have recorded between 200 and 250 news broadcasts a year. We started with CNN's *WorldView*. In 2001 we switched to BBC's *World News*. In this analysis we examine how the global news media handle terror — the globalization of terror. The analysis is in three parts: (1) what terror becomes in global broadcasting; (2) terror and the synchronization of global media; and (3) how terror becomes us.

What Terror Becomes

For a year the world watched the Kosovars living in terror. Finally, the world said that it had enough, a brief war ensued, the terror abated — though the hardships continued. And the world stopped watching.

The Kosovars had no monopoly on terror, of course. Today the Israelis and the Palestinians are living out mutually assured terror. The Afghans lived in terror. The East Timorese, the Eritreans, the Iraqis and the list goes on.

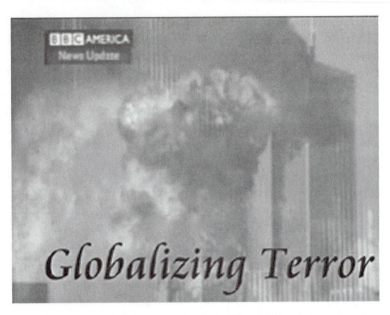

Figure 1. The World Trade Center, September 11, 2001, from BBC America.

The global media are there — at least for a time — making it possible for us to watch. What do they show us? What does terror become in the global media?

Kosovo is one case among many. By looking carefully at this case, one can see the elements that appear over and over in the reporting. Living in terror is told as threat and attack, fear and escape, and shock and mourning.

Here we focus on the threat of terror.

The Yugoslav government construed the Kosova Liberation Army as a terrorist organization. Fighting terrorists is war, and there are no limits on what the government can do. Terrorists hide every- **Terrorists are some of the** where. The government cannot tell a terrorist from a **actors who can now play on** non-terrorist. Hence, every male is a candidate. **a global stage.** There is no limit on who can be rounded up for interrogation. The Yugoslav police went door to door searching for weapons and searching for men. It was the moment the family had dreaded. The man was taken away by the police. "Go inside, don't be afraid," he shouted to his family. But many men did not come back. The threat does not go away because there are no limits on what the government can do. At any moment the police may show up and take anybody away— never to return. 10

There are no limits on what the police may destroy. Any house, any structure is a potential hiding place for KLA fighters. One day, any day, they can destroy. "They came into our main street," the man said, "and then shelled

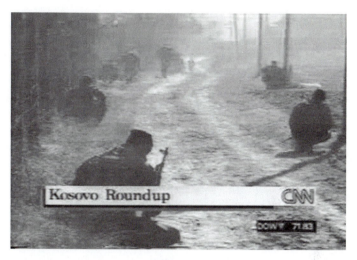

Figure 2. Street fighting in Kosovo, Yugoslavia from CNN.

our house." For everyone whose house had not been destroyed this was the threat. If they did it there, if they did it then, they can do it here and now. The threat is ever present—until you have been destroyed.

There are no limits on whom they can shoot. If anyone may be a KLA terrorist, then anyone can be shot as soon as they do something the least bit suspicious. Trying to escape from the police is definitely suspicious. So the woman was shot. The threat is not so much what they have done to you as it is what they may do to you. It is what you dread; it is what may happen. Terror is living with what may happen.

Figure 3. A shelled building in Kosovo.

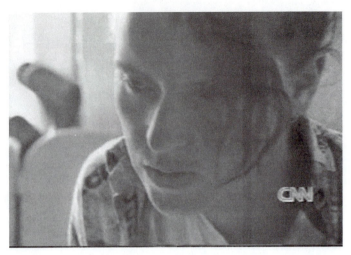

Figure 4. A woman shot by the police in Kosovo.

People tried to escape the threat by hiding in the countryside. That could work in the summer, it could work if you were willing to live without housing and without food. It could work until you were found. Then the survivors mourned.

As the global media tell the story, terror becomes threat, attempting to escape the threat, and mourning when escape fails.

On the Same Page

There are many similarities in news broadcasting around the world. For   15 example, the anchor and the anchor desk are ubiquitous.

Figure 5. Escape to the countryside.

Figure 6. Mourning when escape fails.

Atlanta, Washington, New York, London — China, Croatia, Dubai, Germany, Korea, Russia, Vietnam—the anchor or anchors are managing the broadcast sitting behind a desk and in front of a map and screen display.

In addition to the other similarities, there is the story of the day — the story found in almost every media outlet. The story of the day is well known in the United States. But there is a story of the day in news broadcasting around the world, as well. The world is synchronized in what it is shown as important.

Figure 7. News anchors from around the world.

The day was April 5, 2002. The Israeli invasion of Palestine was nine days old. Around the world the story of the day was the Israeli army terrorizing Palestinians and Palestinians fighting back. Terror was the centerpiece of the news from the Middle East. There were tanks in the streets of Ramallah and Palestinian gunmen firing automatic weapons. There were helicopters attacking and destroying buildings. But the story of the day seemed to be the small arms fire as gunmen ran the length of a street. That one scene was repeated over and over in the news broadcasts we found.

Forest fires in California, flooding in Europe and Bangladesh, an election in Germany—they are all world news. But none synchronizes global broadcasting as terror does. We are all on the same page when terror is the story of the day.

How Terror Becomes Us

Tony Blair said that we watched, and we did.   20

During the first twenty-five seconds, a news reporter explains to anyone who needs explanation what we are seeing. Then we are thrust into a crowd. We are in the midst of shouting, screaming, shock, disbelief. We feel the terror when we see through the eyes of the victims.

It begins with a scream and a replay of the crash into the tower and the tower burning. The images set the story. This is where the grief comes from. The voice of a victim—a telephone message for her husband, recorded as she was waiting for death. And a wedding picture of the victim. Then the picture of a flight attendant—shown over the American flag. And her husband, sitting in front of a flag, recounting her call.

Figure 8. September 11, 2001.

Figure 9. World Trade Center.

The camera moves back to show the large number of lives that have been destroyed. Then it moves in — filling the screen with the face of a wife, then a father. Pictures of searching wreckage, pictures of a victim, then the screen is filled with the face of the wife. Finally, back to the destroyed buildings. The carnage of the lives is reinforced with images of the carnage on the ground.

We cannot miss the terror. Terror becomes us when we are called upon to remember. The news media remind viewers over and over about the event. It becomes a constant point of departure for news, as the sights and sounds are repeated and repeated. And we are called to remember.

The global media brings terror to us all.   25

Figure 10. British Prime Minister Tony Blair.

Project Editor: Richard Meade
Cover Design: Jane Brown
Cover Painting: *Classical Forms Winter*, Grace Cole

Library of Congress Cataloging-in-Publication Data

Chen, Sheying
   Mastering research: a guide to the methods of social and behavioral sciences /
Sheying Chen.
      p.   cm.
   Includes bibliographical references and index.
   ISBN 0-8304-1531-9 (alk. paper)
   1. Psychology—Research—Methodology.   2. Social sciences—Research—
Methodology.   I. Title.
BF76.5.C44   1998
300'.7'2—dc21   98-13338
                                                                                CIP

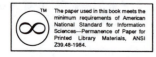

scientific pursuits including biological, psychological, and social investigations, which would give rise to applied research in an even greater variety of professional fields. What you should do, then, is to match your background with the kind of activities that you are most interested in. For instance, if you are training as a social scientist, you may confine yourself mainly to the social, or at most the psychosocial, aspects of aging. By looking at what people mean by "social" or "psychosocial," however, you may find that it is still too broad for your thesis/dissertation project. In real terms, such things as personality, social cognition, education, interpersonal skills, cross-cultural issues, the impacts of immigration, unemployment, social class, life stress, social resources, social support, family and marital problems, parental functions, friendship, political roles, and many more could all be put under the rubric of "psychosocial aspects of aging" (Chen, 1997). Based on your previous experience and interests and after you have gained an overview of the literature, you may want to focus on, say, social support in relation to depression among elderly persons in this country. If you feel that you can study the relationship between social support and depression without further breaking them down, or if you feel that splitting the construct of social support into things like family ties, friend relations and neighborhood interactions is not what you want, you can decide that your research topic is by now pretty well specified.

There are many ways of narrowing a subject area down to a more specific research topic, probably as many as the number of aspects of a research study. In designing a research project, for example, you need to consider your unit of analysis (the research subject, e.g., the elderly individual rather than her family members), your variables that are of focal interest (usually called the "dependent variables," e.g., depression rather than merely poor appetite), the key facts possibly affecting those dependent variables (called the "independent variables," e.g., social support rather than simply marital status), and also the time period and spacial range (e.g., contemporary America rather than ancient China). Always try to be analytic and specific, and your research topic will become clearer and clearer. In such a way your topic will avoid being too vague or too broad, and the issue under study will be reduced to a manageable set of research questions which together form the core of a research problem (you can deal with more than one question in a single study). Note what constitutes a research problem for you is not necessarily a problem in the life of or defined by the research subjects. The process of analyzing your research topic and problem leads to so-called scientific reduction, though there is a controversy as to whether

SHOEBIZ mark might not be able to secure the domain name for its business even though it has a valid trademark registration because the domain name has already been taken by someone else.

Domain names are appearing as assets in sales of businesses and in bankruptcies. The name "business.com" sold for $7.5 million, and the art of establishing a value for a domain name is a burgeoning business. Moreover, at least one state, Virginia, has held that domain names are property and can thus be garnished and sold. *Umbro Int'l, Inc. v. 3263851 Canada, Inc.,* Civ. No. 174388 1999 WL 117760 (Va. Cir. Mar. 12, 1999). Recently, however, "good" domain names have been selling for approximately $1,500, with the drop in price likely due to the flattening of the tech sector — what some refer to as the "dotbomb."

Domain names are registered on a first-come, first-served basis, thus allowing anyone to register a domain such as ford.com, even if the registrant has no connection with Ford Motor Co. The organizations that register domain names, called **registrars,** generally do not prescreen potentially troublesome names (although they typically require domain name applicants to represent that they believe they have a right to use the name and the registration is in good faith). At least one court has held that a domain name registrar cannot be liable for contributory infringement by merely registering an infringing domain name. *Lockheed Martin Corp. v. Network Solutions, Inc.,* 194 F.3d 980 (9th Cir. 1999). Thus, registrars have no duty to police trademarks or to ensure a trademark is not being infringed when they register a domain name.

Internet Corporation for Assigned Names and Numbers (ICANN)

To help resolve the problems in the domain name registration and use process, the U.S. government created the **Internet Corporation for Assigned Names and Numbers (ICANN)** in 1998 to oversee naming policies. ICANN, a nonprofit corporation, has assumed responsibility for overseeing the domain name system in the United States. ICANN is governed by a board of directors elected in part by various members of the Internet community.

Domain names such as www.ford.com can be registered through more than one hundred different registrars that compete with each other. Only registrars accredited by ICANN are authorized to register domain names ending with .com, .org, and .net. Registrations usually last one year, at which time they can be renewed or will expire. Registration requires a representation that the person seeking to register the name is not doing so for an unlawful purpose and does not know of any infringement that will result from his or her registration.

ICANN recently added seven new top-level domains, including .biz (for businesses) and .info (for all uses).

PROTECTING A DOMAIN NAME

Introduction

Over the past several years, one of the biggest issues facing domain name users has been the infringement of their names. In many cases, people register well-known marks as domain names to prey on consumer confusion by misusing the domain name to divert customers from the legitimate mark owner's site. This practice is commonly called **cybersquatting.** The cybersquatter's own site is often a pornography or gambling site that derives advertising revenue based on the number of visits (called "hits") the site receives. In other cases, the cybersquatters offer to ransom back the domain name to the true owner for unreasonable amounts of money.

Conclusion

It begins with technology. The time required to communicate from any-where to anywhere is now measured in seconds. Global communication has always been possible—if you were willing to wait. But waiting only seconds brings new meaning to "global communication" and creates a new human reality.

Kosovo, Israel-Palestine, the twin towers—terror is not a sometime thing. Man's inhumanity toward his fellow men makes terror constant in human affairs. Not very long ago most of the terror was hidden—beyond our will-ingness to wait for the news. That is no longer true. We experience the ter-ror around the world as it happens.

References

Alali, O., and G. W. Byrd. (1994). *Terrorism and the Media: A Selected, Annotated Bibliography.* Jefferson, NC: McFarland.
Greenberg, B. S., and M. T. Thompson, eds. (2002). *Communication and Terrorism: Public and Media Responses to 9/11.* Mount Waverly: Hampton Press.
Hachten, W. A., and J. F. Scotton. (2002). *The World News Prism: Global Media in an Era of Terrorism.* Ames: Iowa State University Press.
Healy, A. F., J. M. Hoffman, F. A. Beer, and L. E. Bourne Jr. (2002). "Terrorists and Democrats: Individual Reactions to International Attacks." *Political Psychology*, 23, 3, pp. 439–67.
Livingston, S. (1994). *The Terrorism Spectacle.* Boulder: Westview Press.
Nacos, B. L. (2002). *Mass-Mediated Terrorism: The Central Role of the Media in Terrorism and Counter-Terrorism.* Lanham: Rowman and Littlefield.
Nelson, J. S., and G. R. Boynton. (1997). *Video Rhetorics.* Urbana: University of Illinois Press.
Norris, P., M. Just, and M. Kern. (2003). *Framing Terrorism: Understanding Terrorist Threats and Mass Media.* New York, NY: Routledge.

Working with the Text

1. Why is it telling that Francis A. Beer and G. R. Boynton begin their article with a discussion of the British—and global—experience of September 11? What role do the international press and international perspectives have in the article?

2. In the first paragraph, Beer and Boynton allude to a famous line in a poem writ-ten by Ralph Waldo Emerson about the Battle of Concord at the outset of the American Revolutionary War: "the shot heard round the world." In what ways is this a fitting line to use, given the argument advanced in the article? Are shots, or bombings, only now heard around the world in a way that is literally true?

3. Beer and Boynton refer to terrorists as global actors who can now play on a world stage, thanks to the globalization of the media. Given the article's discussion of a common narrative or dramatic structure in media broadcasts and the growing synchronization of media events, whose play is being performed? Who controls the now global media?

4. The article by Beer and Boynton is distinctive in that it calls upon multimedia technologies. How does the presentation by the authors change or enhance their ability to make arguments and elicit belief from their readers? With politics and terrorism now a multimedia domain, is it only appropriate, perhaps necessary, for the study of politics and international affairs to draw on multimedia tools?

From Text to Field

1. For their examples, Beer and Boynton draw on terrorist events during the time of their data collection, chiefly those that occurred in Kosovo, Israel, and Palestine, and those of September 11. Consider the applicability and relevance of this article to current or recent terrorist activities that you have been following in the media. Does the global media become synchronized in the fashion Beer and Boynton suggest? Is there a common or generic narrative structure to the media reports? If the media and the world are brought together on the same page, whose page is it and whose story is that page a part of?

2. Although Beer and Boynton focus on how the global media report on and thus disseminate images of terrorism, they also make it clear that terrorists are also actors on the global media stage. To what extent do terrorists use the media as a terrorist weapon— one that can be even more effective than suicide bombings? What are the ethical obligations of the media? When does covering terrorism play into the hands of terrorists?

3. If you find yourself in the midst of an event covered by nearly all media outlets — the story of the day, so to speak — do some channel surfing and catalog how similar and synchronized the coverage might be. What common devices, techniques, and angles become apparent in the coverage, even as you watch different channels?

4. If you have traveled abroad, or have access to foreign media online, comment from your own personal and viewing experience on what Beer and Boynton call the globalization of the media. Is the media really rather homogenous, or are there some cultural and national distinctions that remain? Do those distinctions tend to be erased somewhat when coverage concerns a global event like terrorism?

INTO THE FIELD: Options for Writing Projects

1. Who Is Using This Photograph, and to What End?

This field project encourages you to explore how images, especially photographs, can engender belief and consent, and the purposes to which such belief and consent are put. Speaking of old family photos, David Levi Strauss (p. 728) notes, "People use photographs to construct identities, investing them with 'believability'" (par. 7). And yet Strauss goes on to suggest that this process extends well beyond personal photos. "Of course, advertisers and news-picture editors do the same thing, mimicking the private use of photographs in order to manufacture desire for products and to manufacture public consent. This has caused a great deal of confusion. The first question must always be: Who is using this photograph, and to what end?" (par. 7)

Choose a particular photographic image—or a series of images from a brochure or media campaign, for example—and examine in some detail the ways in which desire or consent is manufactured. What are the cultural codes and conventions that come into play? What pool of experience does the image assume? Who is served by the image, and for what purpose? In what ways can the image you are analyzing develop belief and consent that text alone could never accomplish?

2. On the Cover

Images on the covers of news magazines are chosen for their impact and for their ability to elicit reaction and belief. For example, in his essay David Levi Strauss (p. 728) offers comments on a cover depicting Saddam Hussein as Hitler, published by the *New Republic,* in which he notes the role of visual analogy. For this project, choose a current or recent cover used by a news magazine (such as *Time* or *Newsweek*) and offer an analysis of how the image is meant to draw on the values and beliefs of the magazine's intended audience. You may wish to consult a range of cover images that deal with the same news item or topic. Does the same process apply to the covers of other kinds of magazines, such as publications that deal with lifestyles or fitness or celebrities? To what extent are the values and beliefs culturally determined? How are those beliefs invoked by the image? For insight into the question of culture, you might find it interesting to explore, by way of the Internet, the images and covers used by the press in other countries.

3. Auras of Believability: Images and Beyond

Although works of art have their own "aura," David Levi Strauss (p. 728) asserts that in the more than 150 years that it has been around "photography acquired its own aura—the aura of believability" (par. 1). This field project invites you to read that aura—to analyze the reasons why photos and other means of communication prompt us to believe. Three options for this project suggest themselves:

- Consider a personal photograph, perhaps from a relative who has long since died. In what ways do you invest belief in this photograph, especially since you may not have been around when it was taken? What is it about the photo, both in its material condition and in what and who it depicts, that prompts you to believe?
- Consider a photograph that depicts an event or issue in the world, perhaps as reported in the media. What is it about the image, about its caption, and about when and where it was published that prompts you to consent that this image is real, believable? How much of your belief is determined by the image itself, and how much by the circumstances of its publication and circulation?
- Consider an artifact or an instance of communication that is *not* a photograph, but instead a written text or a speech, for example. What prompts you to believe in it, to lend it credibility? How is believability won? For example, why might a newsletter from a nonprofit organization, a product brochure, a presentation before an audience, or an academic article be thought to be credible? In what ways is the "aura of believability" developed given these different (nonphotographic) kinds of artifacts or examples?

4. Images and Individual Initiative

Because many images are commodified and circulated in the mass media, they often seem beyond our control. Such images are part of a globalized media; you and I seem to have little influence on how they are produced, received, and used. And yet, individual initiative is still possible—either in terms of resisting and questioning images or bringing images to light that would have otherwise remained uncaptured or would have been ignored.

This field project asks that you consider, in some detail, an instance when individual resistance or initiative can or has made a difference. Satiric comment and criticism of the media is one route for such initiative, as in the magazine *Adbusters* or the satiric newspaper the *Onion*. Another route is advocacy, in which committed individuals seek to bring to the public's attention an image or a story that would not likely have received attention were it not for their efforts.

As you analyze and report on your particular case, ask why some images and stories are covered by the mainstream media and others are not. Why might it be important to question some kinds of images? Likewise, are there some images about which it may be difficult, if not taboo, to raise questions? What is the public's right to know, and what limits might there be to such rights?

5. The Intertwined Lives of Image and Text

Although often separate and judged by different standards, image and text are leading an increasingly intertwined life. Witness politics, where the ability to control one's message often depends on one's ability to control images. This field project asks you to explore the relationship between image and text in one particular arena or through one artistic medium. These arenas might include editorial cartoons, politics, advertising, graphic design, and popular culture. You may find it interesting to explore different historical periods or cultures. For example, French poster art of the 1920s and 1930s often combined image and text, as do murals of political protest in Ireland.

As you analyze image and text, ask yourself how and why they function together as they do. How has the genre that permits or invites this interaction developed? What seem to be the limits or boundaries of that interaction? Does the interaction serve aesthetic or utilitarian purposes? What is accomplished by the interaction that could not be accomplished when using text or image separately?

6. Fast Forward: Images of Today's War

This field project asks you to update H. Bruce Franklin's survey of war images (p. 756) from the Civil War to the 1991 Gulf War, focusing perhaps on one specific question or issue. In the years since the Gulf War, new technologies have emerged—both for fighting war and for reporting and waging that war in the media. How is today's technowar different from what Franklin describes? Do images of today's war provide additional evidence for the argument Franklin makes, or do these images call for an adjustment in his argument?

Moreover, since the 1991 Gulf War, war's face has evolved. "Armed combatants" have often replaced uniformed soldiers, and war is now characterized as "conflict." The line between combatants and civilians has grown fuzzy, and terrorism has emerged as a central tool or tactic in armed struggle. How do images of war take into account this new landscape?

What's more, the tools of and the policies regarding news coverage have also evolved. Whereas news reporters were often kept at bay during the 1991 Gulf War, the Iraq War saw the use of embedded reporters, and new technologies, such as satellite phones, made possible the filing of reports from remote areas.

A further development is the increasing globalization of the media. Is the image of war in the United States different from the image of war elsewhere? Do television networks in the Middle East, for example, understand and use the images of war differently from networks in the United States? Or does the globalization of the media tend to erase regional and cultural differences, rendering the image of war generic in its use and effect?

7. Image Ethics

The rich and increasingly complex media culture in which we live places images at the center of our world. We swim in a sea of images; we use them and are used by them. All the more reason to consider the ethics of producing, circulating, and consuming those images.

This field project invites you to explore the practical application of ethics guidelines that have been developed by leading newspapers and broadcast organizations, and by professional associations. For example, the National Press Photographers Association has developed a set of guidelines pertaining to ethics in the age of digital photography. Do you think such guidelines have influenced image making in the news? What guidelines exist or should exist for the use of images in fields removed from the news, such as advertising?

The ethics involved in image making often become the subject of discussion when ethical lines or boundaries have been crossed. Explore one or more cases, in the national press or in your own community, where images have raised ethical questions.

8. The Borrowed Eye and Ear of the Media

As John Durham Peters (p. 736) helps us understand, the act of witnessing is indeed complex, for it has us move back and forth across the threshold between seeing and saying, experience and discourse. Witnessing becomes all the more complex in our media saturated society, where we often witness through what Peters refers to as "the borrowed eye and ear of the media."

This field project has you explore the phenomenon of what might be called secondary witnessing. In what ways is it different to witness an event firsthand than through the media? Is firsthand witnessing always to be preferred? Given that we now witness so much of our world through the media, is the distinction between the two kinds of witnessing beginning to grow unclear? What are some distinctive features of secondary witnessing, such as copresence (witnessing with others or knowing that others have seen what you have witnessed)? How has secondary witnessing created a common vocabulary or a common set of cultural experiences? What problems does secondary witnessing carry with it?

As part of your fieldwork, you may wish to consider controversial events on your campus or in your community that you have witnessed firsthand and that have also been witnessed for you by the borrowed eyes and ears of the media. How widely different are the two witnessings? What might account for the difference? Can both forms of witnessing be credible?

9. Witnessing across the Disciplines

John Durham Peters (p. 736) explores the dynamics of witnessing and suggests that those dynamics speak to difficult issues in the field of communication.

This field project asks you to consider how well Peters's essay travels as it moves into different disciplinary contexts.

In one way or another, all disciplines have to confront the thorny issue of what counts as observation, and how observation becomes credible. What counts as evidence or testimony in different fields? How does your discipline or prospective major think of an ideal witness? What ground rules or conventions does your field of study establish in order to ensure the believability of any one person's observation? Are there some disciplines that seem more self-conscious or reflective about the role of the observer, or does your field seem to place the act of observation within the general scientific method? What counts as observation or witnessing in fields that focus on textual analysis? What does it mean to be a good observer of a text? How do some disciplines deal with the possibility that one might be simultaneously a participant and an observer or a witness?

As you develop your field project, you may wish to refer to exemplary or representative documents in your field or to laboratory guidelines. You may also wish to interview a professor or graduate student in one of your other courses.

10. Witnessing Global Media and New Technology

This field project invites you to develop a media journal, similar to (though on a smaller scale than) the media archiving that Francis A. Beer and G. R. Boynton developed with CNN and the BBC. Follow how one global media event plays itself out over several days.

On the basis of your journal and any taped or downloaded material, examine what role technology played in the media story. Does that technology contribute to a global media? How can that technology be used in the interests of various players on the political stage? What variations did you observe in the coverage of your story or event, or did the globalized press cover the story in similar, if not homogenous, ways?

Given the worldwide reach of new media, how does global media coverage change what it means to witness an event? How does the speed and reach of the global media affect the psychological impact events have on us as viewers?

11. Multimedia Domains

Politics and the press have surely become multimedia domains. Their activities often call upon several traditional media simultaneously and indeed seek out opportunities that are only possible at the intersection of various media. This field project encourages you to consider what other domains are becoming — or ought to become — multimedia domains as well.

You needn't look far afield. Your own classroom experience can be a rich resource for this field project. For example, does the instruction that occurs in your college classes call upon multimedia, and is the effect always positive? In what ways might scholarship become more effective and persuasive if it were pursued with multimedia tools? What kinds of scholarship or what research questions about multimedia occur to you, given its use in your classrooms?

Beyond the educational arena, what other domains are ripe for a multimedia transformation? Why might some domains be resistant to or skeptical about multimedia?

What observational skills does multimedia call for? Are there distinctive or unexpected challenges involved in witnessing the multimedia image? In what ways might multimedia affect how we think of and develop arguments? What is distinctively persuasive about the use of multimedia? Can you recall instances when multimedia tools were not handled well or failed to be persuasive?

As you respond to some of these questions, be sure to draw on concrete instances of multimedia or on specific contexts in which multimedia was used.

Victims of hijacked trademarks can pursue a variety of remedies against cybersquatters. An action for trademark infringement can be brought if likelihood of confusion and use in commerce can be shown. Most victims, however, rely on one of the following three approaches because proving use in commerce by the cybersquatter can be difficult (because the cybersquatter often merely registers the domain name and doesn't use it but rather hopes to sell it to the rightful owner):

1. an action can be brought under the Federal Trademark Dilution Act;
2. a civil suit can be instituted under the recent Anticybersquatting Consumer Protection Act; or
3. an arbitration proceeding can be instituted through ICANN's dispute resolution process.

Cybersquatters and the Dilution Doctrine

If the domain name owner uses its site to promote or offer goods or services confusingly similar to those offered by a trademark owner with prior rights, and the domain name and mark are confusingly similar, the trademark owner can bring an action for infringement under the Lanham Act just as it would for any act of infringement. More difficult issues have arisen, however, when domain names have simply been registered and are used merely for an e-mail address with no web site associated with them (making the name unavailable as a domain name for the rightful owner) or are used in connection with goods or services that are unrelated to those offered by the trademark owner. In such cases, the trademark owner cannot bring an action for infringement inasmuch as the owner cannot show likelihood of confusion or use in commerce. Enter the dilution doctrine.

When the Federal Trademark Dilution Act (15 U.S.C. § 1125(c)) was being considered, Senator Patrick J. Leahy (D. Vt.) expressed his hope that it would be useful in prohibiting the misuse of famous marks as domain names on the Internet. Since the passage of the Act, many trademark owners have in fact relied on the Act in disputes over domain names.

In *Intermatic v. Toeppen,* 947 F. Supp. 1227 (N.D. Ill. 1996), one of the most famous cybersquatting cases, the owner of the well-known mark INTERMATIC® (used on a variety of electronic products) sued Dennis Toeppen, an individual who had registered the domain name "intermatic.com" with NSI. Toeppen did not offer any goods or services on his "intermatic.com" site and acknowledged he intended to "arbitrage" the name, along with more than 240 other names he had registered as domains, including "deltaairlines.com" and "neimanmarcus.com," which he then offered to sell to their owners for sums ranging between $10,000 and $15,000. The district court held that the act of registering a domain name with the intent to resell it constituted "use in commerce" and was therefore covered by the Federal Trademark Dilution Act. Toeppen's acts were held to have diluted the famous INTERMATIC mark by decreasing the owner's ability to identify and distinguish its goods on the Internet because the domain name registration system does not permit two entities to use the same domain name (unlike marketplace conditions in which similar or identical marks may coexist) and it decreased Intermatic's ability to control the association that the public would make with its mark. In mid-1998, the Ninth Circuit Court of Appeals upheld a summary judgment ruling against Toeppen for trademark dilution arising out of similar acts, namely, attempting to sell Panavision's domain name to it for $13,000. *Panavision Int'l, L.P. v. Toeppen,* 141 F.3d 1316 (9th Cir. 1998).

Similarly, in *Hasbro Inc. v. Internet Entertainment Group Ltd.,* 40 U.S.P.Q.2d 1479

Illustrations

Pages 472, 473, 474: Adam and Eve, Conquista, and *Corregidor de minas,* Library of Congress.

Page 694: "Top Hats - In Trouble," 1942 photo by Arthur "Weegee" Fellig, Getty Images.

Page 698: Jimmy Stewart in *Rear Window,* © Bettmann/CORBIS.

Page 705: "Room in Tenement Flat," 1910. Photo by Jessie Tarbox Beals. Museum of the City of New York, The Jacob A. Riis Collection.

Page 710: Plants brought by Thutmose III, limestone relief from the Temple of Thutmose III, The Art Archive/The Picture Desk, Inc.

Page 711: Lion and porcupine, Bridgeman-Giraudon/Art Resource, NY.

Page 712: Locust woodcut, 1556, Wick Collection, Zentralbibliothek, Zurich.

Pages 712, 713: Whale Washed Ashore at Ancona, 1601, engraving; and *Whale Washed Ashore in Holland,* 1598, engraving, Muller Collection, Rijksmuseum, Amsterdam.

Page 714: Rhinoceros by Dürer, Erich Lessing/Art Resource, NY.

Rhinoceros of Africa by Heat, 1789, engraving, The New York Public Library/Art Resource, NY.

Page 714: "African Rhinoceros," Emil Schulthess Erben Photoarchiv.

Page 716: Muscles of the neck, from *Gray's Anatomy.* Henry Gray, *Anatomy of the Human Body.* Philadelphia: Lea & Febiger, 1918; Bartleby.com, 2000. www.bartleby.com/ 107/. 2006.

Page 730: Found photograph of unknown boy, Photographs, © 2003 David Levi Strauss. All images are from the publication *Between the Eyes* © 2003, 2005 Aperture Foundation, Inc.

Page 758: "A Harvest of Death, Gettysburg," photo by Timothy O'Sullivan, 1863, George Eastman House.

Page 765: "General Nguyen Ngoc Loan executing a prisoner," 1968 photo by Eddie Adams, AP/Wide World Photos.

Pages 766, 767, 771: Still from *The Deer Hunter;* Still from *P.O.W.: The Escape,* 1986; and TV sequence of smart bomb destroying an Iraqi building, H. Bruce Franklin.

Pages 768, 769: Cover story of the November 1988 issue of *The 'Nam,* and *The 'Nam* images the photographer as the shooter, *The 'Nam:* TM & © 2006 Marvel Characters, Inc. Used with permission.

Page 779: CNN World View news anchor, CNN Image Source.

INDEX OF AUTHORS AND TITLES

(W.D. Wash. 1996), Hasbro, the owner of the CANDYLAND® mark used in connection with the famous children's board game, was able to enjoin the defendant's use of the domain name "candyland.com" for a web site featuring sexually explicit material. The court held that the defendant's use tarnished the famous CANDYLAND mark under the Federal Trademark Dilution Act.

According to a recent United States Supreme Court case, merely proving the likelihood of dilution is not enough to prevail in an action brought under the Dilution Act—actual dilution must be shown. It is expected that this ruling may make it more difficult for domain name owners to protect their names under the Dilution Act. *Moseley v. V Secret Catalogue, Inc.*, 537 U.S. 418 (2003).

Cybersquatters and the Anticybersquatting Consumer Protection Act

In 1999 Congress enacted the **Anticybersquatting Consumer Protection Act (ACPA)** to bring additional uniformity to the problems associated with domain name registration and cybersquatting. The Act (located at 15 U.S.C. § 1125(d)) makes it illegal for a person to register, traffic in, or use a domain name of another if the domain name is identical to or confusingly similar to the trademark of another and the person has a bad faith intent to profit from the mark. ACPA is the world's first law on domain names.

A registrant's bad faith must be shown for a plaintiff to prevail under ACPA. In determining whether a person has a bad faith intent, a court may consider a number of factors, including whether the person intends to divert consumers from the mark owner's online location either for commercial gain or with the intent to disparage the mark, whether the person has offered to sell the domain name to another for financial gain without having used the domain name, and whether the person has acquired

multiple domain names that are identical or confusing to those of others. Without such a showing of bad faith, recovery will be denied. For example, in *Hasbro Inc. v. Clue Computing, Inc.*, 66 F. Supp. 2d 117 (D. Mass 1999), the court held that the defendant's domain "clue.com" did not infringe Hasbro's famous Clue game because the defendant computing firm had its own trademark rights in the word *clue* and was a legitimate first user.

To prevail in a civil action under ACPA, a plaintiff must prove three things:

1. the plaintiff's mark is a distinctive or famous mark deserving of protection;
2. the alleged cybersquatter's infringing domain name is identical to or confusingly similar to the plaintiff's mark; and
3. the cybersquatter registered the domain name in bad faith.

Parties who prevail in actions under ACPA can obtain actual damages and lost profits as well as attorneys' fees. For plaintiffs who have difficulty proving actual damages, the Act provides for statutory damages in the amount of up to $100,000 per domain name. Additionally, the court can order the wrongful domain name canceled or transferred to the plaintiff.

A standard trademark infringement case requires a plaintiff to prove that the defendant wrongfully used a mark in commerce. ACPA, however, allows recovery if the defendant either wrongfully used or registered the mark. Thus, recovery under ACPA is easier in cases in which the wrongdoer simply registers the domain name and attempts to sell it back to the mark owner without having actually used it.

Cases under ACPA are just starting to emerge from the nation's appellate court system. One of the most famous is *Shields v. Zuccarini*, 254 F.3d 476 (3d Cir. 2001), in which case the defendant registered several misspelled versions of the popular web site http://www.joecartoon.com owned by the plain-

Need more help with writing and research?
Visit our Web sites.

We have a wide variety of Web sites designed to help students with their most common writing concerns. You'll find advice from experts, models you can rely on, and exercises that will tell you right away how you're doing. And it's all free and available any hour of the day. All of these can be accessed at Re:Writing: bedfordstmartins.com/rewriting.

Need help with grammar problems?
Exercise Central (bedfordstmartins.com/exercisecentral)

Want to see what papers for your other courses look like?
Model Documents Gallery (bedfordstmartins.com/modeldocs)

Stuck somewhere in the research process? (Maybe at the beginning?)
The Bedford Research Room (bedfordstmartins.com/researchroom)

Wondering whether a Web site is good enough to use in your paper?
Tutorial for Evaluating Online Sources
(bedfordstmartins.com/onlinesourcestutorial)

Having trouble figuring out how to cite a source?
Research and Documentation Online (bedfordstmartins.com/resdoc)

Confused about plagiarism?
The St. Martin's Tutorial on Avoiding Plagiarism
(bedfordstmartins.com/plagiarismtutorial)

Want to get more out of your word processor?
Using Your Word Processor (bedfordstmartins.com/wordprocessor)

Trying to improve the look of your paper?
Using Your Word Processor to Design Documents
(bedfordstmartins.com/docdesigntutorial)

Need to create slides for a presentation?
Preparing Presentation Slides Tutorial
(bedfordstmartins.com/presentationslidetutorial)

Interested in creating a Web site?
Web Design Tutorial (bedfordstmartins.com/webdesigntutorial)

tiff, a well-known cartoonist named Joe Shields. This practice is a variation of cyber-squatting called **typosquatting.** When visitors attempted to access the plaintiff's site and mistyped a letter or two, they would become **mousetrapped** in Zuccarini's site and need to click on a number of advertisements before they could exit the site. Zuccarini received payment for each click on one of these advertising sites. Shields was awarded damages in the amount of $10,000 for each infringing domain name and nearly $40,000 in attorneys' fees. It was later found that Zuccarini had been making $800,000 to $1 million each year by charging advertisers whose ads appeared after an Internet user mistyped names such as Victoria's Secret or *Wall Street Journal.* In many cases, the advertisers were those promoting gambling and pornography.

Just months later, Zuccarini was still at it and had registered additional misspelled domain names. The court stated that he was a "notorious cybersquatter" and had "boldly thumb[ed] his nose" at the court. Zuccarini was ordered to pay $500,000 in damages and more than $30,000 in attorneys' fees. The Federal Trade Commission later ordered him to stop his scheme and pay almost $1.9 million to victims. Altogether, Zuccarini has lost fifty-three state and federal lawsuits and has had about 200 domain names taken from him.

ACPA has proven to be a potent weapon for trademark owners. Recovery of money damages (and attorneys' fees) and cancellation of the domain name are available under the Act. Its popularity is demonstrated by the fact that in just one six-month period in 2001, over seven hundred federal lawsuits had been filed seeking relief under ACPA.

Resolving Disputes through the Uniform Domain Name Dispute Resolution Policy

In 1999, after assuming control of the domain name registration process, ICANN adopted a **Uniform Domain Name Dispute Resolution Policy (UDRP),** an international policy for resolving controversies relating to domain names. All ICANN-accredited registrars must follow UDRP, and ICANN designated four approved providers to oversee disputes. Of the four, the World Intellectual Property Organization (WIPO), headquartered in Geneva, has emerged as the most popular forum for domain name disputes. As of the end of 2000, about 65 percent of all cases filed seeking relief under the UDRP were filed with WIPO. The UDRP provides a quick and inexpensive alternative to bringing a formal lawsuit under ACPA.

The UDRP establishes an administrative procedure for efficient and inexpensive resolution of a specific category of disputes: those arising from abusive, bad faith registrations of domain names, namely, cybersquatting. Under the UDRP, the holder of a trademark files an online complaint with one of the four approved dispute resolution service providers (often WIPO, as discussed previously). Providers set their own fees, which generally range about $1,500. A decision is usually rendered by a neutral arbitration panel in about two months. Remedies are limited to canceling a wrongful domain name or transferring it to its rightful owner. Neither money damages nor injunctive relief can be obtained under the UDRP. However, if the trademark owner seeks a quick and inexpensive resolution of a domain name dispute, the UDRP provides an excellent forum for cancellation or transfer of a domain name.

To prevail under the UDRP, the trademark owner must establish three things:

1. the allegedly wrongful domain name is identical or confusingly similar to the complainant's trademark;
2. the domain name registrant has no legitimate interest in the domain name; and
3. the domain name is being used in bad faith.

The UDRP resolution process is perceived as complainant-friendly, and statistics show that the arbitrators rule in favor of trademark owners about 70 percent of the time. A party who is unhappy with the result under UDRP can appeal to court; thus, UDRP decisions are not final.

The Future of Cybersquatting

As discussed above, there are a variety of dispute mechanisms available to trademark owners whose marks are hijacked by cybersquatters (see Exhibit 7–1). With the success of the UDRP and increasing awareness that abu-

EXHIBIT 7–1
Remedies for
Cybersquatting

Form of Action	What Plaintiff Must Show	Permitted Recovery	Disadvantages
Infringement Action	Likelihood of confusion and use in commerce must be shown.	Injunctive relief and money damages (including attorneys fees in exceptional cases) are recoverable.	Plaintiff must show use in commerce, which may be difficult if domain name is only registered and not used.
Action under Federal Trademark Dilution Act	Plaintiff must show actual dilution of a famous mark; use in commerce is shown by mere registration of a domain name.	Injunctive relief may be obtained, but if willful intent is shown, money damages (and attorneys' fees in exceptional cases) may be recovered.	Plaintiff must show some empirical evidence that actual dilution has occurred, not merely a likelihood of dilution.
Anticybersquatting Consumer Protection Act	Plaintiff must show bad faith in registration of a confusingly similar or identical domain name; actual use need not be shown. Famous personal names may be protected.	Cancellation of domain name is possible as well as money damages; if money damages are difficult to prove, plaintiff may opt for statutory damages. Injunctive relief may also be ordered.	Court proceeding may be expensive and time-consuming.
Uniform Domain Name Dispute Resolution Policy	Complainant must show identical or confusingly similar domain name (including personal name) is being used in bad faith.	The only possible remedies are cancellation or transfer of domain name to rightful owner.	Money damages are not recoverable; however, process is quick and inexpensive.

sive practices will no longer be tolerated, coupled with the quick and simple UDRP process, many cybersquatters have abandoned their practices.

Many experts also note that the unscrupulous practice of cybersquatting is on the wane as evidenced by the fact that the number of proceedings initiated under the UDRP dropped by one-half in 2001 and 2002 and by nearly 30 percent in 2002 alone. The track record of cybersquatters has been dismal, and thus the potent combination of ACPA and the UDRP may well make domain name piracy a thing of the past, resulting in reliability of domain names on the Internet.

HYPERLINKING AND THE FIRST AMENDMENT

Web page owners frequently provide symbols, called **hyperlinks** (or "links") that designate other web pages that may be of interest to a user. Thus, a trademark owner's mark may be displayed on thousands of different web sites, allowing users to "click" onto the symbol and be transported to a different location, either to a different page within that same web site or to an entirely different web site on the Internet. Links are location pointers and are often shown in blue underscoring.

Most companies have no objection to linking, rightfully believing that linking allows more individuals to visit their sites and thus increases commercial use. Thus, most web site owners have not sought permission from others to link to their site.

A recently enacted Georgia statute prohibited the use of any trademark on the Internet that falsely implied that permission to use the symbol had been granted. In striking down the statute as unconstitutional, the United States District Court for the Northern District of Georgia held that the First Amendment protects the linking function as free speech. *ACLU v. Miller,* 977 F. Supp. 1228 (N.D. Ga. 1997). Many experts analogize linking with library card files or footnoting in written documents, namely, a signal to users that additional information can be sought elsewhere. Linking, however, is not permissible if it points to material with the purpose of disseminating illegal material. Moreover, linking to unsavory web sites could result in liability.

At this time, however, the permissibility of **deep linking,** which allows a user at one site to proceed directly to certain information at another site, bypassing the home page of the second site, is open to debate. Because home pages often provide background information and their owners sell advertising on their home pages, arguments have been made that deep linking that bypasses a home page deprives the second site owner of advertising revenue and is thus impermissible. Most experts, however, believe that deep linking, by itself, without causing confusion, should be permissible.

Another unresolved issue somewhat related to linking is **framing,** the retrieval by one web site of content from another site that is incorporated into the original web site within a frame, often obscuring advertisements and content. Some courts have suggested that because framing "captures" content from another's site and stores it in the user's hard drive, there is infringement.

At this time, due to the uncertainty relating to deep linking or framing, many commentators believe that permission of the original web site owner should be sought by those wishing to deeplink and bypass a home page or those wishing to incorporate others' material by framing. However, those challenged with infringement or other intellectual property violations on the Internet should strongly consider asserting that their acts are protected by the First Amendment. In sum, liability for linking and framing rests on where the linking leads, the content of the linked or framed site, and the likelihood of consumer confusion.

OTHER CYBERSPACE TRADEMARK ISSUES

Asserting Jurisdiction over Web Site Owners

One of the questions that has troubled courts over the past several years is whether by operating a web site accessible in all fifty states, a web site operator becomes subject to the jurisdiction of courts in each state such that it can be sued in that state. In general, a state can only subject a party to personal jurisdiction if the party has had some minimum contacts with the state such that subjecting him or her to jurisdiction does not offend traditional notions of justice. Thus, for example, a company doing business only in Atlanta cannot be sued in Boston.

The most recent analyses of this issue use a three-tier approach in determining whether jurisdiction can be asserted over a nonresident defendant. At one end of the spectrum, if a party merely posts information or advertises its products and services on a passive web site, jurisdiction cannot be exercised over a nonresident defendant. At the other end of the spectrum, if the defendant is actively conducting business or entering into contracts, jurisdiction can likely be exercised. The middle ground, in which a web site owner engages only in some limited interaction with users, is closely scrutinized by courts to determine the specific nature of the interactions. If interaction is significant, jurisdiction can be imposed. *Zippo Mfg. Co. v. Zippo Dot Com, Inc.,* 952 F. Supp. 1119 (W.D. Pa. 1997).

Clandestine Trademark Misuse, Metatags, and Keying

Another area of growing concern is that of clandestine trademark abuse. This involves embedding a trademark into a web site such that it is not visible to the viewer. The search engine, however, registers the presence of the hidden or clandestine trademark and lures the viewer to another web site, generally that of a competitor. The practice is usually accomplished by the use of "metatags," which are special codes whose function is to emphasize key words, making it easier for search engines to locate the web site.

In *Playboy Enterprises, Inc. v. Welles,* 279 F.3d 796 (9th Cir. 2002), the defendant, a former Playboy Playmate of the Year, used the plaintiff's registered trademarks PLAYBOY® and PLAYMATE OF THE YEAR® on her web site both visibly and invisibly through the use of metatags that drew visitors to her site when they entered the term *playboy* into a search engine. The court held that the plaintiff's registered trademarks were being used merely to describe the defendant in an accurate fashion. Because the defendant did not suggest that Playboy Enterprises sponsored or endorsed her, such use was acceptable; however, the court cautioned that its decision might be different if the metatags were so numerous that the defendant's web site would appear before Playboy Enterprises' in searches. While allowing the metatags, the court refused to allow Welles to use the plaintiff's marks as "wallpaper," or background content on her site, because there was no descriptive purpose for such use.

Perhaps the most recent issue relating to Internet trademark use relates to **keying,** an advertising practice in which a preselected banner ad pops up when certain search terms are used. For example, in yet another case involving Playboy Enterprises, when a searcher entered *playboy* as a search term, banner ads for pornography companies were displayed. The court held that such a practice (called "keying" because the banner ad that appears is matched to certain "key" search words) was acceptable and was similar to a store selling one name-brand perfume on the shelf next to another. *Playboy Enterprises, Inc. v. Excite, Inc.,* 55 F. Supp. 2d 1070 (C.D. Cal. 1999). Some experts believe the case is somewhat narrow and hinges on the fact that *playboy* is a common word in the English language. Thus, the ruling may not be applicable if a coined trademark such as KODAK® were used to stimulate pop up ads.

Trademark Policing on the Internet

Although many companies conduct annual or periodic audits and searches to review possible conflicting marks, the proliferation of use of marks and domains on the Internet adds yet another level of complexity to a trademark owner's duty to monitor and protect its marks. Many search companies review lists or databases of domain names, but further investigation may be called for due to the use of hyperlinking and embedded use of marks on others' sites. The database of the top-level domain names administered by perhaps the largest domain name registrar, Network Solutions Inc. (NSI), is located at http://www.internic.net. A tutorial is available to help with searching. Another company, Datalytics, offers monitoring of the NSI domain name registry and access to online discussion groups (see http://www.markwatch.com).

While most search engines (such as Google and Yahoo) can search only for words or text, a new software tool claims it can "see" images and logos in order to locate infringing uses of design marks. This picture research is offered by Cobion, a German company. Finally, a company called Cyveillance Inc. (http://www.cyveillance.com) will scour the Internet looking for false and defamatory statements made about companies and their trademarked products.

In addition to disclosing potential conflicts, periodic monitoring will reveal deadwood domains, namely, those not in actual use, so they may then be applied for and used by others.

Internet Complaint Sites

Irate consumers have frequently set up their own web sites, often called cyber-gripe sites, to complain about certain products or services. In one case, Bally Total Fitness claimed that its BALLY® mark was infringed by a defendant's "Bally Sucks" web site. The court held there was no infringement because consumers would not be confused inasmuch as the addition of the word *sucks* clearly distinguished the defendant's site from Bally's registered mark. The court also held that the web site did not dilute Bally's mark inasmuch as the defendant's use was not commercial and the federal dilution statute was not intended to prohibit noncommercial expression such as parody and satire. There was no tarnishment because the defendant's use was consumer commentary. *Bally Total Fitness Holding Corp. v. Faber,* 29 F. Supp. 2d 1161 (C.D. Cal. 1998). Thus, the use of another's mark on a web site to complain about a product or service is permissible as long as there is no consumer confusion, the remarks are protected parody or noncommercial expression, and the content is neither false nor defamatory. Visitors to the site should know at a glance that the site is a criticism page. If so, the site is likely protected so long as it doesn't tarnish another's mark by associating it with unsavory activity such as sexual conduct or drug use.

If it can be shown that actual harm has occurred from such cyberslander, judges often order Internet service providers to divulge the identity of the "speaker." Unless such harm is shown, the identity of Internet users is generally confidential. Otherwise, valid criticism and free speech would be chilled.

TRIVIA

- The first lawsuit brought under ACPA was filed by actor Brad Pitt against two domain-name holders. Mr. Pitt was successful.
- J. Crew International Inc. won a decision under the UDRP after an individual registered "crew.com" and attempted to sell it to J. Crew. Other successful complainants include NASDAQ and Madonna.
- A federal court has held that an Internet domain name registrar cannot be sued for civil rights violations for refusing to register domain names that included obscene terms.
- By late 2000, Internet users had registered more than 31 million domain names.
- The makers of the movie *Spider Man* were allowed to superimpose digital images on real-life billboards. The makers altered Times Square billboards by superimposing ads from companies such as Cingular Wireless over the real ads for Samsung and NBC. The court ruled that the digital alterations were protected free speech.
- "Dot com" is the most popular domain suffix.

CHAPTER SUMMARY

The Internet has dramatically changed communication. Along with that change, however, has come conflict over use of domain names and trademarks. The assignment of domain names, or Internet addresses, has resulted in disputes between the owners of domain names and the owners of trademarks. Courts have protected the rights of trademark owners as against "cybersquatters," those who register domain names for the purpose of selling them to their rightful owners rather than for some bona fide use or purpose.

If a dispute arises between parties claiming rights to domain names, the aggrieved owner has a variety of avenues in which to pursue relief. Under the new Anticybersquatting Consumer Protection Act, money damages can be obtained in court. Under the Uniform Domain Name Dispute Resolution Policy, a streamlined and inexpensive process, an arbitrator can cancel an abusive domain name or order it transferred to its rightful owner.

Use of the Internet also implicates First Amendment rights to freedom of speech. At present, courts have held that merely providing links to another party's web site is permissible. Deep linking (allowing a party to bypass a home page and proceed directly to relevant material) is subject to dispute. The practice of embedding another party's trademarks on a web site may also constitute trademark infringement. In addition, merely having a passive presence or web site on the Internet will likely not subject a party to personal jurisdiction; however, if goods are offered for sale or contracts are entered into through a web site, a court may subject the web site owner to personal jurisdiction. Finally, use of another's mark on a noncommercial web site for the purposes of satire, parody, or consumer commentary is likely permissible as long as there is no likelihood of confusion.

CASE ILLUSTRATION—DOMAIN NAME INFRINGEMENT

Case: *Victoria's Cyber Secret L.P. v. V Secret Catalogue,* 161 F. Supp. 2d 1339 (S.D. Fla. 2001)

Facts: Plaintiff registered four Internet domain names, each of which incorporated the famous mark VICTORIA'S SECRET and which were used for adult entertainment. The owner of VICTORIA'S SECRET alleged violations of the Anticybersquatting Consumer Protection Act and dilution of its famous mark. The owner of VICTORIA'S SECRET filed a petition under ICANN's policy to prevent further use of the domain names and prevailed. An appeal was taken to federal court.

Holding: The domain names violated the Anticybersquatting Consumer Protection Act and caused dilution by both blurring and tarnishment. The registration of the domain names was done in bad faith to achieve a profit and caused consumer confusion with the famous and celebrated VICTORIA'S SECRET mark. Moreover, incorporating the VICTORIA'S SECRET mark in a domain name for adult entertainment web sites will tarnish and blur the VICTORIA'S SECRET mark. The court ordered the transfer of the domain names, damages under ACPA of $10,000 for each infringing domain name, a permanent injunction, and attorneys' fees.

CASE STUDY AND ACTIVITIES

Case Study.   Watson Inc., the owner of the trademarks FANTASY FUN ADVENTURE® for its amusement park and WATSON® for a variety of goods and services related to the park, recently discovered that Gary Harris has registered the domain name fatasyfunadventures.com for gambling-related activities. Harris has made a significant amount of money from visitors or hits to his site. Additionally, Watson Inc. (the owner of the domain name watson.com, which offers a variety of tickets to the park) discovered that an individual named Jack Watson registered watson.net for his services relating to home repair. Finally, Watson Inc. has a link on its web site http://www.watson.com to United Airlines so customers can find out about favorable airfares to its park. The site also contains a deep link into the web site of a travel agent that offers various vacation packages.

Activities.   What should Watson do to protect FANTASY FUN ADVENTURE® from Gary Harris? Discuss what advantage there is to Watson Inc. in pursuing Harris under the Anticybersquatting Consumer Protection Act rather than initiating a proceeding under the Uniform Domain Name Dispute Resolution Policy. What practice has Harris engaged in? May Watson Inc. bring an action against Jack Watson under ACPA? Finally, discuss the permissibility of Watson's links and whether Watson Inc. can be sued throughout the United States.

reducing a really complicated issue to some simple questions is always scientific and desirable.

You have not yet resolved all the issues by analyzing and specifying your research topic. The framing of a specific research question can be hard since it demands not only language skills but also research experience. You can learn how to ask questions by paying attention to the ways in which people do the same thing in their writings. For the appropriate substance of a research question, however, you need a systematic review of the relevant literature (mainly books and articles in academic journals), to make sure that you are not unwittingly repeating a problem that has already been resolved by others. You may also need to derive a sound rationale as to why the question you ask is so important.

Reading is important to finding a research topic. Reading is also important to getting focused. Do not hesitate to go to the library whenever you feel a need. As a matter of fact, your progress in research depends heavily upon your use of such information resources. If you get an idea for your research project but you do not bother checking it out by examining the relevant literature, you will not be able to go any further, or at least you cannot go with much confidence. You need to learn how to use your library, and this is not hard since the library staff is there to help. If the holdings of your library are limited, you should try to overcome the limitation and expand its capacity by such means as interlibrary loans. Get every book and article you can find that is relevant to your tentative research topic. Since you have a question in mind your first reading of the books and articles can be very fast and effective. When you open a book or start reading an article, first write down the full citation for future reference. Then take notes, and distinguish between quotations and your personal thoughts by using different marks. You may need to learn how to organize your notes either by cards or by computer files/entries. If you use a computer for this task, there are different software packages you can consider for taking and organizing the notes. An ordinary word processor will suffice, which is not very good for such organization tasks as sorting of information but has the advantage of letting you directly work on the material while outlining and drafting your own plan.

Reading and questioning are the main ways of gathering, screening, and organizing the information relevant to your research interests. If you are hesitant about what to do, reading relevant literature will point you to a way out. Nevertheless, literature review is not the only thing that can help you launch your research project. A personal visit to the real research setting could be extremely helpful to you. A consulting session with an expert in the field may also be very

ROLE OF PARALEGAL

Paralegals can assist in enhancing protection for trademark owners in a variety of ways:

- monitoring new developments in cyberspace by reading articles of interest and visiting web sites devoted to areas of trademark concern;
- filing applications for domain name registrations;
- assisting in periodic audits or reviews of uses of conflicting marks in cyberspace;
- reviewing sites of competitors of clients for embedded marks; and
- checking links from and to clients' web sites to ensure that neither the clients' nor third parties' marks are being infringed.

INTERNET RESOURCES

WIPO: http://www.wipo.org (site of World Intellectual Property Organization, offering information and statistics about proceedings under the UDRP)

ICANN: http://www.icann.org (site of Internet Corporation for Assigned Names and Numbers, offering information about domain name registration and the full text of the UDRP)

Information on First Amendment
related issues: http://www.chillingeffects.com (site devoted to examining issues relating to trademark use and the First Amendment and offering sample cease and desist letters and general information about issues such as deep linking and the use of metatags)

DISCUSSION QUESTIONS

1. Al Dyer recently registered the domain name gap.com with Acme Registrars. Mr. Dyer has no relationship with Gap Inc. and has written Gap Inc. a letter offering to sell the domain name to it for $10,000. What is this practice called and what can Gap Inc. do to protect its mark GAP®?
2. Given the facts in question 1, does Acme Registrars have any liability?
3. Sue Trainor is unhappy with her recent experience at Starbucks and created a web site called "hatestarbucks.com." Is the use of the mark STARBUCKS® in the domain name permissible? Discuss.

4. Frank Kimball, a Delaware resident, has a web site that offers sporting goods for sale. Can Frank be sued in California? What if Frank's site merely includes his reviews and critiques of various sporting goods equipment? Discuss.

5. Given the facts in question 4, can Frank provide a direct link from his site to Wilson Sporting Goods? What if Frank bypasses the home page of Wilson Sporting Goods and proceeds directly to Wilson's FAQ (Frequently Asked Questions) page? Is this practice acceptable? Discuss. What is this practice called?

CHAPTER 8

International Trademark Law

CHAPTER OVERVIEW

Foreign nationals who wish to offer their products and services under a trademark or service mark in the United States can seek registration under the Lanham Act. While foreign applicants can seek federal registration on the same bases as U.S. applicants, namely, based on actual use of a mark in commerce, or based on a bona fide intent to use the mark in commerce, two additional bases are available. First, the foreign applicant may apply for registration of a mark in the United States based on a pending application in a foreign country, and if the application was filed in the foreign country within the previous six months, the applicant will be able to use the earlier filing date as its priority date in the United States. Second, the applicant may apply for registration of a mark in the United States based upon a registration issued by a foreign country. The advantage of using either of these latter two bases for registration is that neither requires use in commerce, thus allowing foreign applicants to secure federal registrations for marks that are not in use in commerce in the United States.

Just as foreign nationals may apply for trademark protection in the United States, U.S. trademark owners should give serious consideration to protecting their marks in foreign countries. Because the trademark laws of various foreign countries are complex and often rapidly changing, most U.S. law firms work in tandem with attorneys in the foreign countries who will prosecute the application on behalf of the U.S. trademark owner. The priority date afforded to foreign applicants in the U.S. is also available to United States trademark owners who wish to seek trademark protection in various foreign countries; if the foreign application is filed within six months of the U.S. application, it will retain the earlier filing date for priority purposes.

A new system, called the Community Trademark System, allows U.S. trademark owners to file one single application for the fifteen member nations of the European Union, thereby saving considerable time, effort, and money.

U.S. trademark owners who are considering foreign expansion should consider filing trademark applications in the countries in which they intend to do business to protect their marks and to ensure their marks are not "pirated" by unscrupulous third parties who register marks owned by others and then attempt to sell the marks to the rightful owners.

APPLICATIONS IN THE UNITED STATES BASED ON FOREIGN APPLICATIONS AND REGISTRATIONS

As discussed in Chapter 4, in the United States, application for federal registration of trademarks can be made by anyone based on actual use of the mark or a bona fide intent to use the mark in commerce in the future. In addition to these bases, the United States has assumed certain obligations under international agreements in the trademark field, principally the Paris Convention for the Protection of Industrial Property of 1883, briefly mentioned in Chapter 1. The Paris Convention seeks to afford citizens of each member nation protection against unfair competition and trademark infringement and requires that member nations provide the same trademark protection to citizens of other member nations as they do for their own citizens. More than 175 countries are member nations of the Paris Convention, including Canada, Mexico, most of South America, Europe, and many African and Asian countries. (See Appendix A for a table of treaties and identification of members of the Paris Convention.)

Section 44 of the Lanham Act (15 U.S.C. § 1126) implements these agreements. Section 44 provides significant benefits to any person whose country of origin is a party to a treaty relating to trademarks to which the United States is also a party by allowing the party to file an application for registration of a trade-

mark with the PTO based upon one or both of the following:

- that the applicant filed an *application* in his or her country of origin or a member nation within the previous six months and has a bona fide intent to use the mark in the United States (called a **Section 44(d) Application** after section 44(d) of the Lanham Act); and/or
- that the application in the United States is based upon a *registration* already secured in the applicant's country of origin or in a member nation and the applicant has a bona fide intent to use the mark in the United States (called a **Section 44(e) Application**).

One of the significant benefits of the section 44(d) application is that it affords the applicant a priority filing date; that is, if the applicant files an application in the United States within six months after filing the application in the foreign country, the applicant's priority date in the United States will relate back to the earlier foreign filing date. For example, if Compagnie Le Chat of France files an application in France on March 1, 2003, and files an application under section 44(d) with the PTO anytime before September 1, 2003, the critical date for determining Compagnie Le Chat's priority in the United States with regard to conflicting marks is the foreign filing date of March 1, 2003.

A significant benefit of the section 44(e) application is that it allows those who have secured registrations in a member nation to use that registration as a basis for securing a U.S. registration *even if the mark has not been used in the United States*. The U.S. principle is that the *first to use* a trademark has rights, while most foreign countries provide that the *first to register* a trademark has rights. Thus, many foreign countries allow registration of marks even though the marks have not been used. Once a registration is secured in the foreign country, it may then serve as a basis for securing a

U.S. registration, with no use whatsoever of the mark anywhere in the world (although an intent to use the mark in commerce must be alleged to ensure marks are not warehoused). In this way, foreign applicants receive more favorable treatment than U.S. applicants who can never secure a U.S. registration without a showing of use in commerce. All applicants under section 44, however, must verify that they have a bona fide intent to use the mark in commerce in the United States.

Contents of Applications Made Under Section 44

Applications made under section 44 must comply with a variety of requirements, some of which are identical to those imposed on other applications and some of which are in addition to those imposed on other applications. One additional requirement is that an applicant who relies on a foreign application under section 44(d) must specifically assert its claim of priority by stating either in the application or before the end of the priority period, "Applicant has a bona fide intention to use the mark in commerce on or in connection with the above-identified goods/services, and asserts a claim of priority based upon a foreign application in accordance with 15 U.S.C. § 1126(d), as amended. The application was filed in [country] on [date] and was assigned the serial number [application filing or serial number]."

An applicant who relies on an existing foreign registration under section 44(e) must submit a certified copy of the foreign registration during the prosecution process and state in the application, "Applicant has a bona fide intention to use the mark in commerce on or in connection with the above-identified goods/services and will submit a certification or certified copy of a foreign registration in accordance with 15 U.S.C. § 1126(e), as amended. The mark was registered in [country] on [date] and was assigned the registration number [registration number]." A certified copy of the foreign registration (not merely a photocopy) must be submitted before the PTO will issue a registration. If the foreign registration is not in English, a translation must be provided together with a signature by the translator.

Applications filed under section 44 (for applicants not domiciled in the United States) must also include a "Designation of Domestic Representative," which designates some person in the United States, typically a law firm, as the **domestic representative** to whom the PTO can direct notices and correspondence regarding the mark. (See Exhibit 8–1.) In many instances, law firms in the United States have

EXHIBIT 8–1
Designation of Domestic Representative

The law firm of Bailey & Bailey, L.L.P., 4890 Terrace Place, Minneapolis, MN 09847, is designated the Applicant's representative upon whom notices or process in proceedings affecting the mark may be served, and all prior appointments in connection herewith are hereby revoked.

MAISON BLANC, L.C. of the
United Kingdom _____

By: _____

Title: _____

Date: _____

developed relationships with law firms in foreign countries, generally referred to as "foreign associates." Each firm sends applications and business to the other to assist its own clients in securing trademark protection in foreign countries. Because U.S. lawyers are not experts in the trademark laws and procedures of foreign nations, these relationships allow U.S. law firms to refer business to respected attorneys in other countries. Similarly, the U.S. law firms usually expect that the foreign associates will refer trademark matters to them as well. The Trademark Data Sheet found in Exhibit 3–1 that is used to gather information from domestic applicants can be easily modified to gather information from foreign clients who wish to register their marks.

Applicants under section 44 must submit a drawing of the mark applied for in the United States, just as is required of other applicants, and the drawing must conform to the drawing shown in the foreign application or registration. Applicants under section 44 also must identify the goods and services applied for and specify the international class for the goods or services. Many foreign countries allow applicants to claim all goods in an entire class or allow broad identifications of goods (such as "computer goods in I.C. 9"), but that would not be permissible in the United States, and the examining attorney at the PTO may request a more specific identification in accordance with general PTO policy. Because an application filed under section 44 does not require use of the mark in commerce, such an application will generally not state a date of first use. Similarly, because the mark need not be in use, specimens are not usually filed with the applications.

Examination of Applications Made Under Section 44

Although applications made under section 44(d) (based upon a pending application in a member nation) and section 44(e) (based upon an existing registration in a member nation) are exempt from the actual use requirements of the Lanham Act, they must meet all other requirements for registration set forth in the Lanham Act. Securing registration in the country of origin does not guarantee registration in the United States because section 44 applications are subject to the same review as other applications and may be refused on the basis they are scandalous or immoral, merely descriptive, or confusingly similar to a registered mark or a mark in a pending application. Office actions may be issued and must be responded to in six months, just as is required for other applications. If a mark that is the subject of a section 44 application is refused registration on the basis that it is merely descriptive, the section 44 applicant may assert (just as its U.S. counterpart would) that the mark has acquired distinctiveness or secondary meaning through its long-standing and continuous use such that consumers, upon encountering the mark, recognize it as the applicant's mark and have come to associate the mark with the applicant. However, such a claim of acquired distinctiveness must be based upon use in commerce in the United States; the applicant may not rely on use solely in a foreign country to show the mark has acquired such distinctiveness or secondary meaning that it is not merely descriptive.

For applications filed under section 44(d) (based upon a pending foreign application), the applicant will eventually be required to submit a certified copy of the resulting registration issued by the foreign country before it can be published in the *Official Gazette* and then registered by the PTO. A translation may be necessary if the registration is in a foreign language. If the foreign application is subject to delays, the PTO may suspend action on the U.S. application until the foreign registration is issued. The PTO generally requires that the applicant submit written status reports every six months informing the PTO of the status of the pending application and when registration in the foreign country is expected. Failure to respond will result in abandonment of the U.S. application.

Registration of Marks Applied for Under Section 44

After publication of the mark in the *Official Gazette,* and assuming there is no opposition made to registration of the mark, the mark will proceed to registration. Once issued, the U.S. registration exists independently of the underlying foreign application or registration and is subject to all provisions of the Lanham Act that apply to all other registrations, such as affidavits of use, renewals, assignments, and similar matters. Thus, although the applicant need not have actually used its mark in the United States to obtain a U.S. registration, actual use must occur thereafter because the section 8 affidavit (due between the fifth and sixth years after registration) must verify that the mark is in use in commerce in the United States. When submitting any other documents, the foreign applicant or registrant will be required to designate a domestic representative in the United States upon whom notices and documents affecting the mark may be served (see Exhibit 8–1 on page 146).

SECURING TRADEMARK PROTECTION IN FOREIGN COUNTRIES

Introduction

The globalization of the world economy and ever-expanding markets in other countries for goods and services from the United States has made trademark protection abroad an increasing interest of many U.S. companies. In many instances, a vital part of a company's market strategy includes penetration of foreign markets with a concomitant need to protect the trademarks and service marks under which goods and services will be offered. Similarly, a trademark owner may need to consider registering its marks in countries in which trademark piracy is common so that if and when it decides to enter a foreign market, its name is available to it.

One of the first treaties or "conventions" designed to address trademark protection in foreign countries was the Paris Convention of 1883, adopted to facilitate international patent and trademark protection. As discussed, the Paris Convention is based on the principle of reciprocity so that foreign trademark owners may obtain in member countries the same legal protection for their marks as can citizens of those member countries.

Perhaps the most significant benefit provided by the Paris Convention is that of priority. An applicant for a trademark has six months after filing an application in a member nation to file a corresponding application in other member countries and obtain the benefits of the first filing date. The text of the Paris Convention is available at http://www.wipo.org.

Initial Considerations

Once a decision has been made to adopt a mark, consideration should be given to whether the mark should be applied for in any foreign countries. One of the first factors to consider is the meaning of the mark in various foreign languages. One of the classic international trademark stories is that of Chevrolet's adoption of the mark NOVA® for a compact car. While NOVA connotes "new" or perhaps "star" in English, the literal translation in Spanish of "no va" is "it does not go," immediately dooming the product to ridicule or failure. Thus, if a trademark owner intends to "go global," the assistance of trademark experts in foreign countries is necessary even before a mark is adopted to ensure the mark's translation into the respective foreign language is acceptable.

Once a mark, or perhaps several alternatives, has been selected, international searches should be conducted. Although the search companies identified in Chapter 3 are capable of conducting extensive international searches, many law firms prefer to ask their foreign associates to conduct the search, believing they are most capable of reviewing the results, interpreting the results of the search, and providing an opinion regarding availability of the mark for registration. Once again, the relationships between U.S. trademark counsel and their foreign counterparts can be long-standing and intimate. Some trademark firms have established relationships with foreign law firms that date back for several generations and are based on mutual respect and business interests.

The Foreign Application

Just as foreign applicants can file an application with the PTO and claim priority based on a pending foreign application, so too can U.S. applicants claim such benefits afforded by the Paris Convention. Therefore, upon filing an application for a client, many U.S. law firms confirm the filing particulars and inform the client that if protection for the mark is desired in any foreign country, such a decision should be made within six months from the PTO filing date in order to claim priority in the member nation and secure the benefit of the earlier U.S. filing date. (See Exhibit 8–2.) Similarly, just as foreign applicants can use a foreign registration as a filing basis in the United States, U.S. companies can use registrations issued by the PTO as a basis to secure registration of marks in any of the more than 175 member nations of the Paris Convention.

Trademark owners who are considering global expansion should file trademark applications in any countries in which they anticipate they may do business. Because most countries do not require that a mark be in use to be registered, filing applications in foreign countries allows U.S. trademark owners to protect their marks in anticipation of future expansion and may deter others from using similar marks for similar goods or services. In many countries, because use is not required to secure a registration, third parties often attempt to register marks in anticipation of the entrance of a trademark owner. These "trademark pirates" then attempt to sell the marks to their true owners. Alternatively, pirates register copycat marks, such as registrations secured for "Pizza Hot" and "Sharaton Hotels" in Cambodia. Thus, filing applications in foreign countries preempts trademark piracy and reserves the mark for its rightful owner. Recently, the United States has been pressing its trading partners to strengthen their laws to prevent such acts of piracy and provide stronger protection to the intellectual property rights of U.S. citizens.

The progress of an application filed in a foreign country varies dramatically based upon the country. Some countries have an expeditious procedure, and others take several years. Some countries do not yet recognize service marks. Therefore, if a client is engaged in hotel or restaurant services, rather than forego the opportunity to secure any trademark protection in such a country, the owner may seek registration in I.C. 16 for its printed matter, menus, and brochures relating to the hotel or restaurant services. Some countries, such as Saudi Arabia, have nearly prohibitive filing fees. Others, such as Italy, have more reasonable fees but take nearly three years to process the application. Searching can be speculative inasmuch as many countries lack sophisticated databases and are unable to search for phonetic equivalents of marks and the like. Just as learning the rules and processes of the PTO requires patience and determination, learning the vagaries of international trademark offices requires the same. In almost all instances, the services of reputable foreign counsel should be retained. To determine counsel with experience in trademark matters,

EXHIBIT 8–2
Letter to Client
Advising of Foreign
Priority Dates

March 30, 20xx
Mr. John R. Taylor
Watson Inc.
885 Third Avenue, 24th Floor
New York, NY 10022

   Re: Mark: EXPLORE
         Serial No.: 76/011,193
         Filing Date: January 3, 20xx

Dear Mr. Taylor:

   We are pleased to enclose the official filing receipt issued by the United States Patent and Trademark Office (PTO) in connection with the application filed for EXPLORE on January 3, 20xx. We have reviewed the official filing receipt and it appears to be correct; however, if you notice any errors, please inform us so we can ensure the PTO records are corrected.

   In view of the backlog of applications at the PTO, no action in connection with this application should be expected for approximately four to six months.

   If protection for this mark is desired in any foreign country, or if you plan to expand your business and offer products and services in any foreign country, please notify us immediately. In many countries, it is possible to obtain the benefit of the U.S. application's filing date if the foreign application is filed within six months of the U.S. filing date. In your case, applications in foreign countries must be filed by **July 3, 20xx** in order to claim priority.

   We will continue to keep you informed of any further developments in connection with this application.

                                             Sincerely,

                                             David N. Bailey
                                             Bailey & Bailey, L.L.P.

consult *Martindale-Hubbell Law Directory,* which provides information and biographical sketches of foreign counsel, or contact the International Trademark Association (INTA), an association of approximately 4,000 trademark owners and practitioners from all over the world, at 1133 Avenue of the Americas, New York, NY 10036-6710 (212/768-9887).

   The nature and type of examination of an application pending before a foreign trademark office varies greatly, with some countries subjecting the mark to strict scrutiny and issuing refusals similar to the office actions issued by the PTO, while other countries merely review the form of the application and then issue a registration unless there is a prior identical mark or nearly identical mark. Registrations are usually valid for ten years and may be renewed for like periods. Proof of use often must be submitted after the third or fifth year of registration in many foreign countries. If use is not proved, the registration will be canceled, similar to the U.S. practice of canceling registrations if the section 8 affidavit of continued use is not submitted between the fifth and sixth years after registration.

   If the owner of a foreign trademark registration allows or licenses another to use the registered mark, most countries require that a **registered user agreement** be filed with the foreign trademark office, providing information about the owner of the mark, the licensee, and various other license terms.

The European Community Trademark

In 1996, a new **Community Trademark (CTM) System** was established by the then fifteen member countries of the European Union (Austria, Belgium, Denmark, Finland, France, Germany, Greece, Ireland, Italy, Luxembourg, Netherlands, Portugal, Spain, Sweden, and the United Kingdom). The new system makes it possible for an applicant to file an application for one trademark or service mark that can be protected in each of the member countries of the **European Union (EU).** A single application in a single language may cover any number of classes of goods or services, although the initial fee (975 euros) covers up to only three classes of goods/services. The CTM blanket application covering the member nations of the EU (a market of more than 350 million consumers) provides significant protection at a considerable savings over filing separate applications in the member nations. Consistent with the philosophy of many foreign countries, actual use is not required to secure a registration. The CTM System does not replace the trademark offices in the member nations but coexists with them.

The primary European trademark office for the filing of the CTM application is the Office for Harmonization in the Internal Market, located in Alicante, Spain. An application may, however, also be filed with any one of the national offices of the European Union countries or in the Benelux trademark office, in which case it will then be transmitted to Alicante for prosecution. There is no requirement to be domiciled in any EU member nation or to have actually used the mark anywhere in order to file a CTM application.

Another distinct advantage to the new CTM application is that there is no need to perform a search prior to filing the application. An examining attorney at the central office in Alicante, Spain, is charged with the responsibility of clearing the mark in each of the member countries, providing additional savings of time and money. Moreover, in the event that an examiner's search discloses a conflicting mark in a nation, a separate application can be filed in that nation, using the earlier filing date of the CTM application. After examination, the mark will be published for opposition purposes. If there is no opposition, the mark will proceed to registration. Once registered, the CTM registration is valid for ten years from the date of filing and may be renewed for successive ten-year periods by filing one renewal application that keeps the registration in force in all member countries. Although the mark need not be in use in order to be registered, it must be in use by five years after registration to avoid cancellation by a third party; however, use in any member country constitutes use of the mark for all member countries.

Among the other advantages afforded by the CTM System are the following:

- an attractive fee structure is provided, both in terms of the official fees and the reduction in the number of trademark attorneys required;
- the unitary filing simplifies licensing or assigning the mark;
- a single infringement action may be brought to cover all countries in the European Union and a decision is enforceable in all EU countries;
- priority can be claimed in the CTM application if another trademark application was filed within the previous six months in a member nation of the Paris Convention, allowing the CTM application to capture the earlier priority date;
- protection of a mark is possible throughout all of the EU countries that may not

instructive. In terms of the formal procedure, your research topic as well as your major questions may need to be approved by your advisor and your department chair, though you can request a change later if needed.

Both experience and creativity are important in establishing the research questions. Here your insight and courage are important. Even though you have done a very thorough literature review and have gone through some other forms of tentative exploration, you cannot completely rule out the uncertainty since, after all, you are supposed to do something new. Feasibility is part of the issue in considering research topics and questions. Even if you are confident that you can carry out the research as designed, nobody will nor can he guarantee the results which would lead to a successful thesis or dissertation. Most people would agree that any scientific undertaking is an adventure, though few, if any, would take it as a speculative enterprise. The reality is, however, that chance will play a part in your success, and you have to be prepared for that. Some people falter or quit not because they are unlearned or ignorant of their topic but because they could not take the risk involved. Establishing a research question often involves imagining the way to find the answer to it. Yet oftentimes you do not see a very bright picture, or the topic and the specific question do not appear to be comforting or promising. Since you cannot get rid of the uncertainty, you must take the chance to decide whether or not to further invest your effort. It seems that the only way of minimizing your risk is to gain a thorough understanding of your topic and your field through extensive and effective reading. And you may have to go back and forth to explore different topics and questions. If you finally settle yourself with some research questions on a sound basis, the frustration of having to give up other topics and questions will turn into valuable experience and insights. If you quit without a final decision, however, what you end up with is probably just a nightmare.

The process of searching for suitable research questions can be more complicated than is described in any single flow chart. Unfortunately, the standardized textbooks you read are not prone to showing you the kind of things involved in the research process, such as the uncertainties and risks, beyond some routine procedures and techniques. Only if you are well prepared for the kind of difficulties in research could the likelihood of your faltering or dropping out be reduced.

have previously been possible due to some countries' strict examination of marks (for example, surnames are considered to be *prima facie* distinctive in a CTM application, while these are generally refused registration in the Scandinavian countries);

• use in any one of the member nations of the EU constitutes use of the mark for all member countries and will protect a CTM registration throughout all of the EU against cancellation of a registration due to nonuse of a mark; and

• a user-friendly filing system allows applications to be filed by facsimile or e-mail.

A disadvantage of the CTM System is that a CTM application can be refused if a ground for refusal exists in just one member country or if a confusingly similar or identical registration already exists in any one member country. In such a case, the CTM application fails completely, in an all-or-nothing scenario. As a safety net, however, a party may then convert the CTM application into separately filed applications in the desired countries. The converted applications have the same filing date as the earlier-filed CTM application.

Notwithstanding any disadvantages, in just the short period of time since the CTM System was established, it has proven to be enormously successful, and more than 40,000 CTM System applications are filed each year.

The EU enlarged its membership and accepted ten new member states in mid-2004 (Cyprus, Czech Republic, Estonia, Hungary, Latvia, Lithuania, Malta, Poland, Slovakia, and Slovenia), and will accept two in 2007 (Bulgaria and Romania). Negotiations with Turkey are also in process. If a party had a CTM registration in force at the time of enlargement, protection was automatically extended to the territories of the new member states.

In sum, the CTM system allows a trademark owner to achieve uniform trademark protection in all twenty-five member countries of the EU by filing only one trademark application. A single filing fee, one application, one registration, one renewal, and simplified use and licensing requirements make the CTM System an attractive way to achieve significant protection for a trademark throughout the EU.

The Madrid Protocol

In April 1996, the Madrid Protocol came into existence at the instigation of the World Intellectual Property Organization (WIPO), allowing trademark protection for more than thirty countries and all of the European Union countries by a single trademark application. The United States became a party to the Madrid Protocol in late 2003.

Under the Protocol, the owner of a mark that is registered or applied for with the PTO can file a single trademark application (usually called an international application) in a single language with a single set of fees with the PTO designating in which of the more than 60 Madrid Protocol countries it desires protection. The international application may claim priority rights under the Paris Convention if it is filed within six months of the underlying application. The PTO then forwards the application to WIPO's offices in Geneva, which conducts a review of the application to ensure it complies with certain formalities. WIPO then transmits the application to each country designated in the application. Each country conducts a substantive examination of the application, and each had the independent right to refuse protection. When registered, the international registration under the Protocol is effective only in those countries where the application was not refused or successfully opposed. The registration is valid for ten years in all other designated countries and has one renewal date, making it easy to manage renewal of the registration every ten years.

The Madrid Protocol thus facilitates a one-stop, low-cost, efficient system for the international registration of trademarks by permitting a U.S. trademark owner to file for registration in any or all Madrid Protocol member nations by filing one application with the PTO, in English, with one fee. The previous system required the filing of individual trademark applications in different languages in multiple trademark offices (with different renewal dates as a result).

Developments in Eastern Europe

The disintegration of the Communist Bloc into independent republics greatly changed trademark practices in Eastern Europe and the former Soviet Union. The Soviet Union, once a single nation, has now become fifteen countries, each of which is attempting to achieve some degree of free market economic development. Many of these countries have their own trademark offices, and it is now possible to file applications in each country.

The breakup of Czechoslovakia led to the creation of two trademark offices, one in the Czech Republic and one in Slovakia. Each has adopted its own trademark laws, and each accepts trademark applications. It is also possible to file trademark applications in Croatia, Slovenia, and Macedonia. Some countries, such as Serbia and Montenegro, are presently subject to U.S. embargo, and U.S. citizens are not permitted to file applications there, much as U.S. citizens cannot file applications in other restricted countries, such as Cuba.

EFFECTS OF NEW INTERNATIONAL AGREEMENTS (NAFTA AND TRIPs)

The North American Free Trade Agreement (NAFTA) came into effect on January 1, 1994, and is adhered to by the United States, Canada, and Mexico. The most significant change in U.S. trademark law resulting from NAFTA is that trademarks that are geographically misdescriptive cannot be registered in the United States, even if they have acquired secondary meaning.

The World Trade Organization (WTO) is located in Geneva and is a global international organization dealing with rules of trade between nations. Its primary function is to oversee and administer various agreements entered into by most of the world's trading nations. The agreements are created through a series of negotiations, called "rounds." The WTO was formally created by the Uruguay Round negotiations and was established in 1995, although it is a successor to the General Agreement on Tariffs and Trade (GATT), which itself was established after World War II. More than 140 countries are members of the WTO, and the United States has been a member since January 1, 1995. GATT was both an organization (which was replaced by the WTO) and an agreement (which still exists but which has been amended and incorporated into TRIPs, discussed below).

The Uruguay Round negotiations brought intellectual property rights into the GATT-WTO system for the first time through an agreement called the Agreement on Trade-Related Aspects of Intellectual Property Rights (TRIPs). TRIPs is the most comprehensive multilateral agreement on intellectual property. The first of two key changes to U.S. trademark law resulting from TRIPs is that nonuse of a mark for three years must be shown for a registration to be canceled for such nonuse (prior to TRIPs, the United States followed a rule that two years of nonuse of a mark resulted in a presumption of abandonment). The second change is that TRIPs provides that all signatory countries must prevent the use of a trademark that misleads consumers as to the geographical origin of goods. Even stronger protection is provided for geographical indications for wines and spirits in that TRIPs precludes registration of marks for wines and spirits that contain misleading geographical indicators. For example, a wine bearing the mark SONOMA must originate in that region of the United States.

INTERNATIONAL ASSOCIATIONS

There are a variety of international associations devoted to protecting the rights of trademark owners. The best known are the International Trademark Association (INTA) and WIPO.

International Trademark Association (INTA)

INTA was founded in 1878 as the United States Trademark Association and is dedicated to the advancement and support of trademarks as valuable items of world commerce. It is a not-for-profit association that serves its members and actively pursues private and public policy matters concerning trademarks. More than 4,000 companies and firms in more than 150 countries belong to INTA, together with others interested in promoting trademarks such as law firms practicing in the field of trademarks and advertising agencies that deal with trademarks.

INTA has played a significant role in trademark legislation, including promotion of the passage of the U.S. Trademark Act in 1946 and the 1988 Trademark Law Revision Act, designed to bring U.S. trademark law into conformity with that of the international community. INTA presently advocates that all WIPO member nations adhere to the Madrid Protocol. In 1993, a name change from United States Trademark Association to International Trademark Association was effected to reflect the association's worldwide focus. INTA offers a variety of educational seminars and publica-

tions, including many worthwhile materials available for free on the Internet (see INTA's home page at http://www.inta.org). INTA is located at 1133 Avenue of the Americas, New York, NY 10036-6710 (212/768-9887).

World Intellectual Property Organization (WIPO)

WIPO, founded in 1883, is an intergovernmental organization headquartered in Geneva, Switzerland. Since 1974, WIPO has been a specialized agency of the United Nations. Its purposes are to promote intellectual property throughout the world through cooperation among nations and to administer various multilateral treaties dealing with intellectual property, including the Paris Convention, Madrid Agreement, the Trademark Law Treaty, and the Berne Convention. WIPO encourages new treaties and modernization of national legislative bodies, disseminates information, and provides technical assistance to developing nations. More than 170 nations are members of WIPO. (See Appendix A for identification of WIPO members.)

Additionally, WIPO has an Arbitration and Mediation Center whose purpose is to offer binding arbitration or nonbinding mediation services to resolve intellectual property disputes between parties. These services are available to any person, regardless of nationality. As discussed in Chapter 7, WIPO is the leading dispute resolution service provider for cybersquatting disputes.

WIPO promotes protection of all aspects of intellectual property (trademarks, copyrights, and patents), while INTA is devoted exclusively to promoting trademarks. WIPO offers a variety of useful information on the Internet including the list of international classifications for trademarks, texts of treaties administered by WIPO, and information on publications offered by WIPO (see WIPO's home page, located at http://www.wipo.org).

TRIVIA

- A CTM application may be filed in any one of the languages of the EU nations.
- Approximately 70 percent of all CTM registrations from 1997–2201 issued to non-EU nations were issued to the United States.
- The WTO has estimated that the impact of the 1994 Uruguay Round trade deal was between $109 billion and $510 billion added to world income.
- INTA was established more than 100 years ago by seventeen merchants and manufacturers to protect and promote the rights of trademark owners.
- WIPO administers twenty-three treaties related to intellectual property.

CHAPTER SUMMARY

A foreign national may file an application for trademark registration with the PTO on the basis of actual use of the mark in commerce in the United States, a bona fide intent to use the mark in commerce in the United States, or on the bases of a pending application or existing registration in a foreign country. If the application is filed with the PTO within six months of its filing in the foreign country, it will retain its earlier foreign filing date for purposes of determining priority rights in the mark. Once filed, the application will proceed similarly to other applications, although to secure a U.S. registration, the applicant must submit to the PTO a certified copy of the registration issued by the foreign country. One significant difference is that while U.S. applicants can receive a registration only upon a showing of actual use, foreign nationals can obtain registrations without ever using the mark (inasmuch as their U.S. registration is based upon their foreign registration, which may not have required use).

Just as foreign nationals may seek protection for their marks in the United States, U.S. trademark owners may seek protection for their marks in various foreign countries. The assistance of a foreign associate who is expert in trademark law in the relevant country is nearly always required. As with applications filed by foreign nationals in the United States, applications filed in countries that are members of the Paris Convention filed within six months of the date of a U.S. application retain the earlier U.S. filing date for priority purposes. U.S. trademark owners should file applications in countries in which they intend to do business and in any countries that have a history or tradition of trademark piracy, namely, countries in which third parties attempt to register marks for goods or services they will not be offering in anticipation of the entrance of a foreign trademark owner to whom they can then sell the mark.

A new system called the Community Trademark System allows trademark owners in the United States to file one single trademark application and receive a single registration covering all twenty-five member nations of the European Union, resulting in significant savings of time and money.

CASE ILLUSTRATION—PRESUMPTION OF ABANDONMENT IF NONUSE FOR THREE YEARS

Case: *Citigroup Inc. v. City Holding Co.,* No. 99 Civ. 10115 (RWS) (S.D.N.Y. 2003)

Facts: The plaintiff alleged that defendant had abandoned some of its trademarks because they had not been used in almost five years.

Holding: The Lanham Act establishes a rebuttable presumption that trademarks have been abandoned if they are not used for three years. Although the defendants provided a reasonable business explanation for nonuse of some of their marks (namely, depressed market conditions and economic hardship), they did not rebut the presumption of abandonment by providing evidence of concrete plans to resume use of the marks in the future. Because the marks were not used for three years and because defendant did not show it had plans to resume use of the marks in the foreseeable future, the marks are abandoned.

CASE STUDY AND ACTIVITIES

Case Study.   Watson Inc. filed an application in the United States for its mark PIRATE'S COVE on April 28. Watson is considering opening water parks in Spain, Greece, and France within the next few years and would like to ensure it can use the PIRATE'S COVE mark in those countries in the future.

Activities.   What kind of trademark application should Watson file to protect the PIRATE'S COVE mark for future use in Europe? When should the application be filed? If Watson secures a trademark registration, when must it begin use of the mark? What if Watson uses the mark only in Spain? Must it also use the mark in Greece and France? When will Watson renew the registration?

ROLE OF PARALEGAL

International trademark work can be interesting and challenging. Working with clients and attorneys from foreign countries provides an international perspective on trademark law. Individuals with fluency in other languages should emphasize such skills to potential employers, who are often in need of translations of foreign documents and correspondence.

Among the tasks IP paralegals will undertake in the area of international trademark law are the following:

- assisting clients and foreign associates in completing a trademark data worksheet to determine what marks should be protected in the United States;

- preparing applications based on section 44 and securing either filing particulars about a pending foreign application or a certified copy of the foreign registration;
- monitoring the progress of section 44 applications and corresponding with foreign associates regarding the same;
- notifying U.S. clients of the advantages of filing applications in Paris Convention nations within six months of the date an application is filed with the PTO;
- working with foreign associates in filing applications for marks in foreign countries;
- maintaining dockets to track the progress of foreign applications;
- providing status reports to clients regarding the progress of foreign applications; and
- reviewing registration certificates and docketing same for maintenance and renewal.

INTERNET RESOURCES

Information on section 44 applications:
See TMEP at http://www.uspto.gov/web/offices/tac/tmep/index.html (see Chapter 12).

Texts of Paris Convention and Madrid Protocol:
WIPO's web site at http://www.wipo.org includes basic information about the Paris Convention and the Madrid Protocol and their full texts.

Information about CTM applications:
See web site of Office for Harmonization in the Internal Market at http://www.oami.eu.int.

World Trade Organization:
http://www.wto.org (web site offers information about the WTO and full text of TRIPs and Uruguay Round agreements)

International Trademark Association:
http://www.inta.org

World Intellectual Property Organization:
http://www.wipo.org

DISCUSSION QUESTIONS

1. Galleries Augustin is a French corporation that filed an application for a trademark in France on February 18. The corporation wishes to expand to the United States in the future. What type of application should it file with the PTO? When should the application be filed? Why?

2. If a mark has been registered in Germany, is the PTO obligated to register it in the United States? Discuss.

3. Assume that a United States corporation intends to do business in Denmark, Spain, and Portugal. It filed a trademark application in the United States on March 10. What type of application should it file and when?

4. Given the facts in question 3, if Spain rejects the application, what happens to the application in the other countries? What should the trademark owner do?

5. Can a trademark owner secure a trademark registration for NAPA VALLEY OAK BARREL for wine made in the state of Washington? Discuss.

6. Identify two advantages of securing a CTM registration.

PART III

The Law of Copyrights

CHAPTER 9

Foundations of Copyright Law

CHAPTER OVERVIEW

Copyright is a form of protection arising from the Patent and Copyright Clause of the U.S. Constitution. Copyright protects the works of authors and artists to ensure their products are not unlawfully reproduced, distributed, performed, or displayed, acts that would deprive them of revenue and discourage further creative work. As new technologies have developed, copyright law has evolved to keep pace, thereby affording protection to works not originally contemplated by the framers of the Constitution, such as computer programs.

The present act governing copyrights in the United States is the Copyright Act of 1976, which provides protection upon creation of a work in a fixed form rather than requiring publication of a work as a prerequisite to protection as did the previous Copyright Act of 1909. Rights arise automatically upon creation of a work, and no publication or registration with the Copyright Office is required to secure copyright, although there are several advantages to registration.

INTRODUCTION

Just as medieval merchants in guilds in England used trademarks on their wares to indicate the source of those products, mercantile interests in England prompted the first insistence upon protection for publication of books. When the invention of the printing press in about 1440 resulted in the ability to produce books by machine rather than by hand, bookbinders and printers demanded protection from copying of books. Authors also began to demand protection from unauthorized copying and demanded to share in the financial rewards the publishers were winning. Finally, in 1710, Parliament enacted the first copyright statute, the Statute of Anne, which limited the formerly perpetual rights publishers enjoyed to a period of fourteen years. Under the statute, damages

Two kinds of research

After you take some research courses and read some research books, you may be used to a straightforward or a linear research logic. This logic starts with you articulating one or a few research questions, and then you do some other things like reviewing the literature and formulating the hypotheses. In research practice, however, you cannot appropriately articulate or finalize your research questions until you figure out some plausible and feasible research hypotheses, or unless you do not use any hypothesis at all (in such a case, you may claim it is only a tentative or preliminary study of something). In other words, your research objectives will not be very clear until you know exactly what kind of research hypothesis, if any, you are going to test in your project. And you will have to continue your literature review with substantial effort until your research hypotheses are all set. Before you get to that point, chances are that you may overthrow all or part of your original questions and start over thinking about some new ones.

We will deal with research hypotheses in the next chapter. Here we only take research hypotheses as some tentative answers to the research questions and see, depending on the nature of the questions, what kind of research you will possibly be pursuing.

There are two basic kinds of research you may encounter. One only deals with individual or isolated phenomena, facts, or variables; the other is mainly concerned with the relationship among a set of such things. The former can be called an isolated study or test (measurement), and the latter, a relational research or analysis. You are likely to have been taught about the research of a relational pattern in terms of questioning, hypothesis formulation, and empirical testing. Yet you are unlikely to have been told about any special requirements for this broad category of research as the term "relational analysis" has been used mostly in a narrow sociometric sense. The confusion of the two different kinds of research, however, may lead to such negative consequences as confounding of your results. The measurement tools that are developed mainly from the isolated kind of study, when indiscriminately adopted in your research, may ruin your project if used without special care.

Existing writings on research methodology typically fail to recognize the distinctive features and different requirements for the two kinds of research, although "discovering the relationships among variables" is distinguished from "understanding the variables." On one hand, textbooks on social science research for infringement were set at one penny for every sheet found in the infringer's custody, one-half to go to the author, and one-half to go to the Crown. Authors were thus granted the right to control copying of their books. This grant of rights was called a *copyright.*

Just as trademark law protects the investment by merchants in the marks under which their goods are sold, copyright law protects the creators of books, music, and art by providing them with the exclusive right to reproduce their works and derive income from them. Protecting these rights fosters creative effort—there would be little to be gained from investing and pouring effort into composing a song or writing a novel if others could reproduce the song or book at will without compensating its creator.

Not only is copyright at the center of the creative soul of artists, but it has a significant financial impact in the United States as well. Approximately 5 percent of the gross domestic product in the United States derives from copyright industries, including software, films, music, and television shows. Additionally, copyright piracy costs U.S. businesses an estimated $12.4 billion each year in lost revenues.

Copyright law in the United States stems from the Patent and Copyright Clause of the Constitution, which provides that Congress shall have the power "to promote the progress of science and useful arts, by securing for limited times to authors and inventors the exclusive rights to their respective writings and discoveries." U.S. Const. art. I, § 8. Under this clause, Congress has the power to enact legislation to provide copyright protection for authors for limited periods. Over time, the wording in the clause has been liberally interpreted to incorporate new technologies and protect new forms of expression such as films and video games as varieties of "writings."

Congress enacted the first copyright act in 1790, and the first federal copyright registration was issued that same year to author John Barry for *Philadelphia Spelling Book.* Since 1790, the act has been subject to major revision on four occasions: in 1831, 1870, 1909, and 1976. The 1790 act provided copyright protection to maps, charts, and books, and set damages for infringement of published works in the sum of fifty cents for every sheet found in the infringer's possession, one-half of the damages to go to the copyright owner, one-half to the federal government. Subsequent revisions to the 1790 act reflect a gradual expansion of the categories of works or "writings" that are entitled to protection. Thus, musical compositions, dramatic compositions, photographs, paintings, and sculpture were eventually included within the definition of copyrightable material. The present act provides protection to nearly anything that can be expressed in tangible form, including sound recordings, videotape, and computer software.

Copyright rights are governed exclusively by federal law. Pursuant to 17 U.S.C. § 301, the federal government has preempted all rights relating to copyright. Thus, the individual states cannot grant copyright, and there is no such thing as a state copyright registration. The federal government regulates copyright in two ways: by providing a method of registration of copyright and by allowing access to the federal courts for copyright infringement claims. All cases alleging copyright infringement must be brought in federal court. On the other hand, an allegation that a contract by which one party licensed a copyright to another was procured by fraud would be a matter of standard contractual interpretation and would be governed by state law because copyright issues themselves would not be involved in such a case.

Copyright law strives to balance two competing interests: the interests of authors in protecting their works from unauthorized copying and the interest of the public in having the greatest possible access to works of authorship. U.S. copyright law is intended to stimulate the creation of new works of art, literature, music, sculpture, and other tangible forms of expression.

COMMON LAW RIGHTS AND RIGHTS UNDER THE 1976 COPYRIGHT ACT

Until January 1, 1978 (the effective date of the 1976 Copyright Act), the United States had a dual system of copyright protection in that a distinction was drawn between unpublished works and those that were published. Until 1978, authors had a perpetual common law right to their unpublished works. Thus, the author of an unpublished manuscript could exclude others from copying the material forever. Once the work was published, however, the common law perpetual copyright was extinguished and protection was afforded by virtue of the 1909 act, which then provided a period of protection up to fifty-six years. **Publication** is the distribution of copies of a work to the public for sale or other transfer of ownership, by rental, lease, or lending.

Because this dual nature of copyright protection was complex, and the point at which works became published often led to controversy, the 1976 act eliminated the distinction between unpublished and published works and provides simply that a work is protected from its **creation,** that is, as soon as it is created or fixed in some tangible form. Thus, even an unpublished manuscript is governed by the 1976 act inasmuch as it is created when the author sets the words down onto paper or types them into a computer.

Works published before the 1976 act, for example, Ernest Hemingway's *A Farewell to Arms* (published in 1929), are governed by the act in existence on the date of their publication. Hemingway's book would thus be governed by the 1909 act.

Just as trademark rights arise from use and not from registration with the PTO, copyright rights arise from the creation of a work in fixed form and not from publication or registration or other action in the United States. No permission or application with the U.S. Copyright Office is required to secure copyright protection; however, just as securing a trademark registration from the PTO provides certain advantages to trademark owners, securing a copyright registration from the Copyright Office provides certain advantages to authors of works, including the following:

- registration establishes a public record of the copyright claim;
- before an infringement suit may be filed in court, registration is necessary for works of U.S. origin;
- if made before or within five years of publication, registration will establish *prima facie* evidence in court of the validity of the copyright and of the facts stated in the certificate; and
- if registration is made within three months after publication of the work or prior to an infringement of the work, statutory damages and attorneys' fees will be available to the copyright owner in court actions (otherwise, only an award of actual damages and lost profits is available to the copyright owner).

Copyright protection generally lasts until seventy years from the death of the author. The 1976 Copyright Act is found at 17 U.S.C. §§ 101–1101. (See Appendix E.)

The 1976 Copyright Act has been amended several times. In 1980, specific protection was afforded to computer programs as works entitled to copyright protection. In 1989, the United States joined the Berne Union, an organization now comprising more than 145 nations, by entering into an international treaty called the Berne Convention for the Protection of Literary and Artistic Works. Just as the Paris Convention requires member nations to treat citizens of member nations as they do their own citizens with regard to trademarks, the Berne Convention requires member nations to treat citizens of member nations as they do their own citizens with regard to copyrights. To satisfy our obligations under the Berne treaty,

Congress once again amended the 1976 Copyright Act by eliminating any requirement for a copyright notice (©) to be used with a work (although use of the notice is recommended) and by requiring copyright applicants to submit two copies of a published work in which copyright is claimed when they apply for copyright registration. In 1990, the Copyright Act was again amended to bring U.S. copyright law more into conformity with that of other Berne Union members, particularly with respect to rights of attribution and integrity for certain works of visual arts (see Chapter 11).

The most recent significant amendment to the 1976 Copyright Act was enacted in late 1998, pursuant to the Sonny Bono Copyright Term Extension Act, when Congress extended the duration of copyright to seventy years from an author's death rather than fifty years from death as was previously the case.

Another 1998 amendment to copyright law is the Digital Millennium Copyright Act, which updates copyright law for the digital age by including provisions forbidding individuals from circumventing copyright protection systems and limiting the liability of Internet service providers (such as AOL) for copyright infringement. A number of experts believe that the Digital Millennium Copyright Act of 1998 is the most comprehensive updating of copyright law in a generation. The Act is discussed in detail in Chapters 15 and 16. References in this text to the Copyright Act are references to the 1976 act (with its later amendments).

THE UNITED STATES COPYRIGHT OFFICE

The U.S. Copyright Office is a division of the Library of Congress and is located in Washington, DC. Its address and telephone number are as follows: Register of Copyrights, Copyright Office, Library of Congress, 101 Independence Avenue SE, Washington, DC

20559-6000 (202/707-3000). Its chief officer is the Register of Copyrights, and its powers and procedures are established in the 1976 Copyright Act. The primary function of the Copyright Office is to issue copyright registrations and serve as a depository for materials in which copyright is claimed. The Copyright Office is not permitted to give legal advice and will not offer guidance on matters such as disputes over the ownership of a copyright, suits against possible infringers, or other matters related to copyrights. It does, however, provide a variety of information, publications, circulars (information packets), and forms related to copyright, most of which are provided free of charge. Among the more useful publications and materials are the following:

- forms for copyright registration;
- Circular 1, "Copyright Basics";
- Circular 2, "Publications on Copyright";
- Circular 3, "Copyright Notice";
- Circular 4, "Copyright Fees";
- Circular 15, "Renewal of Copyright";
- Circular 15a, "Duration of Copyright";
- Circular 38a, "International Copyright Relations of the United States"; and
- Circular 61, "Copyright Registration for Computer Programs".

To order copyright publications, write to:

Library of Congress
Copyright Office
Publications Section, LM-455
101 Independence Avenue SE
Washington, DC 20559-6000

Alternatively, you may call the Copyright Office's Forms and Publications Hotline at (202) 707-9100 (twenty-four hours a day). Orders are recorded automatically, and materials will be mailed to you as quickly as possible, usually within two weeks.

Selected circulars and announcements are available via facsimile. Call (202) 707-2600 from any touch-tone telephone. Key in your fax number at the prompt and the document number of the item(s) you want. The item(s) will be transmitted to your fax machine. If you do not know the document number of the item(s) you want, you may request that a menu be faxed to you. You may order up to three items at a time. Copyright applications are not available by fax.

Additionally, frequently requested Copyright Office circulars, announcements, application forms, and the most recent proposed and final regulations are now available over the Internet. To connect through the World Wide Web, enter http://www.loc.gov/copyright or www.copyright.gov. This web site gives you access to information created by the Copyright Office and links to a wide variety of other copyright resources. Internet access is available twenty-four hours a day, and no fees are charged to connect to these Internet resources.

Finally, the Copyright Office provides a free electronic mailing list, "NewsNet," that issues periodic e-mail messages on copyright issues. These messages alert subscribers to hearings, deadlines for comments related to copyright rules and regulations, new and proposed rules and regulations, and other copyright-related matters. To subscribe, send a message to listserv@loc.gov. In the body of the message, type "Subscribe copyright."

The Copyright Office is in the process of implementing an electronic registration system that will enable applicants for registration to file their applications electronically and that will reduce processing time for registration.

TRIVIA

- According to the Department of Commerce, combined copyright and trademark industries represent the second fastest-growing segment of the U.S. economy (behind Internet-related electronic commerce).
- In 2001, the Business Software Alliance estimated that there were 840,000 Internet sites engaged in copyright infringement by selling illegal or pirated software as the real thing.
- The total number of copyrights registered in the United States, through 2001, was more than 29 million.

CHAPTER SUMMARY

In the United States, copyright law arises under the Patent and Copyright Clause of the Constitution. The U.S. copyright laws have been amended several times, and the current governing statute is the Copyright Act of 1976. Copyright ensures that an author or creator of a work will derive benefits from his or her creation and will be protected from unauthorized use or copying of a work. Under the Copyright Act of 1909, a work had to be published to be protected under the act. The 1976 act eliminated the requirement of publication and provides that copyright is secured automatically when the work is created. No publication or registration is necessary to secure copyright protection, although there are certain advantages to registration of a copyright with the U.S. Copyright Office.

CASE ILLUSTRATION—PURPOSE OF COPYRIGHT LAW

Case: *Twentieth Century Music Corp. v. Aiken,* 422 U.S. 151 (1975)

Facts: Defendant played a radio in his small food shop and plaintiff asserted this was a "performance" and a violation of copyright law.

Holding: The immediate effect of copyright law is to secure a fair return for an author's creative labor. The ultimate aim of our copyright law is to stimulate artistic creativity for the general public good. Creative work is to be encouraged and rewarded. The Court held there was no performance and no violation of the copyright act.

(Note: The Court held that it would be impractical to hold such radio transmissions are performances. Moreover, copyright owners would be unable to enforce their claims against the multitude of bars, restaurants, and shops in the United States that play the radio at their premises. The 1976 Copyright Act overturned this case by making virtually all transmissions of copyrighted works "performances." However, Congress specifically allowed small businesses to play the radio and television for the enjoyment of their patrons. The exception allowing small businesses to play radios and televisions and found in the Copyright Act at 17 U.S.C. § 110(5) is commonly known as the Aiken exemption.)

CASE STUDY AND ACTIVITIES

Case Study.   Watson Inc. has decided to issue a series of children's books based on its well-known characters TAYLOR TIGER and BENSON BEAR. Additionally, Watson employees have prepared a series of scripts for a children's television show about the adventures of these two characters. A computer game is also being developed. Finally, Watson employees have written songs for the characters to sing on the television show.

Activities.   Which of the foregoing items is protectable under copyright law? What advantages does Watson secure by registering any copyrights?

ROLE OF PARALEGAL

At this stage of copyright protection and prosecution, IP paralegals will typically be engaged in general legal research relating to copyrightability of clients' works. Additionally, paralegals should contact the Copyright Office and begin creating form files for forms and publications related to copyrights. The files should be maintained in a central location, and indexes to the forms and publications should be circulated to all other IP professionals. Finally, paralegals should routinely monitor the Copyright Office web site to keep informed of new developments in copyright law, check fee schedules, and determine whether the Copyright Office has implemented new procedures.

INTERNET RESOURCES

Federal laws relating to copyright:	http://www.ll.georgetown.edu; http://www.findlaw.com; and http://www.copyright.gov/title17/circ92.pdf
Copyright Office:	http://www.loc.gov/copyright or http://www.copyright.gov
General information:	http://www.law.cornell.edu/topics/copyright.html; (site of Cornell Law School); http://www.findlaw.com; http://www.megalaw.com; and http://www.csusa.org (site of Copyright Society of the United States, a nonprofit corporation organized in 1953 to foster interest in and study of copyright law)

DISCUSSION QUESTIONS

1. Joe Garcia writes a book in 2003. When does copyright protection arise and how long will it last?
2. Is Joe required to seek registration of a work with the Copyright Office to obtain protection of his work? Discuss.
3. Is Joe required to place a copyright notice on his work?
4. Assume an individual discovers an entirely new form of video game based on new technology. Can the work be protected under the current Copyright Act, or would amendment of U.S. copyright law be required to cover this new form of work?
5. Why is copyright protection limited to a certain number of years?

For additional resources, go to www.westlegalstudies.com.

CHAPTER 10

The Subject Matter of Copyright

CHAPTER OVERVIEW

To be eligible for copyright protection, matter must be original, it must be fixed in some tangible form, and it must qualify as a "work of authorship." The requirement of originality does not mean the work must be new or novel; it must merely be created independently by its author. The most common subjects of copyright protection are literary works; musical works; dramatic works; choreographic works; pictorial, graphic, and sculptural works; motion pictures and other audiovisual works; sound recordings; and architectural works. Not all printed or communicable matter can be the subject of copyright protection. For example, useful articles, facts, ideas, titles, and U.S. government works cannot be copyrighted. In some instances, however, material that itself is not copyrightable (such as facts) may be subject to protection if it is arranged or compiled in such a way that shows creativity, for example, arrangement of facts into a book of lists.

INTRODUCTION

The limits of copyrightability are dictated by federal statute. According to 17 U.S.C. § 102, copyright protection exists in original works of authorship fixed in any tangible medium of expression, now known or later developed. Thus, there are three basic requirements for copyrightability:

1. a work must be original;
2. a work must be fixed in a tangible form of expression; and
3. a work must be a work of authorship.

Each of these requirements will be discussed in this chapter.

ORIGINALITY OF MATERIAL

To be eligible for copyright protection, material must be original, meaning that it must have been independently created and must possess a modicum of creativity. The requirement of **originality** should not be confused with novelty, worthiness, or aesthetic appeal. The requirement is rather that the material must be an independent product of the author and not merely some copy or minimal variation of an existing work.

A work can be original even if it is strikingly similar or identical to that of another. The Copyright Act only requires originality, meaning independent creation by the author. Thus, if two photographers each take photographs of the Washington Memorial, each will have copyright protection for the work (as long as one did not copy another). Similarly, if two authors independently write novels that are strikingly similar, each will have copyright protection (again, assuming there was no copying). In a famous copyright case, *Feist Publications, Inc. v. Rural Tel. Serv. Co.,* 409 U.S. 340, 345–46 (1991), the Court held:

> Originality does not signify novelty; a work may be original even though it closely resembles other works so long as the similarity is fortuitous, not the result of copying. To illustrate, assume that two poets, each ignorant of the other, compose identical poems. Neither work is novel, yet both are original, and, hence, copyrightable.

"Originality" thus does not mean "first"; it merely means "independently created."

In regard to the level of creativity required for copyright protection, the threshold is quite low. Even a slight amount of "creative spark" will suffice. In order to be protected by copyright, however, a work must contain at least a certain minimum amount of original expression. Thus, copyright does not extend to blank forms, column headings, names, titles, or lists of ingredients. In *Feist,* the Supreme Court held that telephone white page listings did not satisfy the requirement inasmuch as they lacked

minimal creativity. The Court held that the names, towns, and telephone numbers were all merely facts arranged in alphabetical order, an age-old practice, and thus were uncopyrightable. Although facts are not copyrightable, an author's original selection and arrangement of those facts may be copyrightable as a compilation (see the section in this chapter entitled "Compilations, Collections, and Derivative Works").

FIXATION OF MATERIAL

The Copyright Act protects works of authorship that are "fixed in any tangible medium of expression." A work is "fixed" when it is embodied in a copy or phonorecord and is sufficiently permanent or stable to permit it to be perceived, reproduced, or communicated for a period of more than transitory duration. 17 U.S.C. § 101.

There are thus two categories of tangible expression in which works can be fixed: "copies" and "phonorecords." A **copy** is a material object (other than a phonorecord) from which a work can be perceived, reproduced, or communicated, either directly by human perception or with the help of a machine. Thus, according to the Copyright Act, a famous photograph by Ansel Adams that appears on a book cover, a calendar, a T-shirt, a tie, and a coffee mug is a "copy" in each case. The photograph, calendar, and so forth are copies because they are material objects from which an image can be perceived. The scope of "material object" is broad enough to encompass writings on paper, images on marble, and even designs on fabric.

A **phonorecord** is a material object in which sounds (other than those accompanying a motion picture or other audiovisual work) are fixed and from which the sounds can be perceived, reproduced, or communicated either directly by human perception or with the help of a machine. Thus, a record, a cassette tape, and a CD recording of a song by the Rolling Stones are all considered to be "phonorecords." Thus, for example, a song (the "work") can be fixed in sheet music ("copies") or in a CD (a "phonorecord"), or both.

Because the definition of **fixation** requires that a work be embodied in some sufficiently stable or permanent form to be perceived, an oral presentation, lecture, or live performance is not fixed (unless it is reduced to writing or placed on film or tape). However, by virtue of 17 U.S.C. § 101, which defines the word *fixed,* a live broadcast of a television or radio show is viewed as fixed *if* it is recorded simultaneously with its broadcast transmission. Thus, an impromptu stand-up comedy routine by Jerry Seinfeld is not fixed; however, a recording and transmission of the same routine is fixed. Fixation occurs when a work is reduced to words, numbers, sounds, or shapes and placed on some permanent or stable medium. Thus, literary works are fixed when they are typed or processed into a computer or put onto a disk; sound recordings are fixed when they are recorded and placed on tape; and photographs are fixed when they are captured on film.

Prior to the 1976 act, works were protected only if they were fixed in a form that was perceptible to the human eye (although special rules existed for sound recordings, protecting records). One famous case held that the rolls of music for a player piano were not subject to copyright protection because they could not be read by humans as sheet music could. *White-Smith Music Publ'g Co. v. Apollo Co.,* 209 U.S. 1 (1908). The 1976 act (17 U.S.C. § 102), however, provides that copyright protection subsists in original works of authorship fixed in *any* tangible medium of expression, now known or later developed, from which they can be perceived, reproduced, or otherwise communicated, either directly or with the aid of a machine or device, thus allowing protection for works that are per-

ceived by machines as well as humans, such as CDs, video games, and videotapes.

WORKS OF AUTHORSHIP

The Copyright Act provides that copyright protection subsists in original works of authorship fixed in any tangible medium of expression, *now known or hereafter developed,* from which they can be perceived, reproduced, or otherwise communicated, either directly or with the aid of a machine. 17 U.S.C. § 102. Section 102 then lists eight categories of protectable works. The list is preceded by the phrase that works of authorship "include" those categories, demonstrating that the listed categories are not the only types of works that can be protected, but are illustrative only. Thus, it has been held that fabric designs and toys are copyrightable even though they are not specifically listed in section 102. Moreover, the provision that copyright protection exists in works "now known or hereafter developed" indicates congressional intent to protect new forms of expression that are not yet existent. The eight enumerated categories are as follows:

1. literary works;
2. musical works (including accompanying words);
3. dramatic works (including accompanying music);
4. pantomimes and choreographic works;
5. pictorial, graphic, and sculptural works;
6. motion pictures and other audiovisual works;
7. sound recordings; and
8. architectural works.

Literary Works

A **literary work** is one expressed in words, numbers, or other verbal or numerical symbols, regardless of the nature of the material objects, such as books, periodicals, manuscripts, phonorecords, film, tapes, disks, or cards, in which they are embodied. This broad category includes works of fiction and nonfiction, poetry, catalogs, reports, speeches, pamphlets, and manuscripts. Works such as computer programs are also treated as literary works because they are expressed in letters and numbers. Literary works can include dictionaries, an employee handbook, an instruction manual, or an advertisement. The fact that many people would not regard an advertisement or an instruction manual to be *literary* in the sense the word is usually used is of no significance. If the material is original, in fixed form, and can be expressed in letters or numbers, it is "literary" even though it may be entirely lacking in artistic merit to most people.

Musical Works
(Including Accompanying Words)

A **musical work,** together with its accompanying words, is copyrightable. A musical work or composition may be in the form of a notated copy (such as sheet music) or in the form of a phonorecord (such as a record, a cassette tape, or a CD). The author of a musical work is usually the composer, and the lyricist, if any.

The lyrics or words to a musical composition are not protected as a literary work, but rather as a musical work. Both elements of a composition are separately protected. Thus, if someone writes the lyrics to "Yesterday" in a novel, without permission, it is a violation of the author's copyright. Similarly, an unauthorized performance of the musical arrangement for "Yesterday" on stage, even without singing of lyrics, is also a copyright violation.

Dramatic Works
(Including Accompanying Music)

A **dramatic work** is usually a theatrical performance or play performed for stage, movie, television, or radio. Dramatic works usu-

ally include spoken text, plot, and directions for action. The music accompanying a dramatic work is protected as a dramatic work rather than as an independent musical work. Examples of dramatic works include the well-known plays *Phantom of the Opera, Cats,* and *Death of a Salesman.*

Pantomimes and Choreographic Works

Pantomime or *mime* is a performance using gestures and expression to communicate with no accompanying sound. An impromptu street performance of mime would not be protected (because it is not fixed in some stable or permanent medium of expression), but a filmed performance of the famous mime Marcel Marceau would be protected.

The 1976 act was the first statute to include choreography as a copyrightable work. Choreography is the composition and arrangement of dance movements and patterns. Simple dance routines and social dance steps such as the waltz, the fox trot, and the second position of classical ballet are not copyrightable in and of themselves; however, once these steps are incorporated into an otherwise choreographic work, they are protected, much like words are protected once they are incorporated into a work of fiction or nonfiction. A **choreographic work** does not need to tell a story in order to be protected by copyright; however, the work must be fixed in a tangible medium of expression from which the work can be performed, such as a recorded or notated choreographic work. In one case, still photographs of a George Ballanchine ballet performance were held to infringe his copyrighted choreographic work *The Nutcracker. Horgan v. MacMillan, Inc.,* 789 F.2d 157 (2d Cir. 1986).

Pictorial, Graphic, and Sculptural Works

Pictorial, graphic, and sculptural works include two-dimensional and three-dimensional methods tend to ignore the formulation and testing of such one-variable (univariate) hypotheses as "Less than one percent of the Chinese American elderly will suffer from depression." On the other hand, psychometric theories and procedures derived mainly from the research setting of single-variable testing are indiscriminately applied to the measurement of variables involved in all kinds of relational analyses. This has been an important source of difficulty, frustration and confusion not only to the novice but also to the seasoned researchers (Chen, 1997). Some of these issues will be addressed in chapter twelve of this book. Yet you should be clear from the very beginning as to what kind of questions you are pursuing. If your question is, for example, "How many HIV-positive people are in need of support group service," your research is likely to deal with a single variable rather than focus on the relationship among different variables. But if you ask, "Which age group of HIV-infected persons is in the greatest need of support group service," then your emphasis is put on the relationship between the variable of age and the variable of the need for support group service. If you ask the question in a more generic way, "Which group of HIV-infected persons is in the most urgent need of support group service?" then you will be dealing with a few or a number of factors, such as age, gender and ethnicity, in relation to the need of HIV-infected persons for support group service. The way to formulate and test your hypotheses will depend on the nature of the questions you ask. The research logic and the requirements for a meaningful analysis in different kinds of research may also be very different. In behavioral and social research (equivalent with "psychosocial research" in this book), the relational kind of questions as well as their analysis are most frequently seen and actively pursued. In terms of data analysis, this may also be understood as an issue of statistical control. Univariate analysis is uncontrolled, whereas relational (bivariate or multivariate) analysis is controlled to a certain degree. We will further discuss this in chapter eleven.

works of fine, graphic, and applied art. This category of copyrighted works is extremely broad and includes the following: photographs; prints, posters, and art reproductions; maps; globes; charts; diagrams; artwork applied to clothing; bumper stickers; cartoons and comic strips; dolls; toys; jewelry designs; mosaics; patterns for sewing; record jacket artwork; tapestries; quilts; fabric, floor, and wallcovering designs; games; puzzles; greeting cards, postcards, and stationery; stencils; sculptures (including carvings, figurines, and molds); models; and technical drawings, including blueprints. A minimal threshold of creativity is required. Thus, a simple shape such as a drawing of a circle or square may not be protected; however, even a drawing of a bowl of chili on the label of a can is copyrightable as a pictorial work.

Copyright law does not protect useful articles. A **useful article** is one having an intrinsic utilitarian function. Examples of useful articles are clothing (including costumes), vehicular bodies, furniture, machinery, appliances, dinnerware, and lighting fixtures. Toys, dolls, and stuffed animals are not useful articles and can be copyrighted, even if they portray a utilitarian product. Thus, a toy airplane was held not to be a useful article in *Gay Toys, Inc. v. Buddy L. Corp.*, 703 F.2d 970 (6th Cir. 1983). The intent of Congress was to exclude from copyright protection industrial products such as cars, appliances, and electronic products. Many of these useful objects are protected under patent law. In one case, the court of appeals affirmed that automobile wire-spoke wheel covers were useful and were not subject to copyright protection. The creator argued that the wheel covers were ornamental and were intended to beautify and embellish the wheels, but the court held that the wheel covers were mere utilitarian articles serving to protect lugnuts, wheels, and axles from damage. *Norris Indus. v. Int'l Tel. & Tel. Corp.*, 696 F.2d 918 (11th Cir. 1983).

The Copyright Act provides, however, that the design of a useful article shall be considered a copyrightable pictorial, graphic, or sculptural work if such design incorporates pictorial, graphic, or sculptural features that can be identified separately from and are capable of existing independently of the utilitarian aspects of the article. Thus, the famous statuette that adorns the hood of a Rolls Royce can be protected by copyright inasmuch as it can exist as a sculpture independently from the hood and the car. Similarly, a carving on the back of a chair, animal foot slippers, or a floral relief design on silver flatware is protectable by copyright, but the design of the chair, slipper, or flatware itself is not because these are useful articles.

Motion Pictures and Other Audiovisual Works

A **motion picture** is an audiovisual work consisting of a series of related images that, when shown in succession, impart an impression of motion, together with accompanying sounds. These works are typically embodied in film, videotape, or videodisk. Music accompanying a movie (the motion picture soundtrack) is protected as part of the motion picture.

An **audiovisual work** is a work that consists of a series of related images that are intended to be shown by the use of machines or devices such as projectors, viewers, or electronic equipment, together with accompanying sounds. Thus, a photograph of a mountain is protected as a pictorial work. If the photograph is made into a slide, it remains a pictorial work; however, when the photograph is made into a slide that becomes part of a presentation about mountains of the world, the resulting slide show is an audiovisual work.

Sound Recordings

A **sound recording** is a work that results from the fixation of a series of musical, spoken, or other sounds, regardless of the nature of the material objects, such as disks, tapes, or other phonorecords, in which they are embodied. Thus, a sound recording could be a narration by Meryl Streep of a book played on a cassette tape, a CD of a live performance by Garth Brooks, or an album by Eminem. Sound recordings, however, do not include the sounds accompanying a motion picture or other audiovisual work.

There is a distinction between a "musical work" and a "sound recording." A musical work consists of music, including any accompanying words. The author of a musical work or composition is generally the composer, and the lyricist, if any. A musical composition may be in the form of sheet music or a cassette tape, album, or CD. A sound recording results from the fixation of a series of musical, spoken, or other sounds. The author of a sound recording is the performer whose performance is fixed, or the record producer who processes the sounds and fixes them in the final recording, or both.

For example, the song "You Are the Sunshine of My Life" by Stevie Wonder is frequently recorded by other artists. The original music and lyrics are copyrighted by Stevie Wonder as a musical work. If Celine Dion performs the song "You Are the Sunshine of My Life," she cannot claim copyright in the lyrics and music because she did not create them. However, her particular and unique arrangement of the lyrics and song is copyrightable as a sound recording by her and her record producer. If a later artist wishes to perform "You Are the Sunshine of My Life," permission must be sought from Stevie Wonder (or the present copyright owner). Permission need not be sought from Celine Dion or her record company because the new artist will not be copying Celine Dion's particular arrangement (unless the new artist wishes to extract or "sample" some of the Celine Dion arrangement into the new version, in which case permission must be sought from Celine Dion and/or the record company for the part sampled).

As discussed earlier, sound recordings are embodied in phonorecords, not copies.

Architectural Works

An **architectural work** is the design of a building as embodied in any tangible medium of expression, including a building, architectural plans, or drawings. The work includes the overall form and arrangement and composition of spaces, but not individual standard features such as windows, doors, and other standard components of buildings, which cannot be registered. The term *building* includes not only permanent and stationary structures for human occupancy (such as houses and office buildings) but also gazebos, churches, and garden pavilions. Structures other than buildings (such as bridges, tents, and mobile homes) are not subject to protection.

Before 1990 and the United States's adherence to the Berne Convention, architectural plans and models were protected only as graphic and sculptural works. Because buildings were useful articles, they could not be protected. Protection was allowed only for nonuseful portions, such as decorative moldings, murals, friezes, and so forth.

In 1990, however, Congress passed the Architectural Works Copyright Protection Act and expressly amended the 1976 Copyright Act to provide copyright protection to "architectural works." A claim to copyright in an architectural work is distinct from a claim in technical drawings of the work. If registration is sought for both an architectural work (such as a building) and technical drawings of the work, separate applications must be submitted to the Copyright Office.

If the building is ordinarily visible to the public, anyone can take pictures of it or display it in a painting or movie. 17 U.S.C. § 120(a). One recent case demonstrates the difficulties inherent in protecting architectural works. The recent movie *The Devil's Advocate* with Al Pacino displayed a frieze, which a noted sculptor claimed was an infringement of his work, placed over the doorway of the National Cathedral in Washington, DC. The sculptor sued, alleging copyright infringement. The producers of the movie claimed the frieze was independently created and was merely part of a building ordinarily visible to the public. The case settled out of court, and thus there was no determination of the rights of the parties. Destruction and alteration of works of fine arts is discussed further in Chapter 11.

EXCLUSIONS FROM COPYRIGHT PROTECTION

Not all works are protected by copyright. In addition to articles that are purely useful and that cannot be copyrighted, a number of other works are not protected under copyright law, including ideas, blank forms, short phrases, slogans, titles, works in the public domain, facts, and computing devices.

Ideas, Methods, or Systems

Section 102 of the Copyright Act not only lists eight categories of works that are protected by copyright, but also states that the following are specifically excluded from copyright protection: ideas, procedures, processes, systems, methods of operation, concepts, principles, and discoveries, regardless of the form in which they are described, explained, or illustrated. This statutory prohibition sets out in long form a well-established copyright principle: copyright protects expression, not ideas.

The rule that copyright protection extends only to the expression of ideas, and not to ideas themselves, derives from a famous Supreme Court case, *Baker v. Selden,* 101 U.S. 99 (1879). In that case, Selden published a book explaining a bookkeeping system that included blank forms

with ruled lines and columns for using the new system. Baker later published a book with additional forms for using Selden's system. Selden sued for copyright infringement. The Court denied relief, holding that a copyright on a book explaining a system does not prevent another party from explaining the same system; otherwise, the bookkeeping system or method itself would be monopolized by the first to explain it. The Court held that Baker had copied only Selden's unprotectable idea and not any protectable expression of the idea. The discussion by the Court is often referred to as the **idea-expression dichotomy** and results in a well-known copyright principle: ideas are not protectable, although the expression of those ideas is subject to copyright protection. The Court also held that the forms were not writings and were thus unprotectable, thereby giving rise to the rule that mere blank forms are not copyrightable.

The Copyright Office itself states that copyright protection is not available for the following: ideas or procedures for doing, making, or building things; scientific or technical methods or discoveries; business operations or procedures; formulas of mathematical principles; algorithms; business operations or procedures; or any other concept, process, or method of operation.

Generally, if there are a number of ways of explaining a topic or subject, the original expression will be protected against copying; however, if there are no or few alternative ways of expressing something, only literal copying (rather than mere paraphrasing) will likely result in infringement. In such cases, it is said that the expression merges with the idea, and copyright protection is denied to the merged expression because ideas are not copyrightable. This principle is known as the **merger doctrine.** Thus, in a case involving alleged infringement of contest rules, the court held that because there were a limited number of ways of expressing the rules, given their straightforward nature, only exact copying was prohibited. Otherwise, the first to express the idea in writing would be able to prohibit all later users. *Morrissey v. Procter & Gamble Co.,* 379 F.2d 675 (1st Cir. 1967).

Blank Forms, Titles, Short Phrases, and Common Property

In order to be protected by copyright, a work must contain at least a certain minimum amount of original literary, pictorial, or musical expression. Copyright does not extend to names, titles, short phrases, slogans, clauses such as column headings, or simple checklists. Thus, many books and even movies may share the same title. For example, there are numerous textbooks that share the title *Introduction to Mathematics.* If one person could appropriate a title to the exclusion of others, creativity would be hindered rather than encouraged. Similarly, neither a title nor a slogan such as "You deserve a break today" may be copyrighted (although it may qualify for protection as a trademark or under the law of unfair competition).

Mere variations in typeface, familiar symbols or designs, lettering or coloring, and mere lists of ingredients or contents are not protected by copyright. Similarly, blank forms (such as forms for bank checks, time cards, account books, diaries, scorecards, report forms, address books, and order forms) that are used primarily for recording information rather than conveying information lack sufficient creativity to be copyrightable. Although mere listings of ingredients or contents as in recipes, formulas, or prescriptions are not subject to copyright protection, when the recipe or formula is accompanied by substantial literary expression in the form of an explanation or directions, or when there is a combination of recipes (as in a cookbook), there may be a basis for copyright protection.

Finally, copyright protection does not extend to works consisting entirely of information that is common property containing no original authorship, such as standard calendars, height and weight charts, tape measures and rulers, schedules of sporting events, and lists or tables taken from public documents or other common sources. Thus, a Sierra Club Calendar or Far Side Calendar would be protected to the extent of the photographs or cartoons accompanying the calendars, but the calendars themselves with their standard and readily ascertainable information are not copyrightable.

Public Domain Works

A variety of works are not subject to appropriation by copyright inasmuch as they are said to be in the **public domain,** meaning they are free for all members of the public to use and exploit. The two primary types of works in the public domain are those that arise from expired copyrights and works of the U.S. government.

Expired and Forfeited Copyrights. Copyrights have always been subject to some period of limited duration. Once a copyright expires, or it is forfeited by its owner, it resides in the public domain and is free for all to use. Under the 1909 act, copyrights were subject to an initial period and a period of renewal. Failure to renew the copyright at the appropriate time resulted in a forfeiture of the copyright with the work being placed in the public domain. For works created on or after January 1, 1978, the copyright duration is the life of the author and an additional seventy years. If the work is the product of corporate authorship, it will last for 95 years from publication, or 120 years from its creation, whichever occurs first. These time periods have recently been changed. Until October 1998 and the passage of the Sonny Bono Copyright Term Extension Act, each period of duration was twenty years shorter. In addition to expired or forfeited works being available for all to use, some works are dedicated to public use by their authors. For example, an author could elect not to pursue copyright protection for a work and expressly allow anyone to use it. Some Internet web sites expressly indicate that certain material on the site is so available for all to freely use.

United States Government Works. Pursuant to section 105 of the Copyright Act, copyright protection is not available for any work of the U.S. government or any of its agencies if that work is prepared by an officer or employee of the U.S. government as part of that person's official duties. Thus, federal laws and cases may be freely reproduced and distributed, together with federal regulations, and information and forms from agencies such as the Internal Revenue Service, PTO forms, and forms provided by the Copyright Office.

If the U.S. government commissions special work by an independent contractor, for example, a sculpture for a national park commissioned by an artist not employed by the federal government, the independent contractor will retain copyright in the work (unless he or she agrees that the government can own the copyright). The U.S. government is not precluded from receiving copyrights transferred to it by a third party. Thus, the artist could assign or transfer the copyright to the government.

Works produced by state governments and local governmental bodies are not covered by the Copyright Act, although they may be covered under relevant state law. Thus, because the Copyright Act only refers to the federal government, states and municipalities may own copyrights. Nevertheless, certain information such as cases, statutes, regulations, and ordinances are not copyrightable inasmuch as the public needs free access to such information. In a recent case, however, it was held that Suffolk County, New York, held a copyright in tax maps, even though those maps were compiled and maintained at taxpayer expense. *County of Suffolk v. First American Real Estate Solutions*, 261 F.3d 179 (2d Cir. 2001).

Facts

Facts are not protected by copyright because one who uncovers a fact is not an author or creator. Facts are viewed as "discoveries" and are thus excluded from copyright protection under section 102 of the Act. Moreover, according to *Feist*, facts are not original to a researcher and are not created by a researcher, even if the researcher is the first to reveal them. For example, statistics relating to population, dates of birth and death, and other ascertainable matters cannot be protected by copyright. Thus, the protection afforded to purely factual works, such as books that merely gather statistics or that provide biographies consisting primarily of factual information, is relatively narrow. Although a newscast content may be protected by copyright, the facts recited by newscasters themselves cannot be appropriated by one party to the exclusion of others.

Computing and Measuring Devices

Devices and similar articles designed for computing and measuring cannot be copyrighted. Examples of such uncopyrightable works are slide rules, wheel dials, and perpetual calendar systems. The printed material on the device (numbers, symbols, calibrations, and their arrangements) is not capable of copyright protection because the material is dictated either by the underlying idea (which is uncopyrightable) or some standard formula (which is uncopyrightable). Moreover, a computing or measuring device does not contain a minimum amount of creative authorship—it is merely a means for arriving at a result or reading and does not communicate facts or ideas in and of itself.

Other Copyright Issues: Characters, Scenes a Faire, and Immoral Works

A variety of interesting issues have arisen in copyright law regarding the protectability of characters (both graphical and literary), scenes a faire, and immoral works.

Characters and Scenes a Faire.   Generally, graphical characters, such as cartoon figures like Superman, Mickey Mouse, Dick Tracy, Tarzan, and Doonesbury, are protectable separate and apart from the cartoon strips, films, and books in which they appear. Thus, in one case, a party was enjoined from using a "Wonderman" character on the basis that it infringed the copyright in Superman when the only significant difference between the two characters was the color of their uniforms. *Detective Comics Inc. v. Bruns Publ'ns, Inc.,* 111 F.2d 432 (2d Cir. 1940). On the other hand, the concept of a hero who bravely saves people and the planet from destruction and peril is merely an idea that cannot be protected by copyright. Other heroes with similar characteristics would be permissible as long as they did not appropriate the details of Superman's persona. Cartoon strips, films, and books are also protectable as pictorial works, motion pictures, and literary works, respectively.

In regard to literary characters or characters depicted in a television series or movie, such as James Bond in the Ian Fleming books and movies, Jack Ryan in the Tom Clancy novels, or the Terminator in the *Terminator* movies, if those characters are specifically described and presented, they may be protectable. In 1988, the Ninth Circuit was called upon to determine whether the television series *The A-Team* infringed a screenplay called *Cargo.* Noting that both shared a common approach (adventure actions portraying Vietnam veterans), the court held that this idea alone was unprotectable. There was little similarity in terms of plot, dialogue, or setting. The fact that both involved action-adventure heroes was not sufficient to show infringement. *Olson v. NBC,* 855 F.2d 1446 (9th Cir. 1988). This reasoning is a further illustration of the rule that ideas are not protectable, while the expressions of those

ideas are. In sum, basic character types are not copyrightable; characters that are uniquely developed and display some level of novelty, however, such as Rocky Balboa, are copyrightable.

Certain standard or stereotypical characters and incidents, called **scenes a faire** (literally, "scenes which must be done"), are generally excluded from copyright protection. For example, stock characters, standard literary devices, common expressions, and incidents are viewed as uncopyrightable scenes a faire. For example, in one case involving police fiction, a court held that foot chases, morale problems of police officers, and the "familiar figure of the Irish cop" are common themes in such works and are thus unprotectable scenes a faire. Similarly, the mazes, scoring table, tunnels, and dots of the "Pac-Man" computer game have been held to be scenes a faire, protectable only from identical copying.

Immoral Works.   Although the Trademark Act forbids registration of immoral, disparaging, or scandalous works, no such prohibition exists in the Copyright Act. Generally, Congress has been reluctant to place restrictions on the copyrightability of certain matter believing it would chill First Amendment rights. Thus, even offensive and immoral books, plays, and songs are copyrightable.

COMPILATIONS, COLLECTIONS, AND DERIVATIVE WORKS

Compilations

An author often selects certain items and groups them together in a new presentation. For example, a book may be published that presents lists of Oscar winners or tables of statistics and data that are not themselves copyrightable. Such a work is called a **compilation.** According to section 101 of the Copyright Act, a compilation is a work formed by the collection and assembling of preexisting materials or of data that are selected, coordinated, or arranged in such a way that the resulting work as a whole constitutes an original work of authorship. Compilations are protected by copyright if there is original authorship in the selection or arrangement of the material.

Thus, although the material that comprises the compilation is not original (and therefore is not copyrightable), the manner of its selection and arrangement results in an original work. For example, a type of day planner that consists of calendars, blank forms for appointments, entries, maps, lists of area codes, and time zones may be copyrightable as a compilation due to its unique arrangement, even though the parts that comprise it (calendars, blank forms, and so forth) are not copyrightable because they lack originality or are standard devices. As another example, a book of lists or an information-based almanac is likely comprised merely of facts or raw data that are not copyrightable in and of themselves; however, the unique arrangement of those facts into a select and coordinated system is copyrightable. The author has reviewed certain facts, selected the particular facts to include, and then arranged or presented the facts so that they are interesting or useful to the reader. It is this selection that shows sufficient creativity and originality that copyright protection is provided for that arrangement or selection. The underlying facts themselves, however, remain uncopyrightable.

As seen in *Feist,* in which an alphabetically arranged telephone directory was held not copyrightable, not every selection of facts or compilation will pass muster. As always, a certain level of creativity, namely, "originality," is required. In *Feist,* the Supreme Court recognized that while the requirement of originality is not stringent, the arrangement of facts cannot be so mechanical and routine as to demonstrate no creativity whatsoever. The Court noted that taking data and listing telephone subscribers alphabetically by surname resulted in "a garden-variety white pages directory, devoid of even the slightest trace of creativity."

Collections

According to section 101 of the Copyright Act, the term *compilation* includes collective works. A **collective work** is a work, such as a periodical issue, anthology, or encyclopedia, in which a number of contributions, constituting separate and independent works in themselves, are assembled into a collective whole. Thus, a CD containing musical compositions by various artists and called *The Golden Age of Rock* would be a collective work, as would a book of selected short stories dealing with sports, an anthology of poems by twentieth-century American poets, or selected film clips showing the greatest comedy routines of the 1950s. Even when the works assembled into the collection are public domain works (for example, folk songs or spirituals), the resulting work qualifies for protection as a collection. In the cases in which works that comprise the collection are copyrighted (for example, individual poems or songs), permission must be obtained from the individual copyright owners to reproduce their works by assembling them in the new collection. The new authorship in the collection extends to the particular selection and arrangement of the poems and songs but not to the poems or songs themselves.

The difference between a compilation and a collection is that the matter comprising the compilation is not copyrightable (think lists of facts, such as found in an almanac), while the matter comprising the collective work (think short stories, photos, or poems) is copyrightable.

Derivative Works

A **derivative work** is one that is based on (or derived from) one or more already existing works, such as a translation, dramatization, fictionalization, or any other form in which a work may be recast, transformed, or adapted. Thus, the author of a derivative work transforms or somehow changes a preexisting work (while the author of a compilation or collective work assembles or arranges preexisting materials). The resulting work is copyrightable if it includes original work of authorship and if the original material was not used unlawfully.

Derivative works, also known as *new versions,* include such works as musical arrangements, motion picture versions, abridgments, and condensations. Additionally, any work consisting of editorial revisions, annotations, elaborations, or other modifications that, as a whole, represent an original work, is a derivative work subject to copyright protection.

The following examples show some of the many different types of derivative works:

- a television drama of *The Glass Menagerie* based on the earlier play by Tennessee Williams;
- a motion picture of *Fried Green Tomatoes* based on the earlier novel by Fannie Flagg;
- a play of *In Cold Blood* based on the work by Truman Capote;
- AOL version 8.0 based on earlier versions;
- a television dramatization of *The Gambler* based on the song by Kenny Rogers;
- a novel in English, such as *Doctor Zhivago* (translated from a book originally published in Russian);
- the movie *Chicago* based on the earlier play; and
- the movie *Rocky II* based on the original *Rocky* movie.

To be copyrightable, the derivative work must be different enough from the original to be regarded as a new work or must contain a substantial amount of new material. Making minor changes or additions of little substance to a preexisting work will not qualify the work as a new version for copyright purposes. The new material must be original and copyrightable in itself.

The copyright in a derivative work covers only the additions, changes, or other new material appearing for the first time in the work. It does not extend to any preexisting material and does not imply a copyright in that material. The copyright in the derivative work relates only to the new, independent work and does not affect or extend the nature, scope, or duration of copyright protection for the original work. Thus, if a new preface or foreword is prepared for a new printing of John Grisham's novel *The King of Torts,* only the new material is independently protected and owned by the new author. John Grisham retains the rights in the original work. One cannot extend the length of protection for a copyrighted work by creating a derivative work. A work that has fallen in the public domain (that is, one that is no longer protected by copyright) may be used for a derivative work, but the copyright in the derivative work will not restore or revive the copyright of the public domain material; neither will it prevent anyone else from using the same public domain material for another derivative work.

Only the owner of copyright in a work has the right to prepare or to authorize someone else to create a new version of that work. The owner is generally the author or someone who has obtained rights from the author.

TRIVIA

- Nearly 6 percent of all employment in the United States is in copyright-related industries.
- Between 1977 and 2001, U.S. copyright-related industries' share of the gross domestic product grew more than twice as fast as the remainder of the U.S. economy.
- In *Arden v. Columbia Pictures Industries, Inc.,* 908 F. Supp. 1248 (E.D.N.Y. 1995), the court considered whether plaintiff's novel of a man trapped in a repeating day, forced to live the same day over and over, infringed the famous movie *Groundhog Day,* produced twelve years later. The court held that there was no infringement because the works were not substantially similar. While the *ideas* expressed were the same, the *expression* of those ideas was quite different because the novel was dark and introspective and featured witchcraft while the movie was a romantic comedy. Any similarity between the two related only to unprotectable ideas, concepts, or abstractions.
- Even silence may be copyrightable. Artist John Cage, now deceased, recorded "4'33"" (an entirely silent piece lasting four minutes and thirty-three seconds). Whenever "4'33"" has been recorded by other artists, as it was by Frank Zappa in 1993 (for a tribute album to Cage), royalties have been paid to use the silent work.

CHAPTER SUMMARY

Copyright protects original works of authorship that are fixed in a tangible form of expression such that they can be perceived, communicated, or reproduced either directly or with the aid of a machine or device. The requirement of originality means that the work must be independently created by the author; it need not be the only work of its kind. Copyrightable works include the following categories: literary works; musical works (including any accompanying words); dramatic works (including any accompanying words); pantomimes and choreographic works; pictorial, graphic, and sculptural works; motion pictures and other audiovisual works; sound recordings; and architectural works.

Some matter is uncopyrightable, such as ideas, useful articles, blank forms, titles, short phrases, common property (such as height and weight charts), lists of ingredients, facts, and matters in the public domain, including works whose copyrights have expired and works of the U.S. government.

A compilation of otherwise uncopyrightable material may be protectable (such as a book of lists). Similarly, a collection of other copyrightable material (such as the collection of film clips that made up the movie *That's Entertainment*) may itself be copyrightable as a new work. Finally, a work that is recast (such as a movie made from a book) is copyrightable, in regard to the new material, as a derivative work.

CASE ILLUSTRATION—NONPROTECTABILITY OF IDEAS

Case: *Nichols v. Universal Pictures Corp.*, 45 F.2d 119, 121 (2d Cir. 1930)

Facts: Plaintiff alleged that defendant's motion picture about an Irish family infringed his earlier play about a Jewish family.

Holding: There was no infringement because the parts of the two works that were similar were only general themes, motives, and ideas in which there can be no copyright. "If Twelfth Night were copyrighted, it is quite possible that a second comer might so closely imitate Sir Toby Belch or Malvolio as to infringe, but it would not be enough that for one of his characters he cast a riotous knight who kept wassail to the discomfort of his household, or a vain and foppish steward who became amorous of his mistress. These would be no more than Shakespeare's 'ideas' in the play and as little capable of monopoly as Einstein's Doctrine of Relativity. . . . It follows that the less developed the characters; the less they can be copyrighted; that is the penalty an author must bear for making them too indistinctly."

CASE STUDY AND ACTIVITIES

Case Study.   Watson Inc. has built a new palace to be built at Fantasy Fun Adventure. The structure has a variety of unique features, such as turrets and secret passageways. In connection with the palace, Watson has prepared a brochure that merely lists the different rooms in the palace in alphabetical order. No descriptions of the rooms are provided. A book entitled *Adventures at the Palace* has been prepared and will be sold at the park together with a cassette of songs related to a character called Princess Penny. Watson has a plan to create additional characters that will live at the palace and who will sing a variety of songs. A mime performs street performances at several locations throughout the park during the day. Several brightly painted cars are used in the park to transport characters and the mime to various locations in the park for live performances. Finally, Watson has developed a system for moving people through lines and queues at the park in a more efficient manner.

Activities.   Discuss the copyrightability of each of the above works.

ROLE OF PARALEGAL

The role of paralegals prior to preparing a copyright application will likely be limited to legal research relating to copyrightability so that clients can be advised about whether works created by them qualify for copyright protection and to ensure clients do not infringe the rights of others. Research may focus on any of the following topics:

CHAPTER SIX

Building Your Research Framework

Your literature review, including preparatory reading for the purpose of research, has three major functions: (1) To search for a suitable research topic and establish some specific research questions. While obtaining needed information, you may try to identify the major issues in an interest field, select and narrow down to a particular research problem, articulate your research purpose and objectives, and justify your choice by providing a rationale on the importance of your intended research project. (2) To provide a thorough understanding of the concepts involved in the research questions with the purpose to lay a solid theoretical groundwork for your research. You will also need to synthesize and generalize previous empirical findings in order to derive appropriate hypotheses for further research. (3) To supply some methodological clues by evaluating previous research designs and identifying major technical issues if any.

It is important for your literature review to show the context of scientific knowledge and indicate how well your work will fit in that picture. Your reading assignment, however, is not merely a bibliographic indexing of the substantive research findings in your field. The need to configure your research also requires you to tease out from all the reading some sort of framework, under which you can readily derive meaningful hypotheses and develop innovative approaches to your study. The notes you take during reading, therefore, can be classified into three categories: (1) those about the substantive issues and research findings that are "hot" or of potential interest to you; (2) those concerning the conceptual and theoretical bases of the field; and (3) those regarding methodology and technical problems in conducting related research.

We have talked about how to establish research questions through a thorough

ROLE OF PARALEGAL (cont'd)

- whether a work is an original, fixed work of authorship;
- what type of work of authorship an author's work is, for example, a literary work, dramatic work, musical work, or pictorial work;
- whether the work is subject to protection as an expression rather than a mere idea, system, or process;
- whether the work is excluded from copyright protection because it consists of blank forms, titles, slogans, common property, or facts;
- whether the work is excluded from copyright protection as a work of the U.S. government; and
- whether the author's work is a compilation, collective work, or derivative work.

INTERNET RESOURCES

Federal laws relating
  to copyright: http://www.ll.georgetown.edu
                           http://www.findlaw.com; and
                           http://www.copyright.gov/title17/circ92.pdf

Copyright Office: http://www.loc.gov/copyright or
                           http://www.copyright.gov

General information: http://www.law.cornell.edu/topics/copyright.html (site of Cornell
                           Law School);
                           http://www.findlaw.com; http://www.megalaw.com; and
                           http://www.csusa.org (site of Copyright Society of the U.S.A., a
                           nonprofit corporation organized in 1953 to foster interest in and
                           study of copyright law)

DISCUSSION QUESTIONS

1. Classify the following as likely copyrightable or not copyrightable:
   - a blank form for a redeemable coupon;
   - a live broadcast of a radio program;
   - a speech written for the secretary of defense;
   - a new sculpture of a kitten;
   - the artwork for the cover of a CD;
   - the pagination of a book;
   - a new method of calculating the value of a business;

- a list of the birthplaces of U.S. presidents;
- the slogan, "Just Do It"; and
- the Copyright Act.

2. Would a highly stylized electric mixer be copyrightable? Discuss.

3. An essay has been published in a magazine that contains highly offensive views about various minority groups. Is the essay copyrightable? Discuss.

4. If two artists each paint an oil painting of Niagara Falls, which painting receives copyright protection? Discuss.

5. A writer has written a script for a new sitcom based upon a group of single friends living in a large city and their work and romantic adventures. Would such a script infringe the well-known sitcom *Friends*? Discuss.

6. Identify the following as a compilation, collection, or derivative work:
   - a television drama based upon a novel;
   - a book entitled *Facts about the Presidents* that includes tables of information relating to the birthplaces of the presidents, their likes and dislikes, and families;
   - a book of photographs entitled *The Tragedy of War* and showing photographs of war-torn countries;
   - a sculpture based upon a drawing of a woman;
   - a cookbook entitled *Best Home-made Recipes of the South;* and
   - a directory listing the best colleges in the United States according to several criteria, including SAT requirements, location, and social life on campus.

CHAPTER 11

The Rights Afforded by Copyright Law

CHAPTER OVERVIEW

Under the Copyright Act, a copyright owner has a "bundle" of rights: the right to reproduce, adapt, distribute, perform, and display the work to the exclusion of others. Thus, copyright owners have a full complement of ways to commercially exploit their works. There are, however, some limitations on these exclusive rights. For example, once certain works have been distributed, under the "first sale doctrine," the subsequent owner is free to use or resell the item without liability for infringement. Similarly, some activities do not constitute infringement, for example, uses for certain educational activities, noncommercial fund-raising, or for religious worship. Rights for sound recordings are considerably more limited than rights for other works, such as literary or musical works. Authors of fine arts such as paintings and sculptures may also have "moral rights," meaning rights personal to themselves that survive the sale of their work so that authorship of the work is forever attributed to them and the work is not mutilated or altered, which would prejudice their reputation as artists and creators.

INTRODUCTION

Section 106 of the Copyright Act provides that, subject to certain exceptions, the owner of a copyright has the exclusive rights to do and to authorize any of the following:

- to reproduce the copyrighted work in copies or phonorecords;
- to prepare derivative works based on the copyrighted work;
- to distribute copies or phonorecords of the copyrighted work to the public;
- to perform the copyrighted work publicly (in the case of certain works);
- to display the copyrighted work publicly (in the case of literary, musical, dramatic and choreographic works, pantomimes,

and pictorial, graphic, or sculptural works); and

- to perform the copyrighted work publicly by means of a digital audio transmission (in the case of sound recordings).

Unless exemptions exist, unauthorized exercise of any of these rights by another is an infringement of the owner's copyright in the work, whether or not the owner has secured a copyright registration and whether or not the owner has published the work. Any of these exclusive rights may be transferred and they may be owned separately. For example, the composer of a song may authorize one person to perform it publicly and another to create a television show based on the song. Each right is separately transferable.

These exclusive rights, usually referred to as a "bundle," will be examined in this chapter.

RIGHTS OF REPRODUCTION

The most fundamental of the rights granted to copyright owners is the right to reproduce the work, thereby excluding others from reproducing the work. A violation of the Copyright Act occurs whether or not the violator profits by the reproduction. Consider the warning displayed at the beginning of every video movie you rent that reproduction is a violation of the Copyright Act. Thus, making a copy of the movie *Lord of the Rings* violates the owner's right to reproduction, even if you only intend to view the movie privately.

Only the owner has the right to reproduce the work. Secretly taping a concert, taking pictures at a performance, or recording a simultaneously recorded speech all violate the owner's right to reproduce the work even if there is no later sale or distribution of the work.

At the suggestion of Congress, in 1978 a group of authors, publishers, and users estab-lished a not-for-profit entity called Copyright Clearance Center (CCC) to serve as a clearing-house granting rights to reproduce and distribute books and periodicals. Authors register their works with the CCC, which then grants licenses to academic, government, and corporate users to copy and distribute the works. The CCC grants permission or licenses to use works and then collects royalty fees, which are distributed to the authors. Companies that photocopy articles from journals and magazines often enter into licensing arrangements with the CCC so they can make copies of articles for internal distribution within the company and remain in compliance with copyright law. The CCC is located at 222 Rosewood Drive, Danvers, MA 01923. Its telephone number is (978) 750-8400, and its Internet address is http://www.copyright.com.

RIGHTS TO PREPARE DERIVATIVE WORKS

Section 106 of the Copyright Act provides that the owner of a copyright has the exclusive right to prepare derivative works based upon the copyrighted work. This right is often referred to as the right to adapt the original work.

As discussed in Chapter 10, a derivative work is broadly defined as a work based upon one or more preexisting works, such as a translation, dramatization, fictionalization, motion picture version, abridgment, condensation, or any other form in which a work may be recast, transformed, or adapted. A work consisting of editorial revisions, annotations, elaborations, or other modifications is also a derivative work, if the new material represents original work of authorship.

The copyright owner thus has the right to exclude others from adapting his or her work or creating works based on the owner's work. For example, George Lucas has the right to exclude others from making sequels to his *Star Wars* works. Stephen King can exclude others from making a play or a television movie based upon his books. John Mellencamp can prevent another from making a movie based upon his songs. Of course, if the authors of the works consent, others may be granted rights to adapt a work. Thus, many of author Danielle Steel's works of fiction have been made into television movies, and the novel *The Horse Whisperer* was made into a motion picture. The new derivative work is separately copyrightable in regard to its new elements. Copyright in the derivative, however, does not affect the copyright in the original. Thus, the new elements, lines, characters, and so forth that are added to the movie *The Horse Whisperer* are separately copyrightable as a derivative work, while the original author retains rights to any material in the novel *The Horse Whisperer.*

RIGHTS OF DISTRIBUTION AND THE FIRST SALE DOCTRINE

Section 106(3) of the Copyright Act provides that the owner of a copyright has the exclusive right to distribute copies or phonorecords of the work to the public by sale or other transfer of ownership, or by rental, lease, or lending. A violation of the distribution right can arise solely from the act of distribution itself even if the distributor did not make an unlawful copy or know the copy being distributed was unauthorized. Thus, Blockbuster Video stores can be liable for violating an owner's right to distribute a movie, even if Blockbuster does not know that the movie was placed on videocassette or DVD without the owner's authority. Authors often grant permission to others to distribute their works, including granting licenses through entities such as the CCC discussed earlier.

One limitation on a copyright owner's sole right of distribution is found in section 109 of the Copyright Act, which provides that once the author has parted with ownership of copyrighted material, the new owner of a lawfully made copy can treat the object as his or her own and can then freely use, sell, lease, or lend the work to another. Just as in trademark law (see Chapter 6), where the first sale "exhausts" the trademark owner's right to a mark, in copyright law, the copyright owner's sale of an item exhausts his or her exclusive right to distribute the work. Thus, purchasing a copy of the book *Seabiscuit* or purchasing a videocassette of the movie *Lord of the Rings* gives the new owner the right to lend the book or movie to a friend, resell the work at a garage sale, or even destroy it. The **first sale doctrine** does not apply to or limit the author's exclusive rights to prepare derivative works or rights of public performance and display.

The copyright owner, however, while having parted with distribution rights, retains other rights, such as the right to reproduce the work, adapt it, and prepare derivative works based on it. Thus, in the above example, the purchaser of the book *Seabiscuit* does not have the right to make a movie of the book or to prepare a second updated version of the book based upon the original. The original owner, the author, retains such derivative rights, having lost only the right to distribution through the first sale doctrine.

Courts have struggled with the question whether the first sale doctrine applies to goods imported into the United States. Section 602 of the Copyright Act provides that importing copies or phonorecords of a work acquired abroad into the United States without the copyright owner's authorization is an infringement of the copyright owner's exclusive right to distribute his or her works. In a 1998 decision, the U.S. Supreme Court held that once a first sale occurs, even abroad, the copyright owner's right to distribute is exhausted. Thereafter, the owner of the work or product can resell the item freely, without permission of the copyright owner. *Quality King Distributors v. L'anza*

Research International, Inc., 523 U.S. 135 (1998). See Chapter 16 for further discussion of this topic.

Exceptions to the First Sale Doctrine

There are some exceptions or limitations to the doctrine that once a copyright owner parts with ownership he or she has lost the right to distribute his or her work.

- The first sale doctrine applies only to lawfully made copies and phonorecords. Thus, if Border's Books comes into possession of a pirated or unauthorized version of *Memoirs of a Geisha,* resale to others would violate the author's rights of distribution, even if Border's Books did not know it possessed a pirated version of the book.

- Due to a special statutory exception, enacted largely at the urging of the music industry, the first sale doctrine does not apply to commercial rentals of records and certain computer programs. Those works cannot be commercially rented. Prior to the enactment of 17 U.S.C. § 109, record stores would rent records and CDs to customers who then went home and made copies of the record or CD on a blank tape for a fraction of the price of buying the original. Because of the threat to the music industry, this rental practice is now banned. Thus, Shania Twain can prohibit the purchaser of her records or albums from renting those works commercially, generally because commercial renting of sound recordings would seriously undermine creativity and deprive copyright owners of revenue. Nonprofit libraries and other similar institutions may, however, lend or rent out sound recordings and computer programs. Additionally, if the computer program is

incapable of being copied, it can be rented. Thus, Blockbuster Video can rent out computer video games to consumers because consumers are generally unable to duplicate or copy the video games. Finally, this limitation does not apply to computers that are part of other machines or products. Thus, a car can be rented by a consumer inasmuch as the computer programs, such as an onboard navigational system that makes up part of the car, cannot be readily copied and are integrated into the car itself.

The *Droit de Suite* Doctrine

Droit de suite is a doctrine recognized in many foreign countries, but not generally in the United States, that allows authors of works of fine art to share in the appreciation of the value of a work. Under this doctrine, if a painter sells a painting for $25,000 and the painting is later sold for $100,000, the painter would be able to share in the $75,000 appreciation of the work. California has enacted a statute called the California Resale Royalties Act (Cal. Civ. Code § 986), which accomplishes the same goal, by allowing artists residing in California to collect 5 percent of any resale price for their works, if the work (which must be an original painting, sculpture, drawing, or an original work of art in glass) is sold for at least $1,000 and is sold for more than the reseller paid for it.

Thus, in California, the first sale of a work of fine art does not exhaust the owner's distribution right because the original owner can share in the proceeds of a later sale. Many experts have questioned the constitutionality of the California statute inasmuch as the Constitution provides exclusive authority to Congress (not the individual states) to promote science and arts through copyright law. Moreover, the California law may ultimately damage the California art market if buyers avoid purchasing art in

California in order to circumvent the 5 percent royalty they may later need to pay an artist.

RIGHTS TO PERFORM THE WORK PUBLICLY

Section 106(4) of the Copyright Act provides that in the case of literary, musical, dramatic, and choreographic works, pantomimes, and motion pictures and other audiovisual works, the copyright owner has the exclusive right to perform the copyrighted work publicly. The word *perform* means to recite, render, play, dance, or act a work, either directly or by means of a device or process to show its images in any sequence or to make the sounds accompanying it audible. Thus, if an individual reads the copyrighted novel *Bridget Jones's Diary* on the Oprah Winfrey show, there have been two performances: one in the reading of the work before the live audience and the other in the transmission of it by the television show.

The copyright owner's right to perform is limited to public performances. To perform a work publicly means to perform the work at a place open to the public or at any place where a substantial number of persons outside of a normal circle of a family and its social acquaintances is gathered or to transmit or communicate the work to the public or to a place open to the public (again, outside of a small family or social setting), whether the performance is live or recorded. Performances at places such as clubs, lodges, schools, and summer camps are "public performances" subject to copyright protection. Thus, if Van Morrison sings a song copyrighted by Bob Dylan at a nightclub, theatre, in concert, on Howard Stern's radio show, or on the *Tonight* television show, he has violated Bob Dylan's right of public performance. Note that if Howard Stern's radio show is live in New York City but taped for later transmission in Los Angeles, there have been two separate public performances. The transmission by radio or tele-vision broadcast is a public performance even though listeners receive the transmission at different times and places and in the privacy of their own homes or cars. If Van Morrison sings the same song for a small group of friends and family gathered at his home, there is no violation because there has been no public performance.

If a room or facility is open to the public and a copyrighted movie or song is performed therein, there has been a violation of the owner's exclusive right to public performance of his or her work. Courts have held, however, that a private viewing or transmission of a rented movie in a guest's hotel room is not a public performance, and such a viewing is treated the same as rental of a movie for home viewing. *See Columbia Pictures Indus., Inc. v. Professional Real Estate Investors, Inc.*, 866 F.2d 278 (9th Cir. 1989).

Exception for Sound Recordings

The exclusive right of a copyright owner to perform his or her work publicly does not extend to sound recordings. Recall from Chapter 10 that a sound recording usually protects the arrangement or production of a song, while a musical work is a musical composition and its accompanying words. When a radio station plays or transmits a record of Frank Sinatra singing "My Way," a song written by Paul Anka, there is no violation of Frank Sinatra's or the record company's rights; however, there has been a violation of Paul Anka's right to perform the work publicly because he is the author of the underlying musical composition (assuming Paul Anka did not authorize the performance). The likely rationale for this rule is to ensure that radio stations are not burdened by paying double royalties in order to play most songs.

Other Exceptions

According to section 110 of the Copyright Act, the following performances, many of which relate to nonprofit educational or charitable activities, do not violate a copyright owner's exclusive right to perform his or her work publicly:

- **Face-to-face teaching.** The Copyright Act protects performances or displays of a work by instructors or pupils in the course of face-to-face teaching activities of a nonprofit educational institution and certain instructional or educational broadcasting by governmental bodies or nonprofit educational institutions engaged in systematic instructional activities. Thus, students in a drama class can perform a copyrighted play without liability. The Copyright Office has recommended to Congress that this provision be amended to allow for distance learning as well as face-to-face instruction (see Chapter 15);

- **Religious services.** Performances of a nondramatic literary or musical work in the course of services at a place of worship or other religious assembly are permissible;

- **Promotion of records.** The Copyright Act allows performances of nondramatic musical works (namely, the playing of recorded music) at retail stores, such as record stores and stores that sell radios and CD players, to promote sales;

- **Nonprofit performances.** Live (not transmitted) performances of nondramatic literary or musical works for noncommercial purposes are permissible if there are no admission charges or, if there are charges, the net proceeds are used for charitable purposes and the author is notified so he or she can object prior to the performance (this exception promotes benefit and fund-raising concerts for educational, religious, or other charitable purposes);

- **Veterans and fraternal organizations.** The Copyright Act allows performances of nondramatic literary or musical works at social functions organized by a nonprofit veterans' organization or a nonprofit fraternal organization to which the public is not invited and the proceeds of which are used for charitable purposes and not for financial gain;

- **Agricultural and horticultural fairs.** Performances of a nondramatic musical work by a governmental body or nonprofit agricultural or horticultural association in the course of an annual agricultural or horticultural fair or exhibition are permissible;

- **Small commercial establishments.** The Copyright Act allows transmissions of radio and television broadcasts in small businesses, restaurants, and bars (less than 2,000 square feet for non-eating establishments and less than 3,750 square feet for eating establishments), thus allowing such establishments to play radios and televisions for the enjoyment of their customers without obtaining licenses, as long as no direct fee is charged and there is no further retransmission. Note that this exception applies only to radio and television transmissions—setting up a CD player and playing a tape or CD would be prohibited as a violation of the copyright owner's exclusive rights. Businesses whose square footage exceeds the stated amounts also qualify for the exemption if they use six or fewer speakers or four smaller televisions;

- **Transmissions for handicapped persons.** The Copyright Act allows certain transmissions for the benefit of blind and deaf persons; and

- **Electronic audiovisual games.** Displays of electronic audiovisual games by coin-operated equipment are allowed under 17 U.S.C. § 109(e).

Note that many of the exceptions relate to "nondramatic literary or musical works," meaning books and records and excluding plays, motion pictures, and operas. Thus, showing a motion picture at a religious service (even if it is related to religion) violates the owner's rights of performance and is prohibited.

Performing Rights Societies

Because the playing of music by CDs and radio in theatres, clubs, or large establishments is a public performance (requiring permission of the copyright owner of the music) and because the copyright owner of the music would have a difficult time keeping track of each time his or her musical work is publicly performed to enforce his or her copyright rights, performing rights societies came into existence to reduce the administrative burdens for both those seeking to perform the work and copyright owners.

Composers, lyricists, and publishers usually join one of three performing rights societies that grant licenses to others to publicly perform the works of their members. The societies then collect and distribute royalty fees for the licenses granted.

A **performing rights society** acts as an agent for musical copyright owners and issues licenses in their behalf. The best known of the performing rights societies are ASCAP (American Society of Composers, Authors, and Publishers) and BMI (Broadcast Music, Inc.). ASCAP and BMI are the dominant organizations in the field, and together their repertoires include nearly all the world's copyrighted music. A smaller society is SESAC (Society of European Stage Authors and Composers). These societies issue blanket licenses to commercial establishments, radio and television stations, and clubs, allowing them to play any of the works in the societies' repertoires or inventories for a fixed fee, thus eliminating the

need for a large commercial establishment or radio station to negotiate thousands of separate licenses to play music owned by others. The societies charge license fees and then distribute the collected royalty fees to the thousands of composers, authors, and publishers they represent. ASCAP and BMI monitor and visit radio stations, clubs, restaurants, skating rinks, conventions, shopping malls, gyms, and other commercial establishments to ensure that copyrighted works are not being publicly performed without license. ASCAP, BMI, and SESAC function in granting licenses to perform music the way the Copyright Clearance Center does in granting licenses to others to reproduce and distribute written works. Information about the societies can be found at their web sites, www.ascap.com, www.bmi.com, and www.sesac.com, respectively.

Commercial establishments such as hotels, stores, and other businesses may also be engaged in public performances when they "pipe in" music throughout the establishment or play music when callers are placed on hold, whether the music is from the owner's own record or CD or is music being simultaneously played on the radio. Although smaller commercial establishments are exempt, as discussed earlier, if larger enterprises pipe in such music, there has been a public performance for which permission or a license must be sought. Thus, in *Sailor Music v. Gap Stores, Inc.,* 516 F. Supp. 923 (S.D.N.Y.), *aff'd,* 688 F.2d 84 (2d Cir. 1981), the Gap Stores were held to have publicly performed musical works in violation of the owners' copyrights where two stores had several speakers recessed in their ceilings that broadcast songs and the stores encompassed an average of 3,500 square feet of space.

Generally, fees charged by ASCAP and BMI are determined by square footage, room capacity, revenue generated by the license, or the number of trunk lines a company has coming into its offices that play music on hold.

RIGHTS TO DISPLAY THE WORK PUBLICLY

Section 106(5) of the Copyright Act provides that in the case of all copyrighted works other than sound recordings and works of architecture, the copyright owner has the exclusive right to display the work publicly. A display is "public" under the same circumstances in which a performance is "public," namely, if it occurs at a place open to the public or at a place where a substantial number of persons outside of the normal circle of a family and its social acquaintances is gathered or if it is transmitted or communicated to the public or to a place open to the public (again, outside of a small family or social setting), whether the display is live or recorded.

Exception for Owners of Lawful Copies

Just as the first sale doctrine allows the owner of a lawful copy of a book to sell it or lend it to another, a similar right allows the owner of a lawful copy of a work (other than a sound recording or architectural work) to display that copy publicly, either directly or by the projection of no more than one image at a time, to viewers present at the place where the copy is located. Thus, a museum or gallery that has purchased a painting or sculpture may display that work in the museum or gallery but may not display it by multiple displays, such as displays on multiple computer screens, or by some other method of transmission (for example, closed circuit television transmission) to viewers at another location. By way of illustration, a department store cannot have a bank of screens that display several multiple slide projections of a painting even if it has purchased the painting. Only one image at a time can be displayed to viewers present at the place where the copy is located. Thus, as an exception to the first sale doctrine, the original painter, sculptor, or other author retains the right to display the copy in a way that makes it available either in multiple images or to persons in places other than where a lawfully sold copy is located.

Other Exceptions

Other exceptions to the copyright owner's exclusive right to display are identical to certain of the exceptions to the copyright owner's exclusive right to perform discussed earlier, namely, the following:

- displays in face-to-face teaching activities of nonprofit educational institutions and certain transmissions that are part of systematic instructional activities of a governmental body or nonprofit educational institution;
- displays in the course of religious worship and services;
- displays in small establishments.

RIGHTS TO PERFORM COPYRIGHTED SOUND RECORDINGS

The rights in sound recordings (the author of which is the performer whose performance is fixed or the record producer, or both) are quite limited and are far different from the rights in musical works (composed music including words, on sheet music, in records, or on CDs). The exclusive rights given to owners of copyrighted works in section 106 of the Copyright Act to perform and display their works do not extend to sound recordings. Once a sound recording exists, others may perform the recording without liability. Thus, radio and television stations can play sound recordings without liability (although they likely have entered into blanket licenses with ASCAP and BMI so that the composers and authors of the underlying musical works are being compensated inasmuch as the owners of copyright in musical literature review. In the following, we will discuss how to establish a research framework that will help you maintain conceptual clarity, add theoretical power, and achieve research efficiency. To expedite the building of such a framework, it is a good habit to keep the full citation with the original notes and quotes of important ideas when you review the literature.

The conceptual framework

Your research cannot go well without a clear understanding of the meaning of the concepts you use. The definition and explanation of all the major concepts and constructs constitute a necessary and basic part of your research framework. You need to make sure that the terms you use do not confuse you and your readers. In practice, you are often required to explicate your research terminology in due places of your document (i.e., your thesis, dissertation, or another kind of research report). This is generally referred to as conceptualization in research methodology.

There is more than one definition for almost everything that comes under your study. Your job, then, is to give a full discussion of the various meanings (at least the most commonly used ones) of each key concept in your study. Based on this discussion, you can choose, synthesize, or create a new definition for general use. More often than not, you also need to give some specification in order to use the concept in the particular setting and for your particular research purpose. We will further discuss this in terms of the operationalization of your research ideas and the measurement of your research variables in the next chapter.

If yours is a relational study involving more than one variable (bi- or multi-variate analysis) rather than a single-variable (univariate) test, you should pay special attention to the conceptual relationship between and among different variables. Since you have a particular set of concepts and constructs involved in the study, the way you operationally define them will have a significant impact on your results. You should plan as a whole based on your research purpose and establish a clear understanding of the definitions of the variables in relation to one another. The key point to operationalization in such circumstances is how to avoid potential measurement confounding of the analysis results. We will further explore the issue in chapter eleven.

A concept is a generalized idea of some constant or variable thing. If it is a variable thing, the concept is regarded as representing some kind of "variable."

works are granted exclusive unlimited rights to perform their works).

Although the owner of a sound recording has the exclusive right of reproduction, this right is quite limited and allows the owner merely to produce actual physical copies and thereby prohibits pirates from making bootleg copies of a record.

Some experts believe these limited rights available to the owners of copyrighted sound recordings are meant to relieve those who would pay royalties (such as radio and television stations) from the multiple burdens of having to pay royalties to the composer or author of the underlying musical work as well as to the record companies that produce the sound recording and the performer who performs the work.

In 1995, Congress granted a new and sixth exclusive right to copyright owners, relating strictly to sound recordings. The Digital Performance Right in Sound Recordings Act, 17 U.S.C. § 106(b), provides that owners of sound recordings have the exclusive right to perform their works publicly by means of digital audio transmission. This grant recognized that new technologies, whereby one can easily download a digital transmission of a song and never pay for a tape, record, or CD, needed to be addressed. Thus, the new protection afforded to the owners of copyright in sound recordings is protection against public performances of their sound recordings by subscription services (such as transmission by a cable service that charges recipients for the service) and interactive services (such as services that allow a person to request by telephone or e-mail and then receive a digital transmission of a sound recording). However, the owner of a sound recording cannot preclude others from publicly performing the work (other than by digital audio transmission) because the owner does not have rights of performance. Additional issues relating to the downloading of music through the Internet and music file sharing are discussed in Chapter 15.

OTHER LIMITATIONS ON EXCLUSIVE RIGHTS

In addition to the exemptions to copyright owners' exclusive rights already discussed (namely, exemptions for use of works for certain educational purposes, religious worship, noncommercial charitable purposes, limited transmission for small establishments, performances at fairs, and performances for the handicapped), there are a few other limitations on a copyright owner's exclusive rights to his or her work:

- libraries or archives may reproduce and distribute one copy of a copyrighted work and maintain three copies for preservation if there is no commercial advantage, the library is open to the public, and a copyright notice is placed on the work;
- libraries and archives are not liable for infringement for unauthorized photocopying of copyrighted works as long as a notice is placed on the equipment warning that the making of copies may be subject to copyright law;
- secondary transmissions whereby hotels and other establishments relay radio and television transmissions to private guest rooms without charge are acceptable; and
- radio and television stations that have entered into lawful arrangements to perform works may make one temporary or "ephemeral" recording of the work so that it is easier for them to transmit it and may preserve it for archival purposes (for example, a radio station may copy a compact disc onto a cartridge so it can be readily played).

In addition to the exceptions described, certain uses of copyrighted works are not infringement, for example, quoting lyrics of a song or narrative from a book in reviews of the material or parodying works. Such a use is called a "fair use" and is discussed in Chapter 14 as a defense to copyright infringement.

MORAL RIGHTS AND THE VISUAL ARTISTS RIGHTS ACT

Introduction

Many countries recognize certain personal and noneconomic rights of authors in their works to protect their honor and reputation, even after they have sold their work. Such personal rights are referred to as **moral rights.**

There are two primary moral rights: the right of **attribution** (sometimes called the right of paternity), which ensures the author's right to be known as the author of a work, and the **right of integrity,** which ensures that the work not be distorted, mutilated, or misrepresented in a way that would injure the author's reputation.

The Berne Convention, to which the United States is a signatory, requires that member nations protect authors' moral rights of attribution and integrity. In 1990, Congress enacted the Visual Artists Rights Act (17 U.S.C. § 106A) in order to comply with its Berne Convention obligations. Prior to this legislation, authors generally protected their moral rights through actions for breach of contract, defamation, misrepresentation, or unfair competition.

Definition of Visual Arts

The Visual Artists Rights Act is quite limited and applies only to works of visual arts, namely, paintings, drawings, prints, photographs (produced for exhibition purposes), or sculptures that exist in a single copy or in a limited edition of two hundred or fewer copies, if those copies are signed and consecutively numbered. Works of visual art do not include posters, maps, globes, charts, technical drawings, motion

pictures, books, magazines, newspapers, electronic information services or publications, or merchandising, promotional, packaging material, works made for hire, and works not subject to copyright protection (such as useful articles). Thus, the term *visual arts* generally refers to what is commonly called *fine art.*

Rights of Attribution and Integrity

The author of a work of visual art has the following rights of attribution:

- to claim authorship of the work;
- to prevent the use of his or her name as the author of any work of visual art that he or she did not create; and
- to prevent the use of his or her name as the author of a work of visual art that has been distorted, mutilated, or otherwise modified such as to prejudice his or her honor or reputation.

The author of a work of visual art has the following rights of integrity:

- to prevent intentional distortion, mutilation, or other modification that would be prejudicial to his or her honor or reputation; and
- to prevent any destruction of a work of recognized stature, whether through intentional or gross negligence.

Thus, authors of fine arts have the right to be identified as the creator of their works and to prevent mutilation of their works, such as intentional distortions of their paintings or removal of limbs from sculptures. Modifications that are the result of the passage of time (such as chipping and fading), conservation, or presentation to the public (such as occurs when paintings in museums fade due to exposure to light) are not violations of the statute. The California statute discussed earlier also prohibits the destruction or mutilation of works of fine art and recognizes the right of attribution. Other states, including Massachusetts and New York, also have versions of moral rights statutes.

The removal of works of visual arts from buildings presents special problems. If the works (for example, murals) can be removed without destruction or distortion, removal can proceed if the owner of the building provides notice to the artist and the artist fails to remove or pay for removal of the work. If removal will cause destruction, the owner of the building and the artist must sign a written consent to remove the work. 17 U.S.C. § 113. In a recent case in San Francisco, a famous four-story mural called *Lilli Ann* was whitewashed by the new owners of the building on which it was painted. After more than a year of litigation, the artists were paid $200,000 by way of settlement for the destruction of their work.

Extent and Duration of Moral Rights

The artist who creates the covered work owns the moral rights in it, even after selling the work to another. The moral rights reside with the author and, because they are personal rights, cannot be assigned or transferred to another, although the owner can waive his or her moral rights if the waiver is in writing. Joint authors of a work jointly own the moral rights.

For works created after June 1, 1991, moral rights endure for the author's life. Moral rights in works created jointly last until the death of the last surviving author.

Other Ways to Protect Moral Rights

Because the Visual Artists Rights Act applies to such a narrow category of works, namely, fine arts, authors of other works often use other remedies to achieve a level of protection equivalent to moral rights. Authors can agree by contract when they sell their works

that they are entitled to future attribution and integrity rights. If the purchaser later removes the author's signature from the work or destroys it, a breach of contract has occurred. Authors may also be able to bring an action for violation of their exclusive right to prepare derivative works if a subsequent owner of a work defaces it or edits it. Finally, section 43 of the Lanham Act prohibits persons from making a false designation about the origin of goods. Thus, failure to give attribution by naming the author of a work or implying that an author is the creator of a revised or edited work likely violates this prohibition.

COMPULSORY LICENSES

In the early days of music recording, under the 1909 Copyright Act, once a composer authorized a sound recording, the composer was automatically entitled to a compulsory license or royalty fee of two cents per copy. Another producer was free to copy the sound recording as long as the statutorily set fee was paid. This arrangement, known as a **compulsory license,** allowed certain copyrighted works to be used, provided that the fixed fees were paid, eliminating the need for the user to contact each and every copyright owner for permission to use works. Compulsory licenses are governed by 17 U.S.C. § 115.

The provisions of section 115 of the Copyright Act do not prohibit a party from entering into a voluntary license arrangement with a copyright owner but rather provide a method of licensing when voluntary arrangements are not pursued, the copyright owner is unwilling to negotiate, or the copyright owner cannot be located.

Once a nondramatic musical work (such as a song) has been distributed to the public on a phonorecord under the authority of the copyright owner, any other person may make or manufacture other phonorecords for distribution to the public as long as notice is given and the set fees are paid to the copyright owner. A compulsory license may be obtained only if the primary purpose in making the phonorecords is to distribute them to the public for private (not commercial) use. A compulsory license is not available for phonorecords intended for use in background music systems, jukeboxes, broadcasting, or any other public use. Proprietors of establishments that allow patrons to make selections on coin-operated jukeboxes are required to enter into voluntary (rather than compulsory) license agreements and typically do so through one of the performing rights societies, such as BMI or ASCAP.

Generally, compulsory licensing requires that users register with and pay the royalty fees established by the Copyright Office to the copyright owner or to the Licensing Division of the Copyright Office, which then remits the payments to Copyright Arbitration Royalty Panels administered by the Copyright Office that determine and distribute the royalty fees to the copyright owners.

TRIVIA

- The year 2002 saw a 7 percent drop in global music sales and a 10 percent drop in units sold in the United States, probably due to high-tech piracy and CD burning.
- In fiscal year 2001, the Copyright Office collected and deposited approximately $186 million in royalty fees for various copyright owners.
- In April 2003, the Recording Industry Association of America filed lawsuits against students at Princeton, Michigan Tech, and Rensselaer Polytechnic Institute for copyright infringement for operating song-sharing sites on their university servers.
- John Philip Sousa, Jerome Kern, Irving Berlin, and Victor Herbert were among the first members of ASCAP.

CHAPTER SUMMARY

Owners of copyright are granted a bundle of exclusive rights:

- rights to reproduce the work;
- rights to prepare adaptations or derivative works based on the original work;
- rights to distribute the work;
- rights to perform the work; and
- rights to display the work.

Exercise of any of these rights without permission of the copyright owner will constitute infringement of copyright, even if there is no intent to infringe and the use is innocent. There are, however, certain exceptions to the exclusive rights granted to copyright owners, such as rights to use certain copyrighted works in certain instructional and educational activities, during religious worship services, for noncommercial fund-raising, for the handicapped, and for transmission of works in small commercial establishments. Moreover, according to the first sale doctrine, once a copyrighted work has been lawfully distributed by the owner, the new purchaser is free to further distribute the work by sale or lending.

A copyright owner's rights in sound recordings are significantly more limited than rights granted for other works, especially nondramatic literary and musical works.

Finally, authors of fine arts such as paintings and sculptures are granted "moral rights" in those works, allowing them to be identified as the author of the work and prohibiting destruction or alteration of the work, even after the creator has sold it.

CASE ILLUSTRATION—AUTHORS' MORAL RIGHTS

Case: *Gilliam v. ABC Inc.*, 538 F.2d 14 (2d Cir. 1976)

Facts: Plaintiffs, known as the Monty Python comedy group, sought an injunction to prevent ABC from broadcasting versions of their comedy programs that were significantly edited by the excising of 27 percent of the authors' material, partly to make time for commercials and partly to eliminate allegedly offensive matter.

Holding: The injunction was granted. The editing cuts constituted an actionable mutilation of Monty Python's work. Although American copyright law did not recognize moral rights (the right of artists to have their work attributed to them in the form they created it), it is a form of misrepresentation actionable under the Lanham Act to present an author's work to the public in a distorted form. ABC impaired the integrity of the original work.

CASE STUDY AND ACTIVITIES

Case Study.   Watson has built a large hotel near the grounds of Fantasy Fun Adventure to accommodate guests at the park. The hotel allows guests to select various movies and play them in their rooms. Watson recently purchased some sculptures of various animals from a well-known sculptor and has now costumed them in colorful hats and outfits relating to various Fantasy Fun Adventure characters. Every day at noon, at the Fantasy Stage in the park, singers perform songs from a variety of artists, including Celine Dion, Billy Joel, and Mariah Carey. At a recent birthday party for the park's senior chef, the songs were also performed. Finally, Watson intends to close the park one evening to host a charity event to raise funds for the American Cancer Society. Singers will perform live renditions of hits from Broadway musicals of the last ten years.

Activities.   Consider each activity and determine whether any of the exclusive rights of copyright owners have been violated.

ROLE OF PARALEGAL

Paralegals may need to participate in copyright audits to ensure that clients are not infringing copyrighted works, even innocently. Common activities include the following:

- surveying clients to determine if music is played on hold for telephone callers or if music is piped into clients' business establishments;
- contacting ASCAP and BMI and obtaining sample license agreements and royalty fee schedules so arrangements can be made for performance of copyrighted works; and
- preparing newsletters and copyright fact sheets for distribution to clients advising them of possible copyright violations in the photocopying and distribution of literary works (such as magazine and journal articles), use of copyrighted materials including songs and movie clips in presentations, and playing of music on hold or throughout the clients' places of business.

INTERNET RESOURCES

Federal laws relating to copyright:	http://www.ll.georgetown.edu or http://www.findlaw.com
Copyright Office:	http://www.loc.gov/copyright or http://www.copyright.gov (for information on compulsory licenses and CARP)
Performing rights societies:	http://www.ascap.com, http://www.bmi.com, and http://www.sesac.com
Copyright Clearance Center:	http://www.copyright.com
General information:	http://www.findlaw.com and http://www.megalaw.com

DISCUSSION QUESTIONS

1. A Starbucks coffee shop is playing the radio in the morning hours for the enjoyment of its customers. In the afternoon the store plays a videotape of a recent movie. Have any copyright rights been violated? Discuss.
2. Your cousin is having a family karaoke party at his home the night before his wedding. Have any copyright rights been violated? Discuss.
3. Tower Records would like to rent out copies of Norah Jones's most recent record to determine the level of customer interest in the music. May it do so? Discuss.

DISCUSSION QUESTIONS (cont'd)

4. Your local church has decided to sponsor a showing of the movie *The Pianist* in order to raise funds for an upcoming church event. May it do so? Discuss.

5. If you recently purchased the book *The Founding Fathers*, may you later sell the book to a friend? Discuss. What principle governs your answer?

6. Given the facts in question 5, may you photocopy a chapter of the book to give to a friend who is interested in John Adams? Discuss.

7. A drama class at the local college is rehearsing Arthur Miller's play *The Crucible*. Is this performance a violation of any copyright rights? Assume the drama class performs the play for students at the college. Is this performance a violation of any copyright rights? Discuss.

8. Tower Records plays songs from albums and CDs on the current Top 10 list throughout the store premises. Is this a violation of any copyright rights?

For additional resources, go to www.westlegalstudies.com.

CHAPTER 12

Copyright Ownership, Transfers, and Duration

CHAPTER OVERVIEW

Copyright ownership vests in the author of a work. Special issues arise when more than one person creates a work, when a derivative work based upon an underlying work is created, or when existing works are combined into a collection, such as an anthology. Determining ownership is critical because the exclusive rights of reproduction, performance, display, and so forth belong to the copyright owner. The person who creates a work is the author; however, if a work qualifies as one "made for hire," the author is not the creator but the employer or commissioning party. A work qualifies as a work made for hire if the work is created by an employee within the scope of employment or if the work falls within one of nine enumerated types of works and the parties agree in writing that the work is one made for hire. The exclusive rights ordinarily granted to the work's creator will instead be owned by the employer or commissioning party.

Copyright rights may be transferred. A transfer of exclusive rights must be in writing, while a nonexclusive grant, or license, need not be in writing. To protect copyright authors, even absolute or exclusive transfers can be set aside by the author or certain heirs during a five-year period beginning in the thirty-sixth year after a transfer.

Duration of copyright rights for works created after the 1976 act is for the author's life plus seventy years. For joint works, the duration is for seventy years after the last survivor's death. For works made for hire, the duration is generally 95 years from first publication or 120 years from creation, whichever is shorter. Works copyrighted before the 1976 act are subject to special rules.

COPYRIGHT OWNERSHIP ISSUES

Copyright in a work protected under the Copyright Act vests in the **author** or authors of the work. 17 U.S.C. § 201(a). Issues about ownership arise when more than one person creates a work, when the work has multiple parts (such as a song consisting of a melody composed by one person and lyrics composed by another), or when work is created by an employee. Determining ownership is critical because it affects other rights, such as the ability to transfer or license a work and the duration of the copyright in a work.

Ownership of a physical object is separate and distinct from ownership of the copyright embodied in the material object. 17 U.S.C. § 202. Thus, the purchaser of choreographic notations for a ballet written by Mikhail Baryshnikov acquires only the written document. Baryshnikov, as the copyright owner, retains the exclusive rights granted under section 106 of the act, such as rights to perform the work and prepare derivative works based on it. Similarly, purchasing a manuscript, handwritten lyrics to a song scratched on an envelope, or letters written by a famous person gives the purchaser ownership only of those physical objects. Unless copyright has been explicitly conveyed with those physical articles, the original authors generally retain all other rights associated with the works, including the rights to perform and reproduce them and any other exclusive rights granted to copyright owners under section 106 of the Copyright Act.

JOINT WORKS

Intent to Create a Unitary Whole

A **joint work** is a work prepared by two or more authors with the intention that their contributions be merged into inseparable or interdependent parts of a unitary whole. 17 U.S.C. § 101. Only one copyright exists in the created work. Examples of joint works are books that are coauthored by individuals; plays that are composed of narrative written by one party,

music by another, and lyrics to the music by a third; songs such as "Don't Cry for Me Argentina," in which the music was written by Andrew Lloyd-Webber and the lyrics by Tim Rice; and books comprising narrative written by one person and illustrations by another.

It is the intent of the parties at the time a work is created that determines whether it is a joint work. Thus, if two persons sit at a piano and collaborate on a melody and lyrics, the resulting song is a joint work. More difficult issues arise when parts to a work are created at different times, for example, when a melody is composed by itself and lyrics are added later. The parties' intent governs. If the first composer intended the work to be complete at the time he or she composed it, the copyright in the melody is owned solely by him or her. Merely changing one's mind at some later date and allowing another to add lyrics to a completed work does not convert the work into a joint work. In such a case, the first composer owns the copyright to the melodic composition, and the lyricist has created a derivative work based on the first and owns rights in the newly created lyrics alone. Unless both parties intend at the time they make their contributions that the parts be combined or absorbed into an integrated unit, there is no joint work. Joint works also result when a copyright owner transfers rights to more than one person or the copyright passes by will to two or more persons.

Merely making suggestions or giving directions to one creating a work is not sufficient to make one a joint author. For example, giving an architect instructions that a house to be designed by the architect should have a certain amount of living space and giving other directions does not make one a joint author. Although the contributions of coauthors need not be equal, each must make some significant contribution.

In *Aalmuhammed v. Lee*, 202 F.3d 1227 (9th Cir. 2000), a recent case involving contributions made by an individual to the movie *Malcolm X*, the court held that to be a joint author, it is not enough to make a significant contribution to a work. Joint authors are those who "mastermind" or "superintend" the creative effort. Otherwise, nearly anyone who contributes to a movie or web site design could claim to be a joint author. While the plaintiff made important contributions to the movie, neither Warner Brothers nor the director Spike Lee were bound to accept them. Thus, the plaintiff was not a joint author.

In regard to dividing profits arising out of joint works, courts presume the parties contributed equally unless they provide otherwise. Thus, if three individuals coauthor a book, the profits or royalties will be divided in equal thirds unless the parties agree to some other division. Equal division of profits occurs even when the contributions of the coauthors are not equal. Agreements regarding division of revenue among joint authors should thus be in writing to avoid later disputes.

Ownership Rights in Joint Works

If individuals are authors of a joint work, each owns an equal undivided interest in the copyright as a tenant in common, meaning that each has the right to use the work, prepare derivative works based on it, perform it, display it, and so forth, without seeking the other coauthor's permission. Because each coauthor has rights in the work, one cannot exclude another from using the work or exercising the rights of copyright ownership. Nevertheless, if profits arise out of such uses, an accounting must be made so that each author shares in the benefits or proceeds.

Any coauthor may grant a *nonexclusive* license to another party to use the joint work without permission from the other coauthors; however, the granting of an *exclusive* license (one in which rights are granted solely to one

party with no other party having any rights to use the work) requires consent from all coauthors of a joint work. Similarly, a joint owner cannot transfer all interest in the work without the written consent of the other coauthor(s).

Upon the death of a coauthor, his or her rights pass to heirs who then own the rights in common with the other coauthor(s). Joint ownership of a single work often arises in this fashion. A book may be authored by one person. Upon that person's death, the copyright may pass to several heirs who now own the work jointly.

Duration of Works of Joint Ownership

A copyright generally lasts for the author's life plus seventy years. 17 U.S.C. § 302. If the work is a joint work, however, the copyright lasts until seventy years after the last surviving coauthor's death. Additionally, as discussed in a later section in this chapter entitled "Termination of Transfers of Copyright," each joint author has the ability to terminate his or her transfers.

OWNERSHIP IN DERIVATIVE OR COLLECTIVE WORKS

If a work such as a book is created by one person who intends it to be complete at the time and illustrations are later added to it by another, the work cannot be a joint work because there was no intention of the parties to create a unitary whole at the time of their creation. In such a case, the new work, consisting of text and illustrations, is a derivative work (assuming the original author authorized the illustrator to use the earlier work).

The author of the original book has rights only to his or her work and cannot reproduce or perform the derivative work without permission. Similarly, the author of the derivative

A variable is a characteristic that can change or differ. In other words, it includes more than one state or condition, and each state or condition is called a "value" of the variable. A beginner may mistake a value for a variable. But a variable is a logical grouping of more than one value. Variables are the general objects of scientific study. Although a constant can be considered as a special variable that has only one value, researchers tend not to think this way since they often need to reduce rather than to increase the number of variables involved. Therefore, all constant values tend to be taken as given characteristics of the research population or the research situation, and thus be excluded from research manipulation. Moreover, researchers may even try to remove a real variable or to transform it into more than one constant by fixing its value. They then conduct separate research under each condition represented by each constant, or each fixed value of the original variable whose impact of variation has now been excluded from the study. This is one approach to the key idea of "control" (experimental or statistical) in psychosocial research. Novice researchers, however, may use a one-value variable (i.e., a constant) by mistake. Only after they find out that they cannot manipulate a constant, do they realize they should let an interested variable have at least two values.

Knowing how many variables are involved in your research question is very important. We have discussed two very different kinds of research (isolated vs. relational) according to the number of variables actively involved (single- vs. bi- and multi-variable). The confounding issue in a bi- or multi-variable relational research has much to do with the overlapping of the concepts, as has been indicated earlier in the last chapter. The issue has to be highlighted with clear understanding and resolved by some particular measurement approaches in the process of operationalization.

It is also important to distinguish between two major kinds of variables. One is the sort of simple facts, such as age, sex, and race, among other individual characteristics. The other refers to more or less complicated things, including kinds of theoretical constructs, such as stress, social support, and social adjustment. People tend to call the first kind "observables." But what makes the real difference in theory and measurement is that they are relatively simple. The theoretical constructs, on the other side, are intellectual products derived from observations, which may involve complicated theoretical contents, deliberations, and controversies. The definition and clarification of such variables may involve considerable theoretical work. You should be warned not to engage too many theoretical constructs since this may go well beyond your ability. It should be work cannot create further works based on the original book without permission and cannot reproduce the original work (or exercise other copyright rights) without permission. Each author owns nothing more than his or her original contribution.

Copyright to the first work (the book alone) will last until seventy years after its author's death, and copyright to the derivative work (book and illustrations) will last until seventy years after its author's death.

Multiple ownership rights may also arise if separately copyrightable works are compiled into a collection. For example, if essays written by Jerry Seinfeld, Ellen DeGeneres, and Paul Reiser are collected into a humor anthology by Bill Jones (with permission of the original authors), the original authors retain their exclusive rights (such as rights to reproduce, distribute, and perform) in their respective essays. No joint work is created because there was no intent at the time the separate essays were created to merge them into a unitary whole. No derivative work is created because the original works have not been transformed in any way and nothing new has been added to them. The anthology by the compiler, Bill Jones, is a collective work and pursuant to section 201(c) of the act, Jones acquires only the right to reproduce and distribute the contributions as part of the particular collective work or any revision of the collective work. Jones does not have any ownership interest in the original essays.

WORKS MADE FOR HIRE

Introduction

Although the general rule is that the person who creates a work is the author of that work and the owner of the copyright therein, there is an exception to that principle: the copyright law defines a category of works called **works made for hire.** If a work is "made for hire," the author is considered to be the employer or commissioning party and not the employee or the actual person who created the work. The employer or commissioning party may be a company or an individual.

There are two types of works that are classified as works made for hire: works prepared by an employee within the scope of employment and certain categories of specially ordered or commissioned works.

Works Prepared by Employees in the Scope of Employment

Copyright in works prepared by employees are presumptively owned by their employers. For example, if an employee is tasked with creating a computer program by his or her employer, the resulting work is owned by the employer who is treated as the author of the work for purposes of copyright law. Unless the parties have agreed otherwise in writing, the employer owns all of the rights pertaining to the works created by an employee on the job. Oftentimes, however, questions arise whether the person creating the work is an "employee" (such that his or her creations belong to the employer) or whether the person is an **independent contractor** (such that his or her creations belong to him or her as the owner/author). This question often arises when freelance artists prepare works for others.

In *Community for Creative Non-Violence v. Reid,* 490 U.S. 730 (1989), the Supreme Court held that the term *employee* for purposes of determining authorship of works made for hire should be interpreted according to general common law agency principles. If the person doing the work is an employee under common law agency principles and the work was done in the scope of employment, the employer (not the employee) is the copyright owner/author.

The Court identified certain factors that characterize an employer-employee relationship:

- **Control by the employer over the work.** If the employer has a voice in how the work is done, has the work done at the employer's location, and provides equipment and tools to the person to create the work, such tends to show an employer-employee relationship.
- **Control by the employer over the employee.** If the employer controls the worker's schedule in creating work, has the right to have the worker perform other assignments, determines the method of payment, and/or has the right to hire the worker's assistants, such evidences an employer-employee relationship.
- **Status of employer.** If the employer is in business to produce such works, provides the worker with benefits similar to those received by other workers, and withholds taxes from the worker's compensation, such is supportive of an employer-employee relationship.

These factors are not exhaustive; for example, courts can also consider the duration of the relationship of the parties (a long-term relationship is indicative of employment) and the skill level of the employee. Moreover, no one factor is determinative. All or most of these factors, however, characterize a regular, salaried employment relationship, and works created by employees in the course and scope of such a relationship are works made for hire, authorship and copyright of which vests in the employer (unless the parties agree in writing otherwise).

The Copyright Office has provided the following examples of works made for hire:

- a software program created by a staff programmer for Creative Computer Corporation;
- a newspaper article written by a staff journalist for publication in a daily newspaper; and

- a musical arrangement written for XYZ Music Company by a salaried arranger on its staff.

Note that the work must be created *within the scope of employment* to be a work made for hire. Thus, if the software program was created by a person before joining Creative Computer Corporation, the company has no rights to the work. Similarly, if an employee employed by Creative Computer Corporation writes a book about computers in the evenings and weekends, the work is likely not a work made for hire because it was not created in the course of the employee's duties.

Many employers ask that employees sign agreements acknowledging that works created by the employees will be works made for hire. Such agreements may be considered by courts, but an agreement alone is not controlling. Other factors may be considered in determining the nature of the parties' relationship. One approach to ensure ownership vests in the employer may be to recite in an agreement that the relationship is one of employer-employee, that works created by the employee are works made for hire owned by the employer, and that in the event it is later determined by a court that the work is not one made for hire, the employee irrevocably and immediately assigns all rights to the work to the employer. Such an agreement will likely be given effect by a court. If the employee desires to retain ownership of works created in the course of employment that otherwise would be works made for hire, the parties must expressly agree in a written instrument signed by both parties. (See Appendix D, Form 12, for sample provisions in employment agreements relating to works made for hire.)

Specially Commissioned Works

If the work is not one prepared by an employee but, rather, is one prepared by an independent contractor, it can be deemed a work made for hire and thus owned by the commissioning party if three conditions are met: it is a specially ordered or commissioned work; the parties agree in writing that the work is one made for hire; and the work falls into one of nine specially enumerated categories. 17 U.S.C. § 101. All three of these elements must be satisfied if the work is to be one made for hire. The nine categories of works are as follows:

1. a contribution to a collective work;
2. part of a motion picture or other audiovisual work;
3. a translation;
4. a supplementary work (a work prepared for publication as a secondary adjunct to a work by another author for the purpose of introducing, illustrating, or explaining the work, such as forewords, pictorial illustrations, tables, editorial notes, bibliographies, appendices, and indexes);
5. a compilation;
6. an instructional text (a literary, pictorial, or graphic work prepared for publication with the purpose of use in systematic instructional activities);
7. a test;
8. answer material for a test; and
9. an atlas.

Although the parties can agree in writing that the commissioning party owns the work, this agreement will not convert a work that does not fit within one of the nine statutorily designated categories into one made for hire. Therefore, the safest approach for the commissioning party is for the parties to agree in writing that the work is one made for hire and that if for some reason the work is determined not to be one made for hire, by the same document, the work is automatically assigned and transferred to the person who commissioned the work.

For example, assume that a museum hires a graphic artist to create a painting and an audiovisual slide presentation for a museum opening, and the parties agree in writing that the works are to be owned by the museum and are to be considered works made for hire. While the audiovisual slide presentation is a work made for hire (it was specially commissioned, the parties agreed in writing it would be considered a work made for hire, and it fits the statutory definition), the painting is not a work made for hire despite what the parties agreed because it does not fit the statutory definition. Thus, a safety net clause should be added in written agreements conveying all of the author's rights in the painting in the event it is not a work made for hire. This would allow the museum to create derivative works based on the painting, display it, and so forth.

Effects of Works Made for Hire

There are several effects if a work is classified as one made for hire:

- **Ownership.** The owner/author of a work made for hire is the employer or commissioning party. The artist who created the work has no more rights in the work than any stranger, and the artist cannot reproduce, distribute, or perform the work, or prepare derivatives based on it, without being liable for copyright infringement.
- **Duration.** Copyrights in works made for hire endure for ninety-five years from publication or 120 years from creation, whichever is shorter. Copyrights in other works generally endure for the author's life plus seventy years thereafter.
- **Reversion of transfers.** Rights in works that are not made for hire can be recaptured by the author after thirty-five years, even if there has been an unconditional transfer or sale to another. (See the section entitled

"Termination of Transfers of Copyright" later in this chapter.)

- **Moral rights.** There are no moral rights (rights of attribution and integrity) in works made for hire because they are not defined as works of "visual arts." 17 U.S.C. § 101.

TRANSFERS OF COPYRIGHT

Divisibility of Ownership

Any or all of the exclusive rights of the copyright owner (rights to reproduce, prepare derivative works, distribute the work, and perform and display the work publicly) can be transferred or licensed to another party. 17 U.S.C. § 201(d). Thus, the author of a book may grant the right to prepare derivative works based on the book to one party and yet transfer the rights to distribute the book to another party. The grants or licenses can be perpetual or for limited terms. Similarly, they can be limited to certain geographic areas, such as when one party is granted the right to distribute a work in the western region of the United States and another party is granted the right to distribute the work in the eastern region of the United States.

Copyright rights are divisible, meaning they can be subdivided, such as occurs when the copyright owner of a book carves up his or her rights to prepare derivative works by granting one party the right to translate the book, granting another party the right to make a motion picture based on the book, and granting a third party the right to prepare a sequel to the book.

Granting rights to others is a way for copyright owners to exploit their works to the fullest extent. The copyright owner will grant rights and generally require payment therefor, such as by negotiating a flat fee or by continuing and periodic royalties on the sales of each book or song exploited by the licensee.

Requirement of Writing for Transfer of Exclusive Rights

A transfer of copyright ownership other than a transfer by operation of law is not valid unless the transfer is in writing and signed by the owner of the rights conveyed (or his or her exclusive agent). 17 U.S.C. § 204(a). This requirement of a writing protects copyright owners from inadvertently transferring their copyrights. Granting rights on a nonexclusive basis (for example, allowing several parties to reproduce the work) is not considered a "transfer" under the Copyright Act and thus need not be in writing. Such an arrangement is generally called a license, and although there is no requirement that there be a written document, such is advised because it lends certainty to the terms of the transaction. (See Exhibit 12–1, Assignment of Copyright.)

Like other property rights, copyrights can be transferred by operation of law, generally meaning the law can require a transfer. For example, transfers by operation of law occur when, in a bankruptcy, the bankrupt's property is transferred to the bankruptcy trustee or to a creditor; when a court orders the sale or transfer of a copyright in a divorce proceeding; or when an owner dies without leaving a will and the laws of intestate succession govern who acquires the decedent's property. Copyrights can also pass by will to one's specified beneficiaries.

Just as trademarks can be used to secure obligations, copyrights can serve as secured property. If Sheryl Crow wishes to borrow money from a bank, the bank may require her to pledge certain copyrights in her songs as security for repayment of the debt. If she fails to repay the debt, the bank can seize the copyrights and all rights therein. In fact, some entertainers, including David Bowie and the group Iron Maiden, have sold bonds backed by predicted revenues from future recordings and performances. Bowie financed one of his tours

EXHIBIT 12–1
Assignment of
Copyright

WHEREAS, Kathryn Sherman ("Assignor"), an individual residing at 1010 Canyon Glen Terrace, Phoenix, AZ 22098, is the owner of all copyrights in that literary work entitled *The Challenge* (the "Work") and is the author of such Work; and

WHEREAS, Blake Publishers, Inc. ("Assignee"), a corporation organized under the laws of the State of New York, located and doing business at 555 Avenue of the Americas, New York, NY 96607, desires to acquire all of Assignor's rights in and to the Work;

NOW, THEREFORE, for good and valuable consideration, the receipt and sufficiency of which are hereby acknowledged, Assignor hereby irrevocably sells, assigns, transfers, and conveys to Assignee the entire right, title, and interest in and to the Work, including any copyrights and registrations, the same to be held and enjoyed by Assignee, its successors, assigns, and other legal representatives.

Assignee shall have the right to register the copyright in the Work in its own name and shall have the exclusive rights to develop, exploit, publish, reproduce, distribute, perform, display, and prepare derivative works based thereon throughout the world.

Assignor represents and warrants that she created the Work independently, the Work is the result of her original effort, and that she is the owner of all copyrights and other rights in the Work and that no other party has any rights in or to the Work.

Assignor further assigns to Assignee all right to sue for and receive all damages accruing from past, present, and future infringements of the Work herein assigned.

This Assignment shall be binding upon the parties, their successors and/or assigns, and all others acting by, through, with, or under their direction, and all those in privity therewith.

Assignee agrees to cooperate with Assignor and take any further action and execute any documents required to effect the purposes of this Assignment.

Kathryn Sherman   Blake Publishers, Inc.

_____   By: _____

Date: _____   Title: _____

                                         Date: _____

Recordation of Transfers

There is no requirement that transfers or licenses of copyright or grants of security interests in copyright be recorded with the U.S. Copyright Office. Recordation is prudent, however, because it provides notice of rights in copyrights and may establish priorities of conflicting transfers. The Copyright Office does not make or participate in the transfer but merely records the document in its files. Recordation can be made whether the work is published or unpublished and whether or not it has been registered with the Copyright Office. Other documents pertaining to copyrights can also be recorded. For example, a will that bequeaths a copyright can be recorded with the Copyright Office. The current basic fee for recording a document covering one work is $80. An additional

with the money raised from the sale of such bonds.

charge of $20 is made for each group of ten additional titles or fewer. In certain circumstances (generally when litigation is pending or threatened), special handling may be requested and recordation will be expedited (usually within five business days) upon the payment of an additional fee and a showing of the necessity for special handling.

TERMINATION OF TRANSFERS OF COPYRIGHT

Introduction

In many instances, young artists, songwriters, and other creators transfer or license rights in their copyrighted works at a time when they do not truly have an idea about the value of the works transferred. The works may be exploited by the new owners who may collect astounding amounts of money, and yet the original creators of the works may not realize any economic gain whatsoever from these early works and may not be able to exercise any control with regard to reproduction, distribution, preparation of derivative works, performance, or display of the works. To remedy this situation, section 203 of the Copyright Act provides that transfers of copyrights can be terminated after thirty-five years so that the original author can recapture his or her works.

The Copyright Act's termination of transfer provisions are highly unusual and are contrary to general principles of contract law, which hold that once a valid contract has been entered into, it cannot be set aside (except in extreme cases, such as those involving fraud). When an individual sells a house, he or she is not allowed to cancel the sale and reclaim the house if it later appreciates. Bad decisions made on the stock market cannot be set aside. Yet transfers of copyrights can be set aside or terminated, reflecting Congress's intent to protect artists and authors from exploitation.

Grants Executed After January 1, 1978

Statutory Authority. Section 203 of the Copyright Act sets forth the procedures for terminating grants or transfers of copyrights that occurred after the 1976 Copyright Act became effective on January 1, 1978. Section 203 refers to transfers that occur after January 1, 1978, regardless of when the work was created. Thus, termination of these grants will begin in 2013.

According to section 203(a), in the case of any work *other than a work made for hire*, an exclusive or nonexclusive grant of a transfer or license of a copyright or of any right under a copyright, executed by an author after January 1, 1978, and other than a grant made by will, is subject to termination. Grants of copyright that occur by way of a will cannot be terminated, apparently because Congress saw no exploitation of the author in such cases. The author's right to reach back in time and terminate an earlier transfer cannot be waived, and any provision attempting to waive the protections afforded by section 203 is void.

Who May Effect Termination. In the case of grants by a single author, the author may terminate. If the author has died, his or her termination rights may be exercised by the surviving spouse and his or her children and grandchildren. These successors may terminate in the author's place if they hold more than 50 percent of the author's termination rights.

Section 203(a)(2) sets forth an elaborate scheme for determining who may exercise the rights of a deceased author. In brief, the following apply:

- If a spouse survives the death of the author, and there are no children or grandchildren, the spouse owns all of the termination rights.
- If the author leaves both a spouse and surviving children or grandchildren by a deceased child, the spouse owns one-half

of the termination rights and the surviving children and grandchildren share the remaining one-half.

- If there is no surviving spouse, the author's living children and any children of a deceased child own all of the termination rights.
- Each surviving child gets his or her percentage share. Children of a deceased child of the author take the share that would have gone to their parent and, in casting their votes to effect a termination, must act as a unit. A majority vote controls. Children of surviving children have no rights.
- If the author leaves no surviving spouse, children, or grandchildren, his or her executor owns the author's termination interest.

Example: Author Smith dies, leaving a widow (*W*), one living child (*LC*), and four grandchildren (*GC*) by way of a deceased son. Their termination rights are as follows: *W* owns 50 percent; *LC* owns 25 percent; and the *GC*s collectively own 25 percent. To terminate a transfer, more than 50 percent approval is needed. *W* must be joined either by *LC* or the *GC*s (three of whom must approve the transaction) in order to terminate.

In the case of a transfer by joint authors of a work, the transfer may be canceled by a majority of the authors who made the transfer. If any of the joint authors has died, his or her termination rights are exercised according to the scheme just described.

Effecting a Termination.   Generally, termination of the prior grant may be effected at any time during a period of five years beginning in the thirty-sixth year after the date of execution of the grant. To effect the termination, those who own the rights of termination (or their 'horized agents) must sign and serve a writ-

ten notice to the grantee no less than two and not more than ten years before the transfer is to be terminated. The notice must set forth the date of termination and must describe the grant being terminated. A copy of the notice must be recorded with the Copyright Office. Upon the effective date of the termination, the rights in the work automatically revert to the author or the author's successors (including those who voted against the termination). The author (or successors) must follow this statutory procedure in order to effect a termination. If the author or his or her surviving family fail to take the necessary steps within the appropriate time periods, the original transfer cannot be set aside and it will continue for the remaining term of the copyright.

After the effective date of termination, the author (or successors who have recovered his or her rights) may make a new grant of rights to a different party. If the author (or successors) wishes to regrant rights to the original grantee, such can be done once the notice of termination has been served. In fact, once the notice of termination is served, the grantee will often commence negotiations with the author (or successors) so the grantee can continue to exercise the rights originally granted to him or her. Typically, new fee payments are negotiated. The new grant or regrant must be signed by the same number and proportion of owners as are required to terminate the grant.

Grants Prior to January 1, 1978

Grants or transfers made by copyright authors prior to January 1, 1978, the effective date of the 1976 Copyright Act, are governed by section 304 of the Act. Most of the rules and procedures relating to termination of transfers granted after the Copyright Act of 1976 also apply to transfers granted under the previous 1909 act. One difference, however, is that under the 1976 act, only grants made by the author of a work in his or her lifetime may be terminated. Under section 304, grants made by the author, or certain of his or her beneficiaries or executor if the author was dead, may be recaptured. Most other rules relating to notice, recordation of the notice with the Copyright Office, effect of termination, inability to waive termination rights, and so forth remain the same.

Under section 304, termination can be effected of rights (other than copyrights in works made for hire or those transferred by will) at any point during a five-year period that begins at the end of fifty-six years from the date copyright was originally secured (or beginning on January 1, 1978, whichever is later). For a copyright in its renewal term, if a termination right had expired, under the new Sonny Bono Copyright Term Extension Act, a termination of a transfer may be effected at any time during the five years beginning at the end of seventy-five years from the date copyright was secured. Identical to rights terminated under the 1976 act, rights that have been recaptured may be granted to a new party after the termination is effective, and an agreement to regrant rights to the original transferee may be effected as soon as the notice of termination is served.

DURATION OF COPYRIGHT

Introduction

The duration of a copyright depends upon whether the copyright was created after January 1, 1978, the effective date of the 1976 Copyright Act, or before that date. Under the Copyright Act of 1909, federal copyright protection commenced upon publication of the work. Prior to publication, common law copyright principles controlled. Under the 1976 act, federal copyright protection commences upon creation of the work in a fixed form, whether the work is published or not. Because works under the 1909 act may still be subject to copyright protection, it is important to understand the periods of duration for works created under both acts.

Duration Under the 1909 Copyright Act

Under the 1909 act, the copyright in a work lasted for a first term of twenty-eight years from the date it was secured. During the last year of the term, the copyright was eligible for renewal either by the author or specified heirs. If renewed, the copyright was extended for a second term of twenty-eight years. If not renewed, the copyright expired at the end of the first twenty-eight-year term. Thus, the maximum allowable length of copyright protection under the 1909 act was fifty-six years.

Duration Under the 1976 Copyright Act

For works that are created and fixed in a tangible medium of expression after January 1, 1978, the Copyright Act of 1976 (17 U.S.C. § 302) does away with the burdensome renewal requirements and establishes a single copyright term. There are three basic categories of works:

- for works created after January 1, 1978, copyright extends for the lifetime of the author plus seventy years (this term is similar to that of many foreign countries);
- for joint works, the term lasts for seventy years after the last surviving author's death; and
- for works made for hire and for anonymous works (those in which no natural person is identified as the author on the copies or phonorecords of the work) and pseudonymous works (those in which the author is identified by a fictitious name on the copies or phonorecords of the work), the duration of copyright is ninety-five years from the first publication of the work, or one hundred and twenty years from creation, whichever is shorter (although if the anonymous

or pseudonymous author discloses his or her name to the Copyright Office, the duration will convert to life plus seventy years).

Until recently, duration of each of these copyrights was twenty years shorter. To harmonize U.S. law with that of many foreign countries, Congress passed the Sonny Bono Copyright Term Extension Act in late 1998, which extended the duration of copyright terms as set forth herein. This legislation was subject to much debate, with critics complaining that extending the duration of copyright protection benefits only copyright owners and deprives the public of having works enter the public domain for ready dissemination at the earliest possible date. To respond to fears by libraries and archives that the extended copyright duration would inhibit their educational functions, a provision was added to allow, during the last twenty years of any term of copyright of a published work, a library or archives to make certain uses of copyrighted materials for preservation, scholarship, or research purposes, if those works are not commercially available.

A recent U.S. Supreme Court case considered whether the continual extensions to the term of copyright protection (and, in particular, the additional twenty-year term granted under the Sonny Bono Copyright Term Extension Act) violated the U.S. Constitution, which clearly provides that authors shall have copyright rights for "limited times." In *Eldred v. Ashcroft*, 537 U.S. 186 (2003), the petitioners were those whose products depended on copyrighted works that have entered the public domain. Thus, they objected to an extension of the term of copyright protection an additional twenty years. The Court held that the extension of copyright terms did not exceed Congress's power under the Constitution. The extension reflected a rational judgment of Congress in harmonizing U.S. law with that of most other countries.

Effect of 1976 Copyright Act on Preexisting Works

Any copyright still in its renewal term on October 27, 1998 (the date the new Sonny Bono Copyright Term Extension Act became effective) now has a copyright term of ninety-five years from the date copyright was originally secured.

Works that were in existence but were not published or copyrighted on January 1, 1978 (for example, an unpublished manuscript that had no copyright protection under the 1909 act and was governed by common law principles), are automatically given protection as if they were created after January 1, 1978 (the life-plus-seventy or the ninety-five- and one-hundred-and-twenty-year terms, as applicable), or until December 31, 2002, whichever occurs last. To encourage publication, Congress provided that if the work was published before December 31, 2002, an additional forty-five years of protection would be granted, until December 31, 2047.

In many instances, owners of copyrights that were in their first terms on January 1, 1978, did not apply to renew their copyrights and their copyrights expired after only twenty-eight years. To avoid similar situations, in 1991 Congress amended the Copyright Act of 1976 to provide for automatic renewals for works in their first term. There is now no requirement to file a renewal application to extend the original twenty-eight-year copyright term to the full term of ninety-five years. Although the renewal term is automatically extended, there are a number of incentives that encourage the filing of a renewal application (using Copyright Office Form RE), especially during the twenty-eighth year of the copyright term (for example, the Copyright Office will issue a renewal certificate that constitutes *prima facie* evidence of the validity of the facts stated in the renewal certificate and the copyright in the extended term).

(See Exhibit 12–2 for a chart illustrating duration of copyright.)

Date of Work	Duration of Copyright
Works created on or after 1/1/1978	Author's life plus 70 years (or if a joint work, 70 years after last survivor's death); if work is "work made for hire" (or anonymous or pseudonymous work), copyright lasts for 95 years from publication or 120 years from creation, whichever is shorter
Works created before 1/1/1978, but not published	Author's life plus 70 years or until 12/31/2002, whichever is longer (if work is published before 12/31/2002, copyright extended until 12/31/2047)
Copyright secured under 1909 act and in first or renewal term on 1/1/1978	Term automatically extended to give a total length of copyright of 95 years from publication of work
Works published before 1923	Work is now in the public domain

EXHIBIT 12–2
Copyright Duration

Calculating Dates for Copyright Duration

The act provides that all terms of copyright will run through the end of the calendar year in which they would otherwise expire. For example, if an author of a work created in June 1980 died in June 1990, protection would extend until December 31, 2060.

Restoration of Lost Copyrights

Neither the 1976 act nor any amendments provide for revival or restoration of lost copyrights in works of U.S. origin. If a U.S. work fell into the public domain because its author failed to renew the work under the 1909 act, it is not restored by any statutory provision. However, copyright in foreign works whose U.S. copyright protection had been lost because of noncompliance with formalities of U.S. law were restored as of January 1, 1996, under the provisions of the Uruguay Round Agreements Act. Additional information on these restored foreign copyrights can be found in Copyright Office Circular 38b available at http://www.copyright.gov.

TRIVIA

- In 2001, the Copyright Office registered 601,659 claims of copyright and recorded more than 15,000 documents.
- *To Kill a Mockingbird*, the movie, a derivative work based on Harper Lee's earlier novel, was copyrighted in March 1963.
- The Copyright Office employs approximately 500 staff. Its fiscal year 2001 budget was more than $38 million, approximately $21 million of which was funded by fees charged by the Copyright Office.

noted that a seemingly simple fact may sometimes become as complicated as a theoretical construct. Age, for example, can be simply defined as a calendar or chronological phenomenon, but could also be defined as a state in some complex psychological and social processes. In the latter situation, it could turn into a very sophisticated theoretical construct.

A clear and solid conceptual base is important in directing your research. Especially if your research does not involve any formal theory and/or does not have any articulated hypothesis, this conceptual base would be the mainstay and essential part of your research framework. In an exploratory project of this kind, a clearly laid out conceptual scheme, with various dimensions being identified, can provide you with useful guidance as to how to proceed with your study.

Deductive logic and the role of theory

You have now set up your conceptual framework by defining the key concepts, clarifying their components, structures, and interrelationships, and resolving some of the remaining controversial issues for your particular research purpose. You may articulate a few research hypotheses and/or construct an integrated research model, and back these up with certain theoretical accounts. If you do go further and find some relevant theories and apply them in such a process, then you may indicate in your research document that you have got some sort of theoretical framework.

We usually consider a theory as a body of general statements about the interrelations among a set of variables. Such interrelations, however, are not those caused simply by the overlapping of different concepts, especially those elaborate theoretical constructs. In this regard, the difference between the conceptual part and the theoretical part of your research framework must be highlighted. The former can be used to predict and prevent conceptual overlapping and analytic confounding by clarifying the contents of various individual concepts, while the latter is aimed at discovering the "genuine" interrelations among those concepts that have already been put in place.

Generally speaking, theory may help you think about your research questions. Although you may have to start over sometimes, the theoretical perspectives and viewpoints will provide you with the kind of assurance you need in conducting your research.

Since a theoretical framework has such an important function, do we have to

CHAPTER SUMMARY

Determining ownership of a copyright is critical because a wide variety of rights flow from copyright ownership, including rights to reproduce, adapt, distribute, perform, and display the work. Moreover, the duration of copyright depends upon its ownership. When two or more people create a work with the intent that their separate contributions be merged into the completed work, the work is a joint work and the authors each have rights to distribute, perform, reproduce, or display the work. A derivative work is one based upon an underlying work. The author of the underlying work has exclusive rights in his or her work, and the author of the derivative work has rights in his or her newly created work that exist independently from any rights in the original work.

Although the general rule is that the person who creates a work is the author of that work, there is an exception to that rule: the copyright law defines a category of works called "works made for hire." If a work is one "made for hire," either the employer or commissioner of the work is the author for copyright purposes and possesses the exclusive rights of a copyright owner. A work made for hire is one prepared by an employee in the scope of employment or one of nine specially enumerated types of commissioned works that the parties have agreed in writing will be a work made for hire.

Because copyrights are property, they may be transferred. Moreover, the rights of a copyright owner (including rights to reproduce, adapt, distribute, perform, and display the work) are divisible, meaning that the author may transfer some rights and retain others. Transfers of exclusive rights must be in writing. Transfers of copyright can be terminated either by the author or certain of his or her heirs during a statutorily defined period beginning the thirty-sixth year after the transfer. This unusual provision in copyright law is intended to protect authors who transfer rights before they fully understand the value of their works.

Copyrights created after the 1976 act last for the author's life plus seventy years or seventy years from the last survivor's death in the case of joint works. For works made for hire and anonymous and pseudonymous works, the duration of copyright is ninety-five years from first publication of the work or one hundred and twenty years from its creation, whichever first occurs.

CASE ILLUSTRATION—JOINT AUTHORS

Case: *S.O.S., Inc. v. Payday, Inc.,* 886 F.2d 1081 (9th Cir. 1989).

Facts: S.O.S. provided computer programming services to Payday. Most of the work was performed by two S.O.S. employees. One of Payday's employees, Goodman, was the liaison to the S.O.S. programming team and described Payday's needs to S.O.S. but did not participate in the coding process. The parties agreed in writing that S.O.S. was to retain ownership rights in the work. Payday later asserted that it was a joint author and therefore had copyright rights in the work.

Holding: Payday was not a joint author. Its employee, Goodman, did nothing more than describe the programs that Payday wanted S.O.S. to write. To be an author, one must supply more than mere direction or ideas. One must translate those ideas into a fixed, tangible expression entitled to copyright protection.

CASE STUDY AND ACTIVITIES

Case Study. Watson has asked two of its full-time employees in its creative arts and entertainment department to write a song called "Taylor Tiger's Rag." Two talented animators in Los Angeles who are not Watson employees have been requested in writing to prepare an animated movie relating to various Watson characters. The agreement provides that the movie will be a work made for hire. Watson has also asked one of the employees in the group to prepare illustrations for the cookbook entitled *Mrs. Sweet's Home Made Recipes*, which was published several years ago. Finally, in 1980, Watson transferred the copyright for one of its books called *Empire of the Bears* (created by Watson employees).

Activities. What are the rights of Watson or its employees or others in "Taylor Tiger's Rag," the animated movie, and the newly illustrated cookbook? Discuss ownership rights and the duration of the copyright for each of these works. What are Watson's rights, if any, in *Empire of the Bears?*

ROLE OF PARALEGAL

There are numerous tasks for paralegals to be involved in relating to ownership, transfer, and duration of copyrights. Commonly performed tasks are as follows:

- conducting legal research to determine whether a work is a joint work, derivative work, or collective work;
- drafting agreements between or among joint authors in regard to divisions of royalties and other rights;
- investigating circumstances of employment to determine whether an individual is an employee or an independent contractor;
- drafting provisions for employment agreements relating to ownership of works created by employees;
- drafting agreements relating to specially commissioned works confirming the works are "made for hire," and providing that if they are later determined not to be works made for hire, the creator assigns all rights to the commissioning party;
- drafting agreements transferring or assigning copyright rights to others;
- drafting agreements subjecting copyrights to security interests;
- recording transfers of copyright ownership with the Copyright Office;
- docketing transfers of copyright so dates for termination of transfers can be tracked;
- drafting notices for termination of transfers of copyright and recording notices with Copyright Office;
- docketing dates for duration of copyright so owners can be informed that copyright protection will terminate; and
- renewing copyrights for works protected under the 1909 act to obtain benefits of voluntary renewal.

INTERNET RESOURCES

Federal laws relating to copyright: http://www.ll.georgetown.edu or
http://www.findlaw.com

Copyright Office: http://www.loc.gov/copyright or
http://www.copyright.gov (for forms, circulars, and
information on copyright ownership, works made for
hire, transfers, termination of transfers, and duration)

General information: http://www.findlaw.com and
http://www.megalaw.com

DISCUSSION QUESTIONS

1. Alex orally gives all rights in his copyrighted work to Mario. Is the transfer valid? Discuss.
2. Martin orally commissions Barbara to prepare a test for an engineering class Martin teaches. Is the resulting work one made for hire? Discuss.
3. If Roberto, the owner of a company, instructs one his employees, Chris, to prepare an employee manual for the company, who owns the work? Assume that in the course of writing the manual, Chris becomes interested in workplace issues and, at home and on his own time, writes a novel about sexual harassment in the workplace. Who owns the resulting work? Discuss fully.
4. What is the effect of a determination that a work is one made for hire? Discuss.
5. A publishing company hires Mary to write a student textbook. Does it make a difference if the agreement is oral or in writing? Discuss.
6. Tony and James collaborate on a song together. The two work in Tony's apartment and both contribute significantly to the lyrics and the music. Who owns the copyright? What is the duration of any copyright in the work? May James allow another to perform the work?
7. Sue transfers all of her interest in her copyrighted song to Cal in 2000. Does Sue have any rights in the future with regard to the song? Discuss fully.
8. Provide the period of duration for the following works:
    a. a novel written by Sam in 1980;
    b. advertising copy written by Dave for his employer and created and published in 1995;
    c. a novel published in 1920; and
    d. a novel created in 1970 but not published until 1998.

For additional resources, go to www.westlegalstudies.com.

CHAPTER 13

Copyright Registration, Searching Copyright Office Records, and Notice of Copyright

CHAPTER OVERVIEW

In the United States, copyright protection exists from the time a work is created. Thus, applying for and securing a copyright registration is not a condition of copyright protection. Nevertheless, copyright registration provides several benefits, such as establishing a public record of the claim of copyright, allowing a claim of infringement to be brought in federal court, and resulting in availability of statutory damages and attorneys' fees if a registered work is infringed. The Copyright Office provides all forms necessary for registration, and the process typically takes about sixteen weeks. The Copyright Office also is open for searching of records, and its information specialists will help conduct searches of records for a fee. Although notice of copyright is optional since March 1, 1989, use of a notice is recommended. A copyright notice consists of the symbol © (or the word "Copyright" or the abbreviation "Copr."), the year of first publication of the work, and the name of the copyright owner.

INTRODUCTION

As discussed in Chapter 9, neither publication of a work nor registration or other action in the U.S. Copyright Office is required to secure copyright protection under federal law. Copyright is secured automatically when the work is created. A work is "created" when it is fixed in a copy or phonorecord for the first time. Although not required to provide copyright protection for a work, registration of copyright with the Copyright Office is inexpensive, easy, and provides several advantages, chiefly, that registration is a condition precedent for bringing an infringement suit for works of U.S. origin. The relative ease with which works may be registered is chiefly due to the fact that there is no substantive examination of applications for registration of copyrights (as there is for trademarks and patents). To register a work, the applicant must send the following three elements to the Copyright Office: a properly completed application form, a filing fee, and a deposit of the work being registered. Registration may be made at any time within the life of the copyright.

THE APPLICATION FOR COPYRIGHT REGISTRATION

Parties Who May File Applications

The following persons are entitled to submit an application for registration of copyright:

- the author (either the person who actually created the work or, if the work is one made for hire, the employer or commissioning party);
- the copyright claimant (either the author or a person or organization that has obtained ownership of all of the rights under the copyright originally belonging to the author, such as a transferee);

- the owner of exclusive rights, such as the transferee of any of the exclusive rights of copyright ownership (for example, one who prepares a movie based on an earlier book may file an application for the newly created derivative work, the movie); and
- the duly authorized agent of the author, claimant, or owner of exclusive rights (such as an attorney, trustee, or anyone authorized to act on behalf of such parties).

Application Forms

Types of Forms.   The Copyright Office provides forms for applications for copyright registration. Each form is one 8½- by 11-inch sheet, printed front and back. An applicant may use photocopies of forms. Because the Copyright Office receives more than 600,000 applications each year, each application must use a similar format to ease the burden of examination. The type of form used is dictated by the type of work that is the subject of copyright. For example, one form is used for literary works, while another is used for sound recordings. Following are the forms used for copyright applications.

- **Form TX.** Form TX is used for registration of published or unpublished nondramatic literary works, excluding periodicals or serial issues. This class includes a wide variety of works: fiction, nonfiction, essays, poetry, textbooks, reference works, catalogs, advertising copy, compilations of information, and computer programs.
- **Form PA.** Form PA is used for works of the performing arts (namely, those to be performed before an audience), including plays, pantomimes, choreographic works, operas, motion pictures and other audiovisual works, musical compositions, and songs.

- **Form VA.** Form VA is used for registration of published or unpublished works of visual arts, including two- and three-dimensional works of fine, graphic, and applied art, such as cartoons, comic strips, dolls, toys, fabric and wallcovering designs, games and puzzles, greeting cards, jewelry designs, maps, original prints, photographs, posters, sculptures, and technical drawings including architectural plans and blueprints.
- **Form SR.** Form SR is used for sound recordings.
- **Form SE.** Form SE is used to register each individual issue of a serial, such as periodicals, newspapers, magazines, newsletters, annuals, and journals.
- **Short forms.** The Copyright Office offers a short version of some of its application forms to make registering a copyright claim easier. The information requested is minimal and the instructions are brief. Short forms may be used if the application is by a living author who is the sole author and owner of the work, the work is completely new, and the work is not one made for hire. The following forms are available in short form: Short Form PA (for works of the performing arts), Short Form TX (for literary works), and Short Form VA (for works of the visual arts).
- **Group forms.** Group forms may be used for certain applications comprising several parts, such as the following: Form Group/DN (for registering copyrights in a group of daily newspapers or newsletters); Form Group/CP (for submission with Forms TX, PA, or VA when a group of works such as short stories or a series of sculpture figurines is being applied for); and Form Group/SE (for applying for a group of serials, such as several issues of a magazine).

The Copyright Office provides other forms as well, namely, forms for renewals for works under the 1909 act (Form RE); forms for continuation when, due to length, the application cannot be completed on one page (Form CON); and a form to correct or amplify information given in the Copyright Office record of an earlier registration (Form CA).

Obtaining Application Forms. There are a variety of ways to obtain application forms from the Copyright Office. Application forms are provided free of charge.

- **Forms and circulars hotline.** A person can call the Copyright Office (202/707-9100) and leave a recorded message asking for forms by name and leaving a mailing address. The forms will be sent within a week or two.
- **Ordering by mail.** Copyright applications can be obtained by mailing a request to Library of Congress, Copyright Office, Publications Section LM-455, 101 Independence Avenue SE, Washington, DC 20559-6000.
- **Internet.** All Copyright Office application forms are now available on the Internet. They may be downloaded and printed for use in registering or renewing copyrights. Connect to the Library of Congress home page on the World Wide Web and select the copyright link. The address is http://www.loc.gov. Alternatively, you may connect through the Copyright Office home page at http://www.copyright.gov. You must have Adobe® Acrobat® Reader installed on your computer to view and print the forms. The free Adobe Acrobat Reader may be downloaded from Adobe Systems Incorporated through links from the same Internet site at which the forms are available. Print the forms head to head (the top of page 2 must be directly

behind the top of page 1) on a single sheet of 8½- by 11-inch white paper. Applications may be typewritten or printed by hand in black ink. Applications can be viewed and filled in on the Copyright Office web site and then printed and mailed in. The Copyright Office does not acccept electronic filings.

Preparing the Application Form. Although there are a variety of application forms to be used in applying for registration, the information required of an applicant and the format of the forms are nearly identical from form to form. Generally, there are several sections or "spaces" that must be completed. In order to obtain the information needed for the copyright application, many law firms ask clients to complete copyright questionnaires so information will be complete and accurate (see Exhibit 13–1 for a sample questionnaire).

Space 1: Title. Every work submitted for copyright registration must be given a title to identify it. If the copies or phonorecords of the work bear a title or any identifying phrase that could serve as a title, this wording should be used in its exact and complete form. Indexing of the registration and future identification of the work depends on its title. If the work is a collective work (such as a collection of songs), the overall title of the collection should be given.

The applicant must also indicate if the work has been known under a previous title or if there is an additional title under which someone searching for the registration might be likely to look. For example, if a movie title is changed in the course of filming, the previous title should be given. Similarly, the song "My Heart Will Go On" is also known as the "Theme Song from Titanic." Both titles should be given.

Space 2: Author(s). A variety of information must be given about the author(s) of the work. The fullest form of the author's name should be given, unless the work is a work made for hire, in which case the name of the employer or commissioning party should be given as author. If there is more than one author (such as may be the case in a joint work consisting of a book and its accompanying illustrations), all should be identified.

The application must indicate if the author's contribution is anonymous or pseudonymous. An author's contribution to a work is **anonymous** if a natural person is not identified on the copies or phonorecords of the work. An author's work is **pseudonymous** if the author is identified under a fictitious name, such as the books written by Stephen King under the pseudonym Richard Bachman.

If the author is dead, the application requires that the date of death be given (because copyright protection for most works lasts for life plus seventy years, the author's date of death determines copyright duration). The author's birth date is requested, although it is not required. If the work is one made for hire, the date of birth space should be left blank. The author's nationality or domicile must be given in all cases.

Finally, a brief description of the nature of authorship must be given. For example, the following terms are usually acceptable: *entire text, illustrations, computer program, words and music, sculpture, photographs, lyrics,* and *motion picture.* Conversely, the following terms should be avoided because they suggest lack of copyrightable material: *idea, concept, typeface, title, system, method,* and *layout.*

Space 3: Creation and Publication. Space 3 of each copyright application requires an identification of the year in which creation of the work was completed. Under the Copyright Act, a work is "created" when it is fixed in a tangible form for the first time. Generally, when a work is prepared over a period of time, such as is the case with a novel, the date of creation is the date of completion of the finished project.

EXHIBIT 13–1
Copyright
Questionnaire

The following questions are intended to help determine whether a work is entitled to copyright registration and the particular form to be used in applying for registration. Complete the questions to the best of your knowledge. If you do not know the answer to a question, indicate such and we can address outstanding issues together.

1. Describe your work. Is it a book? A short story? A song? A painting?
2. What is the title of your work?
3. Has the work had any previous or alternative titles? If so, list the titles.
4. Is the work part of a contribution to a periodical, such as a magazine or other serial? Has it been published in the magazine or is it scheduled to be published?
5. Who created the work? Give full name(s). Did anyone else participate in creating the work as a joint effort? If so, identify all joint authors. What part did each author play in the creation of the work (for example, one author may create text and another illustrations for a book or one author may compose a melody and another the lyrics for a song)?
6. Did you create the work in the scope of your employment as an employee of another?
7. Are you an employer whose employee created the work in the scope of employment? Was the creator of the work your employee or was the creator acting as an independent contractor for you?
8. Was the work created as a result of a special order or commission? If so, describe.
9. Give the date(s) of birth, and if applicable, date(s) of death of the author(s) of the work. What is the nationality or domicile of the author(s)?
10. Will the author be identified on the work or is the author anonymous? Is the author known by a pseudonym or fictitious name?
11. In what year was the work created (what year was it fixed in a tangible form)?
12. Has the work been published ("publication" refers to distribution of the work to the public by sale, transfer, sale, lease, or lending, or an offering to distribute it to a group of persons for purposes of further distribution, public performance, or display)? If the work has been published, give the exact date and nation in which it was first published.
13. Who is the owner of the copyright in the work? Has it been transferred by its author to anyone?
14. Have any licenses been granted to others to use the work, reproduce it, distribute it, or perform it? If so, are these licenses exclusive or nonexclusive? Were the licenses in writing?
15. Has registration for this work or an earlier version of this work already been sought in the Copyright Office? If so, please provide a copy of the earlier registration and describe how this version of the work differs from the earlier version.
16. Does the work include contributions by others, such as photographs or text by others? Does the work include any material owned by the U.S. Government?
17. Is this work based upon another work? For example, is this work a translation of another work? Is it based upon another work such as a book, song, movie, or play? Is it a condensation or abridgment of another work? Does it consist of revisions or editorial modifications? Describe.
18. If the work contains both original and preexisting material, identify and describe the new material.

Give the full name, address, and telephone number of the individual completing this questionnaire.

If the work has been published, Space 3 requires that the month, day, and year of the first publication be provided together with an identification of the country in which publication first occurred. "Publication" of a work is the distribution of copies or phonorecords of a work to the public by sale, transfer of ownership, or by rental, sale, or leasing. A work is also published if there has been an offering to distribute copies or phonorecords to a group of persons for purposes of further distribution, public performance, or public display. Thus, a novel is published when it has been offered to bookstores for further sale to the public.

Space 4: Claimant(s). The names and addresses of the copyright claimant(s) of the work must be given even if they are the same as those of the author(s). The copyright claimant is either the author of the work or a person or organization to whom the copyright has been transferred. For example, if Beverly Young is the author of a novel who has sold all rights to the novel to ABC Inc., Beverly Young would be listed as "author" and ABC Inc. would be identified as the claimant. If the claimant is not the author, a brief statement of how the claimant obtained ownership must be given. It is sufficient to state that the claimant obtained ownership "by written contract," "by transfer of all rights by author," "by assignment," or "by will."

Space 5: Previous Registration. The questions in Space 5 are intended to show whether an earlier registration has been made for the work and, if so, whether there is any basis for a new registration inasmuch as only one basic copyright registration can be made for the same version of a particular work.

If the version of the work subject to the application is substantially the same as the work covered by a previous registration, a second registration is generally impermissible.

If the work has been changed and a new registration is being sought to cover the addi-

tions or revisions, a new registration can be sought for these changes. Thus, if a movie is published in 2000 and a new version of it with additional scenes and footage is published in 2003, a second registration can be sought for the new version. Similarly, a new version of a computer program is eligible for copyright registration. The applicant must briefly describe the changes made to the work and give the number and date of the latest registration, if any.

Space 6: Derivative Work or Compilation. Space 6 requires the applicant to indicate if the work is a derivative work or compilation. A derivative work is a work based on a preexisting work (such as a movie based on a novel, a translation, editorial revisions, or a condensation). A compilation is a work formed by collecting and assembling preexisting materials or data that are selected and arranged in such a way that they constitute an original work (such as an almanac or a collection of short stories). If the work is a derivative work, the applicant must identify the preexisting work upon which the derivative work is based, for example, by stating "French translation of *Silent Witness.*" Whether the work is a derivative work or a compilation, the applicant must give a brief description of the new material covered by the copyright claim. For example, the applicant may state "foreword, editing, and annotations" for a derivative work, or may state "compilation of short stories by twentieth-century feminists" for a compilation.

Remaining Spaces. The remaining portions of copyright application forms ask for a variety of miscellaneous information.

- **Deposit account.** Individuals who file many copyright applications (at least twelve transactions each year) can establish a deposit account with the Copyright Office by depositing at least $250, eliminating the burden of sending in a fee with each application filed. If a deposit account is established, the applicant indicates the deposit account number on documents submitted to the Copyright Office so fees can be automatically withdrawn from the account. The Copyright Office sends monthly statements showing charges so individuals can replenish the account. If no deposit account has been established, the applicant merely sends in the fee with the application.

- **Correspondence.** The applicant should provide a name, address, telephone number, fax number, and e-mail address of a person to be consulted in the event correspondence about the application is necessary.
- **Certification.** The application cannot be accepted unless it bears the date and handwritten signature of the author or other copyright claimant or of the owner of exclusive rights or the duly authorized agent of such. The signature certifies to the Copyright Office that the information provided in the application is correct to the best of the applicant's knowledge. Making a false representation of a material fact can subject the signatory to a fine up to $2,500.
- **Address for return of certificate.** The address to which the certificate of registration should be sent must be given. The address space should be completed legibly because the certificate will be sent in a window envelope and this information will appear in the window.

(See Exhibit 13–2 for a sample of a completed copyright application.)

Filing Fee

17 U.S.C. § 708 authorizes the Copyright Office to charge fees. Effective July 1, 2002, the nonrefundable fee for filing an application is $30. Check the Copyright Office web site or call (202) 707-3000 for the latest fee information. The fee for a copyright application may be paid by deposit account or by check or money order payable to Register of Copyrights. Cash is not accepted. Electronic transfers and credit card charges are generally not permissible.

DEPOSIT MATERIALS

Introduction

Section 407 of the Copyright Act requires that the owner of copyright or of the exclusive right of publication in a work published in the United States deposit, within three months after publication, two complete copies of the best edition of the work or, if the work is a sound recording, two complete phonorecords of the best edition. Deposits are to be made into the Library of Congress so that it can continue its tradition of cataloguing and collecting works published in the United States by ensuring that it receives copies of every copyrightable work published in the United States. The Copyright Act presumes that individuals will make the deposit voluntarily.

Although this deposit requirement can be fulfilled through application for copyright registration (because deposit materials are required to be submitted with the application), the requirement is mandatory whether or not an application is ever filed (although certain works such as greeting cards, postcards, stationery, technical drawings, and advertising materials are exempt). Failure to deposit the materials does not cause a loss of copyright protection, but it may subject a party to fine (presently, $250) if the Copyright Office requests the deposit and the copyright owner fails to supply the materials within three months. The deposit requirements in the United States are similar to those in other countries.

have some formal theory in order to conduct research? The answer is: Not really. There are two alternative kinds of research logic. One is called inductive and the other deductive. Only the deductive logic requires a theory as a starting point, and with this logic empirical research takes the form of hypothesis testing. In a narrower sense, both kinds of logic could apply to the process of hypothesis formulation. The inductive approach means the making of a hypothesis on a non- or atheoretical basis, which would include empirical research findings, general observations, or personal experiences. The deductive approach is the reasoning from some general theory or some formal but more specific models, which could also be bolstered by various empirical and practical evidence.

Just as you may conduct an exploratory or tentative study without a formal research hypothesis, you may conduct your research and formulate your hypotheses without an explicit theory. As a matter of fact, it is unlikely that you will always be able to find some formal theory to back up your hypotheses and conclusions in empirical research. The deductive logic, however, may sometimes and somehow be deemed superior to the inductive logic, and in that situation you will be expected to try hard to set up your theoretical framework. It is good for you, therefore, to note the way people deduct from existing theories to their research hypotheses when reading their proposals and reports. In sociology and sociological research textbooks, for instance, there are examples of deducting from such grand theories as functionalism and conflict theory to various specific research hypotheses (e.g., True, 1989). On the other hand, people have spelled out many lower-level or limited-range theories as well as more concrete models. These could all be regarded as various parts of a theoretical system and thus may be used as a theory base of your research.

The requirement for a theoretical framework is often a big headache for a research student. The student may have been reading tons of books but is still uncertain if she can start writing a theory paper. This is probably a matter of a psychological barrier, and misunderstanding may have played a part. You may have come up with a research question simply through some of your random thoughts. Yet you cannot let it go too far without some systematic effort. Preparing the theory part of your research proposal and report is actually a chance for you to show your systematic knowledge of a specific field rather than smattering insights here and there.

The theoretical framework means a systematic review of the theoretical literature. You can write in your research document a concise summary of the theoretical literature as part of your effort to build a research framework. This

EXHIBIT 13–2
Completed
Copyright
Application

Copyright Office fees are subject to change. For current fees, check the Copyright Office website at *www.copyright.gov*, write the Copyright Office, or call (202) 707-3000.

FORM TX

For a Nondramatic Literary Work
UNITED STATES COPYRIGHT OFFICE

REGISTRATION NUMBER

_____

TX _____ TXU _____

EFFECTIVE DATE OF REGISTRATION

_____ _____ _____
Month   Day   Year

DO NOT WRITE ABOVE THIS LINE. IF YOU NEED MORE SPACE, USE A SEPARATE CONTINUATION SHEET.

1

TITLE OF THIS WORK ▼

The Angel in Disguise

PREVIOUS OR ALTERNATIVE TITLES ▼
None

PUBLICATION AS A CONTRIBUTION If this work was published as a contribution to a periodical, serial, or collection, give information about the collective work in which the contribution appeared.   **Title of Collective Work ▼**

If published in a periodical or serial give: **Volume ▼**   **Number ▼**   **Issue Date ▼**   **On Pages ▼**

2

a

NAME OF AUTHOR ▼
Tracy Havermann

DATES OF BIRTH AND DEATH
Year Born ▼   Year Died ▼
12-22-56

Was this contribution to the work a "work made for hire"?
☐ Yes
☑ No

AUTHOR'S NATIONALITY OR DOMICILE
Name of Country
OR { Citizen of ▶ *U.S.A.*
     { Domiciled in ▶

WAS THIS AUTHOR'S CONTRIBUTION TO THE WORK
Anonymous?   ☐ Yes ☑ No
Pseudonymous? ☐ Yes ☑ No

If the answer to either of these questions is "Yes," see detailed instructions.

NATURE OF AUTHORSHIP Briefly describe nature of material created by this author in which copyright is claimed. ▼
Entire Text

NOTE

Under the law, the "author" of a "work made for hire" is generally the employer, not the employee (see instructions). For any part of this work that was "made for hire" check "Yes" in the space provided, give the employer (or other person for whom the work was prepared) as "Author" of that part, and leave the space for dates of birth and death blank.

b

NAME OF AUTHOR ▼

DATES OF BIRTH AND DEATH
Year Born ▼   Year Died ▼

Was this contribution to the work a "work made for hire"?
☐ Yes
☐ No

AUTHOR'S NATIONALITY OR DOMICILE
Name of Country
OR { Citizen of ▶
     { Domiciled in ▶

WAS THIS AUTHOR'S CONTRIBUTION TO THE WORK
Anonymous?   ☐ Yes ☐ No
Pseudonymous? ☐ Yes ☐ No

If the answer to either of these questions is "Yes," see detailed instructions.

NATURE OF AUTHORSHIP Briefly describe nature of material created by this author in which copyright is claimed. ▼

c

NAME OF AUTHOR ▼

DATES OF BIRTH AND DEATH
Year Born ▼   Year Died ▼

Was this contribution to the work a "work made for hire"?
☐ Yes
☐ No

AUTHOR'S NATIONALITY OR DOMICILE
Name of Country
OR { Citizen of ▶
     { Domiciled in ▶

WAS THIS AUTHOR'S CONTRIBUTION TO THE WORK
Anonymous?   ☐ Yes ☐ No
Pseudonymous? ☐ Yes ☐ No

If the answer to either of these questions is "Yes," see detailed instructions.

NATURE OF AUTHORSHIP Briefly describe nature of material created by this author in which copyright is claimed. ▼

3

a YEAR IN WHICH CREATION OF THIS WORK WAS COMPLETED   This information must be given   ◀ Year in all cases.
2003

b DATE AND NATION OF FIRST PUBLICATION OF THIS PARTICULAR WORK
Complete this information ONLY if this work has been published.
Month ▶ *August*   Day ▶ *1*   Year ▶ *2003*   ◀ Nation

4

See instructions before completing this space.

COPYRIGHT CLAIMANT(S) Name and address must be given even if the claimant is the same as the author given in space 2. ▼
Tracy Havermann
120 Elmwood Street
Richmond, VA 22180

TRANSFER If the claimant(s) named here in space 4 is (are) different from the author(s) named in space 2, give a brief statement of how the claimant(s) obtained ownership of the copyright. ▼

APPLICATION RECEIVED

ONE DEPOSIT RECEIVED

TWO DEPOSITS RECEIVED

FUNDS RECEIVED

DO NOT WRITE HERE OFFICE USE ONLY

MORE ON BACK ▶ • Complete all applicable spaces (numbers 5-9) on the reverse side of this page.
                • See detailed instructions.   • Sign the form at line 8.

DO NOT WRITE HERE
Page 1 of _____ pages

EXHIBIT 13–2
Completed
Copyright
Application
(continued)

EXAMINED BY	FORM TX
CHECKED BY	
☐ CORRESPONDENCE Yes	FOR COPYRIGHT OFFICE USE ONLY

DO NOT WRITE ABOVE THIS LINE. IF YOU NEED MORE SPACE, USE A SEPARATE CONTINUATION SHEET.

PREVIOUS REGISTRATION Has registration for this work, or for an earlier version of this work, already been made in the Copyright Office?

☐ Yes ☒ No If your answer is "Yes," why is another registration being sought? (Check appropriate box.) ▼

a. ☐ This is the first published edition of a work previously registered in unpublished form.

b. ☐ This is the first application submitted by this author as copyright claimant.

c. ☐ This is a changed version of the work, as shown by space 6 on this application.

If your answer is "Yes," give: **Previous Registration Number** ▶   **Year of Registration** ▶

5

DERIVATIVE WORK OR COMPILATION

Preexisting Material Identify any preexisting work or works that this work is based on or incorporates. ▼

NA

Material Added to This Work Give a brief, general statement of the material that has been added to this work and in which copyright is claimed. ▼

a 6 b

See instructions
before completing
this space.

DEPOSIT ACCOUNT If the registration fee is to be charged to a Deposit Account established in the Copyright Office, give name and number of Account.

Name ▼   **Account Number** ▼

CORRESPONDENCE Give name and address to which correspondence about this application should be sent.   Name/Address/Apt/City/State/ZIP ▼

Tracy Havermann
120 Elmwood Street
Richmond, VA 22180

Area code and daytime telephone number ▶ (803) 716-4420   Fax number ▶ NA

Email ▶ NA

a 7 b

CERTIFICATION* I, the undersigned, hereby certify that I am the

Check only one ▶

☒ author
☐ other copyright claimant
☐ owner of exclusive right(s)
☐ authorized agent of _____

of the work identified in this application and that the statements made
by me in this application are correct to the best of my knowledge.

Name of author or other copyright claimant, or owner of exclusive right(s) ▲

8

Typed or printed name and date ▼ If this application gives a date of publication in space 3, do not sign and submit it before that date.

Tracy Havermann   Date ▶ August 15, 2003

Handwritten signature (X) ▼

x Tracy Havermann

Certificate
will be
mailed in
window
envelope
to this
address:

Name ▼ Tracy Havermann

Number/Street/Apt ▼ 120 Elmwood Street

City/State/ZIP ▼ Richmond VA 22180

YOU MUST:
• Complete all necessary spaces
• Sign your application in space 8

**SEND ALL 3 ELEMENTS
IN THE SAME PACKAGE:**
1. Application form
2. Nonrefundable filing fee in check or money
   order payable to *Register of Copyrights*
3. Deposit material

MAIL TO:
Library of Congress
Copyright Office
101 Independence Avenue, S.E.
Washington, D.C. 20559-6000

Fees are subject to
change. For current
fees, check the
Copyright Office
website at
www.copyright.gov,
write the Copyright
Office, or call
(202) 707-3000

9

*17 U.S.C. § 506(e): Any person who knowingly makes a false representation of a material fact in the application for copyright registration provided for by section 409, or in any written statement filed in connection
with the application, shall be fined not more than $2,500.

Rev. June 2002—20,000   Web Rev: June 2002   ♻ Printed on recycled paper   U.S. Government Printing Office: 2000-461-113/20,021

Deposit Materials Accompanying Copyright Applications

An application for a copyright registration must be accompanied by a nonreturnable **deposit** of the work being registered. Although the deposit requirements vary in particular situations, the general requirements are as follows:

- if the work is unpublished, one complete copy or phonorecord; or
- if the work was first published in the United States on or after January 1, 1978, two complete copies or phonorecords of the best edition.

The "Best Edition" Requirement

The Copyright Act requires that copies or phonorecords deposited be of the **best edition** of the work. The "best edition" requirement is intended to discourage inferior deposit materials and encourage deposit materials of high quality. Generally, the best edition is one that is larger rather than smaller; color rather than black and white; and printed on archival-quality rather than less permanent paper. For example, for books, hardcover rather than softcover copies are the best edition, and sewn rather than glue-only binding is preferred; for photographs, unmounted rather than mounted photographs are the best edition; for phonorecords, compact digital discs rather than vinyl discs are the best edition; for motion pictures, film rather than videotape formats are the best edition. Copyright Office Circular 7b fully describes the best edition requirements.

If the depositor cannot deposit the best edition, a request for special relief may be made, stating why the applicant cannot send the required deposit and what the applicant wishes to submit in place of the required deposit.

Deposit Requirements for Specific Works

Following are the deposit requirements for specific works:

- **Visual arts materials.** Because it would be impracticable or impossible to submit large sculptures, paintings, and posters, photographs are generally acceptable for these works. For fabrics and wallcoverings, swatches showing the design repeat are acceptable. For games, a complete copy of the game must be submitted unless it is large, in which case a photograph is permissible.
- **Literary works.** Copies of the text, book, advertising copy, and so forth must be submitted.
- **Performing arts works.** For plays, cinema, radio, and television scripts, the scripts themselves should be deposited. For pantomimes and choreographic works, a film or video recording showing the work is permissible, or the works may be described in written text.
- **Architectural works.** The required deposit for an architectural work, whether or not the building has been constructed, is one complete copy of an architectural drawing or blueprint. If the building has been constructed, the deposit must also include photographs showing the work (preferably 8- by 10-inch photos showing interior and exterior views).
- **Motion pictures.** For motion pictures, one copy of the work as first published is required (one of the first prints or tapes made from the master, clear, undamaged, and unspliced). Additionally, a separate description of the work is required, such as a script or summary.
- **Musical compositions.** For vocal and instrumental music, generally the sheet music or full score must be submitted.
- **Sound recordings.** The deposit for sound recordings is two complete phonorecords of the best edition plus any text or pictorial matter published

with the phonorecord (compact discs, albums, or cassettes). Examples of the textual material include all phonorecord packaging, record sleeves, and separate leaflets or booklets enclosed with the phonorecords.

- **Computer programs.** Generally, the first and last twenty-five pages of source code must be submitted as the deposit for computer programs; however, as discussed in Copyright Office Circular 61 and in Chapter 15, the Copyright Office permits authors to "block out" portions of the source code if it constitutes a trade secret.

- **Multimedia works.** A multimedia work is a work that combines forms of authorship, such as a book including charts or a slide presentation to be shown with accompanying narration or music on a cassette tape. A single application can be used if the copyright claimant is the same for each element of the work and the elements of the work, if published, are published as a single unit. Generally, the deposit should be a complete multimedia kit containing all elements covered by the registration.

Recall that in the case of published works, two copies of the best edition are required. For unpublished works, one copy is required.

THE APPLICATION PROCESS AND REGISTRATION OF COPYRIGHT

Filing the Application

After the correct application form has been selected and completed and the correct deposit materials have been identified, the application may be filed with the U.S. Copyright Office. Despite the apparent complexity of the numerous forms and deposit requirements, for those with familiarity with copyright law and procedure, completing the application form often takes thirty minutes or less.

Although not required, it is a good idea to send a cover letter accompanying the application. The cover letter can confirm the contents of the package and provide a name and phone number of a person to contact in the event the Copyright Office has questions. Many applicants also include a "come-back" card, a self-addressed and stamped postcard so the Copyright Office can confirm the filing of the application because the Copyright Office itself does not issue any acknowledgment that an application has been received.

Examination of the Application and Copyright Registration

The Copyright Office will assign the application to a specialist; however, the examination of the application is not substantive, as is the case with trademark and patent applications. Generally, a copyright application is examined only to ensure that the material in which copyright is claimed is copyrightable (for example, a copyright claim in facts, a recipe, or a blank form will be refused) and that the material deposited complies with statutory requirements.

There are four major examining sections in the Copyright Office: one for literary works, one for works of the performing arts, one for works of visual arts, and one for renewals. The examiner will review the application to ensure all information is complete and compare the application and deposit for consistency.

It is nearly impossible to determine the status of an application that has been filed. The Copyright Office Certifications and Documents Section (202/707-6787) may have information, but such information is provided only upon payment of applicable fees. Due to the volume of applications filed each year (more than six hundred thousand), the Copyright Office does not provide free information about the status of an application.

Nevertheless, within approximately sixteen weeks of filing the application, the Copyright Office will either issue a certificate of registration or contact the applicant by letter or phone asking for additional information or explaining why the application has been rejected. If the Copyright Office has questions, the applicant usually has 120 days to respond. Failure to respond within the time required generally results in closing of the file without further notification. If registration is later desired, a new application, deposit, and fee must be submitted.

If the application is acceptable, the Copyright Office will register the copyright by returning a certificate of registration, namely, a copy of the application stamped with a seal, a registration number, and date of registration. A copyright registration is effective on the date the Copyright Office receives a complete application package in acceptable form, regardless of how long it may take to process the application. In general, Copyright Office policy is to resolve questionable cases in favor of the applicant under the **rule of doubt,** meaning that although the Copyright Office has doubts about copyrightability, it will resolve doubts in favor of the applicant and allow a court to make a final determination in the future if questions arise regarding copyrightability.

The Copyright Office is in the process of implementing an electronic filing system called the Copyright Office Electronic Registration, Recordation, and Deposit System (CORDS). The CORDS project aims to develop and implement a totally electronic system of receipt and processing of copyright applications, deposited works, and related documents over communications networks such as the Internet. In early 1996, the Copyright Office received its first electronic application (an unpublished dissertation by a student). The application was completed using a specially developed online form, and the dissertation was transmitted with the application over the Internet in a few minutes. The application and dissertation were "signed" using encryption technology. The CORDS system will enable the Copyright Office to complete its review and processing and issue a registration certificate within a few days or weeks rather than the four-month period usually experienced. Testing and implementation will continue over the next several years. At present, the Copyright Office accepts only literary texts, serials, and musical works in electronic form from a limited number of participants.

Refusal of Registration

If registration is refused by the Copyright Office, reexamination can be requested. The applicant "appeals" the adverse decision by making a written request for reexamination or reconsideration and paying the appeal fee of $200. A response in writing will be made by a Copyright Office section head. Further reconsideration may be requested of the Chief of the Examining Division upon payment of an additional fee of $500. If registration is still refused, the applicant may seek judicial review in the United States District Court for the District of Columbia.

Because copyright registration is a prerequisite for an infringement suit for works originating in the United States, refusal of registration would put a party who believes his or her work has been infringed in the untenable situation of being unable to initiate action in federal court for infringement. Thus, if registration has been applied for and refused, the applicant may still file an infringement action but must provide notice of the action and a copy of the complaint to the Register of Copyrights. The Register may become a party to the court action but only with regard to registrability of the work.

The Copyright Office can cancel a registration if it is determined that a work is not copyrightable or the check for the filing fee is returned for insufficient funds. Prior to cancellation, the Copyright Office will provide notice to the registrant so the registrant has an opportunity to respond to the cancellation procedure.

Special Handling

In some instances, applicants may not be able to wait sixteen weeks to receive notification that a copyright has been registered. For example, before a copyright infringement suit may be filed in court, registration is necessary for works of U.S. origin. Thus, a party who wishes to commence an infringement action upon short notice must have assurance that a copyright has been registered. To expedite the processing of applications for registration (or the recordation of documents relating to copyrights), the Copyright Office has established **special handling** procedures.

Special handling is granted only in special circumstances. These are:

- pending or prospective litigation;
- customs matters; or
- contract or publishing deadlines that necessitate the expedited process.

Special handling is typically requested by a letter stating the reasons why special handling is needed. The request must also include a signed statement certifying that the information contained in the request is correct to the best of the requestor's knowledge. Once a request for special handling is approved, every effort is made by the Copyright Office to process the application or request for recordation within five working days. The present fee for a special handling request for an application is $580 (plus the usual application filing fee of $30 or for expedited recording of documents, $330 plus the usual fee for recording documents).

Supplementary Copyright Registration

If information in a registration is incorrect or incomplete, an application may be filed for **supplementary copyright registration** to correct the error or amplify the information given. Supplementary registration can be made only if a basic copyright registration for the same work has already been issued. Form CA is used, and the filing fee is $100. No deposit materials should be included.

Supplementary registration is not necessary for minor typographical errors or omission of articles, such as the word *the*. Some of the more common reasons a supplementary copyright registration is requested are the following:

- the original application identified an incorrect author;
- the work was registered as published when publication had not yet taken place;
- a coauthor was omitted; or
- a change in the name or title of the work has occurred (for example, a book or movie title has been changed).

If the supplementary registration is issued, there will be two registrations on file with the Copyright Office. The original registration will not be expunged or canceled, but the supplementary registration will direct the public's attention to an error or omission in the basic registration and will place the correct facts or additional information on official record.

Benefits of Securing Registration

Because copyright protection exists from the time a work is created, securing a registration from the Copyright Office is not necessary to protect copyright material. Nevertheless, federal copyright law provides several inducements to encourage copyright owners to secure registration. Among these advantages are the following:

- Registration establishes a public record of the claim of copyright.
- Before an infringement suit may be filed in courts, registration is necessary for works of U.S. origin (except for a suit alleging a violation of the right of attribution or integrity under the Visual Artists Rights Act) and for foreign works not originating in a Berne Union country.
- If made before or within five years of publication, registration constitutes *prima facie* evidence of the validity of the copyright and of the facts stated in the certificate.
- If registration is made within three months after publication or prior to an infringement of an unpublished work, statutory damages and attorneys' fees will be available to the copyright owner in court actions. Otherwise, only an award of actual damages and lost profits is available to the copyright owner.
- Registration allows the owner of the copyright to record the registration with the U.S. Customs Service for protection against the importation of infringing copies.

SEARCHING COPYRIGHT OFFICE RECORDS

It may become necessary to determine whether copyright for a work has been registered or what copyrights are registered to a company or individual. For example, if a company is selling all of its assets to another, the buyer will typically conduct **due diligence** and review records of the PTO and the Copyright Office to determine what patents, trademarks, and copyrights are registered in the seller's name so these can then be transferred to the buyer.

Conducting searches prior to applying for copyright registration is not nearly as critical as conducting searches prior to applying for trademark or patent protection. Because copyright protection exists once a work is created and independent creation is permissible, the fact that another party has a copyright registration for a work will not preclude registration for another similar or identical work (as long as the works do not copy from each other). Nevertheless, although titles are not copyrightable, an author may wish to select a unique title for a book or movie, and a search would reveal similar or identical titles.

There are a variety of ways to search Copyright Office records:

- The records of the Copyright Office are open for inspection and searching by the public. The Copyright Office, however, cannot give legal advice, answer questions on possible infringement, recommend publishers, or enforce contracts. The records freely available to the public include an extensive card catalog (for registrations from 1870 through 1977) and an online catalog (for registrations since 1978) that provide an index to more than 40 million registered copyrights. Searching can be done by the title of the work, author(s), claimant(s), date of publication, or registration number.
- The Library of Congress card catalog can be searched; however, only a portion of the works deposited for copyright are selected for inclusion in the Library's collections, and the Library does not always fully catalog those works it selects. Some searching of Library of Congress records can be done through the Library's web site at http://www.loc.gov. Select "Search Our Catalog" and follow the instructions given.
- Most copyright records since 1978 can be searched by Internet. The Internet site address for the Copyright Office files is http://www.copyright.gov/records.

This is an experimental system best used for short and simple searches.

- The Copyright Office itself will conduct searches for $75 per hour. The Reference and Bibliography Section of the Copyright Office will conduct a search and provide a factual report on the results of the search. Searches can be initiated by writing to this section or by calling (202/707-6850). The Copyright Office will estimate the total search fee and initiate the search upon receiving the fee. Upon payment of additional fees, the search can be expedited. A search request form is provided in Copyright Office Circular 22.
- Private companies can conduct searches. Just as companies will search PTO records and provide reports of trademarks, they will conduct searches of Copyright Office records, file applications and other documents, and provide copies of documents. Contact Thomson & Thomson, 1750 K Street NW, Suite 200, Washington, DC 20006 (800/356-8630, http://www.thomson-thomson.com) or CCH Corsearch, 233 Spring Street, New York, NY 10013 (800/732-7241, http://www.corsearch.com).

OBTAINING COPYRIGHT OFFICE RECORDS AND DEPOSIT MATERIALS

Upon request, the Certificates and Documents Section of the Copyright Office will prepare certified or uncertified copies of certain public records. Applications, registrations, assignments, licenses, and other documents pertaining to copyrights can be obtained. Generally, these records can be obtained for minimum fees (for example, $30 for an additional copy of a certificate of registration). Certified copies are usually requested as evidence of the authenticity of

a document when litigation involving the copyright is involved. Upon payment of additional fees, expedited service is possible.

Obtaining copies of deposit materials is considerably more difficult than obtaining copies of records. Moreover, not all deposits are retained. The Copyright Office policy is to retain deposits for published works for five years (ten years for works of visual arts). Unpublished deposits are generally kept for the full copyright term. Registrants who wish to ensure the Copyright Office retains their published deposits for the duration of a copyright term must pay a fee of $425 to cover storage costs.

Assuming the material is available, the Copyright Office will provide certified or uncertified copies of the actual works deposited with the Copyright Office only when one of the following three conditions has been met:

- written authorization is received from the copyright claimant of record or his or her agent (or the owner of any of the exclusive rights upon written documentation of the transfer);
- a Copyright Office Litigation Statement Form is completed and received from an attorney or authorized representative stating there is actual or prospective litigation involving the copyrighted work, giving assurance that the material will be used only in connection with the litigation, and providing detailed information about the parties, the controversy, and the court; or
- a court order is issued for reproduction of a deposited article that is the subject of litigation.

Rather than providing the actual deposit material, the Copyright Office may provide a reproduction, such as photographs or photocopies or a reproduction of a sound recording. A fee will be quoted by the Copyright Office when the request for deposit material is made.

COPYRIGHT NOTICE

Introduction

Since March 1, 1989 (the date of adherence by the United States to the Berne Convention), use of a **notice of copyright** (usually the symbol © together with the year of first publication and copyright owner's name) is no longer mandatory, although it is recommended and offers some advantages. Use of the notice informs the public that the work is protected by copyright, identifies the copyright owner, and shows the year of first publication. Furthermore, if a work is infringed, if a proper notice of copyright appears on a published work to which the defendant had access, the defendant cannot assert that infringement was innocent (an innocent infringement defense may result in a reduction of damages). Use of the notice is the responsibility of the copyright owner and does not require advance permission from or registration of copyright with the Copyright Office.

Works published before January 1, 1978, are governed by the 1909 Copyright Act. Under that act, if a work was published under the copyright owner's authority without a proper notice of copyright, all copyright protection for that work was permanently lost in the United States. Many works fell into the public domain merely because the owner failed to include the copyright notice. To align the United States with the laws of most other foreign countries, the United States joined the Berne Convention in 1989 and agreed to eliminate any requirement for copyright notice. With regard to works published between January 1, 1978, and March 1, 1989, omission of a notice was generally excused if the notice was omitted from a small number of copies, registration was made within five years of publication, and a reasonable effort was made to add the notice after discovery of its omission. See Exhibit 13–3.

Form of Notice for Visually Perceptible Copies

The form of notice used for visually perceptible copies—those that can be seen or read either directly (such as books) or with the aid of a machine (such as movies)—is different from the form used for sound recordings (such as records or cassettes).

Under 17 U.S.C. § 401, the form for visually perceptible copies includes three elements that

EXHIBIT 13–3
Copyright Notice
Requirements

For works published before 1/1/78	Failure to include notice on published work invalidates copyright, and work will go into the public domain.
For works published between 1/1/78 and 3/1/89	Notice required for all published works. If notice omitted, copyright valid if notice only omitted from a small number of copies, registration is sought within five years, and a reasonable effort is made to add notice.
For works published after 3/1/89	Use of copyright notice is optional. Lack of notice, however, may allow a defendant to assert infringement was innocent and may affect damages.

should appear together or in close proximity. The elements are the following:

1. the symbol © (the letter C in a circle), or the word "Copyright," or the abbreviation "Copr."; and
2. the year of first publication (the year can be omitted when a pictorial, graphic, or sculptural work is reproduced on greeting cards, stationery, jewelry, dolls, or toys); and
3. the name of the owner of copyright in the work, or an abbreviation or alternative designation by which the name can be recognized.

Recall that *publication* is defined as the year of distribution of copies or phonorecords of a work by sale, transfer, rental, lease, or lending or an offering to distribute copies or phonorecords to a group of persons for purposes of further distribution, public performance, or display. If there are joint owners, all of their names should be given. The Copyright Act does not specify the actual order of the elements of the copyright notice but only requires that the notice be placed in such a manner and location as to give reasonable notice of the claim of copyright.

Examples of acceptable copyright notices are "© 1995 John Andrews," "© 2003 ABC Inc.," and "Copr. 1997 Madonna."

Form of Notice for Sound Recordings

Because audio recordings such as audiotapes and phonograph discs are not "copies" but are "phonorecords" under the Copyright Act, the form of copyright notice is different from that used for visually perceptible copies. Copyright in a sound recording protects the particular series of sounds fixed in the recording against unauthorized reproduction, revision, and distribution. Phonorecords may be records (such as LPs and 45s), audiotapes, cassettes, or discs. Notice for phonorecords should contain the following three elements:

1. the letter "P" placed inside a circle; and
2. the year of first publication; and
3. the name of the owner of copyright or an abbreviation or alternative designation by which the owner can be recognized.

Special Notice Requirements

Questions about the form of copyright notice arise in a variety of cases. Some commonly encountered problems are as follows:

- **Contributions to collective works.** A single copyright notice applicable to the collective work (such as an anthology of poems or magazine) as a whole is sufficient protection for all the contributions in the collective work (except advertisements). Nevertheless, the separate contributions to the collective work may bear their own notices of copyright (primarily to inform the public of the identity of the owner of the contribution).
- **Publications incorporating U.S. government works.** Any work published before March 1, 1989, that included government works was required to include a special notice identifying the portions of the work that incorporated government works. Thus, if a 1985 textbook reproduced the U.S. Constitution, the notice should state "© 1985 Penguin Books. Copyright is not claimed as to the U.S. Constitution reproduced in Chapter 14." For works published after March 1, 1989, the notice is not required but is recommended, because including the notice will preclude a defendant from alleging his or her infringement was innocent.
- **Derivative works.** In the case of a derivative work (one based on an underlying work, such as a sequel to a preexisting book), the information in the

Contents

would please your readers, especially those who are eager to see that part. As a student you are not in a position to tell your committee that theory is not necessary for your research. Be prepared and you may benefit from your hard work by even creating a new theory. It should be noted that theorization following inductive logic is also an important category of research. And sometimes the core of the entire theoretical work is the conceptualization of an important behavioral/social phenomenon.

In practice, a major obstacle to students conducting research has not been the lack of theory, but a rigid, dogmatic, and narrow-minded understanding about what is meant by theory. This might not be the fault of the students but of those who read, comment, and grade their papers, theses, and/or dissertations. For the purpose of research, any known statement about the logical and persistent patterns of regularity should be recognized as serving the function of theory. And of course, your hypothesis is part of the theory which needs to be validated or refuted by empirical observations and generalized via statistical means.

The popularity of the deductive logic combined with the difficulty in finding a relevant, well-formulated theory does not mean that you should apply whatever you can find to your study. Here a critical view is very important. Unfortunately, people sometimes mistake this and urge you to hold a skeptical and critical attitude not toward theoretical statements but toward certain subject groups in a given study. These commentators as researchers tend to lose their neutrality, impartiality and objectivity, and are prone to making arbitrary judgments about the issues under study. It should be clarified that here what we attach the primary importance to is a critical view of the way people gain their knowledge and beliefs, including our own research strategies and approaches. Although objectivity and value neutrality are often difficult to achieve and to maintain in social research, social scientists always try to avoid the kind of subjectivity and preference-driven studies by relying on facts and using such substitute principles as intersubjectivity (the agreement of the scientific community).

The formulation of research hypotheses

A research hypothesis is a tentative statement about the condition of a variable or about the relationship between variables. Research textbooks tend to ignore the sort of single-variable hypothesis, yet the students tend to start from making that kind of research hypothesis. The gap often leaves the students at a loss.

notice should relate to the new work, not the underlying work. The symbol © (or the word "Copyright" or the abbreviation "Copr."), the year of first publication of the new work, and the name of the copyright owner of the new work should be given. Only the new material is owned by the new author, and one cannot extend the length of copyright protection by creating a derivative work. On occasion, a copyright notice will indicate a range of years for a work, for example, "© 1998, 1999, 2002 Jane Doe" to indicate the years of publication of the original work and later derivative works.

- **Unpublished works.** There has never been a requirement for use of a copyright notice for unpublished works, although a notice may be used. An example would be "Unpublished work © 1996 Daniel Donoghue."

Location of Notice

The Copyright Act does not dictate exact placement of the copyright notice but requires only that it be placed in such a way that it gives reasonable notice of the claim of copyright. According to 37 C.F.R. § 201.20, the following placements are acceptable:

- **Works published in book form.** The notice may be placed on the title page, the page immediately following the title page, either side of the front or back covers, or the first or last page of the work.
- **Single-leaf works.** The notice may be placed anywhere on the front or back of the leaf.
- **Contributions to collective works.** The notice may be placed under the title or elsewhere on the same page if the contribution consists of one page. If the contribution spans more than one page, the notice may be placed under the title,

on the first page of the contribution, or at the end of the contribution.

- **Works published as periodicals or other serials.** The notice may be placed at any of the locations acceptable on books, near the masthead or on the same page as the masthead, or adjacent to a prominent heading near the front of the issue.
- **Computer programs and works produced in machine-readable copies.** The notice may appear with or near the title or at the end of the work, on visually perceptible printouts, at the user's terminal at sign-on, on continuous display on the terminal, or reproduced durably on a label securely affixed to the copies or to a container used as a permanent receptacle for the copies.
- **Motion pictures and other audiovisual works.** The notice may be placed with or near the title, with the credits information, at or immediately following the beginning of the work, or at or immediately preceding the end of the work. If the work is distributed to the public for private use (such as rental of videotaped movies or DVDs), the notice can also be placed on the permanent container for the videotape or DVD.
- **Pictorial, graphic, and sculptural works.** For works embodied in two-dimensional copies (such as paintings and posters), the notice may be affixed to the front or back of the copies or any backing or mounting material. For works reproduced in three-dimensional copies (such as sculptures, globes, and dolls), the notice may be affixed to any visible portion of the work or any base or mounting for the work. If it is impracticable to affix a notice to the copies directly (such as is the case with jewelry), a notice may be placed on a tag or

label. For sheeting such as fabrics and wallcoverings, the notice may appear on the margin selvage or reverse side of the material in frequent and regular intervals. For games and puzzles, the notice may be reproduced on the container.

- **Sound recordings.** The notice may be placed on the surface of the phonorecord or on the phonorecord label or container.

When a notice does not appear in one of the precise locations prescribed by 37 C.F.R. § 201.20, but a person looking in one of those locations would be reasonably certain to find the notice in another somewhat different location, that notice will be acceptable.

Omission of and Errors in Notice

Under the 1909 Copyright Act (and until March 1, 1989), copyright notices were mandatory; failure to give the notice resulted in permanent loss of copyright. There were no provisions to cure omissions of notice. The 1976 act attempted to lessen the harshness of prior law and allowed for cure of omissions of notice or certain errors as long as cure occurred within five years of publication. For works published after March 1, 1989 (the effective date of the Berne Convention Implementation Act), use of the notice of copyright is optional, and omissions and errors in the notice are less important. Nevertheless, the 1909 act still applies to works published while it was in effect. For example, if copies of a work first published in 1987 omit or have errors in the copyright notice, the owner risks losing copyright protection if the defect is not cured.

Some errors are considered so serious that they are viewed as equivalent to omitting the notice entirely. These errors include failing to include the symbol ©, the word "Copyright," or the abbreviation "Copr."; dating a notice more than one year later than the date of publication; giving a notice without a name; and locat-

ing a notice so that it does not give reasonable notice of the claim of copyright. Omission of a notice does not affect copyright protection and no corrective action is required if the work was published after March 1, 1989.

Under section 406, if an error in the date occurs for works distributed after January 1, 1978, and before March 1, 1989, it may affect copyright duration. For example, if a work for hire is published in 1985 and yet the copyright notice gives the year as 1984, the term will be measured from 1984 and the copyright will last until 2079 (ninety-five years from 1984). If the year date in the notice is more than one year later than the year of publication, the work is considered to be published without any notice.

Surplusage in Copyright Notice

Many copyright owners and publishers place notices or information in addition to the three elements of a copyright notice. For example, the following information is often seen: "Not for reproduction," "All Rights Reserved," and "No portion of this work may be reproduced, displayed, broadcast, or disseminated in any form without prior written consent." Such additional information may be included on the copyrighted work; however, it is mere surplusage and provides no rights beyond those already provided for by the Copyright Act. The phrase *all rights reserved* is often seen inasmuch as it is commonly used in many foreign countries. Surplusage should never take the place of the actual copyright notice and serves primarily to offer a certain level of comfort to the author or copyright owner.

Restoration of Copyright in Foreign Works

Pursuant to the Uruguay Round Agreements Act, effective January 1, 1996, copyright in foreign works whose U.S. copyright protection had been lost due to noncompliance with notice requirements in U.S. law (for example, if the work were published in the United States without a copyright notice) was automatically restored. Works of U.S. origin are unaffected, but foreign works that fell into the public domain in the United States were automatically restored as of January 1, 1996. Additional information is available in Copyright Office Circular 38b at http://www.copyright.gov.

TRIVIA

- The song "White Christmas" was registered by Irving Berlin in 1942. The song is said to be the most valuable music copyright in the world.
- Total copyright registrations in 1990 were 590,700. The total number of copyright registrations in 2001 was 580,800.
- In fiscal year 2001, the Copyright Office web site logged 12.1 million hits. The web site can be searched for copyright registrations and recorded documents from 1978 to the present.
- More literary works are copyrighted than any other type of work. In 2001, 212,100 literary works were copyrighted, 156,300 musical works were copyrighted, and 99,900 works of the visual arts were copyrighted.

CHAPTER SUMMARY

Copyright protection exists from the time a work is created in fixed form. No publication or registration or other action in the Copyright Office is required to secure copyright. There are, however, several advantages to securing registration, namely, the ability to initiate suit in federal court for copyright infringement, the ability to recover statutory damages and attorneys' fees in infringement actions, and the creation of a public record of one's claim to copyright.

Because there are many advantages to copyright registration, copyright owners should be encouraged to complete an application for copyright registration. Three elements are required to register a work: a properly completed application form; a nonrefundable filing fee of $30; and supporting deposit materials. The Copyright Office provides forms for applications. The registration process takes approximately sixteen weeks, although it can be expedited if certain conditions are met. Existing registrations can be corrected or amplified if needed.

Searches of Copyright Office records can be conducted at the Copyright Office, online, or by requesting search assistance from the Copyright Office or a private company. The Copyright Office provides copies (both certified and uncertified) of records upon request and payment of fees.

Although use of a copyright notice is optional for works created on or after March 1, 1989, use of the notice is recommended. The notice consists of three elements: the symbol © (or the word "Copyright" or abbreviation "Copr."); the year of first publication of the work; and the name of the copyright owner. The notice should be affixed to copies or phonorecords in such a way as to give reasonable notice of the claim of copyright.

CASE ILLUSTRATION—DEFECTIVE COPYRIGHT NOTICE AND RELEASE INTO PUBLIC DOMAIN

Case: *Shapiro & Son Bedspread Corp. v. Royal Mills*, 568 F. Supp. 972 (S.D.N.Y. 1983)

Facts: Plaintiff sought an injunction to restrain defendant from making bedspreads that allegedly infringed plaintiff's bedspreads. Defendant asserted that plaintiff did not have a valid copyright because its notice of copyright was omitted. The notice was placed on a flyer in the packaging for the bedspreads.

Holding: The notice placed on the flyer accompanying the goods was defective because it was not affixed to copies of the work; however, omission of a notice is excused if registration is made within five years after publication without notice and a reasonable effort is made to add the notice to copies of the work. In this case, plaintiff presented no evidence that it made a reasonable effort to add the copyright notice after it discovered the omission. Thus, the omission of the notice is not excused, and the legal consequence is forfeiture of the copyright and release of the work into the public domain.

[Note: This holding would not apply to any work published after March 1, 1989, when use of a copyright notice became optional.]

CASE STUDY AND ACTIVITIES

Case Study. Watson is in the process of preparing copyright applications for a variety of works that it will offer in the stores and gift shops at Fantasy Fun Adventure. For example, Watson will offer a cookbook entitled *Mrs. Sweet's Home Made Recipes,* which will feature recipes, descriptions of table settings and hostess ideas, and illustrations. A song entitled "The Taylor Tiger Rag" will be registered as well as a new version of the Taylor Tiger stuffed animal. Charm bracelets featuring various characters will be offered in the park gift stores, the pattern for a new line of wallpaper featuring Watson's most beloved characters is being registered, and a collection of some previously published stories regarding the characters will be combined into a large-size picture book for children. Watson is particularly anxious to register "The Taylor Tiger Rag" because it plans to sue for infringement of the song, the name of which is being changed to "Taylor Tiger's Ragtime Dance." Finally, Watson is interested in viewing its largest competitor's stuffed animals to determine what products its competitor is launching.

Activities. Identify the particular copyright form that Watson will need to use to register each copyright, the location of copyright notice for each item, and the deposit material that must accompany each application. Is there anything Watson can do to ensure prompt registration of the song relating to Taylor Tiger? May Watson obtain its competitors' deposit materials? Discuss fully.

ROLE OF PARALEGAL

Paralegals are more actively involved in applying for copyright registration than in any other aspect of copyright law. Among the many activities in which IP professionals are engaged are the following:

- obtaining forms and circulars from the Copyright Office so the office has a ready supply of application forms and information;
- assisting copyright owners in completing copyright questionnaires so applications can be prepared;
- preparing applications and sending them to clients for review and signature;
- assisting clients in collecting deposit materials to accompany copyright applications;
- establishing deposit accounts with the Copyright Office and monitoring those accounts to ensure they are routinely replenished;
- filing copyright applications with come-back postcards;
- working with clients to determine if special handling is needed for applications;
- docketing dates of filing of applications and monitoring progress of the typical sixteen-week application process;
- responding to requests for information or clarification from the Copyright Office;
- reviewing certificates of registration for errors and preparing supplementary registration to correct or amplify information in copyright records;
- preparing letters confirming registration, indicating duration of copyright, and giving instructions for providing notice of copyright;
- searching or requesting searches of Copyright Office records;
- requesting copies, certified and uncertified, of Copyright Office records;
- reviewing client materials to ensure copyright notices are in compliance with law and are placed properly; and
- monitoring the Copyright Office web site to keep abreast of changes in copyright law and procedure.

INTERNET RESOURCES

Federal laws relating to copyright:	http://www.ll.georgetown.edu or http://www.findlaw.com
Copyright Office:	http://www.loc.gov/copyright or http://www.copyright.gov (for forms, circulars, and instructions and information on filing copyright applications, fee schedules, information on special handling, requesting deposit materials, and other information)

General information: http://www.findlaw.com and
                             http://www.megalaw.com

DISCUSSION QUESTIONS

1. In 2002, Ann, an employee of Gregory Publishers Inc., created a computer program for her employer while on the job. What form should be used to register the copyright for this computer program? Identify the form of copyright notice that should be used. May a short form be used to register this work? Discuss.

2. Bill writes a book on financial management during the 1990s. The book takes Bill a great deal of time to complete, and he finally sends the finished manuscript to his publisher in 1998. What is the year of creation of the work?

3. Sam, a songwriter, bequeathed rights in his songs to his daughter in his will. The songs were not previously registered. Sam died in 2000. The daughter has filed for copyright registration of the songs. Who should be identified as author of the works, and who should be identified as claimant of the works in the copyright registration application forms? What is the duration of copyright for these works?

4. Pablo is the author of a novel published in 2002. Describe the deposit materials that Pablo should provide to the Copyright Office when he seeks to register the copyright for the novel.

5. Tara would like to sue Mike for infringement of a song Tara wrote. Tara did not seek copyright registration for the song. What must Tara do to sue for infringement?

6. Assume the same facts as in question 5. How can Tara obtain copies of allegedly infringing works registered by Mike with the Copyright Office so she can compare the similarity of Mike's works to her works?

7. Give an appropriate copyright notice for the following works by Jane Daniels:
   • a book published in 1968;
   • a sound recording published in 1999;
   • poems published in 2002.

8. A book was first distributed and published in 1981 although the copyright notice for the work mistakenly listed 1980 as the year of copyright. What is the effect of this mistake? What if the copyright notice identified 1984 as the year of copyright? Discuss.

For additional resources, go to www.westlegalstudies.com.

CHAPTER 14

Copyright Infringement

CHAPTER OVERVIEW

A copyright owner who has a registered copyright may bring an action for infringement when any of his or her exclusive rights have been infringed by another. Generally, to prevail in an infringement action, a plaintiff must show ownership of copyright and impermissible copying. Copying is generally proven by demonstrating that the defendant had access to the work and the defendant's work is substantially similar to that of the copyright owner.

There are various defenses a defendant may assert in an infringement action. One of the most common defenses is that the defendant's use of the work is a "fair use." A fair use is generally a use for scholarly, research, or educational purposes. Courts examine four factors in determining whether a defendant's use of a copyrighted work is a fair use: the purpose and character of the use, including whether the use is of a commercial nature or is for nonprofit educational work; the nature of the copyrighted work (with factual works receiving less protection than works of fiction or fantasy); the amount and substantiality of the portion taken by the defendant; and the effect of the defendant's use on the market for the plaintiff's work. Other defenses include laches, unclean hands, and the statute of limitations, which is three years from the infringing act. Remedies available to a plaintiff include injunctive relief, impoundment of the infringing goods, actual damages and the defendant's profits, statutory damages, costs, and attorneys' fees. Criminal sanctions can be imposed for certain willful infringements.

INTRODUCTION

Registration of a copyright is a requirement for initiating an action for infringement, 17 U.S.C. § 411, although registration is not required for works not originating in the United States. Moreover, prompt registration is a prerequisite for certain remedies for infringement. 17 U.S.C. § 412. Thus, although registration is not required to obtain copyright protection for a work, the failure to register will preclude a copyright owner from seeking redress for infringement. If registration of a work is refused by the Copyright Office, an action for infringement may still be brought if the author notifies the Copyright Office of the action. The Register of Copyrights then has the right to become a party to the action with respect to the issue of registrability of the copyright claim. 17 U.S.C. § 411.

Section 501 of the Copyright Act provides that anyone who violates any of the exclusive rights of a copyright owner (rights of reproduction, adaptation, distribution, performance, and display), or of the author (as provided in the Visual Artists Rights Act), or who imports copies or phonorecords into the United States in violation of copyright law, is liable for direct infringement of the copyright or right of the author. For example, the following may constitute infringement: playing copyrighted music in a large department store without permission; failing to provide attribution for a painting or other work covered by the Visual Artists Rights Act; and photocopying material from a copyrighted book.

ELEMENTS OF INFRINGEMENT

Ownership of Copyright

To prevail in an infringement action, a plaintiff must prove two things: his or her ownership of the copyright and copying or some other impermissible invasion by the defendant of one of the exclusive rights afforded to copyright owners. Ownership is usually more easily established than copying. A party may prove ownership by demonstrating that he or she is the author of the work or that the copyright in the work has been transferred to him or her. A certificate of copyright registration (made

before or within five years of first publication of the work) will establish *prima facie* evidence in court of the validity of the copyright and of the facts stated in the certificate, including identity of the author or copyright owner. Ownership issues often arise in the context of work made for hire disputes, particularly when a party claims he or she is not an employee and thus a work cannot be owned by an employer or when a party claims there was no written agreement relating to the status of a specially commissioned work and thus he or she has retained copyright ownership.

If the copyright has been transferred to another, that party is now the owner of the transferred rights and has the right to protect the work by an infringement action. For example, if a copyright author has transferred exclusive rights to perform a work to another and the work is infringed by impermissible performance, the transferee's rights have been infringed. If there has been unauthorized reproduction rather than unauthorized performance, the original copyright author's rights have been infringed and he or she may initiate an infringement action. Courts will insist the plaintiff prove the transfer and show how the plaintiff acquired rights. Additionally, the plaintiff must have been the owner at the time his or her rights were infringed. If a copyright owner has transferred a work to another and yet retains some connection with the work, for example, by receiving periodic royalty payments, the owner as well as the transferee's rights have been infringed because both are affected by an infringement that would reduce the value of the work; therefore, both have standing to initiate an infringement suit.

Upon introduction of the registration (or transfer of copyright) into evidence, the court will presume that the work is protected under copyright law (although that presumption can be rebutted or defeated by the defendant) and that the plaintiff has ownership rights in the work such that he or she is the proper party to bring the infringement action.

Copying

Introduction. Proving copying generally requires that the plaintiff in an infringement action show that there is substantial similarity between his or her work and that of the defendant and that the defendant had access to the copyrighted work. The infringing work must derive from the copyrighted work. An independently created work cannot infringe even if it is identical to the copyrighted work.

Innocent Infringement Is Not a Defense. Infringement does not require an intent to infringe; even **innocent infringement** gives rise to liability. For example, assume *A* is given a book that *B* claims *B* wrote. The book was actually the creation of *C*. If *A* copies the book, *A* has infringed *C*'s copyright even though *A* did not intend to infringe and did not know *C* had any copyright interest in the book. Thus, neither intent to infringe nor knowledge of copyright is required for infringement to occur, although innocence may have a bearing on the amount of damages for which a defendant is liable. Moreover, merely attributing the material copied to the owner by stating that copies of chapters of a text are the product of their author will not protect an infringer. Attribution may reduce damages, but a party cannot escape liability for infringement by merely acknowledging the work is owned by another.

Additionally, infringement can be "subconscious," as was the case in *Bright Tunes Music Corp. v. Harrisongs Music, Ltd.,* 420 F. Supp. 177 (S.D.N.Y. 1976), *aff'd,* 722 F.2d 988 (2d Cir. 1983), in which a court held George Harrison's song "My Sweet Lord" infringed the song "He's So Fine" recorded by The Chiffons. In that case, the court held that Harrison did not deliberately plagiarize the earlier song but that he subconsciously recollected the copyrighted song when he composed "My Sweet Lord." On appeal, the Second Circuit reaffirmed that intent to infringe is not essential and that to allow a defense of innocent infringement would undermine the protections Congress intended copyright owners to possess.

Access. **Access** is generally interpreted to mean that a party had the opportunity to perceive or review a work, either directly or indirectly. Access can be inferred if the copyrighted work has been widely disseminated. Moreover, if the two works are identical or nearly so, it may be presumed that the defendant had access to the plaintiff's work. Generally, the greater the similarity between two works, the less access must be shown. Conversely, if the works are entirely dissimilar, no amount of access will result in a finding of copying.

In some cases, where there has been no evidence of access, courts have nevertheless found infringement if the two works are strikingly similar. Access will be inferred where the works are so similar that the possibility of independent creation or coincidental creation is precluded.

Access has been shown where copies of the plaintiff's work have been sent to the defendant, where the defendant has visited the plaintiff's place of business, where the plaintiff's works have been displayed at events attended by the defendant, and where access occurred through a third party, such as a manufacturer, connected to both the plaintiff and defendant.

Substantial Similarity of Works. Because it is seldom possible to prove copying by direct evidence (such as testimony from a witness who saw the defendant copy from the plaintiff's book), copying is usually proven through circumstantial evidence. Thus, infringement is usually shown by demonstrating that the allegedly infringing work is substantially similar to the copyrighted work. In some instances, map makers and directory authors purposely include fictitious entries in their works; when the same erroneous matter is found in a defendant's work, copying is generally found to exist.

The test used, often referred to as the ordinary observer test, focuses on whether the accused work is so similar to the copyrighted work that an ordinary reasonable person or lay observer would recognize that the copyrighted work was appropriated by the defendant.

The lay observer test has been refined to take into account the intended market for the works. Thus, where infringement of a video game was alleged, and the target market was young men, a court found that the intended purchasers (seventeen-and-a-half-year-old males) were a knowledgeable and discerning group and would not regard the works as substantially similar. *Data East USA, Inc. v. Epyx, Inc.,* 862 F.2d 204 (9th Cir. 1988). Another refinement of the lay observer test occurs when the works are complex, such as computer programs. In such cases, expert testimony is often used to prove or disprove substantial similarity inasmuch as computer programs are highly technical and unfamiliar to most of the general public.

Many courts use a two-step analysis to determine if infringement has occurred. The first step analyzes whether there has been copying. Once copying has been established, the second step requires that a determination be made whether the copying constitutes an impermissible appropriation, namely, whether the copying of the protected material was so extensive that it rendered the offending and copyrighted works substantially similar. In the first stage, some courts compare the works element by element and create lists of similarities and dissimilarities, in essence, "dissecting" the works. Other courts criticize dissection and prefer to focus on the overall similarities or the "total concept and feel" of the works, especially when only some of the work is protectable. For example, *Boisson v. Banian, Ltd.,* 273 F.3d 262 (2d Cir. 2001), a case involving infringement of

quilt patterns, some of which included nonprotectable elements such as alphabet letters, the court relied on the "more discerning observer" test and stated that determining substantial similarity required examination of the total concept and feel of the two works, as instructed by common sense.

Courts have continually struggled in assessing "substantial similarity." In *Nichols v. Universal Pictures Corp.,* 45 F.2d 119 (2d Cir. 1930), Judge Learned Hand commented that copyright protection cannot be limited literally to the text; otherwise a plagiarist would be able to make immaterial variations with impunity. Thus, a party need not copy the entire work to be an infringer. When only a part of a work is taken, such as one scene from a play, Judge Hand stated that the question is whether the part taken is substantial. Even more difficult questions, however, arise when the plagiarist does not copy a block of material but rather abstracts the whole work. In these two instances (**literal copying** of some of a work and nonliteral copying of an entire work), Judge Hand remarked that "Nobody has ever been able to fix that boundary [of protection], and nobody ever can." *Id.* at 121.

If part of a work is copied or taken, courts usually examine not only the quantity of the work taken but also its characteristics and the nature of the work itself. Infringement has been found even if language is not identical when recognizable paraphrases have been taken. There is no precise answer to the question "how much is too much?" In one case, the taking of fragments from three sentences in a book of more than two hundred pages was found to be infringement. Moreover, if the part taken is the "heart" of the material, there may be an infringement. Thus, a love story about lovers from different economic classes with a tragic ending might not infringe the book *Love Story;* however, using the well-known line, "Love means never having to say you're sorry," might

Generally speaking, a research hypothesis is a tentative answer to a specific research question. The research question itself, on the other hand, may remain tentative or even unclear until the hypothesis is established. The formulation of your research hypotheses often involves the modification of your articulated research questions. If your research hypotheses and your research questions are inconsistent, it is the hypotheses that eventually count. In that situation, it is possible that you will leave some of your questions unanswered in your project if you are not prudent, though it is not necessary for all of your questions to be answered through the deductive hypothesis-testing logic.

It seems that you cannot fully specify your research topic until you have established all your hypotheses, or until all the research design issues are resolved. To go a step even further, you probably cannot fully settle these issues until the research is carried out. This gives rise to a question: Do we really need to articulate those questions and hypotheses beforehand? This, indeed, could mean painstaking effort on the part of a novice researcher.

Research questions and hypotheses serve important functions in guiding the planning and implementation of your research. However, it is not that you must have all your questions and hypotheses specified beforehand. That is only one way to go about research, and that approach has limited use indeed. Another way is an inductive one, in which you will first look at the information collected. Oftentimes you will be prompted by the data to form some new hypotheses and test them immediately. In other words, researchers formulate hypotheses and test them when they are doing data analysis, although methodologists' attitude toward this practice is typically ambiguous. No validated information is available on the percentage of such type of hypothesis formulation and testing, though it is frequently seen in practice. The hypotheses contained in various kinds of research reports all appear to be well-established beforehand. It should be noted that the writing of a research report does not have to follow the exact order as it was proposed or carried out. Yet as a student or an applicant for some research funding you may have to meet the expectation for the kind of linear logic starting from the questions and hypotheses that lead to your research designs. Such a kind of logic may be expected from even an exploratory or preliminary study.

In working with the kind of relational hypotheses you can use some diagrams to organize your ideas. For example, you can use an arrow to represent the influence of one variable on another. And multiple pairs of variables connected with the arrows can be incorporated into one general model. This model itself can be considered as a hypothetical structure, or a complicated multivariate well constitute an infringement because the statement is a substantial portion of or the "heart" of the work copied.

Once copying is shown, examination must focus on whether the elements taken were protected by copyright. It is permissible to take ideas but impermissible to appropriate expression of those ideas. Works in the public domain may be examined, and the defendant may attempt to prove that both the plaintiff's work and the defendant's work share elements and similarities with works in the public domain. If all similarities arise from use of common ideas or works in the public domain, there can be no substantial similarity and no infringement.

Some courts use a test known as the "abstraction-filtration-comparison" test to sep-

arate protectable expression from unprotectable ideas in copyright infringement cases. First, a court dissects the allegedly infringing work and isolates each level of abstraction in it. Second, unprotectable elements, such as ideas, processes, facts, and public domain information, are filtered out. Third, a comparison is made of the remaining protectable elements to determine if the second work misappropriates substantial elements of the first. *Gates Rubber Co. v. Bando Chem. Indus., Ltd.*, 9 F.3d 823 (10th Cir. 1993). The abstraction-filtration-comparison test is used most frequently in determining whether infringement of computer programs has occurred and is discussed further in Chapter 15. See Exhibit 14–1 for copyright infringement myths.

EXHIBIT 14–1
Copyright Infringement Myths

There are a number of myths or misconceptions regarding copyright infringement. Some of the more common myths include the following:

- **I can use anything without a copyright notice.** False. Placing a copyright notice on a work is optional since March 1, 1989, and works are protected under copyright law from the time of their creation in a fixed form.
- **If I give credit or attribution to another, there is no infringement.** False. While indicating that material is the product of another may show innocent infringement and help to reduce damages, infringement is not cured by reciting that another is actually the author of a work.
- **I'm only using a little bit, so there can be no infringement.** False. Copyright infringement does not depend on how much is taken. This myth is similar to a common misunderstanding that a musician can use four bars of another's song before infringement will be found. If the amount taken is qualitatively significant, infringement will exist. In one case, the taking of two bars of music was held to be an infringement.
- **If I don't charge for what I took, there can be no infringement.** False. Although a noncommercial use of a work may affect the damages awarded in an infringement case, unauthorized taking constitutes infringement whether or not it is for profit-making purposes.
- **I'm only paraphrasing, so there can be no infringement.** False. Infringement is not limited to exact copying. If two works are substantially similar, copying may be shown.
- **I mailed it to myself and thus copyrighted the work.** False. For some reason, a myth persists that if one mails a copy of one's work to oneself, the work is now protected by copyright. The mailing of the work has no relationship to copyright protection. The work is protected from the time it is created in a fixed form.

CONTRIBUTORY INFRINGEMENT AND VICARIOUS INFRINGEMENT

Courts have held persons and companies liable for the infringing acts of others. If a person, with knowledge of an infringing activity, induces, causes, or contributes to infringing conduct, he or she will be liable for infringement as a contributory infringer. **Contributory infringement** occurs when photo shops reproduce or duplicate photographs bearing a copyright notice, when copy shops reproduce or allow customers to photocopy books and other protected materials, when operators of flea markets or swap meets allow pirated works to be sold, or when an individual sells specially formatted blank cassettes and tape duplicating equipment to pirates with knowledge they are engaging in acts of infringement.

In the famous case *Sony Corp. of America v. Universal City Studios Inc.,* 464 U.S. 417 (1984), the Supreme Court was called upon to determine whether home videotaping of copyrighted works for later private viewing (for example, taping the movie *Shakespeare in Love* shown on television so one can watch it at a more convenient time, commonly referred to as "time-shifting") constituted infringement and whether the defendant Sony was contributorily liable for making the videocassette recorders used to make the allegedly infringing copies. The Court held that time-shifting did not constitute infringement and that the sale of copying equipment, like the sale of other articles of commerce, does not constitute contributory infringement if the product is widely used for legitimate and unobjectionable purposes. Sony was held not liable for contributory infringement. By contrast, in *Elektra Records Co. v. Gem Electric Distributors, Inc.*, 360 F. Supp. 821 (E.D.N.Y. 1973), the defendant stores sold blank tapes and for a fee loaned customers prerecorded tapes containing copyrighted songs.

Customers would then duplicate the entire tapes on the defendants' Make-A-Tape systems at the stores. The defendants were held liable for contributory infringement because they supplied all means necessary to infringe. Moreover, the defendants had a financial interest in the infringement.

Vicarious infringement occurs when one party is responsible for infringement conducted by another when the two parties share a special relationship, such as that of employer-employee. One who is in a position to control the use of copyrighted works by others and authorizes use without permission of the copyright owner will be liable for vicarious infringement, even if he or she had no knowledge the infringement was occurring. For example, universities may be held liable for the infringing activities of teachers who photocopy copyrighted materials for distribution to students. The universities are in a position to control and direct the activities of teachers and should implement policies refusing photocopying unless the teachers obtain copyright releases or permission forms from the authors. Similarly, the operator of a swap meet was held vicariously liable for the sale of counterfeit recordings by a vendor who rented space from the operator on the basis that the operator had the right and ability to supervise the direct infringer and derived a financial benefit from the infringer's activities. *Fonovisa, Inc. v. Cherry Auction, Inc.,* 76 F.3d 259 (9th Cir. 1996).

DEFENSES TO INFRINGEMENT

There are a variety of defenses a defendant charged with copyright infringement may assert. As stated, however, the infringer's intent is not relevant and infringement can be found whether or not the defendant intended to infringe copyrighted works. Intent, however, may be relevant in assessing damages.

Fair Use

Section 107 of the Copyright Act provides that the fair use of a copyrighted work for purposes such as criticism, comment, news reporting, teaching, scholarship, or research is not an infringement. Fair use is thus a privilege to use copyrighted material without permission of the copyright owner. The rationale for allowing certain uses of copyrighted material is to benefit the public and promote the arts and sciences. The fair use defense is the most important defense to an allegation of copyright infringement.

The Copyright Office has given examples of activities that courts have regarded as fair use, including the following:

- quoting excerpts from copyrighted materials in a review or criticism of the work;
- quotation of short passages in scholarly or technical works for illustration or clarification of the author's observations;
- use in a parody of some of the parodied work;
- reproduction of a small portion of a work by a teacher to illustrate a lesson; and
- a summary of an address or article, with brief quotations, in a news report.

Thus, reviewers critiquing a song may quote lyrics from it, and parodies may be made of other works.

The act identifies (and courts consider) four factors in determining whether a use is fair and is thus permissible:

1. the purpose and character of the use, including whether such use is of a commercial nature or whether it is a non-profit educational use;
2. the nature of the copyrighted work;
3. the amount and substantiality of the portion used in relation to the copyrighted work as a whole; and

4. the effect of the use upon the potential market for or value of the copyrighted work.

None of the four factors identified in section 107 are meant to be conclusive. Courts will examine each factor and weigh all considerations in determining whether a use is a permissible fair use or an infringing use. No one test is applied, and each case is determined on its own merits.

The Purpose and Character of the Use. One factor considered by courts focuses on the purpose for which reproduction, adaptation, distribution, performance, or display of a copyrighted work is undertaken and the use that is made of it. Generally, use for comment, criticism, and so forth is acceptable because it benefits the public and advances the public good; however, if a for-profit motive underlies any of these purposes, a different conclusion may be reached. Although commercial use will not automatically defeat a defense of fair use, use of another's work for a commercial purpose is less likely to be permitted than use for a noncommercial purpose. According to *Harper & Row Publishers, Inc. v. Nation Enterprises*, 417 U.S. 539 (1985), every commercial use is presumptively an unfair exploitation of the copyright owner's rights. Thus, commercial use tends to weigh against a finding of fair use.

Courts also examine whether the defendant's use adds something new with a new purpose or different character. Addition of new material or a productive use benefits the public. Failure to transform a work in any way weighs against a finding of fair use.

Finally, a use that is merely incidental is more likely to be determined to be a fair use. For example, if a news reporter stands in front of a copyrighted painting while reporting on theft of works of art, such a use is incidental and may support a finding of fair use, even though it violates the copyright owner's right to display the work.

The Nature of the Copyrighted Work. Courts consider the degree of creativity in the copyrighted work in determining whether a use is fair. Generally, the more creative the work, the more protection it is afforded. Conversely, the more informational or factual the work, the less protection it receives. Thus, the fact that a second work is factual or informational in nature tends to support a finding of fair use. Once again, use and dissemination of factual and informational material tends to advance research and scholarship and is thus encouraged.

Whether the work is published or unpublished is important. Unauthorized use of an owner's work prior to publication severely affects the owner's right to determine the timing of entry into the market and be the first "on the scene." Thus, works that are unpublished generally receive more protection than those that have been published. Nevertheless, 17 U.S.C. § 107 specifically provides that the fact that a work is unpublished shall not itself bar a finding of fair use.

Amount and Substantiality of the Portion Used. In determining whether use of another's copyrighted work is fair, courts consider the quantitative as well as the qualitative portion of the work that is reproduced. Generally, it is not a fair use to reproduce an entire work. When less than all of a work is reproduced, whether the use is fair depends on the importance of the portion used, namely, whether the reproduced portion is the essence or "heart" of the copyright owner's work. Even when the amount taken is quantitatively small, the use may still be impermissible if what is taken is the central or pivotal portion of the work. For example, in *Harper & Row*, although the portion taken was small (only about 300 words out of 200,000 words), the verbatim copy-

ing was the essence of the copyrighted work. This amount was considered excessive.

The Effect of the Use on the Market for the Copyrighted Work. Most courts agree that the effect of the defendant's use on the potential market for the copyright owner's work is the most important of the four factors considered in determining whether a use of another's work is a permissible fair use. If the defendant's use causes or will cause a loss of revenue to the copyright owner, such argues against a finding of fair use. If the work will supplant the market for the copyright owner's work or diminish the potential market, the use is likely not a fair one.

Overview of Fair Use Cases. A brief review of some fair use cases will help demonstrate the balancing of the fair use factors engaged in by courts.

- *Sony Corp. of America v. Universal City Studios, Inc.,* 464 U.S. 417 (1984). In this case, Universal alleged that use of VCRs sold by the defendants violated the 1976 Copyright Act and that sale of the VCR machines constituted contributory infringement. The Court focused on the fourth factor of the fair use doctrine (the effect of the use on the potential market for the copyrighted work). The Court held that the practice of using a VCR to record a program for later private viewing ("time-shifting") was a fair use because it was noncommercial and there was little likelihood of harm to the potential market for the copyrighted works. Moreover, the VCRs had substantial noninfringing uses.
- *Harper & Row Publishers, Inc. v. Nation Enterprises,* 471 U.S. 539 (1985). In this case, former President Ford granted Harper & Row exclusive rights to publish his memoirs and to license

prepublication serialization of those memoirs. *Time* magazine then purchased from Harper & Row the right to publish certain excerpts from the book before its publication. Before *Time* could publish the excerpts, someone provided a copy of the manuscript to *Nation* magazine, which then published an article about the forthcoming book and included approximately three hundred words of direct quotes from the book. Because it had been "scooped," *Time* abandoned its plans to publish excerpts from the book and refused to pay the balance of its license fee to Harper & Row. Harper & Row sued *Nation* for copyright infringement. The Court held that the use was not a fair one: the publication in *Nation* was commercial in nature; the amount copied, though small quantitatively, captured the "heart" of the book; and the publication had an adverse effect on the potential market for the book.

• *Basic Books, Inc. v. Kinko's Graphics Corp.,* 758 F. Supp. 1525 (S.D.N.Y. 1991). For many years, Kinko's, a copy shop, had prepared course packets consisting of photocopies of assigned reading for college students. Publishing houses sued Kinko's, alleging that Kinko's practice of copying portions of books without permission and without payment violated the publishers' copyrights. The court found that Kinko's use was not fair use. Although the students' use of the materials was educational, Kinko's purpose in copying them was commercial. The amount and substantiality of the portions copied also weighed against a finding of fair use, and the potential market for the copyrighted materials was harmed in that Kinko's offered the materials at a lower cost and thus students refrained from buying the books.

• *Consumers Union of United States, Inc. v. General Signal Corp.,* 724 F.2d 1044 (2d Cir. 1983). In *Consumers Union,* the defendant's commercials included excerpts from the magazine *Consumer Reports,* which favorably rated defendant's product. The court held the use was fair and concluded that the purpose of the use was to report factual information and that the commercials made relatively insignificant use of the work. Use of reviews containing significant original analysis and conclusions from the first work rather than primarily factual material, however, might not be a fair use.

• *American Geophysical Union v. Texaco, Inc.,* 37 F.3d 881 (2d Cir. 1994). In this case, publishers of several scientific journals brought suit against Texaco, alleging that the company's practice of copying articles from journals and then routing or distributing the articles to its more than four hundred researchers was infringement. The researchers placed copies of the articles in their files for later use and reference. The publishers alleged the practice infringed their rights in the articles. The court held that Texaco's copying was not a fair use. Although the for-profit motive of Texaco was relevant, the court stated the focus should be on the use of the material itself rather than the user. The fact that the materials were used for an archival purpose—they were merely placed in files and not transformed in any way—weighed against a finding of fair use. On the second factor (the nature of the work), the court found the articles were scientific and factual, and this weighed in favor of Texaco. The third factor (amount of work copied) weighed against Texaco because entire separately copyrighted articles were copied. In regard to the last factor (impact of the copying on the potential market for the copyrighted materials), the court found against Texaco because the publishers lost subscription revenue and because Texaco could have entered into a license with the Copyright Clearance Center (CCC), a central clearinghouse established by publishers at the suggestion of Congress to license the copying of materials, much like ASCAP and BMI license the performance of music. By bypassing CCC, Texaco's copying caused a loss of revenue to the publishers. Texaco appealed to the United States Supreme Court, which granted *certiorari;* however, before the Court heard the case, the parties entered into a settlement with Texaco agreeing to pay more than $1 million and an additional retroactive license fee to CCC. Texaco also agreed to enter into a five-year licensing arrangement with CCC.

The *Texaco* case has caused much consternation inasmuch as it has been common practice for many companies to purchase only a limited number of subscriptions to journals and then copy articles as needed for distribution to employees. Without a ruling by the Supreme Court, users are left with the Second Circuit's holding that the practice is infringement. Many issues remain unresolved, including whether there is a difference between the archiving of articles by researchers funded by government grants and archiving by those funded by private company grants and what result should be reached when copying is done by an institution that serves both the commercial sector and the educational sector. The safest course appears to be to enter into private licensing arrangements with the publishers or to obtain a license through CCC. The CCC also offers guidelines for creating copyright compliance policies. Call (978) 750-8400 or access CCC's web site at http://www.copyright.com.

Parody

Parodies of works of literature, art, and music are viewed as a productive form of social commentary and criticism. Because copyright owners are highly unlikely to grant permission to another to parody their work, parodists often rely on the fair use defense when infringement is alleged by the owner of the parodied copyrighted work. Generally, no more than is necessary to accomplish the parody may be taken from the original work. The parodist's work must "conjure up" the copyright owner's work and link the parody with that of the original to make social comment or criticism. If the parodist merely copies a work to make social comment on some other topic, fair use is not available.

In *Campbell v. Acuff-Rose Music, Inc.,* 510 U.S. 569 (1994), Acuff-Rose, a music company, brought suit against the rap group 2 Live Crew claiming that the group's rap version of the song "Pretty Woman" infringed its copyright in the famous Roy Orbison song, "Oh, Pretty Woman." The Supreme Court held the parody was a fair use. In regard to the first fair use factor, the Court held that although the use was commercial, the new work added something new with a new expression and meaning. The second factor (the nature of the copyrighted work) was held to be of little use in the context of a parody because a parody, by definition, almost always copies known works such as the Orbison song. As for the amount and substantiality of the work copied, the Court stated that even if 2 Live Crew copied the "heart" of the Orbison song, it is the heart that most readily conjures up the original for the parody. Regarding the fourth factor, there was no evidence that the 2 Live Crew song had any impact on the market for nonparody or nonrap versions of the original Orbison song. Persons interested in the original song were unlikely to purchase the parody version in its place.

Conversely, in *Dr. Seuss Enterprises, L.P. v. Penguin Books USA, Inc.,* 924 F. Supp. 1559

(S.D. Cal. 1996), the district court held that a poetic account of the O. J. Simpson double murder trial presented in the style of the famous *Cat in the Hat* rhyming book was not protected parody inasmuch as it did not target or parody that book itself but merely copied its general style to make comments regarding society as a whole. Thus, a parody must comment in some way on the original material in order to satisfy the fair use requirement of criticism.

Reproduction of Copyrighted Works by Educators and Librarians

Pursuant to section 108 of the Copyright Act, libraries can reproduce a work for distribution and for preservation purposes. Similarly, libraries are protected from liability for infringement for unpermitted photocopying by their patrons as long as a notice is displayed on the photocopy equipment that the making of copies may be subject to copyright law.

In 1975, Congress urged educators and publishers to meet to reach an agreement regarding permissible educational uses of copyrighted material. The result was the "Agreement on Guidelines for Classroom Copying in Not-for-Profit Educational Institutions with Respect to Books and Periodicals." These guidelines were made part of the legislative history of the 1976 act. Some of the more notable provisions of the guidelines follow:

- Single copies of copyrighted materials (such as chapters from books, short stories, charts, or articles from a journal) may be made by teachers for scholarly research or use in teaching.
- Multiple copies (not to exceed more than one copy per pupil in a course) may be made if the copying meets specified tests for brevity (the guidelines include stated criteria for the amount of work that may be copied, for example, a poem may be

copied if it is less than 250 words) and spontaneity (the decision to use the material is made so close to the time the material is needed that it would be unreasonable to expect a reply to a request to the author to use the material); each copy includes a copyright notice; and the cumulative effect of the copying is limited (for example, no more than nine instances of multiple copying for one course during one class term can be made).

Similarly, music teachers and publishers met and developed "Guidelines for Educational Use of Music" to state the standards of educational fair use of music. The guidelines for books and for music are available as Circular 21 from the Copyright Office (http://www.copyright.gov).

Other Defenses to Infringement

Although fair use is one of the most widely asserted defenses in actions for infringement, a number of other defenses are also available.

Invalidity of Copyright. A defendant may assert that the material sought to be protected by the plaintiff is uncopyrightable. Even if a certificate of copyright registration has been issued, the defendant may rebut the presumption of validity arising from registration and prove that the work lacks sufficient originality to be protectable and that the Copyright Office erroneously registered the work. Thus, the defendant may assert that the works are useful articles, public domain matter, common facts not subject to copyright protection, or scenes a faire (common or stock themes) that flow naturally from a premise or setting and are thus unprotectable. Moreover, works are not protected merely because they result from hard work. To be protectable, works must contain copyrightable expression. Thus, in *Feist Publications, Inc. v. Rural Telephone Service Co.,* 499 U.S. 340

(1991), the Supreme Court held that although a telephone company had invested a great deal of hard work or "sweat of the brow" into compiling its telephone directory, the directory was unprotectable because it was merely factual. A similar result was reached in 1998 when the Second Circuit held that West Publishing Company's addition of certain features, such as attorney information, parallel citations, and star pagination, to cases in the public domain did not result in original copyrightable work entitled to protection. *Matthew Bender & Co. v. West Publ'g Co.*, 158 F.3d 674 (2d Cir. 1998), *vacated and remanded on other grounds*, 240 F.3d 116 (2d Cir. 2001). A defendant may also show that the plaintiff failed to disclose certain facts to the Copyright Office (such as that the plaintiff's work was a derivative work or a useful article), thus rendering the registration invalid.

Estoppel. A copyright owner who knows of an infringing use and acquiesces in it may be estopped or precluded from later claiming the use is an infringement, particularly when the defendant has expended sums in marketing the work.

Misuse or Unclean Hands. A plaintiff may be precluded from obtaining relief in an infringement action if it is guilty of inequitable conduct, unclean hands, or **misuse** of its copyright. For example, requiring a defendant who licenses one copyrighted work to license another or coupling a copyright license with a restrictive covenant precluding a party from developing its own copyrighted works may be such misuse as to preclude the licensor from later asserting infringement of copyright.

Improper Copyright Notice. Section 406 of the Copyright Act provides a complete defense to infringement if the alleged infringer is misled by a pre-Berne copyright notice (meaning, before March 1, 1989) that misidentifies the copyright owner. In one case, the plaintiff created a video and licensed it to another, the licensee, for use in schools. The video contained a copyright notice that improperly identified the licensee as the copyright owner (rather than the plaintiff, the true owner). The licensee sold copies of the video to the defendant. The defendant successfully defended the action on the basis that the copyright notice identified the licensee as the owner and that he therefore had the right to assume that such party could sell the video to him. The court agreed and found no infringement by the defendant.

Statute of Limitations and Laches. Section 507(b) of the Copyright Act provides a three-year statute of limitations on civil copyright infringement actions. The time period may be tolled or suspended if the defendant has fraudulently concealed his or her copyright infringement from the plaintiff such that the plaintiff did not know to bring an action. The three-year period is measured from the time the infringement occurred. If there are separate acts of infringement or the infringement is continuing in nature, the plaintiff may initiate suit at any time within three years of the last infringing act.

Even if the plaintiff is within the three-year statute of limitations, the defendant may assert a defense of laches, namely, that the plaintiff unjustifiably delayed in bringing suit and this delay caused prejudice to the defendant. Laches typically does not excuse infringement but may preclude a plaintiff from obtaining injunctive relief.

INFRINGEMENT ACTIONS

Generally, a party who believes its copyrighted work has been infringed will send a cease and desist letter to the other party (much like the cease and desist letter used in trademark infringement matters shown in Chapter 6, Exhibit 6–4). If the parties cannot resolve their dispute amicably, they may proceed to arbitration or litigation.

The federal courts have exclusive jurisdiction over copyright infringement cases and any cases arising under the Copyright Act. Thus, infringement cases can be brought only in federal district courts, and not in state courts. Some cases, however, might be heard in state court because they do not "arise under" the Copyright Act. For example, if *A* agrees to pay a license fee to *B* for use of *B*'s copyrighted song but fails to make the required payments, the matter may be heard in state court as a straightforward breach of contract matter.

Like any civil action, a copyright infringement proceeding is initiated by the filing of a complaint by the plaintiff. The clerk of the court must report the action to the Register of Copyrights. The defendant typically answers the complaint and asserts various defenses or challenges to the complaint. If the defendant has claims against the plaintiff, they must be made in the same action. This promotes judicial economy because the court can resolve all differences between the parties at the same time.

The action is governed by the Federal Rules of Civil Procedure. The plaintiff has the burden of proving all elements of an infringement action: ownership of copyright; copyrightable subject matter; and unauthorized use, copying, reproduction, adaptation, performance, or display of material expression by the defendant. Discovery will be scheduled by the court, and the parties may take depositions, propound interrogatories to each other, and request that various documents and other materials be produced. If settlement is not reached, the matter will proceed to trial. Either party may demand a jury trial. Expert witnesses may testify. Ultimately, the fact finder (either the jury or the judge) will render a decision. Within one month after any final judgment, the clerk of the court must notify the Register of Copyrights of the judgment or order. An appeal may be filed in the appropriate U.S. Court of Appeals by the losing party if a prejudicial error of law occurred at the trial. Further review may be sought in the U.S. Supreme Court, although it has discretion to deny *certiorari* and refuse to hear the case.

REMEDIES FOR INFRINGEMENT

Plaintiffs in infringement actions may seek both monetary and nonmonetary relief. In some instances, the plaintiff may be more interested in ensuring the infringing activity ceases than in recovering damages. Courts can use a variety of remedies to ensure the copyright owner is adequately protected:

- **Injunctive relief.** Section 502 of the Copyright Act provides that a court may grant both temporary and final injunctions to prevent or restrain infringing activities. To secure an injunction before trial, generally a plaintiff must prove that it is likely to succeed on the merits of its case, that it will suffer irreparable injury unless injunctive relief is ordered, that the threatened injury to it outweighs possible damage to the defendant, and that monetary damages will not provide sufficient relief. If a plaintiff has delayed in seeking injunctive relief, such tends to show that there is no irreparable harm occurring and injunctive relief may be denied.
- **Impoundment.** Courts can order the **impoundment** of infringing copies during the pendency of an infringement action and may order their destruction as part of a final judgment. The plaintiff usually must post a bond so that if no infringement is found, the defendant is recompensed for the seizure of the goods.

- **Compensatory damages and profits.** Plaintiffs may recover **compensatory damages**—the actual damages suffered as a result of the infringement—and any additional profits received by the defendant arising out of the infringing activities. Actual damages should compensate the plaintiff for lost sales and revenues. To recover the infringer's profits, the plaintiff must present proof of the infringer's gross revenue, and the infringer may then prove deductible expenses and profits attributable to factors other than the infringing work. Even indirect profits may be recovered. For example, in one case, a plaintiff recovered a portion of the defendant's hotel and gambling revenue on the basis that the performance of an infringing show in the hotel drew additional business to the hotel and casino.

- **Statutory damages.** In lieu of actual damages, if the copyright owner has secured registration within three months after publication or, for unpublished works, before the defendant's infringement, a plaintiff may elect an award of **statutory damages** under section 504(c) of the act. The statutory damages are set by the judge or jury in their discretion in a sum of not less than $750 and not more than $30,000 for infringement of one work (all the parts of a compilation or derivative work are viewed as one work). If willful infringement is shown, statutory damages may be awarded in an amount not exceeding $150,000. If the court finds that infringement was innocent (the infringer was not aware his or her acts were infringing and had no reason to know such), the court can reduce statutory damages to an amount not lower than $200. The election to seek statutory damages

rather than actual damages and profits can be made at any time prior to entry of final judgment and is usually made in cases in which the plaintiff has difficulty proving actual damages. In one recent case, it was held that each unauthorized airing of a television series episode by a different station controlled by the defendant was a separate act of infringement. Because the defendant's acts were willful, damages were fixed at just over $70,000 per act multiplied by 440 separate airings, for a total damage award to the copyright owner of $31.7 million (plus costs and attorneys' fees). This award was made by a jury in April 1999 and is believed to be the highest ever award of statutory damages. *Columbia Pictures Television v. Krypton Broadcasting of Birmingham, Inc.,* 259 F.3d 1186 (9th Cir. 2001). The Supreme Court has held that under the Seventh Amendment, if a party demands, there is a right to a jury trial on all issues pertinent to an award of statutory damages, including the amount itself. *Feltner v. Columbia Pictures Television, Inc.,* 503 U.S. 340 (1998).

- **Costs and attorneys' fees.** If registration has been secured within three months after publication of a work (or, for unpublished works, before the defendant's infringement), a court may award reasonable attorneys' fees to the plaintiff. The plaintiff may also recover costs (for example, expert witness fees, court filing fees, photocopy charges). If the defendant prevails, reasonable attorneys' fees and costs may be awarded to him or her in the discretion of the court.

- **Criminal sanctions.** Under the No Electronic Theft Act (the NET Act) signed into law in late 1997 (17 U.S.C. § 506 and 18 U.S.C. § 2319), various hypothesis. The formulation of this kind of hypothesis is called model specification, and it consists of specification of the key constructs and measures as well as relationships between variables. The testing of this kind of hypothesis is called model fitting, and the result may include such indicators as coefficient of alienation, goodness or badness of fit, etc.

For the individual bivariate hypotheses, the language to be used will show different patterns. One is "the more ... the more (or the less)..." format, which can also be translated into such a statement: "there is a positive (or negative) relationship between ...". This pattern applies to variables measured at the ordinal or higher levels (see next chapter for details about measurement levels). For nominal or categorical variables, there is no direction in the relationship. Therefore, the format of the hypothesis only tells "there is difference between (different categories of one variable)... in...(another variable)", which can be translated into such a statement: "there is a relationship between...and...". Whenever possible, however, you should specify the direction of your hypothesis to facilitate its testing.

In terms of the content of a hypothesis, you should pay special attention to its causal implications. Causation is often an issue of debate, and different research designs are considered to have different capacities in making causal inferences. Generally speaking, there are three levels of scientific inquiry: exploratory, descriptive, and explanatory. An exploratory study leads to only tentative or preliminary results and conclusions, and is conducted as a pioneering or inventive effort with emphasis on discovery rather than on validation. A descriptive study describes and confirms the condition of a variable or the relationship between variables, which may go beyond descriptive statistics and involve the use of significance tests. However, it does not tell the reason why such relationship exists, nor strictly distinguish between the causes and the effects. An explanatory study, in contrast, aims to identify specifically the causes and the effects.

A well-controlled experimental design is commonly regarded as the most rigorous form of research and thus has the highest capability of drawing explanatory or causal conclusions. For other forms of behavioral and social science research, such as a cross-sectional survey, researchers tend to keep their research categories at the descriptive or exploratory level by lessening the causal overtone of their hypotheses as well as their conclusions. This may suggest to you just to "play safe." What you should keep in mind is a kind of highly causal logic, however. Your research planning and thinking might involve a series of orderly and very clear causal links. And the language used to describe the criminal penalties can be imposed (with jail terms up to five years) for infringers who reproduce or distribute by electronic means copyrighted works of a certain value (generally, over $1,000). Subsequent offenses can result in jail terms of up to ten years. Fines up to $250,000 can also be imposed under the NET Act. The NET Act strengthens prior criminal provisions to make serious copyright piracy subject to criminal penalties even if there is no profit motive. Its primary purpose was to close the "LaMacchia Loophole," named for David LaMacchia, a student at MIT who set up an electronic bulletin board from which users downloaded approximately $1 million of free software. A copyright piracy case against LaMacchia was dismissed because LaMacchia had received no monetary compensation for the software he distributed. The NET Act also extended the statute of limitations in which criminal action may be brought from three years to five years. The Register of Copyrights testified before Congress in support of enhancing criminal penalties for copyright violations, stating that advances in technology have increased the potential for copyright piracy because it is easy and inexpensive to make and distribute pirated copies without a major investment in equipment and facilities. Thus, more serious penalties were needed to deter infringers.

- **Fines.** A fine up to $2,500 may be imposed when a copyright notice is fraudulently used or removed. Making a knowingly false statement of a material fact in a copyright application may subject a person to a fine up to $2,500.

TRIVIA

- In September 2000, a district court allowed presidential candidate Ralph Nader to continue to criticize the fund-raising tactics of the major parties by parodying MasterCard's "Priceless" ad campaign. The court held that the ad was a protected parody of the MasterCard ad and that Nader had made fun of MasterCard to make a political comment.
- In late 2000, the producers of the Mel Gibson movie *The Patriot* settled a copyright infringement case brought by an individual who claimed the studio misappropriated his designs for uniforms worn by the colonial Minutemen in the movie. While the studio initially negotiated with the artist, the deal later fell apart and the studio allegedly used a design from one of the artist's paintings and paid him nothing. The settlement sum was undisclosed.
- In *SunTrust Bank v. Houghton Mifflin Co.*, 268 F.3d 1357 (11th Cir. 2001), the Court of Appeals reversed a lower court's injunction that prohibited the publication of *The Wind Done Gone*, a parody of *Gone with the Wind*. The appellate court held that the use was

highly transformative and provided social benefit and thus the author of *The Wind Done Gone* was entitled to a fair use defense. After the decision, the parties reached a private settlement and *The Wind Done Gone* was published.

- In 1991, singer Michael Bolton was ordered to pay $5.4 million in damages for infringing a 1964 song called "Love Is a Wonderful Thing" by the Isley Brothers. The court found that Bolton had access to the earlier work and that the two works were substantially similar. *Three Boys Music Corp. v. Bolton*, 212 F.3d 477 (9th Cir. 2000), *cert. denied*, 531 U.S. 1126 (2001).

- Lawsuits for infringement of architectural works are increasing. In 2001, a Virginia jury awarded $5.2 million to an architectural firm whose home designs were used to construct more than 300 homes. The award represented the defendant's profits in the approximate amount of $17,000 for each of the 300 infringing houses.

CHAPTER SUMMARY

An infringement action may be brought by an owner of a registered copyright whenever any of his or her exclusive rights have been violated. Infringement requires that a plaintiff prove copyright ownership and impermissible copying. Copying is usually demonstrated by showing that the defendant had access to the copyrighted work and there is substantial similarity between the copyrighted work and defendant's work.

A defendant in an infringement action may assert a variety of defenses. The most common defense raised is that the defendant's use was a "fair use" of the copyrighted work. The fair use doctrine was developed to promote scholarly and educational use of certain works. Courts examine four factors in determining whether a defendant's use is fair: the purpose and character of the use, including whether the use is for commercial or nonprofit purposes; the nature of the work (with factual and scholarly works receiving less protection than works of fiction or fantasy); the amount and substantiality of the portion of work taken by the defendant (even a small taking may constitute infringement if it is the heart of the work); and the effect of the defendant's activities on the potential market for the copyrighted work. No one factor is conclusive; courts examine and weigh all factors in reaching a conclusion about infringement. Parody is a form of fair use, as are certain uses by libraries and educators.

Other defenses to infringement are invalidity of the plaintiff's copyright; estoppel to allege infringement due to the plaintiff's acquiescence in infringement; misuse or unclean hands by the plaintiff; and the statute of limitations, which provides that a civil infringement action must be brought within three years of the infringing activity.

Remedies available to a plaintiff include injunctive relief, actual damages and the defendant's profits, statutory damages (in lieu of actual damages and profits), costs, and attorneys' fees. Criminal penalties may be imposed in the case of certain willful infringements.

CASE ILLUSTRATION—FAIR USE

Case: *Princeton University Press v. Michigan Document Services*, 99 F.3d 1381 (6th Cir. 1996)

Facts: Defendant was a commercial company that reproduced articles and readings for university students, without permission, and bound them into coursepacks, which were then sold to students. The defendant alleged that its reproduction was a fair use of the copyrighted works.

Holding: The use was not a fair use. Examining the four fair use factors, the court concluded the following: (1) the use was a commercial one done for the defendant to make a profit and there was no transformation of the work; (2) the excerpted works contained creative material rather than purely factual material such as telephone listings, and this cuts against a finding of fair use; (3) in some cases, 30 percent of a copyrighted work was taken and in another instance 5 percent of a copyrighted work was copied—this is not insubstantial; and (4) the copyright owners were deprived of revenue by this copying. This destruction of a revenue stream would have a deleterious effect upon the authors' incentive to publish academic writings.

CASE STUDY AND ACTIVITIES

Case Study.   Watson has noticed that one of its competitors, Griffin Publishing, Inc., has published a children's book that is similar to Watson's book *Adventures at the Palace*. Both books tell the story of a princess who is locked in a palace and relies upon her wiles and the assistance of various animals to escape from her captors. The characters in the two books have different names and wear different costumes. Watson's princess is saved by a prince, while Griffin's princess is saved by her two sisters. Additionally, Watson recently discovered that a university professor wrote a poem that was published in the *New Yorker*, entitled "Crummy Corporate Days," that uses the cadence and rhythm of Watson's children's poem, "Happy Sunny Days," and mocks the Watson theme park and its characters and comments on Watson's use of children's stories and characters as a form of corporate exploitation.

Activities.   Discuss whether these two incidents constitute copyright infringement and what defenses Griffin and the poet are likely to assert.

ROLE OF PARALEGAL

The role of paralegals in infringement matters is similar to the role played by paralegals in other litigation matters. Intellectual property practitioners may be engaged in the following activities:

- obtaining certified copies of certificates of registration or other documents to prove a plaintiff's ownership of copyright;
- obtaining certified copies of applications for registration of copyrights to examine applications for misstatements to prove misuse of the copyright application procedure by a plaintiff;
- conducting research regarding defenses that may be asserted by a defendant, especially the fair use defense;
- preparing a cease and desist letter (or response to same);
- drafting complaints, answers, motions, and other pleadings in infringement actions;
- assisting in the discovery process in infringement actions (summarizing depositions, drafting interrogatories and responses to interrogatories, reviewing documents produced, examining statements related to defendant's revenues, and so forth); and
- assisting at the trial (preparing and maintaining exhibits and lists of witnesses, preparing a trial notebook, preparing jury instructions, and assisting in preparing motions and trial briefs).

INTERNET RESOURCES

Federal laws relating to copyright:	http://www.ll.georgetown.edu or http://www.findlaw.com
Copyright Office:	http://www.loc.gov/copyright or http://www.copyright.gov (for forms, circulars, information on fair use, Guidelines for Classroom Copying, and other materials)
Information on fair use:	http://fairuse.stanford.edu (for links to cases, regulations, treaties, and articles on copyright and fair use)
Crash Course in Copyrights:	http://www.utsystem.edu/ogc/intellectualproperty/cprtindx.htm (information on copyright and fair use)
General information:	http://www.findlaw.com and http://www.megalaw.com

DISCUSSION QUESTIONS

1. Ana Garcia, the owner of an unregistered copyright for a dance, transferred her rights to perform the work to Janice Taylor, in return for which Ms. Taylor pays royalties to Ms. Garcia. The work is being performed by a third party without authorization. Who is entitled to bring an action for infringement?

2. At a large well-attended computer trade show, Velocity Computer Products showcased its new software program that is designed for health care professionals. One year later, Velocity discovered that a competitor, Reynolds Computer Systems, Inc., is marketing a computer program nearly identical to Velocity's. In fact, the Reynolds program includes an error that Velocity intentionally left in its program during the design process. Discuss whether Velocity can prove infringement of the work by Reynolds.

3. Dave, the owner of a photocopy shop located near a university, routinely helps students photocopy sections of books they have borrowed from the university library. In an infringement suit by the authors of the works, Dave has asserted that he is not liable because the students are the actual infringers and that because the copying done by the students does not provide the students with any commercial advantage, there is no infringement. Discuss.

4. Jack is a movie critic for *That's Entertainment Tonight*, a nightly show devoted to show business and entertainment. May Jack show clips from the movies he reviews or must he obtain the owners' permission to use the clips? Why or why not?

5. A community theatre in your area is hosting "open mike" night to encourage individuals in the community to get involved in theatre and the performing arts. Admission fees are charged at the theatre. One performer routinely sings Madonna songs in a way that makes fun of Madonna and her lifestyle. Has infringement occurred? Discuss.

6. Dan recently discovered that a book he wrote was reproduced without permission by another person four years ago. May Dan sue for infringement? Discuss.

7. Paul is the owner of a copyright for a song that has been willfully infringed by Alex. Paul is having difficulty proving actual damages and lost profits due to Alex's infringement. What strategy should Paul consider?

For additional resources, go to www.westlegalstudies.com.

CHAPTER 15

New Developments in Copyright Law and the Semiconductor Chip Protection Act

CHAPTER OVERVIEW

Technological advances have created new forms of copyright authorship that in turn have created new issues relating to protection and dissemination of these new works. Although it is clear that computer programs and automated databases are copyrightable literary works, issues relating to copying computer programs continue to present challenges to the courts. The literal portions of computer programs (source code and object code) are protectable, but the nonliteral portions are often viewed as unprotectable useful articles, scenes a faire, or merged ideas and expressions. Reverse engineering of computer programs to create compatible programs may be acceptable, but creating identical or substantially similar programs may be infringement.

No subject in copyright law is subject to as much debate as copyright in the electronic age. The ease with which works can be viewed, copied, manipulated, reproduced, displayed, and transmitted using electronic means, particularly the Internet, has given rise to serious concern by authors that their works will be subject to wholesale infringement and piracy. Although some advocate that there should be no restrictions on information on the Internet, others are furiously working to develop encryption and metering devices that can track and monitor electronic use of works and charge for that use. The protection and infringement of songs and movies is of critical interest to their authors and industries. For example, just one week after the release of the long-anticipated book *Harry Potter and the Order of the Phoenix*, in June 2003, it could be obtained illegally online. A number of bills are pending in Congress to address these issues. Nevertheless, many experts believe the solutions to technology-related issues lie with technology rather than the courts or the legislature and that copyright protection on the Internet will be advanced by encryption and coding devices rather than piecemeal legislation or court decisions.

In 1998, the **Digital Millennium Copyright Act (DMCA)** became effective to promote electronic commerce and the distribution of digital works by providing tools and remedies to combat copyright piracy and to impose penalties on those who circumvent technological protection measures. This new act has spawned a series of court decisions and significant controversy with regard to whether the act chills innovation and free speech. The DMCA also provides for registration of the designs of original boat vessel hulls.

Protection for semiconductor chips stems from the Semiconductor Chip Protection Act of 1984. The act establishes a new form of intellectual property protection for the stencils or "masks" used to create the electronic circuitry of semiconductor chips. Although this form of protection is said to be *sui generis* (literally, "one of a kind"), mask protection draws upon many copyright principles.

INTRODUCTION

Developments in technology create new industries and opportunities for reproduction and dissemination of works of authorship. A number of new issues have arisen relating to the growth of electronic publishing, distribution, and viewing of copyrighted works. Along with new and expanded markets for works comes the ever-increasing challenge of protecting works from piracy or infringement. For example, in 1998, an advance copy of the first single from Madonna's latest album was released to foreign radio stations. Almost immediately, unauthorized copies were placed on web sites allowing anyone with Internet access to download a copy weeks before the single was released for sale or radio play in the United States. Similarly, in mid-2002, bootlegged versions of the movie *Star Wars: Attack of the Clones* appeared on the Internet within hours of movie house premieres.

Both the courts and Congress continue to be faced with issues that were unimagined just a decade ago. "High-tech" legislation continues to be introduced in Congress. Courts struggle with the complexity and balance between protecting the rights of authors and promoting the progress of science and useful arts as is mandated by the Constitution. This chapter is intended to introduce some of the copyright cutting edge and bleeding edge issues presently confronting authors, users, legislators, and judges.

COPYRIGHT PROTECTION FOR COMPUTER PROGRAMS

Protectable Elements of Computer Programs

Computer programs have been accepted for copyright registration since the mid-1960s. In 1974, Congress created the Commission on New Technological Uses of Copyrighted Works (CONTU) to analyze various technology-related issues and report to Congress on several topics, including copyrightability of computer programs. The CONTU recommended that the 1976 Copyright Act be expressly amended to make clear that computer programs are copyrightable. In 1980, Congress followed CONTU's recommendations and added a definition in the Copyright Act for the term *computer program* and a limitation on the exclusive rights of computer program authors in order to allow users to make certain adaptations to programs and to make archival copies of programs.

According to section 101 of the Copyright Act, a **computer program** is a set of statements or instructions to be used directly or indirectly in a computer in order to bring about a certain result. Copyright protection extends to all of the copyrightable expression embodied in the program. Copyright protection is not available for ideas, program logic, algorithms, systems, methods, concepts, or layouts. Computer programs are copyrightable as literary works, and applicants seeking registration of computer programs should generally use application Form TX (the same form used for books and other literary materials). However, if pictorial or graphic authorship predominates, registration may be made using Form PA (for audiovisual works).

Computer languages are written in specialized alphanumeric languages (such as Basic, C, or Java) called **source code** that are human-readable. In order to operate a computer, source code must be translated into machine-readable **object code,** consisting of only two symbols, 0 and 1, which represent the alphanumeric characters of the source code. Object code cannot be read by humans. Both source code and object code are copyrightable.

Copyright protection extends to screen displays as well, if they possess copyrightable material. Screens consisting of mere menus or blank forms usually are not protectable, either because they lack original expression or because they are useful articles. In *Lotus Development Corp. v. Borland International, Inc.,* 49 F.3d 807 (1st Cir. 1995), *aff'd,* 516 U.S. 233 (1996), the First Circuit held that the menu command hierarchy of the Lotus 1-2-3 spreadsheet was uncopyrightable subject matter inasmuch as it was a mere method of operation. The court held that highlighting a "p" for "print" on a computer screen was really no different from pressing a "play" button on a VCR. Such was not protectable expression.

A single registration is sufficient to protect the copyright in a computer program, including related screen displays, without a separate registration for the screen displays or a specific reference to the displays in the application. Acceptable identifications of the work include "computer program," "entire text of computer program," "entire program code," and "text of user's manual and computer program." These identifications will cover any copyrightable authorship contained in the computer program and screen displays. The Copyright Office will refuse registration if the claim of authorship is based only on "encrypting," "firmware," "formatting," "functions," "printout," "software methodology," or "system."

Because most computer programs are accompanied by user manuals, the manuals may be included as part of the computer program registration, thus eliminating the need for a separate application for the manuals.

Deposit Requirements for Computer Programs

For published or unpublished computer programs, the first twenty-five and last twenty-five pages of source code should be submitted in a form visually perceptible without the aid of a machine or a device. If the program is less than fifty pages in length, all of the source code should be deposited.

Because computer programs often contain proprietary information and trade secrets, the Copyright Office has developed alternative deposit requirements for such works. Where a computer program contains trade secret material, a cover letter should accompany the application, stating that the claim contains trade secrets. One of the following must then be deposited:

- first twenty-five and last twenty-five pages of source code with portions containing trade secrets blocked out; or
- first ten and last ten pages of source code alone, with no blocked-out portions; or

- first twenty-five and last twenty-five pages of object code plus any ten or more consecutive pages of source code, with no blocked-out portions; or
- for programs less than fifty pages in length, entire source code with trade secret portions blocked out.

Some applicants are reluctant to deposit even blocked-out portions of source code. They may therefore apply for a registration under the Copyright Office's "rule of doubt" by submitting object code together with written confirmation that the material does contain copyrightable authorship. The Copyright Office will issue a registration on the basis of the information given by the applicant even though it is unable to examine the deposited material and determine the existence of copyrightability. If questions arise later regarding copyrightability, a court will determine whether the material is copyrightable.

Notice of Copyright

Although the form of copyright notice is the same for computer-related works as for other works (the symbol ©, the year of first publication, and the name of the owner), the location of the notice presents special problems. The Copyright Office has stated the following are acceptable placements of the notice:

- a notice embedded in the copies in machine-readable form in such a manner that on visually perceptible printouts it appears either with or near the title, or at the end of the work;
- a notice that is displayed at the user's screen or terminal at sign-on;
- a notice that is continuously on the screen or terminal display; or
- a legible notice on a label securely affixed to the copies or to a box, reel, cartridge, cassette, or other container used as a permanent receptacle for the copies.

Video Games

Although the ideas underlying some video games (such as a solitaire game) are not copyrightable, certain elements of video games, such as a sequence of sounds and images, are copyrightable as audiovisual works apart from the underlying computer program. Some infringers alleged early on that video games were not copyrightable inasmuch as player participation causes variations in games and different outcomes, and thus the works are not "fixed," but courts have held that many of the game elements remain constant and that the memory devices of games satisfy the requirement of fixation.

Revisions and Modifications to Computer Programs

Computer programs are frequently updated and revised by their authors, generally to provide additional features to users. Substantive revisions will result in a new work for which a new copyright registration should be sought. Thus, each separately published version of a computer program should be separately registered, assuming each contains a sufficient amount of new or revised authorship to sustain a claim of copyright. The Copyright Office will accept the following claims of authorship: "new modules," "revised modules," "revised program," "new routines," and "revised routines."

Copyright owners have the exclusive right under section 106 of the Copyright Act to reproduce their works and to prepare derivative works based on their copyrighted works. Section 117 of the act, relating exclusively to computer programs, limits these exclusive rights by allowing a backup copy to be made and allowing some modifications of programs for an owner's own use, such as improving the program or increasing its speed of performance.

Section 117 provides that notwithstanding the otherwise exclusive rights of a copyright owner, it is not an infringement for the owner of a copy of a computer program to make an additional copy or to adapt a program if the new copy or adaptation is created as an essential step in the utilization of the computer program or is used for archival purposes only. Thus, section 117 authorizes some modifications to computer programs for a purchaser's own use under the theory that having paid for a computer program, the consumer may experiment with the product and create new variations of play, for personal enjoyment, without creating an infringing derivative work. *Lewis Galoob Toys, Inc. v. Nintendo of America, Inc.,* 964 F.2d 965 (9th Cir. 1992). In *Lewis Galoob*, the defendant manufactured a device called Game Genie to be used with Nintendo's videogames that could increase the speed of a character's moves and increase the number of lives of a player's character. The court held that these were merely permissible enhancements to the copyrighted work. The device was not an unauthorized derivative work and did not physically incorporate a portion of the copyrighted work. The Game Genie was useless by itself and did not supplant demand for a component of Nintendo's works. Additionally, converting a program from one language to another to facilitate its use or adding features to a computer program for one's own needs is permissible. *Foresight Resources Corp. v. Pfortmiller,* 719 F. Supp. 1006 (D. Kan. 1989). Section 117 applies to "owners," and thus courts have held that its provisions are inapplicable to licensees of software or those who are in possession of software unlawfully.

Infringement of Computer Programs

Some of the most complex copyright cases involve the extent of protectability for computer programs. A number of litigants have asserted that computer operating systems are not protectable inasmuch as they are uncopy-rightable "processes" or "systems," expressly excluded from protection according to section 102 of the Copyright Act. Courts generally have held otherwise, reasoning that if other programs can be written or created that perform the same functions, then an operating system is an expression of an idea and is therefore copyrightable. If the idea cannot be expressed in any other way, however, then it is purely necessary to the purpose and is functional, and hence not copyrightable. This is the merger doctrine, discussed in Chapter 10, that provides that if an idea in a work can be expressed in only one way or a very limited number of ways, it is unprotectable inasmuch as it would be unfair to allow one party to appropriate an idea and exclude all others from using it. When an idea and its expression are so merged or inseparable that the unprotectable idea cannot be used without also using protectable expression, then use is not infringement.

Courts have struggled with infringement issues in computer-related cases in part because the issues are often technical, unfamiliar, and complex. Thus, experts are often relied upon rather than the "ordinary observer" commonly referred to in other infringement actions. Moreover, unlike songs and books, which are highly creative, computer programs are usually task-oriented, performing very specific and utilitarian functions. Historically, "useful articles" are excluded from copyright protection.

Some courts have expressly recognized that many computer programs are by nature utilitarian articles inasmuch as their purpose is to accomplish tasks. *See Computer Associates International, Inc. v. Altai, Inc.,* 982 F.2d 693 (2d Cir. 1992). Thus, functional commands and aspects are unprotectable. Based on the merger doctrine, courts have held that when specific instructions are the only means of accomplishing a given task, another may use them without infringing the original work.

relationship among different variables often implies this causal reasoning. When you distinguish between a "dependent" variable and an "independent" variable, for example, you suggest some causal relationship even though you claim yours is merely a descriptive analysis. An independent variable is like a cause, while a dependent variable is more like a result or an outcome. You may focus on one or a few dependent variables and try to identify all the independent variables that bear on them. Or you may focus on one or a few independent variables, and your job is to find out their major effects. Sometimes the causal order in your mind is much more complicated than that simple logic. In any case, you will have an ideal in mind which will guide you through the research.

Moreover, many cases involving computer-related works have held that certain elements are unprotectable inasmuch as they are standard or stock scenes a faire (literally, "scenes which must be done"). Thus, hardware and software standards, mechanical specifications, industry programming practices, and compatibility requirements have been held to be unprotectable scenes a faire, since they are expressions dictated by external factors and their creation is the natural product of such external considerations.

Most courts have used the "abstraction-filtration-comparison" test discussed in Chapter 14 in determining whether infringement of computer programs has occurred. A court will abstract or dissect the allegedly infringed program's structure, filter out the unprotectable elements (such as processes, facts, merger material, and scenes a faire), and then compare the remaining protectable elements of the two works to determine whether infringement exists. *Gates Rubber Co. v. Bando Chem. Indus., Ltd.,* 9 F.3d 823 (10th Cir. 1993). Other courts focus on the idea-expression dichotomy and hold that only those elements not necessary to the purpose or function of the work are protectable expression.

Early cases often involved nearly identical copying of code (often referred to as "literal copying"), and courts found it easy to determine that in such cases infringement had occurred. Analogizing computer programs to other textual works, such as books, which could be infringed even without literal copying (namely, by paraphrasing), courts then extended copyright protection to the structure, sequence, and organization of programs, namely the nonliteral elements of a program.

Later cases have involved less clear-cut issues, such as copying functional elements of programs. Many of these cases involve **reverse engineering,** or disassembling a computer program to understand its functional elements. In *Sega Enterprises Ltd. v. Accolade, Inc.,* 977 F.2d 1510 (9th Cir. 1993), the defendant reverse engineered Sega's video game programs in order to make its own video games that would be compatible with Sega's console into which the defendant's game cartridges were inserted. The Ninth Circuit held that such was permissible because the defendant had copied Sega's software solely in order to discover the functional elements for compatibility with Sega's console, elements of Sega's programs that were not protectable by copyright. The court held that where disassembly is the only way to gain access to the ideas and functional elements embodied in a copyright program and where there is a legitimate reason for seeking such access, such disassembly is a fair use of the copyrighted work.

Many experts interpret *Sega* as part of a growing trend of courts to limit the scope of copyright protection for computer programs, particularly for the functional elements of programs. Thus, many owners are now seeking patent protection for their computer programs (see Chapter 21). Nevertheless, although efforts can be undertaken to understand a work's ideas, processes, and methods of operation (all unprotectable functional aspects of a computer program), if the final program produced by the "engineer" is substantially similar to the original work, infringement may be found.

Under section 117 of the Copyright Act, owners of a computer program are specifically authorized to make backup copies of their programs and load the program onto a computer's hard drive from a floppy disk or CD-ROM. They cannot, however, make copies for purposes of commercial distribution.

Licensing of Computer Programs

Due to the ease of copying computer programs (allowing numerous users to share one purchased program) and due to the first sale doctrine (allowing the owner/purchaser of a copy to sell or rent it to others), makers of software programs became concerned over piracy and potential loss of revenues. To remedy the problem, they implemented the practice of licensing their programs. Software purchased over the counter is thus not "sold" by the maker but rather "licensed" by the maker to the user/purchaser. Such a license is often called a **shrink-wrap license** because opening the plastic wrapping on the package immediately subjects the user/purchaser to the terms of the license agreement. A notice to this effect is placed on or in the box or packaging, and a method for returning the software is usually provided if the user/licensee objects to the license terms. Courts generally have held that such licenses are valid contracts enforceable under the principles of contract law unless their terms are objectionable on grounds applicable to contracts in general, for example, if they are unconscionable. *ProCD, Inc. v. Zeidenberg,* 86 F.3d 1447 (7th Cir. 1996).

The license agreements contain warranties and the terms and conditions under which the user/licensee can use the software and make it clear that violation of any of the terms, such as loading the software into more than one computer or decompiling it, constitutes infringement. Because the transaction is a license rather than a sale, no "first sale" concerns are implicated, and the user/licensee cannot resell or rent the software to another inasmuch as there was no sale to him or her in the first instance. In some cases, software is licensed electronically; this license agreement is referred to as a **click-wrap license,** since the license terms and conditions come into existence when the user/licensee clicks an icon displayed on a computer screen to indicate "purchase" or license of the work per the stated terms. Such click-wrap licenses may not be valid unless the computer screens display reasonably conspicuous notice of the existence of the contractual terms and require the user or licensee to unambiguously manifest agreement to those terms. Asking users to show assent by clicking "OK" or

"I agree" before proceeding shows assent to an agreement; however, a process allowing users to download software without first viewing an agreement or even being made aware of its existence does not show assent.

Section 117 of the Copyright Act, allowing owners of copies of computer programs to make a new copy or adaptation if necessary to use the program or to make an archival or backup copy, is limited to "owners" and is thus not applicable to licensees under shrink-wrap or click-wrap license agreements. Most software makers/licensors, however, typically include as a term of the license a provision substantially similar to section 117, allowing the user/licensee to make a new copy or adaptation if necessary to enable the use for which the software was obtained or for archival purposes. The Digital Millennium Copyright Act (discussed below) allows software developers who have lawfully obtained the right to use a computer program to reverse engineer it to analyze the elements necessary to achieve interoperability of an independently created computer program. Additionally, either owners or licensees can make a copy of a computer program for purposes of maintaining or repairing the computer hardware.

Piracy of Software

In addition to the complex legal issues surrounding protection and infringement of computer-related works, there are significant economic issues as well. It has been estimated that software piracy causes a loss of revenue of nearly $3 billion annually in the United States alone. One expert has estimated that there may be nearly thirty thousand sites on the Internet that offer software illegally. Piracy of other content is also rampant. Just the day after the film *Titanic* won several Oscar awards, fifty separate web sites offered illegal video copies of the film. One of the most common types of software piracy is "softlifting," or making unauthorized copies of a licensed software program (often for a home computer, fellow employee, family, or friends). The economic effect of computer piracy is reportedly more than $12 billion worldwide per year, costing 111,000 jobs in the United States alone. Consequently, many companies, notably Microsoft Corporation, are stepping up their crusades against software piracy, both through educational programs and legal action. One counterfeiting operation in early 1999 in California resulted in a seizure of $30 million of pirated MICROSOFT® software.

Software makers often join one of two associations, the Software & Information Industry Association (SIIA, formerly the Software Publishers Association) or the Business Software Alliance (BSA), that exist to educate businesses about copyrights in software and to locate infringers. The SIIA has 1,200 members and represents the software industry. The BSA was formed in the late 1980s, and some of its members are Apple, Borland, Novell, Intel, and Microsoft. Generally, it represents the interests of the leading makers of software for personal computers. It has filed hundreds of lawsuits for software infringement, asking for restraining orders and audits of a company's computers to locate pirated software. Most lawsuits are settled out of court, with the infringers paying the retail value of the software and replacing the pirated software. In other cases, damages have been assessed in the millions of dollars. Both BSA and SIIA have hotline numbers to report infringement, and in many instances, disgruntled former employees report infringement by their former employers. The SIIA reports that it receives about thirty calls per day on its hotline. Visiting technicians to companies and temporary employees also tend to report infringement.

The BSA offers a publication to help businesses implement antipiracy programs. Call (800) 688-2721 (or access http://www.bsa.org) and ask for *Software Management Guide*. The

SIIA offers a free self-audit kit to help determine if a company is in violation of any copyrights. Write to SIIA at 1090 Vermont Avenue NW, Washington, DC 20005.

Although software piracy is of great concern in the United States, it is estimated that most loss from computer piracy arises in foreign countries due to their lax enforcement practices and laws. For example, until 1998, software piracy was not a crime in Argentina or Brazil. The SIIA has rated China as having a piracy percentage of 90 percent, meaning that for every one hundred programs sold, ninety are pirated. Similarly, in May 1998 alone, Hong Kong officials seized more than 10 million pirated CDs. The U.S. Trade Representative attempts to work with these countries to secure their commitment to protect copyrighted works by placing countries on intellectual property "watch lists," which can lead to trade restrictions and sanctions. Countries currently on the priority watch list include India, Russia, Vietnam, and the Philippines. Once a country is placed on a watch list, an investigation is initiated to determine whether tariffs or trade restrictions should be imposed on the offending country. In 2003, the U.S. Trade Representative imposed $75 million worth of sanctions on Ukraine exports for Ukraine's repeated failures to protect intellectual property and noted that such failures could well jeopardize Ukraine's efforts to join the World Trade Organization.

COPYRIGHT PROTECTION FOR AUTOMATED DATABASES

According to the Copyright Office, an **automated database** is a body of facts, data, or other information assembled into an organized format suitable for use in a computer and comprising one or more files. An automated database is a compilation because it is formed by collecting and assembling preexisting materials or data. Although there is no specific reference to automated databases anywhere in the Copyright Act, they are viewed as types of literary works subject to copyright protection. An example of an automated database is WESTLAW's database of federal court cases. Although the cases themselves are government works in the public domain, West Group's arrangement of those cases qualifies for copyright protection as a compilation.

Automated databases will not receive protection if there is no original authorship in the selection and ordering of the data, such as is the case in merely transferring data from hard copy to computer storage. Registration is secured using Form TX. If the material in the database has been previously published, previously registered, or is in the public domain, the claim should be described as "compilation." If the material is original, the claim should be described as "text."

For a single-file database (one in which the data records pertain to a single common subject matter, such as bankruptcy cases), the deposit should consist of the first and last twenty-five pages or data records. For a multiple-file database (one in which there are separate and distinct groups of data records, such as bankruptcy cases, federal regulations, and state statutes), the deposit should consist of fifty data records from each file, or the entire file, whichever is less. The Copyright Office also requires a descriptive statement from the applicant, giving the title of the database, identifying the copyright claimant, describing each separate file in the multiple-file database, and giving information about the nature and frequency of changes within the database and information about the copyright notice to be used. The Copyright Office will consider requests for relief from the deposit requirements if the database contains trade secrets or the applicant is unable to deposit the materials.

The Copyright Office provides specific information about copyright registration for automated databases in its Circular 65, obtainable from the forms hotline (202/707-9100) and on the Internet at http://www.copyright.gov.

In April 1998, the United States sponsored a conference on database protection to discuss providing additional protection to databases. Additionally, on three occasions, Congress has considered legislation that would protect databases created through a substantial investment of time and money (a provision that would effectively overrule *Feist,* which held that a database work, namely, a telephone directory, was not protectable merely because it was the result of "sweat of the brow"). Thus, protection would be provided for realtors' home listings, stock quotations, and certain case reports. Certain databases containing information for educational, scientific, research, and news-gathering purposes would be exempt. Such protection would harmonize U.S. law with that of many of the European Union countries, which provide some protection to noncreative compilations of material. As discussed in Chapter 16, the issue of providing enhanced protection to databases is the subject of both national and international debate and discussion, with no present resolution in regard to the extent to which databases should be protected. Generally, however, companies that have been damaged because their databases were infringed have been successful in court, leading some experts to say this shows that no dramatic new legislation relating to database protection is needed.

COPYRIGHT IN THE ELECTRONIC AGE

Introduction

There is a dynamic tension inherent in copyright law: the rights of authors and creators to protect their works and reap the benefits of their creations must be balanced against the right of the public to have access to information. Nowhere is that tension more pronounced than in the discussion of copyright in cyberspace. It is amazingly easy to make electronic copies of works and then transmit those works to others using digital media. Using our computers, we are capable of retrieving, storing, revising, and disseminating vast amounts of information created by others with a single keystroke. There are few mechanical or economic restrictions precluding or restricting the free flow of information in cyberspace.

On one side of a vigorous debate are the adherents to the "Dyson model," named after Esther Dyson, board member emeritus of the Electronic Frontier Foundation, who believe that "information wants to be free," meaning that the logical product of the Internet and our global communications capacities is unrestricted dissemination of information. Widespread access to information is beneficial to the research, educational, and scientific communities, all benefiting the public interest. On the other side of the debate are authors and creators of works who fear that unrestricted access to their works on the Internet will impair the value of their works, cause a loss of revenue to them, and ultimately discourage creation of work. If authors fear loss of protection, they will not create work, and the public will then receive no benefit.

The Copyright Act has been liberally written to encompass new technologies as seen in the reference in section 102 that copyright protection subsists in original works of authorship fixed in any tangible medium of expression, *now known or later developed.* Nevertheless, although the Copyright Act anticipates emerging technologies, developments of the past several years have been so unexpected and rapid that many experts believe additional amendments to the Copyright Act may be necessary.

Issues Confronting Cyberspace Users

Some of the issues presently facing authors, consumers, and Internet service providers (such as America Online or Mindspring) are the following:

- Should individuals browsing information offered on the Internet be required to obtain the author's permission before viewing the information; saving the information; transmitting it to others; revising the material; making a hard copy of or printing the information; or reproducing the information in another form, such as in a newsletter? At least one court has held that a company that downloaded copyrighted material from a web site to post on an internal intranet was liable for copyright infringement. *Marobie-FL v. National Ass'n of Fire Equipment Distributors,* 983 F. Supp. 1167 (N.D. Ill. 1997).

- Should the owner of a digital version of a copyrighted work be permitted to disseminate that information to another under the "first sale" doctrine? At present, the first sale doctrine has not been expanded to permit digital transmission of copies of copyrighted works.

- Is placing information (or "uploading") on the Internet a dedication to the public domain such that anyone can thereafter use, reproduce, adapt, or display the information for any purpose?

- Is posting information on a bulletin board system a "performance" of a copyrighted work?

- Is quoting material from others in a chat room infringement?

- Should the U.S. government be able to restrict exports of the most powerful encryption software unless the maker of the software provides the government with a decoding key or "back door" so the government can fight organized crime and terrorism?

A common thread running through all of these issues is whether the Copyright Act should be amended to address these issues or whether the courts should resolve these questions on a case-by-case basis.

The National Information Infrastructure

In 1993, President Clinton formed the Information Infrastructure Task Force to study the complex issues posed by posting and disseminating information in cyberspace and to develop guidelines for a National Information Infrastructure (NII). The NII encompasses digital interactive services now available, such as the Internet, as well as those that may be developed in the future.

The NII is not restricted to copyright issues. The NII, combining computer technology and communications technology, can support our education systems by connecting students and educators all over the world, advance cultural and entertainment opportunities, and increase participation in the democratic process by making available speeches, bills, and other government works. However, the NII has a direct impact on copyrighted works. Two-dimensional works are easily converted to digitized form (a series of zeroes and ones) and can then be easily and rapidly reproduced (with each "copy" identical in quality to the original) and transmitted to others with just a few keystrokes. They may be posted on a bulletin board where thousands of individuals can have access to them. These works can be changed by modifications and by combining them with other works (such as the addition of lyrics written by one party to music written by another), blurring ownership rights. Just one unauthorized uploading of an author's work onto a bulletin board could have a devastating effect on the market for that author's work.

Thus, appropriate systems must be put into place to protect authors' rights.

After holding hearings and examining a variety of issues, the task force determined that although some minor modifications and amendments would be needed to the 1976 Copyright Act to reflect the realities of the NII and to take account of current technology, the act was fundamentally adequate and effective. The task force also concluded that no revisions were needed to trademark, patent, or trade secret law at the time. Its final report, however, "The White Paper on Intellectual Property and the National Information Infrastructure," (available at http://www.uspto.gov) has engendered much criticism. Opponents of the recommendations set forth in the White Paper have formed the "Digital Future Coalition," which believes that the White Paper recommends far too much protection to authors at the cost of drying up information that should be freely accessible to the public. The web site of the Digital Future Coalition (http://www.dfc.org) provides information about its activities in the ongoing debate regarding intellectual property law in the digital network environment.

Copyright Notices in the Electronic Age

Authors concerned about unauthorized reproduction and dissemination of their works by electronic means can include notices with their works to remind users that further reproduction or transmission is unauthorized and may constitute infringement. Some notices are as follows:

- © 2003 John Doe. Copying, transmitting, reproducing, or archiving this work in any media or by any means for other than personal use without express permission of John Doe is prohibited and may constitute copyright infringement.
- Access to and use of this web site is subject to the following terms and

conditions: you may browse this site only for information and entertainment use; you may not modify, transmit, or revise the contents of this site without the owner's written permission; any communication you post to this site will be treated as nonconfidential; you may not post or transmit any unlawful or defamatory material; your use of the site constitutes acceptance of these terms.

- This web site contains links to other sites. Such links are not affiliations with or endorsements of other sites or the products or services offered by or through such sites.
- © 2003 Jane Roe. The user or viewer of this work is hereby granted an express nonexclusive license to reproduce the work, display, transmit, and distribute it by all means and in any media.
- Those individuals who post messages or works to this list own the copyrights to the messages or works; however, they grant a nonexclusive license to the list owner to reproduce, transmit, forward, and archive any messages or works posted to this list.

Although these notices will not preclude infringement, they may assist an author in obtaining damages for willful infringement or, alternatively, clarify that the work may be freely disseminated.

Copyright Rights Management

A number of proposals have been advanced to protect works from unauthorized and global reproduction, transmission, and distribution over the Internet. These proposals are generally referred to as "copyright rights management," or "copyright management information," or "digital rights management." Some of the proposals include the following:

- "metering" each use of a copyrighted work so that viewers are required to pay for viewing or distributing the work, with proceeds going to the author and Internet service provider ("metering" works substantially similar to "pay per view" television viewing);
- developing secure processors, encryption techniques, and digital watermarking technologies that preclude copying of digital works unless authorized;
- developing secure containers for digital works, sometimes called "cryptelopes," that operate as lock boxes, requiring users to secure permission or pay a fee before works can be decrypted for use and viewing;
- protecting information through the use of passwords and requiring users to agree to certain terms and conditions (for example, the *New York Times* does not charge a fee for users to access its web site, although it requires users to register by selecting a password and agreeing to abide by the terms of the *Times*'s subscriber agreement);
- developing models based on those used by the Copyright Clearance Center (discussed in Chapter 14) whereby a broad library of information would be preauthorized for digital use and licenses and permissions would be granted to use and reproduce the digital works for preset fees much the same way licenses and permissions are granted by clearinghouses to use works printed in conventional hardcopy form. In this model, clearinghouses would allow customers to purchase software on the Internet through the use of a secure "envelope" that could not be opened until payment is received or confirmed (note that this method allows no protection against downstream infringement because the

first authorized user could readily distribute copies to others, both by electronic and conventional means);

- developing devices that monitor and track digital usage (comparable to the way telephone companies determine telephone charges) by embedding chips into works that meter usage as soon as information is accessed and then produce monthly statements or bills; and

- introducing fingerprint readers or iris-scanning software (the field of biometrics) to recognize authorized users and protect network security.

Specific proposals to deter music piracy are discussed below.

Practical Do's and Don'ts

Because of the uncertainty inherent in viewing, archiving, transmitting, reproducing, downloading, uploading, and otherwise using digital information on the Internet, following are some practical pointers and guidelines for copyright compliance in the electronic age:

- Even attributing quotes to their authors may not protect against a claim of infringement. When on the Internet, do not quote from, transmit, copy, archive, or reproduce others' works without permission (unless such use is a fair use).

- Review material placed on the Internet for permissions; in many cases, authors have already granted limited permissions or licenses for others to use and view the materials. Unless permission is given, all material on the Internet, especially software, should be considered copyrighted work. Therefore, software should not be downloaded or modified without permission from the copyright holder. Similarly, downloading and printing an article you find for your personal use may be appro-

priate; however, printing multiple copies of the article and distributing them to others without permission likely violates the owner's exclusive copyright rights. Although such acts are infringements, copyright violations are common. For example, the developer of the popular computer games "Quake" and "Doom" estimates that 50 percent of the versions of Quake now being played are unlicensed, having been downloaded from unauthorized web sites.

- Do not place any documents or materials from clients or your employer on the Internet without permission and without including a copyright notice.

- Newsgroup and e-mail postings are not always in the public domain. The safest course may be to forward postings only with permission (although a number of people believe that posting messages is an implied license to either archive or to forward those messages to others).

- Do not copy material (whether text or graphics) from another's web page without permission, and do not combine items from others' web pages to create a web page.

- Ask permission before establishing links to others' sites, and indicate that links to unaffiliated sites are so unaffiliated to avoid presumed sponsorship of others.

- Place copyright notices on all web sites and on all original works.

THE DIGITAL MILLENNIUM COPYRIGHT ACT

Introduction

In 1998, Congress enacted the Digital Millennium Copyright Act (DMCA), 17 U.S.C. § 1201 *et seq.*, to move the nation's copyright law into the digital age. Because piracy of digital content is so easily accomplished, Congress sought to expand copyright protection for digital works by ensuring that copyright protection tools (such as encryption technology) could not be circumvented. Additionally, the DMCA seeks to update U.S. copyright law to prepare for ratification of various WIPO treaties (see Chapter 16). Some experts have stated that the DMCA represents the most comprehensive copyright reform in a generation.

Some of the most critical provisions of the DMCA are as follows:

- prohibitions against acts that circumvent technological protection measures;
- provisions forbidding trafficking in products or technology that are used in circumventing copyright protection measures;
- provisions forbidding removal or tampering with copyright management information (for example, removal of digital watermarks); and
- safe harbor provisions insulating online service providers (such as America Online and Yahoo) from liability for acts such as transmitting or linking to unauthorized content (if the provider meets certain criteria such as adopting policies to terminate service of copyright offenders).

The DMCA expressly authorizes reverse engineering of computer programs. Both civil and criminal penalties can be imposed for violations of the DMCA.

The DMCA has met with a great deal of criticism from electronics manufacturers, computer scientists, researchers, and libraries that are concerned that the act may chill freedom of expression. For example, the American Library Association's web site states that under the DMCA, "the doctrine of 'fair use' has never been more threatened. . . ."

Issues Arising under the DMCA

A number of interesting cases and issues have arisen under the newly enacted DMCA, including the following:

- **DeCSS technology.** DeCSS is a software program created by a fifteen-year old computer hacker that enables users to descramble the encryption code that prohibits the copying of DVDs. In *Universal City Studios v. Reimerdes*, 111 F. Supp. 2d 294 (S.D.N.Y. 2000), eight motion picture studios sued a journalist to enjoin him from using his web site to make available the DeCSS software program. The court held that dissemination of DeCSS violated the DMCA. The defendant was not only enjoined from offering DeCSS on his own web site but was enjoined from offering links to other sites where DeCSS could be found. Although the defendant argued that he had a First Amendment right to offer the software program, the court held that disseminating the program violated the antitrafficking and antidecryption provisions of the DMCA. Additionally, the court found that dissemination of DeCSS was neither a fair use nor acceptable reverse engineering under the DMCA.
- **First Amendment issues.** In *Universal Studios, Inc. v. Corley*, 273 F.3d 429 (2d Cir. 2001), another DeCSS case, the court affirmed an injunction prohibiting an individual from posting the DeCSS code on his web site and providing links to other sites that posted DeCSS. Although the court held that computer code, including decryption algorithms, constituted protected "speech" under the First Amendment, the court upheld the DMCA's limitations on such speech, ruling that any restriction on speech was

justified by the government's need to prevent piracy.

- **Online service providers.** In 2000, a San Francisco court held that the online service provider eBay was not liable for auctioning sound recordings on its Internet web site that might infringe copyrights of others. Imposing liability on eBay for the sale of bootleg recordings would place an unjustifiable burden on eBay and would likely force it to cease or restrict its operations. Similarly, in 2002, a California appeals court held that eBay was not liable for the sale of fake sports memorabilia on its auction site. These courts have ruled that eBay does not have the ability or right to control infringing activity, a standard required by the DMCA. Some online service providers, including eBay, engage in voluntary monitoring of their sites to locate infringing material.

- **Webcasts.** The DMCA requires radio stations to pay royalties to music performers and their record labels when broadcasts or **webcasts** are transmitted over the Internet, a practice called **streaming.** In mid-2002, the Librarian of Congress established royalty fees for these Internet radio stations and webcasters. Thus, AM-FM radio broadcasters that simultaneously offer Internet transmission of their radio programs must pay the statutorily set fees (presently set at $0.07 per song per listener). As discussed in Chapter 11, AM-FM stations pay royalties to composers and authors of songs (usually through ASCAP and BMI) but do not pay the record producers for sound recordings. Thus, webcasters have vigorously objected to what they perceive as "double royalty payments" and allege that requiring such fees to be paid for

sound recordings will chill their ability to provide Internet webcasts and drive them out of business. Broadcasters continue to submit proposals to the Copyright Office for decreased royalty fees.

Five years after its passage, the DMCA continues to be a controversial piece of legislation. Court cases continue to challenge its provisions, and Congress has been asked to amend some of its provisions. As of the time of writing of this text, the Library of Congress was holding hearings regarding what changes, if any, should be made to the sections of the DMCA that restrict bypassing copy protection technology. Additionally, the DMCA mandates that various studies and reports be conducted by the U.S. Copyright Office on the effects of the DMCA. These reports are available at http://www.copyright.gov.

MUSICAL NOTES

Introduction

The music industry has likely been the hardest hit by technology that enables consumers to swap or share copyrighted songs over personal computers, thus eliminating the need to buy records or CDs. Surveys suggest that more blank CDs are sold in the United States than recorded ones. Sales of albums and CDs in the United States have continually decreased over the past several years, with the industry posting its worst performance in ten years in 2002.

The battle to stop music piracy is fought principally by the Recording Industry Association of America (RIAA). Initially, the RIAA's strategy focused on peer-to-peer music swapping services, such as Napster, developed in 1999 by a college student. RIAA has since broadened its focus by pursuing companies, universities, and individual users while simultaneously

CHAPTER SEVEN

Measuring the Variables

General reading and focused literature review serve the same function of learning. While you are looking for suitable research questions and straightening the conceptual and theoretical issues, you are also getting the methodological hints if you pay due attention. By appreciating previous research designs and detecting the major technical as well as epistemological issues, you may discover better approaches to the research questions that interest you. If you have a mindset like a methodologist, you may get deep into such issues as modifying a measurement theory and devising a new computational procedure. Generally speaking, the methodological deliberations are also an important part of your research framework. In this chapter, we will concentrate on measurement, or so-called operationalization as a step following the conceptualization of your research. The following two chapters will discuss other methods and issues under the general rubric of research design.

Operationalization and your working hypotheses

Conceptualization in inductive logic is the process through which we move from specific observations to some generalized ideas, or abstract concepts. In deductive logic, it refers to the specification and refinement of such abstract concepts at the inception of research, and operationalization is the move-back process through which we find specific observations to represent those generalized ideas for further analysis. Empirical tests can only be done on the basis of specific observations. Therefore, the process as well as the results of seeking legislative assistance from Congress in stopping piracy. One of RIAA's chief obstacles, however, is that surveys continually show that users who download music from the Internet do not perceive it as "theft" and the widespread practice of music piracy may be nearly impossible to control.

Napster and MyMP3.com

Napster's software enabled users to search the computer drives of thousands of other users for music files. The users could select songs from vast music repertories and download copyrighted songs from one another's computers, a practice often called **peer-to-peer file sharing.** Napster's popularity was immediate, and nearly every college student and teenager was easily able to download copyrighted songs and make their own CDs.

The RIAA and various record labels sued Napster in late 1999 in the U.S. District Court in San Francisco for copyright infringement. After a series of court skirmishes, most of which resulted in rulings against Napster, Napster's site was ordered shut down and it agreed to pay certain damages to some of the plaintiffs. Napster also entered into agreements with some of the record labels in an effort to launch a secure music subscription service. Napster ultimately filed for Chapter 11 bankruptcy in mid-2002 and its assets were later auctioned. Napster was officially shut down in September 2002. In late 2003, Napster was re-established as a paid subscription service.

The RIAA and Universal Music Corp. also sued MP3 Board, Inc., which provided a service called "MyMP3.com," allowing subscribers to develop a digital music "locker" from which they could access sound recordings. In 2002, the U.S. District Court for the Southern District of New York ruled that the service was a violation of copyright law. Court cases involving Napster and MyMP3.com easily found that the services were not fair uses of copyrighted material and that the services were not entitled to the safe harbor provisions immunizing online service providers under the DMCA.

Kazaa, Morpheus, and Grokster

Although the RIAA prevailed in its cases against Napster and MyMP3.com, the offending services were immediately replaced by other music swapping services, among them, Kazaa, Morpheus, and Grokster, which gained millions of users. For example, 1 million people downloaded Kazaa's application (called FastTrack) to enable music swapping in just one week in early 2002. Shutting down these new song swapping services has proven difficult, partly because they operate from overseas and partly because these services do not route traffic through a central server. Instead, each user's computer becomes a "virtual server." Thus, there is no one central network that can be shut down. With about 200,000 sites providing free access to roughly 100 million pirated music files, at any given time more than 3 million people are running the Kazaa program to trade songs.

In mid-2002, the music industry began a multipronged effort to stop piracy and educate consumers about music piracy. After urging by the RIAA, universities developed codes of conduct for users of their computer systems and began monitoring their computer networks for unusual activity levels that might suggest the dissemination of copyrighted material. In early 2003, 300 companies were sent letters by the RIAA notifying them of the risks of allowing their employees to download copyrighted music.

In early 2003, the RIAA sued four college students who were running music-swapping services that searched computers connected to their college networks. They also shared copyrighted music from their own computers. The lawsuits were the first time that RIAA directly sued students rather than companies associated with peer-to-peer file sharing. The students agreed to pay settlements to the RIAA totaling between $12,000 and $17,000 each. At the time of writing of this text, there has been some backlash against RIAA, and some experts have commented that the RIAA is merely antagonizing its own customers.

Copyright Rights Management Approaches

Because many users of copyrighted music do not perceive their activities as stealing and because it is difficult to persuade consumers who currently obtain music for free to sign up for fee-based music subscription services, the industry has developed a variety of technological devices (often called "copyright rights management" or "digital rights management") to thwart piracy, including the following:

- **Digital watermarks.** Digital watermarks contain copy-protection devices that prohibit copying. Similarly, Microsoft recently developed an edge-to-edge hologram covering the entire side of a CD, which verifies the legitimacy of the CD and alerts users to counterfeit copies.
- **No copy technology.** CDs have been released that contain encryption technology that precludes copying and that cannot be played in a computer. After release of the CDs, furious consumers figured out they could defeat the technology with a felt tip marker.
- **Dummy files. "Spoof"** or false files have been posted to the music trading sites. When users download songs, they obtain a spoof, containing either repetitive loops of lyrics or silence. Users have begun outsmarting the spoofed files by using rating systems that push entries for the spoofs to the bottom of search lists.
- **Scoldings.** In mid-2003, the music industry began sending instant copy-right infringement messages that pop up on the screens of consumers who are downloading unauthorized copies of songs. Similarly, consumers who attempted to download music from Madonna's 2003 release "American Life" were greeted with a recording of her voice asking, "What the ___ do you think you're doing?"
- **Digital music services.** Recording and other companies have introduced subscription services allowing consumers to access music files for monthly or per song fees. In fact, Napster was relaunched in late 2003 as a fee-based subscription service. Numerous other subscription services also exist, but many subscribers have complained that the music libaries are not sufficiently extensive.

Legislative and Prosecutorial Efforts to Stop Piracy

Some of the persistent problems with countermeasures designed to stop piracy include the fact that as soon as the music industry introduces a form of protection technology, consumers figure a way to outwit it. Subscription services have been slow to catch on because many users are reluctant to pay fees for what they presently download for free. As a result, the industry has turned to Congress for help. Bills introduced in Congress have ranged from those requiring manufacturers of computers and other electronic devices to incorporate technology that would prevent illegal copying to those that would disrupt or even attack a user's computer drive if a copyright holder has a reasonable basis to believe piracy is occurring on that computer.

The Department of Justice and the Customs Service has launched "Operation Buccaneer" to locate and prosecute copyright pirates. It has resulted in the convictions of more than sixteen defendants, some of whom have been sentenced up to forty-six months in federal prison. The operation has been particularly successful in prosecuting members of the notorious software piracy group DrinkorDie, responsible for copying and distributing more than $50 million of pirated software, music, games, and movies. Information about Operation Buccaneer can be found at http://www.cybercrime.gov. Other prosecutions have been effected under the NET Act.

The *Grokster* Case

In a case shocking to the RIAA, a court ruled in 2003 that the Internet swapping services Morpheus and Grokster were not engaged in contributory or vicarious copyright infringement. The court likened the music-sharing services to the landmark *Sony Betamax* case, in which the U.S. Supreme Court ruled that makers of videocassette recorders were not liable for what consumers did with the products, primarily because the products can be used for legal purposes. Similarly, the court held in *Metro-Goldwyn-Mayer Studios, Inc. v. Grokster, Ltd.*, CV01-08541-SVW (C.D. Cal. Apr. 25, 2003) that the Grokster and Morpheus software could be used for legitimate purposes, and thus absent evidence of active and substantial contributions to infringing activities, the defendants could not be liable for copyright infringement. Moreover, unlike Napster, which provided a network and could monitor and control its users, Grokster and Morpheus merely distributed free software to users over whom they had no control. Grokster and Morpheus did not provide a site or facilities for direct infringement as did Napster but rather provided software connected to a peer-to-peer network (FastTrack in the case of Grokster and Gnutella in the case of Morpheus). The court acknowledged that it was likely that users of the software were engaging in infringing activities but specifically invited Congress to take the lead in addressing copyright infringement issues raised by these new technologies.

The ruling is an upset of the previous victories record labels achieved against MyMP3.com, Napster, and Aimster. The music industry has appealed. If businesses that facilitate music sharing have no liability, the industry may be forced to sue individual infringing users, which is not only a costly and nearly prohibitively difficult effort but also a strategy that risks offending the very customers it relies upon for sales. Most experts believe the *Grokster* case will be appealed to the U.S. Supreme Court, a process that could take years.

Movies

Just as music can be downloaded or pirated, so can movies. Cable modems and digital subscriber lines allow fast and easy downloading of movies. Before the popular movie *Harry Potter and the Sorcerer's Stone* was officially released in China, it was already being peddled on the streets of Beijing. While bootleg videocassettes cause an estimated $2.5 billion annual loss, the movie industry's primary worry is a Kazaa-like scenario of digital copying in which high-quality movies are downloaded and swapped at will. For example, while downloading of movies was previously a time-consuming and frustrating process, the downloading of even a long movie such as *Pearl Harbor* can now be accomplished in less than twenty minutes. Thus, the Motion Picture Association of America is working to develop antipiracy technologies and encryption devices. Another technique uses software called Ranger that scours the Internet looking for illegally copied movies. Additionally, Hollywood is looking to Congress for legislation requiring encryption technology to block illegal copying and transmission of movies.

Conclusion

At the time of writing of this text, no one is sure how to prevent piracy of music and movies. The situation is further complicated by the *Napster* and *MyMP3.com* cases, which held that the defendants were engaged in copyright infringement, and the new *Grokster* case, which held that the providers of peer-to-peer file-sharing software are not engaged in infringing activities. It is likely that Congress will be called upon to settle the difficult issues posed by these emerging and evolving technologies.

RECENT DEVELOPMENTS IN COPYRIGHT LAW

As is apparent from the foregoing discussion, copyright law continues to evolve with technology. Some of the more recent and interesting developments are as follows:

- While acknowledging that clothing is a useful article and thus not subject to copyright protection, a New York federal court ruled that lace designs, copyrighted as writings and incorporated into wedding dresses, were protectable and enjoined another maker of wedding dresses from making or marketing copies. Similarly, detailed embroidery or some other two-dimensional drawing or graphic work affixed to a portion of a garment may be copyrightable.

- A federal court in California recently held that while type fonts themselves are not protectable under copyright law, a software program that generated and created the typefaces was protectable.

- As soon as Stephen King sold his book *Riding the Bullet* exclusively in an Internet format, an individual cracked the copyright protection software and posted free copies of the book on the Internet. The publishers responded by adopting stronger encryption technology. Similarly, in 2000, Mr. King suspended online publication of a serial novel because too many individuals were downloading the work without paying for it.

- As discussed in Chapter 14, in late 1997 President Clinton signed into law the No Electronic Theft (NET) Act (amending 18 U.S.C. § 2319) to enhance criminal penalties for copyright infringement, even if the infringer does not profit from the transaction. The act also extends the statute of limitations for criminal copyright infringement from three to five years, and allows law enforcement officers to use federal copyright laws against online copyright violation, thereby extending the same copyright protection to the Internet that is provided to other media.

- In September 1999, the Clinton administration relaxed government restrictions on the export of encryption products and simultaneously introduced new legislation to give law enforcement agencies greater authority to combat the use of computers by terrorists and criminals and to create a new code-cracking unit within the FBI.

- In mid-2000, President Clinton signed the Electronic Signatures in Global and National Commerce Act, making digital executions, called **e-signatures,** as legally binding as their paper counterparts.

- BMI, the music licensing society, has developed a Web robot (sometimes called a "spider") to track transmission and sales of music on the Internet so it can eliminate electronic infringement of music by requiring users to either cease infringement or enter into licensing and royalty agreements with BMI. Similarly, in 2003, a web crawler deployed by BSA and representing Microsoft and Apple found more than 22,000 infringements of their software.

- As further evidence of the seriousness of copyright piracy, in 1999, a father and son accused of conspiracy to sell more than $20 million in stolen Microsoft software were sentenced to five years and one year in prison, respectively.

- In 2000, federal prosecutors in Chicago indicted seventeen people who called themselves "Pirates with Attitude" for pirating thousands of software programs. The case was brought under the NET Act. Some of the individuals were former employees of Intel and Microsoft.

- In August 1999, the National Conference of Commissioners on Uniform State Laws passed a model law, called the Uniform Computer Information Transaction Act, to regulate electronic commerce, including shrink-wrap and click-wrap licenses. The act, the product of three years of work, is intended to provide a uniform law for software and other computer information transactions and is now being presented to the various state legislatures for consideration and adoption. The act, however, is already subject to much dispute and controversy, with its opponents saying it favors the software, Internet, and banking industries. Attorneys general from twenty-four states oppose the act as presently written, and thus, its adoption in all states is highly uncertain. In fact, at the time of writing of this text, only Maryland and Virginia have adopted UCITA.

- The Copyright Office has recommended that Congress amend section 110 of the Copyright Act to grant educators the right to transmit copyrighted works for distance learning if certain conditions

are met (the educational institution must be nonprofit, only officially enrolled students may view the material, and so forth).

- In *New York Times v. Tasini,* 533 U.S. 483 (2001), the Court held that the conversion of articles that had appeared in the *Times* in print form to electronic form was a republication of the works such as would entitle authors to additional compensation. Similarly, in a second victory for writers, in *Random House, Inc. v. Rosetta Books LLC*, 150 F. Supp. 2d 613 (S.D.N.Y. 2001), *aff'd*, 283 F.3d 490 (2d Cir. 2002), the court held that the right to print and sell works in conventional book form does not include the right to publish the work in digital or electronic formats (unless the author agrees to such).

- The Second Circuit has ruled that West is not entitled to copyright protection for certain elements in its database of judicial opinions. The court held that West's star pagination system and additions of attorney information and parallel citations to cases in the public domain were not sufficiently original to qualify for copyright protection. *Mathew Bender & Co. v. West Publishing Co.,* 158 F.3d 643 and 674 (2d Cir. 1998), *vacated and remanded on other grounds*, 240 F.3d 116 (2d Cir. 2001). As a consequence of this ruling, West and other database publishers are now looking toward Congress rather than the courts, hoping that Congress will pass some form of database protection law (see earlier discussion of "Copyright Protection for Automated Databases" in this chapter) that will result in protection for its compilations of judicial opinions.

- Copyright experts are debating whether file retrieval by "intelligent agents," akin to web robots, that monitor the Internet, search for files on behalf of users, and copy the files for later viewing and use constitutes infringement.

- Many Internet service providers are now introducing privacy policies, allowing customers to prohibit or limit distribution of information about themselves to others and prohibiting collection of information relating to children unless parental permission is granted.

While many authors and copyright owners are justifiably concerned over infringement of their works by electronic means, a number of other experts compare the situation to that faced by the music industry several years ago when it became possible to make copies of tapes and CDs. For years people have been able to borrow books and tapes from friends and libraries, and yet there remains a strong market for the sale of books and music. Thus, many experts believe that although some measures and controls are needed to reduce electronic infringement and piracy, there is no need for panic, at least not yet.

TERMS OF THE TRADE

Following is a glossary of some terms currently used in discussing availability of works in the electronic age:

- **Softlifting.** Loading unauthorized copies of software into other computers, a practice frequently encountered in small businesses that do not wish to incur the expense of buying software for each computer and by consumers who share software with friends and family.
- **Copyhoarding.** Retaining all rights in a work, especially software, and refusing to allow others to view it, reproduce it, display it, or use it in any way.

- **Shareware.** Releasing copyrighted software under the condition that if the user likes what he or she sees, the user will pay a license fee.
- **Copylefting.** Licensing all users of software to have free and unfettered access and rights for any purpose and requiring that any improvements or adaptations they make to the work be similarly treated. This concept is even more permissive than that allowed for works in the public domain, which, although not protected, may serve as the source for derivative works that can then be copyrighted and protected from unauthorized use. Copylefting ensures that any derivative works based on the original work remain as freely available as the underlying work.
- **Freeware.** Allowing others to use software for free but retaining rights to ensure the work is not reverse engineered or disassembled.
- **Downstream infringement.** Infringement by users who obtain copyrighted items from legitimate users. Thus, if a licensee allows X to make an unauthorized copy of a software program, X is a downstream infringer (and the licensee is likely liable for contributory infringement).

VESSEL HULL PROTECTION

Title V of the DMCA, referred to as the Vessel Hull Design Protection Act (17 U.S.C. § 1301 *et seq.*), provides for protection for original designs of boat vessel hulls. Vessel hull design protection draws many of its concepts from both copyright and patent law and affords a new form of intellectual property protection. It is thus said to be *sui generis* (literally, "the only one of its kind"). The new law grants an owner of an original vessel hull design certain exclusive rights provided that an application for registration of the design is made with the Copyright Office within two years of the design first being made public. Registration is made using Form D-VH and the application fee is $140. Deposit material may consist of either drawings or photographs of the design. To ensure that protection is not granted for useful articles, protection is limited to those designs that make the article attractive and distinctive in appearance.

Vessel hull design protection was prompted by a 1989 case in which the U.S. Supreme Court struck down a Florida statute that had protected the designs of boat hulls against copying. The new act affords protection for original vessel hull designs far more quickly and inexpensively than patent protection affords.

Protection of vessel hull designs is not the same as copyright protection, and the term of protection lasts ten years. When any vessel hull embodying a protected design is publicly exhibited or distributed, the hull must carry a notice of the design's protection; omission of the notice would prevent the owner from recovering against a party who infringes before receiving notice of the protection. Generally, the notice consists of the words "Protected Design" or the symbol "D" together with the name of the owner and the year in which protection commenced. In 2002, the Copyright Office registered only thirty-four vessel hull designs under the new act.

SEMICONDUCTOR CHIP PROTECTION

Introduction to the Semiconductor Chip Protection Act

Semiconductor chips (or integrated circuits) are used in a wide array of products, including watches, cardiac pacemakers, microwave ovens, televisions, automobiles, and computers. Development and engineering of the complex chips can cost millions of dollars, yet once created, chips can be easily copied. Copyright law does not provide adequate protection for the chips inasmuch as they are useful products and cannot be copyrighted (although the design drawings of chips are copyrightable). Neither does patent law provide adequate protection because the chips generally do not meet the strict standards that patentable material be nonobvious (see Chapter 17). Furthermore, issuance of a patent typically takes two years, and given the rapidity of technological advances, chips are often nearly obsolete by the time a patent might issue.

In 1984, Congress fashioned a solution to the lack of protection for semiconductor chips by enacting the Semiconductor Chip Protection Act. The act creates an entirely new form of intellectual property right in semiconductor chips, one that is different from either copyright law or patent law. As such, and like vessel hull design protection, it is said to be *sui generis*. Nevertheless, many of the concepts relating to protection, registration, and infringement of chips draw from copyright law. The act is found in title 17 of the United States Code, after the copyright statutes (17 U.S.C. § 901 *et seq.*). The Copyright Office offers Circular 100, entitled "Federal Statutory Protection for Mask Works," to provide information about semiconductor chip protection and registration of mask works. The circular can be downloaded from the Copyright Office's web site.

Protectable Matter

The act protects **mask works,** which are the stencils used to etch, pattern, or encode an electronic circuit on a semiconductor chip. A **semiconductor chip** is defined as any product "having two or more layers of metallic, insulating, or semiconductor material, deposited or otherwise placed on, or etched away or otherwise removed from, a piece of semiconductor material . . . and intended to perform electronic circuitry functions." 17 U.S.C. § 901(a)(1). Protection extends to the three-dimensional images or patterns formed on the layers of metallic or semiconductor material, i.e., the topography of the wafer-thin chip.

To be protected, the mask work must be "fixed," meaning that it must be capable of being perceived or reproduced for more than some transitory period. Additionally, the mask work must be original. It must be original or independently created and cannot consist of some commonplace variation of an already existing design.

Duration of Protection and Exclusive Rights

Eligibility for protection for a mask work commences on the date the mask work is registered with the Copyright Office or on the date on which it is first commercially exploited (generally meaning the written offer, sale, or distribution to the public) anywhere in the world, whichever occurs first. Protection lasts for ten years from the date protection begins.

The mask work owner has the following exclusive rights:

- to reproduce the mask work;
- to import or distribute a semiconductor chip product that embodies the mask work; and
- to induce or knowingly to cause another to do the foregoing acts.

The mask owner's rights are infringed by copying of the work. The House Report relating to the act explicitly recognized that the concepts used to determine infringement of copyright (such as substantial similarity and the protection of expression rather than ideas) are applicable to mask works. Thus, a mask work that is substantially similar to a protected work infringes even if it is not an identical copy.

Limitations on the Rights of Mask Work Owners

There are several notable limitations on the exclusive rights granted to mask work owners.

- Similar to copyright law, there is no protection if another mask work is independently created. The act prohibits copying, not independent creation.
- It is not an infringement to reproduce a mask work for teaching, analyzing, or evaluating the concepts or techniques embodied in the mask work. Moreover, it is not an infringement to incorporate the results of this analysis in another original mask work. Thus, mask works can be lawfully reverse engineered.
- Also similar to copyright law, protection does not extend to ideas, systems, processes, or methods of operation, but only to the expression of those ideas in the mask work.
- In another borrowing from copyright law, the first sale doctrine applies such that a person who lawfully obtains a semiconductor chip product may later use, sell, or otherwise dispose of it (as long as the work is not reproduced). Thus, after lawfully purchasing the product, the owner may thereafter also sell, import, distribute, use, or dispose of the semiconductor chip product.

Registration and Notice of Protection

Registration of a mask work is highly similar to that of registration of copyrights. An application is made with the Copyright Office (using Form MW), and identifying matter must be deposited with the application. The fee is $75. However, an application must be made within two years after the work is first commercially exploited. Protection for a mask work terminates if an application is not made with the Copyright Office within that two-year period. Thus, registration is encouraged by providing a longer period of protection for registered works (ten years) than for nonregistered works (two years).

The registration process for mask works is nearly identical to that for copyrights in that the examination by the Copyright Office is not exhaustive. If the application is correctly completed, the deposited materials are sufficient, and the fee is paid, the registration will be issued, generally within four months. Few refusals are made. In 2002, the Copyright Office issued 508 registrations for mask works.

The mask work owner may affix a notice of protection to the mask work and to masks and semiconductor chip products embodying the mask works. The notice is not a prerequisite for protection, although it constitutes *prima facie* evidence of notice of protection. The notice consists of the words "mask work," the symbol "M," or the letter "M" in a circle, and the name of the owner of the mask work. No date is needed. The notice is usually placed on a label attached to the packaging for the product.

Infringement of Mask Works

A person who violates any of the exclusive rights of a mask work owner may be sued for infringement. To bring an action in federal court for infringement, however, the owner must have registered the mask work (or been refused registration by the Copyright Office). The action must be brought within three years after the claim accrues. Actual damages and the infringer's profits may be awarded to the mask work owner. Alternatively, similar to copyright actions, the owner may elect statutory damages (up to $250,000). A court may enjoin further infringement and may impound and destroy infringing works and the drawings by which infringing chips are reproduced. Attorneys' fees and costs may be awarded.

TRIVIA

- Approximately 2 billion songs are traded online each month.
- The most downloaded album in history (as of the date of this text) is *The Eminem Show*.
- In mid-2000, the Business Software Alliance announced $2.4 million in software piracy settlements with twenty companies.
- The Business Software Alliance estimates that at least one of every four software applications installed on computers around the world is pirated.

CHAPTER SUMMARY

Computer programs and automated databases are copyrightable and may be registered with the Copyright Office as literary works. As original works of expression, computer programs are protectable against infringement. Nevertheless, a number of cases have held that purely functional elements of programs, stock or standard scenes a faire, and merged ideas and expressions cannot be protected. To hold otherwise would grant developers of computer programs a monopoly and would discourage creative expression. Computer programs may be reverse engineered in certain instances, for example, when it is necessary to gain access to unprotected elements of a program.

The ease with which works may be copied, stored, reproduced, and disseminated by electronic means, primarily the Internet, has caused much debate among authors and owners of works who are concerned about infringement of their works and those who believe that information "needs to be free." Some experts believe that technology itself can solve the challenges of the electronic age: devices can be constructed that would encrypt or protect works and prevent them from being copied or transmitted unless permission or royalties are first obtained. In the interim, the Copyright Act is sufficiently muscular to protect works from infringement by electronic means. Thus, copying and transmitting works over the Internet is subject to risk.

The Digital Millennium Copyright Act of 1998 updated U.S. copyright law for the digital age by prohibiting circumvention of copyright protection systems and protecting online service providers from liability for copyright infringements on their services.

The music and movie industries remain concerned about piracy of songs and movies and continue to educate consumers about copyright piracy, prosecute infringers, and push for legislation to protect music and movies from rampant downloading over the Internet. Moreover, the original designs of boat vessel hulls are protectable against infringement under the DMCA.

Because neither patent law nor copyright law afforded sufficient protection for complex and expensively developed semiconductor chips, Congress enacted the Semiconductor Chip Protection Act of 1984. The act creates an entirely new form of intellectual property protection for mask works, the stencils used to pattern or encode semiconductor chips. Mask works may be registered with the Copyright Office and are protected against infringement.

CASE ILLUSTRATION—THE SAFE HARBOR OF THE DMCA

Case: *Hendrickson v. eBay, Inc.*, 165 F. Supp. 2d 1082 (C.D. Cal. 2001)

Facts: Plaintiff claimed that eBay was liable for copyright infringement because it facilitated the sale of pirated copies of plaintiff's documentary movie called *Manson* through its Internet auction site. Although plaintiff broadly notified eBay of the infringing activity, it did not provide detailed information to eBay about the alleged pirated copies.

Holding: eBay is shielded from liability for copyright infringement under the DMCA. The DMCA is designed to facilitate the robust development and worldwide expansion of electronic commerce and communication. Plaintiff failed to give eBay adequate information to enable eBay to determine which alleged copies infringed plaintiff's rights. Unlike traditional auction houses, eBay is not actively involved in the listing, bidding, sale, and delivery of auctioned items. eBay has established it meets the "safe harbor" test provided for online service providers under the DMCA.

operationalization have significant impact on theory development through deductive logic.

It should be noted that many students find it hard to understand and deal with "operationalization." This should not be the case. Operationalization is nothing more than a metaphor. The development of specific research procedures (operations) is a logical process comprising all the things you are supposed to do leading to empirical testing of a theory: narrowing your research topic, specifying your questions and figuring out your hypotheses, defining your concepts and identifying your variables, and selecting or creating some specific measurement items. These measurement items may themselves be called variables, but their purpose is to yield empirical observations representing the original and more abstract variables. For example, the concept of family includes a variable for one of its important functions, that is, family support. Family support can be specified in light of financial support, material aid, care and services, information and guidance, emotional support, etc. These are obviously more specific variables. Yet each will be further operationalized into observable items (also called variables) when taking the measurement. Financial support can be recorded in terms of the amount of money provided in a certain period; material aid can be supplied in the form of food, clothes, housing, a computer, or a bike; services may be provided to satisfy the need of care for the sick, homemaking, or car transportation; information and guidance may include employment assistance, retirement advice, or help with financial arrangements; emotional support may take the form of listening, assuring, or encouraging. In sum, operationalization may refer to all the steps and activities of specification leading to the concrete "operations" or observations that form direct or indirect measurement of the original and abstract variable. In the latter case, further technical treatment will be needed. This may include the application of various scaling methods to construct appropriate composite or multi-item measures.

To grasp the essence of conceptualization and operationalization, you need to think about the following questions: What are the original observations that lead to a definition? What other (potential) observations should also be covered by the definition? And what observations should be selected to represent the entire group (the population) of the observations?

The operationalization of a concept accounting for a simple variable, such as calendar age, may directly translate into a single indicator, such as a respondent's self-report of her birth date. Many variables that you encounter in behavioral and social science research, however, are not so simple as calendar age.

CASE STUDY AND ACTIVITIES

Case Study.   Watson has recently discovered that unauthorized copies of its animated feature film *Adventures at the Palace* are being offered on eBay. One of Watson's competitors made available DeCSS software on its web site and invited users to descramble the encrypted copies of the DVD. The resulting descrambled versions were then offered for sale on eBay's online auction site. Additionally, one of the songs from the film, "Princess Penny's Lullaby," is routinely downloaded over the Internet through peer-to-peer file sharing. Watson has recently developed a computer game called "Saving Princess Penny," which involves various characters who try to save Princess Penny from various villains. The game is "sold" in plastic shrink-wrap, and inside the box is a sheet outlining various terms and conditions that clearly state that the game cannot be modified and that it is not sold to the purchaser but rather licensed for limited uses. One of Watson's competitors has created a device that enhances the speed at which the villains move, making it more challenging for game players to rescue Princess Penny. To create the device, the competitor first reverse engineered the video game to determine how to make its device operate with the video game.

Activities.   Discuss the copyrightability of the works discussed herein as well as any infringement of those works.

ROLE OF PARALEGAL

Because copyright issues confronting users, authors, legislators, and judges are continuing to evolve, the primary task of IP paralegals may be simply to monitor the issues by continuing research. Specifically, practitioners may be involved in the following tasks:

- preparing and monitoring copyright applications for computer programs and automated databases;
- tracking legislation relating to copyright using LEXIS or WESTLAW or the free and accessible Internet sites THOMAS (http://thomas.loc.gov), Government Printing Office Access offering access to public laws and various congressional documents at http://www.access.gpo.gov, or the Senate and House home pages at http://www.senate.gov and http://www.house.gov;
- monitoring articles, bulletin boards, and other postings on the Internet for information relating to copyrights in the electronic age;
- reviewing legal periodicals and journals for articles relating to emerging copyright issues;
- assisting in preparing newsletters and bulletins for clients to inform them of developments in the field;
- assisting clients in developing copyright compliance policies to ensure their employees do not infringe copyrights of others;
- reviewing clients' web sites and other electronic materials to ensure copyright notices are displayed at those sites;

- reviewing web sites of competitors of clients to ascertain whether clients' copyrighted materials are being infringed or whether links to clients' sites are being improperly used;
- preparing and monitoring applications for registration of mask works and vessel hull designs; and
- ensuring that clients' mask works (or the containers therefor) contain the proper mask work notice.

INTERNET RESOURCES

Federal laws relating to copyright: http://www.ll.georgetown.edu or http://www.findlaw.com

Copyright Office: http://www.loc.gov/copyright or http://www.copyright.gov (for forms, circulars on mask works, information on the DMCA and vessel hull protection)

National Conference of Commissioners on Uniform State Laws: http://www.nccusl.org (for text of UCITA)

Business Software Alliance: http://www.bsa.org (information on antipiracy and technology policy)

Software Information & Industry Association: http://www.siia.net (information on protecting and promoting software and digital content)

Recording Industry Association of America: http://www.riaa.org (information on active music issues)

Electronic Frontier Foundation: http://www.eff.org (information on cutting-edge technology issues and links to cases)

Chilling Effects Clearinghouse: http://www.chillingeffects.org (joint project of EFF and various law schools regarding intellectual property and First Amendment issues)

Digital Future Coalition: http://www.dfc.org (information on active issues relating to digital and electronic copyright rights)

DISCUSSION QUESTIONS

1. Davidson Technology, Inc. has developed a highly valuable and proprietary software application. It wishes to acquire as much copyright protection as possible but does not wish to deposit any of its source code or object code with the Copyright Office. Can Davidson obtain a copyright registration for the program? If so, what sort of copyright notice should be used by Davidson?

2. Davidson granted permission to another company to produce an updated version of its computer application discussed in the above question. Is the updated version of the application copyrightable? Discuss.

3. May a competitor of Davidson reverse engineer the application to review the unprotected elements of the program? Discuss.

4. Davidson will offer the application for "sale" over the Internet. May Davidson place terms and conditions relating to use of the program (such as forbidding users to sell copies of it) on the Internet and thereby bind users to these terms? Discuss.

5. May a company purchase one copy of the computer program Microsoft Word from Microsoft Corp., copy the program, and then give copies of the program to its employees for their home use? Discuss.

6. May an individual sell devices that can crack encryption codes used to protect CDs from being copied? Discuss.

7. How would a company achieve the widest scope of protection for an integrated circuit used in the production of its high-tech toasters?

CHAPTER 16

International Copyright Law

CHAPTER OVERVIEW

There is no international copyright law that protects copyrighted works in every country. More than 145 nations, however, adhere to the Berne Convention, the terms of which require members to treat nationals of other member countries like their own nationals for purposes of copyright. By joining the Berne Convention in 1989, the United States was required to make some changes to its copyright laws, notably, eliminating the requirement that works be accompanied by a copyright notice in order to receive protection and allowing owners of works not originating in the United States to sue in federal court for copyright infringement even if they did not possess a copyright registration. New treaties supplementing the Berne Convention ensure that copyrighted works are protected from infringement by any means, including electronic means, and prohibit attempts to defeat encryption or protection of copyrighted works. The United States is also a party to the Universal Copyright Convention and the Uruguay Round Agreements Act. Finally, in 2002, two international treaties adopted by the World Intellectual Property Organization, and often called the "Internet treaties," entered into force to protect copyrighted works in the digital environment. The United States is a party to both of these new treaties, which are viewed as the most important updates to international copyright protection in a generation.

INTRODUCTION

Nearly 1 million books and other literary titles, 5,000 feature films, and 3 million songs are published worldwide each year. Yet there is no such thing as "international copyright" that will protect an author's work throughout the world. Protection generally is afforded on a country-by-country basis. However, most countries offer protection to foreign works under international conventions and treaties. There are two principal international copyright treaties or conventions: the Berne Convention for the Protection of Literary and Artistic Property (Berne Convention) and the Universal Copyright Convention (UCC). These treaties impose certain minimum requirements that each signatory or contracting nation must agree to implement. After instituting these minimum obligations, countries are free to enact other statutes and provide additional protection. Thus, protection for copyright around the world is far from uniform.

Authors who desire protection for their works in foreign countries should first determine the scope of protection available to works of foreign authors in that country. Determination should be done prior to publication of the work in any country inasmuch as the extent of protection afforded to a work may depend on facts existing at the time of first publication anywhere. The laws of most countries provide that copyright protection exists independently of any formalities and that it is not necessary to register a copyright to achieve protection for a work.

If the country in which protection is sought is a party to one of the international copyright conventions, the work generally may be protected by complying with the conditions of that convention. Even if the work cannot be protected under an international convention, protection may still be available under the specific laws of a foreign country. Some countries, however, offer little or no copyright protection to foreign works.

THE BERNE CONVENTION

The Berne Convention was created in 1886 under the leadership of Victor Hugo to protect literary and artistic works and has more than 145 member nations (see Appendix A for a table of nations adhering to the Berne Convention).

In 1989, the United States became a party to the Berne Convention by entering into an international treaty called the Berne Convention for the Protection of Literary and Artistic Works. The Berne Convention is administered by the World Intellectual Property Organization (WIPO), an organization whose objective is to promote the protection of intellectual property throughout the world. The Berne Convention is based on the precept that each member nation must treat nationals of other member countries like its own nationals for purposes of copyright (the principle of **national treatment**).

Moreover, the Berne Convention has established certain minimum levels of copyright protection to which all member nations must adhere (such as specifying that all members must recognize that authors have the exclusive rights to perform, broadcast, adapt, and reproduce their works), ensuring that copyright laws in the member nations will share many features. The Berne Convention also provides that copyright protection cannot be conditioned upon compliance with any registration formalities, thus clarifying that works are automatically protected without requiring notice of copyright or registration. Finally, the Berne Convention provides that works are protected independently of the existence of protection in the country of origin of the work. If a work originates in one of the more than 145 member nations of the Berne Union, it is entitled to protection in all other member nations. A work's "country of origin" is usually the place of its first publication. Generally, works are protected under the Berne Convention for a minimum of fifty years after the author's death, though member nations may provide for a longer term, as has the United States.

In order to fulfill its obligations under the Berne Convention, the United States made certain changes in its copyright laws, effective after March 1, 1989, the date the United States acceded to the Berne Convention. Perhaps the most significant change to U.S. copyright law was that the mandatory notice of copyright (for example, © 1988 John Doe) that was previously required in the United States was abolished so that failure to place a notice on copyrighted works would no longer result in the loss of copyright. Thus, for all works published after March 1, 1989, use of a copyright notice is voluntary (although it is strongly recommended, since use of a notice will preclude a party from asserting its infringement was innocent, which claim might reduce damages in an infringement action).

The Berne Convention also recognizes "moral rights" (the rights of authors to claim authorship of their works and to object to any mutilation or modification of the work that would be prejudicial to the author's reputation or honor). In 1989, in order to become a party to the Berne Convention, the United States for the first time recognized moral rights; however, the scope of moral rights afforded in the United States is less extensive than in many other countries inasmuch as the Visual Artists Rights Act (17 U.S.C. § 106A) provides moral rights only to works of fine arts.

As discussed in Chapter 14, before a copyright infringement suit is brought for a work of U.S. origin, the work must be submitted to the Copyright Office for registration. Works originating in Berne Union countries are exempt from the requirement to register before bringing suit. Authors whose works originate in the United States, however, are still subject to the requirement of registering their work (or showing they attempted to register but registration was refused).

TREATIES SUPPLEMENTING THE BERNE CONVENTION: THE WIPO TREATIES

In December 1996, WIPO convened in Geneva, Switzerland, to work on the first amendment to international copyright laws in twenty-five years, action that was primarily spurred by concern over piracy of copyrighted works through the Internet. Authors, of course, are concerned that the value of their works will be diminished by unauthorized reproduction and transmission, and Internet service providers are concerned they may face liability for contributory or vicarious infringement based on the fact that their services are used to carry out infringing activities.

Two treaties, the WIPO Copyright Treaty and the WIPO Performances and Phonograms Treaty, were adopted at the Geneva conference and were then considered for ratification by individual countries. In order to fulfill obligations under the WIPO treaties, most countries, including the United States, were required to amend their copyright laws in several respects, chief among them to protect against the unlawful circumvention of technologies used by copyright owners to prevent electronic theft of their works. The passage of the Digital Millennium Copyright Act in the United States in 1998 (see Chapter 15) accomplished this goal, and the WIPO treaties came into force in early 2002 when they were each ratified by thirty countries.

The WIPO Copyright Treaty expressly states that computer programs are protected by copyright as literary works and makes it clear that authors' rights of distribution extend to electronic distribution by granting authors the exclusive right to distribute, sell, or rent their works via electronic means. The Copyright Treaty also requires adhering nations to provide remedies against any person who removes or alters electronic rights management information (information about copyright works, authors, and owners that is appended or attached to works in electronic form) and to provide adequate legal protection against the circumvention of security or encryption devices used by authors to protect their works. The act prohibits both the use of circumvention methods and the manufacturing or offering of circumvention devices. Circumvention is permissible for computer security testing, encryption research, certain library uses, and for law enforcement activities. The WIPO Performance Treaty provides similar rights, granting protection to sound recordings first fixed in a treaty member country.

Neither treaty addresses liability of Internet service providers for copyright infringement using the Internet, although legislation passed in late 1998 in the United States (17 U.S.C. § 512(c)) as part of the Digital Millennium Copyright Act clarifies that Internet service providers are not liable for infringement if they do not know of such acts and if they do not profit from them. Upon receiving notification of claimed infringement, the service providers must expeditiously take down or remove access to the material. Finally, although much discussion occurred relating to whether databases resulting from a substantial investment of time and effort should be protected, the parties could not reach agreement; however, they did agree that databases consisting of original work could be protected. Recall that the United States expressly rejected the "sweat of the brow" doctrine in *Feist Publications v. Rural Telephone Service Co.,* 499 U.S. 340 (1991), holding that a telephone directory consisting merely of facts could not be copyrighted even if it was the result of much effort. The conference adopted a recommendation calling for another session to further discuss database protection inasmuch as many experts fear that extending database protection rights to compilations resulting from effort and time would result in sports statistics, weather information, stock market information, and transportation schedules all being monopolized by the first to compile the data. As discussed in Chapter 15, Congress has considered extending copyright protection to databases produced through investment of substantial time and money (although databases generated with govern-

ment funding would likely remain available for all to use, and the fair use of information in databases would be protected). If passed, such legislation would create an entirely new form of copyright protection for databases and would nullify *Feist* to some extent because it would protect collections of information or data that might not otherwise be copyrightable. To date, any proposed legislation relating to databases has been subject to much debate and an uncertain future.

THE URUGUAY ROUND AGREEMENTS ACT

In December 1994, President Clinton signed the **Uruguay Round Agreements Act** (URAA) that implements the Uruguay Round General Agreement on Tariffs and Trade (GATT), which itself includes an agreement on Trade-Related Aspects of Intellectual Property (TRIPs). TRIPs requires all members of the WTO to provide certain minimum standards of protection for trademarks, copyrights, patents, and trade secrets and requires countries to provide effective enforcement of these rights.

The URAA amended federal copyright law in several ways, including the addition of civil and criminal penalties to provide remedies for "bootlegging" sound recordings of live musical performances and music videos. Prior to this amendment, U.S. copyright law generally protected only the fixed work (such as the song being performed) rather than the live performance itself. The new provisions prohibit unauthorized recording or broadcasts of live performances and reproduction or distribution of unauthorized fixations of the work.

Equally important, the URAA also provided for the automatic restoration of copyright in certain foreign works (but not U.S. domestic works) that had fallen into the public domain in the United States but were protected by copyright in their countries of origin. Typically, works from eligible countries had fallen into the public domain because their authors failed to comply with formalities required by the United States, such as including a notice of copyright on the work or renewing the work (during the time when the United States required copyright notice and had a renewal period for copyrighted works).

Eligible copyrights are restored automatically and remain protectable for the term they would have enjoyed had they not entered the public domain. However, the URAA directs that the owner of a restored work notify "reliance parties" (parties who, relying on the public domain status of the work, were using the work prior to its automatic restoration under the URAA) if the owner of rights in a restored work intends to enforce his or her rights. Either actual notice may be given to a reliance party, or constructive notice may be given through filing a "Notice of Intent to Enforce" with the Copyright Office. The reliance party then has a grace period of twelve months to sell off its existing stock, publicly perform the work, or phase out its reproduction, distribution, performance, or display of the work.

The **World Trade Organization (WTO)** was established in 1995 to implement the Uruguay Round Agreements, serve as a forum for trade negotiations, handle trade disputes, and monitor national trade policies. It has more than 140 members. (See Appendix A.) The United States has been a member of the WTO since 1995. The WIPO and the WTO cooperate to provide assistance to developing countries with respect to intellectual property rights and laws.

As discussed in Chapter 8, GATT (the organization) was replaced by the WTO, which oversees various trade agreements.

THE UNIVERSAL COPYRIGHT CONVENTION

The United States became a party to the **Universal Copyright Convention** (UCC) in 1955, more than thirty years before the United States became a party to the Berne Convention; thus, the UCC was the first international convention relating to copyright to which the United States was subject. Similar to the Berne Convention, the UCC is based on the principle of national treatment, requiring that works originating in a member nation must be given the same protection in each of the other member nations as is granted by the laws of the country of origin. The UCC imposes fewer minimum standards on its members than does the Berne Convention. The UCC provides that use of a copyright notice in a prescribed form (the © symbol, accompanied by the year of first publication and the name of the copyright owner) will satisfy notice requirements in all other member nations. Because the Berne Convention imposes requirements that are stricter than those of the UCC, to ensure members would not drop out of the Berne Convention and rely strictly on the UCC, the UCC provides that no Berne member may withdraw from Berne and later rely on the UCC in its relations with other Berne members. Additionally, the Berne Convention takes precedence over the UCC inasmuch as the terms of the Berne Convention, rather than those of the UCC, apply to relationships among Berne members, even though those parties may also be members of the UCC. Some Berne member countries joined the UCC to establish relations with nations that are not members of Berne (such as British Virgin Islands, Gibraltar, and Saint Helena).

TRADE ASPECTS OF INTELLECTUAL PROPERTY LAW

There is a strong correlation between trade policies and intellectual property protection. The International Intellectual Property Alliance has concluded that countries with the poorest records of protecting intellectual property have slower rates of information technology growth.

Similarly, Jack Valenti, the president of the Motion Picture Association of America, has stated that "copyright industries are the jewels in America's trade crown." Thus, the United States favors strong international protection of intellectual property because theft of such intellectual property has a damaging effect on the U.S. economy.

The "Special 301" provisions of the Trade Act of 1974 require that the United States Trade Representative (USTR) identify "priority" foreign countries that deny adequate and effective protection of intellectual property rights. Once countries are identified in the USTR's annual Special 301 review, the USTR can initiate an investigation. If the foreign country is determined to deny adequate protection to intellectual property, the USTR can impose trade sanctions. For example, in 2003, the USTR's Special 301 report stated the following:

> USTR notes with disappointment Ukraine's persistent failure to take effective action against significant levels of optical media piracy and to implement intellectual property laws that provide adequate and effective protection. As a result, Ukraine will continue to be designated a Priority Foreign Country and the $75 million worth of sanctions imposed on Ukrainian products . . . will remain in place. This continued failure to adequately protect intellectual property rights could also jeopardize Ukraine's efforts to join the World Trade Organization (WTO) and seriously undermine its efforts to attract trade and investment.

The full text of USTR reports is available at http://www.ustr.gov.

GRAY MARKET GOODS

Section 602(a) of the Copyright Act bars importation of copyrighted goods into the United States without the authority of the copyright owner (the goods are referred to as "gray market" goods because they are lawfully made as opposed to pirated "black market" goods). In 1998, the Supreme Court held that a copyright holder loses control over subsequent sales of material produced in the United States once a first sale has occurred anywhere. In *Quality King Distributors, Inc. v. L'anza Research International*, 523 U.S. 135 (1998), hair care products affixed with copyrighted labels were manufactured in the United States and then exported for exclusive sale outside the United States. The products were then imported back into the United States without the copyright owner's permission. The copyright owner alleged that such importation violated its exclusive right to distribute the products. The defendant contended that once a first sale of the product occurred abroad, the copyright owner's exclusive right to distribute was exhausted. The Supreme Court agreed that once the first sale occurred, even abroad, the owner of the work or product could resell the item anywhere without permission of the copyright holder.

Copyright holders are concerned over this ruling, and some experts believe they will attempt to use provisions in their contracts barring importation of goods into the United States, move their manufacturing or production abroad, or lobby Congress for a change in the law to ensure their domestic revenues are not undercut by identical goods intended for export only.

SUMMARY OF UNITED STATES RELATIONS WITH FOREIGN NATIONS

The United States is a party to various copyright conventions, agreements, and treaties with other nations. Following is a summary of some of the agreements and treaties to which the United States is a party:

- **Berne Convention.** The United States is a party to the Berne Convention as of March 1989. The Berne Convention provides protection to literary and artistic works, including computer programs.
- **Universal Copyright Convention.** The United States has been a party to the Universal Copyright Convention since September 16, 1955.
- **WIPO Internet Treaties.** The United States implemented the WIPO Copyright Treaty and WIPO Performances and Phonograms Treaty in late 1998, and the treaties entered into force in 2002.
- **World Trade Organization.** The United States has been a member of the World Trade Organization, established to implement the Uruguay Round Agreements, since 1995.

TRIVIA

- It is estimated that 40 percent of all software programs worldwide are pirated.
- Computer and software piracy in the Middle East costs Microsoft at least $100 million each year and $12 billion worldwide.
- In 2001, a French court ordered Yahoo to block French web users from selling Nazi memorabilia.
- Software companies lost more than $4 billion in 2000 due to piracy in the Asia-Pacific region.
- Eastern Europe has had the highest rate of piracy each year, with more than 60 percent of its software being illegal.

CHAPTER SUMMARY

There is no one treaty or agreement governing copyright throughout the world. More than 145 nations, however, belong to the Berne Convention, which is based on the principle of national treatment: each member nation must treat works originating in other member nations as it does its own domestic works. Recent supplements to the Berne Convention clarify that computer programs are protectable literary works, that unauthorized reproduction or distribution of a work by electronic means is infringement, and that devices that defeat copyright security measures such as encryption are prohibited. The international copyright community is struggling with the issues presented by the ease and rapidity of electronic communications, just as is the United States.

To comply with its commitments under the Berne Convention, the United States was required to modify its copyright law, primarily to eliminate any requirement for a copyright notice for a work to be protectable and to allow owners of works not originating in the United States to sue in federal court for copyright infringement even if they did not possess a U.S. registration for their work.

Psychological age and social age, for instance, are each likely to require more than one indicator to measure. Other examples include social adjustment, social attitude, and psychological well-being. The end product of the operationalization of such complex variables would be the specification of a set of indicators of what we have in mind. In such a case, an indicator will mark the presence or absence, or the degree of some phenomenon, in certain aspects of the concept or construct under study.

Even in a relatively simple case, like the variable age, there could be thorny definitional issues setting up hurdles for your research. First, different theories will offer different definitions, and they oftentimes compete with one another. These theoretical definitions would all appear to be the true and accurate representation of the essential nature or some essential attributes of the reality (real entity) under study. The disagreement will make your choice a difficult task. Sometimes theories in a field are underdeveloped, and you may have to create a theoretical definition which you consider would be the most faithful and essential description of the concept. Second, although every definition would seem to have some merit, you may not be able to incorporate all of the meaningful elements. Usually, you choose and specify a working definition for the particular purpose of your research. Such a working definition is sometimes called a "nominal" definition. It may not be very comprehensive from some point of view but may be most definite and pertinent to your research objective. A hypothesis with theoretical definitions of the concepts can be called a theoretical hypothesis. Likewise, a hypothesis based on the working definitions can be called a working hypothesis.

Obtaining working definitions and working hypotheses is your first step in operationalization. You need to further decide what constitutes the particular measure of a variable in your research project. In other words, you need to specify what are the specific operations you will undertake to represent the concept and gauge it as a variable. These designated operations together form a so-called "operational definition" of the concept. Based on such a definition, concrete observations will be generated to yield the needed empirical data.

Operationalization is the process of specification starting from all available theoretical definitions and leading to a specific measure of a concept functioning as a variable in research. The term "operationalization" or "operational definition," however, is merely a metaphor created to aid your understanding. You do not really have to spell out what exactly operationalization is, but you must understand how to narrow down, to be specific, and to make your variables

The United States is also a party to the Universal Copyright Convention and the Uruguay Round Agreements Act that required the United States to amend its copyright law to allow restoration of copyright for works that had fallen into the public domain due to lack of copyright notice or failure to renew the work during the time the United States required renewal.

Finally, the United States is a party to the WIPO Internet treaties, designed to fight Internet piracy by prohibiting devices and services that circumvent technological protection measures for copyrighted works. Both treaties entered into force in 2002. To comply with its obligations under the WIPO treaties, the United States amended its copyright law in 1988 by enacting the Digital Millennium Copyright Act, which imposes penalties for circumvention of copyright projection devices (see Chapter 15).

CASE ILLUSTRATION—TERRITORIAL LIMITS OF COPYRIGHT ACT

Case: *Subafilms, Ltd. v. MGM-Pathe Communications*, 24 F.3d 1088 (9th Cir. 1994)

Facts: The musical group the Beatles, through Subafilms, entered into an agreement with another to produce their animated motion picture *Yellow Submarine.* Eventually, the defendant, the owner of the rights to distribute the film, authorized distribution of the film in foreign countries, in violation of earlier agreements.

Holding: The defendant cannot be liable under U.S. law for authorizing conduct overseas even though the same conduct would have been infringing had it occurred in the United States. U.S. copyright laws do not reach acts of infringement that take place entirely abroad. U.S. copyright laws do not apply extraterritorially, and the bundle of rights owned by copyright owners extend no farther than U.S. borders. To hold otherwise would be contrary to the intent of Congress, contrary to the spirit of the Berne Convention, and might offend other member nations by effectively displacing their laws.

CASE STUDY AND ACTIVITIES

Case Study.   Watson would like to sell many of its previously published books and songs in foreign countries, namely countries that adhere to the Berne Convention and the new WIPO treaties. Watson is concerned, however, because many of its more recent works do not contain a copyright notice. Watson is also concerned that many of its songs, which have been produced with encryption technology in order to prevent piracy, will be downloaded over the Internet in these countries. Finally, Watson is concerned that the length of copyright protection in these foreign countries will be significantly shorter than the length of protection in the United States.

Activities.   Discuss the protection that Watson may be able to secure in these countries for its books and songs.

ROLE OF PARALEGAL

Unless a client sells or distributes its products or works abroad, involvement by IP paralegals with international copyright issues will be minimal. Nevertheless, inasmuch as works can now be sold or distributed in foreign countries merely by the touch of a computer key, some familiarity with international copyright protection is needed. Intellectual property professionals will likely be involved in the following tasks:

- monitoring issues related to international copyright by reading journals, articles, and other materials;
- gathering information and publications from the U.S. Copyright Office related to international copyright protection, such as Circular 38a entitled "International Copyright Relations of the United States" and Circular 38b entitled "Highlights of Copyright Amendments Contained in the Uruguay Round Agreements Act";
- retrieving the text of treaties to which the United States is a party either by locating them in conventional print form at law libraries or locating them on the Internet (the Berne Convention and the WIPO Internet treaties can be located through WIPO at http://www.wipo.org, and the Universal Copyright Convention can be located through the United Nations site at http://www.un.org or http://www.unesco.org); and
- routinely monitoring various web sites (see the resources at the end of this chapter and in Appendix C) related to intellectual property to keep abreast of new developments in the international arena.

INTERNET RESOURCES

Federal laws relating to copyright:	http://www.ll.georgetown.edu or http://www.findlaw.com
Copyright Office:	http://www.loc.gov/copyright or http://www.copyright.gov (for Circulars 38a and 38b, relating to international copyright relations)
United States Trade Representative:	http://www.ustr.gov (annual reports and information on efforts by foreign countries to protect intellectual property rights; identification of foreign priority watch countries)
World Intellectual Property Organization:	http://www.wipo.org (information on international copyright law and the text of the Berne Convention and the new WIPO Internet treaties)

INTERNET RESOURCES (cont'd)

UNESCO:	http://www.unesco.org (text of Universal Copyright Convention)
World Trade Organization:	http://www.wto.org (information on trade and intellectual property issues)
International Intellectual Property Alliance:	http://www.iipa.com (information on intellectual protection of copyrighted materials)

DISCUSSION QUESTIONS

1. Italy, a member of the Berne Convention, would like to require that works originating in other Berne countries require a copyright notice although it does not require works originating in Italy to carry a copyright notice. May Italy impose such requirements? What is the name of the principle that governs your answer?

2. A Berne Convention member nation has decided to allow for a term of copyright protection of sixty years. May it do so? May it allow for a term of protection of forty years? Discuss.

3. How does the Digital Millennium Copyright Act ensure that the United States complies with its obligations under the WIPO Copyright Treaty?

4. Assume that a work owned by a French national (and protected by copyright in France) fell into the public domain in the United States because the work did not have a copyright notice (at the time such notice was required in the United States). Because the work was in the public domain, Kim Smith began reproducing the work. The owner would like to restore the copyright in the United States. What agreement governs this matter, how will the owner restore rights, and what will happen to Kim Smith's rights? What is the term of protection for the work?

For additional resources, go to www.westlegalstudies.com.

PART IV

The Law of Patents

CHAPTER 17

Foundations of Patent Law

CHAPTER OVERVIEW

A patent is a legal right granted by the federal government that permits its owner to prevent others from making, using, or selling an invention. There are three types of patents: utility patents, design patents, and plant patents. The great majority of patents are utility patents, granted for useful objects or processes. Patents are generally granted to the first to invent, assuming the invention or discovery is not known or used by others in the United States or patented or described in a printed publication in the United States or elsewhere.

Not all discoveries or inventions are eligible for utility patent protection. Patent protection is available only for a new and useful process, machine, manufacture, or composition of matter, or any new and useful improvement thereof. Thus, an inventor must demonstrate that the invention or discovery is useful, novel, and nonobvious. Generally, patent law prohibits the patenting of an invention that is merely an insignificant addition to or alteration of something already in existence or already known.

Some items are excluded from patent protection. For example, a mere arrangement of printed matter, a naturally existing substance, some methods of doing business, and a scientific principle are unpatentable subject matter.

Applications for patents are filed with the U.S. Patent and Trademark Office (PTO), and protection begins only when a patent is issued by the PTO (as opposed to trademark protection, which arises from first use rather than registration with the PTO, and copyright protection, which arises from creation of a work rather than from registration with the Copyright Office).

INTRODUCTION

The word *patent* is a shorthand expression for "letters patent." A **patent** is a grant from the U.S. government to exclude others from making, using, or selling another person's new, nonobvious, and useful invention in the United States for the term of patent protection. After this period of exclusive protection (twenty years from filing for utility and plant patents and fourteen years from grant for design patents), the invention falls into the public domain and may be used by any person without permission. This right of exclusion is far different from the rights provided under copyright law. Under patent law, inventors can enjoin the making, using, or selling of an infringing invention *even if it was independently created.* In contrast, copyright law protects only original works of authorship. If two writers independently compose the same poem, both are protected under copyright law. A patent allows its owner to exclude others from using the owner's invention; it does not provide any guarantee that its owner can sell the invention.

To obtain a patent, an inventor must file an application with the PTO, the same agency of the Department of Commerce that issues trademark registrations. The application must describe the invention with specificity. The application will be reviewed by a PTO examiner, and, if approved, the patent will issue. The patent is a written document that fully describes the invention.

Just as U.S. copyright law derives from the Constitution, so does patent law. The U.S. Constitution provides that Congress shall have the power "to promote the progress of science and useful arts, by securing for limited times to authors and inventors the exclusive right to their respective writings and discoveries." U.S. Const. art. I, § 8, cl. 8. The wording applicable to patents is *science, useful arts, inventors,* and *discoveries.*

Patents promote the public good in that patent protection incentivizes inventors. If inventors of useful discoveries could not protect their works from use or exploitation by others, there would be little motivation to expend effort, time, and money in creating inventions. The introduction of new products and processes benefits society. In return for the full disclosure to the public of the specifics of the invention, thus advancing science and technology, the inventor is given a limited period of time within which to exploit his or her invention and exclude others from doing so. Inventors are thus incentivized to create new products, and the public benefits from inventions that ultimately will fall into the public domain.

RIGHTS UNDER FEDERAL LAW

As stated, patent law derives from the Constitution. In 1790, pursuant to the direction provided in the Constitution, Congress passed the first patent statute, which in large part relied upon English law. Just three years later, the statute was replaced with a new act authored by Thomas Jefferson. These early acts provided the structural framework for U.S. patent law and specified the four basic conditions, still existing, that an invention must satisfy to secure patent protection:

1. the invention must be a utility, design, or plant patent;
2. it must be useful (or ornamental in the case of a design patent or distinctive in the case of a plant patent);
3. it must be novel in relation to the prior art in the field; and
4. it must not be obvious to a person of ordinary skill in the field.

Revisions of federal patent statutes occurred in 1836 when the Patent Office was created and again in 1870 and 1897. Thereafter, in 1952, Congress enacted a new patent act, codified in title 35 of the *United States Code.* This was the last major revision to federal patent statutes, although the American Inventors Protection Act of 1999 (discussed in later chapters) resulted in the biggest changes to

U.S. patent law since 1952. Issues relating to patents are resolved solely by federal law. Moreover, development of patent law has evolved primarily through federal court decisions rather than the legislature. Just as seen in copyright law, where the term *writings* has been held to be broad enough to cover emerging technologies such as computer programs, the language in the 1793 act relating to the protectability of machines, manufactures, art (later changed to *process*), and composition is broad enough to cover new developments such as computers and electronics. In 1982, Congress created a new court, the Court of Appeals for the Federal Circuit (CAFC), to exercise exclusive jurisdiction over all cases involving patent issues and to promote uniform interpretation of the U.S. patent statutes, which until then had been interpreted in often inconsistent ways by the various federal courts of appeals throughout the nation.

Unlike trademark and copyright law, both of which recognize common law rights in marks and works of authorship even without federal registration, patent law requires that an inventor secure issuance of a patent to protect and enforce his or her rights against infringers. Inventors, however, may also secure some protection for their works under trade secret law (see Chapter 22). Moreover, some inventions, such as computer programs, are protectable under copyright law as well as patent law.

UNITED STATES PATENT AND TRADEMARK OFFICE

Patents exist only by authority of government grant. The department of the government responsible for granting patents is the Department of Commerce, acting through the PTO. The PTO receives applications, reviews them, and issues or grants patents. The PTO also publishes and disseminates patent information, records assignments of patents, maintains files of U.S. and foreign patents, and maintains a search room for public use in examining issued patents and records. The present address for mailing and most patent-related documents is Mail Stop ____ (insert particular mail stop or box number per PTO web site instructions), Commissioner for Patents, P.O. Box 1450, Alexandria, VA 22313. Correspondence sent via priority mail and express services must use anther address. Because the PTO is in the process of moving to its new Alexandria, Virginia, offices and the addresses may change, always check the PTO web site befre submitting documents or correspondence to the PTO. Additionally, the PTO web site (http://www.uspto.gov) offers a wealth of general information, forms for downloading, patent statistics, news updates about issues affecting the PTO and patent practice, schedules of patent fees, and other valuable information.

As secretary of state, Thomas Jefferson was the first head of the Patent Office. Legend has it that the reason the files in which patents are kept and maintained are called *shoes* is that the first patent applications were stored in Jefferson's shoeboxes.

The rules and regulations relating to examination and issuance of patents are found in the PTO publication ***Manual of Patent Examining Procedure*** (MPEP), which most practitioners keep handy to serve as a reference tool for patent issues and questions. The entire text of the MPEP is available for viewing and downloading at the PTO web site.

A variety of methods for locating patents are available. Pierce Law's IP MALL (http://www.ipmall.fplc.edu) provides links to a variety of patent-related sites, including one listing famous patents, from Eli Whitney's cotton gin, to the application by Orville and Wilbur Wright for the airplane, to the first application for a computer program. Another site identifies the "wacky patent of the month" and references issued patents for oddities such as hay fragrance and eye protectors for chickens.

Numerous other links are provided to articles and information of interest to IP practitioners. Another way of locating and retrieving issued patents is through the PTO patent database, which provides the full text of all patents issued since 1976 and full and full-page images of all patents issued since 1790. Patents from 1790 through 1975 are searchable only by patent number and the current patent classification system of identifying patents. Patents issued after 1975 are searchable through a variety of techniques, including patent number, inventor name, or topic (using Boolean connectors). The PTO web site offers search tips.

Six and one-half million patents have been issued since the first patent in 1790. The patent office is increasingly busy. In 2002, 333,688 patent applications were filed and 162,221 patents were issued. Many experts attribute the onslaught of filings to applications for software and Internet-related inventions.

(See Exhibit 17–1 for a list of famous patents issued in the United States.)

PATENTABILITY

An invention must satisfy four basic requirements to be eligible for patent protection:

1. the invention must be one of the types specified by statute as patentable subject matter (namely, a utility, design, or plant patent);
2. the invention must be useful;
3. the invention must be novel; and
4. the invention must be nonobvious.

Patentable Subject Matter—Utility Patents

There are three distinct types of patents: utility patents, design patents, and plant patents. Utility patents are the most common and cover a wide variety of inventions and discoveries including the typewriter, the automobile, the sewing machine, the geodesic dome, the helicopter, sulfa drugs, gene sequences, and genetically altered mice. Design patents cover new, original, and ornamental designs for useful articles such as furniture and containers. Plant patents cover new and distinct asexually reproduced plant varieties, such as hybrid flowers or trees. Because the vast majority of patents are utility patents, they will be discussed first. Design and plant patents will be discussed later in this chapter.

Federal law establishes the subject matter that can be protected by a **utility patent:** "Whoever invents or discovers any new and useful process, machine, manufacture, or composition of matter, or any new and useful improvement thereof, may obtain a patent therefor . . . ." 35 U.S.C. § 101.

Although ideas are not patentable, processes are. A **process** is a method of doing something to produce a given result. According to *Cochrane v. Deener,* 94 U.S. 780, 787–88 (1877), a process is "an act, or series of acts, performed upon the subject-matter to be transformed and reduced to a different state or thing. If new and useful, it is just as patentable as is a piece of machinery." A patent may be issued for a newly developed process or a new use of an already known process. Some examples of patented processes are the process for chrome plating; the process for making synthetic diamonds; processes for vulcanizing India rubber, smelting ore, tanning, and dyeing; Louis Pasteur's 1873 patented yeast process; and Clarence Birdseye's process for packaging frozen food. In fact, the first patent issued in the United States, to Samuel Hopkins in 1790, was entitled "improved potash process." In some instances, not only the process but also the result of the process is patentable, such as U.S. Pat. No. 5,658,991 for "toner resin composition and a method of manufacturing it," which combines a process (the method of manufacturing) with a composition of matter (the toner resin).

The other types of utility patents (machines, manufactures, and compositions of matter) are all products or items. A **machine** is a device that accomplishes a result, such as a sewing machine or a typewriter. A **manufacture** includes anything under the sun that is made by humans; the

EXHIBIT 17–1
Famous
U.S. Patents

Patent Number	Inventor	Description	Date of Issuance
None	Eli Whitney	Cotton gin	3/14/1794
None	Samuel Colt	Revolver	2/25/1836
1,647	Samuel F.B. Morse	Telegraph	6/20/1840
3,630	Linus Yale	Door lock	6/13/1844
6,281	Walter Hunt	Safety pin	4/10/1849
6,469	Abraham Lincoln	Buoying boats over shoals	5/22/1849
13,661	Isaac Singer	Sewing machine	10/9/1855
22,186	John Mason	Mason jar	11/30/1858
127,568	Richard Chesebrough	VASELINE®	6/4/1872
140,245	Samuel Clemens	Scrapbook	6/24/1873
174,465	Alexander Graham Bell	Telephone	3/7/1876
182,346	Melville Bissell	Carpet sweeper	9/19/1876
223,898	Thomas Edison	Electric light	1/27/1880
388,850	George Eastman	Roll film camera	9/4/1888
473,653	Sarah Boone	Ironing board for sleeves	4/26/1892
504,038	Whitcomb Judson	Zipper	8/29/1893
644,077	Felix Hoffman	Aspirin	2/27/1900
686,046	Henry Ford	Automobile	11/5/1901
775,135	King Gillette	GILLETTE® safety razor	11/15/1904
821,393	Wilbur and Orville Wright	Airplane	5/22/1906
1,102,653	Robert Goddard	Two-stage rocket	7/7/1914
1,242,872	Clarence Saunders	Supermarket	10/9/1917
1,370,316	Harry Houdini	Diver's suit	3/1/1921
2,071,250	Wallace Carothers	Nylon	2/16/1937
2,177,627	Richard Drew	SCOTCH® cellophane tape	10/31/1939
2,682,235	Buckminster Fuller	Geodesic dome	6/29/1954
2,799,619	Seifter, Monaco, & Hoover	Tranquilizer	7/16/1957
4,270,182	Satya Asija	First computer program (software)	5/26/1981

observable without significant distortion or loss of too much information.

Indicators and measurement levels

An indicator is a single data item providing some kind of measurement for a variable. Defining the values of an indicator, usually with numbers, is called coding. Simple variables such as calendar age, sex, and household size are straightforward and need only one-indicator or single-item measurement. Other variables are more complex and require the selection of multiple items for scaling. We will discuss the special issues for constructing such composite measures, or multi-item scaling, in greater detail in the next section.

Measurement is the assignment of values to variables. If measurement leads to the reduction of data to numbers, it means the quantification of research materials. Strictly speaking, quantification starts with the identification of your research variables and is the core of the process of operationalization. It should be noted, however, that quantification or operationalization is not always desired. Qualitative researchers, for example, have been concerned with the danger incurred by the kind of reduction that quantification and operationalization entail. Nevertheless, quantification is an indispensable and powerful tool for scientific inquiry. If used properly, especially when combined with the qualitative approach, operationalization and quantification can serve as the major vehicle for advancing and validating our knowledge and understanding.

A key to understanding quantification is what we call the level of measurement. When the same numbers are assigned to represent the values of different variables with different numeric or mathematical attributes, they may give very different meanings as well as restrictions to mathematical operations. For instance, a yearly income of $100,000 is ten times that of $10,000; but for a number of 1 representing male and a number of 2 representing female assigned to the gender variable, we cannot even tell which value is higher or larger than the other. Different variables have different possibilities for quantification outcomes, and the major difference is in the different levels of measurement. So far, four levels of measurement have been identified in terms of four kinds of variables, that is, the nominal, the ordinal, the interval, and the ratio.

Nominal measures will only yield different classes, groups, or categories as different values, and the numbers assigned to different categories are merely nominal labels for different characteristics. The only mathematical property that term is broad enough to include a pitchfork and the patented Monopoly game. It is often said that the category of "manufactures" is a type of catchall category to encompass devices or items not easily classified as machines, compositions of matter, or processes. A **composition of matter** is a combination of two or more chemical or other materials into a product, such as a synthetic diamond or the fabric known as polyester. An invention can also consist of some new use of a process, machine, manufacture, or composition of matter as long as that new use demonstrates significant change from the original invention. Thus, new and nonobvious uses of old structures and compositions are patentable.

Usefulness

The Constitution itself provides that patent protection is available for "*useful* arts," and 35 U.S.C. § 101, in defining what is patentable, states that patents are available for *useful* processes, machines, manufactures, and compositions of matter. Although **usefulness** is not a stringent standard, the invention must be of some benefit to humanity to be "useful." Mere novelties or inventions that conflict with scientific principles, such as a perpetual motion machine, are not patentable because they are not useful. In brief, such an invention has no usefulness because it does not work. Similarly, inventions whose only purpose is detrimental or dangerous or would promote illegal ends cannot be patented inasmuch as, by definition, they are not useful. For example, a patent was denied for a process of making a low-cost tobacco leaf that resembled a more select leaf on the basis that its only purpose was to deceive consumers. *Rickard v. Du Bon*, 103 F. 868 (2d Cir. 1900). Inventions that serve to amuse or entertain are considered useful. Generally, a small degree of utility is sufficient to show that an invention satisfies the requirement of usefulness.

The usefulness required of an invention must be present usefulness, not usefulness purely for research purposes. Thus, patent protection will be denied to a drug whose usefulness cannot yet be shown or to a process, the result of which produces an article that has no current use. The fact that a drug, invention, or result of a process might show some benefit or usefulness at some time in the future is generally not sufficient and a patent therefor will be denied. Nevertheless, even if an invention or discovery shows no benefit to humans, it will be protected by patent law if usefulness for animals can be shown. Thus, drugs or compounds whose effectiveness has been demonstrated for animals can be patented even though their usefulness for humans cannot yet be shown. *In re Brana*, 51 F.3d 1560 (Fed. Cir. 1995). Applications that claim some drug or other substance is useful for humans must be accompanied by supporting evidence, usually results of tests or trials, and must show the substance is reasonably safe. To be patentable, an invention need not meet the stricter standards of regulatory agencies such as the Food and Drug Administration; it need only be "reasonably safe."

To ensure that the invention is useful, the application must disclose or specify the usefulness of the invention. To allow a patent that does not specify its utility would be to grant a patent on an entire range of unknown applications, thereby allowing an inventor to obtain a monopoly on an entire field of knowledge. Thus, patent applications must describe their specific advantage or usefulness so the public can benefit from the invention. Similarly, a patent will be denied when an invention fails to operate as described or claimed in the application.

Novelty

Section 101 of the Patent Act requires that an invention (or any improvement to an invention) be "new" or novel. Section 102 of the

Patent Act elaborates on the requirement of **novelty** by setting forth certain situations that demonstrate the invention is not novel. Most codify the basic principle that the first to invent will be granted a patent. If an invention is known or used by others, is the subject of an existing patent, or has been described or sold, then it is not novel and, accordingly, is not eligible for patent protection. The seven subsections of Section 102 are as follows:

Section 102(a): Inventions Known or Used by Others. Section 102(a) states that the following acts prior to the actual date of invention will preclude an applicant from obtaining a patent:

- if the invention was known by others in this country;
- if the invention was used by others in this country;
- if the invention was patented in the United States or in a foreign country by another; or
- if the invention was described in another's printed publication in the United States or a foreign country.

In such a case, it is deemed that the applicant's invention was anticipated and an application will be denied. Often called the **doctrine of anticipation,** this principle is intended to ensure that a second or junior inventor does not secure a monopoly on an invention that a senior inventor owns or that is in the public domain.

An invention is "described in a printed publication" when it is printed in nearly any kind of document by any means (including electronic means) and has been made available to the public. Such availability can occur by circulating copies of a document at a conference, releasing advertising brochures, or by disseminating a thesis. Internal business documents or documents provided to others under conditions of confidentiality are not publications within the meaning of the statute.

Section 102(b): Invention Is In Use or On Sale. The following acts occurring more than one year before the filing of a patent application in the United States will preclude the applicant from obtaining a patent:

- the invention was patented in the United States or a foreign country;
- the invention was described in a printed publication in the United States or a foreign country;
- the invention is in public use in the United States; or
- the invention is on sale in the United States.

The requirements of section 102(b), typically called the **on sale bar,** are intended to ensure that inventors act promptly to secure protection for their inventions. Once an invention is in public use or offered for sale or sold in the United States or is patented or described in a printed publication anywhere, the inventor has a one-year **grace period** or statute of limitations to file an application. Failure to file an application in a timely manner will bar issuance of a patent.

An invention is "in use" if it is being used in the manner intended by the inventor without any confidentiality restrictions. An exception allows **experimental use** of the invention so that the inventor can perfect the invention or ascertain whether it will fulfill its intended purpose. Thus, such experimental use will not trigger the one-year grace period. Similarly, private use by the inventor or use for the inventor's own enjoyment will not trigger the one-year limitation period; however, an invention that is "ready for patenting" will start the one-year limitation period if there is a commercial offer for sale of the invention. *Pfaff v. Wells Electronics, Inc.*, 525 U.S. 55 (1998). In *Pfaff*, the one-year on sale bar applied although the inventor had made only engineering drawings and had not yet made the invention although he had accepted an offer to sell the invention.

An invention is deemed "on sale" if it is offered for sale, even though no actual sales occur. Even a single sale may bar patentability. An invention is "described in a printed publication" if it has been printed by any manner (including electronic methods) and described in such a way that a person of ordinary skill in the art could make the invention, just as is the case under section 102(a) described above.

Section 102(b) is often called a "statutory bar," and the one-year grace period is often triggered by the inventor's own acts, such as offering the article for sale, describing it in a promotional literature, and so forth. Thus, inventors should place confidentiality notices on documents to avoid triggering "publication" of the invention.

The on sale bar engenders many refusals by the PTO. It is intended to encourage prompt action by inventors. It would be unfair to allow an inventor to use an invention for profit and delay filing for an application because such a delay has the effect of adding time to the term of protection for the patent and delaying its placement in the public domain.

Section 102(c): Invention Has Been Abandoned. A person cannot obtain a patent if he or she has abandoned the invention. Abandonment is shown when the inventor expressly or impliedly demonstrates an intent to abandon his or her right to a patent. Abandonment usually requires an intentional act. Delay alone in filing an application does not usually constitute abandonment.

Section 102(d): Invention Is the Subject of a Foreign Patent. Section 102(d) establishes four conditions, which, if all are present, establish a statutory bar against the granting of a patent in this country:

1. an application has been filed in a foreign country more than twelve months before the U.S. application was filed;

2. the foreign application was filed by the same applicant as in the United States;
3. the foreign patent must be granted before the U.S. filing date; and
4. the same invention must be involved.

Section 102(e): Invention Is Described in a Prior Published Application or Patent. Pursuant to section 102(e), an application will be denied if it was described in

- another's published U.S. patent application before the invention by the applicant; or
- another's issued U.S. patent granted before the invention by the applicant.

An invention cannot be novel if it is described in an existing patent already granted or an application that has been published. Section 102(e) is meant to provide priority to senior parties.

Section 102(f): Inventor Did Not Invent the Invention. Only the inventor is entitled to a patent for the invention or discovery. The inventor is the person who conceived the specific invention. If the inventor derived the invention from another, a rejection under section 102(f) is proper.

An employee who invents an item while on the job remains the inventor. Although the employer may have a contractual right to own any inventions created by employees, a patent application must be filed by the individual inventor. It can, however, be assigned to the employer or another concurrently with filing. Parties who work jointly on an invention may be joint inventors even though their contributions are not equal or simultaneous. An application for the resulting invention must name all inventors.

Section 102(g): Invention Was First Invented by Others. A person is entitled to a patent in the United States if, before the applicant's invention,

- the invention was made in this country; and
- the prior invention was not abandoned, suppressed, or concealed.

Sections 102(a), (e), and (g) are all intended to ensure patents are granted to the first inventor. The second or junior inventor's product or process is not novel in such circumstances.

Abandonment typically requires an express intention to relinquish rights to a patent. Merely failing to file a patent application does not constitute abandonment, suppression, or concealment. Similarly, use of the product under agreements with others to protect the invention as a confidential trade secret is not necessarily concealment or suppression as long as the public is receiving some benefit from the invention. Typically, inventors are required to engage in diligent efforts to bring the invention to the marketplace. Such efforts will help counter a claim the invention has been abandoned, suppressed, or concealed. Because abandonment, suppression, and concealment of information that could be valuable and beneficial to the public are contrary to patent law policy, patent law punishes such acts by allowing the second inventor to secure a patent even though another previously invented the item or process.

In determining priority of invention, the statute provides that the dates the inventors conceived of the invention, the dates they reduced their inventions to practice, and their reasonable diligence in reducing the invention to practice will be considered. As discussed in Chapter 19, reduction to practice can be actual (making or building the invention or a prototype) or constructive (filing an application for a patent after invention).

Nonobviousness

Merely because an invention is useful and novel does not automatically entitle it to patent protection. To qualify for a grant of patent, the invention must be nonobvious to those having skill in the field or art to which the subject matter pertains. 35 U.S.C. § 103. The subject matter sought to be patented must be sufficiently different from what has been used or described before it may be said to be nonobvious to a person having ordinary skill in the area of technology related to the invention. For example, the substitution of one material for another in an invention and mere changes in size are ordinarily not patentable because they are obvious. A distinct improvement, however, is patentable even if the new invention improves matter in the public domain. Similarly, a new use of a known process is patentable.

Determining whether an invention is nonobvious is one of the most difficult tasks in patent law. After all, a disposable razor, a safety pin, and a retractable tape measure all seem obvious now, yet none of these items were obvious at the time they were invented.

Until the 1952 Patent Act, courts generally required that an invention result from a "flash of genius" or some sudden insight. The view was that an invention must have been so nonobvious that no amount of diligent research would have produced it. The act now states that "patentability shall not be negatived by the manner in which the invention was made." 35 U.S.C. § 103. Thus, whether an invention is produced by dint of arduous research or a flash of genius does not determine whether it is nonobvious. The present method of determining **nonobviousness** is by reference to the prior art.

The *Graham* Factors. In *Graham v. John Deere Co.,* 383 U.S. 1 (1966), the Supreme Court articulated the following factors to consider in determining whether an invention is nonobvious and thus deserving of a patent:

- **Pertinent prior art.** One must review the scope and content of the prior art in the pertinent field to determine if an invention is nonobvious. The term

prior art refers to the circumstances set forth in sections 102 and 103, namely, the generally available public knowledge relating to the invention for which a patent is sought and which was available prior to invention. Thus, information contained in existing patents, printed publications, and inventions that were known and used before the subject invention will be considered.

- **Differences between the prior art and the invention.** In determining whether an invention is nonobvious, consideration must be given to differences between the prior art and the invention at issue. Applicants themselves may include statements in their applications in regard to how their inventions differ from and are improvements over prior art. An invention that achieves superior results is likely not obvious.

- **Level of ordinary skill in the prior art.** If the invention would be obvious to a person having ordinary skill in the art to which the invention pertains, it cannot be patented. A person of "ordinary skill" is neither a highly sophisticated expert or genius in the art nor a layperson with no knowledge of the field of art but rather some hypothetical person who is aware of the pertinent prior art.

Secondary Considerations.   In *Graham,* after enumerating the factors evaluated in determining whether an invention is nonobvious, the Court suggested that some **secondary considerations,** all of which are nontechnical and objective, could be considered in determining nonobviousness. Some of the secondary considerations include the following:

- **Commercial success.** An invention that is a commercial success may be nonobvious because acceptance by the marketplace tends to show that an invention is significant; moreover, if the invention were obvious, someone would already have attempted to commercialize it for his or her own financial gain.

- **Long-felt need and failure of others.** If there has been a long-standing need for a device or process that has gone unresolved despite the efforts of others to solve the problem, and the invention satisfies this need, it tends to show the invention is nonobvious. If the invention were obvious, others would have been able to discover it readily.

- **Commercial acquiescence.** If competitors seek to enter into licenses with the owner so they may use or sell the invention to others, such tends to show nonobviousness because otherwise the third parties would have challenged the patent as invalid based on nonobviousness.

- **Copying.** Copying or infringement of the patent by another suggests nonobviousness because otherwise the infringer would have been able to independently develop the invention.

Conversely, the independent and near-simultaneous invention of like products or processes tends to suggest obviousness. If it is easy for a number of people in the field to invent the same product or process, it is likely obvious to those with ordinary skill in the art.

To ensure that courts do not overrely on the secondary considerations (commercial success, long-felt need, commercial acquiescence, and copying), the Federal Circuit requires that a party demonstrate some link or *nexus* between the secondary characteristic and the invention. For example, if an inventor argues that an invention is nonobvious because it is commercially successful, the inventor must demonstrate that commercial success is due to some property inherent in the invention, rather than due to some external factor such as aggressive marketing or the renown of the inventor.

Combination Patents. One area that has caused debate over obviousness relates to new inventions consisting of a combination of older, known elements. The unique combination of the elements may make the invention novel, but the combination must be nonobvious to receive patent protection. A factor sometimes used in determining whether these patents, called **combination patents,** are nonobvious is *synergism:* the newly combined elements must result in some different function or some result that is different or unexpected such that one who possesses ordinary skill in the art would not have predicted the result of the combination of the known elements. If there is such a new result, the invention is nonobvious and is patentable.

The Patent Act was amended in 1996 to provide preference to inventions relating to biotechnology processes. Section 103(b) expressly provides that a biotechnological process is nonobvious if it uses or results in a novel, nonobvious product or composition. Thus, the process as well as the composition is patentable in the biotechnology field.

There is overlap between the requirements of novelty and nonobviousness. Both depend on examination of prior art. To ensure novelty, one must examine the prior art (what others know, use, and publish) to determine if the invention could have been anticipated. To ensure nonobviousness, one must examine the scope and content of pertinent prior art to determine if the invention would be obvious to a person having ordinary skill in the field.

Exclusions from Patent Protection

There are a variety of items, products, and processes that cannot be patented. The following are excluded from patent protection either by statutory prohibition or judicial interpretation:

- **Products of nature.** Only human-made inventions can be patented. Naturally occurring substances cannot be protected by patent even if they have previously been unknown to others. For example, a new plant or mineral that is discovered cannot be patented. On the other hand, genetically altered living organisms can be patented as "manufactures" or "compositions of matter." In *Diamond v. Chakrabarty,* 447 U.S. 303 (1980), the Court held that a live, human-made microorganism (in that case, a genetically engineered bacterium capable of breaking down crude oil) was patentable as a human-made "manufacture" or "composition of matter," and stated that "anything under the sun made by man" is patentable. Thus, genetically altered oysters and mice have been held patentable. The distinction is not between living and inanimate things but between products of nature (whether living or not) and human-made inventions. *Id.* at 313.

- **Laws of nature.** Laws of nature, physical phenomena, scientific truths, and abstract ideas cannot be patented. As the Court remarked in *Chakrabarty,* "Einstein could not patent his celebrated law that $E = mc^2$; nor could Newton have patented the law of gravity." *Id.* at 310. Generally, mere chemical or mathematical formulas or algorithms cannot be patented as such; however, chemical substances can be patented, systems using formulas can be patented as processes, and items that are produced as the result of formulas can be patented. Thus, a machine or product that depends on some law of physics or the law of gravity can be patented. A process is not unpatentable merely because it contains a law of nature or a pure mathematical algorithm. Similarly, computer programs, although they consist of algorithms, can be patented in many instances. In *Diamond v. Diehr,* 450 U.S. 175 (1981), a patent was upheld for the process of molding rubber products with the aid of a computer. The Court noted that although mathematical formulas as such are not patentable, a process employing a well-known mathematical equation was patentable. Additionally, the use of a computer to improve an otherwise patentable process did not preclude the process from being patented. Thus, incorporating a computer program as a step in a process or as a component in a machine or manufacture may be acceptable. See Chapter 21 for additional discussion on protection of computer programs under patent law.

- **Printed matter.** Printed forms cannot be patented.
- **Atomic weapons.** Under the Atomic Energy Act of 1954, atomic weapons cannot be patented.
- **Business methods and mental steps.** Systems for the operation of businesses cannot be patented unless they produce a useful, tangible, and concrete result. A useful and novel business system or idea is not patentable unless there is a product or process to effect it. Similarly, processes consisting solely of mental steps, meaning human thought and deliberation, cannot be patented. For more than 100 years, the PTO rarely granted a patent for any business method, reasoning that such methods were akin to abstract ideas. Since 1998, however, the PTO has granted a record number of what are usually referred to as business method or software patents so long as the method or software is useful and produces a tangible result. See Chapter 21 for additional discussion.

DESIGN PATENTS

The Patent Act provides that whoever invents any new, original, and ornamental design for an article of manufacture may obtain a patent. 35 U.S.C. § 171. Comparing the scope of this provision to that of section 101 relating to utility patents, it is clear that the requirement of "usefulness" for utility patents has been replaced by a requirement of "ornamentality." The design must be novel and nonobvious. Just as a person may obtain a patent for a chemical compound and one for the process utilizing the chemical compound, a person may obtain a utility patent and a design patent for one article of manufacture because a useful article may be ornamented with a design. A **design patent** can be obtained for articles as diverse as jewelry, furniture, trash receptacles, and clothing.

Recognizing that while authors could seek protection for their works under copyright law and inventors could seek protection for their works under patent law, no protection was afforded for the creators of decorative arts, Congress filled this gap and allowed design patents in 1842. One of the first design patent cases related to a claim by Gorham Manufacturing that its spoon and fork handle design patents had been infringed. *Gorham Mfg. v. White,* 81 U.S. (14 Wall.) 511 (1871). In *Gorham,* the Court noted that the intent of the design patent statute was to encourage the decorative arts.

To be protectable, a design must satisfy the following four requirements:

1. **It must be an "article of manufacture."** An article of manufacture is nearly anything made by a human and may consist of a manufactured article's configuration (the particular shape of a chair), surface ornamentation (the design on the handle of tableware), or a

combination of both (a uniquely shaped fork with two irregularly sized tines, embossed with a leaf design).

2. **It must be new.** The requirements of novelty for utility patents discussed in the previous section on patentability under the heading "Novelty" apply equally to design patents.

3. **It must be original.** The requirement of originality is the equivalent of the requirement of nonobviousness for utility patents. A design cannot be patented if a designer of ordinary skill who designs articles similar to the one applied for would consider the design obvious in view of the prior art.

4. **It must be ornamental.** To be patentable, a design must be primarily ornamental rather than utilitarian. The article may serve a useful purpose (for example, a spoon and a chair serve a useful purpose), but its primary purpose cannot be functional. If there are several ways that an item could be designed and yet still remain functional, then any one design is likely ornamental rather than functional. An article may qualify for design patent protection if at some point in its life cycle its appearance is a factor even if, when ultimately used, the article is hidden. Thus, caskets and artificial hip prostheses have been given design patent protection. Although both are primarily useful, the appearance of the article is of importance at some point even though when put to their intended use, the articles are hidden from view.

The bars to novelty set forth in section 102 and discussed earlier in this chapter apply equally to design patents. Most of the bars aim at ensuring that designs are promptly patented.

There is some overlap between design patents and copyright. It has been held that the same work can qualify for protection under both copyright law and patent law. For example, the drawing of a cartoon character can be protected under copyright law; when the character is embossed on some article, such as china plates, it may be protected under patent law. Similarly, the same item may qualify for protection under trademark law and patent law. For example, in a case involving the shape of a bottle of Mogen David wine, the court stated the design qualified for both patent and trademark protection. *In re Mogen David Wine Corp.*, 328 F.2d 925 (C.C.P.A. 1964). Finally, there is overlap between trade dress protection and patent law such that the ornamental appearance of an item may be protected under trade dress law and as a design patent.

Securing copyright protection is generally the easiest and least expensive method of protecting certain designs. Although copyright registration is not required, a copyright registration may be obtained for a filing fee of $30 within four to five months, and protection will last for the life of the author plus seventy years. Trademark registrations last only as long as they are renewed, and patent protection comes into being only once the patent issues, a process that may take two to three years from the date of application. Moreover, the nonrenewable term of a design patent is fourteen years from the date of issuance of grant. Practical matters should also be considered. If a design will likely be somewhat limited in its appeal or trendy, such as a piece of jewelry, it is far less expensive and far more expeditious to obtain copyright rather than patent protection for the item. Thus, a combination of intellectual property strategies may be needed to secure the broadest possible scope of protection for certain articles.

PLANT PATENTS

Patents for plants have been recognized only since the passage of the Plant Patent Act in 1930. Prior to that time, the philosophy was that plants were natural products not subject to patent protection. Section 161 of the Patent Act now provides that whoever invents or discovers and asexually reproduces any distinct and new variety of plant may obtain a patent therefor. Just as design patents substitute the requirement of "ornamentality" for the "usefulness" required of utility patents, plant patents substitute the requirement of "distinctiveness" in place of "usefulness."

Congress allowed patents for plants to provide the benefits of the patent system that were then available to manufacturing and industry to the agriculture business in order to incentivize growers and protect their plant products from infringement. Without patent protection, copies of plants could be produced by grafting techniques. Thus, a **plant patent** affords its owner the right to exclude others from asexually reproducing the plant. The term of protection is the same as that for utility patents, namely, twenty years from the application date. The term *plant* is construed in its ordinary meaning and does not include bacteria. The use of the term *discovery* means a discovery by asexual propagation; plants discovered in the wild cannot be patented; however, a plant discovered in a cultivated area and later reproduced asexually can be patented. Tubers, such as potatoes, are not eligible for protection under the Plant Patent Act.

There are four requirements that must be satisfied before a plant can be patented:

1. **The new variety must be asexually reproduced.** A grower or discoverer of a new and distinct variety of plant must be able to reproduce the plant by asexual means. Generally, this is accomplished by taking cuttings of the original plant and placing them in soil or by grafting so as to create a new plant. **Asexual reproduction** involves growing something other than from a seed.

2. **The plant must be distinctive.** The new plant must be clearly distinguishable from existing varieties. Features that show distinctiveness are color, odor, flavor, shape, ability of the plant to grow in a different type of soil, its productivity, its factors of preservation, or immunity to disease. The requirement of distinctiveness imposes only a requirement that the plant be different from, rather than superior to, other varieties. A new color of a rose may be different from other roses but may not be better than some other variety. Nevertheless, it may be patented. There is a great deal of overlap between nonobviousness for utility patents and distinctiveness for plant patents. One patent for a variety of bluegrass recites that the plant is a "new and distinct variety of Kentucky Bluegrass characterized by its excellent tolerance to drought, low fertilizer requirements, deep rooting system, excellent tolerance to Fusarium blight, and good to excellent shade tolerance. The plant tolerates a close cut, is highly resistant to most common bluegrass diseases, is extremely aggressive, has a medium to coarse leaf texture and consistently maintains excellent turf quality." U.S. Plant Pat. No. 4,704.

3. **The plant must be novel.** The new variety of plant must not have previously existed in nature. The bars to novelty set forth in section 102 and discussed in the earlier section on patentability under the heading "Novelty" apply equally to plant patents. For example, selling a plant in the United States more than one year prior to filing a patent application for it will bar issuance of a patent for it.

4. **The plant must be nonobvious.** Although section 161 of the Patent Act providing for statutory protection for plant patents does not specifically state that patents for plants must be nonobvi-

ous, the section does provide that the provisions of the act relating to utility patents apply equally to plant patents unless otherwise specified. Generally, the standards set forth in *Graham v. John Deere Co.*, discussed in the earlier section on patentability under the heading "Nonobviousness," apply equally with regard to plant patents.

Although the most common means of securing protection for plants is through application for a plant patent, two other methods of protection exist for plants. In 1970, Congress enacted the **Plant Variety Protection Act** (7 U.S.C. § 2321), allowing quasipatent protection for certain sexually reproduced plants, meaning plants bred through seeds. Sexually reproduced plants could not receive protection under the 1930 Plant Patent Act because new varieties could not be reproduced true-to-type through seedlings. The new variety was not always stable, and its new characteristics could not be passed uniformly from one generation to the next. By 1970, however, it was generally recognized that true-to-type sexual reproduction of plants is possible, and the Plant Variety Protection Act was passed.

These new varieties, produced through the use of seeds, are awarded "plant variety protection certificates" by the Department of Agriculture, rather than letters patents issued by the PTO. The primary purpose of the Plant Variety Protection Act is to encourage the development of novel varieties of sexually reproduced plants. The certificate owner may exclude others from selling, offering, reproducing, or trading infringing plants. The term of protection is generally twenty years from date of issue of the certificate.

Finally, a plant may qualify for protection as a utility patent, even though it also qualifies for protection under the Plant Patent Act as a plant patent or under the Plant Variety Protection Act for patentlike protection. An application for a utility patent for a plant must satisfy the requirements for utility patents generally, namely, usefulness, novelty, and nonobviousness.

In some cases, matters of tactics and strategy may dictate whether an inventor seeks protection for a plant under the Plant Patent Act of 1930, the Plant Variety Protection Act of 1970, or as a general utility patent. Although the most significant determinant is how the plant can be reproduced (asexual reproduction is required under the Plant Patent Act while sexual plant reproduction is protected under the Plant Variety Protection Act), other factors should be considered. For example, the requirement that an invention be nonobvious applies to utility patents and plant patents reproduced asexually, but not to the Plant Variety Protection Act. Thus, an inventor who cannot demonstrate nonobviousness might seek protection under the Plant Variety Protection Act. Similarly, fees to maintain the patent are due on utility patents but not on plant patents. Assuming applications do not claim identical subject matter, it is possible that a patent could be obtained for a plant both under the Plant Patent Act and under the Patent Act as a utility patent. Each statute has different requirements and affords different protections.

DOUBLE PATENTING

The **double patenting** principle prohibits the issuance of more than one patent for the same invention or for an invention that is substantially the same as that owned by an inventor. The intent of this bar is to ensure that inventors do not make some insignificant change to an invention near the end of its term of existence in order to secure another twenty-year monopoly on the invention or discovery. Nevertheless, design and utility patents may coexist because they relate to arguably distinct such numbers or values have is "equal" or "unequal." No value can be considered larger or smaller than another, nor can it be calculated by any arithmetical operation such as addition, subtraction, or multiplication. The variables that can only be measured at this level are sometimes called categorical variables, though the meaning of a categorical variable may be taken differently in other situations. The coding of a nominal indicator should observe the logical requirements for classification or categorization. These are the exhaustiveness and mutual exclusiveness of the classes, categories, or groups represented by all different numbers or values of the variable. Variables such as gender, race, marital status etc. can be assigned numbers for their categories in this way, and the numbers should be treated as nominal measures. Nominal variables are typical categorical variables. They will need special treatment in statistical analysis.

Ordinal measures are also nominal measures, which means that the properties and rules mentioned above all apply to measures at the ordinal level. Neverthe-less, ordinal measures have more or better mathematical properties since the attributes of the variables measured may be logically rank-ordered, not just equal or unequal. The values from measurement at this level can be compared in terms of more or less, higher or lower, etc., yet cannot be added, subtracted, multiplied, and divided since the results will not make exact numeric sense. In other words, what can be determined here is only an order relation or rank relation. A typical example of the ordinal measurement is education level with the following coding scheme: 0 = no schooling; 1 = elementary school; 2 = junior high school; 3 = senior high school; 4 = college or university; 5 = graduate school. Grades for academic performance including the numeric GPA (grade point average) is another example. It has been mathematically proved that ordinal variables are amenable to any monotone increasing transformation, which makes them suitable for certain statistical tests at higher measurement levels (e.g., as interval variables).

In a like manner, interval measures are also nominal and ordinal measures. However, for nominal and ordinal measures the difference or interval between two different numbers or values does not make any sense. The two kinds of measures do not have the required numeric quality, and that is why their values cannot be put into arithmetical operations. The attributes of interval variables, on the other hand, render full numeric meaning to the difference, distance, or interval between any two of their values. Until we get to this level, we do not know whether the difference between 3 and 4 is the same as the difference between 3 and 2, and therefore we do not know what the result means if we add subject matter. A utility patent claims protection for the usefulness of the object while a design patent covers its ornamentality. Inventors often insert a **terminal disclaimer** into their applications, agreeing that the term of protection for a second invention will terminate upon expiration of the patent for the first invention and that the patent claim to the second invention will be valid only as long as both inventions are owned by the same person or entity. Such a disclaimer will enable an inventor to overcome a rejection based on double patenting. Double patenting is discussed further in Chapter 18.

THE ORPHAN DRUG ACT

Just as the Plant Variety Protection Act grants rights somewhat similar to patents, the Orphan Drug Act (21 U.S.C. §§ 360aa–360ee) provides rights for certain drugs that are similar to patent rights, namely, an exclusive right for seven years to market an **orphan drug** that is necessary to treat a disease that affects fewer than 200,000 people. Protection under the act is triggered when the Food and Drug Administration determines that unless such protection is granted, the drug would likely not be made or available to those in need of it. The act applies whether or not the drug can be patented (thus affording protection for drugs that may lack novelty or nonobviousness). The act thus provides incentives to pharmaceutical companies to develop drugs for rare diseases or conditions when otherwise they might not invest the time and effort in developing a drug for a small target group if patentability could not be assured.

TRIVIA

- Most experts attribute the modern concepts of patents to England where, in 1449, King Henry VI granted a patent for manufacturing stained glass to John of Utynam.
- During 2002 and 2001, patent application filings grew at a rate of 12 percent per year.
- George Washington Carver invented more than 300 uses for peanuts.
- The inventor of VELCRO® reported that he thought of the invention while removing burrs from his pet's fur after walking in the woods.

CHAPTER SUMMARY

A patent is a grant from the federal government allowing an inventor to exclude others from producing, using, or selling the inventor's discovery or invention for a limited period of time, generally twenty years from the filing date of a patent application. Patent laws are aimed at fostering and promoting discoveries. There are three types of patents: utility patents, design patents, and plant patents. The vast majority of patents are utility patents, which must satisfy the requirements of usefulness, novelty, and nonobviousness in order to secure protection. An invention or discovery that is merely an insignificant addition to or alteration of something already known or in existence is unpatentable. Protection is allowed for processes, machines, human-made articles of manufacture, and compositions of matter.

Not all inventions or discoveries may be patented. Generally, patents are awarded to the first to invent. Additionally, patents are not available for scientific or mathematical principles, some business methods, printed matter, or substances existing in nature.

Design patents protect original, new, and ornamental designs for articles of manufacture. Plant patents protect new and distinct varieties of asexually reproduced plants.

CASE ILLUSTRATION—REQUIREMENT OF USEFULNESS

Case: *Brenner v. Manson*, 383 U.S. 519 (1966)

Facts: Manson applied for a patent for an allegedly novel process for making certain steroids. The application was denied because it failed to disclose any utility for the chemical compound produced by the process although an adjacent homologue of the steroid yielded by Manson's process showed tumor-inhibiting effects in mice.

Holding: One may only patent that which is useful. The requirement of usefulness is not satisfied by a showing that the compound yielded belongs to a class of compounds that scientists are screening for possible uses. The quid pro quo for granting a patent monopoly is the benefit derived by the public from an invention with substantial utility. "A patent is not a hunting license. It is not a reward for the search, but compensation for its successful conclusion." *Id.* at 536. In this case, there was no showing of usefulness and thus the process was not patentable.

CASE STUDY AND ACTIVITIES

Case Study. Watson is renovating the grounds of the amusement park and is replanting various flower beds. Watson's landscaping staff has managed to asexually reproduce various new flowers with stunning colors. Watson's in-house design team has also designed and made various plastic chairs in the shape of some of Watson's characters. Other chairs are topped with canopies shaped like fanciful hats. In an effort to reduce noise in the park, Watson's engineers have designed new braking systems for some of the roller-coaster rides. These brakes are far quieter than the brakes currently used. Finally, about fifteen months ago, Watson's game developers developed a new arcade game. Watson has been test-marketing the game in the park and allowing children to try out the game in an effort to see which features the children like best.

Activities. Discuss the patentability of the various items and products discussed above.

ROLE OF PARALEGAL

Until patent searching begins and an application is filed, the role of an IP paralegal will be fairly limited. Typically, tasks may consist of conducting research to help assess and satisfy the required elements of usefulness, novelty, and nonobviousness. If a law firm does not have a general information letter available that can be sent to clients who have basic questions about patent law, one should be drafted. Similarly, a "Frequently Asked Questions" sheet can be prepared for distribution to clients. Flowcharts showing the patent process can be made, and charts comparing types of patents (for example, plant patents and utility patents for plants) can be prepared.

An IP paralegal may also be involved in conducting some type of audit of clients to inquire whether they have invented any processes or products that may qualify for patent protection. A questionnaire should be prepared to assess whether clients' intellectual property is being fully protected. See Chapter 24 for sample questions for an intellectual property audit.

INTERNET RESOURCES

Federal laws relating to patents:	http://www.ll.georgetown.edu or http://www.findlaw.com
U.S. Patent and Trademark Office:	http://www.uspto.gov (general information about patents, frequently asked questions, forms, and filing fees)
General information:	http://www.ipmall.fplc.edu (Pierce Law IP MALL with excellent information and articles and links to other IP sources); and http://www.findlaw.com
Absurd patents:	http://www.totallyabsurd.com identifies odd and unusual patents

DISCUSSION QUESTIONS

1. Amy discovers a process that shows a substantial likelihood of usefulness in the future although its present value is speculative. Is the process patentable? Discuss.
2. In June, Ray participates in a well-known online chat room and describes in detail his new invention for an improved flashlight. Two months later, Brian invents the same item. Can Brian obtain a patent? Discuss.

3. In June 2002, Phil advertises his new golf balls for sale. No sales were made. In July of 2003, Phil applies for a patent for the golf balls. Is Phil likely to receive a patent? Discuss.

4. In July 2002, Hillary demonstrates her invention for her new cheese grater to a few friends invited for dinner in her home. In August 2003, Hillary applies for a patent. Is Hillary likely to receive a patent? Discuss.

5. Alex invents a 13-inch television with improved technology and receives a patent. Two years later, Alex makes a 14-inch television with the same components as the earlier patented invention. Is Alex likely to receive a patent for the new 14-inch television? Discuss.

6. Patrick invents a new type of slide for trombones. The slide produces a superior sound than other trombones. Patrick has decorated the slide with engravings. May Patrick obtain a design patent for the new invention? Discuss.

7. Lee asexually reproduces a new type of rose that has a distinctive fragrance. Is the rose patentable? If Lee discovered the rose in the wild, would it be patentable? If the rose produces a compound that is beneficial in the treatment of arthritis, what type of patent should Lee seek?

CHAPTER 18

Patent Searches and Applications

CHAPTER OVERVIEW

Before an application for a patent is filed, a search should be conducted to ensure that the invention is novel and nonobvious. If the search results suggest that an invention may be patentable, an application is then prepared. An application consists of two parts: the specification (describing the invention) and the inventor's oath or declaration. Applications must be filed by individual inventors, although the application can be assigned to another at the same time it is filed. After the application is filed at the PTO, it will be examined for patentability. Application proceedings at the PTO are confidential until the application is published eighteen months after the application filing date. The examiner may issue office actions, requiring amendment of some of the claims of the invention. No new matter can be added to an application. When an application is allowed by an examiner, a notice of allowance is issued and an "issue fee" must be paid to the

PTO for the patent to be granted. The term of utility and plant patents is twenty years from the date of filing of the application therefor. The term of design patents is fourteen years from the date of grant. Maintenance fees must be paid at three intervals during the term of a utility patent to maintain it in force. Once the patent is issued, its owner may exclude others from making, selling, or using the invention for the term of the patent.

PATENT SEARCHING

The Need for a Search

Patentability requires novelty and nonobviousness. The only predictable method of determining whether an invention is new and nonobvious is to conduct a search of the prior art (including patent records and printed publications). The patentability search, sometimes called a **novelty search,** will help determine whether the differences in the subject matter sought to be patented and the prior art are such that the subject matter as a whole would have been obvious to a person having ordinary skill in the art. Moreover, because 35 U.S.C. § 102 excludes from patent protection inventions that have been known or used by others in the United States or patented or described in a printed publication in the United States or elsewhere, a search will disclose whether such bars to protection exist. Finally, if an invention has fallen into the public domain because its patent has expired, anyone can use it and no one can obtain a patent for it. Searching will disclose the existence of such expired patents. Thus, although not required prior to filing a patent application, a search is recommended to determine the feasibility of obtaining a patent. Otherwise, an inventor may incur costs of several thousands of dollars in prosecuting a patent application only to have an examiner determine that the invention fails to satisfy the requirements of novelty and nonobviousness. An additional benefit of conducting a search is that it may provide ideas for drafting the application itself.

A novelty search is somewhat limited in scope and is designed to disclose whether an application will be rejected on the basis of lack of novelty or obviousness. A novelty search can usually be completed for less than $1,000. If an invention is intended for immediate commercial use or sale, an additional search, called an infringement search or investigation, is often conducted concurrently with the novelty search. An invention may be patentable as a significant improvement over an existing invention and yet still infringe a patent. An infringement search or full patentability search is far more extensive than a novelty search and is thus more expensive, often costing between $1,000 and $2,000. Conducting a search and obtaining an opinion relating to infringement is critical inasmuch as persons have affirmative duties of due care to avoid patent infringement. Obtaining advice of

competent counsel may protect a person from having punitive damages imposed against him or her in an action for patent infringement because it demonstrates exercise of the duty of due care (see Chapter 20).

Searching Methods

The PTO provides public search facilities for patent searching. Searching is free and the PTO allows searchers to review issued patents, complete with drawings. The patent search room contains copies of all U.S. issued patents from 1790 to present as well as many foreign patents. Searching can be done either in the main public search room or in the examiners' search areas where examiners will assist in searching.

The PTO employs a classification system that provides for the storage and retrieval of patent documents. Although the system is primarily designed to be used by patent examiners in the course of examining patent applications, the system is also used by searchers. The classification files are divided into smaller searchable units called subclasses. Most classes have approximately three hundred subclasses. One approach divides art on the basis of the industry employing the art or the use to which an art is put. All relevant patents for a given technology are grouped together. For example, all of the materials relating to butchering are grouped together and all of the materials related to bee culture are classed together. Another approach classifies inventions or art based on their function. Thus, all heat exchange devices are grouped together, whether they are milk coolers or beer coolers. The patents are stored in "shoes" stacked one atop the other. Eli Whitney's cotton gin patent was the first patent filed under classification 19161, identified as "Textiles: Fiber Preparation/Seed Boards." Explanations of the Patent Classification System and suggestions for searching are provided on the PTO's web site at http://www.uspto.gov.

Searching can also be done on the Internet. The PTO itself offers free searching at its site (see end of previous paragraph). The PTO has now published every U.S. patent ever issued, more than six and one-half million patents. Patents are searchable by a variety of fields, including inventor name, classification, key words, or patent number. Patents issued from 1790 through 1975 are searchable only by patent number and designated patent classifications. Images can be downloaded and printed. Searching tips are available on the PTO's web site.

In many major cities throughout the United States, public libraries receive copies of issued patents and trademarks. Called Patent and Trademark Depository Libraries, these libraries store patents on microfiche or microfilm, and the collections are available for use by the public free of charge. Unless an inventor is nearly certain that his or her invention is new and nonobvious, searching through the Patent and Trademark Depositories is usually not recommended inasmuch as records are often not updated and review by microfiche or microfilm is cumbersome. Additionally, the scope of the collections varies from library to library, with some offering patents from 1790 and others offering patents only from recent years. Nearly 100 libraries have been designated Patent and Trademark Depositories. See the PTO web site for a listing of the patent and trademark depository libraries.

Patent searching is also offered by Lexis-Nexis. Charges are assessed by time spent online. Access http://www.lexis.com. Dialog, a Thomson Company, also offers searching for a fee. Contact (800) 3-DIALOG or access http://www.dialog.com. Dialog's database is very comprehensive and includes the full text of utility patents in the United States as well as patents issued in several foreign countries.

Because searching is so difficult and typically requires knowledge of the prior art, many inventors employ professional search firms, similar to those that conduct trademark searches, to determine availability of a mark prior to filing an application for registration. The results are usually reviewed by a patent attorney who will then provide an opinion on the possibility of obtaining patent protection and/or the likelihood that an invention infringes another invention. The opinion should disclose the method of search, the databases covered by the search, whether foreign patents were reviewed, any limitations of the search, and the classifications searched. The opinion typically states that apparently favorable results from a search do not necessarily guarantee that a patent can be obtained and that, due to human error and mistakes in filing, it is possible that not all relevant patents were disclosed.

THE PATENT APPLICATION PROCESS

Overview of the Application Process

The process of preparing, filing, and shepherding a patent application through the PTO toward issuance is called "prosecution" (just as is the process of obtaining a trademark registration). An application may be filed by the inventor himself or herself or, as is more usual, by a patent attorney. Only 20 percent of all applications are filed by inventors without the assistance of attorneys. After the application is filed with the PTO, it will be assigned to one of more than 3,500 patent examiners having experience in the area of technology related to the invention who will review the application and conduct a search of patent records to ensure the application complies with the statutory requirements for patents (including novelty, usefulness, and nonobviousness). Generally, there will be some objection made by the examiner, which will be set forth in an office action. The applicant or attorney typically responds to the office action either by telephone or in writing. The process may continue for several rounds. If the rejections cannot be overcome, the application may be abandoned or the examiner's refusal may be appealed to the Board of Patent Appeals and Interferences. Alternatively, the examiner will accept the response(s) to the office action(s) and allow the application. A Notice of Allowance will be sent to the applicant, which specifies an **issue fee** that must be paid to the PTO in order for the patent to be granted. Until 2000, all patent applications were maintained in confidence. Since November 2000, however, most patent applications are published eighteen months after their filing date (although the applicant can avoid publication by certifying that the invention disclosed in the application has not and will not be the subject of an application filed in another country). Once a patent issues, however, the entire application file (the "file wrapper") becomes a matter of public record. Patents are granted for roughly 65 percent of all applications filed.

It generally takes anywhere from one to three years to prosecute a patent (in fiscal year 2002, the average time was twenty-four months), and costs and fees can range from $5,000 to more than $30,000, with fees generally ranging from $10,000 to $12,000. Because of the time and the high costs involved in obtaining a patent, inventors should conduct a cost-benefit analysis to determine whether the invention merits the effort and expense of obtaining a patent. If the invention will have limited application, it may not be worth securing a patent for it. On the other hand, if the invention is likely to be a commercial success, the time and expense involved in obtaining patent protection will be a worthwhile investment.

Patent Practice

While preparing trademark and copyright applications is relatively straightforward,

preparing a patent application requires skillful drafting as well as knowledge in the relevant field, whether that is biotechnology, chemistry, mechanical engineering, physics, computers, pharmacology, electrical engineering, and so forth. Because patent practice is highly technical, law firms that provide patent services to clients generally have a number of attorneys with different skill sets, and the patent department itself may be divided into different groups, such as a mechanical group, a biotech group, and an electrical group. Many **patent attorneys** possess both a law degree and an advanced degree in engineering, physics, chemistry, or the like. Due to the highly skilled nature of patent work, patent attorneys are highly marketable and often command salaries significantly higher than other attorneys. Similarly, other experienced IP professionals are also in high demand.

To represent patent applicants before the PTO, an attorney must be registered to practice with the PTO. An attorney must pass the Patent Bar, which requires the attorney to demonstrate background in science or engineering. The examination is very difficult, and the pass rate tends to hover around one-third. The examination includes a multiple-choice section as well as a written claim-drafting section. Generally, the test-taker can elect to draft a claim for one of three types of inventions: mechanical, chemical, or electrical. In a recent examination, most applicants chose to draft a claim for a mechanical patent for a corkscrewlike apparatus used to remove champagne corks.

In addition to the inventor himself or herself and registered patent attorneys, individuals called registered **patent agents** can prosecute patent applications. Patent agents are not attorneys but rather skilled engineers and scientists who take and pass the patent agent's examination. All are college graduates or must have the equivalent of such a degree. Attorneys may also take the patent agent's examination, which is designed to test knowledge in science and engineering and PTO rules. Although patent agents can engage in patent prosecution, they may not engage in activities that constitute the practice of law, such as representing parties in patent infringement actions or providing legal advice.

A list of attorneys and agents registered to practice before the PTO is available from the Government Printing Office located in Washington, DC. Alternatively, the PTO web site (http://www.uspto.gov/web/offices/dcom/olia/oed/roster/) provides an index to the more than 18,000 attorneys and agents who are licensed to practice before the PTO. Many cities also have attorney referral services that can recommend patent attorneys or agents. Finally, a local or state bar association may have associations of patent attorneys and agents.

Confidentiality of Application Process and Publication of Patent Applications

For more than 200 years, all patent applications filed with the PTO were maintained in strict confidence throughout the entire application process. Only when the patent issued was the file wrapper open to public inspection. Under the American Inventors Protection Act (AIPA) of 1999, however, which took effect in November of 2000, the PTO now publishes utility and plant applications eighteen months after their filing unless the applicant requests otherwise upon filing and certifies that the invention has not and will not be the subject of an application filed in a foreign country. If the applicant later decides to apply for a patent in a foreign country, the applicant must provide notice of this foreign filing to the PTO within forty-five days or the application will be regarded as abandoned.

Basic information about the patent is published and the information is accessible through the PTO's web site.

The intent of the new law is to harmonize U.S. patent procedures with those of other countries, almost all of which publish patent applications after an initial period of confidentiality. Most commercial inventors supported the idea of preissuance publication because it indicates trends in patents and allows inventors to design their new inventions in ways to avoid infringement. The new act protects inventors from having their inventions infringed by providing that patentees can obtain reasonable royalties if others make, use, or sell the invention during the period between publication and actual grant of the patent. In any event, once a patent application matures into an issued patent, the entire file wrapper is available for review by the public.

Types of Applications

Although the prosecution of patents is essentially the same for any type of patent application, there are different types of applications. They are as follows:

- **Provisional application.** Effective in 1995, and as a result of the adherence of the United States to the General Agreement on Tariffs and Trade (GATT), it is possible to file a **provisional patent application** with the PTO. A provisional application is less formal than a full utility patent application. It is intended as a relatively inexpensive and expeditious way of embarking on patent protection. A provisional application need not include any claims, and the filing fee is inexpensive ($160 for large entities and $80 for small entities). The applicant must, however, file for a standard utility patent within twelve months of filing the provisional application or the provisional application will be deemed abandoned. A provisional application is most useful when an inventor is in a race with a competitor and wishes to be the first to file an application. Filing a provisional application allows the inventor to mark the invention with the notice "patent pending." The twenty-year term for a utility patent begins with the filing of the actual utility patent. Thus, filing a provisional application and then filing a corresponding nonprovisional application allows an inventor to delay the start of the twenty-year period of patent protection. Moreover, it provides the inventor a simplified filing with a lower initial investment with one full year to assess the invention's commercial potential before committing to the higher costs of filing and prosecuting a standard utility patent. Although there are obvious advantages to filing a provisional patent application, there are disadvantages as well, primarily that the application will not be reviewed by an examiner during its twelve-month pendency. Thus, the inventor is left without any indication regarding the ultimate protection for his or her invention.

- **Utility application.** An inventor may file a utility application for a new, useful, and nonobvious process, machine, article of manufacture, or composition of matter or some improvement thereof. If a provisional application has previously been filed by an inventor, a **utility application** must be filed within twelve months of the filing date of the provisional application.

- **Design application.** A **design application** protects new, original, and ornamental designs for articles of manufacture.

- **Plant application.** A **plant application** protects new and distinctive asexually reproduced plants.

- **Continuation application.** A **continuation application** claims priority from a previously filed application. There are two types of continuation applications: the *continuation application* or *file wrapper continuation application* (a continuation patent filed when an examiner issues a final office action rejecting some claims in an application and the inventor wishes to allow the permitted claims to proceed and continue to pursue the rejected claims in a separate application) and the **continuation-in-part application** (which contains some matters in common with the original or "parent" application but also adds new matter, usually because an improvement to the invention was developed subsequent to the filing of the parent application).

- **PCT application.** A **PCT** (Patent Cooperation Treaty) **application** allows an applicant to file one application that may be relied upon for later filing in countries that are members of the **Patent Cooperation Treaty,** to which more than 100 nations belong, including the United States. PCT applications are administered by the World Intellectual Property Organization (WIPO). Because section 102 of the Patent Act bars patents that are the subject of patents in foreign countries, an inventor wishing to protect a discovery or invention would be required to file simultaneous applications in every country in which he or she desires patent protection in order to avoid the statutory bar of section 102. Such filings would be an extremely expensive gamble inasmuch as the applications might be denied in various countries or the inventor might discover there is no market for the invention in some countries and might wish to the two differences together even though it looks just as simple as 1+1=2. Only at the interval or higher level do we get to know that the difference between 3 and 4 is the same as the difference between 3 and 2, and adding them together will double the value of either difference or interval. Calendar dates and Fahrenheit or Celsius temperature are examples of interval variables.

Ratio measures not only contain the properties and obey the rules of all other lower levels, but also have a unique feature, that is, a "true" zero point. Therefore, ratios between the numbers reflect ratios of the attribute measured. A scale at the interval level, such as the Fahrenheit or the Celsius temperature scale, may have a zero point. But this only has a relative meaning and does not really mean "nothing." For a variable like age or income, on the other hand, the zero does have such a real, definite meaning. In mathematical terms, only when its zero means "nothing" can we compare the different values of a variable by applying the operations of multiplication and division. In such a case, the results of the comparison will have the full meaning of how many "times" a value is against another value of the same variable. Examples of ratio measures include age, income, and Kelvin degrees of temperature.

Nominal and ordinal variables are not calculable in terms of such mathematical operations as addition, subtraction, multiplication, and division. Most scales of theoretical constructs in psychosocial research, however, are created at the ordinal level. If we stick to the rules of the measurement level, those scales would have very limited use, or even be useless. The common practice in psychosocial research, therefore, is to treat ordinal scales as interval measures and subject them to needed mathematical operations, such as regression. The violation of the measurement rule seems to be tolerated by the research community, though you cannot take the practice for granted unless you really understand certain specific justifications. Whenever possible, you should refine your scales to make the intervals equitable (or at least appear to be equitable).

On the other hand, most simple psychosocial facts have not only equitable intervals but also "true" zero points. Such ratio measures include the indicators accounting for the duration of time, the frequency of events, and the number of objects. Ratio variables are most convenient for use in quantitative research. Sometimes, however, you may want to downgrade the variables by collapsing the detailed scales, or categorizing the whole bunch of scores into some simple categories. The values representing such categories can be at the interval level, the ordinal level, or the nominal level, depending on your research purpose. Generally speaking, you can always use a higher-level measurement result as a abandon the process. The PCT application process allows an inventor to file one application and then postpone prosecuting the applications in other member nations for thirty months. The filing date for each foreign country is deemed to be the date identified in the original application. Although often called an "international application," the application does not automatically result in registration in member nations of the PCT. The application must still be prosecuted separately in each individual nation in which the inventor desires protection. The primary purpose of a PCT application is to allow an inventor to delay filing in foreign countries until a determination is made about whether protection is desirable in those countries. Patent Cooperation Treaty (PCT) applications are discussed in Chapter 21.

- **Divisional application.** After an application is filed, the examiner may determine that the application covers more than one invention. Because each patent application can cover only one invention, a **divisional application** will be created to carve out a new application for the additional invention. The new divisional application typically retains the filing date of the original or parent application.

Preparing the Application

A utility patent application has two required components: a specification and an oath. If needed to understand the invention, a drawing is also required. A filing fee must also accompany the application. Although these elements are few, their importance cannot be underestimated. Drafting the specification (describing the invention) is difficult and painstaking work. For a complex invention, it may take forty hours or more. The level of detail and specificity imposed on applicants is a trade-off: in return for obtaining a twenty-year monopoly during which they may exclude others from selling, making, or using their inventions, inventors must fully disclose to the public what the invention is and exactly how it works.

Specification. The **specification** is the part of the application that describes the invention and the manner and process of making it and using it. It must be made in "such full, clear, concise, and exact terms as to enable any person skilled in the art . . . to make and use the same, and shall set forth the best mode contemplated by the inventor of carrying out his invention." 35 U.S.C. § 112.

Section 112 requires that the specification must be so complete as to enable one skilled in the art to make and use the invention. Thus, a general description such as "the invention is a high-speed drill" will be insufficient. In many instances, an application is rejected because of a **nonenabling specification,** meaning the specification is not sufficient to teach or enable another to make or use the invention. Simply put, stating what the invention is, is insufficient; the application must describe how the invention works. A specification may incorporate by reference other materials such as pending or issued patents, publications, and other documents as part of the enabling requirement.

In addition to the enabling requirement, the application must set forth the "best mode" or preferred method contemplated by the inventor for making the invention.

The specification itself is composed of several distinct elements:

- **Title.** The invention must be given a short and specific title that appears as a heading on the first page of the application. Examples of titles are "Track Ball for Computer System Cursor Control," "Nail Gun," and "Combined Refrigerator and Microwave Oven with Timed Overload Protection."

- **Cross-references to related applications.** If the application seeks the benefit of the filing date of a prior invention applied for by the same inventor or claims an invention disclosed in an earlier application by the same inventor, the second application must provide a cross-reference to the earlier application and identify it by serial number and filing date.

- **Background.** The **background** section of the specification should identify the field of the invention and discuss how the present invention differs from the known art. Generally, this section critiques other inventions and demonstrates the need and worth of the invention being applied for. A typical background section might discuss the shortcomings of existing similar inventions and itemize the benefits of the subject invention.

- **Summary of invention.** The summary section provides a short and general statement of the nature and substance of the invention. Because the summary and the background section are highly similar, some applications merge the two together into one called "Background and Summary of the Invention."

- **Brief description of drawings.** If drawings are included, they should be briefly described. The applicant must include a listing of all figures by number (for example, Figure 1-A) with corresponding statements explaining what each figure depicts.

- **Detailed description of the invention.** In this section, the invention must be explained along with the process of making and using the invention in full, clear, concise, and exact terms. This description must be sufficient so that any person of ordinary skill in the pertinent art or science could make and use the invention without involving extensive experimentation. The best mode contemplated by the inventor of carrying out the invention must also be set forth. Each element of the drawing should be mentioned. This section was previously called "Description of the Preferred Embodiments."

- **Claims.** A specification must include at least one **claim.** The claims define the scope of the invention. Although the language is precise, the inventor's goal is to draft the claims in such a way as to achieve the broadest possible scope of protection for the invention and yet comply with the statutory requirement of specificity. The claims are the most significant part of the application. The claims will be compared against the prior art to determine whether the invention is entitled to be patented. If the inventor later alleges another has infringed his or her invention, a court will compare the claims set forth in the patent with the alleged infringer's invention in determining whether infringement has occurred. There are two types of claims: independent claims, which describe the invention in a general manner, and dependent claims, which are more narrowly stated and incorporate all elements of the more broadly stated independent claim. Claims are often compared to the descriptions of real estate found in deeds that describe the "metes and bounds" of a parcel of property. A patent claim similarly describes the boundaries of the claimed invention. Each claim begins with a capital letter and ends with a period. The first claim listed is usually the least restrictive claim. One specific type of claim, called a **Jepson claim,** is used for improvements to existing inventions and identifies what is new to the invention. Design patent applications have only one claim, for example, "the ornamental design of a child's chair, as shown and described." Plant patents also have only one claim inasmuch as the entire plant is claimed as the inventive material. (See Exhibit 18–1 for a sample of claims.)

- **Abstract.** Strictly speaking, the abstract is not part of the specification but is rather a concise statement of the invention. The purpose of the abstract is to enable the PTO and the public to determine quickly the nature of the technical disclosures of the invention. It points out what is new in the art to which the invetion pertains. The abstract begins on a separate page and should not be longer than 150 words. The **abstract** should be a single short

paragraph. The abstract for U.S. Pat. No. 5,682,931, entitled "Baby Feeding Bottle" is as follows:

> A baby food jar is directly attachable to the top of a squeezable baby bottle so that the baby food jar can be inverted on the squeezable bottle to gravitationally transfer the baby food without spilling. Thereafter, a feeding member includes a nozzle which attaches directly to the squeezable baby bottle. The nozzle terminates in a baby feeding spoon. Squeezing the bottle delivers baby food directly to the spoon.

An abstract for a plant patent might read, "A hybrid tea rose having two-toned blossoms of pink with a white reverse."

Drawings, Models, and Specimens. If drawings are needed to understand the invention, they must be included. Nearly all patent

---

EXHIBIT 18–1
Claims for Utility Patent (U.S. Pat. No. 5,682,931)

> **What is claimed is:**
>
> 1. A baby feeding bottle comprising:
>   - A baby feeding bottle, said baby feeding bottle being made of resilient material so that it is squeezable to help in expelling the contents, said baby feeding bottle having a top and having an opening at said top, said baby feeding bottle being configured so that it can rest on a horizontal flat surface with said opening directed upwardly;
>   - means integral with said baby feeding bottle at said opening being nonremovable therefrom for detachably attaching a baby food jar thereto with the baby food jar in an inverted position when said baby feeding bottle is in an upright position; and
>   - a feeding structure, means for detachably attaching said feeding structure to said squeezable baby bottle at said opening thereof, said feeding structure having a spoon thereon sized for feeding a baby and an opening through said feeding structure from said attachment means to said spoon so that baby food can be delivered from said squeezable baby bottle to said spoon for one-handed feeding of a baby.

applications are accompanied by drawings. The drawings must also be described so that the viewer knows whether the drawing is a cross-section, a side view, and so forth. For example, the drawings might be described as follows: "Figure 3 is a right-hand perspective view of the child's chair. Figure 2 is a front plan view thereof." The PTO has stringent requirements relating to the size, symbols, and format of drawings, and usually a graphic artist or patent draftsperson is retained to prepare the drawings. Many law firms that practice patent law employ draftspersons on a full-time basis. Using new computer-assisted design and drawing software, some patent practitioners can prepare their own drawings. Informal drawings (photocopies) may be submitted if they are legible, but the examiner will usually impose a requirement that formal pen and ink drawings be submitted. The drawings must show every feature of the invention as specified in the claims.

Applicants were formerly required to submit a working model of the invention, but this requirement was eliminated in the late 1800s (although an examiner does have the authority to require that a working model be submitted). If the invention relates to a composition of matter, the PTO may require the applicant to furnish specimens or ingredients for the purpose of inspection or experiment.

Oath of Inventor. The applicant must sign an oath or declaration that he or she believes himself or herself to be the original and first inventor of the process, machine, manufacture, or composition of matter, or improvement thereof. The applicant must also identify his or her country of citizenship and provide an address. The applicant must acknowledge that he or she has reviewed and understands the contents of the application and understands the duty to disclose all information known to be relevant to the application.

The Patent Act requires that the person claiming the patent must be the actual inventor. 35 U.S.C. § 111. The applicant cannot be an assignee of the inventor. Thus, a review of the several million applications on file with the PTO will disclose that in nearly every case, the application has been made by an individual. Applications are not made by General Electric, Ford Motor Company, Westinghouse, or any other corporation or business entity. Although these companies may employ the inventors and may, in fact, own the invention (due to agreement between the parties that the employer will own any invention made by the employee), the application itself must be signed by the individual inventor. This requirement helps to ensure that inventions are not stolen by others. If an inventor cannot be found or refuses to file an application, an assignee may file the application upon showing such facts. If an inventor has died or is subject to some incapacity, his or her estate or legal representative may file the application.

If an invention has been made by two or more persons jointly, they must file the application jointly. A **joint application** may be made even if the inventors did not physically work together at the same time, did not each make the same type or amount of contribution, or did not each make a contribution to the subject matter of every claim in the patent. Accurate records should be kept regarding each inventor's contributions so that if one inventor's contributions are refused or dropped from the claims, he or she can be removed from the application. An application can be assigned to another person or company concurrently with the execution of a patent application or at any time thereafter. Concurrent assignments usually take place when companies own the inventions created by their employees. All assignments should be recorded with the PTO to provide public notice of the owner of the patent rights even though recordation is not required to make an assignment valid.

If anyone other than the actual inventor is filing the application, a power of attorney will be needed to authorize the patent attorney or patent agent to act on the inventor's behalf. The power of attorney may be a separate form or may be included as part of the oath or declaration. The PTO supplies a form for powers of attorney.

The requirements for preparing and filing design and plant patents are nearly identical to those discussed earlier for utility patents. Design patent applications, however, usually include a preamble stating the name of the applicant and the title of the design and a brief description of the nature and intended use of the article, and plant patent applications require the inventor's oath or declaration to confirm that the plant was reproduced asexually.

An oath is made before a notary, while a declaration is a statement by the applicant acknowledging that willful false statements are punishable by law. Either an oath or a declaration is acceptable.

Filing the Application.   After the application has been thoroughly reviewed to ensure it complies with PTO regulations (such as requirements relating to the size of the paper used and that all pages be numbered and one and one-half or double-spaced), the application package should be assembled for filing with the PTO. A transmittal letter should be prepared (the PTO provides a form—see Exhibit 18–2), and it should reference the following documents:

- the application (consisting of the specification, the oath, and drawings, if any);
- the enclosed filing fee (or instructions to the PTO to charge a deposit account maintained by the firm or agent for patent filings); and
- a self-addressed stamped postcard (so the PTO can stamp the filing date and serial number of the application and return it to the applicant for verification of filing).

Applicants may also submit an Application Data Sheet, a sheet supplied by the PTO that contains bibliographic data such as information about the applicant, correspondence information, and information as to whether the applicant is represented by a patent attorney or agent. Use of the Application Data Sheet allows the PTO to input records more accurately by scanning the information and thereby reducing errors in filing receipts. The PTO supplies the format for the Application Data Sheet.

If the application is being simultaneously assigned at the same time it is filed, a recordation form should be included. (The recordation form used for patent assignments is nearly identical to that used for trademarks shown in Chapter 5 as Exhibit 5–3. The PTO also provides a form for the assignment itself.)

To obtain a filing date for an application, all that is needed is the specification (including claims) and drawings, if needed. The oath and fee can be submitted later, although an additional fee will be assessed as a surcharge.

Any document sent to the PTO by regular or express mail should include a certificate consisting of a single sentence verifying the date the document was placed in the mail/express mail. In the event of a later dispute about filing dates of documents, the certificate of mailing will be accepted as proof of mailing on the date alleged. If there is no certificate of mailing, the filing date of the document will be deemed to be the date the PTO received it.

In October 2000, the PTO implemented its **Electronic Filing System (EFS)** for securely submitting utility patent applications and pre-grant publication submissions to the PTO. EFS allows applicants to prepare patent applications and assemble the various parts of the patent application and transmit the application to the PTO over the Internet. The PTO intends to continue expanding its electronic systems so that eventually all patent-related communications can be filed electronically.

PTO/SB/05 (03-01)
Approved for use through 10/31/2002. OMB 0651-0032
U.S. Patent and Trademark Office; U.S. DEPARTMENT OF COMMERCE
Under the Paperwork Reduction Act of 1995, no persons are required to respond to a collection of information unless it displays a valid OMB control number.

UTILITY PATENT APPLICATION TRANSMITTAL

(Only for new nonprovisional applications under 37 CFR 1.53(b))

Attorney Docket No.	
First Inventor	
Title	
Express Mail Label No.	

APPLICATION ELEMENTS

See MPEP chapter 600 concerning utility patent application contents.

1. ☐ Fee Transmittal Form (e.g., PTO/SB/17)
   (Submit an original and a duplicate for fee processing)

2. ☐ Applicant claims small entity status.
   See 37 CFR 1.27.

3. ☐ Specification [Total Pages _____]
   (preferred arrangement set forth below)
   - Descriptive title of the invention
   - Cross Reference to Related Applications
   - Statement Regarding Fed sponsored R & D
   - Reference to sequence listing, a table,
     or a computer program listing appendix
   - Background of the Invention
   - Brief Summary of the Invention
   - Brief Description of the Drawings *(if filed)*
   - Detailed Description
   - Claim(s)
   - Abstract of the Disclosure

4. ☐ Drawing(s) (35 U.S.C. 113) [Total Sheets _____]

5. Oath or Declaration [Total Pages _____]
   a. ☐ Newly executed (original or copy)
   b. ☐ Copy from a prior application (37 CFR 1.63 (d))
      (for continuation/divisional with Box 18 completed)
      i. ☐ <u>DELETION OF INVENTOR(S)</u>
         Signed statement attached deleting inventor(s)
         named in the prior application, see 37 CFR
         1.63(d)(2) and 1.33(b).

6. ☐ Application Data Sheet. See 37 CFR 1.76

ADDRESS TO:
Assistant Commissioner for Patents
Box Patent Application
Washington, DC 20231

7. ☐ CD-ROM or CD-R in duplicate, large table or
   Computer Program (*Appendix*)

8. Nucleotide and/or Amino Acid Sequence Submission
   (if applicable, all necessary)
   a. ☐ Computer Readable Form (CRF)
   b. Specification Sequence Listing on:
      i. ☐ CD-ROM or CD-R (2 copies); or
      ii. ☐ paper
   c. ☐ Statements verifying identity of above copies

ACCOMPANYING APPLICATION PARTS

9. ☐ Assignment Papers (cover sheet & document(s))

10. ☐ 37 CFR 3.73(b) Statement   ☐ Power of
    (when there is an assignee)   Attorney

11. ☐ English Translation Document *(if applicable)*

12. ☐ Information Disclosure   ☐ Copies of IDS
    Statement (IDS)/PTO-1449   Citations

13. ☐ Preliminary Amendment

14. ☐ Return Receipt Postcard (MPEP 503)
    (Should be specifically itemized)

15. ☐ Certified Copy of Priority Document(s)
    (if foreign priority is claimed)

16. ☐ Nonpublication Request under 35 U.S.C. 122
    (b)(2)(B)(i). Applicant must attach form PTO/SB/35
    or its equivalent.

17. ☐ Other: ....

18. If a CONTINUING APPLICATION, *check appropriate box, and supply the requisite information below and in a preliminary amendment, or in an Application Data Sheet under 37 CFR 1.76:*

☐ Continuation   ☐ Divisional   ☐ Continuation-in-part (CIP)   of prior application No.:_____/_____

Prior application information: Examiner:_____   Group Art Unit:_____

For CONTINUATION OR DIVISIONAL APPS only: The entire disclosure of the prior application, from which an oath or declaration is supplied under Box 5b, is considered a part of the disclosure of the accompanying continuation or divisional application and is hereby incorporated by reference. The incorporation <u>can only</u> be relied upon when a portion has been inadvertently omitted from the submitted application parts.

19. CORRESPONDENCE ADDRESS

☐ *Customer Number or Bar Code Label*   *(Insert Customer No. or Attach bar code label here)*   or ☐   *Correspondence address below*

Name	
Address	

City		State		Zip Code	
Country		Telephone		Fax	

Name (Print/Type)		Registration No. (Attorney/Agent)	
Signature			Date

Burden Hour Statement: This form is estimated to take 0.2 hours to complete. Time will vary depending upon the needs of the individual case. Any comments on the amount of time you are required to complete this form should be sent to the Chief Information Officer, U.S. Patent and Trademark Office, Washington, DC 20231. DO NOT SEND FEES OR COMPLETED FORMS TO THIS ADDRESS. SEND TO: Assistant Commissioner for Patents, Box Patent Application, Washington, DC 20231.

EXHIBIT 18–2
Utility Patent Application Transmittal

The PTO also offers its **Patent Application Information Retrieval (PAIR) System,** which allows patent applicants and their representatives to review the status of their pending patent applications online. There is both a "private" side to PAIR, allowing attorneys, patent agents, and inventors securely to access the PTO's internal database and track the status of applications, and a "public" side to PAIR, allowing members of the public to access issued patents and published applications. Access to PAIR's private side requires registration by the inventor or her representative.

Fees and Small Entity Status.   In order to provide encouragement to individual inventors, small entities or businesses, universities, and not-for-profit organizations, fees for these applicants are reduced by 50 percent of the standard fees (except those in connection with PCT or international patent applications). For businesses, a **small entity** is one with fewer than five hundred employees. While the small business cannot be the inventor, it is possible that, due to assignment, it is the owner of the patent rights, including the right to prosecute the application.

To claim the benefit of the reduced fees, the party must make a simple written assertion that it is entitled to small entity status. Specific forms are no longer required by the PTO, and a simple sentence will be sufficient. The assertion can be prepared and filed at the same time as the application and the reduced fee paid at that time. Alternatively, the small entity statement can be prepared and filed later and a refund will be made. If a party's small entity status changes during the prosecution of the application (often due to an outright assignment to a nonqualified party or internal growth of the applicant), full fees will be due from and after the date of change.

Effective January 1, 2004, the filing fee for a utility patent is $770. Small entities will pay $385. If there are independent claims in excess of three, claims in excess of twenty, or multiple dependent claims, additional fees are charged. The fee for filing a design patent is $340/$170, and the fee for filing a plant patent is $530/$265. The PTO web site provides a fee schedule. Because the fees are subject to change, it is a good idea to check the site periodically. (See Exhibit 18–3 for a schedule of patent fees.) Additionally, Congress is considering changes to the PTO fees, which will be included in the president's fiscal year 2004 budget. Among the highlights are a combined filing, search, and examination fee, due upon filing a utility patent application, that will initially total $1,000. Maintenance fees (due during the life of the patent) will be raised, and numerous other increases are contemplated. Thus, routine review of the PTO fee schedules posted at the PTO web site is critical.

Duty of Candor.   Patent applicants (and any individual associated therewith) are subject to a **duty of candor** and good faith in their dealings with the PTO and must therefore disclose to the PTO any information that is relevant to the patentability of a claimed invention. Violation of this duty may result in loss of patent rights. The applicant must therefore disclose prior art references that bear on the novelty or nonobviousness of the invention, printed publications that describe the invention, any possible use or sale of the invention, related domestic or foreign applications or patents, litigation involving the invention, and any other matter that bears on patentability. The PTO does not have the capabilities of fully researching all patent applications and thus relies on applicants to disclose prior art and other matters material to patentability.

Under PTO rules, information is material to patentability when it is not cumulative to information of record and (1) it establishes a *prima facie* case of unpatentability of a claim or (2) it refutes or is inconsistent with a position taken by the applicant. To comply with

Description	Fee	Small Entity Fee
Utility application filing fee	$770	$385
Design application filing fee	$340	$170
Plant application filing fee	$530	$265
Submission of IDS	$180	$180
Reissue filing fee	$770	$385
Provisional application filing fee	$160	$80
Issue fee for utility patent	$1,330	$665
Issue fee for design patent	$480	$240
Issue fee for plant patent	$640	$320
Maintenance fee due at $3^1/2$ years	$910	$455
Maintenance fee due at $7^1/2$ years	$2,090	$1,045
Maintenance fee due at $11^1/2$ years	$3,220	$1,610
Statutory disclaimer	$110	$55
Notice of appeal	$330	$165
Filing brief in support of appeal	$330	$165
Request for oral hearing	$290	$145
Request for *ex parte* reexamination	$2,520	$2,520

EXHIBIT 18–3
Schedule of Patent
Fees (as of 1/1/2004)

this duty, applicants file an **Information Disclosure Statement (IDS)** with the PTO listing and identifying material information. The PTO provides a form (see Exhibit 18–4) for such disclosure. The IDS can be filed with the application or within three months of its filing. If the IDS is not filed during these time limits, it may be filed later, but generally additional fees will be charged and other documents may be required. If a party discovers additional material information during the course of the application process, the new information must be disclosed. In many instances, an application may be withdrawn so the newly disclosed information can be considered in a continuation-in-part application.

Breach of the duty to disclose may result in refusal to issue a patent, invalidity of the patent, and possible sanctions against the patent attorney.

PROSECUTING THE APPLICATION

Examination of the Application

Once the application is filed and a **filing receipt** is sent by the PTO to the applicant (usually within thirty days after the application is filed), the application will be assigned to a patent examiner who is trained in the field to which the invention pertains. Examiners work in specialized groups or technology centers. The examiner will review the application, conduct a search in the patent files of the prior art, and determine if the invention is patentable. If the examiner finds defects in the application or rejects some of the claims, he or she will issue an office action (similar to the office action issued by trademark examiners in rejecting trademark applications). If the examiner determines there are no bars to patentability, a

PTO/SB/08a (05-03)
Approved for use through 05/31/2003. OMB 0651-0031
U.S. Patent and Trademark Office; U.S. DEPARTMENT OF COMMERCE
Under the Paperwork Reduction Act of 1995, no persons are required to respond to a collection of information unless it contains a valid OMB control number.

Substitute for form 1449A/PTO

INFORMATION DISCLOSURE STATEMENT BY APPLICANT

(Use as many sheets as necessary)

Sheet _____ of _____

Complete if Known

Application Number	
Filing Date	
First Named Inventor	
Art Unit	
Examiner Name	
Attorney Docket Number	

U. S. PATENT DOCUMENTS

Examiner Initials*	Cite No.[1]	Document Number	Publication Date MM-DD-YYYY	Name of Patentee or Applicant of Cited Document	Pages, Columns, Lines, Where Relevant Passages or Relevant Figures Appear
		Number-Kind Code[2] *(if known)*			
		US-			
		US-			
		US-			
		US-			
		US-			
		US-			
		US-			
		US-			
		US-			
		US-			
		US-			
		US-			
		US-			
		US-			
		US-			
		US-			
		US-			
		US-			

FOREIGN PATENT DOCUMENTS

Examiner Initials*	Cite No.[1]	Foreign Patent Document Country Code[3] Number[4] Kind Code[5] *(if known)*	Publication Date MM-DD-YYYY	Name of Patentee or Applicant of Cited Document	Pages, Columns, Lines, Where Relevant Passages or Relevant Figures Appear	T[6]

Examiner Signature		Date Considered	

*EXAMINER: Initial if reference considered, whether or not citation is in conformance with MPEP 609. Draw line through citation if not in conformance and not considered. Include copy of this form with next communication to applicant. [1] Applicant's unique citation designation number (optional). [2] See Kinds Codes of USPTO Patent Documents at _____ or MPEP 901.04. [3] Enter Office that issued the document, by the two-letter code (WIPO Standard ST.3). [4] For Japanese patent documents, the indication of the year of the reign of the Emperor must precede the serial number of the patent document. [5] Kind of document by the appropriate symbols as indicated on the document under WIPO Standard ST. 16 if possible. [6] Applicant is to place a check mark here if English language Translation is attached.

This collection of information is required by 37 CFR 1.97 and 1.98. The information is required to obtain or retain a benefit by the public which is to file (and by the USPTO to process) an application. Confidentiality is governed by 35 U.S.C. 122 and 37 CFR 1.14. This collection is estimated to take 2 hours to complete, including gathering, preparing, and submitting the completed application form to the USPTO. Time will vary depending upon the individual case. Any comments on the amount of time you require to complete this form and/or suggestions for reducing this burden, should be sent to the Chief Information Officer, U.S. Patent and Trademark Office, U.S. Department of Commerce, P.O. Box 1450, Alexandria, VA 22313-1450. DO NOT SEND FEES OR COMPLETED FORMS TO THIS ADDRESS. **SEND TO: Commissioner for Patents, P.O. Box 1450, Alexandria, VA 22313-1450.**

If you need assistance in completing the form, call 1-800-PTO-9199 and select option 2.

EXHIBIT 18–4
Information Disclosure Statement

PTO/SB/08b(05-03)
Approved for use through 05/31/2003. OMB 0651-0031
U.S. Patent and Trademark Office; U.S. DEPARTMENT OF COMMERCE
Under the Paperwork Reduction Act of 1995, no persons are required to respond to a collection of information unless it contains a valid OMB control number.

Substitute for form 1449B/PTO

INFORMATION DISCLOSURE STATEMENT BY APPLICANT

(Use as many sheets as necessary)

Complete if Known

Application Number	
Filing Date	
First Named Inventor	
Art Unit	
Examiner Name	
Attorney Docket Number	

Sheet _____ of _____

NON PATENT LITERATURE DOCUMENTS

Examiner Initials*	Cite No.[1]	Include name of the author (in CAPITAL LETTERS), title of the article (when appropriate), title of the item (book, magazine, journal, serial, symposium, catalog, etc.), date, page(s), volume-issue number(s), publisher, city and/or country where published.	T[2]

Examiner Signature		Date Considered	

*EXAMINER: Initial if reference considered, whether or not citation is in conformance with MPEP 609. Draw line through citation if not in conformance and not considered. Include copy of this form with next communication to applicant.
[1] Applicant's unique citation designation number (optional). [2] Applicant is to place a check mark here if English language Translation is attached.
This collection of information is required by 37 CFR 1.98. The information is required to obtain or retain a benefit by the public which is to file (and by the USPTO to process) an application. Confidentiality is governed by 35 U.S.C. 122 and 37 CFR 1.14. This collection is estimated to take 120 minutes to complete, including gathering, preparing, and submitting the completed application form to the USPTO. Time will vary depending upon the individual case. Any comments on the amount of time you require to complete this form and/or suggestions for reducing this burden, should be sent to the Chief Information Officer, U.S. Patent and Trademark Office, U.S. Department of Commerce, P.O. Box 1450, Alexandria, VA 22313-1450. DO NOT SEND FEES OR COMPLETED FORMS TO THIS ADDRESS. **SEND TO: Commissioner for Patents, P.O. Box 1450, Alexandria, VA 22313-1450.**

If you need assistance in completing the form, call 1-800-PTO-9199 and select option 2.

EXHIBIT 18–4
Information Disclosure Statement (continued)

lower-level variable, but the converse is not true. Therefore, it is to your advantage in a major project to record the original data at the highest possible levels since you can always manipulate them at the lower levels. If you record the original data at a lower level than where it could be by using some rougher categories, you will not have the precise measurement even if you need it later. In addition, at a given measurement level you should record the data in good detail, though too much detail may possibly lead to inaccurate information as well. For example, recording age by such rough categories as the aged, the middle-aged, and the young is usually not a good strategy since the measurement level is inappropriately and unnecessarily downgraded. You can go too far by asking for birth time, however, since asking for the hour and the minute of time at which a person was born would very likely yield unreliable and useless information. Recording only the year of birth is a most commonly seen practice, since for some respondents they may not even remember what exactly is their birth date.

There are some special types of measures at so-called log-interval and absolute levels (Sarle, 1996). Social and behavioral science research, however, seldom deals with issues associated with these special types. In refined statistical tests, the most frequently seen minium requirement is measurement at the interval level. It should be noted that this condition is sometimes expressed in terms of a continuous variable as opposed to a categorical variable. Strictly speaking, not all interval variables are really "continuous," and not all categorical variables have to be measured at the nominal level. An interval variable may become a categorical variable through categorization (i.e., the "collapsing" or grouping of values). In terms of the application of statistical procedures, the difference is often in the number of categories. That is, variables treated as categorical often have very few categories, whereas those considered continuous variables should have large enough numbers of categories with equitable intervals.

It should be stressed that quantification does not mean that you can rule out qualitative analysis. A qualitative understanding is indispensable at even the highest quantification level of measurement. Unfortunately, people tend to put "qualitative" against "quantitative," that is, anything qualitative means non-quantitative. They sometimes use the term "qualitative measurement." However, the emphasis should not be put on avoiding the use of numbers but on carrying more substantive meanings wherever possible. As a matter of fact, the lowest quantitative measurement level can at the same time be considered the most qualitative assessment level, with the numeric values allowing for the identificanotice of allowance will be issued for the application. Relatively few applications are allowed as filed. It generally takes about fifteen months for the PTO to issue a first office action.

It is far more likely that at least one office action will be issued, often indicating that based on the prior art, the subject matter claimed is either not novel or is obvious or that not enough information is disclosed in the application to enable another to practice what is claimed. The maximum time limit to respond to an office action is six months. Typically, however, the examiner demands that a response be filed within one, two, or three months. The applicant may then obtain extensions upon filing a petition asking for an extension and payment of a fee. If a written response to an office action is not timely filed, the application will be abandoned. If the final day for a response falls on a nonbusiness day or holiday, the applicant has until the next business day to file the response. The applicant may also request either a telephonic or in-person interview with the examiner to discuss the office action.

An applicant's response to an office action may include amendments to claims, drawings, or portions of the specification. Although amendments may be added to make explicit a disclosure that was implicit in the application as originally filed, amendments adding "new matter" are normally not allowed. Thus, claims may be amended and even added as long as they are supported by the original specifications in the application. If the applicant believes the examiner's rejection of some claims to be sound, those may be canceled and the applicant may proceed on the remainder. Alternatively, the applicant may submit argument attempting to demonstrate patentability and may submit evidence of secondary considerations, such as evidence of commercial success of the invention or its long-felt need.

The process of office action by the examiner and response by the applicant will continue until either the application is allowed or the examiner enters a **final action** rejecting one or more of the claims. An applicant may appeal a final action (or may initiate an appeal when his or her claims have been rejected twice) to the Board of Patent Appeals and Interferences in the PTO. An appeal fee ($330/$165) is required, and the applicant must file a brief to support his or her position. An oral hearing will be held, if requested, upon payment of a specified fee ($290/$145). If the board affirms the examiner's decision, the applicant may file a civil action in the U.S. District Court for the District of Columbia or may file an appeal with the Court of Appeals for the Federal Circuit (CAFC), located in Washington, DC. Many experts believe the Federal Circuit defers too readily to the board, noting that CAFC affirms between 75 and 90 percent of the board's determinations. The Federal Circuit can set aside PTO findings only when the findings are arbitrary, capricious, an abuse of discretion, or unsupported by substantial evidence. *Dickinson v. Zurko*, 527 U.S. 150 (1999). Decisions by CAFC may be appealed to the U.S. Supreme Court; however, the Supreme Court has the discretionary power to deny *certiorari* and refuse to hear the case.

While the PTO ordinarily examines patent applications in the order in which they are received, an applicant can file a **Petition to Make Special** to accelerate the examination process. Common reasons for requesting expedited examination include the age or health of the applicant, applications involving HIV/AIDS and cancer-related patents, applications that contribute to the conservation of energy resources, and applications that will enhance the quality of the environment. Additionally, an expedited procedure is available for applications for design patents in view of their sometimes short economic life. Requests to obtain expedited treatment usually require payment of a fee.

Restriction Requirements

If an inventor claims two or more independent and distinct inventions in one application, the examiner will issue a **restriction requirement,** requiring the applicant to restrict or limit the application to one invention. The other invention may be pursued in a divisional application for which a separate application fee must be paid. Independent inventions are those that are unconnected in their design, operation, or function. For example, combining a shoe with a locomotive bearing, two articles that are not capable of being used together, would result in a restriction requirement. An applicant may argue against the examiner's requirement that an application be restricted to one invention. Such an argument is called a **traverse.**

Divisional Applications

If the applicant agrees with the examiner that the application includes two independent and distinct inventions and agrees to restrict the application to one invention, the second invention is usually protected or covered by the creation of a divisional application, a separate and distinct application. The divisional application retains the filing date of its **parent application.** It is possible that creation of the divisional application may require changes in inventors inasmuch as the claims in the newly created divisional application may be the product of different inventors from those claims set forth in the original parent application.

Continuation Applications

If the examiner continues to refuse some claims in an application while accepting others, the applicant may wish to divide the application and allow the approved claims to proceed to issuance while continuing to do battle with the examiner on the rejected claims. Such a "continuation application" requires a separate filing fee. Because patents cannot be enforced until they are issued, and the period of protection runs for twenty years from the date of application, an applicant should consider the strategy of moving forward with whatever he or she can to obtain patent protection as soon as possible. Filing a continuation application affords the applicant the opportunity to continue argument on the disputed claims while allowing the permitted claims to proceed to issuance. Moreover, because the continuation application retains the same date as the earlier "parent" application, the continuation application may be able to circumvent "prior art" that came into being after the original filing date and that would bar an entirely new application. A continuation application contains no new material.

If an applicant wishes to proceed on allowed claims and pursue rejected and additional matter that differs from that in the parent application, the applicant will file a "continuation-in-part" application. Because the continuation-in-part application includes additional information not in the original application (often, new improvements recently discovered), it requires a new oath and declaration. A continuation-in-part application may have two filing dates: the original filing date for the original material and a new filing date for the newly added material.

As an alternative to filing a continuation application, the **American Inventors Protection Act (AIPA)** of 1999 allows patent applicants to request continued examination of a utility or plant application for a fee without requiring the applicant to file a continuing application. This process, called **Request for Continued Examination,** may be used even if the application is subject to a final rejection, appeal, or notice of allowance. The fee is $770/$385.

The distinction between a continuation application and a continuation-in-part application is that the former contains no new information while the latter includes new matter.

Double Patenting

Another basis for refusal to issue a patent is double patenting. An applicant may not obtain two patents for the same invention. The doctrine prohibiting double patenting is an attempt to ensure that inventors do not apply piecemeal for patents in an effort to extend the term during which they may preclude others from making, selling, or using the invention. A rejection based on double patenting may arise because of an applicant's related application or already issued patent for the same subject matter or subject matter that is an obvious variation of that in the application.

If the subject matter is identical, the applicant must cancel one set of claims. If the examiner states that the subject matter is not identical but is rather an obvious variation of that in another application or issued patent, and the examiner cannot be persuaded otherwise, the applicant may enter a terminal disclaimer, agreeing that the term of the second patent will not extend beyond the term of the first. Both patents will simultaneously terminate. A terminal disclaimer will remedy a refusal based on double patenting only if the refusal alleges that the second invention is an obvious variation of another. A refusal alleging that two identical inventions have been applied for or patented cannot be remedied by a terminal disclaimer. The duplicate claims in the second application must be canceled.

Interference Practice

In the course of examination, an examiner may discover that another party's pending application or issued patent conflicts with the application in that the subject matter claimed in the application under examination is substantially the same as that claimed in a prior application or existing patent. In such cases, an **interference** will be declared or initiated by the PTO, and a determination will be made regarding priority of invention by the Board of Patent Appeals and Interferences. About 1 percent of applications filed with the PTO become involved in an interference proceeding. In many of those cases, interferences are declared because, due to the initial confidentiality of PTO application proceedings, applicants may not know of other conflicting inventions at the time they file their applications. Because patents are typically issued to the "first to invent," a determination must be made by the PTO in regard to which invention has priority.

Generally, the inventor who proves to be the first to conceive the invention and the first to reduce it to practice either by filing the application (constructive reduction to practice) or by making and testing an embodiment of the invention (actual reduction to practice) will be held to be the first inventor. If an inventor is the first to conceive of the invention but the second to reduce it to practice, he or she may still prevail upon a showing that reasonably diligent efforts were made to reduce the invention to practice.

After holding a hearing and receiving testimony, the board will issue a decision. Appeal may be made to CAFC. A dissatisfied party also has the option of initiating a civil action in the U.S. District Court for the District of Columbia to determine the matter. Alternatively, during the course of any interference proceeding, the parties may reach a private settlement that will be binding on the PTO if they file their agreement resolving the matter with the PTO.

Notice of Allowance and Issuance of Patent

If the PTO allows the claims and determines that the applicant is entitled to a patent, a notice of allowance will be sent to the applicant. The notice of allowance will specify a sum for an issue fee, which must be paid for the patent to be granted. The sum specified in the notice of allowance will also include the publication fee, both of which must be paid within three months to avoid abandonment of the application. You will recall that effective November

2000, all utility patent applications are published eighteen months after filing if there is an equivalent foreign filing. At present, the issue fee for a utility patent is $1,330 ($665 for a small entity), $480/$240 for a design patent, and $640/$320 for a plant patent. When the issue fee is paid, the patent will be granted and a patent number and issue date will be given to the application. The applicant, now the **patentee,** may enforce its rights to exclude others from making, selling, or using the invention. Furthermore, once a patent is issued, there is a statutory presumption of its validity. 35 U.S.C.

§ 282. On the date of the grant by the PTO, the entire patent file becomes open to the public. Failure to pay the issue fee when due will result in abandonment of the application (unless late payment was unavoidable or unintentional and a showing is made demonstrating such).

It generally takes between two and three years for a patent to be issued, compared with four to five months for registration of a copyright and approximately eighteen months to secure trademark registration.

(See Exhibit 18–5 for a flowchart illustrating the patent prosecution process.)

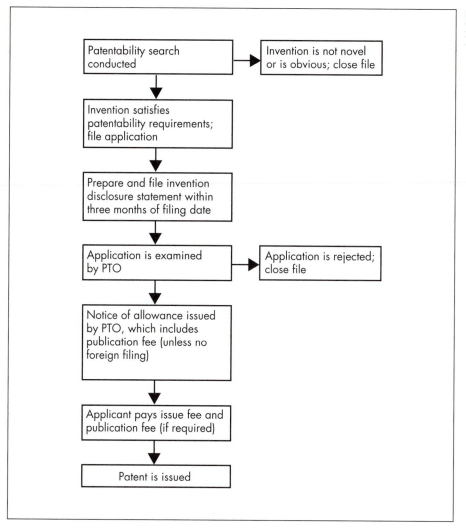

EXHIBIT 18–5
Patent Prosecution
Flowchart

Portions of the issued patent will be published in the *Official Gazette,* the weekly publication of the PTO. While the purpose of publishing trademarks in the *Official Gazette* is to provide notice so those who may be damaged by registration of a mark may oppose registration, publication of patents in the *Official Gazette* is done merely to provide information about patents, including patents that may be available for sale or license. The *Official Gazette* will include a claim and a selected figure of the drawings of each patent granted on that date, notices of patent lawsuits, a list of patents available for license or sale, and other general information such as changes in patent rules.

Utility patents are assigned numbers such as 4,999,904. Design patents are assigned a number as well as the letter "D," such as D339,456. Plant patents are assigned a number and the letters "PP," as in PP4,074.

(See Exhibit 18–6 for a sample of an issued patent.)

Notice of Patent

During the time that the application for the patent is pending, an inventor may mark the invention with the term *patent pending* or *patent applied for.* These notices have no legal effect, although they do provide notice that a patent application has been filed with the PTO. Use of these terms or any other implying that an application for a patent has been made, when it has not, is a violation of statute and is punishable by fine. 35 U.S.C. § 292.

Once a patent has been issued, its owner may give notice that an article or invention is patented by using the word *patent* or its abbreviation *pat.,* together with the number of the patent. The notice may be placed on the article or on a label attached to the article. Use of the notice is not mandatory; however, in the event of failure to use the notice, no damages may be recovered by the patentee in any infringement action, unless it is proved that the infringer was notified of the infringement and continued to infringe thereafter. Marking of the patented invention constitutes such notice. Thus, although use of the notice is not required, it is always recommended. False marking is prohibited and is punishable by fine.

POSTISSUANCE ACTIONS

Correction of Defective Patents: Certificates of Correction and Reissue Patents

Errors occurring through the fault of the PTO, minor errors (such as typographical errors), and errors in the naming of inventors can be corrected by asking the PTO to issue a "Certificate of Correction." Mistakes made by the PTO will be corrected without charge. Mistakes made by the applicant will be corrected upon the payment of a $100 fee.

Errors that are more significant, such as defects in the specifications or drawings, that cause the patent to be partially or wholly inoperative or invalid are corrected by a **reissue patent.** A reissue patent may also be sought for the purpose of enlarging claims. The patentee's attorney may have failed to state the claims broadly enough or the patentee may discover that the claims stated in the issued patent are narrower than the prior art would require the patentee to make. In cases in which the patentee seeks to broaden claims, a reissue application must be filed within two years of the grant of the original patent. A reissue application can be made only if the error was committed without deceptive intent. While claims may be enlarged because the patentee originally claimed less than he or she had a right to claim, no new matter may be allowed.

An oath or declaration must be filed and facts must be set forth showing the grounds for the application for reissue. The filing fee for a reissue application is $770/$385 (the same as that for an original application). A reissue application is examined under the same procedures as any application. If the application is granted, the original patent is surrendered. The reissue patent is identified by the prefix "RE" in the PTO records, for example, RE35,312, and its term is the same as that of the original patent inasmuch as it is granted to replace the original patent.

It is possible that during the two-year period before a reissue application is made, a

EXHIBIT 18–6
Issued Patent

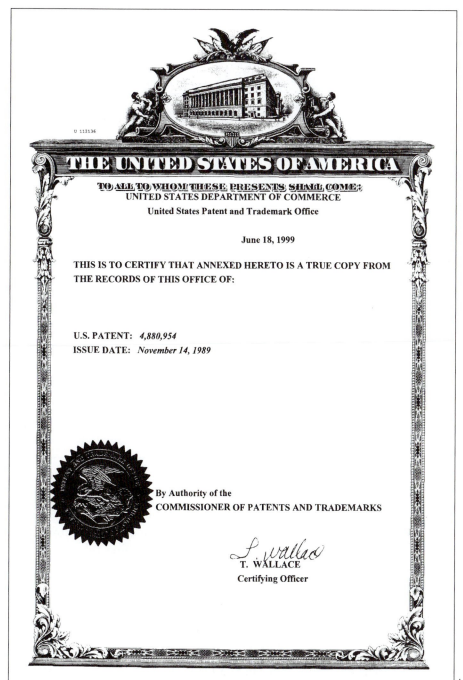

THE UNITED STATES OF AMERICA

TO ALL TO WHOM THESE PRESENTS SHALL COME:
UNITED STATES DEPARTMENT OF COMMERCE

United States Patent and Trademark Office

June 18, 1999

THIS IS TO CERTIFY THAT ANNEXED HERETO IS A TRUE COPY FROM THE RECORDS OF THIS OFFICE OF:

U.S. PATENT: *4,880,954*
ISSUE DATE: *November 14, 1989*

By Authority of the
COMMISSIONER OF PATENTS AND TRADEMARKS

T. WALLACE
Certifying Officer

(continues)

EXHIBIT 18–6
Issued Patent
(continued)

United States Patent [19]

Bennett et al.

[11]   **Patent Number:**   **4,880,954**

[45]   **Date of Patent:**   **Nov. 14, 1989**

[54]   **COMBINED REFRIGERATOR AND MICROWAVE OVEN WITH TIMED OVERLOAD PROTECTION**

[76]   Inventors: **Robert P. Bennett,** 49 Francis Wyman Rd., Burlington, Mass. 01803; **Kunimitsu Ozaki,** 721 Mikan Dr., Richmond, Ind. 47374

[21]   Appl. No.:   **201,903**

[22]   Filed: **Jun. 3, 1988**

[51]   **Int. Cl.⁴** H05B 6/68
[52]   **U.S. Cl.** .... **219/10.55 M;** 219/10.55 B; 219/10.55 R; 221/150 HC; 307/41; 307/30; 361/22
[58]   **Field of Search** .... 219/10.55 B, 10.55 R, 219/10.55 E, 10.55 C, 10.55 M, 10.55 D, 485, 486; 307/38, 41, 35, 30; 221/150 HC; 361/22, 31, 195

[56]   **References Cited**
U.S. PATENT DOCUMENTS

T973,013	8/1978	Ferrara et al.	219/10.55 E X
3,482,509	12/1969	Gardner	219/10.55 R
4,004,712	1/1977	Pond	219/10.55 B
4,045,640	8/1977	McQueen, Jr. et al.	219/10.55 B
4,068,781	1/1978	Toth	219/485
4,129,769	12/1978	Takagi et al.	219/10.55 B
4,225,204	9/1980	Bellavoine	219/386
4,227,062	10/1980	Payne et al.	219/10.55 B
4,398,651	8/1983	Kumpfer	219/10.55 B
4,592,485	6/1986	Anderson et al.	221/150 HC

Primary Examiner—Philip H. Leung
Attorney, Agent, or Firm—Morris Fidelman; Franklin D. Wolffe

[57]   **ABSTRACT**

A microwave oven and a refrigerator are combined in a single cabinet and share line power supplied to the cabinet. Door interlocks and a manually settable time are provided for disconnecting electrical supply to the compressor of the refrigerator during operation of the magnetron of the microwave oven. The circuitry provided ensures that electrical supply is reconnected to the compressor upon expiration of the timer setting, even if the door of the oven is incidentally left open after use.

3 Claims, 2 Drawing Sheets

---

third party has begun offering a device that does not infringe the original patent claims but which now infringes the reissue patent with its broader claims. In such a case, the third party may continue offering the device without liability for infringement. According to 35 U.S.C. § 252, no reissued patent shall affect the right of such an intervening party to continue to use or sell a device or invention unless the device or invention infringes a valid claim of the reissued patent that was in the original patent as well; otherwise, the significant investment an innocent third party might make in bringing a product to market would be lost. The intervening party, however, may continue to make or sell only the same specific thing; no additional devices can be offered.

Reexamination

When trademarks are published for opposition in the *Official Gazette,* third parties who

U.S. Patent Nov. 14, 1989 Sheet 1 of 2 **4,880,954**

Fig.1

Fig.2

EXHIBIT 18–6
Issued Patent
(continued)

(continues)

believe they may be harmed by registration of the mark may oppose registration of the mark. Similarly, even after trademark registration, a registration may be canceled on certain grounds, including confusing similarity to a prior mark. Federal law affords no equivalent rights to a party to oppose the issuance of a patent or to cancel a patent on the basis he or she would be harmed by its issuance. In fact, because pending patent applications are kept confidential until their time of publication eighteen months after initial filing (unless the applicant certifies there is or will be no foreign equivalent to the application), parties seldom know whether an application has been filed for a patent.

Nevertheless, 35 U.S.C. §§ 301 and 302 provide that any person, including either the patent

EXHIBIT 18–6
Issued Patent
(continued)

4,880,954

1

COMBINED REFRIGERATOR AND MICROWAVE OVEN WITH TIMED OVERLOAD PROTECTION

PRIOR ART CROSS REFERENCES

U.S. Pat. No. 3,482,509 Gardner, SANDWICH COOKING AND DISPENSING MACHINE, issued Dec. 9, 1969.

U.S. Pat. No. 4,225,204—Bellavoine, CUPBOARD FOR STORING PREPARED MEALS, WITH COLD-STORAGE AND REHEATING BY MICROWAVES, issued Sept. 30, 1980.

U.S. Pat. No. 4,398,651 Kumpfer, MICROWAVE FOOD DISPENSING MACHINE, issued Aug. 16, 1983.

U.S. Pat. No. 4,592,485—Anderson, et al, MEAL VENDING APPARATUS, issued June 3, 1986.

U.S. application Ser. No. 097,680—Bennett, REFRIGERATOR AND MICROWAVE OVEN AND OVERDEMAND INTERRUPT CIRCUIT, filed Sept. 17, 1987.

BACKGROUND OF THE INVENTION

This invention relates to a refrigerator and microwave oven enclosed in the same cabinet with unique electrical circuitry, so as to provide the convenience of storing and cooking food simultaneously in the same unit, while avoiding the peak power demands of simultaneous operation of the refrigerator compressor and the microwave magnetron. The invention finds particular application in buildings having older wiring and fewer circuits, by minimizing the possibilities of overloading such circuits while providing safe uninterrupted service. It also prevents overloading a more modern circuit which is "dedicated" to the apparatus by preventing start-up of the compressor during operation of the magnetron.

Microwave ovens are now commonly available in quick stop grocery stores and lunch rooms for heating and cooking foodstuffs purchased across the counter and from vending machines. Prior to the above-referenced Bennett application though, it had not been proposed to combine a microwave oven and refrigerator on a smaller scale in the same cabinet, particularly with provision for limiting the peak instantaneous power consumption so as to make the combination useful and attractive for use by students in dorm rooms, resort hotel rooms, tractor trailer cabs, recreational vehicles, so-called pullman efficiencies and the like.

The remaining prior art teaches refrigerated storage and a microwave oven combined in the same vending machine cabinet, and provision for transporting a selected item to the microwave oven for heating and subsequent removal from the machine. In particular, U.S. Pat. No. 4,398,651 discloses a switch, associated with a stack of food containers and actuated upon insertion of the uppermost container from the stack into a microwave oven, which causes a motor to drive a screw which, in turn, raises the stack until the next uppermost container changes the state of the switch. The amount of time that it takes for the switch to be changed by the raising stack determines the time of de-energization of a relay 56 which, in turn, determines how long the refrigerator is off and the microwave oven is on.

It is among the objects of the instant invention to combine prior art appliances into a single more convenient apparatus by utilizing a single molded, insulated shell containing both a microwave oven and a refrigera-

2

tor, while at the same time providing adequate ventilation of both and limiting instantaneous peak power consumption by the combination.

SUMMARY OF THE INVENTION

A microwave oven and a refrigerator are combined in a single cabinet and share line power supplied to the cabinet. Door interlocks and a manually settable time are provided for disconnecting electrical supply to the compressor of the refrigerator during operation of the magnetron of the microwave oven. The circuitry provided ensures that electrical supply is reconnected to the compressor upon expiration of the timer setting, even if the door of the oven is incidentally left open after use.

BRIEF DESCRIPTION OF THE DRAWINGS

FIG. 1 is an isometric view of a microwave oven and refrigerator sharing a common housing.

FIG. 2 is a schematic diagram illustrating an electrical circuit providing features of the instant invention.

FIG. 3 is a schematic circuit diagram of a conventional microwave oven.

DETAILED DESCRIPTION OF THE INVENTION

Referring to the drawings, cabinet 10 houses a microwave oven upper section 12 and a refrigerator lower section 14, with louvers 13 for venting the microwave section and cord 11 for supplying power to the combined refrigerator and microwave device from the standard receptacle.

The basic housing 10 comprises molded inner and outer shells with appropriate insulation therebetween, and these shells may be comprised of several panels defining sides, top, bottom, front and back of the device. The construction of the refrigerator section generally is well known and includes a freezer compartment. Below or at the rear of the refrigerated compartment and above the bottom panel is a refrigeration unit including condenser coils (not shown), while heat transfer mesh or screen is attached at the rear of the unit.

Above refrigerator section 14, and thermally insulated therefrom, is the microwave oven section 12 having the cooking compartment thereof surrounded by an absorptive layer. The absorptive layer is for preventing microwave energy from (1) reflecting from the outer wall and back to the magnetron of the microwave oven and thus damaging the magnetron, (2) warming foodstuffs in adjacent refrigerator compartments, and (3) escaping from the unit to the surrounding environment.

Of particular importance in the invention is the provision of a timing circuit 30 for controlling power to the magnetron and the compressor of the refrigerator.

Referring to FIG. 3, the magnetron of a conventional microwave is supplied with power via a transformer. In FIG. 3, the door of the oven is open and, upon closing thereof, the interlock switches S2 are closed and switch S3 is opened. Thus, the door must be closed in order for line power to be supplied to the timer switch S1 and to the transformer.

However, in order to combine a microwave oven and refrigerator in the same cabinet, while sharing line power supplied to the cabinet in the least costly and most efficient manner, it is necessary to ensure that the magnetron of the oven and the compressor of the refrigerator are not operated at the same time.

(continues)

owner or an accused infringer of a patent, may file a request for reexamination of any claim in an issued patent based upon the prior art, namely, patents or printed publications that may have a bearing on the patentability of a claim. A request for reexamination may be made at any tion of all kinds of qualitative differences.

Composite measures and measurement dimensions

We have noted a major difference among psychosocial research variables in terms of their simplicity or complexity. Race or sex, for instance, is a simple fact and can be measured with a single indicator or question item, of which the value or answer may easily be determined. Other variables, especially such theoretical constructs as "stress," tend to present more than one aspect for a conceptual field, which is broader than what any single item or indicator could cover. In such cases, multiple items or indicators are required to form a composite measure of the construct.

It should be noted that any conceptual field can be regarded as a system containing different levels and subsystems. If we take the entire system as a "black box" and ignore its internal structure, then one general indicator would suffice to provide the needed assessment. This kind of measurement, however, is not always comforting; we oftentimes wish to clarify the elements and components as a base for our measurement. In such cases, multiple indicators are usually required for the construction of a composite measure. From this point of view, the difference between the two kinds of variables (the simple and the complex) may also be interpreted as the difference between two approaches to measurement (the general and the specific). Each approach has its merits and drawbacks, or advantages and disadvantages. How to incorporate the strengths of both approaches and compensate for their weaknesses is an important topic to be addressed in chapter twelve. Here we will further discuss the main issues in the analytic and specific approach. As a matter of fact, few people, if any, would consider that directly adopting a general and simple indicator for the measurement of a complex variable is desirable, accurate, and really comprehensive.

The first issue with the analytic approach to measurement is how to cover a complex conceptual field. You may have encountered this issue in operationalizing a theoretical construct. In establishing your conceptual framework you have clarified the components and elements to a certain degree of detail. In considering the possible items for a limited number of the multiple indicators you will find more, sometimes even countless, choices. Determining which items to use may be overwhelmingly difficult, since any arbitrary selection will likely subject you to some criticism.

EXHIBIT 18–6
Issued Patent
(continued)

4,880,954

3

As seen in FIG. 2, the instant invention provides that the manually settable timer of a microwave oven interrupts line power to the refrigerator compressor by means of switch S4 whenever the timer is operating, while providing that same line power to the microwave oven and magnetron thereof in a manner that ensures the availability of line power to the refrigerator compressor upon completion of the timing function, even if the door of the microwave has been left open. In other words, with the timer manually set and actuated so that power is supplied to the timer motor via switch 54 according to a desired cooking time by the microwave oven, and with the door of the oven closed so that the interlock switches S2 and S3 allow supply of line power to the transformer of the microwave, opening the door of the prior to completion of the timing function will open switches S2 and interrupt power to the magnetron, but not to the timer. Thus, if the door is left open, line power can again be supplied to the compressor via switch S4 at the end of the previously selected timing period.

Having described the invention, it will be seen that the objects set forth above, among those made apparent from the preceding description, are efficiently obtained and, since certain changes may be made in carrying out the above method and in the construction set forth without departing from the scope of the invention, it is intended that all matter contained in the above description or shown in the accompanying drawings shall be interpreted as illustrative and not in a limiting sense.

It is also to be understood that the following claims are intended to cover all of the generic and specific features of the invention hereindescribed, and all statements of the scope of the invention which, as a matter of language, might be said to fall therebetween.

Now that the invention has been described, I claim:

1. In a method of operating a compressor of a refrigerator and a magnetron of a microwave oven, said re-

4

frigerator and microwave oven being combined in a single cabinet, the improvement comprising the steps of:

providing said microwave oven with manually settable means for timing supply of operating power to said magnetron for different, selectable periods of time;

setting said timing means according to each desired period of operation of said magnetron;

starting and operating said timing means according to said setting; and

preventing operation of said refrigerator compressor by and during said operating of said timing means.

2. In an electrical supply control circuit for a compressor of a refrigerator and a magnetron of a microwave oven, said refrigerator and microwave oven being combined in a single cabinet and sharing line power supplied to said cabinet, the improvement comprising:

manually settable means for timing supply of operating power to said magnetron for different, selectable periods of time; and

means for interrupting a power path to said refrigerator compressor during said operating of said timing means.

3. In an electrical supply control circuit for a compressor of a refrigerator and a magnetrom of a microwave oven, said refrigerator and microwave oven being combined in a single cabinet and sharing line power supplied to said cabinet, said microwave oven being provided with a door having interlock means for interrupting power to said magnetron when said door is open, the improvement comprising:

manually settable means for timing supply of operating power to said magnetron for different, selectable periods of time;

means for interrupting a power path to said refrigerator compressor during said operating of said timing means; and

circuitry means for reestablishing said power path upon cessation of said timing means even when said door is open.

* * * * *

time during the term of enforceability of the patent and must be accompanied by a filing fee of $2,520.

Within three months following the filing of a request for reexamination, the PTO will determine whether a substantial new question of patentability affecting any claim of the patent has been raised. If the PTO determines that a substantial question is raised, **reexamination of the patent** will be ordered so the question may be resolved. Reexamination procedure is identical to the procedure for initial examination of a patent application. The patent owner is permitted to amend his or her claims to distinguish them from the prior art, although no new matter enlarging or broadening the scope of a claim is permitted. If a reexamined claim is determined to be unpatentable, it will be canceled. If a reexamined claim is confirmed as patentable, a certificate of confirmation or reexamination certificate will be issued by the PTO. The Patent Act requires that reexamination procedure be conducted with "special dispatch."

The reexamination procedure can provide an alternative to litigation. Prior to commencing an infringement action, either the patent owner or the potential defendant may request reexamination of an issued patent. Reexamination is less expensive and more expeditious than patent infringement litigation, confirms that claims are patentable, and may thus provide impetus for the parties to settle a dispute. Moreover, the AIPA established a reexamination alternative that expands the participation of third parties by permitting those parties to submit a written response each time the patent owner files a response to the PTO. This allows third parties to "weigh in" in reexamination proceedings when they believe a patent is invalid or overly broad.

Disclaimers

A patent owner who discovers that a claim in a patent is invalid may cancel the claim by filing a *disclaimer*. 35 U.S.C. § 253. The other claims remain valid and are unaffected by the disclaimer of the affected claim. A patent owner is not required to cancel an invalid claim, but cannot recover costs in an infringement suit alleging infringement of the valid claims unless the invalid claim is canceled prior to commencement of the lawsuit. 35 U.S.C. § 288.

TERM AND MAINTENANCE OF PATENTS

Term of Patents

For a number of years, the term of a utility patent was seventeen years from the date of issuance. To align the U.S. patent system with that of most European countries and Japan, effective June 8, 1995, the term of utility and plant patents was changed from seventeen years from issuance to twenty years from the date of filing of the application. The new provisions thus encourage inventors to prosecute applications in a timely manner. Under special statutory provisions, patents in existence or issued under applications filed before June 8, 1995, have a term of seventeen years from issuance, or twenty years from filing, whichever is longer. The term for design patents is fourteen years from the date of issuance. After the term for any patent expires, anyone in the public has a right to make, use, or sell the invention or process (assuming no other government agency approval, such as that of the FDA, is required).

There are some rare exceptions to the twenty-year term. For example, if the application has been subject to an interference action, the term is extended for the period of delay (assuming the delay does not extend more than five years). Similarly, because certain patented items, such as drugs, cannot be marketed until they are reviewed by agencies such as the FDA and such review may take considerable time, the patent term may be extended, generally by a time equal to the regulatory review period. Patent terms can also be extended if the patent application was subject to a successful appellate review or if a **secrecy order** (orders generally imposed by the government to protect inventions relating to national security) delayed issuance of the patent.

Additionally, under AIPA, the term of patents was extended to compensate for certain PTO processing delays and for delays in the prosecution of applications pending more than three years. Subtitled, "The Patent Term Guarantee Act of 1999," this portion of the AIPA guarantees diligent applicants a minimum seventeen-year patent term. The term of a patent is extended one day for each day lost (up to a maximum of five years) as a result of various PTO administrative delays or delays caused by interferences, secrecy orders, or successful appeals.

Maintenance Fees

To maintain a utility patent in force, certain fees must be paid to the PTO at three times throughout the term of the patent. **Maintenance fees** are due at the $3\frac{1}{2}$-, $7\frac{1}{2}$-, and $11\frac{1}{2}$-year anniversaries of the date of issuance. If the maintenance fees are not paid on or within six months before the due date or within a six-month grace period thereafter, the patent will expire at the end of the grace period. A surcharge is assessed if payment is made within the six-month grace period. Patents that expire for nonpayment of maintenance fees can be revived only upon a showing of unavoidable or unintentional delay.

At present, the maintenance fees are as follows:

Due Date	Regular Fee/ Small Entity Fee
Due at $3\frac{1}{2}$ years:	$910/$455
Due at $7\frac{1}{2}$ years:	$2,090/$1,045
Due at $11\frac{1}{2}$ years:	$3,220/$1,610

The surcharge for late payments made within six months of the due date is $130/$65. The PTO estimates that most patentees will pay the PTO a minimum of $4,000 over the life of a patent.

No maintenance fees are due for design or plant patents.

TRIVIA

- The youngest person granted a patent was a four-year-old from Texas whose patent was for an aid for grasping round knobs.
- During fiscal year 2001, the PTO became the first intellectual property office in the world to offer electronic filing for patents over the Internet.
- By the end of 2001, there were more than 2,000 patent applications filed electronically at the PTO.
- The design patent for the Congressional Medal of Honor was granted in 1904.

CHAPTER SUMMARY

Once a patent search has been conducted to determine an invention is novel and nonobvious, a patent application can be prepared. The patent application consists of a specification describing the invention and the inventor's oath or declaration. Applicants have a duty of candor in their dealings with the PTO and must disclose anything that bears on the patentability of the invention. Applications filed at the PTO are maintained in confidentiality until their publication. Once a patent issues, the entire file wrapper is available for review and copying. Once the application is filed, it will be examined by an examiner who will review the specification and determine patentability. One or more office actions may be issued to amend or clarify the claims. No new matter can be added to a pending application. Once the examiner allows the application, an issue fee must be paid for the patent to be granted. Utility and plant patents have a term of twenty years from the date of application while design patents have a term of fourteen years from the date of grant. Patentees must pay fees at three different intervals to maintain a utility patent. The invention may be marked with a notice of patent, which will assist the inventor in recovering damages from infringers. After a patent has been issued, the patentee may request reissuance to correct a defective patent or to broaden claims if the application for reissuance is filed within two years after the original patent was granted. Either the patentee or a third party may request reexamination of a patent at any time during its term to determine if the patent or any of its claims are invalid.

CASE ILLUSTRATION—SCOPE OF PATENT CLAIMS

Case: *The Gentry Gallery, Inc. v. The Berkline Corp.*, 134 F.3d 1473 (Fed. Cir. 1998)

Facts: Gentry owned a patent relating to controls placed on reclining sofas. Claim 1 of Gentry's patent application claimed a pair of controls mounted on a fixed console in the sofa. Berkline's sofas, which placed the controls on armrests, seat edges, and so forth, were alleged to infringe the claims in Gentry's patent.

Holding: Gentry's disclosure in its Claim 1 unambiguously limited the location of the controls to the console. Claims may be no broader than the supporting disclosure. Thus, because the disclosure did not support claims in which the location of the recliner controls was other than the console, Berkline's product did not infringe Gentry's patent. Locating the controls anywhere but on the console was outside the stated purpose of the invention.

CASE STUDY AND ACTIVITIES

Case Study. Watson's design engineers recently invented a new style of talking storybooks and filed one application for a patent for this invention and a new closed-circuit television monitoring system for security at the park. The security system is a variation of Watson's original monitoring system patented ten years ago. After the application was filed, the PTO refused some of the claims relating to the talking storybooks although most of the claims were approved. During the prosecution process, the PTO temporarily lost the application file for the talking storybooks.

Activities. Discuss any likely PTO objections to Watson's application and any possible strategies Watson could adopt to obtain patent protection as expeditiously as possible and for the longest possible period of time.

ROLE OF PARALEGAL

Paralegals are involved in a variety of tasks in the patent prosecution process, including the following:

- conducting online searches to locate and retrieve patents that may bar a client's application for a patent;
- drafting claims and preparing patent applications;
- coordinating and assembling drawings for application;
- verifying small entity status;
- assisting in the patent application process by drafting and securing inventor's oath or declaration, drafting descriptions of drawings, and preparing small entity statement, if applicable;
- assembling the application packet and preparing the transmittal letter and the Application Data Sheet;
- preparing assignment of patent application and invention and recordation document for same, if applicable;
- preparing and filing information disclosure statements;
- docketing dates for responding to office actions and preparing requests for extensions, if necessary;
- assisting in preparing responses to office actions;
- amending application to omit inventors if their claims have been dropped from the application;
- notifying clients of status of patent prosecution;
- preparing terminal disclaimers if a double patenting rejection is made;
- assisting in preparing divisional, continuation, and continuation-in-part applications;
- reporting notices of allowance and publication to client and docketing date for payment of issue and publication fees;
- reviewing issued patent and making requests for correction, if necessary;
- assisting in notifying client of issuance of patent, term of duration, and necessity to maintain patent; and
- docketing dates for maintenance fees for utility patents.

INTERNET RESOURCES

Federal laws relating to patents: http://www.ll.georgetown.edu or
                                     http://www.findlaw.com

U.S. Patent and Trademark Office: http://www.uspto.gov (general information about
                                    patents, filing fees, frequently asked questions, forms,
                                    and new rules and regulations)

Manual of Patent
    Examining Procedure: http://www.uspto.gov/web/offices/pac/mpep/index.htm
    (PTO's guide and manual to patent application and
    appeal process)

General information: http://www.ipmall.fplc.edu (Pierce Law's IP MALL
    with excellent information and articles and links to
    other IP sources); and
    http://www.findlaw.com

DISCUSSION QUESTIONS

1. Len is the inventor of a new skateboard. He is concerned that a competitor is nearing completion on a similar invention and wishes to be the first to file a patent application. What should Len do?
2. Assume Len filed a utility application for his invention on August 12, 2003. Len does not wish to have his application published. How can Len avoid publication of his application?
3. Why must Len fully describe his invention in his application?
4. Is Len entitled to any deduction for his patent application filing fee and other fees? If so, why?
5. At the time Len filed his application, he was aware of a few magazines that described improvements to skateboards similar to his newly invented skateboard. What are Len's duties, if any, with regard to this information?
6. The PTO has issued a patent to Len for his skateboard. What is the term of the patent and what are Len's obligations during the term of the patent?
7. After Len's patent was granted, Len realized that he could have stated the claims in the application more broadly. Len would also like to claim a minor improvement to the wheels of the skateboard. What should Len do?
8. One of Len's competitors, Sean, has alleged that Len's patent infringes Sean's earlier patent for a skateboard. Is there any remedy or avenue the parties can pursue without litigating this matter? Discuss.

For additional resources, go to www.westlegalstudies.com.

Patent Ownership and Transfer

CHAPTER OVERVIEW

Because patents have the attributes of personal property, they may be sold, licensed, or made subject to security agreements. Patent applications must be signed by the inventor of the discovery, namely, the person who conceived the invention. In many instances, inventions are the product of more than one inventor. Joint inventorship exists even when the contributions are not equal and the parties do not work in the same physical location. Disputes over ownership of invention are typically determined by the principle that the first to invent is presumed to be the one who first reduced the invention to practice. Laboratory notebooks kept by inventors assist in determining the efforts inventors have made in reducing the invention to practice. Inventions made by an employee are owned by the employee, subject, however, to a "shop right," a nonexclusive royalty-free license to use the invention in favor of the employer. Nevertheless, if an employee is specifically hired to make an invention, the invention will belong to the employer. In most cases, employees and employers enter into written agreements by which employees agree that any inventions will be owned by and assigned to the employer. Patents may be assigned to others (an outright sale) or may be licensed to others, in which case permission to use the invention is granted to another.

OWNERSHIP RIGHTS

Patents are items of personal property and thus may be owned, sold, licensed, or devised by will. Applications for patents must be filed by the actual inventor of the article, process, design, or plant. If there is more than one inventor, the application must be signed by all inventors. Although the application must be signed by the actual inventor(s), it is possible that another party may already own the invention and any rights arising from it. In many instances, employees are required to sign agreements with their employers whereby they agree that any invention or discovery invented by them while on the job will belong to the employer and that they will agree to assist and cooperate in any manner, including signing applications for patents, to ensure the employer's rights are protected. In such cases, although the oath in the patent application is signed by the individual inventor, when the application is filed, a simultaneous assignment is also filed, identifying the employer as the "true" owner of the application and the invention. (See Appendix D, Form 13, for an agreement including provisions relating to ownership of inventions and work product by employers.)

SOLE AND JOINT INVENTORS

Sole Inventors

An invention may be the product of one person or more than one person. If one person conceives of the invention, he or she is the sole inventor. A directive given by an employer to an employee to solve a problem does not make the employer an inventor. It is finding a solution to a problem rather than articulating it that determines whether one is an inventor. Similarly, giving suggestions, making minor contributions, or helping to build a model or embodiment of the invention do not make a person an inventor.

Joint Inventors

When more than one person contributes to an invention, they are **joint inventors.** Persons may be joint inventors even though they do not physically work together or at the same time, do not make the same type or amount of contribution to the invention, or do not make a contribution to the subject matter of

every claim of a patent. Each, however, must have made some contribution of inventive thought to the resulting product.

Joint inventors must apply for a patent jointly and each must make the required oath or declaration in the application. If one of the joint inventors cannot be found or refuses to join the application, the application may be made by the others on behalf of themselves and the omitted inventor. The PTO will grant the patent to the inventor making the application, but the patent will remain subject to the rights of the omitted inventor. Errors in the naming of inventors can be readily corrected by amendment to the application or by correction to an issued patent as long as the errors occurred without any deceptive intent. Similarly, amendments occurring during prosecution that result in deletion of certain claims may require changing the named inventors if certain inventors contributed only to the deleted claims.

DISPUTES OVER INVENTORSHIP

Generally, in the United States, patent rights are awarded to the first to invent. Almost all other countries follow a "first to file" system. Disputes over inventorship are usually determined in interference proceedings, as described in Chapter 18. When a dispute occurs over inventorship, generally, the first to conceive the invention and to reduce it to practice (either actually or constructively) will be held to be the prior inventor. **Conception of an invention** refers to the formation in the mind of the inventor of a definite and permanent idea of the complete invention. **Actual reduction to practice** involves construction of the invention in physical form or making or testing the invention or a prototype thereof. **Constructive reduction to practice** occurs when an application for a patent, completely disclosing the invention, is filed with the PTO.

A person who reduces the invention to practice second may prevail and be found to be the first inventor only by showing that he or she conceived the invention first and made continual diligent efforts to reduce it to practice. Under TRIPs, and effective January 1, 1996, inventive activity abroad may be considered in determining who is the first to invent.

To determine when an invention is reduced to actual practice and which inventors worked on which claims, inventors should keep **laboratory notebooks.** Inventors should make routine entries and sketches in notebooks as work on an invention progresses and as contributions are made by others. The safest course is to have the entries witnessed by the signature of a disinterested third party. Documents relating to the work, such as telephone bills, copying charges, and expenses for materials and supplies, should also be maintained with the notebook. Such notebooks are often critical pieces of evidence in determining conception, reduction to practice, diligence, and collaboration by joint inventors.

An inventor may also file an **Invention Disclosure Document** with the PTO. The invention disclosure document is not a patent application. It is an informal document filed with the PTO that describes the invention and includes sketches or photographs. Its purpose is to provide evidence of dates of an inventor's conception of an invention, the invention's **reduction to practice,** and the inventor's diligent efforts in reducing the invention to practice. The PTO imposes no requirements in regard to the content of the document, and formal claims need not be stated. The PTO filing fee is $10. The document should be signed by the inventor or his or her attorney or agent. The document is kept in confidence by the PTO, although it will be available to the public when an application referencing it matures into an issued patent. While the PTO will retain the document for two years, the inventor is still bound by the one-year grace period and other provisions of 35 U.S.C.

§ 102 requiring an inventor to file an application within one year of using or offering the invention for sale in the United States or describing it in a printed publication anywhere in the world. After two years, the PTO generally destroys the invention disclosure document.

INVENTIONS MADE BY EMPLOYEES AND INDEPENDENT CONTRACTORS

Employers engaged in the business of developing inventions, drugs, processes, and other matter subject to patent protection typically require their employees to sign agreements by which the employees agree that anything discovered or invented by the employee during employment will be owned by the employer. The employee also usually agrees to assign the invention and any patent rights therein to the employer and to cooperate in filing documents and taking any other action to assist the employer in obtaining a patent. If the employee later refuses to sign an application for a patent as the inventor, the employer may do so upon a showing of his or her proprietary interest in the invention, and a patent will issue in the employer's name. (See Appendix D, Form 13).

If an employer and employee do not agree in advance about which party will own inventions conceived by the employee during the course and scope of employment, the general rule is that the employee retains ownership rights, subject to a **shop right** in favor of the employer. A shop right is a nonexclusive, royalty-free, nontransferable license of the employer to make and use the invention in the employer's business whether or not the employee remains employed by the employer. The invention must result from efforts of the employee during his or her working hours and with material belonging to the employer. The employee may grant other licenses, may file a patent application and own any issued patent, and may sue for infringement by parties other than the employer. If an employee is specifically hired to solve a certain problem, however, and an invention results from the employee's work, the employee must assign the invention and any patent rights to the employer, regardless of the existence of any express agreement between the parties.

Companies that engage or commission independent contractors to work on projects or create inventions should always require that the contractor assign all inventions, discoveries, and any other intellectual property rights to the company.

Inventions made by federal employees while working for the U.S. government are generally owned by the employee. Nevertheless, the government will have a shop right to use the invention. Inventions made by companies or individuals working for the federal government pursuant to contract are usually governed by the terms of the contract. Typically, the government has the burden of demonstrating that it owns the invention. In many instances, particularly for educational, not-for-profit, or small business organizations, the government waives its patent rights. Government contracts relating to energy, nuclear propulsion, weapons programs, and other special topics generally provide that the government retains title to inventions arising from such contracts.

ASSIGNMENT OF PATENT RIGHTS

Because patents have the attributes of personal property, they may be transferred or assigned, just as may other items of personal property, and may be bequeathed by will. Patents or applications for patents may be assigned to another; a written instrument is required. 35 U.S.C. § 261. The written instrument should identify the patent by application or issue number, date, and title of the invention. An assignment is a transfer of a party's entire ownership interest or a percentage of that party's ownership interest (see Exhibit 19–1). A few states have prescribed certain formalities to be observed in connection with the sale of patent rights.

Although recording the assignment with the PTO is not required for an assignment to be valid, recording is recommended because an assignment is void as against a subsequent purchaser of a patent or patent application who gave valuable consideration without notice of the earlier assignment unless the first assignment is recorded with the PTO within three months from its date or prior to the time of the subsequent purchase. The PTO provides forms for recording assignments, and the patent recordation form is highly similar to that used for recording assignments of trademarks.

Pursuant to 35 U.S.C. § 262, in the absence of agreement to the contrary, each of the joint owners of a patent may make, use, license, offer to sell, or sell the patented invention without the consent of and without accounting to the other owners. Thus, similar to copyright law, each owner has the right to assign or license the patent to a third party without agreement of the other co-owners. Unlike copyright law, however, which requires accounting of profits, patent law does not require a joint owner to account to the others for monies received from such sale. Thus, it is critical that joint inventors be subject to a written agreement detailing their rights to use, make, sell, and license the invention to others.

LICENSING OF PATENT RIGHTS

A license differs from an assignment in that it is not an outright grant or transfer of ownership. The licensing of a patent transfers a bundle of rights, which is less than the entire

An individual item is also a variable. To distinguish it from the composite variable which it belongs to, we can call it an item variable. The selection of the items for a composite measure is nothing less than a real procedure of sampling (after reading chapter eight you may want to come back here to make a comparison). You first think about all possible items relevant to the measurement of the complex concept (clarifying the item population). You then figure out how many items are needed for constructing the composite measure (determining the sample size). You may want to classify the conceptual contents or the items population into a few categories (stratification). Then you choose certain individual items and/or clusters of items from each stratum, which could be divided into several steps (multistage sampling). And the method of selection is often based on your professional judgment and research purpose (purposive/judgmental sampling). Although people do not seem to favor a random sampling strategy in selecting the items for a composite measure, what you are after here is still the representativeness of the sample, what we call "item sampling adequacy" in scale construction.

Item sampling adequacy is an important idea in guiding the development of any composite measure, although the practice of item sampling is far from perfect. The traditional approach to item sampling adequacy is to base your selection on your own expertise and other experts' advice. And the safest way seems to be making use, with modification if necessary, of some existing and creditable scaling scheme. In considering how many items are needed to measure a complex construct, you need to both ensure the appropriate coverage of the concept field and avoid the kind of redundancy in certain statistical treatment. Generally speaking, parsimony is a principle that goes with the sampling adequacy requirement. As for the internal structure of the item sample, you may want to strike a balance among the different strata that you think is appropriate (no explicit rule to follow at the moment).

It is not yet justified whether a random sampling method should be introduced to item selection in measurement and scaling. This has to do with the second issue, that is, the characteristics of individual items and their quality requirements for the purpose of constructing a good composite measure.

Good item characteristics include both qualitative and quantitative aspects. Your qualitative analysis of the conceptual and theoretical relevance of a data item to the measurement of a complex idea determines what is called the face validity of the item. In addition to such a logical requirement, the quantitative aspect of the item, i.e., its amount of variance among your research population,

EXHIBIT 19–1
Patent Assignment

Sample Form (former PTO/SB/41) (05-01)

ASSIGNMENT OF PATENT	Docket Number (optional)

Whereas, I, _____ of _____, hereinafter

referred to as patentee, did obtain a United Stated Patent for an improvement in _____

_____

No._____ , dated _____ ; and whereas, I am now the sole

owner of said patent, and,

Whereas,_____

of _____

hereinafter referred to as "assignee" whose mailing address is

_____

City of _____, and State of _____

is desirous of acquiring the entire right, title and interest in the same;

Now, therefore, in consideration of the sum of _____dollars ($_____), the receipt whereof is

acknowledged, and other good and valuable consideration, I, the patentee, by these presents do sell, assign and transfer

unto said assignee the entire right, title and interest in and to the said Patent aforesaid; the same to be held and enjoyed

by the said assignee for his own use and behoof, and for his legal representatives and assigns, to the full end of the term

for which said Patent is granted, as fully and entirely as the same would have been held by me had this assignment and

sale not been made.

Executed this _____day of _____, 20 _____,

at _____.

_____
(Signature)

State of_____)

County of _____)   SS:

Before me personally appeared said_____

and acknowledge the foregoing instrument to be his free act and deed this _____day

of _____,20 _____.

_____
(Notary Public)

Seal

This form offers a sample or suggested format for an assignment document. This sample form is not an OMB officially approved form.

ownership interest. A license is merely a permission to use. The permission or license may be limited in its scope, duration, terms, or territory. A patent license is, in effect, a contractual agreement that the patent owner will not sue the licensee for patent infringement if the licensee makes, uses, offers for sale, sells, or imports the claimed invention, as long as the licensee fulfills its obligations and operates within the bounds delineated by the license agreement. Licenses may be exclusive (meaning that only one party has the ability to exploit the invention) or may be nonexclusive (meaning that more than one party may be given rights in the invention or patent). Similarly, they may be for the term of the patent (twenty years from the date of filing) or may be for a limited time period. Licenses may be granted to one party to make the invention and to another party to sell the invention. They may be restricted to specific geographical areas, so that one party has rights west of the Mississippi while another (or the patent owner) has rights east of the Mississippi. Licenses are not usually recorded with the PTO because they are viewed as private contractual relationships between parties that do not affect the ultimate ownership of the patent.

The patent owner may charge a one-time lump-sum payment for the license or may receive royalties or periodic payments during the term of the license. Typically, royalty payments are based upon sales of the invention. For example, an owner might receive 5 percent of the sales price of each patented item sold. Restrictions may be imposed on the licensee requiring the licensee to sell a certain number of units or forfeit the license or pay an increased amount therefor. As a sign of the value of patents, consider that from 1980 to 1999 royalties on patents in the United States increased from $3 billion to nearly $110 billion. IBM alone generates $1 billion in income generated by patent royalties.

Security interests may also be granted in patents to secure an obligation so that in the event of a default, the patent may be seized by the secured party. For example, the owner of a patent may wish to borrow money from a lender. The lender may be unwilling to lend money without some property being pledged as collateral for the loan. If a patent is pledged as collateral, and the patent owner defaults in any payments due to the lender, the lender may

seize all rights in the patent. Although recordation with the PTO of security interests in patents is not required, recordation is advised inasmuch as it provides notice to the public of the various interests claimed in a patent. When the loan is repaid, another document is then filed with the PTO confirming the security interest has been released.

INVENTION DEVELOPERS AND PROMOTERS

Many individual inventors do not have the funds necessary to prosecute a patent application, make the invention, and promote it. To avoid or reduce these costs, many inventors attempt to sell or license their rights to established companies. The invention must be protected during any period of negotiation. (See Appendix D, Form 14, for an Evaluation Agreement that will protect information and inventions disclosed for the purpose of discussing future business transactions.) Alternatively, there are a number of private organizations, usually referred to as **invention developers** or *invention promoters,* that assist inventors in bringing a discovery to market and negotiate with others for assignment or licensing of an inventor's patent rights. Although many of these developers are reputable, others have poor rates of success in bringing an invention to market. Inventors need to exercise caution in dealing with invention promoters or developers, particularly those that demand significant advance payments or guarantee success.

In fact, due to the poor track record of invention promotion firms, the Inventors' Rights Act of 1999, part of the American Inventors Protection Act of 1999, helps protect inventors against deceptive practices of invention promotion companies. The act requires invention promoters to disclose in writing the number of positive and negative evaluations of inventions they have given over a five-year period and their customers' success in receiving net financial profit and license agreements as a direct result of the invention promotion services.

Customers injured by failure to disclose the required information or by any material false or fraudulent representation by the invention promoter can bring a civil action to recover statutory damages up to $5,000 or actual damages. Damages of up to three times the amount awarded are available for intentional or willful violations.

Additionally, while the PTO does not investigate complaints against invention promoters or participate in legal proceedings, it does accept complaints against invention promoters (and provides a form for complaints) and then forwards the complaint to the invention promoter. Both the complaint and the response of the invention promoter are publicly available on the PTO web site.

Additionally, the Better Business Bureau can check the background of an invention promoter or developer. Similarly, the Small Business Administration may be of assistance. Finally, for $25, the PTO will publish a notice in the *Official Gazette* that a patent is available for licensing or sale.

TRIVIA

- The first woman to receive a patent, Mary Kies, received it in 1809 for weaving straw with silk or thread.
- Abraham Lincoln is the only U.S. president to hold a patent (Patent No. 6,469 for "A Device Buoying Vessels Over Shoals," granted in 1849).
- Someone receives a patent in the United States every three minutes.
- In 2000, Qualcomm reported royalty and licensing fees totaling $705 million for its technology used for cell phones.

CHAPTER SUMMARY

Because patents have the attributes of personal property, they may be sold, licensed, or bequeathed by will. A person who conceives of an invention and reduces it to practice is a sole inventor. In many cases, however, more than one person will work on an invention. Those parties may be joint inventors even though they do not contribute equal efforts to the invention and do not physically work together. If a dispute over priority of inventorship arises, the general rule is that the first to invent is the one who conceived of the invention and first reduced it to practice, either actually (by building a model or embodiment of the invention) or constructively (by filing a patent application for the invention). Notebooks describing work done by inventors often assist in determining priority disputes.

Generally, inventions discovered by employees (who are not subject to agreements granting rights to employers) are owned by employees, subject, however, to a "shop right," namely a nonexclusive royalty-free license in favor of the employer to use the invention. In most instances, however, employers require employees to enter into agreements assigning any inventions and rights therein to the employer. Nevertheless, even without a written agreement, if an employee is hired specifically to create a certain work, the employer will own the resulting work.

As items of personal property, patents may be assigned or sold to others, as long as the instrument is in writing. Recordation with the PTO is not required for an assignment to be valid but is recommended. Patents may also be licensed by agreements granting another the right to use, make, or sell the invention for a specified period in a specified territory in return for which the licensee will give consideration (usually in the form of periodic royalty payments) to the licensor. Patents may also be used to secure obligations so that in the event of a default by the patent owner, the secured party may seize the patent and exercise all rights of ownership.

CASE ILLUSTRATION—JOINT INVENTORSHIP

Case: *Kimberly-Clark Corp. v. Procter & Gamble Distrib. Co.*, 973 F.2d 911 (Fed. Cir. 1992)

Facts: In a patent infringement case involving disposable diapers, Procter & Gamble argued that its invention was the product of joint inventors, two employees who worked separately on the invention (and in ignorance of each other) in 1979 and 1982. If the inventors were joint inventors, P&G would capture the 1979 date as its priority date and be the first to invent.

Holding: There was no joint inventorship in this case. Individuals cannot be joint inventors if they are completely ignorant of what each other has done until years after their individual independent efforts. For persons to be joint inventors, there must be some element of joint behavior, such as collaboration or working under common direction. These two inventors had no contact and were completely unaware of each other's work. They cannot be totally independent of each other and be joint inventors.

CASE STUDY AND ACTIVITIES

Case Study. Three engineers employed by Watson in its engineering and security group invented a new security camera for the park. None signed any agreement with Watson regarding ownership of any inventions. One of the individuals has left Watson's employment and cannot be located. Watson also owns a patent for an invention that allows it to count patrons entering and leaving the park. Watson would like to enter into an arrangement whereby it would allow another theme park to use the invention. Finally, Watson would like to borrow a great deal of money to finance expansion of the park. The lender is insisting on obtaining security for the loan.

CASE STUDY AND ACTIVITIES (cont'd)

Activities.   Discuss ownership of the security camera invention and whether a patent application can be filed when one of the inventors cannot be located. What arrangements should Watson enter into with regard to the counting invention and obtaining new funding for planned expansion? Which documents will be recorded with the PTO and why?

ROLE OF PARALEGAL

Paralegals typically engage in the following activities related to ownership of patents:

- monitoring the progress of patent prosecution and the addition and deletion of claims to ensure inventorship is accurate for all claims;
- reviewing issued patents to confirm all inventors are correctly identified;
- preparing and filing invention disclosure documents;
- assisting in drafting clauses for employment or other contracts confirming that inventions developed by employees will be owned by and assigned to employers or the commissioning party;
- reviewing the *Official Gazette* to determine whether clients should be informed of patents offered for sale or license;
- assisting in drafting assignments and security agreements relating to patents and recording same with the PTO and assisting in drafting licenses of patent rights;
- checking the chain of title of records at the PTO to determine ownership of patents; and
- checking the reputation of invention promotion firms and preparing complaints against promotion firms.

INTERNET RESOURCES

Federal laws relating to patents: http://www.ll.georgetown.edu or
http://www.findlaw.com

U.S. Patent and Trademark Office: http://www.uspto.gov (access the MPEP for information about joint inventors, assignment, and licensing; forms are provided for assignments and for recording assignments and for Invention Disclosure Documents; general information about invention promotion firms)

General information: http://www.ipmall.fplc.edu (Pierce Law's IP MALL with excellent information and articles and links to other IP sources); http://www.findlaw.com; and http://www.megalaw.com

DISCUSSION QUESTIONS

1. Karen and Neil have often discussed making a better baby stroller. Discussions have been informal and sporadic. Last year, Karen invented a baby stroller of the type that she and Neil often discussed. Karen has applied for a patent and Neil is now claiming that he is a joint inventor. Discuss.

2. Stan, an individual inventor who has invented a new type of golf club, is concerned that a competitor may file an application before Stan has the opportunity to do so. What should Stan do to ensure that he is the first to invent the new golf club?

3. Kyle, the inventor of a new type of watch, would like to earn income from the sale of the watch. He is therefore considering licensing another company to make and distribute the watch. Will the license agreement be filed with the PTO? Discuss.

4. Raymond was hired by his employer to invent a new type of window shutter. In the process of working on this invention, and while at work, Raymond invented a new type of tieback for draperies. Discuss ownership rights in the invention.

5. Pam, an individual inventor, has decided to use the services of an invention promotion firm to help her market her invention. What protections is Pam afforded under federal statute?

For additional resources, go to www.westlegalstudies.com.

CHAPTER 20

Patent Infringement

CHAPTER OVERVIEW

Any person who, without authority, makes, uses, offers to sell, or sells any patented invention infringes the patent. Innocence is not a defense to a claim of infringement, although it may serve to ensure punitive damages are not assessed. A person can also be liable for encouraging or inducing infringement or for contributory infringement by selling a component of a patented invention knowing it will be used to infringe a patent.

In determining whether infringement has occurred, the infringing device will be compared against the claims of a patent. If the accused invention falls within the language used in a patent claim, infringement is literal. Even if the accused invention differs from the claims in some way, it may still infringe under the doctrine of equivalents if it performs substantially the same function in substantially the same way to reach substantially the same result as the patented invention. A patentee is bound by the prosecution history of the patent process and cannot assert a position inconsistent with one taken during prosecution of the patent. In an infringement action, a defendant may raise a variety of defenses, including asserting that

there was no infringement, that the patent is invalid or was procured by fraud, that the patentee has misused the patent to abuse his or her position, or that the alleged infringer is using the invention solely for research purposes, laches, or estoppel. If infringement is found, a court may order injunctive relief, compensatory damages in an amount necessary to compensate the patentee for injury, costs, interest, and, if bad faith is shown, punitive damages up to three times the amount of compensatory damages and attorneys' fees. If parties cannot resolve infringement disputes amicably, litigation takes place in federal district court and is governed by the Federal Rules of Civil Procedure.

DIRECT INFRINGEMENT, INDUCEMENT TO INFRINGE, AND CONTRIBUTORY INFRINGEMENT

Direct Infringement

A patent issued by the PTO does not grant a party any right to make, use, offer to sell, or sell an invention but rather *excludes* others from engaging in such acts. Under the Patent Act, any person who, without authority, makes, uses, offers to sell, or sells any patented invention within the United States or imports into the United States any patented invention during the term of its patent, infringes the patent. 35 U.S.C. § 271(a). A patent is effective and enforceable only after it is issued. Thus, making, using, or selling devices prior to the time of a patent's issuance do not constitute acts of infringement. Nevertheless, recall from Chapter 18 that under the American Inventor's Protection Act (AIPA) of 1999, patentees may obtain reasonable royalties if others make, use, sell, or import their invention during the period between publication of their patent application (eighteen months after filing of the application) and grant of the patent. Violations of 35 U.S.C. § 271(a), namely, making, using, or selling patented inventions, are referred to as acts of **direct infringement.** Direct infringement can occur even if the infringer does not intend to infringe and is an "innocent" infringer with no knowledge that his or her acts will infringe a patented invention.

The Patent Act prohibits importing into the United States, or selling, offering to sell, or using in the United States a product made abroad by a process patented in the United States. Thus, a company cannot use a patented process abroad to make a product and then bring those products into the United States to compete with the patent owner. Although using the process abroad is not an infringement, subsequent importation of an article produced by a process patented in the United States is infringement. As an alternative to suing for patent infringement, a patent owner may bring a proceeding before the International Trade Commission to block the infringing device from entry into the United States. A patent owner may also order an import survey from the U.S. Customs Service to determine the address of any importer whose goods may infringe a patent. The survey will not stop infringement or importation, but it does provide information relating to the importer, who can then be sued for infringement.

Inducement to Infringe

Liability for infringement can arise indirectly from inducing another to infringe a patent. 35 U.S.C. § 271(b). Thus, if a person actively and intentionally encourages a third party to infringe a patent, and the patent is so infringed, the person who solicited the infringement will be liable. For example, selling a product with instructions on how to use the product in a manner that would infringe is **inducement of infringement.** Similarly, if a corporation encourages and assists an employee in making another's patented invention, the corporation (together with the officer or director who induced the act) will be liable for infringement. Some experts refer to inducement as activity that aids and abets infringement.

The Patent Act also provides that a person who supplies from the United States all or a substantial portion of a patented invention in a manner that actively induces combination of the components abroad is liable for infringement. Liability is also imposed if a person knowingly supplies from the United States a material component of a patented invention that has no substantial use apart from its role in the invention and intends that the component will be combined with other components abroad in a manner that would be infringement if done in the United States. These provisions are intended to ensure that patent laws are not circumvented by shipping parts outside of the United States for assembly abroad into infringing articles.

Contributory Infringement

If a person offers to sell or sells within the United States or imports into the United States a component of a patented invention or process, or material for use in practicing a patented process (and the component has no substantial use apart from use in the patented invention or process), knowing the same to be especially made or adapted for use in an infringement of such patent, he or she will be liable for contributory infringement. 35 U.S.C. § 271(c). Selling some common or staple article that can be used for purposes other than in the invention does not constitute contributory infringement. Thus, a seller may successfully defend a claim of contributory infringement by proving that he or she had no knowledge that the goods sold had no substantial use other than in the patented invention. Moreover, to be liable for contributory infringement, a person must know that his or her component or material will be used by a buyer to infringe a patent.

In sum, while liability can be imposed for direct infringement (making, using, or selling a patented invention) without regard to the infringer's intent, liability for inducing infringement or contributory infringement (both of which are often referred to as "indirect infringement") requires that the defendant infringer know that infringement will occur because of his or her inducement or contribution.

THE FIRST SALE OR EXHAUSTION DOCTRINE

In copyright law, once a copyrighted work, such as a book, is sold, the owner may then resell it or lend it to another without infringing the copyright under the first sale doctrine. The same principle applies with regard to lawful sales of trademarked goods. Similarly, this principle applies to patented inventions. Once the patent owner unconditionally sells a patented item, the buyer has the right to resell it or use it as desired. As in copyright and trademark law, it is said that the **first sale** "exhausts" the rights of the patent owner to control the purchaser's use of the device thereafter. Along with the right to resell the invention, the buyer may repair it in order to prolong its use. Courts generally draw a distinction between repair, which is permissible, and reconstruction, which is

impermissible infringement. While an owner of a patented invention has the right to repair and restore the article, activities that amount to rebuilding it such that the invention is being made anew are infringements. For example, if a party lawfully acquires a television, replacing components or reconditioning it is acceptable as a repair of the invention as long as the complete invention is not reconstructed.

CLAIMS INTERPRETATION

The claims in a patent determine its exclusive rights. The skill required in claims drafting comes into play both before and after a patent is issued. Drafting a claim in a patent application is done to demonstrate patentability of an invention by distinguishing the invention from prior art. If the inventor later believes the invention is being infringed, the claims are again examined for this purpose. Thus, determining infringement requires interpreting the claims language in the patent and then comparing and contrasting the allegedly infringing article against those claims.

Literal Infringement and the Doctrine of Equivalents

If the accused invention, device, or process falls within the language used in a patent claim, there is **literal infringement** because the accused invention is the same as that protected by the grant of patent. For an accused invention to literally infringe a patent, every claim in the patent must be present in the accused device. In some cases, however, a party has made some change to a patented invention, for example, substituting one ingredient known to be an equivalent to that used in the patented invention. Because such a change would not constitute a literal infringement inasmuch as a claim has not been exactly copied, courts developed the **doctrine of equivalents** to protect the true invention from misappropriation and ensure that a fraud is not committed on a patent. Courts will thus examine the accused invention to determine if it is "equivalent to" the patented invention in that it performs substantially the same function in substantially the same way to reach substantially the same result as the patented invention. If so, the two inventions are the same even though they may differ in name, form, or shape, and the second invention will be held to infringe the patent. *See Warner Jenkinson Co. v. Hilton Davis Chem. Co.,* 520 U.S. 17 (1997). Thus, a minor and obvious improvement on a patented invention can be an infringement. The doctrine of equivalents thus protects inventors by ensuring that latecomers do not profit by making an insubstantial alteration to a patented invention. Moreover, if the accused invention has all of the elements of a patent claim, it will be found to infringe; it does not matter that the alleged infringer has added new elements. Adding new features will not negate infringement. Consequently, a broad patent provides its owner with significant protection against not only infringing devices but related and derivative inventions.

For a device to infringe under the doctrine of equivalents, it must have an equivalent of each element of the patented invention. Thus, if one element of a claim in the patented invention is not present in or has no equivalent in the accused invention, there is no infringement, even if the accused device as a whole performs substantially the same function in substantially the same manner as the patented invention.

The doctrine of equivalents reflects the tension between two competing policies. While claims should be drafted clearly and interpreted somewhat strictly so that the patentee is not given a broader scope of protection than that set forth in the patent itself, a patentee's efforts and invention should not be allowed to be circumvented by another person who makes some minor change in the invention or process.

Determining equivalency is a difficult task and generally depends upon the facts of each particular case rather than any set formula or rules. Moreover, the range of equivalents varies according to the significance of the patented invention: a **pioneer patent** (one that is an important advance or significant breakthrough in the art) is usually given a wide range of equivalents so that protection is broader; if the accused invention is generally equivalent to the patented invention, it infringes. Similarly, a patented invention that represents a marked improvement over prior art is given a wide range of equivalents. Conversely, a patented invention that is only a modest improvement is given a limited range of equivalents; the accused invention must be convincingly equivalent to the patented invention for infringement to be found. This theory is somewhat comparable to the one used in trademark infringement cases that holds that distinct and unique trademarks such as XEROX® or EXXON® are given a broader scope of protection than weak or descriptive ones such as TASTEE BITES.

Reverse Doctrine of Equivalents

An accused device may fall within a claim's literal language and yet not infringe if it is so changed in principle from the patented article that it performs the same or similar function as the patented invention but in a completely different way. *Graver Tank & Mfg. Co. v. Linde Air Products Co.,* 339 U.S. 605 (1950). Known as the **reverse doctrine of equivalents,** this theory holds that despite literal infringement of claims, if the resulting device is different from the patented device, there is no infringement. The reverse doctrine of equivalents is not commonly encountered.

Prosecution History Estoppel

During the patent application process, the inventor or applicant may amend his or her is another important criterion for consideration. It should be noted that the value range of a variable is usually an arbitrary matter, depending on how you set up the coding scheme. This shows the assignment of the numeric values to each item, and the selective presentation of the possible measurement outcomes in a pre-coded situation as well, is as important as the selection of the data or question items themselves. The requirement for such metric property of each item, however, is not absolute; it is largely a matter of the applicability of different analytical and statistical procedures you will use later, where various restrictions may be imposed. The procedure of item analysis usually requires the exclusion of items with small variance. However, this again is not absolute, especially if such items have special theoretical and empirical significance. Quantitative procedure, therefore, must be guided by qualitative analysis. If necessary, a procedure of differential weighting can be performed to adjust for the quantitative representation of the qualitative significance.

Beyond the issue of item selection, the construction of a composite measure is also an issue of how to combine different items or individual indicators into a multi-item instrument. For categorical variables, a typological method may be used to combine the categories along different dimensions. For the two dichotomous variables sex and race (white and nonwhite), for example, we can form a composite measure consisting of the following categories: white male, white female, nonwhite male, and nonwhite female. For interval variables, all kinds of mathematical operators may be used to link the individual items, including addition, subtraction, multiplication, and division. If the combination involves only simple multiplication and/or division, the result is called an index, which usually has direct empirical correspondence. More general and complex operations will yield so-called scales.

In the simplest case of scaling, individual items may be just added up and used as a composite score. This is quite natural for a novice researcher. In real terms, this is also a most frequently seen practice among experienced investigators. The well-known Likert-type attitude scale is such a measure (Summers, 1970), which uses a set of statements (usually no more than twenty) with five response categories to each statement ranging from strongly approve to strongly disapprove. Here the ordinal measures are treated at the interval level. The researcher needs to ensure the consistency of the directions of the items, which can be done through the "flipping" of their codings (including signs and values) if necessary. The summated scaling strategy, however, involves risk in situations complicated by such issues as varying metric base, differential weighting, and claims and make various arguments to the examiner relating to the claims in the application. In the course of the patent prosecution, the applicant may omit certain claims or narrow them to avoid rejection on the basis they are precluded by prior art. The inventor/patentee is bound by this prosecution history in a later action alleging infringement under the doctrine of equivalents and is estopped from alleging that the claim was intended to be broader or asserting a position inconsistent with one taken earlier. The principle is inapplicable to literal infringement cases inasmuch as literal infringement exists when the accused invention copies the actual claims in an issued patent; what occurred during the course of prosecution is thus not relevant. For example, during the application process, and in order to satisfy an examiner's objection, a patent applicant may narrow a claim. Once the claim is narrowed to be more specific, any invention that falls within the scope of the initial claims (but not the amended ones) does not infringe. The principle rests on the theory that a patent owner cannot narrow the scope of a claim and exclude certain subject matter in order to obtain a patent and then later recapture the excluded subject matter using the doctrine of equivalents. While the patentee has the right to appeal, a decision not to appeal and submit an amended or narrowed claim is viewed as a concession that the invention as patented does not reach as far as the original claim.

The doctrine, variously called **prosecution history estoppel** or **file wrapper estoppel,** applies not only to prosecution of the original patent but to reissue and reexamination proceedings. Underlying the doctrine is the principle that an applicant who disagrees with an examiner's position should appeal. The applicant is the one who drafts the claims, submits arguments, and makes amendments and should therefore be bound by his or her own actions, even if it is later determined that the examiner's position was incorrect.

The *Festo* Case

In late 2000, the U.S. Court of Appeals for the Federal Circuit sent shock waves through the patent community when it held that any narrowing amendment made by a patent applicant during the patent prosecution process effected a complete bar to the doctrine of equivalents for the amended claim element. *Festo v. Shoketsu Kinzoku Kogyo Kabushiki Kaisha*, 234 F.3d 558 (Fed. Cir. 2000). Thus, applicants who narrowed claims in response to rejections by the PTO subjected those claims to a complete bar and eliminated the doctrine of equivalents for the amended claim elements. Prior to *Festo*, only the particular subject matter surrendered would be lost through estoppel. After *Festo*, the patentee was limited to the strict scope of the amended claim element with no protection against equivalents.

Festo was appealed to the U.S. Supreme Court where it continued to attract attention with more than twenty amicus curiae ("friend of the court") briefs filed. The U.S. Supreme Court vacated the Federal Circuit's decision in *Festo* and held that a narrowing amendment does not effect a complete bar but instead raises a rebuttable presumption that the complete bar applies. *Festo v. Shoketsu Kinzoku Kogyo Kabushiki Kaisha*, 535 U.S. 722 (2002). In fact, the Supreme Court chided the Federal Circuit and reminded the court that "courts must be cautious before adopting changes that disrupt the settled expectations of the inventing community." *Warner-Jenkinson*, 520 U.S. at 28. The Court held that estoppel need not bar suit against every equivalent to the amended claim element. Rather, prosecution history estoppel must be applied in a more flexible manner although the patentee should bear the burden of showing that the amendment does not surrender the particular equivalent in question. In brief, a patentee who amends a patent gives up protection only for those things that were foreseeable by those skilled in the art covered by the patent. Consequently, a patent holder who could not have foreseen that changing the description in a patent application would limit coverage would still be able to sue those making equivalent products.

Patent practitioners have expressed relief at the Supreme Court's confirmation that the doctrine of equivalents is alive and well (although subject to a rebuttable presumption that estoppel applies and that equivalents have been surrendered), and at least one commentator has stated that *Festo* is likely the most significant U.S. Supreme Court patent case in a generation.

DEFENSES TO INFRINGEMENT

Defendants in infringement actions generally assert one or more of several affirmative defenses. The most commonly asserted defenses are noninfringement, patent invalidity, fraud, patent misuse, experimental or research use, laches, and estoppel.

A defendant may assert that its acts do not constitute infringement, either literally or under the doctrine of equivalents. An accused infringer may also assert that the patent is invalid and thus cannot be infringed. An invalidity defense alleges that the invention fails to meet statutory subject matter, is not novel or useful, or is obvious, such that the patent for the invention should not have been issued by the PTO. Because issued patents are presumed to be valid, a defendant asserting invalidity must prove invalidity by clear and convincing evidence. A party using an invention under a license from the patentee may assert patent invalidity and is not estopped from raising such a defense even though he or she has agreed in a license agreement not to contest the validity of the patent, primarily because the policy favoring the negation of invalid patents outweighs contract law policy.

Fraud or inequitable conduct by a patentee during prosecution will render a patent resulting therefrom unenforceable. Such conduct may consist of omissions or material misrepresentations during the patent application process.

An accused infringer may assert **patent misuse,** namely, that the patent owner has abused his or her position to exploit a patent improperly and thus should be precluded from suing for infringement. Common examples of patent misuse include price fixing, tying arrangements (generally, tying or conditioning the sale or license of a patented item to the sale of another item, unless it is a nonstaple item, meaning an item that has no significant commercial use except in connection with the patented invention or process), and other antitrust violations. Other examples of patent misuse that will preclude a patentee from suing for infringement are threatening or initiating patent infringement suits without probable cause or attempting to extend a patent beyond its term by requiring a licensee to pay license fees even after expiration of a patent.

A person accused of infringement may assert that unauthorized making or using of a patented invention was solely for research or experimental purposes. Making or using the patented invention for commercial purposes will defeat this defense.

As will be discussed further in Chapter 21, under the AIPA, in actions involving business methods patents, an accused infringer may assert a defense that he or she had, in good faith, actually reduced the subject matter of the patent to practice at least one year before the effective filing date of the patent and commercially used the subject matter before the effective filing date.

Although there is no statute of limitations in the Patent Act requiring that suits for infringement be instituted within any set time period, 35 U.S.C. § 286 provides that no monetary recovery may be had for any infringement committed more than six years prior to the filing of a claim of infringement. Although action may be initiated for infringement after six years (perhaps to enjoin further acts of infringement), monetary damages cannot be awarded for infringing acts committed more than six years before litigation is begun.

Even if the patentee initiates suit within six years after infringement, an action may still be barred by the doctrines of laches or estoppel. Laches is an unreasonable delay in bringing suit that causes prejudice to the defendant. A laches defense might be successfully asserted if a patentee knew of infringement and its delay in acting allowed the infringer to build up its business, market its accused device, and expend time and money expanding its business. An estoppel defense might be successfully asserted if a patentee knew of infringement and yet led the infringer to believe it would not enforce the patent. Mere silence will not amount to estoppel. In the typical case, a patentee who informs an infringer that it objects to the infringer's activities and then fails to take action, leading the infringer to believe the patentee has decided not to enforce his or her patent rights, may be estopped or precluded from asserting infringement.

Some specific acts do not constitute infringement. For example, 35 U.S.C. § 271(e) allows persons to make, use, offer to sell, and sell certain patented inventions relating to genetic manipulation techniques for the purpose of submitting information to federal regulatory agencies such as the FDA. Thus, using certain patented inventions to perform experiments in order to obtain FDA approval of certain drugs is permissible. This exception allows individuals and companies to position themselves to enter the market as soon as a patent expires for a product. For example, the maker of a drug can engage in acts that would ordinarily be infringement in order to obtain regulatory approval of the drug so the maker can compete with the patented product as soon as the term of the patent expires. Similarly, use of another's patented biotechnical invention is not an infringement if the use is strictly for research purposes. Medical practitioners may perform certain medical activities (such as the performance of medical or surgical procedures) that do not constitute infringement as long as the performance has no commercial application.

REMEDIES FOR INFRINGEMENT

A plaintiff who is successful in a suit for patent infringement may obtain injunctive relief, monetary damages, attorneys' fees, interest, costs of litigation, and, possibly, triple damages.

- **Injunctive relief.** In many instances, a patentee is as interested in ensuring that infringing activities cease as in recovering damages. A court may grant a preliminary injunction pending the final judgment in the case upon a showing that the patentee is reasonably likely to prevail in the action and that irreparable harm would result to the patentee unless an injunction were granted. If a patentee prevails in an infringement action, a permanent injunction is usually issued, enjoining the infringer from further infringing acts.

- **Compensatory damages.** The Patent Act provides that upon finding infringement, a court shall award a claimant damages adequate to compensate for infringement, but in no event less than a reasonable royalty for the use made of the invention by the infringer, together with an award of interest and costs. 35 U.S.C. § 284. If a patentee can prove actual damages, such as lost profits, those damages will be awarded. If such damages are highly speculative or cannot be proven because the infringer has only made rather than sold the invention, courts will then use the reasonable royalty rate as the measure of damages. Amounts paid as royalties by authorized licensees using the invention or other comparable inventions will be used to determine the rate to be paid by the infringer. Under 35 U.S.C. § 287, if a patented product is not marked with a notice of patent, no damages may be recovered by the patentee in an infringement action, unless there is proof that the infringer was notified of the infringement and continued to infringe thereafter, in which case damages are recoverable only for infringement occurring after notice. Filing an action for infringement constitutes notice. The patentee should always mark the invention with a notice of patent so he or she may recover damages from the time the patent is first infringed. To compensate a patentee fully, prejudgment interest is usually awarded, meaning interest from the date of actual infringement rather than from the date judgment is entered by the court. Costs of litigation are awarded to a successful patentee. However, if the patent includes an invalid claim together with a valid claim, no costs may be recovered unless a disclaimer of the invalid claim is entered with the PTO before suit for infringement is commenced. Two fairly new types of damages are often sought: damages for price erosion (damages incurred by a patentee forced to lower its prices to meet competition by the infringer) and collateral sales damages (damages on sales of items that are used with the patented item, for example, recovering damages for sales of patented remote controls when a patented television has been infringed).

- **Punitive damages.** Under 35 U.S.C. § 284, courts are authorized to increase compensatory damages up to three times the amount assessed. An award of such **punitive damages** (those meant to punish the defendant rather than compensate the plaintiff) is made only upon a showing of willful infringement or bad faith by the defendant. Persons have affirmative duties to use due care in avoiding infringement of another's rights. This duty can be satisfied by obtaining advice of counsel that a patent is invalid or that defenses exist to a claim of patent infringement. Thus, reliance on counsel may be used to defend against a claim of willful infringement or bad faith. Bad faith infringement might occur when an infringer duplicates a patented invention or obtains a sham opinion of counsel only for the purpose of using it as a shield against a later charge of willful infringement. Such conduct might justify the imposition of punitive damages. Thus, obtaining an infringement opinion (see Chapter 18) is critical because it may protect an infringer from punitive damages by showing an exercise of due care to avoid infringement.
- **Attorneys' fees.** A court may award reasonable attorneys' fees to the prevailing party "in exceptional cases." 35 U.S.C. § 285. If the patentee is the prevailing party, attorneys' fees might be awarded when the infringer's conduct is willful or in bad faith. If the accused infringer is the prevailing party, he or she may be able to recover attorneys' fees if the patentee instituted or continued the litigation in bad faith or was guilty of inequitable conduct, either in procuring the patent or in the course of litigation. Attorneys' fees awarded in some cases have reached $1 million.

• **Design patents.** In addition to the usual remedies available for infringement, one whose design patent has been infringed is entitled to recover all of the total profit of the infringer (but not less than $250). 35 U.S.C. § 289.

RESOLVING AN INFRINGEMENT DISPUTE

Lawsuits for patent infringement are among the most expensive and time-consuming of all litigation cases. Not only must the acts of the defendant be evaluated, but the entire file wrapper and prosecution history of the patent are open for examination. Moreover, because the subject matter of most patents is highly technical, experts and professionals must be retained for claim interpretation. If infringement is found, damages can run into the millions of dollars. For example, one case relating to a Hughes Aircraft Company patent for satellites produced sixteen separate decisions, took more than twenty-five years to resolve, and resulted in an award of more than $100 million. Thus, many parties try to resolve patent disputes between themselves either before or during the pendency of litigation.

Typically, a party who believes its patent is being infringed will send a "cease and desist" letter to the accused infringer, notifying the infringer of its rights to the patent and demanding that any further infringing activities cease. (The sample cease and desist letter shown in Chapter 6, Exhibit 6–4, may be easily modified for purposes of patent infringement.) Even if the cease and desist letter does not achieve the goal of convincing the infringer to cease his or her activities, it provides actual notice of the patent so that if the patented invention is not marked with a patent notice, the patent owner may recover damages for infringement after the date of letter notice. Moreover, the cease and desist letter generally triggers the accused infringer's duty of due care to avoid patent infringement so that failure to obtain advice of competent counsel in the face of an allegation of infringement might result in the imposition of punitive or increased damages against the infringer if infringement is found. As is the case with trademark-related cease and desist letters, a cease and desist letter should not be sent to a party unless the patentee has carefully evaluated his or her rights because there is a risk that the party receiving the letter may contest the validity of the patent.

The accused infringer often responds to the cease and desist letter by denying its allegations, asserting various defenses, or suggesting a compromise. The parties might agree that the accused infringer should modify the invention in some way or gradually phase the invention out of use. They may enter into a licensing arrangement whereby the accused infringer pays royalties to the patent owner to be able to make, use, or sell the patented invention. One party might acquire the other's rights by outright purchase. The parties may agree to have an arbitrator resolve the dispute rather than go to federal court. One of the parties may initiate a reexamination proceeding before the PTO to have the patent reexamined to determine the validity of any claim in a patent on the basis of prior art. A determination by the PTO that a claim is valid (or, conversely, that it is unpatentable) may give the parties some impetus to settle their dispute inasmuch as the determination constitutes another full review of the patent and its validity. As another alternative to a patent infringement action, either party involved in an actual controversy may initiate an action in federal court for declaratory relief, asking a court to review the matter and declare the parties' respective rights and obligations with respect to the patent.

Finally, as an alternative to patent litigation in the district court, patent rights may be enforced by the U.S. International Trade Commission (ITC). Under section 337 of the

Tariff Act of 1930 (specifically, 19 U.S.C. § 1337), the ITC makes determinations in investigations involving unfair practices in import trade, mainly involving allegations of infringement of U.S. patents and trademarks by imported goods. If it finds a violation of the law, the ITC may order the exclusion of the imported product from the United States or may order the seizure and forfeiture of the infringing imports. Monetary damages are not available. Because ITC proceedings are speedy, the remedies are harsh (a ban on import of the infringing products), and the ITC commissioners are well versed in intellectual property law, section 337 investigations doubled in 2001 over 2000. Decisions may be appealed to the Court of Appeals for the Federal Circuit.

PATENT INFRINGEMENT LITIGATION

If the parties cannot resolve their dispute, the plaintiff will file an action for infringement in federal district court. Federal courts have exclusive jurisdiction over patent law cases, although if the matter only peripherally relates to a patent (for example, a case involving whether a patent licensee has paid its license fees under the terms of a written contract), the matter may be heard in state court. Questions relating to validity of the patent and infringement must be initiated in federal court. Moreover, state regulation of intellectual property must yield to the extent it conflicts with federal patent law. *Bonito Boats, Inc. v. Thunder Craft Boats, Inc.,* 489 U.S. 141 (1989).

The action will be governed by the Federal Rules of Civil Procedure relating to federal civil actions generally. These rules set the times for responding to the complaint, matters pertaining to motions and discovery, and any other litigation-related matters. The action should be filed in the federal district court where the defendant resides or where the defendant committed the acts of alleged infringement and has

an established place of business. After the complaint for infringement is filed, the defendant will respond by filing an answer, usually denying that infringement has occurred and asserting various defenses. If the defendant has a cause of action to assert against the plaintiff relating to the patent, it must be asserted by way of a counterclaim in the litigation so that all disputes between the parties relating to the patent can be resolved at the same time. Claims for inducing patent infringement or contributory infringement may also be asserted.

Within one month after the filing of an action for patent infringement, the clerk of the court must provide notice of the suit to the PTO, identifying the parties, name of the inventor, and the patent number of the patent at issue. Similarly, within one month after judgment is entered in the case, the clerk must provide notice thereof to the PTO.

After the complaint, answer, and counterclaim have been filed, various motions may be made. Discovery will commence. The plaintiff and defendant will take depositions to obtain testimony from those who may have information about the case. For example, the plaintiff may depose individuals in the defendant's company to determine whether they were instructed to copy the patented invention. Interrogatories may be served on either party to obtain information, such as to inquire about experts either side intends to call, how damages such as lost profits were calculated, or to determine the existence of pertinent documents.

Ultimately, if the matter cannot be resolved by private agreement, it will proceed to trial. The patent owner must prove infringement by a preponderance of the evidence. Either party may request a jury trial; otherwise, a judge will render the decision. Although juries determine whether infringement has occurred, the issue of claims construction is determined by the trial judge, not the jury. *Markman v. Westview Instruments, Inc.,* 517 U.S. 370 (1996). The need for uniformity in patent law requires that courts, not juries, interpret patent claims, including terms of art used within those claims. The testimony of witnesses may be received when needed, but per *Markman,* judges, not juries, are "better suited" to find the acquired meaning of patent terms. *Id.* The parties will file their briefs, often called Markman briefs, and the court will hold a Markman hearing outside the presence of the jury to determine the scope of the patent's claims. The losing party in a patent infringement case may appeal the decision to the Court of Appeals for the Federal Circuit, established in 1982 in the District of Columbia to bring about consistency in patent cases, which hears all appeals from infringement cases brought in any of the federal district courts. Thereafter, the matter may be appealed to the U.S. Supreme Court if the Court, in its discretion, grants *certiorari* and decides to take the case.

If the U.S. government has allegedly infringed a patent, action is brought in the U.S. Court of Federal Claims in Washington, DC. Although the patentee is entitled to obtain compensation for use by or for the government, an injunction cannot be ordered against the government to compel it to cease making, using, or selling the invention. If a patent is infringed by a state, a patentee may obtain the same remedies (including injunctive relief) as may be obtained against other infringers.

As technology progresses and the value of certain communication, health-related, and entertainment inventions increases, patent litigation is becoming an increasingly common and high-stakes occupation. Patent infringement cases have increased 80 percent since 1991. Damage awards may run into the millions. For example, in 1997, a court awarded Procter & Gamble Company $178.4 million in lost profits and royalties arising out of the sale of diapers that infringed Procter & Gamble's. Legal fees for both companies exceeded $10 million. In 1994, Microsoft was ordered to pay $120 million in an infringement suit relating to patents for software. Microsoft and the patent owner later agreed to a reduction of damages.

Some experts have questioned whether juries should decide complex patent infringement cases. Because many patent cases involve questions of chemistry, physics, and biotechnology, courts and attorneys are trying a variety of novel approaches to make cases more understandable to jurors. Some courts have limited the number of hours that a plaintiff or defendant may use to present a case, and in one significant case, *Litton Systems, Inc. v. Honeywell, Inc.* (90-0093 C.D. Cal. 1993), attorneys used both a forty-five–second cartoon and a science fair type of experiment to argue that Honeywell had not infringed Litton's patent. Honeywell was ultimately found liable for infringement in the amount of $1.2 billion, the largest patent infringement verdict in the United States. The verdict was later set aside and Honeywell agreed in 2001 to settle the case for $420 million.

Although the role of juries is limited after *Markman*, few experts expect the United States to follow the European model in which juries are not used in patent trials and infringement is decided by a special patent court comprising judges and scientific experts.

To protect against patent suits, which can be costly to a litigant even when no infringement is found, many companies now procure insurance—either to cover the costs of defending a patent infringement suit or for the costs of prosecuting a suit to enforce a patent. Such insurance is extremely expensive, especially for companies owning several patents or patents in high-tech areas.

In July 2001, the American Arbitration Association (AAA) announced it would establish the first National Patent Board Center for Dispute Resolution. The AAA has adopted Patent Arbitration Rules and intends to serve as a forum for out-of-court resolution of patent disputes. More information is available at the AAA's web site at http://www.adr.org.

TRIVIA

- The costs of the average patent infringement trial are estimated at between $1.5 million and $3.5 million.
- Inventors from California apply for more patents than residents of any other state, followed by New York and then Illinois. Residents of Alaska apply for the fewest patents.
- According to some experts, lawyers in patent infringement cases often charge contingency fees as high as 45 percent.
- Although jury verdicts overall increased substantially in 2000, the most significant increase involved IP cases.

CHAPTER SUMMARY

A patent can be infringed even if the infringer does not intend to infringe and does not know a patented invention exists. Liability for inducing infringement or contributory infringement, however, requires intent.

If parties cannot resolve a patent dispute amicably, litigation will be instituted in federal court. The claims of the patent will be construed and the accused invention will be compared against the claims to determine if infringement has occurred. If the accused invention falls within the language used in a patent claim, literal infringement exists. Under the doctrine of equivalents, infringement can also exist if the accused invention performs substantially the same function as the patented invention in substantially the same way to reach substantially the same result. The patentee is bound by arguments made and amendments entered during the history of prosecution of the patent and cannot later argue a position inconsistent with one reflected by the file wrapper.

An accused infringer may assert that there is no infringement, that the patent is invalid, that the patent was procured by fraud, that the patentee is guilty of patent misuse, that the accused device is being used solely for research purposes, or that the patentee is barred by laches or estoppel.

Remedies in infringement actions may include injunctive relief, compensatory damages, costs, interest, and, if bad faith is shown, attorneys' fees and increased damages of up to three times compensatory damages.

CASE ILLUSTRATION—INDUCEMENT OF INFRINGEMENT

Case: *Dawson Chem. Co. v. Rohm & Haas, Inc.*, 448 U.S. 176 (1980)

Facts: Rohm & Hass ("Rohm") owned a patent for a method or process of applying propanil, an herbicide well suited for the cultivation of rice. Dawson sold propanil to farmers and provided them with instructions for application of the propanil in accordance with the method claimed in Rohm's patent.

CASE ILLUSTRATION (cont'd)

Holding: Dawson contributed to infringement by the farmers who purchased and used the propanil and actively inducted such infringement by instructing farmers how to use the herbicide. Propanil is a nonstaple good; it has no commercial use except in connection with the patented invention. The sale of such a nonstaple article with instructions that assisted the farmers in employing a process that infringes a process patent is inducement of infringement. (Note that this case provides an articulate and comprehensive review of the doctrine of patent misuse).

CASE STUDY AND ACTIVITIES

Case Study. Watson has discovered that another amusement park is using a security camera substantially similar to that of Watson's, which is patented although it is not marked with a patent notice. During the patent prosecution process, Watson narrowed some of the claims in the application. The camera, however, represents significant innovation in the industry. Coincidentally, Watson has just received a letter from Golf & Play, Inc. alleging that one of the attractions in Watson's miniature golf course (a large inflated device that bounces golf balls back at players) infringes that of Golf & Play's patented attraction. Watson used the device for a few years but has not used it in at least seven years.

Activities. Discuss the issues facing Watson arising from these facts.

ROLE OF PARALEGAL

Paralegals are typically involved in a variety of interesting and challenging tasks related to patent infringement, including the following:

- ordering and reviewing file wrappers from the PTO to review patent claims and prepare a summary of the prosecution history (because prosecution history will bind a patentee from later taking an inconsistent position);
- reviewing client materials to ensure patented items are properly marked with notice of patent;
- preparing or responding to cease and desist letters;
- preparing requests for reexamination of patents, complaints for infringement, or responses or answers thereto;
- docketing all relevant dates in infringement proceedings, such as dates for close of discovery, submission of written briefs, and so forth;
- assisting in discovery by drafting interrogatories, reviewing documents produced, summarizing depositions, and so forth;

- conducting patent searches and investigations to determine the existence of other patents and whether a patent is a pioneer patent and thus entitled to a broader scope of protection than one that represents only a modest improvement in the art;
- drafting settlement agreements; and
- providing general assistance in infringement trials such as locating witnesses, organizing exhibits and documents, conducting research, and preparing jury instructions.

INTERNET RESOURCES

Federal laws relating to patents:	http://www.ll.georgetown.edu or http://www.findlaw.com
U.S. Patent and Trademark Office:	http://www.uspto.gov (access the MPEP for information about infringement actions and appeals)
Other information:	http://www.bustpatents.com (web site relating to patent issues and providing table listing patent lawsuit awards and patent buyouts by companies);
	http://www.findlaw.com and http://www.megalaw.com offer general information about patents and patent litigation

DISCUSSION QUESTIONS

1. Carlos, an employee of Tech Systems Co., was directed by his employer to develop a new type of golf club that will infringe that of another. Carlos developed the club but it has not yet been marketed. Are any parties liable for infringement? Discuss.
2. Assume that when the grips on the golf clubs become worn, golfers routinely purchase a standard type of tape at sporting goods stores to repair the worn-out grips. Are the golfers and the store liable for infringement? Discuss.
3. A purchaser has bought the patented golf club but has decided to sell the club to her brother. Are any parties liable for infringement? Discuss and identify the name of the principle that governs your answer.
4. During prosecution of a patent application for a new microwave, the applicant, Sarah, narrowed claims 5 and 6. The patent was granted, and Sarah now believes that a similar and equivalent microwave violates claims 6, 9, and 10 of the patent. What is the effect of Sarah's actions during the patent prosecution process? May Sarah sue for infringement? Discuss and identify the legal principles, cases, and doctrines that govern your answer.

multidimensionality. We shall deal with differential weighting and multidimensionality issues in chapter twelve. In research situations suitable for unidimensional treatment, standardization is a useful approach to unifying the initial metric bases of individual items, which can be obtained through various SPSS procedures. The resulting z-scores, however, are not necessary if you wish to retain the weighting of the original values or if all variables already have the same metric base.

The notion of reliability is important in multi-item scaling, which refers to the consistency or stability of measurement results for the same subjects if the same instrument is used repeatedly. By definition, a test-retest method can be used to examine the reliability of any measure instrument, though in practice this will involve such a complication as "contamination" of the first test when a retest is taken. For a unidimensional scale, reliability can be examined through the analysis of its internal consistency among all the items based on a cross-sectional study. The analysis of internal consistency can be carried out via a split-half method, which randomly assigns the items into two sets and then calculates the correlation between their measurement scores. Another frequently used method is the calculation of a reliability coefficient called Chronbach's α, which is based on the number of items in a scale and the average correlation between all pairs of items. SPSS provides a convenient procedure of RELIABILITY, which can be used not only to compute α but also to perform item analysis to help select appropriate items for a unidimensional scale that measure a single aspect of a theoretical construct.

Related to the concept of reliability, the notion of validity plays an even greater role in measurement. It refers to the extent to which an empirical measure adequately quantifies the theoretical concept or construct as a variable. There is no simple statistical procedure offered by SPSS to accomplish this task, however. Researchers may qualitatively achieve a judgment in terms of the face validity of a measure. They may also assess the degree to which a scale covers the range of contents included within the construct in the same manner, which is called content validity of the measure. If they examine the issue in terms of the theoretical or logical relationships among variables, then they are considered dealing with so-called construct validity. If some variables are used to predict some other variables via empirical means, then a criterion-related validity or predictive validity is used. The concepts of content validity, construct validity, and criterion validity are closely related with one another, though their requirements are not always in harmony.

DISCUSSION QUESTIONS (cont'd)

5. Sarah's patented microwave oven was sold without any notice of patent. Sarah has written the alleged infringer, Dave, and requested that he cease and desist from any further infringement of the patented microwave. Dave has ignored the letter and continued making his microwave oven. Do Sarah's and Dave's actions have any effect on remedies they may seek or that may be imposed on them? Discuss.

6. Frank, a patentee, has licensed use of his patented fan to Roy. Roy has failed to pay the agreed-upon royalties to Frank, and Frank would like to sue Roy to recover the unpaid royalties. Frank would also like to sue Rachel, who he believes is infringing the patented item. Frank believes he will have a difficult time proving damages caused by Rachel's infringement. Discuss where Frank should initiate actions to enforce his rights and what damages he should seek from Rachel.

For additional resources, go to www.westlegalstudies.com.

CHAPTER 21

New Developments and International Patent Law

CHAPTER OVERVIEW

Many of the new developments in patent law relate to the increasing number of patent applications filed for computer software, reflecting the somewhat more limited scope of protection afforded to software under copyright law. Other new developments relate to medicine, science, pharmacology, business method patents, and patents for new varieties of seeds and agricultural food products.

In regard to international patent law, because patents granted in the United States have no effect outside U.S. territorial borders, inventors desiring patent protection in foreign countries must comply with the laws of the countries in which they desire patent protection. Alternatively, however, they may rely on three treaties to which the United States adheres. Under the Paris Convention, a U.S. inventor who files a patent application in any of the more than 160 Paris member nations has

twelve months to file applications in any of the other member nations and yet claim the priority date of the first filing. Under the Patent Cooperation Treaty (PCT), an inventor may file one "international" application, thereby receiving the benefit of one centralized filing, searching, and examination process and receiving protection in any PCT member nation, as long as the application is ultimately prosecuted in those nations. Prosecution in the other countries may be delayed for up to thirty months, affording the inventor significant time to gather funds, consider the commercial application of the invention, and evaluate market conditions. Under the Uruguay Round Agreements on Trade-Related Aspects of Intellectual Property Rights (TRIPs), member nations must afford patent protection to citizens of member nations on the same basis they do for their own citizens. Foreign inventors may apply for patents in the United States as long as they comply with the provisions of the Patent Act.

NEW DEVELOPMENTS IN PATENT LAW

The Patent Act has proven remarkably flexible in accommodating changes and developments in technology. Thus, advancements in technology generally have not necessitated changes in the statutes governing patent protection. This situation is somewhat different from that encountered in trademark law with the conflict over domain names creating much turmoil and in copyright law with the ramifications of publication on the Internet creating similar turmoil.

Business Method and Software Patents

Many of the cutting-edge issues in patent law relate to patents for computer software. For several years, the conventional wisdom has been that unless a computer program had significant commercial value and application, patent protection was often counterproductive or ineffective in that the PTO often took two years to issue a patent, roughly the same time it took for the software program to become obsolete. Thus, protection of the program under copyright law was often viewed as the most effective means of protection for software.

Some experts believe that in 1995, when the First Circuit held in *Lotus Development Corp. v. Borland International Inc.,* 49 F.3d 807 (1st Cir. 1995), *aff'd,* 516 U.S. 233 (1996), that Lotus's menu command system did not constitute copyrightable expression (being an unprotectable method of operation), courts clearly signaled that copyright law provides little protection for computer software. Major companies apparently felt the same way: more than one-third of the patents issued to IBM in 1998 were software-related and nearly one-fourth related to network computing. Similarly, in the wake of losing a $120 million patent infringement suit (see Chapter 20), Microsoft received nearly two hundred patents for software in 1997 alone. The PTO has reported that software-related patent applications nearly doubled in just the two years between 1995 and 1997.

The courts have struggled with the issue of patentability for software programs. Programs that are "processes" or "machines" are patentable; programs that are purely mathematical principles or algorithms are not. Nevertheless, in what many observers believe to be a groundbreaking decision, in *State Street Bank & Trust Co. v. Signature Financial Group Inc.,* 149 F.3d 1368 (Fed. Cir. 1998), *cert. denied,* 525 U.S. 1093 (1999), the Federal Circuit held that a data processing system designed to make financial calculations (calculating daily changes in the allocation of certain assets and tracking data relevant to determining year-end income, expenses, and capital gains and losses) was patentable because the calculations produced a useful, concrete, and tangible result. In 1996, guidelines for computer-related inventions (often called "software patents") were adopted by the PTO to aid examiners in determining the patentability of software. Under the guidelines (available at the PTO web site at http://www.uspto.gov), the following are patentable: a machine that is directed by a computer program; a computer-readable memory; and a computer-implemented process. Algorithms that manipulate only abstract ideas remain unpatentable. In brief, patent applications for computer-related inventions must be carefully drafted by attorneys knowledgeable in the art, the developing case law, and the new PTO guidelines.

In sum, *State Street* is seen as a deathblow to the older view that business methods were not patentable. Under *State Street,* software, mathematical algorithms, and business methods are patentable as long as they produce a useful, tangible, and concrete result. In fact, the PTO saw growth rates exceeding 20 percent for software and business method patents in 1997, 1998, and 1999.

The explosion of applications for business method patents and software patents led to the granting of some broad and unusual patents. For example, Patent No. 6,004,596 is for a sealed crustless sandwich; the upper and lower fillings are preferably comprised of peanut butter and the center filling is comprised of at least jelly. In other words, the patent is for a crustless peanut butter and jelly sandwich. Similarly, Patent No. 6,192,323 is for a method of matching golfers with a driver and a ball. IBM received a patent (which it later abandoned) for a "system and method for providing reservations for restroom use." In some instances, these broadly worded patents were used to demand licensing fees by their owners for practices that had long been publicly used. In other instances, inventors merely sought these patents as a defensive measure to thwart efforts by others who might claim rights in similar methods. For example, after Amazon.com initially received an injunction barring Barnesandnoble.com from using Amazon.com's famous "1-click" checkout system, an appeals court vacated the injunction, noting that Barnesandnoble.com had raised a substantial question about the validity of Amazon.com's patent. The parties later settled their dispute out of court.

In 2002, the PTO itself recognized that too many business method patents had been wrongfully awarded in the past and advocated a more careful approach. While previously the PTO was granting approximately 65 percent of the applications for business method patents, the rejection rate was approximately 65 percent by late 2002.

In 2000, the PTO issued a "Business Method Patent Initiative" designed to ensure high-quality patents in this fast-emerging technology field. The PTO hired new examiners, provided additional training to the examiners, held roundtable meetings with patent practitioners, began subjecting business method applications to expanded prior art searches, and imposed a second review, usually called the "second pair of eyes review," for those applications. Coupled with the thorough and detailed PTO Examination Guidelines for Computer-Related Inventions (with numerous training examples), the PTO and many experts believe the PTO has made significant progress in meeting the criticisms directed at the early business method and software patents.

With all of the furor over business method and software patents, it is important to remember that even with the significant growth in their applications over the past few years, they still represent a small portion of patent applications overall. For example, applications in 1999 in Class 705 (the class in which most business method patent applications are filed) represented only about 1 percent of total patent applications filed that year with the PTO. Moreover, perhaps due to the more rigorous examination of those applications at the PTO, applications in Class 705 experienced a decline from 8,700 in 2001 to 5,000 in 2002. Additionally, some large cases have settled out of court (the Amazon.com case discussed above and two lawsuits by Priceline.com against Microsoft and its travel subsidiary, Expedia). Finally, although legislation was introduced in the 106th Congress to curtail business method patents (H.R. 5364, The Business Method Patent Improvement Act of 2000), the legislation did not pass and was not reintroduced in congressional sessions thereafter, perhaps indicating Congress's view that the PTO itself is adequately handling the various challenges presented by these emerging technologies.

In Europe, however, business method patents are not favored, and business methods and software are specifically excluded from the list of patentable inventions by the European Patent Convention, the governing law for the European Patent Organization (EPO). Nevertheless, despite the ban, the EPO has granted patents for computer programs with "technical effects." Likewise, experts predict that the EPO will allow business method patents if they are "dressed up" as another type of invention and specify a technical type of apparatus used to carry out the business method.

Biotechnology Patents

Medicine, science, agricultural, and pharmacology present the other cutting-edge issues in patent law. Research into genes may hold the key to curing disease throughout the world. Agricultural research may hold the key to providing sufficient food for the world's ever-increasing population. The PTO continues to see increases in patents in both these fields. In one interesting case, the PTO issued a patent on Basmati rice lines and grains. The government of India requested reexamination of the patent and submitted 50,000 pages of information to the PTO arguing that the patent should not have been issued because it was not novel. India was concerned that the patent would damage exports from its own farmers to the United States, a type of "biopiracy" that would take the genetic material and biological resources of India. Most of the claims in the patent were declared invalid.

The development of strains of plants and crops that are resistant to drought and disease has also led to an increasing number of patents issued, and attendant litigation, in the field of "agbiotech." Genetically modified varieties of crops have been quickly adopted by U.S. farmers. By 2000, approximately 20 percent of U.S. corn crops were genetically modified to be resistant to insects or herbicides, or both. In *J.E.M. Ag Supply v. Pioneer Hi-Bred International, Inc.*, 534 U.S. 124 (2001), a case involving seventeen corn seed patents, the Supreme Court held that utility patents may be granted for plants even though plants are also protectable under the Plant Patent Act and the Plant Protection Variety Act. The Department of Justice supported the decision, stating that providing such protection would promote incentives for research and development in the agricultural fields.

Because scientific and technological advances now permit researchers to rapidly identify large numbers of gene sequences, and some of the sequences are more than three hundred pages, the prosecution of applications for these gene sequences presents unparalleled search and examination challenges for the PTO. Thus, in 2001 the PTO issued its Final Guidelines for Determining Utility of Gene-Related Inventions. The guidelines are applicable to all areas of technology but they are particularly relevant in areas of emerging technologies, such as gene-related technologies. Genes and other genomic inventions are patentable so long as they meet the requisite statutory criteria of utility, novelty, and nonobviousness and fully disclose the use to which the gene can be put. Isolated and purified DNA is patentable because this form differs from the naturally occurring compound.

The intersection of the Patent Act's requirements that an invention be "useful" with patents in the biotech and chemical fields has led to much discussion. If drugs are experimental, how can their utility be proven to satisfy the Patent Act? Thus, drugs aimed at the most difficult diseases, such as AIDS and cancer, often face the most difficult challenges in meeting the requirements of utility. New PTO guidelines now provide that sufficient utility is shown when a patent application explicitly describes a use for a drug that is credible to a person ordinarily skilled in the art.

Nearly insatiable consumer demand continues to fuel activity in the biotech arena. Just a few years ago, drugs were known by name only to the physicians who prescribed them. Today, patients routinely request or demand prescriptions for PAXIL®, LIPITOR®, or VIAGRA®, all patented products, whose effects are advertised with as much vigor as any other consumer product. Pharmaceutical companies invested approximately $30 billion in 2001 to discover and develop new medicines. Without patent protection for drugs, the pharmaceutical industry could not exist. The process of drug invention is lengthy, costly, and risky. Unless protection were provided by patent, manufacturers would not expend the time and effort in developing drugs that ultimately support public health. Thus, the public is benefited by the limited monopoly a patent gives to pharmaceutical companies.

American Inventors Protection Act of 1999

The AIPA was signed into law in 1999 and represents the most significant changes to patent law in twenty years. Although some of the provisions of AIPA have been discussed earlier, its key subtitles are as follows:

- **Inventors' Rights Act of 1999.** AIPA helps protect inventors against deceptive practices of certain invention promotion companies. The act requires invention promoters to disclose information about their customers' success in receiving financial gain as a result of the invention promotion services and allows injured customers to bring a civil action to recover statutory damages up to $5,000 or actual damages.
- **The First Inventor Defense Act of 1999.** Because many individuals were using business methods prior to the stampede by companies to obtain patents for business methods, the act provides a defense against charges of patent infringement for a party who had, in good faith, actually reduced the subject matter of the invention to practice at least one year before the filing date of the patent and commercially used the subject matter before the filing date. This defense is available only in actions relating to business method patents.

- **The Patent Term Guarantee Act of 1999.** This portion of AIPA extends the terms of patents to compensate for certain PTO processing delays and delays in the prosecution of applications pending for more than three years. Diligent applicants are guaranteed a minimum seventeen-year patent term.
- **The Domestic Publication of Foreign Filed Patent Applications Act of 1999.** This subtitle provides for publication of patent applications eighteen months after their filing unless the applicant requests otherwise upon filing and certifies that the invention has not and will not be the subject of an application filed in a foreign country.
- **The Optional Inter Partes Reexamination Procedure Act of 1999.** This subtitle establishes a reexamination alternative that expands the participation of third parties by permitting those parties to submit a written response each time the patent owner files a response to the PTO. Those third-party requesters who choose to use the optional procedure, however, will not be able to appeal adverse decisions beyond the Board of Patent Appeals and Interferences.

INTRODUCTION TO INTERNATIONAL PATENT PROTECTION

The rights granted by a U.S. patent extend only throughout the United States and have no effect in a foreign country. Therefore, an inventor who desires patent protection in other countries must apply for a patent in each of the other countries or in regional patent offices. Nearly every country has its own patent law, and a person who wishes to obtain a patent in a particular country must make an application for patent in that country, in accordance with its requirements. A directory of more than one hundred foreign patent offices can be found at http://www.piperpat.co.nz, which also provides direct links to the home pages for the foreign patent offices. See also http://www.patents.com for contact information for more than twenty foreign patent offices.

The laws of most other countries differ in various respects from the patent law of the United States. In most foreign countries, publication of the invention before the date of the application will be an absolute bar to the right to a patent, while in the United States, the one-year grace period applies, so that if the invention was described by the inventor in a printed publication, the inventor has one year thereafter to file the patent application for the invention. Most foreign countries require that the invention be manufactured in that country within a certain period of time, usually three years, after grant of the patent or the patent will be void, while in the United States there is no requirement that the invention ever be manufactured, used, or sold. Additionally, nearly all foreign countries grant patents to the "first to file" the application. In the United States, however, a patent is usually granted to the "first to invent."

There are several **international patent** treaties to which the United States adheres, primarily the Paris Convention, the Patent Cooperation Treaty, and the Agreement on Trade-Related Aspects of Intellectual Property Rights.

THE PARIS CONVENTION

The Paris Convention for the Protection of Intellectual Property of 1883 is a treaty adhered to by more than 160 nations and is administered by WIPO, discussed in Chapter 8.

The Paris Convention requires that each country guarantee to the citizens of the other member adherents the same rights in patent and trademark matters that it provides to its own citizens (the principle of "national treatment"). The treaty also provides for the right of priority in the case of patents, trademarks, and industrial designs (design patents). The right of priority means that, on the basis of a patent application filed in one of the member countries, the applicant may, within one year, apply for protection in any of the other member countries. These later applications will then be regarded as if they had been filed on the same day as the first application in the first country, assuming the first application adequately disclosed the invention. (See Appendix A for a table of the countries adhering to the Paris Convention.)

Recall from Chapter 8 that after a trademark application is filed in the United States (or any Paris Convention member country), the applicant has six months to file an application for the same mark in any Paris Convention member country. The later-filed application captures the filing date, called the "priority date," of the earlier-filed application. The same principle is true for patents, although the time period for filing a patent application is one year (six months for a design patent). Thus, a later application will have priority over an application for the same invention that may have been filed during the twelve-month period of time. For example, if an inventor files a patent application in the United States on January 1, 2003, he or she will have until January 1, 2004, to file an application for the same invention in any Paris Convention member country, which application will then be treated as if it were filed in that country on January 1, 2003. Filing either a provisional application or a standard utility patent begins the Paris Convention priority year.

Additionally, the later-filed application, because it is based on the date of the first application, will not be invalidated by some act accomplished in the interval, such as publication or use of the invention. Similarly, the earlier priority date is the date of invention for determining whether prior art precludes granting of a patent for the invention. Finally, for purposes of determining priority of inventorship, the earlier priority date will be deemed to be the date of constructive reduction to practice of the invention.

There are, however, a few conditions that must be satisfied if an applicant is to be allowed to claim the date he or she first filed an application in a foreign country as the priority date in a later-filed U.S. application:

- the foreign country in which the application was first filed must afford similar privileges to citizens of the United States or to applications first filed in the United States;
- no patent will be granted on any application for patent for an invention that has been patented or described in the inventor's printed publication in any country more than one year before the date of the actual filing of the application in the United States or that has been in public use or on sale in the United States more than one year prior to such filing. Thus, if *A* offers an invention for sale in the United States on January 1, 2003, files an application in Spain on April 1, 2003, and then files an application in the United States on February 1, 2004, claiming the foreign priority date of April 1, 2003, the application will be barred because the invention was offered for sale in the United States more than one year prior to the filing of the application in the United States, regardless of the fact that *A* is entitled to the benefit of the priority date of April 1, 2003;
- the applicant must submit a certified copy of the original foreign application,

specification, and drawings to the PTO; and
- the priority application must be for an invention by the same inventor(s) as named in the later U.S. application.

The priority right is based on the filing of the application in the foreign country and timely filing in the United States. The prosecution status or history of the application in the foreign country is irrelevant. If the foreign country refuses to grant a patent, or the applicant abandons the application, such is irrelevant to the later U.S. application.

The Paris Convention affords patent applicants the opportunity to file a patent application in a member country and then take twelve months to determine whether foreign protection will be sought. An applicant may determine that the invention is not marketable in certain countries and thus decide not to apply for patents in those countries. In this way, the Paris Convention saves an applicant the time and expense of having to file simultaneous patent applications in several nations before it has had an opportunity to evaluate the likelihood of obtaining patent protection and exploiting the invention commercially.

THE PATENT COOPERATION TREATY

Introduction to the Patent Cooperation Treaty

While the Paris Convention allows applicants to defer decisions about filing in member countries for twelve months, it still requires that applicants file separate applications in each country in which they desire protection. For an inventor who wishes to market his or her invention on a global basis, this process is time-consuming and expensive in the extreme. The Patent Cooperation Treaty (PCT), which was negotiated in 1970 and came into force in

1978, responds to these concerns by providing a centralized way of filing, searching, and examining patent applications in several countries simultaneously. Moreover, a standardized application format is used, saving applicants substantial time and money that is ordinarily incurred in ensuring that a patent application complies with the procedural and formatting requirements imposed by each country. The PCT is adhered to by more than 120 countries (called "contracting states"), including the United States, and is administered by WIPO. In sum, the PCT allows an inventor to file one "international" application and seek protection for the invention simultaneously in several countries. (See Appendix A for a table of the countries adhering to the PCT.)

The one application filed with the PCT does not automatically mature into a patent that affords patent rights in several countries. The application must designate the countries in which protection is desired, and eventually the applicant must prosecute separate applications in those designated countries (the **national phase**). The PCT process, however, affords a significant window of time for the applicant to keep his or her options open while a determination is made whether protection should be sought in various foreign countries. The PTO web site (http://www.uspto.gov) provides a great deal of information about the PCT process, including a map showing PCT member countries, fee schedules and PCT fees, and tutorials relating to the PCT application process.

The Patent Cooperation Treaty Application Process—Chapter I

The "international" application may be filed with the patent office of the member country of which the applicant is a national or resident or, if the applicant desires, with the International Bureau of WIPO in Geneva, Switzerland. When filed with a national patent office, such as the PTO, the office is said to act as a PCT **receiving office.** The application designates those countries in which the applicant desires patent protection. For example, a citizen of the United States could file a PCT application with the PTO and designate Spain, Brazil, and the United Kingdom as countries in which he or she also desires patent protection. When the application is filed with the PTO as the receiving office, the effect is the same as if the applicant had simultaneously filed applications in Spain, Brazil, and the United Kingdom. Only one filing fee is paid for filing the PCT application, which is called an "international patent application." The amount of the filing fee generally depends upon the length of the application and how many countries are designated in the application. The application is similar in form to utility patent applications in that it contains claims and drawings of the invention.

A PCT application may claim priority, under the Paris Convention, of an earlier patent application for the invention. Thus, if an application was filed in Hungary on January 4, 2003, and an international PCT application was filed with the PTO on June 4, 2003, designating Spain, Brazil, and the United Kingdom, the effective filing date for the PCT application for all of those countries will be January 4, 2003. If priority is not claimed under the Paris Convention (usually because no prior application has been filed in any foreign country), the priority date will be the date the PCT application was filed.

Many applicants file a standard patent application with their home patent office and then, near the end of the twelve-month period afforded by the Paris Convention, file a PCT application with their home office (now acting as a "receiving office"), designating the various foreign countries in which they seek patent protection.

The filing of the international patent application triggers the first phase of the PCT process, called **Chapter I.** During Chapter I, the international application is subjected to an international search by an "international searching authority," experienced patent offices designated by WIPO to conduct searches. The international searching authorities designated by WIPO are the national offices of Australia, Austria, China, Japan, the Republic of Korea, the Russian Federation, Spain, Sweden, the United States, and the European Patent Office. The applicant elects the international searching authority it desires, and it may be different from the office that is serving as the receiving office. The international searching authority will conduct an extensive search of the relevant prior art. The results of the search are set forth in an "international search report" that is provided to the applicant several months after the international application is filed. Although the international search report does not provide an opinion on patentability in the various countries designated in the international patent application, its citations of prior art enable an inventor to evaluate the likelihood of obtaining patents in the designated countries and to amend claims in the international patent application, if necessary to avoid prior art. The applicant is generally given two months to amend its claims. If the report discloses prior art that would bar the application, the applicant may decide to abandon the PCT application.

The PCT application (and the international search report) will be published eighteen months after its filing date or priority date. Publication serves to notify the public that an international patent application has been filed for the invention and affords an opportunity for third parties to obtain copies of the application. This publication date should be docketed so that the inventor can ensure applications are timely filed in countries that are not members of the Paris Convention or are not designated in the PCT application inasmuch as this publication will foreclose patent applications in those countries that bar applications for inventions that have been published (unless they have a one-year grace period such as the United States). Until publication, the application is maintained in confidence. In a later infringement case, in most PCT countries, a patent owner may recover damages arising from the date of publication (rather than the date the patent issues).

The Chapter I phase of the PCT process lasts for twenty months from either the filing date of the international patent application with the receiving office or the claimed priority date if the application claims priority under the Paris Convention. This twenty-month period affords the inventor the opportunity to evaluate the marketability of the invention in the designated countries and gather funds in order to enter foreign markets.

Participation in Chapter I of the PCT process does not require participation in Chapter II.

The Patent Cooperation Treaty Application Process—Chapter II

If the applicant has not yet decided to pursue the patent application in the designated countries and desires examination of the patent application, he or she may elect to enter **Chapter II** of the PCT process. Chapter II must be entered twenty months after the date the PCT application was filed or twenty months after the filing date of an application claiming Paris Convention priority. Upon entering Chapter II, the applicant may demand that the application undergo an "international preliminary examination," a process that takes ten months and requires payment of a fee. Nearly 80 percent of PCT applicants request international preliminary examination. A written opinion on patentability is prepared by an "international preliminary examining authority" having qualifications similar to those of the

Generally speaking, the various kinds of scaling schemes developed by experts in various fields are helpful in selecting the items for your composite measures. The accompanying procedures for translating the different items into a composite score, however, may not be so useful and pertinent to your research project because of the existence of some fundamental issues.

The first issue is called "confounding" in a relational analysis. That is, the association present in the research findings is not the "true" relationship between two variables but the consequence of certain degree of the overlapping of their measurements. Because of this problem, a measurement procedure legitimized in scaling a single, isolated variable may not be applicable to scaling a variable in relation to other variables. In other words, a scaling procedure may have to be readjusted and rejustified based on the specific purpose of a relational analysis. This is especially true for many psychometric products developed mainly for psychological testing purposes. Chapter twelve will further discuss such issues. Generally speaking, you can start your research by selecting all the items you may need to measure a complex construct for data collection. But your final decision as to which data items should be included in a specific scale will not be made until you start thinking about a particular relational analysis. In such sense, the operationalization of your research ideas will not be completed until the measurement items are decided or your data analysis is finally carried out.

The second issue has to do with the dimensionality of your data. A dimension in plain language is a specifiable aspect or facet of a concept. Statistically, a dimension in the data is represented by a principal component, a factor, or a "latent" variable. It has been a major challenge for a researcher to synthesize the different aspects or facets theoretically and to combine the unrelated factors statistically. It is also an unresolved issue as to how to make the conceptual scheme and the factorial structure consistent with each other. Probably for this reason, the methodological literature (e.g., traditional psychometrics) has stressed the requirement for unidimensionality in scale construction, which means that the items you select for a scale should all be parallel. In practice, however, behavioral and social science researchers frequently have to deal with multidimensional measurement. The blind application of unidimensional scaling techniques thus incurs the risk of distorting the reality. With the popularization of computer technology, more and more scholars have started to use multidimensional scaling methods, including factor analysis. The older multiple and partial correlation measures for describing relations among the dimensions are related to the parameters of a multinormal distribution, though this would require a large international searching authorities. The examining authorities are identical to the searching authorities, except that Spain is not an examining authority. The examining authority will review the prior art citations listed in the earlier search report and provide an opinion on patentability, novelty, and usefulness of the invention in the various countries designated in the PCT application. The applicant will have an opportunity to respond to the written opinion and may amend claims or delete claims in the application based upon the examining authority's opinion. The examining authority then issues an "international preliminary examining report," which is a formal report on patentability in the designated nations. Although the report is not binding on any specific nation, it is highly authoritative.

The PCT has experienced a consistent growth rate of 10 percent each year, which growth has generated tremendous increases in the workload for various PCT offices. In many cases, applicants entered Chapter II and demanded an international preliminary examination merely for the purpose of buying time, namely, an additional ten months while the examination was conducted. As a result, the PCT was modified effective April 1, 2002, to provide that the time limit for entering the national phase (and prosecuting the individual patent applications in the desired countries) will be thirty months from the date of filing of the PCT application whether the applicant enters under Chapter I (and foregoes an international preliminary examination) or under Chapter II (and demands the international preliminary examination). Thus, applicants who wish to buy time no longer need to file a demand for the international preliminary examination. WIPO expects that this new modification will result in the fewer demands for international preliminary examinations, which in turn will reduce the workload for the various patent offices.

In brief, until this modification, under Chapter I, applicants entered the national phase twenty months after filing, and the only way to buy additional time was to request an international preliminary examination (whether it was truly desired or not). Effective April 1, 2002, an applicant may enter the national phase thirty months after filing the PCT application whether entry is under Chapter I or Chapter II. Although the United States has adopted the modified rule, not all PCT contracting states have changed their national laws to adopt this new thirty-month period.

The additional time afforded by the PCT process (twenty months from filing of the application plus an additional ten months whether or not a preliminary examining report is requested) is significantly more than the twelve months afforded under the Paris Convention. This additional time is useful for allowing inventors to determine whether the invention is commercially exploitable in various countries and whether protection is needed in certain countries.

The Patent Cooperation Treaty Application Process—The National Phase

If, after the duration of Chapter I (and the international preliminary examining report, if elected through Chapter II), the applicant decides to go forward with the application in the countries designated in the application, the applicant commences the "national phase" of the PCT application process. National fees must be paid to each country in which protection is desired, and often translations must be obtained of the PCT application. In many instances, the applicant will decide to forego protection in some countries and will not pursue the patent application in those countries. Thus, the application will lapse in those countries. Each national office in which the application is pursued will now conduct its own search and examination procedure, although the process is both easier and faster due to the fact that the highly credible international search report and international preliminary examination report have already provided interpretations regarding the patentability of the invention. Each of the countries designated in the PCT application will either grant or reject the application. The term of a patent designating the United States is twenty years from the filing date of the PCT application.

Advantages of the Patent Cooperation Treaty Application Process

The most significant advantage provided by the PCT application process is time. If an application is filed in the United States, and the applicant wishes to file an application for the same invention in Japan, under the Paris Convention, the applicant has only twelve months from the United States filing date to file in Japan. The filing in Japan will require filing fees, translations, and the costs of prosecution as the process proceeds in Japan. On the other hand, under the PCT, the applicant can file one application in the United States and designate Japan in the application. The applicant then has twenty months during Chapter I while a search is done, and, whether or not an examination is requested under Chapter II, a total of thirty months before it must decide whether to pursue the application by entering the national phase in Japan and pay the filing fee, arrange for a translation, and prosecute the application in Japan. In addition to the benefits afforded by this time, the PCT process also affords the benefits of a single application format and a centralized filing, searching, and examination system. The PCT, however, is not applicable to design patents, and therefore, the maximum delay afforded an applicant for a design patent to decide whether to make foreign patent applications is the six months pro-

vided for design patents under the Paris Convention.

The time afforded by the PCT allows an inventor additional opportunity to reflect on whether protection is actually desired in certain countries and to gather funds necessary to prosecute the applications during the national phase and to market and exploit the invention. Additionally, due to the highly authoritative nature of the international search report and international preliminary examination report, the PCT process provides an indication to the inventor about the likelihood whether a patent will be granted in various countries. Finally, the time and costs involved in the national phase are likely to be significantly reduced because much of the searching and examination work required has already been conducted in Chapters I and II.

The success of the PCT process is demonstrated by the fact that in 1979, only 2,625 PCT applications were filed with WIPO's International Bureau, while in 2002, the number had grown to 114,048. The average number of countries designated in each application grew from 6.6 in 1979 to 71.74 in 1998. The United States is the country of origin for approximately 40 percent of PCT applications, followed by Germany (13 percent), Japan (10 percent), the United Kingdom (6 percent), and France (4 percent).

THE EUROPEAN PATENT ORGANIZATION

The **European Patent Organization** (EPO) was founded in 1973 to provide a uniform patent system in Europe. A European patent can be obtained by filing a single application with the EPO headquartered in Munich (or its subbranches in The Hague or Berlin or with the national offices in the contracting nations). Once granted, the patent is valid in any of the EPO countries designated in the application and has the same force as a patent granted in any one of the contracting nations. The EPO contracting nations are Austria, Belgium, Bulgaria, Cyprus, Czech Republic, Denmark, Estonia, Finland, France, Germany, Hellenic Republic (Greece), Hungary, Ireland, Italy, Liechtenstein, Luxembourg, Monaco, Netherlands, Portugal, Romania, Slovak Republic, Slovenia, Spain, Sweden, Switzerland, and the United Kingdom. Although they are not contracting nations to the European Patent Convention, Albania, Latvia, Lithuania, and the former Yugoslav Republic of Macedonia have extension agreements with the convention, allowing them to participate as EPO countries.

After the application is filed, a search will be conducted, the application will be examined, and the application will be published. Within six months after publication, the applicant must decide whether to pursue the application by requesting an examination. It generally takes nearly four years to obtain a European patent. Within nine months following the date of grant of the patent, a party may oppose the grant on the basis the patent does not comply with the substantive provisions of the European Patent Convention. A binding decision will be issued by the opposition division of the EPO. The European patent is valid for twenty years from the date the application was filed. Since the filing of the first European patent application in 1978, more than 300,000 European patents have been granted. In 2001, the EPO received more than 150,000 patent applications.

An applicant who is a national or resident of a nation that is a party to the European Patent Convention may file a PCT application with the EPO. A party from outside the European Patent Convention countries who designates a contracting state in a PCT application may opt for the effect of a European patent application. Thus, if a citizen from the United States files a PCT application and desires patent protection in Germany, the applicant may opt for the effect of a European patent application to cover all of the European contracting nations, rather than merely designating Germany.

As discussed earlier, the EPO takes a far more conservative view in granting patents for software and for business methods than does the United States.

AGREEMENT ON TRADE-RELATED ASPECTS OF INTELLECTUAL PROPERTY RIGHTS

The General Agreement on Tariffs and Trade, Uruguay Round Agreements on Trade-Related Aspects of Intellectual Property Rights (TRIPs) was accepted by the United States in 1994. In addition to providing enhanced protection for trademarks (by requiring all adhering nations to allow registration of service marks as well as trademarks and prescribing an international standard for determining likelihood of confusion of marks) and copyrights (by specifying that computer programs must be protected as literary works), TRIPs also strengthens international patent law.

To comply with its obligations under TRIPs, the United States was required to amend the Patent Act in several respects. The most significant change was the revision relating to the term of a patent. Until adherence to TRIPs, the U.S. utility patent term was seventeen years from the date the patent was issued. Because the term of the patent did not start until issuance, applicants in some instances delayed prosecution of their patents (sometimes called "submarine patents" because they lurked below public view) while they tested the market, gathered funds, and made plans to bring the invention to the marketplace. To harmonize U.S. law with that of most foreign nations, the term of a utility patent was changed to twenty years from the date of filing of the application, thus encouraging applicants to pursue prosecution diligently. Additionally, the publication of patents in the United States within eighteen months of filing avoids the problem of submarine patents. Another significant change in U.S. patent law related to determining the first to invent in priority disputes. Until TRIPs, the United States ignored evidence of inventive activity abroad, thus discriminating against foreign inventors. TRIPs requires the United States to make patent rights available without discrimination in regard to the place of invention. Thus, the United States now generally considers evidence of inventive activity abroad equivalent to evidence of inventive activity in the United States in determining which party is the first to invent for purposes of priority. TRIPs is administered by the World Trade Organization, headquartered in Geneva, Switzerland.

THE PATENT LAW TREATY

Negotiations in WIPO in the latter half of the 1990s produced the Patent Law Treaty (PLT), which was adopted in June of 2000. The goal of the PLT is to harmonize the formal requirements established by the individual patent offices around the world and streamline the procedures for obtaining and maintaining patents. The PLT is primarily concerned with patent formalities. The PLT eliminates overly burdensome requirements and establishes limits on the requirements that can be imposed by the various national patent offices throughout the world. It simplifies and standardizes application procedures that at present vary from nation to nation. For example, the PLT signatories have agreed to a set of standardized forms and have agreed that a failure to comply with various formalities at the time of filing of a patent application will not result in a loss of the filing date. Additionally, the signatories have agreed to offer electronic filing of applications and other communications. These simplified

procedures will make it easier and less expensive for individual inventors to apply for patents. Additionally, the PLT provides that in the event of a late filing (meaning one that is beyond a priority period), restoration is possible if it is found that the failure to file was unintentional or due care was exercised. Finally, the PLT does not require that a representative be employed during all stages of prosecution; however, a legal representative must still be engaged to provide translations, often the costliest part of patent application process.

Although there are numerous signatories to the PLT (including the United States), the PLT will probably not enter into force until sometime in late 2004 (three months after it is ratified by ten countries). The PLT continues the trend of harmonizing patent law throughout the world so that inventors have easier access to patent protection on an international basis.

FOREIGN FILING LICENSES

To ensure that national security is not impaired, a person may not file a patent application in another country for an invention made in the United States unless the Commissioner for Patents grants a license allowing the foreign filing or until six months from the filing of the U.S. application for the invention. The six-month waiting period allows the PTO to review applications that might affect matters of national security.

Filing an application with the PTO is deemed to be a request to the Commissioner for a license to file an application in a foreign country. The official PTO filing receipt will indicate to the applicant whether the license is granted or denied. If the inventor does not wish to file an application in the United States but prefers to file immediately in a foreign country, he or she may file a petition to the Commissioner for Patents requesting that a **foreign filing license** be granted.

If the foreign filing license requirements are violated, any corresponding U.S. application is invalid. Additionally, criminal penalties and fines may be imposed. The violation may be cured, however, and a retroactive foreign filing license may be granted if failure to obtain the license was through error and without deceptive intent.

It is possible that the Commissioner may refuse the applicant permission to file an application in a foreign country and may order that the invention be kept secret. A secrecy order prohibits publication or filing in another country until the order is lifted. No patent can issue on an application subject to a secrecy order. The applicant may, however, obtain compensation from the government for damages caused due to his or her inability to secure a patent for the invention.

APPLICATIONS FOR UNITED STATES PATENTS BY FOREIGN APPLICANTS

The patent laws of the United States make no discrimination with respect to citizenship of the inventor. Any inventor, regardless of his or her citizenship, may apply for a patent in the United States on the same basis as a U.S. citizen. In fact, approximately 45 percent of the patent applications received by the PTO come from abroad. Compliance with U.S. patent law is required; thus, no U.S. patent can be obtained if the invention was patented abroad on an application filed by the inventor more than twelve months before filing of the application in the United States.

If the applicant is a citizen of a Paris Convention nation and has first filed the application in a foreign country, the applicant may claim the filing date of the earlier filed application (as long as the U.S. application is filed within twelve months after the filing of the foreign application). The U.S. application will then be treated as if it were filed on the earlier filing date.

An oath or declaration must be made with respect to the U.S. application. This requirement imposed on all applicants for U.S. patents is somewhat different from that of many foreign nations in that foreign nations often require neither the signature of the inventor nor an oath of inventorship.

TRIVIA

- The top ten best-selling prescription drugs generated worldwide sales of about $42 billion in 2002. The two best-selling drugs in the world are Lipitor® and Zocor®.
- In 2001, only two U.S. companies (IBM Corp. and Micron Technologies) were on the PTO's top ten list of patentees. Seven of the top ten patentees were Japanese companies.
- Since 1996, when the first genetically modified crops were grown, global genetically modified crop areas have increased thirtyfold.
- It costs an average of more than $800 million to bring just one new medicine to patients, with a 1 in 5,000 chance of success.
- During fiscal year 2002, the PTO received approximately 43,000 international or PCT applications.

CHAPTER SUMMARY

The most significant new development in patent law is likely the Federal Circuit's decision in *State Street* to largely discard the business method exception to patentability. So long as they produce a useful, concrete, and tangible result, mathematical algorithms, software, and business methods are patentable. In the wake of *State Street,* patents for Internet business methods, software patents, and e-commerce technologies have been applied for in tremendous numbers. Other new developments in patent law relate to inventions in the areas of medicine, pharmacology, and agbiotech.

Because patents granted by the PTO have no effect in a foreign country, inventors desiring patent protection in other countries must apply for patents in each of the countries in which protection is desired. Because applying for and prosecuting patents on a country-by-country basis is expensive and cumbersome, inventors often rely on the protection afforded by the Paris Convention, a treaty adhered to by more than 160 nations. On the basis of an application filed in one of the member countries, the applicant may, within one year, apply for protection in any or all of the other member countries, and claim as its priority date the date the application was first filed. This twelve-month period of time allows inventors to gather funding and engage in marketing analysis to determine in which countries patent protection should be sought.

Another treaty, the Patent Cooperation Treaty, facilitates the filing of applications for patents in member countries by providing a centralized filing procedure and standardized application format. The filing of an "international" application under the PCT affords applicants an international filing date in each country that is designated in the application and provides a later time period (up to thirty months) within which individual national applications must be filed.

Other international conventions also exist, principally the European Patent Organization (a centralized patent system affording patent protection in as many of the member countries as the applicant designates in a single patent application), and TRIPs, by the terms of which the United States revised the duration of utility patent protection from seventeen years from date of grant to twenty years from the date of filing of a patent application. The new Patent Law Treaty aims to simplify and streamline the process for international patent filings.

Under U.S. law, it is necessary to obtain a license from the Commissioner of Patents before applying for a patent in a foreign country. Filing an application in the United States is equivalent to requesting a license, and when the PTO issues a filing receipt, it will indicate whether the request is granted or denied. The PTO may order an invention to be kept secret if national security concerns are implicated.

CASE ILLUSTRATION—FOREIGN FILINGS

Case: *Beckman Insts. v. Coleman Insts.*, 338 F.2d 573 (7th Cir. 1964)

Facts: Plaintiff applied for one patent in 1951 and later abandoned the application. On November 22, 1952, he filed a second application and stated it was a "continuation in part" of the first application. A patent issued on the second application. On November 7, 1952, and November 24, 1952, he filed foreign

CASE ILLUSTRATION (cont'd)

applications in Great Britain and Germany, respectively, without first obtaining a foreign filing license.

Holding: The Patent Act is clear that an applicant who files an application for a patent in a foreign country must either delay the foreign filing for six months after filing the corresponding U.S. application or obtain a license authorizing such foreign filing in less than the mandatory six-month waiting period. In this case, the question is whether the six-month waiting period began at the time of the filing of the first U.S. application or the second. Because the inventor himself stated that the second application contained subject matter not in the first application (which the inventor abandoned), the inventor was required to obtain a foreign filing license. Failure to do so invalidates the U.S. patent. This holding is consistent with the purpose of the statute, which provides the waiting period in order for officials to ascertain whether the foreign filing might be detrimental to national security.

CASE STUDY AND ACTIVITIES

Case Study.   Watson is considering opening water parks in various countries in Europe and Asia. The parks would use Watson's newly developed wave-making technology, for which Watson filed a patent application two months ago. Watson is in the process of conducting marketing surveys to determine in which countries the water parks would be most successful. The theme parks will also use Watson's newly invented ornamental design for a water wakeboard that will be used at the park and for which Watson filed a design patent application three months ago.

Activities.   What type of strategy should Watson consider to ensure that it has patent protection for its new technology in the various countries in which it may operate its parks?

ROLE OF PARALEGAL

Paralegals may be involved in a variety of activities relating to international protection of patents. Some of the more common tasks include the following:

- docketing filing dates and notifying clients that they have twelve months from the filing date of a patent application in the United States to file applications in Paris Convention nations and claim the earlier filing date as a priority date;
- docketing filing dates and ensuring clients are notified that foreign applications cannot be filed without receipt of a foreign filing license;
- preparing PCT applications and surveying clients for designations of countries to be specified in the PCT applications;

- docketing critical dates involved in PCT applications to ensure rights to pursue patents in foreign countries are preserved;
- reviewing PCT search reports and assisting in reporting results of the reports to clients;
- docketing critical dates to ensure the option to pursue a Chapter II international preliminary examination is preserved, if desired by clients;
- reviewing PCT examination reports and assisting in reporting results of the reports to clients;
- assisting clients in eliminating countries from PCT designation if patent protection is not desired in those countries; and
- assisting in prosecution of national phase for PCT applications in desired countries.

INTERNET RESOURCES

Information about, and text of, treaties: http://www.wipo.org (information about and text of the Paris Convention, PCT, and Patent Law Treaty); http://www.wto.org (information about and text of TRIPs); http://www.european-patent-office.org (information about and text of the European Patent Convention and European Patent Organization)

PTO information about PCT: http://www.uspto.gov (see PCT Home Page and Chapter 1800 of MPEP)

Lists of patent attorneys and patent offices around the world: http://www.piperpat.co.nz

Information about biotechnology: http://www.bio.org (web site of Biotechnology Industry Organization)

Information about agricultural biotechnology: http://www.agbiotech.net

DISCUSSION QUESTIONS

1. Patricia has invented a new twist top for beverage containers. She applied for her patent in the United States on July 1. She would like to file an application in France for the same invention. What is the advantage to Patricia in filing the application in France by July 1 of next year? What treaty or convention governs your answer?

DISCUSSION QUESTIONS (cont'd)

2. Assume that Patricia would like to file applications in several countries for her patent. What advantages does a PCT application afford Patricia?

3. What, if anything, is Patricia required to do before filing an application in any foreign country?

4. Of what advantage is requesting an international preliminary examination during a PCT application process?

5. A resident of Italy filed an application in Italy for a design patent on March 1. What is the latest day that the application can be filed in the United States to capture the filing date in Italy for purposes of priority?

6. Dave has been using a business method for determining accounting practices. Chuck filed a patent application for the same business method thirteen months after Dave began using the business method. Chuck has sued Dave for infringement. What defense should Dave assert?

PART V

The Law of Trade Secrets and Unfair Competition

sample involving few variables with such stringent assumptions as normal distributions of the same variance. However, the use of this kind of multidimensional methods does not lead to the settlement of the scaling issues. Rather, they seem to be used to tear integral theories into pieces, i.e., a set of so-called latent variables. Because most theoretical constructs in social sciences are multidimensional rather than unidimensional, researchers usually need to conduct dimensional analyses of these constructs. Yet they are not well guided as to how to deal with the results of a dimensional analysis with more than one uncorrelated factor. As a result, researchers either forget about the results of dimensional analysis and resort to simple yet inappropriate unidimensional treatment, or ignore the original theoretical construct and turn to those lower-level individual factors or components. The various arbitrary scaling strategies have created tremendous incompatibility of research results. Such issues will further be discussed in chapter twelve.

It should be noted that in psychometrics, the issue of dimensionality is often related to Coombs' (1964) data theory, which is represented by a three-dimensional data matrix for H responses of N persons to K stimuli. Traditional Multi-Dimensional Scaling (MDS) or factor analysis, however, is concerned with the scaling of stimuli or people, and the notion of multidimensionality refers to the groupings of elements along either of the two dimensions of the data matrix. Here concerns such as item response theory are not the primary interest. Applied social research usually focuses on the issue of grouping variables in scaling people, and therefore refers multidimensional scaling technique primarily to factor analysis rather than MDS as a special procedure mainly concerned with scaling stimuli. Principal components analysis is especially important in this regard.

A final note about scaling. Our discussion has not dealt with the issue of the intensity of different items or the pattern of various responses, which is considered separate from or a special case of the dimensionality problem mentioned above. Psychometrics has devoted much attention to such issues in scale development. For example, the well-known Guttman scale that uses cumulative dichotomous response categories attempts to rank-order the degrees of intensity of its statements (Summers, 1970). Thurstone's equal-appearing intervals scale employs a more elaborate method to obtain the values on a scale formed by judges' ratings average for each statement (ibid.). Nevertheless, it is the Likert-type summated scale that has been a most popular and effective scaling method in behavioral and social science research. The summated scale assumes

CHAPTER 22

Trade Secrets Law

CHAPTER OVERVIEW

Trade secrets consist of any valuable business information that, if known by a competitor, would afford the competitor some benefit or competitive advantage. To be protected, trade secrets must be protected by their owner from unauthorized discovery. If properly protected, trade secrets may last forever.

Although many companies and employers require employees to sign agreements promising to keep key information confidential, trade secrets can be protected even in the absence of written agreement if parties occupy a relationship of trust and confidence to each other, as is the case in the employer-employee relationship. Thus, employees who learn trade secrets while in the scope of their employment cannot misappropriate those secrets, even after termination of their employment.

Trade secrets are also protected from being appropriated by improper means, such as theft or espionage. Employers typically require certain employees, generally those with access to the employer's valuable information, to sign agreements promising not to disclose confidential information and not to compete with the employer after leaving the job. Covenants not

to compete restrict an employee's ability to earn a living and are strictly scrutinized by courts to ensure they are reasonable in regard to time, scope, and subject matter.

A company whose trade secrets are misappropriated may seek injunctive relief to prohibit further use or disclosure of the information as well as monetary damages. Defendants typically assert that trade secret protection has been forfeited due to the owner's failure to employ reasonable efforts to protect the information.

INTRODUCTION

Definition of Trade Secret

Legend has it that the formula or recipe for COCA-COLA® is locked in a vault with no one person having access. Whether true or not, this legend illustrates a critical business reality: information that is proprietary to a company and gives it certain advantages over competitors must be protected. Release or dissemination of the information to others may cause economic hardship to (or even total elimination of) the first owner who would then be faced by competitors trading off and using the information to compete with the owner. The type of information that must be kept confidential in order to retain its competitive advantage is generally called a "trade secret." In fact, the secret recipe listing eleven herbs and spices developed by Kentucky Fried Chicken Founder Harlan Sanders "is safe and sound, locked in our vault," according to a spokeswoman for the company. The company has stated that only a few people know the recipe, and they have signed strict nondisclosure agreements.

A trade secret is any information that can be used in the operation of a business or other enterprise that is sufficiently valuable and secret to afford an actual or potential economic advantage over others. Restatement (Third) of Unfair Competition § 39 (1995). A recipe, a formula, a method of conducting business, a customer list, a price list, marketing plans, financial projections, and a list of targets for a potential acquisition can all constitute trade secrets. Even negative information can be protectable as a trade secret. For example, information that a certain operating process or technique is *not* effective or that a product is *not* profitable can qualify for protection. There is no requirement that a trade secret be unique or complex. Even something simple and nontechnical, such as a list of customers, can qualify as a trade secret as long as it affords its owner a competitive advantage and is not common knowledge. Generally, to qualify for trade secret protection, information must

- be valuable;
- not be publicly known; and
- be the subject of reasonable efforts to maintain its secrecy.

The rapid pace of technology advances the ease with which information can now be rapidly disseminated, and the mobility of employees require businesses to devote significant effort to protecting their trade secrets. One survey showed that within 246 responding companies, there were 589 incidents of trade secret theft, representing nearly $2 billion in combined losses.

If trade secrets were not legally protectable, companies would have no incentive for investing time, money, and effort in research and development that ultimately benefits the public at large. Trade secret law not only provides an incentive for companies to develop new methods and processes of doing business but also, by punishing wrongdoers, discourages improper conduct in the business environment.

The Law Governing Trade Secrets

While trademarks, copyrights, and patents are all subject to extensive federal statutory schemes for their protection, there is no federal law relating to trade secrets, and no registration is required to obtain trade secret protection. Most trade secret law arises from common law principles, namely, judge-made case law. The first reported trade secret case in the United States was decided in 1837 and involved manufacturing methods for making chocolate. *Vickery v. Welch,* 36 Mass. 523 (1837). In 1939, the Restatement of Torts adopted a definition of a trade secret, and many states relied on that in developing their body of case law, leading to greater consistency in the development of trade secrets law. Trade secrets are now discussed in the Restatement (Third) of Unfair Competition, which restates in a simple and clear fashion the law relating to trade secrets. Additionally, in 1979, the National Conference of Commissioners on Uniform State Laws drafted the Uniform Trade Secrets Act (UTSA) to promote uniformity among the states with regard to trade secrets law. The UTSA was amended in 1985. The UTSA has been adopted in more than forty states. Although modifications to the UTSA have been made by various states, in general, most states now share similar trade secret legislation largely patterned after the UTSA. There are some differences between the Restatement and the UTSA. For example, the Restatement requires that for trade secret protection, information must be in continuous use, while the UTSA has never imposed such a requirement. Thus, under the UTSA, material can be protected even if it has not yet been used. For the most part, however, the Restatement position and the UTSA are consistent in their treatment of trade secrets law. The following definition of *trade secret* has been adopted by the UTSA:

> Trade secret means information, including a formula, pattern, compilation, program, device, method, technique, or process that:
> (i) derives independent economic value, actual or potential, from not being generally known to, and not being readily ascertainable by proper means by, other persons who can obtain economic value from its disclosure or use, and
> (ii) is the subject of efforts that are reasonable under the circumstances to maintain its secrecy.

In sum, the law related to trade secrets is derived from case law, state statutes modeled after the UTSA, and the various pronouncements made on trade secrets law by the Restatement.

In addition to the various state statutes and cases that provide a body of trade secrets law, additional protection is often gained through contractual arrangements. Companies routinely require employees with access to confidential information to sign agreements promising not to disclose that information to others and to refrain from using that information to compete with the employer, even after employment has terminated. Similarly, companies that enter into business relationships with each other generally require contractual confidentiality obligations to ensure neither party will use confidential information gained through their business relationship for improper purposes. Terms and breaches of those agreements (variously called "confidentiality agreements" or "nondisclosure agreements") are generally governed under standard contract law principles. (See Appendix D, Form 15, for a sample confidentiality agreement.)

Interplay of Trade Secrets Law with Copyright and Patent Law

Copyright rights often intersect with trade secrets. For example, a company may be in the process of developing a new software program. While the program is being developed, any documents or material relating to it are likely trade secrets. Employees of the company might be required to sign agreements promising not to disclose information about the software to others. If software is developed for internal use only or is intended for limited distribution, it may retain its character as a trade secret. Once the program is completed or "fixed," it is automatically protected under copyright law. If the owner wishes to apply for copyright registration, certain deposit materials must be supplied to the Copyright Office. The Copyright Office, however, expressly recognizes that the source code for a computer program might constitute a trade secret and allows the copyright owner to deposit less than all of the source code or to deposit blocked-out portions of the source code, thereby preserving the trade secret status of the program. Similarly, marketing materials for the program might constitute trade secrets while they are being developed. Once created, they are subject to copyright protection and the owner may apply for copyright registration for the written materials and advertisements. Once the marketing materials are distributed to consumers, they will lose their status as trade secrets but will remain protectable as copyrighted works.

In regard to patents, patent applications remain confidential until a patent is published eighteen months after its filing date (unless the applicant certifies there will be no corresponding foreign filing for the invention). Thus, during the first part of the patent application process, an invention might well be protected by trade secrets law. Once a patent is published or issues, however, the invention is fully disclosed, and it cannot be a trade secret. Any protection for the invention arises under patent law. Information that is properly protected as a trade secret may maintain that status indefinitely. In contrast, patents are of a definite duration (twenty years from the date of filing of a utility application). Thus, the formula for COCA-COLA is well protected under trade secret law and protection can last indefinitely, while under patent law, the formula or process would be disclosed upon publication or issuance of the patent and would be protected for only twenty years from the date of filing of the patent application. In fact, Coca-Cola Co. has approximately 800 U.S. patents (primarily in technologies complementary to the beverage industry such as packaging and vending equipment); however, the product formulation for the COCA-COLA beverage is a trade secret.

Thus, trade secrets may be copyrightable or patentable. In fact, during the initial process of development of either copyright material or inventions, the material being developed or invented may well be a trade secret. Once a work is published, copyright protection continues, but trade secret protection is lost. Once a patent is published or is granted, patent protection is available, but trade secret protection is lost. An invention cannot be protected under both trade secret and patent law. Thus, companies should consider a variety of strategies to obtain the most protection for their proprietary materials. Because trade secrets (if properly protected) are eternal, a company may well wish to forego seeking copyright registration or

patent protection and rely on trade secret law to protect the information indefinitely.

Like patents and copyrights, trade secrets can be transferred outright to others or may be licensed to others for use under specified conditions, generally in regard to territory and duration. Such license agreements, however, must contain adequate provisions to protect the confidential nature of the information or its trade secret status will be lost.

DETERMINATION OF TRADE SECRET STATUS

Restatement of Torts § 757 cmt. b lists six factors to be considered in determining whether information qualifies as a trade secret. Courts routinely examine these factors to determine whether a company's information constitutes a trade secret. None of the factors alone are determinative; courts balance these factors and weigh them against each other in determining whether information qualifies as a protectable trade secret:

- **The extent to which the information is known outside the company.** Although information may be known to others outside the company and still qualify as a trade secret, the greater the number of people who know the information, the less likely it is to qualify as a trade secret. Secrecy need not be absolute. The owner of a trade secret may, without losing protection, disclose it to a licensee or a stranger if the disclosure is made in confidence. However, the more widely disseminated the information is, the less likely courts are to protect it. In sum, if information is publicly known or known within a specialized industry, it does not qualify for trade secret protection. Publication of information on the Internet will cause a loss of trade secret status.

- **The extent to which the information is known within the company.** Although an employer or company is permitted to disclose confidential information to those with a demonstrated "need to know" the information, if the information is widely known within the company, especially among those who have no business need to know the information, it may not qualify as a trade secret. Companies should implement policies to prevent the inadvertent disclosure of trade secret information and limit dissemination of the material to those who need it to do their work. Thus, while the information may no longer be technically a "secret," as long as those in possession of the information need to know it to be able to perform their duties, such limited disclosure will not preclude information from trade secret protection.

- **The extent of the measures taken by the company to maintain the secrecy of the information.** One claiming trade secret protection must take reasonable precautions to protect the information. Courts are unlikely to protect information a company has not bothered to protect. A company is not obligated to undertake extreme efforts to protect information, but reasonable precautions are required. Thus, companies that require employees to sign nondisclosure agreements, keep confidential information in locked desks or rooms, restrict access to the information, and mark information with legends relating to its confidentiality are more likely to demonstrate successfully that information is a trade secret than those that fail to take such ordinary and reasonable precautions against inadvertent disclosure.

Some experts predict that courts will likely require advanced security measures to protect trade secrets transmitted via e-mail, including encryption and protocols to ensure confidentiality of messages, authentication of the source of the message, and devices that ensure the recipient cannot deny receiving the message.

- **The extent of the value of the information to the company and its competitors.** If information has little value either to its owner or to the owner's competitors, it is less likely to qualify as a trade secret. Conversely, information that is valuable to a company, such as the recipe for its key menu product, and that would be of great value to the company's competitors is more likely to be a protectable trade secret.

- **The extent of the expenditure of time, effort, and money by the company in developing the information.** The greater the amount of time, effort, and money the company has expended in developing or acquiring the information, the more likely it is to be held to be a protectable trade secret.

- **The extent of the ease or difficulty with which the information could be acquired or duplicated by others.** If information is easy to acquire or duplicate, it is less likely to qualify as a trade secret. Similarly, if the information is readily ascertainable from observation or can be easily reproduced, it is less likely to be a trade secret. If it would be a straightforward matter to reverse engineer the product, it may not qualify for trade secret protection. On the other hand, if it can be reverse engineered only with significant expenditures of time, effort, and money, the product may retain its status as a trade secret.

Not all information qualifies for trade secret protection. In *Buffets, Inc. v. Klinke*, 73 F.3d 765 (9th Cir. 1996), the court held that a restaurant's recipes for barbequed chicken and macaroni and cheese were not trade secrets because they were so basic and obvious that they could be easily duplicated or discovered by others.

LIABILITY FOR MISAPPROPRIATION OF TRADE SECRETS

Misappropriation of a trade secret occurs when a person possesses, discloses, or uses a trade secret owned by another without express or implied consent and when the person

- used improper means to gain knowledge of the trade secret;
- knew or should have known that the trade secret was acquired by improper means; or
- knew or should have known that the trade secret was acquired under circumstances giving rise to a duty to maintain its secrecy.

The term *improper means* includes bribery, theft, misrepresentation, breach or inducement of a breach of duty to maintain secrecy, or espionage through electronic or other means. Thus, misappropriation occurs either when a trade secret is lawfully acquired but then improperly used or when the trade secret is acquired by improper means.

Examples of trade secrets obtained through proper means include independent discovery of the trade secret (such as would occur if a person independently created a recipe or method identical to one protected as a trade secret), discovery by reverse engineering (assuming the product being reverse engineered was lawfully obtained), public observation of the item or method, or obtaining the trade secret from published material.

Absence of Written Agreement

While a written agreement prohibiting misappropriation of trade secrets can be enforced through an action for breach of contract, a company's trade secrets can be protected against misappropriation even in the absence of any written agreement between the parties. A party owning trade secrets can bring an action in tort for breach of the duty of confidentiality, which duty can arise even without an express agreement. Courts will impose a duty of confidentiality when parties stand in a special relationship with each other, such as an agent-principal relationship (which includes employer-employee relationships) or other fiduciary or good faith relationships (such as relationships among partners, or between corporations and their officers and directors, or between attorneys and clients). Courts have consistently held that employees owe a duty of loyalty, fidelity, and responsibility to their employers. Other persons found to be subject to a duty of confidentiality are customers, suppliers, trainees and students, licensees, and independent contractors. In fact, more trade secret cases are brought in tort for breach of confidentiality than in contract for breach of written agreements.

Similarly, courts can find that the parties had an implied contract arising out of their common understanding. For example, if ABC Company is attempting to make a sale to Jones and informs Jones that the ABC product is superior to that of competitors because it involves a new breakthrough in technology and explains the trade secret, courts would likely find that Jones is subject to a duty not to disclose the information. Similarly, if ABC Company explains its trade secrets to its bankers in an attempt to obtain financing, the bankers would likely be precluded from disclosing or using the information. Such implied contracts to protect the information generally arise when the parties' conduct indicates they intended the information to be kept confidential or impliedly agreed to keep it confidential.

Misappropriation by Third Parties

A number of other parties may also have liability for misappropriation of trade secrets if they knew or should have known they were the recipients of protected information. For example, assume Lee is employed by XYZ Company. In the course of his employment with XYZ Company, Lee learns valuable trade secret information. If Lee leaves his employment with XYZ Company and begins working for New Company, Lee and New Company may be prohibited from using the information. Lee may not misappropriate the information because he was in an employee-employer relationship with XYZ Company, and New Company may be prohibited from using the information if it knows or should know that the information was acquired by Lee under circumstances giving rise to a duty to maintain its secrecy or limit its use. In such cases, XYZ Company would generally prefer to sue New Company inasmuch as it is far likelier to have deep pockets, meaning it is more able to pay money damages than is an individual such as Lee.

If New Company has no reason to know the information was secret or that Lee may not reveal it, New Company would not have liability for such innocent use of the information. Similarly, if trade secret information were innocently obtained by New Company by mistake (for example, by a misdirected package or letter), New Company would have no liability for subsequent use or disclosure of the information. However, once New Company receives notice of the secrecy of the information (for example, by a letter from XYZ Company informing New Company of the nature of the trade secret and demanding that New Company cease use), it may not thereafter use the information unless New Company has so

changed its position based on the information that to preclude New Company from further use would be unjust. For example, assume that after acquiring information from Lee, New Company, mistakenly believing it may use the information, incurs great expense in building a new plant facility so it may use the information in a complex manufacturing process. In such cases, courts often attempt to fashion relief for both parties by requiring the party in New Company's position to pay a royalty or license fee to XYZ for continued use of the information. Companies in New Company's position should protect themselves by requiring employees to verify in writing that they will not use information gained in confidence from previous employers.

One who obtains trade secrets by improper means, such as espionage, theft, bribery, or placing one's own employees at a competitor's place of business, cannot use or disclose the information. For example, in one case, a court prohibited a party from using information gained by hiring a plane to make a low-altitude flight over a competitor's half-completed plant to determine its layout and features. While the plane was properly flying in public airspace, the court held that improper means, namely, means that fell below the generally accepted standards of commercial morality and reasonable conduct, subjected the actor to liability. To require the owner of the plant to erect a roof over the half-completed plant would impose an unreasonable burden and expense on the owner, and thus the measures it took to protect its plant at ground level were reasonable and sufficient. *E.I. du Pont de Nemours & Co. v. Christopher*, 431 F.2d 1012 (5th Cir. 1970).

Finally, a recipient of trade secrets may be liable for misappropriation even if modifications or improvements are made to the original confidential information if the resulting product or information is substantially derived from the owner's original trade secret.

EMPLOYER-EMPLOYEE RELATIONSHIPS

Ownership of Trade Secrets in the Absence of Written Agreement

Use or disclosure of trade secrets by employees and former employees is a frequently litigated area. While employers should require employees who will have access to trade secrets to sign agreements promising not to disclose the information, even employees who may not be subject to written nondisclosure agreements have a duty not to use an employer's trade secrets learned by the employee within the scope of employment. Moreover, this duty survives termination of the employment relationship. Generally, the higher the level of expertise possessed by the employee, the more likely it is that a confidential relationship exists between the employer and employee. Thus, senior executives, engineers, and scientists are typically subject to a higher duty of trust and confidence than more junior employees, such as file room clerks. In no event, however, may an employee steal an employer's trade secret.

If confidential information is learned by or disclosed to an employee in the course and scope of employment, the employee is subject to an implied agreement to maintain the information in secret. Information or an invention discovered by the employee on his or her "own time" (for example, on weekends or in the evenings) or before or after the employment relationship is owned by the employee. If an employee is specifically hired to develop certain information or to invent, the employer will own the resulting information or invention. In many cases, courts find that if an employee makes a discovery during employment that is related to his or her duties (even if the employee was not hired for that specific task), the employer is automatically granted a nonexclusive "shop right" in the discovery or trade secret, such that the employer can use the information, royalty-free, both during and after the employee's employment. Because the license to the employer is nonexclusive, the employee is free to market or license the information to others.

Written Agreements

Employers are generally free to require employees, independent contractors, and consultants to sign express agreements relating to the confidentiality of information. These agreements are usually enforced by courts as long as they are reasonable. The agreements usually include four specific topics: (1) ownership of inventions; (2) nondisclosure provisions; (3) nonsolicitation provisions; and (4) noncompetition provisions.

These provisions may be set forth in separate "stand-alone" nondisclosure agreements or they may be included as part of a more comprehensive employment agreement. Provisions relating to the confidentiality of company information should also be placed in the company's employee handbook or manual and employees should be required to confirm in writing that they have received the manual. Departing employees should be reminded of their duties to protect the company's proprietary information.

Ownership of Inventions. Most agreements expressly state that any information, inventions, or material created by the employee in the course of employment are owned by the employer. Better agreements go one step further and state that if for some reason such a clause is not sufficient to vest ownership in the employer, by the terms of the agreement, the employee irrevocably assigns the information or invention to the employer. Some agreements go even further and include a **trailer clause,** whereby an employee assigns to the employer not only the inventions made during the period of employment but those invented for some period thereafter. Typically, reasonable trailer clauses are enforceable. Some states have statutes that restrict an employer's ability to require an assignment of inventions.

Nondisclosure Provisions.   The agreement should prohibit the employee from using or disclosing the employer's trade secrets or confidential information whether during or after employment. The agreement should describe with specificity the information that is to be protected.

Nonsolicitation Provisions.   Most agreements prohibit employees from soliciting or encouraging other employees from leaving the employer's business and from soliciting or attempting to "poach" clients or customers of the employer. Nonsolicitation clauses must be reasonable and should be limited in time.

Noncompetition Provisions.   Most agreements include provisions prohibiting employees from competing against the employer both during and after the term of employment. Noncompetition clauses are also referred to as *restrictive covenants,* and they are enforceable in most states if they are reasonable. Because a covenant precluding an employee from exercising his or her only trade and earning a livelihood can be so detrimental to an employee, restrictive covenants are strictly construed by courts. In California, **noncompetition agreements** are automatically void as a restraint against trade because they preclude people from changing jobs and engaging in their lawful professions (unless they occur in connection with the sale of a business). In fact, in one California case, Aetna Inc. was ordered to pay a former employee $1.2 million after the employee was fired because she refused to sign Aetna's noncompete agreement that it used in all states. The jury found that Aetna knew such covenants were violations of California law but attempted to enforce the agreements anyway.

A variety of factors are taken into account in determining whether such covenants are enforceable.

- **Purpose.** Courts often consider whether the restriction is related to a legitimate business purpose of the employer. A restriction by McDonald's Corporation that its food handlers could not later work for any other restaurants would likely be unenforceable, while a restriction by United Airlines that its senior engineers could not later work for other competitor airlines would likely be enforced by a court. The restriction by McDonald's serves no legitimate public purpose and no legitimate business need of McDonald's. On the other hand, if United Airlines has carefully recruited its top personnel, trained them, and invested time and money in teaching them its techniques and processes, it would be inequitable for a competitor to reap the advantage of this investment of time and money. Thus, only employees with access to proprietary information should be required to sign noncompete agreements.

- **Reasonableness.** The restriction must be reasonable in regard to scope, duration, and geographic area. Thus, a prohibition by United Airlines that its senior engineers could not work for any other airlines in the United States in any capacity for twenty years would likely be struck down as unconscionable. A prohibition that senior engineers could not work for other competitor airlines for one year in a competitive capacity within a one-hundred-mile radius of any United Airlines facility would be more likely to be enforced. In one recent case, a court held that a one-year noncompete agreement was too long in the fast-paced and dynamic technology sector.

equal intensity and relevancy of all items and indifference of response patterns, and it has been found to be just as good as the other types of scaling techniques. However, the issues of confounding and multidimensionality, again, continue to challenge all these techniques, especially the summated scaling approach.

The agreement should carefully define the type of business or competitor for whom the employee may not work.

- **Consideration.** Many states require that a covenant not to compete be supported by adequate consideration. Thus, noncompetition agreements are often entered into when the employee enters the employment relationship. In some instances, when employers award bonuses or salary increases, they use the award as an opportunity to bargain for a noncompetition clause.

If a noncompete clause is struck down by a court (because it is too broad in regard to scope or territory or too long in duration), some courts will reform the covenant (a technique often called **blue penciling**) and enforce it in regard to a more reasonable territory or length, thus making it fit the parties' intentions rather than striking the entire covenant. Many noncompete clauses contain such built-in protection by providing that if the covenant is found to be unenforceable, a court may fashion an appropriate covenant or that if part of the covenant is struck down, the remainder will be valid. In the event of any doubt or ambiguity, the covenant not to compete will be construed against the employer and in favor of the employee.

Even those states that strictly scrutinize noncompete agreements will enforce them in certain situations, such as one bargained for in connection with the sale of a business. For example, if Long purchases Crosby's business at a substantial sum, it would be inequitable to allow Crosby to immediately reenter the market and compete against Long. Thus, a court would enforce a noncompete covenant made by Crosby.

Noncompete clauses must be carefully drafted to ensure they comply with state statutory and case law. Similarly, careful drafting is needed to ensure the employee does not find a loophole to circumvent the restriction. For example, if the covenant merely precludes employment with a competitor, the employee could establish his or her own business or could serve as a consultant to a competitor. Thus, the provisions in a noncompetition agreement or clause should be drafted to afford the employer the protection it needs.

Finally, courts generally will not enforce a restrictive covenant if the employee has left employment due to the employer's breach of the employment agreement. Otherwise, an employer could hire uniquely talented individuals, have them sign covenants not to compete, refuse to pay them, and still reap the benefits of precluding them from working for others. (See Appendix D, Form 13, for a sample nondisclosure and noncompetition agreement.)

PROTECTION FOR SUBMISSIONS

Submissions to Private Parties

In many instances individuals wish to submit an idea for an invention, process, game, or entertainment show to a company or business in the hope that the company will market and develop the idea and the individual will be compensated for the idea. For example, assume that Sanders has developed an idea for a new board game that he believes has great potential. Because Sanders cannot mass-produce and mass-market the game, he decides to write a letter and submit the idea to Milton-Bradley, a well-known company in the game and entertainment field. Because ideas are not protected under copyright law, Sanders faces a dilemma: to pique Milton-Bradley's interest, he must describe the game in sufficient detail that it can fully evaluate the game; yet, by describing the game, he runs the risk that Milton-Bradley will appropriate the idea and develop it on its own, cutting him out of the picture.

Idea submission disputes frequently arise in the entertainment industry. In one case, an individual claimed that the producers of the *Cosby Show* misappropriated her idea for a television program portraying a wholesome and loving African American family. A court held there was no misappropriation inasmuch as Bill Cosby had earlier discussed the concept with a number of other people and the idea was so general as to lack the element of concreteness to be protectable. *Murray v. NBC,* 844 F.2d 988 (2d Cir. 1988). In another case, writer Art Buchwald claimed that the movie *Coming to America* with Eddie Murphy misappropriated his written submission for a similar movie, for which Paramount Pictures had agreed to pay him a royalty if a movie was made based upon his idea. Although the idea was changed slightly by the studio, the court held that the studio had misappropriated Buchwald's submission and entered judgment for Buchwald.

The solution to such a dilemma is for the "inventor" to submit the idea pursuant to an evaluation agreement, or submission agreement, whereby the other party agrees to evaluate the idea only for the purpose of considering a future transaction between the parties and further agrees not to circumvent the submitter or to disclose the idea to others. The parties agree that if the recipient decides to develop and use the idea, the parties will negotiate further for compensation to the submitter. (See Appendix D, Form 14, for a sample evaluation agreement.)

Unsolicited manuscripts and ideas present unique problems. Many producers and companies do not accept unsolicited submissions for fear of lawsuits and often return packages unopened. In many cases involving unsolicited ideas that arrive with no contractual terms or language limiting their future use, courts allow the recipient to develop and market the idea, based on the concept that a person who discloses an idea without first seeking protection has only himself or herself to blame. Other courts find an implied contract exists, and hold that the recipient has impliedly agreed that he or she will compensate the submitter if the idea is used. Still other courts rely on a theory of unjust enrichment, holding that the recipient would be unjustly enriched if he or she could take the idea, develop it, market it, and make a profit from it, all without compensating the submitter. In those cases, courts award some reasonable compensation or royalty to the submitter. Finally, some courts consider industry practice and custom, and if submitters are routinely compensated in the industry, even for unsolicited submissions, courts may find an implied contract to compensate the submitter. In any event, the idea must be sufficiently developed or concrete that it can be protected, and it must be something novel rather than something so ordinary that anyone could have conceived of it. In sum, the only way for a submitter to be assured protection for an idea is by written agreement.

Submissions to Government Agencies

Private companies that present bids to government agencies in the hope of obtaining a government contract are often required to disclose confidential or trade secret information to the agency. Under freedom of information acts (both at the state and federal levels), the proposal might later be released to any member of the public requesting the document, thus resulting in loss of confidential information to possible competitors. To protect companies against such disclosure, many freedom of information acts contain exceptions so that parties can designate certain information as a trade secret and thus prevent its release. The protected information is usually blocked out. If a government agency discloses trade secret information, the owner may have a cause of action for an unconstitutional taking of private property and may be awarded compensation if the owner had a reasonable expectation of confidentiality.

DEFENSES TO TRADE SECRET MISAPPROPRIATION

A variety of defenses may be raised by a party accused of misappropriating another's trade secrets. The most commonly asserted defenses are as follows:

- **Lack of secrecy.** A defendant may assert that the owner of the trade secret failed to take appropriate and reasonable measures to protect the trade secret and the information has thus entered the public domain. Courts will then examine the measures taken by the trade secret owner and determine if they were reasonable under the circumstances. If the information could have been readily protected but was not, courts are likely to hold the owner has lost its rights to the information. Thus, discussions of information at conferences or in publications may result in loss of trade secret protection. Some recent cases have examined whether memorization of information is a defense, holding that reconstruction of a trade secret, such as a customer list, through memorization (as opposed to physically taking or copying the list) is not a defense and is another form of misappropriation.

- **Independent creation.** Just as independent creation is a defense to a claim of copyright infringement, independent creation of information that is a trade secret of another is permissible. As long as a party did not breach a duty of confidentiality or an agreement to hold information in confidence, and did not use improper means in acquiring the information, independent creation will be a defense to a claim of misappropriation. Reverse engineering, namely, the inspection or analysis of a product to determine the method by which it was developed, is generally a protected form of independent creation. An assertion that the information lacks protection because it *could have been* reverse engineered is generally successful only when others have in fact reverse engineered the item or when reverse engineering could be easily accomplished.

- **Privilege.** A party may be compelled to disclose a trade secret in the course of some judicial or administrative action. Such disclosure is privileged and is nonactionable. Many written confidentiality agreements require that one called to testify about a trade secret provide notice to the owner of the trade secret so it may attempt to protect itself by seeking some judicial relief, such as exclusion of bystanders and the media from the courtroom during disclosure.

- **Unclean hands or laches.** A defendant may assert that the trade secret owner's conduct is so reprehensible that its "unclean hands" bars any recovery. Additionally, a defendant may assert that the trade secret owner has so delayed in bringing the action that the defendant has been prejudiced by such delay and thus the action should be barred. Laches (an unreasonable delay that prejudices the other party) is often asserted when a defendant has innocently acquired the trade secret and then expended a great deal of time and money in promoting or marketing the information. To require the defendant to cease use in such circumstances may be inequitable.

REMEDIES FOR MISAPPROPRIATION

A trade secret owner may request a variety of remedies from a court. Among them are the following:

- **Injunctive relief.** In many cases, a trade secret owner is more interested in ensuring the defendant cease use of the trade secret (or is precluded from commencing use) than in recovering damages. In cases in which money damages are not sufficient to protect a trade secret owner, a court may issue an injunction. Injunctions can be issued to prohibit a party from further using or disclosing the information or to ensure the party does not begin to use or disclose the information if disclosure is threatened, imminent, or inevitable. A court may issue a preliminary injunction during the pendency of the action; if the plaintiff prevails, the injunction may be made permanent. Because trade secrets can endure forever, the length of the injunction is often difficult to calculate. A court may also issue an injunction to compel the defendant to surrender or destroy trade secret information. In fact, courts may issue injunctions to prevent **inevitable disclosure,** reasoning that even if a former employer cannot show a particular secret has been taken, it is inevitable that key employees will eventually disclose what they know to a new employer. In such cases, even in the absence of a covenant not to compete, courts have enjoined employees from working on particular projects, imposed time limits during which the new employee cannot work for another, or even prohibited employees from working for a new company in any

capacity. Not all courts acknowledge the inevitable disclosure doctrine.
- **Money damages.** A trade secret owner whose information has been misappropriated may recover money damages from the defendant. The plaintiff may recover its lost profits as well as the profits made by the defendant. Alternatively, the plaintiff may seek and recover a reasonable royalty arising from defendant's use of the trade secret. Punitive damages may also be awarded in cases in which the defendant's conduct is reckless, willful, and intentional. The UTSA provides that punitive damages not exceed more than twice the compensatory damages awarded.
- **Attorneys' fees and costs.** In most cases, the parties bear their own attorneys' fees and costs. The UTSA, however, provides that reasonable attorneys' fees and costs may be awarded to the prevailing party if bad faith or willfulness is shown.

TRADE SECRET LITIGATION

If a trade secret is disclosed in violation of a written confidentiality agreement, and the parties cannot resolve the dispute themselves, an action for breach of contract may be brought, similar to any other breach of contract action. The plaintiff may add other causes of action as well, for example, for misappropriation in violation of a state trade secret law. If no written agreement exists, the plaintiff must rely upon case law or state statutes protecting trade secrets, or both.

To protect itself against a lawsuit by another alleging trade secret violations, companies should require new employees who will have access to confidential information to acknowledge in writing that accepting employment with the new company does not violate any other agreement or violate any other obligation of confidentiality to which the employee may be subject. Additionally, employees should be required to represent that work they perform for the employer will be original work and will not infringe any other party's rights.

If grounds for federal jurisdiction exist (the parties have diverse citizenship and the claim exceeds $75,000), the action may be brought in federal court. If the action also involves copyright or patent, it must be brought in federal court. Otherwise, the action will be brought in a state court. If the action is instituted in federal court, a federal court will apply state law inasmuch as there is no federal trade secret law. The UTSA provides that an action for misappropriation must be brought within three years after misappropriation is discovered or reasonably should have been discovered.

In federal court, the action will be governed by the Federal Rules of Civil Procedure relating to federal civil actions generally. These rules set the times for responding to the complaint, matters pertaining to motions and discovery, and any other litigation-related matters. Most states have rules relating to civil procedure that are modeled substantially after the Federal Rules of Civil Procedure and likewise govern the litigation. After the complaint is filed, the defendant will respond by filing an answer, usually denying that any breach of agreement or misappropriation has occurred and asserting various defenses. If the defendant has a cause of action to assert against the plaintiff relating to the trade secret, it must be asserted by way of a counterclaim in the litigation so that all disputes between the parties relating to the information can be resolved at the same time.

After the complaint, answer, and counterclaim have been filed, various motions may be made. Discovery will commence. The plaintiff and defendant will take depositions to obtain testimony from those who may have information about the case. For example, the plaintiff may depose individuals in the defendant's company to determine whether they were instructed to use the plaintiff's information. Interrogatories may be served on either party to obtain information, such as to inquire about experts either side may intend to call, how damages such as lost profits were calculated, or to determine the existence of pertinent documents.

Ultimately, if the matter cannot be resolved by private agreement, it will proceed to trial. The trade secret owner must prove misappropriation by a preponderance of the evidence. Either party may request a jury trial; otherwise, a judge will render the decision. Appeals may follow.

One of the difficult issues in trade secret litigation arises from the fact that the trade secret sought to be protected often must be disclosed in the litigation so the judge or jury can evaluate whether the information is sufficiently valuable that it affords its owner a competitive advantage. Similarly, the owner's methods of protecting the information often must be disclosed so the fact-finder can determine whether the owner has taken reasonable measures to protect the alleged trade secrets. Thus, the dilemma faced by trade secrets owners in litigation is that they must disclose the very information they seek to protect. Courts can fashion a variety of means to protect the information, from issuing protective orders (prohibiting the parties and their counsel from any further disclosure), to holding private hearings in the judge's chambers, to closing the courtroom to the public, to sealing court records.

As technology progresses and the value of certain communication and entertainment inventions increases, trade secret litigation is becoming an increasingly common and high-stakes occupation. Damage awards may run into the millions. For example, the *National Law Journal* reported in September 1997 that the U.S. Court of Appeals upheld a $45.6 million judgment against Polaris Industries for the theft of a design for a fuel-injection engine for snowmobiles. *Injection Research Specialists, Inc. v. Polaris Indus., L.P.,* No. 90-Z-1143 (D. Colo. 1997).

TRADE SECRET PROTECTION PROGRAMS

Because trade secrets are legally fragile and may be lost by inadvertent disclosure or failure to reasonably protect them, companies should implement trade secret protection programs to safeguard valuable information. While it is common for businesses to assume that only scientific and technical data constitute trade secrets, protection is available for a much broader range of subjects, such as customer lists, marketing plans, hiring tactics, and other information that would be valuable to a competitor, and that are common to many companies, not merely those engaged in scientific endeavors.

Because trade secret protection can last indefinitely, businesses should devote proper attention to the methods used to ensure confidentiality of information. Companies that value their trade secrets should implement trade secret protection programs. Developing programs and measures to protect trade secrets is an easy way to demonstrate to a court that an owner values its information and takes appropriate measures to maintain its secrecy. Such programs consist of several elements.

Physical Protection

There are a variety of tangible measures a company can implement to protect trade secrets, including the following:

- safeguarding information under lock and key;
- protecting the information from unauthorized access;

- forbidding removal of protected information from the company premises or certain rooms;
- retaining adequate security during evenings and weekends either through alarm systems or security services;
- ensuring tours of the company premises do not expose outsiders to valuable processes or information;
- marking materials with legends or stamps such as "Confidential—Trade Secret Information";
- using check-out lists when valuable equipment or information is removed from its normal location;
- monitoring activities of former employees who had access to confidential information and monitoring trade journals for articles that may show a competitor has gained access to company trade secrets;
- ensuring no one person has access to critical information but rather that several people "share" parts of the information;
- implementing inventory control systems (such as numbering each copy of valuable written materials and retaining a log showing which employee received which document);
- securing computers with password or encryption protection;
- requiring use of paper shredders for disposal of sensitive documents;
- designating a responsible person to be responsible for trade secret information and release to others (including the media), and for reviewing bids, proposals, marketing materials, and plans by employees to publish articles or speak at conferences;
- implementing photocopying policies and maintaining log books or electronic monitoring of copying;

- monitoring employees' use of e-mail and the Internet to ensure confidential information is not being disseminated (as long as employees are notified beforehand that use of e-mail and the Internet must be for business purposes only and that the employer may monitor use);
- conducting exit interviews with employees to remind them of their obligations not to use or disclose proprietary company information;
- including notices on facsimile cover sheets and e-mail communications that the communication is intended only for the designated recipient, and if it is received in error, the party who mistakenly received it must return it to the sender;
- using encryption technology and antivirus protection programs to protect information stored on computers;
- educating employees on trade secrets and protection of trade secrets;
- requiring visitors to the premises to sign in and wear badges; and
- ensuring information retained on computers is available only on company networks so that access can be easily tracked.

Most companies will not need to implement all of the measures described above. Courts do not require absolute secrecy or that extreme measures be taken to protect information. Rather, reasonable measures will be sufficient to protect the status of information as trade secrets.

Contractual Protection

Another method of protecting trade secrets is by contract, namely, requiring those with access to the information to agree in writing not to disclose the information to others or use it to the owner's detriment. Similarly, in licensing arrangements, trade secret owners should ensure the license agreements contain sufficient protection for trade secret information. Employers should use noncompetition agreements to ensure former employees do not use material gained on the job to later compete against the employer. Even without formal contracts, a company should include protection policies in its employee handbooks, routinely publish reminders about confidentiality in company newsletters and through e-mail messages, and remind employees of their duties during their initial orientations and during exit interviews conducted when the individuals leave the company's employment.

With the advent of the Internet and the increased ease of electronic communications, employers have become concerned about the loss of trade secrets through dissemination over the Internet. It has been held that "once a trade secret is posted on the Internet, it is effectively part of the public domain, impossible to retrieve." *Religious Tech. Ctr. v. Lerma*, 908 F. Supp. 1362, 1368 (E.D. Va. 1995). Thus, employers have a legitimate interest in monitoring the electronic communications of their employees. Generally, employers have broad discretion to regulate the use of electronic communications in the workplace so long as the employees have been informed that the employer may do so. Many employers now adopt Internet Use Policies (see Chapter 5) to inform employees that their electronic communications may be monitored and to set forth appropriate guidelines for use of the Internet and e-mail.

Intellectual Property Protection

Companies can also rely on other complementary methods of protection to safeguard trade secrets. Any material that qualifies for copyright protection should be protected by registration, or at a minimum, by ensuring a copyright notice is placed on the material or document to afford notice to others of the owner's right and interest in the material. Inventions may be subject to patent protection, and trademarks should be fully protected by applying for registration.

NEW AND INTERNATIONAL DEVELOPMENTS IN TRADE SECRETS LAW

New Developments

Perhaps the newest developments in trade secrets law have arisen out of the ease of electronic communication. Because information can be readily obtained by computer and then similarly disseminated to others with a stroke of the keyboard, companies are investing greater time and money in ensuring their communications systems are secure. While physical methods of protecting trade secrets (such as locked drawers, restricted access to information, marking information with legends, and so forth) have always been favored by courts, companies should now consider protecting their information by electronic security measures. Use of passwords, encryption and coding of documents, and restricting access to information placed on computers are now being examined by courts in attempting to determine whether an owner has taken sufficient measures to protect its proprietary information.

Another newer development in trade secrets law is the use of criminal statutes to punish wrongdoers. In 1996, Congress enacted the Economic Espionage Act of 1996 (18 U.S.C. § 1831), which provides criminal penalties for the theft or attempted theft of trade secret information that will benefit foreign governments and for the theft of trade secrets related to products produced or placed in interstate commerce. Theft of information by physical as well as electronic means is prohibited. The U.S. Attorney General can initiate a civil action to enjoin threatened theft, violators may be imprisoned, and fines can be imposed of up to $10 million for foreign espionage and $5 million

for other trade secret theft. The criminalization of the theft of trade secrets was likely due to the increased incidence of economic espionage. The increasing importance of intellectual property has led to a shift from the theft of tangible physical property to theft of intellectual assets. A 1996 survey by the American Society for Industrial Security reported a 323 percent increase in incidents from 1992 to 1995. Additionally, the FBI reported that during the late 1990s, at least twenty-three foreign governments were stealing or attempting to steal intellectual property from American companies.

Similarly, theft of tangible property containing trade secrets (such as documents or discs) and transporting it across state lines may be a violation of the National Stolen Property Act (18 U.S.C. § 2314). Federal mail and wire fraud statutes are also used to punish theft of trade secrets. Many states have similar statutes that are used to deter and punish misappropriation of trade secrets.

International Developments

Because trade secret information is generally lost once it is disclosed (assuming proper precautions have not been taken), companies intending to do business internationally must ensure that their trade secrets are protected in foreign countries so that inadvertent disclosure abroad does not cause worldwide loss of protection. Just as is the case in the United States, theft of trade secrets is a crime in most foreign countries. Moreover, the North American Free Trade Agreement (NAFTA), entered into by the United States, Canada, and Mexico in 1991, complements U.S. trade secrets law and requires member countries to protect trade secrets from unauthorized disclosure or use. In response to NAFTA, Mexico amended its laws to allow litigants to bring civil actions to enjoin threatened or existing trade secret violations.

In 1994, the General Agreement on Tariffs and Trade (GATT) was concluded by the major industrialized nations of the world, including the United States. GATT provides for adjudication of trade secret disputes, and under TRIPs (Trade-Related Aspects of Intellectual Property Rights), promulgated in accordance with GATT, member countries must provide effective remedies for misappropriation of trade secrets owned by residents of other member countries. Thus, all member nations of GATT have measures similar to those in the United States for protecting trade secrets, thereby ensuring that companies that wish to do business in other GATT member countries can do so with the knowledge that their valuable trade secret information will be protectable.

Note that the Economic Espionage Act of 1996 discussed earlier applies not only to conduct within the United States but also to conduct occurring outside the United States if the offender is a natural person who is a citizen or permanent resident alien of the United States or if an act in furtherance of the offense was committed in the United States.

Additionally, safeguards such as employment and nondisclosure agreements and limiting access to confidential information through both internal and physical measures may help to maintain the status of trade secrets in foreign countries.

TRIVIA

- In 2000, a Florida jury ruled that Walt Disney Co. wrongfully appropriated the idea for a sports theme park from a former baseball umpire and ordered the company to pay $240 million in damages.
- In 2000, a court awarded $25 million in actual damages to an individual whose idea for preparing and serving rotisserie chicken was appropriated by Perdue Farms. The damages were based on the amount of direct costs Perdue Farms saved by using the plaintiff's process.
- According to a 2000 survey by the American Management Association, nearly 70 percent of large U.S. companies actively monitor and review employee e-mail and Internet usage.
- Economic theft cost American companies more than $1 trillion in 2000 according to a study commissioned by the American Society of Industrial Security.

CHAPTER SUMMARY

A trade secret consists of any information that its owner has reasonably protected and that, if known by a competitor, would afford some commercial advantage or benefit. If properly protected, trade secrets may exist forever. Trade secrets are protectable even in the absence of written agreement if the parties enjoy a relationship of trust and confidence (as is the case in employer-employee relationships). Trade secrets are also protected from appropriation by improper means such as theft, bribery, or espionage.

Although trade secrets can be protected even without a written agreement, such an agreement is advisable. Agreements with key employees should also include noncompete clauses. While strictly scrutinized by courts as possible restraints against trade, such noncompete provisions are enforceable in most states as long as they are reasonable in time, territory, and scope.

A trade secret owner may obtain injunctive relief or monetary damages, or both, if a trade secret has been misappropriated. Criminal penalties may also be assessed against the violator. A trade secret, however, will not be protected by a court if its owner has not exercised reasonable efforts to maintain its secrecy.

Companies should implement aggressive trade secret protection programs to ensure the protectability of valuable information. Information can be protected by physical barriers (such as lock and key), contractual provisions prohibiting disclosure, and by taking advantage of protection available under copyright and patent laws.

CASE ILLUSTRATION—THE DOCTRINE OF INEVITABLE DISCLOSURE

Case: *PepsiCo, Inc. v. Redmond*, 54 F.3d 1262 (7th Cir. 1995)

Facts: PepsiCo sought a preliminary injunction to prohibit its former employee, Redmond, from working for Quaker Oats in a similar capacity. Redmond had a high-level position at PepsiCo with access to inside information and trade secrets about PepsiCo's sports drinks. Redmond had signed a confidentiality agreement with PepsiCo.

Holding: Redmond's new employment will inevitably lead him to rely on his former employer's trade secrets. Unless Redmond possessed an uncanny ability to compartmentalize, he would necessarily make decisions about Quaker Oats's sports drink products by relying on PepsiCo's trade secrets. Redmond's inevitable disclosure of these sensitive and important trade secrets justifies an injunction prohibiting him from being employed by Quaker Oats for a period of time in a competitive capacity and preventing him from forever disclosing PepsiCo's confidential and trade secret information.

CASE STUDY AND ACTIVITIES

Case Study. Watson is developing its plans to open at least one amusement park in Europe. It has commissioned a variety of marketing studies and has been consulting with property experts and engineers regarding the planned parks. Watson's plans are known only by a few senior-level employees, all of whom have signed confidentiality agreements. Watson's biggest competitor, ProTheme Inc., has obtained copies of some of Watson's written plans through a computer expert it hired to hack into Watson's

CHAPTER EIGHT

Types of Data and Methods of Collection

Measurement specifies the way by which all kinds of information needed for your research (called data) are obtained. How those pieces of information will form the whole of a data set, however, depends on how you design the structure of your research.

First, your research will have certain coverage. For the kind of questions you ask, you may but do not have to reach everybody or everything affected. You can study only a portion of those targeted, and infer your findings and apply your conclusions to the full range of interest. To do that, however, you must follow certain rules and use certain techniques, and you also need to understand the advantages and disadvantages of different approaches.

Second, your research will have a time dimension. You may just look at the situation at one point in time, or you may want to examine the dynamics of change over time. The latter makes your data set more complicated but has special significance in causation, especially when you choose an experimental design.

Third, your research may have various degrees of intensity of soliciting information about a subject. Accordingly, your data set may be very detailed and complete about a case, or sketchy about many cases, or only deal with certain aspects of all cases.

In addition, there are different approaches to data collection and different techniques of carrying out the measurement and recording the information. The various ways of combining all these different features result in various particular kinds of research. In this chapter, we will explore the major parameters on which research projects differ. We will also examine some most widely used forms of

CASE STUDY AND ACTIVITIES (cont'd)

computer system and from one of the engineers Watson hired to consult on the planned expansion. Recently, one of Watson's most senior employees left Watson to go to work for ProTheme.

Activities.   Discuss whether and how Watson can protect the information relating to its planned expansion into Europe.

ROLE OF PARALEGAL

Paralegals can engage in numerous activities related to trade secret protection, including the following:

- conducting trade secret audits to ensure confidential information is protected;
- drafting guidelines for clients to follow in implementing trade secret protection programs;
- reviewing client documents to ensure materials are clearly marked with notices regarding their confidentiality;
- drafting notices for clients to place in newsletters, near photocopy machines, and in prominent locations throughout offices reminding employees of the need to keep company information confidential;
- reviewing confidentiality clauses and employment agreements entered into with key employees to ensure client information will be maintained in confidence;
- drafting nondisclosure and noncompete agreements; and
- conducting state-by-state research regarding enforceability of noncompete clauses.

INTERNET RESOURCES

Uniform Trade Secrets Act:	http://www.nccusl.org (web site of the National Conference of Commissioners on Uniform State Laws)
Trade Secrets Home Page:	http://my.execpc.com/~mhallign/index.html (web site of attorney Mark Halligan offering excellent information about trade secrets, articles, and links to other resources)
Employment agreements:	http://www.allaboutforms.com (web site offering sample forms for noncompete agreements, confidentiality agreements, and employee invention agreements, which can be used as models and drafting guides)

DISCUSSION QUESTIONS

1. Langley Inc., a large retailer, is the owner of various manuals that outline processes regarding inventory control procedures for inventory in its stores. The processes are known by others in the retail industry but are not known to the public at large. Can the processes constitute trade secrets?

2. Al, an inventor, met with Sid, an attorney, to discuss Al's latest invention, a new type of wine bottle opener. Al later discovered that Sid had applied for a patent for the invention. The parties had no signed agreement. Is Sid liable to Al? Discuss.

3. Sally, a senior employee of Taylor Enterprises Inc., has decided to leave the company and go to work for one of Taylor's competitors. Sally is not subject to any confidentiality agreements. Sally has been able to memorize Taylor's preferred customer list and plans to take this information to her new employer. Discuss whether Sally has misappropriated a trade secret.

4. David, an employee of Gregson Associates Inc., took valuable company information home with him so he could work on a project at home. David left the material on a train and it was discovered by Gregson's competitors. As soon as Gregson realized what had occurred, Gregson sent a notice to the competitor informing it of the valuable nature of the material and demanding its return. The competitor is alleging that the material now belongs to it. Discuss whether the competitor may use the information.

5. Kate, an attorney working on a trade secret trial, neglected to ask the court to protect some of the trade secret information during the trial and it was disclosed to the jury and those in the courtroom. Has trade secret status been lost for the material? Discuss.

6. Lee and Young Inc., a defense consulting firm, requires all of its employees to sign non-competition agreements. Discuss whether the following agreements are likely to be enforceable:
   - an agreement forbidding the clerical staff from working for any similar business for one year anywhere in the United States;
   - an agreement forbidding senior managers from working for competitor companies for one year in the geographical areas in which the company currently conducts business; and
   - an agreement forbidding senior engineers from working for similar companies anywhere in the United States for three years.

7. Renee is an employee of Harris Manufacturing Inc. Renee inadvertently published Harris's customer list on the Internet where the list has been available for two weeks. Has trade secret protection been lost for this material?

For additional resources, go to www.westlegalstudies.com.

CHAPTER 23

Unfair Competition

CHAPTER OVERVIEW

The term *unfair competition* is a broad term covering a wide variety of deceptive practices in the marketplace. The law of unfair competition continues to evolve with changes in the marketplace so that deceptive infomercials and false advertising on the Internet can be prohibited, just as their earlier print counterparts are.

The most commonly alleged forms of unfair competition are passing off (selling one's goods as those of another); misappropriation (the taking of another's intangible commercial property right); infringement of the right of publicity (appropriating another's identity or persona for commercial purposes); false advertising (making false or deceptive representations about the nature of one's own goods or services); product disparagement (making false or deceptive representations about another's goods or services); dilution (weakening or tarnishing the value of another's trademark or service mark even though the use does not cause a likelihood of confusion); and infringement of trade dress (causing confusion with the distinctive product image or overall appearance of another's product or service).

There is considerable overlap in the theories used by injured parties to protect their business property interests against deception and fraud, and the same act may give rise to several causes of action. Thus, a misleading advertisement may constitute passing off, false advertising, and product disparagement. For example, the Fifth Circuit Court of Appeals held in 1998 that a tavern's unauthorized use of the name "The Velvet Elvis" constituted trademark infringement, unfair competition, trademark dilution, and violation of the right of publicity. *Elvis Presley Ent. Inc. v. Capece,* 141 F.3d 188 (5th Cir. 1998). Moreover, section 43 of the Lanham Act (15 U.S.C. § 1125), often referred to as a "national unfair competition statute," also protects against a wide variety of false and misleading commercial practices. Finally, the Federal Trade Commission (FTC) may also take action to protect consumers from false and deceptive trade practices. Thus, injured parties often rely upon a wide variety of theories to protect their business goodwill or intellectual property from unfair tactics in the commercial arena.

INTRODUCTION

The law of unfair competition is based upon the notion that individuals should be protected from deceptive and improper conduct in the marketplace. The law of unfair competition is found in case law, in state statutes prohibiting unfair business practices, in specific federal statutes, and in regulations promulgated by the FTC, the federal regulatory agency charged with protecting consumers from unfair or deceptive acts and practices. The law of unfair competition continues to evolve as new methods of conducting business arise, such as electronic offers and sales through telemarketing, television infomercials, and the Internet.

There are a number of theories and actions that can be used by injured parties to protect against unfair competition. For the most part, the remedies are designed to protect intangible interests, such as one's interest in one's business reputation, goodwill, and so forth. For that reason, unfair competition law often protects "intellectual" property rather than real property or personal property and promotes a well-functioning marketplace.

In many instances, actions for unfair competition will be combined with other actions (such as those alleging trademark, copyright, or patent infringement) to provide a plaintiff a wide array of possible remedies. In other instances, a plaintiff may not have a protectable trademark, copyright, or patent, and thus must rely entirely on unfair competition theories to provide relief against unscrupulous business practices. For example, a designer of scarves imprinted with fanciful designs may decide against applying for a design patent due to the expense involved and the short life cycle of fashion products. Protection against copying of the design may thus be available under the umbrella of unfair competition rather than under design patent law.

Section 43 of the Lanham Act (15 U.S.C. § 1125) provides a federal cause of action to protect consumers against unfair competitive business practices. It is effectively a national unfair competition statute prohibiting a broad range of wrongful business activities and providing a

wide array of remedies to plaintiffs. Moreover, section 43(a) protects unregistered marks and names, such as those that do not qualify for federal trademark registration because they are descriptive or perhaps used only in intrastate commerce.

The most common types of unfair competition are discussed more fully in this chapter but can be briefly summarized as follows:

- **Passing off (or palming off).** "Passing off" occurs when one party attempts to pass off or sell his or her goods or services as those of another.
- **Misappropriation.** Misappropriation exists when one party takes or uses another's property that the original owner created or secured at effort and expense.
- **Right of publicity.** A person's identity, voice, likeness, or persona is protected against unauthorized commercial exploitation through the right of publicity.
- **False advertising.** Making false or deceptive representations about the nature of one's goods or services is actionable as false advertising.
- **Product disparagement.** Making false representations about the nature of another party's goods or services is actionable as product disparagement.
- **Dilution.** Either tarnishing another's mark or causing it to lose its distinctiveness through "blurring" is actionable as dilution.
- **Infringement of trade dress.** Adopting the overall concept of another's distinctive packaging or product image, generally called its "trade dress," so as to deceive consumers is an infringement of trade dress.

Generally, injured parties notify the wrongdoer prior to initiating litigation. A cease and desist letter is usually sent, detailing the wrongdoer's acts and demanding that the wrongdoer cease and desist its activities. (See Chapter 6, Exhibit 6–5, for a sample cease and desist letter used in trademark infringement matters.) If there is no resolution, the injured party may initiate legal action. In many instances, a plaintiff will allege several causes of action. For example, if a competitor of Nike uses a "swoosh" symbol similar to that registered to Nike, Nike may allege trademark infringement, passing off, dilution of its famous mark, and violation of section 43(a) of the Lanham Act, prohibiting a false designation of origin. If another shoemaker sells an athletic shoe that copies the overall appearance or image of Nike's shoes, such conduct may be prohibited as infringement of trade dress.

PASSING OFF

Passing off (also referred to as *palming off*) occurs when one party attempts to pass off its goods under the pretense that they are the goods of another. Passing off may exist when one party affixes another's trademarks to its goods, adopts a trademark or trade name that is so similar to that of another that consumers are deceived about the source of the product or service, or copies features of another's goods so that its goods are confusingly similar to those of the other. The essence of the action is some representation by a defendant, whether direct or indirect, that causes consumers to be deceived about the source of their purchases.

Actions alleging passing off are often brought when a case of trademark infringement does not lie. For example, a business owner may not be able to secure trademark protection for his or her business name because the name is primarily a surname or it is so descriptive it does not qualify for protection as a trademark. The use of a similar name by

another party in connection with similar products and services that causes confusion and deception may thus be remedied by bringing an action alleging that the second party is passing off his or her goods as those of the plaintiff. Passing off may be enjoined and damages may be awarded to compensate the plaintiff for damages suffered, including lost profits.

Passing off is the earliest form of unfair competition, and the term is used to describe a wide variety of deceptive trade practices. Passing off can occur when a party suggests that its products or services are somehow associated with or sponsored by another, as when a retailer advertises that it is "an authorized dealer of Maytag® products," when it is not. Such conduct is harmful to Maytag, which has not only lost a sale but may suffer damage to its reputation inasmuch as improper conduct by the retailer could reflect badly on Maytag. Such a blatantly untrue statement also constitutes false advertising as well as a violation of section 43(a) of the Lanham Act, which prohibits false designations of origin. In fact, because much of the conduct formerly attacked as passing off is also prohibited by section 43 of the Lanham Act, the federal unfair competition statute, fewer actions alleging passing off are brought nowadays, inasmuch as those actions are dependent upon individual state court interpretations of cases. An action brought under the Lanham Act, however, is federal in nature and provides expanded remedies to plaintiffs such as enhanced damages and attorneys' fees, which are generally unavailable under state law.

In brief, passing off one's goods or services as those of another is a form of unfair competition. Actions alleging palming off or passing off are brought less frequently now, since most plaintiffs prefer to bring actions under section 43 of the Lanham Act, which statutorily prohibits such conduct and provides a federal cause of action with expanded remedies.

The most blatant form of passing off is counterfeiting, namely, selling a product with a "fake" trademark that is an intentional copy of the true trademark. Counterfeiting is common with respect to high-end status products, such as Rolex watches, Louis Vuitton and Kate Spade handbags, and certain types of blue jeans. The Lanham Act (15 U.S.C. § 1127) defines "counterfeit" as a spurious mark that is identical with, or substantially indistinguishable from, a registered mark. Thus, the knockoff handbags sold by street vendors as Burberry bags, complete with a trademark or label identical to that used by Burberry, are counterfeits. In some cases, counterfeit goods can be dangerous. For example, in 1995, the FTC warned against the use of counterfeit infant formula labeled as "Similac" formula, but which did not have the nutritional content of the "real" Similac formula. Similarly, the FTC is now concerned about counterfeit drugs sold over the Internet that do not contain the medicinal compounds of their "real" counterparts. Trademark counterfeiting is a federal crime under 18 U.S.C. § 2320, which imposes fines up to $2 million and jail terms up to ten years for individuals who engage in counterfeiting activities. Enforcement of these laws is difficult, however, as street vendors often merely move their location to another corner when confronted. In many cases, trademark owners prefer to deposit their trademark registrations with the U.S. Customs Service (as discussed in Chapter 6) so it can seize illegally imported goods.

MISAPPROPRIATION

The doctrine of misappropriation first arose in *International News Service v. Associated Press*, 248 U.S. 215 (1918), in which the Supreme Court held that an unauthorized taking of another's property, in that case, news information, that it invested time and money in creating was actionable as misappropriation of property. In *INS*, news information originally gathered by the Associated Press relating to World War I was pirated by International News Service and sold to its customers. Because the news itself, as factual matter, could not be copyrighted, the plaintiff could not sue for copyright infringement. Instead it alleged that its valuable property right had been taken or misappropriated by the defendant. The Supreme Court agreed, noting that the defendant was "endeavoring to reap where it has not sown, and . . . is appropriating to itself the harvest of those who have sown." *Id.* at 239–40. Because the defendant was not attempting to convince its subscribers that its news reports were from the plaintiff, an action for passing off would not lie. The defendant was misappropriating rather than misrepresenting.

In recent years, the doctrine of misappropriation has fallen into disfavor due to its somewhat amorphous nature, and many courts have followed *INS* only when nearly identical fact patterns are presented, namely, cases involving the taking of news, event results, mathematical formulae (such as golf handicapping systems), and indices (such as stock market index reports and averages) that are not addressed by copyright or patent law.

RIGHT OF PUBLICITY

Introduction

Some of the most interesting cases in the intellectual property field relate to the rights of individuals to protect their identities from unauthorized commercial use. The **right of publicity** gives individuals, not merely celebrities, the right to control commercial use of their identities or personas. Nevertheless, because the right of publicity protects a commercial interest, the vast majority of cases involve celebrities inasmuch as they can readily show economic harm when their names, photographs, or identities are used to sell products or suggest a sponsorship of merchandise.

Publicity rights are governed by state law. Many states have specific statutes dealing with the right of publicity. Others recognize the right through case law. Some states do not recognize any right of publicity. On the other hand, California, with its large population of celebrities, has extensive statutes and significant case law recognizing the right of publicity.

The right of publicity has evolved from the right of privacy, which protected against unreasonable invasions upon another person's solitude and provided remedies for the disclosure of private information. While the right of privacy, however, protects one's *personal* interests against indignity, hurt feelings, and invasion, the right of publicity protects one's *commercial* interests against wrongful exploitation. The right of publicity allows individuals to protect the marketability of their identities (a property right) and punishes those who would unjustly enrich themselves by appropriating another's fame for profit-making purposes. Unpermitted commercial exploitation of an individual's persona would dilute the value of the persona, making it more difficult for the individual to commercialize his or her identity. Thus, remedies for infringement include injunctions to prevent further exploitation and monetary relief to compensate the individual whose right of publicity has been appropriated (including damages for injury to reputation, recovery of the defendant's profits, and punitive damages in extreme cases).

Courts have articulated a number of reasons for upholding an individual's right to publicity, including the need to protect against confusion that would arise if consumers were led to believe individuals sponsor or approve products when they do not, the need to incentivize performers who provide entertainment and benefit to society and should thus be provided with a protectable property right in their identities, and the need to prevent unjust enrichment of those who seek to profit from another's talent and often hard-earned fame.

The right of publicity does not apply to noncommercial uses; thus, using another's name, likeness, or identity for news reporting, scholarship, or research is permissible (as long as there is no invasion of privacy or defamation). Most cases involve the unauthorized use of another's identity to promote some product or service, thus suggesting that the individual sponsors or approves the item being advertised. It is not necessary to prove falsity, deception, or likelihood of confusion in order to prevail in an action for infringement of the right of publicity.

Appropriation of Identity

Most states protect more than just a person's name. Thus, unauthorized use of a nickname, voice, likeness, portrait, signature, appearance, identity, or personal attribute (such as customary gestures, clothing, or hairstyle) is prohibited if that use is understood to identify a particular person. Neither intent to deceive nor consumer confusion must be proved. The essence of an action for misappropriation of one's right to publicity is that one's identity was used without permission. Nevertheless, wrongfully using a celebrity's name to advertise a product may also be actionable as false advertising and unfair competition.

Although it is clear that unauthorized use of a person's name or picture is actionable, there are a variety of other ways in which the right of publicity or related rights can be infringed.

- **Phrases and nicknames.** In *Carson v. Here's Johnny Portable Toilets*, 698 F.2d 831 (6th Cir. 1983), a court prohibited a portable toilet company from using the phrase "Here's Johnny" in connection with advertising its services, holding that the phrase had become sufficiently identified with the entertainer Johnny Carson to be protected, even though neither his full name nor his picture was used. Disguising a name, such as varying a few letters, will not protect a defendant. Even nicknames are protectable if they are understood to identify the plaintiff. For example, in *Hirsch v. S.C. Johnson & Sons, Inc.,* 280 N.W.2d 129 (Wis. 1979), the use of the word *Crazylegs* to advertise moisturizer was held to infringe the right of publicity of football star Elroy "Crazylegs" Hirsch.

- **Likeness.** A person's "likeness," including a variety of physical features, is protectable against unauthorized use, whether by drawing, cartoons, or look alikes. Thus, in *Ali v. Playgirl, Inc.,* 447 F. Supp. 723 (S.D.N.Y. 1978), a cartoon drawing of a black man in a boxing ring that included the phrase "The Greatest" was held to have identified the boxer Muhammad Ali and violated his right of publicity. Similarly, in *Allen v. National Video, Inc.,* 610 F. Supp. 612 (S.D.N.Y. 1985), Woody Allen was able to prohibit the use of a look-alike's photograph in advertisements for video rental stores inasmuch as the advertisements falsely suggested that Woody Allen endorsed the advertised services. The case was later settled out of court. In yet another case involving a look-alike photo of Woody Allen, a court stated that certain photos could be used only if accompanied by boldfaced disclaimers identifying the person displayed as a look-alike and stating there was no connection with Woody Allen.

- **Voice.** In *Midler v. Ford Motor Co.,* 849 F.2d 460 (9th Cir. 1988), the Ford Motor Company's use of an impersonator to imitate the singer Bette Midler's vocal style in advertisements for Ford's cars was held to be unlawful. The Ninth Circuit held that while it would "not go so far as to hold that every imitation of a voice to advertise merchandise is actionable . . . when a distinctive voice of a professional singer is widely known and is deliberately imitated in order to sell a product, the sellers have appropriated what is not theirs . . . ." *Id.* at 463.

- **Roles and associated objects.** Imitating a distinctive performing style or persona is actionable. Thus, the roles associated with Groucho Marx and Charlie Chaplin (the "Little Tramp" persona) have been protected from unauthorized commercial exploitation. In *White v. Samsung Electronics America, Inc.,* 971 F.2d 1395 (9th Cir. 1992), the use of a mechanical robot wearing a wig, jewelry, and evening wear posed near a game board similar to that used on the television game show *Wheel of Fortune* was held to create a triable issue of fact regarding whether such use violated game show hostess Vanna White's right of publicity because the display evoked her identity. Similarly, Fred Rogers ("Mister Rogers") sued a store for selling T-shirts showing him wearing his well-recognized sweater and bearing a pistol, arguing that the image was wholly inconsistent with his child-friendly persona and violated his right of publicity.

One of the most famous recent right of publicity cases involved robots that appeared to resemble Norm and Cliff from the *Cheers* television sitcom. The robots, named Hank and Bob, were placed at airport bars. The actors who portrayed Norm and Cliff in the television show sued Cheers's trademark and copyright owner for violations of their right of publicity.

After seven years of litigation and an appeal to the U.S. Supreme Court, the parties ultimately settled out of court. The Ninth Circuit Court of Appeals, however, had ruled that the actors' case could proceed and that it was ultimately up to a jury to determine whether the rights of publicity were violated. An earlier court had dismissed the actors' lawsuit but the Ninth Circuit reversed that decision. *Wendt v. Host International Inc.*, 125 F.3d 806 (9th Cir. 1997).

Duration and Descendibility of Right to Publicity

The duration of the right of publicity is subject to much variation. Some states do not provide any protection for deceased individuals. For example, in New York, the right can be asserted only by a living individual. Many experts believe that this view stems from the association of the right of privacy with the right of publicity. Because the right of privacy is personal to the individual and does not survive death, some states similarly hold that there is no postmortem right of publicity.

The majority of states, however, recognizing that the right of publicity is an economic property right, hold that just as one can pass one's other property to one's heirs so that they receive the fruit of one's labors, so too the right of publicity should survive death. To hold otherwise allows others, generally advertisers, to reap a windfall upon the death of a celebrity. Moreover, because an individual can license the right to another to use his or her name or likeness (for example, the use of athletes' names or photos on sporting goods equipment), clearly indicating the nature of the right of publicity as a property right, the better-reasoned view appears to be that of the majority: the right of publicity is a property right, and like other property rights, it can pass to one's heirs upon death.

On the other hand, there is no real need for the right to exist in perpetuity. It serves little purpose today for the heirs of Benjamin Franklin to be able to control the use of his likeness or name. Thus, in most states, the right of publicity survives death for a stated period of time. For example, in California, the right survives for seventy years after a person's death. Other states recognize varying terms for protection, ranging from twenty years to one hundred years. Still other states, however, that recognize postmortem rights allow heirs to allege infringement only when the individual commercially exploited his or her identity during life. In those states, unless a person has exploited his or her likeness or identity during lifetime, heirs cannot sue for infringement after the person's death. This is a minority approach.

State laws that do not recognize postmortem rights of publicity can often be circumvented. For example, New York will apply the law of a deceased individual's domicile at death. Thus, celebrities often make sure to claim California or some other state as their domicile. Indiana, another state that is highly protective of the right of publicity, authorizes application of its law as soon as an advertisement enters the state. Not surprisingly, a company that represents the estates of more than one hundred deceased celebrities is headquartered in Indiana. Similarly, in today's climate of national communication and advertising, heirs of celebrities may be able to avoid states that do not recognize postmortem rights by asserting that the infringing act was committed in some other state and therefore its laws should apply.

Defenses in Right of Publicity Cases

A variety of defenses may be asserted in actions alleging infringement of one's right of publicity. One defense raised is that the plaintiff is not specifically and readily identified by the usage. For example, in *T.J. Hooker v. Columbia Pictures Industries, Inc.*, 551 F. Supp. 1060 (N.D. Ill. 1982), the plaintiff, a woodcarver named T. J.

Hooker, was unable to prove he was the specific person identified in defendant's television program concerning a fictional police officer.

Another defense asserted is that the usage is protected speech under the First Amendment. News reports using a person's name or identity are protected by the First Amendment's freedom of speech clause as long as the use does not extend beyond what is necessary to inform the public of a newsworthy event. Similarly, use in connection with research and scholarship, because it is not commercial use, is permissible. Courts have clearly held that false or misleading commercial speech is not protected under the First Amendment. Thus, once falsity or deception is shown, a First Amendment defense is generally eliminated.

Use of a person's name, identity, or likeness for purposes of satire, commentary, or parody is protected "fair use." Thus, the biting portrayals of President Clinton and Frank Sinatra by the late comic Phil Hartman on *Saturday Night Live* would likely not support actions for infringement of the right of publicity.

In a 2001 case, the California Supreme Court held that T-shirts decorated with an artist's drawing of the Three Stooges violated the rights of publicity of the heirs of the Stooges because the product containing their likeness did not so transform their image that it became the artist's own expression. The work did not contain significant creative elements but was rather a realistic reproduction of their image. The court noted that by contrast, Andy Warhol's famous silkscreens of celebrities are permissible because they go beyond mere commercial exploitation of celebrity images and provide ironic social commentary. *Comedy III Productions Inc. v. Gary Saderup, Inc.*, 25 Cal. 4th 387 (2001).

Because individuals can license the right to use their names, likenesses, and signatures to others, defendants often assert that use was authorized. Actors typically grant studios the right to use their names and identities to promote movies in which they appear. The right generally extends to future re-releases of the movie, even on television, and may extend so far as to allow the studio to use the individual's name or likeness in connection with collateral products, such as toys and other related merchandise. Similarly, athletes often grant or license sporting goods and card companies the right to reproduce their names, signatures, and photos on goods in return for license or royalty fees.

New Developments in the Right of Publicity

As is common with intellectual property rights in today's society, some of the new issues relating to the right of publicity stem from increasing technological advances. Through digital technology, President Clinton appeared in the movie *Contact*, John Wayne sells beer, and Fred Astaire dances with a vacuum cleaner. Some actors, such as Tom Cruise, already insist that their contracts prohibit the modification of their digital images without prior permission. Vanna White's success in presenting a triable issue of fact in seeking to enjoin the use of a robot that evoked her likeness indicates that the right of publicity can extend beyond conventional infringement to misappropriation through digital and electronic means.

In another new development, the International Trademark Association has proposed amending the U.S. Trademark Act to create a federal right of publicity with postmortem rights (although such rights would be limited to some specific period of duration after death). Similarly, the American Bar Association is studying a proposed federal right of publicity. Such federal laws would promote uniformity and eliminate the variation presently existing among the various states.

Another issue is whether the Copyright Act preempts (or takes precedence over) individual social and behavioral science research.

Case, population, and sampling

Behavioral and social sciences are about the persistent patterns of regularity in human life. In the eyes of a scientist, human life is constituted by variables, and the specification of the variables involves scientific reduction. Although reducing real life to a set of variables has incurred criticism from some practical point of view, it seems to be the only way for validating the finding of a regular pattern.

To study variables and the interrelationships among variables, you must first clarify your unit of analysis. There are different analytic units at different levels and in different subsystems of the social system, including an individual, a social group, a community, a social artifact (e.g., a book), a social event, and a social relation. Here you are cautioned not to confuse your unit of analysis with your point of focus to be discussed later.

Your analysis may involve several of the units, but usually you have only one emphasis. A characteristic as a variable may be simultaneously attributed to or reflected in different social units, but most of the time you would only pay attention to your focal unit of analysis. In other words, no matter how many social units are involved in your study, their characteristics tend to be studied through your focal unit of analysis. In behavioral especially psychological studies, the focal unit of analysis tends to be individual persons, who are often called the "subjects." It should be noted that sometimes you may collect information about your focal unit of analysis through other social units (called units of observation). Yet you should avoid confusing your focal unit of analysis with any other social unit. This has been a key issue in drawing research conclusions and clarifying their implications. A sound research logic can only be maintained by ensuring the coincidence between the unit in your analysis and the unit in your conclusion. You should avoid, for example, making assertions about social groups based on the examination of individuals (called atomistic fallacy). It is equally inappropriate to make assertions about individuals based on the examination of social groups (called ecological fallacy).

Scientific reduction focuses your attention on the major interests of your discipline and of your own. Your unit of analysis will be reduced to a number of variables which form a generalized "case." A particular case can be obtained through measurement, or by taking values on those variables, which form a state statutes relating to the law of publicity. In some instances, the two fields coexist. For example, if a scene from a movie with Harrison Ford (protected by copyright) is later used without permission in another movie, Harrison Ford's copyright rights as well as his right to publicity have been violated. At least one court has held that in such a case, federal copyright preempts state laws relating to rights of publicity. *Fleet v. CBS,* 50 Cal. App. 4th 1911 (1996). In the Bette Midler case, because voices cannot be copyrighted, Midler sued solely for misappropriation of her identity and violation of her common law right to publicity. Similarly, names, gestures, and likenesses are unprotectable under copyright law because they are titles or ideas rather than expressions. Thus, in some instances, federal copyright law may control a plaintiff's rights, while in other instances, only the right to publicity will provide protection. In another new development, California recently passed the Astaire Celebrity Image Protection Act (Cal. Civ. Code §§ 3344–3346) to allow heirs of celebrities to block commercial uses of deceased celebrities' likenesses while allowing a "safe harbor exemption" to artistic uses, such as the digital insertion of President Kennedy's image into the movie *Forrest Gump,* or uses for news, public affairs, and so forth.

FALSE ADVERTISING

Introduction

In 1943, the federal trademark law, the Lanham Act, was passed. Section 43(a) of the act (15 U.S.C. § 1125) prohibited false designations of origin, namely, descriptions or representations tending falsely to describe or represent goods or services. Until the passage of the Lanham Act, actions involving unfair competition tended to allege passing off or trade disparagement. Passing off, however, was limited to

instances in which a party misrepresented the *source* of goods or services. Thus, it was not an effective vehicle to use when a party made misrepresentations relating to the *nature* or *quality* of goods or services. Moreover, until the passage of the Lanham Act, plaintiffs were generally required to prove that the defendant's acts were the direct cause of loss of sales and profits, an element that was often difficult to demonstrate. Finally, courts were reluctant to let business competitors bring actions against each other to assert what was often a harm done to consumers and not to them. In *Ely-Norris Safe Co. v. Mosler Safe Co.,* 7 F.2d 603 (2d Cir. 1925), *rev'd on other grounds,* 273 U.S. 132 (1927), Judge Learned Hand stated that the law did not allow a plaintiff-competitor to sue as a "vicarious avenger" of the defendant's customers.

Although the individual states enacted statutes prohibiting **false advertising,** these statutes varied from state to state and were often ineffective to prohibit false advertising that was national in scope. The expansive language of section 43 of the Lanham Act, however, soon began to be used to protect not only against unregistered trademarks but also against nearly all forms of false advertising. In 1989, Congress amended the Lanham Act and broadened the scope of section 43. As presently written, one portion of the statute allows parties to bring actions in federal courts for infringement of trademarks (both registered and unregistered marks) and trade dress, while the other portion of the statute allows the assertion of claims for false advertising and trade libel.

Under section 43(a), whoever uses a false or misleading description or representation of fact or false designation of origin in commercial advertising or promotion or misrepresents the nature, qualities, or geographic origin of his or her or another person's goods, services, or commercial activities is liable to any person likely to be injured by such act (if the act is committed in interstate commerce). Thus, the statute protects competitors as well as perhaps consumers and allows recovery if the plaintiff can show he or she is *likely* to be damaged, thereby eliminating the prior requirement that a plaintiff show *actual damage*. Most plaintiffs are business competitors, injured celebrities, and others who can show direct injury. Most cases that have considered the issue have held that defrauded consumers have no standing to sue for false advertising under section 43(a).

The broad and sweeping scope of section 43 has been used to protect the distinctive uniform of the Dallas Cowboys cheerleaders, the color and shape of a drug capsule, the overall look of a line of greeting cards, and the sound of singer Tom Waite's voice from use by a sound-alike to falsely suggest Waite endorsed DORITOS® chips.

Remedies for false advertising include injunctive relief to prohibit further false statements or to correct falsities as well as monetary relief.

Examples of False Advertising

An advertisement that is literally false is clearly actionable. Even advertisements that are implicitly false or unclear, however, are actionable if they are nevertheless likely to mislead or deceive consumers. False advertising is actionable under section 43 of the Lanham Act, which prohibits advertisements that falsely represent the nature, characteristics, or qualities of one's own or another's goods or services. In many cases, surveys of consumers are used to prove that the message conveyed, even if literally true, is deceptive to the public at large. Courts generally require, in cases involving implicit rather than literal falsity, that an "appreciable" or "substantial" number of consumers must be misled by a claim. If scientific, medical, or technical claims are made in an advertisement, experts are usually called

to demonstrate truth or falsity. Following are some examples of advertising held to be false:

- a failure to disclose that advertised prices did not include additional charges;
- a statement that a pregnancy test kit would disclose results in "as fast as ten minutes" when a positive result would appear in ten minutes but a negative result might take thirty minutes;
- a claim that a certain motor oil provided longer life and better engine protection than a competitor's product when that claim could not be substantiated;
- a claim that orange juice was pure, pasteurized juice as it came from the orange and showing a celebrity squeezing an orange and pouring the juice directly into the carton when the juice was heated and sometimes frozen prior to packaging;
- a false claim that automobile antifreeze met an automobile manufacturer's standards;
- falsely claiming a whiskey to be "scotch" whiskey when it was not;
- covering up a label stating "Made in Taiwan" that appeared on goods; and
- ads for GLAD-LOCK® resealable storage bags that did not accurately portray the leakage rate of a competitor's bags and did not indicate that only a certain percentage of the competitor's bags leaked.

Many cases involve **comparative advertising** claims in which one party claims its products are superior or equivalent to those of a competitor. The competitor need not be specifically identified for an action to lie. In comparative advertising cases, a plaintiff must in fact show that the claimed product is inferior or not equivalent. Claiming that a product is "compatible with" or "works with" another product is permissible as long as the claim is true.

Defenses to False Advertising

Clearly, the truth is a defense to a claim that an advertisement is false or misleading. Truth can be shown by survey evidence (showing consumers are not misled), statistical evidence, or expert opinion. Another common defense asserted in false advertising cases is **puffing.** Puffing is an exaggerated and highly subjective statement upon which no reasonable person would rely. Courts generally hold that such puffing is vague and is opinion only rather than misrepresentation and is thus not actionable. Thus, stating that elves make KEEBLER® cookies is not false advertising because no reasonable person would believe such a statement to be true. Vague statements such as that a product is a "major breakthrough" or represents "new technology" are likewise permissible puffing inasmuch as they are more in the nature of boasting than representation. Similarly, general statements that a product is "superior" are usually held to be nonactionable puffing; however, if a statement purports to rely on test results that demonstrate superiority, such a claim may be false advertising if superiority cannot be proven.

Another defense often raised is that the speech involved in an allegedly false advertisement is protected speech under the First Amendment. Courts have typically held, however, that commercial speech is not constitutionally protected from regulation and that the government has the right to ban deceptive and false speech.

Regulation by the Federal Trade Commission

The **Federal Trade Commission (FTC)** is charged with enforcing a comprehensive law, section 5 of the FTC Act (15 U.S.C. § 45), which prohibits unfair and deceptive acts and practices in or affecting commerce. Similar to section 43 of the Lanham Act and most state statutes relating to false advertising, section 5 requires that objective claims made in adver-

tising and marketing be truthful and substantiated. The FTC will not pursue subjective claims or puffing, such as a claim that a suntan lotion is the "best in the world," but will pursue claims that include an objective component, such as "our suntan lotion lasts longer than other popular brands." Almost all states have statutes similar to section 5 of the FTC Act that prohibit deceptive and unfair trade practices. The state statutes are usually referred to as **little FTC acts.**

Most of the advertising cases challenged by the FTC involve health and safety claims inasmuch as these pose the most risk to consumers. Alcohol and tobacco advertising is subject to particular scrutiny. Many recent cases involve health and nutrient claims for foods and dietary supplements. Health and safety claims typically require competent and credible scientific evidence. Claims such as "clinical studies show that our brand is better than . . ." are permissible only if they are true. If other studies exist that contradict claims or if the methodology of the studies is defective, there is likely a violation of the FTC Act.

The FTC also vigorously pursues fraudulent telemarketing tactics and has been paying increased attention to consumer protection on the Internet, including privacy rights and identity theft. Section 5 of the FTC Act applies to electronic commerce and thus the FTC is charged with prohibiting unfair and deceptive practices on the Internet. FTC staff routinely monitor the Net and online services. In 1995, the FTC brought its first case involving an online scam, and with the cooperation of the Internet service provider (America Online), the FTC shut the scam down and achieved complete redress for injured consumers.

The FTC has a wide array of remedies it uses to protect consumers. While cease and desist orders, injunctions, and monetary penalties are common, the FTC is increasingly using more innovative remedies designed to protect consumers. For example, the FTC often requires that restitution be made to injured consumers, rescinds contracts that are deceptive, and has required corrective advertising and affirmative disclosures about product safety claims. In one case involving false claims relating to sunscreen, the FTC required that the respondent design, produce, and print brochures about the importance of sunscreen usage by children. Similarly, in 2000, the FTC required Bayer Corp. to embark on a $1 million consumer education program to settle charges that Bayer advertisements made unsubstantiated claims that regular aspirin could help prevent heart attacks and strokes in the general population. The FTC itself uses the Internet to protect consumers. By accessing the FTC's home page (http://www.ftc.gov), consumers can obtain consumer protection information electronically and participate in online seminars regarding selected topics.

PRODUCT DISPARAGEMENT

At common law, an action can be brought for making intentional and untrue statements about another company or its products or services that cause monetary harm to the company. The action is variously called **product disparagement,** *commercial disparagement,* or *trade libel.*

The statements, which can be written or oral, must be false and must clearly communicate a disparaging message about the plaintiff. Mere puffing does not give rise to an action for product disparagement. Similarly, merely expressing a negative opinion about a company in an Internet chat room does not constitute disparagement. Most jurisdictions require that the defendant act with intent to injure the plaintiff or, at the least, with a reckless disregard for the truth or falsity of its statements. Finally, specific economic harm must be

pleaded and proven. It is not sufficient for a plaintiff to show that it is likely to be harmed by a defendant's false representations. The plaintiff must generally demonstrate specific economic harm, such as the loss of a contract or loss of customers.

Actions for product disparagement are seen less frequently today inasmuch as plaintiffs would generally prefer to rely upon section 43(a) of the Lanham Act. Relying on section 43 rather than individual state judicial decisions affords a plaintiff several advantages, chiefly that the plaintiff need not prove specific economic harm inasmuch as relief is provided to anyone who is *likely* to be damaged. Moreover, under section 43, a plaintiff need not prove that a defendant had the specific intent to injure the plaintiff or that the defendant acted in reckless disregard of the truth or falsity of misrepresentations.

In defending an action for product disparagement (whether brought under common law or section 43(a)), a defendant may allege that its statements are permissible comparative advertising (as long as the statements are true), that its statements are mere puffing, or that its statements are protected as speech under the First Amendment. As discussed earlier, however, commercial speech is provided a lower level of protection than other forms of speech.

DILUTION

Dilution is another form of unfair competition. Dilution occurs when a famous trademark loses its distinctive quality due to tarnishment or blurring. As previously discussed in Chapter 6, the new Federal Trademark Dilution Act (FTDA) (15 U.S.C. § 43(c)) provides remedies for the dilution of famous marks. Under the act, effective in 1996, the owner of a famous mark is entitled to an injunction against another person's use in commerce of a mark or trade name if such use begins after the mark has become famous and causes actual dilution of the distinctive quality of the famous mark.

The FTDA is intended to provide a remedy for the owners of famous marks when the owners of those marks would not otherwise be able to establish likelihood of confusion and thus avail themselves of the many avenues available to protect marks from confusingly similar uses. In one famous case, the use of TIFFANY for a restaurant was prohibited inasmuch as it diluted the famous TIFFANY® mark used in connection with jewelry. The court noted that confusion was not likely inasmuch as no reasonable person would believe that the restaurant services were somehow affiliated with or sponsored by the jewelers. Nevertheless, the use of the famous mark TIFFANY, even in connection with unrelated services and goods, whittled away or diluted the strong association consumers make between the TIFFANY mark and fine jewelry. The goodwill inherent in the famous TIFFANY mark would evaporate if junior users were allowed to use the mark even on unrelated goods. *Tiffany & Co. v. Boston Club Inc.,* 231 F. Supp. 836 (D. Mass. 1964).

Dilution can occur in two ways: blurring or tarnishment. Blurring occurs when a mark's distinctive quality is eroded through use on dissimilar products. Examples of blurring would be TIFFANY RESTAURANT, KODAK BICYCLES, or CHRYSLER SOUP. Tarnishment occurs when a mark is linked to products of inferior quality or when the mark is portrayed in an unsavory manner, such as a poster reading "Enjoy Cocaine" in the distinctive colors and script used in the famous "Enjoy Coca-Cola" advertisements.

Many of the recent cases involving dilution focus on uses of Internet addresses. For example, the address "http://www.candyland.com" for sexually explicit services and goods was held to dilute the famous CANDYLAND mark owned by Hasbro Toys. *Hasbro Inc. v. Internet Entertainment Group, Ltd.,* 40 U.S.P.Q.2d 1439 (W.D. Wash. 1996). Similarly, the address "http://www.adultsrus.com" used for sexual paraphernalia was held to dilute the famous TOYS "R" US mark owned by Toys "R" Us, Inc. *Toys "R" Us, Inc. v. Akkaouli,* 1996 WL 772709 (N.D. Cal.).

One of the difficult tasks presented to courts is determining what constitutes a "famous" mark. The FTDA provides some factors for courts to consider in determining whether a mark is distinctive and famous, including the following: the degree of distinctiveness of a mark; the duration and extent of use of the mark; the duration and extent of advertising and publicity of the mark; the degree of recognition of the mark; the nature and extent of use of the same or similar marks by third parties; and whether the mark is federally registered. If a plaintiff can show willful intent by the defendant to trade on the plaintiff's famous mark or to cause dilution of a famous mark, a plaintiff can obtain monetary relief, the defendant's profits, costs, and attorneys' fees, in addition to injunctive relief. Some courts have afforded protection even when marks are not nationally famous but have fame in a "limited circle," such as regionally or in a niche market. Thus, in *Wawa Inc. v. Haaf,* 40 U.S.P.Q.2d 1629 (E.D. Pa. 1996), *aff'd,* 116 F.3d 471 (3d Cir. 1997), the court held that the WAWA mark, used for convenience stores in five mid-Atlantic states, deserved protection against dilution.

Under the FTDA, some uses of famous marks are not actionable, such as fair use of a famous mark in comparative advertising, noncommercial use of a famous mark, and use of a famous mark in news reporting and commentary.

INFRINGEMENT OF TRADE DRESS

The total image and overall appearance of a product or service is protectable as its "trade dress." Trade dress, like trademarks, can be registered with the PTO. Trade dress refers to the distinctive appearance of a business or product and may include a product's distinctive packaging, the interior design of a restaurant, the layout of a business, and other nonfunctional features of a product or service. Trade dress may include features such as size, shape, color or color combinations, texture, graphics, and even particular sales techniques. Trade dress protection does not extend to utilitarian or functional aspects of a product or service inasmuch as such would tend to reduce or stifle competition. Functional products may be protected under patent law (assuming they meet the tests of patentability, such as novelty and nonobviousness), which provides a limited period of duration for utility patents. To allow a functional product or service to be protected as trade dress would allow a monopoly on a useful feature or product in perpetuity.

In *Two Pesos Inc. v. Taco Cabana, Inc.,* 505 U.S. 763 (1992), the Supreme Court held that the inherently distinctive trade dress of a Mexican restaurant could be protected under section 43(a) of the Lanham Act against infringement by another restaurant that used confusingly similar décor and design elements. The trade dress included the shape and general appearance of the exterior of the restaurant, the signage, the interior kitchen plan, the décor, the menu, the equipment, servers' uniforms, and other features that reflected the total image of the restaurant. The Court held that as long as a party's trade dress is distinctive (either inherently or upon a showing of secondary meaning), it will be protected against a junior user's use that is likely to cause confusion among consumers. The Court expressly noted that protection of trade dress, like protection of trademarks, serves the Lanham Act's purpose of securing to owners the goodwill of their businesses and protecting the ability of consumers to distinguish among competing goods and services.

In a recent case, *Samara Bros. Inc. v. Wal-Mart Stores, Inc.,* 165 F.3d 120 (2d Cir. 1998), *reversed on other grounds,* 529 U.S. 205 (2000), the plaintiff was awarded $1.2 million against Wal-Mart for selling (under Wal-Mart labels) knockoffs of the plaintiff's children's clothing line. The court held that the clothing, which displayed large collars and bold appliques of hearts and flowers on seersucker, was sufficiently distinctive to be entitled to trade dress protection. Thus, although clothing per se is not protectable under copyright law because it is a useful article, distinctive elements of clothing can be protected under trade dress theory. The Court held that product design is not inherently distinctive, and thus trade dress cases based upon product design must show that the design has acquired distinctiveness through secondary meaning. 529 U.S. 211-13. Moreover, clothing design embellishments, such as the hearts and flowers, can be protected under copyright law, although the scope of protection for such familiar elements will be narrow and only nearly identical copying will be prohibited.

INTERNATIONAL PROTECTION AGAINST UNFAIR COMPETITION

The United States has assumed certain obligations under international agreements in the arena of unfair competition, chiefly under the Paris Convention. The Paris Convention seeks to afford citizens of each of the more than 160 member nations protection against unfair competition and trademark infringement and requires that member nations provide the same level of protection against unfair competition to citizens of other member nations as they do for their own citizens. (See Appendix A for a table of countries adhering to the Paris Convention.)

The Paris Convention expressly prohibits acts that create confusion by any means with a competitor, false allegations that discredit a competitor, and indications that mislead the public in regard to the nature or characteristics of goods.

Section 44 of the Lanham Act (15 U.S.C. § 1126) implements the Paris Convention and expressly provides that any person whose country of origin is a party to any convention or treaty relating to the repression of unfair competition, to which the United States is also a party, is entitled to effective protection against unfair competition, thus affording citizens of Paris Convention member nations the wide variety of protection afforded under section 43 of the Lanham Act.

TRIVIA

- George Foreman has received at least $187 million for lending his name to the marketing of grilling machines, showing the marketability of a celebrity's persona.
- The estimate of losses each year to U.S. businesses due to the counterfeiting of consumer goods is approximately $200 billion.
- In March 2003, Rexall Sundown agreed to pay the FTC up to $12 million to resolve charges that it had made unsubstantiated claims about "Cellasene," a purported cellulite treatment product.
- The FTC currently receives more consumer complaints about identity theft than any other type of fraud.

CHAPTER SUMMARY

The term *unfair competition* refers to a wide variety of acts and practices that constitute improper commercial conduct. Because the property interests being protected are often intangible, such as reputation, image, and goodwill, the interests are classified as "intellectual property."

Injured parties can rely on a host of theories to protect their commercial interests: passing off (selling one's goods as those of another); misappropriation (the taking of another's valuable commercial interests); false advertising (making false representations about the nature or quality of one's own goods or services); the right of publicity (protecting one's image or persona from commercial appropriation); product disparagement (making false representations about another's goods or services); dilution (weakening another's trademark or service mark); or infringement of trade dress (causing a likelihood of confusion with the overall appearance or image of another's product or service). Additionally, section 43 of the Lanham Act provides a federal cause of action for a broad range of anticompetitive activities (including passing off, false advertising, product disparagement, trademark dilution, and infringement of trade dress). Finally, the FTC regulates commercial acts and practices. Under the Paris Convention, the United States is required to protect citizens of member nations against unfair competition, and U.S. citizens are treated in other countries equivalently to nationals of those member nations with regard to unfair competition.

CASE ILLUSTRATION—FALSE ADVERTISING

Case: *Alpo Petfoods, Inc. v. Ralston Purina Co.*, 720 F. Supp. 194 (D.D.C. 1989), *reversed on other grounds*, 913 F.2d 958 (D.C. Cir. 1990)

Facts: Ralston Purina advertisements made certain claims that its Puppy Chow products helped reduce hip joint laxity and reduce chronic hip dysplasia in dogs. A competitor, Alpo, sued for false and deceptive advertising under the Lanham Act.

Holding: Ralston's claims lacked any reasonable basis. In fact, such claims perpetrated a "cruel hoax" on dog owners and disadvantaged Ralston's competitors. With the exception of Ralston's own faulty research, there was no valid scientific support for the proposition that the nutritional balance of a dog's diet could affect hip joint formations. The condition of chronic hip dysplasia is hereditary in nature. Ralston was ordered to disseminate truthful literature to those who had previously received false information and was ordered to pay damages (approximately $12 million) and attorney's fees.

CASE STUDY AND ACTIVITIES

Case Study. Watson's designers have observed that a number of children are carrying backpacks and wearing watches that display Watson's trademarked logo, which is registered with the PTO. The goods are knockoffs and are generally sold by street vendors. Watson has also observed that the overall appearance of a competitor's park is much like Watson's in that its entrance is an "old-fashioned" Main Street that opens onto various themed sections of the park such as a western world, a water park, and a children's section. The competitor's advertising materials state that its roller coasters are "six times faster than" Watson's and that its park is "more fun" and "more adventurous" than Watson's.

Activities. Discuss whether Watson may initiate any actions with respect to the foregoing acts and representations.

ROLE OF PARALEGAL

There are a number of tasks in which IP paralegals are engaged in the unfair competition arena. Some of those activities are as follows:

- reviewing advertisements and publications to alert clients to possible instances of passing off, misappropriation, false advertising, product disparagement, or dilution;
- reviewing the products and services of competitors of clients to ensure that the trade dress of clients is not being infringed;

ROLE OF PARALEGAL (cont'd)

- preparing and responding to cease and desist letters that demand the cessation of unfair competitive practices;
- conducting legal research relating to unfair competitive practices;
- preparing and responding to complaints alleging acts of unfair competition;
- engaging in the discovery process in unfair competition actions, including preparing and responding to interrogatories and requests for production of documents and preparing notices of depositions;
- assisting in trial preparation by preparing exhibits and jury instructions and assisting in the preparation of briefs for court; and
- assisting in the drafting of settlement agreements.

INTERNET RESOURCES

Federal and state laws relating to unfair competition:	http://www.ll.georgetown.edu or http://www.findlaw.com
Federal Trade Commission:	http://www.ftc.gov
General information:	http://www.findlaw.com, http://www.megalaw.com, and http://www.ipmall.fplc.edu

DISCUSSION QUESTIONS

1. PepsiCo. has recently discovered that a competitor is filling empty Pepsi bottles with another type of cola beverage and selling them to consumers. What type of action may PepsiCo bring?
2. An unauthorized picture of Tiger Woods has appeared in the following:
   - an advertisement for golf clubs;
   - a news story about young golfers; and
   - an advertisement for pizza.
   Discuss whether Mr. Woods has any remedies for these uses of his photograph.
3. An advertisement for sports clothing claims "Even His Airness would like these." Have any rights of Michael Jordan been violated by this unauthorized advertisement?
4. The manufacturer of sunglasses has released a television ad in which a model states, "Way cooler than Ray-Bans. I'll never give up these sunglasses." Is such a statement actionable?

5. A company claims that its low-fat cookies contain "less fat per cookie" and "taste better" than those of Nabisco. Are such claims actionable?

6. A company advertises that its blocks "work with" Lincoln Logs. The claim is true and the company that makes Lincoln Logs suffers a loss in its sales. Is the advertisement actionable?

7. Discuss what type of trademark dilution is involved for each of the following:
   • Lexus photocopiers;
   • Nestle pens;
   • Barbie's Sex Toys; and
   • Mattel's Head Shop (for a shop selling drug paraphernalia).

complete "observation" including the whole set of measurement or observational activities. The interrelationship among the variables must be approached through the study of specific cases. Yet the question is, how many cases will be needed for an effective research study?

This question is about the relative scope of a research project. The answer has to do with the homogeneity or heterogeneity of the research population, i.e., all targets of the same unit of analysis, or all potential cases with the same variables in a particular study. If the targets or real cases are all the same or completely homogeneous, then one study case would suffice for the purpose of research. If the targets have nothing in common with one another and each is totally different, or if you do not want to miss any real case, then you would have to study all of them, or take all of them as your study cases. Although researchers sometimes study only one case or a few cases (e.g., case studies), or investigate all the real cases covered by a project (e.g., a census), most of the time they take a middle course selecting a proportion of the total number of the real cases or targets, that is, a sample, to study. It should be noted that although single case design is useful in resolving the issues of individual cases, it has the least generalization power since differences across human subjects tend to be considerable. A sample of relatively large size is often needed to make inference to the study population. In real terms, sampling has become so common that the above two extremes would be considered only as exceptions. In other words, any research project may be termed a sample study, and the study cases and units are considered elements of the study sample. If you want to reach every case in your research population, you would still be considered as taking a "saturation sample" for your study.

Your research population has as much importance as your research question. In choosing a research topic you usually also have an idea as to whom or what to study. In asking a specific question, you need to clarify whom or what you want to draw conclusions about. As a matter of fact, a psychosocial research interest is frequently expressed as a desire to study a certain population (usually people), such as children, women, elderly, alcoholics, or AIDS patients. A further understanding of so-called "points of focus" will help you to narrow down your topic and operationalize your question. There are three main points of focus (Babbie, 1995): characteristics, or states of being including sex, age, race, and marital status for individuals; orientations, such as attitudes and personality traits; and actions, such as voting, going to church, and dropping out of school. Depending on your units of analysis, the examples would be different for the points of focus. All these can be considered as different substantive categories of

CHAPTER 24

Intellectual Property Audits and Due Diligence Reviews

CHAPTER OVERVIEW

Clients are often unaware of the importance of their intellectual property. To help clients realize the value of such assets and exploit them, law firms often conduct intellectual property audits for clients. The audit reveals the intellectual capital owned by a client and assists in developing a strategy so the client can maintain its valuable intellectual capital. Once clients fully understand *what* they own, they can then protect it, license it, or sell it. The audit should be repeated on a periodic basis to reflect the changing nature of intellectual property. Audits are also conducted when a company is sold, when it borrows money, or when it acquires another company. This type of audit is usually referred to as a "due diligence" review.

INTRODUCTION

Clients are often unaware that they own valuable assets: their intellectual property. They may use distinctive names for certain products or services, may possess creative marketing materials, or may have developed a novel method of conducting business. All of these developments are assets that can and should be protected as intellectual property. Distinctive names should be registered as trademarks, written materials should be protected by copyright notices and registration, and trade secrets should be protected so they can endure perpetually.

If intellectual property is not protected, it may be lost. Failure to monitor and police infringing activities may also lead to a loss of rights. Competitors may acquire rights to valuable property that formerly provided a competitive edge to a company, resulting in a loss of market share and profits. Companies not only should protect their intellectual property in order to ensure business survival but also should use their intellectual property to create revenue. Trademarks, copyrights, patents, and trade secrets can all be licensed to others. The owner of intellectual property can achieve a continual revenue stream through licensing of rights to others for either a fixed sum or recurrent royalty payments. Alternatively, intellectual property may be sold outright to another. Intellectual property can also be used as collateral so its owner can secure a loan from a bank or other institution. Just as real property or personal property such as inventory is pledged as collateral when money is borrowed, so too can intellectual property (trademarks, copyrights, and patents) serve as collateral. Intellectual property can also be used as donations. For example, a number of companies have donated patents to universities and other nonprofit institutions. The donors then take an income tax deduction for the donation, although the Internal Revenue Service has begun subjecting such claims to increased scrutiny.

The failure to capitalize on the value of intellectual property is generally caused by a lack of awareness of just what can be protected. Many companies believe that copyright extends only to important literary works and therefore fail to secure protection for their marketing brochures or other written materials. Similarly, companies often fail to implement measures to ensure valuable trade secrets maintain their protectability. Because clients are often unaware of the great potential and value of this property, law firms often offer their clients an **intellectual property audit** to uncover a company's protectable intellectual property. The IP audit is analogous to the accounting audit most companies conduct on an annual basis to review their financial status.

Another type of IP investigation is usually conducted when a company acquires another entity. At that time, a thorough investigation should be conducted of the intellectual property of the target company to ensure the acquiring company will obtain the benefits of what it is paying for and will not inherit infringement suits and other problems stemming from the target's failure to protect its intellectual property. This type of intellectual property investigation is generally called a **due diligence** review inasmuch as the acquiring company and its counsel have an obligation to duly and diligently investigate the target's assets. Due diligence reviews are also conducted when a company offers its securities for public sale inasmuch as potential investors must be informed of the offeror's assets (including its intellectual property) and any claims that may arise against the offeror. Similarly, when a company is being sold, it is generally required to identify its intellectual property and make certain representations and warranties that it owns the property being sold and there are no defects in title or pending claims involving the property. Thus, due diligence must be conducted to ensure these representations and warranties can be made with respect to a seller's intellectual property.

PRACTICAL ASPECTS OF INTELLECTUAL PROPERTY AUDITS

IP audits come in all shapes and sizes. Most importantly, the audit must fit the client and respond to its needs. If a client owns a small retail shop or provides auto repair services from only one location, the sole intellectual property may consist of the business name (which may be protectable as a trademark), any logos or designs used by the client, customer lists, and marketing materials, if any. On the other hand, if a client is engaged in software development, information technology, or telecommunications services, it may possess a wealth of IP assets. For example, in 2002 alone, IBM Corp. was granted 3,288 patents, helping to generate about $10 billion in royalties for IBM over the past ten years.

In many cases, the first IP audit is the most extensive and expensive. Some clients conduct periodic audits, and law firms typically docket the dates for annual reviews and send reminder notices to clients. The annual reviews can focus on changes since the previous audit. While there is some expense involved in conducting any audit, the benefit of the audit outweighs the expense involved. Moreover, there are often intangible benefits to the audit. If the client later wishes to obtain a loan or sell some of its assets, the preceding audit need only be updated, eliminating costly delays in a transaction. If the client is adequately prepared for the audit and actively assists in the audit, costs can be reduced.

Before the audit is conducted, the law firm and the client should agree on its scope and nature. Consideration should be given in regard to whether the firm will conduct the audit on an hourly fee basis or for a fixed fee. In most instances, the law firm will need to send IP professionals to the client site, resulting in disruption to the client's operations. Again, with careful preparation, such disruption can be kept to a minimum.

The following issues should be clearly addressed before the audit begins:

- Who will conduct the audit? Usually, counsel (inside or outside), together with IP paralegals, will conduct the audit, relying on company representatives for assistance. The law firm and the client should each designate a person who will serve as the team leader and to whom questions and concerns can be addressed. If a client is unusually large, it may designate various leaders, for example, one from its research and development department, one from its marketing department, and so forth.
- What scope will the audit have? Should only U.S. rights be explored? Should consideration be given to protecting intellectual property on an international basis?

CONDUCTING THE AUDIT

The first step in the audit should be a face-to-face meeting of the legal team and company managers. The legal team should make a brief presentation on what intellectual property is, why it is important to the company, and why and how the audit will be conducted. Managers will be more likely to cooperate if they fully understand the importance of the audit. Obtaining this kind of "buy in" from the client's managers and employees will speed the audit and reduce costs. Moreover, education about the importance of intellectual property helps ensure that managers consider ways to further protect a company's valuable assets and remain alert to possible infringements of the company's intellectual capital or infringements by the company of others' rights. Finally, having outside counsel involved in the process will ensure that communications related to the audit are protected by the attorney-client privilege.

Once the company's mangers have been advised of the need for the audit, the legal team should provide a worksheet or questionnaire (see Exhibit 24–1) to the company specifying the type of information that the firm is looking for so that company files can be reviewed and materials assembled for inspection by the firm and its representatives. Although it is not strictly necessary that the client do this kind of preparatory work, the more work the client does, the faster, cheaper, and less disruptive the audit will be.

EXHIBIT 24–1
Intellectual
Property Audit
Questionnaire

Identified below is a list of subjects to be covered in connection with our review of the intellectual property rights of your company (the "Company"). Please gather any materials and documents relevant to the subjects listed below so they can be reviewed. If no materials or documents exist with respect to a particular subject, please confirm that in writing next to the relevant question.

For all relevant questions, give the name of the person who assisted in the design, development, or implementation of any intellectual property rights; describe the nature of the relationship between the person and the Company (for example, employee, independent contractor, and so forth); and indicate whether the person signed any confidentiality or nondisclosure agreements with the Company.

A. General

1. Has the Company ever acquired another entity or the business or assets of another entity or person? (This party may have owned intellectual property that is now owned by the Company.)
2. Has the Company ever sold any assets or business to another entity or person?
3. Is the Company engaged in the development or design of any useful products or parts for useful products?
4. Is the Company engaged in the development, design, or modification of computer software?
5. Are there any individuals who may have developed or designed products or software for the Company who have left employment with the Company? If so, indicate whether each such person signed a confidentiality, nondisclosure, or employment agreement with the Company.
6. Does the Company have a web site or are there links from other parties' sites to the Company's site? If so, provide web site addresses.
7. Does the Company use a docketing system or calendar to provide reminders of due dates relating to any of its intellectual property?

B. Trademarks and Service Marks

1. Does the Company use any trademarks, service marks, logos, slogans, or designs (collectively "Marks") in connection with the offer and sale of its products or services? These Marks may have been displayed on products, labels, packaging, letterhead, business cards, in advertisements, brochures, or other marketing materials, including a web site.
2. Has the Company ever applied for registration of any Marks with the United States Patent and Trademark Office (PTO) or any state trademark agencies?
3. Has the Company ever allowed another party (such as an employee, client, vendor, or competitor) to use any of the Company's Marks?
4. Does the Company use any Marks that are owned by any third party? Review Company marketing materials, web site, and other written documents to determine whether the Company displays or uses Marks belonging to another.

C. Copyrights

1. What written materials does the Company use to advertise its products and services? These may be written materials, scripts or copy for radio or television advertisements, or web site materials. Were these developed by Company employees or by independent contractors working for the Company? What agreements exist relating to the development of such materials?

(continues)

2. What written materials does the Company use internally, such as employee handbooks, training materials, company policies, or manuals relating to the way the Company conducts its business?

3. Do Company employees prepare written materials or electronic materials (such as PowerPoint slides) when presentations are made within the Company and outside the Company? If so, describe.

4. Do Company employees submit articles for publication to any journals, periodicals, or other publications? If so, describe.

5. Has the Company ever applied for registration of any copyrights with the U.S. Copyright Office?

6. Are articles from periodicals, magazines, trade journals, and other related written materials photocopied for distribution within the Company?

7. What policies exist regarding reproduction of books, articles, journals, and other materials that may be subject to copyright?

8. Is any music piped in through the Company's offices (whether through the use of CDs or music being simultaneously transmitted by a radio station)?

9. Is music played when callers to the Company are placed on hold?

D. Patents

1. Has the Company or its employees ever invented any useful article, product, method, process, or software? If so, do any inventor or laboratory notebooks exist that document the development of the invention? Does the Company have any present plans for any such inventions?

2. Has the Company ever made any improvements to another party's useful article, product, or invention?

3. Has the Company ever engaged in the reverse engineering or decompilation of another company's product or software?

4. Has the Company ever applied with the PTO for issuance of any patent?

E. Trade Secrets

1. What information does the Company possess that would be harmful to the Company if it were discovered by a competitor? Consider proprietary information relating to research and development plans; calculations and financial data; employee manuals and handbooks and personnel information; information relating to the Company's clients and customers; the Company's methods of recruiting; methods and processes of production; test results for Company products and services; data concerning the pricing for Company products and services; sales forecasts; research information; manufacturing information; marketing materials; surveys and data relating to customer needs and preferences; and business plans and forecasts.

2. Do employment or other agreements exist that protect such proprietary materials?

3. Does the Company conduct employee orientation for new employees and exit interviews for departing employees to ensure employees understand the need to maintain confidentiality of Company trade secrets?

4. What measures does the Company take to protect confidential and proprietary information? Are documents marked "Confidential"? Are proprietary materials kept in locked cabinets? Are restrictions placed on the access to and copying of such materials?

5. What measures does the Company take to ensure electronic communications are protected and secure? Are any encryption methods in place for electronic

EXHIBIT 24–1
Intellectual
Property Audit
Questionnaire
(continued)

communications? Describe restrictions on access to the Company's computer systems.

6. Are any legal notices or disclaimers provided at sign-on when Company employees access the Company server or network?

F. Software

1. Has the Company designed, developed, or modified any software?
2. Does the Company have the right to use any software designed or developed by another party? If so, have licenses been obtained for each user?
3. Does the Company allow its employees to copy any software for their home use?

G. Claims

1. Are there any presently pending claims relating to any of the Company's intellectual property? Has any person alleged or claimed that the Company has violated or infringed its intellectual property rights?
2. What claims have been made (whether or not resolved or compromised) within the past five years against the Company relating to alleged infringement or violation by the Company of the intellectual property rights of others?
3. Has the Company observed or made any claims relating to any possible infringements by others of the Company's intellectual property rights?
4. Does the Company use any methods to detect possible infringing uses of its intellectual property?

H. General Documents

1. Please assemble all applications and registrations, and all license, royalty, security agreements or other agreements relating to trade names, Marks, copyrights, patents, trade secrets, software, licenses, or other similar rights relating to the Company's intellectual property rights.
2. Please assemble all agreements entered into by employees (including officers and directors) and any Company handbooks, manuals, or policies relating to Company employees.
3. Please assemble all agreements entered into between the Company and any consultants or independent contractors.
4. To the extent not already covered, please assemble all agreements or licenses entered into between the Company and any other parties that relate to the Company's intellectual property, which are essential for the operation of the Company's business, or by which the Company is allowed to offer or use another party's Marks, copyrights, patents, processes, software, or other related property.
5. Does the Company offer its products or services in any foreign countries? If no, does the Company have any plans to offer its products or services in foreign countries within the next three years?

Once the materials that are responsive to the questionnaire are gathered, the legal team can review them. The review is generally done at the client site. Files are pulled, brochures gathered, and contracts assembled. The legal team will review these materials and often make copies of pertinent documents, marking them as confidential.

After review of the materials is completed, another face-to-face meeting should be held to ensure that all of the materials were gathered and that there are no other contracts, license agreements, or other documents that should be reviewed. Questions may have arisen during the course of the audit for which the legal team needs responses. For example, the legal team may ask whether a certain brochure or trademark is still in use or whether the company logo was designed in-house or by another company. The legal team will generally check the records of the PTO and the Copyright Office to determine whether there are any records on file showing the company's ownership of trademarks, copyrights, and patents. A follow-up questionnaire may be sent to the client to obtain the answers to questions that arose in the course of the audit.

POSTAUDIT ACTIVITY

After the inspection is completed, the legal team will usually prepare a written report identifying the specific items of IP owned by the company, reviewing their status, and making recommendations for protection. The IP audit team may then proceed to take the following actions: filing applications for registration of trademarks, service marks, copyrights, and patents; drafting contracts to be used when the company retains independent contractors (to ensure that all work created by the independent contractors is "work made for hire" or is owned by or assigned to the company); preparing license agreements so the company can license its intellectual property to others; preparing nondisclosure and noncompetition agreements; and preparing policies for the protection of trade secrets.

The IP audit team may also assist the client's human resources department and provide instructions on conducting exit interviews and may redraft the employee manual to include a trade secret policy, Internet use policy, and instructions regarding use of the company's trademarks. The legal team may also advise the company to engage appraisers and analysts to valuate the IP assets so they can be licensed at appropriate royalties or sold at their fair market value to produce revenue for the company.

The company is usually advised to initiate an aggressive campaign to locate others who may be infringing the company's intellectual property by reviewing competitors' materials and trade publications and by monitoring applications filed at the PTO for marks that may be confusingly similar to those owned by the company. The legal team may help the company initiate a docketing system for reminder dates for renewals of licenses and trademark registrations or may be retained to perform the docketing functions itself.

TRIVIA

- In 2000, the Brookings Institution estimated that at least 50 percent and possibly as much as 85 percent of the value of American companies is attributable to their intangible assets, such as intellectual property.
- As of early 2003, Hasbro had paid filmmaker George Lucas approximately $470 million so that it could sell toys based on the *Star Wars* movies.
- The COCA-COLA trademark is the most recognized trademark in the world and the company values its brands at nearly $70 billion.

CHAPTER SUMMARY

Because clients can be unaware of the value of the intellectual property they own, law firms often conduct intellectual property audits for clients. The audit reveals valuable intellectual property assets that can then be exploited for the client's benefit. Audits should be conducted on a periodic basis to reflect the changing nature of intellectual property. Audits or reviews are also conducted when companies are sold, when they borrow money, or when they acquire other companies. In such instances, the review is often called "due diligence." Because almost all types of intellectual property can be lost through lack of protection (including nonuse, failure to monitor licensees properly, failure to renew or maintain registrations, and failure to protect against infringing activities), the intellectual property audit is a crucial tool that allows a company to understand and exploit the value of its intellectual property portfolio.

CASE ILLUSTRATION—VALUE OF TRADEMARK

Case: *Susser v. Carvel Corp.*, 332 F.2d 505 (2d Cir. 1964)

Facts: Plaintiffs, franchisees of Carvel stores, alleged antitrust violations against Carvel in that they were required to buy certain products only from Carvel.

Holding: There were no antitrust violations. Carvel had the right to impose reasonable restrictions on its franchisees to protect the value of its trademarks and its franchise system. The court noted that the significant growth of the Carvel chain was no doubt attributable in great measure to the increasing value of the Carvel trademarks. An essential element in the Carvel franchise is the trademark license; the cornerstone of the franchise system is the owner's trademark, which in this case, generated significant earning power for the franchisor.

CASE STUDY AND ACTIVITIES

Case Study.   Watson has a variety of characters, books, songs, trademarks, logos, and designs that it seldom uses. It would like to explore the opportunity of either abandoning the rights to these properties or obtaining revenue from their license or sale to others. Additionally, Watson plans to borrow a significant amount of money to fund development of new parks in Georgia and Europe.

Activities.   Given Watson's plans and desires, discuss the advantages of an intellectual property audit for Watson.

ROLE OF PARALEGAL

Paralegals generally play an active and vital role in planning and conducting IP audits. Using nonattorney IP practitioners also helps reduce the costs associated with audits. In many instances, a paralegal serves as the liaison between the law firm and the client and coordinates all activities related to the audit. IP paralegals are generally involved in the following tasks:

- preparing the audit questionnaire and ensuring a company representative completes the questionnaire;
- coordinating the time and manner of the audit by scheduling a convenient date for all team members and ensuring that a conference room or office near a photocopy machine is set aside for the audit team;
- reviewing client files and documents;
- preparing a follow-up questionnaire, if needed;
- reviewing the records of the PTO and Copyright Office to determine if trademarks and copyrights have been applied for or registered and whether patents have been published or have issued;
- reporting the results of IP audit;
- preparing applications for registration of marks, copyrights, and patents; drafting policies for trade secret protection; drafting contracts, licenses, and assignments;
- assisting in setting up a docket or calendar for maintenance of intellectual property; and
- providing reminders to clients of the need for annual or periodic updates to the IP audit.

INTERNET RESOURCES

Statutes relating to intellectual property:	http://www.ll.georgetown.edu and http://www.findlaw.com
General information:	http://www.findlaw.com, http://www.ipmall.fplc.edu, and http://www.megalaw.com

DISCUSSION QUESTIONS

1. What effect does the Federal Circuit's decision in *State Street Bank & Trust Co. v. Signature Financial Group, Inc.*, 149 F.3d 1368 (Fed. Cir. 1998), holding that business methods may be patentable (and which case is discussed in Chapter 21), have on intellectual property audits?

2. In the course of conducting an intellectual property audit, the audit team discovers an unregistered trademark that the client company has not used in several years. Should a trademark application be filed for this mark?

3. In the course of conducting an intellectual property audit, the audit team discovers that few employees are subject to written agreements with the company, although they have access to highly proprietary information. Moreover, the audit team has discovered that the client purchased another company two years ago and has not filed any documents to notify any federal agencies that it is now the owner of various intellectual property assets. What should the audit team advise the client with regard to these matters?

potential research variables. And your job is to think along the line to find out which is your point of focus and what are the specific aspects that you are interested in.

The clarification of your research population, nevertheless, goes in a different dimension. Instead of asking which is your point of focus and what are the interesting aspects, you are attempting to determine who should be covered under your study. You need to clarify the key feature(s) or variable(s) that you want to use to define your research population. For instance, for the aging population and children, you use age, specifically calendar age, as your criterion. For some variables, once they are used as the criteria in determining the research population, they turn into constants and can no longer be treated as variables. Examples for such variables include sex used as a criterion to feature such research projects as women's studies. For some other variables, while they are used as the criteria in determining the research population, they could still be used as variables, but their ranges of variation will be highly limited. Examples for such variables include age used as a criterion to feature such research projects as aging studies. If age as a general human variable has a range from 0 (at birth) to 80+ (the "old old"), in aging studies it would only have a range from 60 or 65, depending on definition of the entry point of old age, to 80 or above. Although aging may begin as soon as one is born, aging studies usually focus on researching "the elderly" (people aged 60 or 65 and above). If no one under 60 is included in a study, then the variable age will not have a range extending below 60 (in fact, if this happens you should double-check your data to correct the errors).

In addition to the above features, you need to delimit the geographic range or the specific locations of your research population. If your topic is aging, you may not be studying elderly persons all over the world, or even of the whole country. You may want to limit your scope, say, to a city. More specifically, you may want to focus on those elderly persons who live in nursing homes within that city. Some people might not want to impose such limitation or additional specification on their research population since they would argue that whatever they study could always be taken as a sample of the unlimited population. It is true if they would like to take it as any kind of sample except that it is representative of what they imply to study. If they want to make any generalization beyond the sample, they must establish a relationship of some validity between the sample and the population. To achieve this, they will have to resort to probability sampling, which is generally recognized as more reliable than nonprobability sampling in

Glossary

A

abandonment: Loss of trademark rights through nonuse coupled with an intent not to resume use; loss of patent rights through express intention to relinquish rights

abstract: A concise statement of an invention

access: Availability of a copyrighted work to a defendant so that the defendant had a reasonable opportunity to copy it

acquiescence: Conduct by a person that leads another to believe the owner will not assert certain claims against the other

acquired distinctiveness: See *secondary meaning*

actual reduction to practice: Construction of an invention in physical form, making or testing an invention or its prototype

actual use application: A trademark application based on an applicant's use in interstate commerce of a trademark

Affidavit of Incontestability: Document filed by the owner of a mark registered on the Principal Register after five years of continuous use that reduces the challenges that may be made to a mark; also called *Section 15 Affidavit*

Affidavit of Continued Use: Document filed by a trademark registrant between fifth and sixth years and every ten years after registration verifying the mark is still in use; also called *Declaration of Use* or *Section 8 Affidavit*

Amendment to Allege Use: Document filed during prosecution of an intent-to-use trademark application, alleging that use of the mark has begun

American Inventor's Protection Act: 1999 federal law providing significant changes to patent law

anonymous work: A copyrighted work in which the author is not identified

anticipation, doctrine of: See *doctrine of anticipation*

Anticybersquatting Consumer Protection Act (ACPA): Federal law intended to deter the practice of cybersquatting

arbitrary mark: A mark using a common dictionary word for an unrelated product, such as APPLE for computers

architectural work: The design of a building as embodied in any tangible medium of expression

article of manufacture: See *manufacture*

asexual reproduction: Growing something other than from a seed, often by grafting or placing cuttings in soil

assignment: Transfer of rights in a trademark, copyright, patent, or other property to another

assignment in gross: A purported transfer of a trademark without the business goodwill that the mark symbolizes; it is insufficient to transfer trademark rights

associates: Attorneys in foreign law firms who work with attorneys in U.S. firms regarding intellectual property matters

attribution: The right of an author to be known as the author of a work; also called *the right of paternity*

audiovisual work: A work consisting of a series of related images intended to be shown by the use of a machine such as a projector together with its accompanying sounds

author: For copyright purposes, a person who creates a work or, if the work is one made for hire, the employer or commissioning party

automated database: A body of facts, data, or other information assembled into an organized format suitable for use in a computer and comprising one or more files

B

background: The portion of a specification in a patent application that discusses how the invention differs from the prior art

Berne Convention: An international convention adhered to by more than 145 nations that requires its members to treat nationals of other countries as their own nationals for purposes of copyright

best edition: The deposit edition of a copyrighted work most suitable for purposes of the Library of Congress; generally, clean, legible, and superior deposit materials

blackout period: The period after approval of an application for publication in the *Official Gazette* within which an amendment to allege use of a mark cannot be filed

blue penciling: The revision of a noncompetition clause by a court to make it enforceable, generally because it is unreasonable in regard to scope, territory, or duration

blurring: A form of trademark dilution that whittles away the value of a famous trademark through its unauthorized use on a dissimilar product or with a dissimilar service

business method patent: A patent allowed since 1998 that covers a business method that produces a useful, tangible, and concrete result

C

cancellation: A proceeding initiated after registration of a trademark seeking to cancel registration of a mark registered on the Principal or Supplemental Register

cease and desist letter: Correspondence sent to a party demanding that it cease and desist from certain action (in the intellectual property context, from further use of a trademark, copyright, patent, or trade secret)

Certificate of Registration: Document issued by the PTO confirming registration of a trademark

certification mark: A word, name, symbol, or device used by one person (or a union) to certify that the goods or services of others have certain features in regard to quality, material, or some other characteristics

chain of title: Documentation of continuity of ownership or title to a trademark, copyright, patent, or other property right

Chapter I: The first phase of a patent application filed under the Patent Cooperation Treaty, consisting of a search of the application and which can now last for thirty months

Chapter II: The second phase of a patent application filed under the Patent Cooperation Treaty during which an International Preliminary Examination is conducted of the application, generally lasting ten months

choreographic work: The composition and arrangement of dance movements and patterns

claim: The portion of a specification in a patent application that defines the scope of the invention

click-wrap license: A license of software that comes into existence by the clicking of a computer keystroke, by which act the licensee agrees to terms governing use of the software

coined mark: See *fanciful mark*

collateral use: Acceptable use of another's trademark, such as in comparative advertising

collective mark: A mark used by a collective membership organization to identify that the person displaying the mark is a member of the organization

collective work: A work such as a periodical issue or anthology in which a number of contributions, constituting separate and independent works, are assembled into a collective whole

combination patents: New inventions consisting of a combination of older, known elements

commerce: See *interstate* and *intrastate commerce*

commercial disparagement: See *product disparagement*

common law trademark: A mark used by a party without any governmental registration

Community Trademark (CTM) System: A trademark system allowing trademark owners to file one single trademark application that covers all members of the European Union

companion application: Related trademark applications by the same applicant

comparative advertising: Advertising that compares one product or service with another or that states that one product works with or is compatible with another

compensatory damages: Damages awarded to a plaintiff to compensate it for injury suffered

compilation: A work formed by the collection of preexisting material arranged in such a way that the resulting work is original; includes *collective works*

composite mark: A mark consisting of words and a design element

composition of matter: In patent law, a combination of two or more chemical or other materials into a product

comprehensive search: A search of trademarks registered or applied for at the PTO, state

trademark registrations, and common law sources such as periodicals, directories, and the Internet

compulsory license: The imposition of a statutorily set fee for use of a copyrighted work

computer program: A set of instructions used directly or indirectly in a computer to produce a certain result

conception of an invention: The completion of the devising of the means for accomplishing an invention's result

concurrent use proceeding: A proceeding initiated at the Trademark Trial and Appeal Board to determine specific geographic areas in which parties with confusingly similar marks can each use the mark

confidentiality agreement: See *nondisclosure agreement*

conflicting application: Trademark applications filed by different parties for conflicting or confusingly similar marks

consent agreement: Private agreement entered into between two trademark owners whereby each consents to the use of the other's mark, generally with some limitations or restrictions; also called *consent to use agreement*

constructive reduction to practice: The filing of a patent application that fully discloses an invention

constructive use: Use of trademark other than actual use; for intent-to-use trademark applications, the application filing date constitutes constructive use of the mark (assuming the mark achieves registration)

continuation application: A patent application that claims priority from a previously filed application and contains no new information

continuation-in-part application: A patent application that adds new matter to a previous patent application

contributory infringement: In the intellectual property context, causing, inducing, or assisting in infringement of another's trademark, copyright, or patent

copy: In copyright law, a material object (other than a phonorecord) from which a work can be perceived, reproduced, or communicated, either by human perception or with the help of a machine

copyhoarding: Retaining all rights in a work and refusing to allow others to use it

copylefting: Licensing users of software to use it for any purpose

copyright: Right protecting original works of authorship, including literary, musical, dramatic, artistic, and other works, from unauthorized reproduction, sale, performance, distribution, or display

counterfeiting: A form of trademark infringement in which a trademark is affixed to goods or services that do not originate with the trademark owner

creation: In copyright law, the fixation of a work in a copy or phonorecord for the first time

cybersquatting: A practice in which a person, without permission, registers another's name or mark as a domain name and then attempts to sell the domain name to its true owner

D

deadwood: Unused marks that the PTO desires to clear from its records

declaration: A statement by an applicant for a trademark registration acknowledging that statements in the application are true

Declaration of Use: See *Affidavit of Use*

deep linking: The process by which an Internet user can proceed directly to certain information at another's web site, bypassing the home page at the second site

deposit: The best edition of a work provided to the Copyright Office in support of an application to register a copyright for the work

deposit account: Prepaid accounts established with the PTO, against which application and other fees are drawn by applicants

derivative work: A work based on one or more preexisting works, such as a translation, fictionalization, revision, or abridgment; also called a *new version*

descriptive mark: A mark that merely describes some characteristic of the goods or services offered under it and is unregistrable unless secondary meaning is shown

design application: An application for a design patent

design patent: A patent covering new, original, and ornamental designs for useful articles

Digital Millennium Copyright Act (DMCA): 1988 law updating copyright law for the digital age

dilution: Unauthorized acts that tend to blur the distinctiveness of a famous mark or to tarnish it

direct infringement: In patent law, making, using, or selling another's patented invention

disclaimer: In trademark law, an acknowledgment by an applicant that exclusive rights in certain wording in a mark, usually descriptive or generic wording, are not claimed; a notice placed on trademarked goods or advertising that the owner of the goods is not affiliated with another; in patent law, the cancellation of invalid claims in an issued patent

distinctiveness: See *secondary meaning*

divisional application: A patent application separated from another application when the original or parent application covers more than one invention

doctrine of anticipation: Theory that an invention was known or used by others such that its invention was anticipated

doctrine of equivalents: Principle that if an accused invention is equivalent to a patented invention in its purpose and achieves the same result, it infringes the patent even if a claim in the patent is not literally copied

domain name: Internet address used by a company or individual

domestic representative: A person or law firm in the United States designated by a foreign applicant to receive documents and notices affecting a trademark application

double patenting: In patent law, a principle prohibiting the issuance of more than one patent for the same invention

downstream infringement: Infringement by users who obtain copyrighted items from legitimate users

dramatic work: A theatrical performance or play performed for stage, movies, television, or radio

drawing: The display of the mark applied for in a trademark application; may be a *typed form* (typewritten display) or *special form* (a design mark or a design mark with words); the display of an invention in a patent application

droit de suite: A doctrine in foreign countries that allows the authors of fine works to share in the appreciation of those works, even after they have parted with ownership of those works

due diligence: A type of audit of intellectual property, usually conducted when a company is sold, when it borrows money, when it offers securities, or when it acquires another company

duty of candor: Requirement that patent applicants disclose to the PTO any information that is material to the patentability of a claimed invention

E

Electronic Filing System (EFS): PTO electronic system allowing secure electronic filing of some documents with the PTO

equivalents, doctrine of: See *doctrine of equivalents*

e-signature: An electronic rather than a conventional paper signature

estoppel: A defense often raised in infringement actions, alleging the plaintiff is precluded from making certain assertions due to the plaintiff's conduct or acquiescence in the infringement

European Patent Organization: An organization with twenty-seven member nations founded in 1973 to provide a uniform patent system in Europe

European Union (EU): An association of twenty-five European nations

Examiner's Amendment: A written communication from the PTO setting forth an agreed-upon clarification or correction to a trademark application

exclusive license: A grant of rights to one party with no other party having any rights

exhaustion theory: In trademark and patent law, the extinguishment or exhaustion of a trademark or patent owner's rights once a lawful first sale has been made of trade-marked goods or a patented invention; in copyright law, the extinguishment of a copyright owner's right to distribute a copyrighted work once a lawful first sale has been made; also see *first sale doctrine*

experimental use: Use of an invention to perfect it and which is not "public use" such as to trigger one-year grace period

F

fair use: A defense asserted in trademark or copyright infringement actions; a noninfringing use of copyrighted work such as a parody or for criticism, scholarly research, or educational purposes

false advertising: False or deceptive representations about one's own goods or services

fanciful mark: A wholly invented mark; also called *coined mark*

Federal Trade Commission (FTC): The federal regulatory agency charged with protecting consumers from unfair or deceptive acts and practices

Federal Trademark Dilution Act: 1995 federal statute that protects famous marks from uses that weaken or tarnish their distinctiveness, even in the absence of likelihood of confusion; actual harm must be shown to prevail against such uses

file wrapper: The official PTO file containing all papers relating to a trademark or patent application

file wrapper estoppel: See *prosecution history estoppel*

filing receipt: Document mailed by the PTO to an applicant to confirm filing and details of an application

final action: Action by the PTO refusing a trademark or patent application; also called *final refusal*

first sale doctrine: In copyright and patent law, the principle that once the owner of copyrighted material or a patented item sells it, the buyer can treat the object as his or her own and freely sell, lease, or lend the work to another; in copyright law, the first sale doctrine only affects the right of distribution; also see *exhaustion theory*

fixation: The embodiment of a work in a sufficiently permanent or stable form to permit it to be perceived, reproduced, or communicated for more than a transitory period

foreign filing license: The grant by the PTO of permission to an inventor to file a patent application in another country for an invention made in the United States, required before a foreign application may be filed

framing: Capture of content from another's web site, often obscuring owner's content

freeware: Software that is allowed to be used for free but in which certain rights are maintained to ensure the work is not reverse engineered

functional feature: A feature that is essential to the use or purpose of the product or affects the cost or quality of the product

G

General Agreement on Tariffs and Trade (GATT): Agreement adhered to by most industrialized nations aimed at increasing international trade and that resulted in some changes to U.S. trademark and patent law, notably relating to the duration of patent protection

genericide: Loss of rights in a trademark occurring when consumers begin calling a product or service offered under a mark by the mark itself

generic mark: An unprotectable common name for a product or service

generic top-level domain: The portion of a domain name to the right of a period, such as ".com" or ".gov"

goodwill: The value inherent in achieving consumer loyalty to a particular product or service through maintenance of consistent quality of the products or services offered under a mark

grace period: A period within which late documents are accepted by the PTO; in patent law, the one-year period within which a patent application must be filed after the invention is in public use, on sale, or described in a printed publication anywhere

gray market goods: Unauthorized importation of goods into the United States for resale after the goods are distributed in foreign markets

H

house mark: A mark used for a wide range of products or services

hyperlink: A symbol designating another's web page

I

idea-expression dichotomy: Doctrine that ideas are not protectable by copyright although the expression of those ideas is copyrightable

idea submission: The submission of an idea for an invention, process, game, or entertainment show in the hope it will be developed and marketed by the recipient

impoundment: Seizure, generally of infringing goods

incontestable: A trademark registered on the Principal Register that is protected from certain challenges after its registrant files a section 15 affidavit alleging continuous use for five years

independent contractor: One who renders services in the course of independent occupation; one who is not an employee of another

inducement of infringement: In patent law, actively and intentionally encouraging another to infringe a patent

industrial property: The term used in some foreign countries to refer to intellectual property

inevitable disclosure doctrine: Principle that if new employment will inevitably lead to disclosure of former employer's trade secrets, employee can be enjoined from working for new employer

Information Disclosure Statement (IDS): A document filed by an inventor with the PTO identifying information material to patentability of an invention

infringement: A violation of some right; in the intellectual property context, a violation of a party's rights in a trademark, copyright, or patent

injunction: A court order prohibiting or compelling some act

innocent infringement: Infringement of another's intellectual property rights without any intent to infringe; not a valid defense in copyright or patent infringement actions

integrity: See *right of integrity*

obtaining a representative sample. However, probability sampling will require the researcher to follow certain procedures and make clear the boundary of his research population, which sets the inferential limit for his sample study findings.

Sampling is the process of selecting a part (the sample) from the whole (the research population) for actual data collection. Social scientists tend to study large-sized populations and it is usually impossible to observe every real case therein. Sometimes they do not want to observe every real case, even if they could, for the purpose of quality control. This is because errors may happen anywhere in the data collection process, including misunderstanding of the interviewee and mistakes of the interviewer. In this regard, the utility or desirability of a so-called dense sample, comprising non-randomly the majority of a population, is questionable. Generally speaking, if you do not follow probability sampling procedures in selecting your sample, statistically it will not make any sense to talk about any research population that goes beyond that sample. From the "qualitative" point of view, nevertheless, you may still be able to argue for the representativeness of your sample, even if it is a small one, based on information you have. That is why some nonprobability sampling methods are still frequently used where probability sampling is impossible, difficult, or deemed unnecessary.

Nonprobability sampling methods include some that are very easy and cheap to use. These are the ones that a beginner would think of when asked to do a project without having learned about more complicated sampling methods. Experienced researchers may also use nonprobability sampling methods especially when (1) they are restricted by available resources; (2) the research population is quite homogeneous; (3) the population sometimes automatically renders randomization; and/or (4) there may be some special controllable research situation.

The first nonprobability approach is called accidental sampling, which takes whatever subjects that are immediately available. The only merit of the method is its ease and convenience, and thus it can be used to facilitate exercises, trials, and pretests in some stages and aspects of the learning and research processes. In practice, this sampling method is frequently exploited and sometimes abused by novice researchers and lay people, who are prone to subject their hypotheses to statistical tests. They should be aware, however, that no matter how refined their design is on such tests, it will prove futile if they do not intend to achieve a group of subjects through random or probability sampling procedures.

The next nonprobability sampling method is called snowball sampling, which

intellectual property: The result or product of human creativity, including trademarks, copyrights, and inventions; generally *intellectual property* comprises the field of trademarks, copyrights, patents, and trade secrets

intellectual property audit: A review of the trademarks, copyrights, patents, and trade secrets owned by a person or company

Intent-to-use application: A trademark application for which no actual use of a mark has been made but rather alleging the applicant's bona fide intent to use the mark in the future

interference: A proceeding before the Trademark Trial and Appeal Board when marks in two pending trademark applications are confusingly similar or when a mark in a pending application may be confusingly similar to a registered mark that is not yet incontestable; a proceeding initiated by the PTO to determine which of two or more patents has priority

International Classes: The categorization of goods and services into forty-five separate topics for trademark purposes; class(es) of goods or services must be identified in a trademark application

international patent: A patent filed under the Patent Cooperation Treaty

International Trademark Association (INTA): A not-for-profit international association devoted to promoting trademarks

Internet Corporation for Assigned Names and Numbers (ICANN): Nonprofit corporation that oversees the domain naming system

Internet Treaties: Two international copyright treaties adopted by WIPO in 2002 to protect copyright works in the digital environment

inter partes proceedings: Literally, "between parties"; proceedings handled by the Trademark Trial and Appeal Board; may be oppositions, cancellations, interferences, or concurrent use proceedings

interstate commerce: Commerce between or among states

intrastate commerce: Commerce conducted within the borders of one state

invention developer: One who assists an inventor in bringing a discovery to market or negotiates with others for assignment or licensing of an inventor's rights; also called an *invention promoter*

Invention Disclosure Document: A document filed with the PTO that describes an invention and is intended to provide evidence of the date of conception and reduction to practice of an invention

invention promoter: See *invention developer*

issue fee: A fee required by the PTO for a patent to be granted

J

Jepson claim: A type of claim in a patent specification used for improvements to existing inventions that identifies what is new to the invention

joint application: An application for a trademark, copyright, or patent registration made by more than one person

joint inventors: Two or more people who contribute to an invention

joint work: A copyrightable work created by two or more authors with the intent that their contributions be merged into a unitary whole

junior user: A party who adopts and uses a mark similar to that previously used by a senior user

K

keying: Practice of forcing an Internet user to view certain preselected ads when certain "key" terms are entered into a search engine

knockout search: A preliminary search of PTO records designed to disclose identical or nearly identical marks; often followed by a *comprehensive search*

L

laboratory notebooks: Books and notes kept by inventors as work progresses on an invention, often used in determining conception of invention and reduction to practice of an invention

laches: An unreasonable delay in asserting one's rights that causes prejudice or harm to another; a common defense asserted in intellectual property infringement actions

Lanham Act: The federal statute found at 15 U.S.C. § 1051 *et seq.* governing the law of trademarks; also called the *United States Trademark Act*

Library of Congress: The agency charged with examining copyright applications, issuing registrations, and maintaining copyright deposits

license: A limited transfer of rights, such as permission to another to use a trademark, copyright, patent, or trade secret subject to some conditions, rather than an outright transfer of all rights

literal copying: Identical duplication or copying of another's copyrighted work

literal infringement: An accused invention that falls within the language used in a claim in an issued patent

literary work: A work expressed in words, numbers, or other verbal or numerical symbols, such as a book or computer program

little FTC acts: State statutes that prohibit deceptive and unfair trade practices

logo: A design used as a trademark

M

machine: In patent law, a device that accomplishes a result

Madrid Protocol: An agreement adhered to by more than forty countries and the E.U. and U.S. that provides an "international trademark registration" that would be valid in all member nations

maintenance fees: Fees due at 3 1/2, 7 1/2, and 11 1/2 years after issuance of a utility patent required to keep it in force

Manual of Patent Examining Procedure (MPEP): A PTO publication containing rules and regulations relating to examination and issuance of patents

manufacture: In patent law, anything made by humans

mark: A trademark or service mark

Markman hearing: Hearing held in front of a judge in a patent infringement case to determine claims construction of a patent; the briefs submitted for the hearing are often called *Markman* briefs

mask works: Stencils used to etch or encode an electronic circuit on a semiconductor chip

merger doctrine: The principle that if there are few alternative ways of expressing something, only literal copying will infringe because the expression merges with the idea and ideas are uncopyrightable

mime: See *pantomime*

misappropriation: The taking or using of property created or secured at great effort by another

misuse: A defense often asserted in patent infringement actions alleging that the patentee has so misused its rights that its patent is unenforceable.

moral rights: Personal rights retained by authors in their works (often works of fine arts) to protect their honor and reputation even after they no longer own the copyright in the work

motion picture: Audiovisual work consisting of a series of related images that, when shown in succession, impart an impression of motion, together with accompanying sounds

mousetrapping: Practice of trapping an Internet user into viewing a series of advertisements

musical work: Original musical compositions or arrangements, including lyrics

N

naked license: Granting permission to another to use a trademark and retaining no control over the nature or quality of the goods or services offered under the mark; a naked license results in a loss of the licensor's rights in a mark

national phase: The final phase of a patent application filed under the Patent Cooperation Treaty consisting of prosecution of the patent in countries designated in the application

national treatment: Principle that member countries adhering to a treaty guarantee to the citizens of other member adherents the same rights in intellectual property matters that they provide to their own citizens

new version: See *derivative work*

noncompetition agreement: An agreement prohibiting an employee from competing against the employer during and after the term of employment; also called *restrictive covenant*

nondisclosure agreement: An agreement requiring a party to maintain information in confidence; also called *confidentiality agreement*

nonenabling specification: A specification in a patent application rejected by the PTO on the basis that it is not sufficient to teach or enable another to make or use the invention

nonexclusive license: A grant of rights to more than one party

nonobviousness: In patent law, the requirement that subject matter sought to be patented be sufficiently different from what has been used or described before such that it may be said to be nonobvious to a person having ordinary skill in the area of technology related to the invention

North American Free Trade Agreement (NAFTA): A trade agreement entered into in 1991 by the United States, Canada, and Mexico

Notice of Allowance: Document issued by the PTO informing a trademark applicant that an intent-to-use application has been allowed and granting the applicant a specified time period within which to begin use of the mark in order to secure registration for it; document issued by the PTO informing a patent applicant that a patent application has been allowed and granting the applicant a specified time period within which to pay an issue fee so a patent will be issued

notice of copyright: A mark informing the public that a work is protected by copyright and identifying its owner and year of publication

Notice of Opposition: The document that initiates a trademark opposition proceeding and that sets forth a short and plain statement of the reasons why the opposer believes he or she will be damaged by registration of a mark

novelty: In patent law, a new invention; one not known or used by another

novelty search: A search of prior art to determine if an invention is new and nonobvious

Nunc Pro Tunc assignment: Assignment prepared on a later date to reflect an earlier transfer

O

object code: A computer language consisting of zeroes and ones that is machine-readable

office action: Written communication from the PTO refusing registration of a trademark or patent and specifying reasons for the refusal

Official Filing Receipt: A document issued by the PTO confirming the filing of a trademark application

Official Gazette: The weekly publication of the PTO that publishes trademarks for purposes of opposition and publishes information about issued patents and patents available for sale or license

on sale bar: The doctrine precluding granting of a patent unless a patent application is filed less than one year from the time the invention is in public use, on sale in the United States, or described in printed publication anywhere

opposition: A proceeding initiated at the Trademark Trial and Appeal Board by one who believes he or she may be damaged by registration of a trademark

originality: In copyright law, a work that is independently created (not copied) and that exhibits a minimal amount of creativity

orphan drug: A drug needed to treat a disease affecting fewer than 200,000 people

P

palming off: See *passing off*

pantomime: A performance using gestures as expression to communicate with no accompanying sound

parallel imports: See *gray market goods*

parent application: An original trademark or patent application that is the source or parent of a later separate application

Paris Convention: An agreement adhered to by more than 160 member nations providing that foreign trademark and patent owners may obtain in a member country the same protection for their trademarks and patents as can citizens of the member country

passing off: Attempting to sell one's goods or services as those of another; also called *palming off*

patent: A grant from the U.S. government permitting its owner to exclude others from making, selling, or using an invention for a limited period of time

patent agent: A nonattorney engineer or scientist who passes a PTO exam testing patent knowledge and may engage in patent prosecution but may not give legal advice or appear in court

Patent and Trademark Depository Libraries: Public libraries throughout the United States that maintain selected trademark and patent records

Patent Application Information Retrieval (PAIR) System: PTO electronic system allowing applicants to review the status of pending patent applications

patent attorney: A licensed attorney who passes a PTO exam testing patent knowledge and who may engage in patent prosecution, give legal advice, and appear in court

Patent Cooperation Treaty (PCT): A 1978 treaty adhered to by approximately 120 countries that provides a centralized way of filing, searching, and examining patent applications in several countries simultaneously

patentee: The owner of a patent issued by the PTO

Patent Law Treaty: WIPO treaty adopted in 2002 to harmonize formal requirements for obtaining patents around the world

patent misuse: See *misuse*

PCT application: A patent application that has applicability and effect in designated member nations adhering to the Patent Cooperation Treaty

peer-to-peer file sharing: Trading of computer files, often songs, from one user's computer to another's

performing rights society: An organization of copyright owners (such as ASCAP or BMI) that licenses the rights to use copyrighted music to third parties, collects fees therefor, and remits those fees to its members, the authors of the works

Petition to Cancel: The document initiating a trademark cancellation proceeding that sets forth a short and plain statement of the reasons a petitioner would be damaged by continued registration of a mark

Petition to Make Special: Request for accelerated examination of patent application due to importance of patent or age or health of inventor

phonorecord: A material object in which sounds (other than those accompanying a motion picture or other audiovisual work) are fixed and from which the sounds can be perceived, reproduced, or communicated by human perception or with the help of a machine

pioneer patent: A patent representing an important advance or significant breakthrough

plant application: An application for a patent for a plant

plant patent: A patent covering asexually reproduced and distinct plant varieties

Plant Variety Protection Act: Federal law allowing quasipatent protection for certain sexually reproduced plants

posting of ports: Monitoring of ports of entry into the United States by the Customs Department for the purpose of seizing unauthorized goods bearing a party's registered trademark

Principal Register: The most preferred roll or register for registration of trademarks conferring wide protection for a mark and indicating that the mark distinguishes the registrant's goods and services from those of others

prior art: In patent law, the generally available public knowledge relating to an invention at the time of its creation

process: A patentable method of doing something to produce a given result

product disparagement: Making false representations about another's goods or services; also called *trade libel*

progressive encroachment: Use of a trademark that becomes infringement although earlier it may have been permissible; often used by plaintiff to defeat a claim of laches asserted by a defendant

prosecution: The process of moving a trademark or patent application through the PTO

prosecution history estoppel: The principle that an inventor or patentee is bound by acts taken and statements made during the prosecution of a patent and cannot later take an inconsistent position; also called *file wrapper estoppel*

provisional patent application: A patent application that is less formal than a utility patent application; within twelve months of its filing, it must be followed by a standard utility patent application at the PTO

pseudonymous work: A copyrighted work in which the author is identified under a fictitious name, such as the name "Mark Twain" used by Samuel Clemens

publication: The distribution of copies of a work to the public for sale or other transfer of ownership by rental, lease, or lending

public domain: A work or invention that is free for all members of the public to use

puffing: An exaggerated and highly subjective statement upon which no reasonable person would rely; generally, nonactionable opinion

punitive damages: Damages intended to punish a defendant rather than to compensate a plaintiff

R

receiving office: A patent office in which a patent application prepared in accordance with the Patent Cooperation Treaty is filed

recordation: Filing of certain documents with the PTO, Library of Congress, or other official body to provide public notice of the contents of a document or a transaction, such as an assignment or transfer of intellectual property, a grant of a security interest in intellectual property, or a change in the chain of title of intellectual property

reduction to practice: Construction of an invention in physical form (called *actual reduction to practice*) or filing a patent application for an invention (called *constructive reduction to practice*)

reexamination of patent: Proceeding initiated at the PTO to review or reexamine a claim in an issued patent to determine its validity

registered user agreement: Agreement by which an owner of a registered mark allows or licenses another to use its mark and is required to be filed by many foreign trademark offices for the grant to be effective

registrant: The owner of a trademark registration issued by the PTO

registrar: Company that assigns domain names

reissue patent: A proceeding to correct defects in an issued patent or to enlarge the claims of an issued patent

renewal: Document filed with the PTO or Library of Congress to maintain a trademark or copyright registration for an additional term

Request for Continued Examination: Request by applicant for continued examination of a utility or plant application

Request to Divide: Request by applicant to create a new trademark application, usually in intent-to-use applications, when applicant can proceed to registration for some goods or services and wishes to retain a separate application for goods or services not yet in use

restriction requirement: Requirement by the PTO that a patent applicant limit a patent application to one invention when two or more distinct inventions are claimed in one application

restrictive covenant: See *noncompetition agreement*

reverse doctrine of equivalents: In patent law, the principle that even if there is literal infringement of claims, if the accused resulting device differs from the patented device, there is no infringement

reverse engineering: Disassembling an object, usually a computer program, to understand its functional elements

right of integrity: A personal right of a copyright author to ensure that his or her work not be distorted, mutilated, or used in a way that would injure the author's reputation

right of publicity: Protection of a person's identity, voice, likeness, or persona against unauthorized commercial exploitation

royalties: Periodic payments paid by one who uses or licenses property owned or created by another, usually based on sales or licenses of the property

rule of doubt: Policy followed by the Copyright Office to resolve doubts about copyrightability in favor of a copyright applicant

S

scenes a faire: Literally, "scenes which must be done"; stock characters and devices in a work that are uncopyrightable

secondary considerations: In patent law, nontechnical and objective factors considered in determining whether an invention is nonobvious, namely, its commercial success, the long-felt need for the invention, commercial acquiescence to it by others, and copying of it by others

secondary level domain: The part of a domain name to the left of a period, such as "ibm" in "ibm.com"

secondary meaning: An association by a consumer who has learned to link a mark with its source; also called *acquired distinctiveness*

secrecy order: An order issued by the PTO requiring that an invention be kept secret and prohibiting publication of it or patent applications for it in another country, generally for national security reasons

Section 8 Affidavit: See *Affidavit of Continued Use*

Section 15 Affidavit: See *Affidavit of Incontestability*

Section 44(d) Application: Trademark application filed with the PTO by a non-U.S. citizen based upon an application filed in a foreign country

Section 44(e) Application: Trademark application filed with the PTO by a non-U.S. citizen based upon a registration secured in a foreign country

security agreement: In intellectual property law, an agreement by which one party grants an interest to another in its intellectual property, usually in order to obtain or secure a loan; if the owner defaults on the loan, the lender usually obtains ownership of the intellectual property

semiconductor chip: A product having two or more layers of metallic, insulating, or semiconductor material placed on or removed from semiconductor material and intended to perform electronic circuitry functions

senior user: The first party to use a mark

service mark: A word, name, symbol, or device used to indicate the source, quality, and ownership of a service

shareware: Copyrighted software that has been released under the condition that if the user likes it, the user will pay a license fee therefor

shrink-wrap license: A license of software that comes into existence by the opening of the plastic wrapping on the software and by which act the licensee agrees to terms governing use of the software

shop right: An employer's nonexclusive royalty-free license to use an invention or trade secret when the employer and employee do not agree in advance about who will own the invention or trade secret conceived by the employee while on company time

small entity: A business with fewer than 500 employees, an individual inventor, a university, or a not-for-profit organization entitled to a 50 percent reduction in many standard patent fees

softlifting: The act of software piracy by which one makes unauthorized copies of computer software

sound recording: A work that results from the fixation of a series of musical, spoken, or other sounds

source code: An alphanumeric computer language that is human-readable

special handling: Expedited processing of copyright applications and other documents for specified reasons upon payment of a fee

specification: The part of a patent application that describes an invention and the manner and process of making and using it

specimens: Samples of tags, labels, packaging, or advertising materials showing how a trademark or service mark is used in commerce

spoof: A dummy file posted on the Internet to frustrate music pirates

Statement of Use: Document filed by an intent-to-use trademark applicant verifying that the mark is in actual use in interstate commerce; required to receive a trademark registration

statutory damages: Damages awarded by a court in an infringement action as specified by statute, generally elected when a plaintiff will have difficulty proving actual damages

streaming: See *webcast*

suggestive mark: A mark that suggests something about the goods or services offered under it; a suggestive mark is registrable without proof of secondary meaning

Supplemental Register: The roll or register for marks not qualifying for registration on the PTO Principal Register; registration on the Supplemental Register is an indication that the mark does not yet distinguish the registrant's goods or services from those of others

supplementary copyright registration: An application to correct an error or amplify information in a copyright registration

T

tarnishment: A form of dilution in which a famous trademark is portrayed in an unsavory or embarrassing manner

terminal disclaimer: An agreement by an inventor that the term of protection for a second patented invention will terminate upon expiration of the term for the first patented invention

trade dress: The overall image of a product or service

trade libel: See *product disparagement*

trademark: A word, logo, phrase, or device used to indicate the source, quality, and ownership of a product or service; technically, *trademark* refers to a mark that identifies a product, while *service mark* refers to a mark that identifies services

Trademark Applications and Registrations Retrieval (TARR): The PTO's online search tool allows searching by application or registration number

trademark compliance policy: A guide to use of a trademark to ensure a mark is not misused or does not become generic or abandoned

Trademark Electronic Application System (TEAS): The PTO's system allowing electronic filing of many trademark documents

Trademark Electronic Search System (TESS): The PTO's online search tool allowing searching of trademarks in the PTO database

Trademark Manual of Examining Procedure: A PTO publication containing rules and regulations related to the prosecution and registration of trademarks

Trademark Status Line: System maintained by the PTO allowing telephonic checking of the status of trademark registrations or applications (703/305-8747)

Trademark Trial and Appeal Board (TTAB): Department of the PTO that resolves inter partes proceedings and other matters affecting trademarks

trade name: A name used to identify a business or company

Trade-Related Aspects of Intellectual Property Rights (TRIPs): Agreement promulgated in accordance with the 1994 General Agreement on Tariffs and Trade providing intellectual property protection for WTO members

trade secret: Any valuable commercial information that, if known by a competitor, would provide some benefit or advantage to the competitor

trailer clause: A clause in an employment agreement requiring employee to assign inventions to employer both during and after employment

traverse: Arguments made in response to objections by the PTO to a trademark or patent application

typosquatting: Variation of cybersquatting in which one registers misspelled versions of others' domain names to attract visitors for profit

U

unclean hands: A defense often raised in infringement actions; an assertion that the plaintiff's own wrongful conduct precludes it from obtaining relief

unfair competition: A branch of law protecting against deceptive and improper conduct in the marketplace

Uniform Domain Name Dispute Resolution Policy (UDRP): Policy adopted by all ICANN registrars, allowing a streamlined and inexpensive dispute resolution procedure for domain name disputes

United States Patent and Trademark Office (PTO): The agency within the Department of Commerce charged with registering trademarks and granting patents

United States Trademark Act: See *Lanham Act*

Universal Copyright Convention (UCC): An international convention relating to copyright requiring that works originating in a member nation must be given the same protection in all member nations as is granted by the country of origin of the work

Uruguay Round Agreements Act: A 1994 act that implemented GATT and amended U.S. copyright law to provide remedies for pirated sound recordings of live performances and to provide automatic restoration of copyright in certain foreign works; amended U.S. trademark law relating to abondonment of marks and geographic designations for wines and spirits; and amended patent law to harmonize term of patent protection with that of most foreign countries

useful article: An article having an intrinsic utilitarian value

usefulness: In patent law, a process or invention that is of some present value to humanity

utility application: A patent application for a new, useful, and nonobvious process, machine, article of manufacture, composition of matter, or some improvement thereof

utility patent: A patent for a useful article, invention, or discovery

V

Vessel Hull Design Protection Act: A portion of the Digital Millennium Copyright Act, providing copyright protection for original designs of boat vessel hulls

vicarious infringement: Liability imposed for infringement on a party due to its special relationship (such as employer-employee) with another infringer

W

watch service: Service provided by a private company, usually a trademark search firm, to review the *Official Gazette* and PTO records for potentially conflicting marks

webcast: The broadcast of a radio program over the Internet; also called *streaming*

work made for hire: A work that is presumed to be authored by an employer because it was created by an employee on company time or authored by a commissioning party when the parties have agreed in writing that the commissioning party will own the copyright and the work falls into one of nine statutorily enumerated categories

World Intellectual Property Organization (WIPO): A specialized agency of the United Nations with more than 175 member nations that promotes intellectual property throughout the world and administers various multilateral treaties dealing with intellectual property, including the Berne Convention

World Trade Organization (WTO): An international organization established in 1995 with more than 140 member countries, created by the Uruguay Round negotiations to handle trade disputes and monitor national trade policies starts from a few available subjects, then expands the sample through referrals, i.e., by having each subject suggest other relevant cases. The sample obtained reflects the structures of various social networks among the subjects. Although this characteristic can be used to facilitate such special kinds of research as sociometric or social networks study, it generally does not represent a research population with any predictable or controllable error and bias.

The third nonprobability sampling method is called judgmental or purposive sampling, which selects subjects based on the researcher's expertise and her research purpose. Although this method can easily be criticized as too subjective, it is not devoid of merit if we recognize the usefulness as well as the limitations of such knowledge sources as practice wisdom and intuition. However, the sampling error is still quantitatively unpredictable and uncontrollable in this case.

The common feature of the nonprobability sampling methods is that they are relatively simple. Probability sampling, on the other hand, tends to involve more complicated considerations and designs. Probability sampling is accomplished by a process of random selection, and thus also called random sampling. The purpose of random sampling is to ensure that each case or unit of the research population has an equal chance to be selected. In order to achieve this, you must be able to identify every case or unit in the research population. That is why it is so important to clarify the boundaries of your research population, although there is a technique called cluster sampling that would allow you to focus only on part of the population.

Note you cannot directly subject human beings to various random sampling procedures under normal circumstances. You will have to obtain or assign an ID, such as a name or a number, from/to each case or unit which you can directly process via various sampling mechanisms. The list of the names or numbers that identify all the cases or units in your research population constitutes your sampling frame. The concept of a sampling frame is extremely important. It requires you to clearly define your research population, and have a means to identify all its individual cases or units. If the list or the sampling frame is incomplete, then your original definition of the research population becomes only nominal. And you should regard the sampling frame as representing the real range of your research population, which finally sets the limit for your statistical inference.

The principles and requirements of probability sampling can be illustrated through what is called the simple random sampling procedure. To obtain a simple random sample, you can assign a number to each case and randomly select a

Index

certain amount (depending on your intended sample size) of the numbers from your sampling frame, or the list of the numbers representing all the cases. But how to randomly select the numbers? You can throw a dice once or a few times to get a random number. Or you can let the computer generate the random numbers, if you have a software package with such a function. You may also make use of existing tables of random numbers, which you can find in the appendices of most research methods and statistics textbooks. You begin anywhere in a random number table and proceed in any direction, take as many digits as you want up to what has been used for your sampling frame to identify the cases in your research population. Each number you obtained represents a case selected from the sampling frame or the actual research population. Eventually, the sum total of the selected cases will constitute a random sample of your research population.

The other way to directly sample from the list, or the sampling frame, is called systematic sampling, which selects cases at predetermined intervals with a random start. The sampling frame need not be made up by numbers. It may be composed of any kind of identifications such as the names of individual persons. However, since the random start is crucial to the whole process, you may want to number each case in the first group with a size equal to the predetermined interval, and then use a random number table to randomly choose a case as the starting point. After sampling a certain number of cases you may need to make a new random start to avoid some patterned biases. But in certain situations, you do not need to make a new start and the effect of systematic sampling may compare to stratified sampling depending on the ordering of the sampling frame. The sampling interval is obtained by dividing the size of the research population and the intended size of the random sample, i.e., the number of cases or units to be included in your sample.

For nonprobability sampling, how large your sample should be is an arbitrary matter, depending on your feeling as to how many you can afford to study and whether increasing the sample size would make a difference. There is no definite rule governing the sample size in nonprobability sampling. For probability sampling, on the other hand, you need to be calculative as you intend to infer your sample results mathematically (statistically) to the whole research population from which the sample was randomly drawn.

It should be noted that people tend to use sampling fraction or proportion, or the ratio of the sample size to the population size, as an indicator of the representativeness of a sample. It is not necessarily the case, however, that you